A Critical Edition of the Hebrew Manuscripts of Ben Sira

Supplements to the Journal for the Study of Judaism

Editors

René Bloch (*Institut für Judaistik, Universität Bern*)
Karina Martin Hogan (*Department of Theology, Fordham University*)

Associate Editors

Hindy Najman (*Theology & Religion Faculty, University of Oxford*)
Eibert J. C. Tigchelaar (*Faculty of Theology and Religious Studies, KU Leuven*)
Benjamin G. Wright, III (*Department of Religion Studies, Lehigh University*)

Advisory Board

A. M. Berlin – K. Berthelot – J. J. Collins – B. Eckhardt – Y. Furstenberg
S. Kattan Gribetz – G. Anthony Keddie – L. Lehmhaus – O. Malka
A. Manekin – S. Mason – F. Mirguet – J. H. Newman – A. K. Petersen
M. Popović – P. Pouchelle – I. Rosen-Zvi – J. T. A. G. M. van Ruiten – M. Segal
J. Sievers – L. T. Stuckenbruck – L. Teugels – J. C. de Vos – Sharon Weisser

VOLUME 217

The titles published in this series are listed at *brill.com/jsjs*

A Critical Edition of the Hebrew Manuscripts of Ben Sira

With Translations and Philological Notes

By

Frédérique Michèle Rey
Eric D. Reymond

BRILL

LEIDEN | BOSTON

The Library of Congress Cataloging-in-Publication Data is available online at https://catalog.loc.gov
LC record available at https://lccn.loc.gov/2024940955

Typeface for the Latin, Greek, and Cyrillic scripts: "Brill". See and download: brill.com/brill-typeface.

ISSN 1384-2161
ISBN 978-90-04-68135-4 (hardback)
ISBN 978-90-04-70080-2 (e-book)
DOI 10.1163/9789004700802

Copyright 2024 by Frédérique Michèle Rey and Eric D. Reymond. Published by Koninklijke Brill BV, Leiden, The Netherlands.
Koninklijke Brill BV incorporates the imprints Brill, Brill Nijhoff, Brill Schöningh, Brill Fink, Brill mentis, Brill Wageningen Academic, Vandenhoeck & Ruprecht, Böhlau and V&R unipress.
Koninklijke Brill BV reserves the right to protect this publication against unauthorized use. Requests for re-use and/or translations must be addressed to Koninklijke Brill BV via brill.com or copyright.com.

This book is printed on acid-free paper and produced in a sustainable manner.

Contents

Preface VII
Introduction IX
   1 History of Research of the Hebrew Witnesses of Ben Sira   IX
       1.1 *The Manuscripts of the Cairo Genizah*   IX
       1.2 *The Dead Sea Scrolls: Discoveries and Editions of the Fragments of Ben Sira*   X
       1.3 *Preceding Editions of the Hebrew Text*   XI
       1.4 *Preceding Translations of the Hebrew Text*   XII
   2 The Hebrew Witnesses   XIII
       2.1 *The Genizah Manuscripts*   XIII
            2.1.1 MS A   XIII
            2.1.2 MS B   XIII
            2.1.3 MS C   XIV
            2.1.4 MS D   XIV
            2.1.5 MS E   XV
            2.1.6 MS F   XV
       2.2 *Dead Sea Scrolls and Masada Scroll*   XV
            2.2.1 2Q18   XV
            2.2.2 11QPs^a [= 11Q5]   XVI
            2.2.3 Masada Scroll   XVI
       2.3 *Quotations of Ben Sira in Rabbinic Literature*   XVI
       2.4 *The "Rhyming" Paraphrase*   XVI
       2.5 *Manuscript Charts*   XVII
            2.5.1 List of Folios and Bifolios of Each Manuscript   XVII
            2.5.2 Images of the Manuscripts   XXI
            2.5.3 Parallels between Manuscripts   XXII
   3 Conventions of the Edition   XXIII
       3.1 *Theoretical Framework of the Edition*   XXIII
       3.2 *Edition of the Hebrew Texts*   XXIV
       3.3 *Critical Apparatuses*   XXV
       3.4 *French and English Translations*   XXVII
       3.5 *Stemma of the Hebrew Manuscripts*   XXVII
   4 Abbreviations and Sigla   XXIX

Critical Edition

   Manuscript A   1
   Manuscript B   69
   Manuscript C   179
   Manuscript D   193
   Manuscript E   205
   Manuscript F   213
   Paraphrase of Ben Sira   221
   2Q18   257
   11QPs^a 263
   Masada Scroll   267

Bibliography   289
Index of Modern Authors   303
Index of Ancient Sources   305

Preface

This edition of the Hebrew text of Ben Sira is the result of almost fifteen years of work, a continuation of Rey's work on 4QInstruction and Reymond's work on the Ben Sira Masada Scroll. When we began work, we recognized that there was no contemporary critical edition of the Hebrew of Ben Sira that met modern standards. The earliest commentaries on the Hebrew were out of date and the more recent editions (e.g., those of Z. Ben Ḥayyim and P. C. Beentjes) had, for different reasons, significant problems. To make their own judgments on specific readings, most scholars (who did not have easy access to the manuscripts themselves) had to rely on the imperfect facsimile edition of the Genizah manuscripts published in 1901 and on photographs published in books and journals. Soon after beginning the project, digital photographs of all the manuscripts became easily available online[1] and it is this development that has allowed us to move forward with the present edition relatively quickly. Moreover, there existed no complete English or French translations of all the Hebrew witnesses.

Many people, friends and institutions have been extremely important in the realization of this project. First of all we would like to thank Hindy Najman and Benjamin G. Wright who greatly encouraged us in the realization of this project and who supported us in submitting it for publication in the series Supplements to the Journal for the Study of Judaism. Our thanks also go to the Ben Sira team of researchers that meets almost each year at SBL for a nice dinner together: Benjamin G. Wright, Elisa Uusimäki, Greg Goering, Frank Ueberschaer, Jeremy Corley, Matthew Goff, Lindsey Askin, Samuel Adams, Gerhard Karner, David Skelton, James Aitken†, Bradley Gregory, Andrew Jordan Schmidt, Marieke Dhont to which we must add Maurice Gilbert and Nuria Calduch Benages. Among these scholars, Émile Puech deserves a special thanks for having accepted to proofread our translations with his usual scrupulousness. This was a precious help. An additional thanks is extended to the anonymous reviewers of our manuscript, who helped to improve it in many ways. It goes without saying that all the remaining errors are our own. A special thanks also goes to Ingo Kottsieper, Annette Steudel, Bronson Brown-deVost and Reinhard Kratz that gave us access to the Qumran Wörterbuch database, their own edition and German translation of the Hebrew manuscripts, as well as morphological analysis and collation of all the preceding readings.[2] It was an incredible help.

Our work has also been supported by numerous institutions. First and foremost libraries that welcomed and supported us: the library of the Jewish Theological Seminary and its curator of manuscripts David Kraemer who was incredibly helpful; the Cambridge University Library and especially Ben Outhwaite, the head of the Genizah Research Unit, who was more than a support; he was a friend and a provider of numerous pieces of advice and suggestions. The Alliance Israélite Universelle Library in Paris and its curators, Jean-Claude Kuperminc and Amaury Toulouse, who have always welcomed us so generously. The Bodleian library of Oxford and in particular César Merchán-Hamann and, finally, the British Library of London.

The project has been financially supported by the laboratoire Écritures (EA3943) and the MSH Lorraine of the University of Lorraine, Yale Divinity School, Yale University, including the Jewish Studies Program and the department of Near Eastern Languages and Civilizations, the ANR/DFG through the PLURITEXT project, the Humboldt Stiftung foundation, which allowed Rey to spend two wonderful years between Berlin and the Martin-Luther Halle-Wittenberg University. We thank them all.

Finally, several postdocs have also actively participated in this project: Marieke Dont with whom we worked on the codicological characteristics of manuscript B and who participated in the English translation of chapters 13 to 16; Myles Schoonover; Jennifer Andruska who worked on the translation into English of all the notes that were written in French and the corrections of the English. Andruska also proposed a first English translation of Rey's French translation, which was completely revised by Reymond. In addition to these, Antonella Bellantuono prepared the critical apparatuses of Masada and 11QPs[a] and verified all the critical apparatuses. She also prepared the codicological and palaeographic description of the Masada manuscript which will be published in the complete introduction.

Finally, we would like to thank our predecessors, those giants, without whom our work could not be what it is: I. Lévi, R. Smend, N. Peters, G. H. Box, W. O. E. Oesterley, M. Z. Segal, P. Skehan, A. Di Lella, M. Kister and W. van Peursen. We have tried to quote our sources as

---

1 See the two websites genizah.org and bensira.org.

2 See now here: https://lexicon.qumran-digital.org/.

systematically as possible; we hope we have not forgotten any, but if we have, please forgive us. By dint of reading and rereading comments of these scholars, it happened that we sometimes have forgotten that a particular solution was already advanced by our predecessors. We owe them so much; without their work nothing of what has been produced here would have been possible.

The work was divided as follows, Rey prepared chapters 3 to 39 and Reymond chapters 40 to 51 (and the corresponding manuscripts) as well as the paraphrase of Ben Sira. Everything has been revised together. (Jan Joosten participated only minimally and only in oral communication with regard to a couple of chapters. After we learned of his conviction, he had nothing more to do with the project.)

I, Eric Reymond, would also like to thank Frédérique Michèle Rey for having invited me to participate in this project. In short, working with her on this edition has been one of the highlights of my career. The many hours we have spent testing our understanding of different words and phrases, puzzling over broken passages, have been not only enlightening, but also exhilerating.

I also wish to thank my friends and colleagues, many of whom have already been mentioned above. I have learned a tremendous amount from them, not only about Ben Sira and ancient Hebrew, but also on the necessity of collaboration. Sam Adams has been a particular boon to me as we are also collaborating on a commentary on Ben Sira together and our conversations have led me to many new interpretations of the text. From Sam's generous readings and observations I have learned so much. In addition, I thank my many colleagues at Yale, especially those I have consulted about Hebrew, Ben Sira, and Wisdom literature, including Joel Baden, John Collins, Jimmy Daccache, Steven Fraade, Jacqueline Vayntrub, Robert Wilson, and Molly Zahn. I also wish to extend a thanks to my students at Yale Divinity School, with whom I have read many chapters of Ben Sira, often sharing with them preliminary versions of this edition. It is, in part, from their instruction that my knowledge of ancient languages has been allowed and encouraged to flourish.

Most importantly, I wish to thank my family. My wife, Robin, and children, Jo and Oliver, have patiently listened to numerous accounts of new readings that Frédérique Michèle and I have made in the course of our work. Few people have had to listen to so many excited descriptions of *vav*s, *yod*s, *bet*s, and *kaf*s. Thank you. Your love means more than all the alphabets of the world.

I, Frédérique Michèle Rey, would also like to thank my companion and friend on this journey, Eric Reymond. We have shared a few hours together, in Adamswiller, Metz, Oxford and New Haven, and a lot of hours in videoconference these last years. Working with him has been one of the most beautiful things one can imagine for a scientific work in common. I learned a lot from him.

I also thank my mother and my sisters, Mary Joly, Rafaëlle and Emmanuelle Rey for their proofreading of the French translation. Many friends accompanied us throughout this journey: Florentino and Annie García Martínez, Émile Puech, Hindy Najman, Stefan Schorch, Noam Mizrahi, Pablo A. Torijano, Andrés Piquer Otero, Corrado Martone, Charlotte Hempel, Katell Berthelot. My colleagues, friends and students from the University of Lorraine deserve special thanks. Being integrated in a Humanities faculty and in a laboratoire where literary scholars, Hispanists, Italianists, Anglicists, philosophers, and art specialists all work together, has radically changed and transformed the way I conceive texts and interact with them. It has been an incredible richness. These exchanges have not only taken place through joint seminars, but above all by sharing a drink on a beautiful terrace in Metz or a good meal in the evening during which we could change the world. Among them, I want to mention, in particular, Claire Placial, Julien Abed, Anthony Feneuil, Fabien Faul, Sylvie Barnay, Magali Myoupo, Marion Deschamp, Julien Léonard, Yves Meessen, Sophie Robert-Hayek and Davide D'Amico.

A special thanks to the École Biblique et Archéologique Française de Jérusalem (EBAF), which is for me more than a school or a library, but a home in which I grew up, in which I feel comfortable and which reassures me. I also spent a lot of time in the Staatsbibliothek zur Berlin in Potsdamer Platz. Like the École, this place has left an indelible mark on my soul. A special thanks also to all the cafés where I spent hours working.

Finally, throughout this work, I have been accompanied by the unconditional love, the benevolence, the unfailing support in everything, the courage, the strength of my spouse, Maryla Strzechodzka Rey, and of my two incredible daughters, Juliette and Clémence. You are the love of my life, my whole.

At the end, we would like to thank Karina Martin Hogan and René Bloch for having accepted this book into the collection Supplements to the Journal for the Study of Judaism. Our thanks go also to Suzanne Mekking, Maaike Langerak, Gera van Bedaf and Marjolein van Zuylen for their patience, their encouragement and their help. The royalties of this book will be given to an association for abused children and women who have suffered sexual violence.

Introduction

Until the end of the 19th century, Ben Sira's book was known mainly through Greek and Syriac translations made from Hebrew *Vorlagen*, as well as secondary translations like the Latin (based on the Greek). Since that time, the Hebrew text of Ben Sira has been partially rediscovered among the manuscripts of the Cairo Genizah and the Dead Sea Scrolls (Qumran and Masada). Although these witnesses were carefully studied during the twentieth century, a complete edition of all the fragments, accompanied by a codicological analysis, a translation and a systematic philological commentary is still lacking. The aim of the present edition is to fill these gaps. In this abbreviated introduction, an expansion of which will be published subsequently as a separate volume, we will present the publication history of the various Hebrew witnesses, a short presentation of each manuscript and the methodology implemented in the project.

1 History of Research of the Hebrew Witnesses of Ben Sira[1]

1.1 *The Manuscripts of the Cairo Genizah*

In 1896, Agnes Smith Lewis and Margaret Dunlop Gibson bought a sheet of paper with Hebrew characters in southern Palestine.[2] Solomon Schechter of the University of Cambridge identified this folio as the original Hebrew text of Ben Sira[3] and published this first fragment in the journal *The Expositor* in July of the same year.[4] It was the manuscript later labeled MS B (Or 1102; Sir 39:15–40:7), which Schechter dated to the eleventh century (though it is now thought to date from around 1000 in Fustat).[5]

In the following year, in 1897, A. E. Cowley and A. Neubauer[6] republished the fragment together with nine new folios which the Bodleian Library had acquired through A. H. Sayce (Ms.Heb.e.62; Sir 40:9–49:11).[7] These first publications gave rise to a series of discoveries over the next three years. Manuscript fragments appeared in Cambridge, Oxford, at the British Museum, in Paris and in private collections.

In 1899, Schechter was authorized to obtain the remaining manuscripts from the Genizah and bring them to the Cambridge library. In that year, he published with Charles Taylor a new batch of Ben Sira fragments, including those from MS B discovered in the Cairo Genizah on August 27th 1897 (T-S 16.312 [Sir 30:11–31:11 and Sir 37:27–38:27], T-S 16.313 [Sir 32:1–33:3 and 35:11–36:21], T-S 16.314 [Sir 49:12–51:30]),[8] as well as two folios of a new manuscript, labeled MS A, discovered on September 2nd and 24th, 1897, respectively (T-S 12.863 and T-S 12.864 [Sir 3:6–7:29 and 11:34–16:26]).[9] At the end of 1898, the British Museum acquired a bifolio of MS B published by G. Margoliouth (Or 5518.2 [Sir 31:12–31:31 and Sir 36:22–37:26]).[10] In 1900, I. Lévi published two new folios acquired by the Bibliothèque du Consistoire Israélite of Paris, which proved to be completely different from the two previous manuscripts A and B.[11] These were two new manuscripts of Ben Sira labeled eventually MS C (ID1 [Sir 6:18b, 19, 28, 35; 7:1, 4, 6, 17, 20, 21, 23–25; 8:7]) and MS D (ID2 [Sir 36:24–38:1]). That same year, Schechter identified and published another bifolio of MS C (T-S 12.727 [Sir 4:23b, 30–31; 5:4–7, 9–13; 36:19a and Sir 25:8, 13, 17–24; 26:1–2a]);[12] Elkan Nathan Adler acquired and published two additional folios of MS A (ENA 2536 [Sir 7:29–12:1]);[13] Moses Gaster edited another folio of MS C (actually lost

---

1 For an overview of the state of research, see Gilbert 2011 and more recently Reymond 2019a. All the bibliographical references and reviews up to 1998 can be found in Reiterer et al. 1998. The introduction to this volume (Reiterer 1998) contains a summary of the history of the publication of the text. For the history of discovery, see also Reif 1997. Finally, for the history of discovery of the Cairo Genizah collection, see in particular Reif 2000.
2 This discovery became public in a letter dated 16 May 1896 sent from Mrs. Lewis to the Academy (Lewis 1896, 405; see also Anonymous 1896, 481–482). For more on these women, see Janet Soskice, *The Sisters of Sinai: How Two Lady Adventurers Discovered the Hidden Gospels* (New York: Knopf, 2009).
3 See the letter of May 13th 1896 from Schechter to Lewis (https://www.bensira.org/schechter_letters.html).
4 Schechter 1896.
5 Olszowy-Schlanger 2018, 92.
6 Cowley and Neubauer 1897. See also Bacher 1897, 543–572. J. Halévy (1897) published the Hebrew text and a French translation of the fragments published by Cowley and Neubauer as well as the fragment of Lewis and Gibson published by Schechter; see also Smend 1897.
7 Cowley and Neubauer 1897, xii. This discovery had already been mentioned by Driver in *The Guardian*, July 1st, 1896, cited in Anonymous 1896, 481–82.
8 The folio T.S. 16.314 (49:12–50:22) had been previously published by Schechter (1898).
9 Schechter and Taylor 1899. See also Bacher 1900a.
10 Margoliouth 1899b. The discovery was announced in *The Times* on 4th April 1899. See also Schechter 1900b.
11 Lévi 1900.
12 Schechter 1900a. The fragment was completed in 1982 by A. Scheiber (1982) with photographs republished in Di Lella 1988.
13 Adler 1900.

[Sir 18:31b–33; 19:1–2; 20:5–7; 37:19, 22, 24, 26; 20:13])[14] which turned out to be the second half (bifolio) of the fragment published by Lévi (ID1). In 1901, all the manuscripts so far discovered were published in facsimile by the Oxford and Cambridge University presses.[15]

Other fragments were identified during the 20th and 21st centuries, both in the Taylor-Schechter collection and in private collections. In 1931, Joseph Marcus discovered a new Ben Sira fragment from the Adler Collection at the Jewish Theological Seminary in New York. It was a new manuscript: MS E (ENA 3597 [Sir 32:16–34:1]).[16] In 1958, and again in 1960, J. Schirmann identified two new folios of MS B (T-S 12.871 [Sir 10:19–11:10] and T-S NS 38a.1 [Sir 15:1–16:7]) and two folios from MS C (T-S 12.867 [Sir 3:14–18, 21–22; 41:16; 4:21; 20:22–23a and Sir 26:2b–3, 13, 15–17; 36:22–26]) in the Cambridge Library.[17] In February 1982, the Hungarian researcher Alexander Scheiber discovered a new fragment that Di Lella identified as a new copy of Ben Sira's book: MS F (T-S AS 213.17 [Sir 31:24–32:7; 32:12–33:8]).[18] In 2007, in a public auction organized by the Bernard Quaritch House in London, a new folio from MS C of the Cairo Genizah was identified. Shulamit Elizur published a first edition of it (Private collection Gifford Combs [Sir 36:24; 6:5–6; 37:1–2; 6:7, 9, 10, 8, 12–15; 3:27; 6:18 and Sir 22:11cd–12; 22:21–22; 23:11; 25:7; 20:30–31; 21:22, 23, 26; 22:11ab]).[19] Finally, in 2011, Sarah Cohen identified a new fragment of MS D in the additional series of the Taylor-Schechter collection. The Hebrew text was edited by Shulamit Elizur and Michael Rand in 2011 (T-S AS 118.78 [Sir 7:18–8:18]) and we re-edited this fragment in 2012.[20]

It is to be hoped that other fragments of Ben Sira are still to be found among the many as yet unidentified (or misidentified) manuscripts of the Cairo Genizah and in particular in the additional series of the Taylor-Schechter Collection.

1.2 The Dead Sea Scrolls: Discoveries and Editions of the Fragments of Ben Sira

The first studies of the Hebrew manuscripts discovered in the Cairo Genizah focused on the question of their authenticity: Were they a form of the original Hebrew text, or a retroversion into Hebrew dating from medieval times?[21] The debate was definitively closed by the discovery of Hebrew fragments of Ben Sira near the Dead Sea, first at Qumran and then in Masada, since these fragments correspond in general to the texts discovered earlier in the Genizah.[22]

At the end of February 1952, two small fragments of a manuscript that contained Sir 6:14–15 (or Sir 1:19–20) and Sir 6:20–31 were identified among the lot of manuscripts found in Cave 2.[23] The text was published by M. Baillet, who dated it to the second half (specifically, to the third quarter) of the 1st century BCE. This first discovery, although very fragmentary, confirmed the authenticity of MS A from the Genizah and the antiquity of the stichometric presentation of MS B.

In February 1956, Bedouins discovered cave 11 which contained, among other things, a scroll of the Psalms (11QPs^a). It was unrolled in November of 1961 and contained, among many psalms known from the biblical book, a portion of Ben Sira (Sir 51:13–19, 30; 11QPs^a XXI–XXII, after Ps 138:1–8 and before the non-Masoretic acrostic poem often labeled "Apostrophe to Zion").[24] Paleography suggested the manuscript dated to the first half of the 1st century CE.

On April 8th, 1964, archaeologists discovered a scroll containing Sir 39:27–44:17 in a casemate in the eastern wall of Masada.[25] The text was published by Y. Yadin in 1965.[26] It contains seven columns of text in stichometry, commonly dated to the 1st century BCE. These fragments are of capital importance, firstly, for their antiquity, dating from just over a century after the text's composition, and secondly, because of the breadth of the preserved text, which overlaps with large portions of MS B. The overlaps coincide with the medieval manuscript (and in particular its marginal notes) as well as the older versions. This witness definitively put an end to the debate over the authenticity of the Cairo Genizah manuscripts.

---

14 Gaster 1900.
15 Anonymous 1901. For more on the context of this early era of Genizah discoveries, one should consult Rebecca J. W. Jefferson, *The Cairo Genizah and the Age of Discovery in Egypt* (London: Bloomsbury, 2022).
16 Marcus 1931.
17 Schirmann 1958 and Schirmann 1960. See also Di Lella 1964.
18 Scheiber 1982 and Di Lella 1988.
19 Elizur 2006, republished in English as Elizur 2010. See also Rey 2008a.
20 Elizur and Rand 2011; Rey 2012.
21 Note, in particular, the controversy between Schechter and D. S. Margoliouth. See D. S. Margoliouth 1899. Note how König (1899a, 1899b, 1899c, 1899d) reacted. Concerning authors who questioned the authenticity of the fragments, see also Bickell 1899; Torrey 1950; Ginsberg 1955.
22 Yadin 1965; Segal 1964; Martone 1997; Puech 1999, 2008.
23 Baillet, Milik and de Vaux 1962. For a review of this edition, see Puech 1999, 413–414.
24 Edition by Sanders 1965, 79–85. For text reconstruction, see Puech 2011.
25 The following verses are not preserved in the scroll: 39:33–40:7; 40:9–10, 22–25; 43:26–28, 30–33.
26 Yadin 1965, 1967, 1999. See also Milik 1966; Baumgarten 1968; Skehan 1968, 1974; Strugnell 1969; Qimron 1999; Reymond 2014.

Actually, we estimate that over two-thirds of the Hebrew text has been recovered through six medieval manuscripts dating from the 10th and 13th centuries, MS A, B, C, D, E and F, and three witnesses from the late Second Temple era, 2Q18, 11QPs[a] and Masada, not to mention the quotations in various other sources like the Mishnah, Talmuds, and the "Rhyming" Paraphrase.

1.3 Preceding Editions of the Hebrew Text

Apart from the preliminary editions published in the various articles and monographs cited above, three major publications contain both an edition of the Hebrew text and a philological commentary:[27] those of Israel Lévi, Rudolf Smend and Norbert Peters.[28] Of these, only the commentary by Lévi focuses specifically on the Hebrew text; the other two consider all the versions with the aim of reconstructing the "original" text. This means that, most of the time, when a form is not considered "original," it is discarded and it is the corrected form that is analyzed and commented on. In addition to these first commentaries, another major contribution was made by M. Z. Segal,[29] whose edition and commentary, in addition to providing a vocalized text of the extant Hebrew fragments, also offers a retroversion of those passages preserved only in Greek and/or Syriac.[30]

After the discovery of the Hebrew witnesses at Qumran and Masada, several new editions of all the witnesses were published. Francesco Vattioni of the University of Naples published a critical edition of the Hebrew text in 1968[31] together with a synopsis of the Greek, Latin and Syriac versions, as well as the rabbinic quotations of Ben Sira. The Hebrew text of the Genizah manuscripts was based on the editions of Lévi, supplemented by observations from the facsimiles.

In 1973, Ze'ev Ben-Ḥayyim[32] published an edition of the Hebrew text with a valuable concordance and analysis of the vocabulary. This high-quality edition follows the order of the chapters and verses of the Greek text, as opposed to the order preserved in the individual Hebrew witnesses. This allows one to compare the Hebrew to the Greek more easily, but obscures the organization and coherence of the individual Hebrew manuscripts themselves, especially MS C, which is an anthology. In any case, although lacking the more recent discoveries,[33] this edition remains the most reliable at the present time.

In 1986, Pietro Boccaccio and Guido Berardi produced a new edition of the Hebrew manuscripts which has not been widely distributed and is not easily accessible. Just over ten years later, in 1997, Pancratius Beentjes published a new edition that aimed to be more complete than the edition of Ben-Ḥayyim, to represent the order of verses in the Hebrew manuscripts and to offer a synoptic presentation of the various witnesses.[34] This was an important innovation in presentation and helped scholars understand the peculiar character of the individual manuscripts.[35] Basing its readings of the Genizah manuscripts on the facsimile edition, it is a rather minimalist edition and offers few suggestions for partially preserved text. Perhaps due to this reliance on the facsimiles, the edition contains numerous errors, despite some corrections that were made in 2002[36] and incorporated into the 2006 edition.[37]

Another edition of all extant Hebrew manuscripts is provided by Martin Abegg in the Accordance module "Ben Sira," also available for the Genizah manuscripts at www.bensira.org, the website created by Gary Rendsburg and Jacob Binstein.[38] The Accordance version allows the user to orient the text according to the verse sequence of the Greek as well as by the sequence of verses attested in the individual Hebrew manuscripts. Abegg's edition is somewhat less minimalist in its approach than Beentjes's, but still does not record many letters and words that are clearly visible in the digital photographs. Due to the fact that the edition is accompanied by a translation (by Abegg) and grammatical tagging (by Abegg and Casey Towes), and can be synchronized with Greek, Syriac, Latin, and other modern translations, it is enormously helpful in making sense of the text. In addition, the website www.bensira.org is also extremely helpful in that it provides easy access to the digital images of the manuscripts

---

27 See in addition: Knabenbauer 1902 (not consulted); Strack 1903.
28 Lévi 1898, 1901; Smend 1906a, 1906b; Peters 1902. See also Lévi 1904; Peters 1905, 1913.
29 Segal 1958.
30 A preceding Hebrew transcription and retroversion was given by A. Kahana 1939 (we thank Noam Mizrahi for this reference). Two retroversions into Hebrew on the basis of Greek and/or Syriac were made in the eighteenth and nineteenth centuries by Y. Leib Ben-Ze'ev 1798 and S. I. Fraenkel 1830. See also Fritzsche 1859.
31 Vattioni 1968.
32 Ben Ḥayyim 1973.
33 Nevertheless, MS F which is not integrated in the edition, is included in the microfiche version of 1988 and available in the database of Maagarim (http://hebrew-treasures.huji.ac.il/).
34 Beentjes 1997a–2006.
35 See the review of the book by Puech 2003a.
36 Beentjes 2002.
37 E.g.: in Sir 3:28, the 1997 edition reads רפואה כי מנטע while the 2006 edition omits כי. In Sir 16:15, the edition of 1997 read לא ידעו; the erasure of the first לא is missing in the 2006 edition.
38 Abegg and Towes 2007–2009; Abegg 2022 (accessed); Rendsburg and Binstein 2022 (accessed).

together with their transliterations and translations by Abegg and other scholars.

Another electronic edition is provided at maagarim .hebrew-academy.org.il, the website of The Academy of the Hebrew Language / The Historical Dictionary Project. This website also provides limited grammatical tagging and translations of Hebrew words. Like Ben-Ḥayyim's edition, on which it is based, it follows the sequence of verses in the Greek translation.

In the final stages of our edition, thanks to Ingo Kottsieper, Reinhard Kratz and Annette Steudel and their Qumran-WörterBuch project, we were able to access the database of texts used to compile their dictionary, *Hebräisches und aramäisches Wörterbuch zu den Texten vom Toten Meer*.[39] The text of Ben Sira has been revised by the dictionary team and is accompanied by a morphological analysis; the variants between the different editions have also been very carefully collated. Renate Egger-Wenzel has most recently (2022) published a synopsis of the different versions of the book, giving each stich its own line and the Hebrew, Greek, Syriac, and Latin versions each their own column. The edition of the Hebrew text presented in this work is minimal in a similar way to Beentjes's, though it does also offer in footnotes a helpful summary of the readings made by past scholars. We are sorry that, due to its late arrival, we were not able to use it.

1.4 *Preceding Translations of the Hebrew Text*

With the exception of the editiones principes and the French translation by Lévi (1899, 1901), very few early works offer a translation directly from the Hebrew manuscripts.[40] Segal (1958) does translate some phrases into modern Hebrew when they are otherwise obscure, and Box and Oesterley (1913) often prioritize the Hebrew text, and, when they do not, they offer a translation of the Hebrew in their notes. Nevertheless, both works seem to be premised on a synthesis of all the versions.

In recent years, more attention has been given to translating the Hebrew itself. For example, Martin Abegg has translated the Hebrew into English in Accordance software (2007, 2009) (≅ www.bensira.org), while Charles Mopsik has translated the Hebrew into French (Mopsik 2003) and Victor Morla the Hebrew into Spanish (Morla 2012).[41] Nevertheless, these translations still present various problems. Abegg's often reflects only the general sense of the Hebrew words, especially where the Hebrew is obscure; the result is a translation that at times does not help to explicate the Hebrew (e.g., והניחתך in Sir 6:3 is translated "And you will be laid low" though the verb is unambiguously third person).[42] Mopsik offers only a single running translation and so does not highlight the peculiarities of individual manuscripts; in addition, he sometimes presupposes a modification of the Hebrew in accordance with Skehan and Di Lella 1987. Morla, for his part, offers perhaps the closest model to our own translation, with each manuscript translated independently, though his readings tend to be much more minimal than ours. Moreover, his notes often reflect an interest in reading the Hebrew according to the interpretation of the versions.

In addition, again with the exception of the early commentaries (including Segal's), very few translations offer consistent, detailed explanations of individual Hebrew words and their syntax. This is a particularly significant gap given the fact that the Hebrew is very often obscure, containing numerous hapaxes, and has experienced various significant alterations during its transmission with the result that many phrases have become enigmatic. Philological commentary is also beneficial given the fact that the Hebrew text has a syntax and semantics characteristic of the Hellenistic period, an era whose Hebrew has received less attention in dictionaries and grammars (though this is gradually changing).[43]

---

39 The lexicon (Kratz, Steudel and Kottsieper 2017, 2019) and a concordance are now available online ("Qumran-Digital," https://lexicon.qumran-digital.org/ [accessed November 24, 2022]).

40 Concerning the French translations of the Hebrew witnesses, mention should be made of the work of J. Halévy 1897 and that of M. J. Touzard 1904.

41 However, it must be acknowledged that Mopsik's as well as Lévi's commentary / translation (1899, 1901) have been of immense help and influence in our work, and we have found in them many extraordinary gems in terms of interpretation and literary innovation.

42 Cf. our translation "and (your appetite would) leave you like a withered tree." Consider also Sir 31:20. Abegg translates: "Refreshing sleep for the inside of the one who is moderate, and rising up with a clear mind." Cf. our translation: "Restorative sleep (comes from) a stomach that is clean. When one rises in the morning, one has an appetite."

43 Since the publication of the texts of Qumran, our knowledge of post-biblical Hebrew has made significant progress, which allows us to better locate and understand the text of Ben Sira. See in particular the various conferences dedicated to the Hebrew of the post-biblical period: Muraoka and Elwolde 1997, 1999, 2000; Joosten and Rey 2008; Fassberg, Bar-Asher and Clements 2013; Tigchelaar and van Hecke 2015; Joosten, Machiela and Rey 2018; Fassberg 2021.

2 The Hebrew Witnesses

2.1 *The Genizah Manuscripts*[44]

The Ben Sira manuscripts from the Cairo Genizah number six, conventionally labeled by letters: A–F. In addition to these, a "Rhyming" Paraphrase of Ben Sira is attested in a separate manuscript. The Genizah manuscripts share certain characteristics. Excluding the Paraphrase, all but MS B are codices "on cheap paper, without ruling or calligraphic efforts," probably intended for personal libraries.[45] MSS B, E, and F are written stichometrically, with each distich being divided into two columns. The other manuscripts (A, C, D, and the paraphrase) are written akin to prose, though verse divisions are indicated by spaces and/or marks (e.g., dots). With the exception of MS C, the manuscripts all exhibit some Tiberian vowels and/or scribal features. The texts in these manuscripts have undergone numerous transformations over time, sometimes as a result of accidental errors or intentional changes, or a combination of both. In addition, doublets to some verses are frequently attested; some are found within the text itself, some as marginal additions. Sometimes the same doublet is found in more than one manuscript, suggesting a common ancestor (e.g., Sir 32:16 in MSS B, E, F). Nevertheless, doublets in the Sirach manuscripts are not all the result of a unique phenomenon. Some are certainly the result of collation of double readings, associated with stylistic creativity and/or retroversion from Syriac.[46]

2.1.1 MS A[47]

MS A consists of three bifolios of Egyptian paper[48] measuring 22.2 × 17.7 cm. The paper is yellowish and has a fairly regular horizontal chain line. There are two rulings on the right and left, probably impressed with a *masṭara* (or ruling board). The justification is rather approximate, the scribe frequently dilates the last or penultimate letter; more rarely they constrict the last letters and on some occasions insert graphic fillers (freely drawn horizontal lines or circles). The scribe of MS A has recently been identified as Abraham ben Shabbetai, who acted as *muqaddam* in Minyat Zifta (Egypt) around 1110.[49] He seems to have come to Egypt from Tyre in the 1090s, perhaps having previously traveled to Tyre from Jerusalem, following the trajectory of the Palestinian yeshiva presumably in the wake of conflict between Seljuks and Fatimids.[50] In any event, he seems to have had some connection to the Palestinian yeshiva and community in Egypt.[51] This implies, all things considered, that the manuscript was copied sometime around the year 1100 CE.[52]

The manuscript contains only a few marginal and interlinear corrections and the scribe is far from being systematic, implementing various means to correct copying errors (words or letters crossed out, cancelation dots, marginal or interlinear corrections and one case of *ketiv / qere* marginal correction [at Sir 8:2]). Some words are supplied with Tiberian vowels and cantillation marks. In rare cases, what seem to be Babylonian cantillation marks have been added (Sir 11:25 and 15:14).[53] The supplementation of words with vowels in some cases seems to have been for the purpose of suggesting alternative pronunciations / interpretations (akin to the *qere / ketiv* distinctions found in the MT); see, for example, Sir 6:22. The scribe used several different means of punctuation: two dots (*sof pasuq*), a suspended dot, spaces (or *vacat*s) and indentations. In many passages MS A seems close to the Syriac translation, an affinity exemplified by the three verses after Sir 1:20 that are known only elsewhere from the Syriac and which seem to reflect an eschatological perspective, otherwise at odds with Ben Sira's theology.

2.1.2 MS B[54]

To date, MS B is comprised of four individual folios and eight bifolios, each folio measuring 19.7 × 17.5 cm.[55] It is distinct from the other manuscripts in that it consists of more carefully ordered lines (18 per folio), ruled with a *masṭara* (or ruling board), on higher quality paper.[56] The text has been written stichometrically, as in the 2Q18, Masada scroll and in MSS E and F. Each manuscript line contains two stichs. The first stich is aligned along the right margin and is not justified. The positioning of the second stich is less systematic, as the spacing between the two stichs on one line is irregular. Sometimes the scribe has tried to adjust the position of the second stich with the intention of aligning its left edge along the

---

44 This section relies on Reymond 2019a.
45 Olszowy-Schlanger 2018, 92.
46 Rey 2021a.
47 For more details, see Rey 2017.
48 Olszowy-Schlanger 2018, 85.
49 See Olszowy-Schlanger 2018, 78–84.
50 See Olszowy-Schlanger 2018, 78–79.
51 Olszowy-Schlanger 2018, 79.
52 The first identification of a connection between MS A and these documents is by Edna Engel in Sirat, Glatzer and Beit-Arié 2002, 32 n. 6; Rey 2017 and Olszowy-Schlanger 2018 further elaborated on this connection.
53 Rey 2017, 106.
54 For more detail, see Rey and Dhont 2019.
55 MS B was composed of six irregular quires made up of the following number of bifolios: 3 + 5 + 6 + 4 + 6 +1 (Rey and Dhont 2019, 99–102).
56 Olszowy-Schlanger 2018, 86.

left margin, but the scribe is not at all consistent in this regard. Letter dilatation is rather rare while the constriction of characters is relatively frequent, especially where the scribe includes an extra stich in the line (i.e., in cases of tristichs).[57]

Words are vocalized only sporadically so that, in contrast to MS A, whole verses are never vocalized (except for the marginal reading of Sir 36:6). In at least three instances, MS B contains Babylonian vocalization (Sir 38:17 margin, Sir 42:3 and Sir 42:18). The divine name is systematically written as three *yod*s.

In three instances the scribe has included titles to introduce a new section (Sir 31:12; 41:14 and 44:1). In a few instances, there are blank lines separating thematic sections and a change in subject (between Sir 10:27, 28; Sir 15:15, 16; Sir 37:31 and 38:1; 38:23, 24; 42:8, 9; 42:14, 15 and 51:12, 13). We also find a marginal *pe* with three dots on top (Sir 36:1; 36:23; 38:13; 51:12a) presumably as an abbreviation for פתוחה "opening."[58]

One of the most characteristic points of MS B is the presence of numerous marginal annotations. The manuscript seems to have served as a kind of critical edition, with alternative readings supplied from at least one other manuscript — one belonging to the same family as MSS A, D, E and F — and perhaps also from ancient translations as well. More so than the other manuscripts, it seems to show affinities with the Babylonian cultural sphere, including scribal notes in the margin that are written in Judeo-Persian.[59] Nevertheless, its paleography has its closest parallels in documents from Egypt, from the late tenth to the early eleventh centuries,[60] implying that MS B is likely the earliest of the Ben Sira manuscripts, dating to around the year 1000.[61]

Unlike MS A, which reflects the work of a single scribe, MS B seems to contain the work of at least two, probably three scribes: 1) the primary scribe who wrote most of the main text and possibly some of the marginal writings; 2) a second scribe who wrote the Judeo-Persian marginal notes (at 32:1; 35:26, 40:26; 45:8), most of the other marginal alternatives and filled in a blank line at Sir 35:26 (a blank line that was left by the primary scribe); 3) a third scribe who wrote a few marginal words scattered across the manuscript, not adhering to the layout of the previous scribes (e.g., writing words at an angle, infra- and supralinear annotations and notes written at the very edge of the paper).[62]

2.1.3   MS C

MS C consists of eight folios and four bifolios. Characterized by a diminutive size (14 × 10 cm) and poor quality paper,[63] it is an anthology of Ben Sira passages. The verses are topically grouped around practical social themes like shame, speech, friendship, and wives. Most philosophical and metaphoric language associated with wisdom and God is avoided. For example, it mentions God only five times.[64] Within the topically organized sections, verses sometimes appear out of the order found in other manuscripts and translations. The verses often seem organized according to a common opening word or catch phrase that links verses together. By virtue of this different sequencing of verses, sometimes the text in MS C expresses ideas distinct from those found in parallel passages.[65]

The scribe of MS C produced other manuscripts found in the Cairo Genizah, including smaller "prayer-books and *piyyuṭim*," though their identity is unknown.[66] Based on paleography, the material seems to date from at least the 13th century.[67]

2.1.4   MS D

MS D consists of two folios. The first folio was initially published in 1900 by Lévi[68] and is conserved at the Bibliothèque de l'Alliance Israélite de Paris (ID 1–2; Sir 36:29–38:1);[69] the second was identified in January 2011 by Sarah Cohen and published by Elizur and Rand in 2011[70] (T-S AS 118.78; Sir 7:18–8:18). The folio is inscribed in dark brown ink on yellowish paper measuring 123 × 165 mm (upper margin 12 mm, lower margin 22 mm, right margin 20 mm, and left margin 12 mm). The manuscript does not seem to have any ruling. The lines are curved and slightly slanted, with a line spacing of 7–8 mm (front 18 lines, back 19 lines). As noticed by Olszowy-Schlanger,[71] the script

---

57   See, for example, Sir 31:16; Sir 31:22; Sir 32:1; Sir 44:16; Sir 46:18. In two cases, there is a doublet of two stichs, that is, a quadristich written as a distich (Sir 43:30 and Sir 45:25). It seems that two cases are simply two long stichs (Sir 50:27 and Sir 51:12 although followed by a blank line).
58   Schechter and Taylor III:10 and Ginsburg 1897, 9–24, esp. 18–19.
59   Olszowy-Schlanger 2018, 87.
60   Olszowy-Schlanger 2018, 91–92.
61   Olszowy-Schlanger 2018, 92.
62   Lévi (1898, xvii) suggests the marginal notes alone attest three different hands. Wright (2018) has recently argued that there are at least two hands.
63   Olszowy-Schlanger 2018, 85.
64   Corley 2011, 22.
65   See, e.g., Corley 2011 and Reymond 2014a.
66   Olszowy-Schlanger 2018, 85.
67   Olszowy-Schlanger 2018, 85.
68   Lévi 1900.
69   We have taken multispectral images of this fragment on June 14, 2022.
70   Elizur and Rand 2011.
71   Olszowy-Schlanger 2018, 84–85.

belongs to the sub-type of the Oriental documentary script developed in the rabbinic courts in Egypt. The specific pronounced waviness and concave bars of MS D, E and F suggest they were copied around the year 1100 CE.[72] Unlike MSS E and F, MS D is not written in stichometry.

2.1.5 MS E

MS E was discovered by Joseph Marcus among the manuscripts of the Adler Collections in the Library of the Jewish Theological Seminary (ENA 3597; Sir 32:16–34:1).[73] The manuscript is now difficult to read. It is particularly dark and a visibility-altering gauze has been glued on top of it.[74]

Only one folio measuring 20 × 17 (?) cm[75] has been recovered. No ruling or pricking is visible and the space between lines is not regular (between 0.8 and 0.5 cm). The text is organized in stichometry presented in two columns. The justification of the right column is very regular for a manuscript that presents no rulings. The justification is ensured either by dilating or constricting last letters, by inscribing words obliquely along the margin or by writing the words / letters in interlinear spacing. Vocalization is rare and limited to לָךְ on recto l. 5 (Sir 32:18), as well as the divine name, which is represented by three *yod*s in a triangular pattern vocalized with a *qamets*. Like MSS D and F, MS E dates to around the year 1100 CE according to paleography and codicological observations.[76]

2.1.6 MS F

In 1982, Scheiber[77] published a new folio of Ben Sira that he erroneously considered to be a folio of MS D. A few years later, Di Lella republished the fragment under the shelfmark "MS F" as it was clearly a new, previously unknown copy of Ben Sira.[78]

The T-S AS 213.17 fragment measures 14.3 × 16.3 cm, but the top of the fragment is missing. In as much as the recto ends with Sir 32:7 and the verso starts with 32:11c, it seems 5 lines should be restored at the top of the fragment on the verso. The line spacing (between two leading lines) is about 11 mm. If one restores a margin equivalent to the lower margin of 2 cm at the head of the fragment, one can estimate the total height of the fragment to be 20.5 cm.

The ink is dark brown on an ochre colored paper with laid lines. Rulings or prickings are not visible and lines are rising. The text is arranged in stichometry (like MSS B, E, Masada and 2Q18) in two columns with right alignment for each. As for the left column, the alignment to the right is quite regular but presents some shifts on the recto (compare lines 5–14 with lines 17–24 and 26; lines 15–16 do not present any intercolumn [for a third stich]). The left margin of the second column is rather irregular, and there is no enlargement of letters to fill the end of lines. Words that exceed the line length are written either between lines or slantwise. The divine name is represented by the sequence of *yod-vav-yod* — along with a decorative element and a *qamets* under the *vav*.[79] On this folio, vocalization is rare, and its only purpose is to clarify certain ambiguous words (e.g., רֵעַ recto l. 14 [Sir 31:31]). MSS E and F present exactly the same text and similar monogenetic errors. Like MS E, MS F is written in stichometry. Additionally, MS F, like MSS D and E, dates to around the year 1100 CE according to paleography and codicological observation.[80] Notably, Böhmisch[81] has recently identified other manuscripts that seem to bear similar characteristics to MS F and may be by the same scribe. He dates the MS F to the mid-1100s CE.[82]

2.2 *Dead Sea Scrolls and Masada Scroll*

2.2.1 2Q18

Two poorly preserved fragments of Ben Sira, numbered 2Q18, were acquired from a Bedouin in 1952 and first published by Maurice Baillet in 1962 in DJD III.[83] Which part of Ben Sira fragment 1 preserves is unclear due to similar language in two different parts of the book. The identification of the text of fragment 2 is clear; the fragment preserves letters that agree with the Hebrew of MS A (Sir 6:20–22, 25, 27–31) and partially of MS C (Sir 6:28). Like Masada, MSS B, E and F, the text of 2Q18 is presented in stichometry.[84] The writing is transitional, between late Hasmonean and early Herodian (i.e. ca. 50–25 BCE).

---

72 Olszowy-Schlanger 2018, 84–85. Compare the writing with Bodl. MS heb. b.12/20 dated to 1100 or T-S NS J17 with a colophon in the hand of Evyatar ha-Kohen b. Elijah Ga'on, dated 1067 CE.

73 Marcus 1931.

74 We were able to take multispectral photos of this manuscript on November 20, 2019 which greatly improved some readings.

75 As the right part of the recto is missing, the supposed size of the folio has been estimated by assuming that the size of the right margin and first column on the recto was roughly the same as the verso.

76 Olszowy-Schlanger 2018, 84–85.

77 Scheiber 1982.

78 Di Lella 1988.

79 See Böhmisch 2020, 150.

80 Olszowy-Schlanger 2018, 84–85.

81 Böhmisch 2020, 150–55.

82 Böhmisch 2020, 155.

83 Baillet 1962. The fragments were photographed in April 1953 (PAM 40.553 [fg. 1]; PAM 40.557 [fg. 2]), in April 1958 (PAM 42.555 [fg. 2]), and in April 1959 (PAM 42.959 [fg. 1 and 2]) by Najib Anton Albina, and in November 2011 by Shai Halevi in Full Spectrum Color Image (frag. 1, B-365815, and frag. 2, B-365809). They are now preserved on plate 644.

84 According to Tov 2004, 19, 156–7, this layout is known almost exclusively for Biblical texts: "That Ben Sira was included in

2.2.2 11QPs^a [= 11Q5]

The manuscript of 11QPs^a is dated to the first half of the first century CE. It is composed of 34 columns with 49 compositions, most of them corresponding to the fourth and fifth books of Psalms, known from the Masoretic Text. 11QPs^a was discovered in 1956, unrolled in 1961 and published in 1965 by Sanders in DJD IV.[85] It contains the text of Sir 51:13–20, 30, located at the bottom of column XXI and at the top of column XXII, between Ps 138:1–8 and the "Apostrophe to Zion." The manuscript is ruled by hard point, generally with 25 lines per column, but some columns may have had 26 lines, as is probably the case for column XXI (as the material reconstruction of the text would suggest).[86] The text of 11QPs^a preserves the alphabetic structure of the poem, in contrast to MS B, which is for the most part a retroversion from the Syriac.

2.2.3 Masada Scroll

The Ben Sira Masada Scroll (MasSir) contains seven columns, which represent Sir 39:27–44:17. The text overlaps entirely with the text of MS B and at points with C (Sir 41:14–15 [// 20:30–31] and 41:16). The preserved length of the scroll is 39 cm and the original height, according to Yadin, was likely around 17 cm, which can be deduced from some portions where both the top and bottom margins have survived (e.g., col. III). The portion of the scroll discovered belongs to two sheets whose common seam had been sewn together in the manner normally found in the Qumran Scrolls. As in MSS B, E, F, and 2Q18, the text is written stichometrically. The scribe in some cases marks the beginning of a new section in different ways. The symbol ׳ occurs always in the right margin and it is used to mark poetic units: in col. II, l. 8; col. III l. 18; col. IV l. 16. At the right top of col. V a ψ is written. An empty line occurs: before l. 24 of col. VII. Paleographically speaking, the date of the scroll can be fixed approximately between 100–75 BCE, in the transitional period between the Hasmonaean and late Hasmonaean script.

2.3 *Quotations of Ben Sira in Rabbinic Literature*

The book of Ben Sira is frequently alluded to or quoted by name in Palestinian and Babylonian Talmuds, as well as in the Palestinian midrashim. It is also quoted in the *Sepher HaGaluy* of Saadia Gaon and in the *Alphabet of Ben Sira*. A list of these quotations can be found in Cowley and Neubauer[87] and in Jenny R. Labendz's study.[88] The influence of the book of Ben Sira on *piyyutim* is also very palpable, and we have tried to reflect this to the best of our ability in the philological notes. Rabbinic literature has been quoted according to the editions provided by *Maagarim*;[89] for the *Sepher HaGaluy* we have used the edition of A. Harkavy,[90] for the *Alphabet of Ben Sira*, the edition of E. Yassif.[91] The English translations are, unless otherwise indicated, our own.

2.4 *The "Rhyming" Paraphrase*

The various fragments of the "Rhyming" Paraphrase of Ben Sira known to us currently have been integrated in this critical edition of Ben Sira. The first pages of the work (ENA 3053.3) were published by Joseph Marcus.[92] In subsequent years further pages were discovered and published, including Frankfurt 177 by Menahem Zulay;[93] T-S NS 108.43 by Hayyim Schirmann;[94] and T-S NS 93.79–80 by Ezra Fleischer.[95] All these discoveries were edited and commented on by Fleischer.[96]

A sixth fragment, HUC 1301, was published by Ezra Fleischer.[97] Recently, Franz Böhmisch[98] has identified more pages of the same manuscript (T-S NS 193.99; T-S AS 137.436; T-S AS 124.103; T-S AS 124.104; T-S AS 133.74). Böhmisch intends to present an edition of the texts illustrating in detail their various correspondences to Ben Sira and other literature and is just beginning this work. In the meantime, we felt it was important to present the manuscript fragments in our edition of Ben Sira (in a more cursory fashion) since the manuscript preserves a Hebrew

---

this group probably implies that this book was considered to be biblical, not necessarily by the Qumran community, but by the scribes of 2QSir and MasSir."

85 Sanders 1965. For a codicological description and reconstruction, as well as bibliography, see Jain 2014 and Dahmen 2003.
86 See Puech 2011, 299 and 324. According to Puech, column IX should also have 26 lines. Jain (2014, 165) and Dahmen (2003, 50) estimate that the text of the poem should have 27 lines but consider this unlikely and, consequently, suggest that the text was shorter than the Greek and Syriac version, though they propose no material reconstruction.
87 Cowley and Neubauer 1897.
88 Labendz 2006. See also Wright 1999.
89 https://maagarim.hebrew-academy.org.il/.
90 Harkavy 1891.
91 Yassif 1984.
92 Marcus 1931a, 238–39; 1931b, 26–27. See also Beentjes 2019.
93 Zulay and Elizur 2004–2005, 185–89. The texts were originally published in articles in *Ha-Aretz*, 16 December 1949; 10 October 1952; for these references, see Fleischer 1990, 42 n. 104.
94 Schirmann 1965, 436–9.
95 Fleischer 1978, 49–54.
96 Fleischer 1990, 264–82.
97 Fleischer 1997, *205–*217.
98 Böhmisch 2017, 197–237.

version of many of the verses that are otherwise unknown in Hebrew and it confirms various readings from the Ben Sira Genizah manuscripts. Note, for example, Sir 35:11a in the Paraphrase (at T-S NS 193.99, verso, line 7) corresponds exactly with the same stich in MS B; similarly, Sir 35:12a in the Paraphrase (idem, line 9) corresponds in all but its preposition to the same stich in MS B (text + margin). This suggests that the Paraphrase can sometimes be used to help reconstruct broken or partially missing text (see, e.g., Sir 39:26 in MS B). More generally, the Paraphrase also exemplifies the broad range of ways that the ancient text was preserved and transmitted during the Middle Ages.

The sequence of fragments is generally organized according to their correspondence to verses in Sirach manuscripts. The correspondences and similarities are remarked on in the list below. It is important to notice that the sequence of fragments does not follow exactly the sequence presented in Fleischer 1990 nor that in Böhmisch 2017. In the chart below, the term "correspondences" indicates a relatively unambiguous correlation between a verse or verses in the paraphrase and the book of Sirach (as evidenced in the Hebrew manuscripts, the Greek translation, and/or the Syriac). Those fragments that are not listed with "correspondences" have a looser association with Ben Sira, at least as far as we can tell. "Similar language" indicates a shared vocabulary and a likely (though not definite) correlation to the book of Sirach. The loosest and least secure associations are those labeled "tentative similarities" and "similar topic."

While most of the fragments are organized according to their apparent correspondences with Sirach, two exceptions are found. First, the last lines of Frankfurt 177 use language also found in Sir 35:12, though that passage more clearly corresponds to lines in T-S NS 193.99. Second, T-S AS 124.103 (with tentative similarities to Sir 31:16, 22, 31) must immediately precede or follow T-S AS 124.104 (with similar language to Sir 44:1–15) based on offset traces (see T-S AS 124.103, verso, line 6 and T-S AS 124.104, recto, line 5). That T-S AS 124.103 should precede T-S AS 124.104 (and not follow it) is based on the fact that the verso of T-S AS 124.104 has a 2 feminin singular pronoun (in line 3) whose antecedent is likely the ארץ "land" found in the recto of T-S AS 124.104, line 1.

Within individual pages, it is clear that the sequence of verses in the paraphrase parallels the sequence of verses in Sirach. Based on this, we may infer in most cases which is the recto and which is the verso (as well as the sequence of fragments themselves). Note that the identification of the recto/verso does not necessarily correspond to what is listed in the Friedberg Genizah website. In order to make comparison with the photographs easier, we have indicated how the website labels "recto" and "verso" in parentheses. Thus, e.g., ENA 3053.3 is labeled "recto (labeled verso)."

The individual verses are labeled sequentially, according to Fleischer 1990 and 1997. Where Fleischer did not label a verse, we have added a label, either as line "zero" or as the last numeral followed by a "+" (e.g., 8+). This is for ease of reference. Since other, future scholars may determine a slightly different verse sequence, we have also indicated the line numbers in the translation and have referred to manuscript and line numbers whenever cross-referencing.

The manuscript contains, as its name implies, a paraphrase of many of Sirach's proverbs in rhyme. However, the manuscript also preserves other verses from the Bible (as well as other texts, presumably) that have been transformed into rhyming couplets. The handwriting is somewhat inconsistent with individual letters sometimes being formed in different ways, with vowels occasionally left out or forgotten.

Most Hebrew words are given vowel symbols.[99] The forms of the symbols are consistent with the Tiberian forms of *hiriq*, *tsere*, *seghol*, *shewa*, *patakh*, *qamets*, *holem*, and *shuruq*. But, there are no *hateph*-vowels and the vocalization corresponds to non-standard Tiberian tradition,[100] where there is no distinction between *seghol* and *patakh*. In addition, matres lectionis are used more frequently than in the Masoretic Text. Previous editions of the fragments present the Hebrew according to the Tiberian model of vocalization and spelling as exhibited in the Masoretic Text. We have, instead, endeavored to present the Hebrew as it appears in the manuscript itself, including its various idiosyncrasies and errors.

2.5 *Manuscript Charts*

2.5.1 List of Folios and Bifolios of Each Manuscript

When quire (or partial quire) can be reconstructed the following tables aim to represent these quires. Bifolios are presented together, for more clarity, the sequence of folios is numbered. Reconstructed folios or bifolios are in grey. A diagram showing the parallels between the different manuscripts is provided in Fig. 1, p. XXII–XXIII.

---

99 See also Schirmann 1965, 436; Segal 1958, 135 n. 2; Fleischer 1997, *207.

100 For the definition of the non-standard tiberian vocalization, see Arrant 2021. We thank G. Khan and E. Arrant for having attracted our attention to this point.

MS A
(Partial ?) quire with three bifolios

Shelfmark of the bifolio	Folio	Content	Folio	Content
T-S 12.863	I recto	Sir 3:6b–4:10b	VI verso	Sir 15:19b–16:26a
	I verso	Sir 4:10c–5:10a	VI recto	Sir 14:11b–15:19a
T-S 12.864	II recto	Sir 5:10b–6:30	V verso	Sir 13:7–14:11b
	II verso	Sir 6:3l–7:29a	V recto	Sir 11:34b–13:6b
ENA 2536	III recto	Sir 7:29a–9:2a	IV verso	Sir 11:11–12:1
	III verso	Sir 9:2a–10:12a	IV recto	Sir 10:12a–11:10

MS B
First quire

Shelfmark	Folio	Content	Shelfmark	Folio	Content
Missing	recto	Sir 3:27b–4:12a?	T-S NS 38a	II verso	Sir 15:17–16:7
	verso	Sir 4:12b–4:28b?		II recto	Sir 15:1–16
Missing	recto	Sir 4:28c–5:10?		verso	Sir 14:11–27?
	verso	Sir 5:11–6:12?		recto	Sir 13:21–14:10?
Missing	recto	Sir 6:13–6:31?		verso	Sir 13:6–20?
	verso	Sir 6:32–7:31?		recto	Sir 12:11–13:5?
Missing	recto	Sir 7:32–8:9?		verso	Sir 11:28–12:10?
	verso	Sir 8:10–9:5?		recto	Sir 11:11–27?
Missing	recto	Sir 9:6–10:17?	T-S 12.871	I verso	Sir 11:3–10
	verso	Sir 10:1–18?		I recto	Sir 10:19–11:2

MS B
Second quire

Shelfmark	Folio	Content	Shelfmark	Folio	Content
T-S 16.312	III recto	Sir 30:11–24a	T-S 16.312	VII verso	Sir 38:13–27b
	III verso	Sir 30:24b–31:11		VII recto	Sir 37:27–38:12
Or 5518	recto	Sir 31:12–21	Or 5518	VI verso	Sir 37:10–26
	verso	Sir 31:22–31		VI recto	Sir 36:22–37:9
T-S 16.313	IV recto	Sir 32:1–13	T-S 16.313	V verso	Sir 36:1–21
	IV verso	Sir 32:14–33:3		V recto	Sir 35:11–26
Missing	α recto	Sir 33:4–19		verso	Sir 34:25–35:10?
	α verso	Sir 33:20–34:3?		recto	Sir 34:4–24?

MS B
Third quire

Shelfmark	Folio	Content	Shelfmark	Folio	Content
Missing		Sir 38:28–39:14?	T-S 16.314	XVIII verso	Sir 50:11–22
				XVIII recto	Sir 49:12–50:10
Or 1102	VIII recto	Sir 39:15–28	MS Heb e. 62.9	XVII verso	Sir 48:24–49:12
	VIII verso	Sir 39:29–40:8		XVII recto	Sir 48:12–23
MS Heb e. 62.1	IX recto	Sir 40:9–40:26	MS Heb e. 62.2	XVI verso	Sir 47:23–48:12
	IX verso	Sir 40:26–41:9		XVI recto	Sir 47:11–23
MS Heb e. 62.3	X recto	Sir 41:10–41:22	MS Heb e. 62.4	XV verso	Sir 46:18–47:10
	X verso	Sir 42:1–11		XV recto	Sir 46:7–18
MS Heb e. 62.5	XI recto	Sir 42:12–43:1	MS Heb e. 62.6	XIV verso	Sir 45:23–46:6
	XI verso	Sir 43:1–16		XIV recto	Sir 45:14–23
MS Heb e. 62.8	XII recto	Sir 43:17–33	MS Heb e. 62.7	XIII verso	Sir 45:5–13
	XII verso	Sir 44:1–16		XIII recto	Sir 44:17–45:4

MS B
Fourth quire

Shelfmark	Folio	Content	Shelfmark	Folio	Content
T-S 16.315	XIX recto	Sir 50:22–51:5	T-S 16.315	XX verso	Sir 51:21–30
	XIX verso	Sir 51:6–12		XX recto	Sir 51:12–20

MS C
Quire of four bifolios

Shelfmark	Folio	Content	Shelfmark	Folio	Content
T-S 12.867	I recto	Sir 3:14–18, 21–22a	T-S 12.867	VIII verso	Sir 36:27b–31(24b–28)
	I verso	Sir 3:22b; 41:16; 4:21; 20:22–23a		VIII recto	Sir 26:2b–3, 13, 15–17; 36:27a
T-S 12.727	II recto	Sir 4:23b, 30–31; 5:4–7a	T-S 12.727	VII verso	Sir 25:20b–24; 26:1–2a
	II verso	Sir 5:7b, 9–13; 36:24a		VII recto	Sir 25:8, 13, 17–20a
G. Combs (Private collection)	III recto	Sir 36:24; 6:5–6; 37:1–2; 6:7; 6:9	G. Combs (Private collection)	VI verso	Sir 22:11cd–12; 22:21–22; 23:11; 25:7
	III verso	Sir 6:10; 6:8; 6:12–15; 3:27; 6:18		VI recto	Sir 20:30–31; 21:22, 23, 26; 22:11ab
BAIU ID 1–2	IV recto	Sir 6:18b–19, 28, 35; 7:1, 4, 6a	Gaster Fragment	V verso	Sir 20:7; 37:19, 22, 24, 26; 20:13
	IV verso	Sir 7:6b, 17, 20–21, 23–25		V recto	Sir 18:31b–33; 19:1–2; 20:5–6

MS D

Shelfmark	Folio	Content
BAIU ID 1–2	recto	Sir 36:24–37:12a
	verso	Sir 37:12a–38:1a
T-S AS 118.78	recto	Sir 7:18–8:1
	verso	Sir 8:1–18

MS E

Shelfmark	Folio	Content
ENA 3597	recto	Sir 32:16–33:14b
	verso	Sir 33:14b–34:l

MS F

Shelfmark	Folio	Content
T-S AS 213.17	recto	Sir 31:24–32:7
	verso	Sir 32:11–33:8

Paraphrase

Shelfmark	Content	Shelfmark	Content
Independent folios			
T-S AS 133.74	Similar to Sir 12:3, 6, 9		
ENA 3053.3	Corresp. to Sir 22:22, 24–27; 23:1–9		
Fleischer 1990, Frag. 1			
Frankfurt 177 Fleischer 1990, Frag. 5	Similar topic to Sir 33:7–15; similar language to Sir 35:12		
Quire of (at least) two bifolios			
T-S NS 108.43 Fleischer 1990, Frag. 2	Corresp. to Sir 34:6–7, 12, 21, 24, 30–31	T-S NS 108.43 Fleischer 1990, Frag. 2	Corresp. to Sir 36:17–19, 21–30; 37:6–7
T-S NS 193.99	Corresp. to Sir 34:31, 35:5–7, 12–14	T-S AS 137.436	Corresp. to Sir 35:15–17, 22–26; 36:1–2, 4, 6, 8, 10, 12–13
One bifolio			
T-S NS 93.80 Fleischer 1990, Frag. 3	Corresp. to Sir 39:26–30, 35; 40:10–11, 17	T-S NS 93.79 Fleischer 1990, Frag. 4	Corresp. to Sir 42:11–12

Paraphrase (*cont.*)

Shelfmark	Content	Shelfmark	Content
One bifolio			
T-S AS 124.103	tentative similarities to Sir 31:16, 22, 31	T-S AS 124.104	similar language to Sir 44:1–15
One bifolio			
HUC 1301, folio 1 Fleischer 1997, Frag. 6	Corresp. to Sir 51:8–12, 20–22	HUC 1301, folio 2 Fleischer 1997, Frag. 6	

2Q18		Masada	
Frag. 1	Sir 6:14–15 or 1:19–20	I	Sir 39:27–32
Frag. 2	Sir 6:20–32	II	Sir 40:11–41:1
		III	41:2–20
		IV	41:21–42:14
11QPsª		V	42:15–43:8
		VI	43:8–30
XXI	Sir 51:13–20	VII	44:1–17
XXII	Sir 51:30		

2.5.2 Images of the Manuscripts

All the images of the Cairo Genizah manuscripts are available online via the websites fjms.genizah.org and bensira.org, this latter also including images of Qumran and Masada manuscripts. We give below the official websites of the libraries that present the most recent and thus the better quality photos. Researchers should also consult the 1901 facsimiles or photos preserved in the first editions of each manuscript. Indeed, manuscripts deteriorate with time and some older photos present a more complete text.

Cambridge University Library

All images are accessible on the Digital Library of the University of Cambridge (cudl.lib.cam.ac.uk). On this website images respect the iiif standard.

T-S 12.863 (https://cudl.lib.cam.ac.uk/view/MS-TS-00012-00863/1)

T-S 12.864 (https://cudl.lib.cam.ac.uk/view/MS-TS-00012-00864/1)

T-S 12.867 (https://cudl.lib.cam.ac.uk/view/MS-TS-00012-00867/1)

T-S 12.727 (https://cudl.lib.cam.ac.uk/view/MS-TS-00012-00727/1)

T-S 12.871 (https://cudl.lib.cam.ac.uk/view/MS-TS-00012-00871/1)

T-S 16.312 (https://cudl.lib.cam.ac.uk/view/MS-TS-00016-00312/1)

T-S 16.313 (https://cudl.lib.cam.ac.uk/view/MS-TS-00016-00313/1)

T-S 16.315 (https://cudl.lib.cam.ac.uk/view/MS-TS-00016-00315/1)

T-S AS 118.78 (https://cudl.lib.cam.ac.uk/view/MS-TS-AS-00118-00078/1)

T-S AS 213.17 (https://cudl.lib.cam.ac.uk/view/MS-TS-AS-00213-00017/1)

T-S NS 38a (https://cudl.lib.cam.ac.uk/view/MS-TS-NS-00038-A-00001/1)

Or. 1102 (https://cudl.lib.cam.ac.uk/view/MS-OR-01102/1)

Jewish Theological Seminary (New York)

ENA 2536, ENA 3597

Images are available on fjms.genizah.org and bensira.org. We took infrared images of ENA 3597. They will be put online soon.

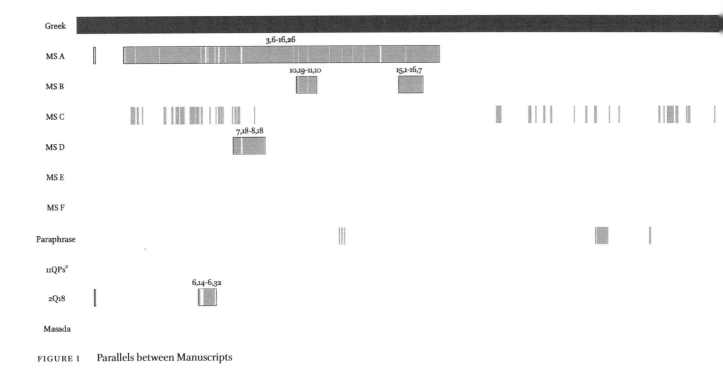

FIGURE 1   Parallels between Manuscripts

British Museum (*London*)
Or 5518 (https://www.bl.uk/manuscripts/Viewer.aspx?ref=or_5518_f001r)

Bodleian Library (*Oxford*)
MS Heb e. 62 (https://digital.bodleian.ox.ac.uk/objects/01bc51ec-80fb-4318-aaf3-bc313692691f/)

G. Combs (*Private Collection*)
Images are available on fjms.genizah.org and bensira.org.

Bibliothèque de l'alliance israélite universelle (*Paris*)
ID 1–2
Images are available on fjms.genizah.org and bensira.org. We took infrared images of MS D. They will be put online soon.

Gaster Fragment
This fragment is at the moment lost. Images are only available on the facsimile of 1901 and in Moses Gaster, "A New Fragment of Ben Sira," *JQR* 12.4 (1900): 688–702.

Paraphrase
All the images are accessible on fjms.genizah.org.

2Q18
PAM 40.553 (frg. 1; Najib Anton Albina, April 1953)
https://www.deadseascrolls.org.il/explore-the-archive/image/B-278289

PAM 40.557 (frg. 2; Najib Anton Albina, April 1953)
https://www.deadseascrolls.org.il/explore-the-archive/image/B-278363
PAM 42.555 (frg. 2; Najib Anton Albina, April 1958)
https://www.deadseascrolls.org.il/explore-the-archive/image/B-283843
PAM 42.959 (frg. 1 & 2; Najib Anton Albina, April 1959)
https://www.deadseascrolls.org.il/explore-the-archive/image/B-284857
Photos from November 2011 by Shai Halevi
Frg. 1 color: https://www.deadseascrolls.org.il/explore-the-archive/image/B-365815
Frg. 1 b&w: https://www.deadseascrolls.org.il/explore-the-archive/image/B-365816
Frg. 2 color: https://www.deadseascrolls.org.il/explore-the-archive/image/B-365809
Frg. 2 b&w: https://www.deadseascrolls.org.il/explore-the-archive/image/B-365810

11QPs^a
PAM 43.788 (https://www.deadseascrolls.org.il/explore-the-archive/image/B-285194)
PAM 43.789 (https://www.deadseascrolls.org.il/explore-the-archive/image/B-285196)
Photos from September 2011 by Shai Halevi
B&W: https://www.deadseascrolls.org.il/explore-the-archive/image/B-314641
Color: https://www.deadseascrolls.org.il/explore-the-archive/image/B-314640

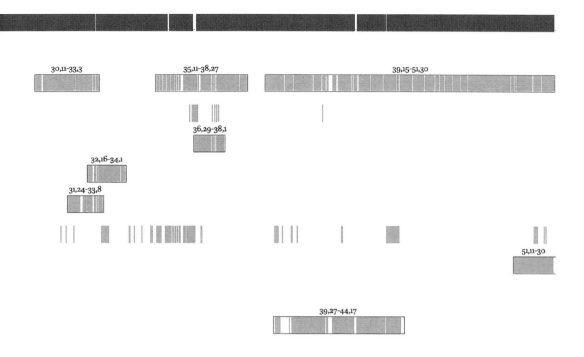

Masada Scroll
Images are available online (at bensira.org), but not available on deadseascrolls.org.il at the present. One may contact the IAA for color and infrared images taken by Shai Halevi. Images in Yadin's edition present some fragments that have now disappeared from the new photographs. Unfortunately images in Yadin's edition are of very poor quality and we were not able to retrieve the original films.

3 Conventions of the Edition

Despite the quality of the previous editions, they have undeniable shortcomings which make their use difficult for the scholarly community and, even more so, for non-specialists. Recent photographs,[101] as well as advances in digital paleography and codicology have allowed us in many instances to present a Hebrew text that more accurately reflects the ancient and medieval manuscripts, including the errors, corrections and additions made by their scribes. Most previous editions (i.e., those of Ben Ḥayyim, Vattioni, Boccaccio, Beentjes and, more recently, Egger-Wenzel) provide the Hebrew text alone, with little or no annotation, even though the manuscripts are often difficult to read; not surprisingly, discrepancies between editions are frequent. The casual reader, unfamiliar with paleography, is forced to choose more or less blindly between the discrepant readings offered in different editions and/or to consult the online digital images, which can still sometimes be hard to read or make sense of (due to the infelicities of handwriting, smudging, offsetting, etc.). Most editions also do not offer a translation of the Hebrew text as it exists in the individual manuscripts, not to mention the many marginal annotations, despite the obscurity of many words and phrases. Because of these difficulties, we have included notes on our readings and translations. We hope that these alleviate some of the difficulties most readers encounter when engaging with the Hebrew versions of Ben Sira.

The structure of our study is that of a trilingual edition, giving on the left page the Hebrew text and, on the right page, its translation into French and English. Three sets of notes complement the text: a critical apparatus, notes on the paleography and an abbreviated philological commentary.

3.1 *Theoretical Framework of the Edition*
When we began this work, we had little idea of the theoretical debates that underlie critical editions. We based ourselves both on strong theoretical intuitions and pragmatic considerations. It was only later, in the course of our philological work, thanks to interactions with colleagues and friends, that we became interested in how the model

---

[101] The photographs of the manuscripts of the Genizah are available on The Friedberg Genizah Project Website (https://fjms.genizah.org/) as well as on https://www.bensira.org.

one uses for a critical edition influences how a text is read, perceived and understood.

In the history of philology, the theoretical frameworks of critical editions are often situated within a spectrum whose two ends are represented by two models: the Lachmannian model (or Neo-Lachmannian)[102] that focuses on the reconstitution of an archetype through the reconstruction of the *stemma codicum* (often focussing on authorial intention), and the Bedierist model (or Neo-Bedierist) that focuses on the "best" preserved manuscript and reports variants of the other manuscripts in an apparatus[103] (often focussing on the scribal version of a text). Exponents of these models are sometimes referred to as eclectic editions (Lachmannian) and diplomatic editions (Bedierist). In the presentation of the Hebrew bible, these two models may be represented by, on the one hand, the *Hebrew Bible: A Critical Edition* that aims to produce an eclectic edition,[104] and, on the other hand, *Biblia Hebraica Stuttgartensia / Quinta*[105] and the *Hebrew University Bible Project*[106] that each edit only one manuscript, the supposed "best" one.

When we conceived the present edition, we wanted to emphasize the pluriformity of Ben Sira's text, the idea of a moving text, which is constantly changing over time. Without being aware of it, we were joining both the debate between Peter Schäfer and Chaim Milikowsky[107] at the end of the 1980s and the so called *New Philology* that emerged in the same years under the influence of Paul Zumthor,[108] Bernard Cerquiglini[109] and Stephen G. Nichols.[110] We recognized ourselves perfectly through Cerquiglini's ideas on text variance, as well as through Schäfer's considerations on the impossible *Urtext*, and again through the emphasis of the *New Philology* on scribes, manuscripts and the world that surrounds them.

One of the intentions of this edition is to present the manuscripts in their diversity, as they are attested, and in particular to represent in some way how the text changed over time; we have not endeavored to reconstruct an *Urtext* or an archetype. We also wanted to avoid implying that the multiple transformations that scribes made to the text through time should necessarily be perceived as a form of degradation or an alteration of a "pure" original and that the "best" reading is always the "earliest." We did not wish to suggest a hierarchization of the different textual forms.

The pluriformity of Ben Sira's manuscripts has often been perceived as an irreducible difficulty,[111] but this pluriformity need not be construed as something that needs solving. Rather, it is an opportunity to see a text transforming itself in the course of its transmission and according to the different contexts in which it was preserved. It is an opportunity to understand how texts, whatever they are and whatever their degree of sacrality, move. In the end, it is this movement that constitutes the life of a text. What we have in the Ben Sira manuscripts is extremely valuable. Certainly, we do not have the text written by Ben Sira himself, its autograph, but we have snapshots of the Hebrew text at different stages of its transmission (from the first century BCE to the 13th century CE) and under different forms (rabbinic quotations and Saadiah's quotations, the anthology of MS C, the Paraphrase, stichometric or non-stichometric presentation, very formal square script in MS B, slightly cursive in MS A, D, E and F, etc.). In fact, the inclusion of the so-called "Rhyming" Paraphrase with the other, more commonly recognized Ben Sira manuscripts is not only because it includes the text of Ben Sira (many verses of which differ from those in MS B no more than the verses of MS C differs from those of MS A), but also because it demonstrates the variety of ways the text has been transmitted.

In addition to expanding our ideas about manuscripts and texts, studying the variants between Ben Sira manuscripts allows us to get a better idea of the practices of the scribes from antiquity to the medieval period and the processes through which they interpreted the words they copied. We may observe, for example, how the scribes of MS B seem to have worked in an inclusive way, presumably trying to preserve as many variants to individual verses as possible. The plethora of doublets in the texts is more evidence for this scribal proclivity toward inclusiveness.

3.2 Edition of the Hebrew Texts

The underlying principle of this edition is to treat each Hebrew witness of Ben Sira with as much integrity as possible. We have chosen to edit, translate and comment on each manuscript independently, one after the other (MSS A, B, C, D, E, F, Paraphrase, 2Q18, 11QPs[a] and Masada).

The text of each manuscript is edited and translated as it is preserved, even if the preserved text does not present a particularly coherent meaning and/or if it could

---

102 Trovato 2017, Maas 1958.
103 Bedier 1928, Duval 2021.
104 Hendel 2013, 2016.
105 Schenker 2013.
106 Segal 2013.
107 Schäfer 1986, Milikowsky 1988, Schäfer 1989, Schäfer and Milikowsky 2010.
108 Zumthor 1987.
109 Cerquiglini 1989.
110 Nichols 1990.

---

111 Segal 1934, 91.

be considered erroneous, secondary, a gloss, or even a back-translation. We have tried to respect the layout of the text and in particular the specific layout of the marginal notes (horizontal, vertical, oblique, interlinear), elongated letters, ligatures, crossed out or deleted words, supra or infra linear notes, vocalization, *teʿamim*, marks of the scribes, etc. As far as possible, we have tried to reproduce the layout of these elements in the edition so that readers can have the best possible idea of the practices of the scribes. However, we have made one important exception: the Hebrew text is always presented in stichometric lines, even when the manuscripts are not organized in this way (as in MSS A, C, D and 11QPsᵃ). We are aware that this adaptation is significant from a hermeneutical point of view and imposes a radically different reading practice for some manuscripts and text conception (on poetry for example). Nevertheless, this decision was made in the interest of producing a text that is easier to read and consult. In addition, this layout does reflect the orientation of the majority of manuscripts (i.e., MSS B, E, F, 2Q18 and Mas).[112]

Unlike Egger-Wenzel's volume, we have not included a synoptic edition of the different manuscripts in the book version of our edition in order that we might preserve the integrity of each manuscript and in particular the order of each of their verses (the case of MS C would have been really problematic). In the future, we plan to produce a digital critical edition of the different manuscripts which will allow, in addition to the visualization of the diplomatic edition (with or without stichometric presentation), a synoptic or evolutionary presentation of the different manuscripts (project SCRIBES, Biblissima+).

For the organization and numbering of the verses, we have followed, as far as possible, the numbering of Ziegler (1980) that follows the Hebrew and Latin order of chapters 30–36, thereby avoiding adding another system to the numerous others.[113] Since we present the sequence of verses as they appear in the Hebrew manuscripts and since the manuscripts do not always align with the Greek, the verse labels sometimes appear out of sequence. For example, in MS C I verso (T-S 12.867 verso), lines 1–6 include the sequence of verses 3:22, 41:16b/c, 4:21, 20:22.

To the right of the verse labels superscript abbreviations have been added to indicate other manuscript(s) where one can find the same verse. We have used the following abbreviations for these superscript cross references. Uppercase letters A–F = MS A, B, etc.; P = Paraphrase; Q = either 2Q18 or 11QPsᵃ [= 11Q5]; M = Masada. Unfortunately, for logistical reasons, it was impossible to add verse labels and cross references to some marginal corrections / alternatives. In addition to verse labels, within the body of the Hebrew text, superscript numerals indicate the individual lines of the manuscript.

For the Hebrew transcriptions, we have used the conventions of the Discoveries in the Judaean Desert, especially as presented by E. Ulrich in DJD XIV, 3–6, (see also DJD I, 44–48 and DJD XXXIX, 18) that distinguishes between certain (א), probable (א̇) and uncertain (א̊) readings, noting possible alternatives in the accompanying paleographic commentary. Reconstructions are sometimes offered within brackets where there is agreement among the manuscripts and/or where it is helpful in making sense of the extant letters. We have avoided any conjectural reconstructions. The purpose is to facilitate the reading of fragmented text. Restorations are limited to: (1) the reconstruction of a few letters when these are evident from the preserved remains and the syntax of the proposal; (2) when the parallel manuscripts allow us to consider a restoration of a few letters or words compatible with available space and physical characteristics of the manuscripts; (3) much more rarely on the sole basis of the ancient versions (Greek and/or Syriac). This last option, which must remain exceptional, is limited to a few particular cases, such as the restoration of chapter 1 on the basis of traces of preserved offset letters.

Readers should note that the cantillation symbol א̊ indicates a *circellus* above a letter in one of the medieval manuscripts. A *circellus* was included by scribes to indicate a correction or alternative reading in the margin of the manuscript.

In addition, in contrast to previous editions, we have presented readings for many partially preserved letters. These include instances where the paper or parchment has become degraded, torn, disintegrated, or is partially missing, where only traces of letters can be made out, for example on the edges surrounding holes or tears as well as where ink has rubbed off onto a facing page (i.e., in cases of offsetting), as in the verses after Sir 1:20. Consulting our readings and then the manuscript images may give some readers pause and may lead to the incorrect impression that these readings are speculative guesses on our part. In fact, our readings in these places are the result of extremely close scrutiny of the extant marks and comparisons with letter forms from other parts of the same manuscript. Using sometimes multispectral images and with image editing software, we have laid images of letters over the partially preserved marks, comparing and contrasting the different possibilities in order to determine which letters

---

112 In the Paraphrase, usually each verse is isolated from other verses by occupying either one or two lines.
113 See Reiterer and Egger-Wenzel 2003.

are those most likely to have been present in the degraded and damaged lines. This work has resulted in many new readings and confirmed many other previous proposals. Ambiguities and alternative possibilities are listed in the notes. In addition, when our readings differ from previous editions, we have often noted this, specifying the choices made by previous editors.

3.3 *Critical Apparatuses*

Each manuscript edition is accompanied by three apparatuses: (1) a critical apparatus, (2) an apparatus with notes on readings, and (3) an apparatus that offers philological commentary on our translation.

(1) As we opt for diplomatic editions, we utilize a neutral critical apparatus that presents the variants attested in the other Hebrew witnesses without hierarchizing them. Greek, Syriac or Latin texts are mentioned only when they are likely to shed light on the Hebrew reading. In general, the notations are self-explanatory, but a few things should be kept in mind. First, the manuscripts are cited in the order in which they appear in the edition (i.e., A, B, Bmg, D, E, F, etc.). The exception is the first element in an entry; the lemma is always a word from the base manuscript. In other words, in the presentation of MS D, the first entry in this apparatus will always be a word from this manuscript. Following this word, then the divergent readings are listed in the order they appear in the edition. Second, to avoid redundancy, marginal notes in the edited manuscript are not collated in the apparatus, except when they agree with another manuscript, since they are directly visible in the edition. Third, where two manuscripts represent basically the same reading with only a minor divergence the apparatus will sometimes indicate the alternative reading in parentheses. This is especially the case where longer phrases are cited. E.g., in MS B at Sir 36:27, the main text has והליל פנים while the margin has יהלל. The marginal reading is clearly intended as an alternative to והליל. In contrast, the reading of the whole phrase in MS C is מכל פנים [יהלל]; in this case, the verb יהלל appears in brackets since it is not attested, though we presume it followed in a now lost portion of the page. All this is represented in the apparatus of MS B in the following manner: 36:27 והליל (יהלל) פנים B Bmg | יהלל] מכל פנים C. Where a manuscript lacks a stich or whole verse, the missing text is introduced by a "+" in the apparatus. In some cases two manuscripts will preserve the same word or phrase, but the word or phrase will only be vocalized in one manuscript; in such cases, the word/phrase is not cited at all. It, however, is cited when a third manuscript attests a different reading; in these cases, the word/phrase is only vocalized if the vocalization is found in the base manuscript. In addition to providing a synopsis of what other manuscripts preserve, we have occasionally noted correspondences to the Greek and Syriac translations, though these are not comprehensive nor provided for every reading.[114] And finally, the text of the paraphrases has not been collated in the respective apparatuses.

(2) The second apparatus aims to justify our readings and reconstructions (or alternative readings and reconstructions), as well as to describe the peculiarities of the fragments and the photographs according to the standard adopted in the Discoveries in the Judaean Desert Series.[115] We have only justified our readings when they diverge from the preceding editions or when the preceding editions diverge between them. The notes are organized according to line number.

(3) The third apparatus is the heart of this edition. It aims to explain our translations and to highlight the Hebrew text which is often polysemic and obscure. These notes are organized according to verse labels.

As far as possible, we have always tried to explain the Hebrew text as it was preserved in the manuscript, even in cases where we were firmly convinced that the preserved form was the result of an obvious accidental error. Although we have avoided prioritizing the readings, the commentary will sometimes trace the history of a particular form of the text. When the Hebrew seemed unintelligible, we either translated a corrected text, the correction being explained in a note, or we did not translate, or, alternatively, we made our translations as unintelligible as the Hebrew. In overlapping passages with the same words, we did not reproduce the philological notes. The reader must refer to the first edited manuscript. Since the philological notes concern only the Hebrew text and given the restricted space of this commentary, we have not been able to overload the text with too many bibliographical references.

---

114 For the ancient versions, we used the following editions: for Greek, the edition of J. Ziegler (1980); for the Syriac text we used the Codex Ambrosianus published by N. Calduch-Benages, J. Ferrer, J. Liesen (2003), the polyglot of B. Walton (1657), P. A. De Lagarde (1861) as well as the critical notes by M. M. Winter (1976); For the Latin text, we used W. Thiele and A. Forte (1987–2005), as well as D. P. Sabatier (1743).

115 See DJD XXXIX, 9.

We have essentially consulted the commentaries of Smend, Peters, Lévi, Segal, the very rich articles of Kister, Rüger and van Peursen. The translations of ancient sources, unless otherwise stated, are our own. Beyond the bibliographical sources mentioned in the body of the notes, for linguistic research in Hebrew, we have made extensive use of Maagarim, which has been an incredible resource. Most of the rabbinic and *piyyutim* quotations were taken from their database. For Aramaic we used mainly the online *Comprehensive Aramaic Lexicon* (CAL).

3.4 *French and English Translations*

As with the critical edition of the Hebrew text, our work as translators was initially an empirical and pragmatic approach before we took a more reflective interest in theories of translation, thanks to our colleague and friend Claire Placial. Since our translation is intended primarily to help the comprehension of the Hebrew text, we have opted for a translation that is as literal as possible (*sourciste*) while avoiding as far as possible falling into slavish translation.

Ben Sira's language is particularly complex in terms of vocabulary and syntax. The choice of vocabulary is often strongly rooted in the context of ancient Jewish literature, and it is often difficult to render the nuances and resonances of the language in translation. In most cases, we have had to highlight these dimensions of the text in the notes.

The Hebrew is also very rich in metaphors. Wherever possible, we have tried to translate the metaphors in a manner that foregrounds the wordplay and semantic interconnections among the Hebrew words. Nevertheless, we have also tried to not be overly literal. For example, we translate Sir 6:2–3: "Do not fall under the influence of your appetite (נפשך), it ... would eat up (תאכל) your leaves and ruin your fruit to its (very) roots (תשרש)." In this case, we translate the common Hebrew noun נפש as "appetite," instead of with the more literal noun "throat" or the more generic "self," in order to emphasize a link with the following verb "eat" and the vegetable imagery that follows (something that the translation "passion" [e.g., in the NRSV and NJB] does not do). The verb אכל "to eat" is used in a metaphoric sense in Sir 6:2–3 to convey total destruction and is parallel to the rarer (presumably *piel*) verb שרש, which seems to convey the same sense (as in Job 31:12), though its etymology implies a connection with the noun שֹׁרֶשׁ "root." With our translation, we have tried to underline the connection between this latter verb and the preceding imagery ("leaves" and "fruit"). One may contrast our translation of the verb שרש with that of the NRSV, which seems more generic: "... your fruit [will be] destroyed."

The fact that we have a double translation in French and English has been incredibly fortunate. It has often led us to rethink our understanding of the Hebrew text in order to adapt it to two different linguistic sensibilities. Generally our translations agree, though in a few rare cases they differ and express two complementary interpretations or visions of the text. We have seen how French and English are two languages that have different perceptions of gender issues. As far as possible, we have tried to opt for a translation that is as gender-neutral and as inclusive as possible. This is why we have translated בן as "child / enfant" (paralleling the Greek translator who translates by τέκνον and not by υἱός) and not as "son / fils," especially in the recurring vocative בני "my child." The same is true of איש and אדם, for example, which we usually render as generic terms. In the English, we have used "they/them" pronouns and the possessive "their" for generic references (e.g., to a "fool" or even a "judge") except where the context implies a specific gender (e.g., in passages implying the pursuit of Wisdom as a future bride as in 4:15–19) and where the text is vague and/or difficult (e.g., 10:13 in MS A).

In the translation, we used italics to indicate a literal translation of what seems, obviously, a corrupted text or conversely when our translation follows a corrected version of the Hebrew text. What is in parentheses is implied by the Hebrew syntax, though it is not explicitly found there; it has been added in the interest of making the translation more comprehensible. Marginal notes in the Hebrew have also been translated, whether they make sense or not. They are added in parentheses in the translation preceded by the abbreviation "mg."

3.5 *Stemma of the Hebrew Manuscripts*

A careful examination of the variances between the different manuscripts allowed us to reconstruct the genealogical tree (*stemma codicum*) of the different manuscript witnesses. We are well aware that the *stemma codicum* is the fundamental basis for reconstructionist editions of the Lachmannian model. However, the reconstruction of an archetype or an authorial version of a text is not the only function of a *stemma codicum*. Rather, it may be used to better understand the relationship between the different textual witnesses and how the text transforms, one could say travels, from one form to another. The risk of an edition like ours that presents each manuscript witness independently is to imply a sort of atomization of texts that are disconnected to any textual tradition and context, each copy becoming a "fragmented electron in an unknowable global tradition."[116] Following Nadia Altschul, we want to consider "an editorial position that may account for the relationships that exist between *scripta* but will not privilege a lost authorial literary text against which extant manuscripts are only imperfect re-presentations."[117]

In this way, the *stemma codicum* is not any more a theoretical model to reconstruct the *Urtext*, but it becomes the fundamental basis for the understanding of the transformation of the text through time. It also becomes a solid basis to study the behavior of scribes when they are copying texts, not for the purpose of creating new typologies of scribal errors (metathesis, homoioteleuton, etc.), what Cerquiglini calls a "treatise of criminology and manual of clinical psychology of the scribe,"[118] but rather to understand how scribes behave as authors in front of the text they are copying.

In several publications and communications,[119] we have reconstructed the following stemma of the medieval manuscripts:

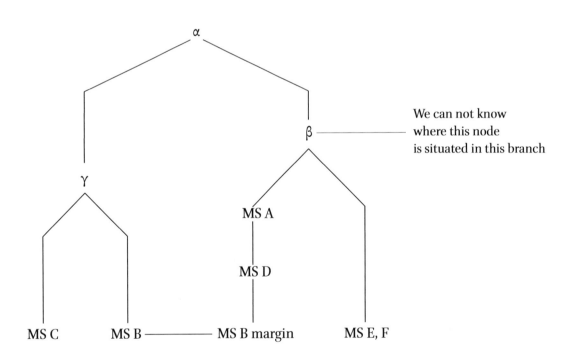

---

116   Camps 2015, 85.
117   Altschul 2006.
118   Cerquiglini 1989, 30.
119   Rey 2021b and Rey 2021c.

4 Abbreviations and Sigla

Where no abbreviations have been specified, the edition follows *The SBL Handbook of Style Second Edition* (Atlanta: SBL Press, 2014) and *The Chicago Manual of Style: Sixteenth Edition* (Chicago: University of Chicago Press, 2010). For the Dead Sea Scrolls, we followed the system for presenting texts described in DJD I, 44–48 and DJD XXXIX, 18–21 (e.g. 1QS III 15–16; 4Q416 1 iii 10–12; etc.). Concerning the Hodayot, we used numbering of lines and columns as defined in DJD XL.

א	Certain letter
א̇	Probable letter
א̊	Possible letter
א̊̊	This cantillation symbol indicates a *circellus* above a letter in one of the medieval manuscripts. A *circellus* was included by scribes to indicate a correction or alternative reading in the margin of the manuscript.
○	A letter which has ink traces remaining but cannot be confidently identified
[ ]	Space between fragments or where the surface of the manuscript is missing
{א}	Scribal correction
[אאא]	Reconstructed text
vacat	Interval, indicating that the writing space was intentionally left blank
+	additional word(s)
>	word(s) lacking
|	Separator in apparatus entry (edited mansucript to left, variants in other manuscripts to right)
·	Separator of apparatus entry
H^A, H^B, H^C ...	Hebrew MSS A, B, C,
H^M, H^{2Q18}	Masada, Qumran Cave 2
H^{Par}	Hebrew MS Paraphrase
SirPar	Paraphrase of Ben Sira
G	Greek text (Ziegler's edition unless indicated otherwise)
S	Syriac text (Codex Ambrosianus unless indicated otherwise)
L	Vetus Latina
3^A	(as a verse label) Verse also attested in MS A
3^B	(as a verse label) Verse also attested in MS B (including marginal alternatives and corrections)
3^C	(as a verse label) Verse also attested in MS C
3^D	(as a verse label) Verse also attested in MS D
3^E	(as a verse label) Verse also attested in MS E
3^F	(as a verse label) Verse also attested in MS F
3^P	(as a verse label) Verse also attested in Paraphrase
3^Q	(as a verse label) Verse also attested in 2Q18 or 11QPs^a [= 11Q5]
3^M	(as a verse label) Verse also attested in MS M
BDB	Brown, Francis, S. R. Driver, and Charles A. Briggs. *A Hebrew and English Lexicon of the Old Testament*
BHS	*Biblia Hebraica Stuttgartensia*
CAL	*Comprehensive Aramaic Lexicon Project* (https://cal.huc.edu/index.html)
CUL	Cambridge University Library
DCH	*Dictionary of Classical Hebrew*. Edited by David J. A. Clines. 9 vols. Sheffield: Sheffield Phoenix Press, 1993–2014
DJD	Discoveries in the Judaean Desert
DNWSI	*Dictionary of the North-West Semitic Inscriptions*. Jacob Hoftijzer and Karen Jongeling. 2 vols. Leiden: Brill, 1995
DSS	Dead Sea Scrolls
ENA	Elkan Nathan Adler

GKC	*Gesenius' Hebrew Grammar*. Edited by Emil Kautzsch. Translated by Arther E. Cowley. 2nd ed. Oxford: Clarendon, 1910
HALOT	*The Hebrew and Aramaic Lexicon of the Old Testament*. Ludwig Koehler, Walter Baumgartner, and Johann J. Stamm. Translated and edited under the supervision of Mervyn E. J. Richardson. 4 vols. Leiden: Brill, 1994–1999
HAWTTM	*Hebräisches und aramäisches Wörterbuch zu den Texten vom Toten Meer. Einschließlich der Manuskripte aus der Kairoer Geniza*. Edited by Reinhard G. Kratz, Annette Steudel and Ingo Kottsieper. 2 vols. Berlin: de Gruyter, 2017–2018
HUC	Hebrew Union College
JM	Joüon, Paul. *A Grammar of Biblical Hebrew*. Translated and revised by T. Muraoka. 2 vols. Rome: Pontifical Biblical Institute, 1991
LAB	*Liber antiquitatum biblicarum* (Pseudo-Philo)
LBH	Late Biblical Hebrew
LCL	Loeb Classical Library
LS	*A Syriac Lexicon: A Translation from the Latin, Correction, Expansion, and Update of C. Brockelmann's Lexicon Syriacum*. Translated by Michael Sokoloff. Winona Lake; Piscataway: Eisenbrauns; Gorgias Press, 2009
LXX	Septuagint
MT	Masoretic Text
NRSV	New Revised Standard Version
par.	parallel
QDTL	Qumran-Digital: Text und Lexikon
TAD	*Textbook of Aramaic Documents from Ancient Egypt*. Edited by Porten, Bezalel, and Ada Yardeni. Texts and Studies for Students. Jerusalem: The Hebrew University, 1986–1999
ThWQ	*Theologisches Wörterbuch zu den Qumrantexten*. Edited by Heinz-Josef Fabry and Ulrich Dahmen. 3 vols. Stuttgart: Kohlhammer, 2011
T-S	Taylor-Schechter
T-S NS	Taylor-Schechter New Series
T-S AS	Taylor-Schechter Additional Series

MANUSCRIPT A

SIR 1:20i–28; 3:6–16:23

Chapter 1

T-S 12.863 recto (offset letters)

[עולם ו]שמחה רבה: כל [דברי שמעו ועשו ותכתבו בס]**פרי**[		¹	20i
[חיים: א]הבו יראת ייי ותנ]ו בה לבבכם ואל תיראו]: [		²	20j
[קרבו אליה ואל תאחרו ו]תמצאו חיים [לרוחכם: וכאשר קרבת]		³	20kl
[כגבור וכאנש חיל: אל תכחש [בירא]ת ייי ות]ג]ע[ליה בלב ולב]		⁴	20l–28

Chapter 3

T-S 12.863 recto

:מכבד אמו [ ]	¹		6
עבור ישיגוך ²כל ברכות:		בני במאמר ובמעשה כבד אביך	8
וקללת אם תנתש נטע:		ברכת אב תיסד שרש	9
כי לא כבוד הוא לך:	³	אל תתכבד בקלון אביך	10
ומרבה חטא מקלל אמו:		כבוד איש כבוד ⁴אביו	11
ואל ⁵תעזבהו כל ימי חייו:		בני התחזק בכבוד אביך	12
ואל תכלים ⁶אותו כל ימי חייו:		וגם אם יחסר מדעו עזוב לו	13
ותמור חטאת היא ⁷תנתע:		צדקת אב לא תמחה	14 ᶜ תנטע
כחם על כפור להשבית עוניך:		ביום צרה תזכר לך	15 ᶜ
ומכעיס בוראו מקלל אמו:		כי ⁸מזיד בוזה אביו	16 ᶜ

יובר A | תזכר C · | > C | AGS צרה 3:15 · C | ותחת ענותו תתנצ]ב[A | ותמור חטאת היא תנתע (תנטע) CGS תשכח | A תמחה · C אל | AGS לא 3:14
ומכעיס CGS · כמגדף העזוב אביו A | כי מזיד בוזה אביו 3:16 · C וכחורב על קרח נמס חטאתיך: | A כחם על כפור להשבית עוניך: | C cor. יזכר · GS עוניך
· CG חזעם אל יסחוב אמו | AS בוראו מקלל אמו

L. 1–4 [1:20i-l; 1:28] The text is only attested as offset traces on the verso of the first folio page of Hᴬ (see Reymond 2015, 83-98 and Karner 2015, 177-203). The Hebrew matches four verses among the twelve verses found in the Syriac translation, but no where else. These twelve verses were, before their discovery in Hᴬ, generally assumed to be unique to the Syriac version. It seems likely that Hᴬ contained the full twelve verses. Their presence in Hᴬ implies some affiliation between the Syriac and Hᴬ. For the heavily reconstructed first chapter of the book, we have presented it as it would have appeared on the page (i.e. not in stichometric units) since this makes our reconstruction easier to understand. We follow the readings and reconstructions of Karner 2015 with some complements and modifications: in line 1, a vertical bar that may correspond to a *waw* is visible (see the note on עבור below), we thank Karner for this solution (personal communication); in line 2, an *aleph* is clearly visible after the reconstruction of חיים:; it should correspond to the *aleph* of אהבו, implying Reymond's reconstruction for the space. On this same line, very faint traces confirm the reconstruction ואל תיראו. On line 3, traces of the *tav* and the *mem* of תמצאו are visible.

L. 1 [3:8] עבור — The line that extends the vertical bar of the *resh* is most likely the trace of an offset letter.

3:6 Only the end of the stich has been preserved. The Hebrew here agrees with the Syriac, against the Greek (except for the recension *b*: τιμήσει μητέρα αὐτοῦ). The variants between the versions do not allow for a reliable restoration of this verse.

3:7 Verse 7 is lacking in Hᴬ, the Syriac and Greek I, and belongs to Greek II (*O L*-694-743 768 La).

3:8 מאמר — The term מַאֲמָר only appears in late Hebrew (Esth 1:15; 2:20; 9:32; Sir 37:16^Bmg,D; 4Q200 2 4; 4Q269 9 8; 4Q270 5 21; 4Q271 3 14) and has predominantly the sense "order." Here, however, one should understand it to mean "word," which reflects the sense of the Aramaic homograph מֵאֲמַר (e.g., Dan 4:14; Ezra 6:9). עבור — The form would be unique in the Second Temple period. It is usually constructed with the preposition ב (ten times in Ben Sira, always in the Hebrew Bible), and its absence here may be a scribal error resulting from the influence of *paytanic* Hebrew. ישיגוך כל ברכות — The phrase is probably inspired by Deut 28:2: וּבָאוּ עָלֶיךָ כָּל הַבְּרָכוֹת הָאֵלֶּה וְהִשִּׂיגֻךָ "All blessings will come upon you (= Greek, Syriac of Sir 3:8) and will reach you (= Hᴬ)." ישיגוך — In late Hebrew, when the subject follows the verb, it is common for the verb to be in the masculine plural even where the subject is feminine in gender (see Qimron 1986, §310.128; Segal 1927, §153; and already in classical Hebrew, see Joüon, §150*b*, *c*, *l*).

3:9 שרש — The term can refer to the root of a plant or a tree, but also to a "foundation, base." In the present verse, the metaphor may evoke origin, stability, rootedness and firm establishment. See for example, Sir 10:16ᴬ about the proud or Sir 40:15ᴮ about the non-believer. Yet, the same image can also allude to descendants (cf. Prov 12:3, 12; Penar 1975, 5), in which case, the father's blessing would be a source of fruitfulness ensuring progeny.

3:10 תתכבד — The *hithpael* of כבד only appears twice in the Hebrew Bible: as a participle in Prov 12:9 and Nah 3:15 with the meaning "to be honored" or "to multiply oneself." The construction התכבד ב... "to glorify in, boast of" appears first in Ben Sira (see 3:10ᴬ, 10:26^A,B, as a participle in 10:27^A,B; 10:31^A,B [2×]) and in 4QInstruction (4Q416 2 ii 20 // 4Q417 2 ii + 23 25: אל תתכבד במחסורכה), and is found repeatedly in later Hebrew, especially in the phrase המתכבד בקלון חבירו (e.g., y. Ḥag. 2:1, 77c; Gen. Rab. 1:5 [see Maagarim]). קלון — Given the context (see 3:10*b*), the term likely refers to dishonor due to old age, rather than disgrace or contempt. לא — For the use of the negation לא in a nominal proposition, see Joüon, §160*b*.

3:11 The omission of a conjunction between the two participial phrases creates ambiguity: we might read "one who multiplies sin curses their mother" or "one who curses their mother multiplies sin." Either way, the construction implies equivalence between the two propositions.

Chapitre 1

20i Écoutez mes paroles [et œuvrez,
 [et vous serez inscrits dans les livres de vie.]
20j [Aimez la crainte de YYY,]
 [et pla]cez votre cœur en elle [et ne craignez pas.]
20k [Approchez-vous d'elle et ne tardez pas,]
 [et] vous trouverez vie [pour votre esprit,]
20l [Et lorsque tu approches,
 (sois) comme un héros et comme un être brave]
28 [Ne renie pas] la crain[te de YYY]
 [et ne l'ap]pro[che pas avec un cœur double.]

Chapitre 3

6 [   ] celui qui honore sa mère.
8 Mon enfant, en parole et en acte, honore ton père,
 afin que t'atteignent toutes bénédictions.
9 La bénédiction d'un père établit une racine
 et la malédiction d'une mère déracine un jeune plant.
10 Ne t'honore pas du déshonneur de ton père,
 car ce n'est pas un honneur pour toi.
11 L'honneur d'une personne, c'est l'honneur de son père
 et il multiplie le péché, celui qui maudit sa mère.
12 Mon enfant, soutiens l'honneur de ton père
 et ne l'abandonne jamais tous les jours de ta vie.
13 De même, si sa raison vient à manquer, secours-le
 et ne le blesse jamais tous les jours de sa vie.
14 La justice envers un père ne sera jamais effacée
 et en échange du péché *elle sera brisée* (mg : plantée).
15 Au jour de la détresse, elle sera rappelée en ta faveur,
 comme la chaleur sur le givre, pour faire disparaître tes iniquités.
16 Car il est insolent celui qui dédaigne son père
 et il offense son créateur celui qui maudit sa mère.

Chapter 1

20i My words, hear [and do them,]
 [so that you will be written in the books of life!]
20j [Love the fear of YYY]
 [and set] your mind to it [and do not fear!]
20k [Approach and do not tarry,]
 [and you will f]ind life [for your spirit!]
20l [When you approach,]
 [(you will be) like heroes and like valiant people.]
28 [Do not act deceitfully] in the fea[r of the YYY]
 [and do not ap]proa[ch with a double heart.]

Chapter 3

6 [   ] one who honors their mother.
8 My child, in word and in deed, honor your father
 that all blessings may reach you.
9 A father's blessing establishes a root
 and a mother's curse uproots a seedling.
10 Do not take pride in your father's disgrace,
 for it is not to your honor.
11 A person's honor is their father's honor
 and the one who curses their mother multiplies sin.
12 My child, uphold your father's honor
 and never abandon him all the days of your life.
13 And even if his mind should fail, help him
 and never humiliate him all the days of his life.
14 Justice towards a father will never be erased
 and in the place of sin *it will be broken* (mg: planted).
15 In the day of distress, it will be remembered for your benefit,
 like heat on frost, to make your sins disappear.
16 For the one who disdains their father is insolent
 and the one who curses their mother offends their Creator.

3:12 התחזק — The *hithpael* of חזק can have a reflexive meaning, "to fortify oneself," which is how the Syriac understood it, or a transitive meaning, "to lend a hand to someone" (cf. Dan 10:21; 1 Chr 11:10 with the preposition ב; 2 Chr 16:9), which is how the Greek seems to have understood it, translating ἀντιλαμβάνομαι. — ואל תעזבהו כל ימי חייך A similar idea is found in Tob 4:3.
3:13 עזב — The verb may have the meaning "rescue, help" here (cf. Neh 3:8), in contrast to its meaning in the preceding line. There is a similar play on the word conveying this double sense in Exod 23:5: "כִּי־תִרְאֶה חֲמוֹר שֹׂנַאֲךָ רֹבֵץ תַּחַת מַשָּׂאוֹ וְחָדַלְתָּ מֵעֲזֹב לוֹ עָזֹב תַּעֲזֹב עִמּוֹ If you see the donkey of the one who hates you fall beneath its load, stop abandoning it and help it." Alternatively, it may retain the meaning "leave, neglect, abandon," as in the previous stich, but in a positive sense, "pardon" (see, for example, the use of עזב in CD V 6 with the meaning "to pardon"); this is how the Greek translator seems to have understood it, translating συγγνώμεν ἕξει τινί.

3:14 צדקת אב — The construct state, "justice of a father," should be understood as an objective genitive ("the justice one owes to a father") rather than as a subjective genitive ("the justice coming from a father"), see Bohlen (1991, 58). In this context the meaning of the word צדקה comes close to "charity, alms" as in the Dead Sea Scrolls (see Zanella 2013, 269–87). תמור — Except here and in Sir 4:10ᴬ, the form is not attested outside *piyyutim* (Lévi 1901, 4–5; Segal 1958, 16). נתע — The verb נתע only occurs once in Biblical Hebrew, in Job 4:10, where scholars think that it is either an Aramaic form of the Hebrew נתץ "to break"(cf. Ps 58:7) or a scribal error that they suggest correcting to נתץ (see DCH 5:815, BDB, HALOT). The verb נתע appears in Syriac with the meaning "to tip the scales." With this sense, the verse could then be understood as: "instead of sin, it will tip the scales." However, this verb is most probably the result of the phonetic confusion between *tav* and *tet*, as is suggested by the marginal correction of Hᴬ. The *niphal* of נטע "plant" is found especially in late Hebrew.

ותאהב מנתן מתנות·	בני בעשרך 9התהלך בענוה· 17 C
ולפני אֵ‍ תמצא רחמים:	מעט נפשך מכל 10גדולת עולם 18 C
11ולענוים יגלה סודו·	כי רבים רחמי אלהים 20
ומכוסה 12ממך אֵ‍ תחקור:	פלאות ממך אל תדרוש 21 C
ואין לך עסק 13בנסתרות:	במה שהורשית התבונן 22 C
כי רב ממך הראית:	וביותר ממך אֵ‍ תמר 23
ודמיונות רעות מתעות:	כי 14רבים עשתוני בני אדם 24
ואוהב טובות ינהג בהם:	לב כבד 15תבאש אחריתו 26
ומתחולל מוסיף עון על עון:	לב כבד ירבו 16מכאביו 27 C
ובאין דעת תחסר חכמה:	באין אישון יחסר 17אור 25
18כי אין לה רפואה	אל תרוץ לרפאות מכ{ל}ת לך 28
	כי מנטע רע נטעו:

3:17 ומאיש מתן תאהב | (חמב ܕܡܗܒܚܠܗ) A S ותאהב מנתן מתנות · C · בענוה הלוך A G S | התהלך בענוה C · את כל מלאכתיך C G · בעשרך A S | ובעיני אלהים A G S | ולפני אֵ‍ C · בני גדול אתה כן תשפיל נפשך A S | מעט נפשך מכל גדולת עולם 3:18 · (אבי‍) C G S · חן A S | רחמים C · 3:21 · תדרוש A | תחקור C · תחקור A | ומכוסה A | ורעים C · 3:22 · במה שהורשיתA | באשר הורשיתה C · ועסק A | ואין לך עסק C · ועסק אל A G · תדרוש C · 3:27 יהי לך C · מכאביו A | כאבן C · יכביד A | ירבו C · חטוא A | ומתחולל A | מוסיף A | יוסיף C · עון על עון A | עון יוסיף C · חוטא · C · חטא על חטא C

L. 13 [3:23] תמר — A *dalet* (תמד) is also possible (see the complete introduction).

L. 17 [3:28] מכ{ל}ת — The *lamed* has been erased and replaced with a *tav*.

3:17 בעשרך — For the expression, "in your wealth...," compare with the converse formulas in 4QInstruction: ברישכה "in your poverty..." (4Q416 2 i 4; 2 iii 6.15.20) or במחסורכה "in your destitution" (4Q416 2 ii 20; 4Q417 2 i 24, 2 ii + 23 5; 4Q418 7b 7). In such expressions, a temporal nuance is sometimes implied, e.g., "when you are wealthy" (see van Peursen 2004, 335). התהלך — For the use of the *hithpael* of הלך in a moral sense, "to behave," see Ps 26:3; 101:2; Prov 20:7 and especially its characteristic use in 4QInstruction (35×, cf. Rey 2009, 34). ותאהב — The verb should be understood as a volitive following the imperative of the preceding stich (cf. van Peursen 2004, 174, 178; Joosten 2005, 334). The *niphal* of אהב is found only in 2 Sam 1:23, Sir 7:35ᴬ and in Rabbinic Hebrew. מנתן מתנות — "More than one who offers gifts." Segal (1953, 16–17) suggests understanding the expression as a designation for God, "and then you will be loved by him who offers gifts," so that verses 17–18 are parallel. For the use of מן to introduce the agent of a passive verb, see Joüon §132c. Hᶜ avoids all ambiguity by using the expression איש מתן.

3:18 The translation of the first stich presents some problems. Most commentators (Box and Osterley 1913, 325; Lévi 1901, 6; Smend 1906a, 28; Segal 1958, 18; Skehan and Di Lella 1987, 158; Mopsik 2003, 72; van Peursen 2004, 194) understand מעט as a *piel* imperative with the meaning found in Rabbinic Hebrew: מעט עצמך "to humble yourself." The expression can be compared to 4Q416 2 ii 6 [+ 4Q417 2 ii + 23 8]: ובדבריכה אל תמעט רוחכה "and by your words do not humble your spirit." For the equivalence between רוחך and נפשך, see Sir 4:9ᴬ. The preposition מן could have a privative meaning (literally, "to make your soul small by depriving it of all the greatness of the world") or a comparative value ("to make your soul smaller than all the greatness of the world"). In light of this difficulty, Smend (1906a, 1) follows the Syriac in correcting מכול to בכול. Another solution would be to understand מעט as a noun (cf. Deut 7:7): "Your soul is smaller than all the greatness of the world, but (yet) before God you will find mercy." עולם — In Ben Sira, as in Biblical Hebrew, the term usually has a temporal value, but here it seems to mean "the world," as in Rabbinic Hebrew and already עלם in Aramaic. The "greatness of the world" may refer to worldly riches, honors or even what follows in v.21, that which "is too marvelous for you" (as Mopsik 2003, 72). תמצא רחמים — This expression is not found in Biblical Hebrew, at Qumran or in the Mishnah, but is found at least nine other times in texts of the 11th century (see Maagarim). The expression seems to replace the frequent idiom מצא חן "to find grace," perhaps under the influence of the following stich and/or the Aramaic idiom שכח רחמים.

3:20 יגלה יגלה — The scribe corrected the dittography by crossing out one of the words. סודו — "his purpose" or "his secret," cf. Prov 11:13; 20:19 and 25:9. This stich is probably inspired by Amos 3:7 and is the source of Luke 10:21–22 // Matt 11:25–29.

3:21–22 These two couplets are referred to several times in rabbinic literature, cf. y. Hag 9b–10a,1 רבי לעזר בשם בר סירה: פליאה ממך מה תדרש עמוקה משאול מה תחקור במה שהורשיתה התבונן אין לך עסק בנסתרות | b. Hag 13a כתוב בספר בן סירא במופלא ממך אל תדרוש ובמכוסה ממך אל תחקור במה שהורשית התבונן אין לך עסק בנסתרות; Gen. Rab. 8 אל תדרוש בחזוק ממך ובל תחקור במופלא ממך בל תדע במכוסה ממך בל תשאל במה שהרשית במופלא ממך: Saadiah Gaon *Sefer HaGaluy*: התבונן אין לך עסק בנסתרות אל תדרוש במכוסה ממך אל תחקר באשר הרשיתה לא יש לך עסק בנסתרות (ed. Harkavy 1891, 178, l. 18), and in a *piyyut* of Eleazar HaQalir מה אשר אנוש הורשה להתבונן לבונין לשנין :זאת בזאת נכתבה פרשה ולאששה.

3:22 ש... במה — The construction מה ש... is the result of Aramaic influence (cf. van Peursen 2004, 316), and in Biblical Hebrew, it is found only in Qohelet (1:9; 3:15; 3:22; 6:10; 7:24; 8:7; 10:14). שהורשית — The verb רשה does not appear in the Hebrew Bible and only here in Ben Sira. It is known in Aramaic and is found twice at Qumran (CD XI 20 // 4Q271 5 i 13; 1QM XII 4), as well as in Rabbinic Hebrew with the meaning "to authorize, permit." עסק — The term is not found in Biblical Hebrew, but exists in Aramaic and Rabbinic Hebrew with the meaning "business, occupation." It may also have the meaning "anxiety, worry." See Sir 7:25ᴬ,ᶜ; 38:24ᴮ; 40:1ᴮ and Sir 11:10ᴬ (spelled עשק). בנסתרות — Cf. Deut 29:28. The *niphal* participle of סתר is particularly frequent at Qumran and, in contrast to Ben Sira, is connected with the motif of revelation: 1QHᵃ XIX 20 // 4Q427 1 1 תרותיכה גליתה לי ונס] "Your hidden things you have revealed to me," 4Q268 1 7 // 4Q266 2 i 5 ויגל ע]יניה[ם בנסתרות "He opens their eyes to hidden things," see also 1QHᵃ XXVI 15 // 4Q427 7 i 19 and 4Q417 1 i 11 // 4Q418 43–45 i 9 ובכושר

17 Mon enfant, dans ta richesse, conduis-toi avec humilité
et tu seras aimé davantage que celui qui offre des présents.
18 Humilie-toi en te privant de toutes les grandeurs du monde
et devant Dieu tu trouveras miséricorde.
20 Car abondante est la miséricorde de Dieu
et aux humbles ~~il révèle~~ il révèle son dessein.
21 Ce qui est trop merveilleux pour toi ne le sonde pas
et ce qui t'est caché ne le recherche pas.
22 À ce qui t'est permis, réfléchis,
mais quant aux choses cachées, ce n'est pas ton affaire.
23 Ne te révolte pas contre ce qui est au-delà de toi-même,
car ce qui t'a été dévoilé est plus grand que toi.
24 En effet, nombreux sont les plans des êtres humains,
mais les imaginations mauvaises égarent.
26 Un cœur endurci, sa fin sera odieuse
et celui qui aime les bienfaits sera guidé par eux.
27 Un cœur endurci, ses douleurs se multiplieront
et celui qui accumule faute sur faute se tourmentera.
25 Faute de pupille, la lumière manque,
faute de connaissance, la sagesse manque.
28 Ne cours pas guérir la plaie du moqueur,
car elle est incurable,
car son plant (vient) d'un plant mauvais.

17 My child, in your wealth, behave humbly
and you will be loved more than one who gives gifts.
18 Humble yourself by refusing all the great things of the world
and you will find mercy before God.
20 For the mercy of God is great,
and ~~he reveals~~ he reveals his purpose to the humble.
21 That which is too wondrous for you, do not investigate,
and what is hidden from you, do not explore.
22 Ponder on what is permitted to you,
but as to hidden things, they are not your affair.
23 Do not revolt against what is beyond you,
for what you have been shown is greater than you.
24 Indeed, many are the plans of humankind,
but evil fantasies lead astray.
26 A hardened heart, its end will be odious,
and the one who loves blessings will be guided by them.
27 A hardened heart, its pains will multiply,
and one who adds sin upon sin will writhe in torment.
25 Without a pupil light is absent,
and without knowledge wisdom is absent.
28 Do not run to treat the wound of the mocker,
for it is incurable,
indeed, thier plant (comes) from an evil plant.

נוד[עו נס]תרי מחשבתו מבינות "And in overflowing comprehension were kno[wn the sec]rets of his purpose." אין לך עסק בנסתרות — Lit., "There is no business for you in the hidden things," which seems to mean that "the hidden things" (which have not been revealed to you) are none of your business.

3:23 ביותר — The substantive יותר "superiority, advantage, excess" is characteristic of late Hebrew (1× 1 Sam, 1× Esth, 7× Qoh, 6× Sir, 3× Qumran and frequent in Rabbinic Hebrew). תמר — The form presents difficulties and several emendations have been proposed. Bacher (1900a, 274) suggests אל תעסק. Smend (1906a, 30) suggests תתור or תתר, from תור ("seek, explore"), or תותר, the *hiphil* of יתר ("leave, eliminate"). Skehan and Di Lella (1987, 158–59) find the form unintelligible and revert to אל תתעסק "meddle not" (cf. 41:22^M). Mopsik (2003, 74) proposes תמרך "do not tire yourself out" (cf. Lev 26:36). Two solutions seem more valid: either a *hiphil* of מרה (Peters 1913, 34), "to be rebellious/disobedient to God or his commandments" (cf. Ps 106:33, 43; Ezek 5:6), or reading a *dalet* in place of the *resh* in the manuscript (Ginzberg 1906, 611; Segal 1958, 18). For the confusion between *resh* and *dalet* in this manuscript, see complete introduction. תמד is a defective spelling of מדד in the *qal* "to measure," so "what is beyond you, do not measure it." הראית — For the *hophal* of ראה, cf. Deut 4:35.

3:24 עשתוני — The term only occurs in Ps 146:4, but is used frequently in the Targums for translating the Hebrew מחשבה. דמיונות — The meaning of this term is not entirely clear, as it only occurs in Ps 17:12 with the meaning "appearance." Segal (1958, 18) argues that, as it is in parallel with עשתון, it means "thoughts" (cf. the *piel* of דמה). Following this same logic, it could also refer to the imagination (see the use of דמה in Rabbinic Hebrew). It is probably used in this sense in 1QM VI 13: כול מראי דמיונים "all imaginable visions" or "every vision imaginable" (see Carmignac 1958, 97–98).

3:26 לב כבד — "A hard heart," cf. Exod 7:14 and the phrase כיבוד לב in 1QS IV 11. תבאש — In the *qal*, באש means "to smell bad, stink" and in the *niphal* "to be made stinking" or "to become odious." Both meanings may apply: "a hard heart, its end will be stinking/odious." Penar (1975, 9–10) refers to the inscription of Nerab from the seventh-century BCE, which says שהר ונכל ונשך יהבאש ממתתה ואחרתה תאבד "May Sahar, Nikkal and Nusk make his death stink/be odious and may his posterity perish" (KAI 226:9–10). It is also possible to understand באש in its Aramaic sense: "to be bad, displeasing, sick," as both the Greek and the Syriac understood it (thus Smend 1906a, 32; Segal 1958, 19). אחריתו — אחרית designates death elsewhere in Ben Sira (see 11:25–27; 16:3), and the terrible death of the impious is a recurrent theme throughout the book (Sir 11:26). ואוהב טובות ינהג בהם — Lévi (1901, 2:10), Skehan and Di Lella (1987, 162–3) find the Hebrew of v. 26b incomprehensible and follow the Greek: "And whoever loves danger will die in it". However, the Hebrew syntax, which is supported by the Syriac, does not really pose a problem, even though its interpretation is ambiguous. טובות can be understood positively (as Segal 1958, 19). The *vav* would then be adversative and this stich would stand in opposition to the preceding one concerning "hard hearts," thus "he who loves the good will be guided by it." However, טובות could also be understood negatively, as the good things that one receives, i.e., material wealth, as in Sir 11:19^A, or "flattering words," as in 2 Kgs 25:28; Jer 12:6; 52:32; and Neh 6:19 (so Mopsik 2003, 76, "gâteries"): "He who loves praise, his life will be led by this need for praise."

3:27 ומתחולל — For the *hithpolel* of חיל, cf. Job 15:20. עון על עון — Cf. Sir 5:5^{A,C} and the similar expression חטאת על חטאת in Isa 30:1.

ואזן מקשבת לחכמה תשמח:	29 לֵב חכם יבין משלי [19]חכמים
[20]כן צדקה תכפר חטאת:	30 אש לוהטת יכבו מים
ובעת [21]מֹוטו ימצא משען:	31 פועל טוב יקראנו בדרכיו

Chapter 4

וא̇ תדאיב נפש [22]ועני ומר נפֹש̇:	1 בני א̇ תלעֹג̇ לחיי עני
וא̇ תתעלם ממִדֶכָדָך [23]נפש:	2 דֶוָה נפש חסירה א̇ תפוח
וקרב עני אל תכאיב:	3 א̇ תחמיר מעי דך
ולא תבזה שאולות דל:	4 א̇ תמנע מתן [24]ממסכינך
	5 ולא תתן לו מקום לקללך:
ובקול צעקתו ישמע צורו:	6 vac. [25] צועק מר רוח בכאב נפשו
ולשלטון עיר הכאף ראש:	7 [26]האהב לנפשך לעדה
והשיבהו שלום בענוה:	8 הט לעני [27]אזנך
וא̇ [28]תקוץ רוחך במשפט יושר:	9 הושע מוצק ממציקיו
ותמור בעל [29]לאלמנות:	10 היה כאב ליתומים
ויחנך ויצילך משחת:	[1]וא̇ יקראך בן
	vacat

T-S 12.863 verso

L. 22 [4:2] דֶוֹה — As in numerous occasions in this manuscript the letter written as a *dalet* may also represent a *resh*. Additionally, the *segol* below the first *vav* may indicate a mistake and the deletion of one *vav*, though we would have expected the *segol* to be upside down. In that case, the letters may represent the word רוח.

L. 26 [4:7] עיר — The reading עיר is assured, with Beentjes (1997, 24), contra Schechter and Taylor (1899, 3), Smend (1906b, 2) who cor-

rects the text in his edition, Peters (1913, 39), Lévi (1901, 2:15), Vattioni (1968, 21) and Ben-Ḥayyim (1973, 4), who read עוד. An ink trace, which is clearly independant from the outline of the letter at the shoulder of the *resh*, misled these previous editors.

L. 29 [4:10] לאלמנות — The scribe was not able to finish the stich on the same page, so he added the last term under the last line, aligning it to the left.

3:30 For the construction of the comparative in this couplet, cf. GKC §161*b* and Sir 13:18. צדקה — As in 3:14, the word may refer here to "charity, alms." כפר — The link between the practice of justice and the expiation of sin is sufficiently rare to justify it being highlighted (cf. Prov 16:6; Dan 4:24). The same idea is expressed in Sir 3:14–15.

3:31 פועל טוב — Segal (1958, 20) understands the phrase as a divine epithet. יקראנו — See HALOT קרא II or קרה "to meet, encounter." Cf. the exact expression (בעת מוטך תמצא מֹ[שען]) in 4Q525 14 ii, 6–7. בעת מוטו — For the construction of the infinitive as *nomen rectum* of a construct state, cf. van Peursen (2004, 270). This form, which is also attested at Qumran, is absent from Rabbinic Hebrew.

4:1 For דאב נפש with the sense "to make languish, despair," see Deut 28:65 [ודאבון נפש] and Jer 31:12, 25. The *hiphil* does not appear in Biblical Hebrew, but is found with נפש as object in b. Ned. 24a, also in the works of Yannai and Qalir. For מר נפש, see Judg 18:25; 1 Sam 1:10, 22:2; 2 Sam 17:8; Job 3:20; 7:11; Prov 31:6; Isa 38:15 and Ezek 27:31.

4:2 דֶוָה — The meaning and reading of this term is not entirely clear (see the note above). By pointing דָוֶה, the scribe may have wanted to indicate that it should be understood as "suffering," and therefore could elucidate the expression מר נפש (see Segal 1958, 21). According to Smend (1906b, 35), Bacher (1900a, 275) and Lévi (1901, 13), דוה is a deformation of רוח that should be attached to the preceding stich as an explanation of the expression מר נפש (read מר רוח, cf. v. 6 and 7:11). The reading רוח may be fully justified if one takes into consideration the fact that the scribe sometimes writes *resh* in the same way as *dalet* (see complete introduction). In this case, the *segol* under the *vav* would not be its vocalization, but rather, would indicate a scribal mistake (dit-

tography of the *vav*), as it does several times in the margin of the manuscript. Assuming this is correct, it is not necessary to attach רוח נפש to the preceding stich. תפוח — The verb פוח should be understood in the sense of "breathe" here (Cant 2:17 and 4:6) and by extension, "exhale, die." In the current state of the text, תפוח is a *qal* jussive, and as such, should have רוח נפש חסירה as subject. Bacher (1900a, 275) suggests correcting the text by reading תפיח in the *hiphil*, so that the formula becomes vetitive, which would fit the context better: "do not make the breath of the needy die/perish." וא̇ תתעלם — The verb may be a 3fs (with רוח as subject) or a 2ms as in the preceding and the next stich. ממדכדך — The *pual* of דכדך is found in Palestinian Aramaic and late Rabbinic Hebrew with the meaning "to be struck, wounded" (see Jastrow 1903, 306; see also Tg. Neof. Gen 44:18, Sokoloff 1990, 149; Lev. Rab. 34:6; 'Abot R. Nat. 43).

4:3 תחמיר — The verb can have several meanings: "to boil (transitive/intransitive), stir up, burn (transitive/intransitive)." The expression is metaphorical. For a similar image, see Lam 1:20; 2:11.

4:4 ממסכינך — The pronominal suffix on"poor/destitute" should be understood as meaning "the destitute who is near you," and similar to the expressions גרך or תושבך (cf. Exod 20:10; Lev 25:6). ולא תבזה — It is difficult to know if passing from a vetitive form like אל תקטל (1*b*, 2*a*?, 2*b*?, 3*a*, 3*b*, 4*a*) to a prohibitive one like לא תקטל (4*b*) results from a confusion of the two formulas or if it implies a modal variation.

4:5 The construction ולא תקטל following the formula אל תקטל has been understood here in a final sense (cf. Joosten 2012, 156–7; Fassberg, 1994, 104–7; Joüon §116*j*; GKC §165*a*). For the construction נתן מקום לקטל, see m. Parah 3:3 and m. Ber. 4:2.

29 Un cœur sage comprendra les sentences des sages
   et une oreille attentive à la sagesse se réjouira.
30 Comme l'eau éteint un feu qui brûle,
   de même, la justice rachète le péché.
31 Celui qui fait le bien le rencontrera dans ses voies
   et lorsqu'il chancelle il trouvera un soutien.

Chapitre 4

1 Mon enfant, ne te moque pas de la vie du pauvre
  et ne fais pas languir l'âme pauvre et amère.
2 Que le souffle de l'âme de l'indigent n'expire pas
  et ne te dérobe pas à l'âme meurtrie.
3 Ne fais pas bouillonner les viscères de l'opprimé
  et les entrailles du pauvre, ne les fais pas souffrir.
4 Ne refuse pas un don à l'indigent qui est chez toi
  et tu ne mépriseras pas les requêtes du misérable
5 pour ne pas lui donner l'occasion de te maudire.
6 Celui qui a le souffle amer crie dans la souffrance de son être
  et son roc entendra le son de son cri.
7 Fais-toi aimer de l'assemblée
  et baisse la tête devant les autorités de la ville.
8 Tends l'oreille au pauvre
  et rends-lui le salut avec humilité.
9 Libère l'opprimé de ses oppresseurs
  et que ton esprit ne soit pas dégoûté de juger selon le droit.
10 Sois comme un père pour les orphelins
   et à la place du mari pour les veuves
   et Dieu t'appellera fils
   et il te fera grâce et t'arrachera de la fosse.

29 A wise heart will understand the sayings of the wise,
   and an ear that is attentive to wisdom will rejoice.
30 As water extinguishes a burning fire,
   so justice atones for sin.
31 The one who does good will encounter it on their paths,
   and when they stumble, they will find support.

Chapter 4

1 My child, do not mock the life of the poor,
  and do not weary a person who is poor or bitter.
2 Let the spirit of the soul of the needy not perish,
  and do not avoid one who is wounded in their soul.
3 Do not inflame the emotions of the oppressed,
  and do not pain the bosom of the poor.
4 Do not refuse a gift to the destitute who is near you
  and you should not despise the requests of the impoverished.
5 so as not to give them occasion to curse you.
6 (When) one of bitter spirit cries out in the pain of their soul,
  their rock hears the sound of their cry.
7 Make yourself beloved by the assembly
  and bow your head before the authorities of the city.
8 Lend your ear to the poor person
  and return their greeting with humility.
9 Free the oppressed from their oppressors
  and let your spirit not loathe a just judgment.
10 Be like a father to orphans
   and a husband to widows,
   and he (God) will call you son,
   and he will have mercy on you and deliver you from the pit.

4:6 מר רוח — The phrase is very close to מר נפש found in 4:1. The two could be synonymous (cf. רוחך in 4:9 as a possible equivalent to נפשך). צורו — Lit., "his rock." The word may also be understood as "his God," since צור in the Second Temple era seems to be used less often in a literal sense (e.g., "rock" in 1QHᵃ XVI 24) and more often in its figurative sense (see the translations of צור in the LXX). Here, it may be used in the sense "his creator," similar to or due to confusion with יֹצֵר (see the Greek ὁ ποιήσας αὐτόν and the Syriac ܒܘܿܗ and note the similar expressions in Prov 14:31 and 17:5).

4:7 האהב — The *hiphil* of אהב is not found in Biblical Hebrew, nor at Qumran, but it does appear in Rabbinic Hebrew. לנפשך — The *lamed* marks the accusative, as in Aramaic. ולשלטון — This is an Aramaism (cf. Qoh 8:8). הכאף — The spelling is surprising since a root כאף is otherwise unknown, though such a root may have existed as a biform of כפף (cf. מאס // מסס) or of כוף (cf. לוט/לאט and רום/ראם; see Segal 1958, 22). Well-attested in Aramaic, the root כוף is possibly found in Hebrew only at Sir 30:12. Alternatively, the *aleph* may be a mater for /ē/ (see Qimron 1986, §100.61; Kutscher 1974, 162; Reymond 2014, 46-47; Qimron 2018, 77-78); both כוף and כפף would be vocalized the same: הַכֵאף. For the expression with the *qal* of כפף, see Isa 58:5.

4:8 והשיבהו שלום בענוה — Literally, "return his peace humbly," that is, answer the poor person's greeting (cf. m. Ber. 2:1; Luke 10:5–6 // Matt 10:12).

4:9 תקוץ — The construction ב + קוץ has the meaning "to be disgusted, loathe," see HALOT, Sir 6:25 and 50:25. The verb can also have a nuance of "fear, dread" (cf. Exod 1:12; Num 22:3; Isa 7:16), but in this case, it is construed with מפני. רוחך seems to be equivalent to נפשך here (cf. Sir 3:18 and the note).

4:10 תמור — See Sir 3:14 and the note. ואל יקראך בן — For the formula, cf. Matt 5:9: "Blessed are the peacemakers, for they will be called sons of God" (NRSV). For the notion of God as father, see Sir 51:1,10 and Puech 2001, 287–310. ויצילך משחת — For the expression, see CD XIV 2. The two terms נצל and שחת have strong eschatological resonances in the Qumran texts, שחת often being synonymous with Sheol (4Q418 69 ii 6; 1QHᵃ XI 19–20; XIII 8; XVI 29–30; 1QS IV 11–14; 1QS XI 13, see also Sir 51:2). For the last stich the Greek has a radically different text.

ותעיד לכל מבינים בה:		חכמות למדה ²בניה	11
ומבקשיה ³יפיקו רצון מיי:		אהביה אהבו חיים	12
ויחנו בברכת יי		ותמכיה ימצאו כבוד מיי	13
ואלהו במא ויהא		⁴משרתי קדשׁ· משרתיה	14
⁵ומאזין לי ייחן בחדרי מבית:		שומע לי ישפט אמת	15
ולפנים ⁶יבחרנו בנסיונות:		כי בהתנכר אלך עמו	17
		ועד עת ימלא לבו בי	
⁷וגליתי לו מסתרי:		אשוב אאשרנו	18
ויסרתיהו באסורים:		אם יסור ונטותיהו	19
ואסגירנו לשדדים:		⁸אם יסור מאחרי אשליכנו	
ואٴ נפשך אٴ תבוש		בני ערٴ ⁹המון שמר ופחד מרע	20
ויש בשת כבוד וחן:		כי יש בٰשׁَאֵרٰ ¹⁰משאת עון	21 ᶜ
¹¹ואל תכשל למכשוליך:		אל תשא פניך על נפשך	22 ᶜ

למכשוליך · C G S | תבוש A | תכשל C · פנים לנَפְשׁَךَ C · פניך על נפשך A | 4:22 · חן וכבוד C | חן וכבוד A G S | בשת C · בَשׂْאֵת A | > C · כי A G S | 4:21
· למכשול לך A | C ·

L. 4 [4:14] קדשׁ — The punctuation after קדש may be wrong (the scribe would have just started tracing a letter; see also what may be a dot after the *shin* of תבאש in Sir 3:26 [T-S 12.863 recto l. 15]).

4:11 חכמות — As Segal (1958, 24) notes, it could be a plural of majesty (as Joüon §134d) or a plural of abstraction. In either case, as in Prov 1:20 and 9:1, the verb is conjugated in the singular. למדה — The *qatal* must have a gnomic value here (Joüon §112d). ותעיד — See Couroyer 1975, 206–17, who proposes to translate the verb "to instruct." מבינים — The *hiphil* participle of בין only appears in late Hebrew (in the plural, see Ezra 8:16; Neh 8:3, 7, 9; 1QHᵃ X 18; 4Q303 1; 4Q372 8 4). At Qumran, and more specifically in 4QInstruction, the participle seems to designate the sage, "they who understand(s)."

4:12 אהביה — The assimilation of Wisdom with a cherished spouse is a *topos* in sapiential literature (cf. Sir 15:2b; Prov 4:6b; Wis 8:2, 9, 16–17). יפיקו רצון מיי — For the expression, see Prov 8:35 and 18:22. The verb פוק is found three times at Qumran, always in a sapiential and cognitive context (4Q424 3 7; 4Q525 5 10; 14 ii 19).

4:13 ויחנו — The form may derive from the root חנה "camp" (as in the Syriac) or from the root חנן, which would be read as וְיָחֻנּוּ, "they will find mercy through God's blessing," i.e., as a passive *qal / hophal* of חנן. Two other attestations occur in Isa 26:10 and Prov 21:10, see Bauer 1922, §286m, and another in Sir 12:13ᴬ. For the analogous construction in the active voice, with חנן followed by the *bet* preposition + ברכה, see 1QSb (1Q28b) I 5 and cf. II 24, 25, 26. See Reymond 2016b for a general treatment of the passive *qal* in Second Temple Hebrew.

4:14 משרתי קדש — The expression may refer to "ministers of the sanctuary," "holy ministers," or even "ministers of the Holy One" (a defective writing of קדוש, as in the Greek). Segal (1958, 25) notes that קדש may also be a name for angels, and refers to y. Ber. 9:4: כבוד לכם המכובדים משרתי קודש). See a perhaps similar expression in 4Q287 2 9. The phrase can be compared to שרי קדש in 1 Chr 24:5; see also משרתי מזבח in Joel 1:13, משרתי הבית in Ezek 45:5 and 46:24, משרתי המקדש in Ezek 45:4, משרתים לבית אלהינו in Ezra 8:17 and Neh 10:37, משרתי דבי]ר in 4Q392 1 9 and משרתי פנים בדביר כבודו in 4Q400 1 i 4. ואלהו במא ויהא — The second stich is often considered to be incomprehensible. According to Schechter and Taylor (1899, 41), Lévi (1901, 17), and Segal (1958, 25), the preserved text could be a corruption of ואל אוהב מאהביה, which would agree with the Greek and Prov 8:17, though it may also be read as a mistake for ואלוה במאיה "God is with those who desire her" (see Habermann 1964, 297 and Reymond 2018a), which has the advantage of preserving the text as it stands.

4:15 אמת — One could read אֱמֶת with an adverbial value, "verily, in truth," (cf. BDB, HALOT) as the Syriac understood it, or less easily אֻמּוֹת "nations," following the Greek, but in this case, the preferred spelling would be אומות, as in 4Q266 11 10, or at least אמות. Van Peursen (2004, 30–31, 34) has demonstrated that the Greek translator of Ben Sira probably had a consonantal text with fewer *matres lectionis* than the Cairo Genizah manuscripts. However, the feminine plural ending in defective script is relatively rare. One example may be found in Sir 48:7, where the Greek has the singular ἐλεγμόν indicating a *Vorlage* of תוֹכַחַת, while Hᴮ has the plural תוכחות. Nevertheless, it is possible that, here again, the discrepancy results from the translator, rather than a different *Vorlage*. ייחן — As in 4:13, the form may come from either חנה (in the *jussive*) "to set up camp, settle" or חנן "to find grace" in the *niphal*, which is found in late Rabbinic Hebrew (יֵחַן). בחדרי מבית — The letters מבית are difficult to interpret. Palestinian Aramaic may preserve a noun מבית "residence" (see CAL 22 Jan., 2022). Alternatively, they may be a mistake for הבית, the expression בחדרי הבית having a parallel in 1Q19 3 5.

4:16 Verse 16 is missing in the Hebrew, although it is attested in the Greek and the Syriac.

4:17 The Greek and the Syriac have five stichs. The Greek deviates significantly from the Hebrew, while the Syriac has retained the content. The Hebrew copyist likely lost a stich and a half by *homoioteleuton* (see stichs c and d in the Syriac: ܒܩܕܡܝܬܐ ܐܣܝܘܗܝ ܘܕܚܠܬܐ, ܐܪܡܐ ܥܠܘܗܝ, ܘܐܒܚܘܪܝܘܗܝ ܒܢܣܝܘܢܝ "At first, I will test him, fear and trembling I will place upon him, and I will examine him through my tests"). בהתנכר — "to pass oneself off as a foreigner" (see Gen 42:7) or "to make oneself unrecognizable" (see 1 Kgs 14:5). יבחרנו — This word should be understood in the sense of "to test," as in Isa 48:10, under the influence of Aramaic. The third person should probably be corrected to the first person singular. The error was already transmitted in the Latin version (*et in primis eligit eum*). בנסיונות — נסיון, "ordeal," does not appear in Biblical Hebrew, but appears three times in Ben Sira, in 4:17ᴬ; 6:7ᴬ and 13:11ᴬ; in 1QHᵃ IV 22 and in Mishnaic Hebrew.

11 La sagesse enseigne ses enfants
et avertit tous ceux qui l'étudient.

12 Ceux qui l'aiment, aiment la vie
et ceux qui la cherchent obtiendront la faveur (qui vient) de YYY

13 et ceux qui la saisissent trouveront la gloire (qui vient) de YYY
et trouveront grâce dans la bénédiction de YYY.

14 Ceux qui la servent, servent le Saint
et Dieu est avec ceux qui la désirent.

15 Et celui qui m'écoute jugera en vérité
et celui qui me prête l'oreille campera dans les chambres intérieures.

17 Car je marcherai avec lui en me faisant passer pour un étranger
et d'abord, *il* le passera au crible par des épreuves
et ce, jusqu'au moment où son cœur sera rempli de moi,

18 et je reviendrai le rendre heureux
et je lui révélerai mon secret.

19 S'il se détourne alors je l'écarterai
et le disciplinerai avec des chaînes.
S'il se détourne de ma suite, je le rejetterai
et je le livrerai aux violents.

20 Mon enfant, au temps du tumulte, sois attentif et redoute le mal,
afin de ne pas avoir honte de toi-même.

21 Car il y a une honte qui amène le péché
et il y a une honte qui est honneur et grâce.

22 Ne sois pas honteux de toi-même
et ne trébuche pas dans tes embûches.

11 Wisdom teaches her children
and warns all those who study her.

12 Those who love her love life,
and those who seek her will obtain favor from YYY,

13 and those who grasp her will find honor from YYY,
and will find grace in the blessing of YYY.

14 Those who serve her are ministers of the Holy One,
and God is with those who desire her.

15 The one who hears me will judge truly
and the one who listens to me will camp in the inner chambers.

17 For I will walk with him while making myself out to be a stranger
and first, *he* will test him by ordeals,
and this, until his heart is full of me,

18 and I will again make him happy
and I will reveal my secret to him.

19 If he turns away, then I will cast him off,
and will discipline him with shackles.
If he turns away from following me, I will throw him off
and will deliver him up to violent people.

20 My child, in time of trouble, be attentive and fear evil,
so you will not be ashamed of yourself.

21 For there is shame that leads to sin,
and there is shame that is honor and grace.

22 Do not feel shame about yourself,
and do not stumble on your own stumbling blocks.

4:18 אאשרנו — The verb אשר may mean "to declare happy" (Gen 30:13; Prov 31:28) or "to guide on the right path" (Prov 23:19), which is how the Greek understood it.

4:19 נטותיהו — The Hebrew presents a problem. It could be corrected to נטיתיהו from נטה with the meaning "to deviate, stray"(see especially Isa 30:11 and Prov 4:27 where it is in parallel with סור) or to נטשתיהו "to leave, abandon," following Bacher (1900a, 275), Lévi (1901, 18), Smend (1906a, 43), and Segal (1958, 26), and agreeing with the Greek. ויסרתיהו באסורים — While unnecessary, some have suggested correcting to אסרתיהו "I bind him with chains" (as Touzard 1904) or ביסורים "I will punish him" (as Lévi 1901, 19). יסור מאחרי — For the expression סור מאחרי, cf. Deut 7:4; 1 Sam 12:20, 21; 2 Sam 2:21, 22; 2 Kgs 18:6; 2 Chr 34:33 and Job 34:27. Note the play on words and the alliteration between סור, יסר and אסור.

4:20 עת המון — An adverbial accusative (see Ps 69:14) or the object of שמר (cf. Job 24:15). ופחד מרע — With פחד, the preposition מן can introduce the object when it is a person (Isa 19:17; Job 23:15; Ps 27:1). Compare with Sir 41:3[B,M] אל תפחד ממות חוקיך and 1QH[a] 4 9 ואני פחדתי ממשפטכה at Qumran. אל תבוש — The vav followed by an indirect volitive expresses finality here (cf. Joüon, §116j, §168b), even though the construction seems strange because we find אל תבוש when we expect לא תבוש and because the object appears before the verb.

4:21 בֹּשֶׁאת — The term is pointed and vocalized this way in the manuscript. The dot in the middle of the *aleph* probably indicates that the letter is erroneous—a scribal error under the influence of משאת, which follows. What seems a mark under the aleph could also be an extended *keraia*. משאת — A *hiphil* participle of נשא with the meaning "to bring" (cf. HALOT) or "to announce" (cf. Jastrow 1903, 938). Alternatively, the word may be a noun מַשָּׂאָה (see Isa 30:27): "there is a shame (that is) a burden of sin" (see Maagarim).

4:22 אל תשא פניך — The suffix of פניך seems redundant (cf. H[C] פנים). The expression נשא פנים (cf. 35:16[B]; 42:1[B,M]) can mean "to show mercy to someone" (Gen 19:21; 1 Sam 25:32), "to show consideration for someone" (Num 6:26; Deut 28:50) or "to be partial to someone" (Lev 19:15; Deut 10:17). Here, the expression may then mean "Do not be partial towards yourself" or "Do not favor yourself." Due to the parallelism with 4:20b (see also 42:1), Kister (1999, 171) suggests understanding the expression as "to be ashamed," and rendering the sentence "Do not be ashamed about yourself and let not shame cause you stumbling." This verse is referred to in Der. Er. Zuṭ. 2:4: אל תשא פנים לעצמך לומר לא שמעתי with the variant אל תבוש לומר לא שמעתי. Another convincing argument to justify this meaning in late Hebrew is its translation by (ἐπ)αἰσχύνομαι in the LXX of Job 32:21 and 34:19 (see also Darshan 2019). על נפשך — The use of the preposition על is surprising and probably stems from a confusion with אל, the two prepositions being interchangeable in late Hebrew. ואל תכשל — The construction כשל + ל is unique, as it is usually כשל + ב.

אל תצפין ¹²את חכמתך:		אל תמנע דבר בעולם	23 c
ותבונה במענה לשון:		כי באומר נודעת חכמה	24
ואל אהים היכנע:		vac. ¹³ אל תסרב עם הא׳	25
¹⁴ואל תעמוד לפני שבלת:		אל תבוש לשוב מעון	26
ואל תמאן לפני ¹⁵מושלים:		אל תצע לנבל נפשך	27
כי כאשר כרצונו תשפט ¹⁶עמו		אל תשב עם שופט עול	
וי׳י נלחם לך˙		עד המות היעצה על הצדק	28
ואל לשונך אל תרגל:		אל תקרא ¹⁷בעל שתים	
ורפי ¹⁸ורשיש במלאכתך:		אל תהי גבהן בלשוניך	29
ומוזר ומתירא ¹⁹במלאכתך:		אל תהי ככלב בביתך	30 c
וקפוצה בתוך מתן:		אל תהי ידך פתוחה לקחת	31 c

Chapter 5

ואל תאמר יש לאל ידי		²⁰אל תשען על חילך	1
²¹ללכת אחר תאות נפשך:		אל תשען על כוחך	
ללכת ²²בחמודות רעה:		אל תלך אחרי לבך ועיניך	2
כי י׳י מבקש נרדפים:		אל תאמר מי יוכל כחו	3

4:23 בעולם A | בעיתו C G S · 4:23 ואל A | אל C G S · תצפין A G S | תקפוץ C 4:30 ככלב A S | כאריה C G · ומזר ומתירא A S | ומתפחז C G (= פחד √?) · ובעת השב קפודה C G · וקפוצה בתוך מתן A S | מושטת לשאת C G S · 4:31 במלאכתך A | בעבודתך C S · פתוחה לקחת A

4:23 The second stich of this verse is absent from Greek I, but is present in Greek II and in the Syriac. בעולם — The form בעולם is surprising here, as the Greek and the Syriac confirm the reading in Hᶜ בעיתו "in his time." עולם may be explained here by its usage in the meaning "life time" in Rabbinic Hebrew. אל תצפין — Note the full spelling of the *jussive*, in place of the biblical form תִּצְפֹּן. The *scriptio plena* of what would be *tsere* (in the Masoretic tradition) coming from the short *i*, is frequent in Hᴬ and Hᴮ (see van Peursen 2004, 46).

4:24 במענה לשון — For the expression, cf. Prov 16:1: לאדם מערכי לב ומיהוה מענה לשון "The plans of the mind belong to mortals, but the answer of the tongue is from the Lord" (NRSV). The expression is particularly frequent in the *Hodayot* at Qumran where it refers to the "proper, appropriate response."

4:25 The verbal form סרב does not appear in Biblical Hebrew; see however the nominal form סָרָבִים in Ezra 2:6. In Aramaic and in Mishnaic Hebrew, it can mean "to be rebellious." This verse is unusual, both in its use of the preposition עם and in its use of the article before אל. According to Schechter and Taylor (1899, 42), a copyist confused האל for האמת (as the Greek and the Syriac): אל תסרב על האמת. The Syriac literally has ܠܐ ܬܚܣܘܡ ܥܠ ܫܪܪܐ. Box and Oesterley (1913, 330) note that in y. San. 2a, אמת is identified with the divine name. היכנע — The spelling requires reading a *niphal* imperative, "humble yourself." With regard to the syntax, the use of (מ)(ל)פני would have been preferable to אל. The variants between versions suggest that the Hebrew is altered here (Skehan and Di Lella [1987, 174–5] propose reading ועל אולתך הכלם "Be ashamed of your own foolishness").

4:26 לשוב — שוב expresses more than simply "turning away from," but rather "repentance, conversion." ואל תעמוד לפני שבלת — Lévi (1901, 21) and Segal (1958, 29) give a series of interesting parallels to this stich: Gen. Rab. 44 כל מי שהוא מעמיד פנים בגל הגל שוטפו "Whoever stands in front of the wave, the wave drowns them"; b. Yeb 121a; Aḥiqar syr. 2:65 "My child, do not argue with a person in their day and do not stand before a river in its cresting" (see also Aḥiqar syr. 2:43) and Ps.-Phoc. 121: "Accommodate yourself to the circumstances, do not blow against the winds" (*OTP* 2:578).

4:27 תצע — This is a short form of the *hiphil* of יצע (תַּצִּעַ). It is unnecessary to correct to תַּצִּיעַ, as Lévi (1901, 22) suggests. The verb refers to the action of spreading materials to prepare a bed (cf. Isa 58:5). . . . כאשר כ — The construction seems needlessly redundant.

4:27c–d These two stichs seem to be borrowed from or paralleled by Sir 8:14. Note the incoherent repetition of כאשר כ.

4:28 היעצה — Note the *scriptio plena* of the imperative *niphal* of עצה, from the Aramaic "to fight, use violence, put pressure on" (Segal 1958, 29). אל תקרא . . . אל תרגל — This couplet is a doublet of Sir 5:14ᴬ. בעל שתים — For the expression (lit. "master of two [tongues]"), see also Sir 5:14ᴬ; Sir 6:1ᴬ (= δίγλωσσος); Sir 28:13 (δίγλωσσος, in the Syriac, ܠܫܢܐ ܬܠܝܬܝܐ) and Sir 28:14, 15 (γλῶσσα τρίτη). אל תרגל — Lit., "Do not let your tongue run on." A similar expression is found in Ps 15:3 לא רגל על לשנו and in 4Q525 2 ii 1 ולוא רגל על לשונו. As in 4:22ᴬ, the use of אל instead of על probably results from an assimilation of the two prepositions (cf. . . . . אל תרגל ב in 5:14ᴬ).

4:29 גבהן — A *hapax* probably formed from the root גבה "to be high, elevated" (See Dihi 2004, 113–6). בלשוניך — Probably the *scriptio plena* of the singular pausal form (cf. pl. לשנות and note van Peursen 2004, 49). ורפי — The *yod* is a mater for the preceding vowel, which would be *segol* in Biblical Hebrew (i.e., רָפֶה; see Num 13:18). רשיש — The word is only attested in Ben Sira (see also Sir 11:12ᴬ) and is either related to the root רשש "to smash, crush," and thus translated "feeble, weak," or to the root רוש (cf. Sir 11:12ᴬ where רשש is translated by νωθρός), and thus translated "impoverished."

4:30 ככלב — "Like a dog," in agreement with the Syriac, whereas Hᶜ and the Greek have "like a lion" (כאריה and ὡς λέων). The earlier

23 Ne retiens pas (ta) parole éternellement,
   ne dissimule pas ta sagesse,
24 car par la parole est connue la sagesse
   et l'intelligence par une réponse de langue.
25 Ne sois pas rebelle avec Dieu
   et humilie-toi devant Dieu.
26 N'aie pas honte de te détourner du péché
   et ne te tiens pas debout face à un torrent.
27 Ne t'aplatis pas pour un insensé
   et ne présente pas un refus devant les gouverneurs.
   Ne t'assieds pas avec un juge inique,
   car selon son bon plaisir tu jugeras avec lui.
28 Jusqu'à la mort, lutte en faveur de la justice
   et YYY combattra pour toi.
   Ne te fais pas taxer de duplicité
   et par ta langue, ne calomnie pas.
29 Ne sois pas hautain par ta langue
   et faible et abattu dans tes actes.
30 Ne sois pas comme un chien dans ta maison
   et oppressé et timoré dans tes actes.
31 Que ta main ne soit pas ouverte pour prendre
   et fermée au moment de donner.

Chapitre 5

1 Ne t'appuie pas sur ta vigueur
   et ne dis pas : « j'en ai le pouvoir ».
   Ne t'appuie pas sur ta propre force
   pour suivre ton propre désir.
2 Ne suis pas ton cœur ou tes yeux
   pour aller vers des convoitises mauvaises.
3 Ne dis pas « qui peut l'emporter (sur) *ma* force ? »
   Car YYY recherche ceux qui sont persécutés.

23 Do not withhold your word forever,
   do not hide your wisdom,
24 For it is by words that wisdom is known,
   and understanding by an answer of the tongue.
25 Do not be rebellious against God,
   and humble yourself before God.
26 Do not be ashamed to turn away from sin,
   and do not stand before a torrent.
27 Do not subordinate yourself to a fool,
   and do not offer refusal before the governors.
   and do not sit with an unjust judge,
   for according to their will, you will judge with them.
28 Until death, fight for justice,
   and YYY will fight for you.
   Do not let yourself be called a hypocrite,
   and do not slander with your tongue.
29 Do not be haughty with your language,
   and feeble and downcast in your acts.
30 Do not be like a dog in your house,
   and oppressed and timid in your actions.
31 Do not let your hand be open to take,
   and closed at the moment of giving.

Chapter 5

1 Do not rely on your own strength,
   and do not say: "I have the power."
   Do not rely on your own strength,
   to follow your own desire.
2 Do not follow your heart or your eyes,
   to go towards evil pleasures.
3 Do not say: "Who can prevail against *my* strength?"
   For YYY seeks those who are persecuted.

reading was probably כלביא, "like a lion" (cf. Smend 1906a, 46; Lévi 1901, 23; Segal 1958, 29), which was mistakenly read as ככלב in H^A and changed to the synonymous phrase כאריה in H^C. ומוזר — Lit., "stranger." This meaning is surprising, given the context. Segal (1958, 29) explains that the term can evoke a "strange" attitude or can be connected to the root זור I (or זרר or even מזר) "to crush, to press, to be smashed" in parallel with רפי and רשיש of the preceding verse (for this meaning, see Job 39:15; Isa 59:5). Cowley and Neubauer (1897, 19) cite b. Git. 6b: לעולם אל יטיל אדם אימה יתירה בתוך ביתו "A person must never bring great terror into their house."
4:31 Lévi (1901, 23) notes a moving parallel with Qoh. Rab. 5:14: כשאדם בא לעולם ידיו הן קפוצות כלומר כל העולם שלי וכשהוא נפטר מן העולם ידיו הן פשוטות כלומר לא נחלתי מן העולם הזה כלום, "When a person comes into the world, their hands are clenched, as if to say, 'all the world belongs to me'; and when they leave the world, their hands are open, as if to say, 'I have possessed nothing of this world.'" לקחת — The verb לקח might also have the meaning "to receive" here. בתוך — בתוך followed by a verb of action literally means "in the midst of an action" (see also Sir 11:8).

5:1 חיל — The term usually means "strength," but can also mean "ability, efficiency," as well as "wealth." יש לאל ידי — For the expression, see Gen 31:29; Deut 28:32; Neh 5:5; Mic 2:1; Sir 14:11; 4Q179 [4QapLamA] 1 1 (ואין לאל ידנו), Watson (1977, 213–215) and Kogut (1988, 435–444).
5:2 אל תלך אחרי — Lit., "do not follow after." Compare with Job 31:7 and Num 15:39. חמודות — The word means "precious things, treasures," or "something desirable," but in the present verse, this desire is negative.
5:3 מי יוכל כחו — כחו should certainly be corrected to כחי, in agreement with the versions, confusion between *vav* and *yod* being frequent in the Genizah manuscripts. The expression seems to be influenced by the Aramaic formula מצא חיל attested in the Syriac. כי — The conjunction could introduce a free citation of Qoh 3:15, the Hebrew of which is obscure. In the old exegetic tradition, this verse is interpreted as: "The Lord will demand justice (תבע) for the poor and the destitute from the wicked ones who persecute them (דרדף ליה)" (Tg. Qoh. 3:15). The verse would then contain a warning to the presumptuous not to profit from the poor. This is how the Syriac understood it: "for the Lord requires justice (ܬܒܥܬܐ) for all of the oppressed."

4 c	⁲³ vac. אל תאמר חטאתי ומה יעשה לי מאומה כי ארך אפים הוא:	
	²⁴אל תאמר רחום י״י	וכל עונותי ימחה:
5 c	אל סליחה אל תבטח	²⁵להוסיף עון על עון:
6 c	ואמרת רחמיו רבים	לרוב עונותי יסלח:
	²⁶כי רחמים ואף עמו	ועל רשעים ינוח רגזו:
7 c	אל תאחר לשוב ²⁷אליו	ואל תתעבר מיום אל יום:
	כי פתאום יצא זעמו	וביום נקם ²⁸תספה:
8	אל תבטח על נכסי שקר	כי לא יועילו ביום עברה:
9 c	²⁹אל תהיה זורה לכל רוח	ופונה דרך שבולת:
10 c	היה סמוך ע̇ל דעתך	¹ואחר יהי דברך:
11 c	היה ממהר להאזין	ובארך רוח השב פתגם:
12 c	²אם יש אתך ענה רעך	ואם אין ידך על פיך:
13 c	כבוד וקלון ³ביוד בוטא	ולשון אדם מפלתו:
14	אל תקרא בעל שתים	⁴ובלשונך אל תרגל רע:
	כי על גנב נבראה בשת	חרפה רעהו ⁵בעל שתים:
15/6:1	מעט והרבה אל תשחת	ותחת אוהב אל תהי שונא

T-S 12.864 recto

5:4 ועל A | ואל C · עוונתי A | עונותי C · רבים רחמיו A G | רחמיו רבים C · יי A | י״י C · 5:6 אל A | > C G · מאומה A S | לו C · לי A G S | ל־ C G S · יעשה A | יהיה C G S · 5:7 ואל תלך לכל שביל A (ܡܒ̈ܠܐ S) | ופונה דרך שבולת A · תהי C · תהיה A | 5:9 ובעת A G S · ליום C S · אל יום A | וביום C G S · יניח A | ינוח C · 5:10 בשמועה טובה C G (+ αγαθη) | נכון C | ממהר A | להאזן A · דברך A G S | דבריך C · יהיה A · ידבר C · 5:11 (ܠܚܠ ܐܒܝܠ S) · דעתך A G S | דברך C · ייהי A | יהיה C · 5:12 ענה תענה נכונה A G S (+ ορθην O L-694-743) La (verum) · רעך A G S | רייעך C · ואם אין A | + (ܠܚܐܒܐ) S (O L'-743) · מפלטו C | מפלתו A · בוטה C | בוטא A · ביד A | ביוד C · 5:13 שים C

5:4 Cf. 6:21ᴬ. מה יעשה לי — This is the same rhetorical question as in Ps 56:12. מאומה — The word, which is absent in Hᶜ, makes the formulation unusual, as it is generally constructed with a negative rather than an interrogative pronoun, except in Num 22:38. Compare with b. Ḥag. 16a: אם יאמר לך יצר הרע חטא והקב״ה מוחל אל תאמן בו "If the evil inclination says to you: 'sin, for the Holy One, blessed be he, is forgiving,' do not believe it." ... אל תאמר — The couplet of 4cd, which appears in the Syriac but not the Greek, seems to be a doublet of 6ab.

5:5–6 These two verses are present in Hᶜ, as well as in Saadiah and Nissim: ואל סליחה אל תבטח להוסיף עון על עון ואמרתה רחמיו רבים לרוב עונותי יסלח. כי רחמים ואף עמו ועל רשעים ינוח עזו (Saadiah, ספר הגלוי, ed. Harkavy 1891, 177); ולסליחה אל תבטח להוסיף עון על עון ואמרת רחמים רבים לרוב עונתיו יסלחה ורחמים עמו ואף עמו על רעים (Nissim, Ḥibbûr Yaphê, ed. Obermann 1933, 148).

5:5 סליחה — In Biblical Hebrew, the term only appears in the singular in Ps 130:4 (the plural occurs in Neh 9:17 and Dan 9:9). בטח אל — The construction with אל is rather rare (cf. 5:8 where the verb appears with על). This may be the consequence of the assimilation of the two prepositions in late Hebrew. להוסיף עון על עון — For the expression "add sin on sin," see Sir 3:27 and the note. A similar concept is found in Tg. Neof. Deut. 29:18–19.

5:6 ואמרת — The couplet 6ab is absent in the Syriac, which has only 4cd. The Greek, which does not have 4cd, retains the two stichs in v. 6, but with the reading καὶ μὴ εἴπῃς "and say not...," as in 4cd in Hᴬ. The weqatal form could be understood as an extension of the prohibition that precedes it (אל תבטח), meaning "do not say..." (as in the Greek), or as an extension of the infinitive (להוסיף). The latter is preferable from a syntactic point of view (cf. Joüon §124q). נוח — The verb is normally constructed with ב- or על (cf. the variant על in Hᶜ and in Saadiah). For the construction with אל, see Ezek 44:30 and the preceding remark on the assimilation of the two prepositions. רגז — "Anger, rage"; cf. Sir 6:11 and Hab 3:2.

5:7 תתעבר — The hithpael of עבר is rare in Biblical Hebrew, and appears only associated with עבר II: "become angry, enrage." Here, however, the verb must mean "to neglect, put off, tarry" (cf. Smend 1906a, 49; Lévi 1901, 26–27; Kister 1990, 318, 321, 328; Joosten 2005, 155–64). See also, Sir 7:10ᴬ; 7:16ᴬ; 13:7ᴬ; 16:8ᴬ and perhaps 4Q438 3 2. This meaning does not seem to be attested in Rabbinic Hebrew. יצא זעמו — "Suddenly his anger will come forth"; cf. Hos 6:5 and Isa 51:5. תספה — In the sense of "remove, take away," and by extension, "to be destroyed, annihilated."

5:8 Cf. Prov 11:4 and 10:2. נכסי — The term belongs to late Hebrew (Josh 22:8; Qoh 5:18; 6:2; Ezra 6:8; 2 Chr 1:11.12). חיל — Cf. נכסי שקר in Sir 40:13ᴹ (syr: ܢܟܣ̈ܐ ܕܚܛܝܐ) and the expression הון רשעה מעול in CD VI 15; VIII 5; XIX 17 and 4Q183 1 ii 5 (see Philonenko 1999, 177–83).

5:9 Note the use of the long form תהיה here (cf. תהי in Hᶜ), rather than the short form תהי used in Biblical Hebrew and elsewhere in Ben Sira (see 4:29, 30, 31). For the periphrastic construction, see van Peursen (1997, 158–73) and Muraoka (1999, 188–204). שבולת — The word probably results from a confusion between שביל "track, pathway," attested by Hᶜ, the Greek and the Syriac, and שבלת "flood" (cf. 4:26). Although the stich seems to have undergone alterations, the participle of פנה agrees with the Syriac, both in meaning and in syntax. Finally, the construction could be compared with Job 24:18: לא יפנה דרך כרמים, "Do not take the path of the vineyards."

5:10 אחר — Certainly read a resh in Hᴬ as in Hᶜ (with Beentjes 1997, 27; contra Smend 1906b, 4; Lévi 1901, 27; Segal 1958, 32; Ben Ḥayyim 1973, 6; compare with the resh of ממהר in the same line or חרפה in

4   Ne dis pas : « J'ai péché et que me fera-t-il ? Rien !
    car Dieu est lent à la colère. »
    Ne dis pas : « YYY est miséricordieux
    et il effacera toutes mes fautes ».
5   Ne te fie pas au pardon
    pour accumuler faute sur faute
6   en disant : « sa miséricorde est abondante,
    il pardonnera l'abondance de mes fautes ».
    Car miséricorde et colère sont avec lui
    et sur les méchants reposera son courroux.
7   Ne tarde pas à retourner vers lui
    et ne diffère pas (ton retour) de jour en jour.
    Car soudainement sortira sa colère
    et au jour de vengeance tu seras happé.
8   Ne te fie pas aux richesses trompeuses,
    car elles ne servent à rien au jour de la fureur.
9   Ne vanne pas à tout vent
    et ne te dirige pas vers le chemin du torrent.
10 Sois assuré de ta connaissance
    et, après, que soit ton discours.
11 Hâte-toi d'écouter
    et avec un esprit patient donne une réponse.
12 Si tu le peux, réponds à ton prochain,
    sinon, (mets) ta main sur ta bouche.
13 Honneur et honte sont dans la *main* du bavard
    et la langue de l'être humain est sa chute.
14 Ne te fais pas taxer d'hypocrisie
    et par ta langue ne calomnie pas un ami.
    Car la honte a été créée pour le menteur
    et le mépris est son compagnon : un hypocrite.
15 Peu ou beaucoup, ne sois pas corrompu
6,1 et d'ami ne deviens pas ennemi.

4   Do not say: "I have sinned but what will he do to me?
    Nothing!
    For God is slow to anger."
    Do not say: "YYY is merciful,
    and he will cancel all my sins."
5   Do not trust in forgiveness,
    adding sin on top of sin,
6   while saying: "His mercy is great,
    he will pardon my many sins."
    For mercy and anger are his,
    and his fury settles on the wicked.
7   Do not delay returning to him,
    do not put (it) off from day to day.
    For, his anger will burst out suddenly,
    and on the day of vengeance you will be taken away.
8   Do not rely upon deceptive riches,
    for they will not help on the day of anger.
9   Do not winnow in every wind
    and do not take the path of a torrent.
10 Be sure of your knowledge
    and afterward, let your speech come.
11 Hurry to listen,
    and with a patient spirit, give a reply.
12 If you are able, answer your neighbor,
    and if not, (put) your hand over your mouth.
13 Honor and shame are in the *hand* of a chatterbox,
    and a person's tongue is their downfall.
14 Do not let yourself be called a hypocrite,
    and do not slander a friend with your tongue.
    For shame has been created for a liar,
    and contempt is their companion: a hypocrite.
15 Little or much, do not be corrupt,
6:1 and do not be an enemy instead of a friend.

line 5). However, according to the hand of this scribe, *resh* and *dalet* are sometimes interchangeable (see complete introduction). The Greek and the Syriac attest to a *Vorlage* with אחד, "may your word be one."
5:11 היה ממהר — For the use of the periphrastic construction (imperative of היה followed by the participle), see van Peursen (1997, 160). This syntax does not really appear in Biblical Hebrew, as the two cases in Exod 34:2 and Ps 30:11 should not be taken into consideration (see the remarks by Joüon §121e and van Peursen 1997, 160). It does not appear at Qumran either, but does occur from time to time in Mishnaic Hebrew (see Segal 1927, §326), as well as in Aramaic (see Greenfield 2001, 56–67). The reading in H^C, היה נכון, echoes Exod 34:2. ארך רוח — The expression appears in Qoh 7:8, "a patient spirit." In our context, it means that one should take time to reply. פתגם — The term, borrowed from old Persian, can signify "message, case, answer, sentence, order, recommendation," and appears exclusively in late Hebrew literature (Qoh 8:11; Esth 1:20; Sir 8:9^A; 4Q161 2–6 26; 4Q420 1a ii-b 2 // 4Q421 1 a ii b 14) and in Aramaic (Deut 3:16; 4:14; Ezra 4:17; 5:7, 11; 6:11; 1Q20 XXII 27; 4Q242 1–3 2.6; 4Q533 3 3; 4Q546 13 4; 4Q550 1 6; 4Q556a 5 i 7; Test. Levi ar. Bodl. b 13; Tg. Job).
5:12 Cf. Sir 9:14^A.

5:13 ביוד — This spelling is without parallel and is probably an error (see H^C and the Syriac; thus Lévi 1901, 28 and Peters 1913, 54). בוטא — For the spelling (H^C has בוטה), see also 9:18. For the meaning, cf. Prov 12:18 and 18:21.
5:14 אל תקרא בעל שתים — See the note for 4:28 and 6:1. תרגל רע — It could also be translated "with your tongue, do not slander in an evil manner" (the object of רגל is usually construed with ב or אל). For the meaning of רגל, see also 4:28 and the note. על גנב נבראה — For the construction and the meaning of ברא + על, see 40:10. גנב usually means "thief," but Kister (1990, 318) thinks that it probably means "liar" here. He refers to t. B. Qam. 7:8 and the expression גנב לב in Gen 31:20, 26–27. חרפה רעהו בעל שתים — This last stich is problematic. The Greek and the Syriac seem to translate a *Vorlage* with חרפה רעה על בעל שתים "evil contempt belongs to the hypocrite."
6:1 The preceding editions differ as to where they begin chapter six. Ben Ḥayyim (1973, 7) and Smend (1906b, 4) open it at 5:15b, while Lévi (1901, 29–30) and Beentjes (1997, 27) open it at 6:2, attaching verse 1 to the previous pericope because of its content. The solution above is based on the indentation of H^A, which seems to indicate a transition.

Chapter 6

1	6 *vac.* שם רע וקלון תוריש חרפה	כן איש רע בעל שתים:	
2	⁷אֿ תפול ביד נפשך	ותעבה חילך עליך:	
3	עליך תאכל ופריך ⁸תשרש:	והניחתך כעץ יבש	
4	כי נפש עזה תשחת בעליה	⁹ושמחת שונא תשיגם:	
5 ᶜ	חיך ערב ירבה אוהב	ושפתי חן ¹⁰שואלו שלום:	
6 ᶜ	אנשי שלומך יהיו רבים	ובעל סודך אחד מאלף·	
7 ᶜ	¹¹קנית אוהב בניסין קנהו	ואֿ תמהר לבטח עליו·	
8 ᶜ	כי יש אוהב ¹²כפי עת	ואֿ יעמוד ביום צרה:	
9 ᶜ	יש אוהב נהפך לשנא	ואת ¹³ריב חרפתך יחשוף:	
10 ᶜ	יש אוהב חבר שלחן	ולא ימצא ¹⁴ביום רעה:	
11	בטובתך הֿא כמוך·	וברעתך יתנדה ממך:	
12 ᶜ	¹⁵אם תשיגך רעה יהפך בך	ומפניך יסתר:	
13 ᶜ	משנאיך הבדל	¹⁶ומאהביך השמר:	
14 ᶜQ	אוהב אמונה אוהב תקוף	ומוצאו מצא ¹⁷הון:	
15 ᶜQ	לאוהב אמונה אין מחיר	ואין משקל לטובתו:	

6:5 בפני A Saadia | > C S · כפי A G | > C S · לבטוח A | לבטח C · בנסיון A | בנסין C · 6:7 שלומך A | שלומך C · 6:6 שואלי C · שואלו A 6:5
רעה A | > C · תשיגנו C | תשיגם A · 6:12 יחשוד A | יחשוף C · לשונא C | לשנא A · 6:9 C Saadia יעמד | יעמוד A C Saadia ולא | ואל A (ܘܠܐ)
אוהב C G · לאוהב A S 6:15 · מצא הוא הון A | + מצא הון C · תקיף A | תקוף (σκέπη ?) · 6:13 נרפך | יהפך C · משנאיך A | משונאיך C · ומאביביך A | ומאהביך C · השמר A C | הזהר Saadia · 6:14 אוהב A S (ܐܘܗܒ) | מגן C G ·

L. 10 [6:5] מאלף — The *aleph* is written over another unidentifiable letter.

6:2 נפשך — The term probably refers to appetite in the broadest sense here (passion, desire, envy, cf. BDB def. 5; see Isa 56:11 and Sir 19:3). Alternatively, while it might be understood as "yourself" and the following verb forms as second person ("Do not fall under your own influence, you would devour your own strength"), the third feminine in v. 3b implies that נפש is the subject. ותעבה — The form is difficult to interpret. (1) It could be the *piel* perfect of תעב "desecrate, to make abominable" (cf. Sir 7:26; 11:2): "(your appetite) would make your strength abominable to you yourself." (2) It could be the *piel* imperfect of the root עבה, meaning "fatten, thicken," thus: "so you might increase your strength for yourself" (by eating, cf. Deut 32:15). (3) It is also possible to postulate a metathesis of תבעה, the *qal* imperfect of בעה, "graze" (as Schechter and Taylor 1899, 20; Smend 1906a, 53; Lévi 1901, 30; Segal 1958, 35). This would explain the Syriac (ܬܪܥܐ) and even, to a certain extent, the Greek (διαρπαγῇ, cf. Isa 5:5, insofar as בער and בעה are synonyms in the Mishnah). This is the solution that we have chosen. The verb is used this way in Sam. Pent. of Exod 22:4, as well as in 4Q158 10–12 6–7 and m. B. Qam. 1:1, again in reference to Exod 22:4 (see also Tg. Ps.-J. Num 22:4).The Greek and the Syriac, but not the Latin, add "like a bull" (ὡς ταῦρος and ܐܝܟ ܬܘܪܐ). A plausible explanation could be the alteration of a primitive reading, ותבער כביער חילך, which would agree perfectly with the Greek; כביער may have disappeared by haplography and עליך, which is clearly redundant here, could be attributed to dittography.
6:3 תשרש — "Would ruin all the way to the root." With a similar context, see Job 31:12. עץ יבש — Cf. Isa 56:3; Ezek 17:24 and 21:3.
6:4 נפש עזה — Cf. Isa 56:11 and Sir 19:3ᶜ, which is a doublet to this verse, and Sir 40:30ᴹ,ᴮ,ᴮᵐᵍ. בעליה — Compare the inverse in Qoh 7:12: החכמה תחיה בעליה, "wisdom makes those who have it live." תשיגם — Here scholars often suggest emending the text (cf. the Greek and Syriac which reflect a similar sense: "it (she) makes him the laughing stock of his enemies." Peters (1902, 21) and Segal (1958, 35) suggest a *Vorlage* like תשימם). Nevertheless, the verb נשׂג not infrequently occurs where various abstractions like righteousness (Isa 59:9), iniquity (Ps 40:13), terror (Job 27:20) may "reach, overtake" someone (see Reymond 2017b, 19–31).
6:5 חיך ערב — Cf. Song 5:16. שפתי חן — Cf. Ps 45:3. שואלו — This should be corrected to שואלי, as in Hᶜ (Smend 1906a, 54; Segal 1958, 36). שואלי שלום — Lit. "those who ask for peace." This idiomatic expression means "those who greet," "those who ask your well-being (or, health)" (cf. Exod 18:7; Judg 18:15; 1 Sam 10:4; 17:22; 25:5; 30:21; Jer 15:5; Cowley 1923, 39:1 ['lhy' kl yš'lw šlmky bkl 'dn "may all the gods seek your welfare at all times"]; Aharoni 1981, Arad 18:2f [YHWH yš'l lšlmk "may the Lord seek your welfare"]; Bresciani and Kāmil 1966, Hermopoli 1:3 [ḥrwṣ š'l šlmhn "Ch. sends them his best wishes / asks after their welfare"] and especially, Sir 41:20ᴮ,ᴹ).
6:6 This verse is quoted in b. Yeb. 63b כתוב בספר בן סירא . . . רבים, יהיו דורשי שלומך גלה סוד לאחד מאלף, "It is written in the book of Ben Sira, Let those who ask your well-being be many (but,) reveal a secret to one out of a thousand"), b. Sanh. 100b רבים יהיו דורשי שלומך גלה סודך לאחד מאלף) and in Saadia Gaon, who presents a text quite close to Hᴬ,ᶜ: רבים יהיו אנשי שלומך גלה סודך לאחד מני אלף) "(Though) your trusted friends are numerous, reveal your secret to one out of a thousand." ספר הגלוי, ed. Harkavy 1891, 178; note the long form of the preposition מן). See also *Alphabet of Ben Sira*: גלה סודך לאחד מאלף אם רבו דורשי שלומך (ed. Yassif 1984, 203). אנשי שלומך — "People of your well-being, your trusted friends," cf. Ps 37:37; 41:10; Jer 20:10 and 38:22 (in Sir 13:18ᴬ, the expression מאיש שלום is probably a corruption of מה יש שלום or of מאין שלום, see Lévi 1901, 96; Kister 1999, 173–75).This expression plays cleverly with that of the preceding stich (שואלי שלום). בעל סודך — Cf. Job 19:19: מתי סודי (LXX: οἱ εἰδότες με).

Chapitre 6

1 Le mépris te fera hériter d'un nom mauvais et d'ignominie,
   c'est ainsi que la personne mauvaise est hypocrite.
2 Ne tombe pas au pouvoir de ton appétit,
   il *dévorerait* ta propre vigueur,
3 mangerait ton feuillage et ruinerait jusqu'à la racine tes fruits
   et te laisserait comme un arbre desséché.
4 Car un appétit vorace détruit son maître
   et la joie de l'ennemi les atteint.
5 Un doux palais multiplie les amis
   et les lèvres gracieuses ceux qui s'enquièrent de (ta) santé.
6 Tes intimes, qu'ils soient nombreux,
   mais ton conseiller, un entre mille.
7 Si tu acquiers un ami par l'épreuve acquiers-le
   et ne te hâte pas de te fier à lui.
8 Car il y a l'ami de circonstance,
   mais il ne restera pas au jour de détresse.
9 Il y a l'ami qui se change en ennemi
   et qui dévoilera ta querelle honteuse.
10 Il y a l'ami, compagnon de table,
   mais il ne sera pas trouvé au jour du malheur.
11 Dans ton bonheur, il est comme toi-même
   et dans ton malheur, il s'éloignera de toi.
12 Si le mal t'atteint, il se retourne contre toi
   et de ta face il se cache.
13 De tes ennemis, sépare-toi
   et de tes amis garde-toi.
14 Un ami fidèle est un ami solide
   et celui qui l'a trouvé a trouvé une richesse.
15 Pour un ami fidèle, il n'y a pas de prix
   et pour sa bonté, il n'y a pas de mesure.

Chapter 6

1 Contempt will make you inherit a bad reputation and disgrace,
   (For) that is how a bad person is a hypocrite.
2 Do not fall under the influence of your appetite,
   it would *devour* your own strength,
3 would eat up your leaves and ruin your fruit to its (very) roots,
   and leave you like a withered tree.
4 For a voracious appetite destroys its master,
   and an enemy's joy overtakes them.
5 A sweet palate multiplies friends,
   and gracious lips, those who ask (your) well-being.
6 Let your trusted friends be many,
   but your counselor one out of a thousand.
7 If you acquire a friend, acquire one by means of a test,
   and do not hurry to trust them.
8 For there is a friend of circumstance,
   but, they will not remain in the day of distress.
9 There is a friend who turns into an enemy
   and who will reveal your shameful quarrel.
10 There is a friend, a mealtime companion;
   but they will not be found in the day of misfortune.
11 In your prosperity, they are like your very self,
   but in your misery, they will be far from you.
12 If evil overtakes you, they will turn against you
   and from your face, they will hide.
13 From your enemies, separate yourself,
   and be wary of your friends.
14 A faithful friend is a solid friend
   and whoever has found one has found wealth.
15 For a faithful friend there is no price
   and for their goodness there is no measure.

6:7 This verse is quoted by Saadia Gaon with few differences from the Genizah texts: ספר הגלוי) קנית אוהב במסה קנהו ואל תמהר לבטח עליו, ed. Harkavy 1891, 178). בניסין — Correct to בנסין, following Lévi (1901, 31), Smend (1906a, 54), Peters (1913, 58) and Segal (1958, 36). The term is found in Aramaic (Sokoloff 1990, 349).
6:8 This verse is quoted by Saadia Gaon, agreeing with H^A: יש אוהב כפי עת ולא יעמד ביום צרה ,ספר הגלוי), ed. Harkavy 1891, 178). יש אוהב — For this formula, which is redundant in the passage (vv. 8, 9, 10), compare with Prov 18:24. ואל יעמד — The expression should certainly be read in a predictive sense (as shown by H^C and the Syriac), rather than in a volitive sense (cf. Qimron 1986, §400.13). יום צרה — Cf. Sir 51:10^B, 12^B.
6:9 נהפך לשנא — Cf. Sir 37:2^D: ריע כנפש נהפך לצר "a friend like your very self who turns into an enemy." ריב חרפתך — Here, as in 6:16–17, the text probably alludes to the episode of Naval and Abigail in 1 Sam 25:39: ברוך יהוה אשר רב את ריב חרפתי מיד נבל "Blessed be the Lord who judged the insult made by Naval" (for the links between Sir 6 and 1 Sam 25, cf. Corley 2002, 46, 52, 60–63). יחשוף — The verb usually has the meaning "discover, reveal;" for a similar sense, see Sir 42:1^(B)M: ומחשף כל דבר עצה "(be ashamed of) laying bare any word of counsel." See also Sir 27:16 and Prov 25:9–10.
6:11 נדה — This verb appears only twice in Biblical Hebrew and always as a *piel* participle, with the sense "to push away, exclude" (Isa 66:5 and Amos 6:3). The *hithpael* appears in Rabbinic Hebrew with the meaning "to be excommunicated" (cf. Jastrow 1903, 876; 4Q512 1–6 17 has a *pual* form). For the sense of the verse, compare Prov 14:20 and 19:4 (and for the inverse advice, see Sir 22:23).
6:12 תשיגך רעה — The word רעה is not found in H^C, the Greek, the Syriac or the Latin. The latter three also presuppose a *Vorlage* with the verb נפל, rather than the נשג of H^A,C. יהפך בך — For the sense conveyed by ב + הפך, see Job 19:19.
6:13 This verse is quoted in Saadia Gaon: משנאיך הבדל ומאוהביך הזהר (ספר הגלוי), ed. Harkavy 1891, 178).
6:14 תקוף — Vocalized with an /o/ after the second consonant (or with /i/; cf. תקיף H^C), the term seems to be borrowed from Aramaic (cf. Sokoloff 2002, 1229–1230); late Hebrew has תוקף.
6:15 ואין משקל — For the expression, see 1 Chr 22:3, 14.

ירא ל׳ ישיגם·		צרור ¹⁸חיים אוהב אמונה	16
¹⁹וכשמו כן מעשיו·		כי כמוהו כן רעהו	17
וקוה לרב ²⁰תבואתה:		כחורש וכקוצר קרב א֜יה	19 C
ולמחר תאכל פריה:		כי בעבדתה מעט תעבוד	
ולא יכלכלנה חסר לב:		²¹ עקובה היא לאויל	20 Q
ולא יאחר להשליכה:		כאבן משא ²²תהיה עליו	21
ולא לרבים היא נכוחה:		כי המוסר כשמה כן ²³הוא	22 Q
וכמהו ²⁴איש על חשבונו:		כלי יוצר לבער כבשן	23 (27:5)
כן חשבון על ²⁵יצר אחד:		על עבדת עץ יהי פרי	24 (27:6)
וא׳ תקף בתחבולתיה:		הט שכמך ושאה	25
והחזקתה וא׳ תרפה:		²⁶דרש וחקר בקש ומצא	26
ונהפך לך לתענוג:		כי לאחור ²⁷תמצא מנוחתה	28 CQ
וחבלתה בגדי כתם:		והיתה לך רשתה ²⁸מכון עז	29 Q
ומוסרתיה ²⁹פתיל תכלת:		עלי זהב עולה	30 Q
ועטרת תפארת תעטרנה:		¹בגדי כבוד תלבשנה	31 Q

T-S 12.864 verso

6:18 + חכמה תשיג שיבה ועד מנוער קבל מוסר בני · S G C   6:19 לרב A | לרוב C · בעבדתה A | בעבודתה C · 6:22 נְכֹ[חָ A | נְבֹ֜ח]   · 6:28 ונהפך | ותהפך C ·   · 2Q18 2 4

6:16 צרור חיים — The Greek and the Syriac have understood this as "an elixir of life," probably reading צרי "balm," but there is no reason to correct the Hebrew, as suggested by Schechter and Taylor (1899, 21), Lévi (1901, 33) and Skehan and Di Lella(1987, 189). For the expression, see 1 Sam 25:29, 1QH^a X 22 (cf. Job 14:17, b. Shab. 52b, b. Meg. 14b and b. Hag.12b). Segal (1958, 37) takes צרור metaphorically to designate where one hides a precious treasure, so that a faithful friend is like a precious treasure of life, similar to v. 14b (מצא הון). ישיגם — The plural pronoun could refer either to life (חיים), or to friendship and the bag of life ("he who fears God will get both a faithful friend and the bag of life").

6:17 The Greek and the Syriac have an additional stich before our stich a which has disappeared from the Hebrew, probably by *homoioarchton* (ירא אל). Stich b is missing in the Greek and in several Syriac manuscripts, while it is present in the *Ambrosianus* codex as a doublet of Sir 2:18. וכשמו — The same phrase (or something very similar) is found in 1 Sam 25:25 (involving wordplay with the name נָבָל), in Sir 6:22^{A,C} (with the noun/participle מוּסָר), and in Sir 43:8^{M,Bm} (with the noun חֹדֶשׁ). Given its repetition in surrounding verses, one assumes that wordplay here would involve the phrase אוהב אמונה, (i.e., a faithful friend is nourishment [אָמְנָה], support [אֲמָנָה], and/or well-established [cf. wordplay in Isa 7:9 and 2 Chr 20:20]); nevertheless, it also seems possible to infer wordplay between רֵעַ "friend" and רַע "thought/desire" (cf. רְעוּת and רַעְיוֹן), if not also an ironic play with רַע "evil."

6:18 This verse is missing in H^A, but present in H^C. Its absence in H^A is likely a mistake, since it contains the antecedent (i.e., "wisdom") for the pronominal suffixes in v. 19.

6:20 עקובה — "winding, uneven," as in Isa 40:4. In Sir 36:25^B, it has the meaning "devious" (לב עקוב, lit. "uneven heart," cf. Jer 17:9 and 4Q418 8a–d 12 [עקוב הלב]). חסר לב — Lit. "who lacks mind," an expression that occurs frequently in the book of Proverbs (Prov 6:32; 7:7; 9:4; 9:16; 10:13; 10:21; 11:12; 12:11; 15:21; 17:18; 24:30).

6:21 אבן משא — משא evokes a "load, weight" (cf. Sir 51:26); for the construction and meaning, cf. Zech 12:3 and perhaps Num 4:47.

6:22 מוסר — The author plays on the double meaning of the expression. As a noun from the root יסר, the word means "discipline" while as a *hophal* participle of סור, it means "what is removed, separate, remote" (cf. Bacher 1900a, 277; Lévi 1901, 34; Reymond 2011, 42). כשמה — One could read a rare writing of the masculine suffix pronoun כְּשָׁמֹה; cf. Joüon §94h; Reymond 2018c; Dan 11:10 and Sir 43:21 (לְבֹנָה). The pronoun could also be feminine and refer to Wisdom (cf. Prov 4:13 where מוסר "instruction" is the antecedent to a 3fs pronoun), which would agree with the pronouns in the following stich, though this would require reading הוא as a mistake for היא. The formula echoes that of v. 17. נְכוֹחָה — The vocalization of the scribe would suggest reading either the preposition נֹכַח "in front of" ("and she was not in front of a large number," see Lévi 1901, 2:35; Sir 8:15^A; 31:16^{Bmg}; 33:14^E), or the *niphal* participle of יכח ("and she was not destined for the many," see the meaning in Gen 24:14, 44 in the *hiphil*; cf. Bacher 1900a, 277; Peters 1913, 60). However, it is certainly preferable to read with the consonants נכוחה, the adjective נָכֹחַ, "straight, right, honest, accessible," agreeing with 2Q18 2 3 (cf. Sir 11:21; 6:22; and particularly, Prov 8:8–9). On this verse, see Calduch-Benages 2013.

6:23–24 The four stichs of H^A do not correspond to the versions or to 2Q18 2 4–5, and are doublets of Sir 27:5–6 (cf. the Greek and the Syriac).

6:23 The language of the comparison is ambiguous: either a person is like a kiln and tests their own thoughts (before speaking them) or human thought is like a kiln that tests the individual. חשבונו — The word חֶשְׁבּוֹן belongs to late Hebrew (2 Chr 25:15; Qoh 7:25, 27, 29; 9:10; Sir 9:15^A; 42:3^{B,M}; 42:4^{Bmg}) and means "reckoning, reflection, account."

6:24 The verse is clearly constructed as a chiasmus. עבדת עץ — Lit., "the work of the tree"; cf. עבדת האדמה "agriculture" in 1 Chr 27:26. For the syntax, cf. Ezek 45:17. על יצר אחד — The Greek and the Syriac read אדם ("a person's inclination") instead of אחד, which may imply singularity, indefiniteness or perhaps could be understood as "(the) one creator" (cf. other expressions of God's oneness, as e.g.

16 Un ami fidèle est un sachet de vie,
   celui qui craint Dieu, les obtiendra.
17 Car tel il est, tel est son ami
   et comme son nom, telles sont ses œuvres.
19 Comme un laboureur et un moissonneur approche-toi d'elle
   et espère en l'abondance de sa récolte.
   Car, à son service, tu serviras peu
   mais le lendemain, tu mangeras ses fruits.
20 Elle est tortueuse pour le fou
   et l'insensé ne la supporte pas.
21 Elle sera sur lui comme une pierre à porter
   et il ne tardera pas à la rejeter.
22 Car la discipline, tel est son nom, ainsi elle est
   et *elle* n'est pas accessible pour la multitude.
23 Le vase du potier doit être brûlé au four
   et, comme lui, une personne à propos de sa réflexion.
24 Grâce à l'arboriculture il y aura du fruit,
   ainsi la pensée grâce à l'inclination unique.
25 Incline ton épaule et supporte-la (s.e. sagesse)
   et ne sois pas effrayé par ses projets.
27 Scrute, sonde, cherche et tu trouveras,
   saisis-la et ne la lâche pas.
28 Car, par suite, tu trouveras le lieu de son repos
   et elle se changera pour toi en délice.
29 Et son filet sera pour toi un appui solide
   et ses cordes, des vêtements d'or.
30 Son joug, des jougs en or
   et ses liens, un ruban de pourpre.
31 Tu la revêtiras, vêtements de gloire,
   tu t'en couronneras, couronne de splendeur.

16 A faithful friend is a bag of life,
   the one who fears God will obtain them.
17 For as he is, so is his friend,
   and as is his name, so are his works.
19 Like a plowman and a harvester, draw near to her,
   and await the abundance of her harvest.
   For, in her service you will serve but little
   and the next day you will eat her fruits.
20 She is convoluted for the fool,
   and the one who has no sense cannot stand her.
21 She will be upon him like a load of stone,
   and they will not delay throwing her off.
22 For discipline, such is her name, so she is
   and *she* is not accessible to the multitude (of people).
23 The potter's vessel must be baked in a kiln,
   and like it, so is a person in relation to their thoughts.
24 It is by arboriculture that there is fruit,
   and so thought, by an inclination.
25 Bend your shoulder and carry her,
   and do not be afraid of her plans.
27 Study, examine, seek and you will find,
   seize her and do not let her go.
28 For afterward you will find her resting place,
   and she will be transformed for you into a delight.
29 And her net will be a firm base for you
   and her ties, golden clothing.
30 Her yoke, golden yokes,
   and her bonds, a ribbon of purple.
31 You will wear her as glorious vestments,
   you will don her as a crown of splendor.

אחד יוצר ואחד בורא Ḥananel ben Ḥushiel, פירוש לתלמוד Sanh. 4:5 [Maagarim]).

6:25 ושאה — The feminine suffixed pronoun suggests that the insertion of the four preceding stichs is a later scribal intervention. The antecedent must refer to the advice (עצה according to the retroversions of Lévi 1901, 36 and Segal 1958, 41) or more generally to wisdom. ואל תקץ — Cf. Prov 3:11: אל תקץ בתוכחתו "Do not be worried by her reproach." בתחבולתיה — The term תַּחְבֻּלוֹת is typically sapiential (Job 37:12; Prov 1:5; 11:14; 12:5; 20:18; 24:6; Sir 32:16; 37:17). It means the art of directing, conceiving plans and strategies. Its use in Rabbinic Hebrew is somewhat divergent. As the Greek is different (τοῖς δεσμοῖς αὐτῆς, "her ties"), Smend (1906a, 59) and Skehan and Di Lella (1987, 192) have felt that the reading of H^A could represent a confusion with בחבלותיה "in her bonds (see 6:29)," under the influence of the preceding stich (absent from H^A, but the Greek of which [τὸν κλοιὸν αὐτῆς] lets one imagine a *Vorlage* similar to that of v. 29). This kind of hypothesis does not seem necessary to us.

6:27 ומצא — The last of the four imperatives could have a purpose and result nuance "so that you will find" (Joüon §116f) with no need to correct to ותמצא (as suggested by Lévi 1901, 36). והחזקתה — The use here of the two antithetical roots חזק, "strong," and רפה, "weak," in the opposition "grab" versus "abandon" is common (cf. Job 27:6, Prov 4:13).

6:28 לאחור — Cf. 12:12. The construction introduces temporality: "then, following, in the future." ונהפך — The *niphal* 3ms (or the participle) of הפך, "change (oneself) into," is senseless in this context, so it seems preferable to correct it to תהפך, like H^C (as Smend [1906b, 6], Lévi [1901, 37] and Segal [1958, 41] do).

6:29 וחבלתה — The feminine of חֶבֶל "ties, cords" does not seem to appear elsewhere. The word might be חֲבִילָה / חֲבָלָה found in Rabbinic Hebrew "band, bond, bundle, luggage" (see Jastrow 1903, 419).

6:30 עלי — It could be vocalized as עֻלֵּי זָהָב, "golden yokes" (as Segal [1958, 42], in opposition to "iron yokes" [Deut 28:48]), or as עֲלֵי זָהָב, "leaves of gold" (as Lévi 1901, 36–37, Mopsik [2003, 100]). This verse is absent from the Syriac. The Greek κόσμος χρυσέος implies a *Vorlage* of עדי זהב, "a golden ornament" (cf. Jer 4:30). עולה — Read עֻלָּה "her yoke." The Greek reads עָלֶיהָ, ἐπ' αὐτῆς. מוסרה — ומוסרתיה "tie" (cf. Ps 2:3; 107:14). פתיל תכלת — For the expression, see Exod 28:28, 37; 39:21, 31 and Num 15:38.

6:31 The Syriac understood: "She will dress you in glorious vestments and she will crown you with a crown of splendor." בגדי כבוד — The only other occurrence of this Hebrew expression, outside of Medieval Hebrew (see, e.g., in דברי הימים של משה רבנו, chap. 19, p. 115 in association with Aaron and his sons) is in Sir 50:11, in reference to the priestly garments of the high priest Simon. ועטרת תפארת — Cf. Isa 62:3; Jer 13:18; Ezek 16:12; Prov 4:9 and 16:31. In verses 30–31, the words "gold, violet, purple, glorious vestments, the crown" evoke a royal image.

ואם תשיים לבד תערם:		אם ²תחפוץ בני תתחכם	32
והט אזנך תוסר:		אם תובא ³לשמע	33
ומשל ⁴בינה ∅ יצאך:		כל שיחה חפוץ לשמע	35 ᶜ
ותשחוק בסיפי ⁵רגלך:		ראה מה יבין ושחריהו	36
ובמצותו והגה תמיד:		והתבוננת ביראת עליון	37
ואשר איותה יחכמך:		⁶והוא יבין לבך	

Chapter 7

הרחק מעון ויט ממך:		∅ תעש לך רעה ⁷וא∅ ישיגך רעה	1–2 ᶜ
פן תקצרהו שבעתים:		∅ תדע חרושי על ⁸אח	3
וכן ממלך ⁹מושב כבוד		∅ תבקש מא∅ ממשלת	4 ᶜ
ופני מלך ∅ תתבונן:		∅ תצטדק לפני מלך	5
אם אין לך חיל להשבית זדון:		¹⁰אל תבקש להיות מושל	6 ᶜ
ונתונה בצע בתמימיך:		¹¹פן תגור מפני נדיב	
וא∅ תפילך בקהלה:		∅ תרשיעך ¹²בעדת שערי ∅	7
¹³כי באחת לא תנקה:		∅ תקשור לשנות חט	8

6:35 לשמע A | לשמוע C · 7:1 לך A | > C · 1 2 רעה A | רע C · 7:2 הרחק A | רחק C · 7:4 ממלך A | כמלך C · 7:6 מושל A | > C ·

6:32 תתחכם — The *hithpael* of חכם occurs five times in Ben Sira (10:26ᴬ; 32:4ᴮ; 38:24, 25ᴮ). In Biblical Hebrew, its sole appearance is in Qoh 7:16. It does not occur at Qumran, but it does in Rabbinic Hebrew and in Aramaic. תשיים לבד — This expression occurs frequently, with the meaning "pay attention" (cf. Sir 14:21ᴬ; 16:20ᴬ, 24ᴬ; Exod 9:21; Deut 32:46; 1 Sam 9:20; 25:25; 2 Sam 18:3; Ezek 40:4; 44:5; Hag 1:5, 7; 2:18; Zech 7:12; Job 1:8; 2:3; 34:14; 4Q525 14 ii 18).
6:33 תובא — For תאבה. תוסר — A verb from the root יסר, similar to the noun מוסר "instruction" (v. 18, 22).
6:35 שִׂיחָה — Feminine noun: "speech of wisdom, meditation, study" (cf. Sir 8:8; 11:8; Job 15:4; Ps 119:97, 99). The feminine is much rarer than the masculine שִׂיחַ. יצאך — The verb יצא is used with a cognitive sense here.
6:36 מה — It does not seem necessary to correct מה to מי; compare with the inverse formula in Sir 37:27: וראה מה רע. Nevertheless, the Syriac and the Greek imply "who is intelligent" (cf. Schechter and Taylor [1899, 45], Smend [1906a, 61], Lévi [1901, 38], Segal [1958, 42] and Mopsik [2003, 101]). This would not be a case where the particles were confused (cf. Sir 12:13; Amos 7:2; Ruth 3:16; see Segal 1958, 80; Van Peursen 2004, 292; Segal 1927, §418 illustrates the confusion of the particles in the Mishnah). יבין — The form could have an active meaning "what (or who) is clever" or a factitive one "what (or who) makes intelligent," cf. the following verse. שחריהו — The *yod* is a mater for what would correspond to a *tsere* in the Masoretic Text. בסיפי — Correct to בסיפו, following the Greek and the Syriac.
6:37 והתבוננת — For the *weqatal* after a series of imperatives, see Joüon §119*l*. ובמצותו והגה — For the syntax, cf. the syntax of Dan 8:25 (ומן־שריו יחזק) and 11:5 (ואל־שכלו והצליח). Alternatively, one can take the *waw* as dittography and correct it to הגה or תהגה (as proposed by Smend [1906b, 6], Lévi [1901, 38] and Segal [1958, 42]). יבין לבך — Lit. "He will teach your heart." For the sense of the expression, see Prov 8:5. The Greek and the Syriac have read יבין "he will strengthen your heart." ואשר — The relative could introduce a conditional, "if you so wish, he will make you wise," but this construction is rare; cf. Deut 11:27 and Joüon §167*j*. יחכמך — The finale probably evokes the gift of wisdom given to Solomon in 1 Kgs 3:11–12.

7:1–17 See Beentjes 1980.
7:1 לך — The pronoun is missing in Hᶜ, the Greek and the Syriac: "Do not do evil and evil will not reach you." ואל ישיגך רעה — For the use of the masculine verb with a feminine subject, see Joüon §150*j-k* (the reading of Hᶜ is therefore not necessary). The proposition can have a predictive meaning, "and evil will not reach you," to the extent that it depends on the previous volitive (Joüon §116*j*). The text seems to be mentioned in rabbinic literature, but in a very different sense, echoing ideas from 12:4ᴬ: מתלא אמ[ר] (בן סירא) טב לביש לא תעבד ובישא לא מטי לך "Ben Sira spoke the proverb: 'Do not do good to an evil person and evil will not reach you.'" (Tanḥ. חקת §1; Gen. Rab. 22:8; Qoh. Rab. 5:10).
7:2 Cf. 1QS I 4; 4Q398 14–17 ii 5 // 4Q399 1 ii 2 (4QMMT) and m. ʾAbot 1:7.
7:3 תדע — For the defective spelling of the /ō/ vowel of the *hiphil*, cf. וישב Sir 10:14ᴬ and תשיבנו 11:1ᴬ. חרושי על אח — For a similar syntax, cf. Judg 5:10. The first stich is clearly corrupt due to confusion with 7:12 (according to Lévi 1901, 39, this is indicated by the marginal sign). The text surely must be corrected according to the Greek and Syriac, perhaps: אל תזרע על חרושי עולה (or חרושי חטא, see the proposals of Lévi [1901, 39] and Segal [1958, 44]). For the image used, see Job 4:8, חרשי און, "the plowmen of misfortunes," and Hos 10:13, חרשתם רשע, "you have plowed wickedness." תקצרהו — חרש, "plow," and קצר, "reap," are regularly associated (cf. 1 Sam 8:12; Job 4:8; Hos 10:13; Amos 9:13).
7:4 אל תבקש מאל — For the construction בקש + מן, "ask of/from," see Neh 5:12. ממשלת — This is the only attestation of the constructed form used for the absolute (but see Ps 136:8). מושב — מושב in the sense of "throne" is similar to its use in 1 Sam 20:25 and 4Q405 20 ii-22 4, 9 parallels. Compare with the expression כסא כבוד in 1 Sam 2:8.
7:5 תצטדק — Among classical Hebrew texts, the *hithpael* of צדק is attested only in Gen 44:16 and Sir 7:5. לפני מלך — The Greek and the Syriac have certainly preserved the correct reading with לפני אל, "before God," thus respecting the same sequence as the preceding verse (just as one should not approach God by presenting oneself as a righteous person, one should not approach a king by presenting oneself as an intelligent person). ופני מלך ∅ תתבונן — If the parallelism with the

32 Si tu le désires, mon enfant, tu deviendras sage
   et si tu appliques ton cœur, tu deviendras judicieux.
33 Si tu veux écouter,
   alors inclines ton oreille, tu t'instruiras.
35 Désire écouter tout discours
   et que la maxime sensée ne t'échappe pas.
36 Vois ce qui est astucieux et recherche-le
   et que ton pied use *son* seuil.
37 Et réfléchis à la crainte du Très Haut
   et dans ses commandements médite sans cesse.
   Et lui, il t'instruira le bon sens
   et il t'enseignera (la sagesse) que tu désires.

Chapitre 7

1 Ne te fais pas de mal et le mal ne t'atteindra pas.
2 Éloigne-toi du péché et il se détournera de toi.
3 *Ne divulgue pas ce qui est médité contre un frère*
   de peur que tu ne le moissonnes au septuple.
4 Ne demande pas à Dieu le pouvoir,
   ni au roi une place d'honneur.
5 Ne te justifie pas devant un roi
   et en présence d'un roi, ne fais pas l'intelligent.
6 Ne cherche pas à être celui qui a le pouvoir
   si tu n'as pas la force de mettre fin à l'arrogance,
   de peur que tu ne prennes peur devant un prince
   et qu'une blessure ne soit infligée à ton intégrité.
7 Ne te déclare pas coupable *dans l'assemblée des portes de Dieu*
   et ne t'abaisse pas dans la communauté.
8 Ne complote pas pour dédoubler un péché,
   car, dès le premier, tu ne resteras pas impuni.

32 If you so wish, my child, you will become wise,
   and if you put your heart into it, you will become judicious.
33 If you are willing to listen
   then bend your ear, you will be instructed.
35 Be eager to hear all discourse
   and may an intelligent maxim not escape you.
36 See what is clever and look for it,
   and may your foot wear out *its* threshold.
37 Contemplate the fear of the Most High,
   and meditate incessantly on his commandments.
   And as for him, he will teach you good sense,
   and he will teach you (the wisdom) that you desire.

Chapter 7

1 Do not harm yourself and harm will not reach you.
2 Keep far from sin and it will turn away from you.
3 *Do not disclose what is devised against a brother,*
   lest you reap it sevenfold.
4 Do not ask God for power,
   nor even the king, a seat of honor.
5 Do not try to present yourself as just before a king,
   do not present yourself as intelligent before a king.
6 Do not try to be someone who wields power,
   if you do not have the strength to end arrogance,
   lest you become afraid before a prince,
   and a wound is left in your integrity.
7 Do not indict yourself *in the assembly of the gates of God*
   and do not put yourself down in the community.
8 Do not scheme to duplicate a sin,
   since, for the first, you will not go unpunished.

previous stich is respected, then one may consider the *lamed* preposition as governing both the end of the first stich and the beginning of the second stich (cf. Miller 2009, 106–9).

7:6 מושל — The verb expresses different types of domination: "the one who governs," "the one who has power," "the one who leads." The Greek and the Syriac seem to have read שופט, "the one who judges, the magistrate." זדון — The term designates "pride," "presumption," "arrogance." A person should not seek to lead if they are unable to put an end to their own arrogance. נדיב — Cf. Prov 25:7. ונתונה בצע — The feminine passive participle of נתן is surprising here, unless בצע is considered feminine (otherwise correct to ונתון). Schechter and Taylor (1899, 45) followed by Smend (1906a, 63–64) and Lévi (1901, 40) propose to correct to ונתתה, in accord with the Greek and the Syriac. The word בצע is likely syonymous with פצע "wound" (note the exchange of bilabials in other words like פזר/בזר and נשף/נשב [see Reymond 2018b, 46], the use of the verb בצע to imply injury in Joel 2:8, and the sense of בצע reflected in Peshitta Jer 51:13). בתמימך — According to Lévi (1901, 40), the plural could be a plural of abstraction (cf. אמונות in Prov 28:20 and Joüon §136*g*); alternatively, this is another example of a plene spelling of the 2ms suffix on a singular form (see לשוניך Sir 4:29).

7:7 תרשיעך — For the use of the pronominal suffix as a reflexive, cf. Ezek 29:3; Sir 7:16^A; 1Q26 1 5, 8 (par. 4Q423 4 1) and perhaps 4Q417 1 ii 13, 14 (see van Peursen 1999, 54 and Rey 2008c, 168–71). בעדת שערי אל — The expression is surprising. The final י אל may be a dittography of ואל, which starts the next stich (see Segal 1958, 45). In that case, the text must be corrected to בעדת שער, "the assembly of the gate," i.e. the place in the city where judgment is made (see the Greek and the Syriac that have "the assembly of the city," which seems to be a modernization of בעדת שער). Alternatively, Segal (1958, 45) suggests to read בעדת אל "the divine assembly" (cf. Ps 82:1, and in particular, 1QM I 10 where the assembly of God עדת אלים and the assembly of men קהלת אנשים are also associated; cf. the following stich). תפיל — See the note for תרשיעך. בקהלה — See Deut 33:4; Neh 5:7; Sir 42:11^{B,M}; 1QM I 10 and 1QH^a X 14.

7:8 תקשור — In the sense of "plot/scheme"; the Greek καταδεσμεύσης has understood קשר in the sense of "link/bind/join." חט — A defective writing of חטא. For this stich's sense, see perhaps Sir 3:27^{A,C} and 5:5^{A,C}. באחת — The feminine form of "one" reflects either confusion over the gender of "sin" (cf. חַטָּאת and חֲטָאָה as well as Aramaic חֲטָאָה) or the use of the feminine to represent a generic antecedent.

הי 14כא נחלקה:	א תאיץ בצבא מלאכת עבדה	15	
ובצדקה א תתעבר:	א תתקצר בתפלה	10	
זכר כי יש מרים ומשפיל:	15א תבז לאנוש במר רוח	11	
וכן על רע וחבר יחדו:	16א תחרוש חמס על אח	12	
כי תקותו לא תנעם:	א תחפץ 17לכחש על כחש	13	
וא תישן דבר בתפלה:	א תסוד בעדת 18שרים	14	
19זכור עכרון לא יתעבר:	א תחשיבך במתי עם	16	
כי תקות 20אנוש רמה:	מאד מאד השפיל גאוה	17 C	
גל א א ורצה דרכו:	א תאיץ לאמר לפרץ		
ואח תלוי בזהב אופיר:	21א תמיר אוהב במחיר	18 D	
וטובת חן מפנינים:	אל 22תמאס אשה משכלת	19 D	
וכן שוכר נותן נפשו:	א תדע – 23באמת עובד אמת	20 CD	

C · שכיר | A D ‖ שוכר C G S · עבד עובד אמת A D ‖ באמת עובד אמת C D G S · אל תרע A ‖ א תדע 7:20 · C לרמה | A רמה C · השפל | A השפיל 7:17

L. 23 [7:20] שוכר — What seems to be a final *nun* corrected into *resh* is in fact an offset letter.

7:15 This verse is placed after verse 14 in the Greek and is not preserved in the Syriac. As Segal (1958, 46) notes, the first stich accumulates synonyms and the following stich seems to be corrupted. The Greek has translated μὴ μισήσῃς ἐπίπονον ἐργασίαν καὶ γεωργίαν ὑπὸ ὑψίστου ἐκτισμένην, "Do not detest hard work, nor the work of the fields created by the Most High," according to which Lévi (1901, 41), followed by Segal (1958, 46), proposes reconstructing the Hebrew text as תאיץ. אל תקוץ בצבא מלאכה כי עבודה מאל נחלקה — Ben-Ḥayyim identifies this as a *hiphil* of אוץ, "hasten/hurry" (see Sir 7:17^A; Isa 22:4). Although Smend (1906a, 65) considers the meaning inappropriate to the context, in this manuscript it fits very well with the following verse (i.e., 7:10). בצבא מלאכת עבדה — The phrase seems redundant and likely the result of expansion, where מלאכת was introduced as a gloss to צבא. Like מלאכה, the word צבא may be used to indicate imposed service (see Isa 40:2; Job 7:1; 14:14); it can also indicate religious service (Num 4:3, 30, 35, 39, 43); note especially צבא עבודה (Num 8:25) in relation to cultic service. The phrase מלאכת עבדה, on the other hand, indicates "submissive, hard, arduous work" and occurs frequently (cf. Exod 35:24; 36:1, 3, etc.). הי כאל — הי could be an Aramaic spelling of the feminine pronoun (cf. הו in 15:19^A), but nevertheless, it is certainly necessary to correct to כי מאל. נחלקה — Cf. Sir 15:9^A: כי לא מאל נחל קה לו "For it has not been apportioned to them by God." The verb חלק holds an important place in Ben Sira and at Qumran and, certainly, it has here the meaning "to create" (See the Greek κτίζω, Kister 1990, 32 and 4Q204 1 vi 12 [En^c], and Bremer, in *ThWQ* 2011, 1:997, art. חלק).

7:10 תתקצר — The *hithpael* of קצר is only attested here in Ben Sira and later in Rabbinic literature (cf. Jastrow 1903, 1408). תתעבר — For the *hithpael* of עבר, cf. 5:7^A and the note.

7:11 מר רוח — See 4:6^A and the note, as well as the expression מר נפש in 4:1^A. בזה — Cf. 4:4^A. For בזה + ל, see 2 Sam 6:16 and 1 Chr 15:29. מרים ומשפיל — Cf. 2 Sam 2:7 and Ps 75:8.

7:12 Cf. Prov 3:29: אל תחרש על רעך רעה.

7:13 לכחש על כחש — לכחש is likely an infinitive *piel* (thus the Greek and the Syriac, which imply לכחש כול כחש, so Smend 1906a, 7; Lévi 1901, 2:42) not a substantive (as in the expression עון על עון, cf. 3:27^A; 5:5^A,C and חטאת על חטאת in Isa 30:1). The construction חפץ + ל + object does not seem to be attested elsewhere (contra Clines [DCH 3:287] who identifies it in 1QS IX 24, where לו is an orthographic variation for the negative particle). If לכחש is understood as a preposition + noun, then it implies the translation "do not desire lie after lie." תקותו — תקוה Lit., "hope," but here figuratively "the aim," "the end," that is to say, "its result/outcome" (synonymous with אחרית; see HALOT §D.a.; Smend 1906a, 65; Lévi 1901, 42; Segal 1958, 46; and the Syriac).

7:14 Cf. Qoh 5:1; Matt 6:7 and b. Ber. 43a. תסוד — The verb סוד is not attested in Biblical Hebrew; it is attested in the Syriac usually in the *ethpaal* with the sense "speak," "converse" and at least once in the *pael*. It is certainly this meaning that is relevant here (in the *piel*: תְּסַוֵּד or *qal*: תָּסוֹד; see Segal 1958, 46; as well as HALOT; Smend 1906a, 66). Ben Sira uses it elsewhere in the *hithpael* (8:17^A; 9:3, 14^A; 42:12^B). For the meaning of the sentence, cf. Sir 32:9^B and Der. Er. Zut. 2.2 אל תדבר בפני מי שגדול ממך בחכמה "Do not speak before one who surpasses you in wisdom" (see Lévi 1901, 42). תישן — *Scriptio plena* of תְּשַׁן. The expression שנה דבר, rather than signifying simply "to repeat speech," implies "to spread gossip," "tell a secret" as in Sir 42:1^M,B and in Prov 17:9. בתפלה — The vocalization of this word is ambiguous. It may be vocalized בִּתְפִלָּה: "Do not repeat in prayer (cf. Matt 6:7)," "do not divulge a word in prayer" which are difficult to situate in the context. Kister (2002, 40–41) proposes that the term be vocalized תִּפְלָה as in Job 1:22 "unworthiness," "in a foolish way," which results in a contextually more relevant sense (cf. the Greek ἀφροσύνην; see also t. Pesaḥ. 8:6 אין עושין חבורה של נשים ועבדים וקטנים שלא לרבות את התפלה "They do not make association with women, slaves or minors so as not to multiply foolishness").

7:16 תחשיבך — The *hiphil* of חשב would be attested in classical Hebrew only here and perhaps in 1QH^a XI 7. However, since the *piel* is comparatively more common, it is easier here to infer a plene spelling of the *piel* (i.e., תְּחַשֵּׁיבְךָ; cf. יְבָרֶכְךָ Ps 134:3), similar to the many other instances where the *yod* functions as a mater for what would be a *segol* in the MT (see van Peursen 2004, 49). For the use of the pronominal suffix as a reflexive, cf. v. 7 and the note. במתי — Cf. 15:7^A, B: מתי שוא "worthless people." עכרון — The term is not attested elsewhere. Segal (1958, 46) understands it as a substantive formed from the root עכר in connection with Josh 7:24–25, having the meaning "trouble, "misfortune." Smend (1906a, 67), Peters (1913, 69) and Lévi (1901, 42) think that it is a corruption of עברון, "anger, punishment, wrath," formed from עבר and thus involving a play on words with יתעבר, which follows. לא יתעבר — See 5:7^A and the note.

7:17ab This verse is quoted in m. 'Abot 4:4 as a saying of Rabbi Levitas of Yavneh: מאד מאד הוי שפל רוח שתקות אנוש רמה. The syntax

15 Ne te hâte pas dans le service d'un travail pénible, *car* il a été créé *par* Dieu.	15 Do not hasten the service of difficult work, *since* it was created *by* God.
10 Ne sois pas trop court dans la prière et dans la justice ne tarde pas.	10 Do not be too brief in prayer, and for justice do not delay.
11 Ne méprise pas la personne au souffle amer, souviens-toi qu'il y a celui qui élève et celui qui abaisse.	11 Do not despise the person who has a bitter spirit, remember that there is one who lifts and who brings low.
12 Ne fomente pas la violence contre un frère, ni contre un prochain et un compagnon ensemble.	12 Do not plot violence against a brother, nor against a neighbor and a companion together.
13 Ne désire pas mentir à propos d'un mensonge, car sa conséquence ne sera pas agréable.	13 Do not desire to lie about a lie, for its consequence will not be pleasant.
14 Ne discours pas dans l'assemblée des princes et ne répète pas une parole insensément.	14 Do not speak idly in the assembly of princes, do not repeat a word foolishly.
16 Ne te considère pas parmi les gens du peuple, souviens-toi que le trouble ne tardera pas.	16 Do not consider yourself among the common people, remember that trouble will not delay.
17 Humilie grandement l'orgueil, car l'espoir de l'humain c'est la vermine. Ne t'empresse pas de parler pour détruire, tourne-toi vers Dieu et mets ton plaisir dans sa voie.	17 Diminish pride deeply, for the hope of humankind is worms. Do not rush to speak in order to undermine, turn yourself to God and desire his way.
18 N'échange pas un ami pour de l'argent, ni un frère *dépendant* pour de l'or d'Ophir.	18 Do not exchange a friend for money, nor a *dependent* brother for the gold of Ophir.
19 Ne rejette pas une femme intelligente, plus belle par la grâce que les perles.	19 Do not reject a prudent wife, more beautiful in grace than pearls.
20 *Ne sois pas mauvais*, en vérité, envers un serviteur fidèle, ni envers un *salarié* qui donne de sa personne.	20 *Do not treat badly*, in truth, a faithful servant, nor a laborer who dedicates themself (to their task).

is adapted to Mishnaic Hebrew and רוח appears for גאוה (as also reflected in the Greek ψυχή, Latin *spiritum* and Syriac ܪܘܚܐ); cf. Sir 10:11ᴬ. תקות — For the meaning of תקוה in this verse, see 7:13ᴬ and the note. Note the graphic wordplay of רמה "worm," which could also be construed as "it (i.e., pride) rises" or "height," the opposite sense of "lower." **7:17cd** The couplet is missing in the Greek, the Syriac and the Latin, perhaps by *homoioarchton* involving אל (Segal 1958, 46). אל תאיץ — Cf. 7:15ᴬ. לפרץ — We have opted to read a defective *qal* infinitive of פרץ (see Qoh 3:3). Alternatively, it could be the preposition *lamed* (indicating time, see, e.g., Gen 3:8) and the noun פֶּרֶץ (see 2 Sam 6:8): "Do not rush to say at (the time of) confrontation: / 'Turn to God and accept his path.'" גל אל אל — Cf. Ps 22:9.

7:18 תלוי — The *qal* passive participle of תלה "suspend" poses some translation problems. The Greek has rendered אח תלוי by ἀδελφόν γνήσιον "a true, sincere brother," while the Syriac translated it as ܐܚܐ ܕܓܐ, corresponding to a *Vorlage* of שֶׁלְּךָ or a confusion with ܕܬܠܐ(ܬ)ܐ, "suspended," which would confirm the reading of Hᴬ,ᴰ. Commentators have considered several solutions: (1) Schechter and Taylor (1899, 46) connect the syntagm אח תלוי with the expression אשם תלוי attested in m. Yebam. 4:2, where it refers to the offering of a sacrifice for sin in the event that there is any doubt as to the reality of that sin. In this case, the expression אח תלוי would refer to an "uncertain," "doubtful," "questionable" friend, but the parallelism of the first stich becomes obscure. (2) According to Bacher (1900a, 277–78), the Syriac, which seems to have a *Vorlage* of שֶׁלְּךָ, could attest to a confusion of the reading אח שלם, "a friend of integrity" (cf. לב שלם in 1 Chr 28:9; 29:9; Isa 38:3), which would explain both the Greek (γνήσιον) and the Syriac (confusion with שֶׁלְּךָ). (3) Nöldeke (1900, 85) considers תלוי to be a corruption of the Aramaic תלים, "blood brothers," as in Tg. Ps.-J., Tg. Neof. and Frg. Tg. of Gen 49:5: אחין תלימין. (4) If one retains the form, it is possible to understand "a suspended brother," that is to say, "a faithful brother," "a very dear brother," or even, following the sense of the Aramaic, תלי "uplifted," "an uplifted brother" or "an esteemed brother," or "a dependent brother" (cf. the cognate verb in Syriac and Hebrew תלא in Deut 28:66). In support of this hypothesis, Peters (1913, 71) notes that in the Sam. Tg., נשא is translated by the Aramaic תלי in Gen 4:7 and Gen 40:13. (5) Finally, Ginzberg (1906, 617) surmises that the expression of the formula in Aramaic derives from the Babylonian Talmud, where it designates a person of great value: כיפי תלא לה (b. ʿErub. 96b; b. Ketub. 81b). תלי would be equivalent to שקול and would refer to weighing something or someone on a scale to estimate its value: "do not trade a friend for money, or a brother who weighs so much/who is worth as much as Ophir's gold"; as regards the meaning, note the parallel with Lam 4:2: בְּנֵי צִיּוֹן הַיְקָרִים הַמְסֻלָּאִים בַּפָּז. (6) Another solution is to assume a text that would more normally read וְאָח תִּלְוֶה with the sense "a brother (to whom) you are attached" (cf. Gen 29:34 and the asyndetic expression of Isa 51:1).

7:19 אל תמאס — The verb מאס, "repel, reject," may also refer to casting off a wife (cf. Isa 54:6).

7:20 אל תדע — Correct to אל תרע with Hᶜ,ᴰ and the Greek. For the confusion between *dalet* and *reš* in this manuscript, see the complete introduction. באמת — "In truth"; this reading is confirmed by Hᴰ, but is not in agreement with Hᶜ, "a servant who faithfully serves," which has the support of the Greek and the Syriac. שוכר — *Qal* participle of שכר, which probably refers to an employer ("the one who hires," cf. Prov 26:10), but perhaps also the employee (cf. 2 Chr 24:12; in CD XI 12, it seems to be synonymous with שכיר). Hᶜ has שכיר, which implies "employee" (cf. Sir 37:11ᴮᵐ,ᴰ). נתן נפשו — The same expression occurs in Sir 29:15ᴸˣˣ, "who gave his life for you" (ἔδωκεν γὰρ τὴν ψυχὴν αὐτοῦ ὑπὲρ σοῦ). See also 4Q416 2 ii 5–6 concerning the bond: נתתה כל חייכה בו "you have given your whole life in (exchange) for it (= your purse)."

[א]ל תמנע ממנו חפש:		חבב כנפש 24עבד משכיל	21 CD
25ואם אמנה היא העמידה:		בהמה לך ראה עיניך	22 D
ושׂא 26לָהֶם נשים בנעוריהם:		בנים לך יסיר אותם	23 CD
ולֹ תאיר 27אֹהם פנים:		בנות לך נצור שארם	24 CD
ולֹ נבון גבר חברה:		הוצא בת ויצא עסק	25 CD
ושנואה לֹ תאמן בה:		28אשה לך לֹ תתעבה	26 D
ואת כהניו הקדיש:		בכל לבך פחד לֹ1	29 D
ואת משרתיו 2לא תעזב:		בכל מאֹדך אֱהֹוב עושך	30 D
ותֶ[ן חֻ]לקם כאשר צֻוותה:		כבד לֹ והדר כהן	31 D
זְבֹחוּ֗ צדק ותרומת קדש:		3לחם אבירים ותרומת ידֹ	
למען תשלם ברכתך:		וגם 4לאביוֹ֗[ן] הֹ[ו]שֹיט יד	32 D
5וגם ממת לֹ תמנע חסד:		תן מתן לפני כל חי	33 D
ועם אבלים 6התאבל:		לֹ תתאחר מבוכים	34 D
כי ממנו תאהב:		לֹ תשא לב מאוהב	35 D
ולעולם לא תשחת:		בכל 7מעשיך זכור אחרית	36 D

ENA 2536–1 recto

7:21 אֹהם A · תאר C | תאיר A D | 7:24 בנים C | בנות A D G S | > C | נשים A D | יסר C D · ישיר A | 7:23 חופש C · חפש A D | אהוב C · חבב A D | 7:21 · ותרומתה A | ותרומת ידֹ D · צויתה A · צוותה D | זבדה A D · חברה C · גבר נבון A D | נבון גבר C · הוציא A D · הוצא C · 7:25 אליהם D · להם C | 7:32 לאביו̇[ן] A G S · לאביו D · 7:34 אבילים A · אבלים D ·

L. 1 [7:30] אֱהֹוב — The reading אֲהַב would be more difficult according to the traces. The *segol* under the *aleph* is not totally clear and could also be interpreted as a *qibbuts*.

L. 3 [7:31] ותרומת ידֹ — *Yod* and *dalet* are read by Ben-Ḥayyim (1973, 10), but not Adler (1900, 468), Beentjes (1997, 31), Vattioni (1968, 39) or Segal (1958, 47), who restores them in brackets. The letters are distorted due to offsetting. Ink from the *sin* of שיחה (Sir 6:35) appears beside the *dalet* of ידֹ; conversely, ink from *yod/dalet* appears in the *sin* of שיחה.

7:21 The first stich is also found at Sir 10:25ᴮ, for which see the note there. עבד משכיל — Cf. Prov 14:35; 17:2 and 4Q418 8a,b,c,d 15 (// 4Q416 2 ii 15). חבב — "To love." Besides Deut 33:3, the word only appears in writings outside the Hebrew Bible (in Ben Sira, Qumran, and later Hebrew). It is attested in Targumic Aramaic (cf. Tg. Onkelos, Neofiti Deut 33:3), in Christian-Palestinian Aramaic and in Syriac (see also in neo-Punic [KAI 121:1; 124:4–6; 162:3] and in Palmyrean; see Hoftijzer and Jongeling 1995, 343–44). The three attestations at Qumran are from fragmentary contexts (4Q498 1 i 1; 4Q502 95 1; 4Q502 96 6). כנפש — "As oneself," cf. Sir 10:25ᴮ; 31:2ᴮ and 37:2ᴮ and especially 31:15ᴮ and the note.

7:22 ראה עיניך — The verb is either רָאָה or רְאֵה, "watch it." We would expect a *bet* preposition, בעיניך, as frequently found elsewhere (e.g., Deut 3:27). אמנה — *Qal* passive participle, cf. Lam 4:5.

7:23 יסיר — The plene form of the *piel* imperative. שׂא — The imperative of נשא in the sense "marry," a meaning attested in late Hebrew (e.g., Ezra 9:12).

7:24 שארם — This use of the masculine suffix in place of the feminine is common in late and Rabbinic Hebrew (cf. Pérez Fernández 1997, 30; Qimron 1986, §200.142). תאיר פנים — The expression is idiomatic (cf. Sir 13:26ᴬ and 35:11ᴮ; see further Num 6:25; Ps 31:17; 67:2; 80:4, 8, 20; 119:135; Qoh 8:1; Dan 9:17; 1QSb IV 27; 1QHᵃ XI 4; XII 6; XII 28; 4Q285 8 4 [par. 11Q14 1 ii 7]; 4Q374 2 ii 8; 4Q393 3 5). Apart from the attestations in Sirach and Qohelet, the expression is always used in a religious context and expresses absolute benevolence. The expression would mean that the father should not be too pleasant, lax, indulgent toward his daughters.

7:25 עסק — See Sir 3:22ᴬ and the note. חברה — The verb חבר is widely used in Sirach to designate all kinds of associations (Sir 12:13, 14; 13:1, 2, 16, 17; 42:3). For the use of this verb in connection with marriage, see 4Q416 2 iii 21 and the use of the substantive in Mal 2:14 and Prov 21:9 par. 25:24.

7:26 תתעבה — The verb is strong and violent, referring to feelings of "horror" and "disgust" (cf. 1 Kgs 21:26; Job 9:31; 19:19; Ps 5:7). ושנואה — The expression generally refers to the unloved woman (Gen 29:31, 33; Prov 30:23), especially in a polygamous couple (Deut 21:15–17), but we can also understand it as "if she is odious, hateful" (cf. Prov 30:23). The Syriac understood it as "if she is bad" (ܘܐܢ ܒܝܫܐ).

7:27–28 Verses 27–28, which are attested in the Greek and the Syriac, are missing in Hᴬ and Hᴰ.

7:29 For Sir 7:29–31 and its links with Deut 6:5, see Kister (1999, 183–6). בכל לבך — The Greek reads בכל נפשך, thus picking up the succession in Deut 6:5: Ἐν ὅλῃ καρδίᾳ (Sir 7:27, בכל לבך), ἐν ὅλῃ ψυχῇ (Sir 7:29, בכל נפשך) and ἐν ὅλῃ δυνάμει (Sir 7:30, בכל מאד). פחד — The verb's use in the sense "worshiping (God)" is rare (cf. Hos 3:5 and perhaps Gen 31:42 as well as 4Q166 [4QpHosᵃ] ii 6, see Kister 1999, 186). הקדיש — In the sense "consider as sacred," "treat as sacred" (cf. Isa 8:13).

7:30 מאֹדך — The *qamets* under the *dalet* instead of under the *kaph* corresponds to the Aramaic vocalization of the pronominal suffix.

7:31 צוותה — *Pual* of צוה (צֻוְּתָה or צֻוְּתָה). The duplication of a geminated letter is typical of later Hebrew spelling (cf. the spelling in Hᴰ, צֻוִּיתָה; for examples of the orthography from the Dead Sea Scrolls, see

21 Un serviteur intelligent, aime(-le) comme toi-même, ne lui refuse pas la liberté.	21 Love a prudent servant as (your) very self, do not refuse them liberty.
22 As-tu du bétail ? Suis-le des yeux et s'il est robuste, conserve-le.	22 Do you have animals? Watch (them) carefully, and if they are sturdy, keep them.
23 As-tu des fils ? Instruis-les et marie-les à des femmes quand ils sont jeunes.	23 Do you have sons? Instruct them, and marry them to women in their youth.
24 As-tu des filles ? Veille sur leur chair et ne leur montre pas un visage radieux.	24 Do you have daughters? Watch over their flesh, and do not show them a radiant face.
25 Fais partir ta fille et le souci partira et marie-la à un homme intelligent.	25 Make your daughter depart and worry will depart too, but marry her to an intelligent man.
26 As-tu une femme ? Ne la prends pas en abomination et (si) elle n'est pas aimée, ne te fie pas à elle.	26 Do you have a wife? Do not consider her an abomination, but if she is unloved, do not trust her.
29 De tout ton cœur, vénère Dieu et sanctifie ses prêtres.	29 With all your heart, venerate God, and sanctify his priests.
30 De toute ta force aime ton créateur et n'abandonne pas ses ministres.	30 With all your strength, love your creator, and do not abandon his ministers.
31 Glorifie Dieu et honore le(s) prêtre(s) et don[ne] leur [par]t selon que tu en as reçu l'ordre : le pain des forts et l'offrande volontaire, les sacrifices de justice et l'offrande de sainteté.	31 Glorify God and honor his priests, and gi[ve] them their share as you were commanded, bread of the strong and the contribution, sacrifices of righteousness and offering of holiness.
32 Et, de même, te[n]ds la main au pauvr[e], afin que ta bénédiction soit parfaite.	32 And, likewise, exte[n]d your hand to the poo[r], so your blessing may be complete.
33 Donne l'aumône à tout vivant et, de même, aux morts, ne refuse pas la charité.	33 Give alms to all the living, and likewise do not refuse charity to the dead.
34 Ne sois pas loin de ceux qui pleurent et avec les endeuillés, porte le deuil.	34 Do not keep apart from those who cry, and with the mourning, mourn.
35 Ne détourne pas (ton) cœur d'un ami, car de lui tu seras aimé.	35 Do not turn your heart from a friend, for you will be loved by them.
36 En toutes tes actions, souviens-toi de la fin et jamais tu ne seras détruit.	36 In all your actions remember the end, and you will never come to ruin.

Reymond 2014c, 61–64). לחם אבירים — "The bread of the strong," the expression comes from Ps 78:25 where it refers to manna, "the wheat of heaven" (for the Greek and the Syriac reading, see Rey 2012b, 411–13). ותרומת יד — See Deut 12:6, 11, 17 where the expression is included in the list of offerings to be brought to the temple. The Syriac, ܘܪܫܝܬ ܐܝܕܝܟ "the first fruits of (your) hands," could confirm the reading, to the extent that the Hebrew תרומה seems to also be translated by ܪܫܝܬ in Sir 45:20B and the LXX often understood the term in the sense of first portion (ἀπαρχή). The reading in the Greek, δόσιν βραχιόνων, is in all likelihood inspired by Num 18:18 or Deut 18:3. The translation of יד by βραχίων is not inconcevable and, therefore, does not require that a different *Vorlage* be assumed (cf. Gen 24:18, 46; Exod 6:1; 32:11; Jdt 15:14; Isa 26:11; Dan 9:15). זבחי צדק — Cf. Deut 33:19; Ps 4:6 and Ps 51:21. תרומת קדש — Cf. Exod 36:6; Lev 22:12 and Num 18:19.

7:33 ממת — The *qal* participle of מות may have a collective meaning.

7:34 תתאחר — The *hithpael* of אחר is not attested in the Hebrew Bible, yet it is found three times in Sirach (Sir 11:11; 32:11); six times at Qumran with the sense "delay, defer, postpone, go back;" as well as in Official Aramaic. It is attested subsequently in the *piyyutim*. The *piel* is found in Mishnaic Hebrew.

7:35 Most commentators agree that v. 35a is corrupt. Lévi (1901, 47) and Segal (1958, 50) propose correcting the text from the versions as follows: אל תשא לבקר מכואב (see Mopsik 2003, 114 and Rey 2012b, 414).

Unfortunately, this verse is too incomplete in HD to either confirm or invalidate the reading in HA. אל תשא לב — The construction נשא לב appears several times in the Hebrew Bible where "heart" is the subject of the verb "to lift," implying a strong emotional response (Exod 35:21, 26; 36:2) or arrogance (2 Kgs 14:10; 2 Chr 25:19). Where לב is the object of נשא (e.g., Lam 3:41) it implies giving attention to something. Here, with the מן preposition, the expression must have the meaning "to turn one's heart away from" or "to forget" (so DCH 5:776).

7:36 אחרית — The term undoubtedly refers to death here, as elsewhere in Sirach (Sir 3:26A; 11:25–27A; 16:3A,B). However, without determination, the word could imply a more general reference: "to remember the end." At Qumran, with rare exceptions where the term refers to descendants (the citation of Ps 36:37–38 in 4Q171 1–10 IV 16.18 and 4Q416 2 iii 16), it is always attested in the form אחרית הקץ, אחרית הימים, or אחרית העת. לא תשחת — The verb שחת can mean "destroy" with an eschatological sense or "corrupt" from a moral perspective. The eschatological color of the term appears quite clearly in the Qumran texts, both through the use of the verb (1QM III 9; 4Q434 1 i 12, 2 2) and the noun, which is often synonymous with Sheol (4Q418 69 ii 6; 1QHa XI 19–20; XIII 8; XVI 29–30; 1QS XI 11–14; XI 13; Sir 51:2); with the meaning of moral corruption, see 4Q222 1 3 (Jub 25:9–12) : [כי אעשה רצונך] וביושר אתהלך ול[א אשחית דרכי לעולם "[For I will do your will, and in righteousness I will walk and n]ever corrupt my ways."

Chapter 8

	למה תשוב על ידו׃	אַ תריב עִם 8איש גדול	1 ᴰ
	9למה תפול בידו׃	אַ תריב עם קשה ממֹּך	
לֹו	פן ישקל מחירך 10ואבדת	אַל תחרש עַל איש לֹא הון	2 ᴰ
קֹ	והן משגה ל[בו]ת[] נ[]דיבים׃	כי רבים הפחיז זהב	
	וא תתן על אש עֵצֵ[י]ם[׃]	11אַ תיניץ עם איש לשון	3 ᴰ
	פן יבוז לנדיבים׃	[אַל] [ת]רגיל עם 12איש אויל	4 ᴰ
	13זכר כי כלנו חייבים׃	אַ תכלים א[י]ש שב מפשע	5 ᴰ
	כִי נמנה 14מזקנים׃	אַ תבייש אנוש ישיש	6 ᴰ
׃	זכר כלנו נאספים׃	אַ תתהלל על גוע	7 ᶜᴰ
	ובחדיתיהם התרטש׃	[א]ַל תטש 15שיחת חכמים	8 ᴰ
	להתיצב לפני שרים׃	כי מֹמנו תלמוד 16ולקח	
	17אשר שמעו מאבתם׃	אַ תמאס בשמיעוֹת שבים	9 ᴰ
	בעת צֹו[ר]ְך להשיב 18פתגם׃	כי ממנו תקח שכל	
	פן תבער בשביב אשו׃	אַ ת{נ}צלח בנחלת רשע	10 ᴰ
	להושיבו כאורב לפני[ך׃]	19וּאַ תזוח מפני לץ	11 ᴰ

C תהֹלל | A D תתהלל 8:7 · D הן | A הןֹ | Amg D לֹו | A לא · D תחרוש | A תחרש 8:2

L. 8 [8:1] יָדֹו — The reading ידו is clear, so Lévi (1901, 2:48), Peters (1902, 336), Vattioni (1968, 41), Elizur and Rand (2011, 204), rather than לבו with Smend (1906b, 8) and Ben-Ḥayyim (1973, 10). The reading על [יד] יֹ proposed by Adler (1900, 468) is impossible.

L. 10 [8:2] והן מִשְׁגֵה — This reading is confirmed by Hᴰ and is perfectly plausible from a paleographic point of view. The horn and left diagonal of the *mem* are visible on the facsimiles from 1901. (Cf. Adler [1900, 468] who reads ישגה ו[ה]ן, Smend [1906b, 8] הִשְׁגֵה [ו]הן, Ben-Ḥayyim [1973, 10] and Vattioni [1968, 41] י[שגה ו[ה]ן, Beentjes

[1997, 31] משגה [ ] ו[ה]). ל[בו]ת[] נ[]דיבים — This reading is confirmed by Hᴰ and is more suitable for the space than the restoration לב נ[דיבים proposed by Ben-Ḥayyim (1973, 10). A trace of ink could indicate a *taw*.

L. 16 [8:9] בשמיעוֹת — The *vav* is embedded in the *ayin* and followed by a trace of a vertical letter that could correspond to the shoulder of the *tav* (thus Elizur and Rand 2011, 205).

L. 17 [8:9] צֹו[ר]ְך — A small trace of the end of the vertical of the *vav* is preserved, joined to the base of the *tsade*. The end of the shaft of the *kaph* is visible.

8:1 Hᴬ has a doublet that is absent in the Greek and the Syriac, but which is also present in Hᴰ. למה — In the sense of פן "lest…" (cf. the use of למה in 1 Sam 19:17; 2 Sam 2:22; Sir 11:33; 12:5, 12; 30:12).

8:2 אל תחרש עַל — Cf. Sir 7:12 and Prov 3:29. לא — The marginal correction invites reading לו, which is confirmed by Hᴰ and the versions. The *qoph* below indicates the *qere* (קרא) reading, as in the Massoretic tradition. הפחיז — The *hiphil* of פחז is only attested clearly in the Hebrew of Ben Sira. The verb appears in Judg 9:4, Zeph 3:4, Sir 4:30ᶜ, 19:2ᶜ and 42:10ᴮ. For the *hiphil*, HALOT gives the meaning "to make high-spirited," "to make reckless," Clines (DCH 6:667) gives "cause to be reckless, cause to be wanton" (but does not record Sir 19:2ᶜ). The verb is also attested in Aramaic in the sense of "to be lewd, reckless" (compare with Tg. Neof. Deut 32:15, Sir 19:2ᶜ, 41:17ᴮ,ᴹ and 4Q184 1 2, 13, 15) and in Syriac in the *aphel* "to become lewd, cause to be lewd." For the meaning of פחז, see also Greenfield (1978, 35–40). ל[בו]ת[] נ[]דיבים — "The noble hearts" or "the hearts of the nobles."

8:4 תרגיל — The verb could be *piel* or *hiphil*. The *hiphil* of רגל is not attested in Biblical Hebrew or at Qumran, but does appear in Rabbinic Hebrew with the meaning "to make familiar, to accustom" (see Jastrow 1903, 1448).

8:5 חייבים — "Guilty," חייב is attested in Aramaic and Mishnaic Hebrew, but not in Biblical Hebrew; see its ambiguous use in 11:18ᴬ.

8:7 גוע — There is a mark between the *gimmel* and *vav* that is commonly interpreted as a *holem* by scholars, but the mark is unlike other *holem* vowels and more like a dot with a circumflex-like mark superimposed on top of it. There are three points drawn in the margin, which usually indicate an error somewhere in the line. The mark between *gimmel* and *vav* is likely the mistake referred to by the three dots. נאספים — As a *niphal*, אסף may mean "to be gathered, assembled" or "to be eliminated, removed, disappear." In a funeral context, it is generally followed by a prepositional phrase: "to be gathered to one's ancestor's / to one's people" (Judg 2:10; Gen 25:8). Used as an absolute, it means "to be removed," a metaphorical reference to dying (cf. Isa 57:1–2, Sir 16:10ᴬ; 40:28ᴮ,ᴹ; 44:15ᴮ; CD XIX 35; XX 14; 1QHᵃ XIV 10–11). In a few rare cases, the absolute verb means "bury" or the passive "to be buried," probably as an extension of the expression "to be gathered to one's ancestors." E.g., see Ezek 29:5, where the LXX translates the *niphal* of אסף with περιστέλλω, and in an even more explicit manner with the *qal* in Sir 38:16ᴮ: כמשפטו אסוף שארו: "according to his custom, bury his body" (LXX : κατὰ δὲ τὴν κρίσιν αὐτοῦ περίστειλον τὸ σῶμα αὐτοῦ).

8:8 תטש — Cf. Prov 1:8; 6:20; Sir 9:10ᴬ; 35:17ᴮ and 47:22ᴮ. שיחה — See 6:35ᴬ and the note. התרטש — In Biblical Hebrew, the root means "to crush," "tear to pieces." In Aramaic, it means "to let run," "abandon," "banish," and in the *ithpe'el* / *ithpa'el* "to be abandoned or to be scattered" (Jastrow 1903, 1472); in the present case, the *hithpael* could have the meaning "to abandon oneself in" and by extension "to occupy oneself with" (thus DCH 7:477). Smend (1906a, 77) and Segal (1958, 53) suggest it is the Aramaic equivalent of the Hebrew נטש with the sense "spread out, invade" in the *niphal* (cf. Tg. Judg 15:9 [Tg. וְאִתְרְטִישׁוּ for MT וַיִּנָּטְשׁוּ] and 2 Sam 5:18, 22). תלמוד — Note the /o/ theme vowel as in Rabbinic Hebrew and in contrast to the /a/ vowel in Biblical Hebrew.

8:9 בשמיעת — According to Smend (1906a, 78) and Segal (1958, 53), שמיעה would be a variant of שמועה with the meaning "teaching," see 5,11ᶜ: ושמועה רעה על שמועה] רעה (cf. 3Q5 [Jub] 1 3: בשמועה טובה).

Chapitre 8

1. Ne te dispute pas avec une personne puissante,
   de peur que tu ne passes en son pouvoir.
   Ne te dispute pas avec plus dur que toi,
   de peur que tu ne tombes en son pouvoir.
2. Ne fomente pas contre une personne qui n'a pas de (mg. a des) richesses,
   de peur qu'elle ne pèse ta valeur et que tu ne périsses.
   Car ils sont nombreux ceux que l'or rend insouciants
   et la richesse fourvoie les cœurs nobles.
3. Ne te querelle pas avec une personne bavarde
   et ne mets pas du bois sur le feu.
4. Ne deviens pas familier avec une personne stupide,
   de peur qu'elle ne méprise les princes.
5. N'offense pas une personne qui se repent du péché,
   souviens-toi que tous nous sommes coupables.
6. N'humilie pas une personne âgée,
   car nous serons comptés parmi les anciens.
7. Ne te félicite pas de celui qui meurt,
   souviens-toi que tous, nous serons ensevelis.
8. Ne néglige pas le discours des sages,
   mais dans leurs énigmes abandonne-toi,
   car à travers cela tu apprendras l'instruction
   pour te tenir devant les princes.
9. Ne dédaigne pas les enseignements des anciens
   qui ont appris de leurs ancêtres,
   car à travers cela, tu acquerras l'intelligence,
   pour retourner, au moment nécessaire, la sentence.
10. N'enflamme pas le patrimoine du méchant,
    de peur que tu ne brûles dans la flamme de son feu.
11. Ne t'écarte pas devant le moqueur,
    de sorte qu'il se tienne en embuscade devant toi.

Chapter 8

1. Do not argue with a powerful person,
   lest you return into their grip.
   Do not argue with (a person) more severe than you,
   lest you fall into their grip.
2. Do not plot against someone who has no (mg. who has) wealth,
   lest they weigh your worth and you perish.
   For there are many that gold has made reckless,
   and wealth leads astray the hearts of nobles.
3. Do not quarrel with the talkative person,
   do not put wood on a fire.
4. Do not become familiar with a foolish person,
   lest they scorn the princes.
5. Do not shame a person who repents of sin,
   remember that we are all guilty.
6. Do not humiliate an old person,
   for we will be counted among the elders.
7. Do not congratulate yourself over someone who is dying,
   remember that we all will be gathered.
8. Do not neglect the discourse of the wise
   rather, in their riddles lose yourself,
   for, through this you will learn instruction,
   in order to stand before princes.
9. Do not despise the teachings of the elders,
   who have heard (them) from their ancestors,
   so, through this you will acquire intelligence,
   in order to produce, when necessary, a response.
10. Do not inflame the legacy of the wicked,
    lest you burn in the flame of their fire.
11. Do not step aside from the mocker,
    so that they set themself up as an ambush before you.

Here, the author plays with the verb שמע from the following stich (cf. m. 'Abot 1:1). שבים — From the Aramaic שב "old" (see Ezra 5:5, 9; 6:7, 8, 14). תקח — For לקח in the cognitive sense, see Sir 16:24^A; 31:22^B; 32:14^B,F; 32:18^B,E,F; 4Q417 2 i 11 // 4Q416 2 i 6; 4Q418 77 2, 4; 4Q418 177 4, 4Q418 197 3 and 4Q418 228 3 (see Lange 1996, 190–192 and Rey 2008b, 129–31). Ben Sira plays on the meaning of the root לקח, which appears in 8:8c with the sense "instruction." צו[ר]ך — The term belongs to late Hebrew and Aramaic (cf. 2 Chr 2:15; Sir 10:26^A,B; 12:5^A; 15:12^ABmg; 32:2^B,F; 32:7^B,F; 32:17^B,E,F; 37:8^B,D; 38:1^B; 38:12^B; 39:16^B; 39:21^B; 39:30^B,M; 39:33^M,B; 42:23^M and 11Q19 XLVII 9). פתגם — The term is borrowed from old Persian; see Sir 5:11^A and the note.

8:10 אל תצלח בנחלת רשע — The first stich presents numerous difficulties. The verb צלח here can mean "to enter," "to thrive, succeed," "to inflame" or "to stir up, arouse" (cf. Amos 5:6). The first is reflected in the translation of Elizur and Rand (2011, 205), who construe נַחֲלָה as "river, torrent" (a feminine form of נַחַל; cf. Ps 124:4): "Do not penetrate the torrent of the wicked." Alternatively, נחלה might mean "inheritance, possession": "Do not enter into the legacy of the wicked." The sense "thrive, succeed" results in the translation "Do not prosper through the possession of the wicked" (cf. צלח [*qal*] + ב in 2 Chr 32:30 and [in Aramaic] צלח [*haphel*] + ב in Ezra 6:14; for the meaning of the root צלח in Hebrew and in Aramaic, see Puech 1971, 5–19). However, due to the following stich, we translate "Do not inflame the legacy of the wicked." Nevertheless, most commentators opt for correcting the text according to the Greek by reading גחלת "coal" in place of נחלת, giving the verse a meaning consistent with the Greek: "Do not ignite the sinner's coals" (μὴ ἔκκαιε ἄνθρακας ἁμαρτωλοῦ). The Syriac ܠܐ ܗܘܝ ܫܘܬܦܐ ܠܓܒܪܐ ܥܘܠܐ, "Do not be the partner of the wholly wicked person (cf. the talmudic expression רשע גמור)," would support the Greek if one accepts the judicious suggestion of Perles 1897, 53-54: ܠܓܒܪܐ ܥܘܠܐ is a confusion of ܓܡܘܪܐ ܕܪܫܝܥܐ "coal of the wicked."

8:11 תזוח — The root זוח (or זחח) may have the meaning "move," "remove," "deviate" (Exod 28:28; 39:21), implied in the translation above. It can also have the meaning "to be proud," attested in Rabbinic Hebrew in the expression תזוח דעתו עליו (b. San. 38a; Segal 1958, 54), which would imply the sense here: "Do not be proud in front of the mocker." להושיבו כאורב — For the meaning, see Judg 16:9, 12 and Job 38:40. The use of the infinitive is surprising here, one would have expected a proposition introduced by פן, and in any case, this seems to be how the Greek and the Syriac understood it.

12 D	א תל[ו]ה[20]ר איש חזק ממך	ואם הלוית כמאבד:
13 D	א תערב יתר ממך	[21]ואם ערבת כמשלם:
14 D	א תשפט עם שופט	כי כרצונו [22]יש[פט]:
15 D	עם אכזרי א תלך	פן תכביד את רעתך:
	כי הוא [23]נוכח פניו ילך	ובאולתו תספה:
16 D	עם בעל אף א תעיז [24]מצח	וא תרכב עמו בדרך:
	כי קל בעיניו דמים	ובאין [25]מציל ישחיתך:
17 D	עם פותה א תסתייד	כי לא יוכל [26]לכסות סודך:
18 D	לפני זר א תעש רז	כי לא תדע מה ילד [27]ספו׃
19	לכל בשר א תגל לבך	וא תדיח מעליך הטוברה:

Chapter 9

1	א[28] תקנא את אשת חיקך	פן תלמד עליך רעה:
2	א תקנא [1]לאשה נפשך	להדריבה על במותיך:
3	אַ־תִקְרַב אֶל־אִשָּׁה זָרָה	[2]פֶּן־תִפּוֹל בִּמְצוֹדֹתֶיהָ:
	עִם זוֹנָה אַ־תִסְתַייָד	פֶּן־תִלָּכֵד בִּלְקוּחֹתֶיהָ:

ENA 2536–1 verso

8:14 תשפט A G ? S ? | תשפוט D · 8:15 נכח A | נוכח D ·

L. 18 [8:10] בשביב — The first letter looks like a *kaph*, though a *bet* is also possible and is supported by H^D, the Greek and the Syriac.

L. 2 [9:3] עִם — Only a trace of the end of the *ayin* is visible (Beentjes [1997, 33] ס[.]).

8:12–13 See Aḥiqar TAD C1.1.130–131: "[130][Do not take] the heavy [l]oan and from a bad person do not borrow. Moreover, [i]f you take the loan, rest to your soul do not put (=give) until [131][you repay] the [l]oan, [for consump]tion of the loan is sweet as ... but repaying it is a houseful" (trans. Porten and Yardeni 1993, 43). See also 4Q417 2 i 19–21 and 4Q416 2 ii 3.18.

8:13 The Hebrew text is not entirely clear. יתר may be a defective writing of יותר, which is how the Greek understood it, "Do not bail out beyond your means" (ὑπὲρ δύναμίν σου; יותר ממך, cf. HALOT, Esth 6:6 and Qoh 12:12). It is more likely that it should read יָתֵר, which is attested in Rabbinic Hebrew and in Sir 10:31^A, and be translated "someone who has more than you," in parallel with the preceding verse. This is how the Syriac understood it.

8:14 An apparent doublet of this verse is found at 4:27c–d^A. תשפט — It is possible the verb is a *niphal*, "enter into judgment with someone" (cf. Joel 4:2), which is how the Greek and the Syriac understood it. It could also be vocalized as a *qal* form, as dictated by H^D: "Do not judge with a judge, for according to his whim, he will judge."

8:15ab עם אכזרי אל תלך — Cf. Ps 1:1; Prov 1:10–15 and Aḥiqar TAD C1.1.99–100: "[99]when a good person [will s]ee a ba[d] person ... [100]he shall [not] join with him on/in ... and a master of wages (=employer) shall not have (=hire) a good person with a [ba]d pe[rson]" (trans. Porten and Yardeni 1993, 39).

8:15cd נוכח פניו — The same idiom occurs in Ezek 14:3–4, 7; Jer 17:16 and Lam 2:19, though in these cases it implies the sense "before," which makes less sense here. Instead, the phrase seems to have the sense "according to himself" or "for his own purposes" (as reflected in the Greek). The phrase is used on analogy to נגד פנים found in Exod 10:10: רעה נגד פניכם "evil (is) your intention" and Isa 5:21 נגד פניהם נבנים "according to themselves they are wise." ובאולתו תספה — For + ספה ב, cf. Gen 19:15 and Num 16:26.

8:16 בעל אף — Cf. Prov 22:24. תעיז — The *hiphil* of עזז is usually constructed with פנים to mean "brazen, bold, shameless, insolent" (cf. Prov 7:13; 21:29). The French "effronté" ("brazen, bold, shameless") correctly renders the meaning of the expression. Surprisingly, the formula תעיז מצח is only attested elsewhere three times in *piyyutim* from the tenth century. The Greek and the Syriac have read תעש מצה "do not engage in dispute." קל בעיניו — For the expression, cf. y. Soṭah 7b, Gen. Rab. 68:4 and 74:14.

8:17 פותה — The "fool," the "naive" (cf. Job 5:2; Qoh 7:11; Sir 16:23^A; 31:7^B; 42:8^{M,B}). תסתייד — Cf. 7:14^A and the note. סודך — Ben Sira plays on the meaning of the verb סוד "discuss" in stich *a* and the meaning of the substantive סוד, which could mean "secret" in stich *b*, as in most cases in his book. Alternatively, the word could refer to "confidential discourse" (see the same sequence and ambiguity in Sir 9:14–15^A).

8:18 זר — The term זר designates the "stranger, foreigner," broadly speaking, not only in an ethnic or nationalistic sense; it is the one who is other, external to a group in a given category (cf. Sir 45:18^B where זר designates the stranger to the priesthood). רז — A term borrowed from Persian to designate "mystery," "secret." The term is attested in Daniel

12 Ne prête pas à une personne plus puissante que toi	12 Do not lend to a person more powerful than you,
et si tu as prêté (tu es) comme celui qui perd.	and if you do lend, (it is) like you are giving (it) up.
13 Ne te porte pas caution pour quelqu'un qui a plus que toi	13 Do not stand as surety for someone who has more than you,
et si tu t'es porté caution, (considère-toi) comme celui qui paiera.	and if you do stand as surety, (it is) like you are repaying.
14 N'aie pas de procès avec un juge,	14 Do not enter into a dispute with a judge,
car selon son bon plaisir, il ju[ge]ra.	for, according to their whim they will ju[dge].
15 Avec un cruel ne marche pas,	15 With someone cruel do not walk,
de peur que tu n'alourdisses ton malheur,	lest you make your misfortune more burdensome,
car, lui, il va où il veut	for, they go where they wish,
et par sa stupidité tu périrais.	but you will be swept away due to their stupidity.
16 Avec un irascible ne sois pas effronté	16 With the irascible do not be brazen,
et ne chevauche pas avec lui sur la route,	and do not ride with them on the road,
car le sang est peu de chose à ses yeux	for blood is a small thing in their eyes,
et sans qu'il y ait de secours, il t'assassinerait.	and when there is no one to help you they will murder you.
17 Avec un sot ne t'entretiens pas,	17 With a fool do not converse,
car il ne pourra pas tenir caché ton secret.	for they will not be able to keep your secret hidden.
18 Devant un étranger ne fais pas de mystère,	18 Before a stranger, do nothing secret,
car tu ne sais pas ce que, finalement, cela produira.	for you do not know what, in the end, it will produce.
19 À toute chair, ne dévoile pas ton cœur	19 Do not reveal your heart to anyone,
et ne repousse pas de toi le bonheur.	and do not push happiness away from you.

Chapitre 9

Chapter 9

1 Ne sois pas jaloux de la femme de ton sein,	1 Do not be jealous of the wife of your bosom,
de peur qu'elle n'apprenne (à) te (faire) du mal.	lest she learn (to do) evil against you.
2 Ne *confie* pas ton âme à une femme,	2 Do not *entrust* your soul to a woman,
de sorte qu'elle marche sur tes hauteurs.	so that she walks on your back.
3 Ne t'approche pas d'une femme étrangère,	3 Do not approach a strange woman,
de peur que tu ne tombes dans ses filets.	lest you fall into her traps.
Ne converse pas avec une prostituée,	Do not converse with a prostitute,
de peur que tu ne sois pris dans ses punitions.	lest you are involved in her punishments.

and more widely at Qumran (on the meaning of this term in the Hellenistic period, see Thomas 2009; in Ben Sira, the term does not seem to have any esoteric connotation). Ben Sira plays on the phonetic chiasmus between זר and רז. ילד — The verb may be impersonal, or has "its end" as subject "for you do not know what its end will produce." ספו — Late Hebrew. For a similar use of the suffix with the synonymous word אַחֲרִית, see Prov 5:4; 14:13; 23:32 and 29:21.

9:1 אשת חיקך — Cf. Deut 13:7; 28:54; 4Q416 2 ii 21 (and par.), 4Q416 2 iv 5.13; 11QT LIV 2 and 11Q20 16 2. תלמד — The form can be interpreted as: (1) a *qal* 3fs imperfect, "Lest she learn (to do) evil against you," or (2) a *piel* 2ms (thus the Greek, Segal 1958, 56 and Lévi 1901, 54), "Lest you teach (her to do) evil against you."

9:2 תקנא — Rather than correcting the text to תתן due to dittography, it seems preferable to see a peculiar spelling of the *hiphil* of קנה, תַּקְנֶה, "to acquire" (Segal 1958, 56). The form could be chosen for stylistic effect with verse 1. להדריכה על במותיך — Lit. "to make her walk on your heights," that is to say, "to rule over you," cf. Deut 33:29 and Hab 3:19.

9:3 תקרב — "To get closer," can be used here to refer to proximity in the sense of "friendship" (1 Kgs 2:7) or as a euphemism for sexual relations (cf. Gen 20:4). אשה זרה — In this context, the "foreign woman," that is to say, the one that is not legitimate, may refer to the prostitute, as the Greek and the Syriac understood it (cf. Prov 2:16; 5:3; etc.). עם זונה . . . בלקותיה — This couplet is missing in the Greek and the Syriac and is likely a doublet of either the previous or the following couplet. תִּסְתַּיָּד — See 7:14^A and the note. For the *hithpael*, cf. 9:14^A and 42:12^B. בְּלְקוֹתֶיהָ — A substantive לקה would be a *hapax*. Various corrections have been proposed: בחלקותיה "by her flatteries" (Lévi 1901, 55; cf. Prov 6:24), בתקלותיה "by her stumbling blocks" (Peters 1913, 82; cf. 31:7), בִּמְוֹקְשֶׁיהָ "in her traps" as an explanation of במצודתיה in the preceding stich (Segal 1958, 56), a variant of לֶקַח "(seductive) speech" attested in Prov 7:21 (Ryssel 1900, 285). However, the fact that the term is vocalized in the manuscript suggests that its form is correct. It seems preferable to understand it either as an infinitive construct from the root לקי "to suffer, be punished" known from early Rabbinic Hebrew texts (for the *yod* mater, see van Peursen 2004, 49), or as a substantive formed from the same root (cf. מַלְקוּת in Rabbinic Hebrew and לקותא in Aramaic). For a similar idea, cf. Qoh 7:26. Stich *b* is quoted together with portions of 9:8–9 in slightly different ways in b. Yeb. 63a; b. Sanh. 100b and the Alphabet of Ben Sira (see the note on 9:8–9 below).

4	[3]עם מְנַגִּינֹת ﭏ תִּדְמוֹךְ	פן יִשְׂרְפֶךָ בְּפִיפִיֹּתָם:
5	בבתולה [4]ﭏ תתבונן	פן תוקש בעונשיה
6	ﭏ תתן לזונה נפשך	פן תסוב [5]את נחלתך:
7	להתנבל במראה עיניך	ולשומם אחר ביתה:
8	[6]העלים עין מאשת חן	וﭏ תביט אל יפי לא לך:
	בעד אשה [7]הֻשחתו רבים	וכן אהביה באשׁ תלהט··
9	עם בעלה ﭏ תטעם:	[8]וﭏ תֻסב עמו שכור:
	פן תטה ﭏיה לב	ובדמים תטה ﭏ שחת:
10	[9]ﭏ תֿטשׁ אוהב ישן	כי חָדָשׁ לא יד[ב]יקנֹו:
	יי[ן] חדש אוהב חדש	[10]וישן אחרֹ תֿ[י]שׁתֵינו:
11	ﭏ תקנאֹ באיש רשע	כי לא תֿדע מה [11]יומו:
12	ﭏ תֿ[קנא] בזדון מצליח	זכר כי עת מֿות לא ינקה:
13	[12]רחקֿ מאיש [שלי]ט להרוֹ[ג]	וﭏ תפחד פחדי מות·
	ואם קרבת [13]לא תאשם	פן יקח אֹת נשמתך:
	דע כי בין פחים תצעד	[14]ועל רשת תתהלֹך:

L. 3 [9:4] A circular mark appears in the right margin.

L. 9 [9:10] יד[ב]יקנֹו — Beentjes (1997, 33) reads יד[..]ק[.], Ben-Ḥayyim (1973, 12) יד[ו]ע[י](ם)[ך] and Vattioni (1968, 47) ◦יד◦◦ק. Nevertheless, the manuscript allows one to read beyond doubt: *yod*, *dalet*, then a space for a large letter, then *yod*, *qoph* (the lobe and the descender fully preserved), a trace of a narrow letter that is very likely a *nun*, then a *vav*. Thus, the reading ידביקנו already proposed by Lévi (1901, 59) seems perfectly assured. תֿ[י]שׁתֵינו — the *tav* is certain and the *shin* is very probable (the last arm often has a characteristic hook). Between the *tav* and the *shin*, there is space left for a narrow letter, probably *yod*.

9:4 מְנַגִּינֹת — The word is misspelled in two ways. The *yod* should be a *vav* and should appear after the *nun*, not before it. תִּדְמוֹךְ — From the Aramaic דמך "to sleep" (according to Lévi 1901, 55, followed by Segal 1958, 56, it results from a confusion of the letters in תתמיד "stay, remain," attested by the Greek). יִשְׂרְפֶךָ — The verb is commonly understood to mean "burn." Cf. Sir 40:30[B,M] and 48:1[B] for metaphors connecting burning and language; note too b. Shab. 88b: ישרפוני בהבל שבפיהם "They will burn me with the breath that is in their mouths." Alternatively the same consonants may be the homophonous verb, "to swallow, suck" found in Rabbinic Hebrew, Syriac, and Jewish Babylonian Aramaic, giving the stich a sense that seems at once contextually sensible and yet unexpectedly explicit. בְּפִיפִיֹּתָם — A plural formed through reduplication of פִּי "mouth." The use of the masculine (pronominal suffix and verb) instead of the feminine is common in late and Rabbinic Hebrew (cf. Pérez-Fernández 1997, 30, Qimron 1986, §200.142). The Syriac ܒܡܡܠܠܗܿ "by his discourse" must be an explanation of the Hebrew.

9:5 Cf. Job 31:1. בעונשיה — The term עונש "fine" may refer to the silver paid to a father of a virgin who has intercourse before marriage (cf. Deut 22:29; Exod 22:15–16; Tg Ps.-Jon. Dt 22:29; m. Ketub. 3:4), which is how the Syriac understood it. Nevertheless, at Qumran, ענש had a broader sense of punishment and could therefore refer to the punishment imposed on the virgin, echoing the stich in 9:3*d* (בלקותיה).

9:6 תסוב — The Greek and the Syriac have presumably read a *hiphil*, תָּסֵיב, rather than a *qal*: "lest you lose your inheritance" (for the meaning of the verse, cf. Prov 29:3, and for the *hiphil* of סבב in the sense of removing, see 2 Kgs 16:18). Nevertheless, the *qal* of סבב could also have the meaning "move on to, transfer to (another)," cf. Sir 10:8[A] and Num 36:7. In this case, the phrase את נחלתך would be the subject of the verb. The particle את sometimes precedes the subject of intransitive verbs in the Hebrew Bible (e.g., Neh 9:19; Dan 9:13).

9:7 Although v. 7 diverges considerably from the versions, and therefore, seems to have undergone several alterations. להתנבל — The infinitive here is epexegetic (Joüon §124o). The *hithpael* of נבל is not attested in Biblical Hebrew or at Qumran. It is found in Rabbinic Hebrew with the meaning "to be degraded, debased, ashamed." According to Segal (1958, 57), the term would mean "to drive oneself crazy, go mad." ולשומם — For the meaning of שמם, cf. Ezra 9:3.

9:8–9 These verses are quoted in b. Yeb. 63b and b. Sanh. 100b. The version in b. Yeb. 63b reads: העלם עיניך מאשת חן פן תלכד במצודתה אל תט אצל בעלה למסוך עמו יין ושכר כי בתואר אשה יפה רבים הושחתו ועצומים כל הרוגיה "Avert your eyes from a graceful woman, lest you be caught in her trap. Do not turn to her husband in order to mix wine and strong drink with him, for many have been destroyed by the appearance of a beautiful woman, though all her victims were strong (Prov 7:26)". The same text appears in b. Sanh. 100b with the following variation: אל תתאצל עם בעלה "do not sit yourself (?) with her husband." The aphorism is almost identical to the version found in the Alphabet of Ben Sira: בתואר אשה יפה רבים הושחתו ועצומים כל הרוגיה (. . .) העלם עינך מאשת חן פן תלכד במצודתה (ed. Yassif 1984, 203–204) "Many have been devastated by the appearance of a beautiful woman, though all those whom she has killed (were) strong / numerous (. . .) Avert your eye from a graceful woman, lest you be caught in her trap." The same sentence is also attested in the Syriac version of the *Proverbes of Aḥiqar* 2:72: ܒܪܝ ܒܐܢܬܬܐ ܕܫܦܝܪܐ ܠܐ ܬܚܘܪ ܥܝܢܝܟ: ܘܠܐ ܬܬܒܩܐ ܒܫܘܦܪܐ ܕܠܐ ܕܝܠܟ: ܡܛܠ ܕܣܓܝܐܐ ܐܬܚܒܠܘ ܒܫܘܦܪܐ ܕܐܢܬܬܐ: ܘܪܚܡܬܗܿ ܐܝܟ ܢܘܪܐ ܕܝܩܕܐ: "My son, let not thine eyes look upon a woman that is beautiful; and be not inquisitive into beauty that does not belong to thee: because many have perished through the beauty of a woman, and her love has been as a fire that burneth" (Harris 1898, 66).

9:8 תביט — This may reflect תַּבִּיט or the plene form of תַּבֵּט. הֻשחתו — Either a *hophal* ("were devestated") or a *hiphil* ("have become corrupt"). For a similar idea, cf. Prov 7:26. אהביה — אהביה may be a plural participle, in which case, it should be translated: "and so she devours her lovers by fire." More likely, it was earlier אהבים "love, lust" (Prov 5:19; 7:18; Hos 8:9) as suggested by the Syriac. In this case, באש

4 Avec des chanteuses, ne dors pas,
    de peur qu'elles ne te brûlent de leurs bouches.
	4 With singers, do not sleep,
	    lest they burn you with their mouths.

5 Ne considère pas une jeune fille vierge,
    de peur que tu ne sois piégé par ses peines.
	5 Do not give attention to a young virgin,
	    lest you are trapped by her fines.

6 Ne te livre pas à une prostituée,
    de peur que ton héritage se détourne,
	6 Do not give yourself to a prostitute,
	    lest your inheritance pass on,

7 en te couvrant de honte par la vision de tes yeux
    et en étant accablé derrière sa maison.
	7 disgracing yourself due to what your eyes have seen,
	    and being desolate behind her house.

8 Cache (tes) yeux devant une femme gracieuse
    et ne regarde pas la beauté qui ne t'appartient pas.
    À cause d'une femme beaucoup furent dévastés
    et ainsi elle brûle ses amants par le feu.
	8 Hide (your) eyes before a graceful woman,
	    and do not look at beauty that is not yours.
	    Due to a woman, many have been destroyed,
	    and thus she burns her lovers in fire.

9 Avec son mari ne mange pas
    et ne t'allonge pas (à table) ivre avec lui,
    de peur que tu n'inclines (ton) cœur vers elle
    et que par le sang tu ne t'inclines vers la fosse.
	9 With her husband, do not eat,
	    and do not sit (at the table), drunk with him,
	    lest you incline (your) heart to her,
	    and by bloodshed you incline to the pit.

10 Ne délaisse pas un vieil ami,
    car un nouveau ne le va[u]dra pas.
    À vin nouveau, ami nouveau
    et lorsqu'il est vieux, alors tu le boiras.
	10 Do not forsake an old friend,
	    for a new one cannot com[p]are with them.
	    A new friend is new wine,
	    so, when it is old, afterwards, you drink it.

11 Ne sois pas jaloux d'une personne méchante,
    car tu ne sais pas quel est son jour.
	11 Do not be jealous of a wicked person,
	    for you do not know when is their day.

12 Ne [sois] pas [jaloux] de l'arrogant qui prospère,
    souviens-toi qu'au temps de la mort il ne sera pas impuni.
	12 Do not [be jealous] of the arrogant who prosper,
	    remember that at the time of death, they will not go unpunished.

13 Éloigne-toi de la personne qui a le pouvoir de tuer
    et tu ne seras pas effrayé des frayeurs de la mort.
    Et si tu t'es approché, ne te rends pas coupable,
    de peur qu'il ne prenne ton souffle.
    Sache que tu marches entre des pièges
    et que tu avances sur un filet.
	13 Keep far from the one with the power to kill,
	    and you will not fear the fears of death.
	    And, if you have approached, be not guilty,
	    lest they take your breath.
	    Know that you step between a thousand traps,
	    and that you advance over a net.

must be corrected to כאש with the Syriac and the Greek.

9:9 This verse is attested twice in the Syriac, in two forms, before and after verse 8. בעלה — It is possible to vocalize בַּעְלָהּ, "her husband," which is supported by the use of the masculine pronoun suffix עמו in the following stich and would also be consistent with b. Yeb. 63b and b. Sanh. 100b. Ben Sira would then be warning his disciples against becoming too familiar with the husband of a graceful woman. However, it is also possible to read a defective spelling of the passive participle בְּעֻלָה, "married woman" (thus the second Syriac version ܐܢܬܬ ܒܥܠܐ, and the Greek μετὰ ὑπάνδρου γυναικός). One could also read בַּעֲלָה, "mistress, matron," which is how the first Syriac version understood it: ܡܪܬ ܒܝܬܐ, "mistress of the house." תטעם — The verb טעם with the meaning "to eat" is attested in Aramaic (cf. Dan 4:22, 29; 5:21), while the Hebrew verb has more the sense of "to savor food, taste," as well as "to perceive by experience." The polysemy of the root reflects the ambiguity of the situation. תסב — The *hiphil* of סבב here has the meaning "to lounge at the table," as in Rabbinic Hebrew and in Sir 31:16B; 32:1B (cf. Jastrow 1903, 948). עמו — If one reads בַּעֲלָה, then עמו should be corrected to עמה; the scribe would have misinterpreted the verse. ובדמים — Literally, "spilled blood." דמים may evoke sin, reflect a link with Ps 51:16, or evoke the violent death of the culprit.

9:10 Compare with the Alphabet of Ben Sira: רחימא קדמאה לית את כפר ביה "As for an old (lit. first) friend, do not reject him" (ed. Yassif 1984, 279); see also Mibchar ha-Peninim: אל תחליף חבר קדמון בחבר חדש "do not replace an old friend with a new friend" (ed. Filipowski 1851, 27–29; cited by Smend 1906a, 86). יד[ב]יקנו — *hiphil* of דבק "to overtake," literally "because the new one will not overtake him (i.e. in value)" (Gen 31:23; Judg 20:42; for the semantic development "overtake" > "compare" cf. נשג in Gen 47:9 [see Reymond 2017b, 19–31]). וישן — The *vav* could introduce a conditional clause, as the Greek has understood it (ἐάν, cf. Sir 13:12, 22; 31:20), but it seems preferable to understand it as a temporal clause (cf. Joüon §166j). The letters may be understood as a *qal* perfect (though very rare and in later Hebrew) or as an adjective.

9:11 Cf. Ps 37:1. כי לא תדע — For the phrase "do not . . . because you do not know. . .," cf. Prov 27:1 and Sir 8:18A,D. יומו — That is to say, the day of his death, his end, as the Greek and the Syriac understood it.

9:12 בזדון — We read as the defective spelling of the adjective זֵדוֹן (cf. Ps 124:5 and the Aramaic זידן), as the versions understood it, but the word could also be read as the substantive זָדוֹן "arrogance."

9:13 ואל תפחד — The formula אל תקטול has here an indicative value (indicating purpose/result), whereas classical Hebrew would have preferred the negation לא after an imperative (Joüon §117j). For the expression, cf. Ps 14:5 and Job 3:25. לא תאשם —Conversely, the phrase לא תקטול seems to have a vetitive sense here when one would have expected the negation אל. פן יקח את נשמתך — Cf. the expression לקח נפש with the meaning "kill" (1 Sam 24:12; Jonah 4:3; Prov 1:19, etc.).

14	ככחך ענה רעך	ועם חכמים הסתייד:
15	^{15}עם נבון יהי חשבונך	וכל סודך בינותם:
16	אנשי צדק בעלי ^{16}לחמך	ובירֹאת אֹהים תפארתך:
17	בחכמי ידים יחשך יושר	^{17}ומוש[ל] [בְּעמו חכם:
18	ביטה נורא בעד איש לשון	ומשא ^{18}על פיהו ישונא׃

Chapter 10

1	^{18}שופט עם יוסר עמו	וממשלת מבין ^{19}סרֹידה:
3	מֹלךְ פרוע ישחית עיר	ועיר֫ נוֹשֶבת בשכל ^{20}שריה:
2	כְשֹופֵט עָם כֵן מְלִיצָיו	וּכְראש עִיר כֵן יוֹשְבָיו׃
5	^{21}ביד אֹהים ממשלת כל גבר	ולפני מחוקק ישית הודו:
4	^{22}ביד אֹהים ממשלת תבל	ואיש לעת יעמד עליה:
6	[ב]כל ^{23}פשע ל̇ תשלֵים רע לריע	ול̇א תהלך בדרך גאוה:
7	^{24}שנואה לאדון ואנשים גאוה	ומשניהם מעל עשק:
8	^{25}מלכות מגוי ל̇ גוי תסוב	בגלל חמס גאוה:

L. 17 [9:17] [בְּעמו ל]ומוש[— A trace of a letter before the *ayin* suggests the presence of a *bet*, as attested by the Syriac.

L. 18 [10:1] יוסר — Adler (1900, 469), Smend (1906b, 10) and Ben-Ḥayyim (1973, 12) read יוסר, whereas Lévi (1901, 62), Beentjes (1997, 34) and Vattioni (1968, 49) read יוסד. The letter is angular and traced in two storkes; this is usually indicative of *dalet* but may also reflect *resh*. For the confusion between *dalet* and *resh* see complete introduction.

L. 19 [10:1] סרֹידה — The second letter is more likely a *resh* than a *dalet*, but see the previous remark (with Ben-Ḥayyim 1973, 12; Beentjes 1997, 34). Smend (1906a, 89; 1906b, 10) reads סדירה, which he corrects to סדורה. Adler (1900, 469) also reads סדורה.

9:14 Cf. 5:12^A. ככחך — Cf. Ezra 2:69 and Qoh 9:10. ענה — "Answer." The parallel with 5:12^A shows that the proposal of Lévi (1901, 60) and Segal (1958, 59) to understand ענה as "to take care of" or "to care about" is unlikely (cf. ענה III; Qoh 1:13). הסתייד — Cf. 7:14^A and the note.

9:15 חשבונך — In Biblical Hebrew, the substantive חשבון is only attested in Qoh 7:25, 27 and 9:10. In Ben Sira, one also finds it in Sir 6:23^A, 24^A (= 27:5, 6) and 42:3^{B,M}, 4^{B,M}. It is much more common at Qumran (26 times in Hebrew and Aramaic). The term refers as much to the notion of calculation, counting, a construction plan (cf 4Q254a 1–2 2) as it does to the notion of thinking, planning, a project (cf. 1QH^a IX 31; 4Q534 1 i 9–13). סודך — The term סוד, attested 19 times in Ben Sira, generally refers to a "secret," but here, it must be closer to "discourse, confidential discussion" in connection with the verb used in 14*b* (see the same succession and ambiguity in Sir 8:17^A). בינותם — The plural pronominal suffix after the singular נבון is surprising and must refer to חכמים from verse 14*b*.

9:16 בעלי לחמך — Lit. "the masters of your bread," that is to say, "your table companions," as in Sir 6:10^A: חבר שלחן (cf. בעל סודך in 6:6^A).

9:17–18 These two verses present a number of difficulties and one can assume that the Hebrew text is corrupt. The versions render the text differently.

9:17 בחכמי ידים — Note the use of חכם with the meaning "skill, experience." It does not seem necessary to understand the term in the negative sense of "manipulator" as proposed by Mopsik (2003, 126) who translates "À cause des manipulateurs la droiture s'obscurcit."

9:18 ביטה — Either a *piel* perfect, "he pronounced inconsiderate/reckless words," or read a *qal* participle, בוטה (as Segal 1958, 60; cf. 5:13^A), "the chatterbox." Although the first word of the verse, ביטה, should be attached to the previous stich, as attested in the versions; the Greek has "the wise in his speech" (σοφὸς ἐν λόγῳ αὐτοῦ), while the Syriac has "wise and intelligent" (ܚܟܝܡ ܘܣܟܘܠܬܢ). To render the meaning of the text as it stands, we have considered ביטה and איש לשון as a dissociated opposition (hyperbate). בעד — This can be read as a defective spelling of בְּעוֹד as sometimes found in the Bible (Jer 15:9 and Ps 39:2). The versions read בעיר (for the confusion between *resh* and *dalet*, see the complete introduction). ישונא — We understand this word as יְשֻׁנָּא, the *pual* of שנא (from שנה)"to change, transform," cf. Qoh 8:1; Sir 12:18^A and Sir 13:25^A. But it may also be read as a rare *pual* from שנא (יְשֻׂנָּא) "to be hated" (see the Greek and the Syriac and 4Q179 1 ii, 3).

10:1 שופט עם — "The judge of the people," in the context of chapter 10, may refer to a broader function (the governor, the king, cf. 1 Sam 8:5, 6). The Greek and the Syriac have read שופט חכם, "the wise judge" or perhaps שופט טעם which became שופט עם due to haplography or sandhi (cf. שופט צדק in Ps 9:5). יוסר — The reading is uncertain, allowing one to read both יוסר and יוסד, and it seems prudent to leave open the two possible interpretations: either יוסר "he instructs, disciplines" (for the *qal* participle of יסר, see Ps 94:10 and Prov 9:7), or יוסד "he establishes." וממשלת — ממשלה can refer both to the action of governing ("the governance of the intelligent"), as well as to the scope of this action ("the domain of the intelligent"). סרֹידה — The term is pointed in the manuscript and the *segol* marked in the margin indi-

14 Selon ta force, réponds à ton compagnon
   et converse avec les sages.
15 Que ton raisonnement soit avec quelqu'un d'intelligent
   et toute ta conversation parmi eux,
16 (que) des personnes justes (soient) tes compagnons de table
   et ton honneur dans la crainte de Dieu.
17 Par les habiles est préservée la droiture
   et celui qui gouverne son peuple (doit être) sage.
18 Le bavard est craint alors que c'est un beau parleur
   et (la) sentence de sa bouche est fluctuante.

Chapitre 10

1 Le juge du peuple discipline/fonde son peuple
   et le domaine de l'intelligent est ordonné.
3 Un roi impulsif ruine une ville
   et une ville est habitable grâce à l'intelligence de ses gouverneurs.
2 Tel un juge du peuple, tels ses médiateurs,
   tel le chef d'une ville, tels ses habitants.
5 Dans la main de Dieu est la gouvernance de toute personne
   et devant le législateur il place sa majesté.
4 Dans la main de Dieu est la gouvernance du monde
   et un humain, pour un temps, présidera sur lui.
6 Quel que soit le péché, ne rends pas le mal au prochain
   et ne marche pas dans le chemin de l'orgueil.
7 Détesté du Seigneur et des humains est l'orgueil
   et des deux (sont détestées) l'infidélité, l'oppression.
8 La royauté passe d'un peuple à un autre,
   à cause de la violence de l'orgueil.

14 According to your strength, answer your companion,
   and converse with the wise.
15 Let your reckoning be among the intelligent,
   and all your conversation among them.
16 Let your table companions be righteous,
   and your glory in the fear of God
17 It is through the skillful that straightness is preserved,
   and the one who rules his people (should be) wise.
18 The talkative person is feared while they are a fine speaker,
   though the utterance on their lips is ever-changing.

Chapter 10

1 The judge of the people disciplines/establishes their people,
   and the domain of the intelligent is ordered.
3 An impulsive king will ruin a city,
   but a city is made habitable through the intelligence of its rulers.
2 As the judge of the people is, so are their ministers,
   as the head of the city is, so are its inhabitants.
5 In the hand of God is the governance of every person,
   and upon the lawgiver he places his majesty.
4 In the hand of God is the governance of the world,
   and a human, for a time, will presider over it.
6 Whatever the sin, do not return evil to your neighbor,
   and do not walk the path of pride.
7 Hated by the Lord and by human is pride,
   and by both (are hated) infidelity, oppression.
8 Kingship passes from one people to another,
   due to the violence of pride.

---

cates that the term is corrupted. It should read סדורה, the *qal* passive participle of סדר attested in Rabbinic Hebrew and in Aramaic: "to position, order, arrange." The Greek τεταγμένη could be understood in this sense. The form could also be understood as a peculiar spelling of the Hebrew שריד "survivor."

10:3 פרוע — Cf. Exod 32:25; Sir 46:7^B and 47:23^B. The verb refers to the idea of acting in a disorderly manner, i.e. being out of control.

10:2 מליץ — This is the only attestation of this verb in the *hiphil* in Ben Sira. Nevertheless, the form is very frequent in late Hebrew, especially at Qumran. In Biblical Hebrew, the conjugated form refers to mockery, while the participle refers to an interpreter or mediator (Gen 42:23; 2 Chr 32,31 in combination with שר). In Job 33:23, the מליץ designates an angelic figure as mediator. It is this meaning that is widespread at Qumran (17 attestations). יֹשְׁבֶיהָ — The masculine pronominal suffix refers to ראש, that is, the inhabitants who depend on the leader of the city. The Greek and the Syriac have a feminine pronoun referring to the city.

10:5 מחוקק — Cf. Isa 33:22 and Sir 44:4^M. הודו — Cf. Ps 96:6 par. 1 Chr 16:27, as well as Num 27:20. The divine splendor dwells in the lawgiver, who then becomes the representative of God to the people. The pronominal suffix could also refer to the splendor of the lawgiver, namely, "all his glory comes to him from God" (cf. 1 Chr 29:25).

10:4 ואיש לעת — While God governs the world, he allows humans, for a given time, to legislate. יעמד — For עמד in the sense of "presiding," see Num 7:2. The Greek and the Syriac both reflect כשר בעתו in place of ואיש לעת: "in his time, he will install over it the one who is suitable."

10:6 רע לריע — This is perhaps a doublet (or a double reading), see the Greek and the Syriac.

10:7 שנואה — For the form, cf. 7:26^A, and for the meaning, cf. Sir 15:11–13^{A,B}. לאדון ואנשים — For a similar formulation, cf. Prov 3:4; Sir 25:1^{LXX}; 45:1^B and Luke 2:52. The *lamed* preposition governs the two coordinated names (see Miller 2009, 106–107). ומשניהם — The מן particle is surprising here. According to Peters (1913, 89), מן may have the meaning of לפני here, as in Num 32:22 and Job 4:17. According to Segal (1958, 62), מן expresses the means here: "by them." מעל עשק — The pair of words are linked by a conjunction *vav* twice in Qumran (מעל ועשק in 4Q525 16 6 and עשק ומעל in 1QpHab I 6) and this matches the Syriac translation. Alternatively, the pair of words in H^A might be construed as a construct phrase "treachery of extortion" (cf. the Greek translation πλημμελὴς ἡ ἀδικία "injustice is wrong" and מעל חטאת in 1QS IX 4). Another possibility would be to understand the words as expressing the idea: "and by both of them, beyond (pride), oppression."

10:8 תסוב — See Sir 9:6^A and the note.

	אשר בחייו יורם גויוֹ׃	מה יגאה ²⁶עפר ואפר	9
	מלך היום ומחר יפול׃	vac שמץ מחלה ²⁷יצהיב רופא	10
	ותולעה כנים ורמש׃	במות אדם ²⁸ינחל רמה	11
ENA 2536–2 recto	וּמַעֲשֵׂהוּ יסור מלבו׃	תחלת גאון אדם ¹מועז	12
	וּמְקוֹרָהּ ²יביע זמה׃	כי מקוה זדון חטא	13
	ויכהו עד כלֵה׃	על כן מלא לבוֹ א[הׄי]םׄ נגעה	רע ויבא 14
	וישב ענים תחתם׃	³כסא גאים הפך אהים	14
	ושרשם עד ארץ קעקע׃	עקבת גוים ⁴טמטם אהים	16
	וישבת מארץ זכרם׃	ו[יׄ]סחם מארץ ⁵ויתשם	17
	ועזות ⁶אף לילוד אשה׃	לא נאוה לאנוש זדון	18
	זרע נקלה ⁷עובר מצוה׃	זרע נכבד מה זרע לאנוש	19ad ᴮ
	וירא אהים בעֵ[יׄ]נָ[יׄו׃]	בין אחים ראשם נכבד	20 ᴮ

10:19c זרע נקלה מׄה זרע לאנוש + B G S · 10:20 בעֵ[יׄ]נָ[יׄו׃] A G (ὀφθαλμοῖς αὐτοῦ) | נכבד ממנו׃ B S ·

L. 26 [10:9] יורם — Read with Smend (1906b, 10), Ben-Ḥayyim (1973, 12), Beentjes (1997, 34) and Vattioni (1968, 51). Adler (1900, 469) and Lévi (1901, 64) read יורש. The final *mem* seems clearly preferable.

L. 7 [10:20] בעֵ[יׄ]נָ[יׄו׃] — The *ayin* is certain and is followed by a trace of a bent letter that could correspond to the angled base of a *nun* which fits the reading בעֵ[יׄ]נָ[יׄו] perfectly and agrees with the Greek ὀφθαλμοῖς αὐτοῦ (Peters 1902, 344; Segal 1958, 65; Rüger 1970, 56; Minissale 1995, 57). The reading בעמו[ן] proposed by Smend (1906a, 11) and Di Lella (1982, 160) is less probable; the *mem* would be too far from the *ayin*. ממנו (Adler 1900, 470; Lévi 1901, 68; Vattioni 1968, 53) is excluded.

10:9 עפר ואפר — A common expression, cf. Gen 18:27; Job 30:19 and 42:6. יורם — The form is difficult to interpret. Morphologically, it could be a *hophal* of רמם, with the meaning "to be eaten by worms, to be rotten" (attested only here according to Maagarim). This is how the Syriac generally understood it (the Greek seems to have read a form derived from רמה "to throw"). In Biblical Hebrew, the verb is attested only once, in the *qal*, in Exod 16:20 (וַיָּרֻם, see also the substantive רִמָּה) where it takes manna as subject. Alternatively, יורם can be understood as the *hophal* of רום, leading to the translation: "so that … its body is exalted." גויוֹ — "His body," from גֵּו (a masculine form of גְּוִיָּה). This form is only attested in *piyyutim*. Segal (1958, 62) mentions the possibility of a substantive corresponding to the Aramaic גֵּו "belly, entrails."

10:10 For the syntax of these two colons, see van Peursen 2004, 352. שמץ — The meaning is not entirely clear. The term is only attested in Sir 18:32ᶜ; Job 4:12 and 26:14, passages where the meaning "small, lowly, weak" seems plausible. Nevertheless, the meaning is poorly attested. In both occurrences in Job, the Targum proposes קצת דאתמצי, "a little bit of what is drained out" (implying the interpretation of שמץ as ש + מצה). The Peshitta rendered the term with ܪܗܓܐ "small" in Job 4:12 and with ܒܝܫ "bad" in Job 26:14, while the Vulgate has *susurrus* and *parvus*. The Greek translated it as μακρός "a prolonged illness" in Sir 10:10 (possibly an error for μικρός), while in 18:32, it is rendered as πολὺς "abundant luxury" (the same as the Syriac ܣܘܓܐܐ). In Rabbinic Hebrew and Jewish Babylonian Aramaic the cognate can have the sense "suspicion," see Jastrow 1903, 1600; Sokoloff 2002, 1136. יצהיב — The meaning of the *hiphil* of צהב is also not entirely clear. In Biblical Hebrew, the verb is only attested in the *hophal* participle in Ezra 8:27 designating the color of bronze (cf. the adjective צָהֹב in Lev 13:30 and in 4Q266 6 i 7 and 4Q272 1 i 16). In Rabbinic Hebrew, Jastrow (1903, 1264) defines the meaning as "to become shining, to be bright" and by extension, "to rejoice." A second root, also attested in Aramaic (צהב/ צהב) and Arabic (ṣhb), has the meaning "to be in pain, distress, afflicted, to anger" (see Ben-Ḥayyim 1940, 75-77, Kister 1983, 130 and Sokoloff 1990, 458, see also Sir 3:16ᶜ). מלך — The Syriac read מהלך: "today it walks, tomorrow it will fall." יפול — "It will fall," either because he is dying (2 Sam 21:9; Ps 82:7) or because his honor is fleeting.

10:11 כנים — Correct to כנים in accordance with the punctuation.

10:12 מועז — Either an abstract noun (akin in form to מוסר) or the *hophal* participle of עזז or its biform יעז (cf. נוֹעָז in Isa 33:19). עזז has already been used in 8:16ᴬ, where it is constructed with מצח (אל תעיז מצח, "do not be brazen"). It is rarely attested in the *hophal* and only in late *piyyutim*. In the *hiphil*, it is always constructed with פנים to express being "brazen." Used in an absolute manner, in the *qal*, it signifies a state of power, force or capability. Thus, the verse could mean that at the root of pride lies power, strength and/or arrogance. מלבו — The form should likely be corrected to לבו or בלבו.

10:13 מקוה — In Biblical Hebrew, מקוה means "gathering place," but it is also found at Qumran with the meaning "source, origin." See the expression מקוי כבוד in 1QHᵃ XX 32 par. 4Q427 3 9 and 4Q511 52+54-5+57-9 2 (in parallel with מקור דעת; 1QM X 13 מקוי נהרות), and also Sir 43:20 where Hᴹ and Hᴮ have מקור, corrected to מקוה in the marginal note of Hᴮ. This is how the Greek and the Syriac understood it. וּמְקוֹרָהּ — The vocalization, as in the following stich (נגעה), indicates the masculine pronominal suffix referring to זדון (see Reymond 2018c, 226–44). יביע — Cf. Prov 15:2 and 15:28. מלא לבו — Could the initial spelling without the suffix imply מָלֵא לֵב "a presumptuous person" (cf. מָלְאוֹ לִבּוֹ "his heart filled him" = "a person filled with presumption" Esth 7:5)? The stich would thus read "therefore, as to a presumptuous person, God strikes him" (inferring נִגְעָה for the last word). רע ויבא — The marginal correction should likely be inserted between "heart" and "God" (מלא לבו רע ויבא א[הׄי]םׄ נגעה "(It is why) his heart is filled with evil [cf. Qoh 8:11 and 9:3], may God bring on his plague"), though the versions give a rather different text. In place of מלא, the Greek and the Syriac seem to reflect a *Vorlage* with הפליא (or הפלה).

9 Pourquoi s'enorgueillirait celui qui est poussière et cendre,
   qui de son vivant voit son corps se décomposer ?
10 Un soupçon de maladie afflige le médecin,
   roi aujourd'hui, demain, il tombera.
11 À la mort, l'être humain héritera des vers,
   d'asticots, de vermine et d'insectes.
12 L'origine de l'orgueil de l'être humain, c'est l'arrogance,
   et depuis *son cœur*, il se détournera de son créateur.
13 Car l'origine de l'arrogance est le péché
   et sa source fait jaillir l'infamie.
   C'est pourquoi Dieu remplit ᵒⁿ cœur de son fléau
   (mg. [C'est pourquoi son cœur est rempli] de mal et
   [Dieu] fait venir [son fléau])
   et le frappe jusqu'à l'anéantissement.
14 Dieu renverse le trône des orgueilleux
   et fait asseoir les pauvres à leur place.
16 Dieu obstrue la ruse des orgueilleux
   et leur racine est détruite jusqu'à la terre.
17 Il les a balayés de la terre et les a supprimés
   et a fait disparaître de la terre leur souvenir.
18 L'arrogance ne sied pas à l'humain
   et l'insolence de la colère à celui qui est né de la femme.
19 Quelle race est digne d'honneur ? La race humaine.
   La race déshonorée : celle qui transgresse le commandement.
20 Parmi des frères, leur chef est honoré,
   mais celui qui craint Dieu (est honoré) à [ses] yeux.

9 Why should one who is dust and ash be proud,
   one who, in their lifetime, sees their body decay?
10 Suspicion of illness afflicts the doctor,
   a king today, tomorrow he falls.
11 When they die, a person inherits worms,
   larva, vermine, and insects.
12 The beginning of human pride is arrogance,
   when *their heart* turns from their creator.
13 For, the origin of arrogance is sin,
   and its source gushes infamy.
   It is why God fills ʰⁱˢ heart with his plague,
   (mg. [It is why his heart is filled with evil and [so God]
   brings forth [his plague],)
   and strikes him to annihilation.
14 God overthrows the throne of the proud,
   and makes the poor sit in their place.
16 God obstructs the guile of the proud,
   and destroys their root down to the ground.
17 He swept them from the earth and uprooted them,
   then made their memory disappear from the earth.
18 Pride is not desirable for a human,
   likewise arrogance for the one born of woman.
19 Which race is worthy of honor? The human race.
   The race dishonored: the one that transgresses the commandment.
20 Among brothers, their leader is honored,
   but the one who fears God (is honored) in [his] eyes.

נִגְעָה — Thus vocalized in the manuscript, it may imply a misspelling of נֶגַע "plague," נִגְעֹה "his plague," or נְגָעָה "he struck him." עד כלה — See 2 Kgs 13:17, 19.

10:14 גאים — "Proud." The Greek translated with ἄρχων "princes." וישב — Note the defective spelling of the *hiphil*, as in Sir 7:3ᴬ and 11:1ᴬ.

10:15 Verse 15 is missing in the Hebrew, either because of *homoioteleuton* with verse 14b or because of *homoioarkton* with verse 16a. One can assume a text like "God has uprooted the roots of the proud and planted the humble in their place."

10:16 עקבת — For עקבה with the meaning "ruse, trick, cunning," cf. 2 Kgs 10:19 and probably Sir 16:3ᴬ,ᴮ. Smend (1906a, 95) and Lévi (1901, 67) prefer the meaning "trace, sign" (see also the Syriac, whereas the Greek has χώρα "territory"). גוים — The Greek ἐθνῶν clearly reflects the reading גּוֹיִם, but the Syriac ܪܡܬ̈ܐ "proud" could correspond to גֵּיִים, both words having a fluctuating spelling (i.e., גֵּאִים "proud" Ps 94:2 and גואים "nations" in 1QM XII 14). Confusion over גוים would not be an isolated case (see Zeph 3:6 where the Septuagint translates the Hebrew גוים with ὑπερηφάνους "proud" and perhaps Sir 35:23ᴮ). טמטם — The root is attested in Rabbinic Hebrew with the meaning "to stop, obstruct," thus "confuse comprehension," i.e. "muddy the waters" (see Jastrow 1903, 532). Nevertheless, most correct טמטם to טאטא "disperse, scatter, sweep away," and in fact, the two dots above the word and the three dots in the margin may indicate an erroneous form. One could then translate: "God sweeps away the trace of the proud."

10:17 ו{י}סחם — The root סחה is rare and seems to have the meaning "to sweep, to rake, to remove," as in Prov 2:22; Ps 52:7 and Ezek 26:4; cf. Sir 48:15ᴮ. וישבת — "To make the memory vanish, to wipe the memory of (someone/something) away," cf. Deut 32:26.

10:18 לא נאוה — Cf. Sir 14:3ᴬ; 41:16ᴹ; Prov 17:7; 19:10 and 26:1. ועזות אף — The phrase occurs only once elsewhere in Hebrew literature, among the medieval *piyyutim*. The word עזות is not attested before Rabbinic Hebrew where it notably appears in similar constructions like עזות פנים or עזות מצח with the meaning "insolence, impertinence, arrogance"; cf. Sir 8:16ᴬ. ילוד אשה — For the expression, see Job 14:1, 15:14; 25:4; 1QS XI 21; 1QHᵃ V 31; XXI 2; XXIII 13–14 (par. 4QHᵇ 14 2); 4Q482 1 4 and 4Q501 1 5.

10:19 The Greek text contains four stichs (*a, b, c, d*) in Ziegler's edition, but the manuscript tradition presents many variations probably by *homoioarkton* (see Ziegler's apparatus [1980, 171]). Hᴬ has only two stichs (*b* and *c*, as some Greek minuscule manuscripts, MS 106 and 545 in Ziegler 1980). Stichs *c* and *d* (labeled after the Greek) are present at the top of the page of Hᴮ, while stichs *a* and *b* (after the Greek) may have been preserved at the end of the previous sheet, though this was not found in the Cairo Genizah. The Syriac contains five stichs. זרע — The term, translated as "race," refers to the "seed" of plants, humans or animals. By extension, it signifies progeny, offspring, and thus, lineage. It is attested 15 times in the Syriac, especially in the praise of the fathers. It always refers to descendants, and thus, the posterity of an ancient figure. The term can also designate a nation whose identity is often defined by descent in Judaism. Naturally, it is translated as σπέρμα in Greek, which broadly covers the same semantic field. מה — For the use of the interrogative in a non-initial position, see Joüon §161k. According to van Peursen (2004, 290), the extraposition of an element in front of the interrogative pronoun is characteristic of Ben Sira and is possibly due to Aramaic influence. לאנוש — The *lamed* marks a genitive relationship here (Joüon §130).

תפארתם י[ר]אָת אהים·		⁸גר וזר נכרי ורש 22 B
⁹ואין לכבד כל איש [ח]כֿם:		אין לבזות דל מֿשֿכיל 23 B
וֿאֿ[י]ן ¹⁰גדול מֿ[י]רא אהים.		שֿ[ר] מושל ושופט נכבדו 24 B
ועבד[] מֿ[שֿ]כיל] לא ¹¹יתאונן:		עבד משכיל הורם 25 B
וא תתכ[בד ב]עֿת ¹²צרכך:		אֿ תתחכם לעֿבֿד חפצֿך 26 B
ממתכבד [ו]חסֿ[ר] מתן:		טוב עובד ויותר הון 27 B
ויתן לך טֿ[ע]ֿם כֿיוֹצֿא בה:		¹³בני בענוה כבד נפשך 28 B
ומי יכבד מקלה נפשו:		¹⁴מרשיע נפשו מי יצדיקנו 29 B
ויש נכבד בגלל עשֿרֿו:		¹⁵יש דל נכבד בגלל שכלו 30 B
ונקלה בעיניו איככה:		¹⁶נכבד בעשרו איככה 31 B

הֿמֿתכבד ¹⁷בדלותו בעשרו מתכבד יתר והנקלה בעשרו ב{ל}דלותו ¹⁸נקלה יותר:

10:22 וזר A | זר B · [ר]אֿת ABG | ביר Bmg S · אלהים A | ייי B · 10:23 כֿם [ח] A | חמס BG? (ἁμαρτωλόν) S? (ܟܡܐ) · 10:24 מושל ושופט A S | עבד משכיל חביב כנפש [...] | עבד משכיל חורים יעבדוהו וג ֿ[...] | עבד משכיל חביב כנפש וגבר מש]...[B G · 10:25 שופט ומושל B G · [...] עבד משכיל חביב כנפש וג ֿ[...] וגבר משֿ[...] B · חורים יעבדוהו B G · ועבד] וגבר A | · 10:26 לעבד A S | לעשות B G · חפצֿך A B | צרכֿך Bmg · 10:28 ויתן לך A S | ותן לה B G · 10:29 מרשיע A G | בני מרשיע B S · 10:30 יש דל A (Bmg?) | דל B · נכבד A | איש עשיר נכבד B G (πλούσιος) S (ܥܬܝܪܐ) · 10:31 נכבד A | יתר B · יותר A | יתר B · ונקלה בעשרו ונקלה בעיניו A | ונקלה בעיניו B · הנכבד בעיניו A

L. 8 [10:22-23] וזר — Most read זר and not דר, though the latter is also possible (for the confusion between *resh* and *dalet*, see the complete introduction). [ר]אֿתֿ — Traces of the diagonal and the second leg of the *aleph* are apparent. מֿשֿכיל — All the letters are clearly visible and certain. For the *mem*, a trace of the angled base, a part of the head and the left diagonal can be seen. For the *shin*, the left arm and part of the base are preserved.

L. 9 [10:23-24] כל איש [ח]כֿם — A trace of a letter touches the *lamed*, so that a *kaph* is possible. Then, before the final *mem*, there is a trace of the head of a letter, probably a *kaph* or a *resh*, so that the reading [יו]רם "high," proposed by Adler (1900, 470), Lévi (1901, 23) and Vattioni (1968, 53) is not excluded. The reading of חמס by Smend (1906b, 11), however, is impossible. [ר]שֿ — The *shin* is certain, as the first two legs and the base are fully preserved. The word is restored on the basis of H^B and the versions. Peters (1902, 344), Smend (1906b, 11), Lévi (1901, 68) and Vattioni (1958, 53) restore [נדיב], which is impossible. וֿאֿ[י]ן — Traces of the *vav* and the end of the diagonal of the *aleph* can be seen.

L. 10 [10:25] [כיל]שֿ[מ] ועבד[] — The ink has faded and all that remains is a trace of a letter that looks like a *samek*, though a *shin* or a *mem* cannot be excluded. The restoration [נו]סֿ[ר] is a little short for the space, while מ[שֿ]כיל fits perfectly.

L. 11 [10:26] וא תתכ[בד ב]עֿת — After the *lamed* that is entwined with the *aleph* there is a trace of the foot of a *tav*, then a *tav* and *kaph*. After the gap, a trace of an *ayin*; after this a *tav* is possible (a trace of the left leg appears in the *facsimile* from 1901). The proposed restoration does more justice to the preserved traces than previous proposals and is in agreement with the versions. [במו]עד, as proposed by Adler (1900, 670), Vattioni (1968, 53), Rüger (1970, 60) and Ben-Ḥayyim (1973, 13) is impossible for the space.

L. 13 [10:28] טֿ[ע]ֿם — A trace of the start of the head of a *mem* can be seen. כֿיוֹצֿא — The manuscript is altered. The *tsade* is almost no longer visible in recent photos, but it is clear in the *facsimile* from 1901 and on the plates in Adler (1900, 670). בה — Read a *he* with certainty, which is elongated to fill in the end of the line (Peters 1902, 344; Smend 1906b, 11; Vattioni 1968, 53), and not בהם (as Segal 1958, 64; Ben-Ḥayyim 1973, 13; Minissale 1995, 57).

L. 16 [10:31] הֿמֿתכבד — The first leg of a *he* and the horn of a *mem* are visible in recent photos (though absent in the *facsimile* from 1901 and on the plates in Adler 1900, 470).

L. 17 [10:31] ב{ל}דלותו — A *lamed* has been erased and corrected to a *dalet*.

10:22 גר — This is a *hapax* in Sirach, though frequent in the Hebrew Bible. It refers to the foreigner staying in the land of Israel, the immigrant. It is usually translated as προσήλυτος in the Septuagint, yet it does not refer to the convert to Judaism; the גר refers to a low and destitute social class (it is often associated with widows and orphans), but its more significant connotation lies in its opposition to אזרח, "the indigenous, the native." זר — "stranger, other, different." The term refers to total otherness. It is the stranger in the broadest sense, not only in an ethnic sense. It is that which is other, outside of a given group or category. For example, in Sir 45:18^B, זר designates the stranger to the priesthood. נכרי — Refers to the stranger who does not reside in the country or who is only passing through.

10:23 [ח]כֿם — Read [ח]כֿם "every wise person" or [יו]רֿם "every elevated person."

10:25 While H^A has only one distich here, H^B has four (*a, b, c, d*). In H^B, the second (*b*), which is inserted interlinearly, resumes the first (*a*). The fourth (*d*), which is the same as *a*, is canceled by dots. These three identical distichs in H^B (*a, b, d*) correspond to Sir 7:21^A,C,D, while the third distich (*c*) is close to 10:25^A, above. The Greek and the Syriac have only one distich, which is equivalent to *d* in H^B. עבד משכיל — See Sir 7:21^A,C,D and the note. הורם — The *hophal* of רום is rather rare in Biblical Hebrew and is usually constructed with מן with the meaning "to collect, levy, remove" (cf. Exod 29:27; Lev 4:10; see also Dan 8:11^Qere; Sir 47:2^B). It is in this sense that the form was most common in Rabbinic Hebrew. In our verse, the meaning should be "to be raised, exalted," yet there are no parallels. In all likelihood, the verse is corrupted and should be read with H^B and the Greek: חורים יעבדוהו "an intelligent servant, the noteworthy serve him." The error could easily be explained by הורם and חורים being very close and יעבדוהו having disappeared by haplography or having been corrupted by ועבד, which now constitutes the beginning of verse 25*b* and is absent from H^B and the versions. ועבד — This is probably not original. H^B has וגֿ[בר], as confirmed by the Greek and the Syriac. יתאונן — The *hithpael* of אנן is only attested in Num 11:1 and Lam 3:39.

10:26 תתחכם — For the *hithpael* of חכם, see 6:32 and the note. לעֿבֿד — According to van Peursen (2004, 337), the *lamed* would intro-

22 Immigré et apatride, étranger et pauvre,
   leur majesté est la c[ra]inte de Dieu.
23 Il ne faut pas mépriser un pauvre intelligent,
   ni glorifier toute personne [s]age.
24 Prin[ce], gouverneur et juge sont honorés,
   mais nul n'est plus grand que celui qui craint Dieu.
25 Un serviteur intelligent est élevé
   et un serviteur in[telligent] ne se plaint pas.
26 Ne deviens pas sage pour accomplir ton désir
   et ne te glorifie pas au temps de ton indigence.
27 Mieux vaut celui qui travaille et qui a une abondante richesse
   que celui qui se glorifie et manque de générosité.
28 Mon enfant, honore-toi avec humilité
   et on te donnera le bon sens selon ta valeur.
29 Celui qui s'incrimine, qui le justifiera ?
   Et qui glorifiera celui qui se déshonore ?
30 Il y a le pauvre qui est honoré en raison de son intelligence
   et celui qui est honoré en raison de sa richesse.
31 Celui qui est honoré, combien plus (le sera-t-il) dans sa richesse ?
   Et celui qui est déshonoré, combien plus (l'est-il) à ses propres yeux ?
   Celui qui est honoré dans son indigence, dans sa richesse, il sera d'autant plus honoré
   et celui qui est méprisé dans sa richesse, dans son indigence, il sera d'autant plus méprisé.

22 Immigrant and stranger, foreigner, and poor,
   their glory is the f[e]ar of God.
23 The intelligent poor person should not be despised,
   nor should (just) any wise person be glorified.
24 Prince, governor, and judge are honored,
   but there is none greater than the one who fears God.
25 The intelligent servant is exalted,
   and an in[telligent] servant does not complain.
26 Do not act like a sage in order to do what you wish,
   and do not boast in the time of your poverty.
27 Better the one who works and has abundant wealth,
   than the one who boasts and lacks alms.
28 My child, with humility honor yourself,
   and you will receive good sense according to your worth.
29 Whoever declares themself guilty, who will ever vindicate them?
   and who will honor the one who disgraces themself?
30 There is one who is poor and honored because of their intelligence,
   and one who is honored because of their wealth.
31 One honored, in wealth how much more so?
   One disgraced, in their (own) eyes how much more so?
   The one honored when destitute, when wealthy, will be greatly honored,
   and the one disgraced when wealthy, when destitute will be greatly disgraced.

duce the temporal clause here, "do not pretend to be wise when you serve your own desire." וא תתכ[בד ב]עת צרכך — Compare with the formula in 4Q416 2 ii 20: אל תתכבד במחסורכה "do not glorify yourself in your destitution." צרכך — Cf. Sir 8:9ᴬ and the note.

10:27 This verse is based on Prov 12:9 in reading עֹבֵד לוֹ (as the LXX and the Peshitta, contra MT עֶבֶד לוֹ, see Kister, 1999, 178). ויותר — Late Hebrew, see Sir 3:23ᴬ and the note. Note here the construction of the comparative, ...מ ... ויותר, which is characteristic of Rabbinic Hebrew. מתן — "Gift, present, charity," cf. Sir 3:17ᴬ; 4:4ᴬ; 7:33ᴬ; 11:17ᴬ and 40:28ᴮ,ᴹ. Lévi (1901, 70) considers מתן a corruption of מזון "food," reflected in both the Syriac(ܠܚܡܐ) and the Greek (ἄρτων), cf. Prov 12:9.

10:28 ויתן לך — Hᴮ has ותן לה in agreement with the Greek and the Syriac, the feminine antecedent referring to נפש from the previous stich. Hᴬ is probably wrong. לך at the beginning of the stich refers to בני, whereas בה at the end of the stich should refer to נפש. ויתן after the imperative of the previous stich can express the consequence (cf. Joüon §116a). The third person can either refer to God or be impersonal. טעם — The noun refers to the notion of "taste" (cf. Sir 25:18ᶜ), but also "discernment" or "common sense" (cf. Job 12:11; Ps 119:66). כיוצא ב... — The expression occurs in 38:17ᴮ but does not appear elsewhere in Ben Sira or other classical texts; it is common in Rabbinic Hebrew with the meaning "in the same way," "in a similar way." As Segal (1958, 64) notes, the expression יוצא ב... has its origin in a commercial context and means "X to the value of Y," see m. Maʿaś. Š. 4:8; m. ʾAbot 5:11.

10:29 מרשיע נפשו מי ... — The extraposition of an element before the interrogative pronoun (casus pendens) could be due to Aramaic influence (van Peursen 2004, 290). יצדיקנו — "who will justify him," that is "acquit him." For the theme of acquitting or justifying, cf. Exod 23:7; Isa 5:23; Prov 17:15 and Sir 42:2ᴮ,ᴹ.

10:30 For the construction יש ... ויש, cf. 4:22ᴬ.

10:31 This verse poses several difficulties. The two Hebrew witnesses (Hᴬ and Hᴮ) each preserve two versions of this verse. In each case, the second version (stichs c and d) is longer than the first (stichs a and b). The Greek and the Syriac present only one version and this corresponds most closely to the first distich of the two Hebrew witnesses. Instead of בעיניו "in his eyes" the Greek and Syriac reflect בעוניו "in his poverty" (for the spelling of עני with mater lectionis, cf. Sir 13:24bᴬ; for a similar confusion, cf. Zech 9:8). The confusion between vav and yod is frequent in the witnesses from the Genizah (see Di Lella 1966, 97–101). In their current condition, the first two stichs of Hᴬ do not really make sense and are probably corrupted. In agreement with the Greek and the Syriac, and with the help of Hᴮ, an earlier version, thus, was most likely similar to: נכבד בעוניו בעשרו איככה | ונקלה בעשרו בעוניו איככה. The two terms בעניו and בעשרו must have disappeared by homoioteleuton.

10:31ab איככה — This interrogative pronoun, meaning "how," belongs to late Hebrew (Song 5:3; Esth 8:6). Here, it must mean "how much more" and this meaning seems to be unique to Ben Sira (cf. the Aramaic היכה; Kister 1999, 161–62). Lévi (1901, 70) proposes rendering it "woe to you, or to him," but without a convincing philological basis.

10:31cd This final distich displays a number of characteristics of late Hebrew: the use of the hithpael (מתכבד) to express the passive in place of the niphal (נעבד) and the use of דלות, which is only attested in Rabbinic and later Hebrew. Di Lella (1966, 115–17) considers these final two stichs as retroversions of the Syriac. However, the use of the hithpael to express the passive and the noun formation with -ות are attested in late Hebrew and at Qumran, so there is no fundamental argument to

Chapter 11

1 B	חכמת דל תשא ראשו		ובין נדיבים תשיבנו:
2 B	[19]אל תהלל אדם בתארו		ואל תתעב אדם מכ[וע]ר במראהו:
3 B	[20]אליל בעוף דברה		וראש תנובות פריה[:]
4 B	בעטה א[ז]ר א [21]תהתל		וא׳ תקלס במרירי יום:
	כי פלאות מעשי י״י		ונעלם [22]אָ[דָ]ם פעלו:
5 B	רבים נדכאים ישבו על כסא		ובל על [23]לב עטו צניף:
6 B	רבים נשאים נקלוּ מאֹד והשפלוּ ֯יַֽחַד		[24]וְגַם נכבדים נתנו ביָֽד:
7 B	בטרם תחקר אֿ֯תסלף		בקר [25]לְפָנִים ואחר תַזְּף:
8 B	בני אֿ֯תשיב דבר טרם תשמע		[26]ובתוך שיחה אֿ֯תדבר:

11:1 קטנה בעוף דבורה וראש + Bmg2 · 11:3 תתעב אדם במ['] | B | מעזב[ר] | A Bmg1 | מכ[וע]ר A | בתוארו B · בתארו A | 11:2 תושיבנו B | תשיבנו A | מא[ ] | A | מֶ[אָ]דָֿ֯ם B = G · וְהָשְׁפָּלוּ A Bmg | והושפלו B · בעוטה B · בעטה A | 11:4 דבורה B · דברה A | תנובות פריה G (μικρά) ·] ... [ ] ... [B · כסא ושפלי לב עטו צניף +: 11:5 נוש A Bmg | וְגַם נכבדים B · ונכבדים נתמו ביד זעירים B · 11:6 כסא ושפלי לב עטו צניף +: נוש B · ונכבדים B · 11:7 This distich is placed after 11:8a–d in B · תֶחְקָר A | תֿח[קוֹ]ר B · 11:8 + אל תשיב ובתוך שיחה [...] : [שְׁ]אול ובקהל טעם שפוט B · טֶרֶם A | בטרם B · אל תדבר:

L. 20 [11:4] בעטה — With Smend (1906b, 12), Ben-Ḥayyim (1973, 14), Beentjes (1997, 36), Rüger (1970, 65). The *bet* is very likely, so that the reading מעטה, proposed by Adler (1900, 470), Lévi (1901, 72), Peters (1902, 345) and Vattioni (1968, 55) should not be retained. א[ז]ר — Different readings and restorations have been proposed: א[ב]ד by Adler (1900, 470), Lévi (1901, 72), Vattioni (1968, 55) and Peters (1902, 345), and א[פ]ר by Smend (1906b, 12), Ben Ḥayyim (1973, 14) and Segal (1958, 65). *Resh* and *dalet* are not always clearly distinguished in this manuscript, so it is difficult to decide between the proposals. A trace of ink appears slightly above the line before the *resh*, so אבד could also be justified with a *bet* having its head pronounced. Still, א[ז]ר, agreeing with H^B, seems most likely.

L. 25 [11:7] לְפָנִים — Note the apparent *rebhia* above the *nun*.

L. 26 [11:8] בְּנִי — Note the apparent *rebhia* above the *nun*. שִׂיחָה — Note the apparent *rebhia* and *geresh* accents.

consider the distich as a retroversion (see van Peursen 2001, 57,61 and 2004, 20–21).

11:1 The *b* stich is cited in y. Ber. 7:2 in combination with a citation from Prov 4:8 then attributed to Ben Sira: בסיפרי דבן סירא כתיב סלסליה ותרוממך ובין נגידים תושיבך, "In the book of Ben Sira, it is written: Exalt her and she will exalt you, and among rulers she will give you a seat." Compare to the sentence from 4QInstruction (4Q416 2 iii 11): כי מראש הרים רואשכה ועם נדיבים הושיבכה, "For out of poverty he has lifted up your head and given you a seat with princes." תשיבנו — Note the defective spelling of the *hiphil* (as at Sir 7:3 and 10:14).

11:2 מכ[וע]ר — The verb כער, "to be ugly, repulsive" does not appear in Biblical Hebrew, though it does occur twice in Ben Sira (cf. Sir 13:22^A), perhaps in 1Q23 26 2 in Aramaic and in Rabbinic literature (e.g., t. Soṭah 2:3). Its variant is כאר which appears in Qumran texts (see below) and Rabbinic literature (e.g., m. Ned. 9:10). Rüger (1970, 64) refers to Nah 3:6: ושמתיך כראי rendered as ושמתך כאורה in 4Q169 (pNah) 3–4 iii 1–2 and translated as ואשוינך מכערא לעיני כל חזך in the Targum.

11:3 אליל — In the plural, the term refers to idols (cf. Sir 30:19^B). The singular is rare in Biblical Hebrew (Job 13:4; Isa 10:10; Jer 14:14; Zech 11:17) and seems to mean "emptiness, nothingness" with a distinctly negative connotation (the etymology is uncertain, perhaps from אלל). The term could then refer to the "smallness, weakness, fragility" of the bee, a meaning that the term later receives in Syriac. Yet, the Syriac translator did not render the Hebrew אליל with its equivalent ܐܠܠ, but with ܒܨܝܪ, which is more in keeping with the original meaning of the Hebrew: "despicable, insignificant." The Greek follows the reading of the doublet in H^B (קטנה, μικρά). Cf. Papyrus Insinger 25:2: "the little bee brings the honey" (see Calduch-Benages 2011, 66–67).

11:4 H^B presents a doublet whose first stich differs radically from that of H^A. א[ז]ר — This restoration, which is supported by H^B2 and perhaps also by the Syriac (ܕܐܡܘܪ), should certainly be preferred over א[פ]ר "the one dressed in ashes" (cf. Esth 4:1), or as Lévi (1901, 72) suggests, א[ב]ד "the one dressed in misery." תהתל — The verb התל + ב is only attested in 1 Kgs 18:27; Sir 13:7^A and then in Rabbinic Hebrew. וא׳ תקלס — For the use of the verb קלס + ב in the *piel* with the meaning "to mock," see also 1QpHab IV 1.3. במרירי יום — The adjective מרירי is clearly attested in Deut 32:24 (קֶטֶב מְרִירִי), and perhaps in the phrase כמרירי יום from Job 3:5 (the targum to which has היך מרירי יום). The adjective or a related noun appears in 1QH^a XIII 36 (במרורי יום). Cf. Amos 8:10 where יום מר is translated by יום מריר in the Targum and by ܝܘܡܐ ܡܪܝܪܐ in the Peshitta. This stich can be understood in various ways: (1) as a continuation of the preceding: "Do not laugh at one whose day is bitter" (similar to the Syriac ܕܒܝܘܡܗ ܡܪܝܪ,

Chapitre 11

1 La sagesse du pauvre relève sa tête
  et le fait siéger parmi des princes.
2 Ne loue personne pour sa beauté
  et n'aie pas horreur d'une personne en fonction de sa répugnante apparence.
3 Insignifiante parmi les volatiles est l'abeille,
  mais son fruit est le premier des produits.
4 Ne tourne pas en ridicule celui qui est vêtu d'un pagne
  et ne te moque pas de celui dont le jour est amer,
  car les œuvres de YYY sont inaccessibles
  et son action est cachée à l'être humain.
5 Beaucoup d'affligés se sont assis sur un trône
  et ceux dont nul ne se préoccupait ont ceint un diadème.
6 Beaucoup de hauts placés ont été grandement méprisés et ont été abaissés ensemble
  et de même des nobles ont été livrés.
7 Avant que tu n'aies examiné, ne rejette pas,
  scrute d'abord et ensuite réprimande.
8 Mon enfant, ne réponds pas avant que tu n'aies écouté
  et au milieu d'un discours, ne parle pas.

Chapter 11

1 The wisdom of the poor will lift their head,
  and give them a seat among princes.
2 Do not praise a person for their beauty,
  and do not abhor a person repugnant in their appearance.
3 Least significant among flying creatures is the bee,
  but its fruit is first among (all) products.
4 Do not ridicule one who wears a loincloth,
  and do not laugh at one whose day is bitter,
  for the works of YYY are inscrutable,
  and his actions are hidden from humanity.
5 Many are the afflicted who sat on the throne,
  and they who no one thought of who wore the diadem.
6 Many of the exalted were thoroughly despised and were brought down together.
  and even the nobles were given over.
7 Before you have investigated, do not reject,
  examine before and afterward you may rebuke.
8 My child, do not respond before you have heard,
  and do not speak in the midst of (another's) discourse.

"... a person whose taste buds are bitter" = "a person who suffers" [see Syriac to Sir 7:11]) (2) "do not laugh at the day's bitterness," (3) or perhaps במרירי יום is an adjunct phrase and קלס is used intransitively: "in the day's bitterness, do not laugh" (cf. Sir 10:26). ונעלם — The *niphal* of עלם means "to be hidden, obscure" (1 Kgs 10:3 // 2 Chr 9:2), or "to be impenetrable, inscrutable" (Job 28:21).

11:5 H^B presents a doublet. ובל על לב — Most critics think that the formula has been altered by *homoioarkton* and that the text should be corrected to ובל עלו על לב (Segal 1958, 68) or ובל עלים על לב (Smend 1906a, 103; Di Lella 1964, 158). However, such a correction is not necessary, especially as H^A is supported here by H^B. Indeed, although the idiomatic phrase עלה על לב is well attested, we also find similar expressions without a verb, as in בל־עליך "there is not (one) above you" (Ps 16:2) and ולבו בל־עמך "his heart is not with you" (Prov 23:7). The expression in 11:5 presupposes an asyndetic relative clause, more literally: "ones who are not worried about." צניף — A mark of royalty, royal headpiece, turban or tiara, cf. 40:4 and 47:6.

11:6 This verse, like the preceding ones, displays some confusion in its textual transmission (see Rey 2021a, 132–3). נְשָׂאִים — The scribe vocalized the *niphal* participle "those who are lifted up" (cf. Isa 2:13). The Greek and the Syriac read נְשִׂיאִים "princes" or "officials," thus presenting the antithesis to נדכאים from v. 5. רבים נשאים נקלו מאד והשפלו יחד — The first stich is abnormally long, and the clause והשפלו יחד appears to be a double reading of נקלו מאד. Indeed, ancient translations represent only one form of the clause. The first form, נקלו מאד, is represented by the Greek (ἠτιμάσθησαν σφόδρα), while the second, והשפלו יחד, agrees—particularly regarding the last word—with the Syriac (ܘܨܥܪܘ ܐܟܚܕܐ, "who suffered dishonor together"); see the variants of this verse in H^B (Rey 2021a, 132–33). Although the *hophal* of שפל is not attested in Biblical Hebrew or at Qumran, the frequent use of the *hiphil* makes its use plausible. Finally, the adverbial use of יחד in a postverbal position is well attested in Biblical Hebrew. נתנו בידך — For the use of the idiomatic expression נתן ביד without a complement, see 1 Sam 26:23 and 2 Chr 25:20.

11:7 H^B displaces v. 7 between two duplicate stichs of v. 8. אל תסלף — The verb סלף renders the meaning of this verse somewhat obscure. In Biblical, Qumran and Rabbinic Hebrew, it often means "to pervert something or someone, to falsify, to distort" and is always transitive. It is in this sense that it is used in Sir 11:34, where it is rendered as διαστρέφω by the Greek. Neither the Greek nor the Syriac give this meaning for the Hebrew סלף here. The Greek translates it as μέμφομαι "reprimand, blame," which is not used outside of Sir 41:7 (where it translates the Hebrew קבב) and 2 Macc 2:7. The Syriac uses the verb ܐܫܬܘܬܦ, an *ethpaal*, "to make a partaker, communicate, to associate with," which usually renders the Hebrew חבר. Lévi (1901, 73) proposes giving the verb the meaning "do not pass rash judgment," which seems consistent with the context (DCH [6:166] "perh. find fault"; Mopsik [2003, 134]: "do not accuse" or "do not cry fraud"). Further complicating analysis is the evidence provided by Jewish Babylonian Aramaic, where סלף in the *peal* appears as a variant of צלף "to whip" (see the magic bowl labeled JBA 64 [line 2] in Shaked et al. 2013, 48 and 273). The meaning "reject," used in our translation, attested in Prov 21:12 and 22:12, seems to be the simplest solution. בקר — With the meaning "scrutinize, reflect" (cf. Prov 20:25). תזיף — This verb, based on the vocalization, derives from the verb נזף, attested in Aramaic and Rabbinic Hebrew, "reprimand, chastise" (thus the Greek ἐπιτίμαω). The consonants alone can be interpreted as expressing זוף also attested in Rabbinic Hebrew, "falsify, denounce as false, refute," but never in the *hiphil*.

11:8 Cf. Prov 18:13 and m. 'Abot 5:7. This verse is cited and attributed to Ben Sira in association with Prov 18:13 in b. B. Bat. 98b: כדכתיב בספר בן סירא . . . וקל מאורה משיב דבר בטרם ישמע שנאמר משיב דבר בטרם ישמע.

9 ᴮ	באין עצבה אל תאחר		וברב זדים ²⁷אֿל תקומם:
10 ᴮ	בני למה תרבה עָׁשקָך		ואץ ⁺ולהרבות לא ינקה:
	²⁸בני אם לא תרוץ לא תגיע		ואם לא תבקש לא תמצא:
11	¹יש עמל ויגע ורץ	ENA 2536–2 verso	וכֵדֿי כן הוא מתאחר:
12	יש רֹשש ואֹבֵד·		²מהלך חסר כל ויותר 🙼 עָני׃
	ועין יי צפתהו לטוב		וינעריהו ³מעפר צחנה׃
13	נשא בראשו וירממהו		ויתמהו עליו רבים׃
14	⁴טוב ורע חיים ומות		ריש ועושר מיי הוא׃
15	חׄכמֿה ושכל ⁵והבין דבר מיי הוא׃		חטא ודרכים ישרים מיי הוא׃
16	שכלות ⁶וחושךֿ לפשעיﾺ נוצרה		ומרעים רעה עמם׃
17	מנֹתֿ צדיק ⁷[לֿעֿ]דֿ [יעֿ]מֿדֿ		ורצנו יצלח לעד [׃]

עשקָך A Bmg | B G אם תברח לא תדביק ול[א ת]מלטנוֹ אם תנוס: + 11:10 · B וברב | A ובריב · B תתור | A תאחר · B עצה | A עצבה 11:9 · B עשק | ולהרבות A להרבות | B לא A | B לוא

L. 27 [11:10] וֿלהרבות — The scribe has traced a *vav*, which he then seems to have effaced by a loop.

L. 2 [11:12] 🙼 עָני: — All the editions transcribe נש[א] (Adler 1900, 471; Lévi 1901, 74-75; Ben-Ḥayyim 1973, 15; Beentjes 1997, 37). Smend (1906b, 12) and Vattioni (1968, 57) restore נש[1]א. However, this reading is impossible. The last three letters are very clearly *ayin*, *nun*, and *yod*, followed by the two end dots of the line. The first traces (🙼) are either a sign by the scribe (see similar ones filling in the end of lines, for example, in codex B19a, and a similar sign in 15:11ᴬ [T-S 12.863 recto l. 25]), or a cancelled *aleph*.

L. 4 [11:15] חׄכמֿה — Two legs of the *khet* are visible.

L. 6 [11:17] מנֹתֿ — The second letter has a vertical stroke and a bent base, which rule out a *tav* and would be perfect for a *nun*. It is followed by a *tav*, visible by its shoulder and its left leg that ends with a foot. Adler (1900, 471) and Vattioni (1968, 57) read צדיק מ[תן]. Smend (1906b, 12) proposes מ[תן]ֿ[יי] צדיק לעֿ[ד יעֿ]מֿד considering יי to be supralinear. The facsimile from 1901 actually shows a stain above the line, which must be a shadow since it does not appear in more recent photographs. Ben-Ḥayyim (1973, 15) follows Smend (1906b, 12) in reading מ[תן] [יי] צדיק [לעֿ] [יעֿ]מד. Although reading מתן is supported by the Greek and the Syriac, it does not fit well with the preserved traces.

11:9 עצבה — The feminine of עצב (see also Sir 38:18ᴮ) is not attested in Biblical Hebrew, but appears in Rabbinic Hebrew (Jastrow 1903, 1101) where it evokes sorrow, toil and pain. The presence of עצבה "pain, sorrow" is supported by the Latin (*quae te non molestat*) and the Syro-Hexapla (ܗܠܐ ܚܡܣܬ). On the other hand, Hᴮ has עצה "counsel." Furthermore, neither עצה nor עצבה "pain, sorrow" is reflected in the Greek (which presupposes a *Vorlage* of אין עסק לך as in Sir 3:22ᴬ) or the Syriac (ܠܝܣ, which presupposes a *Vorlage* of עצמה "strength, force" or עצבה with the sense "strength, health"). Although עצבה "strength, health" is otherwise unknown, it may be reflected in two other places in Ben Sira: in Sir 41:2 where Hᴹ attests עצבה and Hᴮ has עצמה; and in Sir 38:18 where Hᴮ attests עצבה and the Greek has ἰσχύς. Such semantic overlap between the two words would parallel the relationship between the pair עָצְמָה "strength" and עַצֶּמֶת "agony" (cf. Job 7:15). Finally, the hypothetial word עצבה "strength, health" could be related to the Syriac ܚܒܬܐ "healing, cure" or alternatively conceived as a phonetic variant of עזב II "to restore." אל תאחר — The *piel*, "do not delay, postpone" (cf. Sir 5:7), is surprising and one would normally expect the *hithpael*, "do not linger" as in 7:34. Hᴮ is not much clearer, reading תתור "do not examine, observe." The Greek, ἔριζε, and the Syriac, ܠܐ ܬܬܚܪܐ, "do not dispute, argue, fight," seem to have read תֵּתְחַר, which is graphically close to the readings in Hᴬ and Hᴮ. Alternatively, the letters may be interpreted as a *niphal* (תֵּחָר) from the root חרר or חרה with *aleph* as mater lectionis like in הכאף in 4:6 Hᴬ and מארשית in 31:27 Hᴮᵐ, "without pain do not get angry (lit. heated up)." וברב — The form could be vocalized as (בְּרֹב), בְּרֹב "among the many presumptuous," or as בְּרִב, in agreement with Hᴮ and the Greek, "in the quarrel/

trial of the presumptuous" (cf. Ps 1:5). תקומם — The form may be a *hithpolel* with the *tav* assimilated. Cf. the assimilation of *tav* to *kaph* in תְּכַסֶּה in Prov 26:26, and of *tav* to *qoph* in מְקַדְּשִׁין in some manuscripts of m. 'Or. 3:3 (Pérez Fernández 1999, 97).

11:10 למה — The Greek (μή) and the Syriac (ܘܠܐ) have understood the particle למה as a negative particle: "My child, do not multiply your affairs, for the one who . . ." עָׁשקך — Spelled עסק elsewhere in Ben Sira (cf. 3:22ᴬ and the note, 7:25ᴬ,ᶜ; 38:24ᴮ; 40:1ᴮ). The tilde above the word and the three dots in the form of an inverted *segol* in the margin probably indicates that this is a variant spelling. The term is singular, but must have a collective meaning.

11:11 וכֿדֿי כן — The vocalization כְּדֵי has been corrected to כְּדֵי with the *tsere* above the *dalet*. This particle is common in Mishnaic Hebrew and is attested four times in Biblical Hebrew (Lev 25:26; Deut 25:2; Judg 6:5; Neh 5:8). The construction כדי כן does not appear to be attested elsewhere, except in Sir 13:9ᴬ. According to van Peursen (2004, 387), its meaning should be close to the mishnaic expressions כל שכן "so much the more, as a matter of course" and כמו כן "equally, in the same way." מתאחר — For the *hitpael* of אחר see 7:34ᴬ.

11:12 רשש — The verb רשש is only attested twice in Biblical Hebrew (Jer 5:17; Mal 1:4) where it has the meaning "to smash, batter to pieces." It disappears from Rabbinic Hebrew, but reappears sporadically in medieval Hebrew where the roots ששש and רוש "to be poor" (the *polel* of which is attested in Sir 13:5ᴬ and in medieval Hebrew with the meaning "to impoverish") are used together, רשש designating the poor in the sense of being broken (cf. Midr. Prov. XXI רש שהוא מתרושש). Nevertheless, it is necessary to recognize the existence of another verb

9 Là où il n'y a pas de peine, ne tarde pas
   et dans le procès des présomptueux ne te lève pas.
10 Mon enfant, pourquoi multiplies-tu ton occupation ?
   Celui qui s'empresse et̶ de (la) démultiplier ne sera pas sans reproche.
   Mon enfant, si tu ne cours pas tu n'arriveras pas
   et si tu ne cherches pas, tu ne trouveras pas.
11 Il y a celui qui travaille, qui peine et qui court
   et même ainsi il est en retard.
12 Il y a celui qui est pauvre et qui périt,
   il va, manquant de tout et excessivement pauvre,
   mais l'œil de YYY veille sur lui en vue du bonheur
   et il le secoue de la terre puante.
13 Il relève sa tête et l'exalte
   et beaucoup sont stupéfiés à son sujet.
14 Bien et mal, vie et mort,
   pauvreté et richesse viennent de YYY.
15 Sagesse, intelligence et compréhension de la parole viennent de YYY,
   péché et droits chemins viennent de YYY.
16 Folie et ténèbres ont été formées pour les pécheurs
   et ceux qui font le mal, le mal est avec eux.
17 La part du juste [tien]t [pour touj]ours
   et son désir s'accomplit pour toujours.

9 Where there is no pain, do not delay,
   and in the dispute with the proud, do not take a stand.
10 My child, why increase your affairs?
   The one who hurries a̶n̶d̶ to multiply (them) will not be found innocent.
   My child, if you do not run, you will not arrive
   and if you do not seek, you will not find.
11 There is one who labors, toils, and runs,
   and even so they are thwarted.
12 There is one who is poor and wanders,
   they go, lacking everything, excessively poor,
   but the eye of YYY looks over them for (their) benefit,
   and he shakes them from the reeking grime.
13 He lifts their head and exalts them
   so that many marvel at them.
14 Good and bad, life and death,
   poverty and wealth come from YYY.
15 Wisdom, prudence, and comprehension of speech come from YYY,
   sin and straight paths come from YYY.
16 Folly and darkness have been created for sinners
   and as for those who do evil, evil is with them.
17 The portion of the just endures forever
   and their desire prospers always.

with the same root consonants, i.e. רשש (perhaps a biform of רוש), that means "to be poor" in the *qal* and that also occurs in medieval Hebrew (see Maagarim). Alternatively, one wonders if the vowel marks of the participle may be instead interpreted as cancelation dots for the *shin*, implying the reading רש "poor." מהלך — The noun belongs to late Hebrew (Neh 2:6; Ezek 42:4; Jonah 3:3–4; Zech 3:7) and may be the result of Aramaic influence (Rooker 1990, 167–169). Regarding the question of stich length, the term should belong to stich *a* (thus Segal [1958, 69]): "There is the one who is broken and advancing overwhelmed/destroyed." Van Peursen (2004, 213) translates "someone whose guidance, direction has ceased," or with Smend (1906a, 105), "someone whose pursuit of desire has ceased" (cf. Qoh 6:9 and Job 31:7). However, the scribe punctuated after אבד, which means that it is necessary to attach מהלך with stich *b*. The term is not translated in the Greek or Syriac. ויותר — For יותר, see 3:23 and the note. ועין יי צפתהו — Cf. Prov 15:3 and Ps 66:7. צפה does not necessarily have the positive meaning of "to watch out for," as it can also mean "watching, spying on, snooping." וינעריהו מעפר — For the expression, see Isa 52:2, "he shakes it," that is, he "shakes off" the dust. צחנה — The use of this term with the meaning "stink" is surprising, since it is not used anywhere else in Biblical Hebrew except in Joel 2:20. The term is attested in Aramaic and much later in *piyyutim*. The Syriac renders the expression with a stereotypical formula, reflecting מעפר ואפר.

11:13 נשא — One would have expected a *wayyiqtol* rather than a *qatal* at the beginning of the clause (van Peursen 2004, 150). For the construction נשא "to lift" with the ב preposition to introduce the object, see perhaps 1QSb IV 23. Though less likely, the phrase may alternatively be understood "as for the one forgotten (נִשָּׁה = נָשָׂא [*niphal* participle of נשה]) in his poverty, he will exalt him." The *niphal* of נשה appears in Sir 42:10^Bmg (b. Sanh. 100b); Isa 44:21 and perhaps Sir 42:9^B. The spelling of "poverty" (ריש) with a medial *aleph* is found in Ben Sira (37:9^D) and in Qumran (e.g., "in your poverty" בראשכה 4Q416 2 i 4). The *aleph* sometimes is used as a word-final mater for what would be *segol* in the Tiberian tradition, where we would expect *he* (e.g., תובא Sir 6:33). The Greek and Syriac presume the Hebrew נשא ראשו "he lifts his head," which fits the context well, especially with the following verb רום "to exalt."

11:14 Cf. Sir 33:14^E; 37:18^B; 39:24–25^B and Isa 45:7.

11:15–16 These two couplets are absent in Greek I and the Latin version, but are attested in the so called Greek II (see Ziegler 1980, 176 for the list of witnesses) and in the Syriac.

11:15 והבין דבר — Cf. 1 Sam 16:18 and Sir 33:3^B: "comprehension of speech" or "understanding of things." ודרכים ישרים — The expression, as opposed to חטא, has a moral connotation, "right conduct, integrity," cf. Ezra 8:21; Ps 107:7; Prov 14:12; 16:25 and Jer 31:9.

11:16 סכלות — The term סכלות "folly" is only attested in Qohelet, at Qumran in 1QS VII 14 (and par.) and in later *piyyutim*. נוצרה — We would have expected נוצרו (Segal 1958, 71). Nevertheless, a singular verb is sometimes used following a coordinated set of nouns (functioning as subjects), when the two coordinated nouns are considered as a single item (see Joüon §150p). If this is the case here, then חושך "darkness" is being used figuratively for ignorance (see, e.g., Job 37:19 and Qoh 2:14) or something analogous. Note a similar syntax in צרה וחבלים אחזתה "distress and labor pains seized her" (Jer 49:24). ומרעים רעה עמם — The concentrated alliteration of this verse is noteworthy. Segal (1958, 71) thinks that the Greek, which moves away from the Hebrew, has attempted to reproduce this alliteration.

11:17 מנת — See the note on readings. The versions assume a *Vorlage* of מתן or מתת "the alms of the righteous" (cf. 7:33, and for the meaning of the verse, Sir 3:14). ורצנו יצלח — The two words are found in a similar construction in Sir 39:18^B.

18 [יֵ]שׁ מתעשׁר מהתענות	⁸וְיֵ[שׁ] יְחִיּב שְׂכרו:
19 ובעת אָ[מַ]ר מצאתי נחת	ועתה אכל ⁹מ[ט]וּבָ[ת]יֽ:
לא ידע מה קֵ[ץ] יְ[ח]לֹף	וע[ז]בֹּו לאַחֵר ומתֽ׃
20 ¹⁰בְּנִי [עֲ]מַ[ֹ]ד בְּחׇקֶּךָ	ובו הִתְרׇע ובמלַאכתך התישֽׁן [:]
21 [אַ]ל תִּתַ[מַ]הּ ¹¹בּמַבַעֲלֵי עוַ[ל]	[ד]רֻשׁ ליֽי וקוה לאַ[ו]רו:
כי נכח ב[פ]תע פתאם ¹²להַשְׁבִּֽ[י]ע רשׁ[:]	
22 ברכת ל בְּגורל צדיק	ובעת תקותו תפרֽח׃
23 ¹³אַל תאמר מַהּ[ ]לִי[] כי עשיתי חפצִי	ומה עתה יעזב לי:
24 א תאמר ¹⁴דַיִ עַמִֹ	מהׁ דַּ[גַ]ה יהי עָלִי׃
25 טוֹבᵗ יוֹם תְּשַׁכַּח רעָהֺ	ורעת ¹⁵עת תשכח טובה
ואחרית אדֹ ם תהיה עליו:	

L. 8 [11:18] וְיֵ[שׁ] יְחִיּב — The *vav* is visible (so Smend 1906a, 12), then only the *tsere* is preserved, so it is possible to restore וְיֵשׁ, ideal for the space and in agreement with the Syriac, or וְזֶה in agreement with the Greek. The *patakh* under the *khet* transcribed by Vattioni (1968, 59), Ben-Ḥayyim (1973, 15) and Beentjes (1997, 37) is a shadow on the facsimile from 1901.

L. 8 [11:19] אָ[מַ]ר — There is a trace of the diagonal of the *aleph* and the head of the *resh*.

L. 9 [11:19] מ[ט]וּבָ[ת]יֽ: — Adler (1900, 471) restores [בשלום], which is impossible. Smend (1906a, 13), Vattioni (1968, 59) and Ben-Ḥayyim (1973, 16) restore מ[ט]וב[ת]י in agreement with the Greek and the Syriac. [טוב]את (cf. Ezra 9:12) cannot be excluded. מה קֵ[ץ] יְ[ח]לֹף — Adler (1900, 471) reads מה יהיה חלק without indicating the gap, Smend (1906b, 13) מה יוֹם י[ח]לף, Peters (1902, 347) and Vattioni (1968, 59) חקן [יהיה] מה י., and Ben-Ḥayyim (1973, 16) י[ח]לף י. מה. The trace of a slanted letter after מה can hardly correspond to a *yod*, while a *qoph* would be ideal. Then, the *khet* and *lamed* are certain. The final *pe* is perfectly clear on the facsimile from 1901. The reading ח]לף[is therefore assured, and even more so since it is also confirmed by the Greek. We thus propose the reading מה קץ יחלף, which fits perfectly with the preserved traces, as well as with the Greek and the Syriac. וע[ז]בֹּו לאַחֵר ומת: — Adler (1900, 471) reads ועזב לא[חרי]ם ומת, Vattioni (1968, 59) ועזבו לא[חר]ם ומת, yet וע[ז]בו לאחר ומת is preferable (Smend 1906b, 13; Peters 1902, 347, Ben-Ḥayyim 1973, 16). The *vav* after עזב is not certain and a *tav* cannot be ruled out. לאחרים or לאחרם, proposed by Vattioni (1968, 59) and Adler (1900, 471) are impossible for the space.

L. 10 [11:20] בְּנִ[י] [עֲ]מַ[ֹ]ד — The reading [בני ש]לם is excluded. הִתְרׇע — The proposed readings are very divergent: Adler (1900, 471) and Vattioni (1968, 59) have [תה]הגה, Peters (1902, 347) ה[תה]לך, Smend (1906b, 13) and Ben-Ḥayyim (1973, 16) ה[ת]רע, and Abegg (Accordance) ה[ו]שע. The first letter could be a *tav*, a *he* or a *bet*, as there is a trace of an angular shoulder extended by a bent leg. Two faint traces of a letter follow. The first seems to correspond to the end of a trace of a leg, while the second, given its position and inclination, could be the foot of a second *tav*. It is followed by the trace of a down stroke that could be a *resh*, but it would then be very close to the clearly attested *ayin* so that the two letters would be intertwined. התישֽׁן — There is a blurred trace of the *shin*'s base and the end of the shaft of the final *nun*.

L. 11 [11:21] בּמַ[עֲ]שִׂי עו[ל] — After the *bet*, faint traces of ink may correspond to a *mem*. Following this is a trace of ink above the line that may represent a *lamed*. Our restoration, based on the Greek and the Syriac, fits the available space perfectly. Lévi (1901, 78), Vattioni (1968, 59) and Segal (1958, 69) propose to restore און/עול בפעלי אל תתמה. [ד]רֻשׁ — A trace of a horizontal bar is followed by the left arm of a *shin* as well as part of its second arm. Smend (1906b, 13) and Peters (1902, 347) propose reading ק[ד]וֹם (a *hapax* from the Aramaic "to get up early"), which does not agree with the Greek or the Syriac.

L. 12 [11:21] להַשְׁבִּֽ[י]ע רשׁ[:] — According to the versions, one is tempted to restore להעשיר רש, but the third letter is clearly a *shin* (and not an *ayin*) and the next trace most likely corresponds to a *bet*. בְּגורל — A trace of the base of the *bet* is visible (Smend 1906b, 13; Ben-Ḥayyim (1973, 16); Beentjes (1997, 38).

L. 13 [11:23] מַהּ[ ]לִי — The piece of paper must be moved slightly to the left to allow for the restoration of these two letters.

L. 14–15 Supralinear letters may be Babylonian cantilation, Rey (2017, 106).

L. 14 [11:24] דַיִ עַמִֹ מהׁ דַּ[גַ]ה — The editions diverge considerably on the transcription of this stich. Adler (1900, 471), Lévi (1901, 2:78) and Vattioni (1968, 59) do not transcribe anything. Smend (1906b, 13) transcribes עלי יהי א[י]ה א[נ]שׁ דיי. Peters (1902, 348) transcribes דיי עלי יהי א[סו]ן וּמ[א]ה א[סו]ן ישנו; relative to א[סו]ן, he notes that the *aleph* is certain, while the *nun* is uncertain. Ben-Ḥayyim (1973, 16) gives עמי דיי א[..], יהי עלי, and Beentjes (1997, 38) דיי [ ] י[ ] א[ה א] י[ ] יהי עלי. It seems possible to clarify a few things. After דיי, a trace of a slightly curved horizontal letter, which corresponds to an *ayin*, is visible, followed by a *mem* and *yod* that are certain. Then there is a trace of a letter, which is read as an *aleph* by most, but is not clear on the newer photographs, which only show a very faint trace of a letter (the trace that is interpreted as an oblique *aleph* in the *facsimile* from 1901 seems to be a shadow). We propose reading a *mem* followed by a *he* only preserved by traces of its left leg and horizontal bar. Then, it is preferable to read a *dalet* rather than a *he* (there is a trace of the head and of the downstroke). An *aleph* is certain, and after a gap leaving room for a letter, the *he* is also certain. יוֹםᵗ — Adler (1900, 471) has יוֹםᵖ. Smend (1906b, 13), Peters (1902, 348), Vattioni (1968, 59) and Beentjes (1997, 38) note a supralinear *tet*, which is certainly preferable. Ben-Ḥayyim (1973, 16) does not transcribe anything. רעָהֺ — The *he* is not clear, as the second leg is erased. The scribe may have traced a *tav*.

L. 15 [11:25] עֺתᵗ — All editions transcribe [יו] or restore [יום], which is very difficult. The traces favor the reading עת. There are traces of the second arm of the *ayin* (the right arm being partially erased) and the foot of the *tav*). אדֹ — Not אאֹם as proposed by Smend (1906b, 13), Ben-Ḥayyim (1973, 16) and Beentjes (1997, 38). תהיה — The reading תחיה proposed by Smend (1906b, 13) is impossible.

11:18 מתעשׁר — The *hithpael* of עשׁר is attested in Prov 13:7 with the meaning "getting rich." מהתענות — For the use of the *hithpael* of ענה in the sense of "self-inflicted humiliation, mortification," see Ezra 8:21; Dan 10:12; 11QT XXV 12 and XXVII 7. The construction מן followed by the infinitive construct expresses causality here. יש ... ויש — For the construction, see Sir 4:21ᴬ; 10:30ᴬ; 20:5ᶜ; 37:19–20ᴮ; etc. The syntax of יש with a following imperfect does not occur elsewhere in the MT, Mishnah, or Dead Sea Scrolls. We assume an asyndetic relative clause

SIR 11:18–25

18 Il y a celui qui s'enrichit à force de privation
et celui (dont) le salaire (le) condamne.

19 Et, au moment où il dit : « j'ai trouvé le repos
et maintenant je vais profiter de mon bien »,
il ne sait pas comment le temps passe
et il l'abandonnera à un autre et il mourra.

20 Mon enfant, tiens-toi à ce qui t'est prescrit
et prends-y plaisir, et dans ton travail bonifie-toi.

21 [Ne] t'ét[o]nne pas des œ[uvres du perv]ers,
[Ch]erche YYY et espère en sa lum[i]ère,
car c'est aisé ^{aux yeux de YYY} de sub[i]tement rassa[sier le pauvre.]

22 La bénédiction de Dieu est le sort du juste
et au temps voulu son espoir fleurira.

23 Ne dis pas : « combien [ai-je !] Car j'ai réalisé mon désir
et qu'est-ce qui pourrait me secourir maintenant ? »

24 Ne dis pas : « c'en est assez avec moi
[et qu'elle] pei[n]e pourrait m'atteindre ?

25 Le bonheur d'un jour fait oublier le malheur
et le malheur d'un instant fait oublier le bonheur,
mais la fin de l'être humain sera son dû.

---

18 There is one who is enriched through their own privation,
and there is (one whose) salary condemns (them).

19 And, at the moment where they say: "I have found rest,
now, I will enjoy my bounty,"
they do not know how time will pass
and they will abandon it to another and die.

20 My child, persist in what is prescribed for you
delight in it and in your work grow old.

21 [Do] not w[o]nder at in[iquitous dee]ds,
[se]ek YYY and hope in his l[i]ght,
for, it is easy ^{in the eyes of YYY}, at o[n]ce to sati[sfy the poor]

22 The blessing of God is the portion of the righteous,
and at the right time their hope flourishes.

23 Do not say "How much [have I!] for I have done as I wished,
and what now can help me?"

24 Do not say: "I have enough.
What worry could be mine?"

25 A period of prosperity makes one forget suffering,
and a day's suffering makes one forget prosperity,
but a person's end depends on them.

(see van Peursen 2004, 312); cf. the syndetic clauses with יש and verb in Num 9:20 and 21. יְחֹיָּב — The use of the verb חוב makes it difficult to make sense of this stich; the three dots in the margin could indicate an error. In Mishnaic Hebrew, the verb can have the meaning "to owe, to be indebted" (Jastrow 1903, 428). In Biblical Hebrew, it is only attested in Dan 1:10 in the *piel* with the meaning "make guilty, culpable." One could then understand it as the one whose salary, namely wealth, testifies to his guilt, in the sense that it is ill-gotten wealth.

11:19 וּבעֵת אֹ[מ]רֹ — For the construction בעת followed by the infinitive construct, cf. van Peursen (2004, 334), Sir 3:31ᴬ; 4:31ᶜ; 5:7ᶜ and 44:17ᶜ. לא ידע מה — cf. Prov 27:1. קֵ[ץ י]חלוֹף — If the reading that we have proposed is correct, then the expression is subtle. In Ben Sira, קץ can evoke time in a rather general way (see Sir 43:6ᴮ·ᴹ), the end (Sir 41:4ᴹ; 43:27ᴮ), the end times (see Sir 36:10ᴮ) or death (46:20ᴮ). It is this idea of time passing toward the end, towards death, that the term evokes. This idea is reinforced by the use of the verb חלף, which evokes something that slips or slides, that moves on (see Job 9:11, 26 and 11:10). וְעַ[ז]בוֹ — The antecedent of the pronominal suffix is not entirely clear.

11:20 הִתרַע — For the *hithpael* of רעה, see Prov 22:24 and 4Q509 12 i-13 6. The verb should be understood in its Aramaic sense here, "to take pleasure in, to desire" (see Tg. Onq. Num 16:7 and 12:5), while the Greek and the Syriac seem to have understood it in its Hebrew sense, "to make friends with, enter into relationship with." הִתיַשֵן — The *hithpael* of ישן does not occur in Biblical Hebrew or at Qumran, but it is found in Rabbinic Hebrew with the meaning "get older, getting better, improving with age" (cf. Sifre Deut 48: מה יין את טועם טעם מתחילתו וכל זמן שמתיישן בקנקן סופו להשביח "As with wine, you taste (its) flavor when it is young, but the older it gets in the amphora, the better it is.")

11:21 תֹּת[תַּ]מֹהּ — "Do wonder about" (cf. Qoh 5:7). וקוה לא[ו]רו — Cf. Job 3:9; Isa 59:9 and Jer 13:16. נכח — "Right, simple, easy," see 6:22 and the note. בפ[תַע פתאם — For the redundant expression, cf. Num 6:9, 1QHᵃ IV 17; 4Q510 1 6 and 4Q511 10 2.

11:22–26 These verses are missing from the Syriac, probably by *homoioarkton* (cf. ὅτι κοῦφον in 21c and 26a in the Greek).

11:22 בגרל — Cf. Ps 125:3 and 1Q34bis 3 i 2. For the use of the *bet* preposition to introduce the attributive, Smend (1906b, 109) refers to Exod 18:4 and Prov 3:26.

11:23 עָשִׂיתִי חֶפְצִי — The expression implies satisfying one's own desire; cf. 10:26. יעזב לי — עזב in the sense of "rescuing" as in Exod 23:5; Neh 3:8 and Sir 3:13ᴬ.

11:24 דיי — Note the long spelling of די, where יי represents the diphthong -ay. This spelling is well-attested in late Hebrew. דאגה — The term is rather rare in Biblical Hebrew, but well-attested in Ben Sira (Sir 30:24ᴮ; 31:1–2ᴮ; 40:5ᴮ; 42:9ᴹ·ᴮ).

11:25 The organization of the verses seems disrupted. Verse 27 is a doublet of stichs *b* and *c* of verse 25, but this doublet must have been original (involving synonymous parallelism), and in any case, it is attested in the Greek, which adds a verse, 26, that is absent in the Hebrew: "because it is easy with the Lord in a day of death to give back to a person according to his ways (NETS)." The supralinear letters of this verse may be Babylonian cantilation, see Rey (2017, 106) and complete introduction. ואחרית — The term definitely refers to death, as elsewhere in Ben Sira (3:26ᴬ; 11:28ᴬ; 16:3ᴬ·ᴮ). At Qumran, the term has a clear eschatological connotation. Outside the rare exceptions where the term refers to descendants (4Q171 1–10 IV 16.18 citation of Ps 36:37–38; 4Q416 2 iii 16 and see also the Greek of Sir 11:28), it is always attested in the form אחרית הימים, אחרית הקץ or אחרית העת. תהיה עליו — Segal (1958, 73) proposes correcting it to תהוה עליו in accordance with the Greek and in parallel with 27b. However, such a correction is not necessary. The Hebrew is supported by the Syriac, where its verse 27 seems to correspond to the Hebrew verse 25. It is possible to understand the sentence as saying that death is obligatory for every human: "the end of a person is his obligation = i.e., is unavoidable". Or, the preposition על here may have the meaning "according to, in connection with, on the basis of, because of," cf. HALOT 4; BDB 1f. Therefore, one could understand the clause as "The end of a person (i.e. their death) will be according to them (i.e. according to what they have done)" (see van Peursen 2004, 95).

27	עֵת רעה ¹⁶תשכח תענוג	וסוף אדם יגיד עליו:
28	בטרם תחקר אדם ¹⁷אֹ תאש[רה]וֹ	[כי] בְּאַחֲרִיֹתוֹ יאושר אדם:
	לפני מות אֹ תאשר ¹⁸גבר	ובאחריתו ינכר איֹשׁ :
29	לא כל איש להביא אֹ בית	¹⁹ומה רֹבו פְּצָעֵי רוכל:
	כֹּכְלוֹב מלא עֹוֹף	כן בתיהם ²⁰מלאים מִרְמָֹה:
30	כעוף אחוז בכלוב לב גאה	כזאב ²¹אֹרֵב לטרֹףּ:
	מה רבו פשעי בוצע	ככלב הוא באוכל ²²בית:
	וחומס כן בוצע בא	ומשים ריב לכל טֹ[וּ]בֹתם:
	²³אֹורב הרוכל כדוב לבית לצים	וכמרגל יראה עֹרוֹה:
31	vac.²⁴ טוב לרע יהפך נֹרֹגן	ובמחמדיך יתן קשר:
32	מִנִיצוֹץ ²⁵ירבה גחלת	ואיש בליעל לדם יארב:
33	גור מרע כי רע ²⁶יוליד	למה מום עולם תשא:
34ab	לא תדבק לרשע ויסלף ²⁷דרכך	ויהפכך מבריתיך:

L. 17 [11:28] תאש[רה]וֹ [כי] בְּאַחֲרִיֹתוֹ — Adler (1900, 471) transcribes אל תאש[ם] . . . . יד . . . מעושר, Smend (1906b, 13) and Ben-Ḥayyim (1973, 16) אל תאשרהו, Peters (1902, 348) אל תאש[רה]וֹ [כ]ֹי באחריתו, and Vattioni (1968, 59) אל תאש[רה]וֹ [כי ב]אח[רית]וֹ [כ]ֹי באח[רי]תו. The letter traces confirm these last readings with certainty.

L. 20 [11:29] מִרְמָֹה — This reading, based on Jer 5:27, fits perfectly with the available letter traces (as well as Smend 1906b, 13, who leaves the text in notes).

11:27 יגיד עליו — For the construction נגד על with על in the sense of "concerning," cf. BDB, and at Qumran, see 4Q223–224 2 V 21 and 4Q271 3 15.

11:28 This verse presents a doublet, the second quoted by Saadia Gaon: ספר הגלוי, לפני מות אל תאשר גבר כי באחריתו יתנכר איש (ed. Harkavy 1891, 178). — יאושר — The *pual* of אשר is only attested in Ps 41:3 and Prov 3:18. ובאחריתו — The *vav*, as in stich *b* of verse 29, could imply a causal sense. For the meaning of אחרית, see verse 25. ינכר — For the *niphal* of נכר in the sense of recognizing, see Prov 26:24 and Lam 4:8, a meaning also attested in Rabbinic Hebrew.

11:29–32 Several stichs of these verses are quoted in b. Yeb. 63b and b. Sanh. 100b. We give the full text here to highlight the organization, which differs considerably from our witness: רבים היו פצעי רוכל (v. 29b.30c), המרגילים לדבר ערוה (v. 30h), כניצוץ מבעיר גחלת (v. 32a), מנע רבים (v. 29d,e; Jer 5:27), ככלוב מלא עוף כן בתיהם מלאים מרמה (v. 29b, this last stich is cited twice in b. Sanh. 100b).

11:29 Cf. b. Yeb. 63b and b. Sanh. 100b. פצעי — Cf. Prov 27:6: אוהב "the wounds of a friend." רוכל — A *qal* participle from the root

L. 21 [11:30] רבו — Adler (1900, 471) transcribes ירבו, an error that has been reproduced in most editions. There is no *yod*.

L. 22 [11:30] חומס — The *qamets* read under the *mem* by Vattioni (1968, 61) and Beentjes (1997, 38) is actually a stain on the manuscript.

רכל. The majority of commentators give the meaning "slanderer" (Smend 1906a, 111; Segal 1958, 85–86; Dihi 2004, 632–4). The root, which is attested in most northwest Semitic dialects, refers to the action of selling and the possible notion of itinerant trade. The participle רוכל designates the merchant, specifically, the peddler. BDB notes that the primary meaning of the root is "to go about, from one to another," which may have led to the meaning "gossip" found in the derived form רכיל (הולך רכיל) and attested by the Greek, δόλιος, and the Syriac, ܢܟܼܠܐ. Such a meaning is also attested in Medieval Hebrew (see Maagarim). Ben Sira may also target the dishonest peddler, who takes advantage of people's weakness to rob them. Such an interpretation would fit the context, particularly v. 30c, the doublet of this stich where the equivalent of רוכל is בוצע, "the one who is greedy for plunder, who seeks dishonest profits" (cf. Ezek 22:27; Hab 2:9; Prov 1:19; 15:27, though Lévi [1901, 82] translates בוצע as "slanderer" because of its translation as σκάνδαλον in the Greek in Sir 7:6). B. Sanh. 100b and b. Yeb. 63b also go in this direction. The two texts associate the peddler, not with theft, but with illegitimate sexual relations and group this verse with Sir 9:9. They insert the sentence of 30h between stichs *c* and *d* in an attempt to clar-

27 Un temps de malheur fait oublier le plaisir
   et la fin de l'être humain le révèlera.
28 Avant que tu n'aies examiné une personne, ne la déclare pas bien[heu]reuse,
   [car] c'est dans sa fin qu'une personne sera déclarée bienheureuse.
   Avant la mort ne déclare personne bienheureux,
   car c'est dans sa fin qu'une personne est reconnue.
29 Ne laisse entrer personne dans (ta) maison,
   (car) combien nombreuses sont les blessures du calomniateur.
   Comme une cage remplie d'oiseaux,
   ainsi leurs maisons sont remplies de rapines.
30a Comme un oiseau captif dans une cage est le cœur de l'orgueilleux,
30b comme un loup aux aguets pour déchirer.
30c Combien nombreuses sont les fraudes de l'escroc,
30d il est comme un chien qui dévore une maison.
30e En dévastant, ainsi va l'escroc
30f et en mettant la discorde pour tous leurs biens.
30g Le calomniateur épie, comme un ours, la maison des moqueurs
30h et comme un espion, il voit le point faible.
31 Le médisant change le bien en mal
   et dans ce qui t'est précieux il met la conspiration.
32 D'une étincelle, il multiplie la braise
   et le vaurien épie le sang.
33 Prends peur devant le mal car il engendre le mal,
   de peur que tu ne portes une tare éternelle.
34a Ne t'attache pas au méchant, il pervertirait ta voie
34b et te détournerait de ton alliance.

27 A period of suffering will make one forget pleasure,
   a person's end tells their story.
28 Before you examine a person, do not declare them happy,
   for a person is declared happy (only) at their end.
   Before death, do not declare a person happy,
   for, through their end a person is known.
29 You should not let everyone into your house,
   for, how numerous are the wounds of a gossip.
   Like a cage full of birds
   so their houses are full of deceit.
30a Like a bird trapped in a cage is the mind of the arrogant,
30b like a wolf waiting in ambush for its prey.
30c How numerous are the crimes of the crook,
30d they are like a dog who devours the house.
30e By doing violence, the crook comes
30f sowing discord for all their prosperity.
30g The gossip waits in ambush, like a bear, at the house of scoffers,
30h like a spy, they see the weak point.
31 The slanderer changes good to bad,
   and places a conspiracy among those precious to you.
32 From a spark they make embers grow,
   and the sinister waits in ambush for blood.
33 Beware the wicked for they engender wickedness,
   lest you carry an eternal scar.
34a Do not cling to the wicked, (lest) they corrupt your path,
34b and turn you from your covenant.

ify the term רוכל: המרגלים לדבר ערוה כניצוץ מבעיר גחלת "those who are familiar with matters of licentiousness…". ככלוב . . . מרמה — This stich, which is a literal quotation of Jer 5:27, is missing in the Greek and the Syriac versions, but it is attested in the talmudic quotations of Ben Sira (b. Sanh. 100b and b. Yeb. 63b).

11:30 The transmission of this verse must have suffered some disruption, although the Hebrew makes sense. 30b–g are missing in the Greek, while the Syriac retains five stichs more or less corresponding to 30a,c,d,e, and f, and adds another stich, which does not seem to correspond to anything in the Hebrew. כעוף אחוז — Cf. Qoh 9:12. מה רבו פשעי בוצע — A doublet of 29b. Although this doublet does not appear in the Greek, it is attested in the Syriac. פשעי — For the use of פשע in a context of fraud related to theft, see Exod 22:8. בוצע — The one who is greedy for plunder, who seeks dishonest profits (cf. Ezek 22:27; Hab 2:9; Prov 1:19; 15:27). ככלוב . . . בית — The clause is constructed this way in the manuscript, and assumes the *bet essentiae* (see, e.g., BDB I 7). The Syriac, on the other hand, perhaps reflects the *Vorlage* ככלב הוא בא וכל בית וחומס "he is like a dog that comes and devastates the whole house" (so Lévi 1901, 82; Segal 1958, 77). אורב . . . לבית לצים — For ארב ל., cf. Deut 19:11; Josh 8:4. As Lévi (1901, 83) notes, לצים has a pejorative meaning and refers to mockers in Ben Sira (cf. Sir 3:28^A; 8:11^A; 13:1^A; 15:8^A,B; 31:26^B), yet it does not accord well with the context. In light of the absence of parallels in the Greek and the Syriac, it is difficult to propose a solution. וכמרגל יראה ערוה — This final stich also poses difficulties. It is absent from the Syriac, but it is cited in the Talmud between stichs c and d (המרגלים לדבר ערוה) and it is present in the Greek, which has πτῶσις ("like the spy, he watches for the fall"), a meaning that seems more appropriate to the context. For ערוה, usually in the sense of "nudity," see Gen 42:9 and Deut 24:1 (Mopsik [2003, 139] translates "Les parties honteuses" ["private parts"]).

11:32 The first stich is cited in b. Sanh. 100b and b. Yeb. 63b following 30h: כניצוץ מבעיר גחלת. Smend (1906a, 112) and Segal (1958, 76) think that this stich is close to an aphorism in the Alphabet of Ben Sira, but the parallel remains rather loose: נור דליק מוקיד[ן] גדישין סגיאין (ed. Yassif, 1984, 273) "a burning fire kindles many sheaves." מִנִּצוֹץ — The only attestation of ניצוץ in Biblical Hebrew is in Isa 1:31; the word also occurs in Sir 42:22^M. ואיש בליעל — Cf. 1 Sam 25:25; 2 Sam 16:7; 20:1; Prov 6:12 (אדם בליעל); 16:27; 4Q177 2 4; 4Q379 22 ii 9 and 4Q425 1+3 7.

11:33 למה — For למה in the sense of פן, see 1 Sam 19:17; 2 Sam 2:22, Sir 8:1^A; 11:33^A; 12:5^A, 12^A and 30:12^B. מום — The term refers to a moral defect here, as in Prov 9:7; Job 11:15; Sir 33:23^E; 44:19^B and 47:20^B.

11:34 ויסלף דרכך — cf. Prov 19:3. This verse has a doublet that occurs after 12:1. מבריתיך — This is the singular form of the word ברית; the *yod mater* marks what would be a *segol* in the MT in its pausal form (see van Peursen 2004, 49).

Chapter 12

T-S 12.864 recto

28ויהי תקוה לטובתך:		אם טוב תריע למי תטיב	1
1ויִנָּכֵר במחמדיך׃		משוכן זָרֵי זָהִיר דרכיך	11:34cd
אם 2לא ממנו מי׳׃		היטב לצדיק ומצא תשלומת	2
וגם צדקה לא 3עשה:		אין טובה למניח רשע	3
בכל טובה תגיע 4יְאו:		פי שנים רעה תשיג בעת צורך	5de
למה בם יקביל יָדְ:		כלי לחם אֹ תתן לו	5bc
ולרשעים ישיב נקם:		כי גם אֹ 5שונא רָעִים	6
6הקיר מך וא׳ תתן לזד׳		תן לטוב ומנע מרע	4/5a
ולא 7יכוסה ברעה שונא:		לא יודע בטובה אוהב	8
ובְרעתו 8גם ריע בודד:		בטובת איש גם שונא ריע	9
כי כנחשת רועו יחליא:		א׳ תאמן בשונא לעד	10
תן לבך להתירא ממנו		9וגם אם ישמע לך ויהלך בנחת:	11
ולא ימצא להשחיתך		10היה לו כמגלה רז:	
		וְדַע אחרית 11קנאה:	

L. 1 [11:34] וְיִנָּכֵר — It is possible to read a supralinear *waw* and not necessarily a *yod*.

L. 2 [12:3] למניח — It is perfectly possible to read here a *yod* instead of a *vav* as proposed by the preceding editions (see the *yod* of אִן that precedes).

12:1 תריע — The *scriptio plena* of the *hiphil* of רעע. Some have read תדיע (Adler 1900, 471; Ben-Ḥayyim 1973, 17; Beentjes 1997, 38), and this reading is not necessarily to be excluded (for the confusion between *resh* and *dalet*, see the complete introduction), though one would have expected the *qal* תֵּדַע: "If you do good, then you should know to whom you are doing it, so that there may be hope for your goodness." The connection with the following stich then seems clearer, and this is how the Greek understood it (Smend [1906a, 114] proposes correcting to אם תטיב דע, but this is hardly necessary). On the other hand, the Syriac read אם תטיב רע, which demonstrates that the confusion generated by the graphic proximity of the *resh* and the *dalet* existed well before our copy.

11:34cd This doublet of 11:34ab is strangely situated after 12:1 and poses a number of difficulties. משוכן — It could be: (1) a *qal* participle preceded by מן, "of the one who resides," (2) an orthographic error for the noun מִשְׁכָּן "home" (cf. Job 21:28), (3) מִשָּׁכֵן "from a resident, neighbor," or (4) corrected to הַשְׁכֵּן "to take up residence, settle" in agreement with the Greek (ἐνοίκισον, thus Smend 1906a, 114). זָרֵי — The form, vocalized in this way, is without parallel and difficult to explain without making a correction: (1) reading זר or זרים as attested in the Greek (ἀλλότριον), (2) זד / זדים "presumption(s)" in parallel with 11:34a (רשע) (for the confusion between *resh* and *dalet*, see the complete introduction), or (3) as a mistake for זָרִיז "quick, powerful," a word found in Rabbinic Hebrew and in Aramaic. זָהִיר — Here again, the term likely needs to be corrected, probably to הִזָּהֵר "be warned, beware, be careful." דרכיך — According to Segal (1958, 76–77), this word is a doublet of 11:34a and should be deleted. He restores the verse as מִשָּׁכֵן זָר הִזָּהֵר "beware of the foreign resident," but one could also restore as הַשְׁכֵּן זר (ו)הִזָּהֵר דרכיך "(if) you invite the stranger to reside, then beware of your ways, for..." (for the syntax of this type of imperative of condition, see van Peursen 2004, 182–83). וינכרך — In Rabbinic Hebrew, the *piel* of נכר can mean "to treat as a stranger/foreigner, discriminate."

12:2 For the syntax of the first stich, see van Peursen (2004, 182–83), Joüon §116f and 167u. תשלומת — Cf. 14:6ᴬ and תשלומות in 35:13ᴮ and 48:8ᴮ. The term is not attested in this form in Biblical Hebrew or at Qumran, but it does appear in *piyyutim* in the eighth century. Mishnaic Hebrew and Targumic Aramaic attest the form תַּשְׁלוּם with the meaning "payment, indemnity, compensation" and תוּשְׁלָמָה with similar meanings in Judean and Targumic Aramaic (see Dihi 2004, 745–49).

12:3 למניח רשע — On this phrase, see Bacher 1900a, 278. There are two possible interpretations: לְמֵנִיחַ רָשָׁע "to one who gives the wicked rest" and לְמַנִּיחַ רֶשַׁע "to one who permits evil" (reflecting perhaps the Greek: ἐνδελεχίζοντι εἰς κακά). The second stich can also be interpreted to say "nor does he do what is right," which aligns with the first proposal.

12:5–7 The order of these verses does not correspond to that in the Greek manuscripts, but it is consistent with the Syriac.

12:5de/bc פי שנים — A "double share." In Biblical Hebrew, the term means "a double part of a larger whole" (Joosten 1999, 154; cf. Deut 17:6; 19:15; 21:17; 2 Kgs 2:9; Zech 13:8; Sir 18:32ᶜ; 48:12ᴮ). תשיג —Cf. 6:16ᴬ and 6:18ᴬ for the meaning "reap, obtain." On נשג in this verse and in 12:12ᴬ and 31:22ᴮ, see Reymond 2017b. Although some scholars (e.g., Ges¹⁸) interpret the verb here (as well as the same verb in 12:12ᴬ and 31:22ᴮ) as having an abstraction as subject (i.e., "evil"), this seems unlikely for numerous reasons, including the fact that where the verb does take an abstraction as grammatical subject (in the MT as well as in Ben Sira: 3:8ᴬ; 6:4ᴬ, 12ᴬ and 7:1ᴬ,ᶜ), it is always accompanied by an accusative human object, which it would lack here (as well as in 12:12ᴬ and 31:22ᴮ). Our interpretation also agrees with most Greek manuscripts, though a minority of Greek manuscripts and the Syriac reflect the sense "evil will overtake (you)." בעת צורך — See the note in 8:9ᴬ and 10:26ᴬ. לחם — See Judg 5:8. למה — For למה in the sense of פן, cf. 8:1 and the

Chapitre 12

1 Si tu fais du mal au bien, à qui feras-tu du bien ?
  Et y aurait-il un espoir à ta bonté ?
34c (Face) à un résident *puissant*, prends garde à tes voies,
34d ils te rendraient étranger à ce qui t'est précieux.
2 Fais du bien à un juste et tu obtiendras rétribution,
  sinon de lui, de YYY.
3 Il n'y a pas de bonheur pour qui fait perdurer le méchant,
  ni (pour) qui ne pratique pas la justice.
5d Une double part de malheur tu récolteras au temps du besoin,
5e pour tout le bonheur que tu lui auras procuré.
5b Ne lui donne pas des armes de guerre,
5c de peur qu'il ne les retourne contre toi.
6 Car Dieu aussi déteste les mauvais
  et sur les méchants il fait retomber la vengeance.
4 Donne au bon et refuse au méchant,
5a honore le pauvre et ne donne pas au présomptueux.
8 Un ami n'est pas connu dans le bonheur
  et un ennemi n'est pas caché dans le malheur.
9 Lorsqu'une personne est dans le bonheur, même l'ennemi est un ami,
  mais dans son malheur même l'ami se tient à l'écart.
10 Ne fais jamais confiance à un ennemi,
   car, comme le bronze, sa méchanceté s'oxydera.
11 Et même s'il t'écoute et marche paisiblement,
   prends soin de te méfier de lui.
   Sois pour lui comme celui qui dévoile un mystère
   et il ne pourra pas te corrompre,
   et sache la finalité de la jalousie.

Chapter 12

1 If you do evil to the good, to whom will you do good?
  And could there be hope for your prosperity?
34c From a *powerful* resident, guard your ways,
34d (lest) they alienate you from your dear ones.
2 Do good to the just and you will obtain reward
  if not from him, from YYY.
3 There is no benefit for the one who permits evil.
  nor for one who does not do what is just.
5d Twice as much misfortune you will reap in the time of need,
5e for all the good that you extend to them.
5b Do not give them weapons of war,
5c lest they oppose you with them.
6 For God too hates those who are evil,
  and over the wicked he returns vengeance.
4 Give to the good and withhold from the wicked,
5a honor the poor and do not give to the arrogant.
8 A friend cannot be known in prosperity
  and in adversity, the enemy cannot remain hidden.
9 In a person's prosperity, even an enemy is a friend,
  but in their adversity even the friend sits apart.
10 Never trust an enemy,
   for, as with bronze, their wickedness corrodes.
11 And, even if they listen to you and walk along peacefully,
   take care to be wary of them.
   Be to them as though (they were) a revealer of secrets
   and they will not be able to ruin you,
   and keep in mind the result of jealousy.

---

note. יקביל — For the *hiphil* of קבל in the sense of "to use against, in front of" see HALOT; Exod 26:5 and 36:12. See also the Syriac (*aphel*) and Palmyrene.

12:6 ישיב נקם — Cf. Deut 32:41, 43.

12:4/5a מנע מרע — For the use of . . . מ מנע in this way, see Jer 5:25. The object of deprivation is elliptical here (like the object of the gift in the first part of the stich). הקיר — It is possible to read הָקֵיר (cf. הֹקַר in Prov 25:17), a *hiphil* imperative of יקר. The *hiphil* is rare in Biblical Hebrew (Isa 13:12 אוֹקִיר [1QIs^a אוקר]; Prov 25:17) and means "to make rare, precious." The meaning "honor" appears in Rabbinic Hebrew, but is more common in Aramaic (see Aḥiqar TAD C.1.1.112 and DNWSI 467). One could also read a *hiphil* imperative of קרר, הָקֵיר "make fresh, bring freshness." The root קרר appears mainly in Rabbinic Hebrew and in Aramaic, while attestations in Biblical Hebrew are conjectural, though see Jer 6:7. מך — Cf. Lev 25:47 and 27:8.

12:8 Note the parallel construction in these two stichs with the subject appearing after the complement.

12:9 Cf. Prov 19:4. בודד — The verb is rather rare in Biblical Hebrew, where it has the meaning "to stand aside, separate" (Isa 14:31; Ps 102:8; Hos 8:9), while it is more common in Rabbinic Hebrew.

12:10 יחליא — While the biform חלה is much more common, the verb חלא "to get sick" appears in the *qal* in 2 Chr 16:12; in the *hiphil*, only in Isa 53:10 and in a *piyyut* of the sixth century (Yannaï, *Qedoushta'ot*,

354). The meaning "rusting, oxidizing" is only found in this verse, but can be deduced from the noun חלאה in Ezek 24:6, 11.

12:11 תן לבד — For the idiomatic construction נתן לבו + infinitive in the sense of "applying one's heart to something, being attentive to," see Qoh 8:16 and Dan 10:12. The expression belongs to late Hebrew (Qoh 1:13, 17; 7:21; 8:9; 1 Chr 22:19; 2 Chr 11:16). להתירא — The *hithpael* of ירא does not appear in Biblical Hebrew or at Qumran, but it is found in Mishnaic Hebrew with the meaning "to be afraid" (see, for example, m. Šabb. 2:5). כמגלה רז — Cf. Prov 11:13. The phrase may be understood in two ways, either as indicating what the enemy does (as reflected in our English translation) or what the sage should do (as reflected in our French translation). Cf. Mopsik (2003, 143): "devine les vraies intentions de ton ennemi qu'il s'efforce de te dissimuler, décrypte son 'secret'." He argues that the Greek would have paraphrased the Hebrew to make its meaning more comprehensible. ולא ימצא להשחיתך — The use of מצא + infinitive, to express capacity, ability or possibility is characteristic of late and Rabbinic Hebrew (cf. Sir 31:6^B; 1 Chr 17:25 [comp. 2 Sam 7:27]), and corresponds to the common Aramaic formula שכח + infinitive (cf. 1QapGen XXI 13; van Peursen 2004, 259–60). דע — For the syntax of the indirect volitive, see Joüon §116*f* and 167*u*. אחרית — The term must not refer to "the end, death" here as it does elsewhere in Ben Sira (Sir 3:26^A; 11:25–27^A; 16:3^{A,B}), but rather, to the "purpose, outcome, result."

12	ע̇ תעמידהו אצלך	למה יהדפך ויעמד תחתיך·
	י̇ע̇12 תושיבהו לימינך	למה יבקש מושבך:
	ולאחור תשיג 13אמרי	ולאנחתי תתאנח:
13	ע̇ז מה̇ יוחן חובר נשוך	וכל 14הקרב ע̇ חי̇ת שן:
14	כן חובר ע̇ אשת זדון	ומתגלל 15בעונתיו
	לא יעבר: עד תבער בו אש·	
15	כאשר יבוא 16עמד· לא יתגלה לך	ואם תפול לא יפול להצילך
	עד עת 17יעמד לא יופיע	ואם נמוט לא יתבלכל·
16	בשפתיו יתמהמה 18צר	ובלבו יחשוב מהמרות עמוקות:
	וגם אם בעיניו 19ידמיע אויב	אם מצא עת לא ישבע דם
17	אם רע 20קראך נמצא שם	כאיש סומך יתפש עקב:
18	ראש 21יניע והניף ידו	ולרוב הלחש ישנא פנים:

L. 14 [12:13] עז — If the first letter is an *ayin*, it is abnormally written with short horizontal lines crossing its two arms.

L. 20 [12:17] יתפש — Read יתפש (as Smend 1906a, 15; Ben-Ḥayyim 1973, 17; Beentjes 1997, 40) instead of יחפש (as Schechter and Taylor 1899, 48; Peters 1902, 351; Vattioni 1968, 65).

12:12 למה — For למה in the sense of פן, cf. 8:1 and the note. לאחור — Cf. 6:28. תשיג אמרי — Cf. 31:22[B]. For נשג in a cognitive sense, "to reach, grasp, understand," see 1QS VI 14 (ישיג מוסר) and 4Q525 2 ii + 3 3 (אשרי אדם השיג חוכמה), which explains the Greek ἐπιγνώσῃ and the Syriac ܬܕܪܟ. ולאנחתי תתאנח — The *hithpael* of אנח is only attested in Sir 12:12[A]; 25:18[C]; 30:20[B] and 11QT LIX 5, as well as in Aramaic and in Rabbinic Hebrew. The meaning of this polyptoton is obscure: the pupil would later regret not having taken into account the warnings of his teacher (= his present groanings). The Greek (ἐπὶ τῶν ῥημάτων μου) and the Syriac (ܡܐܡܪܝ) seem to have had a *Vorlage* with ולאמרתי, or more likely ולאחותי "my declaration," which has been corrupted to ולאנחתי (cf. Job 13:17; Sir 16:25[A]; 42:19[M,B]). See Smend 1906a, 118.

12:13 יוחן — The form is probably a passive *qal* / *hophal* (two other attestations occur in Isa 26:10 and Prov 21:10, see Bauer and Leander 1922, §286*m*, as well as in Sir 4:13[A]). See the note at Sir 4:13[A]. As Smend (1906a, 118) notes, the interrogative מה would be more in accord with the passive than the correction to מי, which would have more readily involved יחון. But, there are a few cases where מי is used with the meaning of מה or איך (see Amos 7:2). The meaning of the clause could either be "How can the (snake-)charmer who has been bitten be pitied?" or perhaps "Who will be sympathetic (assuming יחון) to the (snake-)charmer who has been bitten?" חובר — The word indicates "snake-charmer" here due to the context (נשך usually refers to the bite of the serpent). חית שן — "Predator." The Hebrew expression occurs only here, in 39:30[B], and in the H[Par] (T-S NS 93.80 line 14). By contrast, in Aramaic, it occurs in the Targum to Hos 13:8 (חֵיַת שִׁינָא) and commonly in Syriac (ܚܝܘܬܐ ܫܢܐ), including in this same Sirach passage and in the Peshitta to Deut 32:24. עז — The margin contains the word עז which must be a correction or alternative to another word in the same line, though it is unclear which one. Graphically, it seems closest to the word שן and, together with חית, would form the otherwise unknown phrase חית עז "strong animal." Semantically, עז is closest to זדון, and would express (with the preceding אשת) the sense "strong woman," which is also unattested elsewhere. Assuming חית to be a mistake, it is also possible that עז, as the adjective, was meant as a correction and that the expression עז שן was intended, with the sense "savage" (though this too is otherwise unknown), in the same way that the adjective is found in construct with פנים and נפש (e.g., Sir 40:30[M,Bm]).

12:14 כן — The construction מה . . . כן . . . (v. 13–14) is used in Mishnaic Hebrew to express the comparative; see Kister (1983, 132–33 and 1988, 43): "As a charmer who gets bitten is not pitied . . . so he who marries an arrogant woman." חובר — In late Hebrew, חבר can refer to marriage (cf. Sir 7:25[A]; Mal 2:14 and 4Q416 2 iii 21). Here it means "one who marries, partner" and resonates with the preceding verse, where the same word referred to the snake-charmer, the implication being that the proud woman is as dangerous as a snake or ferocious animal. By contrast, the Greek and the Syriac have read איש in place of אשת, and this may help explain the masculine suffixal pronoun on בעונתיו in the following stich. ומתגולל — Cf. 2 Sam 20:12. The *hithpolel* of גלל is particularly frequent at Qumran (17 attestations compared to only two occurrences in Biblical Hebrew) and means "to defile oneself, wallow in," always in connection with sin (see, for example, CD III 17 הם התגוללו בפשע אנוש, 1QS IV 19; 1QH[a] XIV 25, and in a sapiential context, 4Q416 1 11 and 4Q525 21 6). בעונתיו — The pronominal suffix can be reflexive, "and who wallows in his own sins," or refer to איש זדון in the preceding stich if one emends the text according to the Greek and Syriac. לא אש . . . יעבר: — The punctuation in the text, here and in the following three clauses, is strange and probably erroneous. In its present state, it should be translated: "He who mires himself in his sins will not pass away. Until the fire devours him; while he comes with you, he does not reveal himself to you." That is, the punctuation is missing until the end of v. 15. Stich *c* is combined with stich *b* in the Syriac, while in the Greek it appears at Sir 23:16. תבער — Note the alliteration: יעבר . . . תבער.

12:15ab Verse 15 contains a doublet. יפול — Ben Sira creates an innovative wordplay with the verb נפל, used first in the ordinary sense of "fall, drop," then in the sense of "pouncing on, rushing on" or "stooping

12 Ne le fais pas se tenir près de toi,
 de peur qu'il ne te pousse et ne prenne ta place.
 Ne le fais pas asseoir à ta droite,
 de peur qu'il ne revendique ton siège
 et plus tard tu comprendras mon discours
 et tu gémiras de mes gémissements.
13 Comment serait pris en pitié un charmeur mordu
 et tous ceux qui s'approchent des prédateurs ?
14 Ainsi celui qui épouse une femme arrogante
 et se vautre dans ses fautes,
 il ne disparaîtra pas jusqu'à ce que le feu le brûle.
15 Tant qu'il avance avec toi, il ne se révèle pas à toi,
 mais si tu tombes, il ne se baisse pas pour te secourir.
 Tant que tu restes debout, il ne se découvre pas,
 mais si tu chancelles, il ne peut plus tenir.
16 Avec ses lèvres un adversaire hésite,
 mais dans son cœur il trame des fosses profondes.
 Et même si un ennemi laisse ses yeux verser des larmes,
 s'il trouve une occasion, il ne se rassasie jamais de sang.
17 Si un malheur t'atteint, il se trouvera là,
 comme quelqu'un te soutenant, il (te) saisira le talon.
18 Il hochera la tête et agitera sa main,
 et, avec force murmure, il changera de visage.

12 Do not let them stand beside you,
 lest they push you away and take your place.
 Do not let them sit on your right side,
 lest they seek your position,
 and you apprehend my words (only) later
 and at my sighs you will sigh.
13 How can a snake charmer, who is bitten, be pitied
 and all those who approach predators?
14 Thus it is with the partner of an arrogant wife,
 the one who mires himself in his iniquities
 will not pass until fire burns him.
15 As long as he goes with you he does not reveal himself to you,
 but if you fall, he will not lower himself to help you.
 While he stands, he does not reveal himself to you,
 but if he is shaken, he will not endure.
16 With his lips, an adversary stalls,
 but in his heart he conceives deep pits.
 Even if an enemy makes tears fall from his eyes,
 if he finds an opportunity, he will not be satisfied with bloodshed.
17 If misfortune meets you, he is found there,
 and (though) acting like someone who supports you he grabs your heel.
18 He will shake his head and wave his hand,
 with much murmuring, his expression changes

to." Most correct יפול to יוכל "he will not be able to rescue you" in accord with the Syriac, but this is hardly necessary.

12:15cd עד — The use of עד with the meaning "while, as long as," rather than "until," occurs in late Hebrew (cf. Job 20:5; Jonah 4:2; Sir 33:21^E) and is probably due to Aramaic influence (note the construction עד ש־ in Mishnaic Hebrew; see van Peusen 2004, 327). עמד — The subject of the infinitive is not explicit. The genitive construction עת + infinitive is well-attested in Biblical Hebrew (e.g., עַד־עֵת בֹּא Ps 105:19), but disappears from Mishnaic Hebrew. יופיע — In Biblical Hebrew, the verb means "to shine, glow, glitter" (Deut 33:2), but it is particularly frequent at Qumran (41 occurrences compared to only 8 in the biblical corpus) where it means "to reveal oneself, manifest oneself" (cf. CD XX 3, 6 בהופע מעשיו and 1QH^a XII 7 הופעתה לי). This meaning for the *hiphil* of יפע is already attested at the time of the Septuagint translation (cf. Ps 50:2 הופיע > ἐμφανῶς ἥξει and Ps 80:2 הופיעה > ἐμφάνηθι) and in the Targums (Deut 33:2 הופיע > אתגלי and Ps 50:2 הופיע > יתגלי). נמוט — Note the use of the participle in place of the *yiqtol* in the protasis of the conditional. Most commentators suggest correcting the participle to תמוט, but this is not necessary; see among other examples Ps 94:9. The absence of the pronoun אתה with the participle is quite frequent in Ben Sira (van Peursen 2004, 222). יתכלכל — The *hithpalpel* of כול does not occur in Biblical Hebrew. One finds it in Sir 43:3^{B,M}, at Qumran (4Q511 1 8 and 4Q405 20 ii + 21–22 2 // 11Q17 VII 4) and in later *piyyutim* of the seventh-century (see, for example, Saadia Gaon, אשא משלי, 8.28). The meaning must come close to the idea of "holding on, persisting." Hence, in 43:3^B לפני חרבו מי יתכלכל "before its heat, who can endure?" (Greek ὑποστήσεται and Syriac ܢܟܠܐ ܟܠܚܕ); 4Q511 1 8 וכול בני עולה לוא יתכלכלו "and none of the children of iniquity will be able to stand/resist" and 4Q405 20 ii + 21–22 2 // 11Q17 VII 4: בח[ו]ק ית[כלכלו לש]רת "by ordinance, they remain in the service of . . ." Note the wordplay with עמד and its different senses.

12:16 יתמהמה — The *hithpalpel* is well-attested in Biblical Hebrew (see also, Sir 14:12^A; 35:22^B) with the meaning "delay, hesitate". Note the alliteration of יתמהמה with מהמרות of the following stich. Segal (1958, 80) proposes reading a form of תמה "to be in awe" (cf. Isa 29:9). The Greek γλυκανεῖ suggests a *Vorlage* of ימתיק or יתמתק "the enemy has sweet words on their lips." יחשוב — The verb indicates conceiving plans inwardly with the intent of harm: "to plot, design, scheme." מהמרות — The "pits," i.e. where the dead are thrown away. ידמיע — The root is well-known in the surrounding Semitic languages, but it is mainly the substantive דִּמְעָה "tears" that appears in Biblical Hebrew. The verb only appears in the *qal* in Jer 13:17 (in an addition of MT absent from the Greek) and in Sir 31:13^B in two closely related formulations (Jer 13:17 וְדָמֹעַ תִּדְמַע and Sir 31:13^B דמעה תדמע). The *hiphil* only appears here and in later ninth century *piyyutim* (7 attestations in Maagarim).

12:17 קראך — See HALOT קרא II or קרה "to meet, arrive." יתפש עקב — "He (you) will grasp the heel," compare with Gen 3:15: ישופך ראש ואתה תשופנו עקב. The phonetic and graphic similarity between the roots תפש and שוף reinforces the allusion.

12:18 ראש יניע — A sign of mockery; cf. 2 Kgs 19:21; Job 16:4; Ps 22:8; 109:25; Isa 37:22 and Lam 2:15. והניף ידו — "Waving the hand" or "making a fist" as a threat, cf. Job 31:21; Isa 10:32 and 11:15. לחש — "Whispering," usually in the context of incantations or spells. The enemy takes on a quasi-diabolical character, mocking, threatening, multiplying incantations and, instead of the friend he pretended to be, he transforms his face to reveal himself as the enemy. ישנא פנים — From good to evil or from evil to good; cf. Sir 13:25.

Chapter 13

וחובר א̇ ליֿ ילמד דרכו׳ *vacat*	נוגע בזפת ²²תדבק ידו	1
וא̇ עשיר ממך מה תתחבר:	*vacat* ²³ כבד ממך מָה תִּשא	2
אשר הוא נוקש בו והוא נשבר:	²⁴מה יִתֿחבר פרור א̇ סיר	
	²⁵או מה יִתֿחבר עשיר א̇ דֿל:	
²⁶ועל דל נעוה הוא יתחנן:	עשיר יענה הוא יתנוה	3
ואם ²⁷תכרע יחמל עליך:	אם תכשר לו יעבד בך	4
וירששך ²⁸ולא יכאב לו׳	אם שלך ייטיב דבריו עמך	5
ושוחק לך והבטיחך:	צָרִיךְ לו עמד והשיע לך	6
פעמים שלש יעריצך	²יעד אשר יועיל יהתל בך׳	7
ובראשו יניע א̇יֿך:	ובכן יראך ²והתעבר בך	
³וא̇ תדמה בַחֲסִיֿרֵי מַדָּע:	השמר א̇ תרהב מאד־	8
וכדי כן ⁴יגישך:	קָרֵב נדיב היה רחוק	9

T-S 12.864 verso

13:1 וחובר — A *vav comparationis*; cf. GKC §161a, Joüon §174h. ילמד דרכו — Literally "learn his way," that is, learn to behave like him. *vacat* — The *vacat* that ends line 22 and marks the beginning of a new paragraph in verse 2 indicates that verse 1 should be connected to the pericope that precedes it. Chapter 13 should then begin with verse 2.

13:2 מה — In its two occurrences in this verse, the pronoun may have a negative connotation, as in 32:4*b*^B and 35:22^Bmg (see also Job 31:1; Cant 8:4; Qoh 6:8), and this is how the Greek and the Syriac translators understood it. If the pronoun retains its interrogative connotation, then the question is rhetorical. יתחבר — For the *hithpael* of חבר, see 4Q416 2 iii 21 // 4Q418 10ab 4 and its occurrences in Rabbinic Hebrew. Without *tav*, the verb could be *qal*. נוקש — The verb נקש "to strike one another" occurs in Sir 41:2^B and in early Rabbinic texts (e.g., m. B. Meṣ. 2:5), and is also cognate with the Aramaic נקש (see, e.g., Dan 5:9).

13:3 These two stichs could be conditional propositions without a particle or *vav* of apodosis (cf. Prov 18:22). The construction, which is rare in Biblical Hebrew, is common in Mishnaic (e.g. m. B. Bat. 5:3). Van Peursen (2004, 348–50) identifies 19 occurrences in Ben Sira. The couplet poses philological problems, even when its antithetical structure is understood. יענה — The *piel* of ענה II means "to humiliate, to oppress," thus "the rich oppresses and is proud of it." The Greek and the Syriac read עוה, "the rich does wrong and is proud of it" (cf. Esth 1:16; Dan 9:5). If this reading is original, then Ben Sira plays on the double meaning of the root עוה in the *qal* (stich a) "to do wrong" and in the *niphal* (stich b) "to be bent, afflicted" (cf. Ps 38:7, where עוה is in parallel with שחת, and Isa 21:3). The *niphal* of עוה is attested several times at Qumran. In 1QS I 24, it means "to be perverted" and is in parallel with the verbs פשע and חטא. In the Hodayot, only the participle is used (10×) with the meaning "perverted" (cf. 4Q400 1 i 16). The antithetical parallelism of the couplet is emphasized by several alliterations. יתנוה — The verb נוה (a biform of נאה) is only attested once in the *hiphil* in Exod 15:2 with the likely meaning "to glorify" (LXX: δοξάσω αὐτόν). The verb is often found in Rabbinic Hebrew with the meaning "to be becoming, pleasing." The *hithpael* means "to make one's self handsome," but also "to be proud, boast of one's beauty" (see m. Soṭah 1:8, Ms. Kaufmann A50). על דל — The preposition על before דל is difficult to explain. Segal (1958, 83) thinks it is an erroneous dittography of דל, or that we must correct נעוה to יעוה (see the Greek ms 248 and the Syriac): "he does evil [as in Esth 1:16] to the poor, and the latter asks grace." In this case, however, the antithetical structure of the two stichs is diminished. Instead, it is possible to read על as a preposition marking the topic of the sentence: "as regards the poor who is afflicted, he pleads for grace" or even as a conjunction marking cause (see BDB III and DCH 6:396): "because the poor is afflicted...." עוה — See above regarding יענה. Box and Oesterley (1913, 362) avoid correcting the text and translate: "While if a wrong is perpetrated upon a poor man he must implore favour," though this requires assuming a sense for נעוה not found elsewhere.

13:4 תכשר — The verb is attested in the *qal* only in Esth 8:5 and Qoh 11:6 with the meaning "to be pleased with, to prosper." Or, read as a defective *hiphil* "if you make him successful" (cf. Qoh 10:10). תעבד בך — For the construction of the verb עבד with the *bet* preposition, see, e.g., Lev 25:46. תכרע — This verb means "to bow down, to kneel down," either as a sign of reverence (cf. Ps 72:9) or as a sign of defeat (cf. Isa 65:12).... יחמל על — "He will have mercy on you," or less positively, "he will spare you." The Hebrew expresses the idea that total submission to the powerful is the only way for the poor to survive. The Greek and the Syriac read "If you have nothing left, he will abandon you." The protasis may correspond to the Hebrew in a figurative sense, but the apodosis may reflect instead לא יחמל עליך "he will not spare/save you," as proposed by Ryssel (1900, 298) and Segal (1958, 83).

13:5 ייטיב דבריו עמך — Cf. Mic 2:7. It is not unusual for an initial verb to appear in the singular followed by a plural subject (see Joüon §150*j*). וירששך — The *polel* of רוש "to empoverish" does not appear in Biblical Hebrew but rather in later Hebrew of the Middle Ages, from the seventh century onwards (Maagarim notes fifteen attestations between the seventh and the eleventh centuries; see, for example, Hekhalot Rabbati 1:2). ולא יכאב לו — "to not feel sorry, have remorse, scruples, an ounce of guilt." For the expression of a reflexive by a preposition followed by a pronominal suffix, see Judg 3:16.

13:6 צָרִיךְ לו עמד — The first word seems to reflect a correction from צָרִיךְ "in need" to צֹרֶךְ "need." Variation between the same words is also found in Sir 32:7^B,F and 39:16^B,Bmg (צורך in 32:7^F and 39:16^B and צריך in

Chapitre 13

1 Celui qui touche la poix, sa main s'englue
  et celui qui s'allie au moqueur apprend sa voie.
2 Comment porter plus lourd que toi ?
  Ainsi ne t'allie pas à un plus riche que toi.
  Comment le pot (de terre) s'allierait-il au chaudron ?
  Qu'il le heurte et il se brise.
  Ou comment un riche s'allierait-il à un pauvre ?
3 Le riche opprime et, lui, en est fier,
  mais, parce que le pauvre est affligé, lui, implore grâce.
4 Si tu lui es utile, il t'asservira
  et si tu fléchis le genoux, il t'épargnera.
5 Si tu as des biens, ses paroles te seront bienveillantes
  et il t'appauvrira sans avoir de remords.
6 A-t-il besoin de toi ? Il te flatte
  et en te souriant, il te met en confiance.
7 Tant qu'il profite, il se joue de toi,
  deux fois, trois fois, il te terrorise
  et après cela, il te regarde et te dédaigne
  et hoche de la tête envers toi.
8 Prends garde, ne sois pas très arrogant
  et ne ressemble pas à ceux qui manquent de savoir.
9 Un prince approche, reste à l'écart,
  et ainsi, de cette façon, il te fera approcher.

Chapter 13

1 As for the one touching pitch, it clings to their hand,
  so the one who associates with a scoffer learns their ways.
2 How can you carry what is too heavy for you?
  So, how can you associate with one richer than you?
  How can the clay pot accompany the kettle?
  For, if it strikes against it, it breaks.
  How can the rich associate with the poor?
3 The rich oppresses and then brags,
  but, since the poor are afflicted, they plead for grace.
4 If you are a benefit to them, they treat you as a slave,
  if you bend your knee, they have mercy on you.
5 If you have means, their words are pleasing to you,
  but they will impoverish you without remorse.
6 Do they need you? They will flatter you,
  and while smiling at you, make you trust them.
7 As long as they profit, they will mock you.
  Two times, three times they will terrorize you.
  And after, when they see you, they will disdain you
  and shake their head at you.
8 Beware, do not be excessively arrogant
  and do not be like someone lacking knowledge.
9 If a prince approaches, stay at a distance,
  and all the more, he will make you come closer.

32:7ᴮ and 39:16ᴮᵐᵍ); cf. the variation between צריך and צרך (presumably the perfect verb) in Sir 42:21ᴮ. For צור, see 8:9ᴬ and the note. For צרך, see 31:4ᴮ and the note. Here, the complementation with the preposition עם to indicate what is needed seems unusual, but this is similar to the use of the preposition את "with" in Sir 32:7ᴮ,ᶠ; both these usages may, in turn, be based on the use of ב elsewhere (with צרך in Sir 15:12ᴬ; 38:12ᴮ,ᴮᵐᵍ and with the Aramaic cognates to both words in, e.g., Tg. 2 Kgs 5:7; Tg. Jer. 14:22; 16:20; and Tg. 1 Chr. 28:12). והשיע — The form is not entirely clear. It could be a *hiphil* of שעע I, "to seal" (see Sir 41:21aᴮ) but this would not fit the context. Instead, it may be a *hiphil* of שעע II, "to flatter someone, take delight in, enjoy oneself, play" (see HALOT and DCH, 8:519), in parallel with שוחק in the following stich. The *hiphil* is not attested elsewhere in Hebrew (according to Maagarim), though the *pilpel*, "to delight in, gladen, enjoy oneself," is well-attested, including at Qumran (see for example 4Q418 69 ii 12). The uniqueness of the *hiphil* form here suggests that this example is perhaps based on analogy to the Syriac *aphel* of ܫܒܒ (found at least once with the sense "flatter," in the Syro-Hexapla to Prov 28:23 with gloss) and/or on analogy to the Hebrew *hiphil* of חלק "to smooth, flatter," which usually occurs with "tongue" as direct object, but which occurs without explicit object in Prov 29:5 as well as in 1QHᵃ XII 8 (where it is complemented by a *lamed* preposition: בדברים החילקו למו). See Reymond 2021a, 276–78. Segal (1958, 83) and Ben-Ḥayyim (1973, 335) suggest reading a *hiphil* of ישע, as in 1 Sam 25:26, a less likely solution given that the verbs in the following stich must belong to the same semantic domain.

13:7 פעמים שלש — As in Job 33:29. יעריץ — The meaning of ערץ in the *hiphil* is usually "to terrify, make someone tremble." Segal (1958, 84) proposes the meaning "to glorify" here, as in Isa 29:23 (cf. Jastrow 1903, 1123 "to proclaim the power of, to praise"). Ironically, the meaning of this verse would then be the same as that of the preceding with glorification implying flattery. ובכן — "After that." The phrase appears in late Hebrew (Qoh 8:9–10; Esth 4:16; Sir 32:2ᴬ; 1QSa I 11; 4Q386 1 ii 8) and is common to Palestinian Aramaic dialects (cf. van Peursen 2004, 331 and the bibliography there). והתעבר בך — The *hithpael* of עבר; see the note in 5:7ᴬ. However, according to Kister (1990, 318), in the present case the meaning would have to be "he will shun/despise you," as the Greek (καταλείψει) and the Syriac (ܢܒܣܐ ܠܟ) understood it (see also the Greek μὴ παρίδῃς in 7:10 and 8:8, and the LXX of Deut 3:26). Kister refers to the parallel formulation in y. ʿErub. 5:1, צרך לך צחק לך לא צרך לך הפליג עליך, where הפליג "to abandon, despise" is used in place of התעבר. ובראשו יניע — A sign of mockery. See 12:18ᴬ and the note. Yet, the verb נוע is not normally constructed with the preposition ב to introduce the object. Nevertheless, the construction is easily explained as based on analogy to נוד "to wander, shake" with ב followed by ראש, as in Jer 18:16.

13:8 אל תרהב — The verb has its Aramaic meaning "to be proud, arrogant" (Jastrow 1903, 1453, Mizrahi 2013, 440–41). אל תדמה — The construction . . . דמה ב does not seem to be attested in Biblical Hebrew, which uses the preposition ל instead, but it does occur at Qumran (4Q418a 4 2 [?]; 4Q431 1 2.3; 4Q491 11 i 8; 4Q525 2 iii 4). This syntactical detail has led Lévi (1901, 94) and Smend (1906a, 124) to suggest reading the *niphal* of דמה III: "and not to perish for lack of intelligence." The use of the full imperfect form reflects late Hebrew usage. בחסירי — Similarly, the spelling and vocalization of the word here match those of Rabbinic Hebrew.

13:9 Cf. Luke 14:8f. As is frequently the case in Ben Sira, the conditional statement is expressed by the asyndetic juxtaposition of two propositions (see 13:3ᴬ and the note). כדי כן — See 11:11ᴬ and the note.

ואל תתרחק פן תשנא:		אל תתקרב פן תתרחק	10
ואל תאמן לרֹב שיחו:		אל 5תבטח לחפש עמו	11
ושחק לך וחקרך:		כי מרֹבות שיחו 6נסיון	
על 7נפש רבים קושר קשר:		אכזרי יתן מושל ולא יחמל	12
ואל תהלך 8עם אנשי חמס:		השמר והיה זהיר	13
וכל אדם את 9הדומה לו:		כל הבשר יאהב מינו	15
ואל מינו יחובר אדם׳ *vacat*		מין כל בשר אצלו	16
כך רשע לצדיק׳		10מה יחובר זאב אל כבש	17
		וכן עשיר אל איש נאצל	
vac. מאין שלום עשיר אל רש:		11מאיש שלום צבוע: אל כלב	18
כן מרעית עשיר דלים:		12מאכל ארי פראי מדבר	19
ותועבת עשיר אביון:		תועבת 13גאוה ענוה	20
ודל נמוט נדחה מרע אל רע:		עשיר מוט בסמך 14מרע	21

13:10 תתקרב — The *hithpael* of קרב is not attested in Biblical Hebrew. It occurs twelve times in the War Scroll with a hostile connotation, "to approach confrontationally" (cf. the Greek ἔμπιπτε). In this stich, it means to approach someone, not confrontationally, but in order to establish a relationship, become intimate or close, as in Rabbinic Hebrew (cf. Deut. Rab. 15; Jastrow 1903, 1410). תתרחק — The *hithpael* of רחק is not attested in Biblical Hebrew or at Qumran, but it does appear in Mishnaic Hebrew with the exact opposite meaning of the *hithpael* of קרב, "to be removed from one's network of friends" (cf. m. Sanh. 3:4 where יתרחק is contrasted with קרוב). Its meaning in stich *a* must be passive and reflexive in *b* (literally "do not make yourself far"). In this case, the wordplay depends on the different nuances not of the root but of the conjugation. The sentence can be compared with Papyrus Insinger 10:12–13: "Do not approach when it is not the time for it, for then your master will dislike you. Do not be far, lest one must search for you and you become a stench to him" (trans. Lichtheim 1980, 3:193).

13:11 לחפש — The verb is only attested in the *qal* in *piyyutim* after the fifth century. However, the meaning "to be free" (cf. Lev 19:20; Sir 7:21) does not seem to pose any difficulties here, "to be free" meaning "to be too familiar." One could also understand it as "Do not trust his freedom (חֹפֶשׁ [see Sir 7:21ᴬ], i.e. the freedom he has with you)." The possessive sense of the expression with עם is similar to the expression in Sir 5:6ᴬ. וחקרך ... כי מהרבות — This verse is quoted in Saadia Gaon: כִּי בְרָב שִׂיחַ מְנַסֶּה אוֹתְךָ וְשָׂחַק לְךָ וַחֲקָרֶךָ (ed. Harkavy 1891, 178). This citation expresses a simplification of the syntax: the adverbial use of the infinitive with the preposition מן is replaced by a noun (רב) with the instrumental preposition ב and the Hebrew נסיון has been changed to a participle: מנסה אותך. Cf. 4:17ᴬ and the note. ושחק — It should probably be vocalized as a participle (וְשֹׁחֵק); the expression is in close parallel to 13:6*b*. וחקרך — "He scrutinizes, unmasks, exposes you"; cf. Prov 18:17 and 28:11.

13:12 The versions, which are no more explicit than our verse, suggest a slightly different *Vorlage*: אכזרי לא ישמר (=ישמר?) דברים (מושל>מילין?), ולא יחמל על רע (>רבים?) וקשרים, while the Syriac seems to have read קושר קשר, leaving out אכזרי יתן שלום ולא יחמל על נפש רבים. Concerning our text, it is not clear whether to punctuate the first stich after מושל, as the Syriac and the Greek do, or after יחמל as the Hebrew suggests. The first stich could be rendered "The cruel brings domination and will be without pity" (cf. Zech 9:10; Dan 11:4) or "The cruel imposes himself as a governor" (Mopsik 2003, 147; Peters's proposal [Peters 1913, 116] to understand מושל in the sense of "mockery" [cf. Sir 50:27, but the meaning there seems different] does not seem appropriate). One could also follow Smend (1906a, 125) in rendering "the governor will bring cruelty and have no pity," if one understands אכזרי in the sense of אכזריות.

13:13 זהיר — The verb זהר with the meaning "to be attentive" is an Aramaism that appears in late Hebrew and in Aramaic at Qumran (cf. Ezra 4:22, Sir 11:34ᴬ; 32:22ᴱ,ᶠ; 42:8ᴹ,ᴮ). The construction היה זהיר is also found in Mishnaic Hebrew (see, for example, m. 'Abot 1:9 והוי זהיר and 2:1 והוי זהיר במצוה בדבריך)

13:15 This verse is cited in b. B. Qam. 92b as part of the Ketuvim: ומשולש בכתובים דכתיב כל עוף למינו ישכון ובן אדם לדומה לו "thirdly, it is written in the Ketuvim: 'every bird resides with its kind and a human close to the one who resembles him.'" This verse is also cited in this form in the Syriac *Testament of Saint Ephrem*, XI: ܕܟܠ ܦܪܚܬܐ ܪܚܡܐ ܒܪ ܓܢܣܗ ܘܒܪ ܐܢܫܐ ܠܕܕܡܐ ܠܗ "For every bird loves its own kind, and man the one who resembles him" (cited by Lévi 1902, 291; see Duval 1901, 257, 292).

13:16 The Hebrew of the first stich is elliptical. One should certainly assume the underlying sense: "all flesh has a species of its own." יחובר — In Ben Sira, the term designates any kind of association, including marriage (cf. 7:25ᴬ; 12:13–14ᴬ). The two verses may allude to Gen 2:18–23, in which case הדומה לו could be an explanation of כנגדו, (Gen 2:18, 20), while אצל calls to mind צלע (Gen 2:22).

13:17 מה ... כך — The conjunction כך is not attested in Biblical Hebrew, but appears frequently in Mishnaic Hebrew (at Qumran, two attestations occur in a very fragmentary context: 4Q384 C 2 and PAM 43.700 frg. 36 1). According to Kister (1983, 132–3 and 1988, 43; cf. Sir 12:13–14ᴬ; 30:19ᴮᵐᵍ; 38:25–27ᴮ), the syntax of these two couplets corresponds to the idiomatic construction of the comparative found in

10 N'approche pas, de peur que tu ne sois écarté,
    mais ne te tiens pas à l'écart, de peur d'être haï.
11 Ne t'aventure pas à être libre avec lui
    et ne te fie pas à l'abondance de ses paroles,
    car de la multiplication de ses paroles (vient) l'épreuve
    et en te souriant, il te scrute.
12 Le cruel apporte domination et n'a pas de pitié,
    contre la vie d'un grand nombre il conspire une conspiration.
13 Prends garde et sois attentif
    et ne marche pas avec des personnes violentes.
15 Toute chair aime son espèce
    et tout être humain celui qui lui ressemble.
16 Toute chair est proche de (son) espèce
    et à son espèce, l'être humain s'allie.
17 Comment le loup s'allierait-il avec l'agneau ?
    Ainsi le méchant avec le juste
    et de même le riche avec une personne démunie.
18 *Comment* la hyène serait en paix avec le chien ?
    D'où (viendrait) la paix du riche avec le pauvre ?
19 La nourriture du lion, ce sont les onagres du désert ;
    de même, la pâture du riche, ce sont les pauvres.
20 L'abomination de l'orgueil : c'est l'humilité
    et l'abomination du riche : c'est le pauvre.
21 Un riche chancelle, il est soutenu par un compagnon,
    mais si un pauvre chancelle, il est repoussé de compagnon en compagnon.

10 Do not approach, lest you are pushed away
    but do not stay afar, lest you are hated.
11 Do not venture to be free with him,
    and do not trust his many words,
    because with the multiplication of his words (comes) a test,
    and smiling at you, he probes you.
12 The cruel will bring dominion and will have no pity,
    against the life of many he conspires a conspiracy.
13 Beware and be careful
    and do not walk with violent people.
15 All flesh loves its own kind
    and every person (loves) one who looks like themself.
16 All living beings are close to (their) kind
    and with their (own) kind, a person associates.
17 As the wolf associates with the sheep
    thus, the evil with the just
    and so the rich with the destitute.
18 *How* could the hyena be at peace with the dog?
    From where (comes) the peace of the rich with the poor?
19 Wild asses of the desert are the food for lions
    likewise, the poor are the feeding-ground of the rich.
20 Humility is the abomination of pride
    and the poor are an abomination to the rich.
21 The rich stumbles and, as soon, is supported by a friend
    but if the poor stumbles, they are pushed from friend to friend.

Mishnaic Hebrew: "As the wolf associates with the sheep, so the wicked with the righteous." The sentence does not emphasize the unlikelihood of such an association ("does the wolf associate himself with the sheep?"), but the danger of the righteous associating with the wicked, who devour the righteous as the wolf devours sheep. For the image of the wolf and the sheep, see Isa 11:16. נאצל — The verb אצל is rather rare in Biblical Hebrew (5×) and is not attested at Qumran or in Mishnaic Hebrew, but does appear in *piyyutim* from the sixth-century onwards. Some, such as Smend (1906a, 127), HALOT, and DCH (1:363), suggest reading רש instead of איש and giving אצל a meaning similar to חבר (cf. the Arabic *wṣl* and the noun אֵצֶל in v. 16*b*): "and likewise the rich who associates with the poor." Segal (1958, 85) follows this correction, but deletes נאצל, which he thinks is an erroneous doublet. Yet, such a correction is not necessary. In Biblical Hebrew, the verb can mean "to take something" (Num 11:17, 25) or "to reduce, shrink something." In the *niphal*, it could then mean "the man who is destitute, who has been deprived (of his possessions)." Cf. Its meaning in Sir 42:21 and 46:8.

13:18 In its current form, the stich *a* does not have a coherent meaning. מאיש — We should probably correct מאיש to מא יש for יש מה, in agreement with the Greek and the Syriac (see, e.g., Lévi 1901, 96; Kister 1999, 173–75). For the orthographic variant between מה and מא, see 4Q381 13 and 27 cases recorded in Maagarim; see also the orthography of this interrogative pronoun in Christian Palestinian Aramaic and in Samaritan Aramaic (Sokoloff 2002, 293). The punctuation after צבוע must also be deleted. Other emendations have been suggested: Lévi (1901, 96) also proposes מה ישלים and Segal (1958, 85) מאין as in the next stich. מאן — Read מֵאַיִן "from where?" though the expression in Mishnaic Hebrew is used like English "how?" The versions have מה יש as *Vorlage*. Segal (1958, 85) proposes that we understand this stich in light of Aḥiqar TAD C.1.1.94: אריא אזל קרב לש[לם חמרא [לם שלם יהוי ל]ך ענה חמרא ואמר לאריא[...] "The lion went, approached (to inquire) about the we[lfare of the ass], saying, "May it be well with you." The ass answered and said to the lion, ["..."]" (trans. Porten – Yardeni, 1993) and Aḥiqar TAD C.1.1.167–168: כי לא [ישא] ל [גמרא] שלם טביא להן למונק דמה "For [the leopard] will not [see]k the welfare of the gazelle but to suck its blood" (trans. Porten – Yardeni, 1993).

13:20 The syntactic construction of these two clauses throws into relief the semantic contrast they express; cf. Prov 3:32; 8:7; 11:1, 20; 12:22; 13:19; 15:8, 9, 26; 16:5, 12; 17:15; etc.

13:21 מוט — The form would seem to be an infinitive absolute or construct, though such a syntax (infinitive + ב + infinitive construct) is unexpected. Proposed solutions vary; Lévi (1901, 96) suggests reading מָט (a participle or perfect), while Maagarim identify the word as an otherwise unattested passive participle. בסמך — The construction ב + infinitive marks the quasi-simultaneous nature of the two propositions: no sooner does the rich person waver than a friend supports them. There is no need to emend to נסמך, as Lévi (1901, 96), Peters (1913, 117), Smend (1906b, 127) and Segal (1958, 86). נדחה — The *niphal* of דחה occurs for certain only once in Biblical Hebrew (Prov 14:32), where it can be hard to distinguish from the biform roots דחח and נדח, but it appears frequently in Rabbinic Hebrew. Here it has the sense of being repelled, rejected or pushed back from friend to friend.

Chapter 13 (continued)

22	עשיר מדבר ועזריו [15]רבים
	דל נמוט גע גע ושא
23	עשיר דובר הכל נסכתו
	דל דובר מי זה יאמרו
24	טוב העושר אם אין עון
25	לב אנוש ישנא פניו
26	עקבת [20]לב טוב פנים אורים

	ודבריו מכוערין מופין:
	ודבר [16]משכיל ואין לו מקום:
	ואת [17]שכלו עד עב יגיעו:
	ואם נתקל [18]גם הם יהדפוהו:
	ורע העוני על [19]פי זדון:
	אם לטוב ואם לרע:
	ושיג ושיח מחשבת עמל:

Chapter 14

1	אשרי [21]אנוש לא עצבו פיהו
2	אשרי איש [22]לא חסרתו נפשו
3	ללב קטן לא [23]נאוה עושר

	ולא אבה עליו דין לבו:
	ולא שבתה תוחלתו:
	ולאיש רע עין לא נאוה חרוץ:

L. 20 [13:26] ושיח — Schechter and Taylor (1899, 8 and 49), as well as Peters (1902, 355) have transcribed ושיח; while Lévi (1901, 2:96), Smend (1906b, 16), Vattioni (1968, 69), Ben-Ḥayyim (1973, 17) and Beentjes (1997, 42) have transcribed ישיח. Both *vav* and *yod* are possible, but *vav* is clearly preferable for the meaning.

13:22 Cf. Qoh 9:16. מדבר — The Greek σφαλέντος suggests a *Vorlage* with נמוט, but the Hebrew, which is paralleled by the Syriac, makes sense as it stands: no sooner does the rich person utter a word than everyone comes to their aid. מכוערין — See 11:2^A and the note. מהופין — The *hophal* of יפה is not attested elsewhere and perhaps is a mistake for an earlier *pual* (attested in Rabbinic Hebrew). The *he* (written above the word) together with the final *nun* (instead of *mem*) give the word an Aramaic appearance. It seems worth mentioning, in this regard, that the Syriac root ܣܦ occurs primarily in the *aphel*, where it means "to come to an end, cease," providing a subversive, if quite subtle wordplay. In any case, the meaning presupposed by the Hebrew root is perfectly coherent in opposition to מכוער: the repugnant, horrible words that he utters are seen as beautiful, sweet, pleasant. נמוט — "The poor stumbles." In parallel with 22a, the Syriac (and the Greek mss 307 ArmII Chr. V 224, which have ἐλάλησε) suppose the verb מדבר as *Vorlage*: "the poor person speaks…" נמוט would have been introduced here under the influence of v. 21b. גע גע — An onomatopoetic expression of mockery: "Ah, Ah!" Although not found elsewhere in Hebrew, it is related presumably to the Syriac interjection ܟܥܐ that indicates contempt and which is found in the Syriac translation to this verse. Cf. Hebrew געגע "to wallow" (in Rabbinic Hebrew) and געה "to low" (in Biblical Hebrew). ושא — The form is enigmatic. The imperative of נשא used alone may mean "get up", or "talk, shout" (with ellipsis of קול, see Num 14:1; Isa 3:7 and 42:2, 11) with an ironic sense "speak up…" (i.e. "as much as you want, we do not care"). It is also possible to correct the Hebrew to ישא "he gets up" or ישאו: "he/they shout, 'Ah! Ah!'" דבר — דבר משכיל could be a noun ("It is a meaningful word, but there is no place for it") or a verb with משכיל either as subject (our translation) or as object ("and although they (i.e., the poor) says (things) that make sense, there is no place for them").

13:23 נסכתו — The verb סכת is only attested once in Biblical Hebrew (in the *hiphil*) and then reappears in later Hebrew in the *qal* and the *hiphil* (attested in *piyyutim* from the sixth-century onwards and twice in b. Ber. 16a and 53b, though not recorded Jastrow 1903 or Levy 1876–89). The *niphal* does not seem to be attested elsewhere. In Deut 27:9, the verb has the meaning "to be silent in order to be attentive, listen." This is certainly the meaning that should be retained here: "all are silent and listen to him." עד עב יגיעו — Cf. Job 20:6 (for יגיע עד, see Isa 8:8; Ps 107:18). The expression is similar to the French "porter aux nues," that is, to give someone undue credit, overrate them. נתקל — The *niphal*, with the meaning "to strike against, stumble" (cf. כשל) is not attested in Biblical Hebrew, but appears twice elsewhere in Ben Sira (15:12^{A,B}; 32:20^{B,E,F}), and in the Mishnah, while in Aramaic the verb occurs (in the *ethpeel*) at Qumran in 11Q10 (Tg. Job) XXV 6. יהדפוהו — The verb carries the sense of aggressive action, pushing or knocking someone down (see, e.g., Num 35:20).

13:24 על פי זדון — "Through, according to, in proportion to" that is to say, the negative feeling about poverty depends on a person's pride. Alternatively, one could read זדון as the adjective (see Sir 9:12^A and note): "but for the proud poverty is repugnant."

13:25 This verse is cited in Gen. Rab. 73:12: בן סירא אמר לב אדם ישנא פניו בין לטוב בין לרע "Ben Sira said: A person's mind changes their face, either for good or bad." A changed face is sometimes indicative of anger, pain, fear or death (cf. Dan 3:19; 5:6; Sir 31:20; Job 14:20) but can also indicate a positive transformation (cf. Qoh 8:1; 4Q462 1 6; Luke 9:29). The biblical construction אם … ואם … has been changed into the Mishnaic form … בין … בין.

13:26 עקבת — Elsewhere in Ben Sira, the term עקבה seems to have the meaning "ruse, trick, cunning" (10:16^A; 16:3^{A,B}), as in 2 Kgs 10:19. Here, however, it must be a feminine form of עקב "trace, imprint" (see Ps 77:20 ועקבותיך, Ps 89:52 עקבות משיחך, m. 'Abod. Zar. 5:7 עקבת יין "a trace of wine"). לב טוב — As Segal (1958, 88) notes, the expression refers to a joyful heart and not to one who has a "good heart" in a moral sense (see Sir 26:4^{LXX}; 30:25^B; 1 Sam 25:36; Esth 1:10; Prov 15:30; Qoh 9:7). פנים אורים — For the expression, see 7:24^{A,D} (and the note) and 35:11^B. ושיג ושיח — As commentators have noted, the expression is influenced by 1 Kgs 18:27. The meaning of the biblical hapax legomenon שיג is disputed. One may render it by "affair, preoccupations, concerns, worries." For שיח in the sense of "complaint, concern, worry" cf. 1 Sam 1:16; Job 9:27 and Sir 35:17^B. In our view, ושיג ושיח must be in antithetic parallelism with לב טוב and not with פנים אורים, as argued by Lévi (1901, 98) and Segal (1958, 88); see also Smend (1906a, 129).

22 Un riche parle, ceux qui le secourent sont nombreux
et ses paroles répugnantes sont trouvées belles.
Un pauvre s'effondre : « Ah, Ah ! lève-toi. »
Et un sage parle et il n'y a pas de place pour lui.
23 Un riche parle, tous se taisent
et ils portent son intelligence jusqu'aux nues.
Un pauvre parle : « Qui c'est celui-là ? » disent-il.
et s'il trébuche, eux-mêmes, ils le repoussent.
24 Bonne est la richesse s'il n'y a pas de péché
et mauvaise est la pauvreté en fonction de l'orgueil.
25 Le cœur d'une personne change son visage,
soit en bien, soit en mal.
26 Le signe d'un cœur bon c'est un visage radieux
et (le signe) de préoccupations et de soucis (ce sont)
des pensées anxieuses.

Chapitre 14

1 Heureuse la personne dont la bouche ne blesse pas
et dont le cœur ne consent pas à se juger lui-même.
2 Heureuse la personne dont l'âme ne la blâme pas,
et dont l'espoir ne s'éteint pas.
3 Au cœur étroit, la fortune ne convient pas
et à la personne avare, l'or ne convient pas.

22 The rich talks, and their helpers are many
and their repulsive words are found beautiful.
The poor stumbles, "Ah ah! Lift yourself!"
and (even if) a sage speaks, there is no place for them.
23 The rich speaks, all are quiet,
their understanding (everyone) exalts to the clouds.
The poor speaks, they say: "Who is that?"
And, if (the poor) stumbles, they themselves push them.
24 Wealth is good if it is without sin
but poverty is bad in proportion to pride.
25 A person's heart changes their face
whether for good or bad.
26 The sign of a joyous heart is a radiant face
and (the sign) of worry and sorrow is anxious thoughts.

Chapter 14

1 Happy is the person whose mouth does not cause harm
and whose heart is unwilling to make judgment against itself.
2 Happy the person whose soul does not shame them
and whose hope does not cease.
3 Wealth does not suit a small heart
and gold does not suit the stingy person.

עמל — This word has quite a wide semantic range: "sorrow, grief, moral suffering, misfortune, toil" (see its use in Qohelet).
14:1 The *b*-stich presents several difficulties and the variants attested in the versions show that it may have undergone some alterations during its transmission process. אבה — The verb אבה, "to be willing," has an awkward but not inconceivable meaning here: "and whose heart is unwilling to make judgment against itself" (with the subject postponed to after the verb). However, most suggest correcting the verb to הביא (Smend 1906a, 130; Segal [1958, 88]; Skehan and Di Lella [1987, 251–52]; van Peursen [2004, 311]) "the one whose heart does not bring him sorrow" (cf. the note for דין) or to אנה (Lévi 1901, 99) "arouse (judgment/sadness)." Similarly, Schechter and Taylor (1899, 49), and Segal (1958, 89) suggest אבל or אנה, but give the latter the sense of "to lament" (Isa 3:26; 19:8) : "the one whose sadness of heart has not tormented him." דין — The letters may be interpreted in two ways: (1) as an infinitive construct (דִּין) "to judge"; (2) as דִּין ? (cf. דָּיוֹן in m. ʾAbot 2:7 MS Kaufmann), an equivalent to דָּוֹן "misery, sadness" (i.e. "And whose heart does not accept sorrow against itself"). Indeed, here and in Sir 30:21ᴮ, 23ᴮ (Syriac ܕܘܢܐ); 37,2ᴮ,ᶜ,ᴰ and Sir 38:18ᴮ, the word has been translated by λύπη in Greek suggesting the Aramaic-derived word דָּוֹן "misery, sadness" as *Vorlage* (See Taylor 1910, 13; Levy 1876–89, 1:384, m. ʾAbot 2:7; 4Q385 4 1 [cf. Dimant 2001, 38]). The number of occurrences of דין as equivalent to דָּוֹן, λύπη in Ben Sira forces us to suppose that it is not a mistake (confusion between *vav* and *yod*), but a true form of the Hebrew cognate (דִּין ?), or a biform of דון (see Reymond 2018a, 165). The verse may be cited in b. Sanh. 100b: בספר דכתיב בן־סירא) לא תעיל דויא בליבך דגברין גיברין קטל יתהון דויא) "Written (in the Book of Ben Sira): Do not let sorrow enter your heart for sorrow has killed many powerful people." In the end, the stich may refer to the happiness of one who is not tormented by guilt or a guilty conscience, or the happiness of one who does not allow themself to be overcome by sadness.
14:2 חסרתו — The use of חסר in the sense of "to decrease, to lessen" results in a strange meaning. With Segal (1958, 89), the proposition may be understood as "Blessed is the person who does not impose on themself deprivation." (cf. Qoh 4:8). Nevertheless, the meaning does not fit the context. It is easier to construe this as an example of the *piel* of חסר in the sense "to disgrace, condemn" (cf. חסר in Gen. Rab. 65:20; 73:5 and the examples cited in Bronznick 1985, 91–105; see also Driver 1934, 277; cf. Arabic *ḥsr* "to grieve, cause pain"). See also Sir 32:12ᴮ for another possible example. Alternatively, given the similarity in form between *dalet* and *resh*, reading חסדתו (proposed as an emendation by Smend 1906a, 130; Peters 1913, 121) also seems possible (cf. חסד "to condemn, shame" in Prov 25:10, Rabbinic Hebrew and Aramaic). In either case, the sense "disgrace, condemn" fits perfectly with the context of the preceding couplet.
14:3 ללב קטן — This phrase, which has no equivalent, must be pejorative because of its parallelism with רע עין. Depending on the context, it might refer to the miser or cheapskate, unless it is brought closer to the more idiomatic phrase חסר לב "fool" (cf. Prov 19:10). Segal (1958, 89) mentions the opposite expressions גודל לבב (Isa 9:8; 10:12), רחב לב (Ps 101:5) and יגדיל בלבבו (Dan 8:25), but all three of these expressions refer to an "inflated heart," that is "the proud." The antonym should then refer to the "humble," but this does not fit the context. נאוה — In the sense of "fitting, appropriate" (cf. Prov 17:7; 19:10; 26:1). רע עין — "evil of eye," that is, the one who is envious, cf. Sir 14:10ᴬ; 31:12–13ᴮ and Prov 28:22.

ובטובתו יתבעבע זר:	4 24יקבץ לאחר • מונע נפשו
25ולא יקרה בטובתו:	5 רע לנפשו למי ייטיב
ועמו תשלומת 26רעתו:	6 רע לנפשו אין רע ממנו
ולוקח חלק רעהו מאבד 27חלקו:	9 בעין כושל מְעַט הוּאֹ חלקו
ומהומה על שלחנו:	10 עין רעֹ עין תעיט על לחם
ומעין יבש יזל מים על השלחן:	28עין טובה מרבה הלחם
ואם יש לך היטיב לך	11 29בני אם יש לך שָׁרוֹת נפשך
	ולאֹ 1ידך הדשן:
ולא מות יתמהמה:	12 זכור כי לא בשאול תענוג
	2וחוק לשאול לא הגד לך
3והשיגת ידך תן לו	13 בטרם תמות היטב לאוהב: vacat
ובה לקח אח 4אל תעבר	14 אל תמנע מטובת יוםֹ
	וחמוד רע אל תחמוד:
5ויגיעך ליודי גורל:	15 הלא לאחר תעזב חילך
כי אין בשאול 6לבקש תענוג	16 תן לאח וְתֵן ופניֹק נפשך
לפני אהים עשה	וכל דבר שיפה: לעשות לפני

T-S 12.863 recto

L. 3 [14:14] אל תמנע — The reading is certain, thus Schechter and Taylor (1899, 50), Smend (1906b, 17), Peters (1902, 356) and Vattioni (1968, 73). The doubts of Ben-Ḥayyim (א[ת מ]נע[ל](י) [1973, 19]) and Abegg (Accordance) concerning the *lamed* and the *tav* are due to offsetting from the previous page.

14:4 לאחר — The word אחר indicates either the "next, subsequent" (i.e. a descendant), or more generally "another"; cf. 33:20E. יתבעבע — A unique form from the root בוע "to rejoice, to exult," which is more common in Aramaic, but also found in the *qal* in Sir 16:2A (see note). זר — The term refers to the stranger, or simply to the one who is other, external to a group or given category. For the meaning of the stich, cf. Qoh 6:2.

14:5 The meaning and the finality of these two verses are similar to Sir 12:1–5A (cf. Prov 11:17). ולא יקרה בטובתו — Most scholars correct the Hebrew according to the versions, but the text makes sense. The verse should certainly be understood in parallel with v. 6 and not in relation to the preceding verse. So, while טובתו referred to "his property, his possessions" in v. 4, it means "his goodness" (or "his happiness") here, as opposed to רעתו in v. 6 (cf. 6:11A, 15A; 11:25A). It should then be understood: "nothing will happen (i.e. he will not get anything) by his goodness," as opposed to 6b where the one who is bad for himself will suffer retribution for his wickedness. The verb קרה "to encounter someone/something," "something happens to someone" makes the sense of this sentence difficult. It is constructed with *bet* in 2 Sam 1:6, but טובתו would more naturally function as the subject of קרה. The letters may also reflect the *niphal* of the root קרא (see Gen 21:12 for its construction with *bet*): "He will not be recalled for his goodness". Finally, reading יקדה is not excluded. Although the verb קדה occurs only once elsewhere in Hebrew (in a medieval text), where it has the sense to "bow," the Syriac verb ܣܓܝ has the sense "to enjoy the possession of" (CAL, 27 Apr., 2021) and may be constructed with *bet* (see Ephrem, *On Genesis and Exodus* 116:5: ܟܒܐܒܬܐ). In addition, note that the Syriac to 5b has this same verb and this sense matches that of the Greek εὐφρανθήσεται "he will enjoy" (though the Greek verb corresponds to Hebrew שמח).

14:6 תשלומת — See 12:2A and the note. ועמו תשלומת רעתו — For the construction, see also Job 12:13, 16.

14:9 בעין כושל — According to Smend (1906a, 132) כושל should have here the meaning "poor, weak" as in Rabbinic Hebrew (Jastrow 1903, 676). According to Segal (1958, 90), the phrase is erroneous and he suggests correcting to עין בוצע "the greedy eye" in accordance with the Greek. Nevertheless, the Syriac ܚܣܡܐ assumes a *Vorlage* with כס(י)ל (cf. Sir 31:30B), which may be a confusion of כש(י)ל and which confirms, at least partially, the Hebrew. In Ben Sira, as in the Qumran scrolls, the verb כשל often has a moral connotation and is closely related to the notion of sin; see Sir 4:22A and 30:21B (in combination with עון), Sir 31:25B ("New wine has made many stumble"); 42:8B,M (שב כושל ענה בזנות), 1QpHab XI 8; 1QS III 24, XI 12 (with עוון); 1QHa IV 35 (ומכשול בכול דברי רצונך); 4Q174 1–2 i, 21 8; 4Q184 1 14 and 4Q509 12 i 13 (with פשע). For the moral sense, see this connotation already in Jer 18:15; Mal 2:8 and Lam 1:14. If "the eye of the one who stumbles" designates the gaze of the one who is inclined towards evil, it also offers a good literary parallel to to the phrase עין רע in verse 10, to which it is the counterpart. The Greek translation "greedy eye" would be explicative. Lévi (1901, 101), Segal (1958, 90) and Mopsik (2003, 152) relate this verse to Der. Er. Zuṭ. 3:3 : אם נטלת ממון שאינו שלך אף שלך יטלו ממך "If you seize wealth that is not yours, then what is yours will be seized from you" (see also t. Soṭah 4:5: מה שבקש לא ניתן לו ומה שבידו ניטל ממנו).

14:10 עין רע עין — The duplication of עין makes the syntax challenging. תעיט — The verb is evocative, designating the hawk swooping down or rushing upon its prey; cf. 1 Sam 15:19 (*Qere* 1 Sam 14:32) and Sir 31:16B. ומהומה — The term usually refers to "panic" in times of war. In Prov 15:16, it illustrates the trouble and worry that great wealth can cause. In the present context, the image of war dominates: the envious one rushes upon the bread and there is nothing left for others (cf. m. 'Abot 5:7, where the term is used in relation to famine). ומעין יבש — The phrase is metaphorical: the good eye (i.e., generosity) makes bread abound, and even from a dried up spring it causes water to gush forth. Alternatively, the phrase indicates that generosity makes even the hard-hearted cry: "From a dry eye, it makes water flow…"

14:11–19 Cf. Qoh 5:17–19.

14:11 Stichs *a* (= Syriac) and *b* (= LXX, b. 'Erub. 54a) form a doublet. This verse and the following one are cited in b. 'Erub. 54a: בני אם יש לך היטב לך שאין בשאול תענוג ואין המות התמהמה ואם תאמר אניח לבני חוק בשאול מי יגיד לך. שָׁרוֹת — Read שָׁרֵ(י)ת, as the vocalisation suggests. ולאֹ ידך — See 5:1A and the note. However, the syntax here is slightly different from the classical usage (see Joosten 1999, 155).

14:12 Stich *a* is a doublet of 16b, but b. 'Erub. has the same sequence of stichs that contrasts with the Greek. לא בשאול תענוג — For the use of the negation לא instead of אין (cf. Sir 14:16A; b. 'Erub. 54a שאין בשאול

4 Qui se prive, amasse pour un autre
   et un étranger se réjouira de son bien.
5 Qui est mauvais pour lui-même, pour qui serait-il bon ?
   Et rien n'arriverait par sa bonté.
6 Qui est mauvais pour lui-même, il n'y a pas pire que lui
   et le salaire de sa méchanceté est à lui.
9 Dans l'œil du faible, maigre est sa part
   et qui prend la part de son prochain, détruit sa part.
10 L'œil de l'avare se jette sur le pain
   et c'est le tumulte à sa table.
   L'œil bon fait abonder le pain
   et d'une source asséchée, l'eau coule sur la table.
11 Mon enfant, si tu as (quelques biens), sers ton âme
   et si tu as (quelques biens), fais-toi du bien,
   et selon tes possibilités, engraisse-toi.
12 Souviens-toi que dans le Shéol il n'y a pas de plaisir
   et que la mort ne tardera pas
   et que le décret pour le Shéol ne t'a pas été révélé.
13 Avant de mourir, fais du bien à un ami
   et si tu as les moyens, donne-lui.
14 Ne refuse pas le bonheur d'un jour
   et ne manque pas d'y emmener un frère,
   et ne désire pas ce qui est désiré d'un compagnon.
15 N'abandonneras-tu pas ta fortune à un autre
   et le fruit de ton labeur à ceux qui jettent le sort ?
16 Donne, *prends* et régale-toi,
   car il n'y a pas, dans le Shéol, de recherche du plaisir.
   Et toute chose convenable à faire,
   fais(-la) devant Dieu.

4 The one who deprives themself amasses for another
   so the stranger will delight in their property.
5 One who is bad to themself, to whom are they good?
   Nothing will happen in exchange for their goodness.
6 One who is bad to themself, there is nothing worse than them
   and the retribution for their evil is theirs (alone).
9 In the eye of the weak, their portion is small
   and who takes a neighbor's share destroys their own.
10 The eye of the stingy person swoops over the bread
   and there is panic at the table.
   The good eye makes the bread abundant
   and from a dry spring, the water flows on the table.
11 My child, if you have the means, serve your soul
   if you have the means, do good to yourself
   and according to your abilities, satisfy yourself.
12 Remember that there is no pleasure in Sheol
   and that death does not delay
   and that the decree of Sheol has not been disclosed to you.
13 Before dying, do good to your friend
   and as much as you are able, give to them.
14 Do not refuse the happiness of a day
   and do not neglect to bring a brother into it
   and do not desire what your companion desires.
15 Will you not leave your fortune to another
   and the fruit of your labour to those who cast lots for it?
16 Give, *take*, and indulge yourself
   because in Sheol, you cannot pursue pleasure
   and everything that is appropriate to do
   do before God.

תענוג); see van Peursen (1999, 226). This usage is also attested at Qumran, in Mishnaic Hebrew, in Job 28:14 and Sir 39:20ᴮ. יתמהמה — The *hithpalpel* of מהה is well-attested in Biblical Hebrew (see also Sir 14:12ᴬ; 35:22ᴮ) with the meaning "to delay." Note the anomalous position of the negative that has been modified in b. ʿErub. 54a (Rey 2015, 173). וחוק לשאול — The term חוק designates the "fixed time" of death here: a person does not know the day of their passing.

14:13 Cf. Prov 3:27–28, where we also find the similar expressions לאל ידך and יש את ידך. והשיגת ידך — השיגה is a verbal noun in construct with the subject (cf. van Peursen 2004, 247). For the idiomatic construction, see Ezek 46:7 כאשר תשיג ידו "according to what he can"; Sir 35:12ᴮ (בהשגת יד); Hᴾᵃʳ Frankfurt 177, 20 (verso, l. 13) (בנשׂיגתו) as well as 1QS VII 8 (ואם לוא תשיג ידו) and 4Q274 2 i 6 (לוא השיגה ידו).

14:14 Smend (1906b, 17) relates this verse to a citation in the Alphabet of Ben Sira: אל הוי טב וחולקיד מן טבתא לא תמנע (ed. Yassif 1984, 267). מטובת יום — Cf. Prov 3:27: אל תמנע טוב. תמנע מטובת יום — Cf. 11:25ᴬ. ובה לקח אח — Puech (personal communication) suggests reading two words (בה לקח) while all the preceding editions have read ובהלקח "And when your brother is seized, do not hand over/transgress." Consequently, they consider the Hebrew as corrupt and propose correcting it to ובחלק תאוה "Do not pass over the desirable share" (= LXX καὶ μερὶς ἐπιθυμίας ἀγαθῆς μή σε παρελθάτω), see Rüger (1970, 19), and also Peters (1913, 123–24), Box and Osterley (1913, 368). Smend (1906a, 134) proposes to correct to ובחלק נאה and Segal (1958, 91) to ובחלק חמד.

Alternatively, ובהלקה may be corrected to ובחלק "Do not transgress your brother's share" (i.e. "do not steal it, do not covet it"), which would form an almost perfect parallelism with the doublet in the next stich: חמוד ... אח. רע = ובחלק and וחמוד = ובחלק — *Qal* passive participle of חמד or the verbal noun חמוד "desire," as attested in Rabbinic Hebrew.

14:15 יגיע — "The fruit of labour." Here, as in Neh 5:13, it has the meaning "property." לידי גורל — *Qal* participle of ידה "to throw," or read יורי (for this scribe's writing of the *resh* in a way identical to the *dalet*, see the complete introduction). For the expression, and the variation between the roots ידה and ירה, see Josh 18:6 (וְיָרִיתִי לָכֶם גּוֹרָל); Joel 4:3; Obad 1:11; Nah 3:10 (יַדּוּ גוֹרָל) vs. 4Q169 [pNah] 3–4 iv 2: יורו גורל).

14:16 תן לאח ותן — Lit. "give to a brother, give." The text, though understandable, must be corrupt. לאח must presumably be corrected to לקח or וקח, and ותן is in all likelihood a dittography (a similar dittography occurs in 14:10ᴬ; cf. Smend 1906a, 135; Gilbert 1998, 173). The three dots in the margin may signal this error. ופניק נפשך — In Biblical Hebrew, the verb פנק is only attested in Prov 29:21; in Rabbinic Hebrew, Aramaic and Syriac, it has the meaning "to spoil." וכל דבר ... עשה — This clause is absent in the Greek and the Latin, but is attested in the Syriac. Its absence in the Greek can easily be explained by *homoioarcton*. The punctuation is incorrect, as לעשות is a complement to יפה. The correction לפני is written interlinearly as well as in the marginal note. For עשה יפה in the sense of "doing the right thing," "what is right, good," see Qoh 3:11 (for the meaning, see also Qoh 9:10).

17	כל הבשר 7כבגד יבלה	וחוק עולם גוע יגועו:
18	כפרח עלה על עץ רענן	8שזה נובל ואחר צומח גֹמֵל :
19	כל מעשיו רקוב ירקבו	ופעל ידיו 9ימשך אחריו:
20	אשרי אנוש בחכמה יהגה	ובתבונה ישעה:
21	vacat 10 השם על דרכיה לבו	ובתבונתיה יתבונן:
22	לצאת אחריה 11בחקר	וכל מבואיה ירצד:
23	המשקיף בעד החלונה	ועל 12פתחיה יצותת:
24	החונה סביבות ביתה	והביא יתריו בקירה:
25	13ונוטה אהלו על ידה	ושכן שכן טוב:
26	וישים קנו בעופיה	14ובענפיה יתלונן:
27	וחוסה בצלה מחרב	ובמעונותיה ישכן:

(marginal: תורת אמת נתן לנו בתורת משה)

Chapter 15

1 B	15כי ירא י'י יעשה זאת	ותופש תורה ידריכנה:
2 B	וקדמתהו 16כאם	וכאשת נעורים תקבלנו:
3 B	והאכילתהו לחם שכל	ומי 17תבואה תשקנו: (תבונה)
4 B	ונשען עליה ולא ימוט	ובה יבטח ולא 18יבוש:

15:3 ומתבואתֿה Bmg · תבונה A | תְּבוּאָה Amg B G S | תְּבוּאָה A

14:17 גוע יגועו — An allusion to Gen 2:17: מות תמות "You will surely die." It is difficult to understand why Ben Sira does not use the verb מות and why he puts the formula in the plural. According to Lévi (1901, 105), the Hebrew is dependent upon the Syriac, where the plural is justified. The Greek and the Syriac are much closer to Gen 2:17 in the Septuagint and the Peshitta than the Hebrew is to the MT. In any case, Ben Sira presents humanity's mortal destiny as an eternal law and not as the consequence of disobedience to the divine order: "You will not eat ... you will certainly die."

14:18 This verse is referred to in b. 'Erub. 54a: בני אדם דומן לעשבי השדה הללו נוצץ והללו נובלין "My child, people are like the grass of the field: some blossom and others wither." פרח — should be an infinitive, but could also be a noun (as in Sir 50:8ᴮ par. Nah 1:4). גֹּמֵל — A scribal error by *homoioteleuton* with the following distich. This may suggest that the scribe was copying a text written stichometrically. אסחות — The form crossed out by the scribe is unknown, unless one reads ארחות, which would be paleographically plausible (see the *resh* of רשע in the interlinear correction to line 21 on this page [15:9]). This might be understood either as "the paths of" or (assuming a metathesis of אחרות) "descendants" (which was subsequently corrected to דורות). בשר ודם — An expression attested in Mishnaic Hebrew (m. Naz. 9:8).

14:19 רקוב ירקבו — A construction based on גוע יגועו of v. 17 (cf. Gen 2:17). Not only will a person die, but what they have done will rot as well. ימשך אחריו — Cf. Job 21:33: the work of their hands will follow them to Sheol.

14:20 This verse, which seems to be constructed based on Ps 1:1–2 (אַשְׁרֵי הָאִישׁ ... בְּתוֹרָתוֹ יֶהְגֶּה יוֹמָם וָלָיְלָה "Blessed is the person ... who meditates on his Torah day and night"), highlights the equivalence between חכמה and תורה (see also Prov 3:13). ובתבונה ישעה — The ב introduces the object rather than the means, cf. Ps 119:117 (ואשעה) and Exod 5:9 (וְאַל יִשְׁעוּ בְּדִבְרֵי שָׁקֶר). שעה — "to observe" in the sense of "practice."

14:21 השם על דרכיה לבו — The expression שים לב על/אל means "to apply one's heart to something," that is, "to reflect on something," "to pay attention to," cf. 6:32ᴬ and the note. ובתבונתיה — "His reasoning," cf. Job 32:11 and Prov 5:1. This is a polyptoton: "who reasons his reasonings" or "who reflects on his reflections" (see the Greek of 14:20: ἐν συνέσει αὐτοῦ = בתבונתה). However, most assume that this is a metathesis and suggest correcting the Hebrew to ובנתיבותיה "who reflects on his paths," in accordance with the Syriac (ܒܫܒܝܠܝܗ̈) and in synonymous parallelism with the preceding stich, as in Prov 3:17. However, this correction is not necessary, especially since polyptotons appear frequently in Ben Sira (see 12:12ᴬ; 14:25ᴬ). The Greek has an alternate reading: ἐν τοῖς κρύφοις αὐτῆς "and reflects on her secrets" (= בנסתרותיה). According to Segal (1958, 93), ἀποκρύφοις is a corruption of ἀτραποῖς (translation of נתיבותיה in Job 24:13), but this is highly conjectural.

14:22 לצאת — The epexegetical infinitive (as in the Syriac, where the copula ܘܠܡܦܩ is added) is justified if v. 22 is understood as a logical continuation of v. 21 and not an independent proposition; see the construction אשרי אדם ... קוטל ... לקטול ... in Prov 8:34. Nevertheless, Puech (1991, 92 and 2011, 318) proposes correcting the infinitive to a participle in order to respect the syntactic structure of the clause: (ha)-qotel X w-X yiqtol. The Greek ἔξελθε assumes a *Vorlage* with יצא, which could be the defective writing of the participle (the reading לצאת would be the result of a supralinear correction of this spelling: < יוצא לאצת). In support of this hypothesis, note that v. 22 is clearly linked to v. 23–25 for semantic reasons: "go out behind ... her entrances ... her window ... her doors ... her house ... her walls ... her home ..." The semantic field evokes the image of the lover who watches and waits for his beloved at her father's house; cf. Sir 42:11ᴮ,ᴮᵐᵍ: "My child, over your [daughter] make strong the bon[d, lest ... she shames you in the assembly of the gate. (In) the place where she dwells, let there not be a window, in (her) room (בית) one looking out to the surrounding (סביב) street (מביא)." These are both direct allusions to Song 2:9–10, one positive (Sir 14:22 in reference to Lady Wisdom) and one negative (42:11 in reference to a daughter). לצאת אחריה — Lit. "to go out after her," that is, "to follow her, to pursue her." (cf. Josh 8:6, 17; 1 Sam 11:7; 17:35; 2 Sam 13:18; etc). בחקר — See Job 38:16. Alternatively, correct to כחקר "like a tracker" on the basis of the Greek and the Syriac. ירצד — Attested only in Ps 68:7; in Aramaic and in Rabbinic Hebrew: "to watch for,

17 Toute chair s'use comme un vêtement
   et le décret éternel est : « ils mourront certainement ».
18 Comme le feuillage pousse sur un arbre verdoyant,
   tandis que celui-ci se flétrit, l'autre ~~mûrit~~ s'épanouit,
   (mg. ~~ainsi ???~~ ainsi les générations de chair et de sang,
   l'un meurt et l'un mûrit.)
19 Toutes ses œuvres pourriront certainement
   et l'œuvre de ses mains sera entraînée derrière lui.
20 Heureuse la personne qui médite la sagesse
   et qui observe l'intelligence,
21 qui applique son cœur à ses voies
   et réfléchit à ses raisonnements
22 pour la poursuivre en profondeur
   et guette toutes ses entrées,
23 qui regarde par sa fenêtre
   et épie à ses portes,
24 qui campe aux alentours de sa maison
   et fixe ses cordes à son mur,
25 et qui tend sa tente à son côté,
   et habite une habitation de bonheur,
26 et qui place son nid dans son feuillage,
   et passe la nuit dans ses rameaux,
27 et qui s'abrite à son ombre de la chaleur,
   et demeure dans ses refuges.

Chapitre 15

1 Car celui qui craint YYY agit ainsi
   et l'expert en la loi la saisit.
2 Et elle va à sa rencontre comme une mère
   et, comme la femme de (sa) jeunesse, elle l'accueille.
3 Et elle le nourrit du pain de discernement
   et elle l'abreuve des eaux ~~du produit~~ de l'intelligence.
4 Et s'il s'appuie sur elle, il ne chancelle pas
   et s'il se fie à elle, il n'aura pas honte.

17 All flesh wears out, like a garment
   it is an eternal law: "they will certainly die."
18 As the bud grows on the green tree
   where one withers, another ~~matures~~ sprouts
   (mg. ~~so ???~~ so the generations of flesh and blood:
   one dies and one matures.)
19 All their works will certainly rot,
   and the work of their hands will be dragged away after them.
20 Happy the one who meditates on wisdom,
   and who observes understanding,
21 who applies his mind to his paths
   and reflects on his reasonings
22 to pursue her into (her) depths
   watch closely her entrances
23 who looks through her window
   and listens at her doors
24 who camps around her house
   and fixes his ropes to her wall
25 and who stretches out his tent by her side
   and resides as a good neighbor
26 and who places his nest in her foliage
   and spends the night in her branches
27 and who shelters from the heat in her shade
   and remains in her refuge.

Chapter 15

1 For the one who fears YYY does this
   and an expert in the law will acquire it.
2 She goes to meet him like a mother,
   and like the woman of his youth, greets him.
3 She feeds him with the bread of understanding
   and she gives him the waters ~~of produce~~ of knowledge.
4 If he leans on her, he will not falter
   and if he relies on her, he will not suffer shame.

---

spy on." For a similar syntax, with an initial infinitive construct (לצאת in stich a) followed by a finite verb (w-X yiqtol), see Prov 5:2.
14:23 המשקיף — "Watching up and down." החלונה — The article is crossed out because of the pronominal suffix. יצותת — צות means "to listen," an Aramaism.
14:24 יתריו — "His ropes"; it is also possible to vocalize "his rope" (for the contraction of the diphthong י- at Qumran see Qimron 1986, §322.141 and Puech, 2011, 318). Alternatively, it is also possible to read יתדיו "his peg."
14:25 ושכן שכן טוב — A polyptoton, as in 14:21ᴬ.
14:26 בעופיה — Scriptio plena and an Aramaism. עפי is only attested in Biblical Hebrew in Ps 104:12, at Qumran in 1QHᵃ XIV 18; 4Q302 2 ii 7, 11 2; 4Q385a 17a-e ii 3 and 4Q433a 2 8, and in Aramaic in Dan 4:9, 11, 18; 1Q20 (apGen ar) XIII 13; Tg. Ezek. 31:3 and Tg. Song 1:16. ובענפיה — "Its branches." Note the alliteration, assonance and semantic proximity to the previous term (בעופיה). יתלונן — For the *hithpolel* of לון, see Ps 91:1; Job 39:28 and 4Q525 22 3.

15:1–6 The verbal succession *yiqtol*, *weqatalti* and (*we*)*X yiqtol* has been rendered by a gnomic present.
15:1 ותופש תורה — There is a similar expression in Jer 2:8. The participle of תפש is used to designate those who practice something, who are expert in something (Jer 50:16; Amos 2:15). ידריכנה — For the *hiphil* of דרך with the meaning "to attain, reach, acquire, comprehend," see Sir 15:7ᴬ,ᴮ (meanings also attested in Aramaic and Syriac).
15:2 וכאשת נעורים — "The woman of (his) youth" or "a young woman," cf. Isa 54:6; Mal 2:14 and Prov 5:18.
15:3 תבונה — The scribe has crossed out תבואה "produce, harvest" and corrected it to תבונה in the margin, which is certainly preferable and in agreement with the Greek and the Syriac. However, the reading תבואה would be supported by the marginal reading in Hᴮ, ומתבואתה, which gives a preferable syntactic structure ("and will water it with its products"). Yet, even if תבואה can refer to the benefits of wisdom in a metaphorical sense (Prov 3:14; 8:19), the term does not accord well with the verb שקה.

ורוממתהו מרעהו	5 B
ששון 19וׄשמחה ימצא	6 B
לא ידריכוה מתי 20שוא	7 B
רחוקה היא מלצים	8 B
לא נאתה תהלה בפי רשע כיׄלא מאׄ נחלקה לו:	9B
בפה חכם תאמר תהלה	10 B
אׄל 22תאמר מאׄ פשעי	11 B
vacat 23תׄאמר פן הוא התקילני	12 B
רעה 24ותעבה שנא יׄיׄ	13 B
אׄלהים מבראשׄית 25 ברא אדםחׄ	14 B
ויתנהו ביד יצרו	
אם 26תחפץ תשמר מצוה	15 B
אם תאמין 27בו	
מוצק לפניך אש ומים	16 B
לפני אדם חיים ומות	17 B

ובתוך קהל תפתח פיו:	
ושם עולם תורישנו:	
ואנשי זדון לא יראוה:	
ואנשי 21כזב לא יזכרוה:	
ומשל בה ילמדנה:	
כי את אשר שנא לא עשה:	
כי אין צורך באנשי חמס:	
ולא יאננה ליראיו:	
וישתיהו ביד חותפו	
ותבונה לעשות רצונו:	
גם אתה תחיה	
באשר תחפץ שלח 28ידיך:	
אשר יחפץ יתן לו:	

כיׄ כל אשר שנא אמׄרׄ לךׄ] [15:11b אל + · B בפי A · 15:10 בפה B · תמצא B | ימצא A Bmg G S · 15:6 בתוך {מ}רעה[Bmg · מרעהו A B G S | 15:5 | A ותעבה · B G | > A Bmg S רעה 15:13 · B אין לי חפץ | A Bmg G S אין צורך B · היא A G S | ההיא B · 15:12 אעש[ה · B תאמר מה פעלתי A G S | עשה: · A ויי̈ | B אלהים · A Bmg S אלהים (- Walton, Mosoul) L | הוא B G S (Walton, Mosoul) · מבראשית A Bmg S | מראש B · וישתיהו A | B וישתיהו · 15:15 ותבונה A Bmg | ואמונה B G S רצונו A, Bmg | רצון אל B · ואם A | אם B · 15:16 אש ומים A G S | מים ואש B · שלח A S | תשלח B | B ישלח B · 15:16 אש ומים · A Bmg G יתן B · ינתן A Bmg G | וכל שיחפץ B · אשר יחפץ A G S | חפץ B · ומת B | ומות A | 15:17 · G

L.23 [15:12] תאמר — An almost complete arc of a circle sits above the *tav*.

15:6 ששון ושמחה ימצא — The construction of the stich is based on 51:3. שם עולם — Cf. Sir 37:26[C,D]; 41:11–13[B,M]; 44:7–14[B,M]; 4Q416 2 iii 7–8 and 4Q417 4 ii 3: שמכה יפרח לעו[לם "your name will flourish forever."

15:7 מתי שוא — Cf. Ps 26:4 and Job 11:11.

15:9 נאתה — From the verb נאה with the meaning "to be decent, proper, pleasant, beautiful, good." The verb appears three times in Ben Sira: here, in 32:5[B] (נואי [HF]) and in 41:16[B,C] (נאוה [HM]). The verb is frequent in Rabbinic Hebrew.

15:10 בפה חכם — "The wise mouth." The reading in H[B] reflects a construct phrase: בפי חכם (cf. Prov 10:14; 14:3; 15:2; Qoh 10:12). ומשל בה — The antecedent of the pronominal suffix is not entirely clear. The logic of the syntax implies that it refers to "praise," thus "the one who masters praise, teaches praise," but one could also understand "the one who masters wisdom teaches praise (or wisdom)."

15:12 פן — According to Smend (1906a, 141), Peters (1913, 130) and Segal (1958, 97), פן has here the meaning of אל, as in Isa 36:18; Job 32:13 and 36:18 (Joüon §168g; Fassberg 1990, 273–94). התקילני — This is the only attestation of the *hiphil* of תקל in Hebrew, though the cognate in Aramaic and Syriac occurs in the *aphel*. For the verb in the *niphal*, see 13:23 and 32:20. צורך — Cf. 8:9 and the note. It does not seem necessary to add לו (Di Lella 2003), which is not attested in the Greek. באנשי חמס — Cf. Ps 140:12; Prov 16:29 and 1QpHab VIII 11.

15:13 יאננה — This is the *piel* of אנה "to allow to happen" with the 3fs energic pronominal suffix "it," presupposing a vocalization like יְאַנֶּנָּה (see Segal 1958, 95). For the meaning, see Ps 91:10 and Prov 12:21 (cf. Gen 20:6). According to Daube (1961, 265), this verse could provide an explanation of the embarrassing verse in Exod 21:13, which legislates

L. 25 [15:14] א ברא — The sign in front of ברא is either a mark of the scribe or a cancelation dot on the *aleph* (see the complete introduction).

the case of an accidental, unpremeditated murder and identifies God as responsible for the death of the victim (see b. Mak. 10b; Mekhilta Exod 21:13).

15:14 The supralinear letters of this verse have been identified as babylonian teamim, see the complete introduction. אׄלהים — The text of H[A] and H[Bmg] is clearly based on Gen 1:1: humanity is presented as the primary work of creation (Bauer [1963], 243–4 also notes the formula in Gen 5:1 [ביום ברא אלהים אדם] and proposes reading בְּרָא, followed by Di Lella [1966, 120]). As Segal (1958, 97) notes, the order of the terms (בראשית ברא אלהים and not אלהים מבראשית ברא) is curiously similar to the corrections that the rabbis attribute to the Greek translators of the Septuagint, see b. Meg. 9b: אלהים ברא בראשית. These corrections may testify to an ancient practice of interpretation of the biblical text. מבראשית — According to Smend (1906a, 142) and Peters (1913, 130), the construction is Aramaic (cf. the Syriac ܡܢ ܒܪܫܝܬ) The introduction of the preposition מן eliminates any instrumental interpretation of the ב of ראשית (cf. 1QH[a] XXVI 13–14; Frg. Tg. Gn 1:1 בחכמה \ בחכמה ברא דיי, Tg. Neof. Gn 1:1 מלקדמין, ברא ה׳ ית שמיא וית ארעא Sir 24:9). Finally, the combination of the two prepositions מן and ב is not attested in Biblical Hebrew (cf. Joüon §133j) or at Qumran, leading one to conclude that the author already considers בראשית to be a word in its own right (Di Lella 1966, 121). וישתיהו ביד חותפו — The presence of this verse, which is absent in the versions, has been understood in various ways. Some have suggested that it is a doublet of stich c, reading צר (= חותף) in place of יצר (Lévi 1901, 110; Fuchs 1907, 37–38; Segal 1958, 97; Rüger 1970, 77–78). Others think that it is the result of doctrinal correction emerging from Qumranian circles (Kearns 2011, 94; Murphy

5 Et elle l'élève au-dessus de son compagnon et au milieu de l'assemblée elle lui ouvre la bouche.	5 She exalts him above his companion and in the midst of the assembly she will open his mouth.
6 Il trouve joie et allégresse et elle lui fait hériter d'un nom éternel.	6 Joy and delight he will find and she will make him inherit an eternal name.
7 Des gens de rien ne la saisissent pas et les personnes arrogantes ne la voient pas.	7 Worthless people do not acquire it and those who are arrogant do not see it.
8 Elle est loin des railleurs et les personnes menteuses ne se souviennent pas d'elle.	8 She stays far from those who scorn and people who lie do not remember her.
9 La louange ne convient pas dans la bouche du méchant, car elle ne lui a pas été donnée en partage par Dieu.	9 Praise does not suit the mouth of the wicked, for it has not been apportioned to them by God.
10 Par la bouche sage, s'exprime la louange et celui qui la maîtrise l'enseigne.	10 By the wise mouth, praise is expressed and the one who masters it, teaches it.
11 Ne dis pas : « ma transgression vient de Dieu », car ce qu'il hait, il ne (le) fait pas.	11 Do not say "My transgression comes from God" for, he does not do what he hates,
12 Que tu ne dises : « c'est lui qui m'a fait trébucher », car il n'a pas besoin de personnes violentes.	12 Do not say "He's the one who made me stumble," for, he does not need the violent.
13 YYY hait le mal et l'abomination et ne (les) occasione pas à ceux qui le craignent.	13 YYY hates evil and abomination and does not allow (them) to befall those who fear him.
14 Dieu, dès le commencement, a créé l'être humain et il l'a placé au pouvoir de son agresseur et il l'a livré au pouvoir de son penchant.	14 God, in the beginning, created a human, and placed them in the power of their captor, and set them in the power of their inclination.
15 Si tu le désires, tu garderas le commandement et l'intelligence pour accomplir sa volonté. Si tu lui es fidèle, alors toi aussi tu vivras.	15 If you wish, you will follow the commandment and understanding to do his pleasure. If you are faithful to him, then you will live.
16 Le feu et l'eau ont été placés devant toi, vers ce que tu désires, étends ta main.	16 Set out before you are fire and water, towards that which you desire, extend your hand.
17 Devant l'être humain sont la vie et la mort, ce qu'il désire, (cela) lui sera donné.	17 Before a person are life and death that which one desires will be given to them.

1985, 335). Di Lella (1966, 123) maintains that it is a retroversion of the Syriac of 4:19b, which is difficult to demonstrate (see van Peursen 2001, 63 and 2004, 24), but also to explain. וישתיהו — The second *yod* may be read as a mater for the vowel of the suffix (corresponding to Tiberian *tsere*), though it is perhaps easier to assume an accidental graphic error for וישיתהו as in H^B. חותפו — The participle חותף only appears in the book of Sirach and in Karaite *piyyutim* of the eleventh-century (Joseph Ibn Abitur, Sa'id Ibn Babshad and Tobiah ben Moshe). The root חתף appears in verbal form in Job 9:12 and 1QH^a XIII 12.29, and in nominal form in Prov 23:28. The root also appears in Sir 32:21^B and 50:4^B, for which see the respective notes. In Aramaic, חתף appears (among other places) in 11QTgJob II 2 (חתפוהי), where the Hebrew has גדודיו "his hordes" (cf. Tg. Job 9:12). In all of these attestations the underlying sense is one of "kidnapping, seizing, capture, stealing," and for the participle "kidnapper, abductor, thief, robber." The root must be a biform of the Hebrew / Aramaic חטף (and the Syriac ܚܛܦ); see Judg 21:21 and Ps 10:9. יצר — For the meaning of this important word, see Patmore, Aitken, Rosen-Zvi, 2021.

15:15 חפץ — The verb is used three times in v. 15–17 and has an ethical dimension implying free choice: "if you want, desire" (cf. Sir 6:32, 35^A; 7:13^A). ותבונה לעשות רצונו — As van Peursen (2004, 253) notes, the infinitive לעשות may have different functions in the clause. It could be the predicate of a nominal clause, having either רצונו for its subject, "his will is to exercise intelligence (H^A) / practice fidelity (H^B)," or תבונה (or אמונה), "intelligence is to do your will." לעשות could also be epexegetic, "you will keep the commandment and intelligence in doing his will," or be an attribute of תבונה (or אמונה), "you will keep the commandment and intelligence (which are required) by doing his will" (Lévi 1901, 110–1). In these two last cases, תבונה (or אמונה) would be the object of תשמר from the preceding stich (as in Prov 19:8), which is uncommon in Ben Sira, as each stich tends to be its own syntactic unit. אם תאמין בו גם אתה תחיה — This stich has been considered an addition based on Hab 2:4. It is absent in the Greek, but its second part is attested in the Syriac of stich b. Di Lella (1966, 128–29) thinks that it is a retroversion of the Syriac. However, while the use of the particle גם in Hebrew to introduce the apodosis of a conditional is rare, it is not inconceivable (cf. Sir 13:23; Gen 13:16; Jer 31:36, 37; 33:21, 26; Zech 8:6; BDB 169b).

15:16 Cf. Deut 30:15, 19 and Jer 21:8. מוצק — The use of the verb יצק in the *hophal* "to be poured out," does not give a clear meaning, so some have proposed correcting to מוצג (Bacher 1900a, 279; Lévi 1901, 111; Segal, 1958, 98; while HALOT proposes correcting to ויצגו). However, יצק in the *hiphil* seems to be attested itself with the meaning "to place, deposit, establish" as a biform of יצג; see 2 Sam 15:24 (LXX: ἔστησαν, Tg: ואקימו) and in Josh 7:23 (LXX: ἔθηκεν); see also Sir 16:22^A in the *qal*. באשר — Complement of שלח; see also 3:22^C. שלח ידיך — ידיך includes the *scriptio plena* of the pausal form יָדֶךָ, and likely alludes to Gen 3:22: פן־ישלח ידו ולקח גם מעץ החיים.

15:17 The verse is based on Deut 30:15 (cf. Deut 30:19; Jer 21:8). ומוות — The spelling ו for the consonantal *vav* in the middle position is characteristic of Rabbinic Hebrew.

	ספקה [29]חכמת יי	18 B
	עיני א̇ יראו מעשיו	19 B
T-S 12.863 verso	לא צוה אנוש לחטא	20 B
	ולא מרחם על עושה שוא	
	אמיץ גבורות וחוזה כל{ם}:	
	[1]והו יכיר עַל כל מפעל איש:	
	ולא החלים [2]אנשי כזב:	
	ועל מגלה סוד:	

Chapter 16

	אֿ [3]תתאוה תואר נערי שוא	1 B
	וגם אם פרו אֿ [4]תעבעם	2 B
	אֿ תאמן בחייהם	3ac B
	כי לא תהיה להם אחרית טובה·	3de B
	ומות ערירי ממי שהיו לו בנים רבים עֿוֿלה [7]ומאחרית זדון:	3gh B
	מאחד ערירי ירא יי תשב עיר	4 B
	ולא תשמח בבני עולה:	
	אם אין אתם יראת יי·	
	ולא תבטח [5]בעקבותם:	
	כי טוב אחד [6]עושה רצון מאלף	
	וממשפחת [8]בגדים תחרב:	

אנוש A | איש B · > A | על A | והוא B · והוא A | אל[הים] A · א B · 15:19 | כל{ם} B : כל A S? | ב̇ כי לו[ה]ב· חכמת יי אל בגבורה ומביט לכל : 15:18 + ואל תבטח B · 16:3b · B S כי A G · אם B · תשמם בם A תבעבם 16:2 | על בני A · בבני B · 16:1 · ולא למד שקרים לאנשי כזב : + 15:20b · B שהיו B · טו[ב] מות A ומות A | ומות ערירי ממאחרית זדון B G · 16:3g | רצון אל A S · רצון B · 16:3f · + בחיליהם B (cf. G πλῆθος αὐτῶν ?) · 16:3e מאחד מ̇[בי]ן תשב עיר + B foll. · בוגדים A | בגדים B · וממשפחות A וממשפחת B · 16:4b | בנים רבים עולה A | בנים רבים בני עולה B · שיהיו B | וממשפחת בוגדים תחרב : A B G ·

L. 28 [15:18] ספקה — Smend (1906a, 18) notes traces of כי above ספקה, but this remains improbable. One can certainly see some traces in the *facsimile* from 1901, which have almost disappeared in the more recent photographs, but these traces are too small and too thin to be considered a supralinear correction.

L. 29 [15:18] כל{ם}: — The final *mem* is partially erased. In the photographs, it is difficult to know whether this is due to wear and tear or time, or if the *mem* has been deliberately erased by the scribe and turned into punctuation (:), which is more likely considering the meaning.

L. 4 [16:2] תבעבם — The two terms are connected in the manuscript, but one should read תבע בם. See, likewise, יתלעבך in Sir 30:13B.

L. 6 [16:3h] עֿוֿלה — The reading is difficult and presuppose a very narrow *ayin* followed by a *vav* that fits into the base of the *ayin*.

15:18 ספקה — The root ספק or שפק means "to be sufficient, abundant." For its use in Biblical Hebrew, see in particular Job 20:20 (שְׂפָקוֹ, LXX πεπληρῶσθαι, cf. 1 Kgs 20:10; Isa 2:6). Although the root is common in Aramaic, the spelling with *sin* is peculiar to the Qumran scrolls; see 4Q201 1 iii 18; 4Q202 1 ii 20; 4Q531 1 5 and 4Q532 2 10. The *qal* participle here must mean "to be great, abundant" (see the LXX πολλή and the Syriac ܘܢܣܓܐ) as in Sir 31:30F, where it has the meaning "make it abound, multiply" (see also 39:16B//39:33B with the meaning "to provide," and in the negative Sir 42:7 [HM: לא הספיקו; HB: לא השפיקו] with the meaning "to not be sufficient, enough," "to not be capable, able"). אמיץ גבורות — "Mighty in deeds" (Lévi 1901, 112), or it can be understood as a superlative, "all-powerful, almighty"; see also the expression אמיץ כח in Isa 40:26 and Job 9:4. For the association of wisdom and power, see Job 9:4 and 12:13. {כל}ם — "Seeing them all," that is, all people, though the antecedent is not explicit, especially as we have the singular suffix in the following stich. Alternatively, read כל (see the palaeographic note), which seems more probable and is in line with HB and the Greek (though the Syriac could confirm the existence of the reading כלם and the lack of punctuation: ܡܛܠ ܕܚܙܐ ܚܝܠܗܘܢ, ܢܢܢ).

15:19 מעשיו — The antecedent of the pronominal suffix is certainly the person of v. 17 rather than God. והו — This rare spelling of the personal pronoun הוא is attested in the *Copper Scroll* (3Q15 X 10, XI 7 and in 1Q20 XX 29; cf. the feminine pronoun הי in 7:15A and the correction הוא in 14:9A). Cf. the spelling of the common personal pronoun in Old Aramaic (see Porten and Muraoka 1998, §5*j*, §11; Kottsieper 1990, 89–93) and occasionally in Nabataean (Cantineau 1932, 2:84–86). It should be noted that this type of spelling is occasionally found in rabbinic literature too, especially in some Genizah texts (see, for example, in Mekhilta de Rabbi Simeʻon ben Yoḥaï 12:12). על — This word has cancelation dots.

15:20 For the textual history of this verse, see Di Lella (1966, 129–34) and van Peursen (2001, 68–72). החלים — For חלם in the *hiphil* with the meaning "to restore, reinforce, strengthen," see Isa 38:16; 4Q222 1 2 (Job 25:10) and 4Q470 3 4. מרחם — For מרחם as a designation for God, see Isa 49:10; 54:10 and Ps 116:5. Concerning the use of the participle in this context, see van Peursen (2001, 72; 2004, 222–3). ועל מגלה סוד: — Cf. Prov 11:13 and 20:19.

16:1 נערי שוא — The term שוא occurs in 15:7A,B (מתי שוא) and in 15:20A,B (עושה שוא). If it designates "emptiness, vanity," then it can have a connotation closely linked to the notion of sin. See, for example, Isa 5:18 (par. עון and חטאה) and its use at Qumran in the phrases סוד שוא (1QHa X 24 par.) and עדת שוא (עדת בליעל) 1QHa XIV 8 par. סוד חמס). This link is supported by the synonymous parallelism of נערי שוא "children of nothing" with בני עולה "children of iniquity." בני עולה — An expression that usually does not refer to actual children, but to people of low moral character (cf. 2 Sam 3:34; 2 Sam 7:10 [par. 1 Chr 17:9]; Ps 89:23; 1QHa XIII 10; 4Q174 1–2 i 1; 4Q418 69 ii 8; 4Q511 1 8).

16:2 תבעבם — The verb בוע (either תָּבַע [cf. יָנַע in 2 Kgs 23:18] or תָּבַע) is here followed by the *bet* preposition. This verb is more common in Aramaic (cf. 4Q196 [4QpapToba ar] 18 2: ובועי בבנ̇[י קשיטיא] "and rejoice in the righteous sons" [cf. Tob 13:15: ἀγαλλίασαι ἐπὶ τοῖς υἱοῖς τῶν δικαίων] and Tg. Isa. 41:16 [trans. of גלל]), but it also occurs in the *hithpalpel* in Sir 14:4A. אתם — The prepositional phrase "with them" expresses possession (see, e.g., BDB 3.a).

16:3 For the complex textual history of this verse, see Di Lella (1966, 134–42) and van Peursen (2001, 73–79). The text has certainly undergone several alterations and received quite a few explanatory glosses.

16:3a-c בעקבותם — Cf. Deut 28:66 and Job 24:22. אֿתאמן בחייהם — The reading is complex, as evidenced by the uncertainty in the versions and the doublet in HB. The term could be understood as "ruse, trick," as in

18 Abondante est la sagesse de YYY, puissant en œuvres et voyant tout.	18 Bountiful is the wisdom of YYY, mighty in deeds and seeing everything.
19 Les yeux de Dieu voient ses œuvres et lui connaît toute l'œuvre de l'être humain.	19 The eyes of God see his works and he recognizes every human work.
20 Il n'a ordonné à personne de pécher et il n'a pas rétabli ceux qui mentent. Il n'a pas pitié de celui qui agit vainement ni de celui qui révèle un secret.	20 He did not command humanity to sin, and he does not sustain those who lie. He has no mercy on those who act falsely nor on those who reveal a secret.

Chapitre 16 / Chapter 16

1 Ne désire pas la beauté de jeunes frivoles
et ne te réjouis pas de fils iniques.

2 Et même s'ils sont féconds, ne te réjouis pas d'eux,
s'il n'y a pas en eux la crainte de YYY.

3a Ne crois pas en leur vie,

3c et ne te fie pas à leurs descendants,

3d car ils n'auront pas une fin heureuse.

3e Car mieux vaut un (seul fils) qui fait la volonté (de Dieu) que mille,

3g et mourir sans enfant que celui qui a des fils nombreux (faisant) l'iniquité

3h et une descendance arrogante.

4 Par un seul sans enfant, craignant YYY, une ville se peuple
et par une famille de traîtres, elle est dévastée.

1 Do not desire the beauty of worthless young
nor rejoice in unjust children.

2 And even if they are fruitful, do not delight in them
if they do not fear YYY.

3a Do not trust in their life

3c and do not be confident in their descendants,

3d for they will not have a happy ending.

3e For one (child) who does the will (of God) is better than a thousand

3g and (better) to die childless than be one who has many children (behaving) iniquitously

3h (than to have) arrogant offspring.

4 From one childless person, fearing YYY, a city is peopled
and by a family of traitors, it is devastated.

10:16ᴬ (see the note), rather than "tracks, footsteps" (Marböck 2010, 199): "do not have confidence in their tricks." However, most commentators (Smend 1906b, 19; Peters 1902, 88; Lévi 1901, 114; Segal 1958, 98–99; Rüger 1970, 82–83) understand it as a synonym for אחרית, which appears in the following stich. Such a semantic development of עקב seems to be attested in antiquity, as in Tg. Onq., which renders עקב in Gen 3:15 with סופא "the end" (which usually translates the Hebrew אחרית). "The end" is also the meaning that Rashi gives the term עְקָבוֹת in Ps 89:52 (see also m. Soṭah 9:15; b. Soṭah 49b). This meaning is also attested in Aramaic and in Syriac. Assuming a metaphorical development for עקב like that of אחרית, the sentence could then be understood: "do not have faith in/trust their descendants (בעקבותם), for they will not have happy descendants (אחרית)." Greek and Syriac translations provide little assistance. The Syriac ends this stich with words that correspond with the end of the following stich, and so does not reflect a translation of עקב. Greek manuscripts attest different phrases here: πλῆθος αὐτῶν "their number," which could render חיליהם "their strength, possessions, fortunes" (cf. Ps 49:7) in Hᴮ (or be a contamination of 16:1ᴸˣˣ, so Rüger [1970, 82–83]), and τόπον αὐτῶν (MS B 46 in Ziegler), which could explain עקבה "tracks, footsteps" (see Sir 10:16ᴬ where עקבת גוים is rendered in Greek with χώρας ἐθνῶν), and κόπον αὐτῶν (679 Latin labores) "their labor," which can be explained as an alteration of τόπον.

16:3d According to Di Lella (1966, 138–9), this stich is a retroversion of the Syriac itself based on a reading of Gr II attested in certain witnesses (Sᶜ, Chrysostom): χρείσσων γὰρ εἷς δίκαιος ποιῶν θέλημα κυρίου ἢ μύριοι παράνομοι "Better one righteous person who does the will of God than ten thousand lawless ones." For the meaning, compare with Aḥiqar (TAD C.1.1.90: "In an abundance of sons let not your heart rejoice and in their fewness [do not mourn]," trans. Porten – Yardeni, 1993).

16:3gh ממי שהיו לו בנים רבים עולה — This second element of the comparison forms a doublet with the syntagm מאחרית זדון at the end of the verse and literally corresponds to the Syriac ܡܢ ܗܘ ܕܗܘܘ ܠܗ ܒܢܝܐ ܕܥܘܠܐ. This element is likely an explanatory gloss. Yet, it remains unclear whether it is a retroversion of the Syriac (Di Lella) or whether the Syriac actually translates a Hebrew witness that already had this addition. ממי שהיו — The construction מי ש (and its analog מה ש) which could be Aramaic in origin (see the bibliography in van Peursen 2004, 316, n. 74), occurs in Sir 3:22ᴬ (מה ש) Sir 30:19ᴮᵐᵍ; in Qohelet (מה ש 7 times, see for example, Qoh 1:19) and in CD XX 4. בנים רבים עוֹלָה — The reading in Hᴬ is more difficult than that in Hᴮ and should imply an implicit verb (i.e. עוֹשִׂים) or, as proposed by van Peursen could be explained as an aposition: "many wicked sons (many sons, wickedness)" (cf. Prov 22:21 אֲמָרִים אֱמֶת; van Peursen [2001, 77–78]). ומאחרית — The term אחרית must have the meaning "progeny, descendants" here (like the term עקב in 3b). For this meaning, see Ps 109:13 (MT אַחֲרִיתוֹ, LXX τὰ τέκνα αὐτοῦ); Sir 11:28ᴬ (Hᴬ ובאחריתו, LXX ἐν τέέ κνοις αὐτοῦ) and Sir 32:21ᴱᶠ (Hᴱᶠ ובאחריתך, LXX ἀπὸ τῶν τέκνων σου).

16:4 Cf. R. Nissim, *Sefer Ma'asiyyot*, Varsovie 1886, 12: וכן אמר בראש בן סירא באחד; *Ḥibbûr Yaphê*, ed. Obermann 1933, 13: אחד תתישב עיר מבין תתישב. This verse in Ben Sira may allude to Abraham, who was childless with Sarah, and his intercession for the city of Sodom (Gen 18:16–33). ערירי — This word is absent in the Greek and the Syriac. All commentators agree that it is a vertical dittography (cf. ומות ערירי in 3e). Yet, as it stands the text reinforces the allusion to Abraham. וממשפחת בגדים — "A family of treacherous traitors" or "the families of treacherous traitors" in defective orthography (see Hᴮ).

5 B	רבות כאלה ראתה עיני	וְעַצֻמוֹת כאלה שמעה ⁹אזני:
6 B	בעדת רשעים יוקדת אש	ובגוי חנף נצתה חמרה:
7 B	¹⁰אשר לא נשא לנסיכי קדם	המורים עולם בגבורתם:
8	ולא ¹¹עׂ חמל על מגורי לוט	המתעברים בגאותם:
9	ולא חמל ¹²על גוי חרם	הנורשים בעונם:
10	כן שש מאות אף רגלי ⸺	¹³הנאספים בזדון לבם:
11	ואף כי אחד מקשה ערף	תמה זה אם ¹⁴ינקה:
	כי רחמים ואף עמו	
12	כרב רחמיו כן תוכחתו	ונושא וסולח· ועל רשעים ¹⁵יגיה רגזו:
לא	¹⁶אׂ ימלט בגזל עול	13 איש כמפעליו ישפט:
	ולא ישבית תאות צדיק לעולם:	
14	כל ¹⁷העושה צדקה יש לו שכר	וכל אדם כמעשיו יצא לפניו:
15	¹⁸יׂי הקשה את לב פרעה	אשר לא ידעו:
	שמעשיו ⸺ ¹⁹מגולין תחת השמים	

· Bmg בגבורֹ[ם ? | A B בגבורתם: B > | A עולם · A | B המורדים | A המורים 16:7 · B רשפה להבה | A Bmg יוקדת אש 16:6 · B ועצומות | A ועצמות 16:5

L. 11 [16:8] עׂ — It is difficult to know whether this is a sign of the scribe (see the reverse sign in T-S 12.863 recto, l. 25, Sir 15:14) or an *ayin* with a cancelation dot ע׳. מגורי — The *vav* is not vocalized with a *holem*; the dot above the *vav* is simply a stain on the manuscript (contra Segal 1958, 99; Ben-Ḥayyim 1973, 23).

L. 12 [16:9] הנורשים — The *resh* is written as a *dalet* (for the confusion between *resh* and *dalet* in the writing of this scribe, see the complete introduction).

L. 13 [16:11] אחד — Smend (1906b, 19), Peters (1902, 361), Lévi (1901, 116) and Vattioni (1968, 81) read אחֹד, while Beentjes (1997, 45) and Ben-Ḥayyim (1973, 23) read אחר. The meaning requires אחד. The letter is clearly written with a rounded shoulder, but the scribe sometimes wrote the two letters identically (see the complete introduction).

16:5 שָׁמַעְתִּי כְּאֵלֶּה — רבות כאלה ראתה עיני — Compare with Job 16:2: רַבּוֹת "I have heard many such things." וְעַצֻמוֹת — A feminine form of עָצוּם (cf. Isa 41:21). עצום is very often used in parallel with רב, "powerful," and can also express a large number (cf. Num 32:1, LXX πλῆθος). **16:6** This verse may be an allusion to Num 11:1–3 and Num 16 (Segal 1958, 99; Skehan and Di Lella 1987, 273; see also Sir 45:18–19ᴮ, Ps 106:18), but it could also be a general statement, exemplified in the following verses (Smend 1906b, 146; van Peursen 2004, 381; Gilbert 2002, 122). אׁש יוקדת — Cf. Isa 65:5 — בעדת רשעים — Cf. 1QM XV 9. בגוי חנף — Cf. Isa 10:6. נצתה חמה — Cf. 2 Kgs 22:17. יָקְדַת כָּל־הַיּוֹם **16:7** For the allusion to Gen 6:1–4, see Goff (2010, 645–655). Gilbert (2005, 92) prefers connecting this verse to the revolt of the Canaanite kings against Chedorlaomer in Gen 14 (cf. Gn 14,4 [מרדו = Hᴮ]; 3 Macc 2:4–5; Jub 20:5). אשר — The particle could have an explanatory function here: "thus, in this way," (see also Sir 45:23ᴮ; van Peursen 2004, 381). נשא ל — For the construction with the meaning "forgive," see for example, Gen 18:26; Num 14:19; Hos 1:6; etc. לנסיכי קדם — The term נסיך with the meaning "prince" is only attested in Josh 13:21; Ps 83:12; Ezek 32:30 and Mic 5:4, as well as in Aramaic (cf. DNWSI 735). The term fell into disuse, but reappears in *piyyutim* of the seventh century. For an analysis of this term and its use in relation to Gen 6:1–4, see the study by Goff (2010, 647–651). **16:8** Cf. Gen 18–19; 3 Macc 2:4–5; Jub 20:5 and Ezek 16:49–50. מגורי — The word refers to a land of domicile, literally "the land of Lot." The phrase is elliptical: "the inhabitants of the land of Lot" (thus the Syriac), "the countrymen of Lot," that is, the inhabitants or citizens of Sodom. המתעברים — The *hithpael* of עבר is rare in Biblical Hebrew and has a rather wide spectrum of meanings in Ben Sira (see 5:7ᴬ; 13:7ᴬ and the respective notes). Here, it must have a similar meaning to Prov 14:16 (as opposed to ירא), "who were arrogant in their pride" (cf. Ezek 16:49). See also, the use of the substantive עברה in conjunction with גאוה in Isa 16:6 (thus Segal 1958, 99).

16:9 גוי חרם — This is an allusion to the Canaanites, cf. Num 21:2–3 and Deut 2:34. The expression reoccurs in Sir 46:6ᴮ (see Josh 16:17, Isa 34:5). הנורשים — Cf. Smend (1906a, 147). Most have read הנדרשים, but the root ירש is not attested. It is not neccessary to conjecture a metathesis and read הנדושים, a *niphal* of דוש, "to be trampled on, crushed, destroyed" as has been proposed.

16:10 This verse evokes the rebellion of the Israelites in the desert with God punishing both the Israelites and the Gentiles; cf. Exod 12:37; Num 11:21, 14:27–38; Deut 2:14 and Sir 46:8ᴮ. הנאספים — For the use of the *niphal* of אסף as a metaphorical representation of death, see Sir 8:7ᴬ (and the note there); 40:28ᴮ; 44:14ᴮ·ᴹ; CD XIX 35; XX 14 and 1QHᵃ XIV 10–11.

16:11ab ואף כי — For the use of כי to introduce a conditional, see 16:2ᴮ and the note. מקשה ערף — This is a common expression (cf. especially Prov 29:1 as well as Deut 10:16; 2 Kgs 17:14; Jer 7:26, etc.) תמה — It could be a substantive (see Sir 36:6ᴮᵐᵍ; 43:25ᴮ; 48:14ᴮ), "it would be an astonishing thing if he went unpunished," or as Segal (1958, 100) proposes, an imperative, תְּמַהּ, "be astonished if he goes unpunished" (see b. Pes. 28a).

16:11d This second stich is particularly long, and it is legitimate to assume that the scribe harmonized the text with Sir 5:6ᴬ. יגיה — The verb נגה (in *hiphil*, "to shed light, illuminate") is generally used in pos-

5 Mon œil a vu beaucoup de choses comme celles-ci
   et mon oreille a entendu quantité de choses comme celles-ci.
6 Dans l'assemblée des méchants brûle un feu
   et contre une nation impie s'est embrasée une fureur.
7 C'est ainsi qu'il n'a pas pardonné aux princes d'autrefois,
   qui se rebellèrent contre le monde par leur puissance.
8 Il n'a pas eu pitié des lieux où Lot a séjourné
   qui furent arrogants par leur orgueil.
9 Et il n'a pas eu pitié des peuples voués à l'anathème
   qui furent dépossédés à cause de leurs péchés.
10 Ainsi en fut-il des six cent mille hommes de pied
   qui furent ensevelis à cause de l'arrogance de leur cœur.
11 Même si un seul raidit sa nuque,
   ce serait étonnant s'il reste impuni.
   Car miséricorde et colère sont avec lui,
   il acquitte et pardonne, mais sur les méchants il fait briller sa colère.
12 Aussi grande que sa pitié est son châtiment,
   il juge chacun selon ses œuvres.
13 Il ne laissera pas s'échapper l'impie avec le butin
   et il ne mettra jamais fin au désir du juste.
14 Quiconque pratique la justice, a une récompense
   et toute personne, selon ses œuvres, paraîtra devant lui.
15 YYY a endurci le cœur de Pharaon
   parce qu'il ~~ne~~ ne l'a pas connu,
   alors que ses œuvres sont dévoilées sous le ciel.

5 My eye has seen many similar things,
   and my ear has heard numerous similar things.
6 In the assembly of the wicked a fire burns,
   and against an impious nation wrath is kindled.
7 For he did not forgive the ancient princes,
   who rebelled against the world in their power;
8 He had no pity on the places Lot sojourned
   which acted arrogantly in their pride;
9 and did not have pity on a people dedicated to the ban
   who were dispossessed because of their sins.
10 Thus, six hundred thousand footmen
   were gathered (to the tomb) because of the arrogance of their hearts.
11 Even if there were just one who stiffens their neck,
   it would be astonishing if they remained unpunished.
   For mercy and anger are with him,
   he acquits and forgives, but on the wicked he makes his anger shine.
12 As great as his pity is his punishment,
   he judges each person according to their works.
13 He will not let the ungodly escape with the spoil
   and he will never end the desire of the righteous.
14 There is reward for the one who practices righteousness
   and everyone according to their works shall appear before him.
15 YYY hardened the heart of Pharaoh
   because he did ~~not~~ not know him,
   that his works might be revealed under the heavens.

---

itive contexts (see 4Q416 2 iii 10: כִּי יגיה אל ת[אר]הו בכול דרכיכה "For God will make his glory shine in all your ways"). Conceivably, the verb is used here ironically, "to shine," not the light, the grace or the splendor, but anger. Alternatively, we might infer a spelling error for יגיה (*qal* or *hiphil* of גיה), "his rage bursts forth over the wicked" (cf. the Greek, which implies *hiphil* "he makes his rage burst forth" [cf. Aramaic גוח in Dan 7:2] and note the confusion of *he* and *khet* in הורם [Sir 10:25ᴬ] for חורים [in Hᴮ]; and similar mistakes in Hᴮ: מהם [Sir 43:4ᴮ] for מחם* and כהניך [Sir 49:14ᴮ] for כחנוך*). Yet another possibility is to correct the verb to יניח as in 5:6ᶜ (in Hᴬ ינוח), "but upon the wicked he will lay his wrath."

16:12 תוכחתו — "Chastisement, punishment," cf. Ps 149:7; 1QHᵃ XV 32 and XVII 24.

16:13 אל ימלט — The jussive (with אל) has been corrected in the margin to the indicative (with לא). The verb מלט could be a *niphal*, in which case עול is the subject, "the godless will not escape with the spoil" (thus the Greek), or a *piel* with the meaning "let escape" (2 Kgs 23:18), in which case God is the subject, "he will not let the godless escape with the spoil" (thus the Syriac). This second option seems preferable in light of the following stich where God is also the subject of ישבית. גזל — The noun usually refers to the act of "theft," rather than to what is gained from theft ("the loot"). ישבית — God will ensure that the desire of the just never ceases (cf. Isa 13:11; 21:2), or as Mopsik (2003, 163) proposes, that their desire is not frustrated (cf. Ruth 4:14).

16:14 יצא לפניו — This verse should be understood as "each one will appear before God according to his works," cf. Ps 17:2. The Greek and the Syriac have read ימצא.

16:15–16 These two verses are attested in Gr II and the Syriac, but are missing in Gr I and the *Vetus Latina*. Verse 15 continues the list of illustrious sinners mentioned in the Pentateuch, "hardening" (קשה) recalls verse 11. For the content of the verse, see 3 Macc 2:6: "You tested the insolent Pharaoh, who enslaved Your holy people Israel with many different punishments and You made known to him Your mighty power" (see Philonenko 1986, 319).

16:15 הקשה — Cf. Exod 7:3. אשר — The word can be used as a relative particle or conjunction indicating cause ("because he did not know him," cf. Smend) or purpose/result (cf. the Greek and the Syriac: "God hardened Pharoah's heart so that he would not know him"). For a theological interpretation of this modality of אשר, and of -ש in the following stich, see Philonenko (1986, 318–19). שמעשיו — The meaning of this second relative clause is not entirely clear. The -ש could introduce a second object of ידע ("he did not acknowledge that his works are manifest"; for the construction ידע + object followed by an object relative clause, cf. Jer 9:23 הַשְׂכֵּל וְיָדֹעַ אוֹתִי כִּי אֲנִי יְהוָה עֹשֶׂה חֶסֶד, thus van Peursen 2004, 303). It is also possible that -ש has a nuance of causal contrast, a concessive clause, "he did not know him although his works." Finally, the possibility of a final nuance is not excluded, "He has hardened … in order that his works might be revealed" (cf. Joüon §168*f*).

16 רחמיו: יראו לכל בריותיו	ואורו [20]ושבחו חלק לבני אדם:
17 אל תאמר מא׳ נסתרתי	ובמרום מי [21]יזכרני:
בעם כבד לא אודע	ומה נפשי בקצות רוחות כל בני [22]אדם:
18 הן השמים ושמי השמים	ותהום וארץ:
ברדתו [23]עליהם עָמוֹדִים	בפקדו וכרגשו:
19 אף קצבי הרים ויסודי [24]תבל	בהביטו איהם רעש ירעשו:
20 גם עלי לא ישים לב	[25]ובדרכי מי יתבונן:
21 אם חטאתי לא תראני עין	או אם אכזב [26]בכל סתר מי ידע:
22 מֶה מעשה צדקי מי יגידנו	ותקות מה כי אצ{י}וק [27]חוק:
23 חסרי לב יבינו אה	וגב׳ר פֹּתֶה יחשב זאת:
24 שמעו [28]אלי וקחו שכלי	ועל דברי שימו לב:
25 אביעה במשקל רוחי	[29]ובהצנע אחוה דעי׳
26 כברא א׳ מעשיו מראש	[על חייהם]

L. 26 [16:22] מֶה — The interrogative is crossed out by the scribe (thus Schechter and Taylor 1899, 10; Smend 1906a, 20; Peters 1902, 94; and Ben-Ḥayyim 1973, 23; contra Vattioni 1968, 83; and Beentjes 1997, 46). צדקִי — A small trace of a letter after the *qoph* could be read as a *yod* (Smend [1906b, 20] and Ben-Ḥayyim [1973, 23] have this reading, which is not transcribed by Schechter and Taylor [1899, 10], Peters [1902, 362], Lévi [1901, 2:120], Vattioni [1968, 83] or Beentjes [1997, 46]). אצ{י}וק — The scribe seems to have written first a *yod* and then extended it into a *vav*.

L. 27 [16:23] חסרי — With Smend (1906a, 20), Peters (1902, 362), Lévi (1901, 2:120) and Vattioni (1968, 83) (contra Ben-Ḥayyim [1973, 23] and Beentjes [1997, 46], who have חסדי). For the confusion between *resh* and *dalet*, see the complete introduction. וגבור — The second *vav* is written above the line, as observed by Smend (1906a, 20), Lévi (1901, 2:120), Ben-Ḥayyim (1973, 23) and Beentjes (1997, 46) and is unlikely to be a trace of the end of the *qoph* of צדק from l. 26 (cf. Peters [1902, 362] and Vattioni [1968, 83]: וגבר).

16:16 רחמיו: — The *Sof Passuq* is misplaced in the manuscript. בריה — "Creation, creature," see 4Q216 5,1.9; 11QT XXIX 9 (4Q529 1 11 in Aramaic) and בריאה in Num 16:30 and at Qumran (see García-Martínez 2005, 49–70 and idem, art. ברא, בריאה in ThWQ, 502–506). ושבחו — "His praise," cf. Sir 44:1ᴮ and 51:30ᴮ. The consideration is therefore radically positive, but perhaps the text initially carried a more antinomic vision that has been preserved in the Greek and the Syriac, which read ואורו וחשכו "He apportioned his light and darkness" (cf. 1QS III–IV; Mopsik [2003, 164] refers to the Midr. Tehilim 27: אמר רבי הושעיא דו פרצופין היו בו אור לישראל וחשך למצרים "Rabbi Hoshaya said: 'There are two faces: light for Israel and darkness for the Egyptians'"). חלק — Cf. Job 39:7, and especially, from a slightly different perspective, Sir 39:25ᴮ. The verb is closely linked to the semantic field of creation (see the translation with κτίζω in Sir 39:25, 40:1, 44,2). For the use of the verb at Qumran, see Bremer, art. חלק II, ThWQ, 996–998.

16:17 This verse is cited by Saadia with few variations: אל תאמר מאל נסתרתי ובמרום מי יזכרני בעם כבד לא אודע מי נפשי בקצות רוחות (ed. Harkavy 1891, 178, l. 12–13). בעם כבד — A similar expression occurs in Num 20:20. בקצות — For the partitive meaning of קצה, see 1 Kgs 12:31; 13:33 (מִקְצוֹת הָעָם); Judg 18:2 and 2 Kgs 17:32 (see the Syriac ܟܢܫܐ). רוחות כל בני אדם — Compare with the formula in Num 27:16: אלהי הרוחת לכל־בשר "The God of the spirits of all flesh," see also at Qumran, for example, the expression רוחי גורלו כל בני אדם (1QS III 24). is missing in the Greek and in the citation from Saadia.

16:18 The syntax of this verse raises a number of difficulties and the text has certainly undergone several alterations (see van Peursen 2004, 336–37). The verse could be related to T. Levi 3:9–10: "So when the Lord looks upon us we all tremble. Even the heavens and earth and the abysses tremble before the presence of his majesty. But the sons of men, being insensitive to these matters, keep sinning and provoking the anger of the Most High." (trans. *OTP* 1:789). See also 4Q416 1 11–133; 1QHᵃ XI 33–35; As. Mos. 10:4 and Sib. Or. 3,675–681. השמים ושמי השמים — The expression is based on Deut 10:14, see also 2 Kgs 8:27 (par. 2 Chr 6:18); 2 Chr 2:5; Neh 9:6; 4Q372 14 2 and [4Q511 30 2]. עָמוֹדִים — As noted by Fassberg, the consonantal text reflects a *qāṭōl* noun patern (*'amodim*), "they stand up." This rare patern in Biblical Hebrew became frequent in Tannaitic Hebrew (Fassberg 1997, 65). The consonantal text, however, has been vocalized according to the common *qōṭēl* participial pattern, reflecting עֹמְדִים. Most commentators follow Perles (1897, 57) in correcting the text to מוֹעֲדִים "When he comes down to them, they tremble," but the Syriac has read עָמְדִים (ܩܝܡܝܢ). The Greek, which only has two stichs, is hardly enlightening; σαλευθήσονται "they will be shaken" can just as easily come from stich *c* (*Vorlage*: בפקדו ירגשו, thus Smend 1906b, 20 and 1906b, 150; Lévi 1901, 118; Segal 1958, 101) as from stich *b* if one corrects to מוֹעֲדִים (σαλεύειν translates מעד in 2 Sam 22:37 and Ps 26:1, thus Schechter and Taylor 1899, 53; Peters 1913, 138; Rüger 1970, 20). For a similar confusion between עמד and מעד, see Ezek 29:7 (MT וְהַעֲמַדְתָּ vs LXX καὶ συνέκλασας, Syriac ܘܐܪܥܠܬ, Vulgate et *dissolvisti*, see Perles 1897, 57; Rüger, 1970, 26). וכרגשו — The use of the preposition -כ before an infinitive to introduce a temporal clause tends to disappear in late Hebrew and at Qumran. For its use in Ben Sira see 16:26ᴬ; 38:23ᴮᵐᵍ and perhaps 46:5ᴮ. This construction is surprising here ("when he visits [them] and when they tremble"), as one would expect a *yiqtol*, ירגשו, in parallel with the preceding stich ("when he visits [them], they tremble"). Van Peursen (2004, 336; cf. Smend 1906a, 150) proposes understanding the verb רגש in the sense of "perceive, feel" as attested in Aramaic, Syriac and Rabbinic Hebrew: "when he visits (them) and perceives (them)."

16:19 קצבי הרים — Cf. Jonah 2:7 (לְקִצְבֵי הָרִים).

16:20 ישים לב — Cf. 6:32ᴬ and the note. ובדרכי מי יתבונן — This stich parallels 16:17ᴬ.

16:21 מי יודע — For the use of the participle in interrogative clauses, see van Peursen (2004, 289 n. 14); GKC §151. מי יודע appears mainly

16 Ses miséricordes sont visibles pour toutes ses créatures ;
    il a donné en partage sa lumière et sa louange à l'humanité.
17 Ne dis pas : « Je suis caché de Dieu
    et d'en haut qui se souviendrait de moi ?
    Dans la foule épaisse, je ne serai pas connu
    et qu'est-ce que ma vie parmi les esprits de tous les êtres humains ? »
18 Voici, les cieux et les cieux des cieux
    et l'abîme et la terre,
    quand il descend au-dessus d'eux, ils se tiennent,
    quand il les visite et qu'ils sont ébranlés.
19 Même, les racines des montagnes et les fondements du monde,
    quand il les regarde, sont complètement ébranlés.
20 « Il ne fait pas non plus attention à moi
    et à mes voies qui y sera attentif ?
21 Si je pèche, nul œil ne me verra,
    ou si je mens en grand secret, qui le saura ?
22 ~~Quelle~~ Mon œuvre de justice qui (la) lui racontera ?
    et quel espoir si j'établis le commandement ? »
23 Les insensés considèrent ces choses,
    et le naïf pense cela.
24 Écoutez-moi et saisissez mon instruction
    et à mes paroles soyez attentifs.
25 Je répandrai avec mesure mon esprit
    et avec humilité j'exposerai ma connaissance.
26 Lorsque Dieu créa ses œuvres au commencement,
    sur leurs vies [il a distribué leur part].

16 His mercy appears to all his creatures;
    he apportioned his light and his praise to humankind.
17 Do not say, "I am hidden from God,
    and in the heights who will remember me?
    In a dense crowd, I will not be known,
    and what is my soul among the spirits of all humankind?
18 Behold, the heavens and the heaven of heavens,
    and the abyss and the earth,
    when he comes down to them, they stand,
    when he visits (them) and when they tremble.
19 Even the roots of the mountains and the foundations of the world,
    when he looks at them, they are completely shaken.
20 So he is not paying attention to me
    and who will consider my ways?
21 If I sin, no eye will see me
    or if I tell lies in secret, who will know?
22 ~~What~~ My work of righteousness, who will recount (it) to him?
    and what hope is there if I establish the statute?"
23 Those who have no sense think these things
    and the person who is naive thinks this (way).
24 Listen to me and grasp my instruction
    and to my words be attentive.
25 I will pour out my spirit in measure
    and with humility declare my knowledge.
26 When God created his works from the beginning,
    on their lives [he set their share].

in late Hebrew and in rhetorical questions (2 Sam 12:22; Joel 2:14; Jonah 3:9; Ps 90:11; Prov 24:22; Qoh 2:19; 3:21; 6:12; 8:1; Esth 4:14).
16:22 For stich a, cf. 11QPsᵃ XXVIII (Ps 151A) 5-7. מעשה צדק֯י — As van Peursen (2004, 290) notes, the extraposition of the complement before the interrogative is possibly due to Aramaic influence (cf. Dan 3:33). אצוק — The use of יצק, usually "to pour, spread, throw," is surprising in this context. As in 15:16^(A,B) (see the note), the verb יצק here may be a biform of יצג with the meaning "to place, deposit, establish" either in the *hiphil* (אציק), or in the *qal* (אצוק). The sense "establish" seems to be found in Job 11:15 וְהָיִיתָ מֻצָק וְלֹא תִירָא "You will be firm and fearless" and (in the *qal*) in Job 41:16 לִבּוֹ יָצוּק כְּמוֹ־אָבֶן וְיָצוּק כְּפֶלַח תַּחְתִּית "His heart is firm (LXX: πέπηγεν; Tg.: מתייסד) as stone, solid (ἕστηκεν) as the bottom grindstone." The LXX repeatedly renders it with τίθημι or ἵστημι, two verbs often used in conjunction with terms like ἐντολή, νόμος or διαθήκη (see 2 Kgs 23:24; 2 Chr 35:19; 1 Macc 2:27; Neh 10:33). See Amos 5:15 for a similar construction with יצג and משפט. However, most correct the text either to אֶצּוֹר "if I keep the commandment" (cf. Ps 119:145, thus Bacher 1900, 280; Segal 1958, 102), to כי ירחק חוק (from the Greek μακρὰν γὰρ ἡ διαθήκη and in Mic 7:11), or to אֲקַוֶּה חוק "waiting for the end" (Ginzberg 1906, 623).
16:23 חסרי לב — Cf. 6:20ᴬ and the note. וגבור פותה — With the supralinear mater, the word reads more literally "the mighty one who is naïve," though without the mater it is more simply "a person (גֶּבֶר) who is naïve." פותה means "the fool, one who is naïve" (cf. Job 5:2; Qoh 7:11; Sir 8:17; 31:7; 42:8).

16:24–25 A characteristic introduction in wisdom discourse; cf. Prov 1:8; 4:1, 10, 20 and 22:17.
16:24 וקחו — For לקח in a cognitive sense, see 8:9ᴬ and the note.
16:25 אביעה במשקל רוחי — This formula is based on Prov 1:23: הִנֵּה אַבִּיעָה לָכֶם רוּחִי "Lo, I will pour out my spirit on you"). Ben Sira adopts the language of personified wisdom (cf. Sir 24:30–33; 50:27ᴮ). ובהצנע — For the use of the infinitive absolute (here, הַצְנֵעַ) in late Hebrew and at Qumran, see Qimron 1986, 47–48; van Peursen 2004, 278. The verb צנע occurs only once in the Bible, in Mic 6:8 (הַצְנֵעַ לֶכֶת "to walk humbly"; cf. Prov 11:2), four times in Ben Sira (31:22ᴮ; 32:3ᴮ; 42:8^(B,M)) and also at Qumran, in 4Q525 5 13 and 4Q424 1 6, and elsewhere (e.g., 1QS IV 5; V 4 [= VIII 2]) quoting the phrase from Mic. In Rabbinic Hebrew, the *hiphil* means "to restrain," hence perhaps here "with restraint." אחוה דעי — The phrase is based on a recurring formula in Elihu's speech in Job (e.g., Job 32:6, 10 and 17). חוה "to declare" is an Aramaism found in the Bible only in the Psalter (Ps 19:3) and Job (Job 15:17; 32:6, 10, 17; 36:2) as well as in Sir 42:19^(M,B). The noun דֵּעַ only occurs in Job 32:6, 10 and 17; 36:3 and 37:16, which also belong to Elihu's speeches.
16:26 כברא — For the use of -כ before an infinitive to introduce a temporal clause, see כרגשו in 16:18ᴬ and the note. על חייהם — The versions diverge at the beginning of this stich (the Greek has καὶ ἀπὸ ποιήσεως αὐτῶν "and from their creation," while the Syriac has ܒܪ̈ܝܬܗ "among his creatures"). Segal (1958, 102) follows the Greek (διέστειλεν μερίδας αὐτῶν), and restores the end of the stich as על חייהם [חלק חלקיהם].

1

²[ול]אֹ יֹרֹ[עבו ו]לֹ[א] יֹצֹ[מ]אֹוֹ [ו]לֹא [ייגעו ולא יעמלו ולא יחסרו גבורתם:]   27cde

³אֹיֹשׁ רֹעֹהֹוֹ [לא יאנסו וע]ד עֹוֹ[לם לא יעברו דברו: ואחר כן]   28

⁴הֹבֹיֹט יֹ[יי אל האר]ץֹ [ו]יֹבֹרֹכֹ[ה]   29

L. 1 The marks are hard to read. Reconstruction of the following lines is based on Karner 2015, though the digital photos available to us reveal some traces not seen by him.

L. 2 (16:27) [עבו]יֹרֹ אֹ[ול — The *aleph* is evidenced by only a small mark from its left leg. A following mark may be the *yod* and next to this, a horizontal bar bending into a vertical stroke looks most like a *resh*. [א]לֹ[מ]אֹ יֹצֹ — The *lamed* is evidenced only by its very slight outline, ascending out of the *lamed* of מגלה (Sir 15:20). The *yod* is only a dark splotch overlapping with the *mem* of מגלה; the *tsade* is clearer with its rounded descending stroke and part of its base line. The *aleph*'s diagonal line is clear and is followed by a vertical mark that is likely a *vav*. [ו]לא — The *lamed* and *aleph* are clearly visible.

L. 3 (16:28) אֹיֹשׁ — The *aleph* is evidenced by its diagonal and its right leg. A following mark may be a *yod*. The *sin/shin* is clear. רֹעֹהֹוֹ — The following mark is possibly the left edge of a *resh*'s horizontal stroke. Following this, the tops of two vertical strokes suggest an *ayin*. A horizontal stroke following these may be part of a *he*, which seems to be, in turn, followed by the downward stroke of a *vav*. וע[ד עו]לם — The offset traces of a *dalet* or *resh* are clearly visible, followed by clear traces of an *ayin*'s diagonal stroke. These are followed, in turn, by a mark that may be the top of a *vav*.

L. 4 (16:29) הֹבֹיֹט — The *he* is evidenced by traces of its right leg and a portion of its horizontal stroke. A portion of the upper right corner of the bet is followed by a mark that may be a *yod*. The *tet* is clear based on its distinctive arms. יֹ[יי — A mark following *tet* is possibly a *yod*. האר[ץֹ — Two offset marks may be the tips of a final *tsade*. [ו]יֹבֹרֹכֹ[ה — A faint offset mark may be the remnants of a *yod*. A following horizontal bar may reflect a *bet*. The *resh* is attested only by a vertical stroke and the *kaph* by the left-most tip of its upper horizontal stroke.

1

27 ²[Et ils n']o[nt n]i fa[im n]i s[oi]f,
[et ils ne se fatiguent pas, et ne peinent pas,
et ne manquent pas de force]
28 ³[Ils ne s'opressent pas] l'un l'autre,
[et pour l'ét]ernité de l'ét[ernité, jamais ils ne transgressent sa parole.]
29 [Après quoi] ⁴Y[YY] observe [la terr]e [et la] bénit.

1

27 ²[They] will n[ot] be hu[ngry o]r thi[r]sty.
[They will not grow weary or toil
and they do not lack strength]
28 ³[They do not harass] each other
[and ne]ver [transgress his word.
29 ⁴[Afterwards,] Y[YY] looks [to the lan]d [and] blesses [it.]

MANUSCRIPT B

SIR 10:19–11:10, 15:1–16:7, 30:11–33:3, 35:11–51:30

Chapter 10

T-S 12.871 recto		זרע נקלה עובר מצוה:	¹זרע נקלה מֹה זרע לאנוש	19cd A
		וירא אלהים נכבד ממנו:	²בין אחים ראשם נכבד	20 A
ביר		תפארתם יראֹת ייי:	³גר זר נכרי ורש	22 A
		ואין לכבד כל איש חמס:	⁴אין לבזות דל משכיל	23 A
		וא[ֹ]ן [גֹד]ול מירא אלהים:]	⁵שר שופט ומושל נכבדו	24 A
	[	[וֹעֹבֹדֹ]	⁶עבד משכיל חביב כנפש	25 A
	[	וגֹבֹ[ר]	⁶ᵃעֹבֹדֹ מֹשֹכֹיֹל חֹבֹיֹב כֹנֹפֹשֹ	
	[		⁷עבד משכיל חורים יעבדוהו	
	[	וגבר משֹ[כיל]	⁸עבד משכיל חביב כנפש	
	[	ואל תתכבֹ[ד]	⁹אל תתחכם לעשות חפֹצך	26 A	צֹרכך
	[	ממתכבד]	¹⁰טוב עובד ויותר הון	27 A
			11	
		ותן לה טעם כיֹצֹ[א] בה:]	¹²בני בענוה כבד נפשך	28 A
		ומי יכבד מֹ[קלה נפשו:]	¹³בני מרשיע נפשו מי יצדיקנו	29 A
		ויש איש עשיר נכבד בגֹלל] עשרו:]	¹⁴דל נכבד בגלל שכלו	30 A	[יש?]
		ונקלה בעשרו בעיניו איככה:	¹⁵הנכבד בעיניו בֹעשרו איככה	31 A
			¹⁶המתכבד בדלותו בעשרו מתכבד יתר והנקלה בעשרו נקלה יתר:	

Chapter 11

	וֹבֹיֹן נדֹ[יֹ]בֹ[יֹ]ם תוֹשׁיבנו:	¹⁷חכמת דל תשא ראשו	1 A

---

⁵A [רֹ]אֹת Bmg S | חזר A | זֹר B | 10:22 · (ὀφθαλμοῖς αὐτοῦ) A G בֹעֹ[יֹ]יו: B S | נֹ]ן B S נכבד ממנו: 10:20 · A > | B G S זרע נקלה מֹה זרע לאנוש 10:19c
B G · ייי B | אלהים A · 10:23 חמס B G ? (ἁμαρτωλόν) S ? (ܕܚܛܐ) | חֹ]ם A · 10:24 שופט ומושל B G | מושל ושופט A S · 10:25 עבד משכיל חביב B G | [...] כנפש A > | B [...] וגֹ]ר A · עבד משכיל חורים יעבדוהו וגֹ]ר [...] · עבד משכיל חביב כנפש וגבר משֹ[כיל...
B S | בני מרשיע A G · 10:30 דל B | יש דל A[Bmg?] · איש עשיר נכבד B G (πλούσιος) S (ܥܬܝܪܐ) | נכבד A · 10:31 נכבד B | הנכבד בעיניו A · ונקלה בעשרו A · בעיניו B | A חורים יעבדוהו וגֹ]ר B G S | וֹעבֹ]ר A · 10:26 לעשות B G | לעבֹ]ד A S · צֹרכך Bmg | חפצך A B · 10:28 ותן לה B G | ויתן לך A S · 10:29 וֹגֹבֹ]ר A · הורם A G מרשיע
A · תושבנו B | תשיבנו A · 11:1 יותר B | יתר A · ונקלה בעיניו B

L. 5 [10:24] וא[ֹן] [גֹד]ון — There is a trace of the diagonal of the *aleph* and its right arm. After the lacuna, there is a trace of a letter corresponding perfectly to *gimel*'s head, then a shoulder and leg of a *dalet* (thus Rüger 1970, 59).

L. 6a [10:25] This line has been inserted between lines 6 and 7.

L. 8 [10:25] The letters of this line have been marked with cancelation dots. משֹ] — There is a trace of the base and the start of the right arm of the *shin*.

L. 9 [10:26] צֹרכך — Only a meager oblique trace of the first letter, close to the leg of the following *resh*, remains. One should most likely read a *tsade*. Consequently, the reading [דֹ]רכך proposed by Vattioni (1968, 53) and Rüger (1970, 60) is impossible.

L. 11 [10:27] The scribe has left a blank line marked with a dot at its beginning.

L. 12 [10:28] כיֹצֹ[א — There is a trace of the angle and the base of a *tsade* and a very faint trace of its right arm.

L. 14 [10:30] דל — The term is preceded by a *circellus*, which implies a marginal correction. It is probable, though no longer visible, that יש was inscribed in the margin (see H^A).

L. 16 [10:31] The two stichs of line 16 are written without a space between them, in slightly smaller and cramped handwriting.

10:22 ביר — The marginal alternative assumes the *bet essentiae* (see, e.g., BDB I 7).

10:25 While H^B has four distichs here (*a*, *b*, c, *d*), H^A has only one. In H^B, the second (*b*), which is inserted interlinearly, repeats the first (*a*). The fourth (*d*), which is also the same as *a*, is canceled by dots. These three identical distichs (*a*, *b*, *d*) correspond to Sir 7:21^A,C,D, while the third distich (c) is similar (but not identical) to 10:25^A. The Greek and the Syriac have only one distich, which is equivalent to *a*, *b*, *d* in H^B.

עבד משכיל — See Sir 7:21^A,C,D and the note. חביב — One could read a noun/adjective ("An intelligent servant is a friend like your very self") or a *piel* imperative. The root appears only in writings outside the Bible (in Ben Sira, Qumran, and later Hebrew).

10:26 צֹרכך — The marginal alternative reflects an idiom found many times in Rabbinic Hebrew "to do what one wants" (see, e.g., y. Ber. 3:4, 6c). The Greek (τὸ ἔργον σου) and the Syriac (ܥܒܕܟ) seem to reflect עבדך as *Vorlage*.

Chapitre 10 / Chapter 10

19c Quelle race est méprisée ? La race humaine.
19d La race méprisée : celle qui transgresse le commandement.
20 Parmi des frères, leur chef est honoré,
mais celui qui craint Dieu est honoré plus que lui.
22 Immigré, apatride, étranger et pauvre,
leur majesté est la crainte (mg. idem) de YYY.
23 Il ne faut pas mépriser un pauvre intelligent,
ni glorifier toute personne violente
24 Prin[ce], juge et gouverneur sont honorés,
mais nul n'est [plus]gr[and que celui qui craint Dieu.]
25 Un serviteur intelligent aime-le comme toi-même
[ ]
Un serviteur intelligent aime-le comme toi-même
et une per[sonne...]
Un serviteur intelligent, les gens importants le serviront
et une per[sonne...]
~~Un serviteur intelligent aime le comme toi~~
~~et une personne intel[ligente...]~~
26 Ne deviens pas sage pour accomplir ton désir (mg. ce que tu veux)
et ne te glori[fie pas]
27 Mieux vaut celui qui travaille et qui a une abondante richesse
que celui qui se glorifie[ ]
28 Mon enfant, honore-toi (s.e. ton âme) avec humilité
et donne lui le bon sens selon[sa valeur]
29 Mon enfant, celui qui s'incrimine, qui le justifiera ?
Et qui glorifiera celui[qui se déshonore ?]
30 (mg. ? Il y a) Le pauvre honoré en raison de son intelligence
et il y a la personne riche honorée en raison[de sa richesse.]
31 Celui qui est honoré à ses propres yeux, combien plus le sera-t-il dans sa richesse !
Et celui qui est méprisé dans sa richesse, combien plus le sera-t-il à ses propres yeux !]
Celui qui est honoré dans son indigence, dans sa richesse, il sera d'autant plus honoré
et celui qui est méprisé dans sa richesse, dans son indigence, il sera d'autant plus méprisé.

Chapitre 11 / Chapter 11

1 La sagesse du pauvre relève sa tête
et le fait siéger parmi des pr[in]ces.

19c Which race is despised? The human race.
19d The despised race: the one that transgresses the commandment.
20 Among brothers, their leader is honored,
but the one who fears God is more honored than them.
22 Immigrant, stranger, foreigner and poor,
their glory is the fear of YYY (mg. idem).
23 The intelligent poor person should not be despised,
nor should any violent person be glorified.
24 Prince, judge and governor are honored.
but there i[s none] gr[eater than the one who fears God.]
25 Love an intelligent servant like your very self,
[ ]
An intelligent servant is a friend like your very self
and a pe[rson...]
An intelligent servant, the noteworthy serve them,
and a pe[rson...]
~~Love an intelligent servant like your very self~~
~~and an intel[ligent] man...~~
26 Do not act like a sage in order to do what you wish (mg. (to do) what you want),
and do not bo[ast].
27 Better the one who works and has abundant wealth
than the one who boasts[ ]
28 My child, honor yourself with humility
and apply discernment accordin[gly].
29 My child, whoever declares themself guilty, who will ever vindicate them?
and who will glorify the one who [disgraces themself?]
30 (mg. There is [?]) one (who) is poor and honored because of their intelligence
and there is the rich person who is honored because of [their wealth].
31 The one honored in their own eyes, how much more when wealthy?
and one disgraced when wealthy, in their own eyes, how much more (will they be disgraced).
The one honored when destitute, when wealthy will be greatly honored,
and the one disgraced when wealthy, when destitute will be greatly disgraced.

1 The wisdom of the poor will lift their head
and give them a seat among pr[in]ces.

	ואל תתעב אדם מעז{ו}ב[ר] במ֯ר֯אהו׃	¹⁸אל תהלל אדם בתוארו	2 ᴬ	[מבוע]ר̇
T-S 12.871 verso	וראש תנובות פריה׃	¹קטנה בעוף דבורה	3 ᴬ	
	וראש תנובות פר֯יה׃	²אלול בעוף דבורה		
	ואל תקלס במרירי יום	³במעוטף בגדים אל תתפאר	4 ᴬ	
	ואל תקלס במרירי יום׃	⁴בעוטה אזור אל תתהל		
	ונעלם מאנוש פעלו׃	⁵כי פלאות מע[ש̇]י י[י]		6e
	ובל על לב עטו צניף׃	⁶[רבים נדכאים ישבו] [על כסא	5 ᴬ	6f
	ושפלי לב יעטו צניף׃	על כסא]⁷		
	ונכבדים נתנו ביד זעירים׃	מ[א̇ד]⁸	6ab ᴬ	
וגם	נכ[לו מאד והושפלו] יחד ונכבדי֯ם̇ נתנו ביד׃	]⁹	6cd ᴬ	
	ובקהל טעם שפוט׃	[שאו֯ל]¹⁰	8ab ᴬ	
	ובתוך שיחה אל תדבר׃	¹¹[בטרם תשמע] אל תשיב	8cd ᴬ	
	בקר לפנים ואחר תזיף׃	¹²[בטרם תח]קו̇ר אל תסלף	7 ᴬ	
	ו̇בתוך שיחה אל תדבר׃	¹³[בני אל]תשיב דבר בטרם תשמע	8ef ᴬ	
[הלוא עטף]	ובריב זדים אל תקומם׃	¹⁴[בא]ן̇ עצה אל תתור	9 ᴬ	[?]
	ול[א ת]מלטנו אם תנוס׃	¹⁵אם תברח לא תדביק	10ab ᴬ	
		16		
	ואיך להרבות לוא ינקה׃	¹⁷בני למה תרבה עש̇ק̇	10cd ᴬ	עשקד

11:2 מבוע[ר] A | בתוארו B | תתעב B Bmg2 · 11:3 קטנה בעוף דבורה וראש תנובות פריה׃ B G (μικρά) | מכ[וע]ר̇ A Bmgı ⟩ מעז{ו}ב[ר] B | [ו]ע̇ר̇ Bmg2 · 11:3 קטנה בעוף דבורה וראש תנובות פריה׃ B G (μικρά) | דבורה A ⟩ דברה A · 11:4 במעוטף בגדים אל תתפאר A ⟩ B | בעוטה B · בעטה A · 11:5 מ̇[א̇]ד̇ A | אד̇ם B | מאנוש B | מעשי A ⟩ B | כסא A · ושפלי לב יעטו צניף׃ B ⟩ A · 11:6 מ̇[א̇ד ונכבדים נתנו ביד זעירים׃ A | ונכבדים B | והשפלו A | נכ[לו... B G ⟩ A · וגם B Bmg · 11:7 תח[A Bmg · 11:8a–d אל תשיב ובתוך שיחה אל תדבר׃ [...] ובקהל טעם שפוט׃ B | שאו̇ל... B ⟩ A · 11:8ef בטרם B | טרם A · קו̇ר B | ת̇ח̇קר̇ A · 11:9 עצה B | עצבה A · תתור B | תאחר A · ובריב B | ובריב A · 11:10ab מלטנו אם תנוס ול[א ת]מלטנו אם תברח לא תדביק B G ⟩ A · 11:10cd עשק B | עשקד A Bmg ·

L. 18 [11:2] מעז{ו}ב[ר] — Schirmann (1960, 130), Rüger (1970, 64), Beentjes (1997, 50) read מעזב. משבר, which is proposed by Di Lella (1964, 156) and Ben-Ḥayyim (1973, 14), is impossible for the *shin*, but the final *resh* is still attested by faint traces that may have been erased by the scribe.

L. 8 [11:6] [א̇]ד̇ — There are oblique traces of the *aleph* and the foot of the left leg.

L. 10 [11:8] [שאו̇ל — There is a trace of the base of the *shin*.

L. 12 [11:7] קו̇ר[— There are traces of the vertical of the *qoph*, then the vertical of the *vav*, and a part of the head and vertical of the *resh*.

L. 14–15 [11:9–10] There is a marginal alternative at the broken edge of the page, which is not mentioned by Di Lella (1964, 158) or Schirmann (1960, 130). It most likely concerns עצה (l. 14) or perhaps תדביק (l. 15), each of which has a *circellus* on it.

L. 16 [11:10] This line is left blank by the scribe, who drew two horizontal caesura lines.

L. 17 [11:10] תרבה̇ — Traces of each of the letters are visible where the fragment is broken, making it possible to restore the reading of Hᴬ with certitude. עש̇ק̇ — The reading [עושק̇] proposed by Di Lella (1964, 158) is impossible. After the *ayin*, the *sin/shin* is certain; there is a trace of the first arm and base, then the start of the second arm. Then most likely read a *qoph*; there are traces of the start of the head, the horizontal and its return into a diagonal line, while the downward stroke seems to have faded.

11:2 According to Rüger (1970, 64), the original form would be the one given in the left margin, אל תתעב אדם במראהו "do not abhor a person for their appearance," as also attested in the Greek. מעזב — This is the *pual* participle of עזב. The *piel/pual* is not attested in Biblical Hebrew or at Qumran, but it does occur in Rabbinic Hebrew with the meaning "to make abominable," and for the *pual* compare the only other attestation (according to Maagarim) "מה עזוב מה הוכארו" in Yannaï (אזירה), קדושתות לשבתות הפורענות והנחמה 27, ימים עם ימים). See also Gen. Rab. 45 מתכערת ומתעזבת.

11:3 אלול — The third letter looks like a *vav* but should be read as a *yod*.

11:4 Hᴮ has a doublet. The first stich (*a*) differs radically from that in Hᴬ, though it is broadly consistent with the Greek, whereas stichs *c* and *d* in Hᴮ and Hᴬ are generally in agreement with the Syriac. The second stich (*b*), although identical to the fourth (*d*), might initially be read with the opposite sense "do not praise..." (i.e., as synonymous to the first stich (*a*) since קלס can also mean "to praise" in Rabbinic Hebrew. Nevertheless, even in stich *b*, the sequence קלס + ב is more likely to have been understood as "to mock, laugh at" given the numerous examples of this construction (once in 1QpHab IV 1, 3 and numerous times in medieval Hebrew [see Maagarim]); by contrast, קלס "to praise" usually occurs with a direct object in Hebrew and Aramaic. במעוטף — The verb עטף with the meaning "to dress oneself" appears in Biblical Hebrew in Ps 65:14 and 73:6 (and perhaps in Job 23:9), but it is mostly used in Rabbinic Hebrew and in Aramaic. In the Targum, it usually translates the Hebrew עטה attested in stich *c* in Hᴮ and Hᴬ. Rüger (1970, 65) thinks that this reading is older, but it seems difficult to justify.

11:5 ושפלי לב — Cf. Isa 57:15. This reading, which is not supported by any of the versions, probably aims to shed light on the expression ובל על לב.

11:6 Hᴮ presents another doublet. The first two stichs seem to be corrected in the margin, in order to match the next two stichs. זעירים — This is an Aramaism (in Biblical Hebrew, see Job 36:2; Isa 28:10, 13), which is absent in Hᴬ, but may correspond to the Greek ἑτέρων (= זרים).

11:7 Verse 7 is incorrectly placed between the two doublets (second and third distichs) of verse 8.

11:8a [שאול — We assume that the word is an infinitive construct, given the /o/ theme vowel and not an imperative, as the context sug-

2   Ne loue pas une personne pour sa beauté
    et n'aie pas horreur d'une personne en fonction de son
    abominable (mg. 1. répugnante) apparence.
    (mg. 2. N'aie pas horreur d'une personne en fonction
    de son apparence.)
3   Petite parmi les volatiles est l'abeille,
    mais son fruit est le premier des produits.
    Insignifiante parmi les volatiles est l'abeille,
    mais son fruit est le premier parmi les produits.
4   En te drapant de vêtements, ne te magnifie pas
    et ne te moque pas de celui dont le jour est amer.
    Ne tourne pas en ridicule celui qui est vêtu d'un pagne
    et ne te moque pas de celui dont le jour est amer.
    [Car les œu]v[res de Y]YY [sont inaccessibles]
    et son action est cachée à l'être humain.
5   [Beaucoup d'affligés se sont assis]sur un trône
    et ceux dont nul ne se préoccupait ont ceint un diadème.
    [sur] un trône
    et les cœurs modestes ceindront un diadème.
6a [grande]ment
6b et les nobles ont été livrés au pouvoir des petits.
6c [   ] grandement [mép]risés
    et ont été abaissés ensemble
6d et les nobles (mg. et de même) ont été livrés.
6e (mg. [… grandem]ent et ont été abaissés ensemble
6f [   ]livrés.)
8a [   ]demande
8b et dans l'assemblée juge avec discernement.
8c [Avant que tu n'aies écouté,] ne réponds pas
8d et au beau milieu d'un discours, ne parle pas.
7   [Avant que tu n'aies ex]aminé, *ne déforme pas*,
    scrute d'abord et ensuite réprimande.
8e [Mon enfant, ne]réponds[pas] avant que tu n'aies écouté
8f et au beau milieu d'un discours, ne parle pas.
9   En l'absence de conseil, n'explore pas
    et dans le procès des présomptueux ne te lève pas.
    (mg. [Là où il n'y a p]as de peine [   ]
    [et dans] le procès [des]présomptu[eux   ])
10a Si tu fuis, tu n'atteindras pas
10b et tu n'y échapperas pas, si tu t'enfuis.

—   —

10c Mon enfant, pourquoi multiplies-tu une occupation
    (mg. ton occupation) ?
10d Celui qui s'empresse de (la) démultiplier ne sera pas
    sans reproches.

2   Do not praise a person for their beauty,
    and do not abhor a person who is abominable (mg. 1.
    repugnant) in their appearance.
    (mg. 2. Do not abhor a person for [their] ap[pear-
    ance…])
3   Small among flying creatures is the bee,
    but its fruit is first among (all) products.
    Least significant among flying creatures is the bee,
    but its fruit is first among (all) products.
4   Draping yourself in clothes, do not glorify yourself,
    and do not mock one whose day is bitter.
    Do not ridicule one who wears loincloth,
    and do not mock one whose day is bitter.
    [For the w]o[rks of Y]YY [are inscrutable]
    and his actions are hidden from humanity.
5   [Many are the afflicted who sat] on a throne,
    and they who no one thought of that wore the diadem.
    [on] a throne,
    and modest hearts will wear the diadem.
6a [gre]atly,
6b and the nobles were given over to the power of the
    small
6c [   ] thoroughly de[spised] and were
    brought down together
6d and as for the nobles, they were (mg. also) given over.
6e (mg. [great]ly were brought down together
6f [   ]delivered.)
8a [to] ask
8b and in the assembly, judge with discernment
8c [My child, before you have heard,] do not respond,
8d and do not speak in the midst of (another's) discourse.
7   [Before you] investigate, do not *distort*
    examine before and afterward you may rebuke.
8e [My child, do not] respond before you have heard
8f and do not speak in the midst of (another's) discourse.
9a Where there is no advice, do not explore
9b and in the dispute with the proud, do not take a stand.
    (mg. [Where there is no]t pain [   ]
    [and in] the dispute of the pro[ud   ]).
10a If you flee, you will not grasp it
10b and you will not escape it if you run away.

—   —

10c My child, why increase affairs (mg. your affairs)?
10d The one who hurries to multiply (them) will not be
    found innocent.

gests, since this would presume an /a/ theme vowel. Nevertheless an imperative is not excluded as the /o/ theme may be found in Jewish Palestinian Aramaic and in Rabbinic Hebrew (e.g., y. Ber. 4:1 [7c]).

11:8c [בטרם תשמע] אל תשיב — For the restoration, cf. Syriac.

11:10ab אם תברח (. . .) תנוס — Although it is possible to make sense of these verbs according to their meaning in Biblical Hebrew, the present context (especially the doublet of 10e–f) suggests that the verbs have the sense here of "pursue." Since this is unexpected, one wonders if they should be interpreted in a different manner, the first as a *hiphil* in the sense "defraud, steal" (as in Rabbinic Hebrew) and the second as the Aramaic verb אנס "rob." On the latter, see, e.g., תנוס "you take by force" in Tg. Ps.-J. Gen 31:31 and חָיְנוּס in Tg. Onq.

¹⁸בני אם לא תרוץ לא תגיע 10ef   ואם לא תבקש לא תמצא[:]

Chapter 15

	¹כי ירא יייי יעשה זאת	ותופש תורה ידריכנה:	T-S NS 38a recto
	²וקדמתהו כאם	וכאשת נעורים תקבלנו:	
	³והאכילתהו לחם שכל	ומי תבונה תשקנו:	ומתבואתה
	⁴ונשען עליה ולא ימוט	ובה יבטח ולא [י]בוש[:]	
בתוך {מ}רעהו	⁵וירוממתהו מרעהו	ובתוך ק[הל תפתח פיו:]	
ימצא	⁶ששון ושמחה תמצא	וש[ם עולם תורישנו:]	
	⁷לא ידריכוה מתי שוא	ואנש[י זדון לא יראוה:]	
	⁸רחוקה היא מליצים	ואנש[י כזב לא יזכרוה:]	
	⁹לא נאתה תהלה בפי רשע	כי לא מא[ל נחלקה לו:]	
	¹⁰בפי חכם תאמר תהלה	ומושל ב[ה ילמדנה:]	
	¹¹ᵃᵇ אל תאמר מאל פשעי	כ[י כל אשר שנא אמר לך] לא תעשה]	
	¹¹ᶜᵈ אל תאמר מה פעלתי	כי את אשר שנא לא אעש[ה:]	
	¹²פן תאמר היא התקילני	כי אין לי חפץ באנשי חמס:	צ[ורך]
רעה	¹³ותועבה שנא אלהים	ולא יאננה לו[יר]אי[ו:]	
[א]ל[ה]ים מבראשית	¹⁴הוא מראש ברא אדם וישיתהו ביד [חו]ת[פ]ו ויתנהו ביד יצרו:		
	¹⁵אם תחפץ תשמר מצוה	ואמונה לעשות רצון אל	ותבונה לע רצונו:
	¹⁶וֹאם תאמן בו	גם אתה תחיה:	
	¹⁷מוצק לפניך מים ואש	באשר תחפץ תשלח ידך:	

15:10 בפי B | בפה A · 15:6 תמצא B | ימצא A Bmg G S · 15:5 מרעהו B A G S | בתוך רעהו Bmg · 15:5 תבואה A | ומתבואתה Bmg | תבונה B Amg G S · 15:3 היא B | הוא A G S · 15:12 עשה A G S | אעש[ה:] B | 15:11d [כי כל אשר שנא אמר לך] לא תעשה] A | > B · 15:11bc A · לי חפץ B | אין צורך A G S · 15:13 רעה + A Bmg S | > B · ותועבה A | ותעבה B · אלהים A | ייי B · 15:14 הוא B G S (Walton, Mosoul) | אהים A Bmg S ואם A Bmg · רצון אל B | רצונו A Bmg · ואמונה B G S | ישיתהו B | וישיתהו A · 15:15 מבראשית A Bmg S | מראש B | L (- Walton, Mosoul) · שלח A S | תשלח B G | ומים ואש A G S | מים ואש B · A · A | B · 15:16

L. 4 [15:4] ולֹ[א י]בוש — Di Lella (1964, 160) has [ו]ל[א ש יבו] [:]. The tops of the letters are preserved along the edge of the fragment. There are traces of the diagonal of the *aleph* and the start of the right arm, then traces of the head of the *bet*, the *vav* and the right arm of the *shin*.

L. 5 [15:5] {מ}רעהו — Schirmann (1958, 442) read רעהו. Di Lella (1964, 160); Ben-Ḥayyim (1973, 20) and Beentjes (1997, 51) read ריעהו which is impossible. The trace of ink beneath the *resh* may be the remnant of a *mem* or perhaps an *ayin*.

L. 15 [15:14] [חו]ת[פ]וֹ — The traces of letters along the edge of the fragment are in agreement with the reading in H^A.

L. 17 [15:15] וֹאם — Di Lella (1964, 160) places these letters in the gap, but traces are preserved that make them certain (the end of the vertical of the *vav*, and the ends of the diagonal and both arms of the *aleph*). תאמֹן — There is a trace of the start of the diagonal of the *aleph*.

15:3 תבונה — This reading is supported by the versions and by the marginal correction in H^A. The marginal correction in H^B, ומתבואתה, does not accord well with the verb שקה even though תבואה can refer to the benefits of wisdom in a metaphorical sense (Prov 3:14; 8:19).

15:5 The marginal correction בתוך רעהו "in the midst of his companion" is not supported by any of the versions.

15:6 תמצא — The second person as in the Greek manuscript 542c (εὑρήσεις). The verb is corrected to ימצא (third person) in the margin, in agreement with H^A. This verb is missing in most Greek manuscripts (except S* A L'-315'-694-743a-613) while the Syriac rendered it with ܬܡܠܝܘܗܝ "she will fill him."

15:10 בפי חכם — Cf. Prov 10:14; 14:3; 15:2 and Qoh 10:12.

15:11 The addition of stichs *b* and *c*, which is specific to H^B, as well as the variant אעשה of stich *d*, are difficult to explain. (The error may have been induced by an *aleph* dittography.) כי כל — A *circellus* indicates a marginal correction that was unfortunately lost in the lacuna.

מה פעלתי — Perhaps compare with the recurring formula מה עשיתי in 1 Sam 20:1; 26:18; 29:8 and Jer 8:6.

15:12 היא — Most probably a confusion between *vav* and *yod*. However, this error may have given rise to verses 11–12 being read as referring to the transgression episode in Gen 2–3, in connection with the origin of evil (though the verb התקילני has been kept in the masculine). The feminine pronoun היא would refer to Eve (cf. Gen 3:12 הָאִשָּׁה אֲשֶׁר נָתַתָּה עִמָּדִי הִוא נָתְנָה־לִּי מִן־הָעֵץ וָאֹכֵל; and Sir 25:24^LXX). Such an interpretation could shed light on the additions in verse 11: "for (concerning) everything he detests, he says to you[, 'do not do it,']" may allude to Gen 2:16–17. "Do not say, 'what did I do?'" may refer to Gen 3:13: מַה־זֹּאת עָשִׂית. לי — Correct לי to לו. This is a confusion between *vav* and *yod* (cf. Di Lella 1966, 97–101).

15:14 הוא מראש — Cf. 16:26^A; 31:28^B; 36:20^B; 39:25^B and 39:32^M,B.

15:16 תשלח — The *yiqtol* can have a volitive sense equivalent to the imperative (Joüon §113m, like שלח in H^A), or express capacity or ability: "you can reach out your hand."

10e Mon enfant, si tu ne cours pas tu n'arriveras pas
10f et si tu ne cherches pas, tu ne trouveras pas.

Chapitre 15

1 Car celui qui craint YYY agit ainsi
 et l'expert en la loi la saisit.
2 Et elle va à sa rencontre comme une mère
 et, comme la femme de sa jeunesse, l'accueille.
3 Et elle le nourrit du pain de discernement
 et elle l'abreuve des eaux de l'intelligence (mg. de ses produits).
4 Et s'il s'appuie sur elle, il ne chancelle pas
 et s'il se fie à elle, il n'au[ra] pas honte[.]
5 Et elle l'élève au-dessus de son compagnon
 et au milieu de l'as[semblée](mg. au milieu de son compagnon)[elle lui ouvre la bouche.]
6 Tu trouves (mg. il trouve) joie et allégresse
 et [elle lui fait hériter d'un]no[m éternel.]
7 Des gens de rien ne la saisissent pas
 et les person[nes arrogantes ne la voient pas.])
8 Elle est loin des railleurs
 et les person[nes menteuses ne se souviennent pas d'elle.]
9 La louange ne convient pas dans la bouche du méchant,
 car elle ne [lui] a pas [été donnée en partage]par Di[eu.]
10 Par la bouche du sage, s'exprime la louange
 et celui qui [la] maîtrise[l'enseigne.]
11a Ne dis pas : « Ma transgression vient de Dieu »,
11b Car tout ce qu'il hait, il te dit : « [ne le fais pas. »]
11c Ne dis pas : « Qu'ai-je fait ?
11d car ce qu'il hait, je ne (le) fais pas. »
12 Que tu ne dises pas : « C'est *elle* qui m'a fait trébucher »,
 car *je* n'ai pas de désir dans (mg. il n'a pas besoin) des personnes violentes.
13 Dieu hait (mg. le mal) et l'abomination,
 et ne (les) occasionne pas à ceux qui le craignent.
14 Lui, dès le début (mg. Dieu, dès le commencement), a créé l'être humain
 et il l'a placé au pouvoir de son agresseur et il l'a livré au pouvoir de son penchant.
15 Si tu le désires, tu garderas le commandement
 et la fidélité pour accomplir la volonté de Dieu (mg. et l'intelligence pour accomplir sa volonté).
 Si tu lui es fidèle,
 alors toi aussi tu vivras.
16 L'eau et le feu ont été placés devant toi,
 vers ce que tu désires, tu étends ta main.

Chapter 15

1 For the one who fears YYY does this
 and an expert in the law will acquire it.
2 She goes to meet him like a mother,
 and, like the woman of his youth, greets him.
3 She feeds him the bread of intelligence,
 and gives him the waters of knowledge (mg. of her products).
4 If he leans on her, he will not falter,
 and if he relies on her, they will not suf[fer] shame[.]
5 She exalts him above his companion,
 and in the midst of the as[sembly] (mg. in the midst of his companions) [she will open his mouth.]
6 Joy and delight you will find (mg. they will find),
 and [she will make them inherit an eternal] na[me.]
7 Worthless people will not acquire it,
 and those who [are arrogant do not see it.]
8 She stays far from those who scorn
 and people who [lie do not remember her.]
9 Praise does not suit the mouth of the wicked,
 for it has not [been apportioned to them] by G[od.]
10 By the wise mouth, praise is expressed,
 and the one who masters [it, teaches it.]
11a Do not say "My transgression comes from God"
11b for (concerning) everything he detests, he says to you, "[Do not do it]."
11c Do not say, "What did I do?
11d for what he hates, I do not do (it)."
12 Lest you say, "She is the one who caused me to stumble."
 for *I* do not desire (mg. do not need) the violent.
13 God hates (mg. evil) and abomination,
 and does not allow (them) to befall those who fear him.
14 He, in the beginning (mg. God, in the beginning), created a human,
 and placed them in the power of their captor and set them in the power of their inclination.
15 If you wish, you will follow the commandment
 and fidelity (mg. understanding) to do God's pleasure
 If you are faithful to him,
 then you will live.
16 Set out before you are water and fire,
 towards that which you desire, you extend your hand.

MANUSCRIPT B

T-S NS 38a verso	יִנָּתֵן	וכל שיחפץ יתן לו׃	¹לפני אדם חיים ומות	17 A
		אל בגבורה ומביט לכל׃	²כי לר[ו]̇ב חכמת ייי	18 A
		אמיץ גבורות וחוזה כל׃	³ספקה חכמת ייי	
		והוא יכיר כל מפעל אנוש׃	⁴עי̇נ̇[י] אל[ה]ים י̇[ר]או מעשיו	19 A
		ולא למד שקרים לאנשי כזב׃	⁵לא צוה אנוש [לחטא	20 A
		ולא מרחם על עושה שוא ועל מגלה סוד׃	⁶ולא] החלים? אנשי] כזב	

Chapter 16

		ואל תשמח על בני עולה׃	⁷[אל תתאוה תואר נע]ר̇י̇ שוא	1 A
		כי אין אתם יראת ייי׃	⁸[א]̇ל תשמח בם	2 A
		ואל תבטח בחיליהם׃	⁹[אל תאמן ב]ח̇ייהם	3ab A
		כי לא תהיה להם אחרית טובה׃	¹⁰[ואל תבטח ב]עקבותם	3cd A
		ומות ערירי מאחרית זדון	¹¹[כי טוב]אחד עֹשה רצון אל מאלף	3ef A
		ב מות ערירי ממי שיהיו לו בנים רבים בני עולה ומאחרית זדון׃	¹²[טו]ב מות ערירי ממי שיהיו לו בנים רבים בני עולה ומאחרית זדון	3g A
		וממשפחות בוגדים תחרב׃	¹³מאחד ערירי ירא ייי תשב עיר	4ab A
		וממשפחת בוגדים תחרב	¹⁴מאחד מ[בי]ן תשב עיר	4cd A
		ועצומות כאלה שמעה אזני׃	¹⁵רבות כאלה ראתה עיני	5 A
			16	
יוקדת אש		ובגוי חנף נצתה חמה׃	¹⁷בעדת רשעים רשפה להבה	6 A

15:17 ומות A ‎| וממות B · 15:17 לו יתן שיחפץ וכל B | יתן יחפץ אשר A G S · יתן A Bmg G · ינתן B 15:18: לכל ומביט בגבורה אל ייי חכמת ב[ו]̇ר לי כי B | A < · כל B ‎| · 15:19 [י]̇נ̇עי A Bmg · אל[ה]ים B | א̇ל A · והוא B | והו A · כל על A כל B · איש A · אנוש B 15:20b: כזב לאנשי שקרים למד ולא B | A < · 16:1 על A · כל}ם S A ? · 15:19 :[ל]G אל A · שהיו A · שיהיו B | טו]ב A ומות A · 16:3g · A < | G B ומות ערירי מאחרית זדון A S · 16:3f רצון בני רבים בנים B | בני עולה A · 16:3e רצון אל B · תבעבם A · כי B S | אם A G · 16:3b תשמח בם A · בבני B · A < 16:2 16:5 ועצומות B G | A < · מאחד מ[בי]ן תשב עיר וממשפחת בוגדים תחרב A · 16:4cd בגדים B · בוגדים A · וממשפחת A · וממשפחות A · 16:4b ועצמות A · 16:6 להבה רשפה B | אש יוקדת A Bmg ·

L. 1 [15:17] יִנָּתֵן — The marks to the right of this verb are the result of the ink bleeding through the paper from the recto.

L. 4 [15:19] [עי̇נ̇[י] אל[ה]ים י̇[ר]או] — Di Lella (1964, 162) reads ורא[. Nevertheless, the ascender of a *lamed* is clearly preserved as well as traces of ink before it. There are traces of the head of the *resh*, as well as the start of the diagonal and the second leg of the *aleph*.

L. 7 [16:1] נע]ר̇י̇ — Di Lella (1964, 162) has נע]ר̇י̇. Faint traces of the head of the *resh* are discernable at the edge of the fragment.

L. 8 [16:2] [א]̇ל תשמח — On the basis of the Greek, Di Lella (1964, 162) restores א]ל תשמח בם ואם הרבו but a restoration similar to H^A is not excluded. תשמח — The scribe wrote a וגם אם פרו א]ל תשמח בם. The scribe wrote a *circellus* indicating a marginal correction that is lost in the gap. Perhaps the correction gave the reading in H^A, as is often the case.

L. 13 [16:4] תשב עיר — Di Lella (1964, 163) notes, "Ms torn between תשב and עיר ; unfortunately, when mounted the ms was not flattened properly . . . Strokes seen before ע belong not to this line but to l. 13b of the opposite side of folio (2a) : they form part of כ, י, and of כי א](ק)."

L. 14 [16:4] מ[בי]ן — The hole outlines a *mem*'s horn. תשב Di Lella (1964, 162) reads תש]ב, but traces of a *bet*'s base are visible.

L. 15 [16:5] כאלה — Di Lella (1964, 163) notes that the first letter should be read as a *bet* and not a *kaph*. In reality, what appears to be an extension of the base on the right is a hole in the manuscript. ראתה עיני — Traces of letters are clearly visible at the edge of the paper. Rightly, Di Lella (1964, 163) notes, "Ms torn before [י]עינ and not flattened properly — same case as in l. 13 above. Marks before ע belong not to this line but to l. 15b of opposite side of folio."

L. 16 [16:5] The scribe left a blank line as paragraph marker.

L. 17 [16:6] חמָּה — Di Lella (1964, 162) reads חמה:, but traces of the letters are clearly discernible.

15:17 וכל שיחפץ יתן לו — For the syntax (כל ש. . .), compare with the Aramaic TAD A.2.4.7: וכעת כל זי תצבה שלח לי "and now, send me everything that you desire" (Muraoka and Porten 1998, 303–304).

15:18 אל בגבורה — For the construction, see Jer 10:6 וגדול שמך בגבורה [missing in the LXX]).

15:20b For the textual history of this verse in H^B, see Di Lella (1966, 131) and van Peursen (2001, 69).

16:1 תשמח על — The reading שמח ב. . . in H^A is more common. The complementation with על only occurs once in Biblical Hebrew, in Isa 39:2 (but // 2 Kgs 20:13 has ישמע, while the LXX and the Vulgate have a *Vorlage* with שמח); see also 4Q223–224 2 ii 19.

16:2 כי — The particle can have a causal meaning (thus the Syriac ܓܝܪ) or introduce a conditional clause (see Isa 1:15, and in Sir 16:11^A; 16:22^A and 35:17^B). In late Hebrew and at Qumran, the particle אם may be used in place of כי (compare Exod 21:37 and 4Q158 10–12 4; Deut 13:2 and 11Q19 LXIV 9; see Muraoka 2000, 212–213), which may explain the reading in H^A.

16:3 בחיליהם — A doublet probably based on Ps 49:7, but which may also have been preserved in the Greek reading τὸ πλῆθος αὐτῶν. רצון אל — The אל explains the ellipsis in H^A and the Syriac. בני רבים בנים עולה — The Hebrew presents two notions in apposition: "many children, iniquitous children."

17 Devant l'être humain sont la vie et la mort
   et tout ce qu'il désire, il lui donnera (mg. cela lui sera donné).
18 Car en ab[on]dance est la sagesse de YYY
   Dieu puissant et observant tout.
   Abondante est la sagesse de YYY,
   puissant en œuvres et voyant tout.
19 [Les yeux de Dieu v]oient ses œuvres
   et, lui, connaît toute l'œuvre de l'être humain.
20 [Il n'a ordonné à personne]de pécher
   et il n'a pas enseigné de tromperies à ceux qui mentent
   [et il n'a pas rétabli ceux qui]mentent.
   Il n'a pas pitié de celui qui agit vainement ni de celui qui révèle un secret.

Chapitre 16

1 [Ne désire pas la beauté de jeu]nes frivoles
   et ne te réjouis pas au sujet des enfants iniques.
2 [ne] te réjouis pas,
   s'il n'y a pas en eux la crainte de YYY,
3a [Ne crois pas en] leur vie,
3b et ne te fie pas à leurs fortunes,
3c [et ne te fie pas à]leurs descendants,
3d car ils n'auront pas une fin heureuse.
3e [Car mieux vaut]un (seul enfant) qui fait la volonté de Dieu que mille,
3f et mourir sans enfant qu'une descendance arrogante.
3g [Mie]ux vaut mourir sans enfant qu'être celui qui a des enfants nombreux, des enfants iniques, et une descendance arrogante.
4a Par un seul sans enfant, craignant YYY, une ville se peuple
4b et par des familles de traîtres, elle est dévastée.
4c Par un seul int[elli]gent une ville se peuple
4d et par une famille de traîtres, elle est dévastée.
5 Mon œil a vu beaucoup de choses comme celles-ci
   et mon oreille a entendu quantité de choses comme celles-ci.
6 Dans l'assemblée des méchants flambe une flamme (mg. brûle un feu)
   et contre une nation impie s'est embrasée une fureur.

17 Before a person are life and death,
   that which they desire he will give to them (mg. will be given to them).
18 For ab[un]dant is the wisdom of YYY,
   almighty God, seeing everything.
   Bountiful is the wisdom of YYY,
   mighty in deeds and seeing everything.
19 [The eyes of God s]ee his works
   and he recognizes every human work.
20 [He did not command humanity] to sin,
   and he did not teach deception to those who lie,
   [and he does not sustain those] who lie,
   He has no mercy on those who act falsely, nor on those who reveal a secret.

Chapter 16

1 [Do not desire the beauty of] worthless [you]ng,
   nor rejoice in unjust children.
2 [do not] rejoice in them,
   if they do not fear YYY.
3a [Do not trust in] their life,
3b and do not be confident of their fortunes,
3c [and do not be confident in] their descendants,
3d for they will not have a happy ending.
3e [For,] one (child) who does the will of God [is better] than a thousand,
3f and better to die childless than (to have) arrogant offspring,
3g [Bett]er to die childless than to be one who has many children, iniquitous children, than (to have) arrogant offspring.
4a From one childless person, fearing YYY, a city is peopled
4b and by families of traitors, it is devastated.
4c From one int[elli]gent (person) a city is peopled,
4d and by a family of traitors, it is devastated.
5 My eye has seen many similar things,
   and my ear has heard numerous similar things.
6 In the assembly of the wicked a flame is kindled (mg. a fire burns)
   and against an impious nation wrath is kindled.

16:4cd The doublet in H^B, which is not attested in H^A, agrees with the Greek (ἀπὸ γὰρ ἑνὸς συνετοῦ), while the Syriac agrees with H^A and H^BI (ܡܢ ܚܕ ܕܕܚܠ ܠܐܠܗܐ "for by one (person) who fears God"). The second form of this sentence is found in a quotation of Sirach by Rabbi Nissim ben Jacob in the text presented by Jellinek's *Beth Ha-Midrash*, V (1967³) 135 (*Ma'asiyoth*): וכן אמר באחד מגין תתיישב עיר and the note in V, 206: וכן אמר בן סירא באחד מגין וכו'; see also VI, 133 (*Ma'asiyoth*): שכן אמר בן סירה, באחד מבין תתיישב העיר. In the first occurence, מגין (hiphil of גנן "to protect," "from one who protects") is without doubt a mistake for מבין as attested in H^B. See Smend (1906a, 145); Segal (1958, 99) and Rüger (1970, 96 n. 108).

16:6 רשפה להבה — Cf. Song 8:6. The use of להבה could allude to the destruction of Heshbon in Num 21:28 (cf. Jer 48:45). The verbal form רשף is not attested before the *piyyutim* of the sixth century (see ref. in Eleazar HaQalir). The verb seems also to be attested in Samaritan Aramaic (see Tal, 2000).

	בגבוֹר[ם]	המורדיםׄ בגׄבּוׄרתם:	ⁱ⁸אשר לא נשא לנסיכי קדם	7 A

Chapter 30

T-S 16.312 recto	מש׳		ואל תשא לשׁחיתותיו:	¹אל תמשילהו בנעוריו	11
			רציץ מתניו שעודנו נער:	²כפתן על חי תפגע	12ab
			ובקע מתניו כשהוא קטן:	³כיף ראשו בנעירותו	12cd
	ילוד ממך		וניֹלדׄ,ילׄדׄ, ממֹנו מפח נפש:	⁴למה ישׁקה ומרה בך	12ef	יקשיח ישקיח
	יתעל		פן באולתו יתׁלעבד:	⁵יסר בנך והכבד עולו	13
			מעשיר ונגע בבשרו:	⁶טוב מסכן וחי בעצמו	14
			ורוח טובה מפנינים:	⁷חיי שֹרׄ אויתי מפז	15	בשר שאר
	שאר:		ואין טובה על טוב לבֹב:	⁸אין עושר על עושר שֹר עצם	16	שאר

16:7 בגבוֹר[ם] ? Bmg · בגבוֹר[ם] B A · בגבורתם: A | המורים עולם B | המורדים 16:7

L. 18 [16:7] בגבוֹר[ם] — Di Lella (1964, 162) reads בנפ, but the *gimel* is certain. Then, there are thin traces of letters that can correspond to the downstroke of a *vav* and a *resh*.

L. 1 [30:11] מש׳ — The *shin* is not drawn in full, as is often the case in this manuscript, where it initiates an abbreviation.

L. 4 ילד —Written *infra linera* in black metallic ink. The reading is ambiguous, the first letter may be either a *vav* (ולד so Lévi [1904, 28]) or a *yod*. The *dalet* has been read as final *kaph* (ולך, "and for you") by Schechter and Taylor (1899, 11-12); Beentjes (1997, 54); Ben-Ḥayyim (1973, 25). ילוד — The reading is ambiguous, the first letter may be either a *yod* or, more probably, a *vav* (Schechter and Taylor [1899, 11-12]; Lévi [1904, 28]; Smend [1906b, 23]; Beentjes [1997, 54]; Ben-Ḥayyim [1973, 25]).

L. 8 [30:16] שאר — Written in black metallic ink.

16:7 בגבורתם — The marginal correction clearly supports בגבורם which seems to be a masculine form of גְּבוּרָה only attested in medieval Hebrew (See Dihi 2004, 116–118); cf. Sir 44:3b (H^B בגבורתם, H^Bmg בגבורם). The word עולם, attested in H^A, is not found in H^B.

30:11 תשא — For the construction ל נשא with the meaning "forgive" or "support," see Exod 23:21 (cf. HALOT §18). לשחיתותיו — The noun שחיתה does not appear in Biblical Hebrew or at Qumran, but it does in Aramaic (cf. Dan 6:5, and perhaps Dan 2:9, as well as 1Q23 3 3). The marginal note (מש׳) may either be the same construction with the preposition מן instead of ל or a substantivised *hiphil* participle with an abstract meaning (cf. HALOT 5b), "his destructions."

30:12 The first stich is enigmatic so we have proposed a fairly literal translation. Stichs *a* and *b* are clearly a doublet of stichs *c* and *d*. Stich *a* should then correspond to stich *c* (see the proposals for corrections in Schechter and Taylor [1899, 53], Lévi [1901, 2:128], Segal [1958, 184], Skehan and Di Lella [1987, 374–375], etc.). Regarding these distichs, see the interesting parallel in Ezek 29:7. רציץ — The *scriptio plena* of the *piel* imperative of רצץ "to tear to pieces." שעודנו — According to the norms of classical Hebrew, one would expect the construction בעודנו. עוד אשר never appears in Biblical Hebrew or at Qumran. כיף — Read כַּיֵּף, a *piel* imperative (not attested elsewhere) of כוף (cf. 4:7), or correct to כפף, the *qal* imperative of כפף. כשהוא — The construction is typical of Mishnaic Hebrew. ישקה — "To provide drink" is certainly incorrect, as is the second marginal correction ישקיח. The first must be a case of metathesis for יקשה in an eliptical form of the expression הקשׁה ערף "to harden one's neck, to become obstinate" (see Job 9:4). The second, ישקיח, must also be a metathesis, in this case for יקשיח as attested in the first marginal alternative. The verb קשח, only attested in Job 39:16 and Isa 63:17, is frequently used in *piyyutim* (see Yannaï and Eleazar HaQalir) in the senses "to harden (the heart)" as well as "to treat harshly." Perhaps, ישקיח is a mistake for ישכיח "(lest) he forget"; in Rabbinic Hebrew the *piel* and *hiphil* of the verb שכח have the same sense as the *qal* "to forget" (see Reymond 2014c, 29 and Qimron 2018, 112 for examples of confusions between velar consonants in the scrolls). מפח נפש — The expression is attested in Job 11:20 where it is used as a synonym of death. Jastrow (1903, 820) gives it the meaning "despair," and in CAL (consulted 11 June, 2021) the feminine מפחה נפש is defined as "expiring, despair"; the same sense is implied by Greek II ἐξ αὐτοῦ ὀδύνη ψυχῆς "(and you will have) from him distress of soul." Note the oxymoron: death/despair is born. ונולד — There are two alternative readings:

7   C'est ainsi qu'il n'a pas pardonné aux princes d'autrefois,
      qui se rebellèrent par leur puissance. (mg. par [leur] puissa[nce.])

Chapitre 30

11 Ne lui laisse aucun pouvoir dans sa jeunesse
      et ne passe pas sur ses méfaits (mg. ses destructions).
12a Comme un serpent, sur une créature tu frapperas,
12b fracasse ses reins pendant qu'il est encore jeune.
12c Courbe sa tête dans sa jeunesse
12d et fends ses reins tant qu'il est petit.
12e De peur qu'il *n'abreuve* (?) (mg. 1. ne (te) traite durement ; mg. 2. *ne t'oublie* (?)) et ne se révolte contre toi
12f et que ne soit engendrée de lui l'expiration du souffle.
      (mg. 1. infralinéaire: que ne soit engendrée)
      (mg. 2. que ne soit engendrée de toi)
13 Corrige ton enfant et appesantis son joug,
      de peur que dans sa folie il ne se moque de toi (mg. ne s'élève (contre toi)).
14 Mieux vaut (être) pauvre et sain dans son être,
      que riche avec une plaie dans sa chair.
15 Je désire la santé du corps (mg. 1. de la chair ; mg. 2. idem) plus que l'or
      et un bon esprit plus que les perles.
16 Il n'y a pas de richesse supérieure à la richesse d'un corps (mg. d'une chair) vigoureux
      et il n'y a pas de bienfait supérieur au bonheur du cœur (mg. de la chair).

7   For he did not forgive the ancient princes,
      who rebelled in their power (mg. in [their] po[wer]).

Chapter 30

11 Do not give him authority in his youth,
      and do not forgive his misdeeds (mg. his destructions).
12a You should strike like a cobra upon an animal,
12b smash his loins while he is still young.
12c bend his head in his youth,
12d and split his loins open while he is still small.
12e Lest he gives (you) drink (?) (mg. 1. treats (you) harshly; mg. 2. *forgets* (*you*) (?)] and revolts against you
12f and despair is born from him.
      (mg. 1. infralinear: is born)
      (mg. 2. born from you)
13 Chastise your son and make his yoke heavy,
      lest in his folly, he mocks you (mg. he rise up (against you)).
14 Better (to be) one poor whose bones are healthy
      than one rich whose flesh has pestilence.
15 I desire the health of the body (mg. 1. of the flesh; mg. 2. idem) more than gold,
      and a good spirit more than pearls.
16 There is no wealth greater than the wealth of a strong body (mg. flesh),
      and there is nothing greater than the happiness of the heart (mg. flesh).

(1) the infralinear note may be read ילד (that could be יָלָד, a passive *qal* participle or יְלָד a *qal* passive participle) or וְלָד "child"; (2) the marginal note may be read ילוד (*qal* passive participle). The reading ולוד would imply a correction to וילוד (Segal [1958, 184]; cf. Peters [1913, 245]).

30:13 יתלעבד — The verb לעב only appears (in the *hiphil*) in 2 Ch 36:16 where it is rendered by the *hithpaal* in the Targum. The *hithpael* of לעב is not otherwise found in Hebrew, though the Aramaic cognate does appear frequently in the *hithpaal* with the sense "to mock," "to be gluttonous" (so CAL 11 June, 2021). One would have expected the formulation יתלעב בך. The text can then be explained either by haplography or as reflecting the phonological assimilation of two *bets* (cf. the assimilation of the two *kaphs* in יברכך to יברך in Kuntillet 'Ajrud 19:7–8 and Ketef Hinnom 2:5). The marginal note יתעל, the *hithpael* of עלה, can be understood in two ways: "Lest in his folly he exalt himself (i.e. boast, take pride in himself)" or "Lest in his folly he rise up against you (יתעל בך)." The reading יתעל is striking since, in classical Hebrew, פן requires the long form of the prefix conjugation (yet, note the exception in Sir 7:3). Note the same basic apocopated form of the verb in an unexpected syntax (i.e., לוא תתעל "you must not lift yourself") in 1QIsaᵃ at Isa 58:7, corresponding to לא תתעלם "do not hide yourself" in MT and 1Q8. Another noteworthy syntactic feature is that פן is not directly followed by the verb (the only other exception is in Num 20:18).

30:14 וחי — While the meaning "to heal" is well attested for the verb חיה, the meaning "healthy" or "well" is rare for the adjective חי (cf. Exod 1:19). בעצמו — Literally, "in his bones," i.e. his being, in parallel with בשר in the following stich.

30:15 שר חיי — The term שר could be a defective spelling of שְׁאָר "flesh," as evidenced by the marginal note, or the noun שֹׁר "navel(?)" (and by extension "body") as seems likely in Prov 3:8 where it is paralleled with עצם; interestingly in Prov 3:8 the Septuagint (τῷ σώματί σου = שאר) and the Peshitta (ܠܒܣܪܟ = בשר) offer two variants exactly similar to those of Hᴮ margin. Segal (1958, 187) sees a connection with the root שרר "to be strong." אויתי — The use of the first person singular to imply the opinion of the author is rare (cf. 16:24–25; 33:16–18).

30:16 שר עצם — As preserved, the letters can be explained in several ways: (1) שר may be a dittography of the last two letters of עושר, though the marginal reading, שאר, would seem to exclude the possibility of a simple mistake; (2) שר may have been understood as the word שֹׁר with the meaning "body," instead of "navel" (as also in the preceding verse and probably in Prov 3:8, see HALOT); (3) עצם could be the noun עֹצֶם "strength, might" (see Deut 8:17) or a deffective spelling of the adjective עָצוּם "robust, powerful" (though we would have expected a mater, עצום, and the adjective usually evokes a multitude rather than power, see Sir 16:5); (4) עצם in the meaning "bone, body" may also be an explanatory gloss for שר (if understood as שאר). טוב לבב — The construction expresses joy and happiness (cf. Deut 28:47), that is, good mental health. The marginal note (שאר) modifies the scope of the verse by limiting it to the register of physical health.

תלד לאשר	מחיים רעים:	וּנוחת עולם מכאב נאֶמן:	⁹טוב למות מחיי שוא	17
	ולוד ושא׳	וליר̇ד̇ שאול מכאב עומד:	¹⁰טוב למות מחיים רעים	
	מצגת גלול:	תנופה מצגת לפני גלול:	¹¹טובה שפוכה על פה סתום	18 פום
	בגל	כן עושה באוֺנס משפט:	¹²כאשר סירים יחבק נערה ומתאנח	20
	ביד{ו̇}	וייי מבקש מידו:	¹³כן נאמן לן עם בתולה	
ל תכשיל עצתך:	בעצתך:	ואל תכשל בעוֺנך:	¹⁴אל תתן לדין נפשך	21
		וגיל אדם האריך אפו:	¹⁵שמחת לבב הם חיי איש	22
		וקצפון הרחק ממך:	¹⁶פת נפשך ופייג לבך	23
		ואין תעלה בקצפון:	¹⁷כי רבים הרג דין	
		ובלא עת תזקין דאגה.	¹⁸קנאה ואף [י̇]קצרו ימים	24
T-S 16.312 verso		ומאכלו יעלה עליו:	¹שנות לב טוב תחת מטעמים	25

L. 9 [30:17] מחיים רעים — Written in black metallic ink.
L. 12 margin [30:19–20] Schechter and Taylor (1899, 11) read מה ימב (ימב being a clear mistake for יטב). The reading לאללי is nonetheless impossible. Smend's reading מה יע[רכו] ל[ג][ל][י]לי is just as impossible (Smend 1906b, 23). After מה, most likely read יעילו in agreement with the traces and the meaning of the Greek (see Hab 2:18). Then, we propose reading פסילי, although reading a *pe* is difficult. Regarding the last word of this line, traces of letters are visible, but impossible to identify with certainty. The last letters of the third line are also extremely difficult to discern.

30:17 ונוחת — The feminine noun נחה appears sporadically in Rabbinic Hebrew (Sifra Nedaba 1:1). נאמן — For the use of the *niphal* participle of אמן in a negative context, see Deut 28:59. ולירד — The form is Mishnaic. The second marginal note, לרד, also reflects Mishnaic Hebrew, but with a different spelling (see 1QIsa^a XXIV 7 [Isa 30:2]: לרדת). The first marginal note, ולוד, is hard to explain. One solution would be to read ילוד (either יָלוּד "born" or יִלּוֹד "new-born": "new-born and Sheol than a stubborn pain"), but it is hard to connect this with the context. Part of a doublet, stich 17d seems to be an interpretation of 17b in which נוחת has been read as the verb נחת "to descend (hence ירד) and עולם has been understood as a reference to שאול.
30:18 פום — Aramaic equivalent for the Hebrew פה. תנופה — The term is translated as "offering," a techinical term belonging to priestly vocabulary. מצגת לפני גלול — As in the text, יצג is usually found with a preposition (see Gen 43:9; 47:2), but in the margin, the *hophal* participle is in construct with גלול (a genitive of place; see Waltke and O'Connor 1991, 148). גלול — The singular form is unusual. The Greek and the Syriac read גולל "tombstone."
30:19 יריחון — Cf. Deut 4:28 and Ps 115:6. נהנה — The verb הנה "to have pleasure, profit" is an Aramaism, and does not appear elsewhere in Hebrew or Aramaic (nor in Syriac) before the Mishnaic period. (For the Hebrew, see Mur 22 6, dated 135 CE [DJD II, 118] and for the Aramaic, perhaps Mur 31 2 1 [DJD II, 148].)
30:20 For a detailed philological analysis of this verse, see Talshir and Talshir (2008). [בעיניו רואה [ומתאנח — Restored on the basis of the Greek, the Syriac and the following parallel. (For the *hithpael* participle of אנה, see the following line and 11Q19 LIX 5.) סירים — "Thorn bushes" or "cooking pots," but correct to סריס "eunuch." באונס — "With force." This is the preposition followed by the abstract noun אוֹנֶס, found frequently in Rabbinic Hebrew. Cf. Esth 1:8. The verb appears eight times at Qumran, always in the participial form. נאמן — The word has the meaning "man of trust" here (see Talshir and Talshir 2008). Syriac has ܡܗܝܡܢܐ; this Syriac word has a double meaning, "faithful" and "eunuch." Several translators interpret the Hebrew word according to the second meaning of the Syriac. מבקש מיד — The expression, which always takes an object in Biblical Hebrew (see Ezek 3:18), seems to have crystallized into an idiomatic expression: "to ask from his hand" (i.e., ask for an account from his hand)."
30:21 לדין — For דין with the meaning "sorrow," see 14:1^A and the note. בעונך — The first marginal correction בעצתך agrees with the Greek and the Syriac. If בעונך is secondary, then it must be strongly influenced by Ps 31:11. כשל — Based on the context, the verb must have a psychological meaning here, as in Ps 31:11.
30:22 שמחת לבב — Cf. Isa 30:29; Jer 15:16 and 4Q185 1–2 ii 12. הם — The plural pronoun here anticipates חיי איש, and this type of construction, while common in Syriac, is rare in Hebrew (Lam 1:8; Song 6:9; Isa 10:5; Muraoka 1999a, 206-208). וגיל אדם האריך אפו — For the meaning, cf. Prov 19:11: שֵׂכֶל אָדָם הֶאֱרִיךְ אַפּוֹ.
30:23 פת — The form must be the apocopated imperative *piel* of פתה, "to persuade" (cf. Joüon §79i). נפש seems to convey mood, desire, appetite here, and the expression פת נפש must refer to the control of that mood. פייג לבך — For the expression, see Gen 45:26. קצפון — The term is attested first in Rabbinic Hebrew. דין — For דין with the meaning "sorrow," see 14:1^A and the note. תעלה — The form may derive from the root יעל "to profit" (see the spelling תועלה in 41:14 of H^B תעלה in H^Bmg]). Such a form, with the meaning "profit," does not seem to be attested elsewhere, except in Sir 41:14 and in two works from the eleventh-twelfth centuries, one of them a Genizah *piyyut* (תועילה); the word is presumably a variation of the more common תועלת "profit." The word may alternatively derive from the root עלה, and could be vocalized תְּעָלָה, which in the Bible means "cure" (see Jer 30:13, 46:11), though in rabbinic literature it has the sense "profit" (see Dihi 2004, 703–704).
30:24 ובלא עת — See Qoh 7:17.
30:25 שנות — For the plural form of שָׁנָה, see Prov 6:10 and 24:33. יעלה עליו — The construction עלה + על means "to rise in value, to be esteemed" (see Jastrow 1903, 1081).

17 Mieux vaut mourir qu'une vie de vanité
   et le repos éternel qu'une peine persistante. (mg. qu'une vie malheureuse.)
   Mieux vaut mourir qu'une vie malheureuse
   et descendre au Shéol (mg. 1. un nouveau-né et le Shéol (?) ; mg. 2. et descendre au Shéol) qu'une peine tenace.
18 Un bienfait versé sur une bouche (mg. bouche) fermée :
   offrande déposée devant une idole (mg. déposée d'une idole).
19 (mg. En quoi pro[fi]tent les idoles des nations qui ne mangent pas et ne se[ntent] pas,
   de même (celui) [qui]a la richesse et n'en profite pas,
20 avec ses yeux[, il voit et soupire,])
   comme un *eunuque* embrasse une jeune femme et soupire,
   ainsi celui qui impose par la force (mg. par escroquerie) le jugement,
   ainsi l'homme de confiance qui passe la nuit avec une vierge
   et YYY lui demande des comptes (mg. idem).
21 Ne livre pas ton âme à la tristesse
   et ne flanche pas à cause de ton péché (mg. 1. ton conseil).
   (mg. 2. que ton conseil ne te fasse pas trébucher.)
22 La joie du coeur, c'est la vie humaine
   et la gaieté de l'être humain ralentit sa colère.
23 Contrôle ton humeur et rends ton cœur impassible
   et éloigne de toi la fureur,
   car la tristesse en a tué beaucoup
   et il n'y a aucun profit dans la fureur.
24 Jalousie et colère abrègent les jours
   et l'anxiété fait vieillir avant l'heure.
25 Le sommeil d'un cœur heureux à la place de mets savoureux
   et sa nourriture lui est profitable.

17 Better to die than (live) a life of vanity,
   and eternal rest than persistent pain (mg. than an unhappy life)
   Better to die than (live) an unhappy life,
   and go down to Sheol (mg. 1. a new born and Sheol; mg. 2. and to descend to Sheol) than (endure) a stubborn pain.
18 A blessing spread for a closed mouth (mg. mouth),
   (such is) an offering placed before an idol (mg. an offering to an idol).
19 (mg. What good would it do for the idols of the nations who do not eat or smell,
   so is someone who has wealth and does not enjoy it.
20 with their eyes [, they see and sigh]).
   Like *a eunuch* embracing a maiden and sighing,
   so is one who imposes judgment by force (mg. by theft),
   so is the trustworthy person who spends the night with a virgin,
   YYY holds them accountable (mg. idem).
21 Do not surrender your soul to sadness,
   and do not stumble because of your sin. (mg. 1. because of your counsel)
   (mg. 2. Do not let your own counsel make you stumble.)
22 Joy of the heart, this is a person's life,
   and a person's joy makes them slow to anger.
23 Control your mood and quiet your heart,
   and put anger far from you
   for sadness has killed many,
   and there is no profit in anger.
24 Jealousy and anger shorten (one's) days,
   and anxiety ages one prematurely.
25 The sleep of a happy heart instead of savory food,
   its food agrees with it.

Chapter 31

	תפריג	דאגת מחיה תפריע נומה :	1	²שקר עשיר ימחה שארו	שקד	
	ומחלה חז תפריג	ומחלי חזק תפריע נומה:	2	³דאגת מחיה תפריג נומה		
		ומסתיר סוד אוהב כנפש:		⁴רע נאמן תניד חרפה	תנוד	
	עמל:	ואם ינוח לקבל תענוג:	3	⁵עמלי עשיר לקבל הון	עמל	
		ואם ינוח יהיה צריך:		⁶יגע עני לחסר ביתו		
		ואם ינוח לא נחה לו:		⁷עמל עני לחסר כחו		
	במח׳	ואוהב מחיר בו ישגה:	5	⁸רודף חרוץ לא ינקה	חריץ	
		והבוטח על פנינים:		⁹רבים היו חבולי זהב	חללי	
		וגם להושע ביום עברה:		¹⁰ולא מצאו להנצל מרעה		
	פתח	וכל פותה יוקש בו:	7	¹¹כי תקלה הוא לאויל		
		ואחר ממון לא נלוז:		¹²אשרי איש נמצא תמים	מצא	

31:1 שקר — The word is most easily understood as the noun שֶׁקֶר "deception, falsehood" (encouraged perhaps by the use of שֶׁקֶר and דאגה together in Sir 42:9) and is often construed as a mistake for the word found in the margin, שקד. Nevertheless, it is also conceivable that the word שקר should be construed as from the rarer root שׂקר which denotes watching, gazing, as in the *piel* in Isa 3:16, often translated "to ogle"; the same verb (spelled with a *samekh*) appears once in the *qal* ("to gaze") in Rabbinic Hebrew (y. Nid. 3:2, 50c) and among the *piyyutim* (in addition to the noun סקר "glance"). The root also appears throughout Aramaic where it carries the additional sense "to envy" (as in the Syriac verb in the *peal*), which seems particularly appropriate to the present context and would lead to the translation "the envying of the rich person . . ." מחה — The verb is forceful, literally "to make disappear, dissolve, erase" (cf. 3:14; 5:4).

31:1b-2a The same idea is expressed in three extremely similar forms, but this is also the case in the Greek and the Syriac. תפריג — According to Maagarim, the verb פרג is only attested elsewhere in Hebrew in Num. Rab. 7:4 where it means "to bud, blossom" as a gloss for the Hebrew פרח, which means not only "to bud, blossom," but also "to fly" and perhaps "to ruin" (cf. in Samaritan Aramaic [Tal 2000, 170] where the verb means "to exchange, to substitute" and "to ruin"). The text of Num. Rab. evokes the germination of a cabbage field, making it unsuitable for consumption and causing the ruin of its owner: בבקר נכנס לראותה ומצא אותה שהפריגה. אמ׳ לה. תיפח רוחך. בערב היית נאה ומשו־ "He בחת ובבקר הרי הפרגת. כך אמ׳ האלהים לישראל ובבקר זרע תפריחי came in the next morning to look at it and found that it had germinated (שהפריגה). 'Woe to you!' he exclaimed, 'in the evening you looked fine and splendid, and in the morning you are ruined (הפרגת)!' In the same strain God said to Israel, 'And in the morning thou didst make thy seed to germinate (תפריחי) (Isa 17:11)'" (trans. Slotki 1961, 186–7). Assuming the sense "ruin" for the verb פרג, the phrase here would have the sense "will disturb one's sleep." Alternatively, given the association of פרג and פרח, the verb פרג might have the sense "to fly" and in the *hiphil* "to put to flight, chase," like פרח. A final possibility is that פרג here may be a phonetic variant of פרק, but with the sense this verb carries in the Syriac *aphel* "to chase away." These last two explanations seem especially apropos given the parallel expressions in Sir 42:9 (in H^M: [תפ]ריד נומה], the *hiphil* of פרד, presumably in the sense "to put to flight" as in Syriac, and in H^B: תפריש נ[ו]ם]). The fact that תפריג is attested three times in this couplet suggests it is not a scribal mistake, but rather was part of the dialect of the author or one of the copyists. The Greek uses the verb ἀφίστημι twice and the verb ἐκνήφω once (Smend [1906b, 24; 1906a, 273] and Segal [1958, 190] assume תפיג or תפריג as a possible *Vorlage* [cf. Lam 2:18]). The Syriac is translated twice with ܪܕܦ "to hunt, chase" (= פרע) and once with ܢܓܕ "to reject."

31:2b מחלי חזק — The particle מן implies that one should understand דאגת מחיה as the subject of תפריע and מחלי חזק as a comparitive expression (thus Segal 1958, 190 and Smend 1906a, 273). The marginal note מחלה חז תפריג gives a slightly different sense, less appropriate to the context, "a violent illness chases sleep away" (thus the Greek and the Syriac).

31:2cd This couplet seems to correspond more or less to Sir 27:16, at least for stich *d*. תניד — A *hiphil* of נוד "to scare off, chase, make tremble." The marginal correction replaces the *hiphil* with the *qal*, which hardly fits the context. אוהב כנפש — Compare with the expression רע עבד משכיל חבב כנפש in Sir 37:2^{C,Bmg,D} (37:2^B has רע כנפשך) and "love a prudent servant as your (very) self" in Sir 7:21.

31:3 עמלי — Here, this word probably has the meaning "labor," as in Qohelet; cf. Sir 13:23^A, in the sense of "sorrow, moral suffering." עמל in the marginal note to 3a can be read as a verb or as a singular noun. תענוג — See 41:1^B. עמל — In 3b, the marginal alternative plays on the meanings of עמל; here, it would have the sense "the fruit of labor." Cf. Ps 105:44 (antanaclasis).

31:4 יגע — This may be a nominal form (in parallel with עמלי עשיר), meaning "toil" (see Job 20:18 and 4Q368 10 ii 5), or more likely a verbal form (in parallel with עמל עשיר). צריך — The term only appears in late Hebrew; see 2 Chr 2:15; Sir 13:6^A; 32:7^B; 39:16^{Bm}; 42:21^B; 4Q372 1 17; Mur 46 2.6 (DJD II, 165–66), and in Aramaic; see 4Q197 3 1 and Naḥal Ḥever 56 7. כחו — The sentence can be understood in two ways: לחסר כחו could imply "the poor person struggles until their strength is exhausted." Or, כוח could refer to "property, assets, product," that is, strength measured in terms of wealth (cf. Gen 4:12; Job 6:22; 31:39; Prov 5:10; Ezra 2:69), so that it is wealth that is drained or exhausted. The sentence would then be parallel to 4a "the poor labors for a lack of wealth." נחה — Read a defective form of the feminine noun נוחה, as in 30:17 (Peters 1913, 252). One could also assume an earlier לאנחה, as Segal (1958, 180) suggests, "And if they rest, it is for their groaning."

31:5 For the meaning of the first stich, see Prov 28:20. חרוץ — The marginal correction חריץ is difficult to interpret. The word is attested in 2 Sam 12:31 and 1 Chr 20:3 in the sense of "iron picks," but the two words חרוץ and חריץ seem to be semantically interrelated in Amos 1:3 (see the Greek and the Targum). לא ינקה — The formula is frequent; cf. Prov 6:29; 11:21; 16:5; 17:5; Sir 7:8; 9:12; 40:15; etc. ואוהב מחיר — The alternative expression in the margin, ואוהב במחיר, may imply that the *bet* was lost due to haplography. Alternatively, ואוהב מחיר may be the earlier expression, the *bet* having appeared by dittography of the final *bet* of אהב. Syntactically, the construction with *bet* is not impossible; cf. Qoh 5:9 for the introduction of the object of אהב with ב. Or, *bet* could be understood as a *bet pretii* "the one who loves for money" (cf. 2 Sam 24:24; Isa 45:13; Mic 3:11).

Chapitre 31

1 Le mensonge (mg. la veille) du riche détruit sa chair,
  l'anxiété de la subsistance détruit (mg. 1. ~~chasse~~) le sommeil,
  (mg. 2. son anxiété chasse le sommeil)

2a L'anxiété de la subsistance chasse le sommeil

2b et plus qu'une maladie violente détruit le sommeil.
  (mg. et une maladie violente chasse le sommeil).

2c La honte fait fuir (mg. fuit) un compagnon fidèle

2d et celui qui garde un secret est un ami comme toi-même.

3 Les labeurs du riche sont (mg. Le riche travaille) pour recevoir la richesse,
  mais s'il se repose, c'est pour recevoir du plaisir (mg. le fruit du travail).

4 Le pauvre peine pour le besoin de sa maisonnée
  et s'il se repose, il sera nécessiteux.
  Le pauvre travaille, épuisant sa force
  et s'il se repose, ce n'est pas du repos pour lui.

5 Celui qui poursuit l'or (mg. un pique (de fer) ?), ne restera pas impuni
  et celui qui aime un salaire (mg. en vue d'un salaire), par lui se fourvoie.

6 Ils sont nombreux les esclaves de (mg. les victimes de) l'or
  et *celui* qui fait confiance aux perles.
  Et ils ne purent se libérer du mal,
  ni se sauver au jour de colère.
  (mg. Et ils ne purent se libérer au jour de colère,
  ni se sauver au jour de malheur.)

7 Car c'est un achoppement pour le fou
  et chaque sot (mg. graveur) s'y laisse piéger.

8 Heureux celui qui est trouvé intègre (mg. qui a trouvé (l'intégrité)
  et qui ne s'est pas perverti en poursuivant l'argent.

Chapter 31

1 The deceit (mg. the watchfullness) of a rich person consumes their flesh,
  anxiety about survival destroys sleep (mg. 1. ~~chases away~~; mg. 2. Their anxiety chases sleep away).

2a Anxiety about survival chases sleep away,

2b and more than a violent illness, it destroys sleep
  (mg: and a violent illness chases sleep away).

2c Contempt will drive away (mg. will flee) a faithful friend

2d and one who keeps a secret is a friend like (your) very self.

3 The labors of the rich are (mg. The rich works) to receive wealth,
  but if they rest, it is to receive pleasure (mg: the fruit of labor).

4 The poor struggles for what their household lacks
  and if they rest, (then) they will be in need.
  The poor labors until exhausted in their strength,
  and if they rest, (then) there is no rest for them.

5 The one who pursues gold (mg. an (iron) pick) will not go unpunished
  and the one who loves reward (mg. for a reward), goes astray in it

6 Many are the slaves of (mg. the victims of) gold,
  and those who rely upon pearls.
  And they are not able to deliver themselves from evil
  nor save themselves in the day of wrath.
  (mg. And they are not able to save themselves in the day of wrath,
  nor save themselves in the day of evil.)

7 For it is a stumbling block for the fool,
  and every simple one (mg. engraver) is trapped by it.

8 Blessed is the person who is found with integrity (mg. who has found (integrity)),
  and who has not become corrupt over money.

31:6ab חבולי זהב — The verb חבל, a *qal* passive participle here, has many senses. In this context, it could mean "to destroy, ruin, corrupt" or "to entrust something as a pledge." The expression could then mean "those who have been ruined or corrupted by gold" or "those who are slaves to gold" (i.e. those who have given themselves in pledge to gold; see Amos 2:8 and 4Q416 2 iii 6 ורוחכה אל תחבל). The marginal alternative, חללי זהב, would reinforce the first interpretation, "the victims of gold." והבוטח — The singular is surprising because of the parallelism of the couplet, and should probably be corrected to והבוטחים (Schechter and Taylor 1899, 55; Lévi 1901, 137; Segal 1958, 180) or והבטחו (Peters 1913, 253), as suggested by the Syriac.

31:6cd ולא מצאו להנצל. For the use of מצא as an auxiliary expressing possibility, see Sir 12:11^A. להושיע — The marginal note could be a *plene* spelling of the *niphal* להושע "to save oneself" (as in the main text) or the *hiphil* להושיע "to save," which does not fit the context. The potential error (seen elsewhere too, e.g., 1QIsa^a XLV 22 והושיעו // MT והושעו) may be due to the more frequent use of the *hiphil* in comparison to the *niphal* (see Kutscher 1974, 360).

31:7 תקלה — The word תַּקָלָה (found in the Mishnah and later literature) does not occur in Biblical Hebrew. The root תקל is more common in Aramaic, though the verbal form also appears in 13:23^A; 15:12^{A,B} and 32,20^{B,E,F} as well as in rabbinic literature. פותה — "Simple person," corresponds to פתה in the margin. The sense "door, opening (פֶּתַח)" does not make sense in the context, so perhaps with the mention of "gold" in v. 6 we should infer "engraver (פַּתָּח)."

31:8 מצא תמים — The form may be impersonal "Blessed is the person that one finds with integrity." One could also understand תמים as a noun (cf. Ps 84:12) and read "Blessed is the person who has found integrity." The form נמצא תמים in the main text is, however, more common (cf. Sir 44:16–17, 20). ממן — The term is not attested in Biblical Hebrew, but appears in an Aramaic inscription from the Assyrian period (Caquot 1971, 9–16, esp. 9.13.15). The term is also attested four times at Qumran, and appears in Greek transcription (μαμωνᾶς) in the NT (Matt 6:24; Luke 16:9, 11), in Mishnaic Hebrew, in Aramaic and in Syriac.

	[:]כי הפליא לעשות בעמו		9	¹³מי הוא זה ונאשרנו	כי הפליא לעשות בעמו
לתפארה	והיה לו שלום והיה לו תפארה		10ab	¹⁴מי הוא זה שנדבק בו	הנדבק
תפארת	אהיה לך לתפארת:		10cd	¹⁵כי ברבות שלום חייו	
	היאׄ לךׄ לתפארת:	אהיה לך להתפאר:	10ef	¹⁶מי ברכו וישלם חייו	
	ולהרע רעה ולא אבֺהֺ:		10gh	¹⁷מי יוכל לסור ולא סר	
Or. 5518.1 (British Museum) recto	ותהלתו יספֹר קהֹל:		11	¹⁸על כן חזק טובו	
	מוסר לחם ויין יחדו		12	¹	
גרון	אל תפתח עליו גרנך:			²בני אם על שלחןׄ גדול ישבתה	איש
דע	זכור כי רעה עין רעה:		12/13a	³אל תאמר ספוק עליו	
	ורע ממנו לא ברא:		13bc	⁴רע עין שונא אל	
תסיע	ומפנים דמעה תדמע:		13de	⁵כי זה מפני כל דבר תזוׄע עין	תזיע
על כל מלפני	על בן מׄפני כל נס לחה:		13fg	⁶רעׄ מעין לא חלק אל	רע מ׳ חלק אׄ
תיחד	ואל דׄיחד עמו בטנא:		14	⁷מקום יביט אל אל תושיט יד	תשית

L. 14 [31:10] תפארה — Read a *he* with Beentjes (1997, 55), rather than a *tav* (תפארת) with Schechter and Taylor (1899, 12); Smend (1906b, 25); Lévi (1901, 138); Vattioni (1968, 163) and Ben-Ḥayyim (1973, 29).

31:9 ונאשרנו — The *weyiqtol* after an interrogative proposition indicates purpose (cf. Joüon §160c). The marginal reading תאשרנו is certainly due to a confusion between נו and ת, but could make sense as expressing a volitive idea, "you should declare him blessed," or as an impersonal use of the second person, "that is declared blessed" (GKC §144h; van Peursen 2004, 176–177). הפליא לעשות — The verb פלא is used as an auxiliary (see Judg 13:19; Sir 50:22^B; van Peursen 2004, 261).

31:10 שנדבק — The form could be a *qal* 1cp imperfect, "that we join him" or a *niphal* 3ms perfect (or participle), "who is the one who is attached to it" (i.e. ממנו) (see the Syriac), although the *niphal* of דבק does not occur outside Sirach before medieval Hebrew. The marginal reading הנדבק attests the use of the *niphal* participle, "Who is the one who attaches themself to it?" The Greek δοκιμάζω assumes a *Vorlage* with בדק "to test, experience." The root is Aramaic but also appears in mishnaic Hebrew, implying the translation "Who is the one who has been tested by it?" (i.e. gold). תפארה — The variant לתפארה does not fundamentally change the meaning "it will be for them a subject of splendor," cf. 10*d,f*. מי ברכו וישלם חייו — For מי in a correlative sense, see BDB, s.v. *g*. ברך may have the meaning "to curse" here (see HALOT, cf. Job 2:9). וישלם must be a *piel* though the exact meaning is not entirely clear. It could mean "he restores his life" or "he finishes his life." היא — Instead of the feminine pronoun which does not make sense in the context, the letters may be read as an orthographic variant for היה (as frequently attested in the Dead Sea Scrolls). מי יוכל לסור — The verb סור is used here without a complement (cf. Sir 4:19^A; Deut 11:16; 17:17). It has a moral meaning in agreement with the following stich, "to turn away" (i.e. from the good). ולהרע רעה — If one reads רֵעָה, the formula may be intentionally redundant for emphasis (cf. Neh 2:10; Jonah 4:1). One could vocalize רֵעֶה, "and (could) harm a neighbor," as understood by the Syriac (ܠܚܒܪܗ "(who could) harm his neighbor").

31:12 The title that is present in the manuscript is absent in the Greek and the Syriac. There is another similar title before 41:16 and 44:1 (see the complete introduction). איש — Because the circellus comes between שלחן and גדול, one should understand the marginal note, איש, as coming between these words ("the table of an important person," cf. the Syriac ܓܒܪܐ ܪܒܐ "a rich person"; the Greek reflects the same *Vorlage* as the text of H^B, translating ἐπὶ τραπέζης μεγάλης "at a great table"). אל תפתח עליו גרנך — The expression is not common, and the construction פתח + על usually indicates an opposition, "to break open against" (cf. Ps 109:2, 4Q372 1 20, CD V 12). The use of גרן "throat" may refer: (1) to gluttony ("do not open your throat wide over it" [i.e. over the table]; cf. Ps 5:10 and 4Q417 2 i 9 // 4Q416 2 i 3–5, and, more importantly, Prov 23:1–2) or, (2) to speech ("do not open your throat wide against him," i.e. "do not speak too much against or speak ill of him"; cf. 32:11). For גרן in context of speaking, see Ps 115:7; 149:6; Isa 58:1. ספוק — The word does not appear in Biblical Hebrew, which only has the noun סֵפֶק "abundance" (see Job 20:22; 36:18), nor at Qumran, though it does appear in Rabbinic Hebrew: ס(י)פוק "sufficiency, abundance." The root derives from Aramaic ספק "to be sufficient" (see also, the Aramaic ספיק, "opportunity").

31:13a This long verse of seven stichs displays, once again, traces of a complex transmission history. רעה עין רעה — Note the *antanaclasis* and the equivalent inverted formula (*diacope*) in 14:10 (עין רע עין). The phrase עין רעה "selfishness, envy" is common in Rabbinic Hebrew. The expression רע עין in the following stich may be synonymous (assuming רֹעַ), literally "the greed of the eye," or it may be interpreted as referring to a greedy, stingy person, assuming the adjective רַע, as in Sir 14:3^A; 14:10^A; Prov 23:6; 28:22; 4Q424 1 10 and 4Q525 13 2.

31:13bc רע עין — One could read "the one with a stingy eye" or "the greed of the eye (רֹעַ עין)."

31:13de כי זה — According to the context, the two particles should mean "that is why," but this construction with this sense is unusual. Instead, we expect the Hebrew על כן of 13*g*, which is also reflected in the Greek (διὰ τοῦτο) and Syriac (ܡܛܠ ܗܢܐ). It is possible that כי זה here reflects a clumsy back-translation of the Syriac ܡܛܠ ܕܗܢܐ (cf. Exod 32:1) (thus Lévi 1901, 141; Smend 1906a, 277 and Segal 1958, 194). תזוע — The verb זוע "to tremble" is only attested in late Hebrew. The marginal alternative תזיע could be a *hiphil* of זוע "to cause to tremble, agitate" (cf. the Aramaic cognate) or the *hiphil* of יזע (found in Rabbinic Hebrew) "to sweat, perspire" (used in the sense of crying in b. Pes. 181a). דמעה תדמע — For the expression, see Jer 13:17. תסיע in the margin should be a *hiphil* of נסע "to make leave, cause to spring up" (said of the wind in Ps 78:26). Note the phonetic harmony with the alternative (תזיע) from the preceding stich.

31:13fg For the last couplet, Kister (1990, 334) refers to Gen. Rab. 79:1: "ר׳ אחא. קשה הוא לשון הרע. שמי שבראו עשה לו מקום שיטמן בו "Rabbi Aha (said): The evil tongue is so severe that the one who created it

9   Qui est-il ? Que nous le déclarions bienheureux !
    Car il fait des merveilles parmi son peuple.
    (mg. Qui est-il ? Déclare le bienheureux !
    Car il fait des merveilles.)
10a Qui est-il ? Que nous nous joignions à lui ! (mg. celui qui se joint à lui ?)
10b Il a la paix et il a la splendeur (mg. 1. idem ; mg. 2. idem),
10c car quand abonde la paix est sa vie.
10d Je serai pour toi une splendeur.
10e Qui l'a béni, rend parfaite sa vie.
10f *C'est* pour toi une splendeur.
    (mg. Je te donnerai l'occasion de te glorifier.)
10g Qui peut dévier et n'a pas dévié
10h et faire le mal mais n'y a pas consenti.
11 C'est pourquoi son bonheur s'est affermi
    et l'assemblée raconte sa louange.
12 Instruction concernant à la fois le pain et le vin.
    Mon enfant, si tu t'assieds à une grande table (mg. la table d'une personne importante),
    N'ouvre pas sur elle ton gosier (mg. le gosier).
    Ne dis pas : « il y a) beaucoup sur elle ».
13a Souviens-toi (mg. sache) que l'avarice est un mal.
13b Dieu hait celui qui est avare,
13c il n'a rien créé de plus mauvais que lui.
13d C'est pourquoi devant toute chose l'œil tremble (mg. fait trembler)
13e et du visage coule (mg. (l'œil) fait tomber) une larme.
13f Dieu n'a rien créé de plus mauvais que l'œil,
    (mg. Dieu a-t-il créé plus mauvais que l'œil ?)
13g c'est pourquoi devant tout (mg. Sur tout, avant tout), son humidité fuit.
14 Le lieu où il regarde, n'y n'(y) étends (mg. pose) pas la main,
    et ne *te joins* (mg. ne te joins) pas à lui dans la corbeille.

9   Such a one we should declare blessed
    for they work wonders in the midst of their people!
    (mg. Who are they? Declare them blessed! For they work wonders.)
10a Who is the one that we might cling to them (mg. the one who attaches themself to it)?
10b Peace will be theirs and splendor will be theirs (mg. 1. idem; mg. 2. idem).
10c for in an abundance of peace is their life,
10d I will be a splendor for you.
10e Who has blessed them will restore their life,
10f *they* are a splendor for you.
    (mg. I will give you an occasion to glorify yourself.)
10g Who could turn aside, but did not turn aside,
10h and do wrong, but did not consent (to do it)?
11 Therefore, their happiness has grown stronger,
    and the assembly recounts their praise.
12 Instruction concerning both bread and wine
    My child, if you sit at a great (mg. person's) table,
    do not open your throat (mg. the throat) over it,
    do not say: "(there is) plenty on it."
13a Remember (mg: know) that selfishness is evil,
13b God abhors selfishness,
13c he did not create anything worse than it.
13d Thus, before all (these) things the eye trembles (mg. it (i.e., selfishness) makes the eye tremble),
13e and from the face a tear flows (mg. it makes (tears) come forth).
13f God has created nothing worse than the eye,
    (mg. Did God create anything worse than the eye?)
13g that is why before (mg. more than anything, in front of) everything, its moisture leaks.
14 The place where they look, do ~~not~~ not extend (mg: put) a hand,
    do not *join* (mg. join) them in the basket.

made for it a place in which to hide it." חלק — For חלק in the sense of "to create" in late Hebrew, see Sir 7:15; 16:16 and the corresponding notes. רע מ׳ חלק אל — This marginal note is surprising because it seems to express the opposite of what the main text expresses, unless as Lévi (1901, 141) proposes, it is an interrogative formula: "Has God created worse than an evil eye?" (see the Greek). נס לחה — The expression derives from Deut 34:7: לֹא־כָהֲתָה עֵינוֹ וְלֹא־נָס לֵחֹה "his eye had not dimmed, nor his vigor fled," where the pronominal suffixes refer to Moses. As Kister (1990, 334) notes, Ben Sira has this text in mind though the suffix in his phrase must be construed as 3fs (לֵחָהּ), referring to the eye. על כל מלפני — The marginal note offers a slight alternative to the phrase of the main text.

31:14 מקום יביט — "The place where he looks." See the similar construction in 42:11^M,B, מקום תגור, "the place where she sleeps." The masculine subject of יביט can only be the "great" of v. 12, unless the canceled אל should be taken as the subject referring to a human "mighty person" (see, e.g., Ezek 31:11). תושיט — Normally, we would have expected the short form תושט as in 31:18 but cf. 7:32, לאביון הושיט יד "extend your hand to the poor," where the yod mater marks what would be a *tsere* in the Tiberian tradition. דיחד — The word can only be a mistake for תיחד noted in the margin. The expression indicates that one should not take a dish or reach for food at the same time as another. Following Schechter (1900, 268), commentators refer to Der. Er. Rab. 7 שנים שהיו יושבין על שלחן אחד. הגדול שבהן שולח ידו תחלה ואחר כך קטן. והשולח ידו בפני מי שגדול הימנו הרי זה גרגרן "If two people are sitting at a single table, the greater person first stretches out their hand and, afterward, the lesser person. And the one who stretches out their hand before one who is greater is a glutton" and t. Ber. 5:7 שנים ממתינין זה לזה בקערה. שלשה אין ממתינין. המברך פושט ראשון. רצה לחלוק כבוד לרבו או למי שג־דול ממנו. הרשות בידו "Two wait for one another [to begin eating] with regard to [partaking of food from] a single plate. Three do not wait. The one who recites the benediction stretches forth his hand first [to partake of the food]. If he wished to honor his master or someone else who is more important than himself [by letting him take the first piece of food], he may do so" (trans. Neusner 2002, 30; see also Kister 1990, 335).

וכל אשר	ובכֹל ששנאת התבונן:		⁸דַּעָה רעך כנפשך	15	רעה
	ואל תעט פן תגעל:		⁹הסב כאיש אשר נבחר	16ab	
	ולא תהיה גרגרן פן תמאס:	¹⁰דע שרעך כמוך ואכול כאיש דבר ששם לפניך		16ef	
	ואל תלע פן תמאס:		¹¹חֹדל ראשון בעבור מוֹסר	17	
	לפני רע אל תושט יד:		¹²וגם אם בין רבים ישבת	18	
יצוריו	ועל יצועיו לא ישיק:		¹³הלֹא די אנוש נבֿ‍ון מזער	19	נכון מועד
ופנים	ופְנֹי הפוכות עם איש כסיל:		¹⁴מכאוב ונדד ושנה וצער ותשניק	20ab	ישנה
	וקם בבקר ונפשו אתֹוֹ:		¹⁵שנות חיים על קרב צֹולֵל	20cd	
	ילין עד בקר ונפשו עמו:		¹⁶שנֻת חִיִּיֹם עִם אֹנֹוֹש נב֗ון קֹם בֹבֹּקֹר	20ef	

Marginal notes (top right): 16c / 16d
אכל כאיש דבר ששם לפניך / לא תהיה גרגרן פן תגעל

L. 15 [31:20] אֹתוֹ — The *tav* is made clear by its right downstroke and a light trace of its foot beneath the lacuna. The *vav* overlaps its foot.

L. 16 [31:20] שנֻת חִיִּיֹם עִם אֹנֹוֹש — The reading שנֻת חִיִּיֹם perfectly fits the traces of letters on the upper edge of the paper, above the hole, suggesting that this line is a doublet of the previous one (see also verse 19). According to the Greek and Syriac, one would expect the following word to be עם and the traces allow for this reading, as there are two small marks before the final *mem*. The following traces perfectly fit the word אנוש. קֹם בֹבֹּקֹר — The remnants of the upper parts of these letters strongly suggest this reading.

31:15 דעה — For the uncommon long imperative in Ben Sira, see van Peursen 2004, 184–186. רעך כנפשך — The expression can have several meanings: (1) "Know your neighbor as (you know) yourself," in connection with the Delphi Inscription (Γνῶθι σεαυτόν) and Lev 19:18 (וְאָהַבְתָּ לְרֵעֲךָ כָּמוֹךָ "love your neighbor as yourself"); (2) "know that your neighbor is like you" (Lévi 1901, 142–143); (3) "know your companion who is like you." Indeed, the formula כנפש following a name or a participle is frequent in Ben Sira; see Sir 7:21 (= 10:25ᴮ) עבד משכיל חבב כנפש "love a prudent servant as (your) very self"; Sir 31:2, ומסתיר סוד אוהב כנפש "and he who keeps a secret is a friend like (you) very self"; and the expression רע כנפש in 37:2ᶜ,ᴮᵐᵍ,ᴰ "the companion as your (very) self" where Hᴮ has רע כנפשך (see Deut 13:7). רעה — The marginal note may be read as an imperative of the verb רעה I in the sense "to honor, take care of, get involved with, attend to" (cf. רעי in Sir 38:1ᴮ, supplemented by רעה in the margin, and the note there); thus Bacher (1900a, 268), who also refers to m. ʾAbot 2:10 (ms. Kaufmann A50): יהי כבוד תלמידך חביב עליך ככבוד חבירך. וכבוד חבירך כמורא רבך. According to the context, the verb may also mean "Feed your neighbor" (see Kister 1988, 51), or even "Associate with you neighbor." ובכל ש — The expression can refer both to things ("all that") and to persons ("all those who"). ששנאת — See Tob 4:15, καὶ ὃ μισεῖς μηδενὶ ποιήσῃς "what you dislike, do not do to a person." התבונן — The construction בין with the particle ב is characteristic of Late Biblical Hebrew, as well as the Hebrew of Qumran and Ben Sira.

31:16ab הסב — In Rabbinic Hebrew, the *hiphil* of סבב can mean "to lounge at the table"; see Sir 9:9ᴬ with this meaning and 32:1ᴮ,ᶠ. It corresponds to the more common אכל that is attested in all the other forms of the sentence, as well as in the Greek (φάγε) and the Syriac (ܠܚܡ). נבחר — The *niphal* of בחר expresses here "election, superiority, a person of choice who is part of the elite." תעט — For the meaning of this verb, see Sir 14:10ᴬ and the note. תגעל — The *niphal* of געל is only attested in 2 Sam 1:21 and in 4Q184 1 3. In the *niphal*, the verb means "to be rejected," which parallels the Greek (μὴ μισηθῇς) and the Syriac (ܕܠܐ ܬܣܬܢܐ). The verb also exists in Aramaic with the meaning "to be defiled."

31:16cd margin נכח — The word could be considered an adjective (as in Prov 8:9; 24:26), semantically parallel to נבחר, namely, a person that is "honest, upstanding"; nevertheless, this adjective does not commonly qualify a person in Classical and Rabbinic Hebrew. נכח may also be understood as reflecting an earlier prepositional phrase: "eat like the person (who is) before you" (= נכחך) or "eat like a person (what is) before you," as the Greek and the Syriac understood it (ܠܚܡ ܐܝܟ ܓܒܪܐ ܕܣܝܡ ܩܕܡܝܟ "Eat as a person what is set before you [= נכחך]"); this would suggest that נבחר may be a misreading of an earlier נכחך. תגעל — The meaning of the marginal reading is unclear and could be explained as a metathesis of תגעל, atttested in the main text. The verb גלע only appears in the *hithpael* in Biblical Hebrew with the meaning "to become irritated, exasperated." In Rabbinic Hebrew, Levy (1876–89, 1:337) considers it as a synonym of גלה "to discover, make known," while Jastrow (1903, 250) gives its meaning in the *niphal* as "to be opened through rubbing or scratching, to be bruised" a meaning that also fits the present context.

31:16ef דע שרעך כמוך — The expression is almost a literal quote of Lev 19:18 וְאָהַבְתָּ לְרֵעֲךָ כָּמוֹךָ "Love your neighbor as yourself"). This doublet of v. 15a is explained as a retroversion of the Syriac (see Rey 2018, 200). ואכול כאיש דבר ששם לפניך — This sentence, which echoes v. 16b and d margin, is very clearly a retroversion of the Syriac: ܘܠܚܡ ܐܝܟ ܓܒܪܐ ܕܣܝܡ ܩܕܡܝܟ "Eat like a person what(ever) is put before you." The same can be said of the second stich written in the margin in very tight handwriting; it matches perfectly the Syriac ܘܠܐ ܬܗܘܐ ܓܪܓܪܢ ܕܠܐ ܬܣܬܢܐ. The syntax and the vocabulary is uncommon in Classical Hebrew and follows isomorphically the syntax and vocabulary of the Syriac: the vetitive לא תהיה, which corresponds perfectly to the Syriac ܠܐ ܬܗܘܐ, is not common and preferably should have been the jussive אל תהי; the noun גרגרן, which is related to the Syriac ܓܪܓܪܢ, is only atttested in Rabbinic Hebrew and Babylonian Aramaic (See Kister 1988, 51; Rey 2018, 200).

31:17 מוסר — In the sense of instruction on how one would behave, "good manners" as Schechter (1900, 269) notes. תלע — The root לעע "to lick, drink greedily" is rare (Obad 1:16; Job 39:30). The same idea of 16b, d, f is repeated here: one should not eat greedily, in a gluttonous manner. תמאס — This verb seems to correspond to the Greek μὴ μισηθῇς and the Syriac ܕܠܐ ܬܣܬܢܐ like the previous verse.

31:18 See also, Der. Er. Rab. 7 and t. Ber. 5:7 mentioned in the note for 31:14.

15 Connais (mg. Honore) ton prochain comme toi-même et considère tout ce que (mg. idem) tu détestes.
16a Allonge-toi comme quelqu'un qui a été élu,
16b mais ne te précipite pas, de peur d'être rendu odieux.
16c (mg. 1. Mange comme une personne honnête,
16d mais ne te précipite pas, de peur que tu ne te révèles (mg. 2. que tu ne sois irrité)
16e Sache que ton prochain est comme toi
16f et mange comme une personne ce qui est placé devant toi et ne sois pas comme un glouton de peur que tu ne sois détesté.
17 Arrête-toi le premier, par éducation, ne te goinfre pas de peur que tu ne sois détesté.
18 Et aussi, si tu t'assieds au milieu de nombreuses (personnes), avant autrui n'étends pas la main.
19 Une personne intelligente (fiable) ne se suffit-elle pas de peu ? (mg. Une fête (n'est-elle pas suffisante pour une personne) fiable ?) et sur sa couche (mg. à propos de ses membres), elle ne vomira pas.
20a Peine et fuite du sommeil, trouble et angoisse,
20b une personne stupide a un visage (mg. idem) tourmenté.
20c Un sommeil vivifiant est sur un estomac vide
20d et en se levant le matin, on a de l'appétit.
20e Une personne intelligente (fiable) a un sommeil vivifiant,
20f se levant le matin, elle dort jusqu'au matin et a de l'appétit.

15 Know (mg: Take care of) your neighbor as yourself, and consider everything that (mg. idem) you detest.
16a Lie back like a person who has been appointed,
16b but do not hasten, lest you be loathed
16c (mg. 1. Eat like an honest person,)
16d (but do not hasten, lest you reveal yourself) (mg. 2. you become irritated.))
16e Know that your neighbor is like you,
16f and eat what is set before you like a person, and do not be a glutton, lest you be loathed.
17 Pause first out of good manners, do not lick up (food), lest you be loathed.
18 And also, if you sit in the middle of a number (of people), do not reach out a hand before (your) companion.
19 Is not a little sufficient for an intelligent (resolute) person? (mg. (Is not) the feast (sufficient for) a resolute (person)) On their bed (mg. Concerning their members), they will not vomit.
20a Pain, fleeting sleep, trouble and anguish,
20b tormented face (mg. idem) belong to the foolish person.
20c Restorative sleep (comes from) a stomach that is clean.
20d When one rises in the morning, one has an appetite.
20e An intelligent (resolute) person has restorative sleep.
20f The one who rises in the morning sleeps until the morning and has an appetite.

31:19 נבון — The confusion between נבון "intelligent" and נכון "firm, established, stable" is repeatedly found in these manuscripts (see the next verse and Sir 36:24 in H^C, H^B and H^Bmg). ישיק — The *hiphil* of שלק/נשק "to burn" is an Aramaism (see Isa 44:15; Ezek 39:9; BDB and HALOT) and may be used in a figurative sense for sickness (fever) or perhaps in the sense "to vomit" (lit. to make go up) as is found frequently with the Syriac cognate (see Reymond 2021a, 269-71; cf. the Targumic idioms: *aphel* סלק with פשר or with גרה "to chew (lit. bring up) the cud"). It may also be the root שוק "to overflow," used in an otherwise unattested figurative sense, "to vomit." Still, it may come from the root שוק "to pant, to gasp" (see the Greek ἀσθμαίνει and Hopkins 2011, 221). יצוריו — For צורים meaning "members," see Job 17:7.
31:20a נדד — Either the *qal* infinitive construct (cf. Ps 55:8) or a rare noun נֵדֶד as in the similar expression בנדד שנת מלך in the *piyyut* of Yannai שמות, קדושתות לשבתות השנה (see Maagarim). ישינה — A verbal noun only attested here, in Lev. Rab. 4:8 and Pirqoi ben Baboï: ולהתענג בעולם הזה אין יכול . . . מפני שיש בה צער וביטול למלאכה ועיר ד[1]ישינה ומנבל עצמו עליה (Maagarim). Cf. Gen 31:40 and Esth 6:1. תשניק — Meaning "anguish, torment," as in 4Q580 4 3 (see Puech, DJD 37 [2009, 423]). The word is from Aramaic (see also, the use of the root שנק in 11QTgJob 33:24 and Tg Onq Ex 14:27). The nominal form appears in Samaritan Aramaic (cf. Tal 2000, 1657), Mandaic, Syriac, as well as twice in Rabbinic Hebrew (though the form תשנוק is more frequent).
31:20b פני הפוכות — The meaning of פנים (here construed as feminine, as sometimes in the Bible) is not entirely clear. It usually means "face," and, construed in this way, might reflect the common idiom of a "changed face" (though this idiom usually uses the verb שנה I "to change"), which can be indicative of anger, pain, fear or even death (cf. Dan 3:19; 5:6; Job 14:20; see also Sir 13:25). Contrast with the more literal היו פני הפוכות "his face was turned away" (e.g., y. Šabb. 1:1). Alternatively, in Rabbinic Hebrew פנים can also mean "inner parts" (cf. the Syriac ܓܘܐ; see Lévi 1901, 144–145; Peters 1913, 257–258; Segal 1958, 196), though usually it occurs in architectural contexts. Segal (1958, 196) refers to the expression פנים של מטה in b. Šabb. 41a as a euphemism for nakedness (see also b. Ber. 24a), but it is difficult to find other examples. עם — The preposition indicates possession (see BDB s.v. 3b).
31:20c שנות חיים — The expression can be translated as "restorative sleep." According to GKC (§124e), variation between singular (see 20e) and plural (see Prov 6:10) with שנה conveys intensification. The phrase may also be translated as "years of life," as in Prov 4:10 and 9:11. As noted by commentators, חיים must have the same meaning as in 30:14-15 (see the note there). צולל — The verb צלל, which means "to tingle, to tremble" in Biblical Hebrew, more likely has here the meaning that it has in Rabbinic Hebrew, Aramaic and Syriac, "to clarify, to be clear."
31:20d וקם — וקם introduces a temporal or conditional sentence here (see van Peursen 2004, 351–352; Joüon §166a). ונפשו — נפש could mean appetite, as in Sir 40:30, or נפשו אתו may refer to the idea of having a clear mind. את expresses possession on analogy to עם.
31:20e-f עם — The preposition expresses possession (see BDB s.v. 3b).

	] ונו ותמצא נחת:	[ ] במ[ט]עמים [ ]וא[ם]	21 17
Or. 5518.1 (British Museum) verso	וכל אסון לא יגע בך:	בכל מעשיך היה צנוע	22ab 1
	ובאחרית תשיג אמֹרִי:	הלא די אנוש נבון מזער וגם אם נאנסתה במטעמים קוה קוה וינוח לך:	22cd 2
	ובאחרית תשיג אמֹרִי:	שמע בני ואל תבוז לי	22ef 3
תלעג	ובאחרית תמצא דברי:	שמע בני וקח מוסרי ואל תלעיג עלי	22gh 4
	עדות טובו נאמנה:	טוב על לחם תברך שפה	23 5
עדות	דעת רועי נאמנה:	רע על לחם ירגז בשער	24 F 6
	כי רבים הכשיל תירוש:	וגם על היין אל תתגבר	25 F 7
ביתן	כן היין למצות לצים:	כור בוחן מעשה לוטש	26 F 8
כי היית מצות			
	כן שכר לריב לצים:	נבון בוחן מעשה	9
	אם ישתנו במתכנתו:	למי היין חיים לאנוש	27 F 10
מארשית מצרו:	שהוא מרֹאשִׁית לשמחה נוצר:	מה חיים חסר היין	11
בעת	יין נשתה בֹעתֹו ודאי:	שמחת לב וששון ועדוי	28ab F 12

31:26 מצות B mg· כי היית מצות B F | כן היין למצות לצים כן שכר לריב לצים B mg· · 31:27 B | > F G S· מארשית B F | מארשית B mg· 31:28ab נשתה B G S | נשאֹר F·

L. 17 [31:21] בֹמ[ט]עמים וא[ם]ֹ — The line begins with a trace that would clearly fit a *vav*. There are some traces of the very bottoms of the following letters. Based on the Syriac and the Greek, one should read ואם. The letter *bet* clearly follows. Again, if one follows the Syriac (ܒܡܐܟܠܬܐ) and the Greek (ἔδεσμα) in forming a reconstruction, one can assume this *bet* is the preposition preceding מטעמים since these words often correspond across the different versions, as in v. 22d. The trace of the letter following *bet* may be a *mem*. Then there is a gap.

ונוֹ — Before the *nun* and the *vav*, there is a trace that could be a *yod*, preceded by the end of a horizontal base, or both traces correspond to a *mem*.

L. 11 [31:27] מארשית — All the preceding editions (Lévi 1901, 148; Smend 1906b, 26; Beentjes 1997, 57; Ben-Ḥayyim 1973, 31) read two words באר שית, but the first letter is clearly a *mem* (with the typical horn continuing into the diagonal). The most straightforward resolution is to consider these letters as one word with a metathesis of *alef* and *resh*. If correct, the scribe, as is often the case, has preserved an erroneous reading in the margin that was attested in another manuscript. The *alef* in this case can be read as a mater for what would be a *tsere* in the Tiberian tradition. Compare with the defective spelling in Deut 11:12 and the spelling in 4Q138 1 33 (מהרשֹׁ[י]ֹת; Qimron 2018, B.3.4).

מצרו — The first letter is preferably a *mem* rather than *nun*+*vav* = נוצרו (against preceding editions). The final letter may be interpreted as a *vav* followed by a *sof pasuq* (see the marginal note for line 15) or as a final *pe* (מַצְרֵף, "crucible," cf. Prov. 17:3).

L. 12 [31:28ab] ודאי — The second letter is preferably a *dalet* rather than a *resh* (against preceding editions).

31:21 The textual situation of this verse is especially complex. The Greek, the Syriac and the doublet in v. 22d attest to a convoluted textual history. Greek manuscripts are divided by two interpretations: (1) reading ἀναστὰς ἔμεσον (πόρρω) "to get up, vomit (a distance away)" (V*, L-248, Sa, [α-534]), which would partially correspond to the Hebrew of v. 22d. The Hebrew קוה could easily be the result of a confusion with קוא קום (= ἀναστὰς ἔμεσον [πόρρω]). (2) reading ἀναστὰς μεσοπορῶν "to get up, being half-way," attested in the main Greek witnesses and which could also reflect the Syriac ܡܢ ܓܘ in the second part of the sentence (ܐܦܩ ܢܦܫܟ ܡܢ ܓܘ ܟܪܣܐ "extract your breath from the midst of the belly"). The Latin translation conflates both readings (*in edendo multum surge e medio et vome et refrigerabit te*). See Lévi (1901, 146–147). The use of the singular מטעם is attested in *piyyutim*.

31:22c This sentence is a doublet of verse 19. See the note there.

31:22d This sentence is a doublet of the fragmentary verse 21. It is construed as a tri-stich written on only one line, in contrast to the stichometric presentation elsewhere. נאנסה — The verb אנס in the *niphal* should mean "to be oppressed, forced" here, as in Aramaic. קוה קוה — For the emphatic double imperative, see Judg 5:12; 2 Sam 16:7 and Nah 2:9. As written, קוה קוה is a double imperative of קוה "keep hoping," but dictionaries (see HALOT and DCH 7:246) record this reference under the entry for קיא "vomit," as translated by several Greek manuscripts (see the preceding note and Jer 25:27). וינוח לך — For the impersonal form of נוח, see Job 3:13 and 23:12.

31:22g Cf. Sir 12:12. תשיג — For the cognitive meaning of נשג, see 12:12 and the note.

31:22h תלעיג — For the *hiphil* of לעג with על, see Neh 3:33. The margin has the regular short form or the *qal*.

31:22i תמצא דברי — The verb מצא has a cognitive meaning here (see Jer 15:16; Qoh 12:10).

31:23–24 טוב על לחם — This seems to be an idiomatic expression, denoting one who is generous with food, just as רע על לחם denotes one who is ungenerous or stingy with food. The expression does not seem to be attested elsewhere. ירגז — This is likely the *qal* "to tremble," and could perhaps result from a confusion with רגן in the *pual* "to be reproached" (see the Greek). בשער — For שער as a metonymy for the people of the city, see Sir 7:7 and 42:11.

31:26ab Lévi (1901, 148) judiciously refers to Theognis (499–502): "Experts recognize gold and silver by fire, but wine reveals the mind of a man, even though he is very prudent, if he takes and drinks it beyond his limit, so that it puts to shame even one who was formerly wise" (Gerber 1999, 245 [LCL]). ביתן — The marginal note ביתן "palace" (only attested in Esth 1:5; 7:7–8 and very rarely in late Rabbinic Hebrew where it is usually an allusion to Esther) is hard to explain. ביתן could be a misspelling of בוטן "that conceives, is pregnant" (see its use in Aramaic; cf. 4Q416 2 iii 17 // 4Q418 9+9a-c 18 המה כֹור הוריכה "they are the furnace that gave birth to you"). מצות — This is the noun "quarrel" (מַצּוּת as in Isa 41:12) or the infinitive construct of מצה "to drain" which

21 Et s[i] par *des m[ets savoureux...]*
[ ] et tu trouveras le repos
22a Dans toutes tes œuvres, sois modeste
22b et aucun malheur ne t'atteindra.
22c Une personne intelligente ne se suffit-elle pas de peu ?
22d Et aussi, si tu as été forcé par des mets savoureux, vomis, vomis, et tu trouveras le repos.
22e Écoute mon enfant et ne me méprise pas
22f et plus tard tu comprendras mes dires.
22g Écoute mon enfant et saisis mon instruction
22h et ne te moque pas (mg. idem) de moi, et plus tard tu connaîtras mes paroles.
23 Les lèvres bénissent celui qui est généreux avec la nourriture,
le témoignage de sa bonté est fiable.
24 Celui qui est mauvais avec la nourriture tremblera à la porte (de la ville)
La reconnaissance (mg. le témoignage) de sa méchanceté est fiable.
25 Et aussi avec le vin, ne sois pas arrogant,
car le vin nouveau en a fait trébucher beaucoup.
26 Le creuset teste (mg. d'un palais est) l'œuvre du forgeron,
ainsi le vin sonde les moqueurs (mg. car tu as été la querelle des moqueurs).
L'intelligent teste chaque œuvre,
ainsi l'alcool pour une dispute des moqueurs.
27 Pour qui le vin est-il vie ? Pour l'être humain,
s'il le boit avec sa mesure.
Qu'est-ce que la vie (pour) celui qui manque de vin,
lequel, depuis le commencement (mg. idem ?), a été créé (mg. sa création est) pour la réjouissance.
28a Joie du cœur et jubilation et plaisir,
28b vin bu en son temps (mg. en temps approprié) et juste assez.

21 And if by *sa[vory food...]*
[...] you will find rest.
22a And in all your affairs, be humble,
22b so no misfortune will touch you.
22c Is not a little sufficient for an intelligent person?
22d And also, if you are overcome by savory food, vomit, vomit, and there will be rest for you.
22e Listen my child and do not despise me.
22f Afterwards you will understand my discourses.
22g Listen, my child, and accept my instruction,
22h and do not mock me, and afterwards you will comprehend my words.
23 Lips will bless the one generous with food,
the testimony of their generosity will be steadfast.
24 The one miserly with food will tremble at the gate,
knowledge (mg. testimony) of their stinginess will be steadfast.
25 And also concerning wine, do not act arrogantly,
for new wine has made many stumble.
26 As the furnace tests (mg. of the palace of) the work of the smith,
so wine is for the measuring of scorners (mg. because you were the quarrel (of scorners)).
As one who is intelligent tests each work,
so alcohol the strife of scorners.
27 For whom is wine life? For humanity,
when they drink it in moderation.
What is life for the one lacking wine,
which was from the beginning (mg. idem) created for jubilation (mg. (was) a creation (for jubilation))?
28a The joy of heart and jubilation and pleasure
28b (is) wine drunk in its time (mg. at the appropriate time) and quantity.

has the figurative sense in Rabbinic Hebrew (in the *piel*) "to sound one's learning" (Jastrow 1903, 825): "thus wine is for examining scorners." כי היית מצות — The marginal note is hard to make sense of and reflects a simple mistake. Yet, מצות as a noun provides a good syntactic complement to the verb בחן and as an infinitive would lead to the translation: "for, you are to examine…"
31:26cd נבון בוחן … לצים — These two stichs are a doublet of words in the preceding couplet. The first stich seems to be the result of letter confusion, while the second is characterized by the use of synonymous variants. מעשה מעשה — One may interpret the repetition in a distributive sense or one may interpret the second מעשה as the particle מן followed by a *qal* participle, "the work from the worker."
31:27 מה חיים חסר היין — The syntax of the sentence is odd. According to Lévi (1901, 149); Smend (1906a, 283–284); Peters (1913, 262) and Segal (1958, 200), one would expect מה חיי or מה חיים לחסר היין. חסר היין. Alternatively, read an asyndetic relative clause: "What is life (when) wine is lacking?" שהוא — (Cf. the Syriac ܕܐܝܬ). This construction, which is frequent in Mishnaic Hebrew, only appears in Qoh 2:22 in the Hebrew Bible (see also Sir 30:12). At Qumran, it is mainly used to introduce a correlation in dating (see 4Q322 1 3a; 4Q324 1 6; 4Q324a 1 i 1; 4Q332 2:3; 4Q333 1:3.7). מראשית — See the note on the reading. מצרו — "Its creation (מִצְרוֹ)."
31:28ab עדוי — In Aramaic and Rabbinic Hebrew, the word עדוי means "pregnancy," which does not fit the context here. The form must be a verbal noun from the root עדה, which according to the context, would be connected to the notion of "pleasure." It is likely that this form is a mistake for a word connected to the root עדן (see the Syriac ܒܣܝܡܘܬܐ). Lévi (1901, 2:149) makes an interesting observation that עדוי "pregnancy" is used to translate עדנה "pleasure" in Tg. Neof. Gen 18:12 (See Dihi 2004, 869). ודאי — The orthography of דַי with aleph is common when it is preceded by the *kaph* or *min* preposition (see Reymond 2017b, 1–16 and for this reading cf. the Greek αὐτάρκης "content, sufficient"). The reading ראי would be difficult to interpret. The most straightforward way to read it is as a *qal* passive participle written defectively, רָאִי "fit, worthy, adapted" (See Lévi 1901, 149; Segal 1958, 200; Dihi 2004, 626–9).

28cd F	¹³חיי מה לחסר תירוש	והוא לגיל נחלק מראש:	
29 F	¹⁴כאב ראש לענה וקלון	יין נשתה בתחרה וכעס:	
30 F	¹⁵מרבה חמר לבסיל מׄוקׄש	מחסר כח ומספק פצׄעׄ:	פחד:	נוקש
31 F	¹⁶במשתה היין אל [תו]כׄח רׄע	ואל תוגהו [בח]דׄ[ו]תׄו:	תחרפהו
17 F	¹⁷דבר חרפה אל [תאמר לו	[ה]]	עמׄו לעיׄני בני אדׄם

Chapter 32

1ab F	¹⁸[ ]	[ ]	[לׄ]	[לׄדׄ] כׄאחׄדׄ] [	T-S 16.313 recto
1/2 F	¹היה להם כאחד מהם: דאג להם ואחד תסוב הכן צרכם ואחׄר תרבץ:	ובכין	אין ניסׄ[ם נ]אׄ אבא אן פסוק איסת נוסכהא דיגר
2 F	²למען תשמח בכבודם	ועל מוסר תשא שכל:		
3 F	³מלל שבׄ כי הׄואׄ לך	והצנע שכלׄ ואל תמנע שיר:	לכת	סבכי שבכי הולך
4 F	⁴במקום היין אל תשפך שיח ובלא מזמר מה תשפך ובל עת מה תתחכם:			
5ab F	⁵כחותם על כיס זהב	שירׄ אל על משתה היין:	שירת	נוב זיר
5cd F	⁶כומז אודם על ניב זהב	משפט שיר על משתה היין:		

31:28cd חיי מה לחסר B חיים למה יחסר F · **31:29** ורוש B וקלון | בתחרה B בחרוׄ] F S (ܟܘܒܐ) · **31:30** חמד F חמר B | מוֹקׁש B נוקש F Bmg · ומספק B ומספיק F · **31:31** היין B יין F | תׄו]כׁחׄ[וׄ] B בח] F | תחרפהו Bmg · בני אדׄם Bmg | כל אדם F · **32:1c** היה להם F | והיה לך B F | שׄכל Bmg2 הולך B F G | הואׄ לך B F G S סבכי Bmg1 שבכי Bmg2 שבט F · **32:3** שב כי B G S | ובכין F ובכן Bmg | ואחר B | הבו F · **32:2** הכן B F | שׄכל B (double reading of B = G) | מה תשפך שיח ובל עת מה תתחכם: F · שׄכל B | היין B · **32:4** לכת Bmg, cf. Mic 6:8 · **32:5ab** שיר B | זהוב F · טס B ניב F Bmg1 זיר Bmg2 | אדם B אודם F · **32:5cd** שירת Bmg F ·

L. 16 [31:31] The line is restored on the basis of H^F, whose text perfectly fits the traces of remaining letters.

L. 17 [31:31] אדׄם — The final *mem* is visible in the crease of the bifolio.

L.1 margin [32:2] אין ניסׄ[ם נ]אׄ אבא — The faint traces of ink on the manuscript perfectly fit the final *mem* and the *alef*. This reading is supported by Wright (2018, 130). Though less probable, it is also possible to reconstruct [ני]מה or [נסׄ]ם, without the negative אׄ. The marginal reading would result in an opposite meaning: "This half (verse) is found with that verse in other copies" (See Wright 2018, 130). Bacher (quoted by Lévi) and Lévi (1901, 152) suggest the reading [אין ני]סׄ פסוק אבא, though it is too long for the available space.

31:28cd חיי מה — For a similar construction, see Sir 16:22^A ותקות מה and Jer 8:9. נחלק — For חלק with the meaning "to create," see 31:13 and the note (See Kister 1990, 334–335).

31:29 לענה — The word refers to the "wormwood" plant, which is used metaphorically in the Hebrew Bible to evoke "bitterness." Here, it may also refer to the effect of the alcohol that wormwood produces (see Lam 3:15). The word seems to have been inspired here by the preceding word ראש, which can refer to a "poisonous plant" and allows for another translation of the sentence: "pain, poison, wormwood and dishonor." For the collocation of ראש and לענה in the Hebrew Bible, see Deut 29:17, Jer 9:14, Amos 6:12 and Lam 3:19. בתחרה — This word is a noun that also appears in 40:5 (the cognate in Aramaic is תחרות) and the root in Jer 12:5.

31:30 חמר — The noun may refer to still fermenting wine or, as in Aramaic, simply to wine. נוקש — This may be a *qal* participle of the Aramaic נקש, which means "to knock" elsewhere in Ben Sira (See Sir 13:2, 41:2). It may also be understood as a *niphal* of יקש "one ensnared" (see Ps 9:17). מספק — For the meaning, see Sir 15:18 and the note.

31:31 במשתה היין — Literally, "banquet of wine," see Esth 5:6 and 7:2, 7–8. חדוה — See 1 Chr 16:27 and Neh 8:10.

32:1 תסוב — For סבב with the meaning "to sit (lie) at the table," see 1 Sam 16:11, and in the *hiphil*, see Sir 9:9 and 31:16.

32:2 For the marginal Persian note, see Wright (2018, 130–1) and the note on the reading. ובכין — See 13:7 and the note. מוסר — For the meaning of מוסר in this verse, see 31:17 and the note. תשא שכל — The expression נשא שכל does not seem to be attested elsewhere. Lévi (1901, 153), Box and Osterley (1913, 424) and Clines (DCH 5:767) understand it as "to obtain consideration, favor" in the light of Prov 3:4; see also נשא חן and חסד in Esth 2:9 and 5:2.

32:3 מלל שב — Both words are typically Aramaic (for מלל in the Hebrew of that period, see 1 Chr 25:4.26 and 1QM XV 11, 4Q171 1–10 i 6, 4Q380 1 i 7, 4Q385 3 3). The two marginal readings are curious. The notations סבכי (Aramaic סַבְּכָא "harp?" סְבָךְ "thicket?" סֵבֶךְ "net? curtain?") and שבכי הולך do not provide sound meaning in this context, unless the first is read as two words and the latter as four words: סב כי and שב כי הו לך (thus Peters 1902, 125). This would result in orthographic variants (for הו in place of הוא; see 15:19 and the note). For the etiology of this form, see Rey 2021b, 14–15. והצנע שכל — Literally, "humble your intelligence," or if צנע is used with its sense in Aramaic and Rabbinic Hebrew, "lay aside your intelligence." For צנע, see 16:25^A and the note. לכת —This marginal reading aims to harmonize the sentence with Mic 6:8: והנצע לכת.

32:4a אל תשפך שיח — Cf. Ps 102:1; 142:3.

32:4b The second stich is abnormally long and actually contains two clauses, which means the entire line represents a tristich. The Greek translates stichs *a* and *c*, while curiously, H^F and the Syriac have stichs *a* and *b*, though these two stichs actually constitute a doublet. מה — The particle מה may be the marker of a rhetorical question or a negation as in the variant in H^F (אל) and in Sir 13:2 (see the note there).

28c Quelle vie pour qui manque de vin nouveau ?
28d et lui, pour l'allégresse a été créé depuis le commencement.
29 Mal de crâne, amertume et déshonneur,
le vin bu à cause d'une dispute ou d'un chagrin.
30 L'abondance de vin est un piège pour (mg. frappe) l'insensé,
il fait manquer de force et multiplie des blessures (mg. l'angoisse).
31 Lors d'un banquet de vin ne [fais] pas de reproche à un compagnon,
et ne le tourmente pas (mg. ne l'outrage pas) [dans] sa [gai]t[é].
Ne [lui dis pas] une parole outrageante[.]
[   ] (mg. avec lui aux yeux des êtres humains.)

Chapitre 32

1a [   ]
1b [   ] (mg.]pour [toi] comme l'un[ ])
1c Sois pour eux comme l'un d'entre eux.
2 Inquiète-toi d'eux et ensuite allonge-toi (s.e. à table),
réponds à leurs besoins et ensuite (mg. et après cela) allonge-toi (s.e. à table)
(mg. [persan] Ce demi (verset) n'est pas attesté avec ce verset dans les autres copies.)
afin que tu te réjouisses de leur honneur
et en raison de ton savoir vivre tu recevras de la considération.
3 Parle vieillard (mg. 1. idem ?), car cela (mg. 2. idem ?) te revient,
sois humble avec ton intelligence (mg. en marchant) et ne refuse pas un chant.
4 Là où il y a du vin, ne te répands pas en discours,
et sans chanson comment te répandrais-tu en discours ? Et quand ce n'est pas le moment, ne fais pas le sage.
5a Comme un sceau sur une bourse d'or,
5b un chant (mg. idem) divin à un banquet de vin.
5c Un pendentif de rubis sur un collier (mg. 1. un collier ; mg. 2. une couronne) d'or,
5d (est) un chant approprié à un banquet de vin.

28c What life is there for one lacking new wine?
28d and it has been created for rejoicing from the beginning.
29 Headache, bitterness, and dishonor
(is) wine drunk because of strife or grief.
30 Abundance of young wine is a snare for the fool (mg. knocks (the fool) down),
decreasing strength and increasing wounds (mg. dread).
31 At a banquet of wine rebuke not a friend
and do not torment them (mg. reproach them) [in th]eir j[o]y.
A reproachful word, do not [speak to them.]
[   ] (mg. with them in the sight of huma[nity].)

Chapter 32

1a [   ]
1b [   ] (mg.]for [you] as one[ ])
1c Be to them as one of them.
2 Concern yourself with them and afterward lie (at the table),
take care of their needs and afterward (mg. then) you may lie down (at the table)
(mg. [Persian]: This half (verse) is not found with that verse in other copies.)
So that you rejoice in their honor,
and that you receive consideration because of your good manners.
3 Speak, old one, because (mg. 1. idem?) it is (mg. 2. idem?) your place,
be humble in your intelligence (mg. walk with humility) and do not withhold a song.
4 In a place of wine do not pour out a discourse,
and without song, how can you pour out a discourse?
and at the wrong time, do not present yourself as wise.
5a Like a seal over a purse of gold,
5b (is) a divine song (mg. idem) at a banquet of wine.
5c A ruby pendant over a necklace of gold (mg. 1. necklace, mg. 2. crown)
5d (is) an appropriate song at a banquet of wine.

תתחכם — For the meaning of the *hithpael* of חכם, cf. 10:26 and the note in 6:32.
32:5a–d שיר אל — The expression is not found elsewhere and its referent is not entirely clear. משתה היין — See 31:31. נוב / ניב זהב — The word ניב "fruit, produce, bud" only appears in Isa 57:19 and Mal 1:12. Here it should refer to a sort of jewelery. Interestingly, Isa 57:19 has נוב as *ketiv* and ניב as *qere*, while this manuscript has the opposite (i.e. ניב in the main text and נוב in the margin). זיר — See זיר זהב in Exod 37:2 (and its targumic translation). This Aramaic word, "ornamental ring," is an explanatory alternative to the obscure word ניב. משפט שיר — The expression may refer to the regulation of songs according to time and occasion, perhaps with a liturgical intention. Lévi (1901, 154; see the Greek σύγκριμα μουσικῶν) and Smend (1906a, 287–8) understood the expression as "concert."

נהפך ספיר	5ef F	⁷כרביד זהב ובו נפך וספיר	כך נאים דברים יפים על משתה היין:
מלא	6 F	⁸מלואות פז וחותם ברקת	קול מזמור על נועם תירוש:
אתך	7 F	⁹דבר נער אם צריך אתה בחזק	פעמים ושלש אם ישאלך: ישא לך
	8	¹⁰כל לאמר ומעט הרבה	ודמה ליודע ומחריש יחדו:
	9	¹¹בין זקנים אל תקומם	ושרים אל תרב לטרד:
	10ab	¹²לפני ברד ינצח ברק	ולפני דכא ינצח חן:
ברד ינצח ברד B| ברד ינצח ברד	cd	¹³לפני ברד ינצח֯ ברק	ולפני בושי חן:
	11 F	¹⁴בעת מפקד אל תתאחר	פטר לביתך ושלם רצון:
		¹⁵בעת שלחן אל תרבה דברים	ואם עלה על לבד דבר:
	12 F	¹⁶פְטֹר לְבִיתְךָ ושלם רצון	ביראת אל ולא בחסר כל:
	13 F	¹⁷מ[ע]ל כל אלה ברך עושך	המרוך מטובתו:
דרש אל חי | קוה רצון	14ab F	¹⁸דוֹרֵשׁ אל [י]קוֹה ר֯צון	ומתלהלה יוקש בו:
	14cd F	¹דורש אל יקח מוסר	ומשחרהו ישיג מענה:
ישא	14ef F	²דורש חפצי אל יקח לקח	ויענהו בתפלתו:

T-S 16.313 verso

32:5ef כרביד B | כדביר F · נפך וספיר B | נהפך ספיר Bmg | נופך וספיר F · כך נאים F · נואי F · דברים F · דברים יפים B · **32:6** מלואות F · מלא B | Bmg | כל מלא F · **32:7** צריך B | אם צריך F · אתה B | אתך Bmg | אותך F · בחזק B | בחזק פעמים F · פעמים F B G | ישאלך F · ישא לך Bmg · **32:14ab** א B | אל F · ומתלהלה B | וגם מתלהלה F · **32:14cd** ומשחרהו ישיג מענה F · > B | דורש אל יקח מוסר | וקוה רצון B | [י]קוה רצון ? F | קוה רצון Bmg F · חי Bmg F · **32:14ef** בכל קצ֯ F · בתפלתו B | מצא F · Bmg ישא B | יקח F ·

L. 13 [32:10] ברד ינצח ברד — The first marginal note is crossed out. In both marginal notes, it is difficult to know whether the scribe varies between ברד "hailstones," ברר "purity" (?) or to read נצח ברד כדדי "(before) bright sparks it hails"; cf. כלפידי כוֹדוד והנצח in Yehuda Ben Koresh's רהיטים ליו״ב (MS Heb.e.35/31r, lines 7–8 [Maagarim]).

32:5e–f נהפך ספיר — The meaning of this marginal reading is difficult to explain, perhaps "twister with saphire." כך — For the use of this conjunction in Ben Sira, see 13:17 and 37:13.

32:6 מלא — Contra Peters (1902, 126), who understands these letters as an abbreviation of the defective reading מלאות, we understand it as מְלָא (see BDB).

32:7 צריך — See 31:4^B and the note. H^F has צורך; on the variation between the two words, see Sir 13:6^A and the note. אתך — The marginal reading may be vocalized as an accusative particle (אֹתְךָ) "one needs you" as in H^F or as the preposition אִתְּךָ "with you" (see Lévi [1901, 154–5] and Segal [1958, 203]); cf. Sir 13:6^A צְרִיךְ לוֹ עִמָּךְ. Confusion between the definite direct object marker and preposition is found in the Bible (e.g., אותם in the Leningrad Codex to Jer 1:16 vs. אתם in other manuscripts; see BHS). בחזק — It is not totally clear in the manuscript whether בחזק belongs to the first stich (so Smend 1906b, 27) or the second. ישא לך — The meaning of this marginal notation is elliptical, perhaps "if he lifts (his word/request) to you" (see Peters [1913, 264]: "wenn man dich anredet") or "if he lifts (his face) to you," i.e. "if someone allows you" (see Lévi [1901, 155]).

32:8 כל — These letters can be understood as an imperative of כלה "stop, finish, complete, vanish" (so Segal [1958, 203]), instead of correcting the text to כלל אמר, as has been suggested (Lévi [1901, 155]; Peters [1913, 264], etc.). מעט הרבה — This is an oxymoron. The phrase can be interpreted as the *piel* imperative (see 3:18 and the note) followed by the *hiphil* infinitive absolute (with an adverbial meaning), "diminish (speech?) greatly" (See also Box and Osterley [1913, 425] "and make little (*piel*) of much") or as the adjective מְעַט followed by the *hiphil* infinitive absolute (used like a noun), "little is (too) much" (see Mopsik [2003, 192] "peu c'est beaucoup"). Alternatively, Lévi [1901, 155] proposes "Dis beaucoup en peu de mots" (*hiphil* imperative of רבה with the adjective מְעַט).

L. 16 [32:12] פְטֹר לְבִיתְךָ — Though damaged, this reading is certain.
L. 17 [32:13] מ[ע]ל כל אלה — All preceding editions restore ו[על] כל, which is clearly too short for the available space. We suggest reading מ[ע]ל, while acknowledging that the base of the *mem* is partially faded. See the Latin *et super his omnibus*.

32:9 תקומם — For the *polel* of קום, see also 11:9^A and 4Q436 1a,b 2. טרד — This verb (also found at Sir 51:20^{11Q5}) is attested in Rabbinic Hebrew, as well as in Aramaic, with the meaning "to be running, to drip, to flow," but also "to trouble, stir up." It is used metaphorically here and has a negative connotation.

32:10ab The overall meaning of this verse is not entirely clear. The author is likely playing on the two meanings of לפני, first in a temporal sense "before" and then a spatial sense "in front of" (yet, see Skehan and Di Lella [1987, 392–3] for a different interpretation). נצח — This verb means "to shine" in Rabbinic Hebrew and in Aramaic (see also 43:5, 13). דכא — See Isa 57:15.

32:10cd בושי — The final *yod* may be an adjectival [ī] ending, see Joüon §88Mg. Bacher (1900a, 281), Lévi (1901, 155) and Segal (1958, 203) explain the *yod* as a possible abbreviation for ינצח or יבוא, but the way the *yod* is written on the manuscript makes it unlikely that it reflects an abbreviation. It is far more likely it is a scribal mistake and one must read בוש ברד ינצח. ברד ינצח ברד — It is very difficult to make sense of the two marginal readings, as *resh* and *dalet* are almost identical in shape, and the *yod* of ינצח may be attached to the preceding word.

32:11 עת מפקד — Read the substantive מִפְקָד "appointed time" (cf. Ezek 43:21) or a *hophal* participle, as suggested by Lévi (1901, 156). Segal (1958, 203) undestood it as "lack, absence" (see Ben Yehuda 6:3217) refering to the end of the banquet (see the opposite in v. 11b בעת שלחן). תתאחר — For the *hithpael* of אחר, see 7:34^A and the note. פטר לביתך — The verb פטר should be understood as a *qal* with its Aramaic (*peal*) meaning here (cf. 4Q549 2 6 [עמרם] פטר לבית עלמה "[Amram] leaves for his eternal house" and similar expressions in Rabbinic Aramaic [e.g., b. B. Bat. 153a] in the context of death). In most later dialects of Aramaic, the verb in the sense "depart" is in the *hithpeel* (and in the *niphal* in the related Rabbinic Hebrew expression), but in Syriac the verb commonly occurs in the *peal*. ושלם רצון — The expres-

5e Comme un collier d'or comprenant turquoise et saphir (mg. [Comme un collier d'or] transformé en saphir),
5f ainsi sont délicieuses les belles paroles lors d'un banquet de vin.
6 Sertissages (mg. enchâssement) d'or fin et sceau d'émeraude,
(sont) la voix d'un psaume sur la douceur du vin nouveau.
7 Parle, jeune homme, si tu le dois (mg. on a besoin de toi), avec fermeté,
deux ou trois fois, si on te demande (mg. si on te le permet).
8 Cesse de parler et peu est (déjà) trop,
ressemble à celui qui, à la fois, sait et garde le silence.
9 Au milieu des anciens ne te lève pas
et ne trouble pas les princes à l'excès.
10a Avant la grêle resplendit l'éclair
10b et devant l'oppressé resplendit la grâce.
10c Avant la grêle resplendit l'éclair,
(mg. 1: (devant) la grêle resplendit la grêle)
(mg. 2: (devant) la grêle resplendit la grêle)
10d et devant le honteux, la grâce.
11 Au temps prescrit, ne tarde pas,
pars pour ta maison et (alors) accomplis (ton) désir.
Lorsque tu es à table, ne multiplie pas les paroles,
même si une parole monte à ton cœur,
12 Pars pour ta maison et accomplis (ton) désir,
dans la crainte de Dieu et ne manquant de rien.
13 Au dessus de tout cela, bénis ton créateur
qui t'enivre de sa bonté.
14a Celui qui cherche Dieu espère une faveur
(mg. Cherche le Dieu vivant et *l'opprimé* espérera),
14b mais le fou furieux y est pris au piège.
14c Celui qui cherche Dieu saisit la discipline
14d et celui qui le scrute comprend la réponse.
14e Celui qui cherche les désirs de Dieu, saisit (mg. idem) l'instruction.
14f Et il lui répond dans sa prière.

5e As a necklace of gold in which there is turquoise and sapphire (mg. [As a necklace of gold] changed into sapphire),
5f so beautiful words are pleasant at a wine banquet.
6 Settings (mg. a setting) of fine gold and emerald seal,
(are) the sound of a psalm with the pleasantness of new wine.
7 Speak firmly, young man, if you are needed (mg. idem), twice or three times, if someone asks you (mg. if someone allows you [?]) .
8 Stop speaking, a little is (too) much,
be like one who knows but at the same time keeps quiet.
9 Among elders do not stand,
and do not disturb princes repeatedly.
10a Before hail, lightning flashes,
10b so favor flashes before the oppressed.
10c Before hail, lightning flashes,
(mg. 1: (before) hail flashes hail)
(mg. 2: (before) hail flashes hail)
10d and before the shameful, grace (flashes).
11 At the appointed time, do not delay,
depart to your house so that you can fulfill (your) desire.
When you are at the table, do not multiply words,
even if a matter arises in your heart,
12 Depart to your house so that you can fulfill (your) desire
with the fear of God and lacking nothing.
13 Above all of these things, bless your creator,
the one who refreshes you from his bounty.
14a The one who seeks God will hope for [his] good will
(mg. Seek the living God and *the oppressed* will hope)
14b but the maniac will be ensnared by it.
14c The one who seeks God will grasp instruction,
14d the one who seeks him diligently will comprehend the response.
14e The one who seeks God's desires will grasp (mg. idem) instruction
14f and he will answer them in his prayer.

---

sion seems to be unique and would at first appear to mean "do what you want," "fulfill your intention" (see the Greek), or, as proposed by Mopsik, "prends-y tes aises." Alternatively, רצון may imply the host or God: "return (the host's) goodwill" (i.e., respect the host's generosity by leaving the party at an appropriate time), or "fulfill (God's) will." עלה על לבך — For the expression, cf. Isa 65:17; Jer 3:16 and 2 Kgs 12:5.

32:12 ביראת אל ולא בחסר כל — See Psa 34:10 and Deut 28:48. The expression ולא בחסר כל "and lacking nothing" corresponds exactly to the Syriac: ܘܠܐ ܒܚܣܪ ܟܠ. Bronznick (1985, 91–105), on the other hand, argues that the noun חסר may mean here "disgrace" (see Sir 14:2ᴬ and the note for the same semantic difficulty). Following others, Lévi (1902, 157) argues that לא בחסר is a mistake for the Aramaic לא בחסד meaning "without shame" (see the Greek λόγῳ ὑπερηφάνῳ). He observes that the Arabic translation of Ben Sira, which is based on the Syriac, translates the word חוסדא "reproach." In any case, it is important to recall the very frequent confusion between *dalet* and *resh* in the transmission of our text.

32:13 המרוך — The *piel* participle of רוה.

32:14 ומתלהלה — The *hithpalpel* participle of להלה, "madman," is only attested in Prov 26:18. It disappears in rabbinic literature and reappears in the tenth-century in the writing of authors like Saadiah Gaon. רצוץ — "The oppressed." This meaning is difficult to accommodate in the context and is most probably a scribal confusion for רצון "and hope in (God's) will." The two words (רצוץ and רצון) also seem to be confused in Sir 35:20ᴮ, where Hᴮ contains רצון though the context suggests perhaps an earlier רצוץ in the phrase "bitterness of (תמרורי) the oppressed." ישיג — For נשג with a cognitive meaning, see 12:2ᴬ and the note. יקח — For לקח with a cognitive meaning, see 8:9ᴬ and the note.

MANUSCRIPT B

	ומתלהלה יוקש בה:	³דורש תורה יפיקנה	15
	ותחבולות מנשף יוציא:	⁴ירא יייֿ יבין משפט	16 EF
וחכמות	וכחׄמות רבות יוציאו מלבם:	⁵יראי יייֿ יבינו משפטו	
וׄיאחר למשוך	ואחר צרכו ימׄשך תורה:	⁶איש חכׄם יטה תוכחות	חמס 17 EF
	ולץ לא ישמר לשונו:	⁷איש חכם לא יכסה כחׄמה	חכמה 18ab EF
	זד ולץ לא ישמר תורה:	⁸איש חכם לא יקח שחד	18cd EF
	ואחר מעשיך אל תתקצף:	⁹בלא עצה אל תפעל דבר	19 EF
	ואל תתקל בנגף פעמים:	¹⁰בדרך מוקשת אל תלך	20 EF
הׄזׄהׄר	ובאחריתך השׄמר:	¹¹אל תבטח בדרך מחתף	רשׄעיׄם 21a/22a
	ובארחתיך הזהר:	¹²אל תבטח בדרך רשעים	21b/22b EF
מצות מצותׄוׄ	כי כל עושה אלה שומר מׄצוה:	¹³בכל דרכיך שמור נפשך	23
	כי עושה זה שומר מצוה	¹⁴בכל מעשיך שמור נפשך	
	ובוטח בייֿ לא יבוש:	¹⁵נוצר תורה שומר נפשו	24 EF

Chapter 33

ושב	כי אם בניסוי שׄבׄ וׄנׄמׄלׄט:	¹⁶ירא יייֿ לא יפגע רע	1 EF

32:15 :דורש תורה יפיקנה ומתלהלה יוקש בה B | > F · **32:16** וכחׄמות רבות B (metat.) | וחכמות E F Bmg · **32:17** חכם B | חמס E F Bmg G (ἁμαρτωλός) · איש | (ܐܢܫܐ) 7a1, ܕܘܢܒܐ, S (73 βουλῆς) B G איש חכם לא **32:18ab** · E F למשך | משך Bmg | משך E F · ימׄשך B | ימשך Bmg E F · ויאחר B | ואחר Bmg E F · **32:18cd** חכם B G (βουλῆς) S (73 ܕܘܢܒܐ, 7a1 (ܐܢܫܐ) | חמס Bmg F · שחד E F · כחׄמה B (metat.) | חכמה Bmg E F · ישמור B E | ישמר Bmg E F · **32:19** תתקצף B | תתקפץ E F · **32:20** יקח מצוה Bmg E F · ישמר תורה B | ישמר שכל Bmg E F G S (ܕܘܢܒܐ) ? G · **32:21a/22a** (הׄזׄהׄר) השמר ובאחריתך מחתף בדרך תבטח אל B | > E F · **32:21b/22b** תבטח B | תתחר F · ובארחתיך B | ובאראחתיך E F · היה זהיר E F · הזהר F · **32:23** > E F · **32:24** נוצר B | שומר E F · **33:1** tr. before 32:24 E F · בניסוי B F | בנסוי E · שב B | ושב Bmg | ישוב E F ·

L. 11 [32:21] רשׄעיׄם — Only a tentative reading, according to the context and the doublet. הׄזׄהׄר — Only a tentative reading, according to the context and the doublet.

L. 16 [33:1] שׄבׄ וׄנׄמׄלׄט — This restoration fits the preserved traces and the available space.

32:16 תחבולות — See Sir 6:25^A and the note. וכחׄמות — The main text clearly presents a metathesis for וחכמות, found in the margin, yet note the same mistake in 32:18^B. For the plural, see 4:11 and the note.

32:17 איש חכם — For the same confusion between חכם and חמס, see Sir 10:23, where the word חמס in H^B (Greek ἁμαρτωλόν and the Syriac ܚܡܠܐ) corresponds to יט[ח]ם in H^A. יטה — Assuming the reading איש חכם (cf. the Syriac ܕܘܢܒܐ "an astute person"), the verb נטה (either in the *qal* or *hiphil*) should have a positive and metaphorical meaning "to extend counsels," which is less common (see ויט אליו חסד with *qal* in Gen 39:21 and ויט עלינו חסד with the *hiphil* in Ezra 9:9). Assuming the marginal alternative איש חמס (see also H^{E,F} and the Greek ἄνθρωπος ἁμαρτωλός), the verb נטה (either in the *qal* or *hiphil*) should have a negative connotation, "to distort counsels," as in Exod 23:6, Deut 16:19, etc. תוכחות — The word תוכחת refers to "reproach, blame," but has a positive meaning in sapiential contexts, "counsel, reproof" (see Prov 1:23, 25, 30; 4Q525 5 10; etc.). ימׄשך — For the construction of משך with אחר, see Song 1:4. Similar to the ambiguity with נטה, if we assume איש חכם to be the subject, then the verb משך should have a positive sense "to grasp": "to suit their need, they acquire the law." For משך in the meaning "to seize," see Job 28:18 and its translation in LXX, and for the close semantic relationship between משך and לקח, see *Mekhilta of Rabbi Ishmael* 11:36 on Exod 12:21). If, on the other hand, we assume איש חמס to be the subject, the expression should imply that the law is turned away due to the individual's own desire: "after their need, they distort the law" (see Levy [1876–89, 3:276] "to attract to oneself"). וׄיאחר צרכו למשוך — The marginal reading changes the ambiguous sentence into an explicitly positive one: "they delay their desire/need to acquire the law." This variant may have been introduced to fit the reading איש חכם instead of איש חמס, yet it also appears in H^{E,F}, which attest the reading איש חמס.

32:18 יכסה — Although *kaph* is certain here and in H^F, the Greek and Syriac (ܒܣܐ) suggest this was earlier יבסה "... will neglect," an Aramaism (cf. ܟܣܐ in Syriac). כחׄמה — A metathesis for חכמה, found in the margin. See the same mistake in 32:16^B. זד ולץ — In the main text, as well as in the margin, the plural subject is followed by a singular verb (see Joüon §150p; Deut 8:13). יקח שכל — Cf. 8:9 "to acquire intelligence" or 16:24 "to grasp instruction."

32:19 תתקצף — The *hithpael* of קצף ("to become enraged") is only attested in Isa 8:21 (see also קצפן in 30:23). It is not used elsewhere before modern times, except for one occurence in the writings of Saadiah Gaon. The Greek (μὴ μεταμελοῦ), the Syriac (ܠܐ ܬܬܘܗ) and the Latin (*non pœnitebis*) translations, as well as the context, invite one to understand it as "do not regret." In Syriac, the cognate root occurs in the *ethpeel* and *ethpaal* with the meaning "to be sad, vexed."

32:20 תתקל — See Sir 13:25 and note. בנגף — The meaning "obstacle" occurs in Isa 8:14, which seems to inspire this text. The term also refers to an obstacle causing stumbling 4Q418 168 2 and 4Q415 11 8.

32:21 מחתף — The same sequence of letters appears in Sir 50:4,

15 Celui qui cherche la loi, la trouvera,
mais le fou furieux y est pris au piège.
16 Celui qui craint YYY comprend le jugement
Et fait sortir des projets de l'obscurité.
Ceux qui craignent YYY comprennent son jugement
et ils font sortir de leur cœur une *sagesse* (mg. sagesse)
abondante.
17 Une personne sage (mg. violent) répand (/biaise) les conseils,
et d'après son besoin, elle détourne/saisit la loi.
(mg. et elle retarde son besoin pour saisir la loi).
18a Une personne sage, comme le soleil, ne se dissimule
(mg. ne dissimule pas la sagesse)
18b et le railleur ne garde pas sa langue.
18c Une personne sage n'accepte pas de présent,
18d l'insolent et le railleur n'observent pas la loi.
(mg. Une personne violente ne saisit pas l'instruction,
l'insolent et le railleur ne saisissent pas le commandement.)
19 Sans conseil, ne fais rien
et après tes actes, n'aie pas de regret.
20 Ne va pas dans un chemin semé d'embûches
et ne trébuche pas sur un obstacle deux fois.
21a Ne fais pas confiance dans la voie du brigand (mg. des méchants),
22a et prends soin de (mg. fais attention à) ta fin.
21b Ne fais pas confiance dans la voie des méchants,
22b et fais attention à tes voies.
23 En toutes tes voies, garde-toi,
Car quiconque fait cela garde le commandement
(mg. 1. les commandements, mg. 2. ses commandements)
En toutes tes œuvres garde-toi,
Car celui qui fait cela garde le commandement.
24 Celui qui veille sur la loi, se garde
et celui qui fait confiance en YYY ne sera pas déçu.

Chapitre 33

1 Celui qui craint YYY ne rencontre pas le mal,
mais s'il retourne dans l'épreuve, alors il sera sauvé
(mg. (s'il est dans l'épreuve) et qu'il se repent (alors il sera sauvé.))

15 The one who seeks the law will find it,
but the maniac will be ensnared by it.
16 The one who fears YYY understands justice,
and will bring out (his) plans from obscurity.
The ones who fear YYY understand his justice,
and will bring out from their heart abundant *wisdom*
(mg. wisdom).
17 A wise (mg. violent) person extends (distorts) counsels
and after their need, they stretch/grasp the law (mg.
They postpone their need in order to seize the law.)
18a The wise person, like the sun, does not conceal themself (mg. [does not conceal] wisdom),
18b and the scoffer does not guard their tongue.
18c The wise person does not accept a bribe,
18d the insolent and the scorner do not keep the law.
(mg. The violent person does not grasp instruction,
the insolent and the scorner do not grasp the commandment.)
19 Do not do anything without advice
and after your actions, do not feel regret.
20 Do not walk down a path of traps,
and do not stumble over an obstacle twice.
21a Do not put your trust in the way of a robber (mg. of the wicked)
22a and take care (mg. pay attention) concerning your end.
21b Do not put your trust in the way of the wicked
22b and pay attention to your paths.
23 In all your ways, guard yourself,
for whoever does so keeps the commandment.
(mg. 1. the commandments, mg. 2. his commandments)
In all your works, guard yourself,
For the one who does this keeps the commandment.
24 The one who observes Torah guards themself,
and the one who trusts in YYY will not be disappointed

Chapter 33

1 The one who fears YYY will not meet evil,
for if they are again put to the test, then they will be
saved (mg. (if they are put to the test) and they repent
(then, they will be saved).

where it is construed as the preposition מן followed by either the *qal* participle of חתף (as in Sir 15:25^A) or the noun חֲתָף (found in Prov. 23:28 and in *piyyutim*). Here, the *mem* may be the same preposition, indicating cause "because of robbery / robber(s)," or part of a *piel* participle (i.e., מְחַתֵּף "one who takes violently" = "robber"). Although the *piel* is rare in Hebrew, the biform in Syriac, ܚܛܦ, occurs not infrequently in the *pael* (including in the Peshitta to Ps 29:5 and Matt 11:12). For a discussion of the root, see Sir 15:14^A and the note there.

32:22b ובאחריתך — This word has a variety of different meanings in Ben Sira. For a similar sentence, cf. 7:36 and the note. It may designate the "future," "death" (see also 3:26) or "descendants" (see 16:3 and the Greek here, καὶ ἀπὸ τῶν τέκνων σου).

32:24 נוצר תורה שומר נפשו — Cf. Prov 19:16. ובוטח ביי לא יבוש — Cf. Ps 22:6.

33:1 יפגע רע — Cf. 1 Kgs 5:18.

במסער	ומתמוטט כמסערה אני:		¹⁷לא יחכם שונא תורה	2 EF
סלסם	ותורתו כאור[י]ן ישרה:		¹⁸איש נבון יבין דבר	3 EF

Chapter 35

T-S 16.313 recto	מעשרך	ובששון הקדש מעשר:	¹בכל מעשיך האר פנים	11 ᴾ
	מעשיך	בטוב עין ובהשגת יד:	²תן לו כמתנתו לך:	12 ᴾ	כמתנו
	וב[ ]הגשת ובה[ ]גיש	ושבעתים ישיב לך:	³כי אלוה תשלומות הוא	13 ᴾ
	ישלם	ואל תבטח על זבח מעשק:	⁴אל תשחד כי לא יקח	14/15 ᴾ
		ואין עמו משוא פנים:	⁵כי אלהי משפט הוא	
	ותחנונים	ותחנוני מצוק ישמע:	⁶לא ישא פנים אל דל	16 ᴾ
	תחבט	ואלמנה כי תרבה שיח:	⁷לא יטש צעקת יתום	17	אנקת
		ואנחה על מרודיה:	⁸הלא דמעה על לחי תרד	18
	צעקתה וצעקתיה	וצעקה ענן חשתה:	⁹תמרורי רצון הנחה	20

33:2 אני ? B G (πλοῖον) | במסער B E F | Bmg אני · 33:3 אזנו E F · כאור[י]ן ישרה B | > E F · איש נבון יבין דבר ותורתו כאור[י]ן ישרה 33:2 במסערה

L. 17 [33:2] כמסערה — According to the remaining traces and H^(E,F), this restoration is almost certain. אני: — While the *yod* is clear and the *aleph* is highly probable, what comes between them is less certain. It is also possible to read אזנו "his ear," as in H^(E,F), though this does not fit the space as well as אני, nor fit the context. אניה, however, is impossible.
L. 18 [33:3] דבר — The traces after דבר are bleed through letters from the recto. כאור[י]ן — Beneath the *aleph* is an offset trace from 36:26. The bottom tip of the *vav* may be attested beneath the hole, while the *resh* is attested only by traces of its upper bar. ישרה — The initial *yod* is a tentative reading, as the bottom edge of paper has more ink than we would expect. Nevertheless, the following traces make clear that the following letter is a *sin/shin* and the letter to the left of this is either a *dalet* or *resh*. The reading of the last letter is again tentative, but seems to be an extended *he*, similar to the extended *resh* seen just above. The word in the margin is harder to read.

33:2 ומתמוטט — The *hithpolel* of מוט, which is only attested in Isa 24:19 in the Hebrew Bible, is frequent at Qumran (1QH^a XIV 21; 4Q176 8–11 12; 4Q424 1 4; 4Q429 4 i 10; 4Q525 14 ii 6) and in Rabbinic Hebrew. כמסערה — Since it is unlikely, though not excluded, that the word combines the two particles כ and מן here, one may suppose a noun מסערה with H^(E,F) or מסער as in the margin (see Ben Yehuda 1948, 6:3132; Dihi, 2004, 858–9), similar to סער (Jonah 1:4) or סערה (Ps 107:25); alternatively, מסערה and מסער may be participles (*pual* [see HALOT]) with אני (fem. in Isa 33:21 and masc. in 1 Kgs 10:11) in apposition: "like a storm-driven ship" (cf. the syntax of מבגדה יהודה "more than the faithless one, Judah," Jer 3:11).
33:3 כאור[י]ן — The word is an Aramaism, meaning "teaching" (see b. Šabb. 88a); cf. the Greek δῆλος, a word used in the LXX to translate אורים "Urim."
35:11 האר פנים — For the meaning of this idiomatic expression, see 7:24^A and the note.
35:12 בטוב עין — Literally "with goodness of eye." This expression is found first in Hebrew here, but then many times among the *piyyutim*. Its opposite is עין רעה in Sir 31:13^B and possibly עין רע (assuming רע) in the same verse. Note also where the initial word is an adjective (עין טוב in Prov 22:9 and the opposite עין רע in Sir 14:3, 10^A and 31:13^B and elsewhere [see the notes to 31:13] for other examples); the unusual anteposition of the adjective in the latter examples should be noted.
השגת יד — The letters השגת are the defective spelling of the same word as in Sir 14:13^A (see the note and Ezek 46:7) if not the related verbal noun found in H^(Par), Frankfurt 177, 20 (verso, l. 13) (בְּנַשָּׁגָתוֹ). The two marginal readings are less clear. The first is a *hiphil* verbal noun of נגש "according to the offering of the hand," which is well attested in the *piyyutim*. The second is a *hiphil* infinitive construct of the same root (see 45:16^B; van Peursen 2004, 271).
35:13 Marginal verse — This verse is attested in the Syriac, but not in the Greek. ייי מלוה — Cf. Prov 19:17. בעל גמולות — Lit. "the master of retribution." This syntagm, attested first here, may derive from Jer 51:56 (אל גמולות translated by מרי גמליא אלהא in the Targum) or from Isa 59:18 where בעל גמולות is translated by בעל גמליא in the Targum. For the expression, see also בעל גמולות אני in Deut. Rab. 17 (ms. Parma, Biblioteca Palatina, 3122 [701]) and בעל הגמול ישלם לכם את גמולכם in b. Ketub. 8b. See also, the sentence כעל גמולות בעל השלום based on Isa 59:18 in Yehuda's poem קרובות לשבתות השנה, במדבר (T-s 8H18.12 [fol. 2v l. 17]). אלוה — This is the only occurrence of אלוה in Ben Sira (though see Sir 4:14^A and perhaps Sir 41^M according to Yadin's restoration). תשלומות — See 12:2^A (and the note) and 14:6^A. The entire verse (especially with the marginal alternative ישלם) is similar to Jer 51:56 (אל גמולות יהוה שלם ישלם).
35:15 אלהי משפט — See Isa 30:18. משוא פנים — See 2 Chr 19:7, the expression נשא פנים in 4:22^A (and the note), 42:1^B and the next verse.
35:16 לא ישא פנים — See 4:22^A and the note. ותחנונים — The marginal reading implies מָצוֹק "from distress" (see Dan 9:25 and Peters 1902, 135) instead of מָצוֹק "distress."
35:17 תחבט — The meaning of this marginal note is not entirely clear. In Biblical Hebrew, חבט is mainly used in agricultural contexts to mean "beat (olives)" or "beat out (the grain)." It seems that the root was also used in rabbinic literature in relation to prayer and as a parallel to התחנן; see especially Deut. Rab. 2:2: עכשיו הוא מתחנן ומתחבט (the verb is used in the *piel* [מחבט] in MS Parma, Biblioteca Palatina, 3122

2 Il n'est pas sage celui qui hait la loi,
mais il est secoué comme un navire battu par la tempête (mg. (il est un navire secoué) dans la tempête).
3 Une personne intelligente comprend la parole
et sa loi est vraie comme un enseignement (mg. ?).

Chapitre 35

11 En toutes tes œuvres, montre un visage radieux
et avec joie consacre la dîme (mg. 1. ta dîme ; mg. 2. tes œuvres).
12 Donne-lui (mg. infr. à Dieu) selon ce qu'il t'a donné (mg. idem),
avec un œil généreux et avec ce que tu peux (mg. 1. dans/selon l'offrande de la main, mg. 2. idem).
13 (mg. Celui qui donne au pauvre prête à YYY
et qui est le rétributeur, sinon lui ?).
Car Eloah est celui qui rétribue
et au septuple il te rendra (mg. il te rétribuera).
14 Ne le soudoie pas, car il n'acceptera pas,
15 Ne te fie pas à un sacrifice (obtenu par) extorsion,
car c'est un Dieu de justice
et il n'a pas de partialité.
16 Il n'est pas partial envers le pauvre
et écoute les supplications (mg. idem) de la détresse.
17 Il ne néglige pas le cri (mg. le gémissement) de l'orphelin,
ni de la veuve qui multiplie (mg. implore) la plainte.
18 Une larme ne coule-t-elle pas sur (sa) joue
alors qu'elle gémit sur ses errances ?
20 Les signaux de (sa) bienveillance la guide
et le cri (mg. 1. son cri) (mg. 2. ses cris) se hâte (vers) les nuées.

2 One who hates the law is not wise,
and they are tossed about like a storm-driven ship (mg. (they are) a ship tossed about in a storm).
3 The intelligent person understands speech,
and his law is true like scholarship (mg. ?).

Chapter 35

11 In all your works, (show) a radiant face
and with joy consecrate the tithe (mg. 1. your tithe; mg. 2. your works).
12 Give to him (mg. to God) according to his gift to you (mg. idem),
with generosity and with what you can (mg. 1. in/according to the offering of the hand, mg. 2 idem).
13 (mg. Whoever gives to the poor lends to YYY,
and who is the one that delivers retribution but him?).
For he is Eloah of rewards,
and seven times over he will give back to you (mg. he will reward you).
14 Do not try to bribe him, because he will not take it,
15 do not rely on a sacrifice (obtained by) exploitation,
for he is a God of justice,
and he has no bias.
16 He shows no bias against the poor,
and listens to pleas of distress (mg. pleas [from distress]).
17 He does not neglect the cry (mg. the moaning) of the orphan,
nor of the widow when she multiplies (mg. pleads) the complaint.
18 Do not tears run down (her) cheek
as she groans over her homelessness?
20 Signposts of (his) favor lead her,
and a scream (mg. 1. her scream) (mg. 2. her screams) hurries (to) the clouds.

---

[701] instead of the *hithpael*; see Schechter and Taylor 1899, 58; Segal 1958, 223).

35:18 דמעה על לחי — Cf. Lam 1:2. ...אנחה על — Cf. Sir 47:20ᴮ. For the verb in *qal*, cf. Aramaic *peal* and Hebrew אנק. מרודיה — See Lam 1:7. The Greek seems to have read מורידה or מרידה implying "and a sigh against the one who caused her to fall."

35:20 תמרורי רצון הנחה — The verse is obviously corrupt but the translation above at least makes sense of the context, especially the preceding stich and its reference to "homelessness." The word תמרור can here be understood as the biblical hapax "signpost" (cf. Jer 31:21) and the verb as הִנְחָה, i.e., the *hiphil* of נחה with a 3fs object suffix (cf. תמת ישרים תנחם "the integrity of the upright guides them" Prov 11:3). Numerous other possible interpretations exist. By itself, the phrase תמרורי רצון seems to be another oxymoronic expression. According to Smend (1906a, 315), it may refer to a positive bitterness (see Isa 58:5). The word תמרור may also be an ellipsis for the expression בכי תמרורים in Jer 31:15 or מספד תמרורים in Jer 6:26, but in that case, it is more difficult to explain the construct state. Another alternative is to consider the phrase akin to מר נפש (see Sir 4:1ᴬ) and מר רוח (4:6ᴬ and notes): "bitterness of spirit" (where רצון has a sense similar to the Syriac ܪܥܝܢܐ "thought, will, spirit"); see the Syriac, which translates ܡܪܝܪܘܬ ܪܥܝܢܗ. It is also possible to imagine that תמרורי רצון is an alteration of an earlier תמרורי רצוץ "bitterness of the oppressed"; note the confusion of רצוץ and רצון in Sir 32:14ᴮ. The verb הנחה may also be understood as a noun הֲנָחָה "rest, ease, relief," a *hiphil* infinitive construct of נוח with a suffix הֲנָחָה (Peters [1902, 135]), or a *hophal* perfect 3fs הֻנְחָה "she (i.e. the widow or the bitterness) has been appeased" (Ryssel 1901, 275). חשתה — The letters reflect the *qal* perfect 3fs of חשה "to be silent." Mopsik (2003, 204) nicely translates "et ses cris de détresse imposent le silence aux nuages", though one would expect the *hiphil*. Based on the context, it is easier to construe חשה as a biform of חוש "to come quickly" (see Job 31:5).

	כי	וְעַד תגיעֹ לא תנוח:		10שועת דל ענֹ חל עם	21	עבים חלפה
עד ה' תגע אל	עושה	ושופט צדק יעֹשה משפט:		11לא תמוש עד יפקוד אל	21/22 P	
תגבה מת יתאמק:	מה	וכגבור לא יתאפק:		12גם אל לא יתמהמה		אדון
		ולגוים ישיב נקם:		13עד ימחץ מתני אכזרי	22/23 P	מפני
	רשעים	ומטה רשֹע גדוע ידע:		14עד יוריש שבט זדון		שבטי
		וגמול אדם כמזמתו:		15עד ישיב לאנוש פעלו	24 P	
	וישמחם	ושמחם בישועתו:		16עֹד יְרִיֹב ריב עֹמוֹ	25 P	
אין פסוק אז נוסכתהא ידיגֹר ואידור זא הישתה בוד ובי נבישתה		כעת חזיזים בעת בצֹורֹת:		17נָ[אָ]ה חֹ[ס]דֹו בזֹמַן מצוקה	26 P	
		כֹעָב חֲזִיזִים בְּעֵת צֹרֶךְ:		18נָאָ[ה] [מִצּוֹק]ָה		

Chapter 36

		פׄ		
T-S 16.313 verso	וְשִׂים פחדך על כל הגוים:		1הושיענו אלהי הכל	1/2 P
	ויראו את גבורתיך:		2הניף על עם נכר	3	יד
בם:	כן לעינֹינוֹ הכבד בנֹו:		3כאשר נקדשת לעיניהם בֹנו	4 P	בם
	כי אין אלהים זולתך:		4וידעו כאשר ידענו	5 P	

L. 10 [35:21] וְעַד — The *circellus* is strangely positioned, as it would require reading כי ועד when ועד כי would be preferable.

L. 16 [35:25] עֹד יְרִיֹב — Only a few traces of these letters are preserved, yet the readings, which are based on the Greek and Syriac, exactly fit these traces.

L. 17 [35:26] Line 17 has been written by a hand that is clearly different from the hand that wrote the main text. The right arm of the *ayin* is more rounded than those in the main text, the *tav* is written differently and the letters are slightly inclined to the left, while they are straight in the main text. The baseline is irregular and the letters are thinner rather than larger (See Olszowy-Schlanger 2018, 91). נָ[אָ]ה חֹ[ס]דֹו בזֹמַן מצוקה — This restoration is plausible (see also Kister 1990, 347 n. 154) but far from certain. The situation is made difficult by the fact that this verse has not been written by the same scribe as the main text and that the Greek and the Syriac translations do not agree. (See also Schechter and Taylor [1899, 15]: [רחמ]ים מיי זמן מצוקה; Peters [1902, 377]: מה [נאה ר[צ][ו][ן] ב[ז][מ]ן מצוקה; Smend [1906b, 30]: נאוה חסד בזמן מצוקה).

L. 17 [35:26] Marginal note — This note is written in Persian; for this tentative translation, see the discussion in Wright (2018, 131–3).

L. 18 [35:26] נָאָ[ה] [מִצּוֹק]ָה — Traces of the upper and lower parts of the letters are preserved. כֹעָב חֲזִיזִים בְּעֵת צֹרֶךְ — The second stich can be fully restored on the basis of preserved letter traces (see Rey 2021a, 140–1).

L. 1 [36:1] פחדך — The vertical of the *dalet* is extended beneath the baseline and then was erased, so that perhaps the word was first accidentally written as פחך "your trap" (see Ps 119:110; 140:6; Prov 29:25).

L. 2 [36:3] גבורתיך — The apparent *circellus* above the *tav* is really an offset trace of the *circellus* above the *tav* of כמתנתו in 35:12.

35:21 This verse is also obviously corrupted. חל עם — Although likely a misrepresentation of חלפה from an earlier manuscript, the first word may be read as a *qal* of חלל "to pierce" attested in medieval Hebrew and found in Aramaic (in the *peal*) as "to pierce" (in Tg. Isa. 10:15); although we expect a 3fs form, proximity to דל may have encouraged the use of the 3ms. The word עם might have been read as related to Syriac ܥܢܢܐ "cloud." ועד כי — Although the combination of particles עד כי is found several times in classical Hebrew (e.g., Gen 26:13; 41:49; 49:10; 2 Sam 23:10; 2 Chr 26:15), it does not occur in the non-biblical Dead Sea Scrolls or elsewhere in Ben Sira. Furthermore, this would be the only occurrence of the phrase preceded by the *vav* conjunction before the modern period. ועד תגיע כי לא תנוח — If one reads the stich with כי between the verbal phrases, then the initial עד is likely not עד but a defectively spelled עוֹד (as in Sir 36:28B and in Gen 8:22; 19:12; and 4Q176 8 13). In this case, the verb תגיע is used intransitively, without an explicit object. תמוש — The verb מוש usually has the sense "to depart" (see, e.g., Sir 23:11C and 38:12B), but here presumably has a more general sense "to cease" (see Jer 17:8 HALOT).

35:22 יתמהמה — See 12:16A and 14:12A, as well as the notes. יתאפק — The *hithpael* of אפק evokes the idea that God cannot restrain himself in dispensing justice. He loses control and becomes like a fearsome warrior.

35:23 ולגוים — Due to the parallel with זדון in the next sentence, it may be preferable to interpret גוים as a misspelling of גאים "the proud, arrogant" as in Sir 10:16A (see the note there). ישיב נקם — Cf. 12:6A and Deut 32:41, 43. יוריש — For the use of ירש with the meaning "to dispossess," see Deut 2:12, 21, 22, etc. ומטה רשע — Alternatively, "a rod of wickedness," as in Ezek 7:11.

35:25 שמחם — Cf. 1 Sam 2:1 and Isa 25:9.

36:1–22 For these verses, see Reymond 2020b.

36:1 אלהי הכל — This expression does not appear in Biblical Hebrew, yet parallels Sir 51:12k+ (יוצר הכול) and Sir 45:23 ([לאלוהי כל). It occurs at Qumran with some variations (4Q403 1 i 28 [ה][אד][ו][ן מל][ך]; 4Q409 1 i 6, 8 אדון הכול; 5Q13 1 2 אלוהי הכול; 11QPsa XXVIII 7–8 [אדון הכול] [Ps 151:4]). It also occurs quite frequently in *piyyutim*, as well as in Aramaic and in Syriac (see Hurvitz 1965, 224–227 and 1967, 84).

36:3 עם נכר — Echoing previous research, Marttila (2012, 135) has noted that the word עם usually refers to Israel and only refers to a foreign nation elsewhere in Ben Sira in Sir 47:17. The reason for its use here is perhaps stylistic. It might also be pointed out that together with the preceding preposition על, the phrase in v. 3 creates a kind of har-

21 Le cri du pauvre *perce* les nuages (mg. traverse les nuées) *avec* (?)
   et il ne se repose pas tant qu'il n'a pas atteint (Dieu). (Mg. 1. idem ; mg. 2. et ainsi il (l')atteint car il ne se repose pas.)
22 Il ne cesse pas, tant que Dieu n'a pas visité
   et que le juste juge n'a pas rendu la justice.
   Aussi Dieu (mg. le Seigneur) ne tarde pas
   et, comme un guerrier, il ne se contient pas (mg. 1. comment ne se contient-il pas ?),
   (mg. 2. et un guerrier que maîtrise-t-il ?)
   jusqu'à ce qu'il brise les reins (mg. la face) du cruel,
23 et que sur les nations il fasse retomber la vengeance,
   jusqu'à ce qu'il dépossède une tribu (mg. les tribus) arrogante(s)
   et rompe définitivement le bâton du méchant (mg. des méchants),
24 jusqu'à ce qu'il rende à chacun son travail
   et la rétribution de chacun selon son dessein.
25 jusqu'à ce qu'il défende la cause de son peuple
   et qu'il les réjouisse (mg. idem) par son salut.
26 Sa co[mp]assion est [ma]gnifique au temps de détresse,
   comme un temps d'orage en période de sécheresse
   (mg. en persan: "Ce verset (vient) des autres copies et avait été omis ici et a été écrit.")
   [. . .]
   Comme un nuage d'orage au temps du besoin.

Chapitre 36

1 Sauve nous, Dieu de l'univers
2 et impose ta crainte à toutes les nations.
3 Lève (mg. une main) sur un peuple étranger,
   qu'ils voient tes puissances.
4 De même que tu t'es montré saint à leurs yeux à travers nous (mg. à travers eux),
   ainsi à nos yeux, sois glorifié à travers nous (mg. à travers eux).
   (mg. De même qu'à leurs yeux tu t'es montré saint par eux, ainsi à leurs yeux, sois glorifié par eux.)
5 Et ils sauront comme nous savons,
   qu'il n'y a pas de Dieu en dehors de toi.

21 The cry of the poor *pierces* the clouds (mg. pierces the clouds),
   and it does not rest until it reaches (God) (mg. 1. idem, mg. 2. (and still it reaches) because (it does not rest)).
22 It does not cease until God visits,
   and the just judge dispenses justice.
   Indeed, God (mg. the Lord) does not delay,
   and like a warrior he does not restrain himself (mg. 1. how (can he restrain himself?), mg. 2. and as a warrior how can he restrain himself?)
   until he breaks the loins of (mg. before) the cruel,
23 and returns vengeance upon the nations,
   until he has dispossessed the tribe (mg. the tribes) of the arrogant,
   and definitively breaks the staff of the wicked (mg. idem),
24 until he has rewarded every person for their work,
   and the compensation of each according to his purpose,
25 until he defends the cause of his people,
   and brings them joy (mg. idem.) with his salvation.
26 His ki[nd]ness is [mag]nificent in the time of distress,
   like a thunderstorm in the time of drought,
   (mg. in Persian: "This verse (is) from the other copies and had been omitted here and written.")
   [. . .]is magnifi[cent   ]of distress,
   like a thunder cloud in a time of need.

Chapitre 36

1 Deliver us, God of the universe,
2 set your terror over all the nations.
3 Lift (mg. a hand) over the foreign people,
   so they may see your might.
4 Just as you showed your holiness before their eyes through us (mg. through them),
   so before our eyes be glorified through us (mg. through them).
   (mg. Just as before their eyes you showed your holiness through them, so before their eyes be glorified through them.)
5 So they know, just as we know,
   that there is no God besides you.

mony with the phrase in v. 17: על עם נקרא "over a people called..." Concerning the phrase עם נכר, which is also attested in 1QH^a XIII 7 (see Stegemann and Schuller, DJD 40, 2009, 167, 170), the use of נכר is also somewhat surprising. It is variously glossed as "foreigner," "foreign land," or simply "that which is foreign, foreignness" (BDB). The word is not used with עם "people" in the Hebrew Bible, where one usually finds עם נכרי "foreign people" (Exod 21:8) instead. Note also איש נכרי "foreign person" in Deut 17:15 and Qoh 6:2. Among the Dead Sea Scrolls, it is quite common to find the analogous expression גוי נכר "foreign nation," though it is not found in the Hebrew Bible (CD XIV 15; 4Q266 10 i 8; 4Q371 1a-b 9; 4Q372 1 11; 4Q524 14 2; 11Q19 57:11 and 64:7).

36:4 The many marginal variants related to suffix pronouns are due to the parallel (and chiastic) construction of the two propositions: us — them versus them — us. For interpretation, see Reymond 2020b. נקדשתה — The *plene* orthography of the second person masculine singular should be noted.

	האדר יד ואמץ זרוע וימין:		⁵חדש אות ושנה מופת	6/7 ᴾ	
וּתֻנֹדוף	והכניע צי והדוף אויב:		⁶העיר אף ושפוך חמה	8/9 ᴾ	
תפעל	כי מי יאמר לך מה תעשׂה:		⁷החיש קץ ופקוד מוֹעֵד	10 ᴾ	מצער
	האומר אין זולתי:		⁸השבת ראש פאתי מואָב	12 ᴾ	אויב
	ויתנחלו כימי קדם:		⁹אסוף כל שבטי יעקב	13a/16b ᴾ	
	ישראל בכור כינתה:		¹⁰רחם על עם נקרא בשמך	17 ᴾ	
	ירושלם מכון שבתיך:		¹¹רחם על קרית קדשך	18 ᴾ	
	ומכבודך את היכלך:		¹²מלא ציון את הוֹדך	19 ᴾ	מהדריך
	והקם חזון דבר בשמך:		¹³תן עדות למראש מעשיך	20	
	ונביאיך יאמינו:		¹⁴תן את פעלת קווֹיך	21 ᴾ	
ברצונך	כרצונך על עמך:		¹⁵תשמע תפלת עבדיך	22 ᴾ	עבדך
	כי אתה אל עוֹלֹם[:]		¹⁶וידעו כל אפסי ארץ		ויראו

L. 9 [36:9] צִי — Preceding editions read צר. Yet, the mark adjacent to the *tsade* can only be explained as the remnant of a *yod*. If the letter were a *resh*, then the vertical mark would have descended slightly further and we would expect to see the *resh*'s top horizontal bar to the left of the hole. וּתֻנֹדוף — The reading is difficult. Most commentators read ותנדוף "you will drive away" (Smend 1906b, 30), though Qimron (1988, 117) has suggested ותרדוף "you will pursue."

L. 16 [36:22] [:] עוֹלֹם — The *ayin* is certain (the left arm, base and part of the right arm are preserved), as well as the *lamed* (its vertical is preserved). However, there is little room for the *vav*. It seems that the latter is very close to the *ayin* and crosses its base.

36:6/7 ושנה — This verbal form may be interpreted in two ways: (1) as the Hebrew root שנה II "to repeat" from etymological *tny, which is supported by the parallel construction of the sentence (// חדש אות שנה מופת), or (2) from the root שנה I "to change" from etymological *šny, which is supported by the *piel* vocalization (וְשַׁנֵּה) of the marginal note, the Greek (ἀλλοίωσον) and the Syriac (ܘܚܠܦ); the root שנה II "to repeat" does not occur in the *piel* in early Hebrew and only rarely in later Hebrew. In Sir 43:8ᴮ, the *hithpael* of שנה, meaning "to change," appears in parallel with the *hithpael* of חדש. See the Greek (ἀλλοίωσις "change") and the Syriac (ܚܘܠܦܐ "change"). The sense "revive" or "renew" for שנה I "to change" (<*šny) may be based on analogy to the *hiphil* of חלף. Note the parallelism in the evening prayer: משנה עתים ומחליף את הזמנים (from, ערבית, ברכה רשונה [St. Petersburg, Russian National Library, Antonin B, 122, 2]; see Maagarim for this and similar examples), which seems to be based on the unambiguous expression from Dan 2:21: והוא מהשנא עדניא וזמניא "he changes ([<*šny], i.e., makes return in a cyclic manner) times and seasons." תמה — An Aramaism; see 16:11ᴬ. זריז — An Aramaism, here in the *piel* "to hasten" or "to strengthen." This marginal reading is not reflected in the ancient versions and likely derives from a misreading of the main text ואמץ זרוע וימין "and strengthen (your) arm, (your) right arm!" (Kister 1999, 164). For the idea of hastening time, see 4Q385 4.2–3 ויתבהלו הימים מהר עד אשר יאמרו האדם הלא ממהרים הימים למען יירשו בני ישראל "Let the days hasten quickly until a person can say: 'Surely the days rush so that the children of Israel may take possession'"), Matt 24:22; Mark 13:20; Epistle of Barnabas 4:3; LAB 19:13; 2 Bar 20:1–2; 83:1; 4 Ezra 4:26 and 4:34.

36:9 צִי — The word צי, "desert-dweller" or "ship" (or "sailor"), forms a pair with the noun אויב "enemy" within the same colon. The only other biblical passage that contains this word pair is Ps 72:9, which also contains the verb כרע "to bow," a verb that is semantically and phonetically similar to the verb in Sir 36:9, כנע "to humble." The apparent allusion or echo of Psalm 72 is important since this psalm was often associated with messianic expectations in later traditions (e.g., Matt 2:11; Pss. Sol. 17:26, 29–30; Justin, Dial. 34:3–6 and 64:6; Tg. Ps. 72). It is significant that the word צי also appears in Num 24:24 וְצִים מִיַּד כִּתִּים וְעִנּוּ אַשּׁוּר "and ships from Kittim will oppress Ashur"), an oracle of Balaam also alluded to in the Hebrew of Sir 36:12. In addition, the word צי also occurs in Dan 11:30 (וּבָאוּ בוֹ צִיִּים כִּתִּים "Kittim ships will come against him"), a text possibly echoed in Sir 36:10 by the word pair קץ "end, time" and מועד "designated time," and with which Sir 36 shares much of its vocabulary. Nevertheless, the Greek and the Syriac translations do not reflect the word צי. Instead, they both seem to support a reading close to צר "enemy." This would seem to suggest that צי appeared through textual transmission.

36:10 החיש קץ ופקוד מועד — The terms קץ and מועד are often associated with the end of time (cf. Dan 8:19; Hab 2:3 // 1QpHab VII 7). The expression החיש קץ seems to be a variation of זריז ימים found in the margin of 36:7. For the meaning of חוש in a temporal context, see 1QM I 11–12; Tg. Onq. and Tg. Ps.-J. on Deut 32:11. For the expression פקוד מועד, compare with 4Q423 5 5 א[יש אדמה פקוד מועדי. (הקיץ ואסוף תבואתכה בעתה). מצער — "Little." This word should be construed as a temporal adverbial accusative: "in a little while, soon"

6 Renouvelle le signe et répète le prodige,
7 Glorifie (ta) main, et fortifie (ton) bras et (ta) droite.
   (mg. Renouvelle (ta) force et change (la) merveille
   étends la main et hâte les jours.)
8 Réveille (ta) colère et répands (ta) fureur,
9 humilie les habitants du désert (ou le(s) navire(s) ou navigateurs) et chasse (mg. expulse) l'ennemi.
10 Hâte le temps et assigne le moment (mg. (visite) rapidement),
   car qui te dira: « que fais-tu (mg. idem) ? »
12 Élimine le chef des gouverneurs de Moab (mg. de l'ennemi),
   celui qui dit : « Il n'est rien en dehors de moi. »
13a Rassemble toutes les tribus de Jacob,
16b et qu'elles héritent comme aux jours anciens.
17 Aie pitié du peuple appelé de ton nom,
   Israël, le premier né (que) tu as désigné.
18 Aie pitié de ta ville sainte,
   Jérusalem, le lieu de ta demeure.
19 Remplis Sion de ta splendeur (mg. de ta majesté)
   et ton temple de ta gloire.
20 Rends témoignage à la première de tes œuvres
   et établis la vision dite en ton nom.
21 Rétribue le travail de ceux qui espèrent en toi
   et que tes prophètes soient confirmés.
22 Écoute la prière de tes serviteurs (mg. ton serviteur),
   selon ta bienveillance (mg. par ta bienveillance) envers ton peuple.
   Et tous les confins de la terre sauront (mg. verront),
   que tu es un Dieu éternel.

6 Renew the sign and repeat (or revive?) the portent,
7 glorify (your) hand and strengthen (your) arm (or, the strength of your arm), your right arm.
   (mg. Renew (your) power and revive the miracle, stretch (your) hand and hasten the days.)
8 Arouse anger and pour forth rage,
9 subdue the desert-dwellers (or, ship(s) or sailor(s)) and thrust off (mg. drive off) the enemy.
10 Hasten time and assign the moment (mg. [punish] soon),
   for who can say to you: "What do you do (mg. do you do)?"
12 Wipe out the leader of the regions (or, rulers) of Moab (mg. the enemy),
   the one who says "there is none but me."
13a Gather all the tribes of Jacob,
16b and let them inherit as (in) days of old.
17 Have mercy on the people called in your name,
   Israel, whom you named first born.
18 Have mercy on your holy city,
   Jerusalem, the place of your dwelling.
19 Fill Zion with your splendor (mg. with your majesty),
   your temple with glory.
20 Set the testimony as the principal of your works,
   confirm the vision spoken in your name.
21 Give the reward (due) those who await you,
   so your prophets might be confirmed.
22 May you hear the prayer of your servants (mg. your servant),
   according to your will (mg. through your will) over your people,
   so all the ends of the earth will know (mg. will see)
   that you are God eternal (or, God of the world).

(see perhaps 4Q385 4 6 and Job 36:2 with זעיר; Dimant 2000, 536). It is likely an alteration of מזער, which in turn, may result from a graphic confusion with מועד in the main text (for exactly the same confusion between מועד and מזער, see 31:19; Kister 1999, 164–65). כי מי יאמר לך מה תעשה — Note the parallels with Qoh 8:4 and Job 9:12.
36:12 השבת — Note the *hiphil* of שבת with similar sense and Moab as direct object in Jer 48:35. פאתי מואב — The expression is found in Num 24:17 (4Q175 I 13); Jer 48:45 and 1QM XI 6. The word פאה is usually interpreted as referring to "the borderlands of Moab," but is understood as "rulers" in the Septuagint, Targums, the Peshitta and elsewhere (see Angerstorfer 2000, 463). The Greek also translates it with ἀρχόντων "rulers" here (the Syriac does not seem to reflect the word).
36:16b כימי קדם — The phrase occurs only twice in the Bible. The first time is in Isa 51:9, in the same verse that includes the phrase "one who cuts Rahab and pierces the dragon." In later *piyyut* and prayers, it is often paired with the phrase חדש ימינו "renew our days."
36:17ss Compare these verses with the Birkat Hamazon or the Amidah: רחם ייי אלהינו ברחמיך הרבים ובחסדיך הגדולים עלינו ועל ישראל עמך. ועל ירושלם עירך ועל היכלך ועל מקדשך ועל (מוע) מעונך ועל ציון

משכן כבודך. ועל הבית הגדול והקדוש שנקרא שמך Birkat Hamazon, 3:3–5, T-S NS 152.35. רחם ייי אלהינו עלינו על ישראל עמך ועל ירושלם Amidah 14 MS Bodleian עירך ועל מעונך ועל היכלך ועל ציון משכן כבודך 1096.
36:18 מכון שבתיך — The expression is frequent, see Exod 15:17; 1 Kgs 8:13, 39, 43, 49; Ps 33:14; etc.
36:19 מלא — In the *piel* of מלא, the *min* preposition indicates the substance that "fills" in Jer 51:34; Ps 127:5 and CD II 11–12. The parallel construction in the second stich makes the syntax of the marginal note preferable. The first את in stich *a* is the preposition "with."
36:20 תן עדות — The expression נתן עדות does not seem to be attested in the Bible but appears in late *piyyutim*. למראש — The expression is not found in the Bible or elsewhere in Ben Sira, but appears in 4Q160 3–4 ii 3 (*plene* spelling למרואש), as well as twice in *piyyutim*. The idea that Israel is the first work of God is based on Ps 74:2 זכר עדתך קנית קדם (see Gen. Rab. 1:4). דבר — The *pual* perfect; cf. קחי חזון דובר עליך "accept the vision spoken about you" 11Q5 XXII 13–14.
36:21 Cf. Isa 49:23 and Ps 25:3.
36:22a Cf. 1 Kgs 8:30; Dan 9:17; 36:22c and Isa 52:20.

אך כל 23		אך יש אוכל מֵאוֹכל נֹעִים:		¹⁷כל מאכל אוכל גרגרת	23 P	פּ̇
מֵאוֹכל נֹעִים		אך יֵשׁ אִשָּׁה מֵאִשָּׁה יָפָה:		¹⁸כֹּל זָכָר תְּקַבֵּל אִשָּׁה	26ab P	
אך יש אשה		אך יש אשה יפה:		19		
מאשה	*Or. 5518.1 recto*	ולב מבין מטעמי כזב:		¹חיך בוחן מטעמי דבר	24 CP	
	ישיבנו	ואיש ותיק ישיבֶנָּה בו:		²לב עקוב יתן עצבת	25 P	
		אך יש מכה ממכה תנעם:		³כל נכר תאכל חיה	26cd	
		ועל כל מחמד עין יגבר:		⁴תואר אשה והלֵיל פנים	27 CP	יהלל
		אין אִשָּׁה מבני אדם:		⁵ועד אם יֵשׁ מרפא לשון	28 CP	בָּהּ
	עיר מבצר	עֹזֵר ומבצר ועמוד משען:		⁶קָנָה אשה ראשית קנין	29 CDP	קונה
		ובאין גדר יבועַר כרם:		⁷באין גדיר יבוער כרם	30 CDP	
		המדלג מעיר אל עיר:		⁸מי יאמן בגדוד צבא	31 CD	
		המרגיע באשר יערב:		⁹כן איש אשֿׁר אֵין קן		אֲשֶׁר אין לו

36:24 חיך B C | חן Bmg · בוחן B Bmg | מטעמי B Bmg | דבר C · ולב Bmg C · וחן Bmg | מבין B | נבון Bmg C · מטעמי B Bmg | יטעם מטעמי Bmg C · כזב B C | זבד Bmg · 36:27 פנים (יהלל) והלֵיל B Bmg | יהלֵל C · מכל פנים C · 36:28 יש בה מרפא B | יש מרפא Bmg C · אִשָּׁה B | אִ]שָׁה C · 36:29 קנה B D | קנה Bmg · עיר מבצר Bmg D · קנה עיר מבצר C (עזר כנגדו) = Gen 2:18.20 ܥܘܕܪܢܐ ܘܒܝܬ ܓܘܣܐ S (cf. G βοηθὸν κατ' αὐτόν) · עזר ומבצר C · ומשען העמיד B D | ומשען משען C · 36:30 גדר CD | גדיר B | יבועֵר D · יבוער B | בצבא גדוד D | בגדוד צבא C · לא B | אין לו Bmg C D · קן B D | קיץ C · באשה יסביב C · באשר יערב B D | C.

L. 17 [36:23] מֵאוֹכֵל נֹעִים — Although the manuscript is quite difficult to interpret, the reading is nevertheless certain. The first letter is clearly a *mem* (with remnants of its head, vertical and base, as well as its diagonal attested). It is followed by an *aleph* whose diagonal is still visible, as well as the end of its right arm and its left leg. Finally, we can clearly distinguish a *vav*, followed by a *kaph* and a *lamed*. The *nun*, which is uncertain, is only preserved by a remnant of its base. After this, one can see the tops of the *ayin*'s arms as well as the end of its base line.

L. 17 Right margin [36:23] Smend (1906b, 31) and others who follow him see several corrections in the right margin, which we cannot discern on either the new photograph or the 1901 facsimile. The marks are indecipherable. Smend states, "Am Rande rechts standen mehrere Varianten, die sich wahrscheinlich auf מאכל und אוכל, sicher auch auf גרגרת bezogen. Neben פ (s. oben) stand ein Wort, das mit א begann (אוכל ?), dann folgte vielleicht eine Variante zum ganzen Stichus. Hierbei steht כ]רש unter פ. Darunter ist noch ein ש erkennbar." (Smend 1906b, 31).

L. 17 Left margin [36:23] כל מֹ[׳] א[כ]לת סוגרת — Very few traces of a *mem* are preserved (its right angle and perhaps its diagonal). It is followed by an oblique trace that may be interpreted as an *aleph* for a reading א[כ]לת or as a *gimel* for a reading גְ[רג]רת which may be a little too long for the space. The trace before the *tav* may be either a *lamed* or a *resh*. The last trace of the line is most probably a final *tav* rather than a *bet* as it has been understood before by Schechter and Taylor (1899, 16) and Lévi (1901, 172) who read כל .. תסוגר בבטן.

L. 18 [36:26ab] כֹּל זָכָר תְּקַבֵּל אִשָּׁה — Only a few traces of the base of the first *kaph* are preserved, then *lamed*. The two next letters are dubious. We read *zayin* and *kaph* in agreement with the Greek (ἄρρενα), but *gimel* and *bet* are also possible though less likely (גבר). The remaining letters do not present difficulties. אך יֵשׁ אִשָּׁה מֵאִשָּׁה יָפָה: — This reading, which is mainly reconstructed on the basis of the Greek text, fits the traces exactly. The *aleph* of אשה and the *mem* of מאשה are the only legible letters after אך.

L. 3 [36:26cd] נכר — Although previous editions present a number of different readings (נבר [Lévi 1901, 174; Di Lella 1987, 426]; נ]בר [Vattioni 1968, 189]; נבֹל [Beentjes 1997, 63]; נבֹר [Lévi 1904, 38]; נכ]ה [Margoliouth 1900, 8]; נכֹל [Smend 1906b, 31; 1906a, 324]; ר̇/נכל [Ben-Ḥayyim 1973, 35]; נכס [Segal 1958, 233]), the text is perfectly clear.

L. 6 [36:29] קונה — The *circellus* and the marginal note seem to come from a different hand. In any case, the ink is clearly darker.

36:23 אוכל גרגרת — The word גרגרת only appears in the plural in Biblical Hebrew, though it appears in the singular in Rabbinic Hebrew. Since the word is feminine, one would expect אוכלת. סוגרת — This word may be a noun, "throat," unattested elsewhere (but cf. Syriac ܓܪܓܪܬܐ "throat" [derived ultimately from the root ܓܪ, see CAL, 27/4/2023] and the Arabic *šajjār* "chin" [Lane 1863, 1507]) or as a participle of the verb "to fill" (סגר II in HALOT). See Reymond 2019b, 184–7.

36:26ab The distich is a doublet of 36:26cd; on this verse, see the comment below. תקבל — For the meaning of קבל in this context, see 15:2^A.

36:24 מבין — The word may be an adjective qualifying לב, "a clever heart" (see the Greek καρδία συνετή and the Syriac ܠܒܐ ܕܣܘܟܠܐ) or a predicate in parallelism with the preceding stich. זבד — The word (attested clearly elsewhere in ancient Hebrew only in Gen 30:20 and Sir 40:29^B) here plays on its two associations, "gift, dowry" and "provision." The word has the sense "gift, dowry" in Gen 30:20 as well as in Aramaic and Syriac. In Samaritan Aramaic and Jewish Palestinian Aramaic, the word has the sense "provision"; note, e.g., in Tg. Neofiti of Gen 42:25, זבדין translates the Hebrew צדה "provision of food," a sense also reflected in the Syriac translation of זבד in Sir 36:24, ܡܐܟܘܠܬܐ "food." The same wordplay with זבד is also found in Sir 40:29^B, where the phrase מטעמי זבד also appears. חן — The term provides an odd meaning and must have appeared during the textual transmission process as a confusion with חך from the preceding stich. נבון — This word could also be נכון. For the confusion of these two words in Ben Sira, see Sir 31:19^B. For the expression לב נבון "intelligent heart," see Gen 41:33; Prov 14:33; 15:14 and 18:15.

36:25 עקוב — For the meaning "sly, crooked," cf. Jer 17:9 and 4Q418 8a–d 12 (עקוב הלב). ותיק — The word is only attested in Rabbinic Hebrew with the meaning "enduring, trustworthy, strong, distinguished." יתן עצבת — See Prov 10:10 for the same phrase. ישיבנה — The suffix is feminine and refers to עצבת while in the marginal note it is masculine and refers to לב עקוב, which must imply something like "corrupt thoughts, ideas." For a syntax similar to that of this stich (i.e., *hiphil* of שוב followed by object and then ב), see Judg 9:57 and Joel 4:4, 7.

36:26cd The verse is difficult to interpret. Strugnell (1972) suggested

23 Le gosier mange toute nourriture,
   mais il y a une nourriture plus délicieuse qu'une autre,
   (mg. la gorge m[an]ge toute nour[riture],
   mais il y a une nourriture plus agréable qu'une autre nourriture)
26a Une femme peut accueillir n'importe quel homme,
26b mais il y a femme plus belle que d'autres.
   (mg. mais il y a une femme (qui est) belle.)
24 Un palais discerne les saveurs d'une parole
   et un cœur comprend les saveurs du mensonge.
   (mg. Un palais éprouve les saveurs d'un présent
   et une grâce comprend les saveurs d'un présent.)
25 Un cœur tortueux procure du chagrin,
   une personne expérimentée le (s.e. chagrin) lui renvoie (mg. le (s.e. cœur tortueux) lui renvoie).
26c Une bête dévore tout ce qu'elle reconnaît,
26d mais il y a une blessure plus plaisante que d'autres.
27 Beauté de femme illumine (mg. idem) le visage,
   et elle surpasse tous désirs de l'œil.
28 Et en plus, si elle a (mg. en elle) une parole apaisante,
   son mari n'a pas (d'égal) parmi les humains.
29 Acquiers [mg: celui qui acquiert] une femme, la meilleure des acquisitions,
   un secours et un rempart (mg. une ville fortifiée) et un pilier solide.
30 En l'absence de clôture une vigne est dévastée,
   en l'absence de femme, on erre et vagabonde.
31 Qui se fiera à une troupe armée
   qui bondit de ville en ville ?
   Ainsi l'homme qui n'a pas (mg. idem) de nid
   est un vagabond lorsque la nuit arrive.

23 The throat eats any food,
   but there is (some) food that is more delicious than (other) food, (mg. the gullet eats any food,
   but there is (some) food that is more delicious than (other) food.)
26a A woman can accept any man,
26b but there are (some) women that are more beautiful than (other) women.
   (mg. but there is a woman (who is) beautiful.)
24 The palate tests a word's flavor
   and the heart understands the flavor of a lie.
   (mg. The palate tests a present's flavor,
   and grace understands a present's flavor).
25 A crooked heart brings sorrow
   but an able person can reverse it (i.e., the grief) in themself (mg. can reverse it (i.e., a crooked heart) in themself).
26c A wild animal devours anything it recognizes,
26d but one wound is more desirable than another.
27 As for a woman's beauty, it brightens the face (mg. (a woman's beauty) brightens (the face))
   and it surpasses every pleasure of the eye.
28 Moreover, if she has (mg. in her is) a soothing tongue,
   her husband has no (equal) among humankind.
29 Acquire (mg: one who acquires) a wife, the best of acquisitions,
   a helper, a fortress (mg. a fortified city) and a supportive pillar.
30 Without a wall, the vineyard is devastated,
   so, without a wife, one wanders vagrant.
31 Who will trust in an armed troop
   that skips from town to town?
   Such is the man who has no (mg. idem) nest,
   who wanders (from place to place) when evening arrives.

"a wild animal eats anything that is recognizable, but one corpse (= מְכָה) is more pleasant than another," though he thought this was perhaps an alteration of an earlier "a wild animal eats anything it digs us (נבר), though one truffle (כמה) is more pleasant than another." Alternatively, it is possible to understand חיה as "army" (as in 2 Sam 23:11, 13) instead of "animal." מכה — "Wound" or read a hophal participle "the one who is struck dead." Segal (1958, 233) refers to מַכּוֹת in 2 Chr 2:9 that corresponds to מַכֹּלֶת "food," in 1 Kgs 5:25 that would make perfect sense: "but some food is more delicious than others."
36:27 והליל — The vav before the verbal form makes the preceding phrase a casus pendens, though the verb is surely a mistake for יהליל, the hiphil of הלל with the meaning "to cause to shine" (or the piel in scriptio plena, as יהלל in the margin). מחמד עין — For this expression, see 1 Kgs 20:6; Ezek 24:16, 21, 25 and Lam 2:4. יגבר — For the combination of גבר with על meaning "to prevail over," see Gen 49:26; 2 Sam 11:23 and Ps 103:11.
36:28 ועד — This is the defective spelling of the adverb עוֹד. The placement of the adverb before אם is, according to Smend (1906a, 325), based on rhythm. Alternatively, it is due to graphic similarity with עַד אִם, which is found several times in the Bible (e.g., Gen 24:19, 33; Isa 30:17; Ruth 2:21). Although the syntax עוֹד אם is not found in classical Hebrew, it is attested in prayers of the Amoraic era and in later literature (see Maagarim). Note the similar sense in H^Par (T-S NS 108.43, page 2, verso [labeled recto; right side], line 7). אין — The word may be the negative particle "there is not" or the interrogative particle "where," found in Rabbinic Hebrew without a preceding preposition (e.g., m. Yebam. 16:7): "Where is her husband?" מרפא לשון — See Prov 15:4.
36:29 Cf. Prov 4:7. עיר מבצר — For this marginal variant, see Jer 1:18.
36:30 נע ונד — Cf. Gen 4:12, 14 concerning Cain.
36:31 בגדוד צבא — For the expression, see 1 Chr 7:4. המרגיע — If the verb is from רגע II "to rest" (see the Greek καταλύοντι), the stich might be translated "He rests when the night comes." Yet, it is also possible to understand it as deriving from the root רגע I "to move from place to place" (See BDB, GKC 1219–20; Jastrow [1903, 1450]; Levy [1876–89, 4:425–426]). This meaning fits the context perfectly and provides a very good parallel with the preceding sentence (המדלג מעיר אל עיר).

Chapter 37

	הֲלֹא דִין מַגִּיעַ אֶל מוֹת רֵעַ כְּנַפְשְׁךָ נֶהְפָּךְ לְצָר׃		¹⁰כל אומר אמר אהבתי	1/2 CD
	למלא פני תבל תרמית׃		¹¹היֹוֹ רֵעַ שֶׁאָמַר מדוע כן נוצרתי	3 D
מנוב	בעת צוקה מנגד יעמד׃		¹²מרֵע אוהב מביט אל שלחן	4 D
	ואל תעזבהו בשללך׃		¹³אל תשכח חביר בקרב	6 DP
	אך יש יועץ דרך אל לך׃		¹⁴כל יועץ יניף יד	7 D
	ודע לפנים מה צורכו׃		¹⁵מיוֹעֵץ שמור נפשך	8 DP
	למה זה אליו יפול׃		¹⁶כֹּ[י גַּ]ם הוּא לנפשו יחשב	
ראשך׃	וקם מנגד להביט רישך׃		¹⁷[ויאמר]לך מַטוֹב דרכך	9 D

(Marginal Hebrew notes at left and right of main text.)

37:1a אך יש א(ו)הב Bmg D G S | > B ר(ע) כל א(ו)הב יאמר אהבתו Bmg D | כל אוהב אומר אהבתו Bmg D | כל אומר אמר אהבתי B · 37:1b + הב שם א(ו)הב C · כל אוהב יאמר יגיע C · הלא בעת יגיע B Bmg D · הלא דין מגיע C · 37:2a על מות B | אל מות C · עד מות D · 37:2b רע כנפשך נהפך לצר B | דין מות כנפש יהפך לצר C · רע כנפשך נהפך לצר Bmg D · 37:3 רע B D | רֵעַ Bmg · שאמר B | יאמר Bmg D · מדוע Bmg | מ׳ D · 37:4 מדוע B D | מרע Bmg · אוהב טוב נלחם (נוחל) עם זר ונגד ערים יחזיק צנה: + 37:5 · מנגד B | ובעת D · בעת Bmg D · על שחת B S | אל שלחן Bmg D · בקרב B | בקֶרֶב Bmg | בקרבו D G (ἐν ψυχῇ σου) S Bmg · חביר B | חבר Bmg D · תשכח B D | תכחש Bmg (metat.) · 37:6a נוחל Bmg2 · נלחם Bmg1 D · (כֱּמֱתכֱבֱא) · 37:6b Bmg ונגד ערים יחזיק צנה B D | ואל תעזבהו בשללך · 37:7 אומר חזה Bmg | אומר חזה D S (וֹהֵי) · אל לך B | עליו Bmg D · יניף יד B | ינוף יד B D G S | מיועץ Bmg · שמר D | שמור B · צורכו D | צרכו B | לנפשו B G (ἑαυτῷ) | נפשו Bmg D · 37:9 מטוב B G (καλὰ) S (ܠܒ) | ראשך Bmg1 | רֵאשֶׁךָ B | רישך D | דרכיך D | דרכך B | להביט Bmg D ·

L. 11 margin [37:3] יֹאמַר — Though the *yod* is possible, as has been proposed by preceding editions, a *shin* seems not excluded.

L. 12 margin [37:4] מנוב — The *vav* is perfectly clear, thus the reading מנגב (Beentjes 1997, 63; Smend 1906b, 34; Lévi 1901, 180) must be rejected.

L. 14 margin [37:7] חזה — The *vav* and the *khet* are clear on the photographs (the small fragment containing a part of the *mem*, *resh* (of אמר) and the right leg of the *khet* must be rotated 40° counter-clockwise), and consequently, the reading חזה (Ben-Ḥayyim 1973,

37:1 כל אומר אמר — As preserved, the letters do not provide a coherent meaning. It is clearly a scribal mistake for כל אוהב אומר (see the other versions) "every friend says: 'I love'".

37:2 דין — Instead of "judgment," this word should probably be understood as having the same meaning as דָּו here, as in Sir 14:1^A (see the note there), Sir 30:21^B, 23^B, and 38:18^B (see Reymond, 2021b, 111-12).

37:2 **margin** רע כנפש — The phrase רע כנפש "a friend (who is) like your very self" in the vertically oriented marginal reading is matched by the semantically identical, but grammatically more explicit, רע כנפשך in the marginal reading to the immediate left of the line. Cf. אשר רעך כנפשך in Deut 13:7. The phrase without pronominal suffix (i.e., רע כנפש or something similar) also occurs in later Hebrew, including the *piyyutim* (e.g., ריע א' [= אשר] כנפש] in Yannai's לאם אשר אומנתו קדושתות לשבתות השנה, ויקרא [line 20] from במעיה יטמא; also ורע כנפש in Solomon Gaon Ben Yehudah's אגרת אל יצחק(?) בן אברהם הכהן [see Maagarim]).

37:3 היו — Since a third person plural of the verb היה is highly improbable, one is forced to understand it as a metathesis for הוי, as documented in the margin and in H^D. רע — It is also possible to vocalize רַע, as in H^D, "Woe to the evil person who says…" The expression הוי רע may also be interpreted as "Woe! Evil! he will say, 'Why was I made?'" See רע רע יאמר in Prov 20:14.

37:4 Cf. Sir 6:10: יש אוהב חבר שלחן ולא ימצא ביום רעה "There is a friend, a mealtime companion; but they will not be found on the day of misfortune." מרע — The word is perhaps the rare Hebrew noun, מֵרַע "evil" (see Dan 11:27), "evil it is when a friend…"; or, it may be the *hiphil* participle of רעע "one who injures is …"; or even an abbreviat-

36; Beentjes 1997, 63; Vattioni 1968, 193), as in H^D, cannot be retained.

L. 15 [37:8] כִּ[י גַּ]ם הוּא — This reading, which is reconstructed on the basis of H^D, fits the traces and the allowed space perfectly. There are very faint traces of the head of the *kaph* and its right elbow and base, as well as traces of the end of the line of the *gimel*. The bottom part of the final *mem* and the *he* have disappeared due to discoloration of the paper.

L. 17 [37:9] לְךָ מַטוֹב — This reading, as already proposed by Lévi (1901, 182) and Smend (1906b, 32), is certain.

ed form of מה רע "how unfortunate (if) …" (see Segal 1958, 235) and note the loss of the *he* of מה in the Bible: e.g., Exod 4:2; Isa 3:15; etc.). מביט אל — For נבט על (cf. mg. and H^D) instead of נבט אל, see Hab 2:15. שחת — The word may be the Rabbinic Hebrew word meaning fodder or animal food (homophonous with the word for "pit, destruction"). In the context, this interpretation implies a friend who covets one's animal food, but who does not share their own produce, even in desperate times. מנגד — See Deut 32:52. מנוב — The word is difficult to interpret, but may be the preposition מן in its privative sense followed by the infinitive construct of נוב: "without producing (anything)" (for the sense, see, e.g., Ps 62:11 and 92:15) and in this context "without sharing"; or it might be the Aramaic noun "growth, bud": "without produce."

37:5 נלחם עם — For the complementation of לחם with עם, see Exod 17:8. זר — The word is usually construed as "stranger" (from *zwr), though the context and the parallelism here suggests the sense "oppressor, enemy" (Jastrow 1903, 411) (perhaps from a different root *ẓwr; cf. the verb זור "to crush" in Job 39:15 and Syriac *zwr* "to strike") or perhaps "hated" from *ḏyr (see the verb זור "to stink, be loathsome" in Job 19:17 and cf. Akkadian *zēru* "hated"). נחל עם זר — From the context, it seems the alternative verb (נחל "to inherit") is used here in the sense "to take possession" (see Exod 34:9) or "to dispossess," a meaning more commonly attested with the synonymous verb ירש. If this is accurate, it suggests reading the following עם as a noun instead of a preposition: "dispossesses a hostile people." ערים — This is the Aramaic equivalent of צר. See, e.g., Dan 4:14 and as a loanword in Hebrew texts: 1 Sam 28:16; Ps 139:20; Sir 47:7.

37:6 בקרב — Based on the context, it seems legitimate to vocalize

Chapitre 37

1 Chacun qui parle dit : « j'aime »
2 N'est-ce pas une tristesse approchant de la mort,
   (qu')un compagnon comme toi-même se change en ennemi ?
1 (mg. Tout ami dit : « j'aime »
   mais il y a l'ami (qui a seulement le) nom d'ami.
2 N'est-ce pas une tristesse approchant de la mort,
   (qu')un compagnon comme soi-même se change en ennemi.)
3 *Malheureux* le compagnon qui dit : « pourquoi ai-je été formé ainsi ?
   (mg. Malheureux le compagnon qui dit : « pourquoi ai-je été formé ?)
   Pour remplir la face du monde de tromperie. »
4 Mauvais est l'ami qui regarde vers la table,
   (mg. Pourquoi l'ami regarde au-dessus de la fosse)
   au temps d'angoisse il se tient à distance (mg. sans rien partager).
5 (mg. Un bon ami se bat contre un ennemi (mg. prend possession d'un peuple ennemi)
   et face à des adversaires, il saisit le bouclier.)
6 N'oublie pas un compagnon dans une bataille (mg. dans la tombe)
   et ne l'abandonne pas lors de ton butin.
   (mg. Ne renie pas un compagnon dans une bataille
   et face à des ennemis, il saisira le bouclier.)
7 Tout conseiller agite la main,
   mais il y a celui qui conseille une voie vers le moqueur.
   (mg. Tout conseiller dit qu'il voit,
   mais il y a celui qui conseille une voie vers cela).
8 D'un conseiller (mg. Du conseiller) garde-toi
   et sache d'abord quel est son besoin.
   Ca[r]lui aussi pense à lui-même (mg. se considère lui-même) :
   « Pourquoi cela lui arriverait-il ? »
9 [Et il]te [dit] : « Que ta voie est bonne ! », (mg. d'observer (ta voie)
   mais il se dresse en face pour contempler ta pauvreté (mg. ta tête).

Chapter 37

1 Everyone who speaks says, "I love."
2 Is it not a sadness approaching death—
   a companion like your very self who turns into an enemy?
1 (mg. Every friend says, "I love"
   but there is the friend (who is only) a friend in name).
2 Is it not a sadness approaching death—
   a companion like your very self who turns into an enemy?)
3 *Woe* to the companion who says, "Why was I made this way—
   (mg. Woe to the companion who says, "Why was I made—")
   to fill the face of the world with deceit?"
4 How unfortunate (when) a friend looks to the table,
   (mg. Why would a friend observe destruction?)
   and at the time of distress stands at a distance (mg. without sharing).
5 (mg. A good friend fights against the enemy (mg. dispossesses (a hostile people)),
   and before adversaries, they seize the shield.)
6 Do not forget a companion in battle (mg. in the grave),
   and do not abandon them for the sake of your spoils.
   (mg. Do not deceive a companion in battle,
   before enemies, they will seize the shield).
7 Every counselor raises a fist
   but there is one who advises a path to scorner(s).
   (mg. Every counselor says (they) see,
   but there is one who counsels a way to (achieve) it).
8 From a counselor (mg. From the counselor) guard yourself,
   and know at first what they need.
   Fo[r], they also think to themself (mg. they themself consider)
   "Why should it happen to him?"
9 [And they will say] to you, "How good is your way!"
   (mg. (you should) watch (your way))
   but they will stand before (you) to contemplate your poverty (mg. your head).

---

the word as בְּקְרָב "in the battle" instead of בְּקֶרֶב "in proximity" (cf. H^D, the Greek ἐν τῇ ψυχῇ σου, and the Syriac ܟܒܣܘܡ). The marginal note בקבר is obviously a metathesis for בקרב. בשללך — This may be a noun with a suffix or an infinitive construct with a suffix. In either case, the expression is elliptical. עָרִים — See preceding note.
37:7 יָנִיף יָד — For the expression, see Sir 12:18; 36:3; and Job 31:21; Isa 10:32 and 11:15. לִיץ — If related to מֵלִיץ "interpreter, envoy" in Gen 42:23; Isa 43:27; Job 33:23 and/or Arabic *lwṣ* "to turn aside," then perhaps "diplomacy." Alternatively, perhaps a defective spelling of לִיץ "scorning" or a mistake for אַלֵּץ "coercing."

37:8 מה יועץ — Literally, "What is a counselor?" Yet, it may perhaps be easier to read מהיועץ. A similar variant appears in the marginal correction of Sir 42:21, where מעולם is replaced with מהעולם in the margin. למה זה אליו יפול — The phrase represents the thought of the counselor, reflecting the sense of נפל in Ruth 3:18. We have interpreted the 3ms suffix of אליו as referring to the person who is counseled.
37:9 מטוב — We assume a contraction from מה טוב. See the note to מרע at Sir 37:4^B. רֹאשֶׁךָ — The vocalization makes clear that the word was interpreted as the word "head," though without the vowels, it is possible to construe it as an alternative spelling of the word in the main text, "poverty" (see H^D and four times in 4QInstruction, e.g., 4Q416 2 iii 11).

Or. 5518.1 verso	ומלוכד ע׳ מלחמֹהֹ	[א]	[° °]18	10 ᴅ	[ ]
	וממקֹנה ע׳ ממכרו	ומדר אל מלחמתו:	¹עם אשה עֿל צרתה	11ab ᴅ	אל
		וממקנהˣ על ממכר:	²עם סוחר אל תתגר	11cd ᴅ	
		ואכזרי על טוב בשר:	³עם איש רע אֿל תגמל חסד	11ef ᴅ	על גמילות
		שומר שוא על מוציא רע:	⁴פועל שוא על מלאכתו	11gh ᴅ	
	מצותיו	אשר̊ תדע שומר מצוה:	⁵אך אם יש מפחד תמיד	12 ᴅ	איש
	יעכר בד:	אם תכשל יגיע אליך:	⁶אשר עם לבֿבו כלבבך		כֿ לבבו
	משבעים	מי יאמין לך אמן ממנו:	⁷וגם עצת לבב הבין	13 ᴅ	
	צפים ע׳ שֿן:	משבעהֿ צופים על מצֿפה:	⁸לב אנוש יגֿיד שעיותיו	14 ᴅ	מגיד
		אשר יכין באמת צעדיך:	⁹ועם כל אלה עֿתר אל אל	15 ᴅ	העתר

37:10 [א] [° °] | B : העלים סוד Bmg · וממקנא אל תועץ עם חמיך D · 37:11ab | אל B ומדר אל מלחמתו Bmg D (G δειλοῦ = דך?, S צר = ܡܢ ܕܚܠܐ?) | ומלוכד על מלחמה Bmg D · 37:11cd | ממקנה B וממקנה Bmg D · 37:11ef | אל תגמל B על גמילות Bmg · ממכרו B ממכרי Bmg D · 37:11gh | שוא B שכיר D · שומר שוא על מוציא רע B צא זרע מ(ו)(א)... D · 37:12ab | יש B איש Bmg D G S · מצוה B D מצותיו Bmg · 37:12cd | לבב הבין B לבֿבו Bmg · יעבד בד D · 37:13 | יגיע אליך B יעכר בד Bmg · ואם B אם D · בלבבו B כֿ לבֿבו Bmg · יכשל B תכשל D · 37:14 | יגיד B משבעה Bmg D משבעים Bmg · צופים B צפים Bmg · מי יאמין לך אמן ממנו B כי אם אמן ממנו Bmg D · לבבו כך B D · 37:15 | העתר B עתר Bmg D · צעדיך B צעדך D · שן B מצפה D ·

L. 5 [Sir 37:12] אשר̊ תדע — The *circellus* does not correspond to a marginal note. מצותיו — This marginal note comes from a different hand.

L. 6 [37:12] יעכר̊ — Although previous editions have fluctuated between reading יעכר and יעבר, the reading יעכר is clear. (What could

be seen as the base of the *bet* extending to the right of the vertical is actually a spot on the paper).

L. 9 [37:15] כֿל — The *circellus* does not correspond to a marginal note.

37:10 This verse, missing in the lacuna, must have contained two introductory phrases, like . . . העלים סוד מן . . . אל תועץ עם "Do not take counsel with . . . hide a secret from . . . ," as in Hᴅ. Stichs 11a, c and e seem to presuppose the first phrase (thus, עם), while stichs 11b and d seem to presuppose the second phrase (thus, מן).

37:11ab ומדר — According to Margoliouth (1900, 29), the word דר "warrior" is a noun, deriving from the root דרר "to fight" and known from Aramaic and Syriac (see more recently Kister 1990, 339–340; Dihi 2004, 189–190). The מן preposition is hard to explain, unless it is assumed to complement the missing phrase העלים סוד "hide a secret" from v. 10 (as in Hᴅ). The same problem pertains to the marginal reading מלוכד, and to ממקנה in the next stich, as well as its marginal alternative וממקנה. — Cf. Prov 16:32. The form may also be interpreted as a *pual* participle מְלֻכָּד (so Peters 1902, 149).

37:11cd אל תתגר — According to the very repetitive construction of v. 11, we should read a noun here preceded by the particle אל, in agreement with the Greek and the Syriac (probably תַּגָּר "merchant," see also Sir 42:5, thus Peters [1902, 149]; or, תִּגְרָה [Aramaic תגרא] "merchandise" or "dispute/quarrel," thus Lévi [1901, 184]; or, מְתַגֵּר as Smend [1906a, 330, see Aramaic מתגרא], the writing of *mem* and *tav* being very close in some scripts). Alternativley, it may be a verbal expression and interpreted in two ways: (1) as a *hithpael* of the root גרה "to get excited, strive" (but the verb is generally constructed with the particle ב), or (2) as a *hithpael* of the Aramaic root תגר "to acquire goods through trade." וממקנה (א) — The strict interpretation of this word depends on whether it is read with a *he* or with the *aleph* superscript. If read with a *he*, then it is more precisely the *hiphil* participle of קנה "the one who

sells, the seller" (as in the *qal*, which is found in the margin and Hᴅ, "the one who acquires," see 1QS XI 2). If read with the *aleph* superscript, then it is the *hiphil* participle of the root קנא "the one who is jealous." In reality, however, the spelling of roots was often not according to etymology and קנה could be spelled with an *aleph* and קנא with a *he*.

37:11ef אל תגמל חסד — Here again, the form is ambiguous. According to the stylistic structure of the verse, it may be preferable to read a noun תַּגְמֻל "benefit" (only attested in Ps 116:12 and in medieval Hebrew; see the similar expression ותגמול חסדים in Shemuel bar Hosha'ana [יוצרות לשבתות השנה, Bodleian e.36 (2715) 22–25] and the expression תגמול אהבתי in Joseph Ibn Abitur [יוצרות לסוכות, T-S H 15.75 verso l. 3]). However, as in the preceding stichs, it is also possible to read a prohibitive statement, "with an evil person do not repay a reproach (or show compassion)." גמילות חסד — The marginal expression (see also Hᴅ) is also found in the Mishnah and later texts (see, e.g., m. Pe'ah 1:1). טוב בשר — The expression does not seem to appear elsewhere, but it may be compared to the similar expression טוב שאר in the margin of Sir 30:15 טוב לבב in the main text; see also חי טוב in 41:13), which expresses physical health. See also Prov 11:17.

37:11gh שומר שוא — Given the sense of the following, it seems easiest to construe this phrase as referring to someone who loves hearing gossip and lies (for שוא in the sense of lies, see, e.g., Prov 30:8). מוציא רע — The expression occurs in b. 'Arak. 15b (Vatican Biblioteca Apostolica ebr., 120); Lev. Rab. 16:1, 2, 3 (British Library, 340) and many times afterwards (see Maagarim) and seems to be an abbreviation of מוציא שם רע which is found more frequently. מצא זרע — The expression is unique, but can be compared with מֹצָא דֶשֶׁא in Job 38:27.

10 [*Ne prends pas conseil auprès de...*   ]
    [*et cache un secret à...*   ]
11a auprès d'une femme à propos de (mg. concernant) sa rivale
11b et à un guerrier concernant sa bataille,
    (mg. et à l'assaillant à propos de la bataille,)
11c auprès du commerçant, ne fais pas d'affaires
11d et au vendeur (mg. 1. le zélateur) à propos de la vente,
    (mg. 2. et à l'acquéreur à propos de sa vente,)
11e auprès d'une personne méchante à propos du bénéfice de la charité (mg. des œuvres de charité)
11f et (auprès) du cruel à propos du bien-être,
11g (auprès) du travailleur paresseux à propos de son œuvre,
11h (auprès) de celui qui s'attache à la fausseté à propos de celui qui profère du mal.
    (mg. (auprès) du travailleur salarié à propos de son œuvre,
    (auprès) du salarié à l'année qui fait pousser la semence.)
12 Cependant, (s.e. prends conseil) s'il y en a un (mg. quelqu'un est) constamment sur ses gardes
    dont tu sais qu'il garde le commandement (mg. ses commandements),
    qui est avec son cœur (mg. comme ᵈᵃⁿˢ son cœur) comme ton cœur,
    si tu trébuches, il s'approche de toi (mg. il sera troublé à cause de toi).
13 Et également, sois attentif au conseil du cœur,
    (celui) qui se fie à toi, y a-t-il plus fiable que lui ?
    (mg. Et aussi le conseil de son cœur est ainsi,
    mais y a-t-il plus fiable que lui ?)
14 Le cœur d'une personne révélera (mg. révèle) ses histoires,
    plus que sept (mg. soixante dix) sentinelles (mg. idem) sur un observatoire (mg. sur un sommet).
15 Et néanmoins implore (mg. idem) Dieu,
    qu'il affermisse tes pas dans la vérité.

10 [*Do not take counsel with.........*]
    [*Hide a secret from.........*]
11a with a woman about (mg. concerning) her rival
11b and (hide a secret) from a warrior concerning his battle (mg. and from an assailant about battle.)
11c With the merchant, do not do business;
11d and (hide a secret) from the vendor (mg. 1. the jealous) about a sale,
    (mg. 2. and from the purchaser about their sale)
11e with a wicked person about the benefit of charity (mg. of charitable works),
11f and (with) the cruel about good health,
11g (with) the lazy worker about their work,
11h (with) one who pays regard to lies about a slanderer,
    (mg. (with) one working for a wage about their work,
    (with) an annually hired-hand about the sprouting of the seed).
12 However, (*do take counsel*) if there is one (mg. if there is a person who is) always in dread,
    who, you know, keeps the commandment (mg. his commandments).
    That which is in their heart (mg. like^within their heart) is like (that which is in) your heart,
    if you stumble, they will approach you (mg. they will be distraught because of you).
13 And also, consider the counsel of the heart;
    whoever trusts you, is there one trusted more?
    (mg. And, indeed, the counsel of their heart is so, but is there one more faithful than it?)
14 A person's heart will tell (mg. tells) their stories,
    more than seven sentries upon a watchtower
    (mg. more than seventy sentries upon a peak).
15 Nevertheless, implore (mg. idem) God,
    that he may establish your steps in truth.

37:12 אם — Lévi (1901, 186); Peters (1902, 150); Smend (1906a, 331) and Segal (1958, 237) all consider אם a mistake for עם, as in the preceding verses. This would be one of the rare errors shared between H^B and H^D; note a similar mistake of אם for עם in H^M at Sir 44:11. מפחד תמיד — Cf. Prov 28:14. עם כ־לבבו — In the margin of H^B and in H^D, the succession of the two prepositions עם and כ/ב could be the result of the conflation of the two readings עם לבבו and בלבבו.בלבבו אליך יגיע — See 1 Sam 14:9.

37:13 מי — The pronoun is used as a relative (as in Rabbinic Hebrew; see Jastrow 1903, 770) or as an interrogative "who will trust you? Is there one more trusted than him?" אמן ממנו — The phrase can be interpreted as an unmarked question made up of the defectively spelled *qal* passive participle and the מן preposition (used in its comparative sense). כך — The meaning of this word is unclear. It may be the particle "thus" (see 13:17 and 32:5) or an error, i.e., a misspelling of בך "the counsel of his heart (is) in you" (so Lévi [1901, 187]; Peters [1902, 332]) or a dittography of a primitive לבבך (so Segal [1958, 238]). Perhaps this first stich continues the idea of the marginal verb phrase (יעכר בך) from 37:12d, implying the companion's dismay. כי אם — As noted by commentators, this is a mistake for כי אין "For there is nothing more reliable than it." As it stands, however, it may mark a contrast: "but" or "rather." Thus, the marginal verse implies that although a companion who shares one's sympathies (v. 12c) might be dismayed at one's stumbling (v. 12d margin), such a companion is still more trustworthy than any other.

37:14 שעיותיו — This form derives from שעיה, also found in 38:25^B, meaning "conversation." Cf. Aramaic שועיתא "story, fairly tale" (Dihi 2004, 683). שן — For the metaphorical use of שן ("crag"), see Sir 40:15.

37:15 ועם כל אלה — The combination of words expresses contrast as with the similar ועם זה in Neh 5:18 (see BDB sub עם, def. 5).

	וראש כל פועל היא מחשבת		10ראש כל מעשה דבר	16 D
שרביטים	ארבעה שבטים יפריחו׃ יֹחֿ		11עִקֶּרֶת תחבולות לב	17/18 D
ומשלח	ומושלת בם כליל לשון׃		12טוב ורעֹה וחיים ומות	
נואל	ולנפשו הוא גֹאֵל׃		13יש חכם לרבים נחכם	19 CD
	ומכל מאכל תענוג נבצר׃		14ויש חכם בדברו נמאס	20 D
	פרי דעתו על גויתו׃		15ויש חכם לנפשו יחכם	22 CD
ישורון	וחיי עַםֿ ישראל יָמֹיֿ אֵיֹן מסֹפֹּרֿ׃		16חיי איש מספר ימים	25 D
	וֹאֹשׁרוֹהוֹ [כל]רֹוֹאָ[יֹ]וֹ׃		17חכם לנפשו יִשְׂבַּע תענוג	24 CD
	[ ] [לֹ] [לֹ]		18[חכם] [כבוד]	26 CD
T-S 16.312 recto	וראה מה רע לה אל תתן לה׃		1בני בחייך נס נפשך	27 D
	לא כל נפש כל זן תבחר׃		2כי לא הכל לכל טובֿ	28 D

Right margin: עקר | נתנה אל | נתן חכמה | לכל הגוי | ובינה שם כלי 23 | ורע | בחמר | כי ל׳ לכ׳ טוב | תענוג

37:16 שרביטים B Bmg D · שבטים B Bmg D · עקר Bmg D · עקרת B | 37:17 פעל D | פעל B Bmg | פועל B Bmg D G (πρό) | לפני B Bmg D G | וראש B | מאמר Bmg D | דבר B | 37:16 ומשלת B G | ומשלח Bmg D · ומשלח Bmg D · 37:19 מות וחיים · D מות וחיים B G (ζωὴ καὶ θάνατος) | וחיים ומות B · ורעה B | ורע Bmg D · 37:18 ירעה B | יפריח Bmg? D G · גואל B Bmg D G (ἄχρηστος) S (ܡܚܒܠ) · 37:20 נמאס B | ימאס D · 37:22 יש B D | יש C · 37:23 + פרי דעתו (יכחם) ויש חכם לעמו יחכם C | נואל Bmg D · גויתהן מספר יש ימים וגוית שם יָמֹיֿ אֵיֿן + Bmg D · יש(ו)רון B | עם ישראל D | ימים מספר B | מספר ימים D · אנוש D | איש B | 37:25 · Bmg D בגויתה׃ · ואל B | אל Bmg D · בחמר B S G | בחייך B · 37:27 C · וכל ראי אשריהו כל רואיהו D ויאשריהו כל רואיהו B G S וֹאֹשׁרוֹהוֹ [כל רֹוֹאָיֹוֹ] · Dmg · 37:24 [כל רֹוֹאָ]יֹוֹ מספר D · 37:28 הכל לכל טוב B G S (ܟܠ ܡܛܠ ܟܠܐ ܛܒ) | לכל טוב תענוג Bmg D | לא B | ולא D | כל B | לכל D ·

L. 11 [37:18] שבטים — Lévi (1901, 188-189; 1904, 42); Margoliouth (1899, 10); Vattioni (1968, 197) and Sauer (2000, 256) read שכמים, which is impossible. יפרֹיֹחֿו — Thin traces of the letters יח are discernible in the margin and may be a correction of the verb (without a *circellus*), implying the singular form יפריח in agreement with H^D.

L. 16 [37:25]: יָמֹיֿ אֵיֹן מסֹפֹּרֿ — Although the remaining marks are very faint, this reading, which is also attested in H^D, perfectly fits the traces and therefore seems certain.

L. 17 [37:24] לנפשו ישבע — Although the traces are very faint, this reading, which is also attested in H^D, perfectly fits the traces. וֹאֹשׁרוֹהוֹ [כל רֹוֹאָיֹ]וֹ — It is preferable to read ואשרוהו, rather than ויאשרוהו as in the preceding editions, since the letter before the *aleph* is clearly a *vav*. The reading in H^C, כל ראיו, fits the preserved traces. The vertical of the *lamed* is not clear, but may have become discolored.

37:16 דבר — Both the marginal alternative and H^D attest to the reading מאמר, in the sense of "word," as in Sir 3:8 (see the note.) ראש — In the sense of "beginning" is well attested in Biblical Hebrew and in Ben Sira (see 11:3). Here, the word contrasts with עקרת "root" of the next verse which has a similar figurative sense to ראש "head," though it represents (in its literal sense) the opposite extreme (top versus bottom). היא — For the feminine pronoun before מחשבת, see Muraoka 1999a, 206-208. See also, 30:22.

37:17 עקרת — The form עֲקֶרֶת is only attested in later *piyyutim* (from the fifth-century according to Maagarim) and is connected to the Aramaic loanword עִקָּר (see the margin) "root" (cf. Dan 4:12, 20, 23), which only appears in the Hebrew Bible in Job 30:3 and at Qumran in 4Q385 6 8. By extension, the word can also mean "the essential part, the essence" (see Jastrow 1903, 1074). תחבולות — Cf. Sir 6:25^A; 32:16^B.

37:18 Cf. Sir 11:14^A. שבטים — The term can refer to a "branch" or "sceptre." The form שרביט in the margin is its Aramaic equivalent. יפריחו — The term seems to be corrected to יפריח in the margin, in accord with H^D. For the *hiphil* internal transitive of פרח, see Ps 92:14 and Prov 14:11. ורעה — The marginal note offers the masculine רע in place of the feminine רעה, thus more accurately reflecting the expression in Gen 2:9, 17; 3:5, 22 and its parallel in Deut 30:15. ומשלת — The verb משל is reflected by the Greek and the Syriac (ἡ κυριεύουσα, ܘܐܫܠܛܗ). The marginal correction and H^D (both ומשלח) surely share a monogenetic error here. משלח may be understood as a *piel* participle of שלח with an impersonal subject or as a *pual* participle (for a similar meaning, cf. the *qal* in Ps 50:19: פיך שלחת ברעה "you let loose your mouth in evil" and the *pual* in Prov 29:15 [and its translation in the Peshitta]).

37:19 נחכם — Apart from this occurrence, the *niphal* of חכם does not appear in Hebrew before the medieval period (cf. Maagarim), where it means "the one who becomes wise" or "the one who is perceived as

16 L'origine de toute œuvre est une parole
et l'origine de toute action, c'est la pensée.
(mg. L'origine de toute œuvre est une parole
et avant toute action, c'est la pensée.)

17 La racine (mg. idem) des projets est le cœur,

18 quatre rameaux (mg. idem) fleuriront (mg. il fera fleurir) :
bien et mal (mg. idem) et vie et mort
mais celle qui les domine (mg. ce qui est livré en eux)
entièrement, c'est la langue.

19 Il y a le sage qui devient sage pour la multitude,
mais qui se hait lui même (mg. il est déraisonnable).

20 Et il y a le sage qui est méprisé par sa parole
et il est privé de toute nourriture délicieuse.

22 Et il y a le sage qui est sage pour lui même,
le fruit de sa connaissance est sur son corps.

23 (mg. Et il y a le sage qui est sage pour son peuple
le fruit de sa connaissance est dans leur corps.)

25 La vie d'un être humain, c'est le nombre de (ses) jours
et la vie du peuple d'Israël (mg: Yeshouroun) des jours innombrables.

24 Le sage pour lui-même se rassasie de délices
et ils le disent bienheureux, tous ceux qui le voient.

26 Un sage[   ]gloire
    [   ]

27 Mon enfant, par ta vie (mg. par le vin), éprouve-toi
et vois ce qui est mauvais pour toi, ne t'y adonne pas.

28 Car tout n'est pas bon pour tous,
(mg. Car un plaisir n'est pas bon pour tous,)
personne ne choisit n'importe quelle sorte de nourriture.

16 The origin of every deed is a word
and the origin of all action is thought.
(mg. The origin of every deed is speech
and before every action is thought.)

17 The root (mg. idem) of (every) plan is the heart;

18 four stems (mg. idem) bloom (mg. it will make bloom):
good and evil (mg. idem) and life and death,
while the tongue rules over them entirely (mg. (the tongue) is given totally free rein (in them)) .

19 There is a sage who becomes wise for the many,
but who loathes themself (mg. who is unreasonable).

20 And there is a sage who is despised because of their word,
and they are deprived of all delicious food.

22 And there is a sage who becomes wise for themself,
the fruit of their knowledge (rests) on their body.

23 (mg. And there is a sage who becomes wise for their people,
the fruit of their knowledge is in their body.)

25 The life of a person is a (fixed) number of days,
but the life of the people of Israel (mg: Yeshurun), days without number.

24 The one wise for themself is satiated with delights,
and [all] who see them will say they are blessed.

26 The sage [   ]glory
    [   ]

27 My child, with your constitution (mg. in wine), test yourself,
and observe what is bad for it; (then,) do not indulge.

28 For not everything is good for everyone,
(mg. For (one) pleasure will not be enjoyed by everyone),
and not everyone will choose the same food.

---

wise". גאל — This reading, which is shared with H^C, at first seems to be the participle of גאל, i.e., "he redeems himself (even though he has others' interests at heart)." Nevertheless, the context and the Greek (ἄχρηστος) suggests two other possible interpretations: (1) the abstract noun גֹּאַל "defilement" (i.e., "he is a defilement to himself") or (2) the participle of געל "to loathe," spelled here with *aleph*. The two roots (i.e., גאל "to defile" and געל "to loathe") already seem to overlap in sense in Biblical Hebrew (cf. געל in the *niphal* "to be defiled" in 2 Sam 1:21) and in Rabbinic Hebrew (cf. געל in the *nithpael* "to be soiled" in b. Zebaḥ. 88a). See HAWTTM 2:3, which characterizes גאל and געל as variants. The confusion or variation between *aleph* and *ayin* within a root is also found in the curiously similar (both phonologically and semantically) root(s) כאר and כער "to be repulsive" (see Sir 11:2^A and note). נואל — The *niphal* of יאל; see, e.g., Isa 19:13.

37:20 נמאס — The variant between the *niphal* participle in H^B and the *yiqtol* in H^D does not seem to have a clear semantic difference (see the next verse).

37:22 גויתו — The word גויה may designate the physical body as well as the person, see Sir 47:19; Gen 47:18; Neh 9:37; 1QH^a XVI 33; 4Q418 167 6 and 4Q416 2 ii 18.

37:25 ישורון — For the use of ישורון to designate Israel, see Deut 32:15; 33:5, 26 and Isa 44:2.

37:24 ישבע — The versions suggest that חכם is the subject of the *qal* verb, though the syntax would allow for תענוג as subject of the *piel* (or *hiphil*): "as for a sage, luxury satisfies his appetite" (cf. Ezek 7:19 and Ps 107:9). Based on the extant consonants and the context, תענוג may be a mistake for תענית "a fast," though the Greek suggests perhaps ברכה "blessing."

37:27 בחמר — The word "wine" is hard to explain in this context, but has perhaps been inserted due to the influence of Sir 31:25-27, which not only mentions wine "testing" (בחן) people but also associates wine with life.

37:28 The dislocation of the negation from the predicate in these two sentences is a particularly rare phenomenon. זן — The Aramaic loan זַן only appears in Late Biblical Hebrew (Ps 144:13; 2 Chr 16:14; Sir 49:8; 4Q371 1a-b 8) and is a generic word meaning "kind." In the Targums, it often translates the Hebrew מין (the construction כל מין is frequent in Rabbinic Hebrew). Nevertheless, in this context, it is preferable to understand the letters as a defective spelling of the Aramaic זָן or זֵן "food," a word not found elsewhere in Hebrew (cf. Maagarim).

MANUSCRIPT B

אחזה		ואל תשפך על כל מטעמים:	³אל תזרע לכל תענוג	29 D	תזר ל
ולא תתנ	והמזיע	והמרבה יגיע אל זרא:	⁴כי ברוב תענוג יקנן חולי	30 D	אוכל ירון
על כל	ובהשמר	והנשמר יוסיף חיים:	⁵ובלא מוסר רבים יגועו וֹעועו	31 D	גועו
מטעמים		vacat	6		

Chapter 38

לכבד	כי	גם אתו חלק אל:	⁷רעִי רופא לפני צרכו	1 D	רעה צרכך
אל אפן		ומאת מלך ישא משאות:	⁸מאת אל יחכם רופא	2	
תתעבר	מלכים	דעת רופא תרים ראשו ולפני נדיבים יתיצב:	⁹	3	
מי כי		וגבר מבין אל ימאס בם:	¹⁰אל מארץ מוציא תרופות	4	ברא שמים
בו פצעו	כוחם	בעבור להודיע כל אנוש כֹחו:	¹¹הלא בֵעץ המתיקו מים	5	מעץ
	בגבורתם	להתפאר בגבורתו:	¹²ויתן לאנוש בינה	6	

37:29 ברוב D · תתחנג על מטעמים Bmg2 | תתחנג אל מטמים B | תשפך על כל מטעמים D · תזד אל Bmg2 | תזרו/ד אל | Bmg1 תזר אל B | תזרע לכל D · 37:30 ברב | D תענוג B אוכל Bmg D G (βρώμασιν) S (ܡܐܟܘܠܬܐ) · יקנן B | ירון Bmg | יקנון D · והמרבה B | והמזיע Bmg D · יגיע אל B | יגוע על B · 37:31 גועו B | יגועו ועועו Bmg D · והנשמר B D ובהשמר Bmg · 38:1 רעי B | רעה Bmg1 | רעה רועה Bmg2 D · לפני B | לפי Bmg2 D ·

L. 3 [37:29] אל תזרע לכל — It is not clear if the words should be divided this way or אל תזר על כל "do not turn toward all" as in the margin and H^D; see Peters 1902, 155). תזרו/ד — The final letter is unclear. It may be a *vav* with an anomalous head (for its length and inclination, see the next *vav* in תענוג) or a *kaph* with a very short head and an anomalous inclination.

L. 6 [37:31] The scribe left a blank line here.

L. 9 [38:3] The scribe did not distinguish between the two stichs by leaving a space.

37:29 תזרע לכל — As noted by most commentators, the words must be divided differently: תזר על כל (see Lévi 1901, 194; Peters 1902, 155). As it stands, the verb seems to be used in a figurative way, as in Hos 8:7 where "wind" is sown but a storm reaped. תזר — This verb may be a *qal* from the root זרה "to scatter, to winnow" or a *niphal* with a reflexive meaning "scatter not yourself upon" = "indulge not excess" (see Box and Oesterley [1913, 448] and Lévi [1901, 193], who translates "Ne te précipite pas sur"). For the *niphal* of זרה, see Ezek 6:8 and 36:19. Another possibility is that the form תזר is a *qal* from the root זור "to be estranged, to turn away" with a meaning very close to that of Ps 78:30 לאזָרוּ (מִתְאַוָּתָם עוֹד אָכְלָם בְּפִיהֶם׃ (see also, Ps 58:4 and Job 19:13; in Aramaic, Tg. Onq. 16:26). With the preposition אל, the verb would be translated "do not turn toward" (cf. זור in Aramaic with the preposition לות in Tg. Judg. 4:18). Segal (1958, 244) understands this verb, as well as the following (שפך), as an allusion to vomiting from excess of food (see Sir 31:22 above). תשפך — As with the preceding verb, this verb, which means "to pour out, to cause to flow," is not semantically well-suited to the context. For its reflexive use in the *niphal*, see Lam 2:11. תזרו/ד — Neither reading of a 3mp תזרו or a 3fs with a 2ms suffix תזרך provides a coherent meaning within the context. It seems preferable to read a 2ms pronominal suffix used as reflexive pronoun (see אל תרשיעך and אל תפיל תפילך in Sir 7:7; אל תחשיבך in Sir 7:16a; Rey 2008c, 168–171). תתחנג — The root חנג is attested in Aramaic with the meaning "to dance, to celebrate," mainly in denominative forms (ex. חִנְגָּא). Yet, the root is also attested in Syriac in the *ethpaal* with the meaning "to desire, to prefer" (see LS 470), and it is certainly this meaning that the word has here. מטמים — This form in the marginal reading, which may be interpreted as a *piel* participle from the root טמא "those things that defile," is clearly a *lapsus calami* for מטעמים.

37:30 אוכל ירון — The reading אוכל here agrees with H^D, the Greek (βρώμασιν) and the Syriac (ܡܐܟܘܠܬܐ). The reading ירון "to rejoice" is more difficult to explain, but it does provide a nice metaphorical sense (for its metaphorical usage, see Isa 44:23; 49:13; Job 38:7). יגיע אל — The verb is most likely נגע in the *hiphil*, though it also seems possible to read the adjective יָגֵעַ "weary (to the point of nausea)" (cf. יָגֵעַ followed by the *lamed* preposition in texts of the medieval era; see Maagarim). המזיע . . . זרא — The reading המזיע, which is also found in H^D, is a *hiphil* of יזע or זוע "to sweat, tremble, be agitated." It is not necessarily a mistake; if we understand the Hebrew word זרא not as nausea, but as cholera (see the Greek χολέρα), then the verb may indicate the symptoms of the disease: cold sweats and tremors (see Smend 1906a, 338 and Num 11:20).

37:31 See Prov 5:23. ועועו — This form, which is usually explained as an erroneous dittography of the preceding word, may be understood as a verbal form of the rare root עוע "to be confused" (see Ben Yehuda 1948, 9:4382) attested in *piyyutim* (cf. DCH [6:311] which gives the meaning "to die").

38:1 This sentence is quoted several times in rabbinic literature: אמ' ר' אלעזר. המשל אומ'. כבד את רופאך עד שלא תצטרך לו (Exod. Rab. 21:7) and א' ר' אלעזר. כבד את רופאך עד שלא תיצרך לו (Pesikta Rabbati 25). It is also known in Aramaic in the Jerusalem Talmud: אמ' ר' לעזר. אוקיר לאסייך עד דלא תצטריך ליה (y. Ta'an. 3:5). רעי — The Aramaic orthography of the imperative רעי is uncommon in Hebrew (van Peursen 2004, 35). The verb could be from the Biblical Hebrew root רעה II (related to רֵעַ "friend"), either in the *qal* "to get oneself involved, to associate with" (see Prov 13:20; 29:3) or in the *piel* "to be a special friend" (Judg 14:20). Assuming this verb, the phrase could be translated "make friends with the physician" (van Peursen 2004, 184). Or, perhaps it is related to Aramaic רעה "to take delight in" (= רצה in Hebrew; see Box and Oesterley 1913, 448). However, it is quite possible that the verb has the meaning "to honor, pay special attention to" (perhaps from רעה I "to pasture, take care of," as a shepherd takes care of their flock.) Both the

29 Ne sème pas pour (mg. 1. ne te tourne pas vers les) tout délice
  et ne te jette pas sur des mets savoureux.
  (mg. 2. Ne te précipite pas vers des délices
  et ne désire pas les choses qui rendent impur).
30 Car dans l'abondance de délices (mg. de nourriture), la maladie fait son nid (mg. se réjouit)
  et celui qui est excessif (mg. celui qui transpire) atteint la nausée.
31 Faute d'instruction, beaucoup périssent (mg. ont péri) *et sont confondus* (?).
  mais celui qui veille sur lui-même prolonge la vie (mg. mais en se surveillant, il prolonge sa vie).

Chapitre 38

1 Respecte (mg. 1 idem) le médecin avant (d'avoir) besoin de lui (mg. 2 ton besoin),
  (mg. 1 car) Dieu l'a aussi créé.
  (mg. 2 Respecte le berger, celui qui guérit, selon ton besoin,
  car Dieu l'a aussi créé (s.e. ton besoin).)
2 De Dieu, le médecin reçoit la sagesse
  et d'un roi, il reçoit des présents.
3 La science du médecin lui élève la tête
  et devant les nobles (mg. les rois) il se tient.
4 Dieu, de la terre, fait sortir les remèdes (mg. a créé les drogues)
  et la personne intelligente ne les rejette pas.
5 N'est-ce pas par un bois (mg. d'un bois) que l'eau fut adoucie,
  afin de faire connaître à tous les humains sa force (mg. leur force).
6 Il a donné à l'être humain la science,
  pour se glorifier par sa force (mg. par leur force).

29 Do not sow (mg. 1. Do not turn to) every delight,
  and do not pour yourself over savory delicacies.
  (mg. 2. Do not scatter yourself towards delights,
  and do not desire those things that defile).
30 For in the abundance of delights (mg. of food), sickness nests (mg. rejoices),
  and the excessive one (mg. the one who sweats) reaches nausea.
31 Without instruction, many perish (mg. have perished) and *are confused* (?)
  but one who watches over themself extends their life (mg. But when they watch over themself, they prolong their life).

Chapter 38

1 Respect (mg. 1. idem) the physician before they are needed (mg. 2. you need them),
  (mg. 1. for) God created them too.
  (mg. 2. Respect the Shepherd, the Healer, according to your need,
  for God indeed created it (i.e., your need).)
2 Through God, the physician becomes wise,
  and through a king, they receive gifts.
3 The physician's knowledge lifts their head,
  and before nobles (mg. kings) they take their place.
4 God brings forth remedies (mg. created medicine) from the earth
  and the person who is intelligent does not reject them.
5 Was it not by wood (mg. from wood) that water was sweetened,
  in order to make known to all people his strength (mg. their strength).
6 He gave humanity understanding,
  to glorify himself in his strength (mg. by their strength).

Greek (τίμα) and the Syriac (ܝܩܪ) translate the verb with the sense "honor," and this is also how it was unanimously transmitted in the rabbinic tradition, whether in its Hebrew (כבד) or Aramaic (אקר) form. See also the margin of Sir 31:15ᴮ for this meaning. As noted by Lévi (1901, 195), this meaning is also well attested in the Arabic cognate (*r'y* in form-I: "to be mindful, regardful of a person or thing" [see Lane 1863, 1109], though the Arabic version of the present verse has instead *'krm* "honor" [see Frank 1974, 70]). רעה רועה רופא — The reading in the margin here, and in Hᴰ, is difficult to explain. If not an erroneous dittography, it may refer to God, as shepherd (cf. Gen 48:15 האלהים הרעה אתי "God is the one who shepherds me") as well as healer (cf. Exod 15:26 אני יהוה רפאך "I am the Lord, your healer"). לפני צרכו — This may be interpreted as "before his need" (so the Greek πρὸς τὰς χρείας αὐτοῦ) or "before you need him" (as the Syriac and rabbinic quotations understood it). חלק — For חלק with the meaning "to create," see Sir 31:13 and the note (see Kister 1990, 334–335).

38:2 ישא משאות — For a similar expression, see Gen 43:34.
38:3 This sentence can be compared with Sir 11:1ᴬ and 4Q416 2 iii 11 // 4Q418 9 11 כי מראש הרים ראושכה ועם נדיבים הושיבכה "For out of your poverty he has lifted up your head, and with the nobles he has seated you." תרים ראשו — The expression is frequent; see Ps 3:4; 27:6; 110:7 and 4Q416 2 iii 11. ולפני נדיבים יתיצב — See 4Q416 2 iii 11.
38:4 בר סירא א' אלוה סמים This verse is quoted in Gen. Rab. 10:6: ברא שמים. שהעלה מן הארץ — The scribe wrote a dot, in order to distinguish the *sin* from a *shin*. In Biblical Hebrew, the word סם is mainly used to refer to "spices, perfumes," while in Rabbinic Hebrew, it means "drug, medicine, poison."
38:5 See Exod 15:25. . . . בעבור ל — The construction בעבור ל + infinitive is attested only in 1 Chr 19:3, is well attested in *piyyutim*, see especially in Yannai, for example, in קדושתות לשבתות השנה, בראשית, 16: קדושתות לשבתות השנה, ויקרא or in בעבור לידעו כי הוא משעו 32: בעבור להודיעם כי ה?ב?ל בצדקם (see Maagarim).

	מבני קרח	וכן רוקח עושה מרקחת:		13בהם רופא יניח מכאוב	7/8
	מפני ארצו	ותושיה מבני אדם:		14למען לא ישבות מעשהו	8	ישכח
	פלל	התפלל אל אל כי הוא ירפא:		15בני בחלי אל תתעבר	9	במחלה
		ומכל פשעים טהר לב:		16סור מעול ומהכר פנים	10	הסיר מ׳ והכר
	ערך הונך וג׳ ישמש מאה כ׳ ג׳ ב׳ צרכיך:	ודשן ערוך בכנפי הונך: ולא ימוש כי גם בו צורך:		17תן ניחח וגם אזכרה 18וגם לרופא תן מקום	11 12	אזכרתה
			פֿ		
T-S 16.312 verso		כי גם הוא אל אל יעתיר:		1כי יש עת אשר בידו מצלחת	13/14a
		ורפאות למען מחיה:		2אשר יצלח לו פשרה	14bc	ימנה
	יסתוגר אלי	יתגבר לפני רופא:		3אשר חוטא לפני עושהו	15
	התמרמר ונה׳ תתחר בגויתם	התמרר ונהה קינה: ואל תתעלם בגויעתם:		4בני על {מ}המת הזיב דמעה 5כמשפטו אסוף שארו	16	כמשפט א׳ שארם

L. 13 [38:8] רעה / צרכך This marginal notation was written by another scribe.

L. 13 [38:8] קרח — The last letter is likely a *khet* with an accidental trace which may be seen as the foot of a *tav*, though it is not actually a *tav*. Whichever the reading, neither makes sense within the context.

L. 14 [38:8] מבני/מפני ארצו — Three successive marginal alternatives, probably drawn from other copies, have been inserted here. ארצו which corresponds to the Greek and the Syriac was written first in the margin as an alternative to אדם. Then, מפני was written above it as an alternative to מבני (see also the Greek and the Syriac). Finally, above מפני, a third marginal reading preserves, מבני, in agreement with the main text. The repetition in the margin of a word that is in the main text is extremely uncommon and would suggest that two alternative manuscripts have been consulted by the scribe.

L. 17 [38:11] תן ניחח וגם אזכרה — The *tav* is clear from its horizontal bar, right vertical and left foot. It is followed by a short final *nun*. One can then see the beginning of the vertical of a *nun* and faint traces of its base, followed by a *yod* attached to the *nun* and two *khets*. Both *khets* are preserved by their horizontal bar and their two legs. The first letter of the next word must be a *vav*, followed by a *gimel*, which is characterized by its vertical going beneath the base line. The last letter is definitely a final *mem* (with its horizontal bar and left stroke). This reading agrees with the Greek, which also has a few supplementary word: δὸς εὐωδίαν καὶ μνημόσυνον σεμιδάλεως.

L. 18 [38:12] This restoration was proposed by Schechter and Taylor (1899, 17).

L. 1 [38:13] פ — For this marginal mark, see complete introduction and Rey and Dhont 2019, 103-105.

L. 3 [38:15] על ידי — It seems that the oblique marginal reading comes from a scribe other than the one who wrote יסתוגר.

38:8 This verse is quoted after v. 4 in Gen. Rab. 10:6: מרפא הרופא בהם — See רוקח עושה מרקחת. את המכה ובהם הרוקח רוקיח את המרקחת. See Exod 30:25 and 1 Chr 9:30. קרח — The marginal notation קרח "ice, frost, crystal" (or "bald head") is very difficult to explain, unless we extrapolate from "frost" the meaning "powder." The alternative reading קרת "city" similarly does not make sense here. ישכח — This marginal notation may have appeared during the textual transmission process, confusing ב with כ and ת with ח (see Lévi 1901, 197).

38:9 בחולי — A *bet* prefixed to a noun can sometimes express a temporal nuance (see van Peursen 2004, 335). Cf. בעשרך in Sir 3:17ᴬ "when you possess wealth" and בטובתך in Sir 6:10ᴬ. תתעבר — For the meaning of the *hithpael* of עבר, see Sir 5:7ᴬ and the note. Here it may have the sense "do not delay" or "do not show yourself angry." פלל — The *piel* of פלל with the meaning "to pray" does not seem to be attested before Rabbinic Hebrew.

38:10 ומהכר פנים סור מעול — Cf. 1QS VI 15: ולסור מכול עול. For the expression נכר פנים with the meaning "to recognize the face, be a respector of persons, be partial," see Deut 1:17; 16:19, with the exact phrase הַכֵּר פנים in Prov 24:23; 28:21. Partiality is especially a concern for the Wisdom tradition and for Ben Sira in particular (cf. 4:22ᴬ,ᶜ; 35:15–16ᴮ; 42:1ᴹ,ᴮ). הסיר מ׳ והכר — In the main text, מהכר is made up of the prefixed preposition מן followed by the *hiphil* infinitive absolute of נכר, though we do not expect a preposition to be prefixed to such an infinitive. Perhaps due to this, the marginal alternative drops the preposition from the infinitive, though its sense is implied from the preceding phrase. The *hiphil* form of סור seems to be used like the *qal* (cf. לאין הסר "without ending" in 1QHᵃ XIV 21 [similar in sense to the *qal* in Isa 11:13]).

38:11 Cf. Lev 2:2. ניחֹח . . . אזכרה — For the association of these two words, see Lev 2:2, 9; 6:8. אזכרתה — For this form in the margin, see Lev 2:2. ערוך — This is most likely the *qal* imperative of the verb ערך "to set in order, to prepare." The text alludes to Lev 1:8, 12 and 6:12 (see also 1QS VI 4 and 1QSa II 17: השולחן לערוך). The vocalized phrase דֶּשֶׁן עֲרוֹך is attested in a medieval *piyyut* by Zerahiah Halevi of Girona in a poem titled יעבור לא פורים זכר, ca. 1186 CE (Russian State Library (Moscow), Guenzberg 198; see Maagarim). The marginal note ערך is the defective spelling of the imperative rather than the noun "equipment, value" (see Lev 5:18; 6:6; 27:3; etc.). בכנפי הונך — The expression is not entirely clear and can have different meanings depending on the semantic value given to כנף. It may refer to the "surplus of your wealth," i.e. what is in excess. In Aramaic, it can mean "gatherings," so that the sentence would be translated "the savings of your subsistence" (so Schechter and Taylor 1899, 61). But preferably, it may also mean "in the limits of your wealth" (Smend 1906a, 341). Most commentators emend the text to כפי "according to your richness."

38:12 וג׳ ישמש מאה — The marginal note is hard to make sense of, unless it derives from an Arabic loan (cf. the Arabic cognate *šms* "to run away, abstain" (Lane 1863, 1597). As noted by Schechter and Taylor (1899, 61) and scholars since, it is likely a mistake for מאתך ימוש לא "May he not depart from you because you also need him." בו צורך — The combination of the preposition ב with the abstract noun צורך is also found in m. Ber. 3:1 and with the Aramaic cognate in Tg. Isa. 9:4.

7	Par eux, le médecin apaise la souffrance
8	et ainsi le chimiste (mg. ?) prépare la mixture, afin que son œuvre ne cesse pas, (mg. ne soit pas oubliée) ni la prudence qui vient des êtres (mg. 1. idem ; mg. 2. à la face [d'Adam]) humains (mg. 3. son pays).
9	Mon enfant, durant la maladie (mg. idem) ne t'irrite pas, prie (mg. idem) Dieu, car c'est lui qui guérit.
10	Détourne-toi de l'iniquité et d'être partial (mg. Détourne-toi de l'iniquité et d'être partial) et de tous péchés purifie (ton) cœur.
11	Offre un parfum apaisant et aussi un mémorial (mg. idem) et dispose (mg. idem) la graisse dans les limites de tes richesses (mg. de ta richesse).
12	Et aussi au médecin, donne une place et qu'il ne soit pas loin car on a aussi besoin de lui. (mg. et qu'il ne serve pas plus qu'un frère car tu as aussi besoin de lui).
13	Car il y a un temps qui prospère par sa main,
14a	car lui aussi implore Dieu, (mg. (Il y a) un temps qui prospère par sa main, car lui, il implore Dieu)
14b	de sorte que lui réussisse (mg. établisse) son diagnostic
14c	et la guérison afin qu'il fasse vivre.
15	Celui qui pêche devant son créateur, fait le fort (mg. 1. est livré) devant (mg. 2. au pouvoir du) le médecin.
16	Mon enfant, sur un mort, verse des larmes, sois amer et entonne (mg. sois furieux et entonne) une plainte. Selon sa coutume, ensevelis son corps (mg. selon la coutume ensevelis leur corps). et ne te détourne pas des mourants. (Mg. ne t'irrite pas concernant leur corps.)

7	Through them, the physician alleviates suffering,
8	and so the apothecary (mg. ?) prepares compounds, so that their work does not end (mg. will not be forgotten). nor the prudence that comes from humankind (mg. 1. idem; mg. 2. from before (humankind); mg. 3. his country).
9	My child, in sickness (mg. idem) do not delay, pray (mg. idem) to God, for it is he who heals.
10	Turn from iniquity and from being partial (mg. turn from iniquity and being partial) and cleanse (your) heart of all sins.
11	Provide a pleasant scent and also a memorial (mg. idem) and present the fat (mg. idem) as much as your wealth allows (mg. idem).
12	And also to the physician, give a place, so that they do not depart for they too are needed. (mg. And do not let them (i.e., the physician) minister (to you) more than a brother for you also need him (i.e., your brother).)
13	For there is a time that prospers through their work,
14a	for they too implore God,
13	(mg. A time (there is) that prospers through their work,
14a	for they implore God)
14b	so that their diagnosis succeeds (mg. (when) they establish (their diagnosis))
14c	and (their) healing (succeeds) for the purpose of saving lives.
15	The one who sins before their maker (is one who) behaves arrogantly (mg. 1. is delivered) before (mg. 2. to the power of) the physician.
16	My child, make tears flow for the dead, be bitter and utter (mg. be furious and utter) a lament. According to their custom, bury their body (mg. according to custom, bury their bodies) and do not turn away from their dying (mg. do not be angry at their bodies).

38:13 עת אשר בידו מצלחת — Given the feminine gender of the participle מצלחת, it seems that עת is its grammatical subject. For the combination of ביד with the verb צלח, see Gen 39:3; Isa 53:10 and Ezra 5:8.

38:14 ימנה — The Hebrew verb "to count" can be interpreted with its Aramaic meaning here, "to reckon as" or "to appoint, fix" in *pael* (see perhaps, in Galilean Aramaic, the word מנייה "expert"; see also 40:29). פשרה — The meaning of this noun is not entirely clear. It can be understood as "diagnosis (and treatment plan)" in connection with the Aramaic root פשר (Dan 5:12.16, and in Hebrew, Qoh 8:1 and at Qumran). Kister (1990, 343) has also suggested a sense related to the same verb's use in Rabbinic Hebrew and Samaritan Aramaic (Tal 2000, 1263): "to rescue, deliver, save."

38:15 יסתוגר — According to Maagarim, neither the *hithpoel* or *hithpael* are attested elsewhere, but the meaning should be the passive to the *piel* of סגר ("to be delivered into the hand of"); see the Greek (ἐμπέσοι εἰς χεῖρας "to fall into the hands of...") and the Syriac (ܬܫܬܠܡ; "to be delivered into the hand of...").

38:16 הזיב — The *hiphil* of זוב is not attested before ninth-century *piyyutim*, though in Aramaic the *aphel* occurs already in 11Q10 XXXV 3 (at Job 40:24). התמרר — The *hithpael* of מרר is only attested in Rabbinic literature with the meaning "to become bitter." By contrast, the *hithpalpel* in the margin, meaning "to become furious," does appear in Biblical Hebrew. קינה — The word refers to a characteristic funeral lamentation. אסוף — For אסף, see 8:7ᴬ and the note there. בגויעתם — This word is a verbal noun from the root גוע, "to die," appearing in b. B. Bat. 16b parallel to אסיפה; see Dihi (2004, 126–127).

	ושית אבלו כיוצא בו:	⁶הָמֵר בנ̇י והתם מספד	17	בכי והֵהֵם
	והנחם בעבור עון:	⁷יום ושנים בעבור דמעה		
	כן רע לבב יבנה עצבה:	⁸מדין יוצא אסון	18	
והכר	פרע זכרו וזכו̇ר אחרית:	⁹אל תש̇יב אליו לב עוד	20	תשית עליו
	לו אתמול ולך היום:	¹⁰זכור חקו כי הו̇א חקך	22	כן
	מה תועיל ולך תריע:	¹¹אל תזכרהו כי אין לו תקוה	21	
	והנחם עם צאת נפשו:	¹²מ̇ושבת̇ מתוש̇בת זכרו	23	כשבות מת ישבות ז'
		vacat	13	
	וחס̇ר עסק הוא יתחכ̇ם:	¹⁴חכמת סופר תרבה חכמה	24	
	ומתפאר בחנית מרע̇יד:	¹⁵מה יתחכם תומך מלמד	25	
	ושעיותיו עם בנ̇י בקֿרֿ:	¹⁶באלוף ינהג יש̇וב̇ב לשדד בש̇ור	26	וישובב בשיר
	לֵב יש̇ית לשד̇ד תלמֹים:	¹⁷ושקידתו לכלות מרבק	26	
ינהג	אשר לילה כֿיֿוֹם מֹנֹהֹגֿ[:]	¹⁸אף עשה חרש וחושב	27	

Chapter 39

Or. 1102 recto	וכן תאמר בתרועה:	¹[ב̇]שֹירות נבל וכלי מינים	15	
לכל צריך	וכל צורך בעתו̇ יספיקו:	²מ̇עש̇י אל כֻלם טובים	16	[הכל ?]
ב' יספיקו:				

L. 12 [38:23] מתושבת — It looks like the *vav* written between מת and שבת has been added afterwards, connecting the two words.

L. 16 [38:25] בנ̇י בקֿרֿ — This reading, proposed by Schechter and Taylor (1899, 18) and Lévi (1904, 46), perfectly fits the traces and corresponds to both the Greek and the Syriac.

L. 17 [38:26] לשד̇ד תלמֹים — The reading תלמים, which agrees with the Greek αὔλακας (see Ps 65:11; Job 31:38; 39:10), is certain; there are traces of the foot of the *tav*, the vertical of the *lamed*, the horn of the *mem*, traces of the head of the *yod* and traces of the horizontal bar of the final *mem*.

L. 18 [38:27] כֿיֿוֹם מֹנֹהֹגֿ[:] — While the first word is easy to reconstruct, the last word is very difficult to read. The reading מנהג, pro-

posed by Cowley (1900, 111), fits the traces. The reading כיומ ז[ו]ע, proposed by Smend (1906b, 36), is impossible.

L. 1 [39:15] [ב̇]שֹירות — The left arm of the *shin* and part of its base are preserved. The *yod* is clearly visible on the original (cf. Smend 1906b, 36). מינים — After the second *yod*, one can distinguish very faint traces of ink that correspond to the missing final *mem*.

L. 2 [39:16] מ̇עש̇י — Traces of the *mem* are preserved (the end of the diagonal and base). The *ayin* is clearly visible on the original and in the photographs. Only traces of ink preserve the *shin* and the *yod*. [הכל] — Ben-Ḥayyim (1973, 40) and Smend (1906b, 35) read הכל (see also Sir 39:32), but there are no traces visible in the margin in the current state of the manuscript.

38:17 According to Kister (1990, 343–344), this verse expresses the idea that the dead must be mourned for an appropriate period of time, but not more; and, it is strongly influenced b. Moʿed Qaṭ. 27b, which is illuminating: "אל תבכו למת ואל תנודו לו". "אל תבכו יותר מדאי. ואל תנודו" יותר מכשיעור. הא כאיזה־צד. שלשה לבכי. שבעה להספד. שלשים לגיהוץ ולתספורת. מכאן ואילך אמ' הקב'ה. אין אתם רחמנים עליו יותר ממני. "Do not weep for one who is dead, nor bemoan them' (Jer 22:10): 'Do not weep' refers to what is excessive; 'nor bemoan them' more than what is appropriate. How so? Three (days) for weeping, and seven for lamenting, and thirty for (not) laundering and for (not) cutting hair. From this point forward the Holy One, Blessed be He, says: 'Do not be more compassionate over one (who is dead) than me.'" הָמֵר — For the sense of the *hiphil* verb, see Zech 12:10. התם — The sense "to finish, stop" is found, e.g., in Isa 33:1. והֵהֵם — This is a *hiphil* imperative from the Aramaic root הום/המם. The root was used in funeral contexts with the same semantic range as קין "to lament" and ספד "to mourn." The parallel with the Nerab Stele 2:5–6 בכוני והום אתהמו is clear (see also, Tg. Onq. Deut 14:1; Talshir 1979, 84–86; Kister 1990, 306). כיוצא בו — For the idiomatic expression יוצא ב..., see 10:28ᴬ. יום ושנים — The expression refers to the duration of mourning and may be understood as one or two days, or even three days. It does not seem necessary to correct the word to דמעה, according to the Greek or the Syriac. See b. Moʿed Qaṭ. 27b, שלשה לבכי. שבעה להספד "three days for crying and seven for lamenting," and Tanḥ. Meqitz 4:1. עון — The Greek read δῶν "sorrow" (see 14:1ᴬ and the note), which is the first word of the next verse, while the Syriac ܚܝܐ presupposes חיים. In the light of b. Moʿed

Qaṭ. 27b, the word עון seems to imply that the dead must not be mourned more than is necessary: אין אתם רחמנים עליו יותר ממני.

38:18 מדין — For דין in the meaning of דון "sorrow," see Sir 14:1ᴬ and the note. רע לבב — See Neh 2:2. יבנה עצבה — For בנה in this context, cf. Ps 89:3 חסד יבנה. For עצבה, see 11:9ᴬ and the note.

38:20 תשית עליו לב — The construction שית ... לב is idiomatic, meaning "to turn one's attention to, to take to heart, to heed, to pay attention"; see Job 7:17 and Ps 62:11. אחרית — See 3:26ᴬ; 7:36ᴬ; 11:25ᴬ and the notes there.

38:22 חקו/חקך — For the meaning of חק here, see 41:2ᴮ and the note.

38:23 מושבת / שבת — The root שבת has the sense "to cease (to exist)" in the *qal* and perhaps the *niphal* in Sir 44:9ᴮ. For the *hophal* here, cf. the use of the *hiphil* to mean "destroy, kill (a person)" in Sir 36:12ᴮ and Jer 48:35. The *hophal* participle of שבת does not seem to be attested before *piyyuṭim*. צאת נפשו — For the expression, see Gen 35:18.

38:24 חכמת סופר ... חכמה — Ben Sira plays on the polysemy of the root חכמ, "skillfull, clever, experienced, wise." חסר עסק — See 3:22ᴬ and the note as well as m. ʾAbot 4:10: הוי מעט עסק ועסוק בתורה "Reduce (your) business dealings, and busy yourself with Torah."

38:25 מלמד — See Judg 3:31 and Jastrow 1903, 793. בחנית — The noun usually has the sense "spear," though here must be instead an instrument for driving cattle. באלוף — Here, the noun is clearly "cattle" as in Ps 144:14, though the root evokes the verb אלף "to learn" (see, e.g., Prov 22:25), which seems to be an ironic use of wordplay (i.e., suggesting a reading "when learning, he leads"). לשדד — The verb שדד means

17 Gémis amèrement, mon enfant, et achève (ta) lamentation (mg. pleure et geins),
   et porte son deuil comme il lui revient.
   Un jour et deux jours, pour les larmes,
   puis console-toi, pour l'iniquité.
18 De la tristesse sort le malheur,
   ainsi le chagrin de cœur crée la douleur.
20 Ne ramène plus l'attention vers lui (mg. Ne fixe plus l'attention sur lui),
   chasse son souvenir et souviens-toi de (mg. examine) la fin.
22 Souviens-toi de son sort, car c'est (mg. ainsi sera) ton sort,
   pour lui (c'était) hier, pour toi, (c'est) aujourd'hui.
21 Ne te souviens pas de lui, car il n'y a plus d'espoir pour lui.
   Quel serait ton profit si tu te fais du mal ?
23 Le mort a cessé (d'exister) et son souvenir cesse
   (mg. Lorsque le mort cesse (d'exister), son souvenir cesse)
   et console-toi avec le départ de son souffle.
24 L'expertise du scribe démultiplie la sagesse
   et celui qui a peu d'affaires, lui, devient sage.
25 Comment deviendrait-il sage celui qui tient l'aiguillon
   et celui qui se vante en brandissant la lance,
   il mène le bétail et ramène ^{(retourne) labourer avec} le bœuf,
   (mg. et retourne avec un chant,)
   et ses discours (sont) avec les jeunes taureaux.
26 Son attention est d'accomplir l'engraissage,
   le cœur s'occupe à labourer des sillons.
27 De même, le travailleur, le graveur et l'artisan,
   lui qui, de nuit comme de jour, gémit (mg. gémira).

Chapitre 39

15 [Par]des cantiques, la lyre et des instruments de toutes sortes,
   et ainsi tu annonceras par des cris de joie :
16 les œuvres de Dieu sont toutes bonnes
   et il pourvoit tout besoin, en son temps.
   (mg. elles pourvoient à tout besoin, en son temps.)

---

17 Show grief, my child, then finish (your) lamentation, (mg. cry and moan),
   mourn over them according to how dear they are (to you),
   one day and two days, for the sake of tears,
   and then console yourself, for the sake of iniquity.
18 From sorrow comes misfortune,
   just as heartache creates injury.
20 Do not turn your mind to them,
   (mg. Do not set your mind on them),
   chase their memory and remember (mg. acknowledge) the end.
22 Call to mind their fate, for (mg. so) it is your fate;
   for them it was yesterday, but for you it is today.
21 Do not call them to mind for there is no hope for them anymore,
   how should you benefit by hurting yourself?
23 The one who has died has been brought to an end and their memory ceases
   (mg. When the one who is dead ceases, their memory ceases)
   so console yourself at the departure of their soul.
24 The expertise of the scribe multiplies wisdom,
   and one who has few business affairs becomes wise.
25 How can the one grasping an ox-goad become wise?
   and the one who glories in waving a prod?
   They drive the cattle and returns ^{to plough} with the ox,
   (mg. and returns with a song)
   and their discourses are with the young bulls.
26 Their attention is devoted to completing the fattening (of calves),
   they set their heart on plowing furrows.
27 Also, the worker, the engraver, and the designer,
   who, by night and by day, moan. (mg. will moan).

Chapter 39

15 [With] songs, the lyre and instruments of all kinds,
   and so you will say with cries of joy:
16 The works of God are all good,
   and any need, in its time, he provides.
   (mg. they provide any need in its time.)

"to harrow, plough," see HALOT. וישובב בשיר — The last word can be read "with song," or perhaps as a misspelling of an Aramaism בסיר "what is unripe" (see Tg. Ps.-J. at Exod 9:31). ושעיותי — See 37:14^B and the note. בֹּנֵי בֹקֶר — See Num 28:11; 29:13 and 1 Sam 14:32.
38:26 ושקידתו — The word שקידה only occurs elsewhere in ninth-century *piyyutim*. לֵב יָשִׁית — For the expression, see Prov 22:17; 24:32 and 27:23.
38:27 חֹרֵשׁ וְחֹשֵׁב — For the association of these two words, see Exod 35:35 and 38:23. מנהג — Although it is possible to read this as the same verb as above in verse 25, the fact that it is here in the *piel* suggests that it is the homophynous Hebrew verb נהג II "to moan," found in the *piel* in Nah 2:8.
39:15 מינים — Note the *plene* writing. Peters (1902, 163) notes that it often occurs before gemination of consonants.
39:16 צורך / צריך — The same two words are confused in Sir 13:6^A; see the note there. For צורך, see 8:9^A and the note. For צריך, see 31:4^B and the note. יספיק — The *hiphil* of ספק, meaning "to supply, to provide," does not appear elsewhere before the rabbinic era.

	ומוצא פיו אוצרו:	³בְּדִבְּרוֹ יעריך נ[ד] מֹ[י]ֹםֹ	17	
	ואין מעצור לתשועתו:	⁴תחתָו רצונו יצליח	18	
מסותר	ואין נסתר מנגד עיניו:	⁵מעשה כל בשר נגדו	19	
	וֹאיןֹ מֹספר לתשועתו:	⁶מעולם ועד עולם יביט	20	
	ואין נפלא וחזק ממנו:	⁷אין קטן ומעט עמו		
בעתו יגבר	כי הכל לצרֹכוֹ נבחר:	⁸אין לאמר זה למה זה	21	
	כי הכל בעתו יגבר:	⁹אין לאמר זה רע מזה		
	וכנהר תבל ריותה:	¹⁰בֹּרכות כיאר הציפה	22	[תו]
	ויהפך למלח משקה:	¹¹וכן זעמו גוים יוריש	23	[???]
	כן לזרים יסתוללו:	¹²א[רחו]תֹ תמים ישרו	24	[א]רחותיו ישׁ[ים]
רע	כן לרעים טוב ורֹע:	¹³[טוב]לטוב חלק מראש	25	
	ואש וברזל ומלח:	¹⁴[ראש]כל חיֹי אדם מים	26 ᴾ	
	דם ענב יצהר ובגד:	¹⁵[סלת/חלב]חטים חלב ודבש		
לזרא	כן לרעים לרעָה נהפכו:	¹⁶כל א[לה]לטובים ייטיבו	27 ᴾᴹ	נֶעְשָׂה?
	]הֹרים יעתיקו:	¹⁷יש ר[וחות לנ]קם יוֹצרו	28 ᴾᴹ	
	[ ]	[ ]¹⁸		

39:27 · M לזרה | Bmg לוזרא | B G לרעה

L. 3 [39:17] בְּדִבְּרוֹ — This reading, which is based on Greek, fits the preserved traces of letters perfectly. נ[ד] מֹ[י]ֹםֹ — The *nun* is clearly visible. It is certainly possible to restore נד מים with Segal (1958, 260), according to the Greek, but there is not enough room for the proposal of Smend (1906b, 36 [Heb]): נר [במ]רֹ[ו]ֹםֹ. Traces of ink correspond to the first *mem* of מים (the horn, diagonal and part of the right shoulder are visible) and the final *mem* (the horizontal bar is visible).

L. 4 [39:18] תחתָו — The reading is assured. The scribe has written a *qamets* under the *tav* to indicate a vocalization corresponding to תחתיו. Cowley and Neubauer (1897, 2) and Lévi (1904, 46) read [תחתי]ו, but there is no space for a *yod*. Smend (1906b, 37) and Ben-Ḥayyim (1973, 40) propose תנגתו, which is impossible.

L. 5 [39:19] וֹאיןֹ — Very faint traces of the head of the *yod* are preserved. Only the end of the *nun*'s vertical stroke is visible.

L. 6 [39:20] וֹאיןֹ — Smend (1906b, 37) and Ben-Ḥayyim (1973, 41) read על כן לא מספר which is absolutely impossible. Cowley and Neubauer (1897, 2) read [הי]ש. Yet, the reading ואין is certain. On the right side of the fracture, one can clearly see a *vav*, and on the left side, the characteristic layout of the left leg of the *aleph*, as well as part of the diagonal. A *yod* is then visible, followed by traces of a letter that matches the *nun*'s head and curve. מֹספר — the *mem* is barely visible, preserved only by meager traces.

L. 10 [39:22] בֹּרכות — A *circellus* is drawn above the *bet*, yet there is no marginal correction visible.

L. 11 [39:23] Smend (1906b, 37) and Ben-Ḥayyim (1973, 41) transcribe the marginal note הוריש, but there is nothing visible on the fragment. כֹן — The *nun* is visible on the original; though the ink is faded, the outline of its head and its entire tail are clearly visible.

L. 12 [39:24] The restoration of the marginal note is challenging, as it is particularly difficult to read, especially the second line. Cowley and Neubauer (1897, 2) and Lévi (1904, 47) transcribe [א]רחותיו (ל)ישרים, while Smend (1906b, 37) and Ben-Ḥayyim (1973, 41) read ארחותיו ב[מיש]רים. The most that can be read is [א]רחותיוֹ, with the *yod* and *vav* questionable, as they are barely visible, follwed by [ים]שר, without any of these letters really being assured.

L. 13 [39:25] רע — Some have read לרע (Smend 1906b, 37; Ben-Ḥayyim 1973, 41; Beentjes 1997, 68), but there is no trace of a *lamed* (thus Cowley and Neubauer 1897, 2; Lévi 1904, 47).

L. 14 [39:26] [ראש]כל חיֹי —The *kaph* is visible (its head and part of its base). There is still a trace of the left leg of the *khet*. The ink-induced paper erosion also follows the form of the letter. Our restoration agrees with Smend's (1906b, 37) reading and restoration and is now confirmed by Hᴾᵃʳ (T-S NS 93.80 recto line 6, verse 2). The restoration כל צרך is less likely. Lévi (1898, 8) suggested ראש כל צרך, in agreement with the Greek and the Syriac, but this is too long for the available space.

L. 15 [39:26] חֹטיםֹ חלב — There are traces of the head of the *khet*. A small trace of the base and left stroke of the *tet* are then preserved. The *yod* and *mem* (or *samek*) are clearly preserved. One can then see the very clear trace of the right leg of the *khet* of חלב. According to the lacuna before this, one can restore either סלת חטים with the Greek (σεμίδαλις πυροῦ, see Exod 29:2) or חלב חטים with the Syriac (ܚܠܒܐ, cf. Ps 147:14 and Exod 23:18 for the translation of חלב with ܚܠܒܐ).

L. 16 [39:27] לטובים — Very faint traces of the upper part of the *tet* are preserved.

L. 17 [39:28] יש ר[וחות לנ]קם יוֹצרו — The *resh* after יש is perfectly clear. Before the *tsade* of יוצרו, one can see very faint traces of ink that may correspond to the proposed reading, in agreement with the Greek and the Syriac and is confirmed by Hᴾᵃʳ (T-S NS 93.80 recto line 10, verse 4). The restoration יש ר[וחות למשפט נוצרו] previously proposed by scholars (Lévi 1904, 47; Peters 1902, 389; Segal 1958, 261; Vattioni 1968, 211) is obviously too long for the available space. הֹרים[ ] יעתיקו: — There are some faint traces of letters before הרים, but it is too difficult to identify them. ובאפם, as previously proposed by scholars, cannot be excluded, but is hard to prove (see the parallel with Job 9:5).

39:17 This sentence seems to be inspired by Ps 33:7: כֹּנֵס כַּנֵּד מֵי הַיָּם נֹתֵן בְּאֹצָרוֹת תְּהוֹמוֹת: "He gathers the sea's waters like a heap, he puts the deeps in storehouses." (כָּל־מוֹצָא פִי־יְהוָה). ומוצא פיו — See Deut 8:3. אוצרו — The term "storehouse" has a cosmological meaning here, where it refers to "heavenly treasure" or "divine reservoirs."

39:18 תחתו — That is, beneath or under God. Alternatively, "on his behalf" (cf. t. Demai 6:4). רצונו יצליח — The same two words are in a similar construction in Sir 11:17ᴬ. ואין מעצור לתשועתו — Cf. 1 Sam 14:6.

39:19 ואין נסתר — The Hebrew syntax supposes אין followed by a participle (see, however, Qoh 8:11), as the marginal notation suggests.

17 Par sa parole, il installe un amon[cellement] d'e[a]u
et ce qui sort de sa bouche est son réservoir.
18 En dessous de lui, son désir s'accomplit,
et il n'y a pas d'obstacle à sa victoire.
19 L'œuvre de toute chair est devant lui
et rien n'est caché (mg. idem) devant ses yeux.
20 Depuis toujours et à jamais, il observe
et il n'y a pas de mesure à sa victoire.
Rien n'est petit ou peu avec lui
et rien n'est plus merveilleux ou plus puissant que lui.
21 Personne ne peut dire : « ceci, pourquoi cela ? »
Car tout a été choisi pour son utilité (mg. prévaut en son temps).
Personne ne peut dire : « ceci est plus mauvais que cela. »
Car tout prévaut en son temps.
22 Les bénédictions débordent comme le Nil
et comme un fleuve abreuvent le monde.
23 Ainsi sa colère dépossède les nations
et il a changé la terre irriguée en saline.
24 Les voies de l'intègre sont droites (mg. Ses voies sont droites),
ainsi s'élèvent-elles pour les étrangers.
25 Depuis l'origine, il a créé [le bien]pour le bon
de même pour les méchants: le bien et le mal (mg. (et pour les méchants ce qui est bien) est mal).
26 [L'essentiel de]toute vie humaine est : l'eau
et le feu, et le fer et le sel,
[la farine/la graisse]du froment, le lait et le miel
le sang du raisin, l'huile et le vêtement.
27 Toutes ce[s choses]font du bien aux bons,
de même elles sont changées en mal (mg. en nausées) pour les méchants.
28 Il y a des v[ents] qui sont formés [pour la venge]ance,
[   ]ils déplacent les montagnes.
[   ]
[   ]

17 And by his word, he arranges a he[ap of] wa[t]er
and what comes out of his mouth is its reservoir.
18 Beneath him, his wish prospers
and there is no obstacle to his victory.
19 The work of all flesh is before him
And nothing is hidden (mg. idem) from his eyes.
20 He has always and forever observed,
and no one can measure his victory.
There is nothing small or little with him,
and nothing more wonderful or more powerful than him.
21 No one can say, "This, why that?"
for everything has been chosen for its purpose.
(mg. (everything) excels in its time)
No one can say, "This is worse than that"
for everything excels in its time.
22 Blessings overflow like the Nile,
and like a river, saturate the world.
23 Thus, his wrath dispossesses the nations
and turns the irrigated land into salt.
24 The paths of integrity are straight
(mg. his paths are straight)
so they rise up against enemies.
25 From the beginning, he created [the good] for the good,
and for the wicked: good and evil (mg. (and for the wicked what is good) is evil).
26 [First of]all things for human life are: water,
and fire and iron and salt,
[flour/fat] of wheat, milk and honey
the blood of the grape, oil and clothing.
27 All t[hese things] are good for the good,
accordingly, they turn out bad (mg. disgusting) for the evil.
28 There are w[inds] that are formed [for ven]geance
[   ] they remove mountains.
[   ]
[   ]

39:21 This is a doublet of Sir 39:34^B and the second stich of the first line (כי הכל לצרכו נבחר) can also be compared to Sir 39:30^B. See the note on נבחר below. The second stich of the second line and the marginal reading for the first line can also be compared to 39:16b^B. לצרכו — "according to its need, use." See 32:7^B. נבחר — The Greek ἔκτισται supposes נברא as its *Vorlage*. The stich should be compared to 39:30^B and its marginal reading גם כל אלה לצורכם נבראו, corrected to אלה לצורכם נבחרו.
39:22 ברכות — Most commentators correct to ברכתו, which may be what the marginal correction said, though it is no longer visible. For the non-agreement between the verb and a plural feminine subject, see JM §150b-c. כיאר — The word יאר may designate any stream, or more specifically, the Nile, as in Sir 24:27^LXX (where the Greek ὡς φῶς seems to be a mistake for כיאר < כאר according to the context; see the same confusion in Am 8:8) and Sir 47:14: ותצף כיאר מוסר "you flowed over like the Nile with instruction." הציפה -- The *hiphil* appears to have the active sense of the *qal*.
39:24 יסתוללו — The *hithpolel* of סלל, which is a *hapax legomenon* in the Hebrew Bible (Exod 9:17), is also attested in Sir 40:28^B, as well as in later *piyyutim*. For the meaning "to exalt oneself (against)," see Ben Yehuda (1948, 4:4071). לזרים — For the possible meanings of the noun or participle זר, see the note to Sir 37:5^B
39:25 חלק — For חלק with the meaning "to create," see Sir 7:15 and the note.
39:26 דם ענב — See Gen 49:11 and Deut 32:14.
39:28 הרים יעתיקו — See Job 9:5.

Or. 1102 verso	להרים	[:]גם אלה למשפט נברֹאֹוֹּ		¹אש וברד רע ודבר	29 PM
חָרֹ֗ב נִקְמת		וחרב נקמות להחרים בֹּם:		²חית שן עקרב ופתן	30 PM
לֹ֗ם בם		והמה באוצר וֹלעת יפקדו:		³כֹּל אלה לצורכם נבראו		גם
בָאֹ֗וֹצרו		ובחקם לא ימרו פיו:		⁴בצוותו אתם יששו	31 M	נבחרו
לעת						
פיהו:		והתבוננתי ובכתב הנחתי:		⁵על כן מראש התיצבתי	32 M	
	צריך	לכל צורך בעתו יספוק:		⁶מעשה אל כלם טובים	33	הכל
	יגבר	כי הכל בעתו יגבר:		⁷אל לאמר זה רע מה זה	34	אין
						מזה
	קדשו	וברכו את שם [הֹ]קֹּ[דֹ]וֹש:		⁸עתה בכל לב הרנינו	35 P	ופה

Chapter 40

	ועול כבד על בנֵי אדם:		⁹עסק גדול חלק אל	1	עליון
אל	עד יום שובו אל אם כל חי:		¹⁰מיום צאתו מרחם אמו		
לובש	עד לשוב עפר ואפר:		¹¹מיושב כסא לגבה	3	
לבש					
עֹדֹ עֹטֹ	ועֹד עוטה שמלת סֹיגֹה[:]		¹²מעוטה צניף וציץ	4	
מ תח רֹיֹב	אימת מוֹת תחרה וֹרֹיֹב[:]		¹³אך קנאה דאגה ופחד	5ab	

L. 1 [39:29] נברֹאֹוֹּ[:] — The *bet* is clearly visible, followed by a horizontal stroke, then traces of the beginning of the right arm of an *aleph* and the left part of its diagonal. The reading נוצרו[:] proposed by Cowley and Neubauer (1897, 4) is impossible.

L. 2 [39:30] ל[ ]ooבם — All the preceding editions read [למשפט], but the traces may hardly agree with such a reading. להרים — As the second *circellus* and the position of the marginal variant show, this annotation is secondary.

L. 5 [39:32] התיצבתי — This reading is certain, despite Lévi's reading התעבבתי (Lévi 1904, 47).

L. 6 [39:33] צריך — It is not clear on the manuscript whether one should read a *yod* or a *vav*.

L. 8 [39:35] [ה]קֹ[דֹ]וֹש — The ink on the manuscript is completely erased.

L. 9 [40:1] בנֵי — The *yod* is clearly visible on the original.

L. 10 [40:1] Mg. אל — Some (Lévi 1904, 48; Beentjes 1997, 69) read ארץ כ׳ ח instead, which seems impossible. The *aleph* is clear, followed by a trace of the *lamed*'s diagonal, ascending vertical stroke and its head. There are no marks that coincide with the letters read by Lévi (1904, 48) et al.

L. 11 [40:3] לבש — The traces are very faint. It may be possible to read לכפר, though this makes less sense.

L. 12 [40:4] סֹיגֹה — Most editions read עור "skin" or [שֹ]ער "hair," yet both are highly unlikely. The first letter is too narrow to be an *ayin* or a *shin* (or a *sin*). The marks fit a *samek* perfectly. The next letter is clearly a *yod*. The following letter has the characteristic bottom of a *gimel*: both the vertical and horizontal strokes are visible. This is followed by the bottom of the left leg of what could be a *he*, visible at the edge of the hole (Reymond et al. 2017). עֹדֹ — Based on firsthand inspection of the manuscript itself, two words were originally written, but the ink is very faded and interpretation extremely difficult. Cowley and Neubauer (1897, 4) read עד עושה, which is possible, though the *he* is not visible. Smend (1906b, 38) and Ben-Ḥayyim (1973, 42) read עֹד עֹט, which is certainly preferable according to the faint traces.

L. 13 [40:5b] וֹרֹיֹב — This is the most likely reading of the traces (cf. Smend 1906b, 38; for the defective writing of ריב, see 11:9b). Another possibility is to read וֹרֹ[:ב]. The last word in the margin is often read as וריב, but the initial *vav* is missing.

39:30 חרב נקמת — See Lev 26:25. להרים — It is more likely that this is the *hiphil* infinitive construct of רום than the plural of הר, "for the mountains." לצורכם — For צורך with this meaning, see 39:21. באוצר — See also 43:14. In this context, as in Job 38:22, אוצר has an obvious cosmic value. יפקדו — The polysemy of the verb makes it difficult to translate. It may be the *hophal* "to deposited, stored" (cf. Lev 5:23), yet its collocation with the word עת may imply that it should be understood as "to punish" (as in Jer 6:15, 49:8, 50:31). It may also be the *niphal* in the meaning "to be commissioned, to be appointed" (Neh 7:1).

39:33 מעשה — The singular of מעשה contrasts with the plural of כלם and טובים and should probably be understood as an error for מעשי; note similar confusions like רֹעה צאן in Gen 47:3 and מקוה מים in 4Q521 7+5 ii 3 (see Qimron 2018, 88). Cf. the similar sentence in 39:16. צורך — It could be the noun "need," or the *qal* active participle "the one who is needy." The marginal reading may be read either as צריך (adjective) or צרוך (Aramaic cognate form). For the same marginal variants see Sir 42:21d and 23a.

40:1 עסק — See 3:22A and the note. חלק — The verb can also mean "to create," see Sir 7:15 and the note there. אם כל חי — The same phrase refers to Eve in Gen 3:20. אל — This marginal reading (in 40:1d), "God," is perhaps influenced by the preceding preposition, which is homographic and homophonous with it.

40:2 This verse is missing in H^B.

40:3 מיושב כסא — In Biblical Hebrew, one would expect יושב כסא. לגבה — This is presumably the preposition + abstract noun (גָּבַהּ), functioning as an adjunct to the participle. The *lamed* limits the field of reference; see BDB 5i (Deut 1:10). לשוב — This form is understood as a preposition and passive participle. The construction of the preposition עד followed by a *lamed* preposition is characteristic of LBH (see, e.g., Ezra 10:14; 1 Chr 28:20). The first marginal reading is the active participle of לבש. The second could be the same or the passive parti-

29 Feu, grêle, malheur et peste,
ces choses-là aussi ont été créées pour le jugement.
30 L'animal carnassier, le scorpion et la vipère
et l'épée des vengeances pour vouer par eux à la destruction (mg. 1. pour élever).
(mg. 2. L'ép[ée qui v]enge pour[   ]par eux (?))
Toutes (mg. aussi) ces choses ont été créées (mg. choisies) selon leur utilité
et elles sont dans un réservoir et seront mises à exécution au moment venu. (mg. elles sont dans son réservoir au moment venu.).
31 Quand il leur commande, ils se réjouissent
et dans leur prescription, ils ne se rebellent pas à sa voix (mg. idem).
32 C'est pourquoi depuis l'origine, je me suis tenu,
j'ai réfléchi et j'ai mis par écrit.
33 Les œuvres de Dieu sont (mg. idem) toutes bonnes,
pour tout nécessiteux (mg. besoin), en son temps, il surabonde.
34 Il ne faut pas dire (mg. idem) : « ceci est mal, qu'est-ce que cela (mg. ceci est plus mauvais que cela). »
Car il magnifiera tout (mg. tout prévaut) en son temps.
35 Maintenant de tout cœur (mg. et de bouche) exultez
et bénissez le nom [du S]a[int.] (mg. son saint nom)

Chapitre 40

1 Dieu (mg. le Très-Haut) a donné en partage un grand souci
et un joug pesant sur l'humanité.
Depuis le jour de sa sortie du sein de sa mère,
jusqu'au jour de son retour vers la mère (mg. le Dieu) de tout vivant.
3 Depuis celui qui siège sur un trône en majesté,
jusqu'à celui qui est retourné (vers) (mg. 1. revêt ; mg. 2. est revêtu de) (la) poussière et (la) cendre.
4 Depuis celui qui porte turban et fleuron
et (> mg.) jusqu'à celui qui porte un vêtement de lin.
5a Seulement jalousie, anxiété, et frayeur,
5b terreur de mort, conflit et dispute (mg. mort, conflit, dispute)

29 Fire, hail, misfortune and plague,
these too were created for judgment.
30 The carnivorous animal, the scorpion and the cobra,
and a sword of vengeance to dedicate to the ban (mg. 1. [to raise]) through them
(mg. 2. the sword that avenges to [   ] by them.
All (mg. also) these were created (mg. chosen) according to their purpose,
and they are in the storehouse and will be assigned when (their) time (comes)
(mg. they are in his storehouse when the time comes).
31 When he commands them, they rejoice
and in their obligation, they do not rebel at his mouth (mg. idem).
32 Therefore, from the beginning I have stood by,
I have reflected and have put (it) in writing.
33 The works of God, all of them (mg. the entirety) are good,
for in its time, every needy one (mg. need) is satisfied.
34 One must not say (mg. idem), "This is wrong. What is this?" (mg. "This is worse than that")
for he will magnify everything (mg. everything prevails) in its time.
35 Now, with all (your) heart (mg. "and mouth") exult,
and bless the name of the Holy One (mg. his holy name).

Chapter 40

1 Great worry God (mg. the Most High) has apportioned
and a heavy yoke over humankind,
from the day they leave their mother's womb,
until their return to the mother (mg. God) of all the living,
3 from the one dwelling on a throne in grandeur,
to the one returned to (mg. the one dressing (in), the one dressed (in)) dust and ash,
4 from the one wrapping themselves in turban and rosette,
and to (mg. to) the one wrapping themselves in linen garments,
5a only jealousy, anxiety, and dread,
5b terror of death, strife and dispute (mg. death, strife, dispute).

---

ciple, as the passive participle is more common, though the active participle is also attested. Note that the active verb occurs with the word "dust" in Job 7:5 and with "ashes" in Esth 4:1.

40:4 צניף — The Hebrew word is associated with a king's head adornment in Isa 62:3; Sir 11:5 and 47:6, and is often used with the verb עטה in these passages. It is also used to describe the head-wear of the high priest in Zech 3:5. Since the accompanying word ציץ is also used in association with the turban (מצנפת) of Aaron in Sir 45:12, it is conceivable that the reference here is to the high priest. שלמת סיגה — See the Greek ὠμόλινον. The word סיגה is attested in Palestinian Aramaic with the meaning "flax, linen" (Sokoloff 1990, p. 373). The contrast is between priestly garments and linen garments, which were common clothing (see the Syriac).

40:5ab תחרה — It is possible to understand this word as a noun, which also occurs in 31:29 (the cognate in Aramaic is תחרות), or as a verbal form, although the latter is less likely in the context. The reading of *he* instead of *khet* results in a verbal form "to conceive." The marginal reading seems to indicate that the word אימת should not be included.

Left margin	Margin	Colon B	Colon A	Verse	Margin	Right margin
	רֹעתֹו	שינת לילה תֹשנהֹ[ ]:	14ועת נוחו על משכבו	5bc		15 נצר חמס לא יכה בו ושורש חנף על שן צור:
		ומבין בחלמֹוֹתֹ[ ]ש:	15מעט לרֹוק כרגע ישקוט	6	[ ]קֹםֹ	
עד כלו◦[ ]		כשריד הֹבֹרֹחֹ[ ] רודף:	16מעט טעמחזון נפשו			
אף עמ[ ]		ומרֹאו ◦[ ]מנוֹחֹ:	17עֹדֹ עודך הֹ[ ]הֹקֹיֹץֹ	7		
			18[ ]לֹ[ ] [ ]	8 M		
MS.Heb.e.62 X recto		שד ושבר רעה ומות:	1[ד]בֹר ודם חרחר וחרב	9		
והשברו	ובֹעבורו ת׳ רעה:	ובעֹבוֹר תמוֹש כלה:	2על רשע נבראֹה רעה	10 P		
	ויש׳	ואשֹר ממרום אל מרום:	3 כל מארץ אל ארץ ישוב	11 PM		
	וכאפיק	ומֹאפיק אדיר בחזיז קולות:	4 מחול אֹל חֹול כנחל איתן	13 M	חיל מחיל	
		כי פתאם לנצח יתם:	5 עםֹ עםֹ שאתו כפים יגילו	14 M	עֹם שאתו	
		כי שורש חנף על שן סלע:	6 נוצר מחמס לא ינקה	15 M		

40:11 מארץ B | מן[M · 40:12 + כל מש]חד M · 40:13 מחול אל חול B | חיל מחיל Bmg | חיל מעול M G · 40:14 עם עם שאתו B | עם שאתו Bmg M · 40:15 נוצר מחמס B | נצר חמס Bmg M · לא ינקה B | לא יכה בו Bmg M · שן סלע B | שן צור Bmg | שֹן צר M ·

L. 14 [40:5] תֹשנהֹ — This word is clearly visible (based on firsthand inspection of the manuscript as well as in the digital photos, but not in the facsimile edition). רֹעתֹו — Though less likely, the first letter has been read as a *dalet*, דעתו "his knowledge" (Cowley and Neubauer 1897, 4; Beentjes 1997, 69). Some (Cowley and Neubauer 1897, 4; Ben-Ḥayyim 1973, 42) think that a *tav* precedes this word in the margin, yet (while not impossible), this is unlikely.

L. 15 [40:6] לרֹוק — The third letter looks like a *vav*, though one would expect a *yod*. Adding to the difficulty of reading the already faint trace of a letter is the offset mark from the curving right arm of the *sin/shin* of אשה at X recto (Ms.Heb.e.62 recto), line 15, Sir 40:23, which intersects with the *vav*. [ ]קֹםֹ — The first letter could be a *qoph* and the second a final *mem*, קם "he arose." Alternatively, the second letter could be a *khet*, קח "?". Others have suggested לקח (Smend 1906b, 38; Ben-Ḥayyim 1973, 42).

L. 16 [40:6] טעמחזון — There is no separation between the *ayin* and the following *mem*, suggesting a possible mis-division of words.

הֹבֹרֹחֹ — The *he* is clearly visible. The crossbar of the following *resh* is visible at the top of the hole, as well as the end of its vertical stroke at the bottom. The next two traces of a crossbar would fit a *he* or a *khet*. Between the word שריד and the following letter are offset marks corresponding to ועז]רֹים] in X recto, line 16 at Sir 40:24.

L. 17 [40:7] עֹדֹ — The *ayin* is only attested by the very tips of its vertical marks above the lacuna. The *dalet* is perceptible due to a portion of its vertical mark, as well as the hole in the paper that matches the shape of the upper crossbar. הֹ — This could just as easily be a *dalet*, a *khet* or a *resh*. הֹקֹיֹץֹ — Only the tops of these letters are visible. Our reading is based on the Greek and fits the traces.

L. 18 [40:8] לֹ — This letter is only attested by a small mark beneath the *dalet* of עודך.

L. 2 [40:10] וֹבשברֹו — The word slants down. Ben-Ḥayyim (1973, 42) also reads the marks in this manner. The reading perfectly fits the cursive marginal writing, and is especially attractive because it provides a good alternative to וֹבֹעבורו.

40:5bc שינת — This *plene* spelling, reflecting /i/, is characteristic of Aramaic, not Hebrew. תֹשנהֹ — The verb שנה primarily means "change, alter," but it also occurs with a negative sense in Lam 4:1; 1 Sam 21:14 and Ps 34:1 (in the last two cases, it is used with the word טעם "judgment, sense" as an accusative object, so that the verb seems to indicate the disturbance of a person's mind). We assume שנה here is used in a similar way, with "distress" as the subject and "sleep" as object.

40:6 ומבין ב — The first word is a *hiphil* participle of the root בין "the one who considers dreams" (cf. the sequence of elements in Dan 1:17: הבין + *bet* + "dreams"). Alternatively, the letters could be interpreted as a sequence of prepositions, as seen in Sir 50:6, with the meaning "from among," but the textual situation of the verse is problematic. טעמחזון — The sequence of letters is difficult to make sense of. The fact that all the letters are written so closely together suggests the possibility of a mis-division of words, as well as haplography: the initial/medial *mem* could go with the preceding letters to make the noun טעם "judgment, sense" (or the verb from the same root), as well as with the following noun. In essence, this understanding presupposes the reading טעם מחזון. One wonders if the underlying text for both the Hebrew and the Greek was something like מעטעט (from עיט) "they dart around from the vision of their soul." Although the verb עיט is only found twice in the Hebrew Bible (1 Sam 14:32 and 15:19), it does occur twice in Ben Sira (14:10; 31:16). Such reduplication is common in verbs that denote "rapidly repeated movement" (GKC §55*f*).

40:7 עֹדֹ עודך — This sequence of letters is also found in 33:21. Here, however, it must be a mistake, the original text having something like ער עוד "they wake again" or עד עורך "until you wake up."

40:9 חרב — The translation is based on the parallel phrase in Deut 28:22; Ezek 5:17 and the Greek (see also 4Q169 3–4 ii 5). This could also be the noun חֹרֶב "drought" or "desolation."

40:10 רשע — The word could be vocalized רָשָׁע "the wicked" or רֶשַׁע "wickedness". תמושֹ — The sentence is very difficult to make sense of. The verb, presumably from the root משש, does not really make sense. According to Rüger (1970, 103–109), משש could have the meaning "to

5b Au moment où il se repose sur sa couche,
5c [....] (mg. son malheur) perturbe le sommeil de la nuit.
6 Un peu, en vain (mg. ?), pour un instant, il se repose
et celui qui comprend les rêves[ ].
(Son) jugement est diminué par sa vision,
comme un réfugié qui fuit[*devant*] un persécuteur.
7 Tant que tu [ ] il s'est réveillé
et sa crainte [...] repos.
8 [ ] (mg. jusqu'à ce que tout[ ] aussi avec[ ])
9 Peste et sang, fièvre et épée,
destruction et dévastation, mal et mort.
10 Le mal a été créé pour le méchant
et afin que l'extermination (avance) en tâtonnant
(mg. 1: et à cause de lui le mal avancera en tâtonnant)
(mg. 2: et de son fait)
11 Tout ce qui est de la terre, à la terre retourne
et ce qui est du ciel, au ciel,
13 du sable au sable (mg. La puissance de puissance),
comme un torrent intarissable
et d'un aqueduc (mg. comme un aqueduc) impétueux
dans un roulement du tonnerre.
14 Lorsqu'il se soulève, les pierres roulent,
mais soudainement il cesse pour toujours.
15 Celui qui est formé à partir de la violence ne sera pas tenu pour innocent,
car la racine de l'impie est sur un pic rocheux.
(mg. Le rejeton violent ne prendra pas (racines) en lui,
la racine de l'impie habite un pic rocheux)

5b At the time of rest over their bed
5c [ ] (mg. their distress) disturbs night-time sleep.
6 A little, for vain (mg. ?), as if a single moment they will rest,
the one who considers dreams[ ].
(Their) sense diminishes from their own vision,
like a refugee who flees[*from*] the pursuer.
7 While yet you are [ ] they woke up,
and their fear [ ] rest.
8 [ ] (mg. until all [ ] also with[ ]).
9 Plague and blood, fever and sword,
destruction and devastation, evil and death.
10 For the wicked evil was created,
and in order that annihilation will grope (forward).
(mg. 1: And on account of it evil will grope forward)
(mg. 2: And for the sake of it)
11 Everything from earth, to earth returns,
and what is from heaven, to heaven.
13 From sand to sand, (mg. Power from strength is) like an ever-flowing wadi,
and from (mg. like) a mighty channel with thunderous noise,
14 when it rises, rocks roll away,
though suddenly it ceases forever.
15 The one formed from violence will not be considered innocent,
for the root of the godless (rests) on a rocky crag.
(mg. The violent scion will not take (root) in it, the root of the godless dwells (on) a rocky crag.)

---

arrive" which would fit the context better, but seems doubtful. The middle weak root מוש "to depart" makes even less sense in the context. Note, however, that H^Par (T-S NS 93.80, lines 8–9) represents the second part of the verse as: "They (the griefs) depart (ימושו) ... when he goes." On the basis of this text, Kister (1983, 135) has proposed reading בעברו "when he passes away," instead of בעבור and בעבורו. וּבְשֶׂכרֹו — The expression בשכר in Rabbinic Hebrew (including in the Mishnah) has the meaning "on account of."

40:11 Note the similarity to Qoh 3:20. ויש׳ — If the marginal reading is an abbreviation, then it could correspond to וישב. If it not, then it might be וְיֵשׁ "and there are (some things) from heaven (that return) to heaven."

40:13 The verse in the Genizah manuscript, including the marginal reading, is corrupt. For a more likely reading, see the Masada text. מחול אל חול — The word חול may also imply here "what is profane, common" (see Jastrow 1903, 433), resulting in an expression parallel to that of Sir 41:10a: מאפס אל אפס "from nothingness to nothingness" (in the main text) and מאונים אל אונים "from iniquities to iniquities" (in the margin [< אָוֶן]). If חול has the sense "profane" here, then the relationship between this word and the corresponding word in H^M (עָוֶל "iniquity") would be similar to the relationship between אפס "nothingness" and אָוֶן "iniquity" in 41:10a. חזיז קולות — The phrase is taken from Job 28:26 and 38:25, but the sense seems to be unique to this passage. That is, in Job it denotes a thunderbolt, while here it likely just implies the sound of thunder.

40:14 עם עם — This is probably a dittography, which is corrected in the margin. עם שאתו — עם with the infinitive construct in a temporal sense is characteristic of post-Biblical Hebrew (see Qimron 1986, §400.04). In a few instances, the verb is intransitive (see Hos 13:1; Nah 1:5; Hab 1:3). יגילו — The root is either גול or גיל, with the meaning "to roll," according to Jastrow (1903, 221), this being a biform of the more expected geminate root גלל. According to Jastrow, the hollow root is found not only in Rabbinic Hebrew, but also in Galilean Aramaic. Alternatively, יגילו is a misspelling of the *plene* form of the geminate root יגולו. In either case, it seems to have an intransitive sense here. For other interpretations of this difficult verse, see van Peursen (2004, 337–338).

40:15 יכה בו — The idiom נכה with the *bet* preposition occurs in 1 Sam 2:14 without an explicit direct object ("he would thrust [the fork] into the pan"). Presumably, the implied direct object in 40:15 is "root," which happens to occur with נכה in Hos 14:6, providing a suitable sense there, "Israel will take root like the trees of Lebanon." In this interpretation, the suffix would then refer to the rock in the next colon, which is atypical in Hebrew. Another possibility is to take the suffix as reflexive, cf. Matt 13:21 and Mark 4:17. ען שן צור — This marginal alternative seems to be the perfect (or participial) form of the rare root "to dwell" (ען), which may occur once (Isa 13:22) or twice (Deut 33:28) in the Hebrew Bible. The following phrase would then be an adverbial accusative.

	לפני נדעכה	מפֿני כל מטר נדעֿכו:	כקרדמות על גפת נחל	7 16 M
		וצדקה לעד תכון:	וחסד לעולם לא ימוט	8 17 PM
יותר שֶׁכל	סימה	ומשניהם מוצא אוצֿר:	חיי יין וֿשכר ימתקו	9 18 M
		ומשניהם מוצא חכמה:	ילד ועיר יעמידו שם	10 19ab M
		ומשניהם אשה נחשקת	שגר ונטע יפריחו שם	11 19cd M
		ומשניהם אהבת דודים:	יוֿן ושכר יעליצו לב	12 20 M
חלִיל		ומשניהם לשון ברה:	ח]לֹ[יֿ]ל ונבל יעריבו שיר	13 21
	שדי:	ומשניהם צמחי שדֿה:	ח]ןֿ[ונעֿ]ם[יעמידו עין	14 22
		ומשניהם אשה משכלת:	אֿ]הב[○○○ ○○[ ]בעֿת ינהגו	15 23
	צדקה	ומשניהם צדק מצלת:	אחי]ם ועז[רֿים בעֿת צרה	16 24
		ומשנֿיֿ[הם]○○○○○○	זהב וכסף] יעמידו רגֿ[ל	17 25
		ומשניהם יֿ]רֿאת אלהים:	חיל וכח יגבֿ]יֿ[הוֿ לב	18 26ab M

40:16 כקרדמות B | כקרמית M · גפת B | גפות M · חצדֿרֿ G M | מטר B | מטֿר M · נדעכו B | נדעך M · נדעכה Bmg   40:17 לעולם B | כעֿד M · ימוט B | תכרת M · תכון B | תכן M ·   40:18 יין ושכר B | יותר שכל Bmg | יתר שכר M · מוֿצאֿ B | מֹצָֿא M · מוצא B | שאר M ·   40:19cd שם B |

L. 13 [40:21] חלִיל — The marginal word is read with a preceding *vav* by Smend (1906b, 39) and Ben-Ḥayyim (1973, 43), which would then distinguish it from the word thought to be present at the beginning of the verse. This *vav*, however, is impossible to read. ח]לֹ[יֿ]ל — It is impossible to determine the initial word of the verse, based on the manuscript alone.

L. 14 [40:22] נעֿ]ם — The base line of the *mem* is visible, as is the top left horn. Such a reading would exclude the reconstructions by Segal (1958, 271) and Peters (1902, 393) (יופי ותאר), suggesting either the reconstruction ח]ןֿ ונעֿ]ם as above or יֿ]פי ונעֿ]ם (Smend 1906b, 39). The former is more likely due to spacing. This reading may reflect the Greek translation (χάριν καὶ κάλλος; for κάλλος see Zech 11:7). יעמידו — The *yod* is fairly easy to see. The *ayin* is clear from the remnants of the right arm angling to the left (see the reconstruction in Ben-Ḥayyim [1973, 43]). The letter cannot be a *khet* (as proposed by earlier scholars).

L. 15 [40:23] אֿ]הב — Extremely faint traces of the top right and bottom right corners of the *aleph* appear at the edge of the hole. It is clear that this is not an *ayin*, as Smend (1906b, 40) reads. Presumably, after this word, there were two other synonyms for "friend," given the remaining traces. The three final traces could conceivably be the remnants of חבר "associate." בעֿת — Only faint traces of the base line of a *bet* are preserved. Smend (1906b, 40) reads a *lamed*, which may be possible, yet one would expect the ascender to be visible. The *ayin* is attested by partial remnants of its base line and the tip of its left most vertical line.

L. 16 [40:24] אחי]ם ועז[רֿים — The *yod* mater of "brothers" is clear, as the curve of the letter makes it unlike the top right arm of a *vav* (as transliterated by preceding editions). The *yod*, final *mem*, and perhaps the *resh* of "helpers" (עוזרים or עזרים could fit the space) are found as offset letters in IX verso (Or 1102 verso), line 16 at Sir 40:6 (see Reymond, 2016a, 132-3). At the least, the absence of ink in the preserved page of MS.Heb.e.62 X recto, 16 does not rule out *resh*. בעֿת — Traces of the *bet*'s base and vertical are visible. The *ayin* is attested by its right diagonal line that finishes at its base, as well as the top of its left vertical line.

L. 17 [40:25] וכסף] יעמידו רגֿ[ל — The *pe* is only attested by a trace of the right side of its descender. The visible traces before the *lamed* are offset marks. Our reconstruction fits the space perfectly and is supported by the Greek and the Syriac.

L. 18 [40:26] יגבֿ]יֿ[הוֿ — Traces of the bottom right corner and base of the *bet* are preserved. The faint traces before the *lamed* fit a *he* and a *vav* well (see the reconstructed word by Cowley and Neubauer [1897, 6], as well as the Greek and the Syriac).

Marginal Note The marginal note runs perpendicular to the text. Apparently, the last two lines are in Persian. Reading the letters of these words is particularly difficult, as they are shaped in a slightly different way than those preceding them (either because of the cramped space or as a result of another scribe's habits). The transliteration of this note was assisted by reference to Wright (2018, 133).

40:16 קרדמות — It seems unlikely that this is the Biblical Hebrew word "axes," and more likely that it is a loanword from Latin or Greek, κάρδαμον, "cress." Presumably, it is a mistake for קרמית "cow wheat," found in the Masada scroll. גפת — While both Hebrew and Aramaic have words with the letters *gimel* and *pe* that mean "side, bank," these words are not feminine and do not have feminine forms. H^M has גפות, so it seems unlikely that this is a mistake due to textual transmission. There may be a confusion here (in the language of Ben Sira) between the Rabbinic Hebrew word for "side," גיף, and the biblical and Rabbinic Hebrew word for "back," גב, which does have feminine forms (Lev 14:9, Ezek 1:18, and in Rabbinic Hebrew). נדעכו — With the prepositional phrase מפני, the verb has its Rabbinic Hebrew meaning "to be crushed" (see Jastrow 1903, 316). The marginal alternative לפני allows the verb to be construed with the meaning "to wither," a sense otherwise only found in Syriac, in reference to vegetation. For 16b in H^Bm, cf. Job 8:12.

40:17 For the first stich, cf. Prov 10:30.

40:18 שכר — In the context of "wine," the consonants presumably reflect the noun שֵׁכָר "beer, strong drink," yet in H^M, where the context is יתר "gain," the same consonants imply the noun שָׂכָר "wages" (Kister 1990, 348–349). The marginal alternative in H^B is either a noun meaning "advantage, excess, plenty" or the *qal* participle meaning "one who abounds with." שכל — The reading in H^M, "a life of plenty and wages is sweet," likely represents the author's original idea. מוצא — The form is likely a participle of מצא (cf. the Greek and the Syriac). However, considering the rhetoric of the entire poem, the word could also be understood as a noun from the root יצא "exit, source, east." אוצר — In this context, the word is likely a metaphoric reference to wisdom. סימה — This word, meaning "treasure," is an Aramaism. It is also found

16 Comme le cresson sur la rive du torrent,
à cause de toute la pluie, il est écrasé (mg. Avant toute pluie, il se fane).
17 Mais la bienveillance ne sera jamais ébranlée
et la justice, pour toujours, sera maintenue.
18 Une vie de vin et de bière (mg. (une vie) pleine de prudence) est douce,
mais plus doux que tous deux, celui qui trouve un trésor (mg. un trésor).
19 Enfant et ville font perdurer un nom,
mais plus que tous deux, celui qui trouve la sagesse.
Bétail et culture font fleurir un nom,
mais plus que tous deux, une femme désirée.
20 Vin et bière réjouissent le cœur,
mais plus que tous deux, des câlins d'amour.
21 [F]l[û]te et lyre rendent mélodieux un chant,
mais plus que toutes deux, une langue pure.
22 G[râce et dou]ceur font se maintenir l'œil,
mais plus que toutes deux, les herbes des champs (mg. des champs).
23 A[mi et] au bon moment ont une conduite adaptée,
mais plus que tous deux, une femme sensée.
24 Frère[s et seco]urs au temps de détresse,
mais plus que tous deux, la justice (mg. charité) qui délivre.
25 Or et argent [assurent le pa]s,
mais plus que tous[deux   ]
26a Richesse et force élèvent le cœur,
26b mais plus que tous deux, la crainte de Dieu.
(mg. « Tous les jours du pauvre sont mauvais » (Pr 15,15). Ben Sira dit : « même la nuit ».
Parmi les toits les plus bas est son toit, et parmi les montagnes élevées est sa vigne,
(ainsi) la pluie des (autres) toits (va) à son (toit),
la terre de sa vigne (va) aux autres vignes.
[En Persan : Il est probable que cela n'était pas dans la copie originale, mais a été transmis oralement.]

16 Like cress on the wadi's bank,
because of all the rain they are crushed (mg. before [any rain] it withers).
17 But piety will never be shaken,
and righteousness will be established forever.
18 A life of wine and beer is sweet (mg. (a life) with plenty of prudence),
But sweeter than both the one who finds a treasure (mg. treasure).
19 Child and city will preserve a name,
but more than both, the one who finds wisdom.
Flocks and crops allow a name to flourish,
but more than both, a desired wife.
20 Wine and beer give joy to the heart,
but more than both, passionate love.
21 [F]l[u]te and lyre sweeten the song,
but more than both, a pure tongue.
22 G[race and ple]santness causes the eye to stand still,
but more than both, the field's produce (mg. field).
23 F[riend and   ] at the proper time behave,
but more than both, a prudent wife.
24 Brother[s and he]lpers, in the time of distress,
but more than both, honesty (mg. charity) delivers.
25 Gold and silver [make the foo]t[stand firm],
but more than [both   ].
26a Wealth and power lift the heart,
26b but more than both, [f]ear of God.
(mg. "All the days of the poor are bad" [Prov 15:15]. Ben Sira says "Even in the night.
Among the lowest roofs is their roof, and on the highest mountains is their vineyard;
(so) the rain of (other) roofs (goes) to their roof and (so) the earth of their vineyard (goes) to (other) vineyards.
[In Persian:] It is likely that this was not in the original copy, but was transmitted orally.)

---

in 4Q523 1 ii 9, and as שימה in 4Q504 (Tobit) 7 9. The word is used as an alternative reading for אוצר in Sir 41:12.

40:19 יעמידו — The verb could also mean "to establish."

40:20 אהבת דודים — Mopsik elegantly translates "calins d'amour" (caresses of love). Indeed, דודים does not refer to friends (אוהב or רע). The plural form indicates the abstraction erotic love (Song 1:2).

40:21 יעריבו — The hiphil of ערב "to cause to be sweet, pleasant" is not attested in Biblical Hebrew and is rare in Rabbinic Hebrew.

40:22 עין יעמידו — The meaning of this phrase is unclear. It recalls the preceding verse 19, יעמידו שם, and perhaps the reconstruction of verse 25 יעמידו רג[ל] (see Lévi 1904, 49). The combination of עמד with עין is unusual and is not attested elsewhere. There are a number of possible meanings: "to fix one's gaze," "bring to the eyes' attention," "to make the eyes rise (a sign of arrogance)," etc. צמחי שדה — Cf. Ezek 16:7. שדי — The word is a biform of שָׂדֶה "field" or an alternative spelling with yod as mater for what would be seghol (cf. חקיק in Sir 41:2ab). Nevertheless, the variant calls to mind the divine name "Shadday," which parallels the expression צמח יהוה in Isa 4:2.

40:23 ינהגו — This verb is understood in its Aramaic, Late Biblical Hebrew and Rabbinic Hebrew sense. אשה משכלת — See Prov 19:14.

40:24 אחי[ם ועוז]רים — The somewhat awkward syntax of the first colon is mirrored in the Greek, in which the nouns are singular. מצלת — The participle of the second colon is implicit in the first. צדקה — The marginal reading not only corrects the gender of צדק, but also changes the meaning of the sentence.

40:26 The passage in the margin is a quotation of Prov 15:15, followed by a Talmud citation (see b. Ketub. 110b; b. B. Bat. 146a; b. Sanh. 100b; Labendz 2006, 376). For the translation of the Persian quote, we follow Cowley and Neubauer (1897, 7).

MS.Heb.e.62 X verso		ואין לבקש עמה משׁען:	¹אֵין בִּירְאַת ייי מחסור	26cd ᴹ
	בّ	וכן כל כבוד חפתה:	²יראת אלהים כעדן ברכה	27 ᴹ
אאין זלה אאין זלה נוקש יןקש בכל כושל וחסר עצמה אוֹנים האח למות כי טוב חקך וּעוֹד בוֹ חל לקבל תענוג האיש שלו ומצליח בכל איש שוקט על מכונתו חַיִּים למות מה מֹר יבֹרך		טוב נאסף ממסתולל:	³מֹנִי חיי מתן אל תחי	28 ᴹ	בני
		אין חייו למנות חיים:	⁴איש משגיח על שלחן זר	29ab ᴹ	
	יסור מזעים	לאיש יודע סוד מעים:	⁵מעגל נפש מטעמוֹ	29cd ᴹ	מעגל נפשו מטעמי זבד עז נפשות מ/תמתיק
	כאש בוערת	בקרבו תבער̈ כמו אש:	⁶לאיש עז נפש תמתיק שאלה	30 ᴹ	

Chapter 41

		לאיש שוקט על מכונתו:	⁷חַיִּים למות מה מֹר יבֹרך	1ab ᴹ	הוי
		ועוד בו חיל לקבל תענוג:	⁸איש שליו ומצליח בכל	1cd ᴹ	
		לאיש אונים וחסר עצמה:	⁹האח למות כי טוב חקֶֹך	2ab ᴹ	חוק חזק חוקו
		סרב ואבד תקוה:	¹⁰איש כושל ינקֹש בכל	2cd ᴹ	ונוקש

יסור מעים Bmg | יסור מזעים B | סוד מעים B • ᴹ ממחצף B | ממסתולל ᴹ • נא[שֹׁף B | נאסף M G S • 40:28 ועל Bmg | בّ B | וכן 40:27
ᴹ • כאש בוערת B | תבער כמו אש B] אש בוערת Bmg | ᴹ • תמתיק B M | ממתיק Bmg • עז [נ]פֹש ᴹ | עז נפש Bmg | עז נפשות B | בפי M G S • לאיש B | 40:30 ᴹ •
כח B | חל ᴹ • עוד B | ועד ᴹ • שלו ᴹ | שליו B • 41:cd ᴹ • שקט ᴹ • שוקט B | ז M G] כֹּרֹך ᴹ • יבֹרך B M G S | הוי Bmg • חיים B | 41:ab ᴹ • כאש תבער ᴹ •
ᴹ • 41:2ab | האה B | הע ᴹ (= הא) • כי טוב B | מה טוב M S • לאיש אוינים B G S | אין אוינים ᴹ • עצמה B | עצבה ᴹ • 41:2cd • כושל B Bmg1 | נוקש
Bmg2 | כשל ᴹ • ינקש B | ונוקש Bmg1 Bmg3 | ומושל Bmg2 | [מֹשֹׁל] ᴹ • סרב B | אפס המראה Bmg1 Bmg2 • אפס המרה ᴹ • ואבד תקוה B Bmg1
Bmg3 | ואבוד תקוה ᴹ •

L. 2 [40:27] בّ — Just after the double dots at the end of the verse, one can see marks, which Smend (1906b, 40) reads as כי על. While כי is possible, על is not preserved. Beneath these is an offset mark from the *lamed* of לכל in the marginal reading of XI recto (Ms.Heb.e.62 recto), line 2, Sir 41:10. The word in the text for which this is presumably an alternative, כן, does not carry a correction circle above it.

L. 4 [40:29] שלחן — The mark above the *lamed* that looks like a *circellus* is actually just due to bleed-through from the other side of the page (which contains a *circellus*).

L. 5 [40:29] יסור — The reading יסוד is also possible. ממתיק — The first letter could also be read as a *tav* (תמתיק), though this would mean that the word in the text is identical to its alternative in the margin, which seems unlikely. For a similarly shaped *mem*, see the *mem* of המראה in the second marginal addition to 41:2c-d (in the left margin of X verso).

L. 7 [41:1] מֹר — The *mem* is clear, attested by marks below and above the small hole. יבֹרך — While the first edition transcribed זכרך (Cowley and Neubauer 1897, 8; Lévi 1904, 50), the *yod* is clearly distinct from the *zayin* in this manuscript and the mark here can only be a *yod*. The *bet* seems likely, though the ink is slightly blurred.

L. 8 [41:1] בו חיל — The *vav* and *het* are clear in the digital photo.

L. 9 [41:2] חוק — The marks to the left of this word in the margin are due to bleed through. אונים — The *vav* is clear and cannot be a *nun*, as Smend (1906b, 41) suggests (i.e., אנים).

L. 10 [41:2] The marginal alternatives run perpendicular to the rest of the text. There are no correction circles in the text to indicate these as marginal alternatives. ואבד (margin) — This word is usually read ואבד, but there is a mark before the *vav* which could be interpreted as a *yod*, יואבד. However this does not make sense according to the context; the mark could be the result of bleed through or offsetting.

40:27 חפתה — Alternatively, this could be understood as a verb and translated: "thus, it (i.e. fear of God) covers all glory." The reading in the margin creates a stronger parallel with Isa 4:5 (Smend 1906a, 379).

40:28 מני — This form is a mistake and is corrected in the margin. נאסף — For the *niphal* of אסף, see 8:7ᴬ and the note there. ממסתולל — The *hithpolel* of סלל appears in Exod 9:17 and in Sir 39:24b. Its meaning in the present verse is problematic (Kister 1999, 166).

40:29 משגיח — In the context, the verb refers to someone looking longingly upon someone else's table. Lévi (1904, 50) and Segal (1958, 275) refer to b. Beṣah 32b: "There are three whose life is not a life: the first one looks to the table of their neighbor" (המצפה לשלחן חבירו). מעגל נפש — Metaphorically, the phrase should refer to the "appetite." Alternatively, following the Greek and the Syriac, it may be a mistake for מגעל "loathing," see Ezek 16:5. מטעמו — The word טעם could be a noun or the *qal* infinitive construct. זבד — The word denotes "provisions," as in Aramaic, and ultimately derives from the root זוד. The same expression is also attested in Sir 36:24. מזעים — The root and stem appear in 43:16ᴮ as well as in the *piyyut* with the sense "to curse, taunt." Note the pairing of this word with the verb טעם many times in the *piyyutim* of the Middle Ages (see Maagarim).

40:30 ממתיק — If the marginal reading is ממתיק, then we should assume that the sentence starts with עז נפשות "A gluttonous person makes sweet their request." Alternatively, the reading with initial *tav* (תמתיק) assumes the sense "to taste sweet" (found in Job 20:12) and is closer to the sense of the Greek and the Syriac, as well as the version in Hᴹ.

41:1 חיים למות — The significance of these letters is hard to determine and this is clearly not what the original text had. למות could be an infinitive, so that we might translate "Life must perish," as above, or a noun, so that we might translate "life belongs to death" or "life is for death." הוי — The marginal alternative presumes a vocative: "O, death ..." The use of *lamed* in vocative expressions is uncommon (see Suderman 2015, 297–312), and the sole example in Ezek 13:18 is ambiguous. The difficulty of making sense of these words is further compounded by the difficulty of the last word. יבֹרך — Although the original word must have been זכרך "memory of you" (i.e., knowledge of death) or something similar, Hᴮ clearly has the verb "to bless" here. It is unlikely that מר is the Aramaic noun "lord." The following *lamed* in the second colon could be understood as marking the object of the verb ("indeed may the lord bless the person ...," see Neh 11:2). The original

26c On ne manque de rien dans la crainte du seigneur
26d et il n'est pas nécessaire de chercher un support en dehors d'elle.
27 La crainte de Dieu est comme un Éden de bénédiction et (mg. car) son dais n'est que gloire.
28 De moi (mg. Mon enfant), ne vis pas une vie de mendiant (lit. d'une vie de don),
mieux vaut celui qui meurt que celui qui s'exalte.
29a Une personne regardant la table de l'étranger,
29b sa vie ne peut pas être comptée comme une vie.
29c Le sentier du gosier (mg. 1. Le sentier de son gosier) est selon son goût (mg. 2. les saveurs des provisions),
29d (il en est ainsi) pour la personne qui connaît le secret de son ventre.
(mg. [pour une personne avisée c'est une épreuve pleine de reproches])
30 Pour une personne avec un appétit vorace (mg. une personne vorace), ce qu'elle demande semble suave (mg. rend suave),
(mais) au milieu d'elle, cela brûle comme un feu (mg. c'est comme un feu brûlant).

Chapitre 41

1 La vie doit mourir (mg. Oh ! mort !), combien amèrement (Dieu) bénit
une personne tranquille dans sa propriété,
une personne paisible qui réussit en tout
et qui a encore de la force pour recevoir du plaisir.
2a Ah ! Mort ! Car ta part (mg. part, force, sa part) est bonne
2b pour une personne triste et manquant de vigueur,
2c une personne chancelante (qui) se heurte à tout (mg. 1 et se heurtant),
(qui) est courbée/obstinée/babillarde et dénuée d'espoir.
(mg. 2 une personne chancelante et se heurtant à tout, perdant la vue et dénuée d'espoir.)
(mg. 3 une personne prise au piège et rabaissée en toute chose
perdant la vue et dénuée d'espoir.)

26c Nothing is lacking in the fear of the Lord,
26d and one need not seek support outside of it.
27 Fear of God is like a blessed Eden,
thus (mg. for), its canopy is entirely glory.
28 From me (mg. My child), do not live the life of begging (lit., the life of a gift),
better one who is dead than one exalting themself (in such a way).
29a As for the person looking upon a stranger's table,
29b their life cannot be counted as a (true) life.
29c The path of the appetite (mg. 1 The path of their appetite) is according to their taste (mg. 2 according to the tastes of provisions).
29d (thus it is) for the person who knows (only) the secret of their belly
(mg. [for a discerning person] (it is) a reproachful disciplining).
30 To a person with a gluttonous appetite (mg. a gluttonous person), the thing asked for seems sweet (mg. sweetens),
(but) inside them it burns like (mg. burning) fire.

Chapter 41

1 Life must perish (mg. Oh! Death!), how bitterly (does God) bless
the person quiet in their estate,
a person at ease, successful in everything,
in whom is still vitality to feel pleasure.
2 Ah, death, for your share (mg. share, strength, its share) is good
to a person of sorrows and lacking strength,
a person stumbling (who) knocks into everything (mg. 1 and knocking),
(who) is crooked/obstinate/blabbering and void of hope.
(mg. 2 a person stumbling and knocking into everything,
lacking sight and void of hope.)
(mg. 3 a person ensnared and brought down in everything,
lacking sight and void of hope.)

---

phrasing of the verse must have been something like "Oh death, how bitter is the thought (literally, "memory") of you, to the person quiet in their place." מכונתו — In Ben Sira, this noun, which also occurs in 44:6, seems to be a feminine form of מכון meaning "place" or "residence." According to the Greek and the Syriac of this passage, the word may have a more abstract meaning like "possessions." קבל — This is a *piel* infinitive construct, meaning literally "to receive."
41:2ab חקיך — The form must be singular, considering the singular form of the preceding adjective/verb. Presumably, the spelling derives from either the frequency of the plural form of this word with the second person masculine singular suffix or from a "pausal" form (i.e.,

ḥuqqekā, akin to רֵעֶךָ "your friend" in Deut 5:21 in the MT). Its meaning seems close to the English "share." The same word and meaning occur in v.3. אונים — The context suggests that this is אֹן "sorrows" (e.g., Hos 9:4), though it could also be the word אוֹן "wealth, vigor."
41:2cd ינקש — The verbal form shoul be understood as an asyndetic relative clause, which is frequent in Ben Sira (see van Peursen 2016, 78). It may be a *piel* or a *niphal* of נקש "to knock," a verb more common in Aramaic. ונוקש — The marginal alternative seems preferable, especially if understood as a *qal* participle from the same verb. Alternatively, it could be a *niphal* from the root יקש "to be ensnared." סרב — This root is attested in Aramaic with the meaning "to refuse, rebel," (see Sir 4:25

	זכֹור כי ראשנים ואחרנים עמך:		¹¹אל תפחד ממות חוקיך	3 ᴹ
	ומה תמאס בתורת עליוֹ[ן]:		¹²זה חלק כל בשר מאל	4ab ᴹ
אין	איש תוכחות בשא[ו]ל חיים:		¹³לאלף שנים מאה ועשר	4cd ᴹ
	ונכד אויל במגו[ר רש]ע:		¹⁴נין נמאס דבר ᵉʳⁱᵐ רעים	5 ᴹ
	עם זרע[ו ת]מֹי[ד] חרפֹה:		¹⁵מבן עול ממשלת רע	6 ᴹ
	כי בגלֹלוֹ הֹ[ ]		¹⁶אב רשע יקובֹ ילד	7 ᴹ
	ע[ ]ליון:		¹⁷אוֹי לכם [ ]o	8 ᴹ
	אם תולידו לאנחה:		¹⁸אם תפרֹתֹו [ע]ל ידי אסון	9ab ᴹ
MS.Heb.e.62 XI recto	ואם תמותו לקללה: לקללתה:		¹אם תכשלו לשמחת עולם:	9cd ᴹ
בן	בֹן חנף מתהו אל תהו:		²כל מאפס אל אפס ישוב	10 ᴹ

(marginal notes: כי נמאס / דבת ערים / מבין ערל; תפרו; כל מאונם / א' אונם)

(right margin, vertical: מותר על כל הוצא על אוילים אין)

M כל [בני אדֹ]ם | B G כל בשר מאל M S קץ | B חלק | 41:4ab M ואחרון | B ואחרנים M קדמון | B ראשנים M זכר | B זכֹור M חֹקך | B חוקיך | 41:3
דבת ערים / רישם | B דבר רעים / ערים | Bmg1/2 כי /כן נמאס | B M נין נמאס | 41:5cd S לאלף שנים מאה ועשר | B לעשר מאה ואלֹף שנים | M G
Bmg1/3 רישם | Bmg2 ת[ל]דות רעים | M G S 41:6 | M מבן עול ממשלת | Bmg מבין ערל | B מבן על[ו] תֹאבֹד ממֹ[ ]שלֹת | M G S ת[מֹ]יד | B ת[מֹי]ד | M חרפ
ה | B חרפה M 41:7 יקוב | M יֹקב ·|]ב[| M בוה | 41:8 אוֹי | M וֹי[| M תולידו | B M מולידו | Bmg + · | 41:9ab אם תפרו על יד אסון ואם מולי[
Bmg 2 · [אפס אל אפס M | בן B M | Bmg · | > B M 41:9cd עולם | B עם M S · לקללה | B M לקללתה | Bmg · 41:10 מאפס אל אפס | B מאונם | א' אונם M | Bmg 1 · מאונם אל אונים

L. 11 [41:3] זכֹור — Faint traces of the upper horizontal mark of the *kaph* as well as its vertical line are discernible in the digital photo.

L. 13 [41:4] בשא[ו]ל — The *aleph* is attested by a trace of the tip of its upper right arm. The *lamedh* is attested by a remnant of its ascender above and just to the right of the *khet* of חיים.

L. 14 [41:5] כן — This is probably a miswriting of בן, which was written as an alternative to נין. The reading כן led to the other alternative כי "because." במגוֹ — The *bet* is suggested by what looks like the upper left tick of an upper horizontal bar, as well as traces of a vertical mark. The marks to the left of this are difficult to read, but seem to be the upper left corner of a *mem*, as well as a trace of its bottom diagonal and the left most part of its base line. The following marks look like the bottom part of a *gimel*. This seems to lend support for Peters's reconstruction as במגור (Peters 1902, 395)

L. 15 [41:6] עם — These first two letters are almost completely faded. ת[מֹ]יד — These three letters are reconstructed on the basis of H ᴹ and fit the preserved traces perfectly.

L. 16 [41:7] Just before the בֹּ, there is a bleed-through mark from the other side of the page, which corresponds to the *he* of צרה in X recto, 16 Sir 40:24. The *kaph* of בֹ is attested by its upper horizontal mark, its vertical line, and its lower baseline. בגלֹלוֹ — The *bet* is attested by its upper and lower horizontal lines. The *gimel* is attested by its top tip, horizontal left leg and the bottom of its descender. The final *vav* is only attested by its lower tip.]ֹ[— The last letter of the line is only attested by the bottom part of its descender and may be a *nun*, a *kaph*, a *pe* or a *tsade*.

L. 17 [41:8] אוֹי לכֹם — Only the tops of these letters are visible. The marks can also be read in other ways.

L. 18 [41:9] תפרֹתוֹ — This is the reading that Smend (1906b, 41) tentatively proposed. Although the top of the *tav* is not clear, the bottom of the letter is visible and has the characteristic left foot. The *pe* is attested by half of its vertical and its full base. According to these features, it is also possible to read a *bet* or a *kaph*, though the context makes these letters less likely. The *resh* is only attested by the bottom tip of its vertical. The *khet* is only attested by the bottom of its left leg, which characteristically lacks all flourish. Just to the left of this mark is another mark, presumably the bottom of a *vav*. The two marks seem too close to be the two legs of a *khet*. A full alternative to this verse is written perpendicularly in the left margin.

L. 2 [41:10] כן — The *kaph* almost looks like a *pe* and the *nun* like a final *tsade*, but this is simply due to an offset *ayin* from the preceding page (עדן from X verso, 2 Sir 40:27).

and HALOT). It could also mean "crooked" (see especially, Tg. Qoh. 1:15, where סרב is used to translate the Hebrew root עות, which means "to twist"). Another possibility is to understand it as "to blabber," as attested in Syriac. ומושל — This word is presumably a *hophal* participle from the root נשל, which occurs in the *hiphil* "to let fall" in Tannaitic and Amoraic Hebrew (see Jastrow 1903, 941), but it is used in various *piyyutim* in the Geonic era with a more generic meaning, "to fall" (*niphal*) or "to make fall" (*hiphil*). It seems particularly significant that the verb appears in close association with a word from the root כשל "to stumble" (see Reymond 2017a, 8–9).

41:3 חוקיך — See v. 2 above. Note the use of the same word to refer to Aaron's priestly service in Sir 45:7.

41:4 איש — This appears to be a simple mistake for אין (found in the margin). חיים — Whether this word is written by the first scribe or another is unclear. The word seems to be misplaced and should reflect the expression תוכחות חיים, as in Prov 15:31, but the *soph passuq* following the word is hard to explain if the word is a marginal notation.

41:5 This sentence is definitely corrupted. In its present state, its meaning is very close to Sir 42:11: the misbehavior of children leads to a bad reputation. All the marginal readings seem to be variations of elements that are close in form and meaning. ערים — The word occurs both in the text (above the line), presumably as a correction to רעים, and in the margin. Its meaning is perhaps "cities," especially in the margin, as the Hebrew דבה is also associated with a bad reputation in a city in Sir 42:11 (H ᴹ and H ᴮ, ᴮᵐᵍ). However, since the word ערים occurs in the context of "the wicked," it may be preferable to understand it as "adversaries," an Aramaic loan word (see HALOT, sub עָר) that is perhaps found in the Hebrew Bible (1 Sam 28:16; Ps 139:20) and also in Sir 37:5, 6 (H ᴮ). רישם — This word is often understood as an alternative reading to a word in the next verse (41:6b), based in part on the Syriac ܡܘܫܡܐ in verse 6b. However, רישם is in the right margin, instead of the left where a correction to v. 6b should be located. Moreover, it is written perpendicularly between 5a and 6a. Since other perpendicular marginal alternatives usually begin from the verse that they offer an alter-

3   Ne crains pas la mort, ta part,
    souviens-toi que les premiers et les derniers sont avec toi.
4   Voici le lot de toute chair devant Dieu ;
    comment rejetterais-tu la loi du Très-Ha[ut].
    Pour mille, cent ou dix ans,
    une personne de (?) (mg. il n'y a pas) reproches dans le Shéol (?)des vivants.
5   Une descendance rejetée est la parole des (adversaires) méchants
    (mg. 1 Ainsi, (mg. 2 car) rejetée
    est la calomnie des adversaires/villes (mg. 3 (mg. de leur misère))
    et une folle lignée est une demeu[re de méchan]ceté.
6   D'un enfant mauvais (mg. Parmi les incirconcis) (vient) la domination du mal,
    [l'opprob]re sera [per]pétuellement avec [sa] lignée.
7   Un enfant maudira un père mauvais,
    car, à cause de lui [...].
8   Malheur pour vous [...],
    [... Tr]ès haut.
9a Si vous vous épanouissez (mg. fructifiez) c'est en [v]ue du malheur,
9b si vous enfantez, c'est pour un geignement,
    (mg. Si vous fructifiez, c'est en vue du malheur,
    s'il l'enfante, c'est pour un geignement,)
9c si vous trébuchez, c'est pour la joie du monde,
9d et si vous mourez, c'est pour être maudit (mg. maudit).
10 Tout ce qui (vient) du rien retourne au rien,
    (mg. 1 Tout ce qui vient de leur néant (retourne) à leur néant)
    (mg. 2 Tout ce qui vient des iniquités (retourne) aux iniquités)
    ainsi (mg. l'enfant de) l'impie (retourne) du vide au vide.

3   Do not fear death, your share,
    remember, those first and last are with you.
4   This is the portion for all flesh from God;
    how can you reject the law of the Most High?
    For one thousand, one hundred, or ten years,
    A person of (?) (mg. there are no) reproofs in Sheol of (?) the living.
5   A rejected offspring is the word of (adversaries) the evil ones,
    (mg. 1 Thus (mg. 2 For,), rejected
    is the slander of adversaries/cities (mg. 3 their poverty))
    and foolish progeny are in a dwellin[g of wicked]ness.
6   From a wicked son (mg. from among the uncircumcised) (comes) bad rule,
    [reproa]ch (remains) [per]petually with [his] seed.
7   A child will curse a wicked father,
    for, on account of him [   ]
8   Woe to you [   ]
    [mo]st high.
9a If you flourish (mg. you are fruitful) it is [f]or misfortune;
9b if you beget (children), it is for moaning.
    (mg. If you are fruitful, it is for misfortune,)
    (if he begets him, it is for moaning.)
9c If you stumble, it is for joy of the world,
9d and if you die, it is (to be) cursed (mg. cursed).
10 All that (derives) from nothing to nothing returns,
    (mg. 1 All that (derives) from their emptiness, to their emptiness (returns).)
    (mg. 2 All that (derives) from iniquities to iniquities (returns).)
    thus, the godless (mg. the child of the godless) from void to void (returns).

native to, one can assume that רישם is an alternative to רעים in 41:5. It is easily explained as a graphic error (ש = עי). The shape of the letters makes it likely that the scribe who added this word is different from the one who added the other marginal alternatives.

41:6 מבן — According to the context, one would assume that this is the compound preposition, though it is also conceivable that it could be the *hiphil* participle of בין. If the latter, then the entire colon could be construed "the uncircumcised knows bad rule."

41:9 Stichs *a* and *b* follow the thought of Job 27:14. על ידי — The phrase expresses purpose here (cf. Jer 18:21; 4Q491 11 ii 20) and is in parallel with (ל)אנחה in the following sentence. מולידו — The marginal reading is clearly due to a confusion between the imperfect and participle forms. The translation above reflects the form as it stands. עולם — H^M confirms Lévi's suggestion (Lévi 1904, 51) that עולם is a mistake for עם, probably due to an assimilation with the common expression שמחת עולם "eternal joy," which may have been understood as the "joy of the world." לקללה — The phrase could be translated more literally as "for cursing," though it implies the cursing of the parent.

לקללתה — The marginal alternative likely has a paragogic *he*, similar to other feminine singular words like בעולתה "in iniquity" in Ps 125:3 (see Joüon §93*j*).

41:10 For the same construction, see 40:11, 13 and cf. Qoh 3:20. מאונם א אונם — און could be a synonym for אפס, as in Isa 41:29. The repetition of the same letters may imply a wordplay, in which the letters can be understood as the same word with different meanings (אָוֶן "disaster, nothingness") or as two different words (אוֹן "wealth, strengh" and אָוֶן). Note the similar repetition of words and the implied wordplay throughout the book (e.g., עזב in Sir 3:12–13^A, חיל in Sir 40:13^Bm). The repetition of אפס and תהו, on the other hand, is probably to emphasize the finality of the returning. מאונים אל אונים — These letters can be understood as the plural form of אוֹן "wealth" or of אוֹנִי "mourning" (see Hos 9:4). The word אָוֶן does not occur elsewhere unambiguously in the plural, but note אונים in Prov 11:7 and the parallel between אָוֶן, אפס and תהו in Isa 41:29. Thus, one cannot discount the possibility of the meaning "from nothingness to nothingness."

		אך שם חסד לא יכרת:	³הבל אדם בגויתו	11 ᴹ	
תומות	חמדה	מאלפי אוצרות חכמה:	⁴פחד על שם כי הוא ילוך	12 ᴹ	
	וטוב	וטוֹבת שם ימי אין מספר:	⁵טוֹבת חי ימי מספר	13 ᴹ	טוב חי מספר ימים
תשׂימה	תעלה	מה תועֳלה בשתיהם:	⁶חכמה טמונה ואוצר מוסתר	14bc // 20:30 ᶜᴹ	וסימה מסותרת
	מאדון	מאישׁ מצפן חכמתו:	⁷טוב איש מצפן אולתו	15 // 20:31 ᶜᴹ	
		מוסר בשת:	⁸מ̇וֹסֵ̇ר בֹּשֵׁ̇ת שֵׁ̇ם	*	
	משפטו	והכלמו על משפטי:	⁹מוסר בשת שמעו בנים	14a/16a ᴹ	
		ולא כל הכלם נבחר:	¹⁰לא כל בשת נאה לשמר	16bc ᶜᴹ	
	ושׂר על	מנשיא יושבׂ אל כחש:	¹¹בוש מאב ואם אל זנות	17 ᴹ	על פחז
		מעדה ועם על פשע:	¹²מאדון וגברת על שקר	18ab ᴹ	
ונגיד על יד:		וממקום תגור על זר:	¹³מ̇ח̇בֹ̇ר̇ ורע על מעל	18c/19a ᴹ	משותף ממקום
		ממטה אציל אל לחם:	¹⁴מ̇[ה̇]פֹ̇ר̇ אלה וברית	19bc ᴹ	

41:11 לא יכרת B | לוא יכרת ᴹ · 41:12 אוצרות B סומות Bmg · שִׁ̇מֹ̇ת ᴹ · חמדה | חכמה B Bmg ᴹ · 41:13 טובת חי B ᴹ | טוב חי Bmg · ימי מספר B | מספר ימים Bmg ᴹ · וטובת B ᴹ | וטוב Bmg · 41:14bc // 20:30 ואוצר B C | וסימה Bmg | ושׂימה ᴹ · מוסתר B | מסותרת Bmg | מסתרת ᴹ · מה B ᴹ | ומה C | תעלה B | תולעת C | תולעֲת Bmg ᴹ · 41:15 // 20:31 מצפן B C | מטמן ᴹ · מאיש B C ᴹ | מאדון Bmg · מצפין B C | יטמן̇ Bmg | מצפן ᴹ · 41:14a/16a משפטי B ᴹ | משפטו Bmg · 41:*: מ̇וֹסֵ̇ר̇ בֹּשֵׁ̇ת שֵׁ̇ם B | > ᴹ · מוסר בשת: ᴹ · 41:16bc בשת B ᴹ | בושת C · נאה B C | נאוה ᴹ · לשמר ᴹ | לשמור B G | לבוש C | לשמר ᴹ · 41:17 על פחז Bmg ᴹ G · 41:18 על זנות B G | אל זנות ᴹ · יושב אל B | ושׂר על Bmg | ישב על ᴹ · קשר ᴹ · שקר B · מעדה B G | מעדם ᴹ · 41:19bc תגור על יד Bmg | ונגיר על יד B | תגור על זר ᴹ | ממקום B G | וממקום ᴹ · ממקום Bmg2 · משותף B Bmgi ᴹ | מ̇ח̇בֹ̇ר̇ B · 41:18c/19a ᴹ · אל ᴹ | על B · וממטה ᴹ | ממטה B ·

L. 4 [41:12] סומות — The marginal alternative is written at an oblique angle to the rest of the text.

L. 7 [41:15] יטמן̇ — This reading is proposed with hesitation. The word is written at an oblique angle to the text and is crossed out. The mark to the left of the *tet* must be a *mem* based on the context.

L. 8 [41:0] מ̇וֹסֵ̇ר̇ בֹּשֵׁ̇[ת] שֵׁ̇ם — The scribe began writing 41:14a in this line, realized their mistake and marked all the letters with cancellation marks. They then wrote the title to the following composition in the middle of the line.

L. 13 [41:18c/19a] מ̇ח̇בֹ̇ר̇ — Only the upper right corner of the *mem* is preserved, while only the top right corner of the *khet* is preserved. The *bet* is attested by its top and bottom horizontal lines. על יד — The reading על זד, as suggested by old editions (Lévi 1904, 52; Smend 1906b, 42), is possible though not probable.

L. 14 [41:19b/19c] מ̇[ה̇]פֹ̇ר̇ — The *mem* is attested by a trace of its right vertical and corner, the *pe* by the end of its base and part of its top, and the *resh* by the tips of its three extremities.

41:12 פחד על שם — In Biblical Hebrew, the verb פחד means "to fear, to tremble, venerate," but it is never constructed with על. Here, על could imply a different nuance ("to be concerned about, to take seriously") or simply be a confusion for אל, which does occur with פחד. In any case, the meaning of this verse contrasts with that of Sir 41:3. חכמה — This is likely a mistake (cf. the margin and Hᴹ). As it stands, the מן particle may mean "without" or "because of, due to." סומות — The marginal alternative should probably be understood as a misspelling of סימה; cf. שִׁ̇מֹ̇ת at Sir 41:12ᴹ and סימה at Sir 40:18ᴮ (and the note) where the word also appears as an alternative for אוצר. In this verse, the variant in the margin offers a much better meaning than the text. חמדה — If this alternative is adopted, then one can translate either "desirous wisdom" or "desirous treasures," the latter making more sense.

41:13 Cf. Sir 37:25. טוֹבת חי — The feminine form in the text implies the noun טוֹבָה, meaning "benefit," which occurs in construct with the following word primarily in Ben Sira (11:25; 12:9; 14:14; 20:13; 41:13) and once in the Hebrew Bible (Ps 106:5). It could also be understood as the feminine adjective. Yet, one would not expect the feminine form of the adjective here since it is usually used in construct with a noun that modifies a feminine entity (e.g., Rebekah in Gen 24:15; Abigail in 1 Sam 25:3; Esther in Esth 2:7). When the reference is to something generic, the masculine adjective is used in construct with a substantive (e.g., טוב־לבנון Ezek 31:16). טוב — The masculine form implies either the noun טוב with the same meaning as the noun טוֹבָה "benefit" or the adjective טוב with the same meaning as the feminine adjective, "a good living person" or "good name." Commentators have suggested that the original phrase was טוב חיים ימי מספר (see Smend 1906b, 41), and that the form חי is due to haplography. If this is correct, then such a mistake would have appeared before Hᴹ. ימי מספר — The opposite sequence מספר ימים found in the margin and Hᴹ is also found in several texts from the Geonic era (three examples in Maagarim). ימי אין מספר — The *status constructus* followed by אין does not seem to be attested other than here and in Sir 37:25 (contrast with Jer 2:32).

41:14 מוסתר — The *hophal* of סתר only appears elsewhere in texts from the sixth-century and later. תועלה — For this word, see the note in Sir 30:23.

41:15 יטמן̇ — This marginal alternative verb, which is crossed out by the scribe, agrees with the partially preserved participle in the first stich of Hᴹ (מטמן̇).

41:16 נאה — The form נאה, attested in Hᴮ and Hᶜ, is the Tannaitic equivalent of the Biblical Hebrew נאוה, attested in Hᴹ.

41:17 The poem is divided into two parts (v. 41:17–42:1d and 42:1e–8). The first part is composed of two different syntactic structures, the first of which (v. 41:17–19a) is characterized by a verb complemented by מן and על, sometimes with אל replacing על. The second structure (41:19b–42:1b) is characterized by a verb complemented by מן. In the second part of the poem, the verb phrase אל תבוש (in 42:1e) is only complemented by על. In verses 41:17–19a, the מן preposition indicates the thing affected by one's wrong behavior (see esp. 19a), and the על preposition introduces the behavior or thing that one should be ashamed of. By contrast, in verses 41:19b–42:1b, it is מן that introduces what one should be ashamed of. Finally, in verses 42:1e–8, as in the first part, the preposition על introduces the person or behavior that causes shame. פחז — See the note for Sir 4:30ᶜ. The noun, also attested in this verse in Hᴹ, most often is associated with lewd and sexually charged behavior, as reflected in its usage in Gen 49:4; 4Q184 1 13 (See Green-

11 L'être humain est éphémère dans son corps,
    mais un nom pieux ne sera pas supprimé.
12 Respecte (ton) nom car il t'accompagnera,
    plus que mille trésors (mg. trésors) de sagesse (mg. désirables).
13 Le bénéfice d'un vivant : des jours comptés,
    (mg. Le bénéfice d'un vivant : des jours comptés)
    mais le bénéfice (mg. idem) d'un nom : des jours sans nombre.
14b Sagesse cachée et trésor enfoui (mg. trésor enfoui)
14c quel profit (mg idem) en ces deux choses ?
15 Mieux vaut une personne qui cache sa folie,
    qu'une personne (mg. un maître) qui cache (mg. qui cachera) sa sagesse.

Instruction sur la honte, écou...
Instruction sur la honte
14a Écoutez, enfants, l'instruction sur la honte,
16a afin que vous soyez confus selon mon précepte (mg. son précepte).
16b Toute honte ne mérite pas d'être observée,
16c ni toute humiliation d'être choisie.
17 Aie honte, à cause d'un père et d'une mère, de la prostitution (mg. de l'arrogance),
    à cause d'un prince siégeant [et d'un ministre], du mensonge,
18a à cause d'un maître et d'une maîtresse, du mensonge,
18b à cause de l'assemblée et du peuple, de la rébellion,
18c à cause d'un compagnon (mg. 1 à cause d'un partenaire) (mg. 2 à cause d'un lieu) et d'un ami, de la trahison,
19a et à cause du lieu où tu séjournes, de l'étranger, (mg. et d'un chef, du pouvoir,)
19b de [bri]ser vœu et alliance,
19c d'étendre le coude vers le pain,

11 Ephemeral is a human in their body,
    but the pious name cannot be cut off.
12 Respect (your) name since it will accompany you,
    more than a thousand (mg. desirous) treasures (mg. treasures) of wisdom.
13 The benefit (that) the living (enjoy) is of limited time,
    (mg. The benefit (that) the living (enjoy) is of limited time,)
    but the benefit (mg. idem) of a name has no such limit.
14b Hidden wisdom and a concealed treasure (mg. concealed treasure)
14c what profit (mg idem) is in either of these two things?
15 Better a person who hides their folly,
    than a person (mg. a master) who hides (mg. who will hide) their wisdom.

Instruction on Shame, hea...
Instruction on Shame
14a Hear, children, the instruction on shame;
16a so as to be chastened according to my precepts (mg. its precepts).
16b Not every shame is worthy of observing,
16c nor should every humiliation be chosen.
17 Be ashamed because of father and mother with respect to prostitution (mg. on account of wantonness),
    because of the sitting prince with respect to lying (mg. and ruler with respect to);
18a because of master and mistress with respect to falsehood,
18b because of congregation or people with respect to rebellion;
18c because of comrade (mg.1 because of partner)(mg.2 because of place) or friend with respect to treachery,
19a because of the place you sojourn with respect to an outsider (mg. and leader with respect to power);
19b of [bre]aking oath or covenant,
19c of stretching the elbow toward food,

---

field 1978, 35–40). However, given the common association between parents and their respect, the noun here would seem to have a more generic sense of "arrogance, presumption." We assume that the normal associations of the noun have led a scribe to exchange פחז for the less ambiguous זנות found in the text. יושב — The word indicates a ruler sitting on the throne (1 Kgs 1:46).
41:18c משותף — The word שותף in the margin, which agrees with H^M, comes from Aramaic (see 4Q563 1 3 and 4Q347 1 6) and is not attested before Ben Sira. ממקום — This marginal alternative perhaps reflects the sense "witness" (cf. Aramaic מקם in TAD B7.2:8, 10).
41:19a זר — The word could be construed as "outsider" or as "something repugnant" (from זור, see Job 19:17). ונגיד — As already noted by Lévi (1898, 41), this form would be the result of a series of graphic confusions: נ for an earlier ת, י for ו and ד for ר. The meaning "leader" is unexpected in this context. The hypothesis that the word has been

preserved because מקום could have meant "Lord" here, as in rabbinic literature (see Lévi 1898, 41 and Gray 1897, 567), is unlikely because, in that case, it would have been המקום. על יד — Literally, "with respect to a hand." יד can have multiple metaphorical meanings: "power" (Exod 14:31), "penis" (Isa 57:8) and "portion of land" (Isa 56:5). The Greek κλοπή interprets it as "theft."
41:19c This half verse raises a number of philological problems and its interpretation is uncertain. מטה — This is probably the *hiphil* participle of נטה used with infinitival force (see Wernberg-Møller 1959, 54–67). The connection with the preceding stich is initially hard to understand, but when manners are addressed in Ben Sira, they usually have larger implications, like the possible rejection of family hierarchy, etc. Alternatively, this may be the noun מַטֶּה "scepter." See also, מֻטֶּה "bending, perversion," in Ezek 9:9. אציל — The word means "elbow," but "edge, border" or "noble" are also possible. לחם — The word can

מי השע פי	מהשבׄ אפי רעֶׄךׄ:	עׄ מׄתׄת שאלה[נ]מׄמׄ15	19d/21a M	מה 19d 21b הוא 20a 21a פני את משיב ומ אשה 20a משאל שאל שפתתיך על ומהתקמם שאלה תנאי אל מתת ומאחרי
משואל	משׄאול שלוםמחׄריש:	[מהש○] [מׄחׄלקות מנה 21b/20a M
[רה̇]	ומהתקׄמׄםׄ עׄלׄ שפׄתֹׄתׄךׄ	17מׄהביט אׄ[○○○○̊ 21c/20b or 22ab M
שאלה	ומאחרי מתת אל תׄנאׄי:	18מאוהב על דברי חרפה 22cd M דבר חסד

Chapter 42

MS.Heb.e.62 XI verso	על סד	ומחסוף כל סׄוד עצה[:]	1משנות דבר תשמע	1 M
		ומצא חן בעיני כל חי:	2והיית בוש באמת	
		ואל תשא פנים וחטא:	3אךׄ עׄל אלה אל תבוש	אל
משפט		ועל מצׄדיק להצדיק רשע:	4עׄל תׄורׄת עליון וחוק	אל 2 M
וישר:		ועל מחלקות נחלה ויש̇:	5על חשבון ב̇ חׄובר ואדון וׄארחׄ	שותף 3 M

41:19d/21a | מחשבות B Bmg2] מהשב B | **41:21b/20a** · M G שארך [רעיך Bmg2 · B רעך] M רעך · M ומהשיב את פני Bmg1 Bmg2 מי השע פי B | מהשב אפי **41:19d/21a** | המחריש Bmg2 · M· המחריש [: מהחריש B · משאל M G ומשאל Bmg1 משואל B Bmg2 משׄאול · M מחלקת B Bmg2 מׄחׄלקות · M מחשות B **41:20b or 22ab** | ומהתקמם B ומהתבונן or ומהתקומם · M ומהתקׄמם B שפׄתׄתךׄ · M עלׄ or עׄלׄ · B שפׄתׄתך] ז[רה B Bmg M or יצעיה · M · **41:22cd** | מאהב B מאוהב · M דברי חרפה B אל תנאי] חרף · M **42:1** | ומחסוף B ומחשף · M · כל סוד] B | חובר **42:3** | משפט Bmg M G מצדיק · M וחק] וחוק · B M אל Bmg · M על B M על **42:2** · Bmg B בוש] M בויש · B M אל Bmg · M G כל דבר] Bmg על סד B | וישר B M וישר] Bmg · M יש B M מחלקות] B מחלקת M · דרך] Bmg וארח · B M ואדון · M Bmg שותף] B

L. 15 [41:19d/21a] מׄמׄ[נ]עׄ מׄתׄת — The traces of letters in H[B] fit the words attested in H[M] perfectly.

L. 15–16 Margin [41:19d.21a–b.20a] The alternative text to 41:19d/21a/21b/20a is written perpendicularly in the right margin. פׄי — The *hireq* may in fact be a *tsere*, as there is a trace of a dot beside the more clearly written dot.

L. 16 [41:21b/20a] משׄאׄול — Traces of the upper and lower horizontal lines of the *mem* are preserved, as well as the vertical line, though the letter could also be read as a *bet* or *kaph*. Only the top tips of the *shin* are attested. The bottom left and bottom right of the *aleph* are preserved. מהחריש — The *khet* looks irregular, as though the scribe first wrote an *aleph* and then corrected the letter to a *khet*. המחריש: (margin) — The letters are often read as a *hithpael* imperative or a perfect. Yet, as Lévi (1904, 52) observes, the second letter is a *mem*. Lévi (1904, 52) reads the last mark as a *vav*, yet this seems unlikely, as the word should be followed by a *soph passuq*, like other cases where whole verses are presented in the margin.

L. 17 [41:21c/20b or 22b] ומהתקׄמם — The second *mem* of the word seems to be attested by traces of its horn and bottom right corner.

L. 18 [41:22c-d] שאלׄה — The *aleph* looks as if the paper has been cut and then re-attached, resulting in the loss of the left side of the letter. The mark beneath the *lamed* is presumably a bleed-through trace of the *mem* from the opposite side of the same page (the second *mem* of משמר in XI verso, 18 Sir 42:11). It is difficult to know whether this is an alternative to מתת or the verbal phrase.

L. 1 [42:1] A smudge of ink appears above the *samek* of סוד.

L. 1 Margin [42:1] The *dalet* of סוד is written in one stroke like a *resh*.

L. 4 [42:2] עׄל תׄורׄת — The ink of these two words is abraded and some ink from the facing page may have worn off onto this page. The *lamed*'s ascender is abnormally inclined to avoid overlapping with the final *kaph*'s descender from the last bicolon.

L. 5 [42:3] ב̇ — The *bet* is cancelled with a slanting line. וׄארחׄ — The interlinear word has what appears to be the Babylonian vowel sign for an /o/ vowel.

mean "bread, food" or "battle, war." These potential meanings can be combined in different ways, for example, "because of the scepter of a noble with respect to fighting" (Lévi 1898, 42) or "and of one extending a border on account of food" (Reymond 2003, 393).

41:21a מתת — This could be a noun in the construct state (e.g., מתת שקר "a false gift" Prov 25:14), but understanding it as תת + מן is preferable. The verb מנע can take a complement introduced with מן (Job 31:16). מהשב אפי — The expression is ambiguous. If אפי is an Aramaism meaning "face," then it is equivalent to the Hebrew השיב פנים "to turn away" (see Tg. 1 Kgs 2:16 and the corresponding Hebrew in the MT). If אפי means anger (see Dan 11:20), a meaning more typical in the singular, then it could mean "to restrain the anger (of your friend)." מי השע פי — The first word is problematic. It could be the interrogative pronoun, but this does not fit the context. It is more likely that it is the abbreviated form of the preposition מן, found in Rabbinic Hebrew (with following *yod*, m. Soṭah 5:5 [ms. Kaufmann]; with following *he*, מיהן "from them" in y. Soṭah 9:10, 24a [Maagarim]). The second word is the *hiphil* infinitive construct of שעע "to seal," used in relation to shutting eyes in Isa 6:10. רעיךׄ: — The marginal word might be a plural, but more likely reflects a pausal form (cf. חקיק Sir 41:2ab).

41:21b/20a מהש○ — Lévi (1904, 52) reconstructs מהשבית "of halting," which fits the available space and remaining traces, and could reflect the Greek ἀφαίρεσις (cf. Isa 30:11). מחשבות מחלקות — The text makes little sense. Our translation above reflects the sense of individual words. משׄאול שלום — See Sir 6:5 and the note. מׄהׄריש — Without the *he*, the form is presumably the מן preposition followed by the *plene* form of the adjective/noun "deaf." With the superscript *he*, it could be the preposition followed by the infinitive construct, the whole colon being translated: "(be ashamed) of being silent with respect to giving a greeting". According to the marginal alternative משואל, one could translate "(be ashamed) of being silent with respect to someone offering a greeting" (see van Peursen 2004, 274–75).

41:20a or 22ab ומהתקׄמם עׄל שפׄתׄתךׄ — The first word seems to correspond to 22b in H[M], while the word שפתתך corresponds to 22a in H[M], but the marginal reading]רה may stand for זרה in H[M] 20b, all of which implies that the scribe of H[B] mixed up 20b and 22ab.]רה — The marginal alternative could be the word נערה "slave girl" or זרה "stranger woman" (as in 20b of H[M]).

19d de re[fu]ser de répondre à une demande,
21a de détourner la face (mg. 1 de fermer la bouche) de ton ami
   (mg. 2 [19d] de re[fu]ser de répondre à une demande,)
   (mg. 2 [21a] de fermer la bouche de ton ami.)
21b de … […]répartitions d'une part,
20a de saluer (mg. 1 de celui qui salue) celui qui est muet.
   (mg. 2 [21b] (des) projets de répartitions d'une part,)
   (mg. 2 [20a] de saluer (celui qui) est muet)
21c de regarder […] (mg. une femme,)
20b/22b de te dresser sur ta servante,
22c à cause d'un ami, de paroles de reproches (mg. une parole honteuse),
22d et après un don (mg. une demande), ne (le) rejette pas ;

Chapitre 42

1 de répéter une parole que tu entends
  et de mettre à nu tout secret d'un conseil. (mg. et de révéler tout ce qui concerne le secret d'un conseil.)
  Tu peux être légitimement honteux (de cela),
  de sorte que tu trouveras grâce aux yeux de tout vivant.
  Mais concernant ce (qui suit), n'aie pas honte
  et n'aie pas honte et (ne porte pas) un péché,
2 de la loi du Très-Haut et de (son) décret,
  de celui qui administre la justice (mg. justice) déclarant juste le méchant,
3 des comptes d'un associé (mg. d'un partenaire) ou d'un maître ^{ou d'un voyageur}
  et du partage d'un héritage ou d'un bien (mg. ou de ce qui est droit/juste),

19d of refu[si]ng to grant a request,
21a of turning away the face of your friend (mg. 1 of shutting the mouth).
   (mg. 2 [19d] of re[fu]sing a requested gift,)
   (mg. 2 [21a] of shutting the mouth of your friend,]
21b of [ ]distributions of a portion
20a of greeting the one who is silent (mg. 1 of one greeting).
   (mg. 2 [21b] reflections on the distributions of a portion,)
   (mg. 2 [20a] of greeting (one who) is deaf.)]
21c of looking a[t   ] (mg. a woman),
20b/22b to raise oneself over your maid servant
22c of a friend with respect to reproachful words (mg. a shameful word)
22d and after (receiving) a gift (mg. a request), do not spurn (them).

Chapter 42

1 of repeating the word you hear,
  and of laying bare any secret of a council (mg. (and of laying bare anything) with respect to secrets (of a council)).
  You may be legitimately ashamed (of these things)
  so that you may find grace in the eyes of all the living.
  But, concerning these (following) things do not be ashamed,
  do not feel shame and (bear) sin:
2 concerning the law of the Most High and (his) statute,
  and concerning the one administering justice (mg. justice), bringing the wicked to justice,
3 concerning the (monetary) account of an associate (mg. partner) or master ^{or traveller},
  and concerning divisions of inheritance or wealth (mg. or what is right),

---

41:22c/d דבר — Despite what looks like a *hireq* under the *bet*, this should be the construct form of "word." חסד — Based on the main text and the context, this is easiest to understand as the rare word "shame, reproach" (found in Lev 20:17; Prov 25:10), a homonym of the more common word "piety, loving kindness."

42:1 משנות — The Greek presumes the root שנה II "to repeat," but it is just as likely that this is the root שנה I "to change, to alter." עצה — The word has the meaning "council" here, as in the Dead Sea Scrolls (1QM III 4) and in Rabbinic Hebrew. ואל תשא פנים — For the idiomatic expression, see 4:22A and the note. Consequently, we understand it as "do not be ashamed (and [do not bear] sin)." The verb נשא takes פנים and חטא as direct objects. Alternatively, it could be interpreted as "do not show partiality," as in Sir 35:15–16. The following verses address situations where it is essential to act impartially (e.g., exonerating the wrongfully accused, wiping down measuring devices, recording financial interactions). וחטא — This may be an infinitive absolute, or more likely, a noun "sin."

42:2 מצדיק — This could be understood in other ways, for example, as "the one who deals strictly" or "the one who deals liberally," based on Rabbinic Hebrew. One can assume that the two *hiphil* verbal forms express slightly different nuances in an attempt at wordplay. משפט — The marginal word gives the entire colon a meaning that is identical to the meaning of H^M: "concerning the exercise of judgment, so as to bring the wicked to justice." להצדיק רשע — Taken at face value, this sentence would translate, "… to declare the wicked righteous," which contradicts Exod 23:7; Deut 25:1; 1 Kgs 8:32; 2 Ch 6:23; Prov 17:15 and Isa 5:23. Presumably, Ben Sira is playing with the reader's expectations here. The word רשע perhaps designates a bad person who can reform (see Isa 26:10 which implies that the רשע can learn צדק); or, הצדיק has the more general sense "to administer justice" (e.g., 2 Sam 15:4) or "to bring justice to" (e.g., Dan 12:3). By contrast, Darshan (2021) explains this unexpected expression as a result of dittography from the following preposition (על) and proposes to read the earlier text להצדיק רש "to maintain the right of the needy." In its entirety, the verse refers to impartial and unbiased judgment.

42:3 חשבון — See 9:15 and the note. שותף — See 41:18B and the note. וישר — Presumably, the word conveys what is rightly due to someone.

תמורת	וְעַל תמהות איפה ואבן:		⁶ועל שחק מאזנים ופלס	4ab ᴹ	
אפה ואפה:					
מוסר	ועל מֽמְחִיר ממכר תגר:		⁷על מקנה בין רב למעט	4c/5a ᴹ	חשבון
	ומקום ידים רפות תפתח:		⁸על אשה רֹעָה חותם : חכם	6 ᴹ	טפשה
ושואה ותתה	ומתת לֹלקח הכל בכתב:		⁹על מקום תפקֹד יד תספור	7 ᴹ	מֹפְקד יד
ועונה בזנות: ושב כושל	וישב וְיֹשיש ונוטל עֵצָה בזנות		¹⁰על מֹוֹסֹר פותה וכסיל	8 ᴹ	תחשוב
	ואיש צנוע לפני כל חי:		¹¹והיית זהיר באמת		מרדות
			vacat	12	
ודאגתה	דְאָגָה תפריש נֹ[וּ]מֹ:		¹³בת לאב מטמנת שקר	9ab ᴹ	מטמון
	ובבתוליה פן תפֹתֹ[ה:]		¹⁴בנעוריה פן תגורי	9cd ᴹ	
	ובבית בעלה לא תנֹשֹה:		¹⁵בבתוליה פן תפֹותה	10ac ᴹ	תתפתה

42:4ab שחק מאזנים B | שחקי מזנים M G · תמהות איפה ואבן B | תמחי איפה ואבן M · תמורת אפה ואפה Bmg | · 42:4c/5a מקנה B M | חשבון Bmg · 42:5bc + מהלמת וצלע רע ועבד M [ ] · 42:6 רעה B G = ר״ Bmg2 | תפ[שת Bmg1 | טפשה Bmg2 | · M חכם חותם · M תפ[שֹת Bmg1 | ממחיר B M | מוסר Bmg · מספר Bmg | תחשוב Bmg | תפקיד M · מֹפְקד יד Bmg | תפקד B | תספור M · תספור B | רבות M G | רפות B | תפתח B | מפתח M · 42:7 תפקד יד Bmg | מֹפְקד M · תפקיד M · תספור B | חותם Bmg M · רפות B | B ונוטל (ושואֹ) עצה M Bmg · וישב וישיש Bmg · מרדות B M | מֹוֹסֹר M · ש[וֹא]וֹת Bmg | · 42:8 ומתת ולקח B G | ושואה ותתה Bmg | ענה M · 42:9ab בת B מטמנת B בש{אֹ}ת M · מטמון Bmg · נומה M · נ[וֹ]מֹ B | תפ[רִי]ד M · תפֹרִיש B | · 42:9cd תגורי B תמאס M · לא M G S ועל אישה Bmg2 | [בבית בע׳ = ובבית בעל B · ובבית בֹעֹלֹה M G S · תחל M G S · Bmg2 תתפתה Bmg1 | תפותה B | · 42:10ac ובבתוליה M G S · ובבעליה M S · תנֹשֹה B = תנשה לֹ Bmg2 | פן תשטה M G S ·

L. 7 [42:4c/5] מֽמְחִיר — The *khet* (see Beentjes 1997, 73), could also be read as a *he* (see Smend 1906b, 43; Ben-Ḥayyim 1973, 47).

L. 10 [42:8] ושוֹאֹ — The word is written beneath ונוטל, as an alternative or complement to it. The *aleph* and *lamed* are written in ligatured form.

L. 13 [42:9ab] תפֹרִיש — The *resh* is fairly clear. The *sin* or *shin* is attested by the tops of its three arms, as well as traces of its right most arm. נֹ[ ]מֹ — The marks are very faint and ambiguous. The space does not allow for נומה, as in Hᴹ. Perhaps the manuscript read נום.

L. 14 [42:9cd] תגורי — The *yod* has been crossed-out with a vertical line. תפֹתֹ[ה — The bottom left foot of the *tav* is preserved, as well as the bottom of its right foot. The following letter is preserved only by traces of a horizontal base, so that a *pe* would be possible. The third trace preserves a horizontal bar that may correspond to a *tav*. Cf. the next stich (v. 10a) which would form a very similar doublet.

L. 15 [42:10ac] וּבבֹיֹת — After this word, there is a vertical line ligatured to the *tav*. This could be a *vav* (implying "and in his house"), the right leg of a *he* ("and in her house"), or conceivably, an offset mark from the *nun* of נאצל of XII recto, 15 Sir 42:21c. All things considered, one can assume that it is an offset mark, followed by traces of the phrase בעלה "her husband," as seems to be presumed in the marginal alternative (see below). לֹאֹ תנֹשֹה — After the *lamed*, we can discern traces of the right arm and the diagonal of an *aleph*, then a faint trace of the foot of a *tav*, followed by a faint trace that can correspond to the base of a *nun*. Finally before the *he*, the base and the left vertical of a *shin* are clear.

42:4 שחק — The expression is borrowed from Isa 40:15 where it functions as a figure of insignificance (see Lévi 1898, 47). תמהות — Literally, "wonders." Presumably, this is a mistake for תמחות or תמחית, an otherwise unknown word meaning "wiping, cleaning, polishing, calibrating" from the root מחה (see Segal [1958, 280] and Dihi [2004, 721–27] for a review of the literature). On scales and their cleaning, see m. B. Bat. 5:10.

42:5a ממחיר — The *mem* is written twice by mistake, perhaps due to the two *mems* in the following word (see Segal 1958, 283). It is strange that the same dittography is found in Hᴹ. Strugnell (1969, 114) suggests reading ל[מחיר, which is unlikely according to the preserved traces in the fragments. The possibility that this is a *hiphil* participle is unlikely, as there is no suitable verb with these consonants in Hebrew or Aramaic. מוסר — The form could be a *qal* participle from the root מסר "to transmit, deliver, hand over." See b. B. Meṣ 8b.

42:5bc The bicolon attested in Hᴹ (and the Greek) is missing.

42:6 This sentence seems to be disconnected from the sequence of prepositional phrases (see the Greek; cf. Prov 1:5 within 1 to 6). טפשה — One wonders if the original text might have had תפשת חותם "who handles a seal" (note the Hᴹ reading and possible reconstruction), see Ahiqar TAD C1.1.3, 19 and Tob 1:22. The more mundane verb was replaced by טפשה in the margin, which was eventually replaced by רעה as a synonym. חכם — After the preceding confusion between תפשת > טפשה > רעה, a scribe could have added the last word חכם to produce a new proverbial sentence. A different scribe added the two dots before חכם, according to their own copy. The second marginal reading attests this version. ידים רפות — See Isa 35:3 and Job 4:3. תפתח — The verb could be a 2ms, or more likely, a 3fs with "the bad wife" as subject.

4a et de la poussière des balances et des bascules,
4b et du *polissage* des mesures et des poids (mg. le changement d'une mesure pour une autre),
4c d'un achat (d'un compte), qu'il soit grand ou petit,
5a et du prix (mg. le pourvoyeur) d'un article d'un marchand.
6 Sur une femme mauvaise (mg. 1 folle), un sceau est sage et à la place de mains languissantes, elle (l')ouvrira. (mg. 2: Sur une femme mauvaise (il faut) un sceau et à la place de mains languissantes, elle (l')ouvrira).
7 Du lieu des dépôts, tu dois compter (mg. Des dépôts tu dois calculer) et des dons et des saisies (mg. son [s.e. main] don et sa saisie), tout doit être par écrit,
8 de l'instruction (mg. de la discipline) du simple et du fou, du grison et du vieillard et de celui qui propose (mg. demande) un conseil à propos de la fornication (mg. du grison qui trébuche et est occupé à la fornication). Alors, tu seras vraiment vigilant et une personne humble devant tout vivant.
vacat
9 Une fille est un faux trésor (mg. trésor) pour un père, l'anxiété (mg. l'anxiété à son sujet) écarte le sommeil : quand elle est jeune, de peur qu'elle n'ait des rapports sexuels, quand elle est vierge, de peur qu'elle ne soit *sédu[ite,]*
10a quand elle est vierge, de peur qu'elle ne soit séduite (mg. qu'elle ne soit séduite),
10c dans la maison de son mari qu'elle ne soit pas oubliée,

4a and concerning dust of scales and balances,
4b and concerning the *wiping* of measure and stone weight (mg. exchange of one measure for another),
4c concerning a purchase (mg. an account), whether big or small,
5a and concerning the price of (mg. the one transmitting) the merchant's wares—
6 On a bad (mg 1. foolish) wife a seal is wise, but in a place of slack hands she will open (it). (mg. 2: On a bad wife (must be) a seal, but in a place of slack hands she will open (it)).
7 As to the place of deposits, you should count (mg. the deposit you should calculate), and (as to) giving and taking (mg. its (i.e., a hand's) taking and giving), everything should be in writing.—
8 concerning the instruction (mg. the chastisement) of the simple and foolish, of the gray-headed and aged and the one offering (mg. the one requesting) advice in fornication (mg. the gray-headed who stumbles and is occupied with fornication). Then, you will be truly vigilant, a humble person before all the living.
vacat
9 A daughter is a false treasure (mg. treasure) for a father anxiety (mg. anxiety over her) chases s[lumb]er away in her youth, lest she has intercourse, when she is nubile, lest she be seduc[ed]
10a when she is nubile, lest she be seduced, (mg. she be seduced),
10c in the house of her husband that she is not forgotten,

42:7 תפקד יד — If the first word is a verb, then it could be a *niphal* with the meaning that it carries in Neh 7:1, "is appointed," or the opposite sense "is missing, lacking" (as in Judg 21:3 and 1 Sam 20:18), resulting in "Don't be ashamed of the place where the hand that takes account is appointed/missing." It could also be a *qal*: "you will appoint as the hand that takes account." More likely, it is the noun תפקיד, which means "command, charge, trust" in Rabbinic Hebrew. Its construction with the following word "hand" would give it a financial sense, "deposit." For a similar construction, see תשומת יד "pledge" in Lev 5:21 where it is parallel to the word פקדן "deposit." מפקד — This word is synonymous with תפקיד and is not attested before the fifth-century CE. ומתת ולקח — These two words convey the sense of commercial exchange. Compare with משא ומתן, "business dealings" in Rabbinic Hebrew. ושואה ותתה — The words are both infinitives construct with 3fs pronominal suffixes, the antecedents of which are "hand." For the form of the infinitive construct of נשא as שוא, see Ps 89:10. For these two words, cf. CD XIII 14 and the interpretation of Kister (1983, 138).

42:8 מרדות — The word is unlikely to be the Biblical Hebrew word "rebellion," but rather a word semantically similar to מוסר, i.e., "chastisement," which is also found in Sir 33:25 and in Rabbinic Hebrew. ושב וישיש — See Job 15:10. ונוטל — The word is presumably the *qal* participle of נטל, used in the same way that it is used in 2 Sam 24:12, that is, "giving." ועונה — The participle could also be construed as "one wretched." צנוע — In Biblical Hebrew, the root often has the sense "to be humble," but in the Dead Sea Scrolls and Ben Sira, it can have the sense "to be careful."

42:9–10 The verses are paraphrased in b. Sanh. 100b: בת לאביה מטמונת שוא. מפחדה לא יישן בלילה. בקטנותה שמא תתפתה. בנערותה שמ' זנה. בגרה שמא לא תנשא. נשאת שמ' לא יהיו לה בנים. הזקינה שמ' תעסוק בכשפים. "A daughter is a worthless treasure for her father. From fear over her, he cannot sleep at night: in her youth, lest she be seduced; in her young adulthood, lest she fornicates; in her adulthood, lest she is not married; as a married woman, lest she has no children; as an elder, lest she engages in sorcery." See also Nissim, *Ḥibbûr Yaphê*, ed. Obermann 1933, 58.60: בת לאביה מטמונת שוא מפחדה לא יישן בלילה.

42:9 זהיר — See Sir 13:13 and the note. מטמנת — This is presumably a nominal form, מטמונת "treasure," with the same meaning as in the margin (see the quotations in the preceding note and אם נקבה תלד מטונת שוא בה תנוחם in the *piyyut*, *The Weeks of the Sabbath of the Year*, §17 [CUL Add. 3374, folio 2, verso, l. 12]). It could also be the *hiphil* participle of טמן "to hide," resulting in "a daughter hides falsehood from a father." תפריש — Cf. Sir 31:1–2. תגורי — The verb גור may have here the meaning "to fornicate" (see Dihi 2004, 128–131 and the quotation in b. San 100b, where תגור corresponds to תזנה).

42:10ac תנשה — This expresses the fear the daughter will be forgotten, though in form it is close to תנשא = תִּנָּשֵׂא in the quotations above.

	ובבית אִשָּׁה פֶּן תֵּע[צַּר:		¹⁶בבית אביה פן תִּוָּנֶה	10bd ᴾᴹ
סרח:	פֶּן[תעשה ל]ךָ שם סרה:		¹⁷בָּנִֿי עַל [ ] [ ]ךָ חֹזֶק מֹוסָֿר	11ab ᴾᴹ
והובישתך	והושבתך בְּעֵדַת שער:		¹⁸דבת עיר וקהִלֿת עם	11cd ᴾᴹ
MS.Heb.e.62 XII recto	ובית מביט מבוא סביב:		¹מָקום תגור אל יהי אשנב	11ef ᴹ
תסתיד	ובית נשים אל תסתוֹיָד:		²לכל זכֿר אל תתן תאר	12 ᴾᴹ
	ומאשה רעת אשה		³כי מבגד יצא עש	13 ᴾᴹ
	ובית מחרפת תביע אשה:		⁴מטוב רוע איש מטיב אשה	14 ᴹ
				5
	וזה חזיתי ואספרה:		⁶אזכר נא מעשי אל	15ab ᴹ
לקח:	ופועל רצונו לקחו:		⁷באומר אלהים רצֿונו	15cd ᴹ

42:10bd תִּוָּשֵׂא B M | תֵּע[צַּר· M | ובעלה · Bmg2 | ובב' א'יש' = B | ובבית אִשָּׁה · G M פן תזריע Bmg1 | פחזה Bmg2 | פן תִּוָּנֶה B | בית · M | בבית B Bmg2 | **42:10obd** בן · Bmg1 | תתן B | תבן M **42:11** בני · M מוסר חזק Bmg2 | משמר החזק · M משמר חזק B | אל יהי · M אל יהי אשנב B | **42:12** זכר B M | תזכר Bmg · תתן B | תבן M **42:11** בני · M מוסר חזק Bmg2 | **42:13** עש B · סס M · S מחפרת B Bmg1 | מחרפת · M ובת · M ובית Bmg M | מטיב Bmg M · מטיב B | רוע Bmg M · רע B | טוב Bmg M | מטוב · B **42:14** אזכר B | אזכרה M Mmg· מעשי אל B M | מעֹ[שׂ]י̇ Mmg אספרה · B G לקח B M | לקחו · M ופעל רצנו B | ופועל רצונו Bmg M G S · רצונו Bmg | אדני · M אלהים B | באמר · M באומר B **42:15cd** ואשננה M Mmg · S Bmg · חרפה B | אשה · M מבול B Bmg | תביע · M מפחדת · G G | מפחדת

L. 16 [42:10bd] פֶּ֯ — The bottom parts of the letters are visible. צַּ֯[— Only the base line of the *tsade* is visible, which means that the mark could also be read in other ways.

L. 15–16 Margin [42:10obcad] תְּנִֻשָׂא — The *nun* is worn away and is lighter in appearance than the other letters. Above the mark that corresponds to a *sin* or *shin* are other marks that may be accidental. The final *he* of תְּנִשָׂה is clear, as can be observed in the manuscript. אִיֽשׁ — These letters are unusual in appearance. The *sin/shin* letter is particularly odd in appearance, looking more like a squashed *pe* followed by a *yod*. One wonders if this originated as the word פן before being altered into a *sin/shin*. Furthermore, each of the letters appears to carry the abbreviation mark above it, as though the scribe kept thinking that they were going to abbreviate the word, but then continued writing all of the letters. If the last is intended as a true abbreviation mark, then it could imply the text found in Hᴹ: אישה. תְּנֻשָּׂאֽ — The *tav* is difficult to read, but the three arms of the *sin/shin* are clear, followed by a vertical line that could correspond to a *nun*. The *aleph* is written above these last letters.

L. 17 [42:11] בָּנִֿי עַל — Only the tops of the letters are preserved. Nevertheless, the remaining marks and their spacing make it very likely that they should be read in this manner. חֹזֶק — The marks are extremely faint. The initial *khet* is attested by the lower part of its two legs. The following *zayin* is attested by its lower half. The *qoph* is fairly clear from its descender and traces of its head. מֹוסָֿר — The *mem* is attested by the lower part of its diagonal, as well as traces of its right bottom corner and a very blurry triangular mark above the lacuna that might be the remnants of the letter's upper left flourish. The *vav* is preserved as a faint vertical line. The *samek* is attested by very faint traces of its right side and perhaps its left vertical. Nevertheless, these letters have also made clear offset traces on the following folio page, XII recto, 17 Sir 42:25b, which makes the proposed reading more certain (see Reymond 2016a, 135). פֶּן[תעשה ל]ךָ — This reconstruction is based on the marginal abbreviations, which assume the same letters in the text.

L. 17 Margin שׁ׳ ס׳ — Beentjes (1997, 73) and Ben-Ḥayyim (1973, 48) read לא׳ מ׳. It seems preferable to read a *sin/shin* based on the marks (the three arms are visible). The next traces are consistent with a *samek*, though the strokes are hard to read, as the paper has become very dark.

L. 18 [42:11] The initial letters of the line are clear, though their top parts are not preserved. The last part of the first stich shows some off-setting from the opposite page (XII recto). Specifically, it seems that the bottom part of the *tsade* and *vav* of צורך in 43:23b appears beneath the *he* of וקהלת, thereby obscuring the bottom part of the *he*. It seems less likely that this obscured letter is a *lamed*, as Segal (1958, 284) suggests. Similarly, the *tav* of וקהלת is obscured by an offset *kaph* from כל in 43:23b.

L. 1 [42:11] מָקום — Only a very small remnant of the *mem*'s diagonal is preserved beneath a hole.

L. 2 [42:12] תזכר — The initial *tav* is clear in the online photo (Beentjes 1997, 74).

L. 7 [42:15] רצֿונו — The first *vav* is only attested by a very small mark beneath the damaged portion of paper (Ben-Ḥayyim [1973, 49]).

42:10 (margin) Notice that the language and sequence of verses in Hᴮ and its margin seem confused. The other textual witnesses have different sequences. תתפתה / תפותה — The verb in the main text is a *pual* and the marginal alternative is the *hithpael* with the same sense that it has in Rabbinic Hebrew. בעל׳ — In the margin, these letters may be read as an abbreviation for בעלה "her husband" (the two dots would be similar to the multiple dots above איש in the next marginal line) or as an abbreviation for two words לא בעלה as in the main text. פחז — See Sir 4:30ᶜ (and the note there) and 41:17. עצר — See Gen 16:2; 20:18 and Prov 30:16. תשנא — In Aramaic documents, the verb שנא can have the meaning "to divorce" (see TAD B2.6.23, 27).

42:11 חֹזֶק מֹוסָֿר — The marks are hard to read. Nevertheless, the text seems to advise applying severe restrictions on a daughter. Alternatively, the letters might be read as advice to "fortify instruction," though this seems less likely. סרה — In Aramaic, the verb may also have the meaning "to stink" as its marginal Hebrew equivalent. מָקום תגור — Compare the use of תגור in v. 9. ובית מביט — The meaning seems to be "(in) a house, (let there not be a window) looking . . .," based on the rules of verbal ellipsis (see Miller 2003, 251–270). If so, then מבוא could have the meaning "alley," as in Rabbinic Hebrew.

42:12 תתן — This could be a 2ms verb (as the Greek) "do not deliver (her) beauty," or the 3fs. ובית — We interpret בַּיִת as the fem. of בַּיִן "between" (cf. also Sir 50:5ᴮ and some five times in Tannaitic and Amoraic texts [see Maagarim], but frequently in Syriac). תסתיד / תסתוד — This

10b dans la maison de son père, de peur qu'elle ne fornique, (mg. de son père, elle a agi lascivement,)
10d et dans la maison de son mari, de peur [qu'elle ne soit sté]rile
(mg. [10b] dans la maison de son père, de peur que [...]
[10c] [et] dans la maison de son mari, elle sera oubliée,
[10a] quand elle est nubile, de peur qu'elle ne soit séduite,
[10d] dans la maison de son homme, de peur qu'elle ne soit détestée.)
11a Mon enfant, sur ta [*fille* (?)] renforce la discipline,
11b de pe[ur qu'elle ne te fasse] une réputation de rebelle (mg. (une réputation) puante),
11c ragot de la ville et de l'assemblée du peuple,
11d et qu'elle ne te fasse asseoir (mg. elle ne te fasse honte) dans l'assemblée de la porte.
(mg. [11a] Mon enfant sur une fille renforce la garde,
[11b] de peur qu'elle ne te fasse une réputation de rebelle,
ragot de la ville et de l'assemblée du peuple
et qu'elle ne te fasse honte dans l'assemblée de la porte.)
11e Là où elle habite qu'il n'y ait pas de fenêtre
11f ni, (dans sa) chambre, de vue sur la rue environnante.
12 Qu'elle n'offre sa beauté à aucun homme (mg. à aucun de ceux qui se souviennent d'elle / à aucun de ceux dont elle se souvient)
et parmi les femmes qu'elle ne converse pas.
13 Car d'un vêtement sort la mite
et d'une femme, la méchanceté de femme.
14 Combien mieux vaut la méchanceté d'un homme que la bonté d'une femme
et au milieu des outrageuses discourt une femme.
(mg. mieux vaut la méchanceté d'un homme
que la bonté d'une femme,
une fille outrageuse (honteuse) proclamera l'outrage.)
vacat
15 Je veux rappeler les œuvres de Dieu
et ce que j'ai vu, je veux le raconter.
Par une parole de Dieu est sa volonté (mg. sont ses œuvres)
et son (mg. omit) enseignement est l'œuvre de sa volonté.

10b in the house of her father, lest she commit fornication (mg. her father she acted lasciviously),
10d in the house of her man lest she be [barr]en,
(mg. [10b] in the house of her father lest [ ]
[10c] [and] in the house of her husband she will be forgotten,
[10a] when she is nubile, lest she be seduced,
[10d] in the house of her man lest she be hated.)
11a My child, over your [*daughter* (?)] make strong the bon[d],
11b le[st she make for you] a reputation for treachery (mg. a stinking (reputation)),
11c the talk of the city and of the congregation of the people,
11d and she causes you to sit (mg. she shames you) in the assembly of the gate.
(mg. [11a] My child over a daughter maintain a guard
[11b] lest she make (for) you a reputation for treachery,
[11c] a talk of the city and congregation of the people,
[11d] and she shames you in the assembly of the gate.)
11e (In) the place where she dwells, let there not be a window,
11f in (her) room one looking out to the surrounding street.
12 To no male (mg. to all by whom she is remembered / to anyone she remembers) may she offer her beauty,
may she not converse among women.
13 For, from a garment a moth comes forth,
and from a woman, wickedness of woman.
14 How much better the evil of a man than the virtue of a woman,
but among reproachful women a woman will pour forth.
(mg. Better the evil of a man
than the virtue of a woman,
a daughter who is reproached (mg. who is shamed)
will pour forth reproach.)
vacat
15 Let me recall the works of God,
and what I have seen, let me recount.
By the word of God is his will (mg. his works)
And his (mg. omit) teaching is the work of his will.

is presumably the middle weak verb סוד (akin to its Syriac cognate) in the *hithpaal* stem with the meaning "to converse with" (see 7:14 and the note).

42:14 This bicolon is clearly corrupted (see the margin and H^M). The translation above is tentative. מטוב רוע איש — We follow Lévi's proposal (Lévi 1898, 54) of understanding מטוב as a contraction of מה and טוב (cf. Ezek 8:6; Isa 3:15; Exod 4:2 and מטוב "how good" in the *piyyut* of HaQalir, שבעתות לשבתות מיוחדות). מטיב — We interpret טיב as a biform of טוב. It could also be understood as the *hiphil* of טוב. מחרפת — In the text, the word functions as a *piel*, while the marginal alternative is a *pual*. חרפה / מחרפת — The repetition of this root in the margin seems to imply that this stich is an independent proverb, though the meaning of the proverb does not really fit the context. מחפרת — A *hiphil* participle of חפר II, this is an alternative reading to the marginal text and allows the last stich to read as a continuation of the preceding comparison, rather than as an independent proverb: "than ... a shamed daughter (who) will pour forth reproach."

42:15 The second stich is an exact repetition of Job 15:17. באומר — The idea conveyed by this phrase, as well as the stich more generally, resembles Ps 33:6.

	וכבוד ייי על כל מעשיו:		⁸שמש זורחת על כל נגלתה	16 ᴹ
גבורתיו:	לספר נפלאות ייי:		⁹לא הספיקו קדושי אל	17ab ᴹ
להחזיק	להתחזק לפני כבודו:		¹⁰אימֿץ אלהים צבאיו	17cd ᴹ אומץ
	ובכל מערומיהם יתבונן:		¹¹תהום ולב חקר	18 ᴹ
	ומגלה חקר נסתרות:		¹²מֿחוה חליפות נֿהיות	19 ᴹ ונהיות
חלף מנ׳ כ׳ דבר:	ולא חלפֿו כל דֿבר:		¹³לֿא נֿעדר ממנו כל שכל	20 ᴹ
מהעולם׳	אחד הוא מעֿולם:		¹⁴גבֿ[ור]ֿת חֿכמתו תכן	21ab ᴹ גבורות
צרך	ולא צריֿך לכל מבין:		¹⁵לֿא גֿ[אסף לא נאצל	21cd ᴹ
לכל צרוך הכל נשמע:	זהֿ על זה חלףֿ טובֿוֿ (v. 23b):		¹⁶הואֿ חֿ[י ו]ֿעֿמֿד לעֿדֿ	23a/25a ᴹ וקים
[לטוֿהרֿ:	תוֿארֿ]		¹⁷וימי ישבֿ[ע] לֿ[הֿ]בֿ[יֿ]טֿ הֿדֿם	25b/43:1a ᴹ

42:16 זורֿחֿת B S | זהרת M G · ייי B | אדני M · על כל B S | מלא M G · 42:17ab הספיקו B | השפיקו M · נפלאות ייי B | גבורתיו Bmg | כל נפלאתיו M G
S · 42:17cd אומץ Bmg | אמֿץ M · אלהים B | אדני M · להתחזק B M | להחזיק Bmg · 42:18 ובכל מערומיהם B | ובמערמיהם M · +42:18cd
רות Bmg · מעולם B M | מהעולם Bmg · 42:21cd צריֿך B | צרך Bmg | צרךֿ] M · 42:23a/25a/23b הואֿ B | הכל M · עֿמֿד B M | וקים Bmg · טובו B | טובֿ M | ומבֿיט אתיות עולם [ ] | כי ידע עליון כל M · 42:20 כל שכל B G S | שכל M · חלפו B | חלף מנו Bmg | עֿבֿרו] M · 42:21ab גבֿ[ור]ֿת B M | גבר
Bmg | תואר M · הֿדֿם B | הֿדֿם Bmg M · 42:25b ומי B | וימי Bmg · והכל נשמר M · הכל נשמע B | הכל נשמע Bmg | כל צרך M | ו]כל צרך B | לכל צרך Bmg | הֿבֿל ישמע M | ולכל צֿוֿרֿ B · טובֿם M· הודם M

L. 8 [42:16] זורֿחֿת — The reading of these letters is clear in the on-line digital image.

L. 11 חֿקר — Note the apparent Babylonian vowel marking /o/, which indicates that this is a participle.

L. 12 [42:19] Verse 18c-d is missing in H^B, though present in H^M, as well as the versions. מֿחוה — The *mem* is faint but legible and clear.

L. 13 [42:20b/20a] לֿא — The *lamed* is faint, but legible and clear. The *aleph* is attested by just a trace of the upper left corner and an even fainter trace of the upper right corner. נֿעדר — The *nun* is attested by a small trace of its top most part. The *ayin* is clear from the tips of its upper arms and lower base line. מנו — The final *vav* almost looks like a *nun*.

L. 14 [42:21] גבֿ[ור]ֿת — The top tip of the *bet* is visible, as is a faint trace of the verticle line. The bottom left foot of the *tav* is visible, as is a trace of the upper left tip. חֿכמתו — The initial three letters are difficult to read. The *khet*'s two vertical strokes can be seen, both their upper tips and their lower tips. The *kaph* has a relatively short top part and a faint base. The top part of the *mem* and its base are visible, as is the lower tip of its diagonal.

L. 15 [42:21] אֿסף — The *aleph* is attested by what would seem to be the foot of its lower left leg and a smudge that is presumably the lower right foot of its diagonal. Given the broadness of the mark that we interpret as the *aleph*'s lower left foot, it seems unlikely that this is the remnant of a *vav*. The *samek* is only attested by its top horizontal bar and perhaps the very slightest trace of its bottom edge.

L. 16 [42:23a/25a] No trace of 42:22 survives in H^B. חֿ[יֿ — The bottom of the two legs of the *khet* are visible, though these could conceivably be interpreted in other ways. עֿמֿד — Only the upper left tip of the *ayin* is seen above the hole, while the lower left tip of its base is found beneath the hole. The *mem* is attested by a trace of its upper right corner, as well as its base (beneath the lacuna) and the lower left tip of its diagonal, just to the left of the base. The *dalet*'s top line is seen above the hole and a trace of the bottom of its leg can be seen beneath the hole. לעֿדֿ — The very tops of the letters are legible, as well as their extreme bottom edges.

The word is followed by offset marks from the preceding folio page (IX verso) that correspond to the phrase ובבית in Sir 42:10d.

L. 17 [42:25b/43:1a] לֿ[הֿ]בֿ[יֿ]טֿ — The *bet* is only attested by the very edge of its top mark. The trace could easily be interpreted as another letter. The *tet* is preserved by two traces of the tops of its arms. Their approximate distance from each other encourages this identification, though in the end, it is difficult to be certain of the letter. The distance between the *lamed* and these traces would fit the reconstruction proposed above exactly, according to the spacing of מרביט in the following line. The next marks could conceivably be read הדם (cf. הודם H^M) or something similar. The very faintest square shape may be the final *mem*, above which is a flourish that seems similar to those found on final *mems*. The marks further to the left seem, in part, to be offset traces from IX verso, 17 Sir 42:11a = חֿזֿקֿ מֿסֿרֿ. The descender of the *qoph* is clearest. Just to the right of this is a squarish mark, which presumably, derives from an offset *mem* (preserved by a short base and traces of its diagonal line). Superimposed on this offset *mem* is a correctly oriented *tav*, the first letter of 43:1a. This *tav* is fully attested and is rather easy to make out (in comparison to the other letters). Based on this identification, one may guess that a correctly oriented *vav* was probably superimposed (and indistinguishable from) the vertical line of the offset *mem* or the vertical line of the offset *qoph*. If one continues looking to the left, then one sees the bottom traces of what could be a correctly-oriented *aleph* or a *resh* (if not another letter) along the bottom edge of the hole. In any case, the foot of the *tav* at the beginning of the stich creates a right angle in the interior of the offset *mem* and makes the offset *mem* look like a final *mem*. The right leg of the *tav* is presumably superimposed on the offset *vav* of מֿוֿם. To the right of this is an offset *samek*, somewhat narrow, but not quite as narrow as the *samek* of סרה in Sir 42:11b at the end of XI verso, 17. Especially clear are the traces of its bottom half. Above the traces of the offset *samek* is what appears to be the flourish of a correctly oriented final *mem*, which may have left faint traces just to the right of the offset *samek*.

16 Le soleil levant se manifeste sur toute chose,
   ainsi la gloire de YYY sur toutes ses œuvres.
17 Les saints de Dieu ne parviennent pas
   à raconter les merveilles de YYY (mg. de ses prouesses).
   Dieu affermit (mg. La force (de Dieu ce sont)) ses armées
   pour résister (mg. pour (les) renforcer) devant sa gloire.
18 Il a sondé l'abîme et le cœur
   et discernera toutes leurs nudités.
19 Il est celui qui déclare les changements, (mg. et) les existants
   et celui qui révèle la profondeur des choses cachées.
20 L'intelligence ne lui fait pas défaut
   et rien ne le surpasse (mg. ne lui échappe).
21 Il a mesuré sa pu[issa]nte sagesse (mg. les puissances (de sa sagesse)),
   depuis toujours (mg. depuis l'éternité), il est un.
   Il n[e s'ac]croît pas, ni ne se rétracte
   et n'a besoin (mg. idem) d'aucun instructeur.
23a Il est vi[vant et] demeure (mg. subsiste) pour toujours,
25a de l'un à l'autre, sa beauté excède.
23b (mg. Pour chaque besoin, tout a été entendu.)
25b Et qui peut se rassa[sier] à l[a] v[u]e de leur gloire ?
1a Beauté[   ]pureté.

16 The rising sun reveals itself over all,
   and the glory of YYY is over all his works.
17 Even God's holy ones do not succeed
   in recounting the wonders of YYY (mg. of his mighty deeds).
   God fortifies (mg. the strength of God) his hosts,
   to withstand (mg. to strengthen (them)) his glory.
18 He probes abyss and heart,
   contemplating all their intimate parts.
19 The one declaring what changes (mg. and) what is to be,
   and the one revealing the depth of hidden things.
20 No insight is lacking from him,
   no matter escapes him (mg. no matter escapes from him).
21 He has measured his mi[gh]ty wisdom (mg. the mighty deeds of (his wisdom)),
   from of old (mg. from of old), he is one.
   He is n[ot ad]ded to or subtracted from,
   he has no need (mg. idem) for any instructor.
23a He is a[live and] remaining (mg. enduring) forever,
25a This one to the next, his beauty is surpassing.
23b (mg. For every need, all is considered.)
25b And, who can get their fi[ll] at [se]eing their glory?
1a Beauty[   ] (are) pristine.

42:17 הספיקו — For the meaning "succeed," see Jastrow (1903, 1016). קדושי אל — The expression designates the angels. See, among other examples, the same expression in 11Q13 II 9.

42:18 מערומיהם — The word is found in 2 Chr 28:15. A similar thought is conveyed in Job 26:6: "Sheol is naked before him" (NRSV). The same word is found in Sir 51:19 in the version from 11Q5, with the same verb as here (בין in the *hithpolel*).

42:19 חליפות נהיות — We assume that this is a simple mistake for חליפות ונהיות as implied by the marginal reading. Alternatively, it is conceivable that the sense of the phrase without *vav* was "future changes." The temporal situation of חליפה is ambiguous, though the Greek and the Syriac imply reference to past time. Similarly, נהיות is ambiguous as to its temporal reference, though the Greek and Syriac imply a reference to the future. Note too that in Sir 48:25, נהיות refers to the future.

42:20 ולא חלפו — Far less likely is the interpretation "no matter changes him," which presumes the rare *piel* of the verb. חלף מנו — One would expect ממנו, but the spelling מנו is very common in *piyyutim* from the sixth-century CE.

42:21 תכן — The verb is understood as the *piel* of תכן here, paralleling the sense of the Greek. However, the same letters could be interpreted as the *niphal* imperfect of כון, meaning "his mighty wisdom will be established," which would parallel the meaning in the Syriac. אחד — For the meaning of this word, see Deut 6:4; Gen 40:5 and Job 31:15. נ[אֹסף] — The *aleph* accords with the reading in the Masada scroll, but is unexpected, given the context. The two roots אסף and יסף are somewhat similar in form and meaning and are occasionally interchanged by scribes. The *niphal* of the root אסף would imply "he is not gathered" or "he does not perish," though in close proximity to נאצל, one would expect the *niphal* of יסף "to add," an interpretation encouraged by the Greek. צריך — The text has the more common adjective, while the margin apparently has the rarer *qal* participle/perfect. Cf. the common variation between צריך, the adjective, and צרך, the noun; see Sir 13:6ᴬ and the note.

42:23b (Margin) The misplacement of this marginal phrase is inspired by the similarity to the last colon of 21. צרוך — This is presumably the Aramaic cognate of the Hebrew צורך, found in the text of line 18.

42:23a קים — This marginal alternative is presumably the adjective "enduring," which is nearly synonymous with the participle עמד in the main text. The expression חי וקים comes probably from Dan 6:27 (in Aramaic) and is frequent in rabbinic liturgy (see among other *Berakhot HaAftarah* 9) as well as in medieval *piyyutim*.

42:23b-24 These verses are misplaced and located at the top of XII verso after 43:1. Verse 23b is also duplicated in the margin after 25a.

42:25a Note that portions of this verse are found in lines 16, 17 and in the margin at the top of XII verso. זה על זה — The construction is frequent in Mishnaic Hebrew with the meaning "each other" (m. ʿErub 6:1; m. B. Meṣ. 6:1; etc.). חלף — Although presumably a *qal* or *piel* verb, the exact nuance of this word is hard to know. Kister (1988, 357–58) suggests a nuance "to bequeath," "to cause to pass," though we prefer a figurative sense of the *qal* similar to that found in Isa 8:8: "to overflow" (where חלף occurs together with שטף and עבר). This fits the context of surpassing beauty, implied in the second stich. טוב — The sense is again ambiguous. Kister (1988, 357–58) suggests a nuance "beauty," though "bounty" also seems possible. וימי — This seems to be a simple graphic mistake for מי (a metathesis and duplication of the mater lectionis). Cf. the alternative in the marginal note on the verso. The meaning "my days" does not make any sense

MS.Heb.e.62 XII verso

	ולכל צוֹרֶךְ הכֹּל ישמע:	¹⁸ וְעֹצֶם שמים מַרביט הדרו	43:1b/42:23b ᴹ
	ולא עשה מהם שיב[:]	¹ כלם שונים זה מזה	42:24 ᴹ

מופיע בצאתוֹᴹ 43:2 / יו הם 25a / 43:1a 43:1b

Chapter 43

	מה נורא מעשי ייי	²שמש מביעֽ בצרתו חמה	43:2 ᴹ	מופיע בצאתו
	לפני חרבו מי יתכלכל:	³ בהצהירו ירתיח תבל	3 ᴹ	
שלוח שׁ׳ יסיק	שׁוֹלח שמש ידלי֗ק הרים:	⁴כור נפוח מהם מצוֹק	4ab ᴹ	מוצק
	ומנורה תכוה עין:	⁵לשׁאון מאור תגמר נושבת	4cd ᴹ	לשון
ינצה	ודבריו ינצ֗ח אביריו:	⁶כי גָ֗דיל ייי עושהו	5 ᴹ	כי גדול עליון עשה
	ממשלת קץ ואות עולם:	⁷וגם ירח ירח עתותֽ שבות	6 ᴹ	עת עת עת עת
	וחפץ עתה בתקופתו:	⁸בם֗ מועד וזמני חוק	7 ᴹ	בו מו׳ וממנו

43:1a תואר B Bmg| תאר֗ M · רקע Bmg | ורקיע M · לטהֹר֗ B | על טהר Bmg| לטהר M · 43:1b/(42:23b) ועצם B Bmg| עצם M · מרביט B| מרביט Bmg M · מביע B G | נהרה Bmg| נהוֹרוֹ M · 42:24 שונים B| שֹ[ני]ם M · מזה B| לעמתו M · 43:2 מביע בצרתו B| מופיע בצאתו M · 43:3 ע[ליו]ן M · ייי B| ולפני M · ולפני B G S| חרבו B G S| תכלבל M · יתכלכל B G S| מעשי M G S· מה M· כלי M G S· נכסה B| חמה B | Bmg M · 43:4cd לשאון B| י֗שיק M · יסיק Bmg G S| ידליק B| שולח Bmg M · שלוח B| מצוק Bmg M · מוצק M G · מעשי B | מהם Bmg M · 43:4ab M· יתכנ[ו]לל B | 43:6 אדני עשהו M · עליון עשה Bmg| ייי עושהו B | גדול Bmg M · גדיל M · 43:5 תג[מ]יר M· תגמר B| לשון Bmg M· לשן B| יר[ח] יאריח B| ירח ירח M · 43:7 בם B| לו M · וזמני B| וממנו Bmg M · חוק B| חג M · Bmg M · עד עת Bmg2 | עד עת Bmg1 | עתות M· עתות שבות B | M·

L. 18 [43:1b/42:23b] שמים — The final *mem* is hard to read. It has a very thick left vertical mark and a base that is actually angled downward. The rightside and top of the letter are particularly faint. מרביט — The *mem* is attested by its right vertical side and its base line. הדרו — Offset marks (specifically the initial *vav* and *he* from והושבתך in XI verso, 18 Sir 42:11d) obscure the *dalet*, *resh*, and *vav* of הדרו, the last word of this colon. ולכל — Offset marks from the word עם in 42:11c can be seen at the base of the *lamed* and *kaph*. צוֹרֶךְ — Offset marks from וקהלת appear amongst these letters. The marginal material appears at the top of the verso, running perpendicular to the text.

L. 1 [42:24] שיב — The last letter is clearly a *bet* not an *aleph*, as others have suggested. The *bet* is attested by traces of its top, vertical side and its base, which angles slightly downward.

L. 4 [43:4a] מהם — The final *mem* looks as though the scribe first started to write an initial/medial *mem* (presumably due to confusion with the first letter in the following word), but then corrected it to final *mem*.

L. 5 [43:4c] תגמר — The leftward bottom extension of the *gimel* looks thicker than other *gimels*.

L. 6 [43:5] ינצה — The last letter is certainly a *he* with a big head.

L. 7 [43:6] ירח ירח — In the second word, the *khet* is written in an awkward way and the marks could also be read ירדו "they go down," though this makes less sense. ואות — There is also some offsetting between the letters of this word. שבות — Although many editions have שכות, the second letter is quite similar in shape to the *bet* of נושבת in 43:4, line 5 above.

L. 8 [43:7] וחפץ — Offsetting from the *resh* of רבה in XIII recto, 8 Sir 43:23a creates a bar that links the *vav* to the *khet*, making it look as if חופץ is the correct reading. עָתה — While Levi (1901, 1:68), Smend (1906b, 45) and Segal (1958, 388) read עשה, our reading is certain.

42:25–43:1 ועצם שמים | לטהר — The same words occur in different order in Exod 24:10.

43:1 מרביט — The word is a mistake for מביט. The *resh* may result from dissimilation of gemination through rhotacization (as with דרמשק for דמשק "Damascus," see Bergsträsser 1918, 1:§20b). If so, then the *resh* is further encouraged by phonetic similarity with the alternative biblical form of שֶׁבֶט, i.e., שַׁרְבִיט "scepter." נבט should have a causitive meaning here (see DCH 5:587; Jastrow 1903, 868; Tg. Sheni Esth. 1:2).

42:23b ישמע — The subject of the verb שמע may be God, "He hears all."

42:25–43:1 (Margin) רקע — Presumably, this word is a verb, as it is missing a *yod* (i.e., רקיע) like that found in Hᴹ. מביט נהרה — This word may be an infinitive with a 3ms pronominal *he* suffix (note נהֹרוֹ in Hᴹ).

42:24 שיב — Presumably, this is a mistake for שוב, with the meaning "again," as in Rabbinic Hebrew.

43:2a בצרתו — If one assumes that the letters represent a Hebrew word, then the phrase is hard to interpret. Neither "in its form" (Rabbinic Hebrew צורה) or "in its distress" (Biblical Hebrew צרה) lend themselves to the context. On the other hand, if this is a loanword from Aramaic, then the letters make perfect sense as an infinitive construct from the root צרה. Note that the verb צרי (usually "to cleave") is used in Syriac, in relation to the sun, with the sense "to shine" (see the example from the Chronology of Elias of Nisibis, listed in LS³, s.v.). Other examples of defectively spelled infinitives construct from etymological III-*vav/yod* roots are found in Hᴮ in 46:16 and 49:7.

43:2b See Psa 66:3. מעשי ייי — The final *yod* would be an orthographic variant for the singular מעשה (Golinets 2020, 53–55).

43:3 בהצהירו — This may be a denominative verb from צהרים "noon." Cf. the *hiphil* of ערב with the meaning "to set" (4Q394 3–7 i 18,; m. Neg. 14:3, cf. HALOT).

43:4 כור נפוח — See Job 41:12 (כְּדוּד נָפוּחַ). The Greek presupposes כור נפוח as *Vorlage*, an expression found in 1QHᵃ V 16 (כור נופחים). מהם — These letters are also difficult to interpret. As they stand, they look like the prepositional phrase "from them," the antecedent being the "works of the Lord" mentioned in 43:2b. However, this reading is surprising given the consistent reference to a single entity, i.e. the sun, in the other stichs. Therefore, it seems better to understand the letters as a mistake for מֵחֵם, the *hiphil* participle of חמם, attested in Rabbinic Hebrew with the meaning "to heat" (for confusion of *he* and *khet* see Sir 16:11dᴬ and note). מצוק — See 1 Sam 2:8. The word is from צוק and is a biform of יצק "to pour". It and the marginal reading מוצק both refer to what is refined in an oven. יסיק — The marginal alternative (*hiphil* of נשק/שלק, see BDB and HALOT) is an Aramaism

1b Sa gloire rend visible le ciel lui-même
23b et pour chaque besoin, il entend tout.
   (mg. [25a] De l'un à l'autre, la beauté excède,
   [25b] et qui peut se rassasier à la vue de (leur) beauté ?
   [43:1a] Il étend la beauté du ciel sur la pureté,
   [43:1b] le ciel lui-même contemple son éclat.)
24 Tous ceux-là diffèrent l'un de l'autre
   et il n'a fait aucun d'eux, de nouveau.

Chapitre 43

2 Le soleil émet de la chaleur par son rayonnement (mg. brille quand il se lève),
   combien redoutables sont les œuvres de YYY ?
3 Lorsque qu'il est à son zénith, il fait bouillir la terre,
   devant sa chaleur, qui peut tenir ?
4 Une fournaise ardente *chauffe* le minerai (mg. idem),
   la radiation (mg. l'irradiation) du soleil embrase (mg. enflamme) les montagnes.
   Au fracas de l'astre, (le monde) habité est anéanti (mg. La langue de l'astre anéantit le monde habité)
   et à sa lumière, l'œil est brûlé.
5 Car grand est YYY son créateur (mg. Car il est grand, le Très-Haut, le créateur)
   et (par) ses paroles, il illumine (mg. fait briller) ses puissants.
6 Et aussi, la lune déambule selon des périodes cycliques (mg. 1. saison après saison ; mg. 2. jusqu'au moment),
   pour gouverner le temps, signe éternel.
7 Parmi eux, les fêtes et les temps légaux (litt. les temps du décret),
   (mg. par elle, les fêtes et à cause d'elle le décret)
   chaque chose en son temps (advient) selon son cycle.

1b His majesty makes the sky itself visible,
23b and for every need, he hears all.
   (mg. [42:25a] This one to the next, beauty is surpassing.,
   [42:25b] and who can get their fill at seeing (their) beauty?
   [43:1a] Beauty of heaven he has spread according to purity,
   [43:1b] The sky itself, contemplates its brightness.)
42:24   All of them are different, this from this,
   he did not make any of them again.

Chapter 43

2 The sun emits heat in its shining (mg. shines when it goes forth),
   how awe-inspiring is the work of YYY.
3 When it is at its peak, it makes the world boil,
   Before its heat, who can endure?
4 A well-fired furnace *heats* the ore (mg. idem);
   the one who sends (mg. the ray of) the sun ignites (mg. sets on fire) mountains.
   At the uproar of the luminary (mg. the luminary's tongue (annihilates)) the habitable world is annihilated,
   and from its fire the eye is scorched.
5 For, great is YYY, its maker (mg. For he is great, the Most High, the maker),
   and (by) his words he lights up (mg. illuminates) his valiant ones.
6 Truly, the moon wanders at recurring seasons (mg. 1. season after season; mg. 2. until the time),
   for the government of time, an eternal sign.
7 Among them (mg. by it) (are) the feast and times that are decreed (lit., the times of the decree) (mg. and from it (the decree)),
   each matter at its time (happens) by its circuit.

(see Isa 44:15; Ezek 39:9) with the same meaning as the verb in the main text. שולח — The active participle indicates either the act of "setting on fire" (e.g. Judg 1:8) or "commanding" (see 1 Kgs 5:23; 20:9). נושבת — Without a preceding noun like ארץ or עיר, the participle means "habitable world" in *piyyutim* (see Maagarim). מנורה — The word נור appears here with the 3ms pronominal *he* suffix with "sun" as antecedent or 3fs with "tongue" as antecedent.

43:5 גדיל — This is either a plene spelling of the *qal* participle, גָּדֵל "high, lofty," or a spelling mistake for גדול. ודבריו — As it stands, דבריו cannot be the subject, but may be a mistake for דברו. We interpreted it as instrumental, yet without a preposition, though this is unusual. ינצח — The verb means "to make shine, glorify" in Rabbinic Hebrew and Aramaic. In Aramaic, the word can also denote the idea of "making victorious," a meaning that is also possible here. ינצה — The marginal alternative is difficult to interpret. It is read as a *piel*, a biform of the Hebrew root נצץ "to shine" (see HALOT, 717, Sir 43:13ᴮ; Ezek 1:7 and the Greek word ἀνάπτω corresponding to נצה in Lam 4:15).

43:6 וגם ירח עתות שבות — The second ירח could be a defective writing of the imperfect of ארח or a denominative form of ירח, implying the translation "the moon moons." Alternatively, the line could be translated "Truly, moon after moon the season returns" but this does not fit the rest of the verse, which clearly speaks about the moon as a heavenly body.

43:7 בם — The translation implies "seasons" as antecedent. Yet, if the antecedent is the sun and moon, then the text may refer to the lunisolar calendar (see Yadin 1999, 187–88). וחפץ עתּה — The words are difficult to interpret in this context. The phrase is interpreted above in light of Qoh 3:1, taking חפץ to mean "matter" and understanding עתה as עת with a 3ms pronominal *he* suffix (cf. Reymond 2018c, 226–244). Alternatively, the line could be translated "Delight, now, in its circuit."

MANUSCRIPT B

בתשובתו	מה נורא בהשתנותו:	⁹חדש בחדשו הוא מתחדש	8ab ᴹ	כשמו והוא
מערץ מש̇ר̇יק ב̇̇׳אל̇׳	מרצׄף רקיע מזהירתו:	¹⁰כלי צבא נבלי מרום	8cd ᴹ	
ישון	ואורׄ מזהיר במרומי אל:	¹¹תואר שמים והדר כוכב	9 ᴹ	
נהדרה	ולא ישׄח באשמרותם:	¹²בדבר אל יעמד חק	10 ᴹ	
לא	כי מאד נאׄדרה בכׄבוד:	¹³ראה קשת וברך עושׄיה	11 ᴹ	עושה
תנצח זלקים	ויד אל נטתה בגבורתׄו[:	¹⁴חוקׄ הקיפה בכבודה	12 ᴹ	הוד הקיפה בכבודו
	ותנצח זיקות במ̇ש̇[פט:]	¹⁵גבורתו תתוה ברק	13 ᴹ	
	ויעף עבים כעיט	¹⁶למׄען ברא אוצר	14 ᴹ	למענו
[ ]		¹⁷גׄבורתׄוׄ [ ]∘∘ [יׄ	15 ᴹ	
	זלעפות צפׄון סופה וסערה:	¹⁸ ᵒᵒקול רעׄמׄו יחול ארצו	17ab ᴹ	

43:8ab בחדשו B | כשמו Bmg M G S · והוא B M | הוא Bmg · 43:8cd מרצף B M | מערץ M · 43:9 תור B | תואר M · והדר B | והוד M · ואורו מזהיר M · B | עשיה M · 43:11 באשמרתם B | באשמרותם Bmg · ישון B M | ישח M | אדני B אל Bmg · במרומי M · במרמ̇י] M · 43:10 B במרומי Bmg M G · עדי משריק Bmg B | עשיה M · עושיה Bmg M · חוק B | הוד Bmg · חוג M G · בכבודה B M | בכבודו Bmg · אל B נהדרה Bmg | נהדר M · בכבוד B · נׄהׄתׄוׄ M · 43:12 נאדרה B | לא Bmg · 43:13 גבורתו B גערתו M Bmg2 · בקר B | ברק Bmg 2 · ברד M G · ותנצח B M | תנצח Bmg 1 | תזנח Bmg 2 · זיקות B M | זלקים Bmg1 | יחול B יחיל Bmg M · זלעפות B | עלעול M יקום Bmg2 · פט] במ̇שׄ B Bmg2 | משפט M · 43:14 למען B | למענו Bmg M · ברא B | פרע M G · 43:17ab Bmg G · צפׄון B G | > Bmg M · 43:16 ובכוחו Bmg | ובכחו M · יזעים Bmg · יניף M · אימתו Bmg · אמרתוׄ M G · תחרף Bmg | תחריף M ·

L. 10 [43:8d] מזהירתו — Offset marks above the *he* and *tav* correspond to the *mem* and *lamed* in the first words of XIII recto, 10 Sir 43:25a.

L. 11 [43:9] משריק — The *qoph* exhibits a corrective widening of its head.

L. 13 [43:11] בׄכׄבוד — The top of the first *bet* is visible, as well as its bottom right corner. The *kaph* is only attested by its top horizontal mark. The second *bet* is attested by its top and bottom horizontal lines.

L. 14 [43:12] לא — The marginal alternative seems to have a *holem* dot above the *aleph*. בגבורתׄו — The initial *bet* is clear based on its edges. The characteristic bottom of the *gimel* is attested beneath the hole, making its identification certain. The following letters are only attested by their tops, and in the case of the second *bet* and *vav*, by a blurry mark beneath the hole. Only the top right corner of the *he* is preserved.

L. 15 [43:13] במ̇ש̇[פט:] — The initial *bet* seems clear from the traces that survive. The left tip of the letter is preserved, as well as its right tip. Beneath the hole, the bottom right corner is preserved, and to the left, the left tip of the base can be seen. According to the marks, the base line seems to be angled downwards. The *mem* is clear from the preservation of the bottom of its diagonal line beneath the hole, and perhaps the bottom right corner. The top edges of the letter can also be seen above the hole. The *sin/shin* is attested by the top tip of its right arm and its middle arm, as well as its base. תנצׄח — This marginal alternative is difficult to read. The initial *tav* seems clear based on its left foot. The *nun* could also be a *zayin*. The *tsade* could also be a *nun*, thus allowing for תזנח, as found in the other marginal alternative. בקר — There is a discoloration in the paper at the center of the *bet*, which is unlikely to be a *dagesh*. There is no *holem* vowel visible (as Ben-Ḥayyim [1973, 51] reads). במׄ — The *mem* can be identified by its short base line. זלקים — While preceding editions read זיקים, the *lamed* is clear (see Reymond, 2019b, 170–80).

L. 16 [43:14] אוצר — The *resh* is only preserved by its top horizontal mark. To the left of a hole are offset marks from the *mem* and *ayin* of the word מעט from XIII recto, 16 Sir 43:32b. עבׄים — The *ayin* is clear. The *bet* is only attested by its top edge and a blurry mark beneath the hole. A mark above the hole may be the remnants of a *yod*. The final *mem* seems more clear, with the characteristic flourish of its upper left corner still visible, as well as traces of all of its sides. כעיט — The remaining traces could accommodate the reading of the Masada text.

L. 17 [43:15] גׄבורתׄוׄ [ ]∘∘ [יׄ — Our reading is based on the Masada text, as the remaining traces fit its reading perfectly. A possible *lamed* in the middle of the line could also just be an offset trace.

L. 18 [43:17ab] רעׄמׄו יחול — Although the bottom traces of the letters are all that is preserved, the reading is certain. The top of the *khet* is preserved as an offset mark on XIII recto, in the space beneath line 17. זלעפות — The *zayin* is preserved by its head and a very faint trace of its vertical. Very faint traces to the right of the *zayin*, which look like a *he/khet* and perhaps a *vav*, are actually the result of bleed through from the recto side of folio XII, where the same marks appear due to offsetting from the word והושבתךׄ in XI verso, l. 18 (Sir 42:11d).

43:8ab חדש בחדשו — Cf. Num 28:14 and Isa 66:23. Alternatively, בחדשו alone could be a distributive phrase, analogous to ביומו in Deut 24:15. כשמו — The marginal alternative makes the pun on the root חדש explicit. בהשתנותו — In Rabbinic Hebrew, the *hithpael* of שנה has a passive sense "to be changed," though here, the stem has a reflexive sense, as is common in Biblical Hebrew. In Biblical Hebrew, the verb in the *hithpael* is translated "to disguise oneself."

43:8cd כלי — The form could be singular, referring to the moon, or plural, referring to the stars. Lexically, it could be a jewel, a weapon or container. נבלי — The phrase נבלי שמים refers to clouds in Job 38:37, but it must refer to luminaries in the present context. Its lexical meaning is uncertain and it could also mean "jars" or "skin-bottle." The word is missing in the Greek and the Syriac, and could have been chosen here as a synonym for כלי. מרצף — This could be an active or passive participle (*piel* or *pual*), or a *mem*-preformative noun. The root can indicate stoking coals (cf. רצפה Isa 6:6), or paving a wall or a ceiling (cf. רצפה Ezek 40:17). מערץ — Based on the attestations of the verb in ancient Hebrew, one may assume that this is a *hiphil*, "inspires with awe" (note the defective spelling of the same participle in Isa 8:13), in which case the "firmament" would be the subject. מזהירתו — This is the *min* preposition followed by a verbal noun from the root זהר "to shine."

43:9 ואורו מזהיר — The antecedent of the pronominal suffix is not

8a Lune après lune (mg. La lune, selon son nom), elle se renouvelle,
8b combien redoutable lorsqu'elle se transforme (mg. lors de son retour) !
8c Joyau de l'armée céleste, harpes d'en haut,
8d qui fait luire (mg. qui rend effroyable) le firmament de son éclat.
9 Beauté du ciel et splendeur d'étoile,
sa lumière brille dans les hauteurs divines. (mg. Parure brillante dans les hauteurs divines.)
10 Par la parole de Dieu, le décret perdure,
il ne faiblit pas (mg. il ne s'endort pas) durant leurs (i.e. les étoiles) veilles.
11 Observe l'arc en ciel et bénis son créateur (mg. le créateur),
car il est extrêmement magnifique (mg. honoré) par sa gloire.
12 Il entoure la limite (s.e. de la voûte céleste) de sa gloire (mg. Il enveloppe la splendeur de sa gloire)
et la main de Dieu (mg. et aucune (main) ne) l'a étendue avec puissance.
13 Sa puissance dessine l'éclair
et illumine des brandons (mg. 1. des éclairs) par décret. (mg. 2. Sa menace dessine le matin,
faisant luire les créatures par dé[cret.])
14 Afin de créer (mg. Pour cela (il a créé)) un réservoir
et faire planer les nuages comme des rapaces.
15 Sa puissance [   ]
[   ]
17a (À) la voix de son tonnerre, sa terre tremble.
17b rafale du nord, tornade et tempête.

8a Moon by moon (mg. is like its name), it renews itself.
8b How awe-inspiring in its changing (mg. in its return)!
8c Jewel of the heavenly host, harps of the heights,
8d it sets aglow (mg. inspires awe) the firmament with its luster.
9 Beauty of sky and majesty of star,
its light shines in God's heights (mg. shining ornament (is) in God's heights).
10 Through the word of God order endures,
it does not weaken (mg. it does not sleep) in their (i.e., the stars') watch.
11 Observe the rainbow and bless its maker (mg. the maker),
for it is exceedingly magnificent (mg. honored) in (its) glory.
12 It encompasses the boundary with its glory (mg. it surrounds splendor with his glory)
the hand of God (mg. no (hand)) stretched it with might.
13 His might scribbles lightning,
it lights up fiery arrows (mg. 1. lightning) in judgment (mg. 2. His rebuke marks morning,
making all that lives glisten in j[udgment]).
14 For the purpose of creating (mg. for its sake (he created)) a storehouse,
and makes clouds soar like raptors[
15 His might [   ]
[   ]
17a At the sound of his thunder, his earth writhes,
17b gusts of the north, storm, and tempest.

God, since this would create redundancy in the stich, but may perhaps be "moon." משריק — See also, 50:7 and Dihi 2004, 695–697.

43:10 ישח — This is likely the *niphal* of שחח with the meaning "to weaken," as in Qoh 12:4. ישן — This form does not occur elsewhere, but it conforms to the tendency in later Hebrew for stative verbs to follow the paradigm of the active verb (see Kutscher 1974, 341–342 and van Peursen 2004, 403).

43:11 עושיה — This is a masculine singular participle with a 3fs suffix (see Isa 22:11; cf. Hos 2:16). עושה — The marginal reading may be grammatically the same (see Isa 45:18; Jer 33:2).

43:12 הקיפה — This is a *hiphil* from the root נקף. חוק — For the meaning "boundary," see Jer 5:22. Alternatively, as already noted by Lévi (1898, 70) and confirmed by H^M, חוק could have the same meaning as חוג, "circle" (see Prov 8:27; Job 26:10).

43:13 תנצח — See the note in 43:5. זיקות — It is conceivable that "comets" or "meteors" is meant. זלקים — The marginal alternative is only attested elsewhere in Syriac, where it means "lightning" (see Reymond 2019b, 169–88). תזנח — The Biblical Hebrew meaning, "to reject," does not fit the context. In Rabbinic Hebrew, another root with the same consonants, זנח, means "to shine," likely a reflex of Aramaic דנח "to shine" (see Jastrow 1903, 406). For the opposite phenomenon,

see 4Q210 1 ii 18 (the Aramaic דרחץ [corrected from ירחץ, pace Milik 1976, 288 who reads שרחץ] reflex of the Hebrew זרחץ).

43:14 למען ברא — Where the compound particle למען is followed by a verb, it is almost always an imperfect or an infinitive construct; the only sure example of a perfect is found with a stative verb in Josh 4:24. למענו — The marginal alternative could also be translated "for his own sake."

43:17ab יחול — One would expect the *hiphil*, as in the marginal reading (cf. the *ketiv/qere* in Ezek 30:16). זלעפות — The word designates a violent emotion, "rage," so that here it would refer to a violent wind.

43:16 Verse 16 is only attested in the marginal text, which follows the sequence of stichs in H^M, namely 17a/16a, 16b/17b. יעים — Note the occurrence of the same root and stem in 40:29. The verb זעם means "to curse, to taunt." The *hiphil* is attested in *piyyutim*. As already noted by commentators, it is likely a mistake for יזיע (for the *hiphil*, see Tannaitic Hebrew) from זוע "to tremble" (see H^M), perhaps due to a misunderstanding of חרף in the following stich. תחרף — The meaning "to annoy, taunt, reproach" fits the context with זעם, but the verb could have the meaning that it has in the Aramaic *pael* "to sharpen" (see also, the Syriac ܚܪܦܘܬܐ) or *aphel* "to urge." עלעול — This word, עַלְעוֹל "hurricane," may also be read as two words עַל עָוֶל ("on account of iniquity").

MANUSCRIPT B

MS.Heb.e.62 XIII recto	רד'	וכארבה ישכון דרתו:	¹בְּרֶ֯שֶׁף יניף שלגו	17cd ᴹ	כר'
		וממטרו יהמה לבב:	²תואר לבנֹה יֻ֯הֻ֯ה עינים	18 ᴹ	יהגה
		ויציץ כספיר ציצים:	³וגם כפור כמלח ישכון	19 ᴹ	ישפך
מקוה		וכרקב יקפיא מקורו:	⁴צינת רוח צפון ישיב	20 ᴹ	
		וכשרין ילבש מקוה:	⁵על כל מעמד מים יקרים		
וצור		ונוֹה צמחים כלהבה:	⁶יבול הרֹים כחרב ישיק	21 ᴹ	
רטב		פורע לדשן שרב:	⁷מרפא כל מערף ענן טל	22	טל פורע
אוצר		ויט בתהום אֹיים:	⁸מחשבתו תשיק רבה	23 ᴹ	משובתו
		לשמע אזננו נשתומם:	⁹יורדי הים יספרו קצהו	24 ᴹ	
		מין כל חי וגבורות רבה:	¹⁰שם פלאות תמהי מעשהו	25 ᴹ	מעשיו

43:17cd בְּרֶ֯שֶׁף B | כר' Bmg = כרשף G M | יניף B | יפרח M | ישכון B | ישכן M | דרתו B | רדתו M G · רדתו = Bmg | 43:18 תור M | לבנה M | תואר B | כסנה M | כספיר B | ויצמח M | ויציץ B | Bmg M | יהמה M | יתמיה M G · 43:19 ישפך B | Bmg M | יהג M | יהגה B | יהגה Bmg | M | לבנו M | B | 43:20 וכרקב B | מקורו M | מקור B | Bmg · מקוה B | M · 43:21 כחרב B | חֹרֶב M · 43:23 אים B M G | אוצר · Bmg | 43:24 אזננו B | צצים M · | נשמתם B | נשתומם M · 43:25 וגבורות B | וֹגְבֻ֯ו֯רֹת M | רבה B | רהב M ·

L. 1 [43:17cd] בְּרֶ֯שֶׁף — The *bet* is suggested by remnants of its top bar and the assumption that the marginal phrase is different than what is in the main text. Offset marks (from ולא עשה XII verso, 1 Sir 42:24b) appear in the middle of the line.

L. 2 [43:18] Offset marks (from חמה XII verso, 2 Sir 43:2) appear in the middle of the line.

L. 3 [43:19] ישכון — The *kaph* almost resembles a *pe* due to an offset mark from the horizontal line of the *lamed* of לפני in XII verso, 3 Sir 43:3b.

L. 5 [43:20] וכשרין — Traces of letters from bleedthrough are present in and around this word. Note especially, what looks like a *sin*, *shin* or *ayin* overlapping with the *shin* of וכשרין (see below). Note also the ascender of the *lamed* extending to the right at a 45 degree angle from the top of the *vav*. Extending to the right from the bottom tip of the *vav* is another mark at a 135 degree angle, which is interpreted as a *mem*. See the discussion at XIII verso, 5 Sir 44:3.

L. 7 [43:22] טל — Although this word likely belongs to the second stich, it is placed with the first. The *circellus* hangs between the stichs.

L. 8 [43:23] מחשבתו תשיק — The final *vav* of the first word and the initial *tav* of the second word are obscured by offset marks from the word עֹתָה in XII verso, 8 Sir 43:7b. Specifically, the *vav* of מחשבתו is obscured by the left foot of the *tav* of עֹתָה. The bottom right leg of the *tav* of תשיק is obscured by the base line of the *ayin* of עֹתָה.

43:17cd ברשף — The word may mean "flame" or "flash of lightning," as in Biblical Hebrew (see Ps 78:48; Song 8:6), or "bird," though the latter only occurs in Rabbinic Hebrew. The form כרשף in the margin allows for this latter meaning. דרתו — Although this seems like an obvious mistake, with its correction in the margin, it is conceivable that a scribe could have read this as the Aramaic word דרה "house, dwelling, settlement," which is fairly common in the dialects and appears in Qumran Aramaic. וכארבה ישכן — This would be translated more literally as "and like locust (that) settle." Note the use of the verb שכן with an adverbial accusative in Isa 33:16. The image of locusts settling (on a field) is also found (with the same vocabulary) in Ugaritic: CTA 14 ii 50–51 and iv 29: k(m) irby tškn šd.

43:18 לבנה — The Masada reading of this word, לבנו, suggests that the *he* may be a 3ms suffix and not the feminine morpheme. If it is the feminine morpheme, then the word is לבנה "white." יהגה — The word is difficult to interpret. The verb גהה is only attested in Hos 5:13 where it can mean "to take away" (see its meaning in Syriac) or "to weaken" (see the Greek and the Targum). The verb could be related to כהה "to weaken," which is often used to refer to the eyes (see Gen 27:1, Deut 34:7; 1 Sam 3:2; for interchanges between כ and ג see Reymond 2018b, 46). Alternatively, the verb could be a mistake for or variation of the *hiphil* imperfect of נגה "to illuminate," or a misspelling of the marginal alternative. יהגה — This verb can also be interpreted in different ways. It may be the less common verb הגה "to remove," which is how Yadin (1999, 190) interprets the corresponding verb in H^M (יהג), essentially "the whiteness turns eyes away." Alternatively, it may derive from the more common Biblical Hebrew verb הגה "to read, mutter, think." If so, then it may be the *piel* "to make think," like the *pael* in Syriac. וממטרו — This form can be understood as the noun "rain" ("his rain") or as an otherwise unattested verbal noun, "its fall" (see the Syriac *peal* ܢܦܠ; cf. the Greek). יהמה — The verb describes agitation, "pounding, wailing moaning," of the "heart" (its subject) in Jer 4:19 and 48:36.

43:19 ישפך — The verb is either in the *qal* with God as subject or in the *niphal* with frost as subject. יציץ — In a similar way, this verb may be either *qal* (with frost as subject) or *hiphil* (with God as subject). Although the Greek presumes that God is the subject in the first stich, the context of the poem suggests the subject is frost. ציצים — The word has numerous associations. In Biblical Hebrew, it is a blossom or a flower-like decoration, while in Rabbinic Hebrew it is also associated with tassels or fringe. Cf. Ugaritic ṣṣ "salt field."

(mg. [17a] La voix de son tonnerre fait trembler sa terre,

[16a] par sa force il raille les montages,

[16b] sa terreur provoque le vent du sud,

[17b] rafale du nord, tornade et tempête.)

17c Avec une flamme (mg. Comme des oiseaux), il répand sa neige

17d et comme une sauterelle, elle se pose sur sa demeure. (mg. et elle descend comme une sauterelle qui se pose.)

18 La beauté de sa blancheur affaiblit (mg. détourne) les yeux

et le cœur palpite à (la vue de) sa chute.

19 Et de même, le givre se dépose (mg. il se déverse) comme du sel

et fleurit comme un saphir de fleurs.

20 Il fait souffler le froid du vent du nord

et comme dans une outre il fige (l'eau de) sa source (mg. (l'eau) d'un bassin).

Il forme une croûte sur toute eau dormante

et comme d'une cuirasse le bassin s'habille.

21 Il brûle la récolte des montagnes comme la sécheresse

et les verts pâturages, comme une flamme.

22 (Mais) les gouttes des nuages guérissent tout,

il libère la rosée pour engraisser la terre brûlée (mg. le vert pâturage).

23 Sa pensée (mg. Son retour) fait déborder le grand (abîme)

et il étend des îles (mg. un entrepôt) dans l'abîme.

24 Les marins racontent ses limites,

à (les) écouter, nous sommes terrifiés.

25 Là sont les merveilles, les miracles de son œuvre (mg. ses œuvres),

les espèces de tous vivants et les puissances du grand (abîme).

(mg. [17a] The sound of his thunder makes his earth writhe,

[16a] with his might he taunts the mountains.

[16b] his terror heckles the south-wind,

[17b] hurricane, storm, and tempest.)

17c With flame (mg. like birds) he scatters his snow,

17d like locusts it settles on his dwelling (mg. its descent is like locusts that alight)

18 The beauty of its whiteness enfeebles (mg. turns away) the eyes,

the heart throbs at its fall.

19 Indeed, frost settles (marg. is poured out) like salt

and blossoms like the sapphire of flowers.

20 The cold of the north wind he causes to blow,

and like in a wine-skin he makes its source (mg. the pool) seize up;

he forms a crust over all still water,

and the pool dresses as though (in) armor.

21 The mountains' produce he burns like a drought,

and the sprouting meadow (mg. rock) like a flame.

22 (But), the cloud's dripping cures everything,

he frees the dew in order to nourish parched ground (mg. fresh crops).

23 His thought (mg. his return) makes the great (deep) overflow,

he spreads out islands (mg. a storehouse) in the deep.

24 Seafarers recount its limits,

at hearing (this), we are astonished.

25 There are the marvels, wonders of his work (mg. his works),

the variety of every living thing and the mighty things of the great (deep).

43:20 ישיב — From the root נשב. וכרקב — Probably not "rottenness," but "wine-skin" as perhaps in Job 13:28 (ἀσκός in LXX; see HALOT). The image of water seizing up as in a wine-skin recalls a widespread interpretation of Exod 15:8 (נֵד translated by זיק "wine-skin" in the Targums, cf. Ps 78:13 Tg, LXX). The relevance of this suggestion is enhanced by the following verb. יקפיא — The verb is used in the *hiphil* to describe "curdling" cheese in Job 10:10. In Rabbinic Hebrew, the *hiphil* is used to describe thickening of liquid by boiling. The *qal* is also used in Biblical Hebrew to describe the "congealing" of the deeps in Exod 15:8. יקרים — In Biblical Hebrew, the verb only occurs twice in the *qal* with an accusative direct object. In Rabbinic Hebrew, it appears in both the *qal* and the *hiphil*, the latter occurring without a direct object with the meaning "to form a membrane" (see Jastrow 1903, 1421). ילבש — This is presumably a *qal*, so that one can assume that the pool is the subject.

43:21 ישיק — The verb is from the root שלק (נשק), cf. Ezek 39:9. Note the homographic verb form in v. 23.

43:22 טל פורע — In the translation, we make an exception and follow the marginal alternative, which attempts to group the word "dew" with the following stich. This seems like a sensible correction, leading to the translation of the second stich as: "he frees the dew…" The root פרע is polysemic ("to neglect," "to pay," "to hasten," "to blossom") and it is difficult to know which meaning applies here. The meaning adopted here follows its usage in 43:14ᴹ.

43:23 תשיק — This is the Biblical Hebrew verb שוק "to overflow" used causatively. משובתו — The Biblical Hebrew word should mean "his apostasy." However, this makes no sense in relation to God. Presumably, the word could mean something more literal, like "turning back, return." In relation to God this might be a "reply" (cf. the Biblical Hebrew תשובה). The use of this word here may have been triggered by the following word שוק, since in Tg. Neof. to Gen 3:16, the word מתב translates the Hebrew תשוקה "desire" (see Joosten 2016, 22–23). רבה — The word רבה is used elliptically to refer to the sea (cf. "waters of the sea" in 4Q511 30, 4; and the expression תהום רבה in Amos 7:4; Gen 7:11; Isa 51:10; Psa 36:7; BDB, s.v., def. 2a).

43:24 יורדי הים — See Isa 42:10 and Ps 107:23. לשמע אזננו — See Job 42:5 and Ps 18:45.

43:25 רבה — See the note above for 43:23.

למענהו למען	26	¹¹לְמַעֲנוֹ יצלח מלאך	ובדבריו יפעל רצון:
	27	¹²עוֹד כאלה לא נוסף	וקץ דבר הוא הכל:
נגלה	28	¹³נִגְדְּלָהּ עוד כי לא נחקור	והוא גדול מכל מעשיו:
	29 ᴹ	¹⁴נוֹרָאִים מאד מאד	ונפלאות דבריו: גבורתו
	30 ᴹ	¹⁵מַגֶּ[ד]לִי יְיָ הרימו קול בכל תוכלו כי יש עוד מרומים תחליפו כח ואל תלאו כי לא ת
	32	¹⁶ורוב סתרי חזק מאלה	מעט ראיתי ממעשיו:
	33 ᴹ	¹⁷את הכל [○○	[ ] [לְ] [חָכְמָה:]

מרומ֯מָיו 30 ה[ת]חזקו אל תלאו כי לא תחקרו

Chapter 44

MS.Heb.e.62 XIII verso

		¹שבח אבות עולם	
	1 ᴹ	²אהללה נא אנשי חסד	ᵃאבותינו בדורותם: את
להם	2 ᴹ	³רב כבוד חלק עליון	וגדלו מימות עולם:
רודי	3ab	⁴דורי ארץ במלכותם	ואנשי שם בגבורתם: בגבורם
יו'	3cd ᴹ	⁵הַיוֹעצים בתבונתם בָּעוֹלָם	וחוזי כל בנבואתם:

43:30 עוד B G | אל ᴹ · 44:1 אבותינו B | (אב)ותינו Bmg ᴹ · את Bmg ᴹ | חלק B ᴹ | להם (חלק) Bmg · וגדלו B | וגדלו ᴹ · 44:3ab > ᴹ · 44:3cd היועצים B | ויעצים ᴹ · בָּעוֹלָם B | > ᴹ G · וחזי B | יו' Bmg | וחזי ᴹ

L. 13 [43:28] נִגְדְּלָהּ — The *nun* is faint, but perceptible. The *gimel* is only attested by its top tip. The *dalet* is attested by its top bar.

L. 14 [43:29] נוֹרָאִים — Traces of the middle three letters are visible on the edges of the lacuna, while the final *mem* seems clear given the presence of its top and base lines.

L. 15 [43:30] מַגֶּ[ד]לִי יְיָ הרימו — The first two letters are most likely a *mem* followed by a *gimel*. The *mem* is recognizable by its curved base, its right shoulder and the end of its oblique stroke. As for the *gimel*, there are traces of the end of the vertical and its leg (see already Cowley and Neubauer 1897, 18; Lévi 1904, 58; Smend 1906b, 47). After the *lamed*, the traces of letters perfectly fit the four expected *yods*. This line contains two verses without spaces, unlike the other lines. The last stich is especially cramped, where the word אל is spelled in its ligatured form. Verse 31 is missing.

L. 15 Margin [43:30] מְרוֹמְמָיו — The tops of the letters are hard to read since they are at the edge of the paper. The letters are also particularly faint. The initial *mem* is attested by traces of its distinctive diagonal line, as well as its base and right vertical mark. The *resh* is attested by its vertical mark, which is unlikely to be a *vav* or *zayin* because of the space between it and the next vertical mark, which is read as a *vav*. The second *mem* is also attested by faint traces of its diagonal, base, and right vertical lines. The third *mem* is the most difficult to read, as it is very faint and only ambiguous traces of it remain. The *yod* is implied by the fact that its mark does not descend like other letters. Its angled bottom touches the *vav*. תחליפו — The bottom of the legs of the *he* are visible, while its top is extremely faint. ואל — The negative particle has its ligatured form. יש — The *sin/shin* is very small and illegible, though it can be inferred from the context. תחקרו[ו] — The *khet* is attested by its right vertical mark and the bottom portion of its left vertical. The *qoph* is comparatively easy to read. Its curved head is separated from its descender. The *resh* is attested by a faint trace of its vertical mark.

L. 16 [43:32] ורוב סתרי חזק מאלה — This reading fits the traces and the available space and explains the Greek translation (πολλὰ ἀπόκρυφά ἐστιν μείζονα τούτων). Lévi (1904, 58) reads נסתרות (followed by Segal 1958, 290 and Vattioni 1968, 235). The reading וחזק נפלא (Smend 1906b, 47) נ֯[פ]ל֯א, followed by Ben-Ḥayyim, 52, by Accordance and QDTL (נ֯[פ]ל֯[א] וחֹזֶק) is too large for the available space. Moreover, the *lamed* would have been visible on the manuscript. Segal (1958, 290) suggested רוב סתרי חקר מאלה as a possible restoration, but there is no space between the trace of the *qoph* and the *mem*.

L. 5 [44:3] בָּעוֹלָם — The letters seem partially erased or worn. In addition, they seem to be written at a downward angle, in comparison to the rest of the line. They do not appear to result from bleedthrough or offsetting. The *bet* is attested by its bottom right corner, directly abutting the left edge of the final *mem*. On the recto to this page (XIII recto, 5 Sir 43:20), the base line of this *bet* appears in the *sin/shin* of וכשרין due to bleedthrough. The mark could also represent a number of other letters, a *kaph*, a *nun*, or a *mem*. The *ayin* on this page is only preserved by the faintest traces of the top tips of its two arms. In addition, bleedthrough traces of the bottom of its right arm are seen in the *sin/shin* of וכשרין in XIII recto, 5 Sir 43:20. The *vav* is fairly clear. At its base is a very short diagonal mark (extending from the upper left to the bottom right). This is an offset trace from the bottom flourish of the *vav* of ובא from XIV recto, 5 Sir 44:20. The *lamed* is clear from its diagonal and ascender, and is also found as a bleedthrough mark on XIII recto, 5 (coming out of the top of the *vav* of וכשרין). The *mem* is squarish and blurred. Its bottom and left lines are thicker than one would expect. Traces of this letter are also visible on the recto, just to the right of the word וכשרין. The marks could also conceivably represent בשלם, "in completing."

43:26 למענו — "Because of him" does not fit the context. The marginal reading למענהו, i.e. the preposition ל with the noun מענה, provides a better parallel with בדבריו. מלאך — Given the consistent references to natural phenomena up to this point (which are available for all to perceive), it seems incongruous for Ben Sira to mention a divine subordinate, "angel/messenger," here. Presumably, "messenger" is a metaphor (as "Rahab" is a metaphor for the deep in v. 25b of the Masada text), referring to one aspect of creation, perhaps "wind" (as "messenger" is used in Ps 104:4). יצלח — Alternatively, the word may mean "to prosper." Some ambiguity is probably intended here, at the end of the sequence of descriptions, so as to imply that God's angels are like the natural phenomena in that both are entirely subordinate to him and successful in all that he wishes them to do. Note also that the notion of hurrying to do God's will is reminiscent of the similar participial expression found several times in the Songs of the Sabbath Sacrifice: נמהרי רצונו "those eager to do his will" (e.g., 4Q403 1 i 20).

26 Grâce à lui (mg. 1. À sa voix, mg. 2. C'est pourquoi) (son) messager se précipite
   et par sa parole (sa) volonté est faite.
27 Comme cela, encore, nous n'ajouterons rien,
   la fin du discours est : il est tout.
28 Magnifions (mg. révélons) encore, car on ne peut pas sonder,
   car il est plus grand que toutes ses œuvres.
29 Immensément prodigieuses
   et merveilleuses sont ses paroles (mg. est sa puissance).
30 (Vous) qui magn[if]iez YYY, élevez la voix,
   autant que vous pouvez, car il y a encore davantage,
   hauteurs, renouvelez (votre) force,
   Ne vous épuisez pas, car vous ne [   ]
   (mg. Vous qui l'exaltez, renouvelez (votre) force,
   ne vous épuisez pas, car vous ne pourrez pas l'appréhender.)
32 De puissants mystères sont plus nombreux que ceux-là,
   j'ai vu bien peu de ses œuvres.
33 [   ] tout.
   [   ] la sagesse.

Chapitre 44

Éloge des pères ancestraux.

1 Je veux louer les hommes pieux,
   nos pères dans leurs générations.
2 Le Très-Haut (mg. leur) a attribué l'honneur en abondance
   et sa grandeur est depuis les jours éternels.
3 Générations (mg. gouverneurs) de la terre par leur royaume
   et hommes de renom par leur vaillance (mg. syn.),
   qui conseillent (mg. conseillers) par leur compréhension du monde
   et visionnaires de tout par leur prophétie,

26 Because of him (mg. 1. At his utterance, mg. 2. So that) (his) messenger speeds
   and by his words (his) will is done.
27 More like these we will not add,
   the end of the matter: he is all.
28 Let us magnify more (mg. reveal) though we cannot fathom
   for he is greater than all his works.
29 terribly awesome deeds,
   his words are (mg. his power is) wonderous.
30 You who ex[al]t the Lord, lift (your) voice,
   in all you are able, for yet there is more.
   O heights, remain strong
   grow not weary though you cannot [ ]
   (mg. O, (you) who praise him, remain strong, grow not weary though you cannot fathom.)
32 Potent mysteries are more numerous than these,
   I have seen few of his works.
   little have I seen of his works.
33 [   ] all.
   [   ] wisdom.

Chapter 44

Praise of the Ancestors of Old

1 Let me praise pious men,
   our fathers in their generations.
2 Abundant glory the Most High apportioned (mg. for them),
   his greatness from days of old.
3 Generations (mg. rulers) of the earth for their dominion,
   and men of renown for their might,
   counselors for their understanding of the world,
   those seeing everything for their prophecy,

43:27 הוא הכל — See 4Q266 11 9. The phrase has inspired a good deal of commentary (see Mattila 2000, 493–495). Based on the context of natural phenomena, it could mean "God is responsible for all the things described in the poem" or "God's presence is perceptible in all the phenomena described."
43:28 נגלה — The marginal note may also be read as נְגִילָה "Let us rejoice," but one would expect a *yod* mater.
44:2 חלק — This could also be construed as a noun, "the portion of the Most High." The marginal addition of a prepositional phrase, להם, suggests that the word was read as a verb by at least some scribes. This follows the sense of the Greek and Syriac. The particle להם is also reflected in the Lucianic recension, 249 and Syrohexapla. וגדלו — This could be interpreted as a noun (גְּדָל) or as a verb: "he exalted him" (וְגִדְּלוֹ) or "they are exalted" (וְגִדְּלוּ). The text of H^M גדלה may be interpreted as a noun with a 3ms pronominal *he* suffix, or as the feminine גְּדֻלָּה.
44:3 במלכותם — This and the following prepositional phrases (through 4d) are translated as complementing the verb of 7a (found in the margin). In this reading, the prepositions indicate cause (see the similar rection of נכבד with *bet* in Exod 14:4, 7, 18 and Sir 10:31^A). Some of the prepositional phrases can also be construed as modifying the preceding participles and some ambiguity seems intended, see Reymond 2001, 2–3. גבורם — This seems to be a masculine form of גְּבוּרָה only attested in medieval Hebrew (see Dihi 2004, 116–118). See 16:7^B.

	ורוזנים במחקרותם:	⁶שרי גוים במזמתם	4ab ᴹ
	ומושלים במשמרותם:	⁷חכמי שיח בספרתם	4cd ᴹ במס׳
	נושאי משל בכתב:	⁸חוקרי מזמור על חֹק	5 ᴹ קו
	ושוקטים על מכונתם:	⁹אנשי חיל וסומכי כח	6 ᴹ
וּבִימֵיהֶם	וּמִיֹּמֵיהֶם תפארתם:	¹⁰כל אלה בדורם	7 ᴹ נכבדו
לְהִשְׁתַּעוֹת	להשתענות בנחלתם:	¹¹יש מהם הניחו שם	8 ᴹ
הַשָּׁעוֹת	וישבתו כאשר שבתו:	¹²ויש מהם אשר אין לו זכר	9 ᴹ
	ובניהם מאחריהם[:]	¹³כאשר לא היו היו	
	ותקותם לֹא תכֹּ[ר]ת:	¹⁴ואולם אלה אנשי חסד	10 ᴹ
	ונחלתם לבנֹ[י]הֹ בֹּ[ניה]ֹם [:]	¹⁵עם זרעם נאמן טובם	11 ᴹ
	וצדקתם לא [תמח]הֹ:	¹⁶עד עולם יעמד זכרם	13 ᴹ
	[וֹ]שֹׁמָֹ חֹ[י] לֹ[דור] ודור:	¹⁷גֹ[וֹ]יֹתֹם בֹשלֹוֹם נֹאסֹ[פה]	14 ᴹ
	והתהלך עם ייי וֹ[נֹ]לקח אות דעת לדור ודור:	¹⁸חנוך נמֹצא תמים	16

44:4ab גוים B | וגוי ᴹ G S · **ורוזנים** B | ורוזנים ᴹ · **במחקרותם** B | במחקק]תם ᴹ · **44:4cd** בספרתם B ᴹ | במס׳ Bmg · **ומושלים** B | ומושלים ᴹ · **44:5** חוֹ־ ᴹ · **חוקרי** B | חוקי B | חוק ᴹ · **נושאי** ᴹ Bmg | ונשאי B | ונשאי ᴹ · **44:6** וסומכי ᴹ | וסמכי ᴹ · **44:7** ושקטים B | ושקטֹ[י]ם ᴹ · **ובדרם** B | בדרם ᴹ · **נכבדו + M** · **44:10** ואולם B | אולם ᴹ G S · **ותקותם** B | וצֹדקתם ᴹ G · **44:9** ימיהם [Bmg ויבימיהם] | מ[ן] אשר אין B | שאין ᴹ · **44:10** ואולם B | אולם ᴹ G S · **ומימיהם** Bmg | ימיהם ᴹ · **ובימיהם** Bmg M G S · **44:12** + אם ᴹ | עם B · **44:13** זכרם B S | זרעם ᴹ G · **בבריתם עמד זרעם וצאצאיהם** ᴹ · **וכבודם** ᴹ G S · **44:14** ודור B | וֹדֹ[שׁ]ת ᴹ · M · **44:15** תשנה Bmg | M · **44:16** > M ·

L. 7 [44:4] בספרתם — A short horizontal mark appears just beneath the top bar of the *resh*, which is an offset mark from the top bar of the *bet* in לברך XIV recto, 7 Sir 44:21. במשמרותם — An offset vertical mark from the *kaph* of כן (XIV recto, 7 Sir 44:21) appears beneath the left tip of the *resh*, thus making the letter look like a *khet* (cf. the alternative transliteration ח̄/ר in Ben-Ḥayyim [1973, 53]).

L. 8 [44:5] קו — Read קו in agreement with H^M, not חק, as proposed by Ben-Ḥayyim (1973, 53); Beentjes (1997, 77) and Lévi (1901, 1:84); there is no trace of *khet* on the manuscript.

L. 14 [44:10] תכֹּ[ר]ת — This reading (Yadin [1999, 194]; Minissale [1995, 128]; Corley [2008, 172]) seems preferable to תשבת (Segal 1958, 302) or תשכח (Skehan and Di Lella 1987, 499) which are paleographically improbable. The *tav* at the beginning of the word is certain, then faint traces of the lower right angle and right shoulder of a *kaph* or *bet* are possible, while a *shin* would be very improbable, and the *tav* is certain at the end of the word.

L. 15 [44:11] [:] לבנֹ[י]הֹ בֹּ[ניה]ֹם — The *bet* is attested by its upper bar with the upper left flourish, as well as its base which is slightly angled. Only a few traces of the lower right angle of the *nun* are preserved. Then a *bet* is possible (faint traces of its lower right angle as well as its head). At the end of the line are faint traces of a final *mem*'s base.

L. 16 [44:13] H^B lacks Sir 44:12. [תמח]הֹ — There is a trace of the second leg of the *he*.

L. 17 [44:14] The text is damaged. Only the upper part of letters is visible. However, the text can be restored with certainty from these traces and with the support of H^M. The reading of the last word נאספה, however, is tentative (the *nun* rises above the horizontal line and a trace of a letter at the end of the stich may suggest a longer reading).

L. 17 margin [44:15] תשנה — The last letter that may look like a *yod*, is *he* with a very short right leg like the *he* of תהלתם in the next line. יספר — The *resh* is written as a *dalet*. For similar writing of *resh* as *dalet* and vice versa, see 31:28 in the main text and 42:1 in the margin.

L. 18 [44:16] נמֹצא — A short horizontal mark appears just to the right of the *tsade*'s base. This is an offset mark from the base of the *sin/shin* of בשר on XIV recto, 16 Sir 45:4. וֹ[נֹ]לקח — Traces of the *vav* and the oblique stroke of the *lamed* are visible.

44:4 במחקרותם — This *mem*-preformative noun (in the feminine form) is not otherwise known in Hebrew (note a masculine form in Ps 95:4). Its translation is based on its etymology and the context. במשמרותם — For this word, used as a metaphor here and as part of a simile in Qoh 12:11, see Skehan (1970, 66–71). ומושלים — "Propounders of parables" or "rulers." במס׳ — According to the practice of this scribe, this note presupposes במספרתם where מספרה should be a neologism more or less synonymous to ספרה (attested one time in a *piyyut* from Eleazar HaQalir).

44:5 בכתב — This prepositional phrase does not make good sense as a complement to the participle, and thus, encourages interpreting all the prepositional phrases as complementing the verb of 7a.

44:8 הניחו שם — Cf. Isa 65:15. להשתענות — This looks like an Aramaized form, the *hithpael* infinitive construct of the Hebrew root שען. The *hithpael* stem of "to lean, support" is not known in Biblical Hebrew or early Rabbinic Hebrew where one usually sees the *niphal* instead (though, it is used one time in a *piyyut* from Eleazar HaQalir). Still, it is conceivable that a confusion between *niphal* and *hithpael* led to the development of a *hithpael* stem for this word by the time of Ben Sira. להשתעות / השעות — The marginal alternatives are more difficult to explain. The first alternative (להשתעות) is likely a Hebraized version of the common Aramaic verb שעי, which in the *hithpael* has an active sense "to tell a story"; here, however, the sense seems to be passive (cf. the Greek version). Alternatively, it could be active with the descendants of the father as implicit subject "for (them) to narrate." It seems less likely that this verb derives from the root, שעה, which is attested in

4 princes des peuples par leur prudence
   et dignitaires par leurs investigations,
   rhéteurs habiles par leurs écrits (mg. syn. ?),
   formeurs de proverbes par leurs (langues) acérées,
5 chercheurs de mélodie selon la métrique (mg. mesure/ligne),
   inventeurs de proverbes par l'écrit,
6 hommes valeureux et soutiens puissants
   et paisibles dans leur résidence,
7 tous ceux-ci, dans leur génération (mg. furent honorés)
   et depuis (mg. durant) leurs jours fut leur splendeur.
8 Certains, parmi eux, laissèrent un nom,
   pour être un soutien (mg. 1 pour être raconté, mg. 2 pour attirer l'attention sur) dans leur héritage.
9 Mais il y en a parmi eux pour lesquels il n'y a pas de souvenir
   et ils se sont arrêtés lorsqu'ils se sont arrêtés,
   ils ont existé comme s'ils n'avaient pas existé
   et (de même) leurs enfants après eux.
10 Inversement, ces hommes pieux,
   leur espérance ne sera pas retranchée.
11 Avec leur descendance, tient fermement leur prospérité
   et leur héritage pour les fil[s] de leu[rs fil]s.
13 Pour toujours se maintiendra leur souvenir
   et leur justice ne sera pas[effac]ée.
14 Leur [co]rps a été ras[semblé] dans la paix,
   [et]leur nom vi[t] de gé[nération] en génération.
   (15 mg. La communauté répétera leur sagesse
   et l'assemblée racontera leur louange.)
16 Hénoch a été trouvé intègre,
   il a marché avec Dieu et il [a été] pris, signe de connaissance de génération en génération.

4 leaders of the people for their cunning,
   and potentates for their investigations,
   meditative sages for their books,
   and propounders of parables for their sayings (lit., nails),
5 those pursuing song according to statute (mg. (over) a chord/string),
   those uttering proverbs for (their) writing,
6 valorous men, those upholding power,
   and those quiet in their homes,
7 All these in their generation (mg. were honored),
   and from their days (was) their glory (mg. in their days (was their glory)).
8 There were among them (those who) left a name,
   being supported in their inheritance (mg. 1 to be talked about; mg. 2 to turn attention to)
9 There were also among them those who are not remembered,
   they disappeared as soon as they perished.
   They are as though they had not been,
   and their children after them.
10 But, as for these pious men (who follow in the poem),
   their hope will not be cut off.
11 With their progeny their prosperity is secure,
   their inheritance belongs to the child[ren] of th[eir children.]
13 Forever their memory will stand,
   their righteousness will not [be wiped o]ut.
14 Their [bo]dies are ga[thered] in peace,
   [and] their name li[ves] from ge[neration] to generation.
   (15 mg. The congregation repeats their wisdom,
   and their praise the assembly recounts.)
16 Enoch was found blameless,
   and walked with the lord, and [was]taken, a sign of understanding from generation to generation.

Biblical Hebrew in the *qal* "to gaze," and perhaps also in the *hiphil* "to turn a gaze away" and the *hithpael* "to gaze about" since this verb makes less sense in the context. Nevertheless, the second marginal alternative (השעות) does seem to reflect this root (in the *hiphil*), perhaps as a way of explaining the previous *hithpael* form.

44:9 וישבתו כאשר שבתו — For שבת with the meaning "to die," see Sir 38:23. The translation presumes some wordplay here between different notions of "ceasing." Specifically, the translation presupposes an initial *niphal* (see Ezek 30:18 and 33:28) followed by a *qal*. Alternatively, it is also possible that two *qals* were intended.

44:10 ותקותם לא תכ[ר]ת: — Cf. Prov 23:18 and 24:14.

44:13 וצדקתם לא [תמח]ה — Cf. Sir 3:14ᴬ.

44:14 נאספה — In the *niphal*, the verb אסף may mean "to be gathered, to assemble" or "to be taken away." The meaning "to be gathered" in connection with death is very common when the verb is complemented, for example, "to be gathered to your ancestors." Compare this verse with 2 Kgs 22:20 (// 2 Chr 34:28): "Therefore, I will gather you to your ancestors, and you shall be gathered to your grave in peace לָכֵן "הִנְנִי אֹסִפְךָ עַל־אֲבֹתֶיךָ וְנֶאֱסַפְתָּ אֶל־קִבְרֹתֶיךָ בְּשָׁלוֹם" (See also Gen 49:29). In a few cases, however the absolute use of the verb seems to mean "to bury" or passively "to be buried" (see Ezek 29:5 or Sir 38:16ᴮ where אסף is translated by περιστέλλω). This absolute use of אסף ("to be buried") is well documented in late Hebrew (see Sir 8:7ᴬ; 16:10ᴬ; 40:28ᴮ·ᴹ; CD XIX 35; CD XX 14; 1QHᵃ XIV 10–11 (= vi 7–8).

44:15 תהלתם יספר קהל — A less likely interpretation would be to take the final *resh* of יספר as a *daleth* and read "the assembly laments their error (תְּהִלָּתָם יִסְפֹּד)."

44:16 חנוך נמצא תמים — The sentence seems inspired by Gen 6:9 concerning Noah (see next verse). והתהלך עם ייי ו[נ]לקח — See Gen 5:24; here, את of the biblical passages is replaced by עם and the verb לקח is made passive.

	MS.Heb.e.62 XIV recto	ב׳	לְעֵת כלה היה תחליף:	17 ¹[נֹ]חֹ צדיק נמצא תמים	M
			ובבריתו חדל מבול:	²בעבורו היה שארית	
כרת			לבלתי תשחית כל בשר:	18 ³באות עולם נכרת עמו	
	דופי		לא נתן לכבודוֹ מום:	19 ⁴אברהם אב המון גוים	
			ובא בברית עמו:	20 ⁵אשר שמר מצות עליון	
			ובניסוי נמצא נאמן:	⁶בבשרו כרת לו חק	
			לברך בזרעו גוים:	21ab ⁷על כן בשבֹועה הקים לו	
			ומנהר ועד אפסי ארץ:	21ef ⁸להנחילם מׄים ועד ים	
כן			בעבור אברהם אביו:	22 ⁹וגם ליצחק הקים בֵּן	
			וברכה נחה על ראש ישראל:	22c/23a ¹⁰ברית כל ראשון נתנו	
ויכנהו בבכורה			ויתן לו נחלתו:	23bc ¹¹ויכוֹנְנהו בברכה	
			לחלק שנים עשר:	23de ¹²ויציבהו לשבטים	
	ומצא		מוצֵא חן בעיני כל חי:	23fg ¹³וֹיוֹצִיא ממנו איש	

Chapter 45

		משה זכרו לטובה:	1 ¹⁴אֹ[הוֹ]בֹ אלהים ואנשים	
ויכ׳ ייי	במוראים	ויאמצהו במרוֹמים:	2 ¹⁵[ויכבֹ]דׄיהוֹ אלהים	

44:17 נ[חֹ] M | נוח B Bmg | לעת B ב׳ | נֹעת M ·

L. 3 [44:18] תשחית — The initial *tav* is clear in the digital photos. It is not a *he*, as most editions read.

L. 7 [44:21ab] בשבֹועה — The second *bet* is attested by its top and bottom horizontal lines. The *vav* has left a very faint trace. Both arms of the *ayin* are clear. לברך — The *resh* is obscured by an offset mark from the interior flourish of the *pe* of בספרתם in XIII verso, 7 Sir 44:4.

L. 8 [44:21ef] מׄים — The horn, end of the diagonal and part of the base of the *mem* are still visible.

L. 10 [44:22c/23a] There is a mark in the right margin that Smend (1906b, 49) understood as a final *nun*, yet judging from the online photos, it could just as easily be a discoloration of the paper.

L. 13 [44:23fg] יֹ[ ]צִׄא — The *vav* is only attested by its upper tip. The *tsade* is attested by the tip of its right arm, a portion of its vertical line and its base. The *yod* is only attested by its upper tip.

L. 14 [45:1] אֹ]בֹ — The *aleph* is clear from traces of its upper right and lower right corners, as well as a much fainter trace of its diagonal line. The *bet* is attested by its upper left corner and its base. אׄלהים — The *aleph* is attested by its four corners.

L. 15 [45:2] [ויכבֹ]דׄיהוֹ אלהים — This reading is confirmed by traces of the upper part of the *dalet* and the *yod*, as well as the upper part and lower part of the *he* and the *vav*.

44:17 See Gen 6:9, 7:1 and Heb 11:7. תחליף — Assuming that the word is a noun in all its occurrences, it appears twice elsewhere in Ben Sira (46:16; 48:8), but nowhere else (according to Maagarim). The noun can have the nuance "successor, survivor, that which springs anew." In the context of the flood, we use the English "survivor" (see Sauer 2000, 303). For a complete discussion of the word, see van Peursen 2008, 133–48.

44:18 נכרת — See Gen 9:17. The *niphal* usually means "to be cut off, destroyed," but at Qumran (4Q225 1 4) it may be attested with the passive sense "(a covenant) was made," as it is in Rabbinic Hebrew. תשחית — We take this as an imperfect verb; it seems unlikely that this is a noun (especially given the *lamed* preposition on בלתי; see Joüon §160l for לבלתי followed by an imperfect). The subject is presumably כלה from the preceding verse.

44:19 אב המון גוים — Note the same expression in Gen 17:4–5. נתן מום ... — The same verb is used with מום "blemish" with a moral meaning in Sir 33:23ᴱ and 47:20ᴮ, and both also occur with the word כבוד "glory." By contrast, the verb is used with מום in Lev 24:19–20 to describe maiming another person.

44:20 אשר — The relative pronoun here introduces a causal proposition (see Joüon §170e). כרת לו חק — The expression is unique and one would expect ברית to be the object according to the common Hebrew idiom, as well as the Greek and Syriac, which both repeat the same word in 20b and c. Still, note that other nouns (דבר, אמנה) are used with this verb in a similar way (in Neh 10:1 and Hag 2:5). Furthermore, one senses a play on the word כרת here that חק might help accent. That is, if the standard idiom כרת ברית were used, then a reader might construe the entire expression as "making a covenant" and miss the point that Abraham's covenant requires not only "cutting" a treaty, but also "cutting" the flesh. ובניסוי נמצא נאמן — The formulation of Sir 44:20d results from the confluence of three biblical quotations: Gen 15:6; 22:1 and Neh 9:8. The text associates the "faithfulness of Abraham" (נמצא נאמן, cf. Neh 9:8) with the trial (בניסוי), which refers to Gen 22. For the link between Abraham's fidelity and the trial of the *aqedah*, see 1 Macc 2:52 ("As for Abraham, in his testing, was he not found faithful, and was it not reckoned to him as righteousness?" Αβρααμ οὐχὶ

17 [N]oé le juste a été trouvé intègre,
   au (mg. idem) temps de la destruction, il a été un rescapé.
   Grâce à lui, il y a eu un reste
   et par son alliance, a cessé le déluge.
18 Par un signe éternel, il a été scellé (une alliance) avec lui
   (mg. il a scellé [une alliance] avec lui),
   afin que (s.e. la destruction) ne détruise pas toute chair.
19 Abraham a été père d'une multitude de nations,
   il n'a infligé à sa gloire aucune tare (mg. reproche),
20 (lui) qui a gardé les commandements du Très-Haut
   et est entré en alliance avec lui.
   Dans sa chair, il a incisé pour lui le commandement
   et dans l'épreuve, il a été trouvé fidèle.
21a C'est pourquoi, par un serment, il lui a garanti
21b de bénir par sa descendance les nations,
21e de leur faire hériter : (de) la mer jusqu'à la mer,
21f et du fleuve jusqu'aux extrémités de la terre.
22 Et aussi pour Isaac, il a suscité un fils (mg. il a garanti la même chose),
   grâce à Abraham son père.
22c Il lui a donné l'alliance de tous les anciens,
23a et la bénédiction qui repose sur la tête d'Israël.
23b Et il l'a établi par une bénédiction (mg. et il le qualifia de premier né),
23c et il lui a donné son héritage.
23d et il l'a établi en tribus,
23e en douze parts.
23f Et il a fait sortir de lui un homme,
23g qui a trouvé (mg. et a trouvé) grâce aux yeux de tous vivants,

Chapitre 45

1 A[im]é de Dieu et des hommes,
  Moïse, son souvenir est bonheur.
2 Dieu (mg. YYY) l'a [glo]rifié
  et l'a affermi dans les hauteurs (mg. par des prodiges terrifiants).

17 [No]ah the just was found blameless,
   in the time of destruction, he was the one who continued on.
   On account of him there was a remnant,
   and at his covenant the flood ceased.
18 With a perpetual sign, it (a covenant) was made with him (mg. he made a covenant with him),
   so that it (i.e., destruction) would not annihilate all flesh.
19 Abraham was father of many nations,
   he set no blemish (mg. reproach) in his glory,
20 he who kept the Most High's commandments,
   and entered into a covenant with him,
   in whose flesh he cut for him a statute,
   and through testing was found faithful.
21a Therefore, in an oath he guaranteed for him
21b to bless nations through his seed,
21e so that they inherit [from] sea to sea,
21f and from the river to the ends of the earth.
22 And also for Isaac he provided a son (mg. [he provided] the same),
   on account of Abraham, his father.
22c The covenant of every ancestor he gave him,
23a the blessing that rests over the head of all Israel.
23b He established him through blessing (mg. he recognized him in (his) first-born status)
23c and gave to him his inheritance.
23d He organized him into tribes,
23e into a twelve-part division.
23f He brought forth from him a man,
23g who found (mg. and has found) grace in the eyes of all the living.

Chapter 45

1 Be[lov]ed by God and humanity,
  Moses, whose memory is a boon.
2 God (mg. YYY) ho[nored] him,
  and strengthened him in the heights (mg. with terrifying acts),

ἐν πειρασμῷ εὑρέθη πιστός, καὶ ἐλογίσθη αὐτῷ εἰς δικαιοσύνην), Jas 2:21; Heb 11:17–19 or Jub 17:15–18.
44:21 The Greek has two additional stichs here (21cd). הקים — Note the use of קום in the *hiphil* in Num 30:14–15. ומנהר — The reference is ambiguous and could refer to either a mythic river that surrounds the ocean or a terrestial river, most likely the Euphrates (as in the Syriac). The same expression occurs in Zech 9:10 and Ps 72:8.
44:22 כן — The word could be construed in several different ways. The expression might mean "he established for Isaac a position" (see Gen 40:13), "he fulfilled what is right for Isaac" (see Prov 11:19), or more likely, "and also for Isaac he guaranteed thus."

44:23 ויכנהו בבכורה — Presumably, this is the verb כנה, which occurs twice elsewhere in this book. In 36:17, the direct object is both "Israel" and the noun בכור: "Israel, (whom) you recognized as firstborn." In 47:6, the same verb, כנה, is modified by *bet* with a similar meaning to the one here: "they acknowledged (David) in (his killing of) ten-thousand" (ויכנוהו ברבבה).
45:2 ויכ' — Given the abbreviation, it is likely that the verb presumed in the margin is the same as that in the text. במוראים / במרומים — The reference to heights is presumably to Mount Sinai, though one would expect the singular form. The "terrors" refer to the terrifying acts of God in Egypt (Deut 4:34), mentioned alongside "signs and wonders."

MS.Heb.e.62 XIV verso

		ויחזקהו לפני מלך:	¹⁶בדבר֯ א֯ותו֯ת מהר	3	בדברו בדבריו
		ויראו֯[הו] ב֯כ֯בו֯ד֯ו֯:	¹⁷ויצוהו ע[ל] ה֯[ע]ם֯		
		בחר בו מכל בשר֯:	¹⁸באמונתו ובענותו	4	ובענותנותו
		ויגישהו לערפל:	¹ויש֯מיעהו את קולו	5	
		תורת חיים ותבונה:	²ויש֯ם בידו מצוה		ויתן
		ועדותיו ומשפטיו לישראל:	³ללמד ב֯יעקב חקיו		לי
		וישימהו לחק עולם:	⁴וירם קדוש את אהרן למטה לוי	6/7	
	ברכה	וישרתהו בכבודו:	⁵ויתן עליו֯ הוד		לו הודו
	תעופה	וילבישהו פעמוני֯ם֯:	⁶ויאזרהו בתועפות ראם		תואר
		ויפארהו בכבוד ועוז:	⁷וילבישהו כליל תפארת	8	תפארות
		ויקיפהו פעמונים:	⁸מכנסים כתנות ומעיל	8c/9a	
		לתת נעימה בצעדיו:	⁹ורמונים המון סביב	9bc	
		לזכרון לבני עמו:	¹⁰להשמיע בדביר קולו	9de	
		מעשה חשב:	¹¹בגדי קדש זהב תכלת וארגמן	10	
		ושני תולעת מעשה ארג:	¹²חשן משפט אפוד ואזור	10c/11a	
		פתוחי חותם במלו֯א֯ים:	¹³אבני חפץ על החשן	11bc	

L. 16 [45:3] בדברי֯ו — The marginal letters are very faint, but are best read as an alternative to whatever was in the text. The *bet* in the middle of the word seems to be ligatured to the final *resh*, which makes the two letters look like a final *mem*. The marks in the middle of the page may reflect a text like that assumed by the Greek, namely אותות "signs." The possible left foot of a *tav* is visible beneath the hole and what may be a very blurred *aleph* is visible at the right edge of the hole. מהר — Offsetting from the first letters of וצדקתם in XIII verso, 16 Sir 44:13 appears after מהר. It seems that offsetting from the final *mem* of וצדקתם occurs to the right of the initial *mem* of מהר as well. At the end of the entire line, one can see bleedthrough traces of הוד from XIV verso 16 Sir 45:12.

L. 17 [45:3] To the left of the clearly visible ascender of the *lamed*, one sees another ascender, which is likely an offset trace from the *lamed* on XIII verso 17 Sir 44:14 (note the lack of any characteristic head to this second ascender). To the left of this offset ascender is a horizontal mark that seems too long to be the horizontal mark of the *lamed* of 44:14 and suggests that a correctly oriented letter like *he* stood here. At the upper edge of the hole, one sees what looks like the upper left corner of a correctly oriented final *mem*. If so, one should perhaps reconstruct the form העם, as in the Syriac (see Smend 1906b, 49).

L. 18 [45:4] בחר — Offset traces from XIII verso, 18 Sir 44:16 intermingle with the letters of this word (and to a lesser degree those that follow), though the letters here are still fairly clear. At the end of the line, the marks are sufficiently vague (especially since it is possbile that some portions of the traces are due to offsetting) to allow for the reconstruction בשר or אדם (cf. 1QH ͣ XVIII, 28). Note the similar expression with חי in Sir 45:15 below.

L. 6 [45:6/7] תואר — The *aleph* is almost totally effaced.

L. 7 [45:8] תפארו֯ת — To the left of the *resh* is a single vertical mark that is not connected to the following vertical mark. We take this as a *vav*. The following vertical mark is connected to a horizontal cross bar, which is connected to another vertical mark that ends with a foot at its bottom. This suggests that this last letter is a *tav*. This reading stands in contrast to תפארתו, which is favored by many other scholars. בכבד — The vertical mark of the *kaph* seems quite close to the vertical mark of the following (and second) *bet*. It is conceivable that what appears to be the vertical mark of the *kaph* and its upper horizontal are really an offset *tav* from מצותיו on XV recto, 7 Sir 45:17. If so, then the *kaph*'s vertical mark is at an angle, just before the hole and the *bet* is attested by very faint traces of its base and upper left corner.

L. 8 [45:8c/9a] מכנסים — Note the diagonal mark extending downward from the bottom of the *samek*. This does not correspond to any marks or letters on XV recto or XIII recto. The mark must either be a mistake by the scribe that was partially erased or a discoloration of the paper.

L. 9 [45:9bc] The marginal letters are a gloss in Persian. For the translation, see Wright (2018, 134).

L. 11 [45:10] In the manuscript, the first five words are grouped together as part of the first colon.

L. 13 [45:11bc] פתוחי — The *vav* is connected to the *khet* by what seems to be a crossbar, which is an offset mark from the *dalet* of כבודו in XV recto, 13 Sir 45:20. במלו֯א֯ים — The bottom part of the *vav* is visible, as well as a very faint trace of its top. The *aleph* is attested by what appears to be its diagonal and a trace of its lower left foot. Within these blurry lines is perhaps an offset mark from the bottom of the first *vav* or *mem* of the word תרומות, reconstructed by Segal (1958, 311) in Sir 45:21 and corresponding to the hole at XV recto, 13. The top tip of the *yod* is attested above the hole.

45:3 מהר — God's rushing to act is noted, for example, in Gen 41:32.

45:5 וישם בידו — For the expression שים ביד, see Exod 4:21, 1 Kgs 20:6 and Isa 51:23. ויגישהו לערפל — The same words appear in Exod 20:21 with Moses as the subject of a *piel* form. מצוה — The singular is used in reference to the whole set of stipulations.

45:6 The fact that what is an entire verse in the Greek and the Syriac is set in one line with 7a suggests that at some point the words of 6ab were a single stich. This suggests that the entire verse was construed as a single clause with קדוש as the subject. The Greek and the Syriac imply that this word is the object of the verb, in syntactic parallelism with the name Aaron. In Ps 106:16, for example, Aaron is called קדוש יהוה. If the words were understood in this way, they would be translated: "He exalted him as a holy one, Aaron . . ." את אהרן למטה לוי — The *lamed* may be used here to introduce the genitive.

45:7 לחק — Note the use of the etymologically related synonym in the phrase לחקת עולם "as a perpetual statute," which refers to the priesthood in Exod 29:9. In Sir 41:2–3, death is called חקך and חקיך "your sentence." תועפות ראם — The expression appears twice in the Bible (Num 23:22, 24:8) in comparisons. The phrase would more literally be "the peaks of the wild ox." The marginal alternative תואר seems to understand תועפות in a metaphoric sense ("extreme"), which is akin to the metaphoric sense "height" in English. תעופה — The word is pre-

SIR 45:3–11   151

3   Par une parole, il a hâté les signes (mg 1. par sa parole, mg 2. par ses paroles)
    et il l'a fortifié devant le roi.
    Il lui a donné des ordres [env]ers le [peu]ple
    et [lui a fait vo]ir *sa gloire*.
4   Par sa fidélité et son humilité (syn. aram.),
    il l'a choisi parmi toutes chairs.
5   Et il lui a fait entendre sa voix
    et il l'a fait approcher de la ténèbre
    et a établi (mg. il lui a confié) par sa main un commandement,
    une loi de vie et d'intelligence,
    pour instruire en (mg. à) Jacob ses décrets
    et ses témoignages et ses commandements à Israël.
6   Le saint a élevé Aaron de la tribu de Lévi
7   et l'a établi par un commandement éternel
    et il a placé sur lui la majesté (mg. sa majesté)
    et il l'a servi par sa gloire (mg. par une bénédiction)
    et il l'a ceint de la force du buffle (mg. d'une éminente beauté)
    et il l'a revêtu de clochettes (mg. d'obscurité)
8   et il l'a revêtu d'une couronne de gloire
    et il l'a honoré de gloire et de force.
8c Caleçons, tuniques et robe
9a et il l'a entouré de clochettes
    [mg. en persan: La copie va jusqu'ici.]
9b et une multitude de grenades autour,
9c pour rendre mélodieux ses pas
9d et faire entendre dans le sanctuaire sa voix,
9e en mémorial pour les enfants de son peuple.
10 Vêtements sacrés d'or, de pourpre violette et pourpre rouge,
    œuvre d'artiste,
10c pectoral du jugement, Ephod et ceinture,
11a cramoisi, œuvre de tisserand.
11b Pierres précieuses sur le pectoral,
11c gravures d'un sceau, dans des enchâssements,

3   By a word (mg. 1 by his word; mg. 2 by his words), he hastened the signs
    and he supported him before the king.
    He commanded him [con]cerning the pe[op]le
    and he sho[wed him] his glory.
4   For his faithfulness, and for his humility (mg humility),
    he chose him from all flesh.
5   He caused him to hear his voice,
    and brought him near to the darkness.
    He set (mg. placed) in his hand the commandments,
    the law of life and understanding,
    to teach in (mg. to) Jacob his statutes
    and his testimonies and judgments to Israel.
6   The holy one exalted Aaron, from the tribe of Levi
7   and established him by an everlasting statute.
    He set upon him majesty (mg. [gave] to him his majesty)
    and had him serve in his glory (mg. with a blessing)
    He girded him in the horns of the wild ox (mg. in exquisite beauty),
    and dressed him in bells (mg. darkness).
8   He dressed him with a crown of glory,
    and glorified him in honor and power.
8c The undergarments, the tunic, the robe,
9a he surrounded him with bells,
    (mg. in Persian:) The copy is until here.
9b and many pomegranates all around,
9c to give a pleasant sound to his steps,
9d to ring out in the holy of holies,
9e as a memorial for his people.
10 Holy garments of gold, purple, and red —
    the work of a craftsman.
10c The breast-piece of judgment, ephod, and loincloth,
11a and red yarn — work of the weaver.
11b Precious stones over the breast-piece,
11c engraved as seals, in settings,

sumably the same as תעפה, which appears in Job 11:17. Although it is often parsed as a verb, "it will grow dark," some also construe it as a misvocalized noun "darkness." Within the context of 45:7, the word is most likely a noun. The sense perhaps is meant to contrast with the darkness into which Moses is led (Sir 45:5*b*). The use of the word here may also be encouraged by the similar sounding תועפות in the preceding stich. **45:8** כליל תפארת — The Greek reads the first word as "perfection," though it could also be a loanword from Aramaic where the same consonants indicate "crown." Note the frequent biblical phrase עטרת כבוד "crown of glory." Furthermore, in the Bible, the word כליל "entirety" is sometimes translated "crown" (e.g., in the LXX and Peshitta of Ezek 28:12, but not in the Targums). The consonants כליל appear in Sir 37:18^(B,D) and 45:14^B with the meaning "entirety." In the DSS, the same consonants occur with the meaning "entirety," but also in construct with כבוד where it is often construed as "crown" (1QS IV, 7; 1QH^a XVII, 25; 4Q257 V, 5), according to the parallelism with another phrase, מדת הדר "garment of majesty," in 1QS IV 7. In Hebrew, עֲטָרָה "crown" does not occur as object of לבש but as object of נתן "to give" (Ezek 16:12, 23:42), עטר "to crown" (Song 3:11), רום "to raise" (Ezek 21:31), שים "to set" (Zech 6:11) and שית "to set" (Ps 21:4). On the other hand, Aramaic כליל "crown" occurs frequently with לבש, including in the *aphel* (see Vayyikra Rabbah 28:6 [as cited in CAL 14 Mar, 2022]).
45:9 נעימה — The word is not attested in Biblical Hebrew, but see in Aramaic in 4Q548 1 ii-2 13 translated by Puech as "suavité." The word is more frequent in Rabbinic Hebrew (see Jastrow 1903, 919). אין נוסכת תא איוד בוד — The translation of the Persian gloss is from Cowley and Neubauer (1897, 25).

11de	¹⁴וכל אבן יקרה לזכרון בכתב חרות	למספר שׄבׄטׄ[יׄ יׄשׄ]רׄאל:
12	¹⁵עטרת פז מעיל ומצנפת	וציץ חׄרׄוׄתׄ] [קׄדׄש:
	¹⁶הוד כבוד ותהלת עז	מחמדׄ עׄיׄן וׄמׄכׄלׄ[ל יׄ]ופי:
13	¹⁷לפׄנׄיׄהׄו לׄ[א היה כׄ]ן	וׄעׄד עׄולם לאׄ] [םׄ זר:
	¹⁸האׄמׄן בׄדׄד לבניו כזה	וכן בניו לדורותם:
14	¹מׄנׄחתו כליל תקטר	וכל יום תמיד פעמים:
15	²וׄיׄמׄלׄא משה את ידו	וימשחהו בשמן הקדש:
	³ותהי לו ברית עולם	ולזרעו כימי שמים:
	⁴לשרת ולכהן לו	ולברך את עמו בשמו:
16	⁵ויבחר בו מכל חי	להגיש עלה וחלבים:
	⁶ולהקטיר ריח ניחח ואזכרה	ולכפר על בני ישראל:
17	⁷ויתן לו מצותיו	וימשילהו בחוק ומשפט:
	⁸וילמד את עמו חק	ומשפט את בני ישראל:
18	⁹ויחרו בו זרים	ויקנאו בו במדבר:
	¹⁰אנשי דתן ואבירם	ועדת קרח בעזוז אפם:
19	¹¹וירא יוי ויתאנף	ויכלם בחרון אפו:
	¹²ויבא להם אות	ויאכלם בשביב אשו:
20ab	¹³וׄיׄשׄתׄ לאהרן כבודו	ויתן לו נחלתו:
20c/21a	¹⁴רׄ[אׄשׄיׄ]תׄ קדש נתן לו לחם	אשי ייי יאכלון:
20d/21b	¹⁵לׄ[חם הׄ]פׄנׄ[יׄ]םׄ חלקו	ומתנה לו ולזרעו:

MS.Heb.e.62 XV recto

L. 14 [45:11de]]ºשׄבׄ — The *sin/shin* is attested by the tops of its three arms. The *bet* is attested by its left corner and a trace of its base.

L. 15 [45:12] חׄרׄוׄתׄ — The upper horizontal parts of the letters are visible above the hole and the lower parts of the legs beneath the hole. The two last letters are only a possible solution that fits the traces. Also possible is חתם "seal" (see Exod 28:36). קׄדׄש — The middle letter should be a *dalet*, but it is unusual since the upper horizontal seems to be written at an angle and the entire letter seems squashed. There is a slight and very faint trace of another vertical mark to the left of the *dalet*.

L. 16 [45:12] וׄמׄכׄלׄ[— The *mem* is attested by its upper part. A reconstruction מבחר "choice" is also possible.

L. 17 [45:13] לפׄנׄיׄהׄו — The reconstruction לׄ[פׄנׄו] proposed by Lévi, (1898, 100) and לפנים by Smend (1906b, 50) are difficult based on the traces. After the *lamed*, we can see the round nose of the *pe*, then the top of a vertical line that may represent the top of a *nun*. The next letter is clearly a *yod*. Then we discern the trace of the top of a right leg as well as a horizontal bar (the *he*). The last mark is the top of a *vav*. This uncommon orthography is attested one time in 1QS VI 26 and more frequently in Rabbinic literature. וׄעׄד — The marks that seem to come at the beginning of the second stich are presumably the remnants of the conjunction and the preposition עד (as suggested by the Greek). If this reconstruction is correct, then the *ayin* is only attested by the top tip of one of its arms and the *dalet* by the left most part of its horizontal bar. עׄולם — The tops of the two arms of the *ayin* and the top of the *vav* are preserved.

L. 18 [45:13] האׄמׄן בׄדׄד — The letters of these two words seems to be very compressed. The *mem* is only attested by its base. The following traces may correspond with בדד that was already restored by Smend (1906b, 50). כזה — Offset marks from the phrase בגבורה on XV recto, 18 Sir 45:23 interfere with the letters of this word. The base of the *he* is from the second *bet* of בגבורה. The left vertical of the *he* intersects with this offset base. To the left of the *he* are more offset marks from the

gimel and the initial *bet*.

L. 1 [45:14] מׄנׄחתו — The initial letter should be a *mem*, but from its traces, it seems to look more like a *kaph* or *bet*, primarily becasue of its upper right corner, which looks less like the short horizontal top of a *mem* and more like the long vertical top of a *kaph* or *bet*. תמיד — One can see offset traces in the *tav* from the bottom left foot of the *aleph* and the right vertical of the *tav* of את at XIV verso, 1 Sir 45:5.

L. 9 [45:18] זרים — An offset mark from the vertical mark of the *dalet* of בצעדיו in XIV verso, 9 Sir 45:9c appears just to the right of the *zayin*.

L. 13 [45:20a] וׄיׄשׄתׄ — The *vav* is clear. It is followed by faint traces of the *yod* and of the three branches of the *shin*, and then by the beginning of the left leg of a *tav* and its foot.

L. 14 [45:20c/21a] רׄ[אׄשׄיׄ]תׄ — The first letter may be a *resh* or a *tav*. Cowley and Neubauer (1897, 26) read *resh*, while most others read *tav*, reflecting תרומות. The letter has a flourish in its upper left corner, characteristic of both *resh* and *tav*. If the letter were *tav*, then we would expect to see a leg descending beneath or slightly to the right of this flourish; instead there is a blank space. At the very edge of the hole, one finds a dark verticle line, which could be due to the tear or remnants of ink from a *tav*'s left leg. On the other hand, the crossbar seems to extend just a touch beyond the right verticle leg, which is more characteristic of a *tav* (as the *tav* of מׄנׄחתו in 45:14, XV Recto, line 1). The reconstruction רׄ[אׄשׄיׄ]תׄ fits perfectly and matches the Greek and the Syriac. The final *tav* is only attested by traces of its top horizontal bar. קׄדש — Although much of the *qoph* is missing, the edge of its long descender is intact. An offset mark from the bottom tip of the vertical mark of the *resh* of למספר in XIV verso 14, Sir 45:11e appears just to the left of the *dalet*.

L. 15 [45:20d] לׄ[חם הׄ]פׄנׄ[יׄ]םׄ — At the beginning of the line, there is a slight trace of a letter just to the right of the hole with no mark on the surviving paper beneath it, suggesting that the initial letter of the line was a *lamed*. The reconstruction לחם הפנים is confirmed by faint traces of the bases of the *pe* and the *nun* (see Peters 1902, 412; Segal 1958, 312).

11d chaque pierre est destinée au souvenir avec inscription gravée,
11e selon le nombre des tribus d'Israël.
12 Une couronne d'or pur, une robe et un turban,
une rosette engravée[   ]sacrée,
splendeur glorieuse et louange puissante,
délice du regard et parfa[ite b]eauté.
13 Avant lui[il]n'[en était]pas[ain]si
et jamais ne [   ] un étranger,
confié de la sorte seulement à ses enfants
et aussi ses enfants pour leurs générations.
14 Son offrande sera entièrement consumée,
deux fois, chaque jour, perpétuellement.
15 Moïse l'a consacré
et l'a oint avec l'huile sainte
et l'alliance éternelle sera pour lui
et pour sa descendance tant que durent les cieux,
pour servir et exercer le sacerdoce pour lui,
pour bénir son peuple en son nom.
16 Et il l'a élu parmi tous les vivants,
pour apporter l'holocauste et les graisses
et pour faire brûler l'odeur agréable et le souvenir,
pour le rachat des enfants d'Israël.
17 Et il lui a donné ses commandements
et il lui a confié l'autorité sur le décret et le jugement.
Il a enseigné à son peuple le décret
et le jugement aux enfants d'Israël.
18 Et des étrangers se sont enflammés contre lui
et ils l'ont jalousé dans le désert,
(c'étaient) les hommes de Datân et Abiram
et l'assemblée de Coré dans leur violente fureur.
19 Mais YYY a vu et s'est irrité
et il les a consumés dans son ardente colère
et il leur a envoyé un signe
et il les a dévorés dans la flamme de son feu.
20a Et il a placé sur Aaron sa gloire,
20b et il lui a donné son héritage,
20c il lui a donné le pr[émi]ce sacré en nourriture,
21a ils mangeront des mets consumés de YYY,
20d le p[ain d'o]ffra[n]de est sa portion,
21b un don pour lui et pour sa descendance.

11d each gem for remembrance with engraved writing,
11e according to the number of tribe[s of Is]rael.
12 A diadem of gold, a robe, and turban,
rosette engraved[...]sacred,
gloried splendor and mightily praised
a desirous thing, a perfec[tion of b]eauty.
13 Before him, [there was] n[ot another the sa]me,
never [   ] stranger.
Entrusted to his children alone in this way,
and thus his children in their generations.
14 His [of]fering will be entirely consumed,
twice each day, perpetually.
15 Moses ordained him,
and anointed him with holy oil,
so that the eternal covenant would be his,
and his seed's, lasting as long as the heavens exist,
to serve and act as priest for him,
to bless his people by his name.
16 He chose him from all the living,
to bring near the burnt offering and the fat,
to offer (incense) as sweet-smelling odor and as a token offering,
to atone for all the children of Israel.
17 He gave to him his commandments,
and granted him authority over statute and judgement.
He taught his people the statutes
and the children of Israel the judgements.
18 Strangers burned with anger at him,
and in the desert, were envious of him,
the people of Dathan and Abiram,
the congregation of Korah, in their intense fury.
19 YYY saw and was enraged,
he destroyed them in his burning fury;
he brought to them a sign,
it consumed them in the flames of its fire.
20a He placed on Aaron his glory,
20b and gave to him his inheritance.
20c Sacred fir[st frui]ts he gave to him as food,
21a offerings by fire to YYY they will eat.
20d the br[ead of the pr]es[e]nce his portion,
21b a gift to him and his seed.

45:13 הָאֵמֹן — The meaning that one would expect should be expressed by the *niphal*. If so, this would be an infinitive absolute used as a finite verb. This does not occur elsewhere in Ben Sira, though it does in the DSS (Smith 2000, 256–268). Alternatively, it is conceivable that this is a *hophal* perfect with the same sense as the *niphal*.

45:16 להגיש עלה — The combination of this verb and object is only found elsewhere in 1 Sam 13:9, though in that passage, the verb describes movement toward Saul, not God. ואזכרה — When this word appears with the verb קטר, it is at least sometimes clearly the direct object (Lev 2:2, 16), whereas ריח ניחח is always construed as an adverbial accusative. Here, we assume that both should be construed as adverbial accusatives.

45:19 ויבא — According to the context, one would expect God to be the subject here. However, when the word אות appears in the context of this verb, אות is usually the subject of the *qal* verb (Deut 13:3; 1 Sam 2:34; 10:7, 9). Thus, "a sign came to them" is also possible. The Greek and the Syriac presume the verb ברא (cf. Num 16:30).

45:20 לֶ֫חֶם הַ[פָּ]נִ֔ים — See Exod 25:30.

22	¹⁶אַךְ בְּ[אַ]רְצָּם לֹא יִנְחַל	ובתוכם לא יחלק נחלה:
	¹⁷אִשִּׁי יְיָ֒ [חֶלְקוֹ] נַחֲלָתוֹ	בְּ[תוֹ]ךְ בְּנֵי יִשְׂרָאֵל [:]
23	¹⁸וגם פנחס בן אלעזר	בגבורה נָחַל ○○○ ○○○:
	¹בקנאו לאלוהי כל	ויעמד בפרץ עמו:
	²אשר נדבו לבו	ויכפר על בני ישראל:
24	³לכן גם לו הקים חק	ברית שלום לכלכל למקדש:
	⁴אשר תהיה לו ולזרעו	כהונה גדולה עד עולם:
25	⁵וגם בריתו עם דוד	בן ישי למטה יהודה:
	⁶נחלת אש לפני כבודו	ונחלת אהרן לכל זרעו:
	⁷ועתה ברכו נא את ייי הטוב	הַמְעַטֵּר אתכם כבוד:
26	⁸ויתן לכם חכמת לב	למען לא ישכח טובכם ואמורתכם לדורות עולם:

MS.Heb.e.62 XV verso

Chapter 46

1	⁹גבור בן חיל יהושע בן נון	משרת משה בנבואה:
	¹⁰אשר נוצר להיות בימיו	תשועה גדלה לבחיריו:
	¹¹להנקם נקמי אויב	ולהנחיל את ישראל:
2	¹²מה נהדר בנטותו יד	בהניפו כידון על עִיר֯:
3	¹³מי הוא לפניו יתיצב	כי מלחמות ייי נלחָֽם:
4	¹⁴הלא בידו עמד השמש	יום אחד כשׁ[נֵי יָמִ]ים֯:
5	¹⁵כי קרא אל אל עליון	כאכפה לפָֽנָ[יִ]ם֯ [:]
	¹⁶ויענהו אל עליון באבני	ברד ואלגב[י]ש:
6ab	¹⁷[וי]חְבֹּט עָל֯ עם אוֹי[ב]	[ ]○○○○○○○○

L. 16 [45:22a] אַךְ בְּ[אַ]רְצָּם לֹא יִנְחַל — This restoration, based on the versions, fits the preserved traces and the available space.

L. 17 [45:22c] There appear to be three *lameds* in the first colon. However, the second (not indicated in the transliteration above) is really an offset *lamed* from the *lamed* following עוֹלָם֯ in XIV verso, 17 Sir 45:13. Our transcription reflects the reconstruction of Lévi (1898, 104) and Segal (1958³, 312) that perfectly fits the numerous traces of letters preserved along the edge of the manuscript.

L. 18 [45:23] אֶלעזר — The distinctive bottom left foot of the *aleph* is preserved. The diagonal mark of the *lamed* is found next to this, as well as a faint trace of the corner where the ascender meets the horizontal bar. נָחַל — Only the bottom of the *nun* and *khet* are preserved. The *khet* could also be a *he*. The trace following the *khet* is certainly the end of the diagonal line of a *lamed*. According to the Greek and the Syriac we would expect to find (בכבוד) שלישי as it has been restored by Lévi (1898, 104) and Segal (1958, 312). But such a reading is incompatible with the traces.

L. 1 [45:23] לאלוהי — The final *yod* is added above the word as a correction.

L. 8 [45:26] Note that the three stichs are written in one line. וְאִמוּרַתְכֶם — The first letters are assured by the traces (see already Smend 1906b, 51; Ben-Ḥayyim 1973, 57); this excludes the restoration גבורתכם proposed by Cowley and Neubauer (1897, 28); Lévi (1898, 108).

45:23 בפרץ — The noun פרץ "breach, gap" is used here in its metaphorical sense "lawlessness," as found in Rabbinic Hebrew.

45:25 אש — This is probably a mistake for איש, "of an individual."

46:3 See Jos 8:18.26.

46:4 See Jos 10:13.

46:5 כאכפה — It is difficult to interpret the letters. The word אכפה is either a noun or an infinitive construct (*qal* or *niphal*) with a third person masculine singular *he* suffix. It may be active or passive. The

L. 12 [46:2] עִיר֯ — The *yod* is extremely faint. The *resh* is faint, but clear.

L. 13 [46:3] נלחָֽם֯: — Although very faded, the upper part of the *khet* and *mem* are preserved on the manuscript.

L. 14 [46:4] כשׁ[נֵי יָמִ]ים֯ — The traces of letters at the end of the verse are very poorly preserved. The *kaph* is preserved by traces of its upper and lower horizontal bars, as well as by traces of its vertical stroke. The next letter may be a *sin/shin*, with the three top tips of the letter leaving only the faintest traces. The final letter of the verse is likely a final *mem*, only preserved by traces of its left bottom corner and upper left corner. The traces seem to exclude Smend's reconstruction, כשנים היה (Smend 1906b, 51) as well as Lévi's היה לשנים (Lévi 1898, 110).

L. 15 [46:5] לפָֽנָ[יִ]ם֯ — The *pe* is attested by the small upper part of the letter, as well as its base, which ends in a downward stroke at the bottom left. The *nun* is preserved by its upper right tip and bottom horizontal mark. The *mem* is only preserved by a portion of its bottom horizontal mark.

L. 17 [46:6ab] [וי]חְבֹּט עָל֯ עם אוֹי[ב] — The *tet* of ויחבט is certain and implies this reconstruction that fits the Syriac (for the reconstruction of the verb חבט, see already Smend 1906a, 441). *Khet* and *bet* fit the existing traces. The end of the restoration follows the versions and fits the space. For the next stich, the reading ובמורד may be possible according to the traces (see the Greek).

Greek can be understood either way, while the Latin implies a passive sense (See Reymond 2018c, 239–241). However, if one assumes that its context is Josh 10:9–10, based, in part, on the mention of "stones" in the next colon, then an active sense may be intended, since Joshua chases the Amorites in this passage. If this is in fact what Ben Sira is describing, then the calling to God referred to in v. 5 is the pleading for the sun and moon to stop their movement alluded to in v. 4.

22 Mais ils n'hériteront pas de leur p[a]ys	22 But in their [l]and, he will not inherit,
et au milieu d'eux, il ne partagera pas l'héritage.	and in their midst he will not share an inheritance.
Les mets consumés de YY[Y]sont sa part et son héritage	The offerings by fire to YY[Y] are his portion
au[milieu]des enfants d'Israël.	in the [mid]st of the children of Israel.
23 Et aussi Pinhas, fils d'Eleazar,	23 Also Phineas, son of Eleazar,
par la puissance il a hérité [ ].	through might he inherited [ ].
Par son zèle pour le Dieu de tout,	When zealous for the god of all,
il a tenu ferme sur la brèche de son peuple,	he remained steadfast in his people's lawlessness,
tandis que son cœur le prédisposait,	whose own heart incited him
il a racheté les enfants d'Israël.	so that he atoned for the children of Israel.
24 C'est pourquoi, pour lui aussi, il (Dieu) a établi un décret,	24 Therefore to him also he (God) established a descree,
alliance de paix, pour soutenir le sanctuaire,	a covenant of peace to sustain the sanctuary,
qui sera pour lui et pour sa descendance,	which will be his and his seed's —
un grand sacerdoce pour l'éternité.	a great priesthood forever.
25 Et aussi, son alliance avec David,	25 Also in his covenant with David,
fils de Jessé, de la tribu de Juda,	son of Jesse, of the tribe of Judah,
un héritage de feu devant sa gloire	an inheritance of fire before his glory,
et l'héritage d'Aaron pour toute sa descendance.	and the inheritance of Aaron to all his seed.
Et maintenant, bénissez YYY, le bon,	So, now, bless YYY, the good,
celui qui vous couronne de gloire.	the one who crowns you with glory,
26 Et qu'il vous donne la sagesse du cœur,	26 so he will give to you a wise mind,
afin que votre bonheur ne soit pas oublié,	so that your boon will not be forgotten,
ni vos discours pour les générations futures.	nor your words by future generations.

Chapitre 46

1 Héros fils de vaillance, Josué fils de Nun,	1 A valiant warrior was Joshua Bin Nun,
serviteur de Moïse en prophétie,	who was serving Moses in prophecy,
qui a été formé pour être en ces jours	who was formed to be in his days
un grand salut pour ses élus,	a great salvation for his chosen ones,
pour exécuter la vengeance contre l'ennemi	to execute vengeance on the enemy,
et pour faire hériter Israël.	and to give Israel its inheritance.
2 Qu'il était resplendissant quand il étendait sa main,	2 How glorious when he stretched his hand
quand il brandissait son sabre contre une ville.	and he waved his sword against a city.
3 Qui aurait pu tenir devant lui ?	3 Who could stand before him?
lorsqu'il combattait les batailles de YYY.	For he fought the battles of YYY.
4 N'est-ce pas par sa main que le soleil s'est arrêté	4 Was it not through his hand that the sun stood still
un jour était comme d[eux jour]s.	and one day was like t[wo day]s.
5 Car il a crié vers Dieu, le Très-Haut,	5 For he called to God, Most High,
lorsqu'il a oppressé dev[a]nt[ ]	when he pressed befo[re . . .
et le Dieu, Très-Haut, lui a répondu par des pierres de grêle et de gré[s]il.	And God, Most High, answered him with stones of hail and hail sto[n]es.
6a [Et il] a secoué sur[un peuple enne]mi	6a [He] beat on [an enem]y [people]
6b [ ]	6b [ ]

	כי צופה ייי מלחמתם:	¹⁸למען דעֹת כל גוי חרם	6cd
MS.Heb.e.62 XVI recto	ובימי משה עשה חסד:	¹וֹגָם כי מלא אחרי אל	6e/7a
	להתיצב בפרע קהל:	²הוא וכלב בן יפנה	
	להשבית דבה רעה:	³להשיב חרון מעדה	
	משש מאות אלף רגלי:	⁴לכם הם בשנים נאצלו	8
	ארץ זבת חלב ודבש:	⁵להביאם אל נחלתם	
	ועד שיבה עמדה עמו:	⁶ויתן לכלב עצמה	9
	וגם זרעו ירש נחלה:	⁷להדריכם על בֹמתי ארץ	
	כי טוב למלא אחרי ייי:	⁸למען דעֹת כל זרע יעקב	10 תֹ'
	כל אשר לא נשא לבו:	⁹והשופטים איש בשמו	11ab
	יהי זכרם לברכה ושמם תחליף לבניהם:	¹⁰ולא נסוג מאחרי אל	11cd/12b
	המשואל מבטן אמו:	¹¹אוהב עמו ורצוי עושהו	13
	שמואל שופט וכמהן:	¹²נָזִיר ייי בנבואה	
	וימשח נגידים על עם:	¹³בֹ[דֹ]בֹר אל הכין ממלכת	
	ויפקד אלהי יעקב:	¹⁴ב[תור]תֹ[ו] צוה עדה	14
	וגם בדברו נאמן רועה:	¹⁵ב[אמונ]ֹת פֹיו דרוש חזה	15
	וֹטֹרֹף לֹ[ו] אוֹיביו מסביב:	¹⁶וגם הוֹ[א] קֹרא אל אל	16ab
	וֹיֹרֹ[ ]עָם [∘∘] [:]	¹⁷בעלתו [טֹ]לֹ[ה ח]ֹלֹ[ב]	16c/17a
	ויכנע נציבי צר ויאבֹ[ד] אֹת כל סרני פלשתים:	¹⁸בפקע אדיר נשמע קולו	17b/18a

L. 18 [46:6c] דֹעֹת — The *dalet* is only attested by the bottom tip of its vertical mark. The *ayin* is attested by the edge of its long base that angles downward.

L. 1 [46:6e] וֹגָםֹ — The bottoms of the letters confirm the reading.

L. 5 [46:8] At the end of the verse, one finds bleedthrough marks from כחלב מורם of XVI verso, 5 Sir 47:2.

L. 8 [46:10] תֹ' — It is unclear whether this is the correct reading of the marks in the margin. It is also unclear how to interpret the marks. למלא — The *mem* is only attested by its top and perhaps part of its bottom stroke.

L. 14 [46:14] ב[תור]תֹ[ו] צוה — Traces of the head and foot of the *tav* are visible, as well as the *tsade*'s base and the top of its branches (see the Syriac). The reconstruction ב[מצו]תו would also fit the space.

L. 15 [46:15] בֹ[אמונ]ֹת פֹיו דרוש — As already noticed by Smend, the reading כאמונת דרוש חזה is too short for the available space. The absence of any base line preceding the *dalet* makes it hard to believe that the word should be reconstructed as the *niphal* participle (against the reconstruction of Lévi [1898, 118] and Segal [1958, 321]; see Smend 1906b, 52 and 1906a, 445). Smend's reading באמונת פיו דרוש חזה is better, though only hypothetical.

L. 16 [46:16] הוֹ[א] קֹרא אל אל — This reading seems to be assured. Traces of the top of the *qoph* and of the horizontal bar of the *resh* are followed by traces of the right arm of the *aleph*, part of its diagonal and the bottom of its left leg. The two last *alephs* are attested by their lower left foot, part of the diagonal and the top of the right arm. A descender appears to the right of the last *aleph*, which is actually due to bleedthrough from the *qoph* of וקֹול of XVI verso, 16 Sir 47:9. The mark to the right of this descender, just to the left of the preserved *lamed*, is presumably another bleedthrough letter, in this case, the second *vav* of וקֹול. One suspects that some of the other traces on this line are also due to bleedthrough. וֹטֹרֹף — The first trace may be interpreted as a *vav*, followed by a *tet* represented by the rounded part of its right arm and the top of its left vertical. The *resh* is only attested by traces of its top bar, including the flourish of its left corner, yet it could also represent another letter. The final *pe* is only attested by a trace of its top curve. For the correspondence between טרף and לכב see Gen 31:39; 37:33; Exod 22:12. אוֹיבֹיו — The *aleph* is only attested by the corner of its bottom left foot. Only the bottom half of the *vav* is visible.

L. 17 [46:17] Marks at the end of the fist colon may be due to bleedthrough.

L. 18 [46:18] Three stichs are again written on this line. אֹת כל — The *aleph* is attested by traces of both feet. The *tav* is attested by a trace of its lower left foot. Next to this is the bottom most part of the *kaph*. The base of the *kaph* rests at an angle. The reason that the *kaph* is written in this way is presumably due to the cramped spacing.

46:6e מלא אחרי אל — Note that the same idiom is used concerning Caleb in Num 14:24 and Josh 14:8.

46:7 דבה רעה — Literally, "evil whispering."

46:8 לכם — Since a preposition with a 2mp suffix would be out of place, scholars often assume that this is a misspelling of לכן "thus." משש מאות אלף רגלי — The "men on foot" are those Israelites who died in the desert for their disobedience, before their children entered the promised land. They (and the number 600,000) are mentioned in Sir 16:10, as well as in various other places in the Bible (e.g., Exod 12:37; Num 11:21).

46:9 עצמה — In Josh 14:11, Caleb is descirbed as חזק and possessing כח.

46:11 בשמו — Literally, "in his name." The same idiom is found at the head of various lists. See, e.g., Gen 25:13; 36:40 and Num 3:17. לא נשא לבו — Given the fact that this is something that the righteous judges did not do, this must be something bad. The sense would seem to be presumption and pride (as also in 2 Kgs 14:10). The same construction, however, can also have a positive association of being inspired (as in Exod 35:21).

46:12 The three stichs are written in one line, which lacks 12a. תחליף — See Zeph 1:6. נסוג מאחרי אל — The same sense pertains to the word's use in Sir 44:17, according to our translation, though the word may indeed also have other connotations. See the note at 44:17.

46:13 אוהב — This is likely a mistake for אהוב, reflected in the Greek and the Syriac. נזיר ייי — See Judg 13:5.7. ממלכת — See also 47:11. This may be a biform of ממלכה with a segolate-like ending in the absolute,

6c afin que chaque nation vouée à l'extermination sache
6d que YYY surveille leur bataille.
6e Et aussi il a parfaitement suivi Dieu,
7a et au temps de Moïse, il a agi avec piété,
   lui et Caleb Ben Yephunneh,
   en tenant ferme lorsque l'assemblée s'était déchaînée,
   en détournant la colère de la congrégation,
   en stoppant la calomnie mauvaise.
8 C'est *pourquoi* eux deux ont été séparés
   d'entre six cent mille hommes de pieds,
   pour les conduire vers leur héritage,
   un pays où coulent le lait et le miel.
9 Et il a donné à Caleb la force
   et jusqu'à la vieillesse, elle s'est maintenue avec lui,
   pour les conduire sur les hauteurs du pays
   et aussi (que) sa descendance prenne possession de l'héritage.
10 Afin que toute la descendance de Jacob sache
   qu'il est bon de suivre parfaitement YYY.
11 Les juges, chacun selon son nom,
   chacun d'eux qui n'a pas élevé son cœur,
   et ne s'est pas détourné de Dieu,
   que leur souvenir soit béni,
12b et que leur nom survive pour leurs enfants.
13 Aimant de son peuple et favori de son créateur,
   appelé depuis le sein de sa mère,
   consacré de YYY par la prophétie :
   Samuel, exerce le jugement et le sacerdoce.
   Sur la parole de Dieu, il a fondé la royauté
   et il a oint des chefs sur le peuple.
14 Par[sa l]o[i], il a instruit la congrégation
   et le Dieu de Jacob (l')a institué.
15 Et en raison de[la vérité]de sa bouche, il fut recherché (comme) voyant
   et en raison de sa parole il fut reconnu (comme) berger.
16 Et aussi i[l] a crié vers Dieu
   et a déchiré pour l[ui-même] ses ennemis alentour,
   lorsqu'il a sacrifié [l'ag]ne[au] de [l]a[it.]
17a Et il ton[na   ]
   dans un puissant éclair, sa voix a été entendue.
18 Il a humilié les gouverneurs de l'ennemi
   et il a détruit tous les princes des Philistins.

6c so that every nation which was devoted to the ban could know
6d that YYY was watching their battle.
6e And also he followed after God faithfully,
7a in the days of Moses he acted piously,
   he and Caleb Ben Yephunneh,
   by taking a stand when the assembly lost restraint,
   turning back wrath from the congregation,
   halting the angry protests.
8 *Therefore*, these two alone were separated
   from the six hundred thousand men on foot,
   in order to bring them to their inheritance,
   a land flowing with milk and honey.
9 He gave to Caleb strength,
   and until old age it remained with him.
   to lead them over the high places of the land,
   and also (so that) his seed would take possession of their inheritance,
10 so that all the seed of Jacob would know
   that it is good to follow after YYY faithfully.
11 The judges, each individual one,
   each one who did not let pride carry them away,
   who did not pull away from God,
   let their memory be a blessing,
12b and their name something that survives for their children.
13 One who loves the people, and is favored by his maker,
   the one called from the womb of his mother,
   one dedicated to YYY in prophecy,
   Samuel, one judging and acting as priest.
   At God's word he established the kingdom,
   and anointed rulers over the people.
14 By [his] l[a]w he commanded the congregation
   and the God of Jacob appointed (him).
15 On account of [the trut]h of his mouth he was sought as a seer,
   and also because of his word he was trusted as a shepherd.
16 Also, h[e] called to God,
   and he tore for [himself] his enemies round about,
   when he offered [a suck]l[ing la]m[b].
17 He th[undered   ]
   in a mighty crack, his voice was heard.
18 He humbled the rulers of the enemy,
   he destroyed all the leaders of the Philistines.

frequent in *piyuttim*, similar to the pairs מחשבה and מחשבת, as well as תפארה and תפארת.

46:14 אלהי יעקב — Although this is presumed in the Greek and the Syriac, it is commonly assumed to be a mistake for אהלי יעקב, "tents of Jacob," the verb פקד indicating not appointment, but rather Samuel's attentiveness (as reflected in 1 Sam 7:16–17).

46:15 רועה — Scholars often assume that this is a mistake for ראה "one seeing" (1 Sam 9:19).

46:17 פקע — The noun presumably refers to the sound of thunder, as attested in Syriac.

46:18 צר — The defective spelling suggests "enemy," not "Tyre," as in the versions. This also fits the biblical context of 1 Sam 7:10–13.

		העיד ייי ומשיחו	וְעֵת נוחו על משכבו[1]	19
MS.Heb.e.62 XVI verso		וכֹּל אדֹם לֹא עָֿנָֿה	כופר וְנֶעלם ממ[ ]תִֿי[○]	
בֹֿ		בעיני ייי ובעֵיֿנִֿי כל חי:	וגם עד עת קצו נבון נמצא[2]	
		ויגד למלך דרכיו נשא קולו מארץ בנבואה:	וגם אחרי מותו נדרש[3]	20

Chapter 47

		להתיצב לפני דוד:	וגם אחריו עמד נתן[4]	1
		כן דויד מישראל:	כי כחלב מורם מקדש[5]	2
		ולדובים כבני בשן:	לכפירים שחק כגדי[6]	3
		ויסֹר חֹרפת עולם:	בנעוריו הכה גֿבור[7]	4
		וישבר תפֿארת גלית:	בהניפו ידו על קלע[8]	
		ויתן בימינו עז:	כי קרא אל אל עליון[9]	5
		ולהרים את קרן עמו:	להדף את איש יודע מלחמות[10]	
		ויכנוהו ברבבה:	על כן ענו לו בנות[11]	6ab
		ומסביב הכניע צר:	בעטותו צניף נלחם[12]	6c/7a
		ועד היום שבר קרֿ[נם]:	ויתן בפלשתים ערים[13]	
		לאל עליון בֿדֿבֿ[ר כ]ֿבֿוד:	בכל מעשהו נתן הודות[14]	8ab	דויד
		ובכל יֿ[ו]ֿםֿ שֿ[בח ב]ֿשֿיֿרֿ:	בכל לבו אוהב עשהו[15]	8d/9c	
וקולו מזמור הנעים	נבל	וקוֹלוֹ הֿנֿעֿיֿםֿ נֿבֿלֿים תיקן:	נגינות שיר לפֿ[נ]ֿיֿ [מֿזֿ]ֿבֿחֿ[16]	9ab	הכין

L. 1 [46:19] Four stichs are found on this single line. The letters at the end of the verse are particularly difficult to read. ממ[ ]תִֿי[○] — The letters are often reconstructed as ממי לקחתי. The proposal has several difficulties. The letter immediately following the second *mem* may be a *sin/shin*, unless the three marks that look like the top tips of the letter are not in fact parts of a letter. There is no clear sign of the *lamed*'s ascender, though there should be. The descender of the *qoph* is not clearly visible, but may be attested in a blurred trace. On the other hand, there is a trace of a vertical mark that might be the left leg of a *khet*. The peculiar shape of the letters is due to the cramped spacing. וכֹּל אדֹם — The *kaph* almost looks as if it has an ascender. The *lamed* almost looks like a straight line, its ascender barely rising above the other letters. The *dalet* is attested by a very short horizontal bar and a smudge that looks like the remnants of a vertical mark. The final *mem* looks like an initial/medial *mem*. לֹא עָֿנָֿה — The *lamed* again looks like a straight line, but this time rising clearly above the other letters. The *aleph* is attested by its diagonal bar and by its upper right arm. The *ayin* is written in the crease; one can barely see the traces of its right edge that becomes the base line, here at an angle. Traces of the left arm also seem to be visible. The *nun* is basically a squat right angle. The *he* is made of two marks, one a rather thick mark that indicates the horizontal bar and the right leg, and another stroke that is the left leg. Curiously, the *nun* and *he* are attested on the same folio page that preserves XI recto, Sir 41:9–22, which raises the question as to how the text of 46:19 came to be written adjacent to Sir 41:9. Were the manuscript pages bound in this incorrect order in antiquity, when these additions to the text were made? Notice that the connection of folio page XVI verso and XI recto is also confirmed later in the marginal alternative to Sir 47:9 where one sees on XI recto the the top of the *lamed* of קול, which is otherwise visible on XVI verso. בֹֿ — These letters are written beneath אדֹם לֹא. The *bet* could also be a *kaph*.

L. 3 [46:20] The line contains three cola. נשא — Most scholars read וישא, but the trace of a low horizontal base line to the right of the *sin/shin* suggests reading *nun*. On the other hand, note the trace of another similar mark beneath the *dalet* of דרכיו, which must reflect an imperfection in the paper or some other cause.

L. 4 [47:1] Bleedthrough letters are clearly visible here and in the next line.

L. 10 [47:5] Note the bleedthrough *bet* (from לבניהם XVI recto, 10 Sir 46:12*b*) to the right of the first letter of the line.

L. 15 [47:9c] יֿ[ו]ֿםֿ שֿ[בח ב]ֿשֿיֿרֿ — The *yod* is clear to the right of the hole. To the left of the hole are traces of what seems to be a final *mem*'s upper and lower bars. Marks immediately to the left of the final *mem* seem too close to be another letter. Perhaps these are the remnants of bleedthrough or offset letters. The following marks are read as a *shin*, perhaps the beginning of the word שבח "he praises" (see the reconstruction of the Greek text of mss 70 and 248 by Segal [1958, 325]). The *shin* is attested by traces of the upper tips of its three arms and by a trace of its lower bar. By overlaying an image of the *sin/shin* of שבר from line 13, Sir 47:7c, it seems clear that these traces fit the form of a *sin/shin*. Given the space above the hole, it is also clear that the reconstruction of the verb הלל is impossible; there is no remnant of a *lamed*'s ascender where one would expect one. According to the last traces and the available space, the reconstruction בֿשֿיר is highly probable.

L. 16 [47:9ab] לפֿ[נ]ֿיֿ [מֿזֿ]ֿבֿחֿ — The *pe, mem, zayin,* and *bet* are only attested by the remnants of their tops. Of these, the *mem* seems the most distinct. The *khet* is difficult to read, in part, because its left leg is so faint, which makes it look like a *resh*. The reading מזמר, however, does not seem possible, given the shapes of the letters above the hole. וקוֹלוֹ הֿנֿעֿיֿםֿ נֿבֿלֿים — What looks like a *lamed*'s ascender in the middle of this series of marks is really due to offsetting from XVII recto 16 Sir 47:22. Our reconstruction is based on the traces and marginal reading (see also y. Šeqal. 48d היה מנעים את קולו "he sweetened his voice"). נֿבֿלֿים — The *nun* and *bet* are only attested by their lower bars. The *lamed* seems clear due to the distinctive bottom form of its diagonal. וקֹלֹ מֿזֿמֹוֿרֿ הנֿעִים — The marginal alternative is written along the extreme left edge of the page.

19 Au temps où il se reposait sur sa couche,
   il a témoigné de YYY et de (son) oint :
   « De qui ai-je pris la rançon et le trésor caché ? »
   Mais personne ne lui a répondu.
   Aussi, au moment de sa fin, il a été reconnu prudent,
   aux yeux de YYY et aux yeux de tous les vivants.
20 Aussi, après sa mort, il a été recherché
   et il a raconté au roi son destin (litt. ses voies),
   il a élevé de la terre sa voix en prophétie.

Chapitre 47

1 Et aussi, après lui, s'est dressé Nathan,
   pour se tenir devant David.
2 Car, comme la graisse prélevée de (l'offrande) sacrée,
   ainsi David (est prélevé) d'Israël.
3 Il jouait avec les lions comme avec des enfants,
   avec des ours comme avec des béliers de Bashân.
4 Dans sa jeunesse, il a terrassé le guerrier
   et a écarté une honte éternelle.
   Lorsqu'il a fait tournoyer sa main avec (litt. sur) la fronde,
   il a brisé la splendeur de Goliath.
5 Car, il a crié vers le Dieu très-haut
   qui a donné à sa main droite la force
   pour repousser l'homme expert en combats
   et pour relever la corne de son peuple.
6 C'est pourquoi les jeunes femmes ont chanté pour lui
   et elles lui ont attribué des myriades.
   Lorsqu'il a enveloppé le turban, il s'est battu,
7a et de toutes parts il a soumis l'ennemi.
   Il a établi des villes chez les Philistins
   et jusqu'à ce jour, [leur cor]ne est brisée.
8a En toutes ses œuvres, il a rendu grâce
8b au Dieu Très-Haut par une paro[le de gl]oire.
8d (mg. David) de tout son cœur aimait son créateur,
9c et chaque j[ou]r il le [louait par] des chants.
9a Instruments à cordes, chant, (mg. qu'il a établi) de[vant
   ]l'autel
9b et il a adouci sa voix et a arrangé les harpes.
   (mg. et il a rendu douce la voix du chant.)

19 At the time he rested over his bed,
   he testified to YYY and his anointed:
   "as for ransom and hidden (treasure), from who[m]
   have I [taken]?"
   And no one answered him.
   Also, at the time of his end, he was found prudent,
   in the eyes of YYY and in the eyes of all the living.
20 Also, after his death he was sought out,
   and he told to the king what would happen (lit., his paths);
   he lifted from the earth his voice in prophecy.

Chapter 47

1 Then, after him, stood Nathan,
   to take his proper place before David.
2 For, like fat lifted from the offering,
   thus is David from Israel.
3 He played with lions as if they were kids,
   with bears as if they were calves from Bashan.
4 In his youth, he struck the warrior,
   and reversed the perpetual disgrace.
   When he raised his hand to his sling,
   he shattered the renown of Goliath.
5 For, he called to God, the Most High,
   and he set strength into his right hand.
   toppling the one expert at battle,
   exalting the horn of his people.
6 Therefore, the young women sing to him
   and acknowledged him in (his killing) of ten thousand.
   When he wrapped his turban on, he fought,
7a and round about subdued his enemy.
   He set cities among the Philistines,
   and until this day [their] hor[n] is shattered.
8a In all his deeds he gave thanks,
8b to God the Most High, with [gl]orious [speech].
8d (mg. David) with all his heart loved his maker,
9c and in every d[a]y, he p[raised (him) with] song.
9a String music, song (mg. he established) be[fore] the altar
9b and his voice he sweetened and harps he arranged.
   (mg. and the sound of song he sweetened.)

46:19 For the same words of the first colon, see above at 40:5. Whereas in that passage the reference is to nightly rest, here the reference would seem to be to Samuel's retirement from public service. Nevertheless, the Greek suggests that his death is intended. The secondary bicolon of 19e-f, which is otherwise unknown, may reflect a similar sense. וּנְעָלַם — The language of these two stichs echoes that of 1 Sam 12:3: וּמִיַּד־מִי לָקַחְתִּי כֹפֶר. Although the Hebrew of that passage immediately follows this phrase with a verbal form, וְאַעְלִים "I will hide," the LXX translates as if it were the word נַעַל "sandal." Here, too, the grandson's translation presupposes the word "sandal" in his *Vorlage*. Although נְעָלָם here in 46:19 might be the plural "sandals," spelled defectively, it seems more likely that it is simply a *niphal* participle used as a substantive, essentially equivalent to "treasure."

47:6b ויכנוהו — The masculine plural is often used with a feminine subject in Late Biblical Hebrew. For כנה with *bet*, see 44:23 margin and the note.

47:7 ויתן בפלשתים ערים — This should indicate some destructive action. Although the Greek suggests a verb like מאס (see, e.g., Judg 9:38), and the Syriac נקם, the form ויתן here suggests that it is perhaps a mistake for ויתץ "he tore down" (see, e.g., Judg 9:45), in which case read עָרִים = "cities," though the Greek implies "enemies" (cf. Sir 37:5 and note). שבר קר[ן]נם — Literally, "he shattered their horn."

	[שָׁנֶה ○[ ]	[	]וֹ○ לֹ[תָ]ן[נ]17	10
	לִפְנֵי בְק[ר] יָרוֹן מִשְׁפָּט: מִקְדַשׁ		18בְהַלְלוֹ○ אֶת שֵׁם קָדְשׁוֹ
MS.Heb.e.62 XVII recto	וִירֶם לְעוֹלָם קַרְנוֹ:		1וְגַם ייי הֶעֱבִיר פִּשְׁעוֹ	11
	וְכִסְאוֹ הֵכִין עַל יְרוּשָׁלָם:		2וַ[יִּ]תֶּן לוֹ חֹק מַמְלֶכֶת
	בֵּן מַשְׂכִּיל שׁוֹכֵן לַבֶּטַח:		3בַּעֲבוּרוֹ עָמַד אַחֲרָיו	12
	וְאֵל הֵנִיחַ לוֹ מִסָּבִיב:		4שְׁלֹמֹה מֶלֶךְ בִּימֵי שַׁלְוָה	13
	וַיַּצֵּב לָעַד מִקְדָּשׁ:		5אֲשֶׁר הֵכִין בַּיִת לִשְׁמוֹ
	וַתָּצֶף כִּיאֹר מוּסָר.		6מַה חָכַמְתָּ בִּנְעָרֶיךָ	14
	וַתִּקְלֹס בַּמָּרוֹם שִׁירָה:		7אֶרֶץ כְּסִית בֹּ[בֹ]יָנְתָךְ	15
	עַמִּים הַסְעָרָתָה:		8בְּשִׁיר מָשָׁל חִידָה וּמְלִיצָה	17
	הַנִּקְרָא עַל יִשְׂרָאֵל:		9נִקְרֵאתָ בְּשֵׁם הַנִּכְבָּד	18
	וְכַעֲפֶרֶת הָרְבִּית כֶּסֶף		10וַתִּצְבֹּר כַּבַּרְזֶל זָהָב
	וַתַּמְשִׁילֵם בְּגֵוִיתְךָ:		11וַתִּתֵּן לְנָשִׁים כְּסָלֶיךָ	19
	וַתְּחַלֵּל אֶת יְצוּעֶיךָ:		12וַתִּתֵּן מוּם בִּכְבוֹדָךְ	20
	וַאֲנָחָה עַל מִשְׁכָּבֶךָ:		13לְהָבִיא אַף עַל צֶאֱצָאֶיךָ
	וּמֵאֶפְרַיִם מַמְלֶכֶת חָמָס:		14לְ[הִיוֹ]תָם לִשְׁנֵי שְׁבָטִים	21

L. 17 [47:10]]וֹ○ לֹ[תָ]ן[נ] — Before the *lamed*, we discern the head and the bottom tail of the *nun*. The *tav* is only preserved as a faint trace of the left edge of its horizontal bar. In the second stich, there are blurred remnants of the tops of letters, but it is impossible to determine even how many letters are represented.

L. 18 [47:10] מִקְדַשׁ: — The word is written above מִשְׁפָּט. Its *mem* is only attested by what appears to be a faint trace of the left most part of its diagonal line. It seems that this note was added by the scribe of the main text as a correction to מִשְׁפָּט because (1) there is no *circellus*, (2) the note includes the *soph pasuq* which is not common for interlinear marginal readings.

L. 1 [47:11] וְגַם — The letters are hard to decipher. The *vav* is a blurry vertical mark. The *gimel* is primarily attested by a trace of the bottom of its leg. There may be a trace of its short lower horizontal stroke, though this is very faint. The *mem* is visible from its bottom horizontal stroke and a portion of its left vertical, as well as traces of its upper left flourish.

L. 3 [47:12] בַּעֲבוּרוֹ — Offsetting from XVI verso, 3 Sir 46:20 makes the letters of this word difficult to read. Note, in particular, offsetting from the *aleph* of נשא that occurs over and between the first *vav* and *resh* in בַּעֲבוּרוֹ.

L. 7 [47:15] בֹּ[בֹ]יָנְתָךְ — The first *bet* is clear, based on the traces, though it could also be a *kaph*. The *yod* and *nun* are attested by just the tops of their letters. There may be a faint trace of the *nun*'s base line, ligatured to the following *tav*, which is attested by portions of its right vertical mark, the upper right corner, and a very small trace of its left foot. וַתִּקְלֹס — The last letter has the characteristic bottom of a *samek*. It seems too narrow to be a *tet*.

L. 8 [47:17] Ms B lacks verse 16, resulting from haplography due to the synonymous words at the end of 15*b* and the beginning of 17*a*. מָשָׁל — Although hardly any ink remains from the *sin/shin*, the hole matches exactly the shape of the letter, leaving no doubt as to its identity. Note also, the indications of the tops of its three arms.

L. 13 [47:20] לְהָבִיא — The *lamed* is only attested by a faint trace of its ascender. The *he* is only preserved by a small trace of its head, followed by traces of the upper and lower part of the *bet*. Then a trace of the *yod* is visible, followed by the distinctive diagonal line of an *aleph* and its left foot.

L. 14 [47:21] לְ[הִיוֹ]תָם — The space is too great to allow for just the reconstruction להיות (see Segal 1958, 327). Only the foot of the *tav* is clearly preserved. Only the lower bar of the final *mem* can be barely seen. The traces before the *lamed* are most likely due to offsetting.

47:10 מִשְׁפָּט — This seems like a simple mistake for the word written above it: מִקְדַשׁ (see the Greek τὸ ἁγίασμα).

47:11 הֶעֱבִיר פִּשְׁעוֹ — A more literal sense is "he caused his transgression to pass by or disappear" see 2 Sam 24:10. מַמְלֶכֶת — For this form, see 46:13 and the note there.

47:14 וַתָּצֶף — The Greek presumes an intransitive *qal* verb, as in the translation above, though the Syriac would presume a *hiphil* transitive verb: "he made the Nile flow…"

47:15 וַתִּקְלֹס — In Biblical Hebrew, the verb has the sense "to mock," while in Rabbinic Hebrew it means "to praise," as in Aramaic. בַּמָּרוֹם שִׁירָה — For the use of the first word, see Isa 58:4. Alternatively, this is a metaphorical use of the noun "height," as, for example, with the Syriac word רומא, hence "in the exaltation through song" (see CAL [9 April, 2015]), or it is a mistake for the Hebrew רומם "glorification," as found in Ps 66:17.

47:17 עַמִּים הַסְעָרָתָה — The *hiphil* of the Hebrew verb סער is not found in earlier sources. Nor is the *hiphil* of any verb with the root consonants שער. Perhaps הסערתה has a sense something like that of the

10 Il[a don]né pour[   ]
   [   ] année,
   lorsqu'[il] a loué son saint nom,
   au petit mat[in,] le jugement (mg. le sanctuaire) a jubilé.
11 Et aussi, YYY a pardonné sa transgression
   et a exalté pour l'éternité sa corne.
   Et il lui a [co]nfié la part de la royauté
   et il a établi son trône sur Jérusalem.
12 Grâce à lui, se dressa après lui
   un enfant intelligent demeurant en sécurité.
13 Salomon a été roi au temps de prospérité
   et Dieu lui a accordé la paix alentour,
   (lui) qui a fondé un temple pour son nom
   et a érigé un sanctuaire éternel.
14 Que tu as été sage dans ta jeunesse,
   tu as fait couler comme le Nil l'instruction.
15 Tu as couvert la terre par ton intelligence
   et tu as loué d'un chant dans les hauteurs.
17 Par des chants, des proverbes, des sentences et des énigmes,
   tu as impressionné les nations.
18 Tu as été appelé d'un nom glorieux
   qui a été invoqué sur Israël.
   Et tu as accumulé l'or comme si c'était du bronze
   et comme si c'était du plomb, tu as multiplié l'argent.
19 Et tu as donné tes reins à des femmes
   et tu les as laissées gouverner sur ton corps.
20 Et tu as mis une tache à ta gloire
   et tu as profané ta couche
   pour faire venir la colère sur tes descendants
   et un gémissement sur ton lit.
21 Pour qu'ils [devien]nent deux tribus
   et que d'Ephraïm (émerge) un royaume violent.

10 He [g]ave for [   ]
   [   ] year,
   When [he] praised his holy name,
   before the morning the place of judgment (mg. the sanctuary) shouted for joy.
11 YYY removed his transgression,
   and exalted his horn forever.
   He gave to him the right to rule,
   and his throne he established over Jerusalem.
12 For his sake, there stood after him
   a wise son, dwelling in security --
13 Solomon, king in the days of prosperity;
   for him, God made things peaceful round about,
   the one who established a temple for his name,
   and erected an eternal sanctuary.
14 How wise you were in your youth,
   you flowed over like the Nile with instruction.
15 You covered the land with your understanding,
   and you offered praise with song in the heights.
17 With song, proverb, riddle, and saying
    you awed the nations.
18 You were called by the gloried name,
   the one called over Israel.
   You accumulated gold as if it were bronze,
   you multiplied silver as if it were lead.
19 But, you gave to women your loins,
   and let them rule your body.
20 You set a blemish in your glory,
   and you profaned your bed,
   bringing anger over your children,
   and groaning over your bed,
21 that they became two tribes,
   and from Ephraim, a violent kingdom (emerged).

piel of סער, "to blow, scatter," but with a causative notion, "to cause X to blow, scatter." If so, then either the blowing is metaphorical, i.e., the nations are made to "blow" (i.e., express themselves) in proverbs that originate with Solomon, or there has been some confusion and the *bet* at the head of the preceding stich should be in front of "nations," so that the verse should read: "you caused song, proverb ... to blow among the nations." Alternatively, the metaphorical sense of "to blow" may be more like "to stir up," similar to the notion of a storm creating anxiety and awe (e.g., Sir 43:17; Ezek 1:4). Such a nuance is also suggested by the Greek and the Syriac, which translate with verbs denoting amazement (the Greek with the nations as the subject and the Syriac with Solomon as the subject). These explanations assume, of course, that the root is סער. Given the Greek and the Syriac, scholars have proposed, instead, that the root is שׁער I "to shudder, be horrified," in essence "you shocked nations with your song ..." Yet, another possibility is that the verb is from the root listed as שׁער III in BDB and HALOT, "to be familiar with," which occurs once in the *qal* in Deut 32:17, though its existence is sometimes doubted. If the verb is from this root, then the *hiphil* would presumably mean "to make familiar with" and might also be attested here: "you made people familiar with your songs ..."

47:18 נקראת בשם נכבד — For the rection of the verb with the preposition, see for example, Isa 43:7 and 48:1. Lévi (1898, 128–129) and others suggest that the reference is to Solomon being called ידידיה in 2 Sam 12:25, a name also applied to Israel in Jer 11:15. However, Segal (1958, 228) and others (see Mopsik 2003, 299) suggest that the reference is to the name of God, something encouraged by the Greek and the Syriac. Such is implied for Israel already in Sir 36:17 (see also Deut 28:10, Isa 63:19). Individual believers in God are said to be "called by his name" in Isa 43:7. Solomon's name is especially connected with the name of God since God is called שלום in Judg 6:24. Note also the rabbinic tradition that connects Solomon's name with God (see Mopsik [2003, 299] for references).

22	ו[ן]אולם [א]ל לא יטוש חסד		ולא יפיל מדבריו ארצה:
	¹⁶לא[ן] יכרית [לבחיריו נין ונכד		וא[ו]הביו לא ישמיד:
	¹⁷ויתן ל[יעקוב שא]רית		ולד[ו]ד [מ]מנו] שור[ש:]
23ab	¹⁸וישכב שלמה מ[ו]אש		ויעזב אחר[יו] [מ]נון
23cd	¹רחב אולת וחסר בינה	MS.Heb.e.62 XVII verso	רחבעם הפריע בעצה עם:
23ef	²עד אשר קם אל יהי לו זכר		ירבעם בן נבט אשר החטי[א] את [י]שראל
23g/24b	³ויתן לאפרים מכשול		להדיחם מאדמתם:
24a/25a	⁴ותגדל חטאתו מאד		ולכל רעה התמכר:

Chapter 48

1	⁵עד אשר קם נביא כאש		ודבריו כתנור בוער:
2	⁶וישבר להם מטה לחם		ובקנאתו המעיטם:
3	⁷בדבר אל עצר שמים		[וי]רד שלש אשות:
4	⁸מה נורא אתה אליהו		אשר כמ[ו]ך יתפאר:
5	⁹המקים גוע ממות		ומשאול כרצון יי:
6	¹⁰המוריד מלכים על שחת		ונכבדים ממטותם:
8	¹¹המושח מלא תשלומות		ונביא תחלי[ף] תחתיך:
7	¹²השמיע בסיני תוכחות		ובחור[ב] משפטי נקם:
9	¹³הנלקח בסערה מעלה		ובגדודי אש מק[די]ח:

L. 15 [47:22a] [א]ולם [א]ל — A *vav* is clearly visible before the hole. Then we can reconstruct an *aleph* based on the traces of the upper left corner of its diagonal and left leg (see also the Greek and the Syriac). The *lamed* is attested by the top of its ascender, just to the left of the hole.

L. 16 [47:22bc] לא[ן] יכרית [לבחיריו — The restoration of יכרית (see Lévi 1898, 130 and Smend 1906b, 54) is possible though a little bit long. The word לבחיריו may be reconstructed according to the preserved traces though the space between the *khet* and the *resh* seems too big for a single *yod*. וא[ו]הביו — The *vav* and the *aleph* are attested by their tops. The *he* is attested by the bottom tips of its legs and a trace of its upper left corner.

L. 18 [47:23ab] מ[ו]אש — The letters are quite clear on the 1901 facsimile edition. מנון — While the letters are incomplete, the reading מנון (with Smend 1906b, 54 and Ben-Ḥayyim 1973, 60) seems to be assured (against קצין proposed by Lévi 1898, 132)

L. 1 [47:23cd] בעצה עם — At the end of the lines, offset letters complicate the reading.

L. 2 [47:23f] ירבעם בן נבט אשר החטי[א] את [י]שראל — The reading is clearer on the 1901 facsimile. The first part, already read by Lévi, is perfectly clear. The restoration ויחטיא את ישראל read by Lévi 1898, 132; Smend 1906b, 55; Ben-Ḥayyim 1973, 60 and QDTL is not possible for the available space. Our reading tries to follow the traces and corresponds to the Greek and the last part of 1 Kgs 14:16.

L. 4 [47:24a/25a] רעה — The word is easier to read on the facsimile.

L. 5 [48:1] כתנור — Only the left half of the *tav* is clearly visible. Its right leg is extremely faint. The left foot is also mostly worn away. A bleedthrough mark (from the *resh* of אשר at XVII recto 5 Sir 47:13) makes it look as if there were a crossbar between the *tav* and the *nun*, so that the left half of the *tav* and the *nun* together look like a *tav*.

L. 7 [48:3] עצר — The *tsade* is only attested by traces of its base and a very blurry and faint trace of its upper right arm. [וי]רד — Where we restored וי there are traces of a letter that may be interpreted as a *pe* that would seem to recommend reading the root נפל "to fall" (ויפל), but it is difficult due to spacing and the other traces. These traces of letters may also be the result of offset letters. The two horizontal upper bars may correspond to *dalet* and *resh* (see Lévi 1898, 134). ש[ל]ש — The initial *shin* is preserved by traces of its right arm and base. Some ink from its middle arm has also survived. Traces of the *lamed*'s ascender are perceptible, as is what looks like the bottom most trace of the letter. The final *shin* is attested by two marks, which must be the top traces of the letter's middle and left arms. In addition, the bottom contour of the hole reflects exactly the shape of *shin*. Puech (2017, 207) reads וגם שלוש הורי[ד] אשות which seems very difficult to us.

L. 8 [48:4] אתה — The *tav* and traces of the *he* are easier to perceive on the facsimile.

L. 12 [48:7] נקם — Only the faintest trace of the upper left corner of the final *mem* is visible.

L. 13 [48:9] מק[די]ח: — The *mem* is attested by its bottom right corner and faint trace of the end of its diagonal. A vertical and the oblique of the *qoph* are preserved. Finally, the end of the left leg of the *khet* is visible on the left part of the hole. Puech (2017, 208) restored [מק[דיחה which is too long for the space. We suggest מק[דיח] which fits the space though אש is rarely masculine. The reconstruction מרום (Lévi 1898, 134) or שמים (Smend 1906b, 55 and Peters 1902, 421) are impossible for the space and the traces (for the latter).

22 Mais [cependant] Dieu n'abandonne pas (son) amour
 et ne laisse pas tomber une seule de ses paroles à terre.
 [Il] n'[anéantit]pas ses élus, les descendants et la postérité
 et il ne détruit pas ceux qui l'a[i]ment.
 Mais il a donné à [Jacob un res]te
 et à D[avid,]de[lui, une]raci[ne].
23a Salomon s'est endormi désespéré,
23b il a laissé après[lui] un rebelle.
23c Largement fou et manquant d'intelligence,
23d Roboam a détourné le peuple par (son) conseil,
23e jusqu'à ce que se lève — qu'il n'y ait aucun souvenir de lui —
23f Jeroboam fils de Nebath qui a fait pécher Israël
23g et qui a mis devant Ephraïm une pierre d'achoppement,
24b pour les bannir de leurs terres.
24a Son péché s'est grandement aggravé,
25a et à tout mal, il se livra.

Chapitre 48

1 jusqu'à ce que se lève un prophète comme le feu
 dont les paroles étaient comme une fournaise ardente.
2 Il a brisé pour eux le bâton de pain
 et dans son zèle, il les a diminués.
3 Par la parole de Dieu, il a fermé les cieux,
 [et il f]it descendre trois feux.
4 Combien redoutable es-tu, Elie ?
 Celui qui est com[me] toi est glorifié.
5 Toi, qui as fait se relever un mort de la mort
 et du Shéol, selon la volonté de YYY,
6 qui as fait descendre les rois dans la fosse
 et les as honorés de leurs couches,
8 qui as oint celui qui accomplit la rétribution
 et un prophète suppléant à ta place.
7 Il a fait entendre des reproches au Sinaï
 et à l'Horeb des décrets de vengeance.
9 (Toi) qui as été emporté en haut par une tempête,
 et par des armées d'un feu ar[den]t.

22 Ho[wever,] God will not abandon (his) devotion,
 and will not let fall to the ground any of his words.
 [He will] not [destroy] his chosen ones, the offspring and progeny,
 [those who l]ove him he will not destroy.
 He gave [to Jacob a remn]ant
 and to D[avid] f[rom him] a roo[t].
23a Solomon lay desparate
23b he left after [him] a rebel.
23c Broad in folly, and absent of understanding,
23d Rehoboam led the people astray with (his) counsel,
23e until one arose who should have no memory,
23f Jeroboam son of Nebat who made Israel sin.
23g He set an obstacle before Ephraim,
24b to banish them from their land.
24a His sin grew very great,
25a for any wicked thing he sold himself,

Chapter 48

1 until one prophet arose who was like fire,
 and whose words were li[k]e a burning oven.
2 He shattered their staff of bread,
 and in his zeal he made them few.
3 With the word of God he bound the heavens,
 [and he] brought down three fires.
4 How awe-inspiring are you, Elijah;
 (who) is glorified, like you?
5 You, who make the dead rise from death
 and from Sheol, according to the will of YYY,
6 who sent kings to the pit,
 and nobles from their beds,
8 who anointed the one who fulfilled retribution,
 and prophet (as) replacement in place of yourself.
7 He proclaimed rebukes in Sinai
 and in Horeb vengeful judgments.
9 (You) who were taken in a storm above,
 in bands of bu[rnin]g fire.

47:22 ולא יפיל מדבריו ארצה — This Hebrew idiom indicates that God will offer support and keep his promises.
47:23 מוֹאָשׁ — The *pual* of יאשׁ is only attested in *piyyutim*.
רחב אולת — Note the wordplay between this phrase and the name of the king, רחבעם, Rehoboam. The sequence of words with רחב at the head of 23c and עם at the end of 23d highlights this wordplay.
הפריע — More specifically, he did not offer the people good counsel.
48:4 אשר — One would expect the interrogative pronoun מי before the relative. Conceivably, the relative belongs to the following verse.

48:7 Not only is the verse out of order, according to the versions, but השמיע also seems at first to reflect the wrong sense: "he proclaimed." The episode involving Elijah and Sinai/Horeb is one in which Elijah listens (1 Kgs 19:8–18; = השומע). He does not proclaim anything. The Syriac translation has a similar meaning for verse 7, though it does not mention Sinai / Horeb and likely refers to a different event in the life of Elijah. Alternatively, it is also possible to read here a plene spelling of the *qal* participle: הַשֹּׁמֵעַ.
48:8 תחליף — See 44:17B. תשלומות — See 12:2A and the note.

	להשבית אף לפני בֹּאׄ[יום יי]ׄ:	10	14הכתוב נכון לעת
	ולהכין שבטֹ[י ישר]אֹל:		15להשיב לב אבות על בנים
	וֹתתן חֹ[יים וי]חׄיה:	11	16אשר ראך ומתׄ
	[וֹ]אֹלישׄ[ע נמל]אׄ[רו]חׄוׄ:	12ab	17אֹלׄ[יׄ]הׄ[וֹ] שׄ[בסערה נ]סֹתרׄ
	ומופתׄ[י]ם כל מוצא פיהו:	12cd	18פי שׄנׄ[י]ם אׄתׄוׄת הרבה
MS.Heb.e.62 XVIII recto	ולא משל ברוחו כל בשר:	12ed	1מימיו לא זע מכל
	ומתחתיו נברא בשרו:	13	2כל דבר לא נפלא ממנו
	ובמותו תמהי מעשה:	14	3בחייו עשה נפלאות
	ולא חדלו מחטאתם:	15	4בכל זאת לא שב העם
	ויפצו בכל הארץ:		5עד אשר נסחו מארצם
	ועוד לבית דויד קצין:		6וישאר ליהודה מזער
	ויש מהם הפליאו מעל:	16	7יש מהם עשו יושר
	בהטות אל תוכה מים:	17	8יחזקיהו חזק עירו
	ויחסום הרים מקוה:		9ויחצב כנחשת צורים
	וישלח את רב שקה:	18	10בימיו עלה סנחריב
	ויגדף אל בגאונו:		11ויט ידו על ציון
	ויחילו כיולדה:	19	12וׄאׄזׄ נׄ[]מוגו בגאון לבם
	ויפרשו אליו כפים:	20	13ויׄ[קר]אׄו אל אל עליון
	ויושיעם ביד ישעיהו:		14ויׄשׄ[מע יי] בׄקול תפלתם
	ויהמם במגפה:	21	15וׄ[ישבר ב]מׄחנה אשור
	ויחׄזק בדרכי דוד:	22	16כי עשה יחׄ[זקיהו את הטוב]
	[ ]		17[ ]
	[ ]	23	18[ ]

L. 14 [48:10] בֹּאׄ[יום יי]ׄ — Our reconstruction follows the Syriac (see also Lévi 1898, 136) and fits well the available space. Puech (2017, 208) suggests to restore [לפנׄ]י יום יי which is too short. Previous scholars have suggested חרון, based on the Greek, though the spacing of the marks seems to discourage this reconstruction. Thus, the reconstruction חרם also seems unlikely. Smend's proposal of [חרון א]ל is also not supported by the surviving marks (Smend 1906b, 55).

L. 16 [48:11] וֹתתן חֹ[יים וי]חׄיה: — The *vav* is only attested by its top. It is followed by a clear foot of *tav*. The second *tav* is preserved by the bottom of its right leg and its left foot. The *nun* is clear, based on its descender. Only very faint traces of the bottom of the two *khet*s are preserved. The reconstruction follows the Greek (see Puech 1990, 81-90 and 2017, 209 n. 12).

L. 17 [48:12ab] Only very faint traces of letters are preserved at the edges of the paper, allowing us to follow Puech's reconstruction (See Puech 2017, 210).

L. 18 [48:12cd] אׄתׄוׄת — Only the very bottoms of the letters are visible.

MS.Heb.e.62 XVIII Recto In order to preserve the page, conservators pasted a blank piece of paper along the lower edge of the manuscript page. The paper masks the lower edge of the recto—including a large section of paper that contained traces of letters—but not the lower edge of the verso. The result is that the shape of the recto does not match the shape of the verso.

L. 13–15 [48:20–21] The first letters are no longer visible on the manuscript due to paper pasted on it, but are transcribed in the first edition (see Cowley and Neubauer 1897, 38; Lévi 1898, 1:140-142; Smend 1906b, 58).

48:10 The missing text at the end of the verse is reconstructed based on the parallel with Isa 49:6, though the wording here is not identical to that biblical verse.

48:11 אשר — We assume this is a mistake for אשרי, the *yod* having been forgotten between the two *resh*es or a haplography of אשרי אשר ראך which is well attested in *piyyutim* and Karaïte literature (see Maagarim).

48:12 The phrase פי שנים echoes Elisha's request to Elijah that he be given a "double portion" of Elijah's prophetic power (2 Kgs 2:9), though here the phrase seems to be used in an adverbial sense (whereas in 2 Kings it is the subject of the sentence).

48:13 נברא — In the context, it seems that the sense of the verb is close to the sense the verb has in Ps 104:30. Most scholars suggest that the original text likely had "prophesied" (נבא), as in the Greek. Comparison is often made to 2 Kgs 13:21, when a man's corpse is thrown into Elisha's grave and the man comes back to life. Here, a simple reading of the words would seem to imply that Elisha came back to life. The language of the biblical passage is sufficiently vague to allow for the interpretation that Elisha came back to life, not the man, though this, of course, would make less sense in the context of 2 Kgs 13:21. In any case, the biblical passage has little to do with prophesying. The revival of the dead is simply one of the acts associated with the prophets Elijah and Elisha. Given the use of בשר in v. 12, one wonders if in v. 13 the same word has been accidentally repeated and a generic reference such as איש, referring to the resurrected man, stood here originally.

48:17 כנחשת — The manuscript preserves a clear *kaph* though this is likely a mistake for *bet*. הרים — We assume that the preposition *bet* is elided (see Miller 2009, 106–9).

10 Selon qu'il est écrit : « il est fixé pour un temps,
   de mettre fin à la colère avant que vienne le jour de YYY.
   pour faire revenir le cœur des pères vers les enfants
   et rétablir les trib[us d'Isra]ël ».
11 Heureux celui qui t'a vu et qui est mort,
   C[ar]tu donnes la vi[e et il vi]vra.
12a E[li]e a été [cach]é dans[une tempête]
12b [et]Elis[ée a été remp]li[de son es]prit.
12c Il a multiplié par deux les signes
12d et les prodiges, tout ce qui sort de sa bouche.
12e Durant ses jours, il n'a tremblé devant rien
12f et aucune chair n'a dominé son esprit.
13 Rien n'était trop merveilleux pour lui
   et en-dessous de lui (s.e. dans la terre), sa chair a été recréée.
14 Durant sa vie, il a fait des merveilles
   et dans sa mort des œuvres prodigieuses.
15 Malgré tout cela, le peuple ne s'est pas converti
   et ils n'ont pas cessé leurs péchés,
   jusqu'à ce qu'ils soient expulsés de leurs terres
   et dispersés sur toute la terre.
   Mais, il restait en Judas un petit nombre
   et encore un chef pour la maison de David, un chef.
16 Il y en a parmi eux qui ont fait ce qui est droit
   et d'autres parmi eux qui ont fait des merveilles de trahison.
17 Ézéchias fortifia sa ville,
   en faisant couler l'eau en son milieu,
   et il a percé les roches avec du bronze
   et il a enfermé un réservoir (dans) les montagnes.
18 En ces jours, s'est levé Sennacherib
   et il a envoyé Rab Schaké
   et il a étendu sa main sur Sion
   et il a blasphémé (contre) Dieu dans son orgueil.
19 [Et alors]ils on[t va]cillé dans l'orgueil de leur cœur
   et ils ont été saisis de contractions comme celle qui enfante
20 et ils [ont cr]ié vers le Dieu Très-Haut
   et ils ont tendu vers lui les mains.
   Et [YYY a écouté] la voix de leur prière
   et il les a délivrés par la main d'Isaïe.
21 Et [il a *brisé*]le camp d'Assur
   et il les a détruits par une plaie.
22 [Car E]zéchias[a fait] ce qui était bon
   et a tenu ferme dans les voies de David.
   [   ]
   [   ]
23 [   ]
   [   ]

10 Thus it is written, at a certain time it is determined
   that anger is to end, before the coming of the day of YYY,
   the heart of fathers is to return to their children,
   and the tri[bes of Israe]l are to be established.
11 Happy the person who has seen you and died,
   f[or] you will give lif[e so that he li]ves.
12a Eli[ja]h is one who was [hi]dden [in a storm],
12b [and] Elisha [one fille]d [with] his [spiri]t.
12c Two fold he increased signs,
12d and wonders (at) every issuance from his mouth.
12e He feared nothing during all his days,
12f nothing of flesh could dominate his spirit.
13 Nothing was too marvelous for him,
   and from his place (in the earth) his flesh was revived.
14 In his life he did wonders,
   and in his death marvelous deeds.
15 Through all this, the people did not turn back,
   and they did not cease from their sinning,
   until they were expelled from their land,
   and scattered throughout the earth.
   There remained a small number in Judah,
   and still a ruler belonging to the house of David.
16 There are among them those who have done what is right,
   and there are among them those who have committed extreme acts of treason.
17 Hezekiah foritified his city,
   extending water into its midst,
   He hewed rocks with bronze,
   and dammed a pool (in) the mountains.
18 In his days, Sennacherib came up,
   and sent the Rab Shakeh.
   He shook his hand at Zion
   and blasphemed God in his pride.
19 [Thus,] they[wav]ered in the pride of their heart,
   and they writhed as one who gives birth.
20 They [call]ed to God, the Most High,
   and spread their palms to him.
   and [YYY]h[eard] the voice of their prayer,
   and delivered them by the hand of Isaiah.
21 [He destroyed] the camp of Assur,
   and crushed them with a plague.
22 [He]zekiah [did] what was good,
   and was steadfast in the paths of David.
   [   ]
   [   ]
23 [   ]
   [   ]

Chapter 49

24	¹ברוח גבורה חזה אחרית	וינחם אבלי ציון:	MS.Heb.e.62 XVIII verso
25	²עד עולם הגיד נהיות	ונסתרות לפני בואן:	

1	³שם יאשיהו כקטרת סמים	הממלח מעשה רוקח:
	⁴בחך כדבש ימתיק זכרו	וכמזמור על משתה היין:
2	⁵כי נחל על משבותינו	וישבת תועבות הבל:
3	⁶ויתם אל אל לבו	ובימי חמס עשה חסד:
4	⁷לבד מדויד יחזקיהו	ויאשיהו כלם השחיתו:
	⁸ויעזבו תורת עליון	מלכי יהודה עד תמם:
5	⁹ויתן קרנם לאחור	וכבודם לגוי נבל נכרי:
6	¹⁰ויציתו קרית קדש	וישמו ארחתיה:
7	¹¹ביד ירמיהו כי ענוהו	והוא מרחם נוצר נביא:
	¹²לנתוש ולנתוץ ולהאביד ולהרס	וכן לבנת ולנטע ולהשׁ֯יׁ֯ב֯[:]
8	¹³יחזקאל ראה מראה	ויגד זני מרכבה:
9	¹⁴וגם הזכיר את איוב	המכלכל כל ד[רכי] צׁדק:
10	¹⁵וגם שנים עשר הנביאׁים	תׁהי עצמתם פר[חות מתח]תם:
	¹⁶אשר החלימו את יעקב	וישׁעֿנוהו כמׁ[ ]
11	¹⁷[מׁה נגׁד֯ל] [	]ל[ ]
12	¹⁸[ ] [	]

ו		¹ויֿרימו היכל קדש	המכונן לכבוד עולם:	T-S 16.314 XIX recto
	13	²נחמיה יאדר זכרו	המקים את חרבתינו:
		³וירפא את הריסתינו	ויצב דלתים ובריח:

L. 12 [49:7] ולהשׁ֯יׁ֯ב֯ — The *sin/shin* is attested by the upper parts of its arms. The letter, at first blush, seems unusually broad with the middle arm much closer to the left arm than normal. However, this understanding is incorrect. What appears at first to be the middle arm is actually the left most arm of the *sin/shin*; the middle arm has been almost totally effaced and appears only as a slight trace. The mark to the far left is likely a *yod*. The *bet* is only visible as a faint trace and could also be read as another letter.

L. 14 [49:9] צׁדק — The *tsade* is only attested by a trace of its base, which is ligatured to the *dalet*, as well as a trace of its vertical mark. The following two letters are easier to perceive in the facsimile.

L. 17 [49:11] מׁה — The upper left flourish of the *mem* is all that is preserved of this letter, though it is sufficiently distinct to make the letter clear. The *he*'s cross bar is partially effaced.

L. 13 [50:6] בימי מועד — These words are written together as one word.

L. 14 [49:9] איוב — Most of the preceding editions read נ[ב]יׁא after איוב (Smend 1906b, 57; Ben-Ḥayyim 1973, 62; Beentjes 1997, 88), but the visible marks are more likely due to bleedthrough from the word ויושיעם of the recto (cf. Skehan and Di Lella 1987, 542).

L. 16 [49:10d] וישׁעֿנוהו — The reading וישעוהו proposed by the preceding editions (Smend 1906b, 55; Ben-Ḥayyim 1973, 62; Beentjes 1997, 88) is impossible for the available traces. After the *shin*, we discern the right arm of the *ayin* as well as its base. To the left of the small hole, one sees a vertical line and a base line that correspond to the shape of a *nun*, followed by the letters *vav*, *he*, and *vav* (cf. Smend 1906b, 55 apparatus). This reading corresponds to the Syriac.

L. 17 [49:11] By shifting the brightness, contrast, and colors, one can see two vertical strokes and the majority of a *dalet* in the dark spot at the bottom edge of the page.

L. 1 [49:12] A *waw* has been inscribed on the upper corner of the inner margin and seems to be the signature of the sixth (ו) folio of the quire (see Schlanger 2018, 72 and complete introduction).

49:1 כקטרת סמים — See Exod 25:6. הממלח — See Exod 30:35 in the same context. The verb means "to salt"; for the use of salt in the production of perfume and incense, see Haran 1960 and Brun 2000.

49:2 נחל — The verb would appear, at first blush, to mean "he took possession," though of course this does not make sense. Scholars have attempted to make sense of the verb by suggesting it is a *niphal* of חלל used in a slightly unusual way ("he was defiled") or a misspelling or biform of the *niphal* of חלה, as reflected in the translation above. In relation to this interpretation, note the *niphal* of חלה used with the על preposition in Amos 6:6.

49:4 תמם — *Qal* infinitive construct of תמם with the 3mp pronoun.

49:5 לאחור — This form is probably the consequence of a confusion between *vav* and *yod*, and so we interpret it as a mistake for לאחיר.

49:6 וישמו — A defective spelling of the *hiphil*, or a *qal* with "its streets" as subject. Cf. ואשמה at 4Q389 6 1.

49:7c This verse quotes Jer 1:10, except for the last word, להשיב, which is missing in Jeremiah (and in the Greek text of Sirach).

49:10 וישׁעֿנוהו — The verb שען, "to support," in the *qal* and the *niphal* does not occur with object suffixes. So, we assume here either a *piel* (extremely rare according to Maagarim) or a defectively spelled *hiphil*.

24 Grâce à un esprit puissant, il a vu le futur (litt., l'après)
   et il a réconforté les endeuillés de Sion.
25 Il a raconté ce qui sera jusque dans l'éternité
   et les choses cachées, avant qu'elles n'arrivent.

Chapitre 49

1 Le nom de Josias est comme un parfum d'encens,
   salé, œuvre de parfumeur.
   Au palais, son souvenir devient doux comme le miel
   et comme une chanson lors d'un banquet de vin.
2 Car il a été bouleversé par nos apostasies
   et a mis fin à nos vaines abominations.
3 Son cœur a été intègre envers Dieu
   et aux jours de violence, il a fait preuve de bienveillance.
4 À l'exception de David, Ezéchias
   et Josias, tous se sont corrompus
   et ont abandonné la loi du Très-Haut,
   les rois de Juda, jusqu'au dernier.
5 Et il a transféré leur pouvoir *à un autre*
   et leur gloire à une nation folle, étrangère.
6 Et ils ont mis le feu à la ville sainte
   et ils ont ravagé ses rues,
7 selon (les paroles de) Jérémie, bien qu'ils l'aient maltraité.
   Mais lui, depuis le sein, il a été formé prophète,
   pour déraciner et renverser et exterminer et détruire,
   mais aussi pour bâtir et planter et restaurer[.]
8 Ezekiel a vu une vision
   et il a décrit les (différents) attributs de chars.
9 Et aussi, il a fait mémoire de Job,
   celui qui a gardé toutes les v[oies]de justice.
10 Et aussi, les douze prophètes
    que leurs ossements fleu[rissent de des]sous eux,
    eux qui ont rétabli Jacob
    et qui l'ont soutenu comme [   ]
11 Comment exalterons-nous[Zorobabel ?]
    [   ]
    [   ]
12 [   ]
    Et ils ont relevé le temple saint
    qui a été établi pour une gloire éternelle.
13 Néhémie, que soit honoré son souvenir,
    lui qui a redressé nos ruines,
    qui a restauré nos décombres
    et qui a mis en place les portes et les verrous.

24 Through his powerful spirit he saw the future (lit., the afterward)
   and comforted those mourning Zion.
25 He spoke of what will be in future times,
   and hidden things, before they happened.

Chapter 49

1 The name of Josiah is like perfumed incense,
   salted, the work of the perfumer.
   On the palate, his memory is sweet like honey,
   and like a song at a banquet
2 For, he was distressed over our apostasies
   and put an end to our vain abominations.
3 His heart was true to God,
   and in the days of violence he did kindness.
4 Apart from David, Hezekiah,
   and Josiah, all of them acted corruptly.
   The kings of Judah abandoned
   the Torah of the Most High, to the last one.
5 So, he gave their power to *another*,
   and their glory to a foolish, foreign people.
6 They set fire to the holy city,
   and destroyed its streets,
7 according to Jeremiah('s words), though they abused him,
   for he was formed from the womb a prophet,
   to uproot, and tear up, and destroy, and annihilate,
   and thus to build, plant, and restore[.]
8 Ezekiel saw a vision,
   and described the qualities of the chariot.
9 Also, he mentioned Job
   the one who continues on p[aths of] righteousness.
10 Also, the twelve prophets
    may their bones sp[rout from] their place (in the grave),
    they who restored Jacob to health,
    and they supported him like [ ].
11 How can we exalt [Zerubbabel]
    [   ]
12 [   ]
    [   ]
    who elevated the holy temple,
    the one established for perpetual glory.
13 Nehemiah, may his memory be honored,
    the one who lifted our ruins,
    who repaired our rubble,
    and set up the doors and bolts.

14	⁴מעט נוצר על הארץ כהניך	וגם הוא נלקח פנים:
15	⁵כיוסף אם נולד גבר	וגם גויתו נפקדה:
16	⁶ושם ושת ואנוש נפקדו	ועל כל חי תפארת אדם:

Chapter 50

1	⁷גדול אחיו ותפארת עמו	שמעון בן יוחנן הכהן:
	⁸אשר בדורו נפקד הבית	וביומיו חזק היכל:
3	⁹אשר בדורו נכרה מקוה	אשיח בם בהמונו:
2	¹⁰אשר בימיו נבנה קיר	פנות מעון בהיכל מלך:
4	¹¹הדואג לעמו מחתף	ומחזק עירו מצר:
5	¹²מה נהדר בהשגיחו מאהל	ובצאתו מבית הפרכת:
6	¹³ככוכב אור מבין עבים	וכירח מלא מבין בימי מועד:
7	¹⁴וכשמש משרקת אל היכל המלך	וכקשת נראתה בענן:
8	¹⁵כנצפענפי בימי מועד	וכשושן על יבלי מים:
8/9	¹⁶כפרח לבנון בימי קיץ	וכאש לבונה על המנחה :
	¹⁷ככלי זהב תבנית אטיל	הנאחז על אבני חפץ:
10	¹⁸כזית רענן מלא גרגר	וכעץ שמן מרוה ענף:
11	¹בעטותו בגדי כבוד	והתלבשו בגדי תפארת:
	²בעלותו על מזבח הוד	ויהדר עזרת מקדש:

T-S 16.314 verso

L. 15 [50:8] כנצפענפי — The letters are written close together so that they appear to be a single word. In addition, as many others have recognized, the fourth letter is a *pe* not a *bet* (as Lévi [1901, 208] reads), though the *pe* is likely a simple graphic or phonetic error for *bet*. The last word (ענפי) in construct with the prepositional phrase is unexpected and presumably reflects another graphic or phonetic error for ענפים.
L. 17 [50:8/9] תבנית — The word is read in different ways by past scholars; e.g., תפילת (Smend 1906b, 58), חפוי (Peters 1902, 427), and הכזית (HAWTTM 2017, sub אטיל). Our reading agrees with that of Ben-Ḥayyim (1973, 63). The letters are clear on the digital photos. The initial *tav* is clear from its left foot beneath the small lacuna. The *bet* is clear from its upper horizontal line and base line that rises to the right toward the lacuna. The final *tav* is also clear from its right vertical leg and left vertical leg with its foot. אטיל — Although the second letter is not transliterated in most editions, it is clearly a *tet* (also in HAWTTM 2017, 76), based on its left most mark, its base line and the top trace of its right horizontal mark.

49:14 כהניך — The second letter is clearly a *he* (not a *khet*) and the penultimate letter is clearly a *yod* (not a *vav*). Nevertheless, the original text presumably read כחנוך "as Enoch" as attested in the Greek and the Syriac. פנים — The absolute use of פנים may mean "inside" as in b. Menaḥ. 9a "inside [the temple]" (see Jastrow 1903, 1190), perhaps evoking here the celestial temple. In its absolute use, the word is often qualifying another word like לחם פנים "bread of the presence," מלאך פנים "angel of the face." Here, it may by association designate the divinity's presence.
49:15 כיוסף אם — For the non-initial position of the interrogative אם, cf. Judg 5:8 (Segal 1958, 340). נפקדה — The meaning of the *nifal* of פקד in the next three verses is unclear. In this verse, the phrase has often been interpreted as an allusion to the transfer of Joseph's bones (see Gen 50:25; Exod 13:19). Kister (1999, 179–82) gives it the meaning "visited by death" in reference to Num 16:29. It may certainly have here, and in the following instances, the meaning "to care for" (see also Tigchelaar 2003, 179–85).
49:16 תפארת אדם — For a discussion of the expression, see Kister 1999, 179–82 and Tigchelaar 2003. The expression may be compared with כבוד אדם in CD III 20; 1QS IV 23; 1QHᵃ IV 27.
50:1–29 For this chapter, see Mulder 2003.
50:1 חזק — We have read חזק as a *pual*, but it may also be vocalized as a *piel* (see the Greek).
50:3 אשיח בם — The words are hard to make sense of. As they stand, they are easiest to construe according to the translation above. This may be a corruption of אשיח כים "a pool (whose abundance is) like the sea" (see the Greek). Although the noun אשי/וח is not attested in Biblical Hebrew or Rabbinic Hebrew, it is found at least four times in the Copper Scroll (3Q15 V 6, VII 4, X 5, XI 12) as well as twice in the Mesha Stele (KAI 181:9,23, see Hoftijzer and Jongeling 1995, 122 and cf. אשחה idem, 123). This passage may be compared with John 5:3–4.
50:4 מחתף — See 15:14ᴬ and the note.
50:5 מה נהדר בהשגיחו מאהל — Note the same expression in relation to the high priest in various *piyyutim* and prayers from the first millennium CE, including a *qedusha* by Johanan Ben Joshua ha-Kohen (e.g., in ms. T-S H.6.42), where the high priest is compared to a number of separate items in language reminiscent of Sir 50: מה נהדר כהן גדול בצאת מן הקודש . . . כיובל כפלגי מים . . . כמור בגבעת הלבונה . . . כקשת מתוחת בענן "how glorious is the high priest when he comes forth from the sanctuary . . . like a stream, like channels of water . . . like myrrh in the hill of frankincense (cf. Song 4:6) . . . like a rainbow stretched in the cloud." מבית הפרכת — As in 42:12ᴮ, we interpret בֵּית as the fem. of בֵּין (compare with Exod 26:33).
50:6 וכירח מלא מבין — The use of מבין is unexpected here, as we suppose it to be followed by a noun. It is possibly a mistake under the influence of the preceding stich.
50:7 משרקת — See also 43:9ᴮ,ᴹ and Dihi 2004, 695–697.
50:8 כנצפענפי — The expression is likely a corruption of כנץ בענפים "like a blossom in branches." Although Hebrew nouns are sometimes found in construct with prepositional phrases (as Peters [1913, 428]

14 Peu ont été formés sur la terre (comme) tes prêtres (= *comme Hénoch*)
　et aussi, il a été pris (dans) la (divine) présence.
15 Est-il né un homme comme Joseph ?
　Et aussi son corps a été visité.
16 Shem et Seth et Enosh ont été visités,
　mais au-dessus de tout vivant est la splendeur d'Adam.

Chapitre 50

1 Grand parmi ses frères et splendeur de son peuple,
　Shime'on ben Yohanan, le prêtre.
　C'est dans sa génération que le temple (litt. la maison) a été visité
　et en ces jours que le temple a été restauré.
3 C'est dans sa génération que le réservoir a été creusé,
　une piscine avec son tumulte en ces (jours),
2 C'est en ces jours que le mur a été bâti,
　pierres d'angles d'une demeure dans le palais du roi,
4 Celui qui s'inquiète pour son peuple à propos des pillards
　et qui fortifie sa ville contre les ennemis.
5 Qu'il était resplendissant quand il regardait hors de la tente
　et lorsqu'il sortait du milieu du voile,
6 comme une étoile de lumière entre les nuages
　et comme une pleine lune au milieu, lors des jours de fête,
7 comme un soleil qui brille sur le palais du roi,
　comme l'arc-en-ciel qui apparaît dans la nuée,
8 comme une fleur sur les rameaux aux jours de fête,
　comme un lys sur des cours d'eau,
　comme une fleur du Liban aux jours d'été,
9 comme le feu de l'encens sur l'offrande,
　comme un vase d'or, un modèle *de repoussé* (?) recouvert de pierres précieuses,
10 comme un olivier verdoyant chargé de fruits
　et comme un arbre à huile qui sature les branches.
11 Lorsqu'il revêtait les vêtements de gloire
　et s'habillait de vêtements magnifiques,
　lorsqu'il montait sur l'autel splendide
　et honorait l'enceinte du temple,

14 Few were those formed over the earth (as) your priests (= *as Enoch*),
　thus, he was taken up (into) the (divine) presence.
15 Has there been born someone like Joseph?
　Whose corpse was even cared for.
16 Shem, Seth, and Enosh were cared for,
　but over all the living is the splendor of Adam.

Chapter 50

1 Greatest of his brothers, the wonder of his people,
　Simon Ben Yochanan, the priest,
　in whose generation the temple precincts (lit., the house) was cared for
　and in whose days the temple was restored,
3 in whose generation the reservoir was dug
　a pool in them (i.e., in those days) with its tumult,
2 in whose days the wall was built,
　the towers of the abode of the king's palace,
4 the one concerned for his people about bandits,
　and fortifying his city against adversaries—
5 how glorious when he looked out from the tent,
　and when he came out from among the curtains,
6 like a star shining from between clouds,
　and like a full moon from between, in the festival days,
7 like the sun shining over the King's palace,
　like the rainbow that appears in the rain clouds,
8 like a blossom in vine-branches in the festival days,
　like a lily over streams of water,
　like a flower of Lebanon in summer days,
9 like burning frankincense (lit., the fire of frankincense) over the offering
　like a golden vessel, a work *of repoussé* (?), covered by precious stones,
10 like a leafy olive tree, full of fruit,
　and like a tree whose oil saturates the branches.
11 When he wrapped himself in glorious clothes,
　dressed himself in wonderful clothes,
　when he ascended over the splendorous altar,
　he brought honor to the temple precinct.

---

observes), the prepositional phrase usually forms a single semantic unit with the preceding noun, as with שמחת בקציר "joy in the harvest" (Isa 9:2), not a separate temporal adjunct, as seems to be the case here.

50:9　אטיל — The Aramaic word אטול occurs in the Aramaic Levi Document at 7:6 (see Greenfield, Stone and Eshel 2004, 167), corresponding to the Greek στρόβιλον "fir." The similar אטל occurs in manuscripts of the Samaritan Targum as a translation to the Hebrew אשרה. These two pieces of data might suggest that the word אטיל here represents a type of wood or tree. Nevertheless, the Greek (ὁλοσφύρητον "solid, beaten metal") and the Syriac (ܚܣܝܢܐ ܫܦܝܪ "beautifully adorned") do not reflect this sense. There are no convincing explanations for אטיל, but perhaps it reflects an earlier הטיל (the infinitive construct of נטל) "lifting" or "pouring," or an *aleph*-preformative noun from the same root (cf. the Aramaic נַטְלָא "ladle"). A "construction of lifting" might refer to repoussé work (cf. the Aramaic נגד "beaten, chased metal"), while a "construction of pouring" would refer to an object made by casting. The same root might also explain the Syriac since the root נטל in the Aramaic *hithpaal* means "to be exalted."

12	³בקבלו נתחים מיד אחיו		והוא נצב על מערכות:
	⁴סביב לו עטרת בנים		כשתילי ארזים בלבנון:
12/13	⁵ויקיפוהו כערבי נחל		כל בני אהרן בכבודם:
	⁶ואשי ייי בידם		נגד כל קהל ישראל:
14	⁷עד כלותו לשרת מזבח		ולסדר מערכות עליון:
16	⁸אז יריעו בני אהרן הכהנים		בחצצרות מקשה:
	⁹ויריעו וישמיעו קול אדיר		להזכיר לפני עליון:
17	¹⁰כל בשר יחדו נמהרו		ויפלו על פניהם ארצה:
	¹¹להשתחות לפני עליון		לפני קדוש ישראל:
18	¹²ויתן השיר קולו		ועל המון העריכו נרו:
19	¹³וירנו כל עם הארץ		בתפלה לפני רחום:
	¹⁴עד כלותו לשרת מזבח		ומשפטיו הגיע אליו:
20	¹⁵אז ירד ונשא ידיו		על כל קהל ישראל:
	¹⁶וברכת ייי בשפתיו		ובשם ייי התפאר:
21	¹⁷וישנו לנפל שנית		כִּי נִבְהֲלוּ מפניו:
22	¹⁸עתה ברכו נא את ייי אלהי ישראל		המפלא לעשות בארץ:
	¹המגדל אדם מרחם		ויעשהו כרצונו:
23	²יתן לכם חכמת לבב		ויהי בשלום ביניכם:
24	³יאמן עם שמעון חסדו		ויקם לו ברית פינחס:
	⁴אשר לא יכרת לו ולזרעו		כימי שמים:
25	⁵בשני גוים קצה נפשי		והשלישית איננו עם:
26	⁶יושבי שעיר ופלשת		וגוי נבל הדר בשכם:
27	⁷מוסר שכל ומושל אופנים		לשמעון בן ישוע בן אלעזר בן סירא:
	⁸אשר ניבע בפתור לבן		ואשר הביע בתבונות:

T-S 16.315 recto

L. 17 [50:21] כִּי — In the second half of the line, these letters are fairly clear. The first letter is unlikely to be a *bet* since it lacks the extension of the base line to the right of the vertical line. נִבְהֲלוּ — The marks are faded, but can still be read. The *nun* is attested by its vertical and base lines, the *bet* by only its base line. Traces of the *he* are also visible; in this case, while the ink has worn away, it has made the paper lighter in appearance than the surrounding paper. The *vav* is attested only by an extremely faint trace of its lower leg.

50:12 נתחים — The word נתח, "portion," designates here the "portion of the sacrifice," see Lev 1:6.

50:14 ולסדר — The verb סדר is not attested in Biblical Hebrew but is quite frequent in 1QM.

50:16 בחצצרות מקשה — The expression is elliptical and presupposes perhaps בחצצרות כסף מקשה which is found in Num 10:2, although in this case, the words belong to two different sentences. For this verse see also Num 10:10.

50:18b The second stich is certainly the result of textual alterations. Most of the commentators correct it according to the Greek (e.g., הירובו רנן or העריבו רנה "and over the multitude they make resound praises of joy"; see Lévi 1901, 212; Smend 1906a, 487–8; Segal 1958, 356; Di Lella 1987, 549). המון can refer to the "crowd" or to the "noise" in this context. For the expression העריכו נרו cf. Lev 24:4. The *hifil* of ערך should have here the same meaning as the *qal* or the *piel* "to prepare, to arrange" (See Moreshet 1976, 249–81; Qimron 2018, 243–44; Reymond 2014c, 192–94).

50:19 ומשפטיו הגיע אליו: — The context suggests some cultic act associated with the altar, though the exact action performed is unclear. The antecedent of the pronoun on משפטיו is the altar. The expression refers to the required sacrifices (see Num 15:24; Segal 1958, 346).

50:21 וישנו לנפל שנית — The redundancy of the verb שנה with the adverb שנית is not encountered in Biblical Hebrew or in the Mishnah.

50:22–24 These verses are similar and can be compared to Sir 45:25–26.

50:22 מפלא לעשות — Note the same phrase in Judg 13:19.

50:23 ויהי בשלום — The space between the second *yod* and the following *bet* is larger than the space between the *bet* and following *shin*, so that we assume that the *bet* goes with the following word. But, given the odd sense that this produces, one wonders if it once read instead ויהיב שלום "and give (an Aramaic like participle יָהֵיב?) peace between you" or "so that peace is set (literally, given, an Aramaic-like passive participle) between you." The verb יהב does occur in the *piyyut* in forms other than the imperative.

50:27 מוסר שכל — These two words can be understood as a consecutive sequence of independent nouns, as we have translated above, or as a construct expression "insightful instruction." ומושל אופנים — The first word may be interpreted as the noun מֹשֶׁל "likeness" as in Job 41:25 or as the participle of משל "the one who rules or makes proverbs." For the noun אופנים "appropriate," see Prov 25:14 and HAWTTM 1:41. Smend (1906a, 492) explains the form as referring to the rhythmic construction of Ben Sira's distichoi. ניבע — The *piel* of the root נבע is otherwise unknown. It may be used here in the sense of the *hifil* or, perhaps, this is a mistake for ניבא "he prophesied," or for יביע or יבע "he will rejoice." לבן — Another presumed mistake for לבו, in which case the sentence may be compared to Sir 16:25A and Prov 1:23.

12 lorsqu'il recevait les morceaux (s.e. du sacrifice) de la main de ses frères et que, lui, se tenait près du bûcher, autour de lui, était une couronne d'enfants, comme des plants de cèdres au Liban et ils l'entouraient comme les saules du ouadi,	12 When he received the portions from the hand of his brothers, he stood by the (altar's) stacks (of wood), round about him a crown of sons like the cedar-plants in Lebanon, they surrounded him like willows of the wadi,
13 tous les enfants d'Aaron dans leur gloire, les sacrifices consumés de YYY dans leur main, devant toute l'assemblée d'Israël.	13 all the children of Aaron in their glory, the fire-offerings to the Lord in their hand before all the assembly of Israel.
14 Lorsqu'il avait achevé son ministère à l'autel et ordonné le bûcher pour le Très-Haut,	14 When he finished ministering at the altar, arranging the stacks for the Most High,
16 alors les enfants d'Aaron, les prêtres, faisaient sonner des trompettes (d'argent) martelées et ils faisaient sonner et retentir un son majestueux, pour faire mémoire devant le Très-Haut.	16 then the children of Aaron, the priests, would give a shout with hammered trumpets, shouting and announcing in a majestic sound to offer remembrance before the Most High.
17 Toute chair ensemble s'empressait de tomber face contre terre, de se prosterner devant le Très-Haut, devant le Saint d'Israël.	17 All flesh together hastened to fall over their faces to the earth, to prostrate themselves before the Most High before the Holy One of Israel.
18 Le chant donnait sa voix et sur le tumulte ils arrangeaient sa lampe (s.e. de l'autel).	18 The song gave its voice, and over the sound they arranged its (i.e., the altar's) lamp.
19 Tous les habitants du pays poussaient des cris de joie dans la prière devant le Miséricordieux. Lorsqu'il avait achevé son ministère à l'autel et fait approcher de lui ses dûs (s.e. sacrifices),	19 All the people of the land shouted, in prayer before the Merciful One. When he finished ministering at the altar, and had brought forward to it its required (offerings),
20 Alors il descendait et levait ses mains sur toute l'assemblée d'Israël. Et par la bénédiction de YYY sur ses lèvres et par le nom de YYY, il était glorifié.	20 he came down and lifted his hands over all the assembly of Israel. By the blessing of YYY on his lips, and by the name of YYY, he was glorified.
21 Ils recommençaient à tomber une seconde fois, car ils étaient terrifiés devant lui.	21 They again fell a second time for they were terrified before him.
22 Maintenant, bénissez YYY, Dieu d'Israël, qui fait des merveilles dans le pays, qui fait grandir l'homme depuis le sein et (qui) l'a façonné selon sa volonté.	22 Now, bless YYY, God of Israel, the one working marvels in the land. The one who causes a person to grow from the womb and who has formed them according to his will.
23 Qu'il vous donne la sagesse du cœur et qu'il soit en paix au milieu de vous.	23 May he give to you wisdom of mind, and may he be in peace among you.
24 Que son amour reste fidèle à Shime'on et qu'il établisse pour lui l'alliance de Pinhas, afin qu'elle ne soit supprimée ni pour lui ni pour sa descendance tant que le ciel subsistera.	24 Let his loving-kindness endure with Shimeon, and let him establish for him the covenant with Phineas, so that it will not be cut off for him or his seed as long as heaven endures.
25 Il y a deux nations que mon âme déteste et une troisième qui n'est pas un peuple.	25 Two nations my soul loathes, and the third is not a people.
26 Ceux qui habitent Séir et la Philistie et la nation folle qui habite à Shichem.	26 The dwellers of Seir and Philistia, and the foolish people who dwell in Shekem.
27 Instruction, intelligence, et similitudes appropriées de Shime'on Ben Yeshua Ben Eleazer Ben Sira, qui répand *son* cœur par l'interprétation et qui répand (son cœur) par l'intelligence.	27 Instruction, insight, and appropriate analogy of Shimeon Ben Yeshua Ben Eleazer Ben Sira, who poured his heart into interpretation and poured out (his heart) with understanding.

28	⁹אשרי איש באלה יהגה	ונותן על לבו יחכם:	
29	¹⁰כי יראת ייי חיים		

Chapter 51

1	אהללך אלהי ישעי אודך אלהי אבי:		
1/2a	¹¹אספרה שמך מעוז חיי	כי פדית ממות נפשי:	
2bc	¹²חשכת בשרי משחת	ומיד שאול הצלת רגלי:	
2de	¹³פציתני מדבת עם	משוט דבת לשון ומשפט שטי כזב:	
2f/3a	¹⁴נגד קמי הי'תה לי	עזרתני כרוב חסדך:	
3bc	¹⁵ממוקש צופי סלע	ומיד מבקשי נפשי:	
3d/4a	¹⁶מרבות צרות הושעתנ{ו}י	וממצוקות שלהבה סביב [:]	
4b/5a	¹⁷מכבות אש לאין פחה	מרחם תהום לאמ'[טה]:	
5b/6	¹⁸משפתי זמה וטפלי שקר	וחצי לשון מרמה:	
1	ותגע למות נפשי	וחיתי לשאול תחתיות:	T-S 16.315 verso
7	²ואפנה סביב ואין עוזר לי	ואצפה סומך ואין:	
8	³ואזכרה את רחמי ייי	וחסדיו אשר מעולם:	
	⁴המציל את חוסי בו	ויגאלם מכל רע:	
9	⁵ואריב מארץ קולי	וממעמקי שאול שועתי:	
10	⁶וארומם ייי אבי אתה	כי אתה גבור ישעי:	
	⁷אל תרפני ביום צרה	ביום שואה ומשואה:	
11	⁸אהללה שמך תמיד	ואזכרך בתפלה:	
	⁹אז שמע קולי ייי	ויאזין אל תחנוני:	
12 ᴾ	¹⁰ויפדני מכל רע	וימלטני ביום צרה:	
	¹¹על כן הודיתי ואהללה	ואברכה את שם ייי:	
a-b	¹²הודו לייי כי טוב	כי לעולם חסדו:	פ

L. 16 [51:3/4] הושעתני — The final *yod* was originally written as a *vav*, but then corrected to a *yod*. שלהבה — The final letter seems unlikely to be a *tav* since the top cross bar extends beyond the right vertical bar as is the case regularly with *he* and only very rarely with *tav* (see, e.g., the last *tav* of תחתיות in Sir 51:6c). Maagarim records only one other instance of the spelling שלהבה in a work dated to the era "before 1050," in a context where the feminine ending is dictated by the rhyme. סביב — Only the tops of the letters are visible above the hole, though they are distinct enough to suggest this reconstruction, which agrees with the Greek and Syriac.

L. 17 [51:4/5] מכבות — The *kaph* seems to have a *dagesh* or other mark in its center. The fact that it might be read as a slash-like mark perhaps suggests that it is meant as a correction mark, indicating that the base line of the *kaph* should be erased and the word read as in the first stich of the line above, מרבות. לאמ'[טה] — The marks after the *mem* may be read as *yod*.

51:1 אלהי ישעי — The same expression is found five times in the Masoretic Text (e.g., Ps 18:47). אלהי אבי — This expression appears in another four verses in the Masoretic Text (e.g., Gen 31:5).

51:2 רגלי — The word may be singular (cf. Ps 116:8) or plural (cf. Ps 56:14). שטי — The verb is שׂוט and occurs in this same expression in Ps 40:5. היתה לי — Cf. Isa 43:1 where God says to Israel "you are mine." But, here, עז "(you were my) strength" likely has been lost through haplography (cf. the syntax of Ps 61:4 and the metaphor of Isa 49:5).

51:3 סלע — Perhaps a mistake for צלע "stumbling" (Schechter and Taylor 1899, 66 and cf. Jer 20:10), or a mistake for an Aramaism סלעמות "destruction" (cf. Tg. Ps. 52:6), due to haplography, which would explain the Syriac and perhaps even the Greek the Bible.

51:4 מכבות — Although this word is usually construed to mean "from extinguishing (inf. of כבה)," this does not fit the context. Instead, this seems more likely to be the word כְּאֵבָה "pain" spelled defectively without the *alef*. This word occurs among the *piyyut* and later literature, but is related to the masculine noun כְּאֵב "pain" known from the Bible. לאין — The construction is typical of Late Biblical Hebrew. פחה — The word is hard to make sense of, but it may be interpreted as the *qal* passive participle of פוח "to blow" (Peters 1902, 302), used in a manner like the *pual* of נפח in Job 20:26 and like in Sem. 8:12 (see Mies 2005, 264–65 [who lists the passage from Sem. as 47b]). Alternatively, it may be cognate to the Samaritan Aramaic פחה "inflammation" found in the Samaritan Targum to Lev 13:55 (Tal 2000, sub פוח).

51:5 [טה]לאמ' — From the Aramaic "dark cloud," found in Tg. Onq., this word translates the Hebrew עֲרָפֶל "thick darkness" in Exod 20:21. וטפלי שקר — The same phrase appears in Job 13:4, with a similar expression in Ps 119:69.

51:6 לשאול תחתיות — To our knowledge, the exact expression does not occur elsewhere in ancient Hebrew. Together, the words usually show agreement in number/gender such that the last word appears in the singular (see Deut 32:22 and Ps 86:13). Nevertheless, note similar expressions with the plural like ארץ תחתיות in Ezek 26:20.

51:10 אל תרפני ביום צרה — A similar expression, occurs in Prov 24:10 התרפית ביום צרה "if you faint in the day of adversity" (NRSV).

28 Heureux l'homme qui médite cela
   et celui qui les garde en son cœur deviendra sage.
29 Car la crainte de YYY est vie.

Chapitre 51

1 Je veux te louer, Dieu de mon salut, je veux te rendre grâce, Dieu de mon père,
   je veux raconter ton nom, forteresse de ma vie,
2a car tu as racheté ma vie de la mort,
2b tu as préservé ma chair de la fosse
2c et de la main du Shéol, tu as délivré mon pied.
2d Tu m'as délivré de la calomnie du peuple,
2e du fouet de la calomnie de la langue et de la lèvre des fauteurs de mensonge.
2f Devant ceux qui se dressent contre moi, tu étais mien,
3a Tu m'as secouru, selon l'abondance de ton amour,
3b du piège de ceux qui épient le roc,
3c de la main de ceux qui cherchent ma vie.
3d D'une multitude de détresses, tu m'as sauvé,
4a et des angoisses d'une flamme alentour,
4b des douleurs d'un feu qui n'a pas été allumé,
5a depuis les entrailles de l'abîme jusqu'aux ténèbres.
5b des lèvres infâmes et de ceux qui répandent le mensonge,
6 et des flèches de la langue trompeuse.
   Et mon âme s'approchait de la mort
   et ma vie du Shéol des profondeurs.
7 Et je me suis tourné de tout côté, pas de secours pour moi
   et j'ai guetté un soutien : rien.
8 Et je me suis souvenu des compassions de YYY
   et de ses amours qui sont éternels.
   Celui qui sauve ceux qui se réfugient en lui
   et les délivre de tout mal.
9 Et j'ai fait monter de la terre ma voix
   et des portes du Shéol, mon cri.
10 Et j'ai exalté YYY : « mon père, c'est toi »,
   car tu es le héros de mon salut.
   Ne faiblis pas au jour de la détresse,
   au jour de dévastation et de la désolation.
11 Je veux louer ton nom perpétuellement
   et me souvenir de toi dans la prière.
   Alors YYY a écouté ma voix
   et a prêté l'oreille à mes supplications.
12 Il m'a racheté de tout mal,
   et m'a sauvé au jour de détresse.
   C'est pourquoi je rends grâce et je loue
   et je bénis le nom de YYY.
a-b Rendez grâces à YYY, car il est bon,
   car éternel est son amour !

Chapter 51

28 Happy the person who meditates on these things,
   and sets (these) upon their mind (so that) they become wise.
29 For the fear of YYY is life.

Chapter 51

1 Let me praise you, God of my salvation; let me thank you God of my father.
   Let me recount your name, stronghold of my life,
2a for you redeemed my life from death.
2b You spared my flesh from the pit,
2c from the power of Sheol you delivered my foot.
2d You delivered me from the people's slander,
2e from the whip of the slanderous tongue, from the lip of those turning away due to lies.
2f Before those standing up to me you were mine,
3a you helped me according to your great kindness,
3b from the trap of those watching the rock
3c from the hand of those seeking my life.
3d From the multitude of distresses you delivered me,
4a and from the distresses of flame round about,
4b from the pains of fire without a burn,
5a from the womb of the deep to darkness
5b from wicked lips to those spreading lies
6 and arrows of deceitful tongues.
   My soul approached death,
   my life to lowest Sheol.
7 I turned around and I had no helper,
   I looked for my supporter and there was none.
8 I recalled the compassion of YYY,
   and the kind acts which are eternal.
   (He is) the one delivering those who seek refuge in him,
   and he will redeem them from every evil.
9 I raised my voice from the earth,
   my cry from the gates of Sheol.
10 I exalted YYY: "You are my father,
   for you are the mighty one of my deliverance.
   Do not leave me in the day of distress
   in the day of destruction and desolation.
11 Let me praise your name continually,
   let me remember you in prayer.
   Then, YYY heard my voice
   and he gave ear to my supplications.
12 He redeemed me from every evil,
   and saved me in the day of distress.
   Therefore, I thank and praise
   and bless the name of YYY.
a-b Give thanks to YYY for he is good,
   for his loving-kindness is forever.

c-d P	¹³הודו לאל התשבחות	כי לעולם חסדו:	
e-f	¹⁴הודו לשומר ישראל	כי לעולם חסדו:	
g-h	¹⁵הודו ליוצר הכל	כי לעולם חסדו:	
i-j	¹⁶הודו לגואל ישראל	כי לעולם חסדו:	
k-l	¹⁷[ה]ודו למקבץ נדחי ישראל	כי לעולם חסדו:	
m-n	¹⁸הודו לבונה עירו ומקדשו	כי לעולם חסדו:	
o-p	¹הודו למצמיח קרן לבית דוד	כי לעולם חסדו:	T-S 16.315 recto
q-r	²הודו לבוחר בבני צדוק לכהן	כי לעולם חסדו:	
s-t	³הודו למגן אברהם	כי לעולם חסדו:	
u-v	⁴הודו לצור יצחק	כי לעולם חסדו:	
w-x	⁵הודו לאביר יעקב	כי לעולם חסדו:	
y-z	⁶הודו לבוחר בציון	כי לעולם חסדו:	
aa-bb	⁷הודו למלך מלכי מלכים	כי לעולם חסדו:	
cc-dd	⁸וירם קרן לעמו תהלה לכל חסידיו	לבני ישראל עם קרבו הלליה:	
	⁹ vacat		
13 PQ	¹⁰אני נער הייתי	וחפצתי בה ובקשתיה:	
15 Q	¹¹באמתה דרכה רגלי	אדני מנעורי חכמה למדתי:	
14/16 Q	¹²ואתפלל תפלה בנערותי	והרבה מצאתי דעה:	
17 Q	¹³עלה היה לי לכבוד	ולמלמדי אתן הודאה:	
18 Q	¹⁴חשבתי להיטיב	ולא אהפך כי אמצאנו:	
19ab Q	¹⁵חשקה נפשי בה	ופני לא אהפך ממנה:	
19cd Q	¹⁶נפשי נתתי אחריה	לנצח נצחים לא אטה ממ[נ]ה̊: [

51:13 לקח | דעה B · 51:16 כי | אדני B · ידעתיה | חכמה למדתי B 11Q5 · במישור | באמתה B 11Q5 · 51:15 בטרם תעיתי | הייתי וחפצתי בה 51:13 זמותי ואשחקה קנאתי בטוב | חשבתי להיטיב B 51:18 הודו | הודאה B 11Q5 · ולמלמדי | ולמלמדי B 11Q5 · ועלה היתה | עלה היה 51:17 11Q5 טרתי נפשי | נפשי נתתי אחריה B 51:19cd 11Q5 · לוא השיבותי̊ | ולא אהפך B 11Q5 · חריתי | חשקה 51:19ab · ולוא אשוב | ולא אהפך B 11Q5 · וברומיה לוא אשלה | לנצח נצחים לא אטה ממ̊נ̊[ה] B 11Q5 · ה בה 11Q5 ·

L. 15 [51:12g-h] הו̇ד̇ו̇ — Only the tops of the first three letters are preserved.

L. 16 [51:19cd] ממ̊נ̊[נה]:אטה — The *he* of the first word exhibits strange features, including a right leg that angles to the right and a very short upper bar. Yet, perhaps these are due to cramped spacing. The two *mem*s of the following expression also seem to be narrower than the same letters just above it on the manuscript. Despite the unusual forms, there are few other possibilities.

51:13–30 The version of this poem in H^B (especially its first half) is considered by most scholars a retroversion from Syriac, based on numerous factors including the disruption of the acrostic structure and the close correspondence between this text and the Syriac (in contrast to the version in 11Q5 which contains a good acrostic structure and fewer correspondences with the Syriac). For the idea of retroversion, see, e.g., Bickell 1899; Lévi 1901, xxi-xxvii and van Peursen 2003, 357–74.

51:17 ולמלמדי — In the context of the preceding imagery of "yoke," the present word might also call to mind the word מַלְמָד "ox-goad" (Judg 3:31).

c-d Rendez grâces au Dieu des louanges,
    car éternel est son amour !
e-f Rendez grâces au gardien d'Israël,
    car éternel est son amour !
g-h Rendez grâces au créateur de tout,
    car éternel est son amour !
i-j Rendez grâces au rédempteur d'Israël,
    car éternel est son amour !
k-l Rendez grâces à celui qui rassemble les dispersés d'Israël
    car éternel est son amour !
m-n Rendez grâces à celui qui bâtit sa cité et son temple,
    car éternel est son amour !
o-p Rendez grâces à celui qui fait pousser la corne de la maison de David,
    car éternel est son amour !
q-r Rendez grâces à celui qui choisit les fils de Tsadoq pour prêtre,
    car éternel est son amour !
s-t Rendez grâces au bouclier d'Abraham,
    car éternel est son amour !
u-v Rendez grâces au roc d'Isaac,
    car éternel est son amour !
w-x Rendez grâces au puissant de Jacob,
    car éternel est son amour !
y-z Rendez grâces à celui qui choisit Sion,
    car éternel est son amour !
aa-bb   Rendez grâces au roi du roi des rois,
    car éternel est son amour !
cc-dd   et qui a élevé la corne de son peuple, louange pour tous ses fidèles,
    pour les enfants d'Israël, peuple proche de lui, Halleluya.

vacat

13 Moi, j'étais jeune
    et je l'ai désirée et je l'ai cherchée,
15 Mon pied a marché dans sa vérité,
    Adonaï, depuis ma jeunesse, j'ai appris la sagesse,
14 Et j'ai prié une prière dans ma jeunesse,
16 et j'ai trouvé beaucoup de science.
17 Son joug était pour moi une gloire
    et je rends grâce à celui qui m'enseigne.
18 Je suis déterminé à faire le bien
    et je ne me détournerai pas car je la trouverai.
19a Mon âme s'est éprise d'elle
19b et je ne détournerai pas mon visage d'elle.
19c J'ai livré mon âme à sa suite,
19d d'âge en âge, je ne m'écarterai jamais d'elle.

c-d Give thanks to the God of praises
    for his loving-kindness is forever.
e-f Give thanks to the guard of Israel
    for his loving-kindness is forever.
g-h Give thanks to the one shaping everything
    for his loving-kindness is forever.
i-j Give thanks to Israel's redeemer
    for his loving-kindness is forever.
k-l [G]ive thanks to the one gathering Israel's scattered
    for his loving-kindness is forever.
m-n Give thanks to the one building his city and sanctuary
    for his loving-kindness is forever.
o-p Give thanks to the one making the horn of the house of David sprout
    for his loving-kindness is forever.
q-r Give thanks to to the one choosing the children of Zadok as priest
    for his loving-kindness is forever.
s-t Give thanks to the shield of Abraham
    for his loving-kindness is forever.
u-v Give thanks to the rock of Isaac
    for his loving-kindness is forever.
w-x Give thanks to the mighty one of Jacob
    for his loving-kindness is forever.
y-z Give thanks to the one choosing Zion
    for his loving-kindness is forever.
aa-bb   Give thanks to the king of the king of kings
    for his loving-kindness is forever.
cc-dd   He has raised the horn of his people, praise for all his pious ones
    for the children of Israel, a people close to him, Halleluya.

vacat

13 I was a boy
    when I desired and sought her.
15 In her truth my foot walks;
    my Lord, from my youth I have learned wisdom.
14 I prayed a prayer in my youth
16 and I found much knowledge.
17 Her yoke is my glory,
    I give praise to my teacher.
18 I determined to do good
    and I would not turn so that I might find her.
19a My soul longs for her
19b and I will not turn my face from her.
19c My soul I have given (to go) after her,
19d never will I divert myself from her.

19ef Q	¹⁷ידי פתחה שעריה	ולה אהֹדֹר ואביט בהֹ[׃]
20bcd PQ	¹⁸בטהרה מצאתיה ולב קניתי לה מתחלתה בעבור כֹן
21 P	¹מעי יהמו כתנור להביט בה	בעבור כן קניתיה קנין טוב׃
22 P	²נתן ייי לי שכר שפתותי	ובלשוני אהודנו׃
23	³פנו אלי סכלים	ולינו בבית מדרשי׃
24	⁴עד מתי תחסרון מן אילו ואילו	ונפשכם צמאה מאד תהיה׃
25	⁵פי פתחתי ודברתי בה	קנו לכם חכמה בלא כסף׃
26	⁶וצואריכם בעלה הביאו	ומשאה תשא נפשכם׃
27	⁷קרובה היא למבקשיה	ונותן נפשו מוצא אתה׃
27	⁸ראו בעיניכם כי קטן הייתי	ועמדתי בה ומצאתיה׃
28	⁹רבים שמעו למודי בנערותי	וכסף וזהב תקנו בי׃
29	¹⁰תשמח נפשי בישיבתי	ולא תבושו בשירתי׃
30 Q	¹¹מעשיכם עשו בצדקה	והוא נותן לכם שכרכם בעתו׃
	¹²ברוך ייי לעולם	ומשובח שמו לדר ודר׃
	¹³עד הנה דברי שמעון בן ישוע	שנקרא בן סירא׃
	¹⁴חכמת שמעון בן ישוע	בן אלעזר בן סירא׃
	¹⁵יהי שם יײ מבורך	מעתה ועד עולם׃

T-S 16.315 recto

בטהרה מצאתיה ולב 11Q5 | כפי הברית אליה 11Q5 | וֹבמערמיה אתבונן 11Q5 51:20ab · 51:19f ולה אהֹדֹר ואביט בה B | בי[אתֹהֹ] 11Q5 · 51:19e שעריה B | קניתי לה B ·

L. 17 [51:19ef] אהֹדֹר — The whole word is partially effaced from off-setting; it corresponds in its spacing to the word נדחי in 50:12k-l. The second letter of אהֹדֹר is more likely a *he* than a *khet* since it seems that the left leg ends before it reaches the top horizontal bar. Confusion has arisen since the *khet* of נדחי has left traces on the *he* of אהֹדֹר; specifically, the right leg of the *khet* of נדחי partially overlaps with the left leg of the *he* of אהֹדֹר. Only the legs of the following two letters are preserved. בה — Only the right most edge of the *he* is preserved.

L. 18 [51:20] כֹּן — The first letter has a strange appearance in the photos, apparently, due to the paper having folded and thus bringing the base line closer to the top line. The *nun* is preserved only by its right edge. The ligature between letters would seem to confirm the reading.

51:19ef אהֹדֹר — The verb seems to be הדר "to honor, glorify," seen multiple times in Ben Sira. A similar association between seeing someone and praising them is found several times in the Hebrew Bible, though with the words ראה and הלל (Gen 12:15; Judg 16:24; Songs 6:9). The verb הדר is unexpected since the entire poem is usually explained as deriving from a back translation of the Syriac translation, where we have the verb גגי "I was surrounded by her." It is conceivable that although the verb here in Ms B is probably written with a *he*, a *khet* was intended (or the two verbs were confused) such that we should instead understand the verb to be in the *qal* "I surround her" or in the *niphal* "I am surrounded by her." Given the preceding colon, one wonders if the original reading was אחדר "I penetrated her" (Jastrow 1903, 506) which of course, would be a sexual innuendo even more pronounced than that found in the 11Q5 version. HALOT defines the root חדר I as "to penetrate, to enter."

51:20 The words of this verse are written without a space between the stichs so that it is unclear where exactly the break between them should be. The phrase מתחלתה belongs syntactically to the preceding words, but could have been included in the second stich. A similar kind of syntactic linkage stretches across the stich boundary in Sir 47:8ab and 47:12. Alternatively, the line represents three separate stichs. בטהרה — These letters may be read as the noun טהר (as in Sir 43:1ᴮ) with the 3fs pronominal suffix, or as the feminine noun טהרה.

51:22 שכר שפתותי — Literally, the expression can be rendered "wage of my lips."

51:23 בית מדרשי — The phrase appears first in texts of the Amoraic era (e.g., b. Meg. 27a) in the sense "school" or "study hall." Here, of course, it could mean something more literal "house of my instruction."

51:24 תחסרון — This form contains one of three instances of the paragogic *nun* among the Ben Sira manuscripts (see also 30:19ᴮ; 45:21ᴮ). אילו ואילו — Literally, "these and those." See, e.g., m. Ned. 3:4. The pronoun is attested only in the Mishnah and later texts.

51:25 ודברתי בה — The phrase may express the sense "I spoke with her" (see the idiom in Num 12:6, 8), but the context suggests perhaps an instrumental nuance for the preposition, similar to the idiom found in 2 Sam 23:2 "the spirit of the Lord speaks through me" and elsewhere (e.g., 1 Kgs 22:28). Alternatively, the idiom ב + דבר might express the sense "to speak about" as in Deut 6:7; 1 Sam 19:3; Ps 119:46.

51:29 ישיבה — The word is used in the sense of "council" in texts of the Amoraic era (e.g., b. Yoma 28b). See Dihi 2004, 318–20.

19 Ma main a ouvert ses portes
   et je l'honorerai et je la contemplerai.
20 Dans sa pureté, je l'ai trouvée et j'ai acquis du sens pour
   elle dès son origine, car ainsi [   ]
21 Mes entrailles rugissaient comme une fournaise pour
   la contempler,
   car, ainsi, je l'ai acquise, bonne possession.
22 YYY m'a donné le salaire de mes lèvres
   et par ma langue, je lui rends grâce.
23 Tournez-vous vers moi, insensés
   et logez dans ma maison d'enseignement.
24 Combien de temps manquerez-vous ceci et cela,
   et votre âme sera grandement assoiffée ?
25 J'ai ouvert ma bouche et j'ai parlé d'elle :
   « acquérez, pour vous, la sagesse sans argent.
26 Faites passer vos cous sous son joug
   et que votre gorge/âme soulève son fardeau.
   Elle est proche de ceux qui la cherchent
   et celui qui consacre sa vie, la trouve.
27 Voyez de vos yeux comme j'étais insignifiant
   mais j'ai tenu ferme avec elle et je l'ai trouvée.
28 Nombreux, écoutez mes enseignements dans ma jeunesse
   et vous acquerrez argent et or grâce à moi.
29 Mon âme se réjouit de mon académie,
   et vous n'aurez pas honte de mon chant.
30 Accomplissez vos œuvres avec justice
   et, lui (s.e. Dieu), vous donnera votre salaire en son
   temps. »
   Que soit béni YYY pour toujours
   et que soit loué son nom d'âge en âge.
   Jusqu'ici ont été les paroles de Shime'on Ben Yeshua
   qui est appelé Ben Sira
   Sagesse de Shime'on Ben Yeshua'
   Ben Elé'azar Ben Sira.
   Que le nom de YYY soit béni,
   maintenant et pour l'éternité.

19d My hand opened her gates
19f and I will glorify her when I look on her.
20bcd   In her purity I found her and I acquired a mind
   for her from her beginning, because thus [
21 My inner self roared like a furnace to see her
   for thus I acquired her as a good possession.
22 YYY gave me my lips as wage,
   and with my lips I thank him.
23 Turn to me, fools,
   and lodge in my house of instruction
24 How long will you lack all these things
   your soul thirsting greatly?
25 I opened my mouth and I spoke of her:
   acquire for yourselves wisdom without silver.
26 Bring your necks into her yoke,
   and your throat/soul will lift her burden.
   She is near to those seeking her,
   and the one giving himself finds her.
27 See with your eyes that I was insignificant
   but I remained with her and I found her.
28. Many heard my teachings in my youth
   and silver and gold you will acquire through me.
29 My soul rejoices in my council,
   you will not be ashamed in my song.
30 Do your deeds with righteousness
   and he (God) will give you your wage in its time.
   May YYY be blessed forever,
   and his name praised by every generation.
   Up to this point are the words of Shimeon Ben Yeshua
   who is called Ben Sira
   Wisdom of Shimeon Ben Yeshua
   Ben Eleazar Ben Sira.
   May the name of YYY be blessed
   from now until eternity.

MANUSCRIPT C

ANTHOLOGY OF SIR 3:14~7:25; 18:31~37:26

MANUSCRIPT C

T-S 12.867 recto	ותחת ²עינותו תתנצ[ב:]	¹צדקת אב אל תשכח	3:14 ᴬ
	³וכחורב על קרח נמס חטאתיך:	ביום יזבר לך	3:15 ᴬ
	וזועם ⁵אל יסחוב אמו·	⁴כמגדף העוזב אביו	3:16 ᴬ
	ומאיש ⁷מתן תאהב·	בני את כל ⁶מלאכתיך בענוה הלוך	3:17 ᴬ
	ובעיני אלהים ⁹תֹּמצא חן	בני גדול אתה ⁸כן תשפיל נפשך	3:18 ᴬ
	ורעים ממך אל ¹¹תֹּדרוש:	פלאות ממך ¹⁰אל תחקור	3:21 ᴬ
T-S 12.867 verso	ועסק אל יהי לך בנסתרות·	באשר הורשיתה ¹התבונן	3:22 ᴬ
	³ולא כל הכלם נבחר·	²לא כל בושת נאה לשמור	41:16bc ᴮᴹ
	ויש בשת ⁵חן וכבוד·	יש ׆ ⁴בשת משאת עון	4:21 ᴬ
	ובאולת ⁷פנים יורישנה·	יש מאבד ׆ ⁶את נפשו מבושת	20:22
	וקונהו שונא ⁹חנם·	יש נכלם ⁸ומבטיח רעהו	20:23
	¹⁰ואל תבוש למכשול לך·	אל תשא פנים לנפשׁך	4:22 ᴬ
T-S 12.727 recto	ואל ¹תקפוף את חכמתך·	¹¹אל תמנע דבר בעיתו	4:23 ᴬ
	ומתפחז בעבודתך·	אל תהי ²כאריה בביתך	4:30 ᴬ
	⁴ובעת השב קפודה·	³אל תהי ידך מושטת לשאת	4:31 ᴬ

3:14 יזכר C cor. יזבר C | ביום צרה A G S · ביום C | ותמור חטאת היא תנתע C | ותחת ענותו תתנצ[ב] A · תמחה C | תשכח C G S | לא A G S | אל C 3:15 ביום C | יזבר A G S · יזכר: A | וכחורב על קרח נמס חטאתיך: C | כחם על כפור להשבית עונך: A 3:16 כמגדף העוזב אביו C G S | כי מזיד בוזה אביו A · תזכר: A | וזועם אל A · ומכעיס בוראו מקלל אמו C G · יסחוב אמו C G S 3:17 את כל מלאכתיך A S · בעשרך C G | בענוה הלוך A G S · התהלך בענוה C | ומאיש מתן תאהב A S · תאהב מנותן מתנות C G S (ܢܣܒ ܡܬܢܘܬܐ) 3:18 בני גדול אתה כן תשפיל נפשך C G | מעט נפשך מכל גדולת עולם A S · ובעיני A S · ולפני ׅ A G S · אלהים C | רחמים C G · רחמים A S 3:21 תדרוש A · תחקור C | תחקור A · תדרוש C | ומכסוה A · ורעים C | במה C | באשר הורשיתה A 3:22 לבוש B | לשמר C | לשמור B M · נאוה M · נאה B C | בשת C M · בושת 41:16 · אין לך A · עסק C | ועסק אל יהי לך A · שהורשית A · כי יש C 4:21 למכשוליך C | למכשול לך A · תבוש C G S | פניך על נפשך C | פני לנפשך A G S · 4:22 כבוד וחן A G S · חן וכבוד C | בֹּשֶׁת A · בשת C | A G S 4:23 בעיתו C G S | בעולם A · ואל C G S | אל A · תקפוף C | תצפין A G S · 4:30 כאריה C G | ככלב A S · ומתפחז C (G = √ פחד?) | ומתירא A · ומוזר A S · וקפוצה בתוך מתן C G | פתוחה לקחת A · ובעת השב קפודה A · במלאכתך A · בעבודתך C S | 4:31 מושטת לשאת C G S | לקחת A S

L. 11 [3:21] תֹּדרוש — While some traces of ink on the manuscript do not agree with our reading, they are likely the result of ink bleeding through the paper or of ink rubbing off from the opposite folio of the codex.

L. 3 [41:16] In order to justify the text on the left side, the scribe completed the end of the empty line with a sign that resembles an uncompleted *shin*.

3:14 אל תשכח — The variation between לא תמחה (Hᴬ) and אל תשכח (Hᶜ) could be the result of a semantic confusion between the formulas אל תקטול and לא תקטול, which appears in Late Biblical Hebrew and Qumran Hebrew (cf. Qimron 2018, §H.4.1). Indeed אל תשכח may be either a *niphal* 3fs (אַל תִּשָּׁכַח), "May justice towards a father never be forgotten," as in Hᴬ or a *qal* 2ms (אַל תִּשְׁכַּח), "Do not forget justice toward a father." ענותו — The form raises some difficulties: (a) it is most likely the result of a metathesis between ענותו, "his humility", and עונות, "the sins" (so Hᴬ, the Greek and the Syriac); (b) but it could also be a *piel* infinitive, "in place of his humiliation," or a *pual* infinitive, "in place of the hardships he endured" (cf. Ps 132:1). [תתנצ[ב — Following Rüger (1970, 27) and Bohlen (1991, 59), we propose restoring to the Aramaic verb נצב "to plant, to erect" (cf. the *hithpeel* in Qumran [e.g., 4Q204 1 v 8] and other ancient dialects; note that the *hithpaal* is not attested). The related Hebrew root נצב "to set, establish" never occurs in the *hithpael*, for which Hebrew uses the root יצב.

3:15 ביום יזבר — Two corrections seem necessary here: inserting (after ביום) the word צרה, which seems to have been forgotten (see Hᴬ, the Greek and the Syriac), and correcting יזבר to יזכר. — In v. 15a (as well as in v. 15b), the *niphal* masculine contrasts with the feminine in Hᴬ that refers to the צדקה of the preceding verse. The subject of the verb is not expressed, though, stich *b* implies that it is God. נמס — The verb in the *niphal* singular participle has a plural subject, חטאתיך, which is understood in a collective sense. This syntactic peculiarity is common in Late Biblical Hebrew.

3:16b וזועם אל — In this sentence, אל may be understood as the object of זעם, "the one who curses God," or its subject (see Num 23:8; Ps 7:12), "God reproves the one who afflicts his mother". יסחוב — The use of the verb סחב, "to drag" (see Jer 15:3; 22:19; 48:20; 50:45), is highly unusual in this context since it must be construed in a metaphoric sense not explicitly found in earlier literature. Furthermore, we would have expected the theme vowel to be /a/ due to the *chet* as second root consonant. Therefore, another possibility is to infer that this is an Aramaic biform of סחף, "to sweep away, exile" which is found relatively commonly with the /o/ theme vowel (so Segal 1958, 320). Alternatively, Kister (1983, 130) suggests that the form may be connected to the root צחב / צהב "to be in pain, distress, afflicted, to anger" (see the Greek ὁ παροργίζων and the Syriac ܚܒ as well as Sir 10:10ᴬ).

3:17 מלאכתיך — Hᶜ agrees with the Greek here, while בעשרך in Hᴬ corresponds to the Syriac.

3:18 For the construction of the comparative, cf. GKC §116*b* and Isa 55:9.

3:21–22 For the rabbinic quotations of these two verses, see the notes for Hᴬ.

3:21 ורעים — The reading רעים ("that which is worse than you") has been interpreted by Segal (1959-1960, 321) as an error for רמים ("that which is higher than you"), see 4Q405 23 i 11. Rüger (1970, 31) suggests correcting to ורים, but this seems less consistent with the Greek. It seems also possible that the word רעים derives from the singular participle "high" or "exalted" in an Aramaic-like form, with a confusion of

3,14	N'oublie pas la justice envers un père et à la place de sa peine elle sera plan[tée].	3:14	Do not forget justice towards a father and in place of his meekness, it will be plant[ed.]
3,15	Au jour (de détresse), *il sera fait mémoire* de toi et comme la chaleur sur la glace, tes péchés fondent.	3:15	In the day (of distress), it will be *remembered* for your benefit and, like heat on ice, your sins will melt away.
3,16	Il est comme un blasphémateur, celui qui abandonne son père et celui qui maudit Dieu, afflige sa mère.	3:16	The one who abandons their father is like one who blasphemes and the one who curses God afflicts their mother.
3,17	Mon enfant, conduis toutes tes œuvres avec humilité et plus que celui qui donne, tu seras aimé.	3:17	My child, behave in all your work with humility and you will be loved more than one who (brings) gifts.
3,18	Mon enfant, autant tu es grand, autant tu dois t'abaisser et aux yeux de Dieu tu trouveras grâce.	3:18	My child, great as you are, so you should humble yourself and in the eyes of God you will find grace.
3,21	Ce qui est trop merveilleux pour toi ne le cherche pas et ce qui est plus *haut* que toi, ne le sonde pas.	3:21	That which is too wondrous for you, do not explore, that which is *higher* than you, do not investigate.
3,22	Sur ce qui t'est permis, réfléchis, mais tu ne dois pas t'occuper des choses cachées.	3:22	Ponder on what is permitted to you, but you should not occupy yourself with hidden things.
41,16b	Toute honte ne mérite pas d'être observée,	41:16b	Not every shame is worthy of observing,
41,16c	ni toute humiliation d'être choisie.	41:16c	nor should every humiliation be chosen.
4,21	Il y a une honte qui amène le péché et il y a une honte qui est grâce et honneur.	4:21	There is a shame that leads to sin, and there is shame that is grace and honor.
20,22	Il y a celui qui s'anéantit lui-même à cause de la honte et qui, par la folie, se ruine.	20:22	There is one who destroys himself due to shame, he ruins himself in folly.
20,23	Il y a celui qui est humilié et qui fait confiance à son prochain et il s'en fait un ennemi pour rien.	20:23	There is one who is humiliated and reassures his friend, and (in turn) makes himself an enemy for nothing.
4,22	Ne sois pas honteux de toi-même et n'aie pas honte de ton trébuchement.	4:22	Do not feel shame about yourself, do not be ashamed at your stumbling.
4,23	Ne retiens pas (ta) parole quand c'est le moment et ne réfrène pas ta sagesse.	4:23	Do not withhold your word at its proper moment, do not stifle your wisdom.
4,30	Ne sois pas comme un lion dans ta maison et arrogant dans ton ouvrage.	4:30	Do not be like a lion in your house, and arrogant in your work.
4,31	Que ta main ne soit pas tendue pour recevoir et refermée au moment de rembourser.	4:31	Do not let your hand be extended to take but clenched in the time of returning.

ayin for an intended *aleph*, the earlier form being ראים (*rāʾēm*) (see Reymond 2017a, 10-11). Cf. confusion of רועה for רואה in 46:15ᴮ.

3:22 ועסק אל יהי לך — The modal value of the nominal clause in Hᴬ (ואין לך עסק) is made explicit in Hᶜ (cf. van Peursen 2004, 196).

4:21 See notes in Hᴬ.

20:22 באולת פנים — For this expression, cf. בשת פני in Ps 44:16 and ברע פנים in Qoh 7:3. יורישנה — The verb ירש is not clearly reflected in the Greek or Syriac, which seem to presuppose the verb אבד. Nevertheless, note the *hiphil* of ירש with the sense "dispossess, destroy" in Exod 15:9 (cf. Syriac ܚܪܒ "to become a ruin, to destroy").

20:23 וקונהו — We understand the suffix pronoun as a reflexive dative: "he buys for himself an enemy for nothing" (see the Syriac). Yet, the sentence may also be understood as "the one who acquires him for nothing is an enemy."

4:22 אל תשא פנים — For the expression, see the notes in Hᴬ. פנים seems preferable to the redundant פניך in Hᴬ. בוש — Hᶜ has the support of the Greek and the Syriac, against Hᴬ.

4:23 בעיתו — I.e. "Do not hold back your word when it is the time you should give it."

4:30 כאריה —The most ancient version probably had כלביא; see the note in Hᴬ. ומתפחז — The *hithpael* of פחז is not attested elsewhere. In the *qal*, the root expresses "arrogance, indiscipline." Greenfield (1978, 35-40) gives it the meaning "fornication, lechery, passion, lasciviousness," referring to Sir 23:5; 41:17 and 4Q184 1 2, 13, 15. According to Lévi (1901, 23) and Segal (1958, 29), it should be corrected to מתפחד, "to be afraid," which is attested in Rabbinic Hebrew and in accordance with the Greek (and מתירא of Hᴬ).

4:31 קפודה — Most propose correcting to קפוצה, "be closed," in agreement with Hᴬ and the versions (Schechter and Taylor 1899, XIX; Smend 1906b, 8; Lévi 1901, 23; HALOT). Nevertheless, the verb קפד can also be understood metaphorically here: the hand is rolled up, i.e. closed.

	6כי ייי ארך אפים הוא:	אל 5תאמר חטאתי ומה יהיה לו	5:4 A
	להוסיף עון 8על עון·	אל 7סליחה אל תבטח	5:5 A
	לרוב עוונותי יסלח·	ואמרת רבים 9רחמיו	5:6 A
	ועל רשעים 11יניח רגזו·	10כי רחמים ואף עמו	
	ואל תתעבר מיום ליום·	אל תאחר לשוב 12אליו	5:7 A
T-S 12.727 verso	ובעת נקם 2תספה·	1כי פתאום יצא זעמו	
	ואל תלך לכל שביל·	אל תהי זורה לכל 3רוח	5:9 A
	ואחר 5יהיה דבריך·	4היה סמוך על דברך	5:10 A
	ובארך 7ענה תענה נכונה·	היה נכון 6בשמועה טובה	5:11 A
	ואם 9אין שים ידך על פיך·	אם 8יש אתך ענה ריעיך	5:12 A
	ולשון אדם 11מפליטו·	כבוד 10וקלון ביד בוטה	5:13 A
Frag. G. Combs recto	1ולב נבון יטעם מטעמי כזב·	חיך יטעם מטעמי זבד	36:24 BP
	ושפתי 3חן שואלי שלום·	2חיך ערב ירבה אוהב	6:5 A
	ובעל 5סודך אחד מאף·	אנשי 4שלומיך יהיו רבים	6:6 A
		כל אוהב 6יאמר אהבתו	37:1 BD
	דין מות רע 8כנפש יהפך לצר·	הלא בעת 7יגיע עליו·	37:2 BD
	ואל 10תמהר לבטוח עליו·	קנית 9אוהב בנסיון קנהו	6:7 A
	ואת 12ריב חרפתך יחשוך·	יש 11אוהב נהפך לשונא	6:9 A
Frag. G. Combs verso	ולא ימצא 2ביום רעה·	יש 1אוהב חבר שלחן	6:10 A
	3ולא יעמד ביום צרה·	יש אוהב בפני עת	6:8 A
	ומפניך יסתר·	אם 4תשיגנו נרפך בך	6:12 A

5:4 ואל | ועל A C · עוונתי C עוונותי A G · רחמיו רבים C רבים רחמיו A G 5:6 · אל A C · ייי A S · מאומה A S + לו C · לי A G S · יעשה A · יהיה C G S | 5:7 אליו A · ליום C S ובעת C G S · וביום A · 5:9 תהי C תהיה A · ואל תלך לכל שביל C G (S ܠܟܠ) ופונה דרך שבר· | 5:10 דבריך C דברך A · יהיה C יהיה A · דעתך A G S · 5:11 נכון C ממהר A · בשמועה טובה C (+ αγαθη O L'-743) A · יניח C · ינוח A · 5:7 ליום C S ובעת C G S · וביום A · 5:9 תהי C תהיה A · ואל תלך לכל שביל C G (S ܠܟܠ) ופונה דרך שבר· | 5:10 דבריך C דברך A · יהיה C יהיה A · דעתך A G S · 5:11 נכון C ממהר A · בשמועה טובה C (+ αγαθη O L'-743) A · רוח השב פתגם A G S · 5:12 ריעיך A G S · רעך C | שים C > (ܠܡܐܙܢ S) להאזין A · ענה תענה נכונה C G (+ ορθην O L-694-743 La [verum]) A · 5:13 ביד C · ביוד A · בוטה C בוטא A · מפלטו C מפליטו A · מפלתו A · 36:24 חיך C B | דבר C Bmg | ולב C B · זבד C Bmg | יטעם C | בוחן B Bmg · חך B Bmg | כזב C B | זבד Bmg | > B Bmg · יטעם C | מבין B · נבון C Bmg | וחן Bmg | 37:1a שלומך A · שלומיך C | שואלו A · שואלי C 6:6 · אך יש A(ו)הב שם A(ו)הב Bmg D G S | > C B · 37:2a הלא בעת יגיע C | 37:1b + הב A · אומר אהבתי B | כל אוהב אמר אהבתי C אהבתו C · 37:2b D · עד מות Bmg | על מות B | אל מות C עליו B Bmg D · הלא דין מגיע ר(י)ע כנפש B | רע כנפשך נהפך לצר C | דין מות רע כנפש יהפך לצר Bmg D · 6:7 בנסיון C בניסין A · לבטח C לבטוח A · 6:9 לשונא C לשנא A · יחשוך C יחשוף A · 6:8 יש C S | כי A G · בפני C S נהפך Bmg D · נרפך C | יהפך A · (רעה) > C G S L · רעה A תשיגך רעה C תשיגנו 6:12 · יעמוד A · יעמוד C Saadia · ואל A · ולא C Saadia · כפי (ܟܐܦܝ) A Saadia

5:4 לו — This certainly must be corrected to לי with H^A, the Greek and the Syriac.

5:6 יניח — The spelling here implies that one should read a *hiphil*, while H^A has a *qal* (ינוח). Confusion between *yod* and *vav* is quite frequent in these manuscripts.

5:9 שביל — This term for "path, way" is attested twice in biblical Hebrew (Ps 77:20; Jer 18:15), and is further attested in Rabbinic Hebrew.

5:10 דברך — This is probably a dittography from the end of the following stich (which suggests that the scribe was copying a manuscript written in stichometry, as attested by Masada).

5:11 H^C has a different text here from H^A, Greek and Syriac It adds two terms, טובה in the first stich and נכונה in the second. These two additions are also attested in some Greek witnesses (O L'-743 adds αγαθη and O L-694-743 La [verum] adds ορθην).

5:13 מפליטו — "Protects him from evil" (Isa 5:29; Mic 6:14), but according to Lévi (1901, 28) and Segal (1958, 34), it is a miswriting for מפלתו.

36:24 יטעם — In the second stich, H^C adds the verb טעם, which is not reflected in any of the versions, and is probably a harmonization with the previous stich.

37:1 אהבתו — The reading of H^C, אהבתו, "his love," is certainly an error for אהבתי, "I love," in all the Hebrew witnesses and ancient translations.

37:2 The punctuation of H^C is faulty. The scribe has placed a period after עליו, which does not offer a coherent meaning and is not supported by any version. The manuscript presents an original reading in relation to the other witnesses and versions by adding a temporal proposition and constructing דין (here construed as "judgment" in contrast to "sorrow" in H^{B,Bmg,D}) with מות. It connects this stich with the next one, and like the Syriac, emphasizes the faithfulness of the friend. The unfaithful friend turns into an enemy at the moment of death, that is, at the time of trial. The perspective is markedly different from that of H^{B,Bmg,D} and the LXX, which limit themselves to one observation: it is sad to see a friend turn into an enemy. The interpretation of H^C fits well with the context of 37:5-6 and seems more consistent than H^{B,Bmg,D} and the LXX, but it is also possible that it is an explanatory correction.

6:9 יחשוך — This verb is certainly a misspelling of יחשוף in H^A and the LXX. The final *pe* has been confused with a final *kaph*. This stich is missing in the Syriac.

6:8 בפני — The phrase, which occurs with a following noun only here in texts before the Common Era, usually indicates a spatial relation "in the presence of," though it does seem to appear sometimes in place of the more common לפני (see, e.g., m. 'Abot 4:11 in the Kaufmann Ms, which has לפני, and the same passage in the Vilna 1913 edition, which has בפני). If its use here corresponds to that of לפני "before," then עת would have the sense "a (trying) time."

5,4	Ne dis pas : « j'ai péché et que *m*'arrivera-t-il ? » car YYY est lent à la colère.	5:4	Do not say: "I have sinned, but what will come of it? for YYY is slow to anger.
5,5	Ne te fie pas au pardon, pour accumuler faute sur faute,	5:5	Do not trust in forgiveness, adding sin on top of sin,
5,6	en disant : « abondante est sa miséricorde, il pardonnera l'abondance de mes fautes ». Car miséricorde et colère sont avec lui et sur les méchants il fera reposer son courroux.	5:6	while saying: "Great is his mercy, he will pardon my many sins." For mercy and anger are his, and his fury he settles on the wicked.
5,7	Ne tarde pas à retourner vers lui et ne diffère pas de jour en jour. Car soudainement sortira sa colère et au temps de vengeance tu seras happé.	5:7	Do not delay returning to him, and do not put (it) off from day to day. For, his anger will burst out suddenly, and at the time of vengeance you will be taken away.
5,9	Ne vanne pas à tout vent et ne va pas par n'importe quel sentier.	5:9	Do not winnow in every wind, do not follow just any path.
5,10	Sois assuré de ta parole et après, que soient tes paroles.	5:10	Be sure of your speech, and afterward, your words should come.
5,11	Sois ferme dans une bonne écoute et avec patience réponds juste.	5:11	Be steadfast in hearing well and patiently you should really answer steadfastly.
5,12	Si tu le peux, réponds à ton prochain, sinon, mets ta main sur ta bouche.	5:12	If you are able, answer your neighbor, and if not, put your hand over your mouth.
5,13	Honneur et honte sont dans la main du bavard, mais la langue de l'être humain le préserve.	5:13	Honor and shame are in the hand of a chatterbox and a person's tongue can deliver them.
36,24	Le palais savoure les saveurs d'un présent, mais le cœur intelligent savoure les saveurs du mensonge.	36:24	The palate perceives a present's flavor but an intelligent mind perceives the flavor of a lie.
6,5	Un doux palais multiplie les amis et des lèvres gracieuses, ceux qui s'enquièrent de (ta) santé.	6:5	A sweet palate multiplies friends and gracious lips, those who ask (your) well-being.
6,6	Tes intimes qu'ils soient nombreux, mais ton conseiller, un entre mille.	6:6	Let your trusted friends be many, but your counselor one out of a thousand.
37,1	Tout ami dira son amour,	37:1	Every friend will speak their love.
37,2	n'est-ce pas au moment où s'approche de lui le jugement de la mort, qu'un compagnon comme lui-même se change en ennemi ?	37:2	Is it not at the time when a mortal judgment reaches them, a friend like oneself turns into an enemy.
6,7	Si tu acquiers un ami par l'épreuve acquiers-le et ne te hâte pas de te fier à lui.	6:7	If you acquire a friend, acquire one by means of a test, and do not hurry to trust them.
6,9	Il y a l'ami qui se change en ennemi et qui détournera ta querelle honteuse.	6:9	There is a friend who turns into an enemy and will withhold your shameful quarrel.
6,10	Il y a l'ami compagnon de table, mais il ne sera pas trouvé au jour du malheur.	6:10	There is a friend, a mealtime companion; but they will not be found in the day of misfortune.
6,8	Il y a l'ami avant le temps (d'épreuve), mais il ne reste pas au jour de détresse.	6:8	For there is a friend before a (trying) time, but, they will not remain in the day of distress.
6,12	Si tu l'approches, il se retourne contre toi et de ta face il se cache.	6:12	If you approach them, they turn against you, and from your face, they will hide.

6:12 רעה — The word רעה is missing in H^C, but the association of verses 8 and 12 in this manuscript allows this elision: "if it (i.e. the distress) reaches us". תשיגנו — H^C confirms the reading of H^A with the verb נשג, "to reach," against the Greek, the Syriac and the Latin, which suppose the *Vorlage* תפול. Yet, the third person singular pronominal suffix gives a radically different meaning to the couplet. The friend will turn away if distress strikes him. The statement is legitimate, but it doesn't fit the context of describing the unfaithful friend very well. נרפך — As the root רפך is not attested elsewhere, it should certainly be corrected to נהפך, as in H^A (יהפך) the Greek and the Syriac. The second leg of the *he* has been omitted by the scribe. For the meaning of הפך + ב, see Job 19:19.

6:13 A	משונאיך הבדל⁵		⁶השמר· ומאוהביך
6:14 AQ	אוהב אמונה מגן ⁷תקיף		ומוצאו מצא הוא הון·
6:15 AQ	⁸אוהב אמונה אין מחיר		ואין ⁹משקל לטובתו·
3:27 A	לב כבד ¹⁰יכביד כאבן		וחוטא יוסיף ¹¹חטא על חטא·
6:18 A	בני מנוער ¹²קבל מוסר	BAIU ID1 recto + frag. Gaster recto	ועד שיבה ¹תשיג חכמה
6:19 A	כחורש וכקוצר ²קרב אליה		וקוה לרוב תבואתה
	³כי בעבודתה מעט תעבוד		⁴ולמחר תאכל פריה
6:28 AQ	כי ⁵לאחור תמצא מנוחתה		⁶ותהפך לך לתענוג
6:35 A	כל שיחה ⁷חפוץ לשמוע		ומשל בינה ⁸אל יצאך
7:1 A	אל תעש רע		⁹ו[ל]א ישיגך רע·
7:2 A	רחק מעון ¹⁰[ו]ט ממד·		
7:4 A	אל תבקש מאֵל ¹¹ממשלת		וכן כמלך מושב ¹²כבוד·
7:6 A	אל תבקש להיות	BAIU ID1 verso + frag. Gaster verso	¹אם אין לך חיל להשבית זדון·
7:17 A	²מאד מאד השפל גאוה		כי ³תקות אנוש לרמה·
7:20 AD	אל תרע ⁴עבד עובד אמת		וכן שכיר ⁵נותן נפשו·
7:21 AD	עבד משכיל ⁶אהוב כנפש		אל תמנע ממנו ⁷חופש·
7:23 AD	בנים לך יסר ⁸אותם		ושא להם בנעוריהם·
7:24 AD	⁹בנים לך נצור שאר[ם]		ו[א]ל ¹⁰תאר להם פנים·
7:25 AD	הוציא [ב]ת ¹¹{ooo} ויצא עסק		ואל גבֿר ¹²נבון זבדה·
8:7 AD	[ ] אל תהֹלל		
18:31		Frag. Gaster + BAIU ID1 recto	¹שונא· [ ]

6:13 משונאיך | C משנאיך A · ומאוהביך | C ומאהביך A · השמר A C הזהר Saadia · 6:14 מגן C G (σκέπη?) | אוהב A S (ܢܣܒܐ) · תקיף | C תקוף A · מוסיף | C יוסיף A · ומתחולל | C G S ומתחולל A · חוטא | C G S וחוטא A · מכאביו | C כאבן A · ירבו | C יכביד A · 3:27 כביד | A S לאהוב | C G אוהב 6:15 A· > | A · הוא A· 6:18 בני מנוער קבל מוסר ועד שיבה תשיג חכמה | C G S > | A · 6:19 לרב | C לרוב A · לרב | A · בעבודתה | C בעבודתה A · 6:28 ותהפך | A 7:6 ממלך | C ממשל A + | A 12 לך | C רע A · רעה | C הרחק | A · 7:2 רחק | C אל תדע A · אל תרע | C D G (S) 7:4 כמלך | C מושל + | C | A לרמה | C S רמה A · 7:20 עבד עובד אמת | C G (S) באמת A עובד אמת | C השפל | C השפיל A · 7:17 D · שכיר | C D A · שוכר | C אהוב A D · חבב | C חופש A D · חפש | C חפשי A D · 7:23 יסר C D · יסיר A · להם | C + נשים A D · 7:24 בנים | C בנות A D G · תאיר | C תאר A D · להם | C אהם A אליהם D · 7:25 הוציא | C הוצא A D · הוצא | C גבר נבון A · נבון גבר C G S · חברה A D · 8:7 תהלל C | S · תאר A D · תהללו A D ·

Fragment BAIU + Gaster The fragment on the right, as it is presented on the plate of the library of the Bibliothèque de l'Alliance Israélite Universelle, is upside down. In addition, a fragment visible in the 1901 facsimile has become detached and disappeared.

L. 9 [7:1] ו[ל]א — The head of the *vav* and the right arm of the *aleph* are visible in the 1901 facsimile.

L. 10 [7:2] [ו]טֹ — The bottom left corner of the *tet* is visible. There is an ink trace in the right margin that cannot be identified.

L. 11 [7:4] ממשלת — The diagonal line of the *mem* is visible on the Gaster fragment.

L. 9 [7:24] שאר[ם] ו[א]ל — The head of the *vav* and the diagonal line of the *lamed* are still visible on the fragment present in the 1901 facsimile.

L. 10 [7:25] הוציא [ב]ת — The end of the diagonal of the *aleph* is visible. The characteristic foot of the *tav* is visible on the Gaster fragment.

L. 11 [7:25] גבֿר — The upper corner of the *bet* is visible at the break in the BAIU fragment. The head of the *resh* is clearly visible on the Gaster fragment.

L. 12 [8:7] תהֹלל — הלל is clearly visible on the Gaster fragment (not transcribed in Ben-Ḥayyim [1973, 10]).

6:14 מגן — "Shield" may agree with the Greek (although σκέπη never translates מגן in the LXX), while H^A has אוהב, which agrees with the Syriac (ܢܣܒܐ).

3:27 Elizur (2010, 24) hesitates to identify this verse with Sir 3:27. Nevertheless, although H^C presents variants to H^A and the versions, its association with Sir 3:27 seems fully assured. יכביד — The verb is likely a *hiphil* with an intransitive sense (cf. the *hiphil* form in 2 Chron 25:19 that corresponds to the *niphal* in 2 Kgs 14:10; see also Jastrow 1903, 607). Alternatively, it could be a plene spelling of the *niphal*. כאבן — is easily explained as a graphic alteration of מכאביו, attested in H^A and reflected in the Greek and the Syriac.

6:18 This verse is missing in H^A.

7:1 The reading in H^C agrees with the Greek and Syriac, while H^A has a different reading: "Do not harm yourself, and evil will not reach you".

7:2 רחק — The use of the *qal*, instead of the *hiphil* attested in H^A, does not seem to have any influence on the meaning of the sentence.

7:6 להיות — The absence of מושל, attested in H^A, the Greek and the Syriac (ܫܘܦܛ), is in all likelihood, an oversight from when the scribe turned the page.

7:20 עבד עובד אמת — H^C certainly presents the best reading, in agreement with the Greek (μὴ κακώσῃς οἰκέτην ἐργαζόμενον ἐν ἀληθείᾳ) and the Syriac (ܠܟ ܠܥܒܕܐ ܕܦܠܚ ܒܩܘܫܬܐ), against H^{A,D}.

6,13	De tes ennemis, sépare-toi et de tes amis, garde-toi.	6:13	From your enemies, separate yourself, and be wary of your friends.
6,14	Un ami fidèle est un bouclier solide et celui qui l'a trouvé a trouvé une richesse.	6:14	A faithful friend is a strong shield and whoever has found one has found wealth.
6,15	Un ami fidèle n'a pas de prix et il n'y a pas de poids à sa bonté.	6:15	As for a faithful friend, there is no price and for his goodness there is no measure.
3,27	Un cœur lourd s'alourdit comme de la pierre et celui qui pèche accumule péché sur péché.	3:27	A hardened heart will be heavy like a stone and a sinner will add sin upon sin.
6,18	Mon enfant, dès la jeunesse, reçois l'instruction et à la vieillesse, tu atteindras la sagesse.	6:18	My child, from your youth accept instruction, and when old, you will attain wisdom.
6,19	Comme un laboureur et un moissonneur approche-toi d'elle. et espère en l'abondance de sa récolte. Car, à son service, tu serviras peu, mais le lendemain, tu mangeras ses fruits.	6:19	Like a plowman and a harvester, draw near to her, and await the abundance of her harvest. For, in her service you will serve but little and the next day you will eat her fruits.
6,28	Car, par la suite, tu trouveras le lieu de son repos et elle se changera pour toi en délice.	6:28	For afterward you will find her resting place, and she will be transformed for you into a delight.
6,35	Désire écouter tout discours et que la maxime sensée ne t'échappe pas.	6:35	Be eager to hear all discourse and may an intelligent maxim not escape you.
7,1	Ne fais pas le mal et le mal n[e] t'atteindra pas.	7:1	Do no evil and evil will not reach you.
7,2	Éloigne-toi du péché et [il se détour]nera de toi.	7:2	Keep far from sin and it will turn away from you.
7,4	Ne demande pas à Dieu le pouvoir, ni, comme un roi, une place d'honneur.	7:4	Do not ask God for power, nor like a king, a place of honor.
7,6	Ne cherche pas à être (*celui qui a le pouvoir*) si tu n'as pas la force de mettre fin à l'arrogance,	7:6	Do not try to be (*someone who wields power*), if you do not have the strength to end arrogance,
7,17	Humilie grandement l'orgueil, car l'espoir de l'humain est pour la vermine.	7:17	Diminish pride deeply, for the hope of humankind is worms
7,20	Ne sois pas mauvais envers un serviteur qui sert fidèlement, ni envers un salarié qui donne de sa personne.	7:20	Do not treat badly a servant serving faithfully, nor a laborer who dedicates themself (to their task)
7,21	Un serviteur intelligent aime(-le) comme toi-même, ne lui refuse pas la liberté.	7:21	Love a prudent servant as (your) very self, do not refuse them liberty.
7,23	As-tu des fils ? instruis-les et pardonne leur quand ils sont jeunes.	7:23	Do you have sons? Instruct them, and forgive them in their youth.
7,24	As-tu des fils, veille sur [leur] chair et [ne] leur montre pas un visage radieux.	7:24	Do you have sons? Watch over their flesh, and do not show them a radiant face.
7,25	Fais partir (ta) [fil]le et le souci partira et donne-la à un homme intelligent.	7:25	Make [your] daughter depart [. . .] and worry will depart too, but give her to an intelligent man.
8,7	Ne te fé[li]cite pas [de celui qui meurt,]	8:7	Do not congratulate yourself [over someone who is dying,]
18,31	[ ]ennemi.	18:31	[ ] enemy

7:21 עבד משכיל — Cf Prov 14:35; 17:2 and 4Q418 8a,b,c,d 15 (// 4Q416 2 ii 15). אהוב כנפש — The construction אהב + נפש is also attested in Sir 4:7ᴬ (ומסתיר סוד אוהב), as well as in 31:2ᴮ (האהב לנפשך לעדה), and seems to be inspired by 1 Sam 18:1 and 20:17.

7:23 ושא להם — The absence of נשים, attested in Hᴬ,ᴰ, is clearly accidental (cf. the Syriac). Without נשים, the verb נשא may take here the meaning "to forgive" (see Gen 18:24; Ps 99:8). The Greek renders a totally different stich, which it seems to borrow from Sir 30:12ᴮ (כוף ראשו בנעורתו, cf. Isa 58:5).

7:24 בנים — According to Lévi (1901, 45), the reading בנות in Hᴬ,ᴰ was erased and replaced by בנים because of the following pronouns with masculine suffixes. Yet, the variant in Hᶜ can also be explained as a vertical dittography (Rüger 1970, 47).

7:25 זבדה — The only attestation of this word is in Gen 30:20, where it is translated by δωρέω in Greek and by יהב in Tg. Onq., precisely as the Greek and the Syriac translate in Sir 7:25, whereas חבר, as attested by Hᴬ,ᴰ, never corresponds with these translations.

	אשר פי שנים רישו	אל תשמח אל שמך ²תענוג	18:32
	ומאומ[ה] ⁴אין בכיס·	³אל תהי זולל וסובא	18:33
	ובוזה מעוטים ⁶יתערער:	פועל זאת ⁵לא יעשיר	19:1
		יין ונשים ⁷יפחיזו לב	19:2
		ונפש עזה ⁸ת[שׁ]חית בעליה·	19:3
	[וי]¹⁰שׁ נמאס בריב שׂ[יח]	יש ⁹מ[חריש]ׁ ונחשב̇ חכם	20:5
	¹²ויש מחריש כי ראה עת	¹¹יש מחריש מאין מענה	20:6
Frag. Gaster + BAIU 1D1 verso	²וכסיל לא ישמור עת	¹חכם יחריש עד עת	20:7
	ולנפשו ⁴הוא גואל·	יש ³חכם לרבים נחכם	37:19 BD
	פרי דעתו ⁶על גויתו·	יש חכם ⁵לנפשו יחכם	37:22 BD
	וכל ראיו ⁸יאשרוהו·	חכם לנפשו ⁷ישבע תענוג	37:24 BD
	ושמ[ו] ¹⁰עומד בח[י]ׂ עולם·	חכם ע[ם] ⁹ינ̇ח[ל] כבוד	37:26 BD
	וטובת ¹²כסילים ישפוך	חכם ¹¹במעט דבר נפשו	20:13
Frag. G. Combs recto	ומה תולעת בש[תיהם·]	חכמה ¹טמונה ואוצר מ[וסתר]	20:30 // 41:14bc BM
	⁴מאיש מצפין חכמ[תו·]	³טוב איש מצפין̇ אולתו̇	20:31 // 41:15 BM
	וכבוד לאיש בחז[ק] ⁷יעמוד·	רגל נבל ממהרת אל ⁶בית	21:22a/23b
	ואיש מזמות ⁹יכניע פנים·	כסיל מפתח ⁸יביט אל בית	21:23a/22b
	ובלב חכמים פיהם	בפי כסילים ¹⁰לבם	21:26
	¹²ועל כסיל לבכות כי חדל בינה	¹¹על מת לבכות כי חדל אורו	22:11
Frag. G. Combs verso	ור[עים] ²[ממות חיים רעים·]	[אין ל]בׂכות על מת כי נח	[1]

ויאשריהו B G S | ואׁשׁרוׁהוׁ [כל ר]וׁאיׁ[י]ו C | וכל ראיו יאשרוהו C 37:24   ויש B D | יש C 37:22   (ܬܟܫܐ) S (ἄχρηστος) Bmg D G   נואל Bmg | גואל C B 37:19   מאיש C מטמן M | מצפן C B | מצפן Bmg 20:31 // 41:15   מצפן C B ואוצר | וסימה Bmg ושימה M | תולעה C תועלה B תעלה Bmg M · 20:30 // 41:14   כל רואיהו D · ישטׁמׂן Bmg | מצפן C B יטמן Bmg · מאדון Bmg · B M

L. 2 [18:32] רישו — The last letter can also be read as a final *kaph* with the horizontal bar slightly faded.

18:32 שמך — The meaning of this word within the context is unclear. It is translated by πολύς in the Greek "great luxury," and similarly in the Syriac (ܐܣܓܐ). For our translation, see Sir 10:10ᴬ and the note. פי שנים — See 12:5ᴬ and the note, as well as 48:12ᴮ. רישו — See the note on the reading.

18:33 זולל וסובא — This verse is a subtle combination of Deut 21:20 where the two participles are coordinated and Prov 23:20 which attests the vetitive syntax. See also Puech's restoration in 4Q525 25 4.

19:1 מעוטים — This is either the passive participle of the root מעט "to be few, small" or the rabbinic substantive מיעוט "narrowing, limitation." In either case, it would seem to have a figurative sense here, either "austerity" or "sobriety." יתערער — The form is rare and may be the *hithpalpel* of ערר or ערער "to strip, lay bare, knock down, destroy," see Jer 51:58 and 4Q416 1 12. See also the noun ערער in Ps 102:18 which seems to mean "the poor" based on ancient translations.

19:2 יפחיזו — For the meaning of the verb פחז in the *hiphil*, see 8:2ᴬ. Here, it is associated with לב and could mean "to lose one's mind," as in Hos 4:11 זְנוּת וְיַיִן וְתִירוֹשׁ יִקַּח־לֵב "fornication and wine and new wine carry away understanding"). See also, the use of the noun פחז concerning Reuben in Gen 49:4.

19:2-3 The Greek and the Syriac add two stichs here (19:2*b* and 19:3*a*).

19:3 This stich is a doublet of Sir 6:4ᴬ (see the note there).

20:5 בריב — "By a strife." All commentators (Lévi 1901, 123; Smend 1906b, 21; Segal 1958, 120) consider it to be a misspelling of ברוב "by abundance." [שׂ]יח — One may restore שיח with the Greek (λαλιᾶς) or שיחו with the Syriac (ܡܡܠܠܗ).

20:13 טובת — The word can have the sense "inclination, intention" (see Jastrow 1903, 521 and Levy 1876–89 3:144). ישפוך — Although the

L. 12 [22:11] The last line is written with an indentation and in smaller characters.

subject (טובה) is feminine, the verb is masculine, presumably due to the immediately preceding noun (cf. זנונים התעה רוח Hos 4:12). The sense seems to be intransitive (as in some Aramaic dialects like Late Jewish Literary Aramaic; see CAL 15 May, 2021).

20:30 // 41:14 תולעת — The word "worm" does not make sense here and is clearly a metathesis for תועלה/ת, attested in the other manuscripts (see 30:23 for this word).

21:22-23 According to Cowley and Neubauer (1897, xxiii), this verse is quoted in חידוש דרבינו פרקא 14*a*: לבית חבירו אדם יהמר אל ולעולם שכך כתוב בספר בן סירא רגל נבל ממהרת אל בית ואיש מזמות יכניע רבים ולעולם אל יסתכל אדם לשער חבירו שכן בספר בן סירא אויל מפתח יביט אל בית וכבוד לאיש בבית עמיו. "Let a man never hasten into the house of his neighbor; for thus it is written in the book of Ben Sira: The foot of a senseless man hastens to (another's) house, but a prudent man will subdue many. Let a man never look in at the door of his neighbor; for thus (it is written) in the book of Ben Sira: A foolish man gazes from the door into (another's) house, but a man's honor is in the house of his own kinsmen (trans. Cowley and Neubauer, ed. Schönblum)." The Greek, the Syriac and the rabbinic tradition invert the second stich of v. 22 with the second stich of v. 23.

21:22 There are several allusions to this verse in rabbinic literature. See b. Nidda 16b–17a: וארבעה שנאתי שלשה סירא בן בספר כתיב לכד לא אהבתי סר הנרגל בבית המשתאות ואמרי לה סר הנרגן והמושיב שבת במרומי קריה ואוחז באמה ומשתין מים והנכנס לבית פתאום א' ר' יוחנן אפילו לביתו שמע א'ר ארבעה הקב'ה שונאן ואף אני אינו אוהבן הנכנס לביתו פתאום ואין צריך לומ' לבית חברו והאוחז באמה ומשתין מים ומש' "... according to what is written in the book of Ben Sira: Three things I have hated, and four

18,32	Ne te réjouis pas de petits plaisirs qui (seraient) une double part de sa/ta pauvreté.	18:32	Do not rejoice in the least of pleasures whose poverty is double.
18,33	Ne sois ni glouton ni ivrogne, alors qu'il n'y a rien dans la bourse.	18:33	Do not be a glutton or a drunk with nothing in your purse.
19,1	Qui fait ainsi ne s'enrichira pas et celui qui méprise la sobriété sera dépossédé.	19:1	One who does this will not grow wealthy; the one despising austerity will become destitute
19,2	Le vin et les femmes rendent déraisonnable	19:2	Wine and women corrupt the mind,
19,3	et un appétit vorace détruit son propriétaire.	19:3	the voracious appetite destroys its master.
20,5	Il y a [le silencie]ux (qui) est considéré[sage] [et il] y a le méprisé par *l'abondance* de disc[ours.]	20:5	There is [one who is sil]ent and considered [wise] [and] another rejected for *constant* pr[attle.]
20,6	Il y a le silencieux (car) il n'a pas de réponse et il y a le silencieux car il guette le (bon) moment.	20:6.	There is one who is silent for they have no reply, and another who is silent watching for the right moment.
20,7	Le sage se tait jusqu'au (bon) moment, mais l'insensé n'observe pas le (bon) moment.	20:7	A wise person stays silent till the right moment, the fool does not observe the right moment.
37:19	Il y a le sage qui devient sage pour la multitude, mais qui se hait lui même.	37:19	There is a sage who becomes wise for many, but who loathes themself.
37,22	Il y a le sage qui est sage pour lui même, le fruit de sa connaissance est sur son corps.	37:22	There is a sage who becomes wise for themself and the fruit of their knowledge (rests) upon their body.
37,24	Le sage pour lui-même se rassasie de délices et tous ceux qui le voient le diront bienheureux.	37:24	The one wise for themself is satiated with delights and all who see them will say they are blessed.
37,26	Le sage du pe[uple héri]tera de gloire et [son]nom[tiendra dans la v]ie éternelle.	37:26	The sage of the peo[ple will inhe]rit glory and [their] name [will endure in] eternal [lif]e.
20:13	Le sage avec peu (de mots) dit son désir, mais l'intention des insensés se répand.	20:13	A sage with few (words) speaks their desire but the intention of fools spills forth.
20,30	Sagesse cachée et trésor en[foui,] quel profit en ces deux choses ?	20:30	Hidden wisdom and con[cealed] treasure, what profit is in either of these two things?
20,31	Mieux vaut une personne qui cache[sa folie] qu'une personne qui cache [sa] sages[se.]	20:31	Better a person who hides [their folly] than a person who hides [their] wisd[om.]
21,22a	Le pied de l'insensé se hâte vers la maison,	21:22a	The foot of a fool rushes into a house,
21,23b	mais l'honneur est pour celui qui se tient à l'extérieur.	21:23b	though it is proper for a person to wait outside.
21,23a	L'insensé, depuis la porte, regarde vers la maison,	21:23a	A fool looks into the house from the doorway,
21,22b	mais la personne discrète incline la face.	21:22b	while a discrete person bows their face.
21,26	La raison des insolents est dans leur bouche, mais la bouche des sages est dans leur raison.	21:26	The mind of the fool is in their mouth, while the mouth of the wise is in their mind.
22,11	Sur un mort, il faut pleurer, car sa lumière a cessé et sur un fou, il faut pleurer, car l'intelligence a cessé. [Ne Ple]ure [pas] sur un mort, car il se repose, [mais pire]que la mort, une vie mauvaise.	22:11	Over the dead one should weep, for their light has ceased, and over a fool one should weep, for their reason has ceased. [One should not] weep over the dead, for they are at rest, [but worse] than death is a wicked life.

I have not loved: a minister who frequents the bar-houses-and some say, a minister who grumbles, and one who sets up a seat in the highest [part] of a city, and one who holds his member and urinates, and the one who enters a house suddenly (R. Yohanan says also his own house). R. Simon said: Four things the Holy One, blessed be He, hates, and even I do not love them: One who enters his house suddenly-and it goes without saying, his friend's house-and who holds his member and urinates, and one who urinates before his bed naked, and one who has intercourse [lit. uses his bed] before any living thing [i.e., in view of others]" (text and translation slightly adapted from Labendz 2006, 377–78). See also Chuppah of Eliyahou, 201: ואל תכנס לעיר ולא לביתך פתאום וכל שכן לבית חבירך "And do not enter a city or your house suddenly, and all the more, the house of your neighbor." See Der. Er. Rab. 5:2: לעולם אל יכנס אדם פתאום לבית חבירו "A person never suddenly enters the house of their neighbor."

22:12	[אבל ג]וע שבעת ימים		4[ואבל]רש כל ימי חייו·	
22:21	אל 5[או]הב אל תשלוף חרב		6אל תגור כי יש כופר·	
22:22	אל 7אוהב אל תפתח פה		אל 8תדאג כי יש תשובה·	
23:11	איש שבועות ימלא אשמה		10ולא ימוש מביתו הנגע·	
25:7	11אשרי איש שמח באחריתו		12חי וראה בשבר צריו·	
25:8	1אשרי שלא נפל בלשון		ולו 2עבד נקלה ממנו·	T-S 12.727 verso + T-S AS 213 recto
	אשרי 3בעל אשה משכלת		ולא 4חורש כשור עם חמור[·]	
25:13	5כל מכה ולא כמ[כת] לב		כל רעה ולא כרע[ת אשה]	
25:17	7רע אשה ישחיר 8מראה איש		ויקדיר פנ[י]ו 9לדוב·	
25:18	9בין רעים ישב בעלה		ובלא טעמו יתאנח·	
25:19	מעט 11רעה כרעת אשה		גורל 12חוטא יפול עליה·	
25:20	כמעלה 1חזק לאיש ישיש		אשת 2לשון לאיש מך·	T-S 12.727 recto + T-S AS 213 verso
25:21	אל תפול 3אל יופי אשה		ועל יש לה 4[א]ל תמהר·	
25:22	4כי בערה 5[ ] [ו]בושת		אשה מכלכלת 6[את] בעלה·	
25:23	רפיון ידים 7[וכ]שלון ברכים		אשה לא 8תאשר את בעלה·	
25:24	מאשה 9תחלת עון		ובגללה גוענו 10יחד·	
26:1	אשה טובה אשרי 11בעלה		ומספר ימיו כפלים:	

L. 5 [25:22] בערה — The third letter, read as a *dalet* in preceding editions, may also be a *resh* (already Schechter 1900, 465; see the *resh* of רע on TS 12.727 verso l. 7).

L. 5-6 [25:13] The restoration of this verse is based on the Greek and the Syriac, which present the same repetitive pattern.

22:12 [אבל ג]וע . . . [רש]אבל — The restoration of אבל and גוע is mainly based on the Syriac (see Elizur 2010, 27).

22:21-22 Unlike the Greek and the Syriac, the Hebrew does not have a conditional particle. Verses 21 and 22 have the same construction: two successive asyndetic vetitive formulas (v. 21: "Do not draw a sword, do not be afraid . . . " v. 22: "Do not open your mouth, do not worry . . .") followed by an explanation introduced by כי (21*b*: "because there is a redemption;" v. 22*b*: "because there is a return"). It implies that one should understand the second vetitive formula as a conditional formula "otherwise," thus, "Do not draw a sword, (but if you have drawn the sword, then) do not be afraid, because there is a redemption." The same type of argumentation is found in Sir 8:12, 13 and 9:13 (see also, 4Q417 2 i 19-22; 4Q416 2 ii 3-6, 2 ii 6-9, 2 iii 5-8 and Aḥiqar TAD C.1.1, 130-131), as well as in the preceding verse in the Syriac version (without parallel in the Greek): ܠܐ ܬܫܬܚܠܦ ܥܠ ܚܒܪܟ ܘܐܢ ܬܫܬܚܠܦ ܠܐ ܬܣܒܪ ܕܐܝܬ ܠܟ ܪܚܡܘܬܐ ܥܡܗ "Do not act differently (i.e., be changed) towards your friend and if you do act differently, do not hope that you have friendship with him." The fact that these two proverbs are cut off from their context considerably alters their meaning. Indeed, the Greek (and the Syriac) complete the sentence with an antithesis: "with the exception of reproach, arrogance, revealing a secret and a treacherous blow—in these cases any friend will flee" (NETS). In this case, the purpose of verses 21-22 is to show that an open quarrel (drawing a sword or opening one's mouth) can always lead to reconciliation, while pride, revelation of a secret, treachery and hypocrisy will destroy friendship.

25:8 ולו — As it is written, this verse clearly echoes Prov 12:9: טוב נקלה ועבד לו ממתכבד וחסר־לחם "Better to be despised and have a servant, than to be self-important and lack food (NRSV)." Yet, the Greek and the Syriac seem to imply that it is a misspelling of ולא, as in the next stich: "And the one who does not serve (one) less honorable than himself."

25:13 Cf. b. Šabb 10a: כָּל חֳלִי, וְלֹא חוֹלִי מֵעַיִם. כָּל כְּאֵב, וְלֹא כְּאֵב לֵב. כָּל מֵיחוֹשׁ, וְלֹא מֵיחוֹשׁ רֹאשׁ. כָּל רָעָה, וְלֹא אִשָּׁה רָעָה, Chuppat Eliyahu Rabbah 131: דברים קשים זה מזה: מכת הלב קשה ממכת הגוף, חולי מעיים קשה ממכת הלב, אשה רעה קשה משניהן, וחסרון כיס קשה מכולן and Qoh. Rab. 7:26:2 (. . .) אָמַר רַבִּי יְהוּדָה אַרְבָּעָה עָשָׂר דְּבָרִים קָשִׁין זֶה מִזֶּה (. . .) וְאִשָּׁה רָעָה קָשָׁה מִכֻּלָּן.

25:17 לדוב — Instead of "bear," Kister (1983, 134) interprets the letters as דאב "sorrow." Indeed, this spelling may be compared with תֹּאַר in H[B], written תור in H[M], in Sir 43:18. See also, יפי התור in 11QPs[a] XXVIII 9 (Ps 151:5) compared with יפה תאר in Gen 29:17 and 39:6 (see Sanders, DJD 4 [1965, 49.57]). The Greek (ὡς ἄρκος) and the Syriac (ܐܝܟ ܕܘܒܐ) assume a *kaph* preposition before דוב. The divergence between the Hebrew דוב "bear," as understood by the Greek, and the Syriac ܕܘܒܐ, is well documented in the Greek and Latin textual traditions. While most of the Greek manuscripts have ὡς ἄρκος, some have ὡς σακκον (B La Sa Aeth). The Old Latin (*ursus et quasi saccum*) and the commentary of the monk Malachias (σάκκος ἢ ὡς ἄρκος ὡς ἐν ἑτέροις) attest both forms. These variations can easily be explained by a scribal confusion between Greek letters: ὡς αρκος > ὡς σαρκος (MS 336) > ὡς σακκος (B). This suggests that the Syriac translator used the Greek version for his own translation here.

22,12	[Le deuil d'un m]ort : sept jours, [mais le deuil]du pauvre : tous les jours de sa vie.	22:12	[Mourning for the d]ead (lasts) seven days, [but mourning for] the poor all the days of their life.
22,21	Contre un ami, ne dégaine pas une épée, (si tu l'as fait,) ne redoute pas, car il y a un rachat.	22:21	Do not draw your sword against a friend, (if you do,) do not despair, for there is a chance for repentance.
22,22	Contre un ami, n'ouvre pas la bouche, (si tu l'as fait,) ne t'inquiète pas, car il y a un retour.	22:22	Do not open your mouth against a friend, (if you do,) do not fear, there is still the chance for reconciliation.
23,11	Une personne de serments sera rempli de culpabilité et l'affliction ne s'éloignera pas de sa maison.	23:11	A person who makes many oaths will be filled with guilt and affliction will not turn from their house
25,7	Heureuse la personne qui se réjouit de ses descendants, vivant, il verra la ruine de ses ennemis.	25:7	Happy is the person who rejoices in their descendants, alive, they will see the destruction of their enemies.
25,8	Heureux qui ne tombe pas par (sa) langue et qui possède un serviteur moins estimé que lui. Heureux l'époux d'une femme intelligente et qui n'a pas labouré *avec* un bœuf et un âne.	25:8	Happy the one who does not fall by their tongue, whose servant is less esteemed than them. Happy is the husband of an intelligent wife and who does not plow *with* ox and donkey (together).
25,13	De toutes blessures, rien n'est comme une bles[sure] de cœur, de tout mal, rien n'est comme un mal de femme.	25:13	Of all wounds, there is nothing like a wo[und] of the heart, of all evils, there is nothing like the evil of a woman.
25,17	La méchanceté d'une femme assombrit l'apparence de son mari et obscurcit son visage par désespoir.	25:17	The wickedness of woman darkens (her) husband's appearance and obscures his face with sorrow.
25,18	Au milieu des compagnons, siège son mari et, n'ayant plus goût à rien, il gémit.	25:18	Among companions, her husband sits and moans without his reason.
25,19	Peu de mal est comparable au mal d'une femme que le sort du pécheur tombe sur elle.	25:19	(All other) wickedness is minor compared to a woman's wickedness, may the fate of the sinner fall upon her.
25,20	Comme une forte montée pour une personne âgée, ainsi une femme bavarde pour un homme modeste.	25:20	Like a steep slope to an aged person, thus is a talkative woman to the modest.
25,21	Ne succombe pas à la beauté d'une femme et sur ce qu'elle possède, ne te précipite pas.	25:21	Do not succumb to the beauty of a woman and do not hasten to what is hers.
25,22	Car, colère [ ] et honte, une femme qui entretient son mari.	25:22	For, anger [ ] and shame (belong to) a wife who supports her husband.
25,23	Mains défaillantes et genoux fléchissants: une femme qui ne rend pas heureux son mari.	25:23	Feeble hands and failing knees: a wife who does not make her husband happy.
25,24	D'une femme est le commencement du péché et à cause d'elle, nous mourrons tous ensemble.	25:24	From a woman is the beginning of sin and because of her we die together.
26,1	Une femme bienveillante, heureux est son mari et le nombre de ses jours est doublé.	26:1	A good wife—happy is her husband, the number of his days is double.

25:18 רעים — The letters may be vocalized רֵעִים "companions" (so the Greek and the Syriac) or רָעִים "evildoers." טעמו — "N'ayant plus goût à rien" with Mopsik (2003, 172). The word טעם may have the meaning "ground, cause" here, as attested in Rabbinic Hebrew (see Peters 1902, 100). יתאנח — See 12:12 H^A and the note.
25:21 תמהר — Alternatively, read: "(do not) pay the bride price." See, e.g., Exod 22:15 and Ps 16:4.
25:22 בערה — "Fire, conflagration" (See Exod 22:5 and Jastrow 1903, 183) from the root בער "to burn" which is associated with anger as in Jer 44:6 (see the Greek ὀργή "wrath" which may also represent the word עברה "anger, rage" by metathesis). The Syriac presupposes the Hebrew עבודה "enforced labor."
25:23 רפיון ידים — See Jer 47:3.
25:24 This verse has caused a lot of ink to flow.
26:1 This verse is quoted in b. Sanh. 100b and b. Yeb. 63b: אשה יפה אשרי בעלה מספר ימיו כפלים.

MANUSCRIPT C

26:2	¹²אשת חיל תדשן לבעלה	¹ושנות֯ חיי ב[שׂמח]ה ימלא·[	T-S 12.867 recto
26:3	²אשה טׄובה מנה [טׄובה]	³ובחלק ירא ייי תנתן֯·[	
26:13	⁴אשה מׄטיב בעלה [חן֯]	⁵ידשן שכלה·]∘ۭ[ז֯ׄ	
26:15	⁶אשה ביישת חן על חן֯[ ]	ואין משׁקׄל ⁷לצרורות פה:	
26:16	שמש זׄורׄחׄת ⁸במרומי מעל	יפה א[שה] ⁹בדביר בחור·	
26:17	נר שׂרׄף֯ ¹⁰על מנורת קדש	הוד ¹¹פנים על קומת תוכן:	
36:27 BP	¹יהלל]תואר אשה מכל פנים	ו]עַ֯לׄ֯ בׄלׄ֯] מחמד [עַ֯ןׄ יׄגׄבׄ]רׄ[	T-S 12.867 verso
36:28 BP	²וׄעׄוׄד אׄם [יׄשׁ בה מ[רׄ]פׄא לשון	³אׄ[ין א]ישה מבני אדם֯·	
36:29 BDP	⁴קׄונה [א]שה ראשיׄת קנין	⁵קׄנׄהׄ עיר מבצרׄ צׄינה ⁶ומשען העמיד·	
36:30 BDP	באין גדר ⁷יׄבו]ׄער כרם	ובאין אשה ⁸ג֯]עׄ ונד·	
36:31 BD	מי יאמין בצבא ⁹גדוד	המדלג מעיר אׄלׄ עׄיׄרׄ	
	¹⁰וכן איש אשר אין לו קין	¹¹המרגיע באשה יסביב·	
27:17?	[נסה	[	

36:27 עזר ומבצר C | קׄנׄהׄ עיר מבצרׄ צׄינה B (cf. B) | אׄשָׁה B · 36:29 C אׄ[ישה] · > B | C Bmg בה 36:28 · B Bmg והליל (יהלל) C פנים | C מכל פנים [יהלל 36:27
גדר C D | B D · ועמוד משען C ומשען העמיד Bmg D · עיר מבצר (עזר כנגדו) = Gen 2:18.20 ܥܘܕܪܢܐ ܥܡܗ, ܗܘܐ S κατ' αὐτὸν βοηθὸν G
גדיר · 36:31 באשר יערב C באשה יסביב B D קן B D · קין C קץ B · לא B D · בגדוד צבא C בצבא גדוד C Bmg D אין לו B D ·

T-S 12.867 recto The photos in Schirmann (1960, plate) and Di Lella (1964, plate), although of poor quality, offer a more complete text than the recent photos, which reveal a deterioration of the manuscript.
L. 1 [26:2] ב[שׂמח]ה — The photos in Schirmann (1960, plate) and Di Lella (1964, plate) still clearly preserve the *mem* and part of the right leg of the *khet*. [ושנות֯ חיי ב[שׂמח]ה ימלא — This restoration is based on the Syriac and perfectly fits the space. The last word may be ישלם (see the Greek πληρώσει ἐν εἰρήνῃ = ימלא בשלום). The restoration proposed by Di Lella (1964, 166), [ושנות֯ חיי ב[שׂמח]ת:], is too short to be aligned with the left margin. The lacuna is smaller than it appears on the photos, so that the fragment on the left must be shifted to the right.
L. 3 [26:13] [חן֯] אשה — It is necessary to restore a word after תנתן at the end of line 3 (see the Greek Χάρις γυναικός).
L. 4 [26:13] מׄטיב — The *mem* and the *tet* are still visible on the photos in Schirmann (1960, plate) and Di Lella (1964, plate). [ ]∘ۭ — The restoration עצמותי, suggested by Schirmann (1960, 133), is impossible for the space. Di Lella (1964) restores עצמי, which would fit the space, but the *ayin* is impossible according to the traces.
L. 1 [36:27] יהלל] ו]עַ֯לׄ֯ בׄלׄ֯] מחמד [עַ֯ןׄ יׄגׄבׄ]רׄ[— The restoration of יהלל is only based on the text of H^Bmg. The first preserved traces can only correspond to *ayin, lamed* and *kaph, lamed* (see the plates in Schirmann 1960 and Di Lella 1964), and not to מחמד, as proposed by Abegg and Towes in the Accordance module. Indeed, the space between מחמד and עַ֯ןׄ would be far too great. The *ayin* and the *nun* are both visible on new photographs.
L. 5 [36:29] צׄינה — The *tsade* with a low right arm is possible (Schirmann 1960, 133). This reading would be preferable paleographically, as well as for the meaning, over against the reading קינה proposed by Di Lella (1964, 166).
L. 6 [36:29] ומשען — The first two letters are clear in old photos.
L. 11 [36:31] באשה — The first letter resembles a *kaph*, but a *bet*, easier for the meaning, is not excluded. The last letter is clearly a *he* (with Beentjes 2006, 357–58), against Schirmann (1960, 134) and Di Lella (1964, 166) who read כאשר.

26,2	Une femme valeureuse engraissera son mari et [il passera]les années[de sa vie dans] la joie.	26:2	A valorous wife will make her husband fat [and he will pass] the years of [his life] in joy.
26,3	Une femme bienveillante est une [bonne] part et elle est accordée dans le lot de celui qui craint YYY,	26:3	A good wife is a [good] portion, she is set in the lot of the one who fears YYY.
26,13	[La grâce] d'une femme fait du bien à son mari, son intelligence engraissera [ ].	26:13	[The grace] of a wife will make her husband glad, [ ] her intelligence will make fat.
26,15	Grâce sur grâce, une femme modeste et nul ne peut peser celle qui a la bouche scellée.	26:15	Grace beyond grace is a modest wife, beyond measure is one whose mouth is sealed.
26,16	Un soleil levant dans les hauteurs d'en haut, une femme belle dans une chambre sacrée de choix.	26:16	A sun rising in the heights above (such is) the beauty of a woman in the chamber of a young man.
26,17	Une lampe qui brûle sur un candélabre du sanctuaire, la splendeur d'un visage sur une haute taille.	26:17	A lamp that burns on the lampstand of the sanctuary (such is) the splendor of a face upon a perfect stature.
36,27	Beauté de femme [illumine] plus que tout visage, [et] elle surpas[se] tous [désirs] de l'œil.	36:27	The beauty of a wife [illuminates] more than any face [and] it surpas[ses] every [desire] of the eye.
36,28	[Et en plus, s']il y a en elle une parole apaisante, son [m]ari n'a [pas] (d'égal) parmi les humains.	36:28	[Moreover, if] she has a calming tongue her [hus]band has [no] (equal) among humankind.
36,29	[Celui qui acquiert] une femme, la meilleure acquisition, a acquis une ville fortifiée, un bouclier et un appui (qui le) raffermit.	36:29	[The one who acquires] a wife, the best of acquisitions, acquires a fortified city, a shield, and a support that bears him up.
36,30	En l'absence de clôture la vigne [est déva]stée, en l'absence de femme, on [er]re et vagabonde.	36:30	When there is no fence, the vineyard is destroyed, when there is no wife, one ceaselessly [wan]ders.
36,31	Qui peut se fier à une troupe armée qui bondit de ville en ville ? Ainsi l'homme qui n'a pas de nid, en se reposant chez une femme, vagabonde autour.	36:31	Who will trust an army of troops who hop from city to city? Thus, the man who has no nest, who reposes with a woman, will wander around.

26:2 אשת חיל — Cf. Prov 12:4 and 31:10. תדשן — The verb דשן means "to make fat," but figuratively, "to make happy, prosper." See Prov 15:30 where it is in parallel with שמח and Deut 31:20.

26:3 This verse is quoted in b. Sanh. 100b and b. Yeb. 63b: אשה טובה מתנה טובה בחיק ירא אלהים תנתן לו.

26:15 ביישת — The word is not attested elsewhere in Hebrew literature (as far as we know). Maagarim classifies it as the feminine of the qattāl adjective בַּיָּשׁ with the meaning "modest, bashful," as understood by the Syriac ܒܗܬܢܝܬܐ and the Greek αἰσχυντηρός, though this is the only occurrence of the adjective. According to Qimron (2001, 362-75), the form was initially בוישה, the feminine participle of the root בוש, as with the form בויש in Sir 42:1 H^M (see also Dihi 2004, 95). ואין משקל ל . . . — See Sir 6:15 H^A where it is in parallel with אין מחיר "is beyond price."

26:16 במרומי מעל — Surprisingly, this tautology is also attested in Eleazar HaQalîr, 124, סדרי דיברין לשבועות, as a comment on Prov 8:28: מתאמצת הייתי במרומי מעל.

36:31 קין — Note the unusual plene writing. כאשר יסביב — This reading, which has no parallel in the ancient translations, is hard to explain.

27:17 נסה — According to Corley (2002, 174–75; 2011, 4), this last word of the folio may represent Sir 27:17 (see the Syriac ܢܣܐ ܠܚܒܪܟ "test your friend").

MANUSCRIPT D

SIR 7:18–8:18; 36:29–38:1

Chapter 7

T-S AS 118.78 recto

ואח תלוי בזהב אופיר:	א]ל תמיר אוה[ב במחיר	18 ᴬ ¹
וטובת חן מפנינים:	אל תמאס אשה ²משכ]לת	19 ᴬ
[וכ]ן שוב֯ר נותן נפשו:	אל תרע [ב]א֯מ[ת] עוב֯[ד ³אמת]	20 ᴬᶜ
אל תמנע ממנו חפש	עבד משכ֯יל חבב /// ⁴כנ[פש	21 ᴬᶜ
⁵ואם] אמנה היא העמידה:	בהמה [ל]ך֯ ראה עיניך	22 ᴬ
ושא ⁶לה]ם נשים בנעוריהם:	בנים לך [י]ס֯ר אותם	23 ᴬᶜ
⁷ואל ת]א֯יר אליהם פנים:	בנות לך [נ]צ֯ור שא[רם]	24 ᴬᶜ
וא]ל נבון גבר חברה: ⁸	ה]וצא בת ויצא עסק]	25 ᴬᶜ
[ושנואה ⁹א]ל תאמן בה:	אשה לך אל [תתעבה]	26 ᴬ
ואת כהנ]יו [הק]ד֯יש:	בכל לבך פחד אל	29 ᴬ
ואת משרתיו לא תעז֯ב:	¹⁰[בכל] מא̇ודך אהוב עושך	30 ᴬ
ותן חלקם כאשר צויתה:	¹¹כב]ד אל והדר]כה̇ן	31 ᴬ
זב]ח֯י [צ֯ד֯ק] ותרו]מת [ק]ד֯ש:	¹²לחם אבירים ותרומתה	
למען תשלם ברכתך:	¹³וגם לאביו הושיטה יד	32 ᴬ
וגם ממת [א]ל תמנע חסד:	¹⁴תן מתן לפני כל חי	33 ᴬ
ועם אבילים התאבל:	¹⁵אל תתאחר מבוכים	34 ᴬ
[כי ממנו תאהב:	¹⁶אל] תשא לב מאוהב]	35 ᴬ
[ולעו]לם לא ת[שחת:]	[בכ]ל ¹⁷מעשיך זכור אחרית]	36 ᴬ

7:20 אל תרע D C G S | א̇ תדע A · ב[א̇מ]ת עוב̇[ד אמת D A | עבד עובד אמת C G S · שוב̇ר D A | שכיר C · 7:21 חבב D A | אהוב C · חפש D A | חופש C · 7:23 יסר D C | יסיר A · נשים D A | > C · 7:24 בנות D A G S | בנים C · תאיר D A | תאר C | אליהם D | אהם A | להם C · 7:25 הוצא D A | לאבז̇ן D | לאביו A G | וצא D A | נבון גבר D A | גבר נבון C · זבדה A D | חברה C G S · 7:31 צויתה D | צווית A · תרומתה D | תרומת יד A · 7:32 לאביו D C G S · 7:34 אבלים D | אבילים A · S

L. 1 [7:18] אל תמ̇א̇ס̇ אשה — Traces of letters are clearly visible on the photograph, particularly the two *alephs* and the *shin*, which are beyond doubt.

L. 2 [7:19] אל תר̇ע̇ — The upper parts of the last three letters are visible, so that the reading תרע is certain (contra תדע in Hᴬ). Concerning the *ayin*, the tips of its two arms are visible.

L. 3 [7:20] [וכ]ן שוב̇ר נות̇ן — The end of the vertical of the *nun* is perceptible at the break of the fragment. Then, there are traces of the *shin*, *waw*, *kaph* and *resh*. In any case, the restoration שכיר (as in Hᶜ) is impossible given the space and remnants of letters. Finally, the reading נותן is ensured by the preserved traces. משכ̇יל חבב — Traces that may correspond to a *kaph* (its right shoulder and the end of its base line), *yod* (its head and end of its verticle stroke), *lamed* and *khet* are possible.

L. 4 [7:21] כנ[פש̇ — Traces of the end of the base line of the *pe* and the lower part of the *shin* are visible. [ל]ך̇ — There is a trace of a letter on the left part of the break that may correspond to the head of the *kaph* and part of its shaft.

L. 5 [7:23] [י]ס̇ר — There is an ink trace that may correspond to a *samek* before the *resh*.

L. 6 [7:24] [נ]צ̇ור — Before the *resh*, there is a characteristic trace of the start of a *tsade*, then a trace of a narrow letter, which may correspond to a *vav*.

L. 8 [7:26] לך̇ אל — An ink trace corresponding to part of the *lamed*'s mast and the end of its curve is preserved, though very blurred. Then there is a very clear trace of the shaft of the final *kaph*. This is followed by traces of letters consistent with אל, which is restored from Hᴬ.

L. 9 [7:26] [א]ל̇ — The end of the trace of the *lamed* touches the right side of the *tav*.

L. 10 [7:30] ואת משרתיו — The *vav* and *aleph* are clearly legible. The right part of the *mem* appears after *tav*, and then at the break in the fragment, one sees traces of the three branches and the base of the *shin*. תע̇ז̇ב — There are traces of letters at the break in the fragment that could correspond to the succession of *tav*, *ayin* and *zayin*.

L. 11 [7:31] כה̇ן — Only a few faint traces are preserved on the fragment. ותן — The final *nun* is ligatured to the foot of the *tav*.

L. 12 [7:31] זב̇]ח̇י — In spite of the erasure of ink, one can distinguish between the *zayin* and the *bet*. Traces of a *khet* and *yod* also seem to be visible.

L. 16 [7:34] אבילים — Note the plene spelling of the adjective, which is spelled defectively in Hᴬ. The plene spelling is found commonly in Rabbinic Hebrew texts.

L. 16 [7:35] אל] — The *aleph* and *lamed* can be distinguished at the beginning of the line. Then, some traces of the upper parts of letters are visible where the fragment is broken, but it is difficult to distinguish one from the other.

Chapitre 7

18 [N'échange pas un am]i pour de l'argent,
   ni un frère *dépendant* pour de l'or d'Ophir.
19 Ne rejette pas une femme [intelli]gente,
   plus belle par la grâce que les perles.
20 Ne sois pas mauvais, [en] véri[té,] envers un servite[ur fidèle],
   [n]i envers un *salarié* qui donne de sa personne.
21 Un serviteur sensé aime(-le) [comme (ton) â]me,
   ne lui refuse pas la liberté.
22 As-[tu] du bétail ? Suis-le des yeux
   [et s]'il est robuste, conserve-le.
23 As-tu des fils ? [ins]truis-les
   et marie-[le]s à des femmes quand ils sont jeunes.
24 As-tu des filles ? [Ve]ille sur [leur c]hair,
   [et ne]leur mont[re pas] un visage radieux.
25 Fais[partir ta fille et le souci partira]
   [et]marie-la [à] un homme intelligent.
26 As-tu une femme ? Ne [la prends] pas [en abomination]
   [et (si) elle n'est pas aimée, ne] te fie pas à elle.
29 De tout ton cœur, vénère Dieu
   et sanc[tifie ses]prêtres.
30 [De toute] ta force aime ton créateur
   et n'abandonne pas ses ministres.
31 Glori[fie Dieu et honore]le(s) prêtre(s)
   et donne leur part selon que tu en as reçu l'ordre :
   le pain d[es] forts et son offrande,
   les sacri[fices]de justice[et l'offra]nde de [sain]teté.
32 et, de même, tends la main au pauvre,
   afin que ta bénédiction soit parfaite.
33 Donne l'aumône à tout vivant
   et, de même, aux morts, [ne] refuse pas la charité.
34 Ne sois pas loin de ceux qui pleurent
   et avec les endeuillés, porte le deuil.
35 Ne [détourne pas (ton) cœur d'un ami],
   [car de lui tu seras aimé.]
36 [En tou]tes [tes actions souviens-toi de la fin]
   [et jam]ais tu ne seras dé[truit]

Chapter 7

18 [Do not exchange a frien]d for money
   nor a dependent brother for the gold of Ophir.
19 Do not reject a [prud]ent wife,
   more beautiful in grace than pearls.
20 Do not treat badly, [in] tru[th, a faithful] serva[nt]
   [no]r a laborer who dedicates themself (to their task),
21 Love a prudent servant [as (your) very s]elf,
   do not refuse them liberty.
22 Do you [have] animals? Watch (them) carefully,
   [and if] they are sturdy, keep them.
23 Do you have sons? [Ins]truct them,
   and marry [the]m to women in their youth.
24 Do you have daughters? Watch over their flesh,
   and do not show them a radiant face.
25 M[ake your daughter depart and worry will depart too],
   [but] marry her t[o] an intelligent man.
26 Do you have a wife? Do not [consider her an abomination],
   [but if she is unloved, d]o not trust her.
29 With all your heart, venerate God,
   and sa[nctify his] priests.
30 [With all] your strength, love your creator,
   and do not abandon his ministers.
31 Glori[fy God and honor] the priest(s),
   and give them their share as you were commanded,
   bread of the strong and its contribution,
   sacri[fices of] righteousness [and offe]ring of holiness.
32 And, likewise, extend your hand to the poor,
   so your blessing may be complete.
33 Give alms to all the living,
   and likewise [d]o not refuse charity to the dead.
34 Do not keep apart from those who cry,
   and with the mourning, mourn.
35 [Do] not [turn your heart from a friend],
   [for you will be loved by them.]
36 [In a]ll [your actions remember the end],
   [and] you will [ne]ver [come to ruin].

7:20 שכר — It is difficult to know if H^D is a defective spelling for the reading of H^A (שוכר) or that of H^C (שכיר "the employee").

7:21 עבד משכיל — Cf Prov 14:35, 17:2 and 4Q418 8a,b,c,d 15 (// 4Q416 2 ii 15).

7:31 תרומתה — "Its offering," with לחם as antecedent (feminine as in Gen 49:20 and where כִּכָּר is presumably elided as in m. Menaḥ. 11:1); or, the *he* is paragogic, as in ישועתה Ps 3:3 (see JM §93i-j). Nevertheless, the reading is likely an error for תרומתם (see Elizur and Rand 2011, 204).

7:32 לאביו — An error for לאביון, which is restored in H^A ([ן]לאביו) and is reflected in the Greek and the Syriac. The *vav* and final *nun* are sometimes similar in appearance (cf. כן in Sir 36:31 and אוהב in 37:1), which perhaps led to the scribe's accidental omission of the final *nun*.

Chapter 8

T-S AS 118.78 verso

	למ֗ה תשׁוב על ידו֗	אֶל 18תֹ֗ר]יב עִם איש ג֗[דֹ֗ול	1 A
	למה תפול בידו:	אֶל 1תריב ע֗[ם קש]ה ממך	
	פֶן [יש]קֹל [מ]חֹ[י]ר֗ך ואבדת:	אל תחרוש עַל 2אִיש לו הן	2 A
	3וֹהן משׁגה לבות נ֗דיבים:	כִי רבִים הפחו֗[ז זהב]	
	וֹאל [תתן] 4על אש עצים:	אל תיניץ עם איש לֹ[ש]ון	3 A
	פן יבוז לנֹדיבֹים	אל֗ תרגיל עם איש אוֹיל	4 A
	זכר כי כלנו חייבים:	5אל תכלים אי֗[ש] שׁב מפשע	5 A
	כי נמנה מזקנים:	אֶל 6תבייש אנוש י֗[ש֗]י[֗]שׁ	6 A
	[זכר כלנו נאספים:]	[אל תתהלל על 7גוע]	7 A
	[8ובחידתיהם התרטש:]	אל תטש שיחת חכמים	8 A
	[להת]יצב 9לפני שרים:	כי ממנו תלמוד לקח	
	[אשר שׁמ֗ע]וֹ 10מאבתם:	[אל ת]מֹאֹס בשמיעות שבִֹים	9 A
	[בע֗ת צ֗ורך להשיב פ֗]תגם:	[כִי] ממנ֗וּ תקַח שֹכל	
	פ֗]ן תבע֗ר כ֗/בשבֹיֹב אש֗[וֹ:]	11אל תצ֗[לח] בנֹ֗ח֗[ל]ת רשׁע֗	10 A
	ל]הושיבו כארב ל[פ]נֶיך	[א]ל֗] תזוח 12מֹפֹנוֹ לִיך֗	11 A
כמֹאֹבד	13vacat וֹאם הלוית כמאo̊o̊	אֶ[ל] ת֗[לוה] אִ[י]ש חֹ֗זק מֹמך	12 A

8:2 תחרוש D | תחרש A · לו D Amg | לא A · 1הן D | הן A ·

L. 18 [8:1] תֹ֗ר]יב — There are traces of very erased letters: the hook of the left foot of the *tav*, then the shoulder and vertical of the *resh*. ג֗[דֹ֗ול למה — Although the ink is very faded, one can distinguish a few traces. The two *lameds* and the *mem* are certain.

L. 1 [8:1] ע֗[ם קש]ה — There are traces of the right diagonal of the *ayin*, then traces of the left leg and right shoulder of the *he*. עַל — The traces of letters may correspond to the right diagonal of the *ayin*, as well as part of its left diagonal. Although very faded, one can distinguish the hook-shaped top of the *lamed*'s shaft.

L. 2 [8:2] פֶן [יש]קֹל — The base and rounding of the beginning of the head of the *pe* are clearly visible, then the final *nun*. There are traces of a letter that may correspond to the head and the end of the shaft of the *qoph*, but this is uncertain. רבִים הפחו֗[ז — The leg and base of the *bet* are visible, as well as the end of a trace of the *yod*. The loop that is characteristic of the head of the *pe* is completely preserved, then traces of letters that could correspond to a *khet* and *yod*.

L. 3 [8:2] נ֗דיבים — A trace of a letter is visible at the break, which may correspond to a *nun*. אי֗ש — The *aleph* is fully preserved, and following this, there are traces of the *yod* and two diagonal lines of the *shin*. לֹ[ש]ון — There is a trace of the start of the shaft of the *lamed*, then after the lacuna, a trace of the *vav* and final *nun*. וֹאל — There is no doubt about these three letters: a *vav*, then the top right diagonal and part of the verticle of a cursive *aleph* are visible, followed by the mast of a *lamed*.

L. 4 [8:4] אל֗ — There is a trace of the start of the shaft and the lower loop of the *lamed*. לנֹדיבֹים — The lower parts of the series of letters is visible on the fragment.

L. 5 [8:5] תכלים — The *tav* is certain, as there is a trace of the upper part and the foot.

L. 6 [8:6] י֗[ש֗]י[֗]שׁ כי — There are traces of the branches of the two *shins* at the break in the fragment, then the *kaph* and a trace of ink corresponding to a *yod*.

L. 7 [8:8] תטש — There are traces of the upper part, the shoulder and the foot of the *tav*. חכמִם — Contra Elizur and Rand (2011, 203), all the letters are visible: a trace of ink that can correspond to a *khet*, then the upper part of the *kaph*, the *mem*, a trace of a narrow letter and the upper right part of a final *mem*.

L. 8 [8:8] כִי — There are traces of the *kaph*: part of its head and base. להת]יצב — The reading is based on H^A, and from some hardly identifiable letter traces.

L. 9 [8:9] ת]מֹאֹס — Some letter traces are visible, yet only the *mem* can be identified. שבִֹים — There are traces of the head and the base of the *bet*, then traces of ink of a narrow letter, so that a *yod* would be possible. שׁמ֗ע]וֹ — Only the *shin* is identifiable. The *mem* and *ayin* are reconstructed from traces of ink and H^A.

L. 10 [8:9] ממנ֗וּ תקַח שֹכל — The manuscript is badly damaged, but traces of the upper parts of the letters are preserved where the fragment is broken, making it possible to reconstruct the reading in H^A with certitude. בע֗ת צ֗ורך — After the *bet*, there is a trace of the lower curve of the *ayin* and the start of the left slant, then a trace of ink corresponding to the *tav*. This is followed by a trace characteristic for *tsade*, then a *vav* with a very narrow head. להשיב פ֗תגם — The *yod* is concave, rather than convex, and without the start of its head. It is followed by a trace of the winding of the *pe*.

L. 11 [8:10] אל תצ֗[לח] בנֹ֗ח֗[ל]ת רשׁע֗ — There are traces of the right arm of the *tsade*, then of its elbow towards the base. After the lacuna, the first letters cannot be a medial *mem* as read by Elizur and Rand (2011, 203), but should be read as a *bet* followed by a *nun*. פ֗]ן תבע֗ר כ֗/ בשבֹיֹב אש֗ — There is a trace of the *pe* (head and base), then traces of clearly visible letters, so that we can restore a *tav* and *bet* according to H^A. This is followed by traces of the two arms of an *ayin*, then the characteristic head of a *resh*, a *kaph* (less likely *bet*), a *shin*, a *bet*, then traces of letters, so that a *yod* and *bet* are possible. Before the break, the *aleph* is certain, followed by the first arm of a *shin*.

L. 12 [8:11] מֹפֹנוֹ לִיך֗ — Although the ink is very blurred, the *lamed*, final *tsade* and *lamed* are certain. ל[פ]נֶיך — Apart from the final *kaph*, only a few unidentifiable traces of ink are preserved.

L. 12 [8:12] אֶ[ל] ת֗[לוה] — There is a trace of the *aleph*, then a trace of a leg at the break, so that the first leg of a *tav* is possible. אִ[י]שׁ — Only a few unidentifiable traces of ink are preserved at the break. חֹ֗זק

Chapitre 8

1 Ne te dis[pute] pas [avec une personne puis]sante,
   de peur que tu ne passes en son pouvoir.
   Ne te dispute pas avec plus [d]ur que toi,
   de peur que tu ne tombes en son pouvoir.
2 Ne fomente pas contre une personne qui a des richesses,
   de peur qu'il ne [pè]se [ce que] tu [v]aux et que tu ne périsses.
   Car ils sont nombreux ceux [que l'or rend in]souciants
   et la richesse fourvoie les cœurs nobles.
3 Ne te querelle pas avec une personne bavarde
   et ne [mets] pas du bois sur le feu.
4 Ne deviens pas familier avec une personne stupide,
   de peur qu'elle ne méprise les princes.
5 N'offense pas une person[ne] qui se repend du péché,
   souviens-toi que tous nous sommes coupables.
6 [N'humilie]pas une perso]nn[e âgé]e,
   car nous serons comptés parmi les anciens.
7 Ne te félicite pas de [celui qui meurt],
   [souviens-toi que tous, nous serons ensevelis.]
8 Ne néglige pas le discours des sages,
   [mais dans leurs énigmes abandonne-toi,]
   car à travers cela tu apprendras l'instruction
   pour te te[nir devant les princes].
9 [Ne dé]daigne pas les enseignements des anciens
   qui ont app[ris de leurs ancêtres],
   [car] à travers cela, tu acquerras l'intelligence,
   pour retourner, au moment nécessaire, la sen[tence.]
10 N'en[flamme] pas le *patrim*[*oine* du méchant,]
   de pe[ur] que tu ne brûles dans la flamme de [son] feu.
11 [Ne t'écarte] pas devant le moqueur,
   de sorte [qu'il se tienne en embuscade de]vant toi.
12 [N]e [prête pas] à une person[ne] plus puissante que toi
   (*vacat*) et si tu as prêté, (tu es) comme celui qui perd.

Chapter 8

1 Do not ar[gue with a po]werful [person],
   lest you return into their grip.
   Do not argue wi[th (a person) more seve]re than you,
   lest you fall into their grip.
2 Do not plot against someone who has wealth,
   lest they [wei]gh your [w]orth and you perish.
   For there are many that gold has made reckless,
   and wealth leads astray the hearts of nobles.
3 Do not quarrel with the tal[ka]tive person,
   [do] not [put] wood on a fire.
4 Do not become familiar with a foolish person,
   lest they scorn nob[l]es.
5 Do not shame a person who repents of sin,
   remember that we are all guilty.
6 D[o not humiliate an o]ld [person],
   for we will be counted among the elders.
7 Do not congratulate yourself over [someone who is dying],
   [remember that we all will be gathered.]
8 Do not neglect the discourse of the wise
   [rather, in their riddles lose yourself,]
   for, through this you will learn instruction,
   in order to st[and before princes].
9 [Do not] despise the teachings of the elders,
   who have heard [(them) from their ancestors],
   [so,] through this you will acquire intelligence,
   in order to produce, when necessary, a re[sponse].
10 Do not in[flame] the lega[cy of the wicked,]
   lest you burn in the flame of their fire.
11 [Do no]t [step aside] from the mocker,
   so that [they set themself up as an ambush be]fore you.
12 Do no[t lend] to a person more powerful than you,
   (*vacat*) and if you do lend, (it is) like you are giving (it) up.

מֹמֹךְ — The left leg of the *khet*, then the head and vertical of the *zayin* and *qoph* are visible. Then, there are traces of the two *mem*s and the shaft of the final *kaph*.
L. 13 [8:12]   ○○כמא — The last letters of the word are especially difficult to read due to what seems to be smeared ink. The first three letters are clear, even the *aleph*. To its left, we see traces of letters, though they are too obscure to be identified. Perhaps due to a smearing of ink or a misspelling, the scribe has made a zig-zag line, canceling the word. We assume the cancellation mark starts at the base of the *aleph*'s vertical stroke, descending to the left before moving up through the next letter and then down through the following letter. An apparent *raphe* line is clearly visible above the last letter. The word is corrected in the margin (though this was not transcribed by Elizur and Rand 2011, 203).
יֹתֹר — The traces of letters are very blurred.

8:10   בֹּחֹלֹ]ת — On the difficulties of this verse, see the note in H^A and Rey (2012b, 418). Although a more difficult reading, גחלת "coal," in agreement with the Greek and the Syriac is not excluded (following the correction of Perles 1897, 53-54). כ/בשביב — With regards to reading the fragment, a *kaph* seems preferable, though a *bet* cannot be excluded. H^A has כשביב, which should be corrected to בשביב in agreement with the Greek and the Syriac.

ואם ¹⁴ערבת כמשלם:	13 ᴬ אל תערב יתר ממך
כי כרצונו ישפט:	14 ᴬ אל תשפוט עם שופט
פן תכביד את רעתך:	15 ᴬ ¹⁵עם אכזרי אל תלך
ובאולתו תספה:	כי הוא נכח ¹⁶פניו ילך
ואל תרכב עמו בדרן[:]	16 ᴬ עם בעל אף אל תעיז ☙ ¹⁷מצֹה
¹⁸ובאין מצֹל ישחיתך	[כי קל בעיניו דמי]ֹם
[כי לא] ¹⁹יוכל לכסות סודך:	17 ᴬ עם פותה אל] תסתי[יד]
[כי] לא תדע	18 ᴬ לפני זר אל תעש ר[ז]

Chapter 36

BAIU ID2 recto

עיר מבצר ועמוד משען:	29 ᴮᶜᴾ ¹קנה אשה ראשית קנין
ובאין אשה נע ונד:	30 ᴮᶜᴾ ²באין גדר יבער כרם
המדלג מעיר אל עיר:	31 ᴮᶜ מי יאמן ³בגדוד צבא
המרגיע באשר יערב:	כן איש אשר ⁴אין לו קן

Chapter 37

אך יש אהב שם אהב:	1 ᴮᶜ כל אוהב אומר ⁵אהבתי
ריע כנפש נהפך לצר:	2 ᴮᶜ הלא דין מגיע ⁶עד מות
למלא ׀ פני תבל תרמית:	3 ᴮ הוי רע יאמר מדוע ⁷נוצרתי
ובעת צוקה מנו יעמוד:	4 ᴮ מרע אוהב ⁸מביט על שחת
ונגד עריִם יחזיק צנה:	5 ᴮ ⁹אוהב טוב נלחם עם זר
ואל תעזבהו בשללך:	6 ᴮᴾ ¹⁰אל תשכח חבר בקרב
אך יש יועץ דרך עליו:	7 ᴮ כל ¹¹יועץ אומר חזה

8:14 תשפוט D תשפט A G ? S · ? · 8:15 נכח D נוכח A · 36:29 קנה D B קונה Bmg · עיר מבצר D Bmg | קנה אשה מבצר צינה C | עזר ומבצר B (cf. G βοηθὸν κατ' αὐτοῦ S ܗܘܐ ܠܗ ܥܘܕܪܢܐ = Gen 2:18-20 עזר כנגדו) · ומשען העמיד D B | ועמוד משען C · 36:30 גדר D C | גדיר B · יבער D | יבוער B · באשה יסביב C · באשר יערב D B · 37:1a כל אוהב אומר אהבתי D | כל אוהב אמר אהבתי Bmg · קין D B | קן B · לא D B | אין לו C Bmg | לא B · בצבא גדוד C · בגדוד צבא D B · 37:1b הב(ו)א ש(ם) א(ו)הב D Bmg G S | > B C · 37:2a הלא דין מגיע D B Bmg | הלא דן B · כל אומר אמר Bmg | כל אוהב יאמר אהבתו B · כל אוהב אהבתו C · 37:2b ר(י)ע כנפש נהפך לצר D Bmg | רע כנפש יהפך B · עד מות D | אל מות B | על מות Bmg · עליו C · בעת יגיע C · 37:3 רע D B | ריע Bmg · יאמר D Bmg | שאמר B · מדוע כן D B | מ' Bmg · 37:4 מרע D B | מדוע Bmg · מדוע Bmg · על שחת D Bmg | אל שלחן B · חביר B · חבר D Bmg | (metat.) Bmg תשכחה D B · תכחש Bmg · 37:6a חבר D Bmg | חביר B · בקרב B · מנגד D Bmg | מנוב S · 37:5 D Bmg | > B · נלחם D Bmg1 | נוחל Bmg2 · 37:6a תשכחה D B · תכחש Bmg · 37:6b Bmg · בקרב B | בקרב S (ܟܡܘܒ) S (ὄντος ἐν ψυχῇ ἐν) G D · 37:7 אומר חזה D S (ܣܘܢ) | ונגד ערים יחזיק צנה D B | ואל תעזבהו בשללך Bmg · 37:7 אומר חזה Bmg · עליו D Bmg | לך B · אל לך B · אומר חזה Bmg · יניף יד B

L. 16 [8:15] ובאולתו — The *aleph* is certain.

L. 16 [8:16] תעיז — The *zayin* is clearly visible and is followed by a half-circle dotted to fill the space at the end of the line (☙).

L. 17 [8:16] Traces of letters around the break in the fragment allow us to read the stich on the basis of the text of Hᴬ.

L. 18 [8:16] ובאין — The final *nun* is clearly visible under the line to the left of the *yod*. מצֹל — The traces of ink are very blurred, yet allow one to perceive traces of a *tsade* (the start of a trace and its base) and a *yod*.

L. 18 [8:17] Traces of letters beneath the tear allow one to read the stich based on the text of Hᴬ.

L. 19 [8:18] תעש ר[ז] — The *tav* is visible, then the oblique of the *ayin*, traces of the arms of the *shin*, and then the vertical of the *resh*.

8:14 תשפוט — Hᴰ requires reading a *qal*, "Do not judge with a judge, for he will judge according to his pleasure," while Hᴬ may vocalize a *niphal*, "enter into judgment with someone" (cf. Joel 4:1), as understood by the Greek and the Syriac.

37:2 ריע כנפש נהפך לצר — Cf. Sir 6:9ᴬ: יש אוהב נהפך לשנא "there

לא — The distinctive lower hook of the *lamed* is visible beneath the tear, as is the vertical stroke of the *aleph*.

L. 1 [36:29] The text of Hᴮ perfectly fits the traces of ink preserved in Hᴰ.

L. 2 [36:30] יבעֹר — Despite Levi's reading (Lévi 1901, 176), there is no space to restore a *vav* between the *bet* and the *ayin*.

L. 3 [36:31] The scribe has drawn a line across the page that begins with a hook and crosses over the first three lines, probably inadvertently.

L. 6 [37:3] הוֹי — There is a dot above the *he*.

L. 8 [37:4] מנוב — Lévi (1900, 3) reads a מנגב, but the *vav* is clear (Ben-Ḥayyim 1973, 36; Beentjes 1997, 101; Abegg Accordance).

is a friend who turns into an enemy."

37:6 בְּקֶרֶב — The vocalization is curious, as בְּקֶרֶב would have been expected. The sense is also obscure. Either it is an elliptical phrase "in the midst of (battle)" (cf. 1 Kgs 20:39) or is a phrase similar to the Syriac ܟܡܘܒ "who is near."

13 Ne te porte pas caution pour quelqu'un qui a plus que toi
et si tu t'es porté caution, (considère-toi) comme celui qui paiera.
14 N'aie pas un procès avec un juge,
car selon son bon plaisir, il jugera.
15 Avec un cruel ne marche pas,
de peur que tu n'alourdisses ton malheur,
car, lui, il va où il veut
et par sa stupidité tu périrais.
16 Avec un irascible ne soit pas effronté
et ne chevauche pas avec lui sur la route[,]
[car le san]g[est peu de chose à ses yeux]
et sans qu'il n'y ait de secours, il t'assassinerait.
17 Avec le sot ne [t'entretiens] pas,
[car il ne] pourra [pas] tenir caché ton secret.
18 Devant un étranger ne fais pas de mys[tère,]
[car] tu ne sais pas [...]

Chapitre 36

29 Acquiers une femme, la meilleure des acquisitions,
une ville fortifiée et un pilier solide.
30 En l'absence de clôture une vigne est dévastée,
en l'absence de femme, on erre et vagabonde.
31 Qui se fiera à une troupe armée
qui bondit de ville en ville ?
Ainsi l'homme qui n'a pas de nid,
erre lorsque la nuit arrive.

Chapitre 37

1 Tout ami dit: « j'aime »
mais il y a l'ami (qui a seulement) le nom d'ami.
2 N'est-ce pas une tristesse approchant jusqu'à la mort
(qu')un compagnon comme soi-même se change en ennemi ?
3 Malheur au mauvais (qui) dit : « pourquoi ai-je été formé ?
Pour remplir la face du monde de tromperie. »
4 Mauvais est l'ami qui regarde au dessus de la fosse,
au temps d'angoisse il se tient sans rien partager.
5 Un bon ami se bat contre un ennemi
et face à des adversaires il saisit le bouclier.
6 N'oublie pas un compagnon proche
et ne l'abandonne pas lorsque tu amasses ton butin.
7 Tout conseiller dit : « observe »,
mais il y a celui qui conseille une voie (menant) à lui-même).

13 Do not stand as surety for someone who has more than you,
and if you do stand as surety, (it is) like you are the one repaying.
14 Do not judge with a judge,
for, according to their whim they will judge.
15 With someone cruel do not walk,
lest you make your misfortune more burdensome,
for, they go where they wish,
but you will be swept away due to their stupidity.
16 With the irascible do not be brazen,
and do not ride with them on the road[,]
[for blo]od [is a small thing in their eyes],
and when there is no one to help you they will murder you.
17 With a fool do not [talk,]
[for they] will [not] be able to keep your secret hidden.
18 Before a stranger, do nothing se[cret,]
[for] you do not know [...]

Chapter 36

29 Acquire a wife, the best of acquisitions,
a fortified city and a supportive pillar.
30 Without a wall, the vineyard is devastated,
so, without a wife, one wanders vagrant.
31 Who will trust in an armed troop
that skips from town to town?
Such is the man who has no nest,
who wanders (from place to place) when evening arrives

Chapter 37

1 Every friend says: "I love"
but there is a friend (who is only) a friend in name.
2 Is it not a sadness approaching death—
a friend like your very self who turns into an enemy?
3 Woe to the evil person (who) will say, "Why was I made—
to fill the face of the world with deceit?"
4 How unfortunate (when) a friend observes destruction?
and at the time of distress stands without sharing.
5 A good friend fights against the enemy
and before adversaries, they seize the shield.
6 Do not forget a close companion
and do not abandon them for the sake of your spoils.
7 Every counselor says (they) see
but there is one who counsels a way to (achieve) it

8 BP	מִיּוֹעֵץ ¹²שמר נפ{ש̇}ךָ		ודע לפנים מה צרכו:
	כי גם הוא ¹³נפשו יחשב		למה זה אליו יפול:
9 B	ויאמר לך להביט ¹⁴דרכיך		וקם מנגד להביט ראשך:
10 B	אל תועץ עם ¹⁵חמיך		וממקנא העלים סוד:
11ab B	עם אשה אל צרתה		¹⁶ומלוכד על מלחמה:
11cd B	עם סוחר אל תתגר		ומקונה ¹⁷על ממכרו:
11ef B	עם איש רע על גמילות חסד		¹⁸ואכזרי על טוב בשר:
11gh B	פועל שכיר על מ̇לאכת[ו̇]		¹⁹שכיר שנה על מוצא זרע:
12 B	אך אם איש מפחד ²⁰תמיד		¹אש̇ר תדע שומר מצוה	BAIU ID2 verso
	אשר עם בלבבו כלבבך		²ואם יכשל יעבד בך:
13 B	וגם עצת לבבו כך		כי אם ³אמון ממנו:
14 B	לב אנוש מגיד שעיותיו		משבעה ⁴צפים על שן:
15 B	ועם כל אלה העתר אל אל		⁵אשר יכין באמת צעדך:
16 B	ראש כל מעשה מאמר		⁶לפני כל פעל היא מחשבת:
17/18 B	עקר תחבולות ⁷לבב		ארבעה שרביטים יפריח:
	טוב ורע מות ⁸וחיים		ומשלח בם כליל לשון:
19 BC	יש חכם לרבים ⁹נחכם		ולנפשו הוא נואֿ:
20 B	ויש חכם בדברו ימאס		¹⁰ומכל מאכל תענוג נבצר:
22 BC	ויש חכם לנפשו ⁱ̇יחכם		¹¹פרי̇ דעתו על גויתו:
23 B	ויש חכם לעמו יחכם		פרי ¹²דעתו בגויתם:
25 B	חיי אנוש ימים מספר		וחיי ישרון ¹³ימי אין מספר:
24 BC	חכם לנפשו ישבע תענוג		ויאשריהו ¹⁴וכל רואיהו:

G מטוב B | D Bmg | 37:9 להביט B G (ἑαυτῷ) | D Bmg לנפשו | B נפשו | B צרכו | D צורכו | B שמור | D שמור | Bmg מה יועץ | D B G S מיועץ 37:8
(καλή) S (ܠܒ̈) | D דרכיך | B ראשך | D Bmg 2 רישך | Bmg1 רֵאשֶׁךָ | 37:11ab אל D Bmg | B על | D Bmg ומלוכד על מלחמה | D Bmg ומדר אל
B | 37:11gh שכיר D Bmg שוא | B שוא | D Bmg (מ)וצא זרע | D Bmg שומר שוא על מוציא רע | B 37:12ab איש D Bmg G S | יש B | D B מצוה |
Bmg מצותיו | D Bmg כלבבו | B לבבו | D אם | B יכשל | D תבשל | B יעבד בך | D יגיע אליך | Bmg יעכר בך | 37:13 לבבו
ראש | G (סף) B Bmg לפני | B דבר | D Bmg מאמר | 37:16 צעדיך | D צעדך | B עתר | D Bmg העתר | 37:15 מצפה | B שן | D Bmg צופים | B ראש B | D Bmg משבעים | D B משבעה | Bmg צפים | D Bmg
B | פועל | D B Bmg 37:17 עקר | D Bmg עקרת | B שרביטים | D Bmg שבטים | B יפריח | D Bmg? G יפריחו | B 37:18 ורע | D Bmg מות
ומות D וחיים | B G (ζωὴ καὶ θάνατος) | ומשלח D Bmg | ומשלת B G | 37:19 נואל D Bmg G (ἄχρηστος) S (ܡܐ) | גואל B C | 37:20 ימאס D
D | ימים מספר B · איש D אנוש D | 37:25 > | D Bmg ויש חכם לעמו יחכם (יחכם) פרי דעתו בגויתם | · C | 37:23 נמאס B | יש D B ויש | 37:22
B < ים וגוית שם ימ̇י אין מספר · | B עם ישראל D Bmg ישרון B מספר ימים גויתהן מספר יש ים · | D ויאשריהו C וכל ראיו יאשריהו | B G S וְאַשְׁרוֹהוּ | [כל]ר̇וֹאֹ[י] D

L. 12 [37:8] נפ{ש̇}ךָ — The supralinear *shin* seems to be intended as a replacement for the letter beneath it, but in all likelihood, it was also a *shin*.

L. 20 [37:12] תמיד — The word תמיד is added to line 19 and aligned to the left.

L. 2 [37:13] לבבו — The final *kaph* proposed by Ben-Ḥayyim (1973, 37) is not possible, as only a *vav* could fit the space and the preserved traces. Lévi (1900, 4; 1901, 186) just reads לבב, but the trace of the head of the *vav* is clear.

L. 10 [37:22] יחכם — The manuscript is stained here.

L. 13 [37:24] ויאשריהו — The scribe wrote the word diagonally in the space between lines, in order to respect the alignment to the left.

37:10 חמיך — Lévi (1901, 183) thinks that this word only refers to the father-in-law of the wife. Yet, while this may be the case in biblical Hebrew, it is not the case in Rabbinic Hebrew (see m. Ketub. 1:5; Segal 1958, 236). The word coincides with the Latin (*cum socero tuo*), while the Greek reads τοῦ ὑποβλεπομένου σε "the one who views you with suspicion," which seems to derive from the Aramaic root חמי "to see," and the Syriac reads ܒܥܠܕܒܒܟ "your enemy," which as noted by Segal (1958, 236), should refer to the first word of the next stich (ממקנא).

37:12 אשר עם בלבבו — Here, H^D combines two prepositions that usually do not appear together, paralleling the confusion found in H^B.

37:15 העתר — The *hiphil* of this root has the same sense as the *qal*, which is found in H^B.

37:22 יחכם — Confusion of *kaph* and *khet* is found in earlier manuscripts of the Dead Sea Scrolls (see Reymond 2014c, 111). Less likely is that this should be construed as a doubly defective *hiphil* form of יכח "he should reprove them (יכחם)."

37:25 ימים מספר — Literally, "days, (a small) number," that is, only a few days (see GKC §131e and Num 9:20). גויתהן . . . מספר — The word גויה in the second stich of the marginal addition (or doublet) must have a figurative sense "essence" (cf. גוף "body, corpse, essence" in Rabbinic Hebrew). The text itself is not entirely transparent. What appears to be the 3fp suffix is hard to explain here and may be a graphic mistake for גויתם, which would perfectly fit the context of the preceding verse 22, or it is a defective Aramaic 3mp suffix -הן.

37:24 ויאשריהו — For the verb in the singular with a collective subject, see Joüon §150e.

8 D'un conseiller garde-toi,
   et sache d'abord quel est son besoin.
   Car lui aussi, pense (à) lui-même :
   « Pourquoi cela lui arriverait-il ? ».
9 Et il te dira d'observer ta voie,
   mais il se dressera en face (de toi) pour observer ta pauvreté.
10 Ne prends pas conseil auprès de ton beau-père,
   et du jaloux cache un secret.
11a auprès d'une femme à propos de sa rivale
11b et de l'assaillant à propos de la bataille.
11c auprès du commerçant, ne fais pas d'affaires
11d et de l'acquéreur à propos de sa vente,
11e auprès d'une personne méchante à propos des œuvres de charité,
11f et (auprès) du cruel à propos du bien-être,
11g auprès du travailleur salarié à propos de son œuvre,
11h auprès du salarié à l'année à propos de la pousse de la semence.
12 Cependant, (s.e. prends conseil) si quelqu'un est constamment sur ses gardes,
   dont tu sais qu'il garde le commandement,
   qui est avec/dans son cœur comme ton cœur,
   et s'il trébuche, il t'asservira.
13 Et aussi, le conseil de son cœur est ainsi,
   mais y a-t-il plus fiable que lui ?
14 Le cœur d'une personne révèle ses histoires,
   plus que sept sentinelles sur un sommet.
15 Et avec tout cela implore Dieu,
   qu'il affermisse tes pas dans la vérité.
16 L'origine de toute œuvre est une parole
   et avant toute action est la pensée.
17 La racine des projets est le cœur,
18 Il fera fleurir quatre rameaux:
   Bien et mal, mort et vie,
   et celle qui les libère complètement, c'est la langue.
19 Il y a le sage qui devient sage pour la multitude,
   mais pour lui même, il est déraisonnable.
20 Et il y a le sage qui est méprisé par sa parole,
   et il est privé de toute nourriture délicieuse.
22 Et il y a le sage qui est sage pour lui même,
   le fruit de sa connaissance est sur son corps.
   Et il y a le sage qui *est sage* pour son peuple
   le fruit de sa connaissance est dans leur corps.
25 La vie d'un être humain, c'est peu de jours,
   mais la vie de Yeshouroun des jours innombrables.
   (mg. Leur corps, c'est peu de jours,
   mais le corps de la renommée, des jours innombrables.)
24 Le sage pour lui-même se rassasie de délices
   et ils l'ont dit bienheureux, tous ceux qui le voient.

8 From a counselor guard yourself
   and know at first what he needs
   For, he also considers himself:
   "Why should it happen to him?"
9 He will say to you "(You should) watch your ways
   but he will stand before (you) to watch your poverty.
10 Do not take counsel with your father-in-law
   and from the jealous hide a secret.
11a with a woman concerning her rival
11b and (hide a secret) from an assailant about battle.
11c With the merchant, do not do business
11d and (hide a secret) from the purchaser about their sale,
11e with a wicked person about charitable works,
11f and (with) the cruel about good health,
11g (with) one working for a wage about [their] work,
11h (with) an annually hired-hand about the sprouting of the seed.
12 However, (*do take counsel*) if there is a person who is always in dread,
   who, you know, keeps the commandment,
   that which is with in their heart is like (that which is in) your heart,
   and if they stumble, they will enslave you.
13 And, indeed, the counsel of their heart is so,
   but is there one more faithful than it?
14 A person's heart tells their stories,
   more than seven sentries over a peak.
15 And with all these, implore God,
   that he may establish your steps in truth.
16 The origin of every deed is speech
   and before every action is a thought.
17 The root of (every) plan is the heart;
18 which will make bloom four stems:
   good and evil, death and life,
   while the tongue is given totally free rein in them.
19 There is a sage who becomes wise for the many,
   but who, to themself, is unreasonable.
20 And there is a sage who is despised because of their word,
   and they are deprived of all delicious food.
22 And there is a sage who becomes wise for themself,
   the fruit of their knowledge (rests) on their body.
   And there is a sage who *becomes wise* for their people,
   the fruit of their knowledge is in their bodies.
25 The life of a person is a few days,
   but the life of Yeshurun is days without number.
   (mg. As to their body, there is a (fixed) number to their days,
   but the body of a name has days without number.)
24 The one wise for themself is satiated with delights,
   and all who see them will say they are blessed.

26 BC	חכם עם ינחל כבוד	ושמו עומד [15]בחיי עולם:
27 B	בני [b]חמר נס נפשך	וראה:מה רע [16]לה ואל תתן לה:
28 B	כי לא לכל טוב תענוג	ולא לכל [17]נפש כל זן תבחר:
29 B	אל תזד אל תענוג	ואל ⫽ [18]תתחנג על מטעמים:
30 B	כי ברב אוכל יקנן [19]חולי	והמזיע יגוע על זרא:
31 B	בלא מוסר רבים [20]גועו	והנשמר יוסיף חיים:

Chapter 38

1 B	[20]רעה רועה רופא לפי]

לכל B · לא D | ולא B · (ܠܗ ܡܬܚܫܒܢ) B G S ? | הכל לכל טוב D Bmg · לכל טוב תענוג 37:28 · B אל | D ואל · B S G בחייך | D Bmg בחמר 37:27
D | כל B · 37:29 · D תזד אל | D תזרע לכל | B תזר אל | Bmg1 אל | Bmg2 תזרו/ך · D תתחנג על מטעמים | B תשפך על כל מטעמים · ג׳ מטמים | תתחנג
Bmg2 · 37:30 ברב D | ברוב B · אוכל D Bmg G (βρώμασιν) S (ܡܐܟܠܐ) | תענוג B · יקנן D | יקנן B ירון Bmg · והמזיע D Bmg | והמרבה B · יגוע
B · לפני D Bmg2 לפי B · רעי Bmg1 רעה D Bmg2 | רעה רועה 38:1 · Bmg · והשמר D B | ובהשמר · B יגועו ועועו · B גועו D Bmg | יגיע אל D | על

L. 13 [37:25] ספרْ: — The *sof passuq* has a swoosh above it.

L. 15 [37:27] וראה:מה — The scribe wrote two dots to separate these two words and to avoid reading וראהמה.

L. 18 [37:29] ואל /// — The scribe added three dashes to fill the space and respect the alignment to the left.

37:28 ולא לכל ... תבחר — In comparison with H[B], the presence of the *lamed* preposition before כל modifies the syntactic structure of the proposition, requiring one to interpret the verbal form תבחר as a second person masculine singular.

37:29 תזד — The word is from the root זוד "to behave presumptuously," thus "be not excessive" (so Box and Oesterley 1913, 448), or it may mean "to plan evil, act with premeditation, in full consciousness of doing wrong" (Jastrow 1903, 391).

38:1 רעה רועה — The possibilities to translate this sentence are numerous: "Respect the one who respects the healer," "the one who respects the healer respects according to," "respect the Shepherd, the Healer, according to."

26 Le sage du peuple héritera de gloire, Et son nom tiendra dans la vie éternelle.	26 The sage of the people will inherit glory and his name will endure in eternal life.
27 Mon fils, par le vin, teste-toi, et vois ce qui est mauvais pour toi, et ne t'y adonne pas.	27 My child, in wine, test yourself, and observe what is bad for it; (then,) do not indulge.
28 Car le plaisir n'est pas bon pour tous, et tu ne peux pas choisir pour toute personne n'importe quelle sorte de nourriture.	28 For (one) pleasure will not be enjoyed by everyone, and you cannot choose for every person every kind of food.
29 Ne sois pas excessif envers les délices, et ne désire pas des mets savoureux.	29 Do not act excessively toward delicacies, and do not desire savory delicacies.
30 Car dans l'abondance de nourriture, la maladie fait son nid, et celui qui tremble mourra de la nausée.	30 For in the abundance of food, sickness nests, and the one who sweats will perish due to cholera.
31 Faute d'instruction, nombreux ont péri, mais celui qui veille sur lui-même prolonge la vie.	31 Without instruction, many perish but one who watches over themself extends their life

Chapitre 38 / Chapter 38

1 Honore celui qui honore le médecin selon [

1 Respect the Shepherd, the Healer, according to [

MANUSCRIPT E

SIR 32,16–34,1

Chapter 32

ENA 3597 recto

ותחבולות מנשף יוציא:	יֵרָא יְיָ י]בין משפט:	¹	16 BF
וחכמות יוצי]או[מלבם:	יראי יְיָ יבי]נו משפטו:	²	
ויאחר צרכו למשך תורה:	איש חמס י]טה תוכחות:	³	17 BF
ולץ לא ישמר לשונו:	איש לא יכ]סֹה חכמה:	⁴	18 BF
זד ולץ לא יקח מצוה:	איש חמס]לא יקח שכל:	⁵	
ואחר מעשיך א֗ל תתקפץ:	בלא עצה אל]תפעל דבר:	⁶	19 BF
ואל תתקל בדרך נגף:	בדרך מוקש]ת אל תלך:	⁷	20 BF
ובאחריתך היה זהיר:	אל תתחר?]בדרך רשעים:	⁸	21b/22b BF
כי אם בנסוי ישוב ונמלט:	יֵרָא יְיָ לא י]פגע רע:	⁹	33:1 BF
ובוטח בי֗י֗ לא יבוש:	נוצר תור]ה נוצר נפשו:	¹⁰	24 BF

Chapter 33

אזנו:			
ומתמוטט כמסערה	לא יחכם] שונא תורה:	¹¹	2 BF
ובית מנוח ואחר תגיה	הכין אמ]ר ואחר תעשה:	¹²	4 F
ואופן חוזר מחשבותיו:	גלגל ק]ל לב נבל:	¹³	5 F
תחת כל [אוהב] יצהל:	כסוס מוכן]אוהב שונא:	¹⁴	6 F
אור ש֗נה על שמש:	מה על יו]ם יום כי כלו:	¹⁵	7 F
ויש מהם מועד:	אבל בחכ]מת בחכמת יְ֗יָ נשפטו:	¹⁶	8 F

32:16 למשך E F | למשך B · ואחר B | ויאחר E Bmg F · וחכמות E Bmg F | וכחמות רבות B (metat.) · **32:17** חמס [E] Bmg F G (ἁμαρτωλός) | חכם B · ישמר E B | ישמר Bmg F · כחמה B | חכמה E Bmg F · 7a1 (ܚܟܡܬܐ) S (βουλῆς) B G איש חכם לא [F] | איש לא B · **32:18ab** ימשר · B Bmg · **32:18cd** שכל E F Bmg G S (ܚܟܡܬܐ) 7a1 (βουλῆς) B G שחד | B שכל F · חמס [E] Bmg F G (βουλῆς) S (ܚܟܡܬܐ) 7a1 · יקח מצוה E Bmg F | ישמר B · תורה B · **32:19** תתקפץ E F | תתקצף B · **32:20** בדרך נגף E F G? | בנגף פעמים S B + השמר ובאחריתך (רֹשעֹים) מחתף בדרך תבטח אל · **32:21b/22b** B (הֹזהֹר) · B | הזהר E F | היה זהיר E F · באחריתך B | ובאחריתך E F · **32:23** מצות (ר]מצוה שומר אלה עשה כל כי נפשך שמר דרכיך בכל · **32:24** נוצר E F | שומר · Bmg ושב | שב E F | ישוב F B · בנסוי E | בנסוי F · 33:1 B | 2-מצותו]: בכל מעשיך שמור נפשך כי עושה זה שומר מצוה · **33:2** כמסערה E B F Bmg במסער · **33:3** אזנו E F אני | B G (πλοῖον) ? · B · איש נבון יבין דבר ותורתו כאוֹ[ר י]ֵי ישֹרָה + :

L. 1–16 [32:16–33:8] Restorations are based on H^F, which presents a similar text (see complete introduction).

L. 3 [32:17] [טה חמס איש] — It is difficult to know whether one should restore חמס איש in agreement with H^F,Bmg and the Greek, or חכם איש in agreement with the Syriac and cohering with v. 17b (see the note for 32:17 in H^B).

L. 4 [32:18] [חכמה יכ]סֹה לא איש] — Given the space available, we restore יכסה לא איש according to H^F, instead of חכם איש as in H^B.

32:18 יקח שכל — See 8:9 in H^A and the note.

32:19 תתקפץ — The *hithpael* of קפץ ("to shut" in the *qal*, see Sir 4:31 and 4:23) is not attested elsewhere in Hebrew before the Middle Ages. However, the form is attested in Aramaic with the meaning "to contract" (see 11QTgJob 9:1 = 24:24) or "to jump back and forth." The Syriac equivalent ܩܦܣ means "to draw oneself back" (See Payne Smith 1901, 2:3696; Driver 1937, 37), and it is probably this meaning that should be retained here according to the context: "After your actions do not draw back."

32:20 נֹגֶף — See Isa 8:14.

32:21 היה זהיר — For זהיר as adjective, see 11:34 in H^A and the same construction in Sir 42:8.

33:4 ובית מנוח — Cf. 1 Chr 28:2, where the expression designates the place for the ark of the covenant. We have to suppose that the verb הכין

L. 7 [32:20] נֹגֶף — Marcus (1931, 226) reads פְּעָמִים in agreement with H^B, but this reading is impossible. First, as the final two dots are clearly visible, this reading is too long for the available space. Second, the *nun*, *gimel* and *pe* are visible on the new multispectral photographs.

L. 16 [33:8] מועד — Marcus (1931, 231) and Ben-Ḥayyim (1973, 34) read מועדים, but this is improbable in light of the enlarged *ayin* and *dalet*. The trace of ink after the *dalet* should be the *sof passuq*.

from the preceding sentence is implied. Driver (1937, 37) suggests reading בִּית as the imperative of the Hebrew בָּת, which is identical with the Aramaic/Syriac בות, "passed the night," thus: "And pass the night in rest, and afterwards you shalt be bright." תגיה — For the verb נגה, see 16:11 in H^A and the note.

33:5 חוזר — The verb is also attested in 4Q468bb 1 2 (and eventually in 4Q124 8 4) and becomes common in Rabbinic Hebrew.

33:6 כסוס מוכן — See Prov 21:31. יצהל — The verb צהל plays on two registers here: according to the context, it may mean "to neigh" (see Jer 5:8; 50:11), but also to "to rejoice, to cry aloud." The sentence is polysemous.

33:7 As it stands, the verse is very hard to understand. Our translation is tentative. Previous scholars were not able to resolve the problem without correcting the Hebrew according to the Greek and the Syriac.

Chapitre 32

16 [Celui qui craint YYY c]omprend le jugement
   et fait sortir des projets de l'obscurité.
   [Ceux qui craignent YYY comp]rennent son jugement
   et ils font sortir de leur cœur la sagesse.
17 [Une personne violente]biaise les conseils,
   et elle retarde son besoin pour saisir la loi.
18 [une personne ne dis]simule[pas] la sagesse
   et le railleur ne garde pas sa langue.
   [Une personne violente]ne saisit pas l'instruction,
   l'insolent et le railleur ne saisissent pas le commandement.
19 [Sans conseil, ne] fais rien
   et après tes actes, ne reviens pas en arrière.
20 Ne va pas [dans un chemin semé d'embûches]
   et ne trébuche pas dans un chemin semé d'entraves.
21b [Ne t'irrite pas] contre la voie des méchants,
22b et sois attentif à ta fin
1 [Celui qui craint YYY ne] rencontre pas le mal,
   mais s'il retourne dans l'épreuve, alors il sera sauvé.
24 [Celui qui veille sur la lo]i, veille sur lui-même,
   et celui qui fait confiance en YYY ne sera pas déçu.

Chapitre 33

2 [Il n'est pas sage] celui qui hait la loi,
   mais son oreille est secouée comme une tempête.
4 [Prépare une par]ole et ensuite tu agiras
   et (prépare) une maison de repos, et après tu illumineras.
5 Le cœur du fou est [une roue rapide]
   et ses pensées, un disque tournoyant.
6 Un ami haineux est [comme un cheval équipé,]
   il hennira/se réjouira à la place de quelque [ami].
7 [Qu'en est-il de cha]que jour ? Car (tous) s'achèvent,
   la lumière change à cause du soleil.
8 [Cependant, ~~par la sage~~]sse par la sagesse de YYY, ils ont été jugés
   et il y a parmi eux (des jours) de fête.

Chapter 32

16 [The one who fears YYY un]derstands justice,
   and will bring out (his) plans from obscurity.
   [The ones who fear YYY under]stand his justice,
   and will bring out from their heart wisdom.
17 [A violent person] distorts counsels
   and postpones their need, in order to seize the law.
18 [A person should not con]ceal wisdom,
   while the scoffer does not guard their tongue.
   [The violent person] does not grasp instruction
   while the insolent and the scoffer do not grasp the commandment.
19 [Do not] do anything [without advice]
   and after your actions, do not draw back.
20 Do not walk [down a path of trap]s,
   and do not stumble down a path of obstacles.
21b [Do not be anxious over] the way of the wicked,
22b but pay attention to your end.
1 [The one who fears YYY will not] meet evil,
   for if they are again put to the test, then they will be saved.
24 [The one who observes Tor]ah guards themself,
   and the one who trusts in YYY will not be disappointed.

Chapter 33

2 One who hates the law is not wise,
   and their ear is tossed about as from a storm.
4 Prepare your speech and afterward you should act,
   and (prepare) a place of rest and afterward you will shine.
5 The mind of a fool is a fast-[spinning wheel],
   their thoughts are a rotating disk.
6 A hateful friend is [like a saddled horse],
   under any [friend] they neigh / rejoice.
7 [What comes of every] day? For, they (all) end,
   light changing due to the sun.
8 [But, ~~in the wisd~~]om of in the wisdom of YYY they are judged,
   and there are among them festival days.

Segal (1958, 210) suggests reading: למה יום מיום יבדל / וכל אור ימות שנה משמש "Why a day is distinguished from another day, all light of the days of the year (comes) from the sun." שונה — The root שנה may mean "to change," thus "The light changes because of the sun," or "to shine, be beautiful, be exalted," thus "The light shines on the sun" (see Driver 1937, 38). As noticed by Cowley and Neubauer (1897, xxvi) this verse may be compared with b. Sanh. 65b: וזו שאלה שאל טורנוס־רופס הרשע את ר' עקיבה. אמ' ליה. מה יום מיומים. אמ' ליה. ומה גבר מן גוברין (Maagarim). "The גוברין. אמ' ליה. דמארי צאבי. שבת נמי דמארי [צ]בי

wicked Turnus Rufus asked this question to Rabbi Aqiba, he said to him: 'Why is a day (different) from another day?' He said to him: 'and, why is one person (different) from another?' He said to him: 'Because my Lord desires it. Shabbat too, because my Lord desires it.'"

33:8 נשפטו — The use of שפט in this context is not clear, unless one understands it in the sense of "(judging) to distinguish" (see DCH 8:536). מועד — The plural, מועדים, would have been preferable (as the Greek and the Syriac presume).

9	מהם] בֵּרַךְ והקדיש:	ומהם שם לימי מספר:
10	וְכל איש] כְּלִי חמר:	ומן עפר נוצר אדם:
11	אבל חכמָ]ת יְיָ תבדילם:	וישם אותם דרי האָרֶץ:
12	בֵּרַךְ והרים מָ]הֵמָּה:	מהם הקדיש ואל]יו הקריבֿ:
13	ומהם קלל וֹ]הִשְׁפִּיל:	ו○○פם ממעבד יָהֹ]ם:
	כחומר בי]ַד יוצר	לאחוז כרצון:
	כן אדם ביד עֹ]וֹשֵׂהוּ	להתיצב מפני חלק:
14	נוכח רע]טֹוֹבֿ	ונוכח חיים מות:
15	נֹוֹכַֿחֿ איש טֹוֹבֿ רשע	ונוכח האור חֹ]שֶׁךְ[:
	הַבִּטֿ אל כל מעֲשִׂי אל כלם שניםשנים	זה לעומת]זה[:
16	וֹגַםֿ אני אחריו שקדתי:	וכמו עולל אחרֵ]י בוצרים[:
17	בֵּרַֿכְֿתִּ אל גם אני קמתי:	וכבוצר מלאתי]ֿקביֿ[:
18	רָאֹֿו כי לא לבדי עלמתי:	כי לכל מבקשיֿ] חכמה[

ENA 3597 verso

L. 17-end [33:9-] When possible, the restorations are based on the Greek and the Syriac, as well as the available space.

L. 17 [33:9] והקדיש — Marcus (1931, 232) reads והקדשו, but what he reads as a *vav* is certainly either the *sof passuq* or the sign that fills the end of the line before the *sof passuq*.

L. 19 [33:11] [אבל חכמָ]ת — Marcus (1931, 232) and Prato (1975, 14) restore חכמת, but it is too short for the space. We suggest adding אבל to respect the parallel with v. 8; see the Syriac. הָאָרֶץ — Traces of the shoulder of the *resh* and of the vertical and right arm of the final *tsade* are visible. [וִישֹׂ]ה — The word is very difficult to read.

L. 20 [33:12] [מָ] — We would be tempted to restore [מהם ברך והרי]ם מה, "[He has blessed and exalt]ed [some of them]," with Marcus (1931, 232) and Lévi (1932, 140), in agreement with the Greek and the Syriac and because of the parallelism with verse 9. Yet, the disadvantage of this restoration is that one must suppose that the מה at the end of the line is a mistake (the beginning of a dittography of מהם). Segal (1958, 206) suggests reading and restoring [מהם ברך וה]רמה, but as noted by Lévi (1932, 140), the *resh* is difficult to read. It would be preferable to read מ]המה (attested at Qumran and in Jer 10:2 and Qoh 12:12), and to suppose a chiastic construction with the second stich. מהם — Marcus (1931, 232) and subsequent editions read ומהם, but there is no place for a *vav*. [יו ואל] — The restoration proposed by Marcus (1931, 232), ואל]יו הקריבם "and made them close," is too long for the constrained space due to the marginal reading. הקריב seems preferable, according to the parallel with verse 9 and the Greek (also Segal 1958, 206).

L. 21 [33:12] [ומהם קלל ו]השפיל. The restoration is short for the space, but the size of letters may vary significantly in the hand of this scribe. The final *mem* (השפילם), transcribed by Marcus (1931, 232) and subsequent editions, is not visible on the manuscript. The faint traces that Marcus noticed must be the *sof passuq*. The reading השפיל is preferable for the space and for the syntax that is in parallel with the preceding verse (see the preceding note on הקריב). ו○○פם — Marcus (1931, 232) and the following editions read ודחפם, but the *dalet* is very difficult to read and the *khet* is impossible. A *resh* followed by another *pe* seems to be more probable.

L. 22 [33:13] יוצר — The reconstruction ה]יוצר (Marcus 1931, 233; Lévi 1932, 140; Prato 1975, 14) is highly improbable. A trace of a letter far on the right of the *yod* of יוצר should be the beginning of the horizontal of the *dalet* of ביד.

L. 23 [33:13] מפני — Marcus (1931, 233) reads a *vav* מפניו, but this *vav* is no longer visible.

L. 2 [33:15] מעֲשִׂי — Marcus (1931, 233) and subsequent editions read מעשה, but there is no space for a *he*. The traces of letters are very faint and almost illegible. כלם — Marcus (1931, 233) and subsequent editions read כולם, but there are neither traces nor enough space for a *vav* between the *kaph* and the *lamed*.

L. 3 [33:16] אחריו — This reading is preferable to אחרון, as the final *nun* usually starts at the bottom of the line and then clearly goes under the line.

L. 4 [33:17] קמֿתִּי — Marcus (1931, 234) reads קדמתי, but the succession of *dalet*, *mem* and *tav* does not fit the available space. It is preferable to read קמתי (see the Syriac). The two traces of letters that are read as a *dalet* and a *mem* by Marcus (1931, 234) may in fact be a *mem* (the right vertical and the horn, the diagonal having disappeared).

33:9 בֵּרַךְ והקדיש — The defective reading of הקדיש is hard to explain here. For the benediction and sanctification of days, see Gen 2:3 and Exod 20:11 in relation to the Sabbath. See especially, Jub 2:19–24 // 4Q216 VII 10–16. לימי מספר — The expression also occurs in Sir 41:13 where it means "limited time." According to the context, Marcus (1931, 232) and Segal (1958, 210) understand the expression as "ordinary days," in opposition to the festive days. The "counted days" are the days counted between each Sabbath (see Mekhilta Exod. 20:8: רבי יצחק אומר: תהא מונה כדרך שאחרים מונין, אלא תהא מונה לשם שבת "R. Yitzchak says: Do not be one who counts (days) according to how others count (days), rather be one who counts according to the Sabbath.")

33:10 כלי חמר — For the motif of the potter and the vessel of clay, see Jer 18:1–6. For the comparison of men with clay, see Job 10:9 and 33:6. The motif is recurrent in the Hodayot (1QH[a] IX 21; XI 23–24, 30; XIX 6–8; etc.). ומן עפר נוצר אדם — This sentence is clearly a reformulation of Gen 2:7.

33:11 דרי האָרֶץ — The form דרי may be interpreted as a noun, דור "generation" (for the plural דורים, see Ps 72:5; 102:5; Isa 51:8; 1QH[a] IX 18), or as a *qal* participle from the root דור "to live, to dwell" (see Ps 84:11; Sir 33:11[E]; 50:26 הדר בשכם, and the same expression in Aramaic in Dan 4:32).

33:12 ו○○פם — Marcus (1931, 232) reads ודחפם. In Biblical Hebrew, the verb דחף is attested in the *qal* passive participle in Esth 3:15 and 8:14, and in the *niphal* in Esth 6:12 and 2 Chr 26:20 with the meaning "to hasten, to hurry." In Aramaic and in Rabbinic Hebrew, it means "to push, to thrust, to knock down." However, a reading ורפפם seems more probable, though the verb usually has an intransitive meaning "to tremble". ממעבד יָהֹ]ם — As noticed by previous commentators, this reading may be a mistake for ממעמדיהם "from their places" (see the Greek and the Syriac).

33:13*ab* For the potter metaphor, see Jer 18:1–6. לאחוז — The verb אחז means "to seize, to grasp." In this context, it should mean "to mold."

9 [certains d'entre eux,]il (les) a bénis et sanctifiés
   et certains d'entre eux, il a établi pour (eux) un nombre fixé de jours.
10 [Et toute personne est]un vase d'argile
   et de poussière l'humain est formé.
11 [Mais la sages]se de YYY les séparera
   et il les établira habitants de la te[r]re
   (mg. et il différen[ciera] leurs voies.)
12 [Il a béni et exaltés cer]tains d'entre eux
   et certains d'entre eux, il (les) a sanctifiés et *pr*[*ès de lui
   *(les) *a fait approcher.*]
   [*certains d'entre eux, il* (*les*) *a maudits et*]abaissés
   et il les a renversés de leurs lab[eur]s.
13 [Comme l'argile dans la ma]in d'un potier
   à modeler selon (sa) volonté,
   [ainsi l'humain dans la main] de celui qui le fait
   pour se tenir devant (son) créateur.
14 [En face du mal], le bien,
   et en face de la vie, la mort,
   en face d'un homme bon, un mauvais
   et en face de la lumière, les tén[èbres.]
15 Observe toutes les œuvres de Dieu,
   toutes sont deux par deux,
   celle-ci vis-à-vis de [celle-là.]
16 Et moi aussi, après lui, j'ai veillé,
   comme un glaneur après les vendangeurs.
17 Par la bénédiction de Dieu, moi aussi, je me suis levé,
   comme un vendangeur j'ai rempli [mon pressoir].
18 Voyez, ce n'est pas pour moi seul *que j'ai peiné,*
   mais pour tous ceux qui cherchent[la sagesse].

9 [Certain of them] he has blessed and sanctified,
   and certain of them he has established (for them) a fixed number of days.
10 [Every person]is a vessel of clay,
   and from dust a human is formed.
11 [But the wisdo]m of YYY will distinguish them,
   and he will establish them as residents of the earth.
   (mg. and he will distingu[ish] their paths.)
12 [*He has blessed and exalted so*]*me of them*,
   and some of them he has sanctified and [*brought near*]
   to [*himself*],
   [*and some of them he has cursed and*] brought low,
   and driven them from their wor[k]s.
13 [Like clay in the han]d of the potter,
   to mold according to (their) will,
   [so are humans in the hand of] their maker,
   so they may stand before (their) creator.
14 [Opposite evil] (is) good
   and opposite life, death,
   opposite a good person, the wicked,
   and opposite the light, da[rkness].
15 Observe all the works of God,
   all of them, two-by-two,
   this one opposite [that].
16 Even I, after him (God?), I watch,
   like a gleaner after [the grape pickers].
17 By the blessing of God I too arise
   and like the grape picker I fill [my] pr[ess].
18 See, it is not for myself *I labor*,
   but for all those who seek [wisdom].

33:13cd This verse is very difficult to understand. להתיצב — The *hithpael* of יצב in connexion with חומר may be borrowed from Job 38:14. See similarly, b. Sanh. 38a: והקב״ה טבע את כל העולם בחותמו שלאדם הראשון ואין אח׳ מה׳ דומ׳ לחבירו שנ׳ תתהפך כחומר חותם ויתיצבו כמו לבוש "But the Holy One, blessed be he, stamps everyone in the world with the seal of the first person (i.e., Adam), but there is not one similar to the next. As it is said: 'they are changed like clay (beneath) a seal and they emerge like a garment' (Job 38:14)." מפני — The interpretation of the sentence depends on the reading: מפני versus מפניו (see the reading note). The former implies translating "to stand in front of a portion/creation" or "… (their) creator," and the latter implies "To stand in front of him he created (him [= a human])." חלק — The word can be read as a noun or a verb (*qal* 3ms perfect or ms participle), depending on whether מפניו or מפני is read. As is often the case in Ben Sira, the word should refer to the idea of creation here (see Sir 7:15 and 16:16, and the corresponding notes). See Segal (1958, 212), who understands the word as the thing that is created and also Driver (1937, 38) for this verse.

33:15 Cf. T. 12 Patr. T. Ash. I,4: "Therefore all things are by twos, one over against the other." (trans. Charles 1913, 343). b. Hag. 15a: "(Rabbi Meir) said to him: 'Everything which the Holy One, blessed be he, created, he created that which corresponds to it (כנגדו). He created mountains; he created hills. He created seas; he created rivers.' (Aḥer) said to him: 'Akiva, your teacher, did not say thus, rather (he said): 'he created the righteous; he created the wicked. He created the Garden of Eden; he created Gehenna. To each person there are two portions, one in the Garden of Eden and one in Gehenna. If one is innocent, as a righteous person, they take their portion and the portion of their companion in the Garden of Eden; if one is guilty, as a wicked person, they take their portion and the portion of their companion in Gehenna.'" Sefer Yetsira 60: גם כל חפץ זה לעומת זה ברא אל״ים. טוב לעומת רע. רע מרע וטוב "Indeed, every desire, one opposite the other, God has made (Qoh 7:14). Good (he made) opposite evil, evil from evil, good from good. Good makes evil distinct, and evil makes good distinct. Good is reserved for the good." זה לעומת זה — This is a quotation of Qoh 7:14 and also appears at Sir 42:24 H^M.

33:16 עולל — The word most naturally would be read as "child," though this does not accord with the sense of the versions, which instead imply interpreting the word as a *qal* participle with the sense "gleaner." Usually, where the root עלל has the sense "glean" it appears in the *poel* conjugation (hence perhaps an earlier כמעולל became כמו עולל in H^E [as suggested elsewhere, e.g., Box and Oesterley 1913, 430]). Maagarim records one other text from before 1050 where the *qal* also has this sense.

33:18 עלמתי: — The verb עלם does not make any sense here. This is undoubtedly a metathesis for עמלתי.

19	⁶שמעו אלי שרי עם רב:	ומשלי קהל ה]אזינו[	
20ab	⁷בן ואשה אהב ורע:	אל תמשיל בחייך[:]	
21	⁸עד עודך חי ונשמה בך	אל תשלט בך כל ב]שר[	
20cd	⁹אל תתן שלך לאחר:	לשוב לחלות א]ת פניו[:	
22	¹⁰כי טוב לחלות בָּנֶיךָ ᵖ נידָ:	מהביטך על ידי]בניך[:	
23	¹¹בכל מעשיךָ היה עליון:	ואל תתן מום בכבֹ]ודך[:	
24	¹²בעת מספר מצערֹ ᵐידָ:	וביום המות הנחֹ]ל נחלה[:	
25	¹³מספוא ושוט ומשא לחמור:	ומרדות מלאכה לע]בד[:	
26	¹⁴העבדֹ עבדך שלא יבקש נֹחֹת	ואם נשא ראשו יבג]ד[	
28	¹⁵העבד עבדך שלא ימרוד:	כי הרבה רעה עוֹ[	
27	¹⁶על וע]בות חוטר תומכו	על עבד רע הרבֹ]ה[	
30	¹⁷אל תֹוֹתר על כל אדם:	ובלא משפט]אל תעש דבר[	
31	¹⁸אֹחֹדֹ עבדך]י[הֹי בֹ]נ[פֹשְׁךָ	כי כנפשׁךָ [	
19	¹⁹אחד עבדך כאח חשבהֹוֹ	א]ל תֹקֹנֹא בֹ[	
32	²⁰כי אם עניתו יצא ואבד	באיזֹה דרֹךְ[	

Chapter 34

1	²¹רק תֹדרֹשׁ תֹּחִלֹּת כזב	וחלומֹוֹת [	[

L. 8 [33:21] כל ב]שר[:] — This is a restoration according to the Syriac.

L. 14 [33:26] יבקש: — The yod is written above the aleph.

L. 15 [33:28] עוֹ[— Marcus (1931, 236) and Lévi (1932, 142) restore עו]שה עצלה[, which is too large for the space. One would expect only one word here.

L. 16 [33:27] על וע]בות — Traces of the *bet*, *vav* and *tav* are clearly visible on the manuscript.

L. 17 [33:30] תֹּוֹתר — The traces are very faint. ובלא משפט]אל תעש דבר[— Our reconstruction follows the Syriac.

L. 18 [33:31] As Marcus (1931, 237) notes, from this line on, the traces of letters are very faint and difficult to read. בֹ]נ[פֹשְׁךָ — Very faint traces of ink may correspond to this reading, which is suggested by the Greek and the Syriac. כֹנֹפֹשֹׁךָ — Marcus (1931, 237) and subsequent editions read במשך, which does not make any sense. The reading כנפשך fits the faint traces of letters perfectly.

L. 21 [34:1] רק — There is no trace nor space for a *yod* between the *resh* and the *qoph*. תֹדרֹשׁ — After the *dalet*, a vertical line is visible that would perfectly fit a *resh*. The *shin* is only preserved by an unidentifiable faint trace. תֹּחִלֹּת — There is no trace nor space for a *vav* between the *tav* and the *khet*. However, as Marcus (1931, 237) notes, there is space for one or two letters before this word.

33:19 The succession of imperatives, "Hear... Give ear" is typical in Hebrew, see Judg 5:3; Job 34:2; Ps 49:2; etc.

33:21 עודך חי — See Gen 46:30.

33:20d לחלות א]ת פניו[: — The construction is normally חלה פנים without the particle את; see 33:22.

33:22 מהביטך על ידי — The expression does not seem to be attested elsewhere and should evoke the idea of dependence on children.

33:23 בכל מעשיךָ — The formulation is recurrent in Ben Sira, see 7:36; 31:22; 32:23 and 35:11. עליון — The word, used elsewhere in Ben Sira in reference to God, presumably refers to a distinguished person. In the Bible, it qualifies various architectural features as well as humans (e.g., Ps 89:28). מום — Cf. Sir 44:19 concerning Abraham.

33:24 הנחֹ]ל נחלה[— Cf. Isa 49:8.

33:25 מרדות — It is unlikely that this is the biblical Hebrew word "rebellion," but rather a word semantically similar to מוסר, i.e., "chastisement," also found in Sir 42:8ᴮ (as an alternative to מוסר) and in Rabbinic Hebrew.

33:26 יבקש נֹחֹת — For the absolute usage of בקש, see Neh 5:12. The final word agrees with the Greek 248 [καὶ ζητήσει ἀνάπαυσιν] and the Latin.

33:27 וע]בות חוטר תומכו — As in v. 25, the form תומכו is surely a singular participle of תמך with a plural subject (unless one vocalizes as תומכי, which would not be impossible). תמך should mean "to uphold, to support" here, as in Isa 41:10; Exod 17:12 and Ps 41:13 (i.e. the servant works only because of yoke, rope and rod). This verse can also be understood differently if the word חוטר is interpreted as a participle from the Aramaic root חטר "to strike (with a stick), fence in, impede, block" (see Tg. Job 19:8 where אסרטי חטר translates the Hebrew ארחי גדר).

19 Ecoutez moi, princes d'un peuple nombreux, et dirigeants de l'assemblée, pr[êtez l'oreille.]	19 Listen to me, princes of a numerous people, gi[ve ear,]rulers of the assembly.
20a Enfant et femme, ami et compagnon, 20b ne (les) laisse pas gouverner ta vie.	20a Child and wife, friend and companion 20b do not let them rule over your life.
21 Tant que tu es vivant et qu'il y a un souffle en toi, ne laisse per[sonne] dominer sur toi.	21 So long as you are alive and there is breath in you do not let any[one] dominate you.
20c Ne donne pas ce qui est à toi à ton prochain, 20d tu devrais revenir le flat[ter.]	20c Do not give what is yours to another, 20d so that you must make repeated [appeals].
22 Car mieux vaut que tes fils te flattent, que tu ne doives regarder les mains [de tes enfants.]	22 For it is better for your children to appeal to you, than for you to look to the hands of [your children].
23 Dans toutes tes œuvres sois au sommet et n'inflige aucune tare à [ton] hon[neur.]	23 Be on top of all your affairs, and do not set a blemish in [your] hono[r].
24 Au temps du décompte du petit nombre de tes jours, et au jour de la mort, distribue l'héritage.	24 At the time when your days are very few, and in the day of death, distribu[te an inheritance].
25 Fourrage, fouet et fardeau sont pour l'âne, et correction, travail sont pour le serviteur.	25 Fodder, whip, and burden are for the donkey, and punishment, work for the slave.
26 Fais travailler ton serviteur qu'il ne cherche pas le repos, mais s'il relève sa tête, il (te) trahira.	26 Make your slave work so they will not seek rest, for if they lift their head they will betray (you).
28 Fais travailler ton serviteur qu'il ne se révolte pas, car [ ] fait se multiplier le mal.	28 Make your slave work so they do not rebel, for [ ] increases evil.
27 [Joug et cor]dage, une baguette le motive, sur un serviteur mauvais multiplie [ ].	27 [Yoke and ro]pe, a rod motivate them, increase (these) over a wicked slave.
30 Ne sois indulgent envers personne et [ne fais rien] de contraire au droit.	30 Do not be indulgent with any person, and without justice [do (not) do anything]
31 Tu as un seul esclave, qu'il soit comme toi-même, car comme toi-même [ ] Tu as un seul esclave, considère-le comme ton frère, [N]e sois pas jaloux de[lui]	31 Do you have only one slave? Let them be like yourself for, like yourself [ ] Do you have only one slave? Consider them like a brother, do [n]ot be jealous of [ ]
32 Car si tu l'humilies, il partira et périra, par quel chemin[ ]	32 For, if you mistreat them, they will go forth and be lost, in what path …

Chapitre 34 / Chapter 34

1 En vain tu cherches un espoir mensonger, et les songes[ ]	1 In vain you will search a false hope, and dreams …

In this case, the next word, תומכו, would refer to the neck (i.e. what supports the yoke and rope): "yoke and rope impede what supports them (i.e. the neck)." See Driver (1937, 38–39) and the Greek. על עבד רע הרבֿ֯ה — The restoration of the end of this line is hard to determine. Marcus (1931, 236), followed by Lévi (1932, 144) and Segal (1958, 215), restores על עבד רע הרבֿ֯ה אסוריו "on an evil servant multiply his fetters," borrowed from the Syriac of the next verse (ܪ̈ܣܘܪܘܗܝ ܐܣܓܐ).
33:30 תותר — The verb here is the *piel* of יתר, known from Rabbinic Hebrew, with the sense "to be liberal, indulgent" (see Jastrow 1903, 376). The *hiphil* (or *niphal*) of יתר should mean "do not have superiority

over" or "exceed, surpass" here (see. Gen 49:4; 4Q416 2 ii 10; Sir 10:27; 11:12; 32:1). The *piel* also has the meaning "to add, do too much" (see Jastrow 1903, 604), which would imply the translation "do not abuse (them) beyond all (other) people."
33:31 באיזֿה֯ — The preposition ב followed by the particles אי־זה has the meaning "by what, how."
34:1 רק — It may be adverbial or the object of תדרש. In the latter case, the verse may be translated, "A false hope seeks after vanity." תוחלת אונים — Cf. Prov 11:7 תֹּחֶלֶת כזב.

MANUSCRIPT F

SIR 31:24–33:8

Chapter 31

[4–1]

T-S AS 213.17 recto	[ ]	[בִּשְׁעָרֹ]·[ ]	24 B 5]
	[רַבִּים]	אל תתג[בר·	25 B 6]
	כן היין למצ[ות	[מ]עשה לוטש·	26 B 7]
	אם ישתנו]	חיים לאֱנוֹש [ ]	27 B 8]
	שה[וא] מרא[שית נוצרו:	[מה חיי]ֹם חסר היין·	9]
	[ ]	[שמ]חֹת לב וששון ועדוי	28 B 10]
	יין נשאֹרֹ בֹ[ ]		
	והוא לגיל]	חיים למה יחסר תירוש·	11]
	יין נשתה בחר[ֹן]	כאב ראש לענה ורוש·	29 B 12]
	מחסר כח ומספיק [ ]	מרבה חמד לכסיל נוקש·	30 B 13]
	וא תוגֵהו בחדותו:	במשתה יין אֹ תוכח רֵע·	31 B 14]
לעיני כל אדם:	דבר חרפה אֹ תאמר לו· וֹאֹ תקמיעהו בנגשה וֹאֹ תריב עמו	15]

Chapter 32

לך כאחד מהם:	תסתורה והיה אֹ עשירים ובראש· תותר אֹ סמוך ראש	16 1 B
	הבו צרכם ובכן תרבץ:	דאג להם ואחר תסוב·	17 1c2a B
	ועל מוסר תשא שכל:	למען תשמח בכבודם·	18 2bc B
	והצנע שכל וֹאֹ תמנע שיר:	מלל שבט הוא לך·	19 3 B
	ובלא מזמור אֹ שיח תשפך:	במקום שכל אֹ תשפך שיח·	20 4 B

31:26 כן היין למצ F | כן היין למצות B כי היית מעשה מצות Bmg · +31:26cd נבון בוחן מעשה מעשה כן שכר לריב לצים Bmg · 31:27 מרא F | מרֹאשִׁיֹת B | מראשית B · 31:28 נשאֹרֹ F | נשתה B G S | חיים למה יחסר F | חיי מה לחסרֹ B · 31:29 ורוש F | וקלון B | בחרֹ[ֹן F S (ܟܣܘܐ) בתחרה B · 31:30 חמד F | כל אדם B · בני אדֹם F | תתרפהו B בחדותו F | תרחיעהו Bmg · 32:1 והיה F | חמר F | נוקש Bmg · מֹקש B · ומספיק F | ומספק B · 31:31 יין F | היין F | בחדותו F | חמר F | הולך F B G | הוא לך F B · Bmg2 שבכי Bmg1 שבכי | שב כי F | סבכי B G S · 32:3 ובכן F | ואחר F | הכין B · הבו F | תרביץ B לך F S | היה להם B · 32:4 שכל F | לכת B cf. Mic 6:8 · Bmg cf. B F שכל | היין B · שיח תשפך F אֹ מה תשפך שיח ובל עת מה תתחכם: B (double reading of B = G) · Bmg2

L. 9 [31:27] שה[וא] מרא[שית נוצרו — According to the space available in the left margin, the restoration מראשית לשמחה נוצר in H^B is impossible, unless one imagines that נוצר was written in the margin. As elsewhere in this manuscript, it is likely that the text of H^F had the same reading as the margin of H^B.

L. 10 [31:28] [שמ]חֹת — There is a thin trace of ink corresponding to the end of the left leg of the khet, then traces of the head and foot of the tav. נשאֹרֹ — The preceding editions (Di Lella 1988, 231; Scheiber 1982, 182) read נשתה according to H^B, but this reading is totally impossible. The last letter is clearly a resh (the head and vertical are preserved).

The trace before it most likely corresponds to the end of the vertical of an aleph.

L. 12 [31:29] בחרֹ[ֹן — Preceding editions erroneously read בתחרה according to H^B. Yet, the tav is impossible and it must be a khet, followed not by a khet, but a resh. The small trace of a letter at the break of the fragment could be a yod (for this reading compare the Syriac ܟܣܘܐ, and to some extent the Greek ἐρεθισμῷ).

L. 13 [31:30] חמד — The scribe clearly wrote a dalet, though the context, H^B and the ancient versions clearly presuppose חמר ("still fermenting wine"). For the similarity between resh and dalet in the writing of this scribe, cf. צרכם at l. 17.

31:28 חיים למה — In this construction, חיים may be understood as a casus pendens or one may suppose an implied conditional sentence: "life is for what (if) new wine is missing?"

31:30 חמד — See reading note.

31:31 תקמיעהו — The verb קמע, an Aramaism in Rabbinic Hebrew, means "to press, squeeze, tie" in the qal (cf. the Biblical Hebrew קמץ and קמט). The hiphil appears only once elsewhere, in a text dated by Maagarim to 1204. בנגשה — The root נגש fits the context either with its Hebrew meaning "to approach," or its Galilean Aramaic meaning (נגס) "to eat, to dine." But, the grammatical form is obscure, unless one reads the final he as a 3ms suffix (for other cases, see 10:13 נֵגְעָה, וּמְקוֹרָה).

32:1 סמוך — Greek and Syriac suggest this is an alternative spelling of שָׁמוּךָ "they set you," though it may formally be a qal passive participle (cf. niphal in Rabbinic Hebrew). תותר — The hiphil (or niphal) of יתר should mean "do not show superiority" or "exceed, surpass" here (see Gen 49:4; 4Q416 2 ii 10; Sir 10:27; 11:12; 32:1). תסתורה — The form is obscure since the qal of סתר "to hide" is not clearly attested. It may be the root סתר II "to upset, tear down," or "contradict, disprove" as found in Rabbinic Hebrew. Or, it may be a misspelling of תשתורה, a would-be Syriacism, "exalt yourself" (see Payne Smith 1901, 2:4105).

Chapitre 31

24 [　　　　　　　　　　　　]à la porte (de la ville)
   [　　　　　　　　　　　　　　　　　　　　]
25 [　　　　　　　　　　　　　　ne sois pas arro]gant,
   [car] beaucoup [　　　　　　　　　　　　]
26 [　　　　　　　　　　　　　　]l'œuvre du forgeron,
   ainsi le vin son[de　　　　　　　　　　　]
27 [　　　　　　　　　　　　] la vie ? Pour l'être humain,
   s'il le boit [　　　　　　　　　　　　　　]
   [Qu'est-ce que la vi]e (pour) celui qui manque de vin,
   lequel, depuis le com[mencement est sa création.]
28 [Jo]ie du cœur et jubilation et plaisir,
   le vin conservé en[　　　　　　　　　　　]
   (Pendant) la vie, pourquoi le vin nouveau manquerait-il?
   Et lui, pour l'allégresse [　　　　　　　　]
29 Mal de crâne, amertume et poison,
   le vin bu à cause d'une colère [　　　　].
30 L'abondance de désir frappe l'insensé
   il fait manquer de force et multiplie [　　]
31 Lors d'un banquet de vin ne fais pas de reproche à un compagnon
   et ne le tourmente pas dans son bonheur.
   Ne lui dis pas une parole outrageante
   et ne le presse pas lorsque tu l'approches et n'entre pas en conflit avec lui ^aux yeux de tout être humain^.

Chapitre 32

1 (Es-tu) établi chef, ne te montre pas dominant,
  et (es-tu) à la tête des riches ? Ne le cache pas ;
  sois ^comme l'un d'entre eux^.
1c Inquiète-toi d'eux et ensuite allonge-toi (s.e. à table),
2b apporte ce dont ils ont besoin et sur ce allonge-toi (s.e. à table)
2b afin que tu te réjouisses de leur honneur,
2c et en raison de ton savoir vivre tu recevras de la considération.
3 Parle, sceptre, cela te revient,
  sois humble avec ton intelligence et ne refuse pas un chant.
4 Là où il y a de l'intelligence, ne te répands pas en discours,
  et sans chanson, ne te répands pas en discours.

Chapitre 31

24 [　　　　　　　　　　　　　] at the gate (of the city).
   [　　　　　　　　　　　　　　　　　　　　]
25 [　　　　　　　　　　do not act arro]gantly,
   [　　　] many [　　　　　　　　　　　　]
26 [　　　　　　　　] the work of the smith,
   thus wine the quar[rel　　　　　　　　　]
27 [　　　　　　] life? For humanity,
   when they drink it [　　　　　　　　　　]
   [What is lif]e for the one lacking wine,
   which was from the begin[ning created.]
28 The [jo]y of heart and jubilation and pleasure
   (is) wine left in [　　　　　　　　　　　]
   As for a life, why should new wine be lacking?
   It is for rejoicing [　　　　　　　　　　　]
29 Headache, bitterness, and poison
   (is) wine drunk because of strife [　　　]
30 Abundance of desire knocks the fool down,
   decreasing strength and increasing [　　]
31 At a banquet of wine rebuke not a friend
   and do not torment them in their joy.
   a reproachful word, do not speak to them,
   and do not press them when approaching them and do not contend with them ^in the sight of any human being^.

Chapitre 32

1 (Are you) established as the head (of a feast)? Do not be dominant.
  (Are you) at the head of the wealthy? Do not hide it; be ^like one of them^.
1c Concern yourself with them and afterward lie (at the table),
2a provide for their needs and then you may lie down (at the table).
2b So that you rejoice in their honor,
2c and that you receive consideration because of your refined manner.
3 Speak, scepter, because it is your place,
  be humble in your intelligence and do not withhold a song.
4 In a place of intelligence, do not pour out a discourse,
  and without song, do not pour out discourse.

32:3 שבט — "Scepter" (or less probably "tribe") used as a metonymy for a respectable and responsible person. This reading, as opposed to שב בי in H^B, is the result of two phenomena: (1) the wrong word division of שבבי, as attested in the H^B margin, and (2) the misreading of *kaph* and *yod*, as a *tet*, which is understandable in semi cursive script.

See, e.g., the *tet* of משפט in H^E (Sir 32:16, ENA 3597 l. 1), which resembles בי. Confirmation of this error is found in Sir 32:5, where the scribe confused כיס זהב "purse of gold" with טס זהב "plate of gold."

32:4 אל שיח תשפך — For a similar case of dislocated negation, see 4Q417 2 i 9 [// 4Q416 2 i 3–5] and Rey (2015, 171).

5ab B	²¹כחותם על כיס זהב·	שירת א׳ על משתה היין:
5cd B	²²כומז אדם על טס זהוב·	משפט שיר על משתה היין׃
5ef B	²³כדביר זהב בו נופך וספיר·	נואי דברים על מש׳ היין׃
6 B	²⁴כל מלא פז וחותם ברקת·	קול מזמור על נועם תירול׃
25		
7 B	²⁶[דב]ר נער צורך אותך·	פעמים ושלש אם ישאך:
[8–11] B	[¹⁻⁵]	[
11cd B	[ ]י̇ [ז] [	]
12 B	[ ]ר[צון] [בי]תך ושל[ם]	בירא]ת
13 B	[ ]א]לה ברך עושך·	המרוך מטו]בתו׃
14ab B	[ ]א]ל חי וקוה רצון·	וגם מתלהלה י̇ [
14ef B	¹⁰[דורש ח]פצי̇ [אל י]מצא לקח·	ויענהו בכל קצ̇י עד׃
16 BE	¹¹[ירא יי י]בין משפט·	ות{ת}חבולות מנשפ̇ יוצ̇יא:
	¹²[יראי] יי יבינו משפטו·	וחכמות יוציאו מלבם׃
17 BE	¹³איש חמס יטה תוכחות·	ויאחר צרכו למשך תורה:
18ab BE	¹⁴איש לא יכסה חכמה·	ולץ לא ישמור לשונו:
18cd BE	¹⁵איש חמס לא יקח שכל·	זד ולץ לא יקח מצוה:
19 BE	¹⁶בלא עצה א׳ תפעל דבר·	ואחר מעשיך א׳ תתקפץ:
20 BE	¹⁷בדרך מוקשת א׳ תלך·	וא׳ תתקל בדרך נגף:
21b/22b BE	¹⁸אל תתחר בדרך רשעים·	ובאחריתך היה זהיר:
33:1 BE	¹⁹ירא יי לא יפגע רע·	כי אם בניסוי ישוב ונמלט:
24 BE	²⁰נוצר תורה נוצר נפשו·	ובוטח ביי לא יבוש:

T-S AS 213.17 verso

32:5ab שירת F Bmg | שיר B · **32:5cd** אדם F | אודם B · טס F | ניב B | נוב Bmg1 | זיר Bmg2 | זהב B · זהוב F | **32:5ef** כדביר F · כרביד B · נופך וספיר B · נהפך ספיר Bmg · נופ̇ף וספיר F | **32:6** דברים יפים B · כך נאים F | נואי F | דברים F · מלואות F | מלא Bmg | מלא B · **32:7** צורך F | אם צריך F | וקוה רצון F | [י̇]קוה רצון | א]ל F Bmg | אל B · אתה B | אתך Bmg · בחזק פעמים F | פעמים F B G | ישאך B · ישא לך Bmg · **32:14ab** א]ל חי F Bmg | [י̇]קוה רצון B ? | **32:14cd** וגם מתלהלה F | ומתלהלה B · ומשחרהו ישיג מענה:+ **32:14ef** [מצא F | יקח B | ישא Bmg · בכל F | קצ̇י B | בתפלתו B · **32:15** + : יוקש בה· ומתלהלה ויפיקנה תורה דורש · **32:16** וחכמות F Bmg E | רבות (metat.) B · **32:17** חמס F Bmg G (ἁμαρτωλός) | חכם B · ויאחר F Bmg E | ואחר B · למשך F E | ימשך B | למשוך Bmg · **32:18ab** לא איש F | לא חכם B G (βουλῆς) S (7h3) 7ai | **שכל F Bmg E G | חכם B G (βουλῆς) S (7h3) 7ai | חכמה F Bmg E | כחמה B · ישמור B E | ישמר F | **32:18cd** חמס F Bmg | חכם B G (βουλῆς) S (7h3) 7ai | יקח מצוה F Bmg E | שחד B | S · **32:19** תתקפץ F E | תתקצף B · ישמר תורה F Bmg E | **32:20** בדרך נגף F E G? | בנגף פעמים B S · **32:21a/22a** + הזהר F E | ובארחתיך B · ובאחריתך F E | תבטח B · תתחר F | אל תבטח בדרך מחתף (רשעים) (הזהר) · **32:21b/22b** · **33:1** בניסוי B · בכל דרכיך שמור נפשך כי כל עושה אלה שומר מצוה (1⁻ מצוה 2⁻ מצות): + **32:23** B · **32:24** נוצר · Bmg שב B | ישוב E F בנסוי B · שומר B · F E | F B

L. 10 [32:14] מצאי̇ — Di Lella (1988, 234) and Scheiber (1982, 183) read מוצא, which is impossible. The preserved traces perfectly correspond to a *mem* (the horn, diagonal and base), and not a *vav*. קצ̇[ה:] — Di Lella (1988, 234) and Scheiber (1982, 183) read בכל תפ̇לתו, probably under the influence of H^B, but the *tav* is impossible. The reading of *qoph* followed by a non-final *tsade* is certain.

L. 15 [32:18] חמס — The last letter looks more like a final *mem* than a *samek*, but חמם would not provide a sound meaning, and in this manuscript, final *mem* and *samek* look similar.

L. 19 [33:1] יי̇ — Above the divine name is a semi-circular hoop. On this writing of the divine name, see Böhmisch 2020, 150.

32:5 טס This reading is the result of the combination of two phenomena: (1) as in the preceding note (Sir 32:2 on שבט), the misreading of the two letters, *kaph* and *yod*, as a *tet* (see כיס זהב in MS B), and (2) a mistake by homoioteleuton with the words of the preceding line, כיס זהב "purse of gold." זהוב — The *qal* of זהב is quite rare, and as here, is mainly used as a passive participle. כדביר זהב — Obviously, the scribe has inverted the two letters *resh* and *dalet*, creating a beautiful semantic innovation. See, however, 2 Chr 4:20. נואי — This is the abstract noun (sometimes spelled נוי), known from Rabbinic Hebrew, in contrast to the adjective נאים (plural of נָאֶה) in H^B.

32:7 צורך — For this word, see see 8:9^A and the note. H^B has צריך, for which see 31:4^B and the note. For the variation between these words, see Sir 13:6^A and the note.

5a Comme un sceau sur une bourse d'or,	5a Like a seal over a purse of gold,
5b un chant divin à un banquet de vin.	5b (is) a divine song at a banquet of wine.
5c Un pendentif de rubis sur un plateau doré,	5c A ruby pendant over a place of gold,
5d Un chant approprié à un banquet de vin,	5d (is) an appropriate song at a banquet of wine.
5e Comme un sanctuaire d'or comprenant turquoise et saphir,	5e As an inner sanctuary of gold in which there is turquoise and sapphire
5f la beauté des belles paroles à un banquet de vin.	5f are pleasant words at a wine banquet.
6 Tout enchâssement d'or fin et sceau d'émeraude (est) la voix d'un psaume sur la douceur du vin nouveau.	6 Every setting of fine gold and emerald seal, (are) the sound of a psalm with the pleasantness of new wine.
vacat	*vacat*
7 [Par]le, jeune homme, si on a besoin de toi, deux ou trois fois, si on te demande.	7 [Spea]k, young man, if one needs you, twice or three times, if one asks you.
[8-11]	[8-11]
12 [ ]ta maison et accomplis (ton) [d]ésir, dans la crain[te]	12 [ ] your house so that you can fulfill (your) [d]esire, with the fear [of]
13 [c]ela, bénis ton créateur qui t'enivre de[sa]bon[té.]	13 [ ] these things, bless your creator, the one who refreshes you from [his] boun[ty].
14a [Di]eu vivant et espère une faveur,	14a [ ] the living God and hope for [his] good will
14b mais aussi le fou furieux [ ]	14b but also the maniac will [ ].
14e [Celui qui cherche les d]ésirs [de Dieu,]trouvera l'instruction,	14e [The one who seeks God's de]sires will find instruction
14f Et il lui répondra en tout temps [d'éternité.]	14f and he will answer them at all times.
16 [Celui qui craint YYY c]omprend le jugement et [fait sortir] des projets de l'obscurité [.] [Ceux qui craignent] YYY comprennent son jugement et ils font sortir de leur cœur une sagesse.	16 [The one who fears YYY un]derstands justice, and [will bring out] (his) plans from obscurity. [The ones who fear] YYY understand his justice, and will bring out from their heart wisdom.
17 Une personne violente biaise les conseils et elle retarde son besoin pour saisir la loi.	17 A violent person distorts counsels and postpones their need, in order to seize the law.
18 Une personne ne dissimule pas la sagesse et le railleur ne garde pas sa langue. Une personne violente ne saisit pas l'instruction, l'insolent et le railleur ne saisissent pas le commandement.	18 A person should not conceal wisdom, and the scoffer does not guard their tongue. The violent person does not grasp instruction, while the insolent and the scoffer do not grasp the commandment.
19 Sans conseil, ne fais rien et après tes actes, ne reviens pas en arrière.	19 Do not do anything without advice, and after your actions, do not draw back.
20 Ne va pas dans un chemin semé d'embûches et ne trébuche pas dans un chemin (semé) d'entraves.	20 Do not walk down a path of traps, and do not stumble down a path of obstacles.
21b Ne t'irrite pas contre la voie des méchants,	21b Do not be anxious over the way of the wicked,
22b et sois attentif à ta fin	22b but pay attention to your end.
33:1 Celui qui craint YYY ne rencontre pas le mal, mais s'il retourne dans l'épreuve, alors il sera sauvé.	33:1 The one who fears YYY will not meet evil, for if they are again put to the test, then they will be saved.
24 Celui qui veille sur la loi, veille sur lui-même, et celui qui fait confiance en YYY ne sera pas déçu.	24 The one who observes Torah guards themself, and the one who trusts in YYY will not be disappointed.

Chapter 33

2 BE	²¹לא יחכם שונא תורה·	ומתמוטט כמסערה אזנו[	:
4 E	²²הכין אומר ואחר תעשה·	ובית מנוח ואחר תגיה	:
5 E	²³גלגל קל לב נבל·	ואופן חוזר מחשבותיו	:
6 E	²⁴כסוס מוכן אוהב שונא·	תחת כל אוהב יצהל	:
7 E	²⁵מה על יום כי כלו·	אור שונה על שמש	:
8 E	²⁶אבל בחכמת ייי נשפטו·	ויש מהם מוע[ד[	

B · איש נבון יבין דבר ותורתו כאור[י]ן ישרה: + 33:3 · (πλοῖον) B G ? אני E F | אזנו Bmg · כמסער F B E | כמסערה 33:2

33:4   הכין — This is a plene spelling of הָכֵן.

Chapitre 33

2 Il n'est pas sage celui qui hait la loi,
mais son oreille est secouée comme une tempête.

4 Prépare une parole et ensuite tu agiras
et (prépare) une maison de repos, et après tu illumineras.

5 Le cœur du fou est une roue rapide
et ses pensées, un disque tournoyant.

6 Un ami haineux est comme un cheval équipé,
il hennira/se réjouira à la place de quelque ami.

7 Qu'en est-il de chaque jour ? Car (tous) s'achèvent,
la lumière change à cause du soleil.

8 Cependant, par la sagesse de YYY, ils ont été jugés
et il y a parmi eux (des jours) de fête.

Chapitre 33

2 One who hates the law is not wise,
and their ear is tossed about as from a storm.

4 Prepare your speech and afterward you should act,
and (prepare) a place of rest and afterward you will shine.

5 The mind of a fool is a fast-spinning wheel,
their thoughts are a rotating disk.

6 A hateful friend is like a saddled horse,
under any friend they neigh / rejoice.

7 What comes of every day? For, they (all) end,
light changing due to the sun.

8 But, in the wisdom of YYY they are judged,
and there are among them festival da[ys].

PARAPHRASE OF BEN SIRA

T-S AS 133.74

T-S AS 133.74, recto

1 ^{1}רַגְלֵהֶם חַדְרֵי מָוֶת יוֹרְדוֹת   וְאֶל שְׁאוֹל תַּחְתִּית
   ^{2}מוֹרִידוֹת:
2 ^{3}כָּל רוֹאָם יָרִיחוּ בְעֶשְׁנָם   וְכָל רוֹאָם
   ^{4}יִלְבְּטוּ בְאוֹנָם:
3 ^{5}כִּי הֵם בְּכוּר הַבַּרְזֶל יוֹקַד [וְכָ]ל [רוֹאָ]ם
   ^{6}וּפָחִים שׁוֹקֵד:
4 ^{7}הַמַּקְרִיב עֲלֵהֶם יְכַוֶּה בְגַחֲלֵי[ם]
   ^{8}וְיִשָּׂרֵף בְּלֶהָב נִצוֹצֵי שַׁלְהֶ[בֵ]ם:
5 ^{9}הַרְחֵק מֵעֲלֵהֶם [
   ^{10}יִיקַר מְקוֹמְךָ וְאֶ[   ]
   ^{11}וְתַשְׁקִיט נַפְשֶׁךָ [   ]
6 ^{12}כִּי אַתָּה בֶן דֵּעָ[ה   ]
   ^{13}תִּשְׁכַּב בַּהֲנָחָה [   ]
7 ^{14}נַפְשֶׁךָ בּוֹשָׁה [   ]
   ^{15}יִרְכֵי שׁ[   ]
8 ^{16}ה[   ]

T-S AS 133.74, verso

9   ^{1}הֲרוֹג הַנֶּפֶשׁ הָרָעָה תַּנִּיחֶנָּה
    ^{2}וְיִנָּפְשׁוּ הַנְּפָשׁוֹת אֲשֶׁר הִיא תְעַנֶּנָּה:
10 ^{3}כִּי הַנְּפָשׁוֹת הָרָעוֹת נִשְׂנָאוֹת
    ^{4}וְאִם הֵם כִּנְחָשִׁים מַשִּׂיאוֹת:
11 ^{5}[   ][הַ]רְחֵק מֵרָע וְאַל יְהִי לָךְ רֵעַ:
    ^{6}[   ] וּ תִּנָּכֵר וְתִוָּדֵיעַ:
12 ^{7}[   ]נוּ וְאַל יְהִי לָךְ עֲמִית
    ^{8}[   ]לוֹ הֲרוֹג וְהָמִית
13 ^{9}[   ]בְּמַלְכּוּדָתוֹ וְתִלָּקַח
    ^{10}[vacat
14 ^{11}[   ]אִישׁ וְיְכַחֵשׁ
    ^{12}[vacat
15 ^{13}[   ]בַּמְּרֵעִים
    ^{14}[רְ]שָׁעִים:
16 ^{15}[   ]קְ בָּאֵשָׁם יְלַהֲבוּךָ
    ^{16}[   ]○ בִּישָׁעוֹתָם יַצִּיבוּךָ:
17 ^{17}[   ]לֹ○רִיתָם
    ^{18}[   ]:

L. 5 [3] [וְכָ]ל [רוֹאָ]ם — The reconstruction is based on the phrase from the preceding lines.

L. 3 [10] הַנְּפָשׁוֹת — The *patakh* appears to be two dots that are smeared horizontally.

L. 5 [11] [הַ]רְחֵק — After the hole, only the lower dot of the *shewa* is found; the *resh* is not attested at all.

L. 16 [16] יַצִּיבוּךָ — The word is placed above and to the left of the preceding word.

---

1 The first stich combines language from Prov 5:5 (רַגְלֶיהָ יוֹרְדוֹת מָוֶת) and Prov 7:27 (חַדְרֵי־מָוֶת). The second stich seems to restate the same idea with different words (cf. שְׁאוֹל תַּחְתִּית in Deut 32:22).

3 בְּכוּר הַבַּרְזֶל יוֹקַד — The expression is similar to the description of Elijah's words as כְּתַנּוּר בּוֹעֵר in Sir 48:1, though here, of course, it is not Elijah's words but rather the wicked who are in the furnace.

5 וְתַשְׁקִיט נַפְשֶׁךָ — The sense of the phrase seems to be echoed in the following manuscript of the paraphrase, Frankfurt 177, recto, line 3.

9 The first stich includes language reminiscent of Sir 12:3 in H^A (אין טובה למנוח רשע), if one presupposes למנוח should be connected with the root נוח "to rest." The verse also recalls the language of Sir 22:11^c: [אַל] [Do not] weep over the dead, for they are at rest." הֲרוֹג — The infinitive construct presumably refers to execution or other legal forms of killing. Note the idiom הרג נפש in Num 31:19. תַּנִּיחֶנָּה — In Biblical Hebrew, the *patakh* beneath the verbal prefix presupposes the figurative senses "to set down, let lie, leave, abandon, allow." In Rabbinic Hebrew the verb occurs in the context of burial. The 3fs pronominal suffix takes as antecedent נפש "soul." תְעַנֶּנָּה — The verb is assumed to be the *piel* of ענה "to humble, afflict" with a paragogic *nun* + 3fs pronoun, the antecedent being הַנְּפָשׁוֹת. Formally, the

T-S AS 133.74

1 ¹Leurs pieds descendent aux chambres de la mort
et vers le Shéol, en bas, ²ils (les) font descendre.
2 ³Tous ceux qui les voient sentent leur fumée
et tous ceux qui les voient ⁴sont perdus par leur injustice.
3 ⁵Car ils sont dans un creuset de fer brûlant,
[et tou]s les [voient] ⁶et remarquent les pièges.
4 ⁷Celui qui s'approche d'eux est brûlé par de[s]charbons,
⁸et il est brûlé par la flamme d'étincelles de feu.
5 ⁹Tiens-toi loin d'eux [...] ¹⁰ta place sera estimée
et [...] ¹¹et tu apaiseras ton âme.
6 ¹²Car tu es un enfant de la connaissance [...].
[...] ¹³tu te coucheras dans le repos.
7 ¹⁴Ton âme [...]
[...] ¹⁵les côtés de [...]
8 ¹⁶[...]
9 ¹La mise à mort d'une personne mauvaise, laisse-la tranquille,
²et les personnes qui ont été affligées seront réconfortées.
10 ³Car les personnes mauvaises sont détestées,
⁴et, en effet, elles sont comme des serpents trompeurs.
11 ⁵[é]loigne-toi du mal et qu'il ne soit pas pour toi un compagnon,
⁶[   ] tu seras reconnu et tu te feras connaître.
12 ⁷[   ] et qu'il ne soit pas pour toi un compagnon,
⁸[   ] tuer et mettre à mort.
13 ⁹[   ] dans son piège et tu seras pris.
¹⁰[   ] vacat.
14 ¹¹[   ] une personne et il sera faible
¹²[   ] vacat.
15 ¹³[   ] parmi ceux qui font le mal
¹⁴[m]échants.
16 ¹⁵[   ] dans leur feu ils t'enflammeront
¹⁶[   ] par leur délivrance, ils te feront tenir.
17 ¹⁷[   ]
¹⁸[   ]

T-S AS 133.74

1 ¹Their feet descend to the chambers of death,
and to Sheol, below, ²they bring (them) down.
2 ³Each who sees them smells their burning stench,
and each who sees them (sees that) ⁴they are captured in their wickedness.
3 ⁵For, they are in a burning iron-smelter,
and each sees them ⁶and notices the traps.
4 ⁷The one who approaches them is burned by coals,
⁸and is scorched in the blaze of flaming sparks.
5 ⁹Keep far from them [...] ¹⁰your place will be honored,
and [...] ¹¹and you will make your soul at ease.
6 ¹²For you are the child of know[ledge ..]
[...]¹³you will dwell in rest.
7 ¹⁴Your soul [...]
[...] ¹⁵sides of [...]
8 ¹⁶[...]
9 ¹As for the killing of an evil person, you should leave it alone,
²the people whom (the evil person) afflicted are refreshed.
10 ³For, wicked souls are hated,
⁴indeed, they are like deceiving snakes.
11 ⁵Keep far from the wicked and let them not be your friend,
⁶[   ] you will be recognized and well-known.
12 ⁷[   ] and let it not be your companion,
⁸[   ] killing and putting to death.
13 ⁹[   ] in his trap, and you will be taken,
¹⁰[   ] vacat.
14 ¹¹[   ] a person, and he will be weak
¹²[   ] vacat.
15 ¹³[   ] among those doing evil,
¹⁴[w]icked.
16 ¹⁵[   ] in their fire they will burn you
¹⁶[   ] through their deliverance they will make you stand.
17 ¹⁷[   ]
¹⁸[   ]

---

verb could also be a 3fp imperfect, though this would leave הִיא unexplained.

10   The sentiment that the wicked are hated is expressed in Sir 12:6ᴬ, though in a different way (אֵל שׂוֹנֵא רָעִים "God hates the wicked"). The association between deception (נשׁא) and snakes (נָחָשׁ) recalls Gen 3:13, though an association between deceptive enemies and snakes is also drawn in the analogy of Sir 12:13–14, reflected clearly in the Greek and Syriac, but only partially in Hᴬ. Significantly, both Hᴬ and Syriac indicate that such association will lead to being burned by fire (see v. 16 below).

11   [הַ]רְחֵק מֵרָע — The expression is similar to הרחק מעון in Sir 7:2ᴬ (cf. רחק מעון Hᶜ]) and even closer to the Syriac ܐܘܚܩ ܡܢ ܒܝܫܐ. Cf. also Sir 6:13ᴬᶜ. Ben Sira plays on the words for "evil" and "friend" in at least two places: Sir 10:6 (אל תשלם רע לריע) and 12:9 (וברעתו גם ריע בודד).

16   יְלַהֲבוּךָ — The verb appears first in the *hiphil* in texts from the era of 500–700 CE (see Maagarim). בִּישְׁעוּתָם — We assume that the dot in the *vav* should really go above and that this is simply the plural form of the *noun*.

ENA 3053.3

ENA 3053.3, recto (listed as verso)

1 ^{1}הוֹצָאַת סוֹד חֶרְפָּה גְדוֹלָה
   וּמַכַּת סֵתֶר ^{2}[ת]בִיא קְלָלָה :
2 ^{3}לִפְנֵי אֵשׁ תִּימְרוֹת עָשָׁן
   וְלִפְנֵי שְׁפָךְ דָּם ^{4}צָרָה תֶעְשַׁן :
3 ^{5}מַסְתִּיר סוֹדוֹ לֹא יֵ{א}יֵבוֹשׁ
   וּמַטְמִין דִּבָּה ^{6}רֵעָתוֹ יְכַבּוֹשׁ :
4 ^{7}אִם גָּלָה לְךָ רֵעֲךָ סוֹדוֹ אַל תְּגַלֵּהוּ
   ^{8}פֶּן תְּהִי כִנְבָל בְּהוֹצִיאוֹ וְיִזָּהֵר מִמְּךָ שׁוֹמְעֵהוּ :
5 ^{9}שִׂים עַל פִּיךָ מִשְׁמָר
   וְעַל שְׂפָתֶךָ ^{10}חוֹתָם נִגְמָר :
6 ^{11}לְמַעַן לֹא תִּדָּמֶה בִמְגַלִּים סוֹדוֹת
   ^{12}וְלֹא תִתֵּן לְנִבְלוּת אֶךָ אוֹדוֹת :
7 ^{13}תַּשְׁחִית נַפְשְׁךָ בְּגִילוּי סוֹדֶךָ
   ^{14}וְרֵעֲךָ אֲשֶׁר הֶאֱמִינְךָ וְהָבֵא עָדֶךָ

ENA 3053.3, verso (listed as recto)

8 ^{1}אֱמוֹ{ל}ר לְיוֹצֶרְךָ אֵל אָבִי וֵאדוֹן חַיָּי
   ^{2}אַל תַּפִּילֵנִי בַעֲצָתִי וּמְאַוָּיַי
9 ^{3}רְדֵנִי עַל יִצְרִי
   וְהַצִּילֵנִי מִמְּגוּר[י]
10 ^{4}וּמְחֹל עַל חֲטָאַי
   כִּי אַתָּה בּוֹרְאִי
11 ^{5}לְמַעַן לֹא יִרְבֶּה פִּשְׁעִי
   וְלֹא יוֹסִיף רֶשַׁע[י]
12 ^{6}אַל תְּשַׂמַּח עָלַי אוֹיְבִי
   וְאַל יְנַחֲמוּנִי רֵעַי וּקְרוֹבַי :
13 ^{7}גֹּבַהּ עֵינַיִם אַל תִּתְּנֵנִי
   וְלֵב פַּחַז הַרְחֵק מִמֶּנִּי :
14 ^{8}נֶפֶשׁ עַזָּה אַל תִּמְשֹׁל בִּי
   וְטַהֵר ^{9}רַעְיוֹן לְבָבִי וְקִרְבִּי :

L. 1 [1] הוֹצָאַת — The right corner of the manuscript is torn and only the left half of the *he* is preserved. The *patakh* under the *aleph* was first a *qamets*, but the dot beneath the line has been cancelled with a diagonal stroke.

L. 3 [2] תִּימְרוֹת — There is an unusual dot above the first *tav*. דָּם — The word is written above שְׁפָךְ. The *mem* appears to have been written in its initial/medial form and then changed to its final form as a correction.

L. 5 [3] יֵ{א}יֵבוֹשׁ — The scribe first wrote an *aleph* and then cancelled it with a stroke. The *sere* appears under the *aleph*, though presumably it belongs under the *yod*.

L. 6 [3] רֵעָתוֹ — Under the *qamets* is an unidentified diagonal line. The *qamets* that should go under the *ayin* is missing due to a tear.

L. 7 [4] אִם — To the right of the *aleph* are unidentified marks.

L. 11 [6] תִּדָּמֶה — We assume a *niphal* verb. A *segol* appears under the *dalet* where we might expect a *qamets*. The *he* seems to have been written first as a *tav* with a *raphe* symbol above it.

L. 12 [6] נְבֹלוֹת — The first vowel appears to be a *hireq*, though we might expect a *patakh*.

L. 13 [7] בְּגִילוּי — A horizontal bar appears above the last letter, likely to indicate it is not a *mater*. סוֹדֶךָ — A mark follows the word to fill out the rest of the line.

L. 1–2 [8] חַיָּי and וּמְאַוָּיַי — The last vowel of each was first written as *segol* and then the bottom dot was cancelled with a diagonal line.

L. 5 [11] רֶשַׁע[י] — The word sits above the verb יוֹסִיף and is not vocalized, though presumably it would have the same vowels as פִּשְׁעַי.

L. 6 [12] וּקְרוֹבַי — The word sits above רֵעַי and is difficult to read due to crumpling of the paper.

L. 7 [13] מִמֶּנִּי — The initial *mem* is smudged. The other letters are difficult to read due to the crumpled paper.

1 The verse corresponds to Sir 22:22c–d in the Syriac and is similar to Sir 27:16 (in both Greek and Syriac); see too the extra verse following Sir 31:2^B.

2 The verse corresponds to Sir 22:24.

3 The vocabulary reflects that of Sir 22:25, though the expression here is not exactly the same as that reflected in the versions. יְכַבּוֹשׁ — The word ("he will conquer") can also have the sense "to forgive" with the object עון (see Jastrow 1903, 610) as well as "to hide."

4 The verse corresponds to the Syriac of Sir 22:26; the Greek reflects a different sense for the first stich.

5 The verse corresponds to Sir 22:27a–b.

6 The verse corresponds to Sir 22:27c–d. תִּדָּמֶה — For the idiom of דמה "to be like" in the *niphal* with a *bet* preposition, see note to Sir 13:8^A. אוֹדוֹת — The exact sense of the word is unclear. Maagarim identifies it in general terms "a matter, thing, word," though the word has a masculine form where it occurs in medieval texts (once expressed

ENA 3053.3

1. Dévoiler un secret est une grande honte
   et une blessure (faite) secrètement apporte le déshonneur.
2. Devant un feu, des colonnes de fumée
   et devant le sang versé, l'angoisse fume.
3. Celui qui cache son secret ne sera pas honteux,
   celui qui cache un ragot vaincra sa propre méchanceté.
4. Si ton prochain te révèle son secret, ne le révèle pas,
   de peur que tu ne deviennes comme un insensé en le divulguant et que ceux qui l'entendent soient avertis à ton sujet.
5. Place sur ta bouche une sentinelle
   et, sur tes lèvres, un sceau complet.
6. Ainsi, tu ne ressembleras pas à ceux qui révèlent des secrets
   et tu ne laisseras pas place aux infamies contre toi.
7. Tu te détruis toi-même par la révélation de ton secret,
   ainsi (que) ton prochain qui t'a fait confiance et qui est venu à toi.
8. Parle à ton créateur: « Dieu, mon père et Seigneur de ma vie,
   ne me laisse pas tomber par mon conseil et mes désirs.
9. Gouverne-moi à propos de mon inclination,
   sauve-moi de [ma] peur.
10. Pardonne mon péché,
    car tu es mon créateur.
11. Afin que mon péché ne se multiplie pas
    et que [mon] impiété ne s'accroisse pas.
12. Que mon ennemi ne se réjouisse pas à mon sujet
    et que mon prochain et mon compagnon ne me rejettent pas.
13. Ne me donne pas des yeux hautains
    et éloigne de moi un cœur insolent.
14. Ne laisse pas un appétit vorace me gouverner
    et purifie les préoccupations de mon cœur et mes entrailles.

ENA 3053.3

1. ¹Exposing a secret (brings) great shame,
   a wound (made) through deceit brings dishonor
2. ³Before a fire (there are) whisps of smoke,
   and before the spilling of blood anguish smolders.
3. ⁵One who hides their secret will not be embarrassed,
   one who secrets a dispute will conquer their (own) wickedness.
4. ⁷If your friend reveals their secret to you, do not reveal it,
   ⁸lest you become like a fool when (you) expose it so that those who hear it will be wary of you.
5. ⁹Set a guard over your mouth,
   over your lips a total seal!
6. ¹¹So you will not seem like one who reveals secrets,
   ¹²(so) you will not give a reason for obscenities (being expressed) against you.
7. ¹³And you destroy yourself with the revelation of your secret,
   ¹⁴as well as your friend who trusted you and who came to you.
8. ¹Say to your creator: "God, my father, and master of my life,
   ²do not make me fall by my counsel and my desire.
9. Chastise me over my inclination,
   rescue me from [my] fear.
10. ⁴Pardon my sin,
    for you are my creator.
11. ⁵So that my transgression does not multiply,
    and [my] wickedness does not increase.
12. ⁶Do not cause my enemy to rejoice over me,
    and do not let my friends and relatives reject me.
13. ⁷Do not give me haughty eyes,
    keep a reckless mind far from me.
14. ⁸Do not let a voracious appetite rule me,
    and purify ⁹my mind's thoughts and my emotions.

---

together with שאלה "request"). In this verse, it seems most likely to be the nominal use of the lexeme that appears with the preposition על in the Bible with the force "because" (Gen 21:11, 25, etc.). Here, it seems to have the sense "a cause, a reason" (cf. Fleischer 1990, 267). Together with וְלֹא תִתֵן, the sense is more literally "do not give a reason." Note, on the other hand, Kena'ani (1960, sub אודה) lists the feminine word with the gloss "a song of praise."

8   The verse corresponds to Sir 23:1 in the Greek or to 23:4 in the Syriac.

9   The verse corresponds to Sir 23:2a–b, though it is very different from the versions. רְדֵנִי — The expression seems to have the sense "chastise me" or "punish me," though more literally perhaps it would be rendered "rule me!" It seems like a combination of expressions like הרודה את יצרו "the one ruling his inclination" (b. Meg. 15b [Maagarim] and cf. b. Sot. 12b) and מלוך על יצרך "rule over your inclination" (Deut. Rab. 33 ואתחנן). Typically, the construction על with יֵצֶר is used with some form of התגבר "to make oneself master (over)" (e.g., b. San. 111b).

10 The verse corresponds to Sir 23:2c–d. Here it follows the Syriac, not the Greek.

11 The verse corresponds to Sir 23:3a–b.

12 The first stich corresponds to Sir 23:3c–d.

13 The verse corresponds to Sir 23:4c–5a.

14 The first stich corresponds to Sir 23:6b; the other does not correspond to any specific verse in Ben Sira.

$$
\begin{array}{rl}
15 & \text{10}\text{פַּחַז יֵצֶר אַל יַחְפִּיזוּנִי} \\
& \text{וּמְלִיצֵי רָע אַל יְלִיצוּנִי :} \\
16 & \text{12}\text{בִּשְׂפָתַי אַל תַּפִּילֵנִי} \\
& \text{וְלִשׁוֹנִי אַל יִלְכְּדֵנִי :} \\
17 & \text{13}\text{לִשְׁבוּעָה אַל תְּאַלְּפֵנִי} \\
& \text{וְלִפְנֵי שׁוֹפְטִים }\text{14}\text{אַל תּוֹשִׁיבֵנִי :} \\
18 & \text{15}\text{מוסר}
\end{array}
$$

Frankfurt 177

Frankfurt 177, recto

$$
\begin{array}{rl}
1 & \text{1}\text{אִם תִּיקַר נַפְשׁוֹת בְּעֵ[י]נֶ}\text{ךָ} \\
& \text{2}\text{תִּיקַר נַפְשְׁךָ לְמוּל אֲדוֹנֶךָ :} \\
2 & \text{3}\text{וִיהִי לִבְּךָ שַׁאֲנָן} \\
& \text{וְקִרְבְּךָ וּמֵעֲךָ תּוּחְנָן} \\
3 & \text{4}\text{כִּי רְצִי}\{\text{ה}\}\text{תָ בְּמַתַּת יָדוֹ} \\
& \text{5}\text{וּבָטַחְתָּ עַל כְּבוֹדוֹ וְהוֹדוֹ} \\
4 & \text{6}\text{אָבֶן אֱלֹהִים עֶזְרֶךָ} \\
& \text{וְעַל עֲשִׁירִים וְשָׂרִים הַדְרֶךָ :} \\
5 & \text{7}\text{יֵשׁ עָשִׁיר אוֹצְרוֹתָיו מְלֵאִים} \\
& \text{8}\text{כְּרֶגַע יְסוּפוּ בַּעֲבָדִים וּנְשִׂיאִים :} \\
6 & \text{9}\text{ooooכְּלָיו רֵקִים} \\
& \text{וְעוֹשֵׂה דָּתוֹת וְחוּקִים :} \\
7 & \text{10}\text{זֶה יֶעְדַּר לוֹ סִפְקוֹ} \\
& \text{וְזֶה שָׂמֵחַ בְּחֶלְקוֹ :} \\
8 & \text{11}\text{זֶה בְּיָדַיִם חוֹתָה} \\
& \text{וְזֶה אוֹכֵל : וְשׁוֹתֶה :} \\
9 & \text{12}\text{זֶה טוֹב לֵב וְחוֹדֶה} \\
& \text{וְזֶה זְמָנוֹ }\text{13}\text{עָלָיו רוֹדֶה :} \\
10 & \text{14}\text{זֶה יוֹלִיד בָּנִים וּבָנוֹת} \\
& \text{15}\text{וְזֶה דָּתוֹתָיו מִכָּל עַם שׁוֹנוֹת :} \\
11 & \text{16}\text{זֶה [ ] ◦ב בְּכָל אוֹנוֹת} \\
& \text{17}\text{וְזֶה א◦[ ] טוֹבוֹת וַחֲנִינוֹת :}
\end{array}
$$

L. 10 [15] פחז — The word would be vocalized פַּחַז or פֶּחֶז "recklessness." יַחְפִּיזוּנִי — Fleischer represents this as a mistake for יַפְחִיזוּנִי "make me wreckless" (based on the Syriac version of Sir 23:6: ܢܦܚܙܢ [cf. Schirmann 1965, 438]).

L. 12 [16] בִּשְׂפָתַי — The *sin* seems to be on a small piece of paper that has slipped from its original position, so that the *sin* looks like it sits beneath the base line of the other letters.

L. 15 [18] מוסר — The word is placed on the lower left side of the page, indicating that the next proverb (on the following page) begins with this word. In addition, the *resh* was written twice, one *resh* on top of the other.

L. 1 [1] נַפְשׁוֹת — The vowel beneath the *pe* seems to be a *shewa* that was been corrected to a *qamets*. בְּעֵ[י]נֶךָ — Only the vowel beneath the *nun* and the tail of the *kaph* are visible; the rest of the letters are in the hole.

L. 4 [3] רְצִי{ה}תָ — The word seems to have been written רצה before being corrected with a *yod* and the *he* being changed to *tav*.

L. 9 [6] וְחוּקִים — The word is written above and to the left of דָּתוֹת.

L. 10 [7] יֶעְדַּר — The reading is very conjectural, but makes sense of the remaining traces. If this is correct, then the right arm and base of the *ayin* are visible, as well as the bottom of the *dalet*'s vertical line. The *patakh*, however, is clear. Only traces of the upper horizontal lines of the *dalet* and *resh* are preserved.

L. 11 [8] בְּיָדַיִם — The reading follows Fleischer 1990, 280. וְאוֹכֵל : וְשׁוֹתֶה — The scribe wrote the *soph pasuq* prematurely and then wrote וְשׁוֹתֶה above and to the left of וְאוֹכֵל.

L. 14 [10] יוֹלִיד — The reading follows Fleischer's (1990, 280) reconstruction and makes sense of the remaining traces.

L. 17 [11] וְזֶה — The reading follows Fleischer 1990, 281.

15 The first stich corresponds to Sir 23:6a; the other does not correspond to any specific verse in Ben Sira. פחז יצר — More literally this would be "recklessness of inclination." Given the plural verb form that follows, Fleischer (1990, 268) suggests haplography פחזי יצר, though the plural form is not otherwise attested in Hebrew (see Maagarim).

16 The verse corresponds loosely to Sir 23:8, though it is not exact.

17 The verse corresponds to Sir 23:9, the second stich reflecting the Syriac translation but not the Greek.

18 מוסר — This is the catch word for the following page. Perhaps it corresponds to Sir 23:7 (see Fleischer 1990, 268).

15 ¹⁰Qu'une inclination arrogante ne m'anime pas
et que les mauvais moqueurs ¹¹ne se moquent pas de moi.
16 ¹²Ne me laisse pas chuter par mes lèvres
et que ma langue ne me piège pas.
17 ¹³Ne m'apprends pas à jurer
¹⁴et devant des juges ne me laisse pas siéger.
18 ¹⁵Instruction

Frankfurt 177

1 ¹Si les âmes sont précieuses à tes yeux,
²(alors) ton âme est précieuse devant ton seigneur
2 ³et ton cœur sera imperturbable
et tes entrailles et tes viscères seront graciés.
3 ⁴Car tu as plaisir au don de sa main,
⁵et tu tu as confiance en sa gloire et sa splendeur.
4 ⁶Ainsi, Dieu est ton secours
et il t'honore plus que les riches et les princes.
5 ⁷Il y a (une personne) riche dont les trésors sont pleins,
⁸mais en l'espace d'un instant, ils disparaissent dans les nuages et la brume.
6 ⁹[ ] ses jarres sont vides
et celui qui fait les règles et les statuts.
7 ¹⁰Celui-ci sera dépouillé de son abondance
et celui-là se réjouit de sa part.
8 ¹¹Celui-ci creuse avec ses mains
et celui-là mange et boit.
9 ¹²Celui-ci a le cœur content et se réjouit,
celui-là, son temps domine sur lui.
10 ¹⁴Celui-ci engendre des fils et des filles,
¹⁵celui-là ses règles diffèrent de tous les peuples.
11 ¹⁶Celui-ci [ ] par tous les deuils,
¹⁷celui-là [ ] faveurs et grâces.

15 ¹⁰Do not let reckless inclination(s) provoke me,
or let wicked scoffers ¹¹scorn me.
16 ¹²Do not make me fall by my (own) lips,
do not let my tongue trap me.
17 ¹³Do not teach me to swear,
¹⁴do not cause me to sit before rulers."
18 ¹⁵Instruction

Frankfurt 177

1 ¹If souls are precious in your eyes,
²(then) your soul is precious before your Lord,
2 ³then your heart will be at ease,
and your midst and inner being will be graced.
3 ⁴For you are pleased with the gift of his hand,
⁵and you trust in his glory and honor.
4 ⁶Thus, God is your help,
and he honors you more than the rich and princes.
5 ⁷There is a rich person whose treasuries are filled
⁸but in an instant they come to an end in cloud and mists.
6 ⁹[ ] his vessels are empty
and the one who made laws and statutes.
7 ¹⁰This one will lack sustenance,
while this one rejoices in their portion.
8 ¹¹This one scrapes embers with their hands,
while this one, they eat and drink.
9 ¹²This one is cheerful, as one rejoicing
while this one, their festival ¹³dominates themself.
10 ¹⁴This one engenders sons and daughters,
¹⁵while this one, their customs are different from all people.
11 ¹⁶This one [ ] with all mourning,
¹⁷while this one [ ] favors and mercies.

---

1 תִּיקַר — The verb in the first and second stichs is clearly a *qal*, not a *piel* as reflected in Fleischer (1990, 279). We assume in the first stich it takes "souls" as subject, despite the disagreement in number. The theme reflected in this verse (i.e., care for others), then, is similar to that in, e.g., Sir 4:4–5, 8–10, 31; 7:33. That one will be rewarded in kind is reflected in various places, e.g., Sir 3:31 and 4:10. נַפְשׁוֹת בְּעֵי[נֶ]ךָ — The initial vocalization נַפְשׁוֹת presupposes that the word is in construct with the prepositional phrase and would more literally be translated "souls which are in your eyes." לְמוּל — The compound prepositional phrase appears in *piyyutim* and seems to appear once in Late Biblical Hebrew, in the form לְמוּאל (Neh 12:38), though elsewhere in Biblical Hebrew one finds אֶל־מוּל (e.g., 2 Sam 11:15). אֲדוֹנֶךָ — The reference is likely God, as presupposed by the reference to God in verse 4.

2 For the first stich, notice the similar expression in T-S AS 133.74 recto, line 9. וּמֵעֲךָ — We would expect instead a *segol* beneath the *ayin*. תֻּחְנָן — Although the *hophal* of חנן is found in Sir 4:13; 12:13, the form with two *nuns* is not found in texts until the *piyyut* (see Maagarim).

4 The idea that the glory of the pious is superior to that of the wealthy and powerful is found in different places in Ben Sira (e.g., Sir 40:26–27), but perhaps most prominently in the prelude to the Praise of the Ancestors (Sir 44:1–15).

5 The idea of wealth suddenly vanishing is reflected in, e.g., Sir 11:21.

7 The contrasting of the fortunate with the unfortunate is found in Sir 33:7–15. זֶה יֶעְדָּר לוֹ סִפְקוֹ — Literally, this is "this one will lack for himself his sufficiency."

9 זְמַנּוֹ — The word can mean both "time" and more specifically "a festive season" (see Jastrow 1903, 404).

Frankfurt 177, verso

12 ¹זֶ֥ה נוֹדַע בַּאֲנָשָׁיו וּקְהָלוֹ
וְזֶה בָּאוֹשׁ ²וְנִלְכַּד בַּעֲמָלוֹ :
13 ³זֶה הוֹלֵךְ בְּתוּמּוֹ
וְזֶה בְגַאֲוָתוֹ וְרוּמוֹ :
14 ⁴זֶה נוֹתֵן וְלוֹקֵיחַ
וְזֶה כֹהֵלֶךְ וְאוֹרֵיחַ :
15 ⁵זֶה נוֹתֵן וְלֹא יֶחְסַר
וְזֶה חוֹשֵׂךְ וּמְחוּסָר :
16 ⁶לֹא יִפָּתֵר זֶה הָעִנְיָן
וְלֹא יִתָּכֵן לוֹ ⁷ מִסְפָּר וּמִנְיָן
17 כִּי לֵאלֹהִים לְבַדּוֹ
⁸כִּי אֶפֶס אֵן עָדוֹ :
18 ⁹רָאִיתִי אֶחָד מַטְרִיף נַפְשׁוֹ
וּבְפֶתַע יוֹדַע רֻשׁוֹ :
19 ¹⁰וְאַחַר יוֹסִיף כְּמֵתָתוֹ
וּבְרִכַּת יְיָ ¹¹תָּנוּחַ אִתּוֹ :
20 ¹²וְהוּא שָׂמֵחַ כְּאָ°ר°ס°וֹתוֹ בַאֲרוּחָתוֹ
וּלְבָבוֹ חוֹדֶה ¹³בְנַשָּׁהשְׁגָתוֹ :
21 ¹⁴וְהוּא יוֹתֵר מֵעֲשִׁירִים
וְנִשָּׂא עַל מְלָכִים וְשָׂרִים :
22 ¹⁵וּגְבִיר עַל גְּבִירִים
וְגִבּוֹר בְּגִבְרִים :
23 ¹⁶וְחָכָם עִם חֲכָמִים
וּמֵאִיר לְעֵנֵי כָל עַמִּים
24 ¹⁷אֵן בּוֹ עַצְלוּת
וְלֹא [ ] שְׁפָלוּת
°נִי

L. 1 [12] זֶ֥ה — Only the vowel beneath the *zayin* and what appears to be the tip of the bottom left leg of the *he* are preserved. בָּאוֹשׁ — The word is written above זֶה. Only the vowel beneath the *bet* is preserved.

L. 5 [15] וּמְחוּסָר — The word is written above and to the left of חוֹשֵׂךְ.

L. 8 [17] עָדוֹ — Fleischer (1990, 281) reads גֵדוֹ, though this is not possible. The initial letter is clearly *ayin*; there is no *raphe* symbol above the second vertical mark, which we would expect, and the base line is flat, unlike that of a *gimel*.

L. 10 [19] כְּמֵתָתוֹ — Fleischer reads בְּמֵתָתוֹ, but an initial *kaph* makes more sense.

L. 12 [20] כְּאָ°ר°ס°וֹתוֹ בַאֲחוֹרָתוֹ — The scribe initially spelled the word on the line, but recognizing some error, seems to have erased it and then spelled it again above the misspelling.

L. 13 [20] בְנַשָּׁהשְׁגָתוֹ — The letters at the beginning of the word are difficult to read. The *shin* is particularly difficult to see. The scribe recognized a mistake and then seems to have crossed out the *nun* and *shin* (perhaps also erasing the *shin*) before writing a cramped *he* and the rest of the letters.

L. 14 [21] עַל מְלָכִים וְשָׂרִים — The word מְלָכִים is written above עַל and וְשָׂרִים is written above מְלָכִים.

L. 16 [23] וּמֵאִיר — The initial letters are difficult to decipher; the reading follows the reconstruction of Fleischer (1990, 282). עַמִּים — The word is written above and to the left of כָל.

L. 17 [24] °נִי — The letters appear beneath the lacuna as perhaps a correction to a word lost in the lacuna.

12 ¹Celui-ci est connu de ses hommes et de sa communauté,
   celui-là pue ²et est piégé par son labeur.
13 ³Celui-ci marche dans sa perfection,
   celui-là (marche) dans son orgueil et son mépris.
14 ⁴Celui-ci donne et prend,
   celui-là est comme un voyageur qui est sur la route.
15 ⁵Celui-ci donne et ne manque de rien,
   celui-là est pingre et est dans la nécessité.
16 ⁶Ceci est l'affaire qui ne peut pas être expliquée
   et ⁷aucun chiffre ou nombre ⁶ne peut lui être assigné.
17 ⁷Car Dieu est le seul Dieu,
   ⁸car, finalement, il n'y a rien au-dessus de lui.
18 ⁹J'ai vu une (chose) qui nourrit son être
   et, subitement, sa pauvreté s'est fait connaître.
19 ¹⁰Et une autre qui fait croître par son don
   et la bénédiction de YYY ¹¹repose avec lui.
20 ¹²Et, lui, se félicite de ses vivres
   et son cœur se réjouit ¹³de ses moyens.
21 ¹⁴Il est plus riche que les riches
   et est élevé au-dessus des rois et des princes.
22 ¹⁵Il est le maître au-dessus des maîtres
   et un héros parmi les hommes.
23 ¹⁶Un sage avec les sages
   et celui qui illumine les yeux de tous les peuples.
24 ¹⁷Il n'y a pas de paresse en lui
   et pas [   ] mollesse.

12 ¹This one is well-known among their men and their congregation,
   while this one stinks ²and is captive to their labor.
13 ³This one goes in their integrity,
   while this one (goes) in their pride and self-importance.
14 ⁴This one gives and takes,
   while this one is like a traveler and goes about.
15 ⁵This one gives and does not lack,
   while this one is stingy and (yet) in need.
16 ⁶This (whole) matter cannot be explained,
   and ⁷no number or figure can be assigned to it.
17 But, God is God alone,
   ⁸for, in the end, there is nothing beyond him.
18 ⁹I have seen one who feeds themself
   but suddenly their poverty makes itself known.
19 ¹⁰But, another increases (praise) according to his (i.e., God's) gift,
   and the blessing of the Lord ¹¹stays with them.
20 ¹²And, they rejoice in their food,
   and their heart celebrates ¹³(what) is in their means.
21 ¹⁴He is wealthier than the rich,
   and is lifted higher than kings and princes.
22 ¹⁵He is lord over lords,
   and a hero among men.
23 ¹⁶A sage among sages,
   and one shining light for the eyes of all peoples.
24 ¹⁷There is no indolence in him,
   and not [   ] laziness.

17 אֶפֶס — The word ("end, only") is interpreted in its adverbial sense and translated "in the end." אָן עָדוֹ — We assume the phrase is simply a variation of בלעדי "apart from, except, without," עָדוֹ being the preposition with the 3ms pronominal suffix (though we might have expected עָדָיו as in Isa 45:24). The entire stich echoes the language and sentiment of Isa 45:6.
18 מַטְרִיף נַפְשׁוֹ — The hiphil of טרף means "to feed" in Prov 30:8 and in Rabbinic Hebrew, though in other stems the verb denotes violent actions like tearing apart, disfiguring (in qal, piel) and with the object נפש appears in the qal in Job 18:4 "those who tear themselves to pieces." Given the context here, presumably the image is of one who only looks after themself, but still falls into poverty.
19 This verse and the following use language also found in Sir 35:12. יוֹסִיף בְּמִתָּתוֹ — The object of the verb יסף is ambiguous, though the context suggests the image is of a person who increases their own wealth and power. Note, however, the similarity in syntax to Sir 35:12 (with marginal alternative): תן לו כמתתהו. In Sir 35:12, the sense would appear to be the opposite (i.e., here the person looks after themself and in Sir 35:12, God is the focus of giving). Were we read the initial letter of כְּמִתָּתוֹ as a kaph, then we perhaps should infer that the object of the verb יסף is praise of God: "but, another increases (praise) according to his gift."
20 בארוחתו — The word ארוחה is found frequently in later Hebrew meaning "food, meal." בְּנַשָּׁהִשְׂגָּתוֹ — We assume that this is an inflected form of הַשָּׂגָה "having the necessary means" (Jastrow 1903, 369). The same word appears in Sir 35:12.
24 שִׁפְלוּת — The word can mean both laziness and humility (see Jastrow 1903, 1618).

T-S NS 108.43

T-S NS 108.43, folio 1, recto (left side)

1 ¹אִם [לֹא מַר]אוֹת מֵא֒ נִפְקָדוֹת
²אָ֒ חָשָׁ֒ב בְּמָחוּגָה לַחֲדוֹת :
2 ³רַבִּים תָּעוּ דֶּרֶךְ בַּחֲלוֹמוֹת
⁴וַיִּכָּשְׁלוּ בַהֲלִיכָתָ֒ם עַד מוֹת :
3 ⁵מָקוֹם שֶׁאֵין חֵטְא אֱלֹהִים רוֹצֶה בּוֹ
⁶וּמְקוֹם צִדְקוּת וְיוֹשֶׁר הוּא אֲהֵבוֹ :
4 ⁷חֲכַם פֶּה כְּלִיל לָשׁוֹן
וַחֲכַם לֵב ⁸הוּא רִאשׁוֹן:
5 ⁹רַב מְזִמּוֹת עִם עוֹשֶׁ{ה}ר
יַשִּׂיג כָּל תַּאֲוָ֒ה ¹⁰וְכֹשֶׁר:
6 ¹¹כֹּל אֲשֶׁר דִּבַּרְתִּי בְּנִסּוּי בָּהּ אֵ֒י
¹²וּמֵרֻבִּית שִׂיחִי עָבֹ[ר] עָלַי :
7 ¹³פְּעָמִים רַבּוֹת לַמָּוֶת הִגַּעְתִּי
¹⁴וּבְכָל שׁוֹחָה וּתְהוֹם אֲזַי נָפַלְתִּי :
8 ¹⁵בָּטַחְתִּי עַל אֱלוֹהַּ וְהִצִּילַנִי
וּמִבּוֹר[ ] ¹⁶שִׂיחִים מִלְּטַנִי :

T-S NS 108.43, folio 1, verso, (right side)

¹יַסֹּר יִסְּרַנִי יָהּ וְלַמָּ[וֶת לֹא] נְתָנָנִי [:]
9 ²אֶבֶן עָשָׂה רְצוֹנוֹ
וְהִ{שְׁ}שְׁלִ{שְׁ}{ה}ם חֵפֶץ רֵעֵיוֹנוֹ :
10 ³מַחְרֻב סְתָרַי בְּאֶבְרָתוֹ
וּמִמָּוֶת ⁴וּמִנֶּגַע הֱחֲבִיאַנִי בְּצִלּוֹ וִישׁוּעָתוֹ :

L. 2 [1] חָשָׁ֒ב — The vowel marks under the letters appear at first to be *shewas*. This, however, does not make sense morphologically, even for the system employed in this manuscript. Upon closer inspection, the upper mark under the *tav* seems to be a very short line, perhaps consisting in reality of two dots closely written together. In either case, it seems that the vowel symbol is a *qamets*. For a *qamets* that looks similar, see the first *qamets* of אָכְלָה in T-S NS 108.43, verso, right side, line 11 The opposite problem of a *segol* appearing as a *qamets* is exemplified by וְנֶגַע from T-S NS 108.43, verso, right side, line 13. Under the *shin*, the upper dot seems to be juxtaposed to another dot beside it, the effect of which is to make the two upper marks look like a *segol*, though perhaps here too the intention was to correct an initial *shewa* into a *qamets*. In the context of the verse, a *qamets* seems to make more sense. The *metheg* appears between the vowels but likely should go with the former. בְּמָחוּגָה — The final letter is oddly shaped. It looks like it was initially written as a *resh*, but then the left leg of a *he* was clumsily added as a diagonal line.

L. 4 [2] וַיִּכָּשְׁלוּ — Beside the *qamets* is what appears to be a cantillation mark.

L. 5 [3] בּוֹ — The word is written above רוֹצֶה.

L. 9 [5] עוֹשֶׁ{ה}ר — The word was first written as the participle עשה "one who does." תַּאֲוָ֒ה — The word is written above כָּל and has a *raphe* mark above the *vav* to indicate it is not a *mater*.

L. 12 [6] עָבֹ[ר] — The rightmost edge of the *bet's* base line is visible, as is the *raphe* symbol.

L. 2 וְהִ{שְׁ}שְׁלִ{שְׁ}{ה}ם — The letters are difficult to make sense of due to a hole in the paper that obscures the true nature of the *shin* / *ayin* and the *sin*. Nevertheless, it would appear that the scribe first wrote והעשה "and he caused to do" (*hiphil* of עשה) but then corrected this to וְהִשְׁלִם by making the initial *ayin* into a *shin* (with dot), adding a *lamed*, canceling the *sin* with a diagonal stroke (going from the upper left to the lower right), changing the *he* to a final *mem*, and then finally adding the vowel symbols. That the first letter began as an *ayin* is clear based on how the middle arm intersects with the base line. For *shins*, the middle arm does not intersect with the base line, but instead with the left arm. The reading of *sin* is implied by its left edge. A diacritic dot is visible above the vertical line; this line bends at its bottom to the right and this fits the writing of *sin* / *shin*. The cancellation mark seems to be attested partially in the upper left corner of the letter and more clearly beneath the *lamed*. Finally, the last letter is square, which is unlike how most other final *mems* are written (like circles or triangles). It seems likely, therefore, that this letter began as a *he* and then was corrected to a final *mem*. The confusion between different words is due, in part, to the use of the verb עשה in the preceding stich, and to the biblical and early post-biblical precedents of the verb עשה (Isa 48:14) and שלם (Isa 44:28) taking the object חֵפֶץ, the former verb even with רָצוֹן וחפצי רצונו אשר יעשה (CD III 15). רֵעֵיוֹנוֹ — The word is written above and to the left of חֵפֶץ.

L. 3 [10] וּמִמָּוֶת — Ligatured to the *holem* is what appears to be a *raphe* line above the *vav*; the mark is unexpected here since elsewhere in the manuscript it indicates that the *vav* is not a *mater*. הֱחֲבִיאַנִי — Ligatured to the *nun*, here, the final *yod* looks like a *vav*.

T-S NS 108.43

1 ¹Si [ce ne sont pas des visi]ons envoyées par Dieu,
   ²ne retourne pas dans un cercle pour (leurs) énigmes.
2 ³Nombreux se sont perdus en chemin dans les songes
   ⁴et ont trébuché dans leurs voies jusqu'à la mort.
3 ⁵Dieu désire pour lui-même un lieu où il n'y a pas de péché
   ⁶et, lui, aime un lieu de justice et de droiture.
4 ⁷Sage de bouche et parfait de langue,
   mais le sage de cœur ⁸est premier.
5 ⁹Nombreux sont les stratagèmes avec la richesse,
   on acquiert tout désir ¹⁰et succès.
6 ¹¹Tout ce dont j'ai parlé à propos de l'épreuve, m'est arrivé
   ¹²et l'abondance de mon discours m'a traversé.
7 ¹³De nombreuses fois j'ai approché la mort
   ¹⁴et dans chaque fosse et abîme, de la sorte, je suis tombé.
8 ¹⁵J'ai eu confiance en Dieu et il m'a délivré
   et de la fosse ¹⁶des citernes, il m'a sauvé.
   ¹Yah m'a puni sévèrement, mais il [ne] m'a pas livré à la [mo]rt.
9 ²Certainement, il a fait sa volonté
   et accomplit le désir de sa pensée.
10 ³De la chaleur, il m'a caché avec ses ailes
   et de l'outrage ⁴et de la plaie il m'a recouvert par son ombre et par son salut.

T-S NS 108.43

1 ¹If [(these) are not visi]ons determined by God,
   ²do not return in a circle back to (their) riddles.
2 ³Many have lost the path through dreams
   ⁴and stumbled in their going until (their) death.
3 ⁵God desires a place without sin,
   ⁶a place of justice and uprightness he loves.
4 ⁷(There is) one wise of mouth, one flawless in tongue,
   but the one wise in mind ⁸is first.
5 ⁹Many are the schemes (of those) with wealth,
   (such a person) acquires every desire ¹⁰as well as propriety.
6 ¹¹All which I speak about a trial, comes (back) to me,
   ¹²and the increase in my talk passes against me.
7 ¹³Many times I have approached death,
   ¹⁴and in every pit and depth then I fell.
8 ¹⁵I trusted God and he delivered me,
   and from the pit of ¹⁶ditches he rescued me.
   ¹Yah punished me severely, but to de[ath did not] deliver me.
9 ²But, he does his will
   and fulfills the desire of his thought.
10 ³From the heat, he hid me with his wing,
   and from defect ⁴and plague he concealed me in his shade and his salvation.

---

1   The verse corresponds to Sir 34:6, which is preserved in Greek and Syriac, but not Hebrew. The reconstruction follows Fleischer (1990, 269). The previous understanding of the second stich, reflected in Fleischer's vocalization (though this matches neither the vowels nor the consonants on the manuscript page) אַל תֵּשֵׁב [בְּ]מְחוּגָּתָ[ם] לַחֲדוֹת, is obscure: "do not dwell in their circle (i.e., in their secrets) to rejoice." Far better, it seems, is to assume a defective spelling of "riddles" (usually חידות), which spelling is found a handful of times in medieval literature and once (in Aramaic) in Tg. Onq. Num 12:8. This makes better sense of the letters and vowels themselves, as well as the context.

2   The verse corresponds to Sir 34:7 and the first stich matches the Syriac quite closely. וַיִּכָּשְׁלוּ בַּהֲלִיכָתָם — The phrase parallels (though not exactly) the expression of Nah 2:6.

3   The verse corresponds to Sir 34:7 and is again quite close to the Syriac, while differing from the Greek.

4   The verse does not clearly correspond to another verse in Sirach, though the idea that wisdom and discernment are more important than accurate speech is found elsewhere, especially Sir 20:27, in both Greek and Syriac (cf. also Sir 5:13^{A,C}; 21:7 [Greek]). כליל לשון — The words occur also in Sir 37:18^{B,D}, though with a different syntax and meaning. Cf. too the expression לשון ברה "pure tongue" in Sir 40:21b^B.

5   The verse does not clearly correspond to another verse in Sirach, though it is at least reminiscent of Sir 31:3.

6   The vocabulary of the verse is similar to that presupposed by the *Vorlage* of Sir 34:11 (in both Greek and Syriac), though the sentiment is different. The underlying idea (i.e., what you say can be used against you) seems closer to various statements on the importance of silence (e.g., 5:15; 6:1; 19:16). בָה — This is presumably an alternative spelling of בָא.

7   The verse corresponds to Sir 34:12. See also 51:2, 6.

8   The verse does not clearly correspond to another verse in Sirach, though the idea of trusting God is expressed elsewhere, as in Sir 32:24^{B,E,F}; and, the promise of deliverance from the pit is found in Sir 4:10^A. בור שיחים — As Fleischer notes, the expression is reminiscent of the phrase בורות שיח ומערות "pits, ditches, and caves" found repeatedly in Rabbinic Hebrew, though the word בור here in verse 8 seems to be in construct with שיחים while in the rabbinic expression it is simply in coordination with the following two words. Some wordplay is no doubt intended with the word from verse 6, שִׂיחַ "talk, speech." The continuation of the verse on the next manuscript page is interpreted as a third stich based on the rhyme, though it is an independent verse in the Bible: Ps 118:18.

9   There is no clear parallel for this verse, but the vocabulary and idea of 9a are similar to those in Sir 50:22e^B.

10 Similar vocabulary and idea are found in Sir 14:27^A, which concerns Wisdom's protection, though the verse here reflects the idea of Sir 34:19c–d.

5כָל אֵלֶה וְכִפְלֵהֶם עָשָׂה עַמִּי בְּצוּקִים 11
6וְכָהֵנָּה רַבּוֹת תֵּאוֹת לַצַּדִּיקִים :
7לֹא יִרְצֶה אֵ׳ פְּעוּלַת חוֹמְסִים 12
8וְלֹא בִּפְעוּלַת זֵדִים וּפָרִיצִים :
9כִּי מַגִּישׁ מִנְחָה מֵחֵיל דַּלִּים 13
10כְּזוֹבֵחַ בָּנָיו לְשֵׁדִים וַעֲוֵלִים :
11פַּת רְשָׁעִים לֹא תִישַׁר אָכְלָה 14
12וְלֹא תֵיט[ב] נְפָשׁוֹת לְקַבְּלָה :
13מִתְרַחֵץ מִשֶּׁרֶץ וְשָׁב וְנָגַע בְּגֻוִיָּתוֹ 15
14מָה הוֹעִילוּ רְחִיצָתוֹ וּשְׁטִיפוֹתוֹ :
15כֵּן אִישׁ צָם עַל חַטָּאתוֹ 16
וְהִכְפִּילוֹ 16[עוֹנוֹ] וְאַשְׁמָתוֹ
17מָה 17

T-S NS 193.99

T-S NS 193.99, recto (labeled verso)

1מָה הוֹעִילָה תְּפִלָּתוֹ 1
וּקְרִיאָתוֹ וַעֲמִידָתוֹ :
2דַּע כִּי רְצוֹן יְיָ סוּר מֵרַע וּדְרָכֶיהָ 2
3וְחֶפְצוֹ חֲדַל מִפֶּשַׁע וְאוֹרְחוֹתֶיהָ :
4וְלֹא תֵרָאֶה פָּנָיו רֵקָם מִבִּרְכָתוֹ 3
5אֲשֶׁר נָתַן לְךָ לְקַיֵּים בָּהּ מִצְוָתוֹ :
6אִם הָיִיתָ פָּקִיד נֶאֱמָן עַל פְּקוּדָתוֹ 4
7עָשָׂה רְצוֹנוֹ וְקַוֵּה אֲמִירָתוֹ :
8כִּי יְיָ יַפְקִיד פְּקִידִים בִּיצִירָתוֹ 5
9שֶׁיַּעֲשׂוּ רְצוֹנוֹ כָּל עַמּוֹ וּמַרְעִיתוֹ :

L. 5 [11] עֲמִי — This is presumably a mistake for עַמִּי. The second *hireq* seems to be written twice (i.e., one very close and touching the other) and perhaps a similar double-writing has created the initial *sere*.

L. 9 [13] וַעֲוֵלִים — The *raphe* mark above the *vav* indicates it is not a mater. There are two final *mems* superimposed on each other; the first has been partially erased and seems to have been slightly too small.

L. 10 [13] פַּת — The first letter is clearly a *pe* (not a *bet* [Maagarim]; and not a *kaph* [Fleischer 1990, 271]). The *tav* is legible and clear, though its left edge is lost in a hole; it is clearly not a *pe* (as in Fleischer 1990, 271).

L. 11 [14] תֵיט[ב] — The *tav* and *sere* are somewhat awkwardly written. The *sere* is written along a diagonal axis, as though the two dots are part of a *qibbuts* symbol. The lack of a third dot and the relatively short following letter (i.e., a *yod* not *vav*), suggests reading the vowel as *sere*. Nevertheless, this is somewhat unexpected, as explained in the translation notes.

L. 13 [15] וְנָגַע — The *segol* looks more like a *qamets*, due to the merging of the upper two dots.

L. 15 [16] [עוֹנוֹ] — The spacing and context suggest the reconstruction, which is suggested by Fleischer (1990, 271).

L. 16 [16] מָה — The word is placed on the lower left side of the page, indicating that the next proverb (on the following page) begins with this word.

L. 3 [2] מִפֶּשַׁע — We would expect a *patakh* instead of a *tsere*.

L. 7 [4] אֲמִירָתוֹ — This is presumably a misspelling of אֲמִירָתוֹ.

11 As Fleischer (1990, 270) points out, the same idea and language are reflected in an addition to the Syriac of Sir 34:21: ܟܠܡ ܚܠܡܝ ܐܚܒܐ ܟܠ ܘܬܐܬܐ ܬܐܬܐ "all these doubly will come to the righteous." The Syriac text uses the verb, ܐܬܐ "to come, enter," which is suspiciously similar in shape to the verb in the second stich, תֵּאוֹת, though the latter is clearly a different verb, אות in the *niphal*. The similarity between the Hebrew of the paraphrase and the Syriac implies that the paraphrase is in some way dependent on the Syriac translation or a Hebrew text that is similar to the Syriac (see Böhmisch 2017, 197–235).

12 Note the unusual rhyme of *samek* and *tsade* (see Fleischer 1990, 271). The language and sentiment echoes Sir 34:23. See also Sir 15:12.

13 The verse corresponds to Sir 34:24. מֵחֵיל דַּלִּים — The phrase is reflected in the Greek and is typical of Ben Sira's oxymoronic style (cf. יש בשת כבוד Sir 4:21ᴬ). The second stich is more literally: "like one sacrificing his children to demons, as well as young ones." The same motif and language of sacrificing (זבח) children to the demons (שֵׁדִים) is found in Deut 32:17 and Ps 106:37. עֲוֵלִים — "young ones." The last word in 13b is found in Job 21:11 as well as among the *piyyutim*, alternatively (and perhaps not coincidentally) the word can also be read as the homophone "evil ones."

14 The general idea of this verse is remotely similar to the idea of Sir 34:25, which speaks of the evil in depriving the poor of food. אָכְלָה — Graphically, this may be interpreted as the feminine abstract noun "food," the masculine noun אֹכֶל with the 3fs suffix, or the *qal*

11 ⁵Tout cela, et (même) le double, il l'a fait, avec moi, dans (mes) détresses
⁶et de la même manière, de nombreuses choses sont gratifiées pour les justes.
12 ⁷Dieu n'a pas plaisir dans les œuvres des violents,
⁸ni dans les œuvres des orgueilleux et des furieux.
13 ⁹Car celui qui apporte une offrande (tirée) de la richesse du pauvre
¹⁰est comme celui qui sacrifie ses enfants et les plus jeunes aux démons.
14 ¹¹La portion des méchants n'est pas propre à la consommation
¹²et ce n'est pas bon pour les gosiers de la recevoir.
15 ¹³Celui qui se lave du (contact avec un) reptile impur reviendra et sera atteint dans son corps,
¹⁴en quoi son bain et son ablution lui sont-ils profitables ?
16 ¹⁵De même une personne qui jeûne à cause de son péché,
pourtant ¹⁶[son iniquité] et sa culpabilité ¹⁵sont doublés,
17 ¹⁷ en quoi

T-S NS 193.99

1 ¹en quoi sa prière lui est-elle profitable ?
Sa récitation et son Amidah ?
2 ²Sache que la volonté de YYY est de se détourner du mal et de sa voie
³et d'endiguer son désir de la transgression et de ses sentiers.
3 ⁴Tu ne devrais pas apparaître devant lui vide sans sa bénédiction,
⁵celle qu'il t'a donnée pour ériger par elle le commandement.
4 ⁶Si tu es officier, (sois) celui qui est fidèle à son office,
⁷fais sa volonté et espère en sa parole.
5 ⁸Car YYY fait officier (ses) officiers dans sa création,
⁹(afin) que tout son peuple accomplisse sa volonté et son contentement.

11 ⁵All of these and (even) double he did with me in (my) straits,
⁶like these, many things are enjoyed by the righteous.
12 ⁷God does not delight in the work of the violent,
⁸nor in the work of scoffers and the lawless.
13 ⁹For the one who brings an offering from the wealth of the poor
¹⁰is like one sacrificing their children and young ones to demons.
14 ¹¹The portion of the wicked is not right for eating,
¹²nor is it good for throats to receive it.
15 ¹³The one who washes themself from creeping things, will return with plague in their body,
¹⁴what does their washing and cleansing profit them?
16 ¹⁵Thus, a person fasts due to their sin,
though ¹⁶[their iniquity] and their guilt are doubled.
17 ¹⁷What

T-S NS 193.99

1 ¹How is their prayer beneficial?
their reading or their Amidah?
2 ²Know that the will of YYY is turning from evil and its ways,
³his desire is ceasing from transgression and its ways.
3 ⁴You should not appear before him empty, without his blessing,
⁵because he has set for you to maintain with it his commandment.
4 ⁶If you are appointed, (be) one trustworthy according to his ordinance,
⁷do his will and hope (in) his speech.
5 ⁸For YYY appoints (his) officers in his creation
⁹that all his people should do his will and his satisfaction.

---

infinitive construct of אכל with the 3fs suffix as reflected in Fleischer (1990, 271). [תֵיטַ]ב — The subject of the verb is assumed to be the preceding פַּת, though we might have expected a preposition before נְפָשׁוֹת. Alternatively, the following noun נְפָשׁוֹת could be the subject (cf. the numerous cases where לֵב is subject of יטב like Ruth 3:7); the disagreement in gender between the verb and following subject is not infrequent (see, e.g., 1 Kgs 22:49 [*ketiv*]; Jer 12:4; 51:56). לְקַבְלָה — We understand this as the *piel* infinitive construct plus 3fs suffix.

15 The verse corresponds to Sir 34:30. In the Sirach passage, the complement is "from the dead," whereas here it is "from creeping things" (מִשֶּׁרֶץ). As Fleischer (1990, 271) notes, the impurity conveyed on a person who holds creeping things is described in b. Taan. 16a where it is stated that washing does not cleanse. This situation is used as an analogy to those who persist in sin.

16 The verse corresponds to Sir 34:31a–b.

17 מה — The catch word is the first of the page that follows in the codex.

1 The verse corresponds to Sir 34:31c–d.

2 The verse corresponds to Sir 35:5.

3 The verse corresponds to Sir 35:6–7.

4 Verses 4–7 do not correspond to any in Sirach. אֲמוֹרָתוֹ — We assume אֲמִירָתוֹ.

6	¹⁰מֵהֶם שֶׁיְּעַשֶׂה אֱמוּנָה לְטוֹבָה
	¹¹וּמֵהֶם פּוֹעֵל כָּל רָעָה וְאֵיבָה :
7	¹²זֶה עוֹשָׂה רְצוֹנוֹ וְנַחַל שְׂפָתוֹ
	¹³וְזֶה פּוֹעֵל אֲשֶׁר לֹא אֲמָתוֹ
8	¹⁴oo

T-S NS 193.99, verso (labeled recto)

9	¹וּבְקוּמוֹ לַמִּשְׁפָּט מִתְנָאֲצוֹ יִתְפָּרַע
	²וּבְעֵיתּ הַדִּין יְדִינוֹ עַ{שפ}{ל}ט} טוֹב וָרַע רַע :
10	³אִם מַזְהִיב יְיָ הוֹנֶךָ
	⁴וְהַרְחֵב נָא לְבָבְךָ וְעֵינֶךָ :
11	⁵כִּי נְעִים oo מִתְבָּרָךְ בְּשָׁעֲלוֹ
	⁶וְיִתְהֲלֵךְ בְּיוֹשֶׁר דְּרָכָיו וּשְׁבִילוֹ
12 B	⁷וּבְכָל מַעֲשֶׂךָ הָאֵר פָּנִים
	וּבְשָׁשׂוֹן ⁸תִּתֵּן מַתְנָן :
13 B	⁹תֵּן אֵלָיו כְּמַתְּתוֹ
	וַעֲשֵׂה ¹⁰כְּמוֹ כְּעָשִׁיר[יְתוֹ] :
14 B	כִּי לֹא תוּכַל ¹¹וְכֵן שָׁלֵם תַּשְׁלוּמָיו
	כִּי לֹא תְסַפֵּר נָעֱמ[יו]
15 B	¹²וּמַלְוֹה {מלוה} יְיָ נוֹתֵן לָאֶבְיוֹן
	כִּי הוּא בַעַל ¹³גְּמוּלוֹת שׂוֹכֵן חֶבְיוֹן
16 B	¹⁴כִּי לֹ֯ הוּא אֱלוֹהַּ תַּשְׁלוּמוֹת
	¹⁵וְיָשֵׁב לְךָ שִׁבְעָתַיִם כְּפִלוֹת :
17 B	¹⁶לֹא ooם תִּשְׁחֲדוֹ
	כִּי הַכֹּל בָּרָא ¹⁷לְחַד[וֹ] :
18	¹⁸לְבָבוֹתוֹ

T-S AS 137.436

T-S AS 137.436, recto

1 B	¹כִּי אֱלֹהֵי מִשְׁפָּט הוּא לְבַדּוֹ
	וְאֵין מַשָּׂא פָּנִים עִמּוֹ :
2 B	²לֹא יִשָּׂא אֶל דַּל פָּנִים
	כָּל אַנְקַת כִּי יִשְׁמַע ³עַל אֶבְיוֹנִים

L. 10 [6] שֶׁיְּעַשֶׂה — The scribe wrote a dot for a *shin* and then wrote the dot for *sin* without canceling the first dot.

L. 2 [9] עַ{שפ}{ל}ט} — The letters are hard to make sense of. It would appear that the word was שפט "judge" or "he judged," but then the letters were reformed into the preposition עַל "according to." וְרַע רַע — The scribe seems to have written the word initially, crossed it out, and then wrote it again above the initial word. The mistake in the first word is hard to perceive.

L. 4 [10] : וְעֵינֶךָ — The *soph pasuq* is beneath the *kaph* of הוֹנֶךָ.

L. 7 [12] וְיִתְהֲלֵךְ — The last letter appears to be an initial/medial *kaph*, not a final *kaph*.

L. 9 [13] אֵלָיו — Only the bottom of the final letter is visible and has a curved form, like the bottom of a *tsade* or the left leg of a *tav*. In addition, a *tsere* vowel appears beneath the *vav*.

L. 11 [14] : כְּשֶׁעָשִׁיר[וֹ] — The first letter may also be *bet*. Note the *soph pasuq* under the following כִּי.

L. 12 [15] {מלוה} וּמַלְוֹה — The scribe wrote the word once and then, presumably due to some mistake, wrote the word again beneath it.

L. 13 [15] גְּמוּלוֹת — The letters are very difficult to make sense of, though they can be reconstructed based on the parallel in Sir 35:13[Bmg].

L. 14 [16] לֹ֯ — The marks after the *lamed* (whose ascender is lost in a fold) are hard to make sense of. One expects a *kaph*, but it is hard to understand how the lines could form a *kaph*.

L. 15 [16] כְּפִלוֹת — The *sere* dots are placed so that one sits just under the *yod* and one at the end of the *pe*'s horizontal line, the effect of which is to make the *yod* look more like a *vav*.

L. 17 [17] לְחַד[וֹ] — Only the bottoms of the letters are preserved; the *lamed* is attested only as a dot. Together, the marks look more like the phrase לְחַי "for the living." This obviously does not fit the rhyme, however. It seems conceivable that here we have a form akin to the Aramaic particle לחוד "alone" used like the Hebrew לְבַדּוֹ. Note the *soph pasuq* under the *vav* of תִּשְׁחֲדוֹ.

L. 18 לְבָבוֹתוֹ — The *tav* is missing its left leg.

L. 1 [1] עִמּוֹ — The word is written above the preceding word. The *ayin* is faint but clear; the distinctive "horn" of the *mem* is clear.

L. 2 [2] כָּל אַנְקַת — The reading is very tentative. Only faint traces of most letters remain.

6	¹⁰Parmi eux, il y a celui qui pratique la fidélité en vue du bien ¹¹et parmi eux, il y a celui qui accomplit tout mal et toute haine.	6	¹⁰Among them is one who acts trustworthy for the good, ¹¹and among them is one who does every evil and disgusting thing.
7	¹²Celui-ci fait sa volonté et hérite de ses lèvres, tandis que celui-là accomplit ce qui n'est pas sa vérité.	7	¹²This is one who does his will and inherits his lip ¹³while this one does that which is not his truth.
8	¹⁴	8	¹⁴
9	¹Et lorsqu'il se lève pour le jugement, celui qui a été outragé sera remboursé, ²et au temps du jugement, il le jugera selon le bien et le mal.	9	¹And when he arises for judgment, he who is blasphemed will be paid back, ²and in the time of judgment, he will judge him according to good and evil.
10	³Si YYY fait scintiller ta richesse, ⁴élargis ton cœur et tes yeux.	10	³If the Lord gilds your wealth, ⁴broaden your heart and your eyes.
11	⁵Car, c'est plaisant [ ] celui qui est béni par le creux de sa main, ⁶et qui marche dans la droiture de ses voies et de son sentier.	11	⁵For, it is pleasant [ ] one blessed by his hand, ⁶and he will go in the straightness of his paths and his way.
12	⁷En toutes tes œuvres montre un visage radieux et, avec joie, ⁸donne (tes) dons.	12	⁷In all your works show a radiant face, and in joy ⁸you should give (your) gifts.
13	⁹Donne-lui selon son don (s.e. ce qu'il te donne) et agit ¹⁰selon [sa dî]me.	13	⁹Give to him according to his gift (to you), and do ¹⁰according as [his] tith[e.]
14	Si tu ne peux pas, alors accomplis ses rétributions, car [sa] grâce ne peut pas être mesurée.	14	If you are not able, ¹¹then he fulfills his rewards (to you), for [his] kindnesses cannot be measured.
15	¹²Celui qui prête à YYY donne au pauvre, car il est le ¹³rétributeur, celui qui dresse sa tente cachée.	15	¹²Whoever lends to YYY gives to the poor, for he is the one who delivers ¹³retribution [ ] the one dwelling in hiding.
16	¹⁴Car [ ] il est Eloah, celui qui rétribue, ¹⁵et il te rendra le double au septuple.	16	¹⁴For [ ] he is a God of rewards, ¹⁵and will give back to you seven times twice-over.
17	¹⁶[ ] ne le soudoie pas, car il a créé la totalité ¹⁷par lui-même.	17	¹⁶[ ] you should not try to bribe him, for the whole he has created ¹⁷by himself.
18	¹⁸ ses cœurs	18	¹⁸ his hearts

T-S AS 137.436

1	¹Car c'est un Dieu de justice, lui seul et il n'y a pas de partialité en lui.	1	¹For he alone is a God of justice, and he has no bias.
2	²Il ne montre pas de partialité envers le pauvre, tous les cris qu'il écoute concernent les pauvres.	2	² He shows no bias against the poor, every moan (is one) that he hears ³as regards the poor.

6   The contrast of two particular sets of individuals or things is quite common in Sirach, often expressed with a repetition of מֵהֶם, like here. See, e.g., Sir 33:9[E, Syriac], 12[E, Syriac]; 44:8–9[Mas,B]; 48:16[B]. The last passage (48:16) is also similar in sense to verse 6.

7   The idea of receiving one's speech from God is not unique (e.g., Isa 50:4), nor is the idea of receiving songs and poems from God (e.g., Ps 40:4); cf. to Sir 51:22[B].

9   The verse does not correspond to any known verse in Ben Sira. מִתְנָאֲצוֹ — Literally, "his (i.e., God's) blasphemed one."

12   The verse corresponds to Sir 35:11a.

13   The verse corresponds to Sir 35:12a. The idea that everyone might not have the means to give to God in proportion to what they have received from God is expressed obliquely in Sir 35:12b. [כְּעֲשִׂירָ]יָתוֹ — The preserved qamets that should follow the resh (though it is actually placed under the yod) and the necessity to rhyme with כְּמַתְּתוֹ from the preceding line imply the Aramaic ordinal numeral עֲשִׂירָיָה, though presumably here with the meaning "tithe."

15   The verse corresponds to the marginal alternative to Sir 35:13[B, Syr] (similar to the expression in Prov 19:17).

16   The verse corresponds to the text of Sir 35:13[B, Gr, Syr].

17   The verse corresponds to Sir 35:14

18   לִבְבוֹתוֹ — We would expect לִבְבוֹתָיו. This is the catchword for the next folio, though T-S AS 137.436, recto does not begin in this way. This implies, of course, that at least one more page came between T-S NS 193.99 and T-S AS 137.436. It is perplexing because T-S AS 137.436 begins with 35:15 which, naturally, follows 35:14 in H[B].

1   The verse corresponds to Sir 35:15.

2   The verse corresponds to Sir 35:16.

3 ᴮ לֹא יִטּוֹשׁ אַנְקַת יָתוֹם
⁴בַּשְׁלֹנֶּר וְאַלְמָנָה בֶּאֱמֶת יְחַתוֹם :
4 ᴮ ⁵לֹא יִתְמַהְיָהּ לַעֲשׂוֹת צֶדֶק
וְלֹא יִתְאַפָּק ⁶לְהַצְדִּיק צַדִּיק :
5 ᴮ ⁷וְאַכְזָרִים יִמְחַץ מָתְנֵיהֶם
וְיָשִׁיב צוּרֵב {רֶשַׁע} ⁸עַל גְּוִיּוֹתֵיהֶם :
6 ᴮ ⁹וְשִׁבְטֵי זָדוֹן יְצַבֵּת וְיוֹרִישׁ
וּמַטֵּה רֶשַׁע ¹⁰יְאַבֵּד וְיַפְרִישׁ :
7 ᴮ ¹¹עַד יָשִׁיב לְכָל אֲנֻ[וֹ]שׁ תִּגְמוּלוֹ
וּפֹעַל ¹²אָדָם יְשַׁלֵּם לוֹ :
8 ᴮ ¹³וְיָרִיב רִיב סְגֻלָּתוֹ
וְחָ ooooo ¹⁴בִּישׁוּעָתוֹ וּפָעֳלוֹ :
9 ᴮ ¹⁵מַה יָּפָה תְשׁוּעָה בְּתוֹךְ בּוּקָה
וּבְעֵית חֲזִיזִים ¹⁶רֶחַ מַנְזִיקָה

T-S AS 137.436, verso

10 ᴮ ¹אָמְרוּ אֱלֹהֵי כֹל הוֹשִׁיעֵנוּ בְּחַסְדֶּךָ
²וְעַל כָּל הַגּוֹיִים שִׂים פַּחְדֶּךָ :
11 ᴮ ³כַּאֲשֶׁר נִקְדַּשְׁתָּ {ם}בָּם לְעֵינֵיהֶם
⁴כֵּן לְעֵינֵנוּ הַכְבִּידָם וְהַפְלֵיהֶם :
12 ᴮ ⁵וְיֵדְעוּ כַּאֲשֶׁר יָדַעְנוּ כִּי אֵין אֱלֹהִים זוּלָתֶךָ
⁶וְאֵין פּוֹעֵל וּמַאֲמָר כִּי מֵחָכְמָתֶךָ :
13 ᴮ ⁷חַדֵּשׁ שִׁבְטְךָ עַל זָרִים
⁸וְהַאֲרִיךְ יָדְךָ וּזְרוֹעֲךָ עַל כָּל נָכְרִים :
14 ᴮ ⁹הָעֵר עֲלֵיהֶם אַפֶּךָ
וּשְׁפֹךְ זַעְמְךָ וְקִצְפֶּךָ :
15 ᴮ ¹⁰וְהַשְׁבֵּת רֹאשׁ אוֹיֵב יְלִיצֵנִי
הָאוֹמֵ[ר] ¹¹אֵין זוּלָתִ[י] כָמ[וֹ]נִי :

L. 3 [3] יָתוֹם — The word is written above the preceding word.
L. 5 [4] צֶדֶק — The last letter looks at first like a *holem-vav*, but a faint trace of a curve at its base suggests it is instead *qoph*.
L. 6 [4] צַדִּיק — The spelling is unexpected, but perhaps demanded by the rhyme.
L. 7 [5] וְיָשִׁיב — The top dot of the initial *shewa* overlaps with the bottom of the *vav*. Only the top of the *gimel* is preserved. The line above it is either a mistaken *raphe* line or part of a cancellation mark. צוּרֵב — The *vav* is extremely light and hard to perceive. {רֶשַׁע} — The *resh* and *shin* are very tentative. The word is spelled in very small letters beneath צוּרֵב and above וְיָשִׁיב probably as a mistake from the following line.
L. 8 [5] תרב — The word is written above the preceding word.
L. 9 [6] יְצַבֵּת — A *raphe* line appears above the *tsade*, though presumably belongs over the *bet*. The *tsade* appears closer to its final form than its initial/medial form. רֶשַׁע — The word appears above the preceding word.
L. 16 [9] רֶחַ — We would expect רוּחַ in Biblical Hebrew.
L. 1 [10] בְּחַסְדֶּךָ — The word is written above and to the left of the preceding word.
L. 4 [11] לְעֵינָיִן — The word should have a final *mem*, not *nun*, which makes it appear Aramaic.
L. 5 [12] זוּלָתֶךָ — The word is written above and to the left of the preceding word.
L. 9 [14] אַפֶּךָ — A *qamets* appears beneath the *aleph* and a *patakh* beneath the *qamets*. וְקִצְפֶּךָ — The word is written above and to the left of the preceding word.

3	Il ne néglige pas le gémissement de l'orphelin, ⁴concernant l'immigré et la veuve, en vérité, il pose un sceau (sur eux).	3	He will not neglect the moaning of the orphan, ⁴on account of the sojourner and the widow he will seal (them) in (his) truth.
4	⁵Il ne tarde pas à faire ce qui est juste et il ne se contient pas ⁶pour rendre justice au juste.	4	⁵He will not delay to do what is right, he will not restrain himself ⁶from declaring right what is right.
5	⁷Et quant aux cruels, il leur brise les reins et fait croître {un mal} une brûlure sur leurs corps.	5	⁷As for the cruel, he strikes their loins, and increases {evil} burning ⁸over their bodies.
6	⁹Et il saisit les tribus orgueilleuses et (les) déposséde et le bâton du méchant, ¹⁰il (le) détruit et (le) supprime.	6	⁹And the tribes of the arrogant he will seize and dispossess and the staff of the wicked ¹⁰he will destroy and remove.
7	¹¹Jusqu'à ce qu'il rende à chacun son bienfait et (selon) l'œuvre de l'être humain, il le rétribue.	7	¹¹Until he returns compensation to each person, and (according to) the work of ¹²(each) human he will repay them.
8	¹³Il défend la cause de sa part personnelle, [ ] ¹⁴dans son salut et son œuvre.	8	¹³He defends the cause of his possession, [ ] ¹⁴in his salvation and work.
9	¹⁵Combien est magnifique la délivrance au milieu de la dévastation et au temps d'orage ¹⁶la délivrance du danger.	9	¹⁵How beautiful is success in the midst of desolation, and in the time of thunderstorms, ¹⁶relief from danger.
10	¹Parle, Dieu de tout, sauve-nous par ton amour, ²impose ta crainte sur toutes les nations.	10	¹Speak, God of all, deliver us in your kindness, ²set your terror over all the nations.
11	³De même que tu t'es montré saint à travers eux à leurs yeux, ⁴ainsi à nos yeux, honore-les et fais-leur des merveilles.	11	³Just as you were sanctified through them before their eyes ⁴so before our eyes honor them and awe them.
12	⁵Et ils sauront, comme nous savons, qu'il n'y a pas de dieu en-dehors de toi ⁶et qu'il n'y a aucune œuvre ni parole en-dehors de ta sagesse.	12	⁵So they know just as we know that there is no god besides you, ⁶and no one does (anything) or speaks except from your wisdom.
13	⁷Renouvelle ton bâton contre les étrangers ⁸et étends ta main, ton bras, contre tous les étrangers.	13	⁷Renew your staff against the strangers, ⁸and stretch your hand, your arm against all the foreigners.
14	⁹Reveille contre eux ta colère et répands ta fureur et ton courroux.	14	⁹Arouse against them your anger, and pour out your indignation and your wrath.
15	¹⁰Elimine la tête de l'ennemi qui se moque de moi, celui qui di[t] ¹¹ «il n'y a personne excepté moi et (personne) comme moi.»	15	¹⁰Wipe out the leader of the enemy who mocks me, the one who says ¹¹"there is none but me (and none who are) like me."

3   The first stich corresponds to Sir 35:17. The second stich does not correspond to any known verse in Ben Sira. בְּשַׁלֵּג — For the construction of bet-shin-lamedh, cf. Jon 1:7, 12 and T-S NS 93.80, verso (labeled recto), line 4. יְחִתּוֹם — The verb presumably has a figurative sense "to protect, keep secure."

4   The verse corresponds to Sir 35:22.

5   The first stich corresponds to the last stich of Sir 35:22. The second stich is reminiscent of some of the words in Sir 35:23: ולגוים ישיב נקם. The word תרב seems like the Aramaic word "fat." וִישַׂגֵּב — The verb presumably was originally vocalized as a hiphil: וְיַשְׂגִּיב. The verb, usually translated "exalt," has a more martial usage in Isa 9:10 (in the piel), where it takes as object צָרִים "enemies." It occurs in the hiphil only in Job 36:22 and then in later piyyut, from the era close to 1000 CE (see Maagarim).

6   The verse corresponds to Sir 35:23b–c. יְצַבֵּת — The verb צבת appears in Rabbinic Hebrew and Aramaic in the Palestinian Talmud (e.g., y. Ketub. 30a [see CAL, 22 Jan., 2021]) with the sense "to join, associate"; in the present context, however, it seems likelier that the verb is simply a variant of צבט "to grab, seize." וְיַפְרִישׁ — The word is presumably from the root פרשׁ in the sense "to set aside," as in Rabbinic Hebrew and in Aramaic, though note פרשׁ "to sting" in Prov 23:32.

7   The idea of the verse corresponds to Sir 35:24 in its entirety. For the first stich, the wording follows that of H^B, but for the second stich, the scribe has quoted Job 34:11. צרב — The root is relatively rare, but occurs both in the Bible and in post-biblical literature.

8   The verse corresponds to Sir 35:25.

9   The verse corresponds to Sir 35:26. בּוּקָה — See Nah 2:11. מְזִיקָה — The word נְזִיקָה "damage, injury" occurs only four times in Maagarim (the first time in m. 'Abod. Zar. 1:9).

10 The verse corresponds to Sir 36:1–2.

11 The verse corresponds to Sir 36:4. וְהַפְלֵיהֶם — The verb is פלה, the biform of פלא.

12 The first stich corresponds to Sir 36:5.

13 The verse corresponds to Sir 36:6–7.

14 The verse corresponds to Sir 36:8.

15 The verse corresponds to Sir 36:12.

16 ᴮ	¹²הָחֹשׁ [קֵ]ץ וּפְקֹ[וֹ]ד מוֹעֵד	
	וְיֵעֵד ¹³בְּבֵית הֵיעֵד :	
17 ᴮ	¹⁴∘∘ אֱסוֹף כָּל בְּנֵי יַעֲקוֹב שְׁבָטֶ[יָ]ךְ	
	¹⁵יֶהֱרֹס בְּכָל גּוֹיִים דָּנֶךָ וּמִשְׁפָּטֶיךָ :	

T-S NS 108.43

T-S NS 108.43, folio 2, recto (labeled verso; left side)

18 ᴮ	¹[רַחֵם עַ]ל נַחֲלָתְךָ וְעַמְּךָ
	הַנִּקְרָאִים ²[ ] בִּשְׁמֶךָ
19 ᴮ	³יִשְׂרָאֵל בְּכוֹר כִּנִּיתוֹ
	וְיַעֲקוֹ{ד}ב אֲשֶׁר בְּחַרְתָּה בּוֹ :
20 ᴮ	⁴וְרַחֵם עַל קִרְיַת קָדְשָׁךְ
	יְרוּשָׁלַיִם ⁵מְכוֹן מִקְדָּשֶׁךָ :
21 ᴮ	⁶מַלֵּא צִיּוֹן מֵהַדָּרְךָ
	וְהֵיכָלָךְ מִפְאֵירְךָ :
22 ᴮ	⁷לְמַעַן יֵאָמְנוּ בוֹטְחֶיךָ
	וְיִתְאַמְּתוּ ⁸בְּפָעֳלְךָ קוֹוֶיךָ :
23 ᴮ	⁹וְשֶׁמַע תְּפִלַּת עֲבָדֶךָ
	¹⁰הַשׁוֹחֲחִים הֲדַר כְּבוֹד הוֹדֶיךָ
24 ᴮ	¹¹וְיֵדְעוּ כָּל יוֹשְׁבֵי הָאֲרָצוֹת כִּי אַתָּה שׁוֹכֵן חֶבְיוֹן
	¹²וְכִי אֱמֶת אַ{ה}תָּה אֶחָד וְעֶלְיוֹן
25 ᴮ	¹³כָּל מַאֲבָל נָכוֹן לְעָם
	¹⁴אַךְ מַאֲבָל מִמַּאֲבָל יִנְעָם :
26 ᴮ	¹⁵יִיטַב לִזְכָר כָּל אִישָׁה
	וְיָפָה טוֹבַת ¹⁶יְרוּשָׁה

T-S NS 108.43, folio 2, verso (labeled recto; right side)

27 ᴮᶜ	¹חַךְ בּוֹחֵן כָּל אוֹבֶל וּ∘∘[ ] [
	²וּלְזָכָר יֵיטְבוּ יָפִים בַּתֹּאַר ∘∘ [∘] [
28 ᴮ	³לֵב עָקֵב יִתֵּן עַצְבוֹנוֹת
	⁴וְיַרְבֶּה דְאָגוֹת בַּלְּבָבוֹת וְאוֹנוֹת :
29 ᴮᶜ	⁵וְתֹאַר בְּאִישָׁ{ם}ה יְהַלֵּל פָּנִים
	וְעַל כָּל מַחֲמַדֵּי ⁶עַיִן יִישַׁר בָּרַעְיוֹנִים :
30 ᴮᶜ	⁷וְכָל שֶׁכֵּן אִם יְהִי לָהּ רַכּוּת לָשׁוֹן
	⁸וְיֹפִי תֹּאַר וּמַרְאֶה כְּאִישׁוֹן :

L. 14 [17]   It is unclear if the first marks are part of an effaced word or are due to offsetting or bleedthrough. שְׁבָטֶ[יָ]ךְ — Only the bottom of the *kaph*'s tail is visible.

L. 15 [17]   יֶהֱרֹס — Given the preserved shape of letters it is difficult to be sure of the reading and difficult to make sense of the word itself. Could it be a mistake for יהלך?

L. 1 [18]   [רַחֵם עַ]ל נַחֲלָתְךָ — The reconstruction follows Fleischer (1990, 271–72) and the assumption that the text here is similar to that of Hᴮ. Only a single dot of ink remains of the *lamed*, which is otherwise lost in the lacuna. The *nun* itself is not visible, though a *patakh* is found beneath the hole. Only the bottom legs of the *khet* are visible. וְעַמְּךָ — The *qamets* after the final *kaph* is missing, though the letter seems otherwise well preserved. Presumably the scribe forgot to write it.

L. 3 [19]   וְיַעֲקוֹ{ד}ב — The final letter seems to have been written as a *dalet* and then corrected to a *bet* by a single horizontal line. בְּחַרְתָּה בּוֹ — These words sit above וְיַעֲקוֹ{ד}ב אֲשֶׁר.

L. 4 [20]   קָדְשָׁךְ — The scribe uses the pausal form of the 2ms pronominal suffix here, though just above, at line-end, the scribe used the contextual form.

L. 8 [22]   קוֹוֶיךָ — The *holem* dot appears as a vertical line close to the *shewa* mark of יֵאָמְנוּ.

L. 11 [24]   שׁוֹכֵן חֶבְיוֹן — The words are written above כִּי אַתָּה.

L. 13 [25]   נָכוֹן — The word can just as easily be read נָבוֹן.

L. 1 [27]   ו∘∘ — The consonants are lost but the vowels are legible on the edge of the paper.

L. 2 [27]   בַּתֹּאַר — The following letters are lost, though a *hireq* is found beneath the edge. בַּלְּבָבוֹת — Under the second *bet*, the scribe wrote a *qamets* and crossed it out.

L. 5 [29]   כָּל — The second letter almost resembles a final *mem* in its triangular form, though this is a *lamed* whose top ascender has been bent to fit the space. Cf. the word כָּל in T-S NS 9380 recto (labeled verso), line 4

L. 8 [30]   וְיֹפִת — The *hireq* beneath the *vav* was first written as a *shewa*, but then the bottom dot was canceled with a diagonal stroke.

16   ¹²Hâte le temps et assigne le moment
     et rassemble ¹³dans la maison de rassemblement.
17   ¹⁴[ ] rassemble tous les enfants de Jacob, tes tribus,
     ¹⁵et que ton jugement et ta justice détruisent toutes les nations.

T-S NS 108.43

18   ¹[Aie pitié d]e ton héritage et de ton peuple,
     ceux qui sont appelés ²[   ] de ton nom.
19   ³Israël, le premier né (que) tu as nommé
     et Jacob que tu as choisi.
20   ⁴Et, aie pitié de ta ville sainte,
     Jerusalem, ⁵le lieu de ta sainteté.
21   ⁶Remplis Sion de ta splendeur
     et ton temple de ta parure.
22   ⁷Afin que ceux qui se fient à toi soient fidèles
     et ⁸ceux qui espèrent en toi soient convaincus par ton œuvre.
23   ⁹Ecoute la prière de tes serviteurs,
     ¹⁰de ceux qui contemplent la splendeur de la gloire de ta majesté.
24   ¹¹Et tous les habitants des pays sauront que tu demeures en un lieu caché
     ¹²et que véritablement tu es un et Très-Haut.
25   ¹³Toute nourriture convient pour le peuple,
     ¹⁴mais il y a une nourriture plus délicieuse que d'autre.
26   ¹⁵Toute femme convient à un homme,
     mais la beauté est le bénéfice ¹⁶de la propriété.
27   ¹Un palais éprouve toute nourriture et [ ]
     ²et pour un homme conviennent les belles apparences [ ].
28   ³Un cœur tortueux procure des chagrins
     ⁴et multiplie anxiétés dans les cœurs et lamentations.
29   ⁵Beauté de femme illumine le visage
     et, au delà de tous plaisirs de l'œil, c'est droit parmi les désirs.
30   ⁷À plus forte raison, si elle a une langue douce,
     ⁸alors belle forme et (beau) visage sont comme la prunelle (des yeux).

T-S NS 108.43

18   ¹[Have mercy o]n your inheritance and your people,
     those who were called ²[   ] in your name.
19   ³Israel, whom you named first born,
     and Jacob whom you chose.
20   ⁴And, have mercy on your holy city,
     Jerusalem, ⁵the place of your holiness.
21   ⁶Fill Zion with your majesty,
     and your temple with your splendor.
22   ⁷So that those who trust in you will believe,
     and ⁸those hoping in you will be convinced by your work.
23   ⁹Hear the prayer of your servants,
     ¹⁰those contemplating the glory of the honor of your majesty.
24   ¹¹So all who dwell in the lands will know that you dwell in hiding
     ¹²and that in truth you are one and the Most High.
25   ¹³All food is established for the people,
     ¹⁴but there is (some) food that is more delicious than (other) food.
26   ¹⁵Any woman can be good for a man,
     but the benefit of ¹⁶heirs is beautiful.
27   ¹The palate tests all food and [ ]
     ²and for a man those handsome in form make good [ ].
28   ³A crooked heart brings sorrows,
     ⁴and multiplies anxieties in hearts, as well as mourning.
29   ⁵Beauty in a woman brightens the face,
     and beyond every pleasure of ⁶the eye it is secure among desires.
30   ⁷All the more so, if she has a tender tongue,
     ⁸then supreme beauty and looks is like the apple of the eye.

---

16   The verse corresponds to Sir 36:10.
17   The verse corresponds to Sir 36:13.
18   The verse corresponds to Sir 36:17a.
19   The verse corresponds to Sir 36:17b. For the second stich, Fleischer (1990, 272) notes the similarity to Ps 135:4, though the syntax and vocabulary matches Isa 44:2 more closely.
20   The verse corresponds to Sir 36:18.
21   The verse corresponds to Sir 36:19.
22   The verse corresponds to Sir 36:21. וְיִתְאַמְּתוּ — The denominative of אמת is only attested in Hebrew after the first millennium.
23   The verse corresponds to Sir 36:22a–b.
24   The verse corresponds to Sir 36:22c–d.
25   The verse corresponds to Sir 36:23.
26   The verse corresponds to Sir 36:26.
27   The verse corresponds to Sir 36:24.
28   The verse corresponds to Sir 36:25.
29   The verse corresponds to Sir 36:27.
30   The verse corresponds to Sir 36:28. וְכָל שֶׁכֵן — For the construction, see Jastrow 1903, 638, sub כֹּל. רַכּוּת — This word is only attested in late *piyyutim* after the 7th c.

⁹רֵאשִׁית קִנְיָן קָנֵה אִשָּׁה כְּשֵׁירָה 31 BCD

¹⁰תִּהְיֶה לָךְ ᵉⁱʳ כְּחוֹמָה בְּצוּרָה וְעֶ{נ}{זו}{שׁ}רָה :

¹¹ כִּי הַכֶּרֶם יְבֹעַר בְּאֵין גָּדֵר 32 BCD

וְכֵן הָאִ[ישׁ] ¹²יְנוֹדַד מֵאֵין אִשָּׁה בַּחֶדֶר :

¹³אַל תִּשְׁכַּח חֲבֶרְךָ בַּקְרָב 33 BD

¹⁴וְאַל תַּעַזְבֵיהוּ בִּשְׁלָל רָב

¹⁵מִיּוֹעֵץ שְׁמוֹר נַפְשֶׁךָ 34 BD

עַד שֶׁתֵּידַע צָרְכוֹ ¹⁶לָךְ :

T-S NS 93.80

T-S NS 93.80, recto (labeled verso)

[ ]¹
[ ]²
[ ]³ 0
[⁴לְשֶׁלֶּ] 1
[⁵כָּל אֶחָד כְּוֶן [○ לֹ]
⁶רֹאשׁ כָּל חַיֵּי אָדָם מַ[יִ]ם [וְאֵ]שׁ 2 B
⁷וְיִצְהָר וּבֶגֶד וּדְבָשׁ :
⁸כָּל אֵלֶּה לַטּוֹבִים יֵיטִיבוּ 3 BM
וְרָעִים לְזָרָה ⁹עֲלֵהֶם יֵהָפֵכוּ :
¹⁰יֵשׁ רוּחוֹת לְנָקָם יוּצָרוּ 4 BM
וּלְאָסוֹן ¹¹וְצָרוֹת נִכְרְאוּ :
¹²אֵשׁ וְדֶבֶר וְצָרוֹת וְרָעוֹת 5 BM
לְמִשְׁפָּט ¹³רְשָׁעִים הֵם נוֹגָעוֹת :
¹⁴חַיּוֹת שֵׁן פֶּתֶן וְעַקְרָב 6 BM
וּלְנָקְמוֹת כְּלִי זַן וּקְרָב :
¹⁵כָּל אֵלֶּה לְצָרְכָם נוֹעָדוּ 7 BM
וְהֵמָּה לְעִתָּם ¹⁶יִפָּקֵדוּ :

T-S NS 93.80, verso (labeled recto)

[ ]¹
[ ]²
[ ]³

L. 10 [31] וְעֶ{נ}{זו}{שׁ}רָה : — The second letter is clearly an *ayin*, not a *samekh* as Fleischer (1990, 274) implies with סְגוּרָה. The third letter seems to have been initially a *nun* but then canceled with a vertical line and/or (based on the context) changed to *zayin*, whose head is lost in the other lines. That this letter was initially a *nun* (and is not *gimel*) is suggested by the trace of a vertical line as well as a relatively straight lower horizontal bar, both of which are unlike those of the *gimel*. For a similar sequence of *ayin-nun*, see עֲנַיִים in ENA 30533 verso, line 7; for a *nun* with a straight lower horizontal bar, see נוֹגָעוֹת T-S NS 9380 verso, line 11. The fifth letter was initially a *shin*, upon which a *resh* has been superimposed. Although the *resh* is more worn than the *shin*, the *resh* is presumably the correction since this makes sense with the rhyming word in the first stich. The *resh* is unusual in that it seems to have been made with two separate strokes. The initial reading was presumably ענוש. The *he* seems too far away from the *shin* to assume that it was written following the letter, though perhaps the scribe recognized the mistake before finishing the spelling with *he*: ענושה "treasured" (?).

L. 11 [32] יְבֹעַר — Reading the second letter as a *kaph* is also possible: יְכֹעַר "is unsightly."

L. 12 [32] בַּחֶדֶר — A *qamets* was written initially under the *resh*, but then canceled with a diagonal line.

L. 15 [34] צָרְכוֹ — The word sits above the preceding שֶׁתֵּידַע.

L. 3 [0] Only a *shewa* is visible from the first preserved line. Based on the regularity of 16 lines per page, one would assume that there are two further lines above this one that are lost.

L. 4 [1] לְשֶׁלֶּ] — The second *lamed* is only attested by its lowest part, specifically by part of the v-like bottom mark and a vertical line that intersects with it.

L. 5 [1] כָּל — A horizontal line appears above this word. כְּוֶן — The second letter is unlikely to be *lamed* (so Fleischer 1990, 274) since there is no indication of a separate v-like mark of the *lamed*, which even appears where it merges with the ascender (as with לְמִשְׁפָּט T-S NS 93.80, recto [labeled verso], line 10). לֹ — The remaining trace appears to be the bottom v-like mark of the *lamed*.

L. 6 [2] מַ[יִ]ם [וְאֵ]שׁ — The bottom and diagonal mark of the *mem* are followed by various vowel marks just beneath the tear. Only the *hireq* is preserved, not the *yod* of [מַיִ]ם; only the bottom dot of the *shewa* beneath the *vav* is preserved, together with the following *tsere*. Nevertheless, due to the parallels with Sir 39:26, we might expect the sequence of words in the reconstruction though it does not rhyme with the next stich.

L. 14 [6] וּקְרָב — The word is written on top of זַן.

31	⁹La meilleure des acquisitions : acquiers une honnête femme ¹⁰elle sera pour toi ᵘⁿᵉ ᵛⁱˡˡᵉ comme une muraille inattaquable et {précieuse} fortifiée.	31	⁹The best of acquisitions, acquire an honest wife ¹⁰she will be to you ᵃ ᶜⁱᵗʸ like a fortified and protected wall.
32	¹¹Car la vigne brûlera en l'absence de clôture et ainsi l'ho[mme] ¹²vagabonde en l'absence d'une femme dans (sa) chambre.	32	¹¹For the vineyard will burn without a wall, and thus a per[son] ¹²wanders (who is) without a wife in (their) chamber.
33	¹³N'oublie pas un compagnon dans la bataille ¹⁴et ne l'abandonne pas lorsqu'il y a un important butin.	33	¹³Do not forget your companion in battle, ¹⁴and do not abandon them for the sake of great spoils.
34	¹⁵D'un conseiller garde-toi, jusqu'à ce que tu sache (pourquoi) il a besoin ¹⁶de toi.	34	¹⁵From a counselor guard yourself, until you know why they need ¹⁶you.

T-S NS 93.80

0	3	0	3
1	⁴Pour... ⁵Chacun...	1	⁴to... ⁵every one...
2	⁶L'essentiel de toute vie humaine, c'est l'e[au,] le fe[u,] ⁷ l'huile, le vêtement et le miel.	2	⁶First of all things for human life are wat[er], fir[e], ⁷oil, clothing, and honey.
3	⁸Toutes ces choses font du bien aux bons, mais quant au méchant elles se changent en nausée pour eux.	3	⁸All these things are good for the good, but as for the wicked, these things ⁹turn loathsome against them.
4	¹⁰Il y a des vents qui sont formés pour la vengeance et pour le malheur et les détresses ¹¹ils sont reconnus.	4	¹⁰There are winds that are formed for vengeance, and ¹¹are recognized for disaster and tribulations.
5	¹²Feu, peste, détresse et malheurs, ¹³ils adviennent ¹⁰pour le jugement ¹¹des méchants.	5	¹²Fire and plagues, troubles and evils ¹³they come for the judgment of the wicked.
6	¹⁴L'animal carnassier, la vipère et le scorpion, l'instrument de guerre et de conflits sont pour la vengeance.	6	¹⁴The carnivorous animal, adder, and scorpion instruments of armor and war are for vengeance.
7	¹⁵Toutes ces choses adviennent pour leur utilité et elles, en leur temps, ¹⁶seront mises à exécution. [...]	7	¹⁵All these were appointed for their purpose, and these, when their time (comes), ¹⁶ will be assigned. [...]

---

31 The verse corresponds to Sir 36:29. וְעֶ{נ}זֻ{שׁ}וֹרָה — The initial reading was presumably supposed to be ענושה "treasured" (?). Although the root of this word is associated with punishment and fines, it was perhaps also associated with the result of assessing fines, that is wealth. Note the related noun from Palmyrene Aramaic ענשא "treasury" and perhaps also the Hebrew noun עונש often translated "punishment," but which in Hᴬ (Sir 9:5) corresponds to Syriac ܗܕܘܬܐ "dowry." Note too that the Hebrew text to this verse in Hᴮ,ᶜ contains the phonetically similar משען "support." The secondary reading, עזורה is likely the *qal* passive participle of the root עזר "to help, protect." The dot appears above the *vav mater* due to sloppy writing. The *soph pasuq* is located above this word, instead of directly to its left. Kister (1983, 127) wonders if the initial rhyme was between אשה and the initial word of this stich (what we read as -ענוש), but that then כשירה was added to the first stich necessitating a change in the second.

32 The verse corresponds to Sir 36:30. יְנוֹדֵד — The *polel* of נוד occurs only one other time in ancient / medieval literature, in a text dated to 942 by Maagarim.

33 The verse corresponds to Sir 37:6.

34 The verse corresponds to Sir 37:8.

1 The verse that this might correspond to in Ben Sira is not known.

2 The verse corresponds to Sir 39:26.

3 The verse corresponds to Sir 39:27. Alternatively, translate "but as nausea, wicked acts overwhelm them" and cf. the syntax of 1 Sam 4:19. לזרה — The word is spelled with final *aleph* (זָרָא) in the Hebrew Bible at Num 11:20.

4 The verse corresponds to Sir 39:28.

5 The verse corresponds to Sir 39:29.

6 The verse corresponds to Sir 39:30a–b. זֵי — For this word, see Jastrow 1903, 393, sub זֵיי.

7 The verse corresponds to Sir 39:30c–d. The first stich is more literally: "all of these are appointed for their need."

⁴עַתָּה בְּכָל לֵב וָפֶ[ה] הַרְנִינוּ	8 ᴮ	נוּ∘∘
⁵וּבָרְכוּ אֶת שֵׁ{מ} קָדְשׁוֹ וְלִקְרָאתֹ[וֹ]		
⁶עַל רָשָׁע נִבְרְאוּ כָל רָעוֹת	9 ᴮ	כִּי אֵ[ל] אוֹ 14
⁷וּבְשָׁלוֹ כָל צָעַרִים נוֹגָעוֹת : ∘		מִתְקַ[לֵּל] מֵאָבִיו וְאָבִיו אִתּוֹ לַחֹבְרָה
⁸יָבוֹאוּ עַמּוֹ בְּבִיאָתוֹ	10 ᴮ	
וְיָמוּשׁוּ אֶצְלוֹ ⁹בְּהֲלִיכָתוֹ :		
¹⁰רוּחַ רָעָה תָשׁוּב אֶל נִדְנָהּ	11 ᴮᴹ	
וְרוּחַ יְשָׁרָה ¹¹תָּשׁוּב אֶל הָאֱלֹהִים אֲשֶׁר נְתָנָהּ :		
¹²אֲשֶׁר לַמָּרוֹם לַמָּרוֹם	12 ᴮᴹ	
וַאֲשֶׁר לָאָרֶץ ¹³מִצְדָּקוֹת עָרוּם :		
¹⁴וְהַחֶסֶד לֹא יָמוֹט לָעַד	13 ᴮᴹ	
וַאֲשׁוּרָיו ¹⁵לְעוֹלָם לֹא תִמְעַד :		
¹⁶חונן	13+	

T-S NS 93.79

T-S NS 93.79, recto (labeled verso)

[מֵ]¹	0	
[ ]∘הֵ תִּפְנֶה²	1 ᴮᴹ	
[ ] ³תִּישַׁר בְּבִיאָתָהּ		
⁴נִשְׁחֲרַת בְּבֵית הַחֲזַק מִשְׁמְרָהּ :	2 ᴮᴹ	
⁵עַד נְ[יְשׂוּ]אָהּ אִם תִּתְחַבְּרָה :		

L. 4 [8] עַתָּה בְּכָל לֵב וָפֶ[ה] הַרְנִינוּ — Reconstruction follows Fleischer 1990, 276.
L. 5 [8] קָדְשׁוֹ — A single dot under the *qoph* has been extended into a line to make a *qamets*.
L. 7 [9] וּבְשָׁלוֹ — What we read as *vav* is preserved only in its top, just above a hole. : ∘ — An open circle appears after the last word of the line, but before the *soph pasuq*. Most likely this indicates that the marginal text should be placed after this verse.
L. 7 Margin [14] יְלָכֵד — In the margin, the second line is difficult to make sense of. The *yod* and *lamed* (together with their vowel marks) are easy to discern; although only the bottom v-like mark of the *lamed* is preserved, it is unlike other letter shapes. If the next letter is a *kaph*, it is attested only by the faint traces of the tip of its bottom left line. Only a faint trace of what might be the vertical line of the *dalet* is attested (if this is indeed the letter). It is also conceivable that we should read instead יְלֻקַּח "it will be taken." מִנְחָתוֹ — Here, the *mem* is attested only by the tip of its "horn," which appears just above an ink spot; the ink spot is presumably part of the *mem*'s diagonal line. Alternatively, the ink spot is intended to cancel the underlying *mem*. The vertical stroke of the *nun* is clear, though what might have been an accidental slip of the pen or a broad cancellation mark sweeps through the *nun*'s base line and a *qamets* beneath the base line. The broad sweeping mark contributes to the impression that this group of lines represents a *shin* (cf. Fleischer 1990, 277). However, this is unlikely; the right-most stroke of a *shin* is usually a single curved line, while the right-most stroke in this group of lines (interpreted here as the vertical line of the *nun*) is straight up and down and at its bottom it appears to exhibit a right angle. The following *khet* is somewhat unusual in form and perhaps started too as another letter. The *tav* appears as though it was first written like a final *kaph*, though a peculiar *resh*-like shape is super-imposed on the right shoulder of the *tav*. Was the letter first written as a *resh* or *he*, then corrected to a final *kaph*, before then being changed into a *tav*? We assume the *qamets* beneath the *nun* is a mistake and that the expression reflects the sense "his offering." If we assume that the *qamets* should be preserved, then the word might be the *min* preposition plus נוּחָה "rest" spelled defectively (with *qamets hatuf*), though perhaps the cancellation mark through the *nun* hides a *holem* dot; the noun נוחה appears also in Sir 30:17. The stich would read: "and he will be captured from his rest and his strength."

L. 8 [10] עַמּוֹ — The *patakh* beneath the *ayin* seems to be written twice, though perhaps the second super-imposed line is meant to be a cancellation or is an offset trace. A large dot to the left is presumably the intended correction. אֶצְלוֹ — The word is written above וְיָמוּשׁוּ.
L. 10 [11] יְשָׁרָה — The word appears above וְרוּחַ. The *shin* has almost entirely been lost to a hole, though a trace of its upper left corner remains, as does the diacritic dot, and the *qamets*. The second *qamets*, under the *resh*, looks more like a *segol*, but this just reflects the wearing away of the ink of the top line of the *qamets*.
L. 12 [12] אֲשֶׁר — In this word that starts the verse, a *segol* was initially written beneath the *aleph*, but then it was erased and a *patakh* was super-imposed upon it.
L. 14 [13] לָעַד — The *dalet* is preserved only as faint traces. Clearly visible vowel marks appear beside the *qamets* and *patakh* of this word, reflecting presumably an erased word or offset traces. A *shewa* appears to the right of the *qamets* and a second (fainter) *qamets* appears to the right of the *patakh*. וַאֲשׁוּרָיו — Beneath this word are another sequence of vowel marks, from right to left, *hireq, patakh, segol*.
L. 16 [13+] חונן — The word appears at the bottom left corner of the page, indicating that the next verse begins with this word.
L. 2 [1] הֵ∘[— The reading is very uncertain.
L. 3 [1] בְּבִיאָתָהּ — Only traces remain of the first *bet*, though the *shewa* is clear. Even less is preserved of the second *bet* (only the left tip of the bottom line); here too the vowel is clear. No other word fits the remaining letters and context.
L. 4 [2] נִשְׁחֲרַת — The *patakh* under the *resh* is obscured due to a crease in the paper. מִשְׁמְרָהּ — The word sits above the preceding הַחֲזָק.
L. 5 [2] נְ[יְשׂוּ]אָהּ — "Her marriage." The reconstruction is tentative, though the word fits the space and remaining traces, as well as the context. Only traces of the *nun* and *hireq* remain; only the left vertical line

8	⁴Maintenant, de tout (ton) cœur et de (toute ta) bou[che], exultez, (mg. [ ]lui.) ⁵et bénissez son saint nom à [sa] rencontre.
9	⁶Les méchancetés ont été créées pour le méchant, ⁷et à cause de lui toutes les peines adviennent.
14	(mg. Malheur au méchant et malheur à son voisin car son offrande et sa richesse seront saisies.)
10	⁸Ils viennent avec lui dans ses allées et venues et s'écartent de son côté ⁹dans ses va-et-vient.
11	¹⁰Un esprit mauvais retourne dans son fourreau et un esprit droit ¹¹retourne au Dieu qui l'a pourvu.
12	¹²Ce qui est d'en haut est d'en haut et ce qui est terrestre ¹³est dénué de la justice.
13	¹⁴Le pieux jamais ne trébuche et ses pas ¹⁵jamais ne chancellent.
13+	¹⁶Celui qui fait grâce

T-S NS 93.79

0	¹[ ]
1	²Elle tournera [ ] [ ] ³elle agira correctement dans ses relations intimes.
2	⁴Renforce la garde sur (une fille) qui demeure dans (ta) maison, ⁵jusqu'à son ma[riage,] si tu la donnes en mariage.

8	⁴Now, with all your heart and mouth, exult (mg. [ ] him) ⁵and bless his holy name and towards [him].
9	⁶For the wicked all these evil things were created, ⁷and on account of them all griefs come.
14	(mg. Woe to the wicked, woe to his neighbor for his offering and his wealth will be seized.)
10	⁸They come with him in his entering, and they depart beside him ⁹when he goes.
11	¹⁰An evil spirit returns to its sheath, and an upright spirit ¹¹returns to God who gave it.
12	¹²What belongs to the height (goes) to the height, and what belongs to the earth ¹³is stripped from righteousness.
13	¹⁴But piety will never be shaken, and its steps ¹⁵never falter.
13+	¹⁶One favoring

T-S NS 93.79

0	¹
1	²She will turn … [ ] ³she will have intercourse in the correct manner.
2	⁴Fortify the watch over the (daughter) who remains in the house, ⁵until her ma[rriag]e, if you marry her off.

and *segol* of the *aleph* remain. תִּתְחַבְּרָה — "You marry her." The second letter is effaced and could have been a *gimel*, a *nun*, or perhaps even another letter, though certainly not a *shin* since it is far too narrow. Furthermore, the mark that seems to have been interpreted as the diacritic mark of a *shin* is actually the left most tip of the preceding *tav*'s top horizontal line (cf. Fleischer 1990, 278). The reading *khet* provides the best sense for the word in its context. The *soph pasuq* at the end of the line seems smeared.

8   The verse corresponds to Sir 39:35.
9   The verse corresponds to Sir 40:10. וּבְשֶׁלּוֹ — For the construction of *bet-shin-lamed*, cf. Jon 1:7, 12 and T-S AS 137.436, recto, line 4.
14 The verse does not correspond easily to any in Ben Sira, though the first stich is a phrase found repeatedly in Rabbinic Hebrew (see, e.g., m. Neg. 12:6), as Fleischer (1990, 277) notes.
10 This verse seems to continue the idea of verse 9 (i.e., Sir 40:10).
11–12 These verses correspond to Sir 40:11, though verse 11 in the H^Par seems to reflect an interpretation of the verse. נְדָנָה — An Aramaism, found clearly only seven other times in medieval Hebrew (see Maagarim); for the word with this articulation, see Dan 7:15.
13 The verse corresponds to Sir 40:17.
13+ חונן — The catch word is the first of the page that would have followed in the codex.
1   תִּישַׁר בְּבִיאָתָהּ — More literally, this would be "she goes straight in her intercourse." The similarity of בְּבִיאָתָהּ with בית אביה from

Sir 42:10 (H^B,M), together with the use of זנה "to fornicate" in that same verse suggests perhaps the present text corresponds to Sir 42:10. The association of correct sexual practices with Ben Sira is reflected in b. San. 100b (read from the Maagarim database): אורח ארעא קא משמ' לן דלא תבעול שלא כדרכה "he (Ben Sira) teaches us (about) regular practice: that you (or she) should not have intercourse in an unnatural manner." Immediately following in the Talmudic passage is a discussion and quotation of Ben Sira's sayings about daughters (Sir 42:11–14).
2   The verse corresponds to Sir 42:11a. נִשְׁחַרַת — The phrase is likely related to the Syriac verb ܚܫܚ, which occurs exclusively in the *ethpeel* "to be left, remain" (as in Sir 23:27 ܟܠ ܕܡܫܬܚܪܝܢ "all who remain in the world"). תִּתְחַבְּרָה — The sense of marriage for חבר is found in Sir 7:25 (H^A,D). The verb is usually assumed to be in the *piel*. Nevertheless, the *qal* does appear with a direct object elsewhere (see, e.g., Deut 18:11; in Eleazar HaQalir's קדושתא וזאת הברכה at מי גבר יחיה ולא יראה מות סילוק, line 102 [see Maagarim]).

3 BM	⁶פֶ[ן] ○○ [רֶעְשְׁךָ
	וְתָשִׂים ⁷עֵדֹ[ן] בֹּ[ךָ] [בָּ]שֹׁחַדֹ לְדַשְׁשְׁךָ :
4 BM	⁸וְדִיבָּה תִהְיֶה בִּקְהִילוֹת
	וְעֵדַת שַׁעַר ⁹וּמַקְהֵלוֹת :
5 BM	¹⁰אַל תִּתֵּן תּוֹאַר לִזְכָרִים
	¹¹וְאַל תִּסְתַּיֵּדֹ לִפְנֵי נָשִׁים :
6 BM	¹²כִּי רָעַת אִשָּׁה מֵאִשָּׁה
	וְיֵשׁ חֲבֶרֶת ¹³הֲבִיאָה בוּשָׁה :
6+	¹⁴קֹ○

T-S NS 93.79, verso (labeled recto)

7	¹[○○○○] [ ]○[ ] [דְּמָתָ○○ וְרִבָּה
	²וְעֻמְּקַ{וּ}ים עַד תְּהוֹם רַבָּה :
8	³הֲמַשִּׂיג מֵהֶם תַּאֲוָה
	יִפֹּל בַּחֹשֶׁק וְהוֹוָה :
9	⁴וְאִשָּׁה רָעָה צָרַעַת בָּ[בָשָׂר]אִישָׁה
	⁵כִּי רָדָה עַל עָרְפּוֹ עַד לֹא יוּכַל לְגָרְשָׁה :
10	⁶אִם יוּכַל לְגָרְשֶׁנָּה וְיִתְרַפֵּא
	וְאִם לָאו ⁷יְרִצִּיעַ אָזְנוֹ עַד יְסֻפֶּ{נּ}ה :
11	⁸אוּלַי תִּישַׁר אַחֲרִיתוֹ וְתִקְוָתוֹ
	⁹וְלוּ יוֹם אֶחָד יִתְרַפֵּא מִצָּרַעְתּוֹ :
12	¹⁰כִּי שְׁכִיבָה בֶּעָפָרִים
	וּשְׁכִינָה בְּתוֹךְ ¹¹קְבָרִים :

T-S AS 124.103

T-S AS 124.103, recto (labeled verso)

1	¹[ ] [ ]○○○[ ]○□
2	²[ ]לְבָבוֹת
3	³[ ]○ה בְּעוֹלָמִֹםֹ וְיִבְחִין [ ]○○○

L. 6 [3] רֶעְשְׁךָ — "Your quaking." Note that the diacritic dot above what must be the *shin* is really above the letter's left arm.

L. 7 [3] עֵדֹ[ן] בֹּ[ךָ] [בָּ]שֹׁחַדֹ לְדַשְׁשְׁךָ — The reconstruction is an educated guess. The *dalet* is preserved as just faint traces of the vertical and horizontal lines and could be another letter. The prepositional phrase בֹּ[ךָ] is partially based on the sense and spacing. Only a portion of the *kaph*'s descender is visible. Ordinarily it would not be possible to assume this letter, but note how the final *kaph* in לְדַשְׁשְׁךָ is almost entirely effaced (except for its lower bend), though the *raphe* line and *qamets* are clearly legible. The curvature of the hole suggests a missing *bet* or *kaph*. Only the tip of the *shin* is visible, though a dot which might be the *holem* of שֹׁחַדֹ "bribe" or the misplaced diacritic of the *shin* (cf. רֶעְשְׁךָ in line 6) is clear above the hole. The *khet*'s top and left leg are visible, while the *dalet* is fairly clear, though faint. As for לְדַשְׁשְׁךָ "to crush you," the first *shin* is faint, though one can see the left arm as well as a trace of the middle arm. A single mark is all that remains of the right arm. As mentioned above, only the bottom bend of the final *kaph*'s descender is visible, though the *raphe* line and the *qamets* are clear. The reading of *kaph*, of course, seems confirmed by the rhyme. We assume the *piel* infinitive construct.

L. 8 [4] שַׁעַר — The word sits above וְעֵדַת.

L. 14 [6+] קֹ○ — The *qoph* is identifiable primarily based on its long descender, which is followed by another letter as part of the same word. The marks are located on the bottom left corner of the page and indicate that the next verse began with a *qoph*.

L. 1 [7] [דְּמָתָ○○]○[ ]○○○○ — Various vowel marks are preserved beneath the tear. The first trace should be either a *dalet* or *resh* given the space between the vertical mark and the beginning of the *mem*. The *shewa* is clear. The marks following the *tav* are difficult to make sense of in the context.

L. 3 [8] וְהוֹוָה — The word appears just above the word בַּחֹשֶׁק.

L. 4 [9] בָּ[בָשָׂר]אִישָׁה — The reconstruction is based on context. Note that under the *bet* is clearly a *hireq*. This suggests that the following vowel is likely a *shewa*. That is, בָּ[בֵית] is not possible.

L. 5 [9] לְגָרְשָׁה — The phrase appears just to the left and slightly above the preceding word so that the expected *shewa* beneath the *lamed* has been obscured.

L. 6 [10] לָאו — The word appears just above וְאִם.

L. 7 [10] יְסֻפֶּ{נּ}ה — The initial spelling (with *shewa* presumably under the *pe*: יְסֻפְּנוּ) reflects "they will be respected" or "they will be hidden/covered" (and perhaps in this context "buried"?), while the correction reflects "he will be swept away."

L. 10 [12] וּשְׁכִינָה בְּתוֹךְ — The *he* of וּשְׁכִינָה appears to bear a *raphe* symbol, which perhaps suggests that the letter was initially written as a *dalet* (though such a spelling does not reflect a known word). Some unidentifiable marks also appear to the left of the *he*. The word בְּתוֹךְ appears just above and to the left of וּשְׁכִינָה.

L. 1 [1] Multiple traces can be made out, though it is difficult to make sense of them.

L. 3 [2] בְּעוֹלָמִֹםֹ — The *qamets* beneath the *lamed* is secure as is the following *mem*. Based on the traces, the most likely readings would seem to be either the one given above or בְּעוֹלָמִֹת "ever." וְיִבְחִין — Based on the preceding line-final word and the presence of another verse in the line that follows, one assumes that some word ending in -*ot* has been lost from the end of this line.

3	⁶De peur que [ ] ton tremblement et qu'elle place ⁷un témoin [contre] toi pour te briser [par] un présent.	3	⁶Lest [ ] your quaking, and she set ⁷a witness [against] you [with] a bribe to crush you.
4	⁸Et tu seras (l'objet) de rumeur dans les assemblées et à l'assemblée de la porte ⁹et des congrégations.	4	⁸And a byword you will be in the assemblies, in the congregation of the gate ⁹and gatherings.
5	¹⁰Qu'elle n'offre pas sa beauté aux hommes ¹¹et qu'elle ne converse pas devant les femmes.	5	¹⁰May she not offer (her) beauty to males, ¹¹may she not converse before women.
6	¹²Car la méchanceté d'une femme vient d'une femme et il y a un compagnon ¹³qui fait venir la honte.	6	¹²For the evil of a woman (comes) from a woman and there is a companion ¹³that brings shame.
6+	¹⁴ [ ]	6+	¹⁴ [ ]
7	¹et [ ] [ ] ... et davantage ²et les profondeurs jusqu'au grand abîme.	7	¹And, ... and much ²and deeps until the great abyss.
8	³Celui qui obtient d'eux le désir tombera dans le désir et la destruction.	8	³The one who attains his desire from them, will fall in (their) desire and destruction.
9	⁴Une femme mauvaise est une lèpre dans [la chair de son mari, ⁵car il domine sa (propre) nuque tant qu'il est capable de la diriger.	9	⁴An evil woman is leprosy in [the flesh of] her husband, ⁵for he has control over his body until he is not able to drive her away.
10	⁶S'il est capable de la diriger alors il sera guéri, sinon ⁷il percera sa (propre) oreille (et deviendra esclave) jusqu'à ce qu'il périsse.	10	⁶If he is able to drive her away, then he will be healed, if not, ⁷then he pierces his (own) ear (and is a perpetual slave) until he is gathered up.
11	⁸Peut-être que son avenir et son espoir seront droits ⁹et peut-être qu'un jour il sera guéri de sa lèpre.	11	⁸Perhaps his future and his hope will be all right, ⁹and perhaps one day he will be healed from his leprosy.
12	¹⁰Car son repos est dans les poussières et sa demeure est au milieu ¹¹des tombeaux.	12	¹⁰For, his lying down will be in dust and his dwelling in the midst of ¹¹graves.

T-S AS 124.103

1	¹[ ]	1	¹[ ]
2	²[ ] cœurs	2	²[ ] hearts.
	³[ ] et dans l'éternité et il discernera [ ]		³[ ] and ever and he will distinguish [ ]

---

3 The verse seems to correspond to Sir 42:11b.
4 The verse corresponds to Sir 42:11c–d. וְדִבָּה — For our translation, see Deut 28:37; דיבה may also be the subject of תהיה, "A rumor will be in the assemblies."
5 The verse corresponds to Sir 42:12.
6 The verse corresponds to Sir 42:13.
7 וְרָבָה — The word should be vocalized with a *patakh* under the *resh* or with a *raphe* line above the *bet*.
8 This and the following verses do not have a direct correspondence in Ben Sira, though they clearly develop the theme of daughters found in Sir 42.

10 לֹאו — The negative particle appears frequently in Rabbinic Hebrew preceded by אִם. יְרְצִיעַ אָזְנוֹ — The image and language are drawn from Exod 21:6.
11 אַחֲרִיתוֹ — Literally, "his end," the word might also connote "his progeny."
2 בְּעוֹלָמִם — Although the *qamets* is secure as well as the *bet*, *ayin*, and *mem*, the other letters are hard to decipher. The *bet* preposition is surprising and does not commonly occur with עוֹלָמִים or עוֹלָמִית. Instead, we might expect a word meaning "youth" (עוּלָמִים) or "strength" (עוּלָמִית). וְיַבְחִין — The *hiphil* of בחן is found in Tannaitic and later texts.

PARAPHRASE

3	[4] שְׁמַע בְּנִי אִמְרֵי פִי
	[5]]ס[יבָה חוֹרְפַי וּמְגַדְּפִי :
4	[6]]ס[וּלְבָבְךָ טַהֵר
	וּבְדַרְכֵי יוֹשֶׁר]ס[7]נָה וּמַהֵר :
5	8יַשֵּׁר נָתִיב וּמַעְגָּל
	וְסוֹדְךָ 9לְאַחֵר אַל תְּגַל
6	10חֲמוֹל עַל אָח וְרֵיעַ
	וְאַל תְּהִי 11לְסוֹדוֹ כְפָרִיעַ :
7	12בְּחַ[ר] מִבְחַר עָרִסס
	[13]ר נְתִיבֵי נְסִיכִים
8	סִסס14 נְסִיכִים זַכִּים [ ]
9	[1] סססס]ס[נו]ססדוֹש̇ס
	[2]ב̇יו יִירִישׁ :
10	[3 אִם צָמֵה אִיבְךָ הַשְׁקֵהוּ]
	4א[ם רָעֵב הַאֲכִילֵהוּ :]
11	5וְהֵטִיב לֹא פָעַל בְכַדְּבָה
	וְהָסִיר 6תַּחֲרוּת וְאֵבָה :
12	7אִם רָבַץ חֲמוֹרוֹ תַּחַת מַשָּׂאוֹ
	[א] 8תִּמָּנַע לְעָזְרוֹ וּלְנַשְּׂאוֹ :
13	9הִלֵּךְ בְּדַרְכֵי חֲכָמִים
	10כִּי הֵם יָפִים וּנְעִימִים :
14	11בְּחַר בָּהֶם [יֹ]שֶׁר דַּרְכָּם
	כִּי יִמְתַּק לְךָ 12[ ]ח[ ] :
15	[13]תָּבֹן וְתֶחְכַּם
	וּבְדַעְתֶּךָ 14[ ]חכם :
16	[15]ס[ ]ססס

T-S AS 124.103, verso (labeled recto)

T-S AS 124.104

T-S AS 124.104, recto (labeled verso)

1	1כֵּן אַשְׁרֶךָ אֶרֶץ שֶׁיְּהוּ אוֹ[ ]
	2שָׂרִים וַעֲבָדֶיךָ חוֹרִים
2	מש[ס] 3מַשְׂכִּילִים בַּצָּהֳרָיִם
	וּמֹשְׁל[חִים] 4לֶח[ ]ם עַל פְּנֵי הַמָּיִם :

L. 7 [4] וּמַהֵר — Although the entire word is obscured by an ink splotch, the rhyme makes the reading of the last two consonants clear.

L. 11 [6] כְפָרִיעַ — The *holem* dot actually appears over the *resh*.

L. 12 [7] מִבְחַר עָרִסס — The *resh* of the first word is irregularly shaped and we might expect a *patakh*, not *tsere*, if the word were in construct. A black splotch obscures the letters that follow.

L. 13 [7] נְסִיכִים — The dark splotch obscures the letters again and the reconstruction is tentative.

L. 1 [9] ססס]נו[— Offset marks or effaced letters appear above and to the left of the *vav*. ש̇ד̇וֹש]ס[— The marks are difficult to read. The last letter has a tail.

L. 3 [10] צָמֵה — The vowel mark beneath the *tsade* actually looks like a *tsere*, but this is likely due to the effacing of ink.

L. 5 [11] פָעַל בְכַדְּבָה — The two words are surprisingly close together and there is perhaps a better way to read the first letters.

L. 6 [11] תַּחֲרוּת וְאֵבָה — Offset traces of these words are found at T-S AS 124.104, recto, line 5. This correspondence suggests that T-S AS 124.103 recto and T-S AS 124.104 verso were originally facing each other.

L. 2 [1] חוֹרִים — The *khet* was first written as two letters. A heavy horizontal bar created the *khet*.

3	⁴Écoute, mon enfant, les paroles de ma bouche, ⁵[ ] celui qui m'outrage et qui m'insulte.
4	⁶[ ] et purifier ton cœur et dans des voies de droiture ⁷[ ] et en hâte.
5	⁸Rends droit un sentier et une route et ton secret ⁹ne le révèle pas à un autre.
6	¹⁰Aie pitié d'un frère et d'un compagnon et ne sois pas ¹¹comme celui qui dévoile son secret.
7	¹²Fa[is] un choix [ ] ¹³[ ] des sentiers de princes [ ]
8	¹⁴[ ] de pures libations [ ] ¹⁵[ ]en eux [ ]
9	¹[ ]son [ ] ²[ ]ses [ ] il héritera.
10	³Si ton ennemi a soif, abreuve-[le], ⁴si il a faim, nourris-le.
11	⁵Il fait le bien celui qui ne travaille pas au mensonge et qui se détourne ⁶de la colère et de l'animosité.
12	⁷Si son âne s'affale sous sa charge, [ne]⁸refuse [pas] de le secourir et de le relever.
13	⁹Marche dans les voies des sages, ¹⁰car elles sont belles et plaisantes.
14	¹¹Choisis-les, redresse leurs voies, car ce sera doux pour toi ¹²[ ].
15	¹³[ ]tu comprendras et tu deviendras sage et dans ta connaissance ¹⁴[ ] sage.
16	¹⁵[ ]

T-S AS 124.104

1	¹Ainsi, heureuse es-tu, Ô terre, [ ] qui seront[ ] ²des princes et tes nobles serviteurs.
2	[ ] ³ceux qui sont stériles en plein midi et ceux qui jet[tent du pai]n à la surface des eaux.

3	⁴Hear, my child, the words of my mouth, ⁵[ ] the one who reproaches me and who reviles me.
4	⁶[ ] your heart purify, and in straight paths ⁷[ ] and hurry!
5	⁸Make straight the path and trail, and ⁹do not reveal your secret to another.
6	¹⁰Have pity over brother and friend, and do not be ¹¹as one uncovering his secret.
7	¹²Ma[ke] a choice [ ] ¹³[ ] paths of princes [ ]
8	¹⁴[ ] pure libations [ ] ¹⁵[ ]
9	¹ ²his [ ] he will inherit.
10	³If your enemy is thirsty, give him drink, ⁴if he is hungry, feed him.
11	⁵He has done good who does not deal in lies, and (instead with) turning away ⁶anger and animosity.
12	⁷If his donkey lies down under its load, do [not] ⁸keep from helping him and lifting it.
13	⁹Walk in the path of the sages, ¹⁰for they are beautiful and pleasant.
14	¹¹Choose them, straighten their path, for it will be sweet to you ¹²[ ].
15	¹³[ ]you will understand and you will be wise, and in your knowledge ¹⁴[ ] wise.
16	¹⁵

T-S AS 124.104

1	¹Thus, you are happy, O land, that [ ] they will be ²princes and your servants nobles.
2	[ ] ³those bereaving at noon time, and those sen[ding] ⁴[brea]d over the face of the water.

3   The verse expresses an idea similar to that of Sir 31:22.
5   A close parallel to the expression of the second stich is found in Prov 25:9b. As for Ben Sira, the theme of keeping a secret is frequent, but an exact parallel to this expression and to that of the next verse is not attested. Perhaps most relevant are Sir 27:16–17 (in the Syriac ܪܓܠܐ ܕܓܠܐ ܘܪܕܦ ܢܦܫܗ. ܘܡܢ ܕܡܓܠܐ ܐܪܙܐ ܐܘܒܕ ܗܝܡܢܘܬܐ. ܘܠܐ ܡܫܟܚ ܪܚܡܐ ܕܫܘܐ ܠܗ. ܐܚܒ ܪܚܡܟ ܘܗܝܡܢܝܗܝ. ܐܢ ܕܝܢ ܓܠܐ ܐܪܙܟ ܠܐ ܬܐܙܠ ܒܬܪܗ "One who reveals a secret destroys their trustworthiness and will find no friend like himself. Test your friend and trust them, but if they reveal a confidential secret do not go after them") or 31:31 (best preserved in H^F). תגל — The word is presumably the *piel* jussive; the expected *patakh* is a *qamets*.
6   כפריע — This is the *kaph* preposition plus the *qal* participle.
7   The verse might be compared to Sir 31:16, where one also finds the verb בחר and the advice (at least according to one interpretation of the words) to eat what has been prepared. מבחר — Under the *khet* we would have expected a *qamets* or *patakh* instead of a *tsere*.

9   יירש — We would expect instead יִרַשׁ. The theme vowel for the verb here is likely connected to the theme vowel of the Aramaic verb ירת in Jewish Babylonian Aramaic (cf. the vocalization יָרֵית in Jastrow 1903, 598, sub ירת).
10 The verse corresponds to Prov 25:21. צמה — Based on the MT, we would expect the spelling צָמֵא.
11 בכדבה — The word כְּדָבָה is an Aramaism. The pairing of speaking truth and avoiding anger is reminiscent of Sir 46:7 (... להשיב חרון להשבית דבה רעה).
12 The verse corresponds to Exod 23:5.
13 The first stich is reminiscent of Prov 13:20. הֵלֵךְ — This is the *piel* imperative.
1   אַשְׁרֵךְ אֶרֶץ — The phrase comes from Qoh 10:17. In the second stich, the juxtaposition of "servants" with "nobles" is reminiscent of Qoh 10:7 as well as Sir 10:25 (in H^B and Syriac).
2   The first stich seems reminiscent of the expression עַל־אֵם בָּחוּר שֹׁדֵד בַּצׇּהֳרָיִם from Jer 15:8. The second stich corresponds to Qoh 11:1.

3	[⁵] [בֵּ]ינֵיהֶם שִׂנְאָה
	[⁶]°[אָה] מָלֵא תַחֲרוּת :
4	⁷וַחֲכָמֶיךָ מְכֻבָּדִים
	וְתַלְמִידֶיךָ ⁸יְדִידִים :
5	⁹וּזְקֵנֶיךָ הַדּוּרִים
	וְשׁוֹפְטֶיךָ ¹⁰מְיֻקָּרִים :
6	¹¹וּבְצֶדֶק וֶאֱמֶת יָדַי°°
	[ ]¹² ירוֹשׁ °[ ] וְיוֹשֶׁרׄ :
7	[ ]¹³[נִבְחָרִים] [ ]
	]¹⁴[°°°°°] [
8	]¹[°[ ]° [חָכְ]מָה
	וּסְגֻלָּה°°[ ]²[ ]אֲ[נָ]שִׁים בְּעָרְמָה :
9	]³[°בָּרִיךְ בְּשֵׂכֶל וּבִינָה
	[וַחֲנִינָה]⁴ [ ] וְתִישַׁרׄ :
10	⁵זֶה דּוֹר אֱלֹהִים בֵּרְכוֹ
	וְחָכְ[מוֹ]⁶ וְהַעֲרִיכוֹ :
11	⁷דּוֹר אַנְשֵׁי מְזִמָּה
	וִיסוֹדוֹ כֵּן [ ]°⁸ בְּחוֹמָה :
12	⁹דּוֹר נְגִידָיו נְבוֹנִים
	וְקוֹרְאִים ¹⁰הֲלָכָה וְשׁוֹנִים :
13	¹¹[אֱ]לֹהִים°° וְחוֹשְׁבֵי שְׁמוֹ
	וּבְחוּרֵי ¹²[ ]ת וּקְדוֹשָׁיו °°לוֹ ׄ :
14	]¹³[לְלָשׁוֹן] [°] [ ]

T-S AS 124.104, verso (labeled recto)

HUC 1301

1	¹וְאָשׁוּב בְּכָל לְבָבִי אֵלָיו
	וּבְ°[ ]
2	²וְאֵדַע כֵּן אֵן לִי סוֹמֵךְ בִּלְתּוֹ
	°[ ] [ ]³ אֵן זוּלָתוֹ :
3	⁴כִּי הוּא בְרֶחֶם הֱתִיכַנִי
	[וּבְמֵ] [
4	⁵וּמִבֶּטֶן הוֹצִיאַנִי
	וּכְדֵי מַחְסוֹרִי הֵ°[ ]
5	⁶וְאָבִי וְאִמִּי לֹא הוֹעִילוּנִי
	וְאָחִי וְאַחְיוֹתַי ⁷לֹא הִצִּילוּנִי :

HUC 1301, folio 1, recto

L. 5 [3] תַחֲרוּת — Curiously, the same word is found in offset letters just beneath this word. The offset traces correspond to the word on T-S AS 124.103 verso, line 6 and suggests that these two pages faced each other in the book.

L. 11 [6] יָדַי°° — One would imagine the word being read יָדִין "he will judge" (cf. Ps 9:9) or יָדֶיךָ "your hands," but there appear to be two letters in the dark splotch, not just one. ירוֹשׁ — The word appears above and to the left of וְיוֹשֶׁרׄ and appears to be canceled with a diagonal line.

L. 3 [9] °בָּרִיךְ[ ] — The 2fs pronominal suffix likely has as antecedent the earth (אֶרֶץ) found in line 1 of the recto.

L. 5 [10] [מוֹ]וְחָכְ — This is an educated guess, based on context and the preserved marks.

L. 2 [2] כֵּן אֵן — Fleischer (1997, 213*) suggests [אֵן] כִּי, which makes sense semantically, though the marks are impossible to read in this way. The mark following the kaph is a final nun, ligatured to the kaph. This is presumably a mistake for כִּי. As for the following letters, the aleph's right and left vertical marks are visible, as is the tsere. Only the top and bottom of the final nun are visible. בִּלְתּוֹ — A hireq is canceled by a diagonal line under the tav.

L. 5 [4] הֵ°[ ] — The marks are written above and to the left of מַחְסוֹרִי. The letter is clearly a he, not a khet as in Fleischer 1997, *213.

3	⁵[ ]la haine entre eux, une pleine colère ⁶[ ]	3	⁵[ ]between them hate, fulfillment of anger ⁶[ ]
4	⁷Et tes sages sont honorés et tes enseignants ⁸bien aimés.	4	⁷And your wise ones are honored, and your scholars ⁸loved.
5	⁹Tes anciens respectés et tes juges ¹⁰estimés.	5	⁹Your elders respected, your judges ¹⁰valued.
6	¹¹Dans la justice et la vérité [ ] et prendre possession de la droiture ¹²[ ]	6	¹¹In righteousness and truth [ ] and to inherit uprightness ¹²[ ]
7	¹³[ ] ceux choisis [ ]	7	¹³[ ] those chosen [ ]
8	¹[ ] sagesse [ ] et amasse [ ] ²[ ] des personnes par la ruse.	8	¹[ ] wisdom [ ] treasure [ ] ²[ ] men in prudence.
9	³[ ] ta [ ] par discernement et intelligence et tu as aplani ⁴[ ] et la grâce.	9	³[ ] your [ ] with insight and understanding, and you will go straight ⁴[ ] and grace.
10	⁵c'est la génération que Dieu a béni et qu'il a ren[du sa]ge ⁶et qu'il a estimé.	10	⁵This is the generation that God blessed, and he tau[ght them] ⁶and compared them.
11	⁷Une génération de personnes réfléchies, dont la fondation est comme[ ] ⁸par une muraille.	11	⁷A generation of cunning people, whose foundation is like [ ] ⁸in a wall.
12	⁹Une génération de chefs établis qui lisent ¹⁰la *halakha* et (la) répète.	12	⁹A generation of established rulers who read ¹⁰the law and repeat (it).
13	¹¹[ ] Dieu [ ] et ceux qui contemplent son nom et ceux qui choisissent ¹²[ ] et sa sainteté [ ].	13	¹¹[ ] God [ ] and those contemplating his name, those chosen ¹²[ ] his holy ones [ ].
14	¹³[ ] à une langue [ ]	14	¹³[ ] to a tongue [ ]

HUC 1301

1	¹Et je retournerai vers lui de tout mon cœur et dans [ ]	1	¹I will return to him with all my heart, and in [ ]
2	²et je saurai ainsi qu'il n'y a pas de secours pour moi en dehors de lui, [ ] ³il n'y a rien, en dehors de lui.	2	²and I know thus I have no support without him, [ ] ³there is not beside him.
3	⁴Car lui m'a déversé dans le sein et dans [ ]	3	⁴For he has poured me into the womb, and in [ ]
4	⁵et depuis les entrailles, il m'a fait sortir et selon mon indigence [ ]	4	⁵and from the belly he has drawn me out, and according to my need [ ]
5	⁶Et mon père et ma mère ne m'ont pas été utiles et mon frère et ma sœur ⁷ne m'ont pas sauvé.	5	⁶My father, my mother, did not benefit me, and my brothers and my sisters ⁷do not deliver me.

8ff These verses do not individually parallel the language of any specific verse in Ben Sira, but their idea and vocabulary collectively reflect Sir 44:1–15, the prelude to the Praise of the Ancestors. In Sir 44:1–15, the word דּוֹר appears in three verses at the beginning (44:1), middle (44:7), and end (44:14). In addition, the construct form "generations of" appears at 44:3 in Hᴮ (also reflected in the concluding words of the Syriac to 44:2), though in the margin of Hᴮ one finds רודי "rulers of" which agrees with the Greek. Other words and roots are also shared among this and the Sirach text, including אִישׁ (Sir 44:1, 3, 6, 10 // vv. 8, 11); אֵלֶּה (Sir 44:7, 10) // זֶה (v. 10); חָכָם (Sir 44:4) //וְחָכְ[מוֹ] (v. 10); חָכְמָה (Sir 44:15 // v. 8); מְזִמָּה (Sir 44:4 // v. 11); מְכוּנָּה (Sir 44:6) // נְבוֹנִים (v. 12); שנה (Sir 44:15 // v. 12); תבונה (Sir 44:3) // בִּנָה (v. 9). Beyond this, there are obvious synonyms between the two texts, e.g., רֹזֵן/שַׂר(Sir 44:4) // נָגִיד (v. 12); נָשָׂא מָשָׁל (Sir 44:5) and קרה (v. 12).

1 Similar expressions to the first stich are found in Deut 30: 2, 10; 1 Sam 7:3; 1 Kgs 8:48; and especially Jer 24:7; 2 Chr 6:38; and 4Q398 14–17 i 7.

2 A similar idea, though not exact, is found in Ruth 4:4 and Sir 36:5, though perhaps (given the clear parallels to Sir 51 below), we should see here an echo of Sir 51:7, which also contains the phrase סומך ואין "a support, but there was not." The negative particle plus 3ms suffix בִּלְתוֹ is found first in texts dating to 400–600 CE according to Maagarim.

3 Fleischer (1997, *213) notes the similarity in language to Job 10:10. In Sir 51:5a, the word רחם "womb" also occurs.

5 Cf. Ps 27:10. Here the theme of God's exclusive benefit to the speaker is taken up, as in verse 2 and in Sir 51:7.

6	⁸וְאָרִים מֵאֶרֶץ קוֹלִי
	וּבִקַּשְׁתִּי רוּחֹת[י] בְּכָל יָכְלִי :
7	⁹כִּי רַחֲמָיו עֲזָרוּנִי מִנְעוּרַי
	וְלֹא ¹⁰הוֹעִילוּנִי אָבֹתַי וּמוֹרַי :
8	¹¹וְאַזְכְּרָה אֶת רַחֲמָיו הָעֲצוּמִים
	¹²וְטוֹבוֹתָיו הָרַבִּים וְהַקְּדֻ[וּ]מִים :
9	¹³וְאֲרוֹמֵם אָב ה]∘[
	¹⁴כִּי בֶאֱמֶת חֵ] [
10	¹⁵וְאֶזְכְּרַהוּ בְתֹ[פלה
11	[¹][קוֹלִי]
	וַיַּעַן שׁוְעָתִי וּפְלוּלִי :
12	²[מִכֹּל ר]עוֹת פְּדָאַנִי
	וּמִכָּל צָרוֹת חִלְּצַנִי :
13	³[מִכָּל]מוֹקֵשׁ הִצִּילַנִי
	וּמִבּוֹר שְׁאוֹן הֶעֱלַנִי :
14	⁴וְלֹא נָתַן לַמּוֹט רַגְלִי
	וְהָפַךְ מִסְפְּדִי לְמָחוֹל לִי:
15	⁵וַיָּכוֹנֵן אֲשׁוּרַי בְּדֶרֶךְ יוֹשֶׁר
	וַיִּתֵּן רַגְלַי בְּאָרְחוֹת כּוֹשֶׁר :
16	⁶וַיָּשֶׂם בְּפִי שִׁירִים לְהַלְלוֹ
	וּלְהוֹדוֹת לוֹ ⁷כִּטּוּב פָּעֳלוֹ :
17 ᴮ	⁸אֲבָרְכָה שְׁמוֹ כִּיָכְלִי
	כִּי הוּא חֶלְקִי וְחֶבְלִי :
18 ᴮᵠ	⁹וְכִי הוּא מִנְּעוּרַי אִוִּיתִי
	¹⁰וְעַל רַחֲמָיו וְטוּבוֹ קִוִּיתִי :
19 ᴮᵠ	[¹¹] אַחֲרָיו
	[¹²]יוֹ וְלָנֶצַח
20 ᴮ	[¹³] הָמוּ וְרוּחִי בַאֲמָרָיו
	[¹⁴]לֹ[ ]
21	¹יִמְתּוֹק לְפִי עֵת אַזְכְּרֶנּוּ
	וְרוּחִי וְנִשְׁמָתִי ²מְאֹד תֶּחְמְדֶנּוּ :

HUC 1301, folio 1, verso

HUC 1301, folio 2, recto

L. 8 [6] רוּחֹת[י] בְּכָל יָכְלִי — The words בְּכָל יָכְלִי are written above and to the left of רוּחֹת[י]. The latter sequence of letters is difficult to make sense of; Fleischer (1990, 213*) reads בּוֹרְאִי, though the first mark cannot be a *bet*; the following mark we assume to be a *vav* with *dagesh* to mark it as a consonant. The following marks could reflect numerous different letters. We assume that the vertical stroke is the right leg of a *khet*; a dot of ink is all that is preserved of the top of the left leg while a faint mark preserves the bottom of the left leg. The *tav* is attested only by the left most part of its horizontal bar and a trace of the left leg. Alternatively, the word might be read רוּמְיָה "objection," an Aramaism drawn from Jewish Babylonian Aramaic (b. Git. 61b), though the word is masculine there and otherwise unknown in Hebrew. Perhaps, alternatively, we should read רוֹמִי "one on high" (another potential Aramaism, found in Galilean Aramaic, see CAL 4 Jan., 2021).

6 The verse corresponds to Sir 51:9. [י]רוּחֹת — The word is assumed to be an inflected form of רְוָחָה often spelled with two *vavs* in Rabbinic Hebrew and having the sense "relief" or, as in Lam 3:56, an "appeal for relief." — יָכְלִי — The infinitive construct of יכל is found in similar phrases (with בכל) in texts dating from ca. 900 CE (see Maagarim).
8 The verse corresponds to Sir 51:8.
9 The verse corresponds to Sir 51:10.
10 The preserved portion of text seems to correspond with Sir 51:11b.

L. 15 [10] Reconstruction follows the Hᴮ version of Sir 51:11b, though (as Fleischer [1997, *214] notes) the versions reflect בתהילה.
L. 2 [12] [מכל ר]עוֹת — The reconstruction is based on Sir 51:12a (see Fleischer 1997, *214). חלצני — The word is written above and to the left of צרות.
L. 3 [13] הִצִּילַנִי — We would expect a *patakh* under the *lamed*. הֶעֱלַנִי — The word is written above and to the left of שׁאון.
L. 8 [17] וְחֶבְלִי — The word is written above and to the left of חֶלְקִי.
L. 9 [18] מִנְּעוּרַי — The *shewa* looks more like a *meteg*. We expect a *patakh* beneath the *resh*, instead of a *hireq*.
L. 1 [21] יִמְתּוֹק — The word is written with two theme vowels. Presumably the *patakh* was written after the *shureq* and represents the revision of the scribe.

11 The verse corresponds to Sir 51:11c–d. For וּפְלוּלִי, see Jastrow 1903, 1163, sub פִּילּוּל.
12 The verse corresponds to Sir 51:12a–b.
13 מוֹקֵשׁ — The word appears in Sir 51:3b, though the other language and images are not identical. מִבּוֹר שְׁאוֹן הֶעֱלַנִי — The same image and vocabulary are found in Ps 40:3.
14 As Fleischer (1997, *214) notes, the language of the first stich matches Ps 66:9 and the second matches Ps 30:12.

6	⁸Et j'ai élevé ma voix depuis la terre	6	⁸I raised my voice from the earth,
	et j'ai poursuivi [mon] appel au secours de tout mon possible.		I pursued (my) appeal for relief with all my ability.
7	⁹Car sa miséricorde m'a secouru depuis ma jeunesse	7	⁹For, his mercy has helped me from my youth,
	et ¹⁰mes ancêtres et mes instructeurs ne m'ont pas été utiles.		though ¹⁰my ancestors and my teachers have not benefitted me.
8	¹¹Que je fasse mémoire de ses puissantes miséricordes	8	¹¹Let me recall his numerous mercies
	¹²et de ses bontés nombreuses et anciennes.		¹²and his many former good deeds.
9	¹³J'exalterai le père de [ ]	9	¹³I will exalt the father of [ ]
	¹⁴car en vérité [ ]		¹⁴for in truth [ ]
10	¹⁵Et je ferai mémoire de lui dans la pr[ière]	10	¹⁵I recall him in pr[ayer]
11	¹[ ] ma voix	11	¹[ ] my voice,
	et il a répondu à mon cri et ma plainte.		and he answered my cry and my pleading.
12	²[De tout m]al, il m'a racheté	12	²[From every e]vil he ransomed me,
	et de toute détresse, il m'a délivré.		and from every distress delivered me.
13	³[De tout]piège il m'a sauvé	13	³[From every] trap he rescued me,
	et de la fosse tumultueuse il m'a retiré.		and from the pit of destruction lifted me.
14	⁴Il n'a pas laissé mes pieds chanceler	14	⁴He did not allow my foot to slip,
	et il a changé mes lamentations en danse.		he turned my lament to my rejoicing.
15	⁵Et il a établi mes pas dans le droit chemin	15	⁵He established my steps in the straight path,
	et il a mis mes pieds dans des sentiers légitimes.		and set my feet in the right ways.
16	⁶Il a placé dans ma bouche des chants pour le louer	16	⁶He set in my mouth songs to praise him,
	et pour le célébrer ⁷selon la bonté de son œuvre.		and to give thanks to him ⁷according to the goodness of his actions.
17	⁸Je veux bénir son nom selon m(es) capacité(s),	17	⁸Let me bless his name according to my ability,
	car il est ma part et mon lot.		for he is my portion and my allotment.
18	⁹Et parce que, lui, depuis ma jeunesse, je l'ai désiré	18	⁹And because he (was the one that) from my youth I desired
	¹⁰et en ses miséricordes et en sa bonté, j'ai espéré.		¹⁰for his mercy and his good deed I hoped.
19	¹¹[ ] après lui	19	¹¹[ ] after him
	et pour toujours ¹²[ ] his [ ].		and forever ¹²[ ] his [ ].
20	¹³[ ] ils ont rugi comme mon esprit à ses paroles	20	¹³[ ] they roar as does my spirit through his words
	¹⁴[ ]		¹⁴[ ]
21	¹Il est doux le temps où je me souvenais de lui	21	¹The time I remember him is sweet,
	et mon esprit et mon souffle ²le désiraient immensément.		my spirit and my breath ²greatly desire him.

15 The expression of the first two words is like that of Ps 40:3.

16 The verse seems to correspond to Sir 51:12c, though really the similarity is based on the shared use of the verbs הלל and ידה. Note also that the words שׂים "to set," בפה "in the mouth of," and שׁירה "song" occur together in Deut 31:19.

17 This verse corresponds to Sir 51:12d. יְכָלִי — See the note on HUC 1301, page 1, recto, line 8 above. The second stich contains language reminiscent of Deut 32:9, though the idea is slightly different.

18 In its general idea, the verse seems closest to Sir 51:13, though the specific phrase מנעורי "from my youth" is found in Sir 51:15 (in both 11Q5 and H^B).

19 Although much of the verse is missing, it corresponds to Sir 51:20a–b, especially given the sequence in H^B: אחריה ולנצח.

20 The first stich seems to condense Sir 51:21–22. Note the presence of the verb המה in 51:21 and God's gift of lips and tongue in 51:22.

21 More literally, the stich can be translated: "It is sweet, according to how long I remember him." The verse does not clearly correspond to any in Ben Sira. יְמְתַוּק — The two theme vowels preserved in the spelling here reflect the two possible theme vowels found in Rabbinic and medieval Hebrew (see, e.g., Jastrow 1903, 864). There seems to be no semantic distinction between the two forms. לְפִי עֵת — For the construction, cf. כפי עת in Sir 6:8^A.

22	³אוֹדֶה יְיָ מְאֹד בְּפִי
	וּבְתוֹךְ רַבִּים אֲהַלְלֶנּוּ :
23 ᴮ	⁴אוֹדֶה לוֹ בְּכָל הַתּוּשְׁבָּחוֹת
	כִּי הוּא ⁵יוֹצֵר כָּל רוּחוֹת :
24	⁶אֱ׳ לֵאלֹהֵי הָאֱלֹהִים
	הַשּׁוֹכֵן מְרוֹמוֹת וּגְבוֹהִים :
25	⁷אֱ׳ לַאֲדוֹנֵי הָאֲדוֹנִים
	הַשָּׂם כִּסְאוֹ בִּמְעוֹנִים :
26	⁸אֱ׳ לְעוֹשֵׂה נוֹרָאוֹת לְבַדּוֹ
	כִּי לְעוֹלָם חַסְדּוֹ :
27	⁹אֱ לְעוֹשֵׂה הַשָּׁמַיִם בִּתְבוּנָה
	וְהוּא נִפְרָד בַחֲנִינָה :
28	¹⁰אֱ לְרוֹקַע הָאָרֶץ
	וְשָׁכְנוּ בְרוּם עֶרֶץ :
29	¹¹אֱ לְעוֹשֵׂה אוֹרִים
	וִישִׂימֵם לְמֶ"שֶׁלֶת וּמַזְהִירִים :
30	¹²אֱ אֶת הַשֶּׁמֶשׁ לְמֶמְשֶׁלֶת
	וְעַל הַיּוֹם הִיא מוֹשֶׁלֶת
31	¹³אֶת הַיָּרֵחַ וְכוֹכָבִים לְמֶ[מְשֶׁ]לֶת בַלַּיְלָה
	¹⁴וְאוֹתוֹ תָּמִיד אֲיַחֲלָה :
32	¹⁵אֱ לְמַכֵּה מִצְרַיִם בִּבְכוֹרֵהֶם
	וַיָּשֶׂם לְדָם ¹⁶כָּל אַגְמֵהֶם
33	¹וַיוֹצִיא יִשְׂרָאֵל מִתּוֹכָם
	וּבְאֲרָצוֹת רַבּוֹת הִדְרִיכָם :
34	²לְגוֹזֵר יַם סוּף לִגְזָרִים
	וַיוֹלִיכֵם בִּדְרָכִים יְשָׁרִים :
35	³וְהֶעֱבִיר יִשְׂרָאֵל בְּתוֹכוֹ
	לָכֵן אֲהַלְלוֹ וַאֲבָרְכוֹ :
36	⁴וְנִעֵר פַּרְעוֹ וְחֵלוֹ
	וְנִתְבָּאֲרָה אוֹתוֹתָיו וּפָעֳלוֹ :
37	⁵לְמוֹלִיךְ עַמּוֹ בַמִּדְבָּר
	אֲהַלֵּל בְּלָשׁוֹן יָפֶה וּבָר :
38	⁶וַיַּהֲרוֹג מְלָכִים אַדִּירִים
	לְעוֹלָם בְּשַׁבָּ{ת}חֲוָותָי קוֹלִי אָרִים :

HUC 1301, folio 2, verso

L. 3 [22] אֲהַלְלֶנּוּ — The word is written above רַבִּים.

L. 6 [24] וּגְבוֹהִים — The word is written above and to the left of מְרוֹמוֹת.

L. 7 [25] בִּמְעוֹנִים — The word is written above the line.

L. 8 [26] חַסְדּוֹ — The word is written slightly above the line.

L. 9 [27] בַחֲנִינָה — The word is written above and to the left of נִפְרָד.

L. 10 [28] עֶרֶץ — The word is written above and to the left of בְרוּם.

L. 11 [29] מַזְהִירִים — The word is written above and to the left of לְמֶמְשֶׁלֶת. The reading מַזְהִירִים is certain. The slight smudging of the *shewa* has made the *zayin* look like a final *nun* (cf. וּמַן שָׂרִים as read by Fleischer 1997, 216).

L. 12 [30] מוֹשֶׁלֶת — The word is written above הִיא.

L. 15 [32] לְמַכֵּה — The *tsere* is smeared and looks like a *patakh*.

L. 16 [32] אַגְמֵהֶם — The reading follows the suggestion of Fleischer 1997, 216.

L. 1 [33] הִדְרִיכָם — The word is written above רַבּוֹת.

L. 2 [34] יְשָׁרִים — The word is written above בִּדְרָכִים.

L. 3 [35] וַאֲבָרְכוֹ — The word is written above וּפָעֳלוֹ of the following line, which is itself above the line. This suggests that the scribe thought initially that the second stich ended with אֲהַלְלוֹ. Only after completing the following line did they complete the second stich of v. 3 with וַאֲבָרְכוֹ.

L. 4 [36] וּפָעֳלוֹ — The horizontal bar of the *qamets* lies on top of the lower line of the *pe*.

L. 5 [37] בַמִּדְבָּר — The word is written above and to the left of עַמּוֹ.

L. 6 [38] בְּשַׁבָּ{ת}חֲוָותָי — It seems that the scribe wrote an initial *tav* followed by a *vav* and the rest of the word, but then revised the spelling by writing another *vav* on top of the foot and the left most part of the upper horizontal bar to make the *tav* a *khet*.

22	³Je veux rendre grâce à YYY immensément par ma bouche et au milieu des nombreux, je veux le louer.	22	³Let me give thanks to the Lord greatly with my mouth, and in the midst of many, let me praise him.
23	⁴Je veux lui rendre grâce par toutes louanges, car, lui, ⁵est le créateur de tous les esprits.	23	⁴Let me give thanks to him with every acclaim, for he is ⁵the creator of all spirits.
24	⁶Je veux (rendre grâce) au dieu des dieux, celui qui habite dans les hauteurs et les hauts lieux.	24	⁶Let me (give thanks) to the God of gods, the one dwelling in the heights and high places.
25	⁷Je veux (rendre grâce) au seigneur des seigneurs, celui qui place son trône parmi les refuges.	25	⁷Let me (give thanks) to the Lord of lords, the one who set his throne among the dwellings.
26	⁸Je veux (rendre grâce) à celui qui fait, seul, des merveilles, car pour toujours est son amour.	26	⁸Let me (give thanks) to the one who, alone, does wondrous acts, for his kindness if perpetual.
27	⁹Je veux (rendre grâce) à celui qui fait les cieux avec intelligence et qui se distingue par sa grâce.	27	⁹Let me (give thanks) the one who made the heavens with understanding, and he who is distinct with his mercy.
28	¹⁰Je veux (rendre grâce) à celui qui étend la terre et qui habite dans la hauteur céleste.	28	¹⁰Let me (give thanks) to the one who spreads the land and whose dwelling is in the height of heaven.
29	¹¹Je veux (rendre grâce) à celui qui fait les luminaires et qui les place pour gouverner et pour qu'ils brillent.	29	¹¹Let me (give thanks) to the maker of lights, who set them for dominion and as shining things.
30	¹²Je veux (rendre grâce à celui qui fait) le soleil pour qu'il domine et qu'il gouverne sur les jours,	30	¹²Let me (give thanks to the maker of) the sun for dominion, for it rules over the day.
31	¹³(à celui qui fait) la lune et les étoiles pour gou[ver]ner la nuit, ¹⁴et je veux espérer en lui perpétuellement.	31	¹³(to the maker of) the moon and stars, for dominion in the night, ¹⁴let me hope in him continually.
32	¹⁵Je veux (rendre grâce) à celui qui a frappé l'Égypte en leurs premiers nés et a changé en sang ¹⁶tous leurs étangs	32	¹⁵Let me (give thanks) to the one who struck Egypt in their first born, and turned ¹⁶all their pools into blood.
33	¹et qui a fait sortir Israël d'au milieu d'eux et qui les a conduits dans de nombreux pays.	33	¹He brought forth Israel from their midst, and through their many lands he led them.
34	²(Je veux rendre grâce) à celui qui coupe la mer des joncs en deux parties et qui les a fait marcher dans de droits chemins	34	²(Let me give thanks) to the one splitting the sea of reeds into parts, and (the one who) made them go in straight paths.
35	³qui a fait traverser Israël en son milieu. C'est pourquoi, je veux le louer et le bénir.	35	³He caused Israel to pass in its midst, therefore, let me praise and bless him.
36	⁴Il a précipité Pharaon et son armée et ses signes et son œuvre ont été manifestés.	36	⁴He threw Pharaoh and his army and his signs and his work were revealed.
37	⁵(Je veux rendre grâce) à celui qui mène son peuple au désert. Je (le) louerai par une langue magnifique et pure.	37	⁵(Let me give thanks) to the one causing his people to go in the desert. I will praise (him) with a beautiful and pure tongue.
38	⁶Il a tué des rois redoutables, — pour toujours j'élèverai ma voix à ses louanges —,	38	⁶He killed mighty kings, forever I raise my voice in his praises,

22 Here begins a poem that parallels both the poem found in H^B after Sir 51:12 and Ps 136. Like the poem after Sir 51:12, here the verb ידה repeats at the beginning of verses (up through HUC 1301, page 2, recto, line 13). Unlike both the poem after Sir 51:12 and Ps 136, the refrain כי לעולם חסדו is not repeated here. Most of the phrases are drawn from Ps 136, though here, the verse duplicates Ps 109:30.

23 The first stich recalls Sir 51:12c.

27 נִפְרָד — Literally, the one who separates himself.

28 וְשִׁבְנוֹ — See Deut 12:5. עֲרֶץ — The word is used in the *piyyut* as a synonym for heaven (see Fleischer 1997, *216; cf. מערץ in Sir 43:8d^Bmg).

36 וְנִתְבָּאֲרָה — The *hithpael* of באר is found first, according to Maagarim, in the tenth century CE.

38 בְּשִׁבְ{ת}חֲוֹותָי — The word שְׁבָחָה appears for the first time, according to Maagarim, in *Shir ha-Shirim Rabbah*.

39 ⁷לְסִיחוֹן מֶלֶךְ הָאֱמוֹרִי
עַד אֲשֶׁר נְצָרַנִי וְעָזְרִי :
40 ⁸ וּלְעוֹג מֶלֶךְ הַבָּשָׁן
עַד הִצִּילַנִי מֵאוּר הַכִּבְשָׁן :
41 ⁹וְנָתַן אַרְצָם לְנַחֲלָה
נַחֲלָה לְעַם סְגֻלָּה :
42 ¹⁰שֶׁבְּשִׁפְלֵנוּ זָכַר לָנוּ
וּלְעוֹלָם תָּמִיד אֲהַלְלֶנּוּ :
43 ¹¹וַיִּפְ׳ קֵנוּ מִצָּרֵנוּ
עַד עוֹלָמִים אֲיַחֲדֶנּוּ :
44 ¹²נוֹתֵן] לֶחֶם] לְכָל בָּשָׂר
וְטוּבוֹ לָעַד לֹא יֶחְסַר :
45 ¹³אוֹדֶה לְאֵל הַשָּׁמְםַיִם
יוֹצֵר אֵשׁ וְעָפָר ¹⁴רו[חַ] וּמַיִם :

L. 7 [39] וְעָזְרִי — The word is written above נְעָרָיו.

L. 10 [42] אהללנו — The word is written above and to the left of תָּמִיד.

L. 12 [44] [לֶחֶם] — Following Fleischer 1997, 217. לֹא יֶחְסַר — The words are written above and to the left of לָעַד.

L. 13 [45] הַשָּׁמְםַיִם — The scribe wrote a final *mem* after the non-final *mem* and then corrected the spelling without canceling the first final *mem*.

L. 14 [45] רו[חַ] — Following Fleischer 1997, 217.

39	⁷Sihon, roi des Amorites,
	— jusqu'à ce que (Dieu) me sauve et me secoure —,
40	⁸et Og, roi de Bashân,
	— jusqu'à ce que (Dieu) me délivre de la flamme de la fournaise —.
41	⁹Il a donné leur terre en héritage,
	un héritage pour le peuple, un trésor.
42	¹⁰Celui qui dans notre abaissement se souvient de nous
	et pour toujours, perpétuellement, je le louerai.
43	¹¹Il nous a sauvés de nos adversaires,
	jusqu'à l'éternité, je le déclarerai un.
44	¹²Il donne du pain à toute chair
	et sa bonté ne manquera jamais.
45	¹³Je veux rendre grâce au Dieu des cieux,
	le créateur du feu et de la poussière, ¹⁴du vent et des eaux.

39	⁷Sihon, king of the Amorites,
	until he (God) saved me and helped me,
40	⁸Og, king of Bashan,
	until he (God) delivered me from the flame of the kiln.
41	⁹He gave their land as an inheritance,
	an inheritance for the people, a possession.
42	¹⁰Who, in our lowly state, remembered us?
	Forever, continually I will praise him.
43	¹¹He rescued us from our enemies,
	for eternity, I will declare him one.
44	¹²He gave food to all flesh,
	and his good acts never are missing.
45	¹³Let me give thanks to the God of the Heavens,
	the creator of fire and dust, ¹⁴wind and water.

39 וְעֹזְרִי — We would expect וְעָזְרֵנִי but the rhyme has necessitated an unusual form.

MANUSCRIPT 2Q18

SIR 1:19–20 OR 6:14–15 AND SIR 6:20–32

2Q18 frag. 1

^{1}] [ת][[
^{2}] [ה א∘∘] [
Bottom margin

2Q18 frag. 1 – Reconstruction of Sir 6:14-15 according H^A

6:14 AC ^{1}[אוהב אמונה אוהב ת]קוף   ומוצאו מצא הון[
6:15 AC ^{2}[לאוהב אמונ]ה אי[ן מחיר   ואין משקל לטובתו]
Bottom margin

2Q18 frag. 1 – Reconstruction of Sir 6:14-15 according to H^C

6:14 AC ^{1}[אוהב אמונה מגן ת]קוף   ומוצאו מצא הוא הון[
6:15 AC ^{2}[אוהב אמונ]ה אי[ן מחיר   ואין משקל לטובתו]
Bottom margin

2Q18 frag. 1 – Reconstruction of Sir 1:19-20

1:19 ^{1}[שכל ודעת תביע   וכבוד תומכיה ת]רים]
1:20 ^{2}[שרש חכמה יראת יהוה   וענפי]ה ארך] ימים]

2Q18 frag. 2

6:20 A ^{1}[עקובה היא לאויל   ולא יכלכלנה חסר ל]ב
6:21 A ^{2}[כאבן משא תהיה עליו   ולא יאחר להשליכה]
6:22 A ^{3}[כי המוסר כשמה כן הוא   ולא לרבים הוא נ]כח
6:23 ^{4}] [
6:24 ^{5}] [
6:25 A ^{6}[הט שכמך ושאה   ואל תקץ בתחבולתיה]
6:26 ^{7}[בכל נפשך קרב אליה   ובכל מאדך שמר דר]כ[י]ה

6:22 נ]כ[ח 2Q18 | נְכוֹחָה A ·

Frag. 1. L. 2]ה א∘∘[— The *he* is clear by the traces of the crossbar, head of the right leg and the end of the left leg. After the *alef* a vertical downstroke slightly angled to the right is preserved. Finally, the last trace belongs to a long final letter like, *kaph, nun, pe* or *qoph*. The distance between the two last letters is difficult to determine with precision, as well as the inclination of the last trace corresponding to the final letter. Indeed, the two parts of the fragment could have been moved (compare, for example, their positions in PAM 42.959 and B-365816).

Frag. 2. L. 3 נ]כח — Only a part of the base of the *kaph* has been preserved, and it would permit other reconstructions (*bet, pe* or with more difficulty *mem, nun* or *tav*). The *khet* is certain and cannot be confused with *he*.

Frag. 2. L. 7 דר]כ[י]ה — A meager trace of ink is visible at the edge of the fragment and could correspond to the end of a letter's base.

2Q18 frag. 1   Baillet (1962, 75-77) proposed two alternative readings of the fragment and consequently suggested two concurrent identifications. The first reading would correspond to Sir 6:14-15. Baillet's reconstruction was based on the Hebrew text of H^A (T-S 12.864 recto ll. 16-17). He had not at his disposition H^C, that would suggest a slightly different restoration. The word מגן, "shield," in H^C seems to be preferable for the meaning and the context and would agree with the Greek σκέπη while אוהב in H^A would agree with the Syriac ܪܚܡܐ. It would also slightly reduce the length of line 1. Indeed, one of the weaknesses of this identification is the restoration of line 2 (Sir 6:15) that requires a *vacat* due to a defect of the surface, or larger letters, or an erasure or a dittography, etc, to adjust the right margin. Our reconstruction of Sir 1:19 differs slightly from that of Baillet. The preserved *tav* of line 1 must be that of תרים and not the *tav* of תומכיה. The weakness of this identification is that it is based on the Hebrew retroversion of Segal (1958, 3) since this passage was not preserved in the Cairo Genizah manuscripts. The retroversion based on the Greek translation can only be tentative whereas the Syriac presents a very different text especially for verse 19. If this identification is right, and if this Hebrew text agrees with the Greek I, then the column of this manuscript would have 18 lines. In line

2Q18 frag. 1 (Sir 6:14-15 H^A)

14 [Un ami fidèle est un ami] so[lide]
   [et celui qui l'a trouvé a trouvé une richesse.]
15 [Pour un ami fid]èle, il n'y a pas[de prix]
   [et pour sa bonté, il n'y a pas de mesure.]

2Q18 frag. 1 (Sir 6:14-15 H^c)

14 [Un ami fidèle est un bouclier] so[lide]
   [et celui qui l'a trouvé a trouvé une richesse.]
15 [Un ami fid]èle n'a pas[de prix]
   [et il n'y a pas de poids à sa bonté.]

2Q18 frag. 1 (Sir 1:19-20)

19 [Elle répand intelligence et connaissance,]
   [et elle exal]te[l'honneur de ceux qui la possède.]
20 [La racine de la sagesse, c'est la crainte du Seigneur]
   [et]ses [branches]prolongent[les jours.]

2Q18 frag. 2, Sir 6:20-32

20 [Elle est tortueuse pour le fou]
   [et l'inse]nsé [ne la supporte pas.]
21 [Elle sera sur lui comme une pierre à porter,]
   [et il ne tardera pas à la rejeter.]
22 [Car la discipline, comme son nom, ainsi elle est]
   [et elle n'est pas ac]cessible[pour la multitude.]
23 [   ]
   [   ]
24 [   ]
   [   ]
25 [Incline ton épaule et supporte-la (s.e. la sagesse),]
   [et ne sois pas effrayé par ses projets.]
26 [De toute ton âme approche-toi d'elle]
   [et de toute ta force garde ses vo]i[e]s.

2Q18 frag. 1 (Sir 6:14-15 H^A)

14 [A faithful friend is a] sol[id friend]
   [and whoever has found one has found wealth.]
15 [For a faith]ful friend there is no[price]
   [and for their goodness there is no measure.]

2Q18 frag. 1 (Sir 6:14-15 H^c)

14 [A faithful friend is a] str[ong shield]
   [and whoever has found one has found wealth.]
15 [As for a faith]ful friend, there is no[price]
   [and for his goodness there is no measure.]

2Q18 frag. 1 (Sir 1:19-20)

19 [She pours out insight and understanding,]
   [and] she [exalts the glory of those who grasp her.]
20 [The root of wisdom is fear of the Lord,]
   [and] her [branches] lengthen [one's days.]

2Q18 frag. 2, Sir 6:20-32

20 [She is convoluted for the fool,
   and the one who has no se]nse [cannot stand her.]
21 [She will be upon him like a load of stone,]
   [and he will not delay throwing her off.]
22 [For discipline, such is her name, so she is]
   [and she is not ac]cessible[to the multitude (of people).]
23 [   ]
   [   ]
24 [   ]
   [   ]
25 [Bend your shoulder and carry her,]
   [and do not be afraid of her plans.]
26 Draw near to her with all your soul,
   And with all your strength keep]her[wa]ys

2, the two readings, אֵיךְ and אָדֹן, are both paleographically plausible. The first reading has been defended by Puech (1999, 413-414) who considers it paleographically secure. However the new photographs make the second hypothesis highly preferable: the size, as well as the curve of the stroke of the first trace would fit better for a *resh* (see the *resh* in תעטרנה or תפארת frag. 2 12) than for a *yod*. In that case, our second fragment would represent Sir 1:19-20 which does not simplify the reconstruction of the scroll.

6:22 נ[כֹ]ח. H^A reads נְכוֹחָה with a corrective vocalization. The word נכח could be the preposition נֹכַח "in front of" (for the construction with *lamed*, see Jos 15:7), the adjective נָכֹחַ "right, straightforward, accessible" (see the feminine נכוחה in H^A), or the participle נוֹכַח. These last two cases impose restoring the masculine pronoun הוא in the pre-ceding lacunae (and not היא with H^A) in agreement with the masculine pronoun of the preceding stich. The Greek φανερά and the Syriac , which suppose a *Vorlage* נבחרה, are not helpful.

6:23-26 The manuscript presents four lines (i.e. 4 distichs), where H^A has only three distichs. In H^A, verse 25 agrees with the Greek and the Syriac versions, while verses 23-24 are borrowed from Sir 27:5-6 and verse 26 is missing. As noticed by Baillet, the preserved text confirms the sequence of verses attested in the Greek and the Syriac, as against H^A: lines 4-5 should have contained verses 23-24, equivalent to the Greek and Syriac, line 6 verse 25 according to H^A, and line 7 verse 26 which is missing in H^A. This latter can be reconstructed on the basis of the Greek and the Syriac with a certain degree of confidence. The proposed restoration is based on Lévi (1904, 8) and Segal (1958, 39).

6:27 A	8[דרש וחקר בקש ומצא והתחזקתה ואל תר]פֿה	
6:28 AC	9[כי לאחור תמצא מנוחתה ותהפך לך לת]עֿנג	
6:29 A	10[והיתה לך רשתה מכון עז וחבלתה]בֿגֿדֿי כתם	
6:30 A	11[עלי זהב עולה ומוסרתיה פתיל תכ]לת	
6:31 A	12[בגדי כבוד תלבשנה ועטר]ת תפארת תעטרנה	
6:32 A	13[	]

6:26 > A ·   6:28 לת]עֿנג 2Q18 | לתענוג A C ·

Frag. 2. L. 8 תר]פֿה — The base of the *pe* is only attested by a small trace of ink on the edge of the fragment.

Frag. 2. L. 9 לת]עֿנג — The left arm and the end of the right arm of a small *ayin*, similar to the *ayin* of תעטרנה line 12, are preserved.

Frag. 2. L. 10]בֿגֿדֿי — A trace of the base of the *bet* is preserved. The next traces at the edge of the fragments represent the right and left legs of a *gimel* similar to the *gimel* of לת]עֿנג line 9.

Frag. 2. L. 12 ועטר]ת — The fragment attesting the foot of the *tav* is misplaced in B-365816, see PAM 42.959.

Frag. 2. L. 13 No letters of this line have been preserved, but the dot of the marginal line and the horizontal rule are well attested. There would also be space for a 14th line, unless this is the bottom of the column.

Frag. 2. L. 9 לת]עֿנג — The defective writing תענג seems not to be attested elsewhere in ancient Hebrew; H^A and H^C have the *scriptio plena*, לתענוג. However, Samaritan Hebrew knows the form תענג, *tānnåg*. In consequence, it seems more legitimate to consider the writing תענג, in 2Q18, as a dialectal variant (*taʿnāg*) also attested in the Samaritan, rather than an odd defective writing.

27	[Scrute, sonde, cherche et tu trouveras,] [saisis-la et ne]la[lâ]che[pas.]	27	Study, examine, seek and you will find, seize her and do not let h]er go.
28	[Car, par suite, tu trouveras le lieu de son repos] [et elle se changera pour toi en d]élice.	28	[For afterward you will find her resting place,] [and she will be transformed for you into a d]elight.
29	[Et son filet sera pour toi un appui solide] [et ses cordes,]des vêtements d'or.	29	[And her net will be a firm base for you] [and her ties,]golden clothing.
30	[Son joug, des jougs en or] [et ses liens, un ruban de pour]pre.	30	[Her yoke, golden yokes,] [and her bonds, a ribbon of pur]ple.
31	[Tu la revêtiras, vêtements de gloire,] tu [t'en couronne]ras, couronne de splendeur.	31	[You will wear her as glorious vestments,] you [will don her]as a crown of splendor.
32	[ ] [ ]	32	[ ] [ ]

MANUSCRIPT 11QPSᴬ

SIR 51:13–30

Chapter 51

		11Q5 XXI	
תעיתי ובקשתיה		¹¹אני נער בטרם	13 BP
ועד ¹²סופה אדורשנה		באה לי בתרה	14 B
ענבים ישמחו לב		גם גרע נץ בבשול	15 B
כי מנעורי ידעתיה		¹³דרכה רגלי במישור	
והרבה מצאתי לקח		הטיתי כמעט ¹⁴אוזני	16 B
למלמדי אתן ¹⁵הודו		ועלה היתה לי	17 B
קנאתי בטוב ולוא אשוב		זמותי ואשחקה	18 B
ופני לוא השיׄבותיׄ		חריתי ¹⁶נפשי בה	19ab B
וברומיה לוא ¹⁷אשלה		טרתי נפשי בה	19cd B
וׄבׄמערמיה אתבונן		ידי פתחׄ[ה בי]אׄתׄהׄ	19ef B
¹⁸[ובטהר]הׄ [מצאתיה]		כפי הברותי אליׄהׄ	20ab BP
ל[כן לוׄ אׄ אׄעׄ[ז]בׄנׄהׄ		[לב קניתי עמה מר]אׄשׄ	20cd B
		11Q5 XXII	
		¹[...] שכרכם בעתו	30 B

51:13 11Q5 לקח] לקח 51:16 B · אדני] אדוני 11Q5 · כי] כי 11Q5 · חכמה למדתי B ידעתיה 11Q5 · באמתה B במישור 11Q5 · 51:15 הייתי וחפצתי בה B בטרם תעיתי 11Q5 · 51:13 חשבתי] 11Q5 זמותי ואשחקה קנאתי בטוב 51:18 B · הודאה B הודו 11Q5 · ולמלמדי B למלמדי 11Q5 · עלה היה B ועלה היתה 11Q5 · 51:17 דעה B · דעה 11Q5 להיטיב B ולא אשוב ולא אהפך B · ולא אהפך B · חשקה 11Q5 חריתי 51:19ab לוא השיׄבותיׄ 11Q5 · ולא אהפך B 51:19cd 11Q5 טרתי נפשי בה נפשי | 11Q5 וׄבׄמערמיה אתבונן B · שעריה 11Q5 בי]אׄתׄהׄ 51:19f · לנצח נצחים לא אטה מׄמׄנׄהׄ B 51:19e · וברומיה לוא אשלה 11Q5 נתתי אחריה B אהדׄרׄ ואביט בה 51:20ab 11Q5 כפי הברותי אליׄהׄ ולב קניתי לה 11Q5 בטהרה מצאתיה B ·

L. 16 [51:19] השיׄבותיׄ — The *yod* is clear in the new digital photographs, just to the left of the traces of the *shin*'s left arm.

L. 17 [51:19] פתחׄ[ה בי]אׄתׄהׄ — For this reading, see Puech 2011, 307.

L. 17 [51:20] הברותי אליׄהׄ — This reading proposed by Puech is now clear according to the new photos. The traces of letters after אליה that must be read מעול]ם should be a marginal correction belonging to Ps 93:2 of the next column (Puech, personal communication).

L. 18 [51:20] For these readings and reconstruction, see Puech 2011, 308.

Chapitre 51

Col. XXI

13 (Lorsque) j'étais jeune, avant
 que j'erre, je l'ai cherchée,
14 Elle est venue à moi dans sa beauté
 et jusqu'à la fin, je la rechercherai.
15 Si la fleur s'étiole lorsqu'elle atteint la maturité,
 les raisins réjouissent le cœur.
 Mon pied a marché dans la plaine,
 car dès ma jeunesse, je l'ai connue.
16 J'ai à peine tendu l'oreille
 et en abondance j'ai trouvé l'instruction.
17 Elle a été une nourrice pour moi,
 à celui qui m'enseigne, je (lui) rendrai sa gloire.
18 J'ai projeté de jouer,
 j'ai été zélé pour le bien et je ne me détournerai pas.
19a Moi-même, je me suis enflammé pour elle,
19b et je n'ai pas détourné ma face.
19c Moi-même, je me suis épuisé pour elle
19d et dans ses hauteurs, je n'aurai de cesse.
19e Ma main a ouve[rt]son[en]trée,
19f et j'ai considéré ses intimités.
20a J'ai purifié mes paumes pour elle
20b [et dans la pure]té[je l'ai trouvée,]
20c [Depuis le dé]but[j'ai acquis l'intelligence avec elle]
20d C'est[pourquoi je [n]e l'aba[ndon]nerai [p]as.
 (...)

Col. XXII

30 [Il (vous) donnera] votre récompense en son temps.

Chapter 51

Col. XXI

13 (When) I was a boy, before
 I wandered, I sought her.
14 She came to me in her beauty
 and until the end, I will seek her.
15 While the blossom withers with the ripening,
 grapes gladden the heart.
 My foot treads a plain
 since from my youth I have known her.
16 I stretched my ear just a little
 but I have found great learning.
17 She is a nurse for me,
 to my teacher I give (to him) his glory.
18 I conceived that I would play
 I was excited by goodness and would not turn away.
19a I, myself, burned for her,
19b I did not turn my face away.
19c I wearied myself with her,
19d and in her heights I will not relax.
19e My hand access[ed]her[en]trance,
19f that I could consider her intimate parts.
20a I purified my palms to[her]
20b [and in puri]ty[I found her,]
20c [From the begin]ning[I acquired a mind with her,]
20d Th[us I will n]ot ab[and]on her
 (...)

Col. XXII

30 your wage in its time.

13-30 For more thorough notes on this version of the text and its readings, see Reymond 2011, 29-39 and Puech 2011.
51:13 תעיתי — Or read the infinitive תעותי. בטרם may be followed either by the infinitive (see the Greek here) or the perfect *qal* (see Ps 90:2 and Prov 8:25 and the DSS were it is frequent).
51:14 בתרה — The *aleph* of תאר has been elided here (See 43:9 in H^M). This is an abbreviated form of the word usually spelled with *aleph* (and no mater) in the Leningrad Codex: תֹּאַר. Among the DSS, this kind of spelling is typical of those words whose medial *aleph* had quiesced (e.g., רוש for ראש "head").
51:15 בשול — This is either the *qal* infinitive construct or the related noun בְּשׁוּל "ripening," known from Rabbinic Hebrew. במישור — The word means "plain" evoking a place of "safety comfort and prosperity"

(BDB); metaphorically it may also evoke "rectitude, righteousness."
51:17 ועלה היתה — The first word may be interpreted as the feminine participle of עול "to nurse." Another possibility is to read the form as an infinitive absolute used as a noun "elevation" (עֲלֵה, see Puech 2011, 304–305). Alternatively, if the *he* is due to dittography, one can translate "a yoke she was to me" (see the Syriac and H^B). למלמדי — Assuming the preceding emendation, there seems to be a word play here, the word being either interpreted as "my goad" or "my teacher."
51:19 טרתי — It is assumed that this is the root טרד with the *dalet* assimilated into the *tav* or lost due to haplography. Alternatively, this would be a defectively spelled Aramaic loan טרי "to throw," the whole stich to be translated "I threw myself at her." בי[אתה — Cf. בָּאָה in Ezek 8:5. וֹּבמערמיה — See Sir 42:18^B.

MANUSCRIPT MASADA

SIR 39:27–44:18

Chapter 39

Col. I

27 BP	]²	[	[ ] לזרה נ[ה]פכו
28ab BP	]³	[	[ ] הר]ים יעתיקו
28cd P	]⁴	[	[ ] הם יניחו
29 PB	]⁵	[	[ ] נב]ראו
30ab PB	]⁶	[	[ ] ב̇ם ̊[
30cd PB	]⁷	[	[ ] ו̇[
31 B	]⁸	[	[ ] י̇ו̇פ̇[
32 B	]⁹	[	[ ] ת̇י̇[
22–10	(. . .)		

Chapter 40

8 B	]²³	[	[̊ס̊ס̊ל̇

Col. II

11 BP	¹כל מ[ן אר]ץ	[	[ ]
12	²כל מש[נה ח]ד	[	[ ]
13 B	³חיל מעול [	[	[ת̇
14 B	⁴עם שאתו כפ[י]ם̊	[	[ס̊
15 B	⁵נצר חמס לא יכ̇ה̊ ב̇[	[	[שׁ̇ן צ̇ר
16 B	⁶כקרמית על גפות נחל		[לפני כ]ל̇ חצ̇י̇ר̇ נדעך
17 BP	⁷חסד כע̇ד̇ לא תכרת		וצ̇דקה לעד̇ תכ̇ן
18 B	⁸חיי יתר שכר ימתקו		ומ̇שניהם מ̇צ̇א̇] [

ד̇‎

39:27 לזרה M | לרעה B G | לזרא Bmg · 40:12 כל מש]חד M | > B · 40:13 חיל מעול M G | מחיל אל חול B | מחיל Bmg · 40:14 עם שאתו M Bmg · 40:15 שן צור B | שן סלע M | שן צר B · לא ינקה B | לא יכ̇ה̊ ב̇[ו M Bmg | נוצר מחמס M Bmg | נצר חמס B · עם שאתו Bmg · 40:16 כקרמית M | תכ̇ן M | ימוט B · נדעכה B | נדעבו M | נדעך M · מטר B · חצ̇י̇ר̇ M G | לעולם M | כעד̇ M · תכרת B · לעולם B · גפות M | גפת B · כקרדמות M | B · מוצא M | מ̇צ̇א̇ Bmg · יותר שכל B | יין ושכר M | יתר שכר B · 40:18 B

L. 2 [39:27] נ[ה]פ̇כו — The bottom corner of the nun is preserved.

L. 3 [39:28] יעתיקו — Portions of all the letters are visible. The tav, however, is only attested by the tip of its bottom foot.

L. 6 [39:30b] ̊[ב̇ם — The second-to-last letter is clearly a bet (as Strugnell reads) and not a ligatured ayin-yod (as Yadin 1999, 171 reads). The preceding letter is attested only by a small mark, approximately centered at the halfway point of the bet's vertical mark.

L. 8 [39:31] פ̇י̇ו̇ — No horizontal stroke is visible to bolster Yadin's preference for]הו. Both spellings (i.e., פיו and פיהו) occur in the medieval Ben Sira manuscripts, as well as in contemporaneous manuscripts of the Dead Sea Scrolls. For more on this and other readings from the Masada scroll, see Reymond 2014b, 327–46.

L. 4 [40:14] ס̊[— Only the bottom left corner of the final mem is attested on a corner of the parchment. This small mark is only visible in the photographs from the *editio princeps*; the digital photographs reveal that the corner of parchment on which this mark was preserved has broken off.

L. 5 [40:15] יכ̇ה̊ ב̇[— The second letter may be either a kaph or a nun, though the apparently extended base line suggests kaph. The following letter seems to be a he; the bottom of the left leg is preserved, as may be a small portion of the right, just above the end of the kaph base line. If it is not a hole, a dot of ink to the left of the he's left leg may be the remnant of a following bet, though it is difficult to be sure. The reading ינ̇ק̇ה̇, therefore, seems less likely. צר — The reading without a vav mater is certain.

L. 6 [40:16] חצ̇י̇ר̇ — On the top of the tear, a relatively thin mark is presumably the left most top mark of the tsade, followed by a mark that is likely the top of the yod, and two marks that are presumably the top most tips of the resh.

L. 8 [40:18] In the right margin is a large symbol, resembling something like a medieval-era dalet or backward Greek gamma followed by a dash or maqqeph-like symbol. מ̇צ̇א̇] — So Strugnell (1969, 112), the traces also allow for the possible reading מוצא (Yadin 1999, 173).

Chapitre 39

Col. I

27 [   ]
   [   ]ils sont c[h]angés en nausée.
28a [   ]
28b [   ]ils déplacent [les mon]tagnes
28c [   ]
28d [   ] eux [ ] ils déposent.
29 [   ]
   [   ]ils [ont été cr]éés.
30a [   ]
30b [   ] par eux.
30c [   ]
30d [   ]ils[   ]
31 [   ]
   [   ]sa [bouche]
32 [   ]
   [   ]j'ai[   ]

Chapitre 40

8 [   ]
  [   ]l[   ]

Col. II

11 Tout ce qui est de[la terre   ]
   [   ]
12 Tout ce qui est d'un pré[sent   ]
   [   ]
13 La richesse provenant de l'iniquité [   ]
   [   ]t.
14 Lorsqu'il se soulève, les pierr[es   ]
   [   ]m.
15 Le rejeton violent ne prendra pas (racines) en [ ],
   [   ]pic rocheux.
16 Comme la sarriette jaune sur les rives du torrent,
   [avant tou]te herbe il (le rejeton violent) est flétri.
17 La bienveillance, comme l'éternité, ne sera jamais détruite
   et la justice, pour toujours, sera maintenue.
18 Une vie d'abondance (et) de salaire est douce,
   mais plus que les deux, celui qui trouve[   ]

Chapter 39

Col. I

27 [   ]
   [   ] are [tu]rned to something disgusting.
28 [   ]
   [   ] they remove [moun]tains.
   [   ]
   [   ] their [   ] they settle.
29 [   ]
   [were] created.
30 [   ]
   [   ] with them
   [   ]
   [   ]they[   ].
31 [   ]
   [   ]his [mouth]
32 [   ]
   [   ] I [   ]

Chapter 40

8 [   ]
  [   ]l[   ]

Col. II

11 Everything from [the earth   ]
   [   ]
12 Everything from a b[ribe   ]
   [   ]
13 Wealth from injustice [   ]
   [   ]
14 When it lifts rock[s,   ]
   [   ]
15 The violent scion will not take root [   ]
   [   ] a rocky crag.
16 Like cow wheat on the wadi's banks,
   [before a]ll (other) grasses it (the violent scion) withers.
17 Piety, like eternity, will never perish,
   righteousness for eternity is secure.
18 A life of plenty <and> (a life) of wages is sweet,
   but more than both, finding [   ]

39:27 לזרה — We would have expected a final *aleph* as in H^B here and in 39:29, as well as in Num 11:20.

39:30 בם[— This is likely the preposition *bet* followed by the 3mp suffix, as reflected also in the H^B text and margin. The preposition presumably has an instrumental sense here, the pronoun referring back to the snakes, scorpions, and sword.

40:12 מש]חד — The reading משחד is based on the Greek δωρον "gift, bribe" (see Peters 1902, 177), though the Syriac would perhaps suggest משקר, "lie" (see Smend 1906a, 372).

40:17 כעד — The expression is otherwise unknown in ancient or medieval Hebrew. תכרת — The feminine form is likely attributable to the context with the following feminine noun and verb. Note a similar idiom in Sir 41:11 where the verb is masculine.

ומשניהם מוֹצׄ[	]	⁹ילד ו[עיר יעמ]ידו שם	19ab B
וֹמִשֺנֵיׄ[הם אשה נ]חֹשקת	]ו שאר[	¹⁰	19cd B
דו[דׄ]ם[	]	]¹¹	20 B
[	]	]¹²	21 B
[	]	]¹³	22 B
[	]	]¹⁴	23 B
[	]	]¹⁵	24 B
[	]	]¹⁶	25 B
[ום]שֺנֵיׄהֺםׄ] [	]¹⁷	26ab B
[אׄיֹן לבקש עמה משען	]¹⁸	26cd B
ועל כל כבׄ[וׄ]דׄ חפתה	]¹⁹	27 B
טוב [נא]שֺף ∘ממחצף	]²⁰	28 B
[אין חייו ל]מׄנות חיים	]²¹	29ab B
[לא]יׄש יודע יסור מעים	[מׄטׄ]עֹמו	]²²	29cd B
[בקרב]וׄ כאש תבער	²³בפי עז [נ]פֹשׄ ת[מתיק שאלה]	30 B

Chapter 41

לאיש שקט על מכונתו	²⁴הוֹ[יׄ] ל[מות מה מר ז]כׄרׄךׄ	1ab B	דׄ
עוד בו כח לקבל תענוג	²⁵שלו ומצׄלׄיׄחׄ בכל	1cd B	

Col. III

[ל]אין אוינים וחסר עצבה	¹הע למות מה טוב חׄ[קׄךׄ]	2ab B
אפס המרה ואבוד תקוה	²איש כשל {מׄשֺלׄ} ונוקש בׄ[לׄ]	2cd B

כל ימי עני רעים בן סירא אום אף בלילא בשפל גגים גגו במרום הרים כרמו. ממטר גגים לגגו מעפר כרמו לכ־ + 40:26ab · B שם | M שאר 40:19cd
יסור | B סוד מעים | M יסור מעים · 40:29cd B · ממסתולל M · ממחצף M · נאספ B · נא[שׄף M · 40:28 Bmg· בׄ[| B וכן | M G S ועל · 40:27 Bmg· רמים
B · תבער כמו אש | M כאש תבער · Bmg ממתיק | M B ת[מתיק · Bmg עז נפשות | B עוד נפש | M עז נפ[שׄ · עזׄ | M G ויברד · B · שקט M שוקט · 41:1cd M שלו · שליו · M עוד · ועוד · כח M · 40:30 בפי · M G S לא[יש B · Bmg מזעים
M עצבה · B G S לאיש אונים | M ל[אין אוינים · Bmg חוק חזק חוקן | B חקיד | M חׄ[| B · כי טוב M S מה טוב · B · האח | (הׄא = M) הע · 41:2ab חׄיל
אפס B סרב | M אפס המרה | Bmg 2 ומושל · Bmg 1 Bmg 3 ונוקש | B ינקש | M {מׄשׄל} | Bmg 2 וקש | B Bmg 1 כושל | M כשל · 41:2cd B · עצמה
המראה · Bmg ואבוד תקוה | M ואבד תקוה | B Bmg | יואבד תקוה · Bmg ·

L. 9 [40:19b] מוֹצׄ — Strugnell suggests to read the defective [מצ], but the traces encourage the plene writing.

L. 10 [40:19d] חׄשקת — In the photograph of column II, the leather on which these letters are preserved sits below the word שאר of line 10. Furthermore, the letters run at an angle to the other lines in column II. Based on these factors, as well as the fact that the sequence שקת– corresponds most closely to the end of vs. 40:19d, it is assumed that the parchment on which these letters sit is a fragment that has been misplaced and should be re-positioned so that the letters חׄשקת are the end of line 10 and follow a small lacuna after שאר (see Reymond 2014b, 329–30).

L. 11 [40:20] דו[דׄ]ם[— The reading of the *dalet* and *yod* here is based on the repositioning of the fragment as described above (see ibid.). The remnants of the letters are found just beneath חׄשקת.

L. 19 [40:27] ועל כל כבׄ[וׄ]דׄ — The letters are found on a fragment represented in the *editio princeps* but absent from the digital photographs.

L. 20 [40:28] טוב — This too is attested only on the fragment described in the note to line 19. שֺף[— The first letter after the break is clearly a *sin* and not a *samek*. An angled line intersects midway down the left vertical stroke; this is the middle arm of the *sin*, the right most arm having been abraded. ממחצף — Before the initial *mem* there is a mark that looks like it could be the head of a *bet* or perhaps the upper part of a *mem*. Or, perhaps, it is just a discoloration in the leather. The reading ממחצף would reflect dittography.

L. 22 [40:29c] מׄטׄ — These letters are found on a fragment pictured in the *editio princeps* but not the digital photographs. Before the *yod* of יסור one can perceive a small mark above the tear. This may be the left arm of the *ayin* or a *vav*, in which case we should read ויסור and interpret the *vav* as a *vav* of apodosis.

L. 23 [40:30] בפי עז [נ]פֹשׄ ת — These letters are part of the same fragment mentioned in the note to line 22.

L. 24 [41:1] הוֹ[יׄ] לׄ — The letters, together with the *dalet*-like symbol in the margin, are part of the same fragment mentioned in the note to line 22. זׄ]כׄרׄךׄ — Only the bottoms of the letters are found beneath the tear.

L. 1 [41:2ab] חׄ[קׄךׄ] — Only a small portion of the right leg is perceptible. עצבה — The third letter is clearly a *bet* and not a *mem*.

L. 2 [41:2cd] {מׄשֺלׄ} ונוקש — Three letters following כשל have been erased. The first seems to have had a squarish appearance and may have been an erroneous final *mem*, a *samek*, (initial/medial) *mem*, or *bet*. The following letter is clearly *sin/shin* and the last letter may have been a *lamed*, whose ascender would overlap with the descender of the *qoph* of ונוקש which is written above and to the left of the erased letters. בׄ[לׄ] — Only a trace of the upper right corner of the *kaph* is visible.

19a Enfant et[ville font perdu]rer un nom,
19b mais plus que tous deux, celui qui tr[ouve   ]
19c [   ] la parenté,
19d mais plus que tous d[eux, une femme d]ésirée
20 [   ]
   [a]mo[urs]
21–25 (...)
26 [   ]
   [Mais p]lus que tous deux, [   ]
   [   ]
   [et]pas besoin de chercher un support en dehors d'elle.
27 [   ]
   son dais est au-delà de toute g[loi]re.
28 [   ]
   mieux vaut celui qui meurt que celui qui agit insolemment.
29a [   ]
29b [sa vie ne peut pas être] comptée comme une vie.
29c [   ]de [son] go[ût   ]
29d [pour une pers]onne avisée c'est une épreuve pour son ventre.
30 Dans la bouche d'un [ap]pétit vorace, [ce qu'elle demande semble]su[ave.]
   [(mais) au milieu d']elle c'est comme un feu brûlant.

Chapitre 41

1 O[h]! M[ort! Combien amère est]ton [so]uvenir,
  pour la personne tranquille dans sa propriété,
  [une personne]paisible et qui réussit en tout,
  qui a encore de la force pour recevoir du plaisir.

Col. III

2a Ah! Mort! Combien bonne est [ta pa]rt,
2b pour celui sans vitalité et qui manque de soin,
2c Une personne chancelante et {rabaissée} se heurtant à to[ut,]
2d perdant la vue et dénuée d'espoir.

19a Child and [city will pre]serve a name,
19b but more than both, one who fi[nds   ]
19c [   ] a family [   ]
19d but more than [both is a de]sired [wife]
20 [   ]
   [l]ov[e]
21–25 (...)
26 [   ]
   [but m]ore than both [   ]
   [   ]
   [ ] one need not seek support outside of it.
27 [   ]
   its canopy (is) above every g[lor]y.
28 [   ]
   better one who is dead than one acting insolently (in this regard).
29a [   ]
29b [his life cannot be] counted as a (true) life.
29c [   ] from ta[sting   ]
29d [to] a discerning [per]son (it is) a distress to the stomach.
30 In the mouth of a glutton [the thing asked for] se[ems sweet,]
   [but in] his [midst] it burns like fire.

Chapter 41

1 Ah, [death! How bitter (is) the th]ought of you
  to the person quiet at their estate,
  [a person]at ease, successful in everything,
  in whom is still strength to feel pleasure.

Col. III

2a Lo! Death, how good (is) [your] sha[re]
2b [for] one without vitality and lacking healing,
2c (to) a person stumbling {one brought [down?]} and knocked down by every[thing]
2d one lacking vision, void of hope.

40:27 The same expression is almost identical to Isa 4:5 (כי על־כל־כבוד חֻפָּה), though here the final word has a pronominal suffix.
40:28 ממחצף — The verb חצף occurs in the Talmud, usually as the *qal* passive participle; its first use in the *hiphil*, where it has the sense "to act impudently," appears in Qohelet Rabbah and later texts. The verb is more common in Aramaic, occurring in the *aphel* in Tg. Ezek 13:6 and elsewhere (מחצף Prov 21:29). The spelling here would seem to presuppose the *piel*, though this is otherwise unknown in Hebrew; correspondingly, the *pael* is rare in Aramaic. It is conceivable that the spelling here is a mistake for the *hiphil*, influenced perhaps by the spelling of the Aramaic *aphel*.
41:2ab הע — This seems to be a phonetic variant of הא "lo." The Masada scroll attests the confusion of *aleph* and *ayin* also in the writing of עדם (Sir 41:18) for what was presumably intended אדם "person, individual" and אם (Sir 44:11) for עם "with." אוינים — The word is an otherwise unknown *qitlān* noun from the root אוה "to desire" or a *qatīl* form from the root אן, related to the noun אֹן "wealth, vigor." עצבה — Although the *Vorlage* may have had עצמה "strength," עצבה would, by itself, seem to suggest the opposite sense "pain" or "grief" (cf. עצב "to hurt"; see Strugnell 1969, 112). Obviously, this does not fit the context. One wonders, therefore, if the word might be a phonetic variant of עזב II "to restore" or related to Syriac *ṣābā* "healing, cure." See 11:9ᴬ and the note.
41:2cd {מֻשׁל} — The erased word is perhaps the *hophal* participle of נשל "to drop off." The defective writing of a short /u/ is common in the scroll (see Reymond 2014b, 332). ונוקש — The supralinear word is, as in Hᴮ, either to be construed as a *qal* participle ("one knocking") or a *niphal* participle of יקש ("one ensnared"). המרה — The spelling is defective for המראה, which is found in Hᴮ.

3 B	³אל תפחד ממות חׄקך	זכר קדמון ואחרון עמך
4ab B	⁴זה קץ כל [בני אד]ֹם	[ומה תמאס ב]תוֹ[רת] עליו[ן]
4cd B	⁵לעשר מאה ואלף שנים]	[
5 B	⁶נין נמאס ת]ל[דות רעים	]ר[שׁע
6 B	⁷[מבן עו]ׄל תֹאֹבֹד ממ]שלת	עם זרעו[תמׄי]ד [חרפה
7 B	⁸א]ב רשע] יקב יל[ד [	[כי ב]גׄללו היו בז
8 B	⁹ה]וי [אׄנשׁׄי ∘∘ [	עזבי תורת עליון
9ab B	¹⁰[ ]ל∘[ ]	ואם תולידו לאנחה
9cd B	¹¹אם תכש]לוׄ [ל]שׄמחת עׄם	ואם תמותו לקללה
10 B	¹²כל מ]אפס אל אפס ישוב	כן חנף מתהו אל תהו
11 B	¹³הׄב]ל אד]ֹם ∘∘	[אך]שם חסֹד ללא יכרת
12 B	¹⁴פחד על שם כי הוא ילוך	מׄאׄלפי שׂיׄמׄת תׄמׄדה
13 B	¹⁵ט]וׄבת חי מספר ימים	וטובׄת שם ימׄי אין מספר
14bc//20:30 BC	¹⁶ח]כמה טמונה ושימה מסתרת	מה תעלה ב∘תיהם
15//20:31 BC	¹⁷טוב איש מטמן אׄולתו	מאיש מצפן חכמתו
14a/16a B — ד	¹⁸מוסר בשת שמעו בנים	[וה]כׄלמו על משפטי
16bc BC	¹⁹לא כל בשת נאוה לבוש	ולא כל הכלם נבחר
17 B	²⁰בוש מאב ואם על פחז	מנשיא ושר על כחֹשׁ

41:3 חׄקך M | חוקיך B · זכר M זכור B · קדמון M ראשנים B · ואחרון M ואחרנים B · 41:4ab בני אד]ֹם B | חלק M S | קץ M S · כל בשר מאֹל]ה M S · 41:4cd לעשר מאה ואלף שנים M G · B · לאלף שנים מאה ועשר G · 41:5 נין נמאס B | כן נמאס M / כי Bmg1/2 · ת]ל[דות רעים M G S | ת]מׄי[ד M | דבר רעים B G · 41:6 ממ]שלת M G S | מבן עו]ׄל תֹאֹבֹד B | מבן עול ממשלתב M Bmg · ערל Bmg · רישם Bmg2 · Bmg1/3 דבת ערים / רישם B | ערים M | ת]מׄי[ד M | חרפה M | 41:7 יקב M | יקוב B · בוז M | [ ]B · 41:8 הׄ]וי M | אׄנשׁׄי B · 41:9ab תולידו M B | מולידו Bmg · 41:9cd עׄם M S B · עולם B · לקללה M B · מוֹד · 41:10 לקללתה Bmg | כן M B | אפס מ]אפס אל אפס M B | מאונג א' אונם Bmg 1 | מאונים אל אונים Bmg 2 | לא יכרת M | ללא יכרת Bmg · 41:11 מספר ימים M Bmg · 41:12 שׂיׄמׄת M | אוצרות B | סומת Bmg · חמדה M Bmg · חכמה B · 41:13 טובת חי M B | טוב חי Bmg · ימי מספר B · תוׄ] Bmg | מה M B | ומה C · תעלה M Bmg · 41:14bc // 20:30 מסוׄתרת M | מוסתר B | מסתרת B Bmg · וסימה C | ואוצר M | ושימה M B | וטוב Bmg · עלה B | תולעת C · 41:15 // 20:31 מטמן M | מצפין B C · מאיש M B C · מאדן Bmg · מצפן M | מצפן B C · יטׄמׄן Bmg · 41:14a/16a + מׄוסׄרׄ בׄשׁת שׁמׄ · M על פחז B | מוסר בשת: M B משפטי · Bmg · 41:16bc בשת M B | בושת C | נאוה M | נאה B C | לבוש M | לשמר B G · לשמוׄר C · B · יושב אל M Bmg G | ושר על B G · אל זנות Bmg |

L. 4 [41:4a] כל [בני אד]ֹם — The restoration כל [בשר מאלו]ה suggested by Yadin (1999, 176) is not possible for the space. We suggest to read the traces as a final *mem* which is paleographycally better and to restore כל [בני אד]ם (see the Syriac).

L. 4 [41:4b] [ב]תוֹ[רת] — Only the top tips of the letters are preserved above the lacuna.

L. 6 [41:5] ר[שׁע — The letters are preserved on a fragment pictured in the *editio princeps* but absent from the digital photographs.

L. 7 [41:6] עו]ׄל תֹאֹבֹד ממ]שלת — The letters are preserved on another fragment pictured in the *editio princeps* but absent from the digital photographs. חרפה — The letters are preserved on the same fragment as שׁע from line 6.

L. 8 [41:7] א]ב — The bottom half of the *aleph* appears clearly on the misplaced fragment of col. II (containing נ]חשקת etc. at 40:19). יקב — יל[ד — The letters are preserved on the same fragment as עו]ׄל תֹאֹבֹד ממ]שלת from lines 6 and 7.

L. 9 [41:8] הׄ]וי — A vertical mark on the edge of the misplaced fragment of col. II (containing נ]חשקת etc. at 40:19) is likely the remnant of a *he* at the beginning of this line (see col. II, lines 10–11; Reymond 2014b, 330). אׄנשׁׄי — The letters are preserved on the same fragment as עו]ׄל תֹאֹבֹד ממ]שלת from line 7; Yadin (1999, 176) also reads a following עׄ though these are impossible to read from the photographs in the *editio princeps*.

L. 10 [41:9ab]]ל∘[— From the photos in the *editio princeps*, the ascender is clear in the fragment that also contains עו]ׄל תֹאֹבֹד ממ]שלת from line 7. A small mark on the edge of the tear may be the remnant of another letter.

L. 11 [41:9c] תכש]לוׄ — The vav is clear; only the bottom tip of the *lamed* is preserved but since this is the only letter that terminates above the base line, its identity is clear. עׄם — Though Yadin 1999, 177 reads a *lamed*, there are just two letters here, as Strugnell (1969, 113) recognized.

L. 13 [41:11] הׄב]ל — The two letters are on a piece of leather that is bent so that it runs perpendicular to the rest of the lines. Althouth Yadin (1999, 177) reads a following *lamed*, this is not visible in the photographs. The following letters of this colon are either lost in a hole in the leather or have been effaced from the surface so that they are difficult to read. חסֹד ללא יכרת — Except for the aleph which is complete, only the tops of the letters are preserved.

L. 14 [41:12] פחד — Due to the warped leather, the letters run perpendicular to the rest of the line. ילוך — The initial *yod* is somewhat large, owing to the fact that the two strokes of the letter actually do not meet at the top tip, but instead are separated by a small space. The *vav* and *kaph* are written tightly together, so much so that it is hard to decide if the *vav* is even present. שׂיׄמׄת — The letters are very faint. Three dots correspond to what would be the heads of the three arms of a *sin/shin*. A dark splotch is the approximate shape and position of a *yod*. The top and right side of the *mem* are visible, while just a dot remains of the *tav*.

3   Ne crains pas la mort, ta part,
    souviens-toi, le premier et le dernier sont avec toi.
4a C'est la fin de tout [être humai]n
4b [Comment rejetterais-tu la]lo[i]du Très-Hau[t.]
4c Pour dix, cent, ou mille ans,
4d [   ]
5   Une descendance rejetée : des générations de mauvais
    [m]échant.
6   D'un enfant mauvais l'au[torité] est anéantie,
    l'opprobre sera perpétuellem[ent avec sa lignée.]
7   Un enf[ant] maudira un pè[re mauvais,]
    car, à cause de lui, ils seront (objet de) mépris.
8   Mal[heur   ] hommes de [   ]
    (vous) qui abandonnez la loi du Très-Haut.
9a [   ]l[   ]
9b et si vous enfantez, c'est pour un geignement,
9c [si vous tréb]uchez c'est [pour]la joie du peuple,
9d si vous mourez, c'est pour être maudits.
10 Tout ce qui (vient) du rien retourne au rien,
    ainsi l'impie (retourne) du vide au vide.
11 L'être [humain est éphè]mère[   ]
    mais un nom pieux ne sera pas supprimé.
12 Respecte (ton) nom car il t'accompagnera,
    plus que mille trésors désirables.
13 [Le bé]néfice d'un vivant : des jours comptés,
    le bénéfice d'un nom : des jou[r]s sans nombre.
14b Sagesse cachée et trésor enfoui,
14c quel profit en ces deux choses ?
15 Mieux vaut une personne qui cache sa folie,
    qu'une personne qui cache sa sagesse.
14a Écoutez, enfants, l'instruction sur la honte,
16a [afin que] vous soyez [c]onfus selon mon précepte.
16b Toute honte ne mérite pas d'être honteuse,
16c ni toute humiliation d'être choisie.
17 Aie honte, à cause d'un père et d'une mère, de l'arrogance,
    à cause d'un prince et d'un ministre, du mensonge.

3   Do not fear Death, [your] share;
    remember those first and last are with you.
4a This is the end of all [the children of Ada]m,
4b [how can you reject] the l[aw of] the Most High?
4c For ten, one hundred, or one thousand years
4d [   ]
5   Rejected offspring (are) the gen[erat]ions of the wicked,
    [of the wi]cked.
6   [From a wicked so]n aut[hority] is lost;
    reproach (remains) [with his seed] perpetual[ly].
7   A [wicked] fat[her] chil[dren] curse
    [because on] account of him they are scorned (lit., an object of contempt).
8   O[   ] unrighteous men,
    (you) who abandon the law of the Most High.
9a [   ] (it is) by [   ]
9b and if you beget (children), it is for moaning.
9c [If you stum]ble, (it is) for the joy of the people,
9d and if you die, it is (to be) cursed.
10 [All (that derives) from] nothing to nothing returns,
    thus, the godless (who are) from a void to a void (return).
11 Epheme[ral (is) a huma]n their [   ]
    [but] a pious name is not destroyed.
12 Respect (your) name since it will accompany you
    more than (would) a thousand desirous treasures.
13 [The b]enefit (that) the living (enjoy is) of a limited time (lit., days),
    but the benefit of a name has no s[u]ch limit (lit. is da[y]s without number).
14b Hidden [w]isdom and concealed treasure —
14c what profit (is) in these two things?
15 Better the person who hides their folly
    than the person who hides their wisdom
14a Hear, children, the instruction on shame;
16a [so as to be] chastened according to my precepts.
16b Not every shame merits shameful feelings (lit., feeling ashamed),
16c nor should every humiliation be chosen.
17 Be ashamed because of father or mother with respect to wantonness,
    of a prince or ruler with respect to lying,

L. 15 [41:13]   וטובֿת שֹׁםֿ יֹמֹי — Only the top of the *tav* is preserved. The *shin* is attested only by its bottom corner, where one sees the joint of the vertical mark and the right arm. Following this is a single mark that seems to be the remnant of a final *mem*. A similar mark that follows is likely a *yod*. A single mark seems to be the remnant of the *mem*.

L. 17 [41:15]   מטמן — A very small vertical line, joined to the diagonal line of the *mem*, is all that remains of the *nun*. The defective spelling is implied by the spacing that does not allow room for a *yod* mater.

L. 18 [41:14a/16a]   [וה]כֿלֹמֹוֹ — The head of the *kaph* is visible pressed next to the *lamed*; its base line is also clear beneath the hole. The narrow top of the *mem* is visible (cf. the narrow *mem* of מעדם in line 21), as well as the left tip of its base line. The *vav* is fairly clear.

L. 20 [41:17]   כֿחֿשׁ — The top of the *kaph* is clear, while only a single mark remains of the following letter. The lower arm and the bottom part of the *sin/shin*'s left vertical mark is preserved.

21 18ab B	מאדון וגבר[ת] על קשר	מעדם ועם [ע]ל [פ]שׁע
22 18c/19a B	משותף ורע על מעל	ממקום תגור על יד
23 19bc B	מהפר אלה וברת	וממטה אציל על לחם
24 19d/21a B	ממנׄ[ע]מתת שאלה	ומשיב את פני שארך
25 21b/20a B	מׄשׁ{א}ות מחלׄקת מנה	ומשאל שלום החריש

Col. IV

1 21c/20b B	מהביט אׄ[ ]	ומתבונן אל זרה
2 22ab B	מהתעשק עׄ[ם שפ]חה לך	ומהתקומם על יצעיה
3 22cd B	מאהב על דברי חסד	ומאחר מתת חרף

Chapter 42

4 1 B	משנות דבר תשמע	ומחשף כל דבר עצה
5 B	זׄהׄ[י]ית בוש באמת	ומצא חן בעיני כל חי
6 B	[אד] על אלה אל תבוש	ואל תשא פנים וחטא
7 2 B	על תורת עליון וחק	ועל משפט להצדיק רשע
8 3 B	על חשבון שותף ודרך	ועל מחלקת נחלה ויש
9 4ab B	על שחקי מזנים ופלס	ועל תמחי איפה ואבן
10 4c/5a B	על מקנה בין רב למע[ט]	[ועל]מׄמחיר ממכר תגר
11 5bc B	[על מוסר בנים מא]דׄה	ועבד רע וצלע מהלמת

תגור על יד M G | וממקום M | ממקום B G | וממקום Bmg · ממקום M | מֿתֿבּרׄ B | מֿתֿבּרׄ M Bmg | משותף 41:18c/19a · מעדה B G | מעדה M | מעדם B · שקר M | קשר 41:18ab | מי השע פי B | מהשב אפי M | מהשיב את פני 41:19d/21a · אל M | אל B · על M Bmg · וממטה M | וממטה B | Bmg · ונגיר על יד B | תגור על יד M Bmg 1 Bmg | משאלׄ B Bmg | ומשאל M G | רעד B | רעיד Bmg2 · 41:21b/20a · מחשות M | מחשבות B | מחלקת M | מחלקותׄ B Bmg2 · משואל M G | שארך 2 | זרה M Bmg or אלׄ M | על B · ומהתקׄמׄמׄ M | ומהתקומם B or ומתבונן 41:21c/20b · Bmg2 · המחריש B | מחריש M | החריש Bmg 1 · משואל 2 | אלׄ תׄנאׄץׄ B · שׁפֿחֿתֿך M | יצעיה 41:22cd · דברי חרפה B G | דֿבּרי חרפה M | ומאחר B · מאחרי M | מתת B | מתת M | שאלה Bmg · חרף M | וחק M | חוק B · Bmg · ומחסוף M | ומחשף · 42:1 | ישר M | בוש M Bmg · בוש M | על על M B | אל Bmg · 42:2 · על M B | אל Bmg · חק B · כל דבר MG | כל סוד B | על סוד Bmg | ומשפט M | משפט B · מצדיק B · מצדיק M Bmg G | ישר Bmg · 42:4ab | ויש B | מחלקות M | ואדם B · ואדם M | דרך B | שותף M Bmg | חובר B · 42:3 | ממחיר M B | חשבון Bmg · 42:4c/5a · מקנה M B | תמהות אפה ואפה B | תמחי איפה ואבן M | תמהי איפה ואבן B | שחק מאזנים G | שחקי מזנים M B | מוסר Bmg | 42:5bc · [ ]דׄה ועבד רע וצלע מהלמת M | > B ·

L. 25 [41:21b/20a] מחשות — Presumably due to confusion with the following half-line, the word was initially written משאת, before being corrected. A *khet* is written above and between the *mem* and *sin/shin*. A *vav* is superimposed on the right edge of the *aleph*.

L. 5 [42:1] זׄהׄ[י]ית — Only the tops of the letters are preserved.

L. 10 [42:4c/5a] מקנה — The *mem* lacks the top stroke above its long diagonal arm. [למע]ט — The top and part of the right stroke of the *mem* is visible above the tear, while only the tip of the right arm of the *ayin* is preserved. מׄמחיר — All that remains of the first *mem* is the left most tip of the diagonal arm and a trace of the base line.

L. 11 [42:5] [ ]דׄה — The *dalet* is very uncertain and could also be a *resh*. All that is preserved is the very bottom tip of its vertical mark, though the empty space to the left of it suggests only *resh* or *dalet*.

41:18 מעדם — The characteristic form and shape of the final *mem* could not be clearer. This reading does not make good sense, especially in light of the H[B] text that has מעדה. Presumably the combination of *ayin* and *mem* in the following word ועם "and people" has led the scribe to write a final *mem* instead of a *he*. Alternatively, this is another mistake of an *ayin* for an *aleph* (see הע for *הא in Sir 41:2[M] [III:1] and cf. אם for *עם in Sir 44:11[M] [VII:18]) and we should understand מאדם as intended and conclude that the initial colon of the verse juxtaposes "lord" and "lady" while the second juxtaposes "an individual" and "people." The words אדם "person" and עם "people" are in parallel in two places in the Hebrew Bible (Ps 22:7 and especially 2 Chr 6:29). Nevertheless, the Greek and Syriac translations of Ben Sira presume עדה here.

41:22 מהתעשק — We interpret the verb here as the root עשק "to quarrel" (see Gen 26:20), but used in the sense "to occupy oneself with, attend to" as found in Rabbinic Hebrew and Aramaic. דברי

18a à cause d'un maître et d'une maîtresse, du mensonge,
18b à cause d'un humain et du peuple, de la rébellion,
18c à cause d'un partenaire et d'un ami, de la trahison,
19a à cause du lieu où tu séjournes, du pouvoir,
19b de briser vœu et alliance,
19c et d'étendre le coude sur le pain,
19d de refu[ser]de répondre à une demande,
21a et de détourner le visage de ta propre chair,
21b de se taire lors de la répartition d'une part,
20a et de saluer le muet,

Col. IV

21c de regarder une fe[mme   ]
20b et de considérer l'étrangère,
22a d'avoir des occupations avec ta servante,
22b et de te dresser sur sa couche,
22c de l'ami à propos de paroles honteuses,
22d et de tarder à faire un reproche,

Chapitre 42

1   de répéter une parole que tu entends
    et de mettre à nu toute parole d'un conseil,
    Tu peux légitimement être honteux (de cela).
    de sorte que tu trouveras grâce aux yeux de tout vivant.
    Mais concernant ce (qui suit), n'aie pas honte
    et n'aie pas honte et (ne porte pas) un péché,
2   de la loi du Très-Haut et du décret,
    de celui qui exerce le jugement déclarant juste le méchant,
3   des comptes d'un partenaire ou d'un voyageur
    et du partage d'un héritage ou d'un bien,
4a des poussières des balances et des bascules,
4b et du polissage des mesures et des poids,
4c d'un achat, qu'il soit grand ou petit,
5a [et du]prix d'un article d'un marchand,
5b [de l'instruction intensi]ve [des enfants]
5c et d'un serviteur mauvais et boiteux des coups,

18a of lord or lad[y] with respect to conspiracy,
18b of man or people [with] respect to [tr]ansgression,
18c of comrade or friend with respect to treachery,
19a of the place where you sojourn with respect to power (lit., a hand),
19b of breaking oath or covenant,
19c and of extending a border with respect to food,
19d of withhol[ding] a requested gift,
21a and of turning away one of your family (lit., face of your flesh),
21b of keeping silent (at) a portion's division,
20a and of greeting the deaf,

Col. IV

21c/20b   of looking at [   ],
          and of noticing a foreign woman,
22   of arguing [with] your [hand]maid,
          and of climbing up into her bed,
          of befriending (someone) on account of shameful words,
          and of delaying giving a reproach (lit., reproaching),

Chapter 42

1   of repeating the word you hear,
    and of laying bare any word of counsel.
    You may [be] legitimately ashamed (of these things)
    so that you may find grace in the eyes of all the living.
    [But,] concerning these (following) things do not be ashamed,
    yet, do not feel ashamed and (bear) sin:
2   concerning the law of the most high and (his) statute,
    or concerning the exercise of judgment so as to bring the wicked to justice,
3   concerning the (monetary) account of friend or traveler,
    or concerning divisions of inheritance or wealth,
4a concerning the dust of scales and balance(s),
4b or concerning the polish of measure and stone weight,
4c concerning the purchase of much or li[ttle,]
5a [concerning] the price of the merchant's wares,
5b [concerning the intensi]ve [instruction of children,]
5c or of a servant, wicked and limping from beatings,

חסד — Based on H^B (דברי חרפה) and the context, this is easiest to understand as the rare word "shame, reproach" (found in Lev 20:17; Prov 25:10), a homonym of the more common word "piety, loving kindness." ומאחר — This is the preposition followed by the *piel* of אחר.
42:1 בויש — This is a unique word, apparently of an adjectival *qattīl* or *qatīl* base.
42:4 שחקי מזנים — The phrase is based on Isa 40:15, where we find the singular noun שחק, as in H^B. In the plural, the noun has the sense "clouds" or "heaven"; rarely, it also has this sense in the singular (as at

Ps 89:7, 38). By analogy, it is likely that the plural could also simply have the sense "dust." תמחי איפה — The first word is otherwise unknown and is assumed to be a mistake for תמחות or תמחית "wiping" (see H^B).
42:5 וצלע מהלמת — The phrase might also be interpreted as "whose side is beaten (מַהֲלָמֹת)," (lit. "and a side of beatings"). The extreme rarity of the *piel/pual* and *hiphil/hophal* of the root הלם would seem to discourage interpreting מהלמת as a participle "beaten," though this admittedly also remains a remote possibility, giving the following translation "... or of a side that is struck."

276 MANUSCRIPT MASADA

6 ᴮ	¹²[שת חותם תפ]שת אשה על	ומקום ידים רבות מפתח	
7 ᴮ	¹³[קום] מ[על תפקיד מספר	ש[וא] ותת הכל בכתב	
8ab ᴮ	¹⁴על מו[סר פ]ותה וכסיל	[וש]ב כושל ענה בזנות	
8cd ᴮ	¹⁵והיית זהיר באמת	[ואיש צנו]ע לפני כל חי	
9ab ᴮ	¹⁶בש{א}ת לאב מטמון שק[ר]	[דאגתה תפ]ריד נומה	ר
9cd ᴮ	¹⁷בנעוריה פן ״מאס	ובעליה פן ת[פת]ה	
10ac ᴮ	¹⁸בבתוליה פן תחל	ועל אישה[פן] תשטה	
10bd ᴮᴾ	¹⁹בית אביה פן תזריע	ובעלה[פן תע]צ֯ר [	
11ab ᴮᴾ	²⁰[בני] ע֯ל בת חזק משמר	[פ]ן תע[]שה [	
11cd ᴮᴾ	²¹דבת עיר וקהלת עם	] שע[ר	
11ef ᴮ	²²מקום תגור אל יהי	] סב[י	
12 ᴮᴾ	²³לכל זכר אל תבן תאר	] [	
13 ᴮᴾ	²⁴כי מבגד יצא סס	[ומא]שה רעת אשה	
14 ᴮ	²⁵טוב רע איש מטוב אשה	ובת מפחדת מבול חרפה	

42:6 שת[תפ M רעה]ר' = B G | Bmg 2 טפשה Bmg 1 · חותם M Bmg · חותם חכם B · רפות M G | רבות B · מפתח M | תפתח B Bmg · 42:7 תפקיד M מרדות M B | מו[סר 42:8ab · Bmg ושואה ותתה B G | ומתת ולקח M ש[וא]ותת · Bmg מספר M | מספור B | תספור B Bmg · תחשוב Bmg ·]ותת M ש[וא]ותת · Bmg מ֯פ֯ק֯ד יד B | תפקד יד | תפ[ריד B · מטמנת B מטמון M Bmg | בת B · בש{א}ת M | בש{א}ת 42:9ab · Bmg ועונה B · ונוטל B | (ושוא) עצה M | ענה B · ושב וישיש M Bmg | וש[ב] כושל Bmg · M | תפריש B · נומה M | נ[ו]מ֯ M · 42:9cd תמאס M S | תגורי B · ובעליה M G S | ובבתוליה B · 42:10ac תחל M G S | תפותה B | תפתתה Bmg 1 Bmg 2 · ועל M G S | אישה ובת B = Bmg2 בבית בעי בבית בעלת = Bmg2 | בבית ב֯ע֯ל֯ת B · תשטה M G S | פן תשטה B תנשא B · 42:10bd בית M | בבית B Bmg2 · פן תזריע M G | תנשא ל' תנשא · Bmg2 · 42:11 ומשמר M G S | ומוסר B 42:12 זכר M G | ת֯נ֯ז֯ה B | פן תחזה Bmg1 · ובעלה M | ובבית אשה B = Bmg2 ובב' א'ר"ש B | תע[]צ֯ר M B | ת֯ש֯נ֯א֯ ובית M | ובת B · מטיב B · מטיב M Bmg | מטוב B · רוע M Bmg | רע M Bmg | מטוב B · טוב M Bmg · 42:14 עש M · סס M Bmg · 42:13 תתן B | תבן M S | תזכר Bmg · M B B · מפחדת M | מחפרת B Bmg 1 · מבול Bmg 2 G | תביע M Bmg · חרפה M Bmg G | אשה B ·

L. 13 [42:7] ש[ו — There seems to be a mark near the base of the *sin/shin* that may be the bottom tip of a *vav* or *aleph* (if not another letter). ותת — The initial letter does not appear to be a *mem* (as Yadin reads). The only apparent mark is the bottom of a vertical stroke, though this could also be a tear in the leather.

L. 14 [42:8] פ[ותה — The initial letter looks more like a *vav* than a *pe*, as it lacks the characteristic head of the *pe* and any remnant of a base line. כושל — The initial letter looks like a *yod*, though its right edge curves in the opposite direction of most *yod*s. Due to this last factor as well as the fact that no known root easily corresponds to the reading יושל, we read the first letter as *kaph*, which does sometimes show a concave right edge. However, it should be noted that no base line is visible, though the leather is preserved.

L. 15 [42:8] צנו[ע לפני — Only the tops of the letters are preserved.

L. 16 [42:9ab] ר — The mark is neither *dalet* nor *resh*, but most probably a Greek *gamma* (see the *psy* in the margin of col. V line 1). בש{א}ת — The *bet* is written bigger than other letters. It is followed by a *sin/shin* with a cancellation dot above it. The next letter is more probably an *aleph* that the scribe has reshaped into a *tav*. It suggests that the scribe first wrote בשא perhaps confusing the spellings of Hebrew בושת "shame" and Aramaic באשה "evil." תפ[ריד — The *resh* is represented by only the left most tip of its horizontal bar, touching the head of the *yod*; the mark could also be read in different ways.

L. 17 [42:9cd] ובעליה — Only the bottoms of the first four letters are visible, though these are distinctive enough to be sure of the reading. ת[ה — The *tav* is conjectural as its top lacks the distinctive mark that stands above the left leg and horizontal bar. Only the left part of the top bar of the *he* is visible.

L. 18 [42:10] תשטה — Only the right most part of the *he* is visible.

L. 19 [42:10] ובעלה — Only the bottom tip of the *he*'s right leg is visible. תע[צ֯ר — Only the top left stroke of the *tsade* is visible, followed by the top right corner of another letter. The top stroke of this letter seems partially effaced.

L. 20 [42:11ab] ע֯ל בת — Only the left most tip of the *tav* is visible now in the digital photographs; the other letters are visible on a fragment seen in the photographs in the *editio princeps*. In these earlier photographs, only the bottom parts of the *ayin*, *lamed*, and *tav* are visible. [פ]ן תע[]שה — Only the tops of the letters are visible.

L. 21 [42:11d] שע[ר — Only the bottom most part of the letter is preserved.

L. 22 [42:11f] סב[י — Only the very slightest trace of the left most head of the *yod* is visible.

L. 24 [42:13] א֯שה — Only the bottom most part of the right leg of the *aleph* is visible.

L. 25 [42:14] מבול — This is a mistake for מכול (see Reymond 2014b, 334–35).

6 [d'une femme qui dét]ient un sceau,
 ou d'une clé en un lieu (où il y) a des mains nombreuses.
 7 du li[eu] du dépôt de comptes,
 saisie et don, le tout par écrit
 8a de l'ins[truction du si]mple et du stupide,
 8b et du grison qui trébuche, occupé à la fornication.
 8c Alors, tu seras vraiment vigilant,
 8d [et une personne hum]ble devant tout vivant.
 9a Une fille est un faux trésor pour un père,
 9b [l'anxiété à son sujet éca]rte le sommeil:
 9c quand elle est jeune, de peur qu'elle ne soit détestée,
 9d quand elle est mariée, de peur qu'elle ne soit [sédu]ite
 10a quand elle est vierge, de peur qu'elle ne soit profanée
 10c et[de peur] qu'elle ne se détourne de son mari,
 10b dans la maison de son père, qu'elle ne soit enceinte,
 10d et dans (la maison) de son mari[, de peur qu'elle ne soit sté]rile.
 11a [Mon enfant,] sur une fille renforce la garde,
 11b [De] peur qu'elle ne[te]fa[sse   ]
 11c ragot de la ville et de l'assemblée du peuple,
 11d [   ]
 11e Là où elle habite qu'il n'y ait pas
 11f [envir]onnante.
 12 Qu'elle ne révèle (sa) beauté à aucun homme,
   [   ]
 13 Car d'un vêtement sort la mite
   [et d'une fe]mme, la méchanceté de femme.
 14 Mieux vaut la méchanceté d'un homme que la bonté d'une femme,
   (ou) qu'une fille qui redoute *tout* reproche.
	6 [concerning a woman hol]ding a seal,
	 or a key in a place of many hands,
	 7 concerning [the place] of registered accounts (lit., the deposit of a number),
	 wa[ges] and giving, everything in writing,
	 8a concerning the ins[truction of the si]mple and stupid,
	 8b [and of the old] man, stumbling, occupied with fornication.
	 8c Then, you will be truly observant,
	 8d [and a pruden]t [person] before all the living.
	 9a A daughter (is) a decepti[ve] treasure to (her) father;
	 9b [anxiety over her divi]des (his) slumber;
	 9c in her youth, lest she be rejected,
	 9d in her married state, lest she be [seduc]ed
	 10a in her virginity, lest she be defiled,
	 10c and [lest] she be faithless toward (or: against) her husband;
	 10b (while still in) her father's house, lest she bear children,
	 10d and (while in) [ ] husband('s house) [lest she be ba]rr[en.]
	 11a [My son,] over a daughter maintain (your) vigilance (lit., watch),
	 11b [le]st she m[ake]
	 11c the talk of the city and of the congregation of the people,
	 11d [gat]e
	 11e (In) the place where she dwells, let there not be
	 11f [aro]und
	 12 May she not make (her) beauty discernible to any male,
	   [ ]
	 13 Indeed, from a garment a moth comes forth,
	   [and from a wo]man, women's wickedness.
	 14 Better a man's wickedness than a woman's virtue,
	   (better even) than the daughter who dreads *every* reproach.

42:6 תפ[שת] — We propose to reconstruct תפשת "one holding" and assume the author is referring to powerful women who possessed seals and keys, women which a scribe might encounter in the course of their administrative work. Note the presence of many seals of women from the first temple era onward (Marsman 2003, 643–59). Another possibility is to assume that the marginal word טפשה "foolish" in H^B had been spelled here with a final *tav*. The phrase would be curious since it (and similar constructions) could be read as essentially saying: "(do not be ashamed)… concerning a woman foolish in regard to a seal" (cf. Jezebel's use of Ahab's seal in 1 Kgs 21:8), an idea Ben Sira would never express. Other reconstructions are conceivable: e.g., על אשה רעה [שת חותם "[concerning a wicked woman] (over whom) you have set a seal." Still, this is unparalleled in H^B.

42:9 וּבְעלִיה — The word is interpreted above as an abstract noun akin to בתולים and זקונים (see Reymond 2014b, 334). Alternatively, perhaps it could be read as "in the roof chamber" (עלִיה), a metaphor for domestic life as a married person. תֹּ[ ]תֹּ — The missing letters can be reconstructed as either תנשה "(lest) she is forgotten" or תשנה (for תשנא*) "(lest) she be hated" as the Syriac, or again תשטה as in 10c.

42:14 מבול — The second letter is a mistake for a *kaph* and the phrase should be read מכול, as in the translation above.

Col. V

15a אזכרה נא		
מעֿ[שׁ]וׄ 15b זה		
חזיתי ואשננה		

¹אזכרה נא מעשי אל	15ab B	ψ
²באמר אדני מעשיו	15cd B	
³שמש זהרת על כל נגלת[ה]	16 B	
⁴לא השפיקו קדשי אל	17ab B	
⁵אמץ אדני צבאיו	17cd B	
⁶תהום ולב חקר	18ab B	
⁷[ ] כי ידע עליון כל [	18cd B	
⁸מחוה חליפות [ונהיות]	19 B	
⁹לא נעדר ממנו שכל	20 B	
¹⁰גבורות חכמֿ[תו	21ab B	
¹¹לא נאסף [ול]אׄ נׄ[אֿצֿ]לׄ	21cd B	
¹²הלוא כל מעשיו נחמד[ים]	22	
¹³הכל חי ועמֿ[ד] לעד	23 B	
¹⁴[ ] וכלם שׁנׁ[י]ם	24 B	
¹⁵ולא עשה מהם [שוא]		
¹⁶זה על זה חלף טובם	25 B	

וזה חזיתי ואשננה
ופעל רצנו לקחו
[וכ]בוד אדני מלא מעשיו
לספר כל נפלאתיו
להתחזק לפני כבודו
ובמערמיהם יתבונן
[ו]מֿביט אתיות עולם
[ו]מֿגלה חׁקר נסתרות
ולאׄ עב[רׄ]ו כל דבר
אחד הׄ[ו]אׄ [מעׄ]ולם
[ו]לׄ[א צריׄ]ךֿ לבל מבין
עדני ציץ וחזות מראה
[ו]כל צרך והכל נשמר
[זה] לעמת זה
vacat
[ו]מי ישבע להביט הודם

אלהים M | אדני B · באומר M | באמר M · 42:15cd · ואספרה B G S · ואשננה M Mmg | ואשננה Mmg · מעֿ[שׁ]וׄ M B | מעשי אל B · אזכר M Mmg | אזכרה M 42:15ab · עלׄ M G | ייי M · אדני M · זורׄחׄת B S · זהרת M G 42:16 · לקח M B | לקחו Bmg · ופעל רצונו M | ופעל רצנו B · רצוׄנו B · רצנו M Bmg G S מעשיו B · אלהים M | אדני Bmg · אומץ B | אימץ M אמץ M · 42:17cd · גבורותיו B | נפלאות ייי M G S | כל נפלאתיו B · הספיקו M | השפיקו 42:17ab · BS · כל חלפו M | עבֿ[רׄ]ו B · כל שכל M G S | שכל 42:20 · B · < 42:18cd · B · ובכל מערומיהם M | ובמערמיהם Bmg · 42:18ab · להחזיק M B | להתחזק B · B | חלף מנו Bmg · 42:21ab גבורת M B | גבורות Bmg · מעׄ[ו]לם M B | מהעולם Bmg · 42:21cd צרך M | צריךׄ M | צרך B | צרך Bmg · 42:23 הכל M G הוא B שונם M | שֿנֿיׄם M 42:24 · Bmg הכל נשמע B | הבׄלׄ ישמע M | והכל נשמר M | וכל צרך M | ולכל צוׄרךׄ B | לבל צרך Bmg · 42:24 וקים Bmg | וקים M B | ועמד B · הודם M | לה[ה]בֿ[י]טׄ M Bmg | להביט B · ישבׄ[ע] M Bmg | ישבע B · ומי M Bmg | ומי B · טוב Bmg | טובי S | טובו M | טובם B · 42:25 · מזה M | לעמת זה תואר B | תׁאׄם Bmg

L. 1 margin [42:15] On the right margin what looks like a Greek *psy* has been written. And on the left margin of the column, a scribe inserted a marginal note. אזכרה — An erased *mem* is visible more or less over and just beneath the *zayin*, and a much more faint *sin/shin* can be made out beneath the *resh* and *he*. Presumably, the scribe wrote "his works" from the following line, before erasing it. מעֿ[שׁ]וׄ — See Qimron (1999, 230). The *mem* is extra dark and larger than the other letters, suggesting perhaps that this and following letters were written over another erased word. The letters מעֿ[שׁ]וׄ are not followed by the word אל, as in the main text and this suggests that the final letter is the 3ms pronominal suffix.

L. 8 [42:19] חׁקר — In the digital photos, one can see a tear that bisects this word, with the vertical strokes of the *qoph* and *resh* misplaced to the right. Only the top of the *khet* and a portion of its right leg is visible. The entire letter seems narrowed. נסתרות — The initial *nun* is written above the *samek* (as a correction) such that the *nun*'s lower bar intersects with the top bar of the *samek*.

L. 9 [42:20] ולאׄ — The *aleph* is not attested by ink, but by the distinctive shape of the hole in the leather that reflects the bottom right, bottom left, and upper left arms of the letter.

L. 10 [42:21] מעׄ]ולם — Traces of the first two letters may be hidden by a small piece of leather that hangs from the preceding line and covers a portion of this word.

L. 11 [42:21]]לׄ — Only two dots of ink are visible, both part of an upper horizontal stroke.

L. 12 [42:22] נחמד[ים] — The *mem* and *dalet* are visible in the *editio princeps*, though in the digital photos the leather of the second part of the column is covering a part of the *mem* and all of the *dalet*.

Col. V

15a Je veux rappeler les œuvres de Dieu
15b et ce que j'ai vu, je veux l'enseigner.
   (mg. [15a] Je veux rappeler son œu[vre]
   [15b] et ce que j'ai vu, je veux l'enseigner).
15c Par une parole de Dieu (sont) ses œuvres
15d et son enseignement est l'œuvre de sa volonté.
16 Le soleil brillant se manif[este] sur tout,
   [et la gl]oire d'Adonaï remplit ses œuvres.
17a Les saints de Dieu ne parviennent pas
17b à raconter toutes ses merveilles,
17c Adonaï affermit ses armées,
17d pour résister devant sa gloire.
18a Il a sondé l'abîme et le cœur,
18b et discernera leurs nudités.
18c Car le Très-Haut connaît tout [   ]
18d [et]observe ce qui arrivera pour toujours.
19 Il est celui qui déclare les changements[et les existants]
   [et]celui qui révèle la profondeur des choses cachées.
20 L'intelligence ne lui fait pas défaut
   Et rien ne le dépasse.
21a [Sa]puissante sages[se   ]
21b depuis toujours, il est un.
21c il ne s'accroît pas, ni ne se [rét]ra[cte]
21d [et n]'a [beso]in d'aucun instructeur.
22 Toutes ses œuvres ne sont-elles pas désirables,
   délices cristallins et visions merveilleuses ?
23 Tout est vivant et demeure pour toujours,
   [et]tout besoin, tout est préservé.
24 Tous ceux-là diffè[rent   ]
   [celui-ci] vis-à-vis de celui-là,
   et il n'a fait aucun d'eux [en vain.]
   vacat
25 De l'un à l'autre, leur beauté excède,
   [et]qui peut se rassasier de leur bonté ?

Col. V

15a Let me recall the the works of God;
15b what I have seen, let me teach.
   (mg. [15a] I shall remember his wo[rks]
   [15b] and what I have seen, shall I teach.)
15c By the word of the Lord (come) his works,
15d his teaching (is) the work of his will.
16 The sun, shining over all, reveals itself;
   and the glory of the Lord fills his works.
17a Even God's holy ones do not succeed
17b in recounting all his wonders.
17c The Lord fortifies his hosts
17d to withstand his glory.
18a He probes abyss and heart,
18b contemplating their intimate parts.
18c The Most High knows all [   ]
18d observing what transpires throughout eternity.
19 The one declaring what changes [and what is to be]
   and the one revealing the depth of hidden things.
20 Insight he does not lack;
   no matter pas[s]es him by.
21a [His] mighty wisdom [   ]
21b [of] old, h[e] is one and the same.
21c He is not added to n[or sub]trac[ted from]
21d [and he does] not n[eed] any instructor.
22 Are not all his works desirable,
   shining delights and wonderful of appearance?
23 All live and endure forever;
   [and] (their) every need—everything is provided for.
24 All of them, diff[erent   ]
   [this] opposite that
   he made none of them [in vain]
   vacat
25 This one to the next, their beauty is surpassing
   [and] who could be sated at seeing their splendor?

42:15 מֹ[שׁ]יֿ — The defective spelling is unexpected, but not unprecedented. The spelling may also be explained as a case of haplography, where the final letter would be read as a *yod* (i.e., זה <ı>ˢ[שׁ]מֹע). ואשננה — This is the verb שנן "to teach," also found in Deut 6:7.
42:18 The second distich in this verse is not found in H^B, but is reflected in the Greek.
42:20 עב]ר]וֿ — The verb might have the sense it bears in Aramaic, "to overtake, surpass" (cf. Tg. Zech. 9:8).
42:22 עדני ציץ — For the division of words, see Strugnell 1969, 117. Alternatively one may read עד ניצוץ "even a spark." Strugnell's translation "delightful to gaze upon" is unlikely since the root צוץ or ציץ has the sense "to gaze" only in the *hiphil*. וחזות מראה — The phrase is more literally "vision of an appearance." The word חזות is used to indicate a preceding noun's prominence in Dan 8:5 (חזות קרן "a prominent horn"), though here perhaps we should infer a superlative expression (see, e.g., Waltke and O'Connor 1990, 267–68). Alternatively, it might indicate the reflection of a mirror (reading מְרָאָה). The translation of Strugnell (1969, 117), "a joy to behold," requires understanding וחזות as a mistake for וחדות, which seems unlikely.
42:24 [שוא] — This is conjectured based on the Greek and Syriac. Tangentially, this reading might also be supported by the word שב in H^B, a presumed mistake for שוב, which is phonetically similar to שוא.

Chapter 43

1 B	¹⁷תאר מרום ורקיע לטהר	עצם שמים מֹ[בי]עַ֯ נֹהוֹרֹו
2 B	¹⁸שמש מופיע בצאתו נכסה	כלי נורא מעשה [ע]ליון
3 B	¹⁹בהצהירו ירֹ[תי]ח תבל	ולפני חרב מי יתכ[ו]לל
4ab B	²⁰[כ]ור נפוח מעשי מוצק	של[וח ש]מֹש [י]שֹׁיֹק
4cd B	²¹לשון מאור תֹ[ג]מיר נושבת	[ ]
5 B	²²כי גדול אדני עשהו	ודברֹ[ ]
6 B	²³וגם [י]רח יאריח עתות	מֹמ[שלת]
7 B	²⁴לו מֹ[ע]ֹד וממנו חג	[ ]
8ab B	²⁵חֹדש כשמו הוא מתֹ[חדש]	[ ]

Col. VI

8cd B	¹וכלי צבא נבלי מרום	מרצֹףׂ [ ]
9 B	²תור שמים והוד כוכב	עדי משריק במרמֹ[י אל]
10 B	³בדבר אדני יעמד חק	ולא ישח באשמרתם
11 B	⁴ראה קשת וברך עשיה	כי מאד נהדר נֹהֹרֹתֹה
12 B	⁵הוֹגֹ [ ] בכבודה	[ו]יד אל נטתה בגבֹ[רה]
13 B	⁶גערתו תֹ[תו]ה ברד	ותנצח זיקות משפט

נֹהוֹרֹו Bmg · מביט B מֹרביט M | מֹ[בי]עַ֯ M ועצם Bmg · עצם B Bmg | עֹצם M על טהרֹ B לטֹהֹוֹרֹ Bmg · לטהר M ורקיע M רקע Bmg · תואר B Bmg | תאר M | 43:1 תאר | עֹ[ע]ליון B מעשי M מעשה M G S | מה · B כלי · B חמה · M נכסה · B מביע בצרתו M מופיע בצאתו M Bmg · 43:2 | נהרה B G | הדרו M | 43:3 ולפני B G S | לפני · B חרב M חרבו B G S | יתכ[ו]לל M יתכלכל · B מוצק M Bmg | מצוק · B מהם · B מעשי M G | מעשי B · ייי M Bmg | יֹדליק B יסיק Bmg G S | 43:4cd לשון M Bmg | לשאן B · תֹגמר M תֹ[ג]מיר B · 43:5 גדול M Bmg | גדיל B · אדני B עשיהו M עושיו · B ייי עושה עליון Bmg · 43:6 י]רֹח יאריח M י]רח ירח B · עתות M עתות שבות B עת עת Bmg1 · עד עת Bmg2 · 43:7 לו M | בם B ו]ממנו M Bmg | וזמני B · חֹק M חוק · B 43:8ab כשמו M Bmg G S בחדשו B · הוא M B והוא Bmg · 43:8cd מרצֹף M B מעריץ Bmg · ישח B יסח M | אל M אדני · B במרומי · B במרמֹ[י M ואורו מזהיר · B עדי משריק M Bmg G והוד · B והדר M והד B · תואר M תור Bmg · 43:9 חוז · 43:12 בֹ֯כֹבֹ֯וֹדֹ M נֹהֹרֹתֹה Bmg · נהדרה B נאדרה M נהדר B · 43:11 עשיה M עשיה B עושה Bmg · באשמורתם M באשמרתם Bmg · ישון Bmg · תנצח M Bmg1 תזנח Bmg2 זיקות M B זלקים Bmg1 · יקום Bmg2 · משפט M [פט]בֹמשֹׁ B Bmg2 · גערתו M Bmg2 גבורתו · B ברד M G | ברק B בקר Bmg2 · בכבודו M B בכבודה · Bmg אל M B לֹא Bmg · 43:13 חוק · B הוד M G |

L. 17 [43:1] שמים — In the digital photos, the word is split lengthwise by a tear. The upper parts and lower parts of the letters are not aligned such that the bottom halves of the letters are located to the left of the upper parts. מֹ[בי]עַ֯ — Only the tops of the *mem, ayin* are visible. It might also be reconstructed מֹ[פי]עַ "cause to shine" or even perhaps מֹ[ציא] "bring forth" (see Reymond 2014b, 336). נֹהוֹרֹו — The word is difficult to read due to the tear in the manuscript that splits it in two lengthwise. When the upper and lower parts are joined, the spelling of the word is clear. The vertical line of the *nun* is clear, as are the legs and top bar of the *he*. The bottom part of the *vav* is visible. The distinctive left tip of the *resh*'s upper bar is clear, as is part of its leg. Only the top of the final *vav* is visible.

L. 18 [43:2] מעשה — Only the right leg of the *he* is visible, making it appear as a *vav* or *yod*.

L. 19 [43:3] יתכ[ו]לל — Qimron (1999, 230) suggests that the word could perhaps be read יסת[ו]לל citing the curved nature of the second letter, though this implies that the *tav* has an extra long foot.

L. 20 [43:4] [י]שֹׁיֹק — Extremely faint traces of the *sin, yod*, and the leg of the *qoph* are visible to the left of שמש.

L. 23 [43:6] [י]רֹח — Only the upper left stroke of the *resh* is preserved. מֹמ[שלת — Only the right most vertical stroke of the second *mem* is visible.

L. 24 [43:7] מֹ[ע]ֹד — Only the bottom tip of the *vav* is preserved. As for the *dalet*, only the bottom tip of its vertical stroke and the left most part of its horizontal stroke are preserved.

L. 25 [43:8a] חֹדש — Only the upper left tip of the *khet* is visible. The top of the *dalet* is preserved above the tear, but not the vertical stroke. מתֹחדש — Only the upper stroke of the *tav* is preserved above the tear.

L. 1 [43:8d] מרצֹףׂ — Only the bottom tips of the *tsade* and *pe* are visible.

L. 2 [43:9] במרמֹ[י — The last letter before the hole is likely a *mem*, not a *vav* as Yadin reads.

L. 4 [43:11] נֹהֹרֹתֹה — Only the tops of the letters are visible. The first vertical mark perfectly resembles a *nun* (or a *zayin*). It is followed by a *he* (a two stroke horizontal line and the top of the right leg) and a *resh*. The last marks may be read as a *tav* (the right shoulder and the top of the left leg) followed by a *he* (a trace of the top of its right leg).

L. 5 [43:12] בגבֹ — Only a trace of the bottom of the *vav* remains.

L. 6 [43:13] תֹ[תו]ה — Only a dot remains of the foot of the *tav*. Only the left most stroke of the *he* is visible.

Chapitre 43

1 La beauté des hauteurs (célestes) et la pureté du firmament,
   le ciel lui-même répand son éclat.
2 Le soleil illumine, lorsqu'il se lève, ce qui est caché,
   un instrument redoutable est l'œuvre du [Trè]s-Haut,
3 Lorsqu'il est à son zénith, il fait bouillir la terre
   et devant la chaleur, qui pourrait tenir.
4a Une fournaise ardente, œuvres en fusion,
4b l'irr[adiation du soleil   ]
4c La langue de l'astre anéantit le monde habité,
4d [   ]
5 Car grand est Adonaï son créateur
   et [ses] paroles[   ]
6 Et aussi la lune fait déambuler les saisons,
   pour gou[verner   ]
7 Par lui (les) fête(s) et de lui le(s) solennité(s),
   [   ]
8a La lune, selon son nom, se reno[uvelle,]
8b [   ]

Col. VI
8c Joyau de l'armée céleste, harpes d'en haut,
8d qui fait luire [   ]
9 Beauté du ciel et splendeur d'étoile,
   parure brillante dans les hauteur[s divines.]
10 Par la parole d'Adonaï, le décret perdure,
   il ne faiblit pas durant leurs (i.e. les étoiles) veilles.
11 Observe l'arc-en-ciel et bénis son créateur,
   car son éclat est extrêmement honoré,
12 La voûte (céleste) [   ] par sa gloire,
   [et] la main de Dieu l'a tendue avec puis[sance.]
13 Sa menace dessine la grêle
   et illumine des brandons de jugement

Chapter 43

1 The beauty of the (heavenly) height(s) and of the firmament (is) pristine indeed (lit., for purity);
   heaven itself em[it]s its shining.
2 In its coming forth, the sun illumines what is hidden;
   a fear-inspiring instrument is the work of the [Mo]st High.
3 When it shines, it makes the world b[oi]l;
   who can endure (its) parching heat?
4a [As a we]ll-fired furn[ace] (ignites) cast objects,
4b so, the bea[m of sun   ] sets [on fire   ]
4c The luminary's tongue con[su]mes the habitable world,
4d [   ]
5 For, great is the lord, its maker;
   [(by) his] word[s   ]
6 Truly, [the m]oon carries (lit., causes to travel) time forward,
   for the gove[rnance   ]
7 According to it (are the) fe[a]st(s) and from it (come the) festival(s);
   go[vernance of   ]
8a The new moon, as its name (implies), re[news] itself;
8b [   ]

Col. VI
8c Jewels of the heavenly host and the harps of the heights,
8d [   ] is paved [   ]
9 Beauty of sky and splendor of star,
   shining ornament, (all are) in [God's   ] heights.
10 Through the word of the Lord order endures;
   it does not weaken in their (the heavens') watch.
11 Observe the rainbow and bless its maker;
   for its brightness is much celebrated.
12 [   ] heaven's vault with its glory,
   [and] the hand of God stretched it with (his) mig[ht.]
13 His rebuke s[tamp]s the hail,
   lighting up the fiery arrows of (his) judgment.

43:1 לטהר | עצם שמים — The absence of the conjunction *vav*, makes the allusion to Exod 24:10 clearer than in MS B. נְהוֹרוּ — This is an Aramaic word and it occurs only three times in Hebrew texts from the Middle Ages according to Maagarim.

43:2 נכסה — We have understood the word as a *niphal* participle "what is hidden" and not as a word traced back to the root א/כָּסֵה (See Yadin 1999, 186).

43:3 יתכולל — This is the only attestation of the *hithpolel* conjugation for the root כול, which more regularly appears in the *hithpalpel* conjugation (e.g., Sir 12:15A and 43:3B).

43:4 תגמיר — The word may also be read as תגמור "it will consume" or "burn." As HAWTTM indicates, the root here may have the more specific sense "burn" (as found in Aramaic and Syriac; see CAL 16 March, 2021).

43:6 יאריח — The *hiphil* of ארח does not occur elsewhere. Dihi (2004, 82–84) gives to it the meaning "to fix the date" (cf. Arabic *'arraḫa* 'to date').

43:9 תור — The *aleph* of תאר has been elided here (See 51:14 in 11QPsa). This is an abbreviated form of the word usually spelled with *aleph* (and no mater) in the Leningrad Codex: תֹּאַר. Among the DSS, this kind of spelling is typical of those words whose medial *aleph* had quiesced (e.g., רוש for ראש "head").

14 B	⁷למענו פרע אוצר		ויעף עבים כעיט
15 B	⁸גבורתו חזק ענן		ותגדע אֿבֿני ברד
17a/16a B	⁹קול רעמו יחיל ארצו		ובכחו יניף הרים
16b/17b B	¹⁰אמרֿתֿו תחריף תימן		עלעול סופה וסערה
17cd B	¹¹כרשף יפרח שלגו		וכארבה ישכן רדתו
18 B	¹²תור לבנו יהג עינים		וממטרו יתמיה לבב
19 B	¹³[וגם] כֿפֿוֿר כמלח ישפך		ויצמח כסנה צצים
20 B	¹⁴[צנת רו]חֿ צֿפֿוֿן ישיב		וכרגב יקפיא מקור
21 B	¹⁵[על כל מע]מֿדֿ מֿיֿם יקרֿ[ים] חֿרֿב		[ ]
21 B	¹⁶[ ]יבול הרי[ם יש]יֿקֿ [		[ ]
22 B	¹⁷[ ]		[ ]
23 B	¹⁸[ ]		[ ]אֿיֿם
24 B	¹⁹[ ]		לשמע אזנינו נשמתֿםֿ
25 B	²⁰[ ]		מֿןֿ כֿ[ל חי וֿ]גֿבֿוֿתֿ רהֿב
26 B	²¹[ ]		[ ]
27 B	²²[ ]		[ ]
28 B	²³[ ]		[ ]
29 B	²⁴[ ]		[ת/יֿוֿ]

43:14 למענו M Bmg | למען B · ברא M G | פרע B · 43:17a/16a יחיל M Bmg | יחול B · ובכוחו M | ובכחו Bmg · יניף M G | יעים Bmg · 43:16b/17b אמ־ ישכן B · יניף M | יפרח B · ברֿשֿף B · כרשף M Bmg G · 43:17cd צֿפֿוֿן B G · + זלעפות B · עלעול M Bmg G · תחרף Bmg | תחריף M | אימתו Bmg | אמרֿתֿוֿ M G | M ישפך 43:19 · יהמה B · יהג M Bmg · יתמיה M G · יגהה B · יהגה M | לבנה B · לבנו M | תואר B · תור M | דרתו M Bmg G | רדתו B · ישכן M Bmg | חֿרֿב 43:21 · מקוה Bmg | מקורו B | מקורו M | מקור B | וכרגב M | וכרגב B · 43:20 וציצים M | ציצים B · ציצים M | כסנה B · כספיר B · ויצמח M | ויציץ B · ישכן B · Bmg B · רבה M | רהֿב M | וגבורות M | וֿגֿבֿוֿרות 43:25 · נשתומם B · נשמתם M | נשמתמ B · אזנונו M | אזנינו B · 43:24 אוצר Bmg | אֿיֿם M B G · 43:23 · כחרב B · M

L. 8 [43:15] אֿבֿנֿיֿ — Only the right most part of the *aleph* is preserved. Only the base line of the *bet* is visible, ligatured to the *nun*.

L. 10 [43:16b/17b] אמרֿתֿוֿ — Only the bottom tips of the *resh* and *vav* are preserved, while the *tav* is attested only by its foot.

L. 13 [43:19] כֿפֿוֿר — Only the traces of the tops of the first three letters are preserved.

L. 14 [43:20] צֿפֿוֿן — Again, only the traces of the tops of the first three letters are preserved. ישיב — The tops of the letters are clear above the tear. In addition, in a fragment printed in the *editio princeps*, but lacking in the digital photographs, the bottoms of the letters are also visible (according to the placement on plate 8 of Yadin's edition). The same fragment is placed further down the column in plate 6. It seems clearly to belong with lines 14–16 (as implied by the placement in plate 8 of the *editio princeps*; see also Skehan 1966, 261–62).

L. 15 [43:20] מֿעֿמֿדֿ מֿיֿם יקרֿים — The letters are visible on a fragment printed in the *editio princeps* but which is absent from the digital photographs. Only the left most tip of the base line of the first *mem* of מיֿם is preserved. The spelling of the final *mem* with a initial/medial letter is not unprecedented among the Dead Sea Scrolls.

L. 16 [43:21] יבול הרי[ם חֿרֿב ישֿ]יֿקֿ — One can see these letters on the same fragment as mentioned in the preceding line. In the supralinear word, the right vertical stroke of the *khet* is visible but nothing else. The *resh* is attested by just the left most tip of its horizontal stroke. The *sin/shin* of ישֿיֿקֿ is nearly entirely missing, but the tips of the three arms are visible making the identification of the letter relatively certain.

L. 19 [43:24] לשמע אזנינו — These words are only visible on another fragment printed in the *editio princeps*, but not pictured in the digital photographs.

L. 20 [43:25] מֿןֿ כֿלֿ — Only traces of the letters can be made out. וֿגֿבֿוֿרות — The *gimel*, *bet*, and *vav* are visible on the same fragment mentioned in the preceding note. Although only the tops of the letters are visible, the distinctive shape of the *bet* and *vav* leave little question as to their identification. רהֿב — The second letter is damaged at the top and it could conceivably be read as *khet*, though there is the smallest trace of a *he*'s heavy left mark above the effaced surface.

L. 24 [43:29] A small fragment of the scroll, attested in Yadin's photos, is missing from the digital images. It contains two marks that belong to this line. The reading above is that of Yadin (1999, 192).

SIR 43:14–29

<table>
<tr><td>

14 Pour lui-même il libère le réservoir
   et fait planer les nuages comme des rapaces.
15 Sa puissance intensifie les nuages
   et abat des pierres de grêle.
17a La voix de son tonnerre fait trembler sa terre
16a et par sa force il agite les montagnes.
16b Sa parole provoque le vent du sud,
17b rafale du nord, tornade et tempête.
17c Comme des oiseaux, il fait virevolter sa neige
17d et elle descend comme une sauterelle qui se pose.
18 La beauté de sa blancheur détourne les yeux
   et le cœur s'émerveille de sa chute.
19 Et de même, le givre se déverse comme du sel
   et germe comme un buisson de fleurs.
20 Il fait souffler [le froid du vent]du nord
   et comme une motte (de terre) il fige la source.
   [   ]
   Il forme une cro[ûte sur tout]eau dorm[ante,]
   [   ]
21 La sécheresse brû[le la récolte des montag]nes,
   [   ]
22 [   ]
   [   ]
23 [   ]
   [   ]îles
24 [   ]
   à (les) écouter, nous sommes terrifiés.
25 [   ]
   les espèces de to[us vivants et]les puissants de Rahab
26 [   ]
   [   ]
27 [   ]
   [   ]
28 [   ]
   [   ]
29 [   ]
   [   ]

</td><td>

14 For himself he unleashes storms (lit., loosens the storehouse),
   and makes clouds soar like birds of prey.
15 His might intensifies the clouds
   and splinters hailstones.
17a The sound of his thunder makes his earth writhe,
16a shaking mountains with its force.
16b His word sharpens the south wind,
17b hurricane, storm, and tempest.
17c His snow flies like the birds;
17d its fall is like descending locust(s).
18 The beauty of its whiteness turns away eyes;
   the mind marvels at his rain.
19 [Indeed,] frost is poured out like salt
   and sprouts like a flowering bush (lit., like a bush of flowers).
20 [The cold of the] north [wind] he causes to blow;
   like a clod of earth, he (or: it) freezes (lit., thickens) the spring.
   he forms [a crust over all st]ill water,
   [   ]
21 [The mountain]s' [produce] drought bu[rns],
   [   ]
22 [   ]
   [   ]
23 [   ]
   [   ] islands [   ]
24 [   ]
   our ears hearing (this), we are astonished.
25 [   ]
   the variety of ev[ery living thing and] the mighty things of Rahab
26 [   ]
   [   ]
27 [   ]
   [   ]
28 [   ]
   [   ]
29 [   ]
   [   ]

</td></tr>
</table>

43:15 גבורתו חזק ענן — The syntax of the stich can be explained in different ways. Assuming חזק is a verb, one can construe it as a *piel* infinitive absolute (see Jer 4:18 for a similar syntax: noun + suffix followed by infinitive absolute). Alternatively, the disagreement in gender between subject and verb might be a result of a phonetic confusion *ḥizzəqā 'ānān > ḥizzeq 'ānān*.

43:18 יהג — This is the jussive form of the verb הגה (on which, see the note on the corresponding verse in H^B). The form does not express a jussive sense but instead is simply used in place of the imperfect. While it is possible that this is due to phonetic confusion (i.e., יהגה עינים *yehge 'ēnayim > yeheg 'ēnayim*), similar jussive forms occasionally appear among the DSS where we must assume an indicative sense and where phonetic confusion seems less likely (e.g., ופלגיו יעל קוץ *ūpalgō ya'al qōṣ* "and its middle will send up a thorn" 1QH^a XVI 25–26 and ורעבים יעשר "and the hungry he will enrich [*hiphil*]" 4Q521 2 ii + 4, 13 [see Reymond 2020a, 31 and 39–40]).

43:24 נשמתם — The sublinear final *mem* suggests that the intended word is, as in MS B, נשתמם. However, one wonders if the spelling נשמת reflects an initial reading נְשַׁמֹּת "(hearing this, our ears) are appalled."

30 B	]25	[	]	[	ש אל[

Col. VII

31	]1	[	]	[
	]2	[	]	[
32 B	]3	[	]	[
33 B	ש̇]4	[	]	[
	]5	[	]	[

Chapter 44

1 B	[אהללה נ]א̇ אנ[שי] חסד	6	את אב[ותינו] [
2 B	רב כבוד חלק עליון	7	וגדלה מי[מות עולם]
3cd B	וֹיועצים בתבונתם	8	וחזי כל בנבו[אתם]
4ab B	שרי גוי בםזמתם̇	9	ורזנים במחקק[תם]
4cd B	חכמי שיח בספרתם	10	ומשלים במ̇[שמרותם]
5 B	חקרי מזמור על קו	11	ונשאי משל̇ [בכתב]
6 B	אנשי ̇חיל וסמכי כח	12	ושקט̇[ים [
7 B	וכל א̇ ה בדרם נכבדו	13	[מ̇]ן ימיהם תפארתם[
8 B	יש מהם הניחו שם	14	לה] [
9 B	ויש מהם שאין לו זכר	15	] [
	כאשר לא היו היו	16	ו] [
10 B	אולם אלה אנשי חסד	17	וצ]דקתם [
11 B	אם זרעם נאמן טובם	18	ונחל]תם [
12	בבריתם עמד זרעם	19	וצאצאיהם] [

43:30 אל M | עוד B G   44:1 את M Bmg | > B ·   44:2 חלק M B | להם (חלק) Bmg · וגדלה M | וגדלו B ·   44:3ab + במלכותם ארץ (רודי) דורי גוים M G | גוי M G ·   44:4ab ו̇חזי M | וחזי B · בֹעולם B · > M Bmg G Bmg · ב̇עולם B · יו[ר̇ B | היועצים M | ויעצים B Bmg G ·   44:3ab ואנשי שם בגבורתם (בגבורם):   קו B · חוקרי M | חקרי 44:5 · ומושלים M | ומשלים Bmg · במס̇ M B | בספרתם 44:4cd · במחקרותם B · במחקק]תם M | ורוזנים B · ורזנים M Bmg | > B ·   [מ M Bmg G S | > B · נכבדו B בדורם | M בדרם 44:7 · וסמכי M | וסומכי B · ו̇שקט̇]ים M | ו̇שוקטים B ·   44:6 וסמכי M | סמכי B · חוק B · חזק M Bmg | נשאי B · ונשאי M   44:10 אולם M G S | ואולם B · וצ̇]דקתם M G S | ותקותם B ·   44:11 אם M | עם   B · 44:9 שאין M | אשר אין B · 44:10 וביומיה B | ו̇מימיה Bmg 44:9 ומימיה M | ימיהם B ·   44:12 > B ·

L. 4 [43:33] ש̇] — In the digital image of column VI, at line 4, at the far left, one sees what appears to be the rightmost tip of a *sin/shin* where line 4 of column VII should begin. That this is part of a *sin/shin* is implied not only by the angle of its two strokes, but also by its relative height compared to the letters of the same line in column VI.

L. 6 [44:1] נ]א̇ אהללה — Only the left side of the *aleph* is preserved and the mark may, instead, be the left leg of a *he*.

L. 9 [44:4] במזמתם̇ — A tear in the leather cuts through the *bet* and *mem* and the leather above covers a portion of the leather below. The effect is that the *bet*, whose head and base line is still visible, appears quite a bit shorter than normal. Only the bottom right leg of the *tav* is visible, together perhaps with a trace of the left foot (unless this is simply part of the edge of the leather). The bottom half of the final *mem* is clear. ורזנים — A fold in the leather results in the top of the *nun* being obscured, though the bottom is clear, ligatured to the following *yod*.

L. 10 [44:4] חכמי — The *khet* looks as though it was corrected from an *aleph*, since its top bar sinks diagonally into the right leg and its left leg looks unusually thick.

L. 11 [44:5] משל — Only the slimmest trace of the *lamed*'s right corner is visible.

L. 12 [44:6] ושקט̇]ים — Only the traces of the top of the *tet* are preserved.

L. 13 [44:7] [מ̇]ן — The *nun* is attested only by its descender, which nearly touches the top of the *lamed* from the preposition in the following line.

L. 18 [44:11] ונחל]תם — Only a slight trace of the right corner of the *lamed* is preserved.

30 [   ]
   [e]st Dieu   ]

Col. VII

[   ]
[   ]
31 [   ]
   [   ]
32 [   ]
   [   ]
33 [   ]
   [   ]

Chapitre 44

1 [Je veux louer] les hom[mes] pieux,
  nos pè[res   ]
2 Le Très-Haut leur a attribué l'honneur en abondance
  et sa grandeur est depuis les jours éternels.
3c conseillers par leur intelligence
3d et visionnaires de tout par leur prophétie,
4 princes du peuple par leur prudence
  et dignitaires par leurs décrets,
  rhéteurs habiles par leurs écrits,
  formeurs de proverbes par leurs piques,
5 chercheurs de mélodie selon la mesure,
  inventeurs de proverbes par l'écrit,
6 hommes valeureux et soutiens puissants
  et paisibl[es   ]
7 Tous ceux-ci, dans leur génération, furent honorés
  [dep]uis[leurs jours fut leur splendeur.]
8 Certains, parmi eux, laissèrent un nom,
  pour[   ]
9 Mais il y en a parmi eux pour lesquels il n'y a pas de souvenir
  [   ]
  ils ont existé comme s'ils n'avaient pas existé
  et[   ]
10 Inversement, ces hommes pieux
   et[leur]ju[stice   ]
11 avec leur descendance, tient fermement leur prospérité
   et[leur]héritage[   ]
12 Par leur alliance s'est maintenue leur descendance
   et leur postérité[   ]

30 [   ]
   [   ] God [i]s.

Col. VII

[   ]
[   ]
31 [   ]
   [   ]
32 [   ]
   [   ]
33 [   ]
   [   ]

Chapter 44

1 [Let me praise] pious me[n],
  [our] father[s   ]
2 Abundant glory the most high apportions,
  greatness, from [the days of old]
3c and counselors for their understanding,
3d and those seeing everything for [their] prophec[y,]
4 leaders of the people, for their cunning,
  and potentates, for [their] decree(s),
  meditative sages, for their book(s),
  and propounders of parables, for [their sayings]
5 those pursuing (lit., examining) song(s) over a chord,
  and those uttering prover[b(s) for their writing]
6 valorous men and those wielding power,
  and those quiet [   ] --
7 all these in their generation were honored;
  [fr]om [their days was their glory.]
8 There were among them (those who) left a name,
  [   ]
9 There were also among them those who are not remembered;
  [   ]
  They are as though they had never been,
  and (likewise) [   ]
10 But as for these pious men (who follow in the poem),
   [their] ri[ghteousness   ]
11 With their progeny, their good (reputation) is secure;
   and [their] inheri[tance   ]
12 Through their covenant, their progeny endures,
   as do their offspring [   ]

44:4 מחקק]תם — The word is assumed to be the feminine (singular or plural) *pual* participle of חקק, based in part on the feminine forms in preceding and following verses; cf. מְחֹקֵק in Prov 31:5.

44:10 וצ]דקתם — The reading agrees with the Greek and Syriac, in contrast to ותקותם of H^B.

44:11 אם — This is a mistake for the preposition עם. See the similar confusion in 41:2ab and the comment there.

44:12 This verse is entirely absent from H^B.

13 B ‏²⁰עַ֯ד עולם יעמד זרעם‏	‏וכבודם לא ימח[ה]‏
14 B ‏²¹גִ֯וִ֯[ת]ם בשלום נאספה‏	‏[ו]שמם חי לדור ודר‏
15 B ‏[ ]²² ת[שׁ֯] עדה‏	‏ותהלתם יספר קהל‏
23 vacat	
17 B ‏²⁴נוח צדיק נמצא תמים‏ [	‏ב[עת כ]ל[ה]‏ [
‏²⁵בֹ֯עֵ֯[ת] בורו‏ [	] [

44:13 זרעם M G | זכרם B S · וכבודם M G S | וצדקתם B · 44:14 ודור M | ודר B · 44:15 ת[שׁ֯] M | תשני Bmg · 44:16 + חנוך נמצֹא תמים והתה־ Bmg ב' B | לעת M | ב]עת B · ח[נ֯ M | נ]ח֯ B · 44:17 נוח M | לך עם ייי וֹ[נ]לקח אות דעת לדור ודור:

L. 20 [44:13] עַ֯ד — Only the upper right arm of the *ayin* is preserved, together with half the horizontal stroke of the *dalet*. ימֹח[ה] — The bottom right leg of the *khet* is visible, as is the bottom tip of the left leg.

L. 21 [44:14] גִ֯וִ֯[ת]ם — The *gimel* is only preserved by a faint trace of its top, followed by a complete *vav* and a vertical that may correspond to a *yod*. ודר — The word is clear and the spelling is obviously defective.

L. 22 [44:15] ת[שׁ֯] — The reading is conjectural and tentative; the tops of the *sin/shin*'s three arms are visible just to the left of the tear. The mark just to the right of this is straight and looks more like a *zayin*, though this seems less likely in the context. While a *he* might be expected (see Yadin), there is no trace of an upper horizontal stroke.

L. 24 [44:17] נוח צדיק — Once again, the letters are preserved on a fragment printed in the *editio princeps* but absent from the digital photographs.

L. 25 [44:17] בֹ֯עֵ֯[ת] בורו — The marks are found on the same fragment mentioned in the preceding note.

13 pour toujours se maintiendra leur descendance
   et leur gloire ne sera pas effa[cée.]
14 Leur c[orp]s a été rassemblé dans la paix,
   [et]leur nom vit de génération en génération.
15 Que la communauté [ré]pète[   ]
   et que l'assemblée raconte leur louange.
   vacat
17 [N]oé le juste a été trouvé intègre,
   au [temps de la des]tru[ction   ]
   Grâ[ce à lui   ]
   [   ]

13 Forever their progeny will endure;
   their glory will not be wiped [out.]
14 [Their] bo[dies] in peace were gathered (to their graves),
   [but] their name (is) alive from generation to generation.
15 Let the congregation [re]peat [   ]
   and praise of them let the assembly recount.
17 Noah was found righteous, blameless
   in [the time of   ]
   Be[cause of him   ]
   [   ]

Bibliography

Abegg, Martin G. 2022. "Manuscripts A–F." On "The Book of Ben Sira." *bensira.org*. Edited by Gary A. Rendsburg and Jacob Binstein.

Abegg, Martin G., and Casey Towes. 2007. "Ben Sira." *Accordance*. Altamonte Springs: Oak Tree Software.

Adams, Samuel L., Greg S. Goering, and Matthew J. Goff, eds. 2021. *Sirach and Its Contexts: The Pursuit of Wisdom and Human Flourishing*. Supplements to the Journal for the Study of Judaism 196. Leiden: Brill.

Adler, Elkan Nathan. 1900. "Some Missing Chapters of Ben Sira." *JQR* 12:466–80.

Aharoni, Yohanan. 1981. *Arad Inscriptions*. Judean Desert Studies. Jerusalem: Israel Exploration Society.

Aitken, James K. 2019. "The Synoptic Problem and the Reception of the Ben Sira Manuscripts." Pages 147–68 in *Discovering, Deciphering, and Dissenting: Ben Sira manuscripts after 120 years*. Edited by James K. Aitken et al. Deuterocanonical and Cognate Literature Yearbook 2018. Berlin: de Gruyter.

Aitken, James K., Renate Egger-Wenzel, and Stefan C. Reif, eds. 2018. *Discovering, Deciphering and Dissenting: Ben Sira Manuscripts after 120 years*. Deuterocanonical and Cognate Literature Yearbook 2018. Berlin: de Gruyter.

Anderson, Francis I. 1978. *Hebrew Verbless Clause in the Pentateuch*. Journal of Biblical Literature 14. Nashville: Abingdon.

Angerstorfer, Andres. 2000. "פאה." Pages 461–63 in *Theological Dictionary of the Old Testament*. Edited by Gerhard J. Botterweck et al. Vol. 11. Cambridge: Eerdmans.

Anonymous. 1896. "Notes of Recent Expositions." *The Expository Times* 7:481–87.

Anonymous. 1901. *Facsimiles of the Fragments hitherto recovered of the Book of Ecclesiasticus in Hebrew*. London: Oxford University Press; Cambridge University Press.

Arrant, Estera 2021. *A Codicological and Linguistic Typology of Common Torah Codices from the Cairo Genizah*. PhD diss., University of Cambridge.

Argall, Randal A. 1995. *1 Enoch and Sirach: A Comparative Literary and Conceptual Analysis of the Themes of Revelation, Creation and Judgement*. Society of Biblical Literature Early Judaism and Its Literature 8. Atlanta: Scholars Press.

Avishur, Yitzhak, and Joshua Blau, eds. 1978. *Studies in Bible and the Ancient Near East: Presented to Samuel E. Loewenstamm on His Seventieth Birthday*. Jerusalem: Rubinstein's Publishing House.

Bacher, W. 1897. "The Hebrew Text of Ecclesiasticus." *JQR* 9:543–62.

Bacher, Walter. 1900a. "Notes on the Cambridge Fragments of Ecclesiasticus." *JQR* 12:272–90.

Bacher, Walter. 1900b. "Notes sur les nouveaux fragments de Ben Sira." *REJ* 40:253–55.

Baillet, Maurice. 1962. "Textes des grottes 2Q, 3Q, 6Q, 7Q à 10Q." Pages 45–166 in *Les "Petites Grottes" de Qumrân: exploration de la falaise. Les grottes 2Q, 3Q, 5Q, 6Q, 7Q à 10Q. Le rouleau de cuivre. 1. Textes*. By Maurice Baillet, Joseph T. Milik, and Roland de Vaux. Discoveries in the Judaean Desert of Jordan 3. Oxford: Clarendon.

Baillet, Maurice, Joseph T. Milik, and Roland de Vaux. 1962. *Les "Petites Grottes" de Qumrân: exploration de la falaise. Les grottes 2Q, 3Q, 5Q, 6Q, 7Q à 10Q. Le rouleau de cuivre. 1. Textes*. Discoveries in the Judaean Desert of Jordan 3. Oxford: Oxford University Press.

Balla, Ibolya. 2011. *Ben Sira on Family, Gender, and Sexuality*. Deuterocanonical and Cognate Literature Studies 8. Berlin: de Gruyter.

Bauer, Hans, and Pontus Leander. 1922. *Historische Grammatik der Hebräischen Sprache des Alten Testamentes*. Halle: von Max Niemeyer.

Bauer, Johannes-Baptist. 1963. "Sir. 15,14 et Gen 1,1." *VD* 41:243–44.

Baumgarten, J. M. 1968. "Some Notes on the Ben Sira Scroll from Masada." *JQR* 58:323–27.

Beentjes, Pancratius C. 1980. "Jesus Sirach 7:1–17." *Bijdr* 41:251–59.

Beentjes, Pancratius C. 1997. *The Book of Ben Sira in Hebrew: A Text Edition of All Extant Hebrew Manuscripts and a Synopsis of All Parallel Hebrew Ben Sira Texts*. Supplements to Vetus Testamentum 68. Leiden: Brill.

Beentjes, Pancratius C, ed. 1997. *The book of Ben Sira in Modern Research: Proceedings of the First International Ben Sira Conference, 28–31 July 1996*. Zeitschrift für die alttestamentliche Wissenschaft 255. Berlin: de Gruyter.

Beentjes, Pancratius C. 1999. "The Hebrew Texts of Ben Sira 32[35].16–33[36].2." Pages 53–67 in *Sirach, Scrolls, and Sages. Proceedings of a Second International Symposium on the Hebrew of the Dead Sea Scrolls, Ben Sira, and the Mishnah, held at Leiden University, 15–17 December 1997*. Edited by Takamitsu Muraoka and John F. Elwolde. Studies on the Texts of the Desert of Judah 33. Leiden: Brill.

Beentjes, Pancratius C. 2002. "Errata et Corrigenda." Pages 375–77 in *Ben Sira's god: Proceedings of the International Ben Sira Conference, Durham — Ushaw College 2001*. Edited by Renate Egger-Wenzel. Beihefte zur Zeitschrift für die alttestamentliche Wissenschaft 321. Berlin: de Gruyter.

Beentjes, Pancratius C. 2006. *"Happy the One Who Meditates on Wisdom" (Sir. 14,20), Collected Essays on the Book of Ben Sira*. Leuven: Peeters.

Beentjes, Pancratius C. 2019. "The Prayer in Ben Sira 22:27–23:6 and the Prosodic Version in MS ENA 3053.3." Pages 21–36 in *On Wings of Prayer: Sources of Jewish Worship; Essays in Honor of Professor Stefan C. Reif on the Occasion of his Seventy-fifth Birthday*. Edited by Nuria Calduch-Benages, Michael W. Duggan, and Dalia Marx. Berlin: De Gruyter.

Ben Yehuda, Eliʿezer. 1948. *Thesaurus totius hebraitatis et veteris et recentioris: A Complete Dictionary of Ancient and Modern Hebrew by Eliezer Ben Yehuda of Jerusalem*. Popular edition. 17 vols. Jerusalem: Ben Yehuda.

Ben-Ḥayyim, Zeev. 1940. "חקרי מלים. Philological Notes." *Tarbiz* 12:75–77.

Ben-Ḥayyim, Zeev. 1973. ספר בן־סירא, המקור, קונקורדנציה וניתוח אוצר המלים (*The Book of Ben Sira: Text, Concordance and Analysis of the Vocabulary*). The Historical Dictionary of the Hebrew Language. Jerusalem: The Academy of the Hebrew Language and the Shrine of the Book.

Benoît, Pierre, Joseph T. Milik, and Roland de Vaux. 1961. *Les grottes de Murabbaʿât*. DJD 2. Oxford: Clarendon Press.

Bergsträsser, Gotthelf. 1918. *Hebräische Grammatik mit Benutzung der von E. Kautzsch bearbeiten 28. Auflage von Wilhelm Gesenius' hebräischer Grammatik*. Leipzig: Vogel.

Bezzel, Hannes, Louise Hecht, and Grit Schorch. 2019. "Die Anfänge moderner Bibelwissenschaft in der Wiener Haskala." Pages 171–94 in *Deutsch-jüdische Bibelwissenschaft: Historische, exegetische und theologische Perspektiven*. Edited by Daniel Vorpahl et al. Europäisch-jüdische Studien — Beiträge 40. Berlin: De Gruyter.

Bickell, Gustav. 1899. "Der hebräische Sirachtext eine Rückübersetzung." *WZKM* 13:251–56.

Boccaccio, Pietro, and Guido Berardi. 1986. *Ecclesiasticus: textus Hebraeus secundum fragmenta reperta*. Roma: Pontificio Istituto Biblico.

Bohlen, Reinhold. 1991. *Die Ehrung der Eltern bei Ben Sira. Studien zur Motivation und Interpretation eines familienethischen Grundwertes in frühhellenistischer Zeit*. Trierer Theologische Studien 51. Trier: Paulinus-Verlag.

Böhmisch, Franz. 2017. "Die Vorlage der syrischen Sirachübersetzung und die gereimte hebräische Paraphrase zu Ben Sira aus der Ben-Ezra-Geniza." Pages 197–237 in *Texts and Contexts of the Book of Sirach. Texte und Kontexte des Sirachbuches*. Edited by Gerhard Karner et al. Septuagint and Cognate Studies 66. Atlanta: Society of Biblical Literature.

Böhmisch, Franz. 2020. "Die Sirachhandschriften aus Kairo und das Umfeld von Ms. F." *PZB* 29:142–55.

Botterweck, Gerhard J., Helmer Ringgren, and Heinz-Josef Fabry, eds. 2021. *Theological Dictionary of the Old Testament*. 17 vols. Cambridge: Eerdmans.

Box, George H., and William Oscar E. Oesterley. 1913. "Sirach." Pages 268–517 in *The Apocrypha and Pseudepigrapha of the Old Testament in English with Introductions and Critical and Explanatory Notes to the Several Books*. Vol. 1. Edited by Robert H. Charles. Oxford: Clarendon Press.

Braun, Oskar. 1901. "Ein Brief Des Katholikos Timotlieos I Über Biblische Studien Des 9 Jahrhunderts." *OrChr* 1:299–313.

Bresciani, Edda, and Murād Kāmil. 1966. *Le lettere aramaiche di Hermopoli*. Atti della Accademia Nazionale dei Lincei, memorie, classe di scienze morali, storiche et filologiche 8. Roma.

Brockelmann, C. 2009. *A Syriac Lexicon: A Translation from the Latin, Correction, Expansion, and Update of C. Brockelmann's Lexicon syriacum*. Translated by Michael Sokoloff. Winona Lake: Eisenbrauns; Piscataway: Gorgias Press.

Bronznick, Norman M. 1985. "An Unrecognized Denotation of the Verb HSR in Ben-Sira and Rabbinic Hebrew." *HAR* 9:91–105.

Brown, Francis, Samuel. R. Driver, and Charles A. Briggs, eds. 1906. *A Hebrew and English Lexicon of the Old Testament*. Oxford: Clarendon Press.

Brun, Jean-Pierre. 2000. "The Production of Perfumes in Antiquity: The Cases of Delos and Paestum." *AJA* 104:277–308.

Brutti, Maria. 2006. *The Development of the High Priesthood during the Pre-Hasmonean Period: History, Ideology, Theology*. Supplements to the Journal for the Study of Judaism 108. Leiden: Brill.

Calduch-Benages, Nuria. 1991. "La sabiduría y la prueba en Sir 4,11–19." *EstBib* 49:25–48.

Calduch-Benages, Nuria. 2011. "Animal Imagery in the Hebrew Text of Ben Sira." Pages 55–71 in *The Texts and Versions of the Book of Ben Sira: Transmission and Interpretation*. Edited by Jan Joosten and Frédérique Michèle (J.-S.) Rey. Supplements to the Journal for the Study of Judaism 150. Leiden: Brill.

Calduch-Benages, Nuria. 2012. "Poligamia in Ben Sira?" *RB* 60:221–32.

Calduch-Benages, Núria. 2013. "A Wordplay on the Term mûsar (Sir 6:22)." Pages 13–36 in *Weisheit als Lebensgrundlage: Festschrift für Friedrich V. Reiterer zum 65. Geburtstag*. Edited by Renate Egger-Wenzel et al. Deuterocanonical and Cognate Literature Studies 15. Berlin: de Gruyter.

Calduch-Benages, Nuria, Joan Ferrer, and Jan Liesen. 2003. *La sabiduría del escriba. The Wisdom of the Scribe*. Biblioteca midrásica 26. Estella: Verbo Divino.

Camps, Jean-Baptiste. 2015. "Copie, authenticité, originalité dans la philologie et son histoire." *Questes* 29:35–67.

Cantineau, Jean. 1930. *Le nabatéen. I. Notion générales — Ecriture — Grammaire*. Paris: Ernest Leroux.

Cantineau, Jean. 1932. *Le nabatéen. II. Choix de textes — Lexique*. Paris: Ernest Leroux.

Caquot, Albert. 1971. "Une inscription araméenne d'époque assyrienne." Pages 9–16 in *Hommages à André Dupont-Sommer*. Edited by Albert Caquot and Marc Philonenko. Paris: Librairie d'Amérique et d'Orient Adrien-Maisonneuve.

Caquot, Albert, and Marc Philonenko, eds. 1971. *Hommages à André Dupont-Sommer*. Paris: Librairie d'Amérique et d'Orient Adrien-Maisonneuve.

Carmignac, Jean. 1958. *La Règle de la guerre : Des fils de lumière contre les Fils de Ténèbres. Texte, restauré, traduit, commenté*. Paris: Letouzey & Ané.

Cerquiglini, Bernard. 1989. *Éloge de la variante. Histoire critique de la philologie*. Des travaux. Paris: Seuil.

Charles, Robert H. 1913. "The Testaments of the XII Patriarchs." Pages 282–83 in *The Apocrypha and Pseudepigrapha of the Old Testament in English with Introductions and Critical and Explanatory Notes to the Several Books*. Volume 2. Edited by Robert H. Charles. Oxford: Clarendon Press.

Clements, Ruth A., and Daniel R. Schwartz, eds. 2009. *Text, Thought, and Practice in Qumran and Early Christianity: Proceedings of the Ninth International Symposium of the Orion Center for the Study of the Dead Sea Scrolls and Associated Literature, jointly sponsored by the Hebrew University Center for the Study of Christianity, 11–13 January, 2004*. Studies on the Texts of the Desert of Judah 84. Leiden: Brill.

Clines, David J. A., ed. 1993. *Dictionary of Classical Hebrew*. 9 vols. Sheffield: Sheffield Phoenix Press.

Conybeare, Frederick C., Rendel Harris, James, and Agnes Smith Lewis, eds. 1898. *The Story of Ahikar from the Syriac, Arabic, Armenian, Ethiopic, Greek and Slavonic Versions*. London: C. J. Clay and Sons.

Corley, Jeremy. 2002. *Ben Sira's Teaching on Friendship*. Brown Judaic Studies 316. Providence: Brown Judaic Studies.

Corley, Jeremy. 2008. "Sirach 44:1–15 as Introduction to the Praise of the Ancestors." Pages 151–81 in *Studies in the Book of Ben Sira: Papers of the Third International Conference on the Deuterocanonical Books, Shime'on Centre, Pápa, Hungary, 18–20 May 2006*. Edited by Géza G. Xeravits and József Zsengellér. Supplements to the Journal for the Study of Judaism 127. Leiden: Brill.

Corley, Jeremy. 2011. "An Alternative Hebrew Form of Ben Sira: The Anthological Manuscript C." Pages 3–22 in *The Texts and Versions of the Book of Ben Sira: Transmission and Interpretation*. Edited by Jan Joosten and Frédérique Michèle (J.-S.) Rey. Supplements to the Journal for the Study of Judaism 150. Leiden: Brill.

Corley, Jeremy, and Vincent Skemp, eds. 2005. *Intertextual Studies in Ben Sira and Tobit: Essays in Honor of Alexander A. Di Lella, O.F.M.* The Catholic Biblical Quarterly Monograph Series 38. Washington: The Catholic Biblical Association of America.

Couroyer, Bernard. 1975. "Un égyptianisme dans Ben Sira IV, 11." *RB* 82:206–17.

Cowley, A. E., and A. Neubauer. 1897a. "Prof. Smend's Emendations." *JQR* 9:563–67.

Cowley, A. E. 1897b. *The Original Hebrew of a Portion of Ecclesiasticus (XXXIX, 15 to XLIX, 11) Together with the Early Versions and an English Translation Followed by the Quotations from Ben Sira in Rabbinical Literature*. Oxford: Clarendon Press.

Cowley, Arthur E. 1900. "Notes on the Cambridge Texts of Ben Sira." *JQR* 12:109–11.

Cowley, Arthur E. 1967. *Aramaic Papyri of the Fifth Century B.C.* Oxford: Clarendon Press.

Cross, Frank M. 2003 *Leaves from an Epigrapher's Notebook: Collected Papers in Hebrew and West Semitic Palaeography and Epigraphy*. Harvard Semitic Studies 51. Leiden: Brill.

Dahmen, Ulrich. 2003. *Psalmen- und Psalter-Rezeption im Frühjudentum: Rekonstruktion, Textbestand, Struktur und Pragmatik der Psalmenrolle 11QPsa aus Qumran*. Studies on the Texts of the Desert of Judah 49. Leiden: Brill.

Darshan, Guy. 2019. "The Semantic Shift of נשא פנים and בשת in Ben Sira in its Hellenistic Context." *Biblica* 100:173–86.

Darshan, Guy. 2021. "Do Not be Ashamed of Rendering Judgment to Acquit the Wicked? On Sirach 42:2." *Vetus Testamentum* 72:173–182.

Daube, David. 1961. "Direct and Indirect Causation in Biblical Law." *VT* 11:246–69.

Delcor, Mathias. 1968. "Le texte hébreu du Cantique de Siracide LI,13 et ss. et les anciennes versions." *Textus* 6:27–47.

Di Lella, Alexander A. 1964. "The Recently Identified Leaves of Sirach in Hebrew." *Biblica* 45:153–67.

Di Lella, Alexander A. 1966. *The Hebrew Text of Sirach: A Text-Critical and Historical Study*. Studies in Classical Literature 1. The Hague: Mouton.

Di Lella, Alexander A. 1982. "Sirach 10:19–11:6: Textual Criticism, Poetic Analysis, and Exegesis." Pages 157–64 in *The Word of the Lord Shall Go Forth: Essays in Honor of David Noel Freedman in Celebration of His Sixtieth Birthday*. Edited by Carol L. Meyers and Michael P. O'Connor. Winona Lake: Eisenbrauns.

Di Lella, Alexander A. 1988. "The Newly Discovered Sixth Manuscript of Ben Sira from the Cairo Geniza." *Bib* 69:226–38.

Di Lella, Alexander A. 2003. "Free Will in the Wisdom of Ben Sira 15:11–20: An Exegetical and Theological Study." Pages 253–64 in *Auf den Spuren der schriftgelehrten Weisen: Festschrift für Johannes Marböck anlässlich seiner Emeritierung*. Edited by Irmtraud Fischer et al. Beihefte zur Zeitschrift für die alttestamentliche Wissenschaft 331. Berlin: de Gruyter.

Di Lella, Alexander A., and Patrick W. Skehan. 1987. *The Wisdom of Ben Sira: A New Translation with Notes*. The Anchor Bible 39. New York: Doubleday.

Dihi, Haim. 2004. *The Morphological and Lexical Innovations in the Book of Ben Sira*. PhD diss. Beer-Sheva.

Dimant, Devorah. 2000. "Resurrection, Restoration, and the Time-Curtailing in Qumran, Early Judaism and Christianity." *RevQ* 19:527–48.

Driver, Godfrey R. 1934. "Notes on the 'Wisdom of Jesus Ben Sirach.'" *JBL* 53:273–90.

Driver, Godfrey R. 1937. "Ecclesiasticus: A New Fragment of the Hebrew Text." *ExpTim* 49:37–39.

Duval, Frédéric. 2021. *"La tradition manuscrite du Lai de l'ombre" de Joseph Bédier ou la critique textuelle en question. Édition critique et commentaires.* Textes critiques français 4. Paris: Honoré Champion.

Duval, Rubens. 1901. "Le Testament de Saint Éphrem." *JA* 18:234–319.

Egger-Wenzel, Renate, ed. 2002. *Ben Sira's God: Proceedings of the International Ben Sira Conference, Durham — Ushaw College 2001.* Beihefte zur Zeitschrift für die alttestamentliche Wissenschaft 321. Berlin: de Gruyter.

Egger-Wenzel, Renate, ed. 2022. *A Polyglot Edition of the Book of Ben Sira with a Synopsis of the Hebrew Manuscripts.* Contributions to Biblical Exegesis and Theology 101. Leuven: Peeters.

Egger-Wenzel, Renate, and Ingrid Krammer, eds. 1998. *Der Einzelne und seine Gemeinschaft bei Ben Sira.* Beihefte zur Zeitschrift für die alttestamentliche Wissenschaft 270. Berlin: de Gruyter.

Egger-Wenzel, Renate, Karin Schöpflin, and Johannes F. Diehl, eds. 2013. *Weisheit als Lebensgrundlage: Festschrift für Friedrich V. Reiterer zum 65. Geburtstag.* Deuterocanonical and Cognate Literature Studies 15. Berlin: de Gruyter.

Elizur, Shulamit. 2006. "קטע חדש מהנוסח העברי של ספר בן סירא (A New Hebrew Fragment of Ben Sira (Ecclesiasticus))." *Tarbiz* 76:17–28.

Elizur, Shulamit. 2010. "Two New Leaves of the Hebrew Version of Ben Sira." *Dead Sea Discoveries* 17:13–29.

Elizur, Shulamit and Michael Rand. 2011. "A New Fragment of the Book of Ben Sira." *DSD* 18:200–205.

Elwolde, John F. 1994. "The Use of 'ēt in Non-Biblical Hebrew Texts." *VT* 44:170–82.

Fabry, Heinz-Josef, and Ulrich Dahmen, eds. 2011. *Theologisches Wörterbuch zu den Qumrantexten.* 3 vols. Stuttgart: Kohlhammer.

Fassberg, Steven, ed. 2021. *Hebrew Texts and Language of the Second Temple Period: Proceedings of an Eighth Symposium on the Hebrew of the Dead Sea Scrolls and Ben Sira.* Studies on the Texts of the Desert of Judah 134. Leiden: Brill.

Fassberg, Steven E. 1990. "Negative Final Clauses in Biblical Hebrew: ולא יקטל and פן יקטל." Pages 273–94 in *Studies on Hebrew and Other Semitic Languages: Presented to Professor Chaim Rabin on the Occasion of his seventy-fifth birthday.* Edited by Moshe H. Goshen-Gottstein et al. Jerusalem: Akadom.

Fassberg, Steven E. 1994. *Studies in the Syntax of Biblical Hebrew* (סוגיות בתחביר המקרא). Jerusalem: Magnes Press.

Fassberg, Steven E. 1997. "On the Syntax of Dependent Clauses in Ben Sira." Pages 56–71 in *The Hebrew of the Dead Sea Scrolls and Ben Sira: Proceedings of a Symposium held at Leiden University, 11–14 December 1995.* Edited by Takamitsu Muraoka and John F. Elwolde. Studies on the Texts of the Desert of Judah 26. Leiden: Brill.

Fassberg, Steven Ellis, Moshe Bar-Asher, and Ruth Clements, eds. 2013. *Hebrew in the Second Temple Period: the Hebrew of the Dead Sea Scrolls and of Other Contemporary Sources: Proceedings of the Twelfth International Symposium of the Orion Center for the Study of the Dead Sea Scrolls and Associated Literature and the Fifth International Symposium on the Hebrew of the Dead Sea Scrolls and Ben Sira, jointly sponsored by the Eliezer Ben-Yehuda Center for the Study of the History of the Hebrew Language, 29–31 December, 2008.* Studies on the Texts of the Desert of Judah 108. Leiden: Brill.

Fischer, Irmtraud, Johannes Marböck, Ursula Rapp, and Johannes Schiller, eds. 2003. *Auf den Spuren der schriftgelehrten Weisen: Festschrift für Johannes Marböck anlässlich seiner Emeritierung.* Beihefte zur Zeitschrift für die alttestamentliche Wissenschaft 331. Berlin: de Gruyter.

Fleischer, Ezra. 1978. "עיון חדש בספרות המשלים העברית הקדומה." *Criticism and Interpretation* 11–12:19–54.

Fleischer, Ezra. 1990. משלי סעיד בן באבשאד. *The Proverbs of Sa'id ben Bābshād.* Jerusalem: Yad Ben Zvi.

Fleischer, Ezra. 1997. "Additional Fragments of the 'Rhymed Ben Sira.'" Pages 205–17 in *Tehillah le-Moshe: Biblical and Judaic Studies in Honor of Moshe Greenberg.* Edited by Mordechai Cogan et al. Winona Lake (Ind.): Eisenbrauns.

Fraenkel, Seckel Isaac. 1830. כְּתוּבִים אַחֲרוֹנִים הַנּוֹדָעִים בְּשֵׁם אֲפּוֹקְרִיפָא. *Hagiographa posteriora denominata Apocrypha. Die Apocryphen des Alten Testaments nach dem griechischen Texte ins Hebräische übertragen.* Leipzig: Fridericum Fleischer.

Freedman, Harry, Maurice Simon, S. M. Lehrman, Israelstam, J., and J. J. Slotki, eds. 1961. *Midrash Rabbah.* 9 vols. London: The Soncino Press.

Gafni, Chanan. 2019. "'They are ours!' Reclaiming the Apocrypha as Jewish Texts." *Wissenschaft des Judentums Beyond Tradition: Jewish Scholarship on the Sacred Texts of Judaism, Christianity, and Islam.* Edited by Dorothea M. Salzer et al. Berlin: De Gruyter.

García Martínez, Florentino. 2005. "Creation in the Dead Sea scrolls." Pages 49–70 in *The Creation of Heaven and Earth: Re-interpretations of Genesis I in the Context of Judaism, Ancient Philosophy, Christianity, and Modern Physics.* Edited by George H. van Kooten. Themes in Biblical Narrative 8. Leiden: Brill.

Garr, W. Randall, and Steven E. Fassberg, eds. 2016. *A Handbook of Biblical Hebrew.* Vol. 1. Winona Lake Indiana: Eisenbrauns.

Gaster, Moses. 1900. "A New Fragment of Ben Sira." *JQR* 12:688–702.

Gerber, Douglas E. 1999. *Greek Elegiac Poetry: From the Seventh to the Fifth Centuries BC*. Loeb Classical Library 258. Cambridge: Harvard University Press.

Gesenius, Wilhelm. 1910. *Gesenius' Hebrew Grammar*. Edited by Emil Kautzsch. Translated by Arthur E. Cowley. 2nd ed. Oxford: Clarendon Press.

Gilbert, Maurice. 1998a. "Prêt, aumône et caution." Pages 179–89 in *Der Einzelne und seine Gemeinschaft bei Ben Sira*. Edited by Renate Egger-Wenzel and Ingrid Krammer. Beihefte zur Zeitschrift für die alttestamentliche Wissenschaft 270. Berlin: de Gruyter.

Gilbert, Maurice. 1998b. "Qohelet et Ben Sira." Pages 161–79 in *Qohelet in the Context of Wisdom*. Edited by Antoon Schoors. Bibliotheca Ephemeridum Theologicarum Lovaniensium 136. Leuven: Peeters.

Gilbert, Maurice. 2002. "God, Sin and Mercy: Sirach 15:11–18:14." Pages 118–35 in *Ben Sira's God: Proceedings of the International Ben Sira Conference, Durham — Ushaw College 2001*. Edited by Renate Egger-Wenzel. Beihefte zur Zeitschrift für die alttestamentliche Wissenschaft 321. Berlin: de Gruyter.

Gilbert, Maurice. 2003. "Venez à mon école (Si 51,13–30)." Pages 283–90 in *Auf den Spuren der schriftgelehrten Weisen: Festschrift für Johannes Marböck anlässlich seiner Emeritierung*. Edited by Irmtraud Fischer et al. Beihefte zur Zeitschrift für die alttestamentliche Wissenschaft 331. Berlin: de Gruyter.

Gilbert, Maurice. 2005. "Ben Sira, Reader of Genesis 1–11." Pages 89–99 in *Intertextual Studies in Ben Sira and Tobit: Essays in Honor of Alexander A. Di Lella, O.F.M.* Edited by Jeremy Corley and Vincent Skemp. The Catholic Biblical Quarterly Monograph Series 38. Washington: The Catholic Biblical Association of America.

Gilbert, Maurice. 2011. "Où en sont les études sur le Siracide ?" *Bib* 92:161–81.

Ginsberg, Harold L. 1955. "The Original Hebrew of Ben Sira 12:10–14." *JBL* 74:93–95.

Ginsburg, Christian D. 1897. *Introduction to the Massoretico-Critical Edition of the Hebrew Bible*. London: Trinitarian Bible Society.

Ginzberg, Louis. 1906. "Randglossen zum hebräischen Ben Sira." Pages 609–25 in *Orientalische Studien. Theodor Nöldeke zum Siebzigsten Geburtstag*. Edited by Carl Bezold. Gieszen: Töpelmann.

Goering, Greg S. 2009. *Wisdom's Root Revealed: Ben Sira and the Election of Israel*. Supplements to the Journal for the Study of Judaism 139. Leiden: Brill.

Goff, Matthew J. 2010. "Ben Sira and the Giants of the Land: A Note on Ben Sira 16:7." *JBL* 129:645–55.

Golinets, Viktor. 2020. "Some Considerations on Questions Philology Cannot Solve while Reconstructing the Text of the Hebrew Bible." *Philology and Textual Criticism of the Hebrew Bible*. Edited by Innocent Himbaza and Jan Joosten. Forschungen zum Alten Testament 2. Reihe. Tübingen: Mohr Siebeck.

Gray, G. Buchanan. 1897. "A Note on the Text and Interpretation of Ecclus. XLI. 19." *JQR* 9:567–72.

Greenfield, Jonas C. 1978. "The Meaning of פחז." Pages 35–40 in *Studies in Bible and the Ancient Near East: Presented to Samuel E. Loewenstamm on His Seventieth Birthday*. Edited by Yitzhak Avishur and Joshua Blau. Jerusalem: Rubinstein's Publishing House.

Greenfield, Jonas C. 2001a. *Al Kanfei Yonah: Collected Studies of Jonas C. Greenfield on Semitic Philology*. Edited by Shalom Paul, Avital Pinnick, and Michael Stone. Jerusalem: Magnes Press.

Greenfield, Jonas C. 2001b. "The 'Periphrastic Imperative' in Aramaic and Hebrew." Pages 56–67 in *Al Kanfei Yonah: Collected Studies of Jonas C. Greenfield on Semitic Philology*. Edited by Shalom Paul et al. Jerusalem: Magnes Press.

Greenfield, Jonas C., Michael Stone, and Esther Eshel. *The Aramaic Levi Document*. Studia in Veteris Testamenti Pseudepigrapha 19. Leiden: Brill, 2004.

Gregory, Bradley C. 2010. *Like an Everlasting Signet Ring: Generosity in the Book of Sirach*. Deuterocanonical and Cognate Literature Studies 2. Berlin: de Gruyter.

Habermann, Abraham M. 1964. "עיונים בבן ספר." Pages 296–99 in *Sefer Segal: Studies in the Bible, Presented to Professor M. H. Segal by His Colleagues and Students*. Edited by Jehoshua M. Grintz and Jacob Liver. Israeli Society for Biblical Research 17. Jerusalem: Kiryat Sepher.

Hadot, Jean. 1970. *Penchant mauvais et volonté libre dans la sagesse de Ben Sira (L'Ecclésiastique)*. Bruxelles: Presses universitaires de Bruxelles.

Halévy, Joseph. 1897. *Étude sur la partie du texte hébreu de l'Écclésiastique récemment découverte*. Paris: Ernest Leroux.

Haran, Menaḥem. 1960. "The Uses of Incense in the Ancient Israelite Ritual." *VT* 10:113–29.

Harris, James Rendel. 1898. *The Legend of Ahiqar from a Syriac MS. in the University of Cambridge*. Edited by Frederick C. Conybeare, Rendel Harris James, and Agnes Smith Lewis. London: C. J. Clay and Sons.

Hart, John H. A. 1909. *Ecclesiasticus. The Greek Text of Codex 248 Edited with Textual Commentary and Prolegomena*. Cambridge: Cambridge University Press.

Hendel, Ronald. 1016. *Steps to a New Edition of the Hebrew Bible*. Text-Critical Studies 10. Atlanta: SBL Press.

Hendel, Ronald. 2013. "The Oxford Hebrew Bible: Its Aims and a Response to Criticisms." *HeBAI* 2:63–99.

Hildesheim, Ralph. 1996. *Bis dass ein Prophet aufstand wie Feuer: Untersuchungen zum Prophetenverständnis des Ben Sira in Sir 48,1–49,16*. Trier: Paulinus.

Himbaza, Innocent, and Jan Joosten, eds. 2013. *Philology and Textual Criticism of the Hebrew Bible*. Forschungen zum Alten Testament 2. Reihe. Tübingen: Mohr Siebeck.

Hoftijzer, Jacob, and Karel Jongeling. 1995. *Dictionary of the North-West Semitic Inscriptions*. Handbuch der Orientalistik 21/2. Leiden: Brill.

Hopkins, Simon. 2011. "Hebrew tešuqā and Arabic šawq 'Desire' — an Etymological Study." *WZKM* 101:213–31.

Hurvitz, Avi. 1965. "התואר הבתר־מקראי ״אדון־הכל״ — והופעתו במזמור קנא מקומראן." *Tarbiz* 34:224–27.

Hurvitz, Avi. 1967. "The Language and Date of Psalms 151 from Qumran." *ErIsr* 8:82–87.

Ibn Gabirol, Salomon. 1851. *Mibḥar ha-Peninim*. Edited by Hirsch Filipovski. London: The Jewish Antiquarian Society.

Jain, Eva. 2014. *Psalmen oder Psalter? Materielle Rekonstruktion und inhaltliche Untersuchung der Psalmenhandschriften aus der Wüste Juda*. Studies on the Texts of the Desert of Judah 109. Leiden: Brill.

Jastrow, Marcus. 1903. *A Dictionary of the Targumim, the Talmud Bavli and Yerushalmi, and the Midrashic Literature*. Leipzig: Drugulin.

Jellinek, Adolph. 1853. *Bet ha-Midrasch*. 2nd ed. Vol. 1–6. Jerusalem: Bamberg & Wahrmann.

Joosten, Jan. 1999. "Pseudo-Classicisms in Late Biblical Hebrew, in Ben Sira, and in Qumran Hebrew." Pages 146–59 in *Sirach, Scrolls and Sages. Proceedings of a Second International Symposium on the Hebrew of the Dead Sea Scrolls, Ben Sira, and the Mishnah, Held at Leiden University, 15–17 December 1997*. Edited by T. Muraoka and J. F. Elwolde. STDJ 33. Leiden: Brill.

Joosten, Jan. 2005a. "Source-language Oriented Remarks on the Lexicography of the Greek Versions of the Bible." *ETL* 81:152–64.

Joosten, Jan. 2005b. "The Distinction between Classical and Late Biblical Hebrew as Reflected in Syntax." *HS* 46:327–39.

Joosten, Jan. 2012. *The Verbal System of Biblical Hebrew. A New Synthesis Elaborated on the Basis of Classical Prose*. Jerusalem Biblical Studies 10. Jerusalem: Simor Ltd.

Joosten, Jan. 2016. "Pseudo-Classicisms in Late Biblical Hebrew." *ZAW* 128:16–29.

Joosten, Jan, Daniel A. Machiela, and Frédérique Michèle (J.-S.) Rey, eds. 2018. *The Reconfiguration of Hebrew in the Hellenistic Period: Proceedings of the Seventh International Symposium on the Hebrew of the Dead Sea Scrolls and Ben Sira at Strasbourg University, June 2014*. Studies on the Texts of the Desert of Judah 124. Leiden: Brill.

Joosten, Jan, and Frédérique Michèle (J.-S.) Rey, eds. 2008. *Conservatism and Innovation in the Hebrew Language of the Hellenistic Period: Proceedings of a Fourth International Symposium on the Hebrew of the Dead Sea Scrolls & Ben Sira*. Studies on the Texts of the Desert of Judah 73. Leiden: Brill.

Joüon, Paul, and Takamitsu Muraoka. 1991. *A Grammar of Biblical Hebrew*. 2 vols. Roma: Ed. Pontificio Istituto Biblico.

Kahana, Abraham. 1937. "דברי שמעון בן־סירא." Pages 435–530 in 2. הספרים החיצונים לתורה לנביאים לכתובים ושאר ספרים חיצונים. Tel Aviv.

Karner, Gerhard. 2015. "Ben Sira Ms A fol. I recto and fol. VI verso (T-S 12.863) Revisited." *RevQ* 27:177–203.

Karner, Gerhard, Frank Ueberschaer, and Burkard M. Zapff, eds. 2017. *Texts and Contexts of the Book of Sirach / Texte und Kontexte des Sirachbuches*. Septuagint and Cognate Studies Series 66. Atlanta: SBL Press.

Kearns, Conleth. 2011. *The Expanded Text of Ecclesiasticus: Its Teaching on the Future Life as a Clue to Its Origin*. Deuterocanonical and Cognate Literature Studies 11. Berlin: de Gruyter.

Kena'ani, Ya'aqov. 1960. אוצר הלשון העברית לתקופותיה השונות. Jerusalem: Masada.

Kister, Menaḥem. 1968. "Al-Ḥīra: Some Notes on Its Relations with Arabia." *Arabica* 15:143–69.

Kister, Menaḥem. 1983. "בשולי ספר בן־סירא." *Lěšonénu* 47:125–46.

Kister, Menaḥem. 1988. "נוספות למאמר 'בשולי ספר בן־סירא'." *Lěšonénu* 53:36–53.

Kister, Menaḥem. 1990. "לפירושו של ספר בן־סירא" (A Contribution to the Interpretation of Ben Sira)." *Tarbiz* 59:304–78.

Kister, Menaḥem. 1999. "Some Notes on Biblical Expressions and Allusions and the Lexicography of Ben Sira." Pages 160–87 in *Sirach, Scrolls and Sages. Proceedings of a Second International Symposium on the Hebrew of the Dead Sea Scrolls, Ben Sira, and the Mishnah, held at Leiden University, 15–17 December 1997*. Edited by Takamitsu Muraoka and John F. Elwolde. Studies on the Texts of the Desert of Judah 33. Leiden: Brill.

Kister, Menaḥem. 2000. "Some Observations on Vocabulary and Style in the Dead Sea Scrolls." Pages 137–65 in *Diggers at the Well. Proceedings of a Third International Symposium on the Hebrew of the Dead Sea Scrolls and Ben Sira*. Edited by Takamitsu Muraoka and John F. Elwolde. Studies on the Texts of the Desert of Judah 36. Leiden: Brill.

Kister, Menaḥem. 2002. "Genizah Manuscripts of Ben Sira." Pages 36–48 in *The Cambridge Genizah collections: Their contents and significance*. Edited by Stefan C. Reif and Shulamit Reif. Cambridge University Library Genizah series 1. Cambridge: Cambridge University Press.

Kister, Menaḥem. 2004. "Wisdom Literature and its Relation to Other Genres: From Ben Sira to Mysteries." Pages 13–47 in *Sapiential Perspectives: Wisdom Literature in Light of the Dead Sea Scrolls: Proceedings of the Sixth International Symposium of the Orion Center for the Study of the Dead Sea Scrolls and Associated Literature, 20–22 May, 2001*. Edited by John Joseph Collins et al. Studies on the Texts of the Desert of Judah 51. Leiden: Brill.

Kister, Menaḥem. 2009. "Divorce, Reproof, and other Sayings in the Synoptic Gospels: Jesus Traditions in the Context of 'Qumranic' and other texts." Pages 195–229 in *Text, Thought, and Practice in Qumran and Early Christianity: Proceedings of the Ninth International Symposium of the Orion Center for the Study of the Dead Sea Scrolls and Associated Literature, Jointly Sponsored by the Hebrew University Center for the Study of Christianity, 11–13 January, 2004*. Edited by Ruth A. Clements and Daniel R. Schwartz. Studies on the Texts of the Desert of Judah 84. Leiden: Brill.

Kister, Menaḥem. 2013. "Ben Sira." *Encyclopedia of Hebrew Language and Linguistics*. Edited by Geoffrey Khan and Shmuel Bolozky. Leiden: Brill.

Knabenbauer, Joseph. 1902. *Commentarius in Ecclesiasticum. Cum Appendice: Textus "Ecclesiastici" Hebraeus descriptus secundum fragmenta nuper reperta cum notis et versione litterali Latina*. Paris: Lethielleux.

Koehler, Ludwig, and Walter Baumgartner. 1958. *Lexicon in Veteris Testamenti Libros*. 2nd ed. Leiden: Brill.

Koehler, Ludwig, and Walter Baumgartner, eds. 1994. *The Hebrew and Aramaic Lexicon of the Old Testament*. 4 vols. Leiden: Brill.

Kogut, Simcha. 1988. "The Biblical phrase 'יש/אין יד לאל'." *Tarbiz* 57:435–44.

König, Eduard. 1899a. "Professor Margoliouth and the 'Original Hebrew' of Ecclesiasticus." *ExpTim* 10:512–16.

König, Eduard. 1899b. "Professor Margoliouth and the 'Original Hebrew' of Ecclesiasticus." *ExpTim* 10:564–66.

König, Eduard. 1899c. "Professor Margoliouth and the 'Original Hebrew' of Ecclesiasticus." *ExpTim* 11:31–32.

König, Eduard. 1899d. "Professor Margoliouth and the 'Original Hebrew' of Ecclesiasticus." *ExpTim* 11:69–74.

König, Eduard. 1900. "The Origin of the New Hebrew Fragments of Ecclesiasticus." *ExpTim* 11:170–76.

Kratz, Reinhard Gregor, Annette Steudel, and Ingo Kottsieper, eds. 2017. *Hebräisches und aramäisches Wörterbuch zu den Texten vom Toten Meer: einschliesslich der Manuskripte aus Kairoer Geniza*. Vol. 1–2. Berlin: de Gruyter.

Kutscher, Edward Yechezkel. 1974. *The Language and Linguistic Background of the Isaiah Scroll (1QIsaᵃ)*. Studies on the Texts of the Desert of Judah 6. Leiden: Brill.

Labendz, Jenny R. 2006. "The Book of Ben Sira in Rabbinic Literature." *AJS* 30:347–92.

Lagarde, Pauli Antonii. 1861. *Libri Veteris Testamenti Apocryphi Syriace*. Leipzig: Brockhaus.

Lavoie, Jean-Jacques. 2000. "Ben Sira le voyageur ou la difficile rencontre avec l'hellénisme." *Science et Esprit* 52:37–60.

Leib Ben Ze'eb, Yehouda. 1798. חכמת יהושע בן סירא נעתק ללשון עברי ואשכנזי ותרגום ארמית. Breslau: Grassische Stadt Buchdruckerey.

Lévi, Israël. 1898. *L'Ecclésiastique, ou la Sagesse de Jésus, fils de Sira. Première partie (ch. XXXIX, 15, à XLIX, 11)*. Bibliothèque de l'École des hautes Études. Sciences religieuses 10.1. Paris: E. Leroux.

Lévi, Israel. 1900. "Fragments de deux nouveaux manuscrits hébreux de l'Ecclésiastique." *REJ* 40:1–30.

Lévi, Israël. 1901. *L'Ecclésiastique, ou la Sagesse de Jésus, fils de Sira*. Bibliothèque de l'École des hautes Études. Sciences religieuses 10.2. Paris: E. Leroux.

Lévi, Israël. 1902. "Quelques citations de l'ecclésiastique." *REJ* 44:291–94.

Lévi, Israël. 1904. *The Hebrew Text of the Book of Ecclesiasticus*. Leiden: Brill.

Lévi, Israel. 1932. "Un nouveau fragment de Ben Sira." *REJ* 92:136–45.

Levy, Jacob, ed. 1876–89. *Neuhebräisches und Chaldäisches Wörterbuch über die Talmud und Midraschim*. 4 vols. Leipzig: Brockhaus.

Lewis, Agnes. 1896. "Discovery of a Fragment of Ecclesiasticus in the Original Hebrew." *The Academy* 49:405.

Lichtheim, Miriam. 1980. *Ancient Egyptian Literature: a Book of Readings. Volume III: The Late Period*. Berkeley: University of California Press.

Liesen, Jan. 2008. "A Common Background of Ben Sira and the Psalter. The Concept of תורה in Sir 32:14–33:3 and the Torah Psalms." Pages 197–207 in *The Wisdom of Ben Sira: Studies on Tradition, Redaction, and Theology*. Edited by Angelo Passaro and Giuseppe Bellia. Deuterocanonical and Cognate Literature Studies 1. Berlin: de Gruyter.

Maas, Paul. 1958. *Textual Criticism*. Translated by Barbara Flower. London: Oxford University Press.

Mack, Burton L. 1985. *Wisdom and the Hebrew Epic: Ben Sira's Hymn in Praise of the Fathers*. Chicago Studies in the History of Judaism. Chicago: University of Chicago Press.

Marböck, Johannes. 1999. *Weisheit im Wandel: Untersuchungen zur Weisheitstheologie bei Ben Sira*. Zeitschrift für die alttestamentliche Wissenschaft 272. Berlin: de Gruyter.

Marböck, Johannes. 2010. *Jesus Sirach 1–23*. Herders theologischer Kommentar zum Alten Testament. Freiburg: Herder.

Marcus, Joseph. 1931a. "A Fifth MS. of Ben Sira." *JQR* 21:223–40.

Marcus, Joseph. 1931b. *The Newly Discovered Original Hebrew of Ben Sira (Ecclesiasticus xxxii, 16–xxxiv, 1) the Fifth Manuscript and a Prosodic Version of Ben Sira (Ecclesiasticus xxii, 22–xxiii, 9)*. Philadelphia: The Dropsie College for Hebrew and Cognate Learning.

Margoliouth, David S. 1899. *The Origin of the "Original Hebrew" of Ecclesiasticus*. London: James Parker.

Margoliouth, David S. 1904. "The Destruction of the Original of Ecclesiasticus." *ExpTim* 16:26–29.

Margoliouth, G. 1899a. *Catalogue of the Hebrew and Samaritan Manuscripts in the British Museum. Part. 1.* London: British Museum.

Margoliouth, G. 1899b. "The Original Hebrew of Ecclesiasticus XXXI. 12–31, and XXXVI. 22–XXXVII. 26." *JQR* 12:1–33.

Margolis, Max L. 1931. "Notes on 'A Fifth MS. of Ben Sira.'" *JQR* 21:439–40.

Marsman, Hennie J. 2003. *Women in Ugarit and Israel: Their Social and Religious Position in the Context of the Ancient Near East.* Society of Biblical Literature. Leiden: Brill.

Martone, Corrado. 1997. "Ben Sira Manuscripts from Qumran and Masada." Pages 81–94 in *The book of Ben Sira in Modern Research: Proceedings of the First International Ben Sira Conference, 28–31 July 1996.* Edited by Pancratius C. Beentjes. Beihefte zur Zeitschrift für die alttestamentliche Wissenschaft 255. Berlin: de Gruyter.

Marttila, Marko. 2012. *Foreign Nations in the Wisdom of Ben Sira: A Jewish Sage Between Opposition and Assimilation.* Deuterocanonical and Cognate Literature Studies 13. Berlin: de Gruyter.

Mattila, Sharon L. 2000. "Ben Sira and the Stoics: A Reexamination of the Evidence." *JBL* 119:473–501.

McNamee, Kathleen. 1992. *Sigla and Select Marginalia in Greek Literary Papyri.* Papirologica Bruxellensia 26. Bruxelles: Fondation Égyptologique Reine Élisabeth.

Mermelstein, Ari. 2014. *Creation, Covenant, and the Beginnings of Judaism: Reconceiving Historical Time in the Second Temple Period.* Supplements to the Journal for the Study of Judaism 168. Leiden: Brill.

Meyers, Carol L., and O'Connor, Michael P., eds. 1982. *The Word of the Lord Shall Go Forth: Essays in Honor of David Noel Freedman in Celebration of His Sixtieth Birthday.* Winona Lake: Eisenbrauns.

Mies, Françoise. 2005. "« De la brûlure d'un feu … » - Ben Sira 51,5a (hébreu)." *Bib* 86:260–68.

Mies, Françoise. 2009a. "Le psaume de Ben Sira 51,12a–o hébreu: l'hymne aux noms divins (Deuxième partie)." *RB* 116:481–504.

Mies, Françoise. 2009b. "Le psaume de Ben Sira 51,12a–o hébreu: l'hymne aux noms divins (Première partie)." *RB* 116:336–67.

Milik, Józef T. 1966. "Un fragment mal placé dans l'édition du Siracide de Masada." *Bib* 47:425–26.

Milik, Józef T. 1976. *The Books of Enoch: Aramaic Fragments of Qumrân Cave 4.* Oxford: Clarendon Press.

Milikowsky, Chaim. 1988. "The Status Quaestionis of Research in Rabbinic Literature." *JJS* 39:201–11.

Miller, Cynthia L. 2003. "A Linguistic Approach to Ellipsis in Biblical Poetry: Or, What to Do When Exegesis of What Is There Depends on What Isn't." *BBR* 13:251–70.

Miller, Cynthia L. 2009. "A Reconsideration of "Double-Duty" Prepositions in Biblical Poetry." *JANES* 31:99–110.

Miller, Cynthia L., ed. 1999. *The Verbless Clause in Biblical Hebrew: Linguistic Approaches.* Linguistic Studies in Ancient West Semitic 1. Winona Lake: Eisenbrauns.

Minissale, Antonino. 1995. *La versione greca del Siracide: confronto con il testo ebraico alla luce dell'attività midrascica e del metodo targumico.* Analecta Biblica 133. Roma: Editrice Pontificio Istituto biblico.

Mizrahi, Noam. 2013. "The Textual History and Literary Background of Isa 14,4." *ZAW* 125:433–47.

Mopsik, Charles. 2003. *La Sagesse de ben Sira.* « Les Dix Paroles ». Lagrasse: Verdier.

Moreshet, Bar-Ilan. 1976. "The Hifʻil in Mishnaic Hebrew as Equivalent to the Qal." *Bar-Ilan* 13:249–81.

Morla, Víctor. 2012. *Los manuscritos hebreos de Ben Sira: traducción y notas.* Asociación Bíblica Española 59. Estella: Verbo Divino.

Mulder, Otto. 2003. *Simon the High Priest in Sirach 50: An Exegetical Study of the Significance of Simon the High Priest as Climax to the Praise of the Fathers in Ben Sira's Concept of the History of Israel.* Supplements to the Journal for the Study of Judaism 78. Leiden: Brill.

Muraoka, Takamitsu. 1999. "The Tripartite Nominal Clause Revisited." Pages 187–214 in *The Verbless Clause in Biblical Hebrew: Linguistic Approaches.* Edited by Cynthia Lynn Miller. Linguistic Studies in Ancient West Semitic 1. Winona Lake: Eisenbrauns.

Muraoka, Takamitsu, and John F. Elwolde, eds. 1997. *The Hebrew of the Dead Sea Scrolls and Ben Sira: Proceedings of a Symposium held at Leiden University, 11–14 December 1995.* Studies on the Texts of the Desert of Judah 26. Leiden: Brill.

Muraoka, Takamitsu, and John F. Elwolde, eds. 1999. *Sirach, Scrolls, and Sages. Proceedings of a Second International Symposium on the Hebrew of the Dead Sea Scrolls, Ben Sira, and the Mishnah, held at Leiden University, 15–17 December 1997.* Studies on the Texts of the Desert of Judah 33. Leiden: Brill.

Muraoka, Takamitsu, and John F. Elwolde, eds. 2000. *Diggers at the Well. Proceedings of a Third International Symposium on the Hebrew of the Dead Sea Scrolls and Ben Sira.* Studies on the Texts of the Desert of Judah 36. Leiden: Brill.

Murphy, Roland E. 1985. "'Yeṣer in the Qumran Literature." *Bib* 39:334–44.

Neusner, Jacob, ed. 2002. *The Tosefta: Translated from the Hebrew with a New Introduction.* Peabody: Hendrickson Publishers.

Nichols, Stephen G. 1990. "Introduction: Philology in a Manuscript Culture." *Speculum* 65:1–10.

Nissim ben Yaqob. 1886. ספר מעשיות. Edited by Meir Yechiel Holstock. Varsovie.

Nissim ben Yaqob. 1933. *Studies in Islam and Judaism. The Arabic original of Ibn Shâhîn's Book of Comfort known as the Ḥibbûr Yaphê of R. Nissîm b. Yaʻaqobh.* Edited by Obermann, Julian.

Yale Oriental Series — Researches 17. New Haven: Yale University Press.

Nöldeke, Theodor. 1900. "Bemerkungen zum hebräischen Ben Sīrā." *ZATW* 20:81–94.

Olszowy-Schlanger, Judith. 2018. "The 'Booklet' of Ben Sira." Pages 67–96 in *Discovering, Deciphering, and Dissenting: Ben Sira manuscripts after 120 years*. Edited by James K. Aitken et al. Deuterocanonical and Cognate Literature Yearbook 2018. Berlin: de Gruyter.

Passaro, Angelo, and Giuseppe Bellia, eds. 2008. *The Wisdom of Ben Sira: Studies on Tradition, Redaction, and Theology*. Deuterocanonical and Cognate Literature Studies 1. Berlin: de Gruyter.

Patmore, Hector M., James K. Aitken, and Ishay Rosen-Zvi, eds. 2021. *The Evil Inclination in Early Judaism and Christianity*. Cambridge: Cambridge University Press.

Payne Smith, Robert, ed. 1901. *Thesaurus Syriacus*. 2 vol. Oxford: Clarendon Press.

Pérez Fernández, Miguel. 1999. *An Introductory Grammar of Rabbinic Hebrew*. Translated by John F. Elwolde. Leiden: Brill.

Perles, Félix. 1897. "Notes critiques sur le texte de l'Ecclésiastique." *REJ* 35:48–64.

Peters, Norbert. 1902. *Der jüngst wiederaufgefundene hebräische Text des Buches Ecclesiasticus*. Freiburg im Breisgau: Herdersche Verlagshandlung.

Peters, Norbert. 1905. *Liber Iesu Filii Sirach sive Ecclesiasticus Hebraice*. Freiburg im Breisgau: Herder.

Peters, Norbert. 1913. *Das Buch Ben Sirach oder Ecclesiasticus*. Exegetisches Handbuch zum Alten Testament 25. Münster: Aschendorf.

Peursen, Willem van. 2001. "The Alleged Retroversions from Syriac in the Hebrew Text of Ben Sira Revisited: Linguistic Perspectives." *KUSATU* 2:47–95.

Peursen, Willem van. 2003. "Sirach 51:13–30 in Hebrew and Syriac." Pages 357–74 in *Hamlet on a Hill: Semitic and Greek Studies Presented to Professor T. Muraoka on the Occasion of his Sixty-fifth Birthday*. Edited by Martin F. J. Baasten and Willem Th. van Peursen. Orientalia Lovaniensia Analecta 118. Leuven: Peeters.

Peursen, Willem van. 2004. *The Verbal System in the Hebrew Text of Ben Sira*. Studies in Semitic Languages and Linguistics 41. Leiden ; Boston: Brill.

Peursen, Willem van. 2007. *Language and Interpretation in the Syriac Text of Ben Sira. A Comparative Linguistic and Literary Study*. Monographs of the Peshitta Institute 16. Leiden: Brill.

Peursen, Willem van. 2008. "The word תחליף in Ben Sira." Pages 133–48 in *Conservatism and Innovation in the Hebrew Language*. Edited by Frédérique Michèle (J.-S.) Rey and Jan Joosten. Studies on the Texts of the Desert of Judah 73. Leiden: Brill.

Peursen, Willem van. 2016. "Ben Sira." Pages 69–82 in *A Handbook of Biblical Hebrew*. Vol. 1. Edited by W. Randall Garr and Steven Ellis Fassberg. Winona Lake Indiana: Eisenbrauns.

Philonenko, Marc. 1986. "Sur une interpolation essénisante dans le Siracide (16, 15–16)." *Orientalia Suecana* 33–35:317–21.

Philonenko, Marc. 1999. "De l'intérêt des deutérocanoniques pour l'interprétation du Nouveau Testament : l'exemple de Luc 16, 9." *RevScRel* 73:177–83.

Porten, Bezalel, and Ada Yardeni, eds. 1993. *Textbook of Aramaic Documents from Ancient Egypt. 3. Literature, Accounts, Lists*. Texts and Studies for Students. Jerusalem: The Hebrew University.

Prato, Gian Luigi. 1975. *Il problema della teodicea in Ben Sira*. Analecta Biblica 65. Roma: Pontificio Istituto Biblico.

Puech, Émile. 1971. "Sur la racine 'slh' en hébreu et en araméen." *Sem* 21:5–19.

Puech, Émile. 1991. "4Q525 et les péricopes des Béatitudes en Ben Sira et Matthieu." *RB* 98:80–106.

Puech, Émile. 1999. "Le livre de Ben Sira et les manuscrits de la mer Morte." Pages 411–26 in *Treasures of Wisdom: Studies in Ben Sira and the Book of Wisdom*. Edited by Jacques Vermeylen and Núria Calduch-Benages. Bibliotheca Ephemeridum Theologicarum Lovaniensium 143. Leuven: Peeters.

Puech, Émile. 2001. "Dieu le père dans les écrits péritestamentaire et les manuscrits de la mer Morte." *RevQ* 20:287–310.

Puech, Émile. 2003a. "Review of Masada VI: The Yigael Yadin Excavations 1963–1965, Final Reports; Hebrew Fragments from Masada and The Ben Sira Scroll from Masada by Shemaryahu Talmon and Y. Yadin." *RevQ* 21:125–28.

Puech, Émile. 2003b. "Review of The Book of Ben Sira in Hebrew, by P. C. Beentjes." *RevQ* 21:128–29.

Puech, Émile. 2008. "Ben Sira and Qumran." Pages 79–118 in *The Wisdom of Ben Sira: Studies on Tradition, Redaction, and Theology*. Edited by Angelo Passaro and Giuseppe Bellia. Deuterocanonical and Cognate Literature Studies 1. Berlin: de Gruyter.

Puech, Émile. 2011. "La sagesse dans les béatitudes de Ben Sira : Étude du texte de Si 51,13–30 et de Si 14,20–15,10." Pages 297–329 in *The Texts and Versions of the Book of Ben Sira: Transmission and Interpretation*. Edited by Frédérique Michèle (J.-S.) Rey and Jan Joosten. Supplements to the Journal for the Study of Judaism 150. Leiden: Brill.

Puech, Émile. 2017. "Élie et Élisée dans l'Éloge des Pères: Sira 48,1–14 dans le manuscrit B et les parallèles." *RevQ* 29:205–18.

Qimron, Elisha. 1986. *The Hebrew of the Dead Sea Scrolls*. Harvard Semitic Studies 29. Atlanta: Scholars Press.

Qimron, Elisha. 1988. "New Readings in Ben Sira." *Tarbiz* 58:117.

Qimron, Elisha. 1999. "Notes on the Reading." Pages 227–31 in *Masada VI: The Yigael Yadin Excavations 1963–1965, Final*

Reports. *Hebrew Fragments from Masada and the Ben Sira Scroll from Masada*. Edited by Shemaryahu Talmon and Yigael Yadin. Jerusalem: Israel Exploration Society.

Qimron, Elisha. 2001. "ויו לסימון הגה מעבר (Waw as Marker for a Glide)." Pages 362–75 in תשורה לשמואל: מחקרים בעולם המקרא (*Homage to Shmuel. Studies in the World of the Bible*). Edited by Zipora Talshir et al. Jerusalem: Bialik Institute.

Qimron, Elisha. 2018. *A Grammar of the Hebrew of the Dead Sea Scrolls*. Between Bible and Mishnah. Jerusalem: Yad Yizhak Ben Zvi.

Reif, Stefan C. 1997. "The Discovery of the Cambridge Genizah Fragments of Ben Sira: Scholars and Texts." Pages 1–22 in *The Book of Ben Sira in Modern Research: Proceedings of the First Proceedings of the First International Ben Sira Conference, 28–31 July 1996, Soesterberg, Netherlands*. Edited by Pancratius C Beentjes. Beihefte zur Zeitschrift für die alttestamentliche Wissenschaft 255. Berlin: de Gruyter.

Reif, Stefan C. 2000. *A Jewish Archive from old Cairo: The History of Cambridge University's Genizah Collection*. Culture and Civilisation in the Middle East. Richmond; Surrey: Curzon.

Reiterer, Friedrich V., ed. 1996. *Freundschaft bei Ben Sira: Beiträge des Symposions zu Ben Sira Salzburg 1995*. Beihefte zur Zeitschrift für die alttestamentliche Wissenschaft 244. Berlin: de Gruyter.

Reiterer, Friedrich V., and Renate Egger-Wenzel. 2003. *Zählsynopse zum Buch Ben Sira*. Fontes et Subsidia ad Bibliam pertinentes 1. Berlin: de Gruyter.

Reiterer, Friedrich Vinzenz, Núria Calduch-Benages, Renate Egger-Wenzel, Anton Fersterer, and Ingrid Krammer. 1998a. *Bibliographie zu Ben Sira*. Beihefte zur Zeitschrift für die alttestamentliche Wissenschaft 266. Berlin: de Gruyter.

Reiterer, Friedrich Vinzenz et al. 1998b. "Text und Buch Ben Sira in Tradition und Forschung. Eine Einführung." Page 1–77 in *Bibliographie zu Ben Sira*. BZAW 266. Berlin: de Gruyter.

Rendsburg, Gary A. 2015. "The Nature of Qumran Hebrew as Revealed Through Pesher Habakkuk." Pages 132–59 in *Hebrew of the Late Second Temple Period: Proceedings of a Sixth International Symposium on the Hebrew of the Dead Sea Scrolls and Ben Sira*. Edited by Eibert J. C. Tigchelaar and Pierre van Hecke. Studies on the Texts of the Desert of Judah 114. Leiden: Brill.

Rendsburg, Gary A., and Jacob Binstein. 2013. "The Book of Ben Sira." bensira.org.

Rey, Frédérique Michèle (J.-S.). 2008. 2009. *4QInstruction : sagesse et eschatologie*. Studies on the Texts of the Desert of Judah 81. Leiden: Brill.

Rey, Frédérique Michèle (J.-S.). 2008. "Quelques considérations sur le vocabulaire sapientiel de Ben Sira et de 4QInstruction." Pages 119–34 in KUSATU: *Kleine Untersuchungen zur Sprache des Alten Testaments und seiner Umwelt*. Edited by Johannes F. Diehl and Reinhard G. Lehmann. KUSATU 9. Waltrop: Spenner.

Rey, Frédérique Michèle (J.-S.). 2008a. "Quelques particularités linguistiques communes à 4QInstruction et à Ben Sira." Pages 155–74 in *Conservatism and Innovation in the Hebrew Language of the Hellenistic Period: Proceedings of a Fourth International Symposium on the Hebrew of the Dead Sea Scrolls & Ben Sira*. Edited by Jan Joosten and Frédérique Michèle (J.-S.) Rey. Studies on the Texts of the Desert of Judah 73. Leiden: Brill.

Rey, Frédérique Michèle (J.-S.). 2008b. "Un nouveau bifeuillet du manuscrit C de la Genizah du Caire." Pages 387–416 in *Florilegium Lovaniense: Studies in Septuagint and Textual Criticism in Honour of Florentino García Martínez*. Edited by Hans Ausloos et al. Bibliotheca Ephemeridum Theologicarum Lovaniensium 224. Leuven: Peeters.

Rey, Frédérique Michèle (J.-S.). 2009. *4QInstruction : sagesse et eschatologie*. Studies on the Texts of the Desert of Judah 81. Leiden: Brill.

Rey, Frédérique Michèle (J.-S.). 2012a. "Les différentes versions du livre de Ben Sira : évolution et transmission d'un texte juif de l'antiquité." Pages 27–39 in *Corpus anciens et bases de données*. Edited by Marie-Sol Ortola. ALIENTO 2. Nancy: Presses Universitaires de Nancy.

Rey, Frédérique Michèle (J.-S.). 2012b. "Si 10,12–12,1: nouvelle édition du fragment Adler (ENA 2536–2)." *RevQ* 100:575–603.

Rey, Frédérique Michèle (J.-S.). 2012c. "Un nouveau feuillet du manuscrit D de Ben Sira : notes de philologie et de critique textuelle." *RevQ* 99:395–422.

Rey, Frédérique Michèle (J.-S.). 2015. "'Dislocated Negations': Negative אל Followed by a Non-verbal Constituent in Biblical, Ben Sira and Qumran Hebrew." Pages 160–74 in *Hebrew of the Late Second Temple Period: Proceedings of a Sixth International Symposium on the Hebrew of the Dead Sea Scrolls and Ben Sira*. Edited by Eibert J. C. Tigchelaar and Pierre van Hecke. Studies on the Texts of the Desert of Judah 114. Leiden: Brill.

Rey, Frédérique Michèle (J.-S.). 2017. "Scribal Practices in the Ben Sira Hebrew Manuscript A and Codicological Remarks." Pages 99–114 in *Texts and Contexts of the Book of Sirach. Texte und Kontexte des Sirachbuches*. Edited by Gerhard Karner et al. Septuagint and Cognate Studies 66. Atlanta: SBL Press.

Rey, Frédérique Michèle (J.-S.). 2018. "Reflections on the Critical Edition of the Hebrew Text of Ben Sira. Between Eclecticism and Pragmatism." *Text* 27:187–204.

Rey, Frédérique Michèle (J.-S.). 2021a. "Doublets in the Hebrew Manuscript B of Sirach." Pages 126–48 in *Sirach and its contexts: the pursuit of wisdom and human flourishing*. Edited by Samuel L. Adams et al. Supplements to the Journal for the Study of Judaism 196. Leiden: Brill.

Rey, Frédérique Michèle (J.-S.). 2021b. "The Relationship Between Manuscripts A, B, D and the Marginal Readings of Manuscript B of Ben Sira." *JJS* 72:240–56.

Rey, Frédérique Michèle (J.-S.). 2021c. "The Relationship Between the Hebrew Manuscripts B, (B Margin), E and F of Ben Sira." *RevQ* 33:5–17.

Rey, Frédérique Michèle (J.-S.), and Marieke Dhont. 2019. "Scribal Practices in Ben Sira Manuscript B." Pages 97–124 in *Discovering, Deciphering and Dissenting: Ben Sira Manuscripts after 120 years*. Edited by James K. Aitken et al. Deuterocanonical and Cognate Literature Yearbook 2018. Berlin: de Gruyter.

Rey, Frédérique Michèle (J.-S.), and Jan Joosten, eds. 2011. *The Texts and Versions of the Book of Ben Sira: Transmission and Interpretation*. Supplements to the Journal for the Study of Judaism 150. Leiden: Brill.

Reymond, Eric D. 2001. "'Prelude to the Praise of the Ancestors, Sirach 44:1–15.'" *HUCA* 72:1–14.

Reymond, Eric D. 2003. "Remarks on Ben Siras Instruction on Shame, Sirach 41,14–42,8." *ZAW* 115:388–400.

Reymond, Eric D. 2011. *New Idioms Within Old: Poetry and Parallelism in the Non-Masoretic Poems of 11Q5 (= 11QPs^a)*. Early Judaism and Its Literature 31. Leiden: Brill.

Reymond, Eric D. 2014a. "Fast Talk: Ben Sira's Thoughts on Speech in Sir 5:9–6:1." *RevQ* 26:253–73.

Reymond, Eric D. 2014b. "New Readings in the Ben Sira Masada Scroll (Mas 1h)." *RevQ* 26:327–43.

Reymond, Eric D. 2014c. *Qumran Hebrew: An Overview of Orthography, Phonology, and Morphology*. Resources for Biblical Study 76. Atlanta: Society of Biblical Literature.

Reymond, Eric D. 2015. "New Hebrew Text of Ben Sira Chapter 1 in Ms A (T-S 12.863)." *RevQ* 27:83–98.

Reymond, Eric D. 2016a. "New Readings in Ben Sira 40:9–49:11 Ms B (MS.Heb.e.62 and Or. 1102)." *RevQ* 28:127–40.

Reymond, Eric D. 2016b. "The Passive Qal in the Hebrew of the Second Temple Period, Especially as Found in the Wisdom of Ben Sira." Pages 1110–27 in *Sibyls, Scriptures, and Scrolls: John Collins at Seventy*. Edited by Hindy Najman et al. Leiden: Brill.

Reymond, Eric D. 2017a. "New Readings and New Senses in the Hebrew to the Wisdom of Ben Sira." *JANES* 54:1–16.

Reymond, Eric D. 2017b. "The Verb נשׂג in Second Temple Hebrew." *ZAW* 129: 19–31.

Reymond, Eric D. 2018a. "Gibberish?: Sir 4:14 in Ms A (T-S 12.863) Verso, Line 4." Pages 164–77 in *Figures Who Shape Scriptures, Scriptures Who Shape Figures: Essays in Honour of Benjamin G. Wright III*. Edited by Géza G. Xeravits and Greg Schmidt Goering. Deuterocanonical and Cognate Literature Studies 40. Berlin: De Gruyter.

Reymond, Eric D. 2018b. *Intermediate Biblical Hebrew Grammar: A Student's Guide to Phonology and Morphology*. Resources for Biblical Study 89. Atlanta: SBL Press.

Reymond, Eric D. 2018c. "Reflections on Orthography and Morphology in Ben Sira's Hebrew: The 3ms Heh Pronominal Suffix." Pages 226–44 in *The Reconfiguration of Hebrew in the Hellenistic Period. Proceedings of the Seventh International Symposium on the Hebrew of the Dead Sea Scrolls and Ben Sira at Strasbourg University, June 2014*. Edited by Jan Joosten et al. Studies on the Texts of the Desert of Judah 124. Leiden: Brill.

Reymond, Eric D. 2019a. "4.2 Hebrew (Ecclesiasticus/Ben Sira)." Pages 199–213 in *Textual History of the Bible: The Deuterocanonical Scriptures. Vol. 2B: Baruch/Jeremiah, Daniel (Additions), Ecclesiasticus/Ben Sira, Enoch, Esther (Additions), Ezra*. Edited by Armin Lange et al. Leiden: Brill.

Reymond, Eric D. 2019b. "A New Hebrew Word (zlq "lightning") and Other New Readings in the Hebrew Manuscripts of Ben Sira (MS B: MS heb.e.62 and T-S 16.313)." *RevQ* 31:169–88.

Reymond, Eric D. 2019c. "The Poetry of Ben Sira Manuscript C." Pages 221–42 in *Discovering, Deciphering, and Dissenting: Ben Sira manuscripts after 120 years*. Edited by James K. Aitken et al. Deuterocanonical and Cognate Literature Yearbook. Berlin: de Gruyter.

Reymond, Eric D. 2020a. "Divergences in the Hebrew of the Scrolls: A Review of Elisha Qimron's A Grammar of the Hebrew of the Dead Sea Scrolls." *RevQ* 32:3–42.

Reymond, Eric D. 2020b. "Thoughts on the Language of Sirach 36:1–22." *DSD* 27:455–74.

Reymond, Eric D. 2021a. "Geminate Verbs in the Hebrew of the Wisdom of Ben Sira." Pages 260–79 in *Hebrew Texts and Language of the Second Temple Period: Proceedings of an Eighth Symposium on the Hebrew of the Dead Sea Scrolls and Ben Sira*. Edited by Steven Fassberg. Studies on the Texts of the Desert of Judah 134. Leiden: Brill.

Reymond, Eric D. 2021b. "Vav and Yod in the Hebrew Manuscripts A and B of Sirach." Pages 104–24 in *Sirach and Its Contexts: The Pursuit of Wisdom and Human Flourishing*. Edited by Samuel L. Adams et al. Supplements to the Journal for the Study of Judaism 196. Leiden: Brill.

Reymond, Eric D. 2022. "The 3ms Suffix on Nouns Written with a Heh Mater." Pages 417–33 in *"Like 'Ilu Are You Wise": Studies in Northwest Semitic Languages and Literatures in Honor of Dennis G. Pardee*. Edited by Eric D. Reymond et al. Chicago: Oriental Institute.

Reymond, Eric D., Frédérique Michèle (J.-S.) Rey, and Jan Joosten. 2017. "A New Hebrew Word in Ben Sira 40:4 (Ms B IX verso, line 12 = Or. 1102): סיגה." *RB* 124:103–10.

Rüger, Hans P. 1970. *Text und Textform im hebräischen Sirach: Untersuchungen zur Textgeschichte und Textkritik der hebräischen Sirachfragmente aus der Kairoer Geniza*. Beihefte zur Zeitschrift für die alttestamentliche Wissenschaft 112. Berlin: de Gruyter.

Rundgren, Frithiof, Tryggve Kronholm, and Eva Riad, eds. 1986. *On the Dignity of man: Oriental and Classical Studies in Honour of Frithiof Rundgren*. Orientalia Suecana. Stockholm: Almqvist & Wiksell International.

Ryssel, Victor. 1901. "Die neuen hebräischen Fragmente des Buches Jesus Sirach und ihre Herkunft." Edited by D. Ullman and D. Umbreit. *TSK* 1:269–94.

Saadiah Gaon. 1891. *Sefer Ha-Galuy*. Edited by Abraham Harkavy. Saint Petersbourg.

Salzer, Dorothea M., Chanan Gafni, and Hanan Harif, eds. 2019. *Wissenschaft des Judentums Beyond Tradition: Jewish Scholarship on the Sacred Texts of Judaism, Christianity, and Islam*. Berlin: De Gruyter.

Sanders, J. A. 1965. *The Psalms Scroll of Qumran Cave 11 (11QPsa)*. DJD 4. Oxford: Clarendon.

Sauer, Georg. 1996. "Freundschaft nach Ben Sira 37,1–6." Pages 123–31 in *Freundschaft bei Ben Sira: Beiträge des Symposions zu Ben Sira Salzburg 1995*. Edited by Friedrich V. Reiterer. Beihefte zur Zeitschrift für die alttestamentliche Wissenschaft 244. Berlin: de Gruyter.

Sauer, Georg. 1998. "Der Ratgeber (Sir 37,7–15)." Pages 73–85 in *Der Einzelne und seine Gemeinschaft bei Ben Sira*. Edited by Renate Egger-Wenzel and Ingrid Krammer. Beihefte zur Zeitschrift für die alttestamentliche Wissenschaft 270. Berlin: de Gruyter.

Sauer, Georg. 2000. *Jesus Sirach, Ben Sira*. Alte Testament Deutsch Apokryphen 1. Göttingen: Vandenhoeck & Ruprecht.

Schäfer, Peter. 1986. "Research into Rabbinic Literature: An Attempt to Define the Status Quaestionis." *JJS* 37:139–52.

Schäfer, Peter. 1989. "Once again the Status Quaestionis of Research in Rabbinic Literature: An Answer to Chaim Milikowsky." *JJS* 40:89–94.

Schäfer, Peter, and Chaim Milikowsky. 2010. "Current Views on the Editing of the Rabbinic Texts of Late Antiquity: Reflections on a Debate after Twenty Years." Pages 79–88 in *Rabbinic Texts and the History of Late-Roman Palestine*. Edited by Martin Goodman and Philip Alexander. Oxford: The British Academy.

Schechter, Solomon. 1896. "A Fragment of the Original Text of Ecclesiasticus." *The Expositor. Fifth Series* 4:1–15.

Schechter, Solomon. 1898. "Genizah Specimens." *JQR* 10:197–206.

Schechter, Solomon. 1900a. "A Further Fragment of Ben Sira." *JQR* 12:456–65.

Schechter, Solomon. 1900b. "The Hebrew Text of Ben Sira. The British Museum Fragments of Ecclesiasticus." *JQR* 12:266–72.

Schechter, Solomon, and Charles Taylor. 1899. *The Wisdom of Ben Sira: Portions of the Book Ecclesiasticus from Hebrew Manuscripts in the Cairo Genizah Collection Presented to the University of Cambridge by the Editors*. Cambridge: Cambridge University Press.

Scheiber, Alexander. 1982. "A Leaf of the Fourth Manuscript of the Ben Sira." *JQR*:179–85.

Schenker, Adrian. 2013. "The Edition Biblia Hebraica Quinta (BHQ)." *HeBAI* 2:6–16.

Schenker, Adrian, Jan de Waard, Peter B. Dirksen, Yôḥānan Gôldman, Rolf Schäfer, and Magne Sæbø, eds. 2004. *General introduction and Megilloth. Ruth, Canticles, Qoheleth, Lamentations, Esther*. Biblia Hebraica Quinta 18. Stuttgart: Deutsche Bibelgesellschaft.

Schirmann, Hayyim. 1965. שירים חדשים מן הגניזה. Jerusalem: Israel Academy of Sciences and Humanities.

Schirmann, J. 1958. "דף חדש מתוך ספר בן־סירא (A New Leaf from the Book of Ben Sira)." *Tarbiz* 27:440–43.

Schirmann, J. 1960. "דפים נוספים מתוך ספר בן־סירא (Additional Leaves from the Book of Ben Sira)." *Tarbiz* 29:125–34.

Schnabel, Eckhard J. 1985. *Law and Wisdom from Ben Sira to Paul. A Tradition Historical Enquiry into the Relation of Law, Wisdom and Ethics*. Wissenschaftliche Untersuchungen zum Neuen Testament 2. Reihe 16. Tübingen: Mohr Siebeck.

Schwartz, Seth. 2010. *Were the Jews a Mediterranean Society?: Reciprocity and Solidarity in Ancient Judaism*. Princeton: Princeton University Press.

Segal, M. H. 1964. "ספר בן־סירא בקומראן (Ben Sira in Qumran)." *Tarbiz* 33:243–46.

Segal, M. Z. 1931. "כתב־היד החמישי של בן סירא העבר (The Fifth Manuscript of Ben Sira)." *Tarbiz* 2:295–307.

Segal, M. Z. 1958. ספר בן־סירא השלם (*Sefer Ben Sira ha-Shalem*). Jerusalem: Bialik Institute.

Segal, M. Z. 1960. "Additional Leaves From Ecclesiasticus in Hebrew' (J. Schirmann, Tarbiz XXIX, 125–134)" / "דפים נוספים מתוך ספר בן־סירא (ח. שירמן, תרביץ, כט, עמ' 125–134)." *Tarbiz* 29:313–23.

Segal, Michael. 2013. "The Hebrew University Bible Project." *HeBAI* 2:38–62.

Segre, Cesare. 2016. "Lachmann et Bédier. La guerre est finie." Pages 15–27 in *Actes du XXVIIe Congrès international de linguistique et de philologie romanes (Nancy, 15–20 juillet 2013)*. Edited by Eva Buchi et al. Nancy: Éditions de linguistique et de philologie.

Shaked, Shaul, James Nathan Ford, and Siam Bhayro. 2013. *Aramaic Bowl Spells: Jewish Babylonian Aramaic Bowls. Volume 1*. Manuscripts in the Schøyen Collection 20. Leiden: Brill.

Sirat, Collette, Mordechai Glatzer, and Malachi Beit-Arié. 2002. *Codices Hebraicis Litteris Exarati Quo Tempore Scripti Fuerint Exhibentes, Tome III de 1085 à 1140*. Turnhout: Brepols.

Skehan, P. W. 1968. "Sirach 40:11–17." *CBQ* 36:570–72.

Skehan, P. W. 1974. "Sirach 30:12 and Related Texts." *CBQ* 36:535–42.

Skehan, Patrick W. 1970. "Staves, and Nails, and Scribal Slips (Ben Sira 44:2–5)." *BASOR* 200:66–71.

Slotki, Judah J. 1961. *Numbers I*. Edited by Harry Freedman et al. *Midrash Rabbah*. Vol. 4. London: The Soncino Press.

Smend, Rudolf. 1897. *Das hebräische Fragment der Weisheit des Jesus Sirach*. Abhandlungen der Königlichen der Gesellschaft der Wissenschaften zu Göttingen, Philologisch-Historische-Klasse. Neue Folge Band 2. No. 2. Berlin: Weidmann.

Smend, Rudolf. 1906a. *Die Weisheit des Jesus Sirach, erklärt*. Berlin: George Reimer.

Smend, Rudolf. 1906b. *Die Weisheit des Jesus Sirach, hebräisch und deutsch*. Berlin: Georg Reimer.

Smith, Mark S. 2000. "The Infinitive Absolute as Predicative Verb in Ben Sira and the Dead Sea Scrolls: A Preliminary Survey." Pages 256–68 in *Diggers at the Well. Proceedings of a Third International Symposium on the Hebrew of the Dead Sea Scrolls and Ben Sira*. Edited by Takamitsu Muraoka and John F. Elwolde. Studies on the Texts of the Desert of Judah 36. Leiden: Brill.

Sokoloff, Michael. 1990. *A Dictionary of Jewish Palestinian Aramaic of the Byzantine Period*. 2nd ed. Ramat Gan: Bar Ilan University Press.

Sokoloff, Michael. 2002. *A Dictionary of Jewish Babylonian Aramaic of the Talmudic and Geonic Periods*. Ramat-Gan: Bar Ilan University Press.

Stadelmann, Helge. 1980. *Ben Sira als Schriftgelehrter: Eine Untersuchung zum Berufsbild des vor-makkabäischen Sōfēr unter Berücksichtigung seines Verhältnisses zu Priester-, Propheten- und Weisheitslehrertum*. Wissenschaftliche Untersuchungen zum Neuen Testament 2. Reihe 6. Tübingen: Mohr Siebeck.

Stegemann, Hartmut, and Eileen Schuller, eds. 2009. *Qumran Cave 1.III: 1QHodayot^a: with Incorporation of 1QHodayot^b and 4QHodayot^{a-f}*. Discoveries in the Judaean Desert 40. Oxford: Clarendon Press.

Strack, Hermann L. 1903. *Die Sprüche Jesus', des Sohnes Sirachs. Der jüngst gefundene hebräische Text mit Anmerkungen und Wörterbuch*. Schriften des Institutum Judaicum in Berlin 31. Leipzig: A. Deichert'sche Verlagsbuchhandlung.

Strugnell, John. 1969. "Note and Queries on 'The Ben Sira scroll from Massada.'" *ErIsr* 9:109–19.

Strugnell, John. 1972. "Of Cabbages and Kings — or Queens: Notes on Ben Sira 36:18–21." Pages 204–9 in *The Use of the Old Testament in the New and Other Essays: Studies in Honor of William Franklin Stinespring*. Edited by James F. Efird. Durham: Duke University Press.

Suderman, Derek W. 2015. "The Vocative 'Lamed' and Shifting Address in the Psalms: Reevaluating Dahood's Proposal The Vocative 'Lamed' and Shifting Address in the Psalms: Reevaluating Dahood's Proposal." *VT* 65:297–312.

Tal, Abraham. 2000. *A Dictionary of Samaritan Aramaic*. Handbook of Oriental Studies. Section 1. The Near and Middle East 50. Leiden: Brill.

Talshir, Zipora. 1979. "תתערדוך בפשיטתא'." *Tarbiz* 49:84–86.

Talshir, Zipora, and David Talshir. 2008. "כן נאמן לן עם בתולה (Ben Sira 20,4; 30,20) Meaning and Transmission." Pages 193–232 in *Conservatism and Innovation in the Hebrew Language of the Hellenistic Period: Proceedings of a Fourth International Symposium on the Hebrew of the Dead Sea Scrolls & Ben Sira*. Edited by Jan Joosten and Frédérique Michèle (J.-S.) Rey. Studies on the Texts of the Desert of Judah 73. Leiden: Brill.

Talshir, Zipora, Shamir Yona, and Daniel Sivan. 2001. תשורה לשמואל: מחקרים בעולם המקרא (*Homage to Shmuel. Studies in the World of the Bible*). Jerusalem: Bialik Institute.

Taylor, Robert. 1910. "The Originality of the Hebrew of Ben Sira in the Light of the Vocabulary and the Versions." PhD diss., University of Toronto.

Thiele, Walter. 1987. *Sirach (Ecclesiasticus)*. Vetus Latina. Die Reste der Altlateinischen Bibel 11/2. Freiburg im Breisgau: Herder.

Thomas, Samuel I. 2009. *The Mysteries of Qumran: Mystery, Secrecy, and Esotericism in the Dead Sea Scrolls*. Early Judaism and Its Literature 25. Atlanta: Society of Biblical Literature.

Tigchelaar, Eibert J. C., and Pierre van Hecke, eds. 2015. *Hebrew of the Late Second Temple Period: Proceedings of a Sixth International Symposium on the Hebrew of the Dead Sea Scrolls and Ben Sira*. Studies on the Texts of the Desert of Judah 114. Leiden: Brill.

Torrey, C. C. 1950. "The Hebrew of the Geniza Sirach." Pages 585–602 in *Alexander Marx Jubilee Volume, English Section*. Edited by Saul Lieberman. New York City: Jewish Theological Seminary of America.

Touzard, Jules. 1904. "Traduction française du texte hébreu de l'ecclésiastique avec les variantes du grec et du latin." Pages 885–971 in *La Sainte Bible polyglotte contenant le texte hébreu original, le texte grec des septante, le texte latin de la vulgate, et la traduction française de M. Labbé Glaire. Ancien Testament. Tome v. L'Ecclésiastique. – Isaïe. – Jérémie. – Les lamentations. – Baruch*. Edited by Fulcran Vigouroux. Vol. 5. Paris: A. et R. Roger et F. Chernoviz Libraires-éditeur.

Tov, Emanuel. 2004. *Scribal Practices and Approaches Reflected in the Texts Found in the Judean Desert*. Studies on the Texts of the Desert of Judah 54. Leiden: Brill.

Trovato, Paolo. 2017. *Everything You Always Wanted to Know about Lachmann's Method: A Non-Standard Handbook of Genealogical Textual Criticism in the Age of Post-Structuralism, Cladistics, and Copy-text*. Translated by Federico Poole. Storie e linguaggi 7. Padova: Libreriauniversitaria.it edizioni.

Turner, Eric G. 1971. *Greek Manuscript of Ancient World*. Oxford: Clarendon Press.

Tyrtaeus, Solon, Theognis, and Minnermus. 1999. *Greek Elegiac Poetry: From the Seventh to the Fifth Centuries BC*. Translated by Douglas E. Gerber. The Loeb Classical Library 258. Cambridge, MA: Harvard University Press.

Ueberschaer, Frank. 2007. *Weisheit aus der Begegnung: Bildung nach dem Buch Ben Sira*. Beihefte zur Zeitschrift für die alttestamentliche Wissenschaft 379. Berlin: de Gruyter.

Vaccari, Alberto. 1961. "Ecclesiastico, 37,10–11: critica ed esegesi." *Miscelanea Biblica Andrés Fernández*. Edited by Andrès Fernández et al. Madrid: Instituto Español de Estudios Eclesiásticos.

Vattioni, Francesco. 1968. *Ecclesiastico: testo ebraico con apparato critico e versioni greca, latina e siriaca*. Pubblicazioni del seminario di semitistica Testi 1. Napoli: Istituto Orientale di Napoli.

Vermeylen, Jacques, and Núria Calduch-Benages, eds. 1999. *Treasures of Wisdom: Studies in Ben Sira and the Book of Wisdom*. Bibliotheca Ephemeridum Theologicarum Lovaniensium 143. Leuven: Peeters.

Waltke, Bruce K., and Michael P. O'Connor. 1990. *An Introduction to Biblical Hebrew Syntax*. Winona Lake; Ind: Eisenbrauns.

Walton, Brian, Thomas Roycroft, Shute Barrington, James G. K. (James Gore King) McClure, and E. B. McClanahan. 1657. *Biblia sacra polyglotta : complectentia textus originales, Hebraicum, cum Pentateucho Samaritano, Chaldaicum, Graecum. Versionumque antiquarum, Samaritanae, Graecae LXXII Interp., Chaldaicae, Syriacae, Arabicae, Aethiopicae, Persicae, Vulg. Lat. quicquid comparari poterat : cum textuum, & versionum orientalium translationibus latinis : ex vetustissimis mss. undique conquisitis, optimísque exemplaribus impressis, summâ fide collatis : quae in prioribus editionibus suppleta, multa antehac inedita, de novo adjecta, omnia eo ordine disposita, ut textus cum versionibus uno intuito conferri possint : cum apparatu, appendicibus, tabulis, variis lectionibus, annotationibus, indicibus, &c. opus totum in sex tomos tributum / edidit Brianus Waltonus*. Londini: Imprimebat Thomas Roycroft.

Watson, Wilfred G. E. 1977. "Reclustering Hebrew l'yd." *Bib* 58:213–15.

Wernberg-Møller. 1959. "Observations on the Hebrew Participle." *ZAW* 71:54–76.

Winter, Michael M. 1976. *A Concordance to the Peshiṭta Version of Ben Sira*. Monographs of the Peshiṭta Institute 2. Leiden: Brill.

Wright, Benjamin G. 1999. "B. Sanhedrin 100b and Rabbinic Knowledge of Ben Sira." Pages 41–50 in *Treasures of Wisdom: Studies in Ben Sira and the Book of Wisdom*. Edited by J. Vermeylen and N. Calduch-Benages. Bibliotheca Ephemeridum Theologicarum Lovaniensium 143. Leuven: Peeters.

Wright, Benjamin G. 2008. "The Use and Inerpretation of Bibical Tradition in Ben Sira's Praise of the Ancestors." Pages 183–207 in *Studies in the Book of Ben Sira: Papers of the Third International Conference on the Deuterocanonical Books, Shime'on Centre, Pápa, Hungary, 18–20 May 2006*. Edited by Géza G. Xeravits and József Zsengellér. Supplements to the Journal for the Study of Judaism 127. Leiden: Brill.

Wright, Benjamin G. 2011. "Translation Greek in Sirach in Light of the Grandson's Prologue." *The Texts and Versions of the Book of Ben Sira: Transmission and Interpretation*. Edited by Jan Joosten and Frédérique Michèle (J.-S.) Rey. Supplements to the Journal for the Study of Judaism 150. Leiden: Brill.

Wright, Benjamin G. 2012. "Conflicted Boundaries: Ben Sira, Sage and Seer." Pages 229–53 in *Congress Volume Helsinki 2010*. Edited by Martti Nissinen. Supplements to Vetus Testamentum 148. Leiden: Brill.

Wright, Benjamin G. 2018. "The Persian Glosses and the Text of Manuscript B Revisited." Pages 125–46 in *Discovering, Deciphering, and Dissenting: Ben Sira Manuscripts after 120 years*. Edited by James K. Aitken et al. Deuterocanonical and Cognate Literature Yearbook 2018. Berlin: de Gruyter.

Yadin, Yigael. 1965. *The Ben Sira Scroll from Masada* / מגילת בן־סירא שנתגלתה במצדה. Jerusalem: Israel Exploration Society.

Yadin, Yigael. 1967. "מגילת בן־סירא שנתגלתה במצדה" (The Ben Sira Scroll from Masada)." *Eretz-Israel* 8:1–45.

Yadin, Yigael. 1999. "The Ben Sira Scroll from Masada." Pages 151–225 in *Masada VI: The Yigael Yadin Excavations 1963–1965, Final Reports; Hebrew Fragments from Masada and The Ben Sira Scroll from Masada*. Edited by Shemaryahu Talmon and Yigael Yadin. Jerusalem: Israel Exploration Society; the Hebrew University of Jerusalem.

Yassif, Eli. 1984. *Tales of Ben Sira in the Middle-Ages. A Critical Text and Literary Study*. Jerusalem: Magnes Press; Hebrew University.

Zanella, Francesco. 2013. "Between 'Righteousness' and 'Alms': A Semantic Study of the Lexeme צדקה in the Dead Sea Scrolls." Pages 19–34 in *The Hebrew of the Dead Sea Scrolls and of Other Contemporary Sources*. Edited by Steven Fassberg et al. Studies on the Texts of the Desert of Judah 108. Leiden: Brill.

Ziegler, Joseph. 1980. *Sapientia Iesu Filii Sirach*. 2nd ed. Vol. 12,2 of *Septuaginta. Vetus Testamentum Graecum*. Göttingen: Vandenhoeck & Ruprecht.

Zulay, Menahem, and Shulamit Elizur. 2004. מפי פייטנים ושופכי שיח. Jerusalem: Ben Zvi.

Zumthor, Paul. 1987. *Essai de poétique médiévale*. Collection Poétique. Paris: Éditions du Seuil.

Index of Modern Authors

Abegg, M. G. 40, 54, 198
Adler, E. N. 22, 24, 30, 32, 34, 36, 38, 40, 42, 44
Aharoni, Y. 14
Aitken, J. 59
Angerstorfer, A. 101

Bacher, W. 5–6, 9, 16, 21, 44, 59, 67, 86, 90, 92
Bauer, H. 8, 46
Bauer, J.-B. 58
Beentjes, P. C. 6, 12–13, 18, 22, 24, 26, 28, 30, 32, 36, 38, 40, 42, 44, 46, 52, 62, 64, 72, 74, 78, 84, 88, 102, 104, 116, 118, 120, 131, 134, 146, 166, 190, 198
Ben-Ḥayyim, Z. 6, 12–13, 22, 24, 28, 30, 32, 34, 36, 38, 40, 42, 44, 46, 49, 52, 54, 62, 64, 72, 74, 78, 84, 88, 102, 104, 114, 116, 118, 120, 122, 131, 134, 140, 144, 146, 154, 162, 166, 168, 184, 198, 200, 206
Ben Yehuda, E. 92, 96, 110, 117
Bergsträsser, G. 138
Bickell, G. 174
Bohlen, R. 3, 180
Böhmisch, F. 216
Box, G. H. 4, 10, 48, 55, 90, 92, 110, 202, 209
Bremer, P. L. 20, 65
Bresciani, E. 14
Bronznick, N. M. 53, 93
Brun, J.-P. 166

Calduch-Benages, N. 16, 36
Cantineau, J. 60
Caquot, A. 83
Carmignac, J. 5
Charles, R. H. 209
Corley, J. 15, 146, 191
Couroyer, B. 8
Cowley, A. E. 11, 14, 114, 116, 118, 120, 122–124, 144, 151–152, 154, 164, 186, 207

Darshan, G. 9, 131
Daube, D. 58
Dhont, M. 112
Dihi, H. 10, 42, 44, 78, 80, 89, 96, 106–107, 113, 132–133, 141, 145, 168, 176, 191
Di Lella, A. A. 4–5, 10, 16–17, 32, 35, 37, 53, 58–61, 63, 72, 74, 76, 78, 92, 102, 146, 166, 170, 190, 214, 216
Dimant, D. 53, 101
Driver, G. R. 53, 206–207, 209, 211
Duval, F. 50

Elizur, S. 24–25, 184, 188, 195–197
Eshel, E. 169

Fassberg, S. 6, 58, 65

Fleischer, E. 225–228, 231–233, 238–240, 242–243, 248–250, 252–254
Fuchs, A. 58

García Martínez, F. 65
Gerber, D. 88
Gilbert, M. 55, 63
Ginzberg, L. 5, 21, 67
Goff, M. J. 63
Golinets, V. 138
Gray, G. B. 129
Greenfield, J. 13, 24, 128, 169, 181

Habermann, A. M. 8
Haran, M. 166
Harkavy, A. 4, 12, 14–15, 42, 50, 65
Harris, J. R. 28
Hoftijzer, J. 22, 168
Hopkins, S. 87
Hurvitz, A. 98

Jastrow, M. 6, 9, 17, 20, 24, 29, 32–33, 38, 41, 49–50, 52, 54, 80, 86, 89, 103–104, 107–108, 114, 121–122, 137–138, 151, 168, 176, 184, 186, 189, 202, 211, 224, 227, 229, 239, 241, 247, 250–251
Jongeling, K. 22, 168
Joosten, J. 4, 6, 12, 44, 54, 143
Joüon, P. 2, 4, 6, 8–9, 12–13, 16–19, 28–29, 33, 35, 44–45, 48, 58, 64, 74, 80, 84, 87, 92, 94, 127, 148, 200

Kāmil, M. 14
Karner, G. 2, 66
Kearns, C. 58
Kena'ani, Y. 225
Kister, M. 9, 12–14, 20, 22, 32, 35, 46, 49–51, 84–86, 90, 98, 100–101, 106, 111, 113–114, 121–122, 124, 133, 137, 168, 180, 188, 241
Kogut, S. 11
Kottsieper, I. 60
Kutscher, E. Y. 7, 83, 141

Labendz, J. R. 123, 187
Lane, E. W. 102, 111–112
Lange, A. 25
Leander, P. 46
Lévi, I. 3–6, 8–20, 23–24, 27–28, 30, 32–38, 40, 42–43, 49–54, 56, 58–62, 64–65, 78, 83–93, 102, 104, 106–108, 110–112, 114, 116, 118, 123–124, 127–130, 132, 135, 138, 141, 144, 146, 152, 154, 156, 161–162, 164, 168, 170, 174, 181–182, 185–186, 198, 200, 208, 210–211
Levy, J. 52–53, 86, 94, 103, 186
Lichtheim, M. 50

Marböck, J. 61
Marcus, J. 206, 208, 210–211
Margoliouth, D. S. 102, 106, 108
Marsman, H. J. 277
Marttila, M. 98
Mattila, S. L. 145
Mies, F. 172
Milik, J. T. 141
Miller, C. 19, 31, 134, 164
Minissale, A. 32, 146
Mizrahi, N. 49
Mopsik, C. 4–5, 17–18, 23, 30, 37, 43, 45, 50, 54, 64–65, 92, 97, 161, 188
Moreshet, B. 170
Mulder, O. 168
Muraoka, T. 12, 60, 76, 80, 108
Murphy, R. E. 58

Neubauer, A. 11, 116, 118, 120, 122–124, 144, 151–152, 154, 164, 186, 207
Neusner, J. 85
Nissim ben Yaqob 61, 133
Nöldeke, T. 21

Obermann, J. 12
O'Connor, M. P. 80, 279
Oesterley, W. O. E. 4, 10, 48, 55, 90, 92, 110, 202, 209
Olszowy-Schlanger, J. 98, 166

Patmore, H. 59
Payne Smith, R. 206, 214
Penar, T. 2, 5
Pérez-Fernández, M. 22, 28, 38
Perles, F. 25, 65, 197
Peters, N. 5–6, 13–16, 20–21, 24, 27, 31–32, 34, 36, 40, 42, 46, 50–55, 58, 61–62, 64–65, 79, 82–83, 87, 89–90, 92, 96–98, 106–107, 110, 115–116, 122, 126, 152, 162, 168, 172, 188, 269
Philonenko, M. 12, 64
Porten, B. 26, 51, 60–61, 76
Prato, G. L. 208
Puech, É. 7, 25, 55–57, 87, 162, 164, 264–265

Qimron, E. 2, 7, 15, 22, 28, 57, 67, 78, 88, 100, 118, 121, 170, 180, 191, 278, 280

Rand, M. 24–25, 195–197
Rey, F. M. 4, 19, 23, 25, 37, 40, 55, 86, 90, 98, 110, 112, 197, 215
Reymond, E. D. 2, 7–8, 14, 16, 19, 23, 29, 32, 44, 49, 53, 78, 87, 89, 98–99, 102, 104, 118, 122, 126, 130, 134, 139–142, 145, 154, 170, 181, 200, 265, 268, 270–272, 276–277, 280, 283

Rooker, M. F.   39
Rosen-Zvi, I.   59
Rüger, H. P.   32, 34, 36, 55, 58, 61, 65, 70, 72, 77, 120, 180, 185
Ryssel, V.   27, 48, 97

Sanders, J. A.   188
Sauer, G.   108, 148
Schechter, S.   6, 8, 10, 14, 16, 18–19, 21, 46, 52–54, 64–65, 78, 80, 83–86, 97–98, 102, 112, 114, 172, 181, 188
Scheiber, A.   214, 216
Schirmann, J.   72, 74, 190, 226
Schuller, E.   99
Segal, M. Z.   2–22, 24–25, 27–28, 30–32, 34–37, 39–44, 47–49, 51–54, 56, 58–59, 61–63, 65, 67, 77–79, 82–84, 87, 89, 92, 97, 102–104, 107, 110, 116, 122, 124, 132, 134, 138, 144, 146, 150, 152, 154, 156, 158, 160–161, 168, 170, 180–182, 186, 200, 207–209, 211
Shaked, S.   37
Skehan, P.   4–5, 10, 16–17, 53, 63, 78, 92, 146, 166, 282

Slotki, J. J.   82
Smend, R.   4–6, 9, 11–15, 17–20, 24, 29–30, 32–34, 36–44, 46, 49–55, 58, 60–65, 67, 77–78, 80, 82, 84, 88–89, 91–92, 97–98, 100, 102–104, 106–107, 110, 112, 114, 116, 118, 120, 122, 124, 126, 128, 131, 138, 144, 148, 150, 152, 154, 156, 162, 164, 166, 168, 170, 181, 186, 269
Smith, M.   153
Sokoloff, M.   6, 15, 32, 51, 119
Stegemann, H.   99
Stone, M.   169
Strugnell, J.   102, 132, 268, 271–272, 279
Suderman, D.   124

Tal, A.   77, 82, 87, 113, 172
Talshir, Z.   80, 114
Talshir, D.   80
Taylor, C.   6, 8, 10, 14, 16, 18–19, 21, 46, 52–54, 64–65, 78, 80, 83–86, 97–98, 102, 112, 114, 172, 181, 188
Thomas, S. I.   27
Tigchelaar, E. J. C.   168
Touzard, J.   9

van Peursen, W.   4, 6, 8, 10, 12–13, 18–20, 27, 32–36, 38–39, 41, 43–45, 47–49, 53, 55, 59–61, 63–65, 67, 76, 84, 86–87, 96, 110, 112, 121, 125, 130, 141, 148, 174, 181
Vattioni, F.   6, 22, 24, 28, 30, 32, 34, 36, 38, 40, 42, 46, 52, 54, 62, 64, 70, 84, 102, 104, 108, 116, 144

Waltke, B.   80, 279
Watson, W. G. E.   11
Wernberg-Møller, P.   129
Wright, B. G.   90, 98, 122, 150

Yadin, Y.   139, 142, 146, 268, 272, 276, 280, 282, 286
Yardeni, A.   26, 51, 61
Yassif, E.   14, 28–29, 43, 55

Zanella, F.   3
Ziegler, J.   33, 39, 61

Index of Ancient Sources

1 **Hebrew & Aramaic Bible**

Genesis (Gen)
   1:1 58
   2–3 74
   2:3 208
   2:7 208
   2:9 108
   2:16–17 74
   2:17 56, 108
   2:18 50, 102
   2:20 50, 102
   2:18–23 50
   2:22 50, 108
   3:5 108
   3:8 21
   3:12 74
   3:13 74, 223
   3:15 47, 61
   3:20 118
   3:22 59
   4:7 21
   4:12 82, 103
   4:14 103
   5:1 58
   5:24 147
   6:1–4 63
   6:9 147–148
   7:1 148
   7:11 143
   8:22 98
   9:17 148
   12:15 176
   13:16 59
   14 63
   14:4 63
   15:6 148
   16:2 134
   17:4–5 148
   18:16–33 61
   18–19 63
   18:24 185
   18:26 63
   18:27 32
   19:12 98
   19:15 26
   19:21 9
   20:4 27
   20:6 58
   20:18 134
   21:11 225
   21:12 54
   22 148
   22:1 148
   24:14 16
   24:15 128
   24:18 23
   24:19 103
   24:33 103
   24:44 16
   24:46 23
   25:8 24
   25:13 156
   26:13 98
   26:20 274
   27:1 142
   29:17 188
   29:31 22
   29:33 22
   29:34 21
   30:13 9
   30:20 102, 185
   31:5 172
   31:20 13
   31:23 29
   31:26–27 13
   31:29 11
   31:39 156
   31:40 87
   31:42 22
   35:18 114
   36:40 156
   37:33 156
   39:3 113
   39:6 188
   39:21 94
   40:5 137
   40:13 21, 149
   41:32 150
   41:33 102
   41:49 98
   42:7 8
   42:9 43
   42:23 31, 105
   42:25 102
   43:9 80
   43:34 111
   44:16 18
   45:26 80
   46:30 210
   47:2 80
   47:3 118
   47:9 29
   47:18 109
   48:15 111
   49:4 128, 186, 211, 214
   49:5 21
   49:10 98
   49:11 117
   49:20 195
   49:26 103
   49:29 147
   50:25 168

Exodus (Exod)
   1:12 7
   1:19 79
   4:2 104, 135
   4:21 150
   5:9 56
   6:1 23
   7:3 64
   7:14 5
   9:17 117, 124
   9:21 18
   10:10 26
   12:21 94
   12:37 63, 156
   13:19 168
   14:4 145
   14:7 145
   14:18 145
   14:31 129
   15:2 48
   15:8 143
   15:9 181
   15:17 101
   15:25 111
   15:26 111
   16:20 32
   17:8 104
   17:12 210
   18:4 41
   18:7 14
   20:10 6
   20:11 208
   20:21 150, 172
   21:6 245
   21:8 99
   21:13 58
   21:37 76
   22:4 (Sam. Pent.) 14
   22:5 189
   22:8 43
   22:12 156
   22:15 188
   22:15–16 28
   23:5 3, 41, 247
   23:6 94
   23:7 35, 131
   23:18 116
   23:21 78
   24:10 138, 281
   25:6 166
   25:30 153
   26:5 45
   26:33 168
   28:28 17, 25
   28:36 152
   29:2 116
   29:9 150
   29:27 34
   30:25 112
   30:35 166

Exodus (cont.)
- 31 17
- 32:1 84
- 32:11 23
- 32:25 31
- 34:2 13
- 34:9 104
- 35:21 23, 156
- 35:24; 36:1, 3 20
- 35:26 23
- 35:35 115
- 36:2 23
- 36:6 23
- 36:12 45
- 37 17
- 37:2 91
- 38:23 115
- 39:21 17, 25

Leviticus (Lev)
- 1:6 170
- 1:8 112
- 1:12 112
- 2:2 112, 153
- 2:9 112
- 2:16 153
- 4:10 34
- 5:18 112
- 5:21 133
- 5:23 118
- 6:6 112
- 6:8 112
- 6:12 112
- 7:6 169
- 13:30 32
- 13:55 172
- 14:9 122
- 19:15 9
- 19:18 86
- 19:20 50
- 20:17 131, 275
- 22:12 23
- 24:4 170
- 24:19–20 148
- 25:6 6
- 25:26 38
- 25:45 45
- 25:46 48
- 26:25 118
- 26:36 5
- 27:3 112
- 27:8 45

Numbers (Num)
- 3:17 156
- 4:3 20
- 4:30 20
- 4:35 20
- 4:39 20
- 4:43 20
- 4:47 16
- 6:9 41
- 6:25 22
- 6:26 9
- 7:2 31
- 8:25 20
- 9:20 41, 200
- 9:21 41
- 10:2 170
- 10:10 170
- 11:1 34
- 11:1–3 63
- 11:17 51
- 11:20 110, 241, 269
- 11:21 63, 156
- 11:25 51
- 12:6 176
- 12:8 176
- 13:18 10
- 14:1 52
- 14:19 63
- 14:24 156
- 14:27–38 63
- 15:24 170
- 15:38 17
- 15:39 11
- 16 63
- 16:26 26
- 16:29 168
- 16:30 65, 153
- 18:18 23
- 18:19 23
- 20:18 79
- 20:20 65
- 21:2–3 63
- 21:28 77
- 22:3 7
- 22:38 12
- 23:8 180
- 23:22 150
- 24:8 150
- 24:17 101
- 24:24 100
- 27:16 65
- 27:20 31
- 28:11 115
- 28:14 140
- 29:13 115
- 30:14–15 149
- 31:19 222
- 32:1 63
- 32:22 31
- 35:20 52
- 36:7 28

Deuteronomy (Deut)
- 1:10 118
- 1:17 112
- 2:12 98
- 2:14 63
- 2:21 98
- 2:22 98
- 2:34 63
- 3:16 13
- 3:26 49
- 3:27 22
- 4:14 13
- 4:28 80
- 4:34 149
- 4:35 5
- 5:21 125
- 6:4 137
- 6:5 22
- 6:7 176, 279
- 7:4 9
- 7:7 4
- 8:3 116
- 8:13 94
- 8:17 79
- 10:14 65
- 10:16 63
- 10:17 9
- 11:12 88
- 11:16 84
- 11:27 18
- 12:5 253
- 12:6 23
- 12:11 23
- 12:17 23
- 13:2 76
- 13:3 153
- 13:7 27, 86, 104
- 16:19 94, 112
- 17:6 44
- 17:15 99
- 17:17 84
- 18:3 23
- 18:11 243
- 19:11 43
- 19:15 44
- 21:15–17 22
- 21:17 44
- 21:20 186
- 22:29 28
- 24:1 43
- 24:15 140
- 25:1 131
- 25:2 38
- 27:9 52
- 28:2 2
- 28:10 161
- 28:22 120
- 28:32 11
- 28:37 245
- 28:47 79
- 28:48 17, 93
- 28:50 9
- 28:54 27
- 28:59 80
- 28:65 6
- 28:66 21, 60
- 29:17 90
- 29:28 4
- 30:2 249
- 30:10 249
- 30:15 59, 108

INDEX OF ANCIENT SOURCES

Deuteronomy (cont.)
- 30:19   59
- 31:19   251
- 31:20   190
- 32:9   251
- 32:11   100
- 32:14   117
- 32:15   14, 24, 109
- 32:17   161, 232
- 32:22   172, 222
- 32:24   36, 46
- 32:26   33
- 32:41   45, 98
- 32:43   45, 98
- 32:46   18
- 32:52   104
- 33:2   47
- 33:3   22
- 33:4   19
- 33:5   109
- 33:19   23
- 33:26   109
- 33:28   121
- 33:29   27
- 34:7   85, 142

Joshua (Jos/Josh)
- 4:24   141
- 7:23   59
- 7:24–25   20
- 8:4   43
- 8:6   56
- 8:17   56
- 8:18   154
- 8:26   154
- 10:9–10   154
- 10:13   154
- 13:21   63
- 14:8   156
- 14:11   156
- 15:7   259
- 16:17   63
- 18:6   55
- 22:8   12

Judges (Judg)
- 1:8   139
- 2:10   24
- 3:16   48
- 3:31   114, 174
- 5:3   210
- 5:8   44, 168
- 5:10   18
- 5:12   88
- 6:5   38
- 6:24   161
- 9:4   24
- 9:38   159
- 9:45   159
- 9:57   102
- 13:5-7   156
- 13:19   84, 170

- 14:20   110
- 16:9   25
- 16:12   25
- 16:24   176
- 18:2   65
- 18:15   14
- 18:25   6
- 20:42   29
- 21:3   133
- 21:21   59

Ruth
- 2:21   103
- 3:7   233
- 3:16   18
- 3:18   105
- 4:4   249
- 4:14   64

1 Samuel (1 Sam)
- 1:10   6
- 1:16   52
- 2:1   98
- 2:8   18, 138
- 2:14   121
- 2:34   153
- 3:2   142
- 4:19   241
- 7:3   249
- 7:10–13   157
- 7:16–17   157
- 8:5   30
- 8:6   30
- 8:12   18
- 9:19   157
- 9:20   18
- 10:4   14
- 10:7   153
- 10:9   153
- 11:7   56
- 12:3   159
- 12:20   9
- 12:21   9
- 13:9   153
- 14:6   116
- 14:9   107
- 14:32   54, 115, 120
- 15:19   54, 120
- 16:11   90
- 16:18   39
- 17:22   14
- 17:35   56
- 18:1   185
- 19:3   176
- 19:17   24, 43
- 20:1   74
- 20:17   185
- 20:18   133
- 20:25   18
- 21:14   120
- 22:2   6
- 24:12   29

- 25   15
- 25:3   128
- 25:5   14
- 25:25   16, 18, 43
- 25:26   49
- 25:29   16
- 25:32   9
- 25:36   52
- 25:39   15
- 26:18   74
- 26:23   37
- 28:16   104, 126
- 29:8   74

2 Samuel (2 Sam)
- 1:6   54
- 1:21   86, 109
- 1:23   4
- 2:7   20
- 2:21   9
- 2:22   9, 24, 43
- 3:34   60
- 5:18   24
- 5:22   24
- 6:8   21
- 6:16   20
- 7:10   60
- 7:27   45
- 11:15   227
- 11:23   103
- 12:22   67
- 12:25   161
- 12:31   82
- 13:18   56
- 15:4   131
- 15:24   59
- 16:7   43, 88
- 17:8   6
- 18:3   18
- 20:1   43
- 20:12   46
- 21:9   32
- 22:37   65
- 23:2   176
- 23:10   98
- 23:11   103
- 23:13   103
- 24:10   160
- 24:12   133
- 24:24   82

1 Kings (1 Kgs)
- 1:46   129
- 2:7   27
- 2:16   130
- 3:11–12   18
- 5:18   95
- 5:23   139
- 5:25   103
- 8:13   101
- 8:30   101
- 8:32   131

1 Kings (cont.)
   8:39   101
   8:43   101
   8:48   249
   8:49   101
   10:3   37
   10:11   96
   12:13:33   65
   12:31   65
   14:5   8
   14:16   162
   18:27   36, 52
   19:8–18   163
   20:6   103, 150
   20:9   139
   20:10   60
   20:39   198
   21:8   277
   21:26   22
   22:28   176
   22:49   233

2 Kings (2 Kgs)
   2:9   44, 164
   8:27   65
   10:19   33, 52
   12:5   93
   13:17, 19   33
   13:21   164
   14:10   23, 156, 184
   16:18   28
   17:14   63
   17:32   65
   18:6   9
   19:21   47
   20:13   76
   22:17   62
   22:20   147
   23:18   64
   23:18   60
   23:24   67
   25:28   5

1 Chronicles (1 Chr)
   7:4   103
   9:30   112
   11:10   3
   15:29   20
   16:27   31, 90
   17:9   60
   17:25   45
   19:3   111
   20:3   82
   22:3   15
   22:14   15
   22:19   45
   24:5   8
   25:4   90
   25:26   90
   27:26   16
   28:2   206
   28:9   21
   28:20   118
   29:9   21
   29:25   31

2 Chronicles (2 Chr)
   1:11   12
   2:5   65
   2:9   103
   2:15   25, 82
   4:20   216
   6:18   65
   6:23   131
   6:29   274
   6:38   249
   9:2   37
   11:16   45
   16:9   3
   16:12   45
   16:14   109
   19:7   96
   20:20   16
   24:12   21
   25:15   16
   25:19   23, 184
   25:20   37
   26:15   98
   26:20   208
   28:15   137
   32:30   25
   32:31   31
   34:28   147
   34:33   9
   35:19   67
   36:16   79

Ezra
   2:6   10
   2:69   30, 82
   4:17   13
   4:22   50
   5:5   25
   5:7   13
   5:8   113
   5:9   25
   5:11   13
   6:7   8, 25
   6:8   12, 25
   6:9   2
   6:11   13
   6:12   67
   6:14   25
   8:16   8
   8:17   8
   8:21   39–40
   8:27   32
   9:3   28
   9:9   94
   9:12   22, 40
   10:14   118

Nehemiah (Neh)
   2:2   114
   2:6   39
   2:10   84
   3:8   3, 41
   3:33   88
   5:5   11
   5:7   19
   5:8   38
   5:12   18, 210
   5:13   55
   5:18   107
   6:19   5
   7:1   118, 133
   8:3   8
   8:7   8
   8:9   8
   8:10   90
   9:6   65
   9:8   148
   9:17   12
   9:19   28
   9:37   109
   10:1   148
   10:33   67
   10:37   8
   11:2   124
   12:38   227

Esther (Esth)
   1:5   88
   1:8   80
   1:10   52
   1:15   2
   1:16   48
   1:20   13
   2:7   128
   2:9   90
   3:15   208
   4:1   36, 119
   4:14   67
   4:16   49
   5:6   90
   6:1   87
   6:6   26
   6:12   208
   7:2   90
   7:5   32
   7:7–8   88, 90
   8:5   48
   8:6   35
   8:14   208

Job
   1:8   18
   1:22   20
   2:3   18
   2:9   84
   3:5   36
   3:9   41
   3:13   88
   3:20   6
   3:25   29
   4:3   132

Job (cont.)
    4:8   18
    4:10   3
    4:12   32
    4:17   31
    5:2   26, 67
    6:22   82
    7:1   20
    7:5   119
    7:11   6
    7:15   38
    7:17   114
    8:12   122
    9:4   60, 78
    9:5   116–117
    9:11   41
    9:12   59, 101
    9:26   41
    9:27   52
    9:31   22
    10:9   208
    10:10 143, 249
    11:10 41
    11:11 58
    11:15 43, 67
    11:17 150
    11:20 78
    12:11 35
    12:13 54, 60
    12:16 54
    13:4   36, 172
    13:17 46
    13:28 143
    14:1   33
    14:14 20
    14:17 16
    14:20 52, 87
    15:4   18
    15:10 133
    15:11 38
    15:14 33
    15:17 67, 135
    15:20 5
    16:2   63
    16:4   47
    17:7   87
    18:4   229
    19:13 110
    19:17 104, 129
    19:19 14–15, 22, 183
    20:5   47
    20:6   52
    20:12 124
    20:18 82
    20:20 60
    20:22 84
    20:26 172
    21:11 232
    21:28 44
    21:33 56
    23:9   72
    23:12 88

23:15   9
24:13   56
24:15   9
24:18   12
24:22   60
25:4   33
26:6   137
26:10   141
26:14   32
27:6   17
27:14   127
27:20   14
28:14   55
28:18   94
28:21   37
28:26   121
30:3   108
30:19   32
31:1   28, 48
31:5   97
31:7   11, 39
31:12   14
31:15   137
31:16   130
31:21   47, 105
31:38   114
31:39   82
32:6   67
32:10   67
32:11   56
32:13   58
32:17   67
32:21   9
33:6   208
33:23   31, 105
33:29   49
34:2   210
34:11   237
34:14   18
34:19   9
34:27   9
36:2   67, 72, 101
36:3   67
36:18   58, 84
36:22   237
37:12   17
37:16   67
37:19   39
38:7   110
38:14   209
38:16   56
38:22   118
38:25   121
38:27   106
38:37   140
38:40   25
39:7   65
39:10   114
39:15   11, 104
39:16   78
39:28   57
39:30   86

40:24   113
41:12   138
41:16   67
41:25   170
42:5   143
42:6   32

Psalms (Ps)
    1:1   26
    1:1–2   56
    1:5   38
    2:3   17
    3:3   195
    3:4   111
    4:6   23
    5:7   22
    5:10   84
    7:12   180
    9:5   30
    9:9   248
    9:17   90
    10:9   59
    14:5   29
    15:3   10
    16:2   37
    16:4   188
    17:2   64
    17:12   5
    18:45   143
    18:47   172
    19:3   67
    21:4   151
    22:6   95
    22:7   274
    22:8   47
    22:9   21
    25:3   101
    26:1   65
    26:3   4
    26:4   58
    27:1   9
    27:6   111
    27:10   249
    29:5   95
    30:11   13
    30:12   250
    31:11   80
    31:17   22
    33:6   135
    33:7   116
    33:14   101
    34:1   120
    34:10   93
    36:7   143
    36:37–38 23, 41
    37:1   29
    37:37   14
    38:7   48
    39:2   30
    40:3   250–251
    40:4   235
    40:5   172

Psalms (cont.)
- 40:13 14
- 41:3 42
- 41:10 14
- 41:13 210
- 44:16 181
- 45:3 14
- 49:2 210
- 49:7 61, 76
- 50:2 47
- 50:19 108
- 51:16 29
- 51:21 23
- 52:7 33
- 55:8 87
- 56:12 12
- 56:14 172
- 58:4 110
- 58:7 3
- 61:4 172
- 62:11 104, 114
- 65:11 114
- 65:14 72
- 66:3 138
- 66:7 39
- 66:9 250
- 66:17 160
- 67:2 22
- 68:7 56
- 69:14 9
- 72 100
- 72:5 208
- 72:8 149
- 72:9 48, 100
- 73:6 72
- 74:2 101
- 75:8 20
- 77:20 52, 182
- 78:13 143
- 78:25 23
- 78:26 84
- 78:30 110
- 78:48 142
- 80:2 47
- 80:4 22
- 80:8 22
- 80:20 22
- 82:1 19
- 82:7 32
- 83:12 63
- 84:11 208
- 84:12 83
- 86:13 172
- 89:3 114
- 89:7 275
- 89:10 133
- 89:23 60
- 89:28 210
- 89:38 275
- 89:52 52, 61
- 90:2 265
- 90:11 67
- 91:1 57
- 91:10 58
- 92:14 108
- 92:15 104
- 93:2 264
- 94:2 33
- 94:9 47
- 94:10 30
- 95:4 146
- 96:6 31
- 99 18
- 99:8 185
- 101:2 4
- 101:5 53
- 102:1 90
- 102:5 208
- 102:8 45
- 102:18 186
- 103:11 103
- 104:4 144
- 104:12 57
- 104:30 164
- 105:19 47
- 105:44 82
- 106:5 128
- 106:16 150
- 106:18 63
- 106:33 5
- 106:37 232
- 106:43 5
- 107:7 39
- 107:9 109
- 107:14 17
- 107:18 52
- 107:23 143
- 107:25 96
- 109:2 84
- 109:13 61
- 109:25 47
- 109:30 253
- 110:7 111
- 115:6 80
- 115:7 84
- 116:5 60
- 116:8 172
- 116:12 106
- 118:18 231
- 119:46 176
- 119:66 35
- 119:69 172
- 119:97 18
- 119:110 98
- 119:117 56
- 119:135 22
- 119:145 67
- 124:4 25
- 124:5 29
- 125:3 41, 127
- 127:5 101
- 130:4 12
- 132:1 180
- 134:3 20
- 135:4 239
- 136 253
- 136:8 18
- 139:20 104, 126
- 140:6 98
- 140:12 58
- 142:3 90
- 144:13 109
- 144:14 114
- 146:4 5
- 147:14 116
- 149:6 84
- 149:7 64
- 151:5 188

Proverbs (Prov)
- 1:5 17, 132
- 1:8 24, 67
- 1:10–15 26
- 1:19 29, 42–43
- 1:20 8
- 1:23 67, 94, 170
- 1:25 94
- 1:30 94
- 2:16 27
- 2:22 33
- 3:4 31, 90
- 3:8 79
- 3:11 17
- 3:13 56
- 3:14 57, 74
- 3:17 56
- 3:18 42
- 3:26 41
- 3:27 55
- 3:28 55
- 3:29 20, 24
- 3:32 51
- 4:1 67
- 4:6b 8
- 4:7 103
- 4:8 36
- 4:9 17
- 4:10 67, 87
- 4:13 16–17
- 4:20 67
- 4:27 9
- 5:1 56
- 5:2 57
- 5:3 27
- 5:4 27
- 5:5 222
- 5:10 82
- 5:18 57
- 5:19 28
- 5:23 110
- 6:10 80, 87
- 6:12 43
- 6:20 24
- 6:24 27
- 6:29 82
- 6:32 16

Proverbs (cont.)
- 7:7   16
- 7:13   26
- 7:18   28
- 7:21   27
- 7:26   28
- 7:27   222
- 8:5   18
- 8:7   51
- 8:8–9   16
- 8:9   86
- 8:17   8
- 8:19   57, 74
- 8:25   265
- 8:27   141
- 8:28   191
- 8:34   56
- 8:35   8
- 9:1   8
- 9:4   16
- 9:7   30, 43
- 9:11   87
- 9:16   16
- 10:2   12
- 10:10   102
- 10:13   16
- 10:14   58, 74
- 10:21   16
- 10:30   122
- 11:1   51
- 11:2   67
- 11:3   97
- 11:4   12
- 11:7   127, 211
- 11:12   16
- 11:13   4, 45, 60
- 11:14   17
- 11:17   54, 106
- 11:19   149
- 11:20   51
- 11:21   82
- 12:3   2
- 12:4   190
- 12:5   17
- 12:9   2, 35, 188
- 12:11   16
- 12:12   2
- 12:18   13
- 12:21   58
- 12:22   51
- 13:7   40
- 13:19   51
- 13:20   110, 247
- 14:3   58, 74
- 14:11   108
- 14:12   39
- 14:13   27
- 14:16   63
- 14:20   15
- 14:31   7
- 14:32   51
- 14:33   102

- 14:35   22, 185, 195
- 15:2   32, 58, 74
- 15:3   39
- 15:4   103
- 15:8, 9, 26   51
- 15:14   102
- 15:15   123
- 15:16   54
- 15:21   16
- 15:27   42–43
- 15:28   32
- 15:30   52, 190
- 15:31   126
- 16:1   10
- 16:5   82
- 16:5, 12   51
- 16:6   6
- 16:25   39
- 16:29   58
- 16:31   17
- 16:32   106
- 17:2   22, 185, 195
- 17:3   89
- 17:5   7, 82
- 17:7   33, 53
- 17:9   20
- 17:15   35, 51, 131
- 17:18   16
- 18:13   37
- 18:15   102
- 18:17   50
- 18:21   13
- 18:22   8, 48
- 18:24   15
- 19:3   43
- 19:4   15, 45
- 19:8   59
- 19:10   33, 53
- 19:11   80
- 19:14   123
- 19:16   95
- 19:17   96, 235
- 20:7   4
- 20:14   104
- 20:18   17
- 20:19   4, 60
- 20:25   37
- 21:9   22
- 21:10   8, 46
- 21:12   37
- 21:29   271
- 21:31   206
- 22:9   96
- 22:12   37
- 22:17   67, 115
- 22:21   61
- 22:24   26, 41
- 22:25   114
- 23:1–2 84
- 23:6   84
- 23:7   37
- 23:18   147

- 23:19   9
- 23:20   186
- 23:28   59, 95
- 23:32   27, 237
- 24:6   17
- 24:10   172
- 24:14   147
- 24:22   67
- 24:23   112
- 24:26   86
- 24:30   16
- 24:32   115
- 24:33   80
- 25:7   19
- 25:9   4, 247
- 25:9–10   15
- 25:10   53, 131, 275
- 25:14   130, 170
- 25:17   45
- 25:21   247
- 25:24   22
- 26:1   33, 53
- 26:10   21
- 26:18   93
- 26:24   42
- 26:26   38
- 27:1   29, 41
- 27:6   42
- 27:23   115
- 28:11   50
- 28:14   107
- 28:20   19, 82
- 28:21   112
- 28:22   53, 84
- 28:23   49
- 29:1   63
- 29:3   28, 110
- 29:5   49
- 29:15   108
- 29:21   27, 55
- 29:25   98
- 30:8   106, 229
- 30:16   134
- 30:23   22
- 31:5   285
- 31:6   6
- 31:10   190
- 31:28   9

Qohelet (Qoh)
- 1:9   4
- 1:13   30, 45
- 1:15   126
- 1:19   61
- 2:14   39
- 2:19   67
- 2:22   89
- 3:1   139
- 3:3   21
- 3:11   55
- 3:15   4, 11
- 3:20   121, 127

Qohelet (*cont.*)
    3:22   4
    4:8   53
    5:1   20
    5:7   41
    5:9   82
    5:17–19   54
    5:18   12
    6:2   12, 54, 99
    6:8   48
    6:9   39
    6:10   4
    7:3   181
    7:8   13
    7:11   26, 67
    7:12   14
    7:14   209
    7:14   209
    7:16   18
    7:17   80
    7:21   45
    7:24   4
    7:25   16, 30
    7:26   27
    7:27   16, 30
    7:29   16
    8:1   22, 30, 52, 67, 113
    8:4   101
    8:7   4
    8:8   7
    8:9   45, 49
    8:11   13, 32, 116
    8:16   45
    9:3   32
    9:7   52
    9:10   16, 30, 55
    9:12   43
    9:16   52
    10:7   247
    10:10   48
    10:12   58, 74
    10:14   4
    10:17   247
    11:1   247
    11:6   48
    12:4   141
    12:10   88
    12:11   146
    12:12   26
    17   45

Song of Songs (Song)
    1:2   123
    1:4   94
    2:9–10   56
    2:17   6
    3:11   151
    4:6   6, 168
    5:3   35
    5:16   14
    6:9   80, 176
    8:4   48
    8:6   77, 142

Isaiah (Isa)
    1:15   76
    1:31   43
    2:6   60
    2:13   37
    3:7   52
    3:15   104, 135
    3:16   82
    3:26   53
    4:2   123
    4:5   124
    5:5   14
    5:18   60
    5:21   26
    5:23   35, 131
    5:29   182
    6:6   140
    6:10   130
    7:9   16
    7:16   7
    8:8   52, 137
    8:13   22, 140
    8:14   94, 206
    8:21   94
    9:2   169
    9:8   53
    9:10   237
    10:5   80
    10:6   63
    10:10   36
    10:12   53
    10:32   47, 105
    11:13   112
    11:15   105
    11:16   51
    13:11   64
    13:12   45
    13:22   121
    14:31   45
    16:6   63
    17:11   82
    19:8   53
    19:13   109
    19:17   9
    21:2   64
    21:3   48
    22:4   20
    22:11   141
    24:19   96
    25:9   98
    26:10   8, 46, 131
    26:11   23
    28:10   72
    29:9   47
    28:13   72
    29:23   49
    30:1   5, 20
    30:2   80
    30:11   9, 130
    30:17   103
    30:18   96
    30:27   9
    30:29   80

    33:1   114
    33:16   142
    33:19   32
    33:21   96
    33:22   31
    34:5   63
    35:3   132
    36:18   58
    37:22   47
    38:3   21
    38:15   6
    38:16   60
    39:2   76
    40:2   20
    40:4   16
    40:15   132, 275
    40:26   60
    41:10   210
    41:12   88
    41:21   63
    41:29   127
    42:2   52
    42:10   143
    42:11   52
    43:1   172
    43:7   161
    43:27   105
    44:2   109, 239
    44:15   87, 139
    44:21   39
    44:23   110
    44:28   230
    45:6   229
    45:7   39
    45:13   82
    45:18   141
    45:24   229
    48:1   161
    48:10   8
    48:14   230
    49:5   172
    49:6   164
    49:8   210
    49:10   60
    49:13   110
    49:23   101
    50:4   235
    51:1   21
    51:5   12
    51:8   208
    51:9   101
    51:10   143
    51:23   150
    52:2   39
    52:20   101
    53:10   45, 113
    54:6   21, 57
    54:10   60
    55:9   180
    56:3   14
    56:5   129
    56:11   14
    57:1–2   24

INDEX OF ANCIENT SOURCES

Isaiah (*cont.*)
- 57:8   129
- 57:15 72, 92
- 57:19 91
- 58:1   84
- 58:4   160
- 58:5   7, 10, 97, 185
- 58:7   79
- 59:5   11
- 59:9   14, 41
- 59:18 96
- 62:3   17, 119
- 63:17 78
- 63:19 161
- 65:5   63
- 65:12 48
- 65:15 146
- 65:17 93
- 66:5   15
- 66:23 140
- 74:14 26

Jeremiah (Jer)
- 1:10   166
- 1:16   92
- 1:18   103
- 2:8   57
- 2:32   128
- 3:11   96
- 3:16   93
- 4:18   283
- 4:19   142
- 4:30   17
- 5:8   206
- 5:17   38
- 5:22   141
- 5:25   45
- 5:27   42–43
- 6:7   45
- 6:15   118
- 6:26   97
- 7:26   63
- 8:6   74
- 8:9   90
- 9:14   90
- 9:23   64
- 10:6   76
- 11:15 161
- 12:4   233
- 12:5   90
- 12:6   5
- 13:16 41
- 13:17 47, 84
- 13:18 17
- 14:14 36
- 15:3   180
- 15:5   14
- 15:8   247
- 15:9   30
- 15:16 80, 88
- 16:20 49
- 17:8   98
- 17:9   16, 102

- 17:16 26
- 18:1–6 208
- 18:15 54, 182
- 18:16 49
- 18:21 127
- 20:10 14, 172
- 21:8   59
- 22:10 114
- 22:19 180
- 24:7   249
- 25:27 88
- 30:13 80
- 31:9   39
- 31:12 6
- 31:15 97
- 31:21 97
- 31:25 6
- 31:36 59
- 31:37 59
- 33:2   141
- 33:21 59
- 33:26 59
- 38:22 14
- 44:6   189
- 46:11 80
- 47:3   189
- 48:20 180
- 48:35 101, 114
- 48:36 142
- 48:45 77, 101
- 49:8   118
- 49:24 39
- 50:11 206
- 50:16 57
- 50:31 118
- 50:45 180
- 51:13 19
- 51:34 101
- 51:56 96, 233
- 51:58 186
- 52:32 5

Lamentations (Lam)
- 1:2   97
- 1:7   97
- 1:8   80
- 1:14   54
- 1:20   6
- 2:4   103
- 2:11   6, 110
- 2:15   47
- 2:18   82
- 2:19   26
- 3:15   90
- 3:19   90
- 3:39   34
- 3:41   23
- 3:56   250
- 4:1   120
- 4:2   21
- 4:5   22
- 4:8   42
- 4:15   139

Ezekiel (Ezek)
- 1:4   161
- 1:7   139
- 1:18   122
- 3:18   80
- 5:6   5
- 5:17   120
- 6:8   110
- 7:11   98
- 7:19   109
- 8:5   265
- 8:6   135
- 9:9   129
- 13:6   271
- 13:18 124
- 14:3–4 26
- 14:7   26
- 16:5   124
- 16:7   123
- 16:12 17, 151
- 16:49 63
- 16:49–50 63
- 17:24 14
- 21:3   14
- 21:31 151
- 22:27 42–43
- 23:42 151
- 24:6   45
- 24:11 45
- 24:16 103
- 24:21 103
- 24:25 103
- 26:4   33
- 26:20 172
- 27:31 6
- 28:12 151
- 29:3   19
- 29:5   24, 147
- 29:7   65, 78
- 30:16 141
- 30:18 147
- 31:11 85
- 31:16 128
- 32:30 63
- 33:28 147
- 36:19 110
- 39:9   87, 139, 143
- 40:4   18
- 40:17 140
- 42:4   39
- 43:21 92
- 44:5   18
- 44:30 12
- 45:4   8
- 45:5   8
- 45:17 16
- 46:7   55, 96
- 46:24 8

Daniel (Dan)
- 1:10   41
- 1:17   120
- 2:9   78

Daniel (cont.)
- 2:21   100
- 3:19   52, 87
- 3:33   67
- 4:9   57
- 4:11   57
- 4:12   108
- 4:14   2, 104
- 4:18   57
- 4:20   108
- 4:22   29
- 4:23   108
- 4:24   6
- 4:29   29
- 4:32   208
- 5:6   52, 87
- 5:9   48
- 5:12.16 113
- 5:21   29
- 6:5   78
- 6:27   137
- 7:2   64
- 7:15   243
- 8:5   279
- 8:11   34
- 8:19   100
- 8:25   18, 53
- 9:5   48
- 9:9   12
- 9:13   28
- 9:15   23
- 9:17   22, 101
- 9:25   96
- 10:12 40, 45
- 10:21 3
- 11:4   50
- 11:10 16
- 11:20 130
- 11:27 104
- 11:30 100
- 12:3   131
- 36:22 101

Hosea (Hos)
- 1:6   63
- 2:16   141
- 3:5   22
- 4:11   186
- 4:12   186
- 5:13   142
- 6:5   12
- 8:7   110
- 8:9   28, 45
- 9:4   125, 127
- 10:13 18
- 13:1   121
- 13:8   46
- 14:6   121

Joel
- 1:13   8
- 2:8   19
- 2:14   67
- 2:20   39
- 4:1   198
- 4:2   26
- 4:3   55
- 4:4   102
- 4:7   102

Amos
- 1:3   82
- 2:8   83
- 2:15   57
- 3:7   4
- 5:6   25
- 5:15   67
- 6:3   15
- 6:6   166
- 6:12   90
- 7:2   18, 46
- 7:4   143
- 8:8   117
- 8:10   36
- 9:13   18

Obadiah (Obad)
- 1:11   55
- 1:16   86

Jonah
- 1:4   96
- 1:7   237, 243
- 1:12   237, 243
- 2:7   67
- 3:3–4 39
- 3:9   67
- 4:1   84
- 4:2   47
- 4:3   29

Micah (Mic)
- 2:1   11
- 2:7   48
- 3:11   82
- 5:4   63
- 6:8   67, 90
- 6:14   182
- 7:11   67

Nahum (Nah)
- 1:4   56
- 1:5   121
- 2:6   231
- 2:8   115
- 2:9   88
- 2:11   237
- 3:6   36
- 3:10   55
- 3:15   2

Habakkuk (Hab)
- 1:3   121
- 2:3   100
- 2:4   59
- 2:9   42–43
- 2:15   104
- 2:18   80
- 3:2   12
- 3:19   27

Zephania (Zeph)
- 1:6   156
- 3:4   24
- 3:6   33

Haggai (Hag)
- 1:5   18
- 1:7   18
- 2:5   148
- 2:18   18

Zechariah (Zech)
- 3:5   119
- 3:7   39
- 6:11   151
- 7:12   18
- 8:6   59
- 9:8   35
- 9:10   50, 149
- 11:7   122
- 11:17 36
- 12:3   16
- 12:10 114
- 13:8   44

Malachi (Mal)
- 1:4   38
- 1:12   91
- 2:8   54
- 2:14   22, 46, 57

2 New Testament

Matthew (Matt)
- 2:11   100
- 5:9   7
- 6:7   20
- 6:24   83
- 10:12 7
- 11:12 95
- 11:25–29 4
- 13:21 121
- 24:22 100

Mark
- 4:17   121
- 13:20 100

Luke
- 2:52   31
- 9:29   52
- 10:5–6 7
- 10:21–22 4
- 14:8f 49

Luke (cont.)
   16:9 83
   16:11 83

John
   5:3–4 168

Hebrews (Heb)
   11:7 148
   11:17–19 149

James (Jas)
   2:21 149

3 Apocrypha and Pseudepigrapha

As. Mos. 10:4 65

Bar 83:1 100

2 Bar 20:1–2 100

4 Ezra 4:26 100
4 Ezra 4:34 100

Judith (Jdt)
   15:14 23

Jubilees (Jub)
   2:19–24 208
   17:15–18 149
   20:5 63
   25:9–12 23

1 Maccabees (1 Macc)
   2:27 67
   2:52 148

2 Maccabees (2 Macc)
   2:7 37

3 Maccabees (3 Macc)
   2:4–5 63
   2:6 64

T. Ash. 1:4 209
T. Levi 3:9–10 65

Tobit (Tob)
   1:22 132
   4:3 3
   4:15 86
   13:15 60

Sib. Or. 3,675–681 65

Sirach (Sir)
   1:19 258
   1:19–20 259
   2:18 16

2:20 2
2:72 28
3:8 2, 44, 108
3:10 2
3:12–13 127
3:13 41
3:14 6–7, 39, 82, 147
3:14–15 6
3:15a 180
3:15b 180
3:16 32
3:17 35, 112
3:17–18 4
3:18 7, 92
3:21 4, 67
3:22 22, 38, 59, 61, 114, 118
3:23 35, 39
3:26 8, 23, 41, 45, 95, 114
3:26b 5
3:27 12, 19–20, 184
3:28 43
3:31 41, 227
4:1 7, 20, 97
4:4 20, 35
4:4–5 227
4:6 6, 20, 97
4:7 78, 185
4:8–10 227
4:9 4, 7
4:10 55, 227, 231
4:11 94
4:13 8, 46, 227
4:14 96
4:17 8, 50
4:19 59, 84
4:20 9
4:21 40, 232
4:22 10, 35, 54, 96, 112, 131
4:23 206
4:25 125
4:26 12
4:27 26
4:28 13
4:29 19
4:29–31 12
4:30 24, 128, 134
4:31 41, 206, 227
5:1 54
5:2 90
5:4 12, 82
5:5 5, 19–20
5:6 12, 50, 64
5:7 20, 38, 41, 49, 63, 112
5:8 12
5:11 25
5:12 30
5:13 30, 231
5:14 10
5:15 231
5:15b 13
6 15
6:1 10, 13, 231

6:2 13
6:4 44, 186
6:5 130
6:6 30
6:8 183, 251
6:9 198
6:10 30, 104, 112
6:11 12, 54
6:12 183
6:13 223
6:14 16
6:14–15 258
6:15 54, 191, 258
6:16 44
6:16–17 15
6:17 16, 60
6:18 44
6:18 18
6:20 67
6:21 12
6:22 16, 18, 41
6:23 30
6:23–24 259
6:24 30
6:25 7, 94, 108, 259
6:26 259
6:28 46
6:29 17
6:30–31 17
6:32 34, 56, 59, 67, 91
6:33 39
6:35 22, 24
7:1 44
7:2 223
7:3 33, 36, 79
7:5 18
7:6 42
7:7 20, 88, 110
7:8 82
7:10 12, 20, 49
7:11 6, 37
7:12 24
7:13 21, 59
7:14 20, 26–27, 30, 135
7:15 21, 60, 85, 117–118, 209
7:16 12, 19, 110
7:17 20
7:21 34, 50, 70, 82, 86
7:24 52, 96
7:25 4, 38, 46, 50, 185, 243
7:26 14, 31
7:27 22
7:27–28 22
7:29 22
7:29–31 22
7:30 22
7:32 85
7:33 35, 39, 227
7:34 38, 92
7:35 4
7:36 95, 114, 210
8:1 43–44, 46

Sirach (cont.)
  8:2   186
  8:5   24
  8:7   63, 113, 124, 147
  8:8   18, 25, 49
  8:9   13, 35, 44, 49, 58, 67, 93–94, 115, 206, 216
  8:11   24? 43
  8:12   188
  8:13   188
  8:14   10
  8:15   16
  8:16   32–33
  8:17   20, 30, 67
  8:18   29
  8:28   47
  9:3   20, 28
  9:5   241
  9:6   31
  9:7   28
  9:8   29
  9:8–9 27
  9:9   42, 86, 90
  9:10   24
  9:12   52, 82
  9:13   188
  9:14   13, 20, 27, 30
  9:14–15 26
  9:15   16, 131
  9:18   13
  9:32   2
  10   30
  10:6   223
  10:8   28
  10:10 32, 180, 186
  10:11 21
  10:13 214
  10:14 18, 33, 36
  10:15 33
  10:16 2, 33, 52, 61, 98
  10:23 94
  10:25 22, 34, 64, 70, 86, 247
  10:26 2, 18, 25, 37, 41, 44, 91
  10:27 2, 211, 214
  10:28 114
  10:30 40
  10:31 2, 26, 145
  11:1   18, 33
  11:2   14, 52, 109
  11:3   108
  11:5   18, 37, 119
  11:7   37
  11:8   11, 18, 72
  11:9   92, 114, 118, 271
  11:10 4, 73
  11:11 23, 49
  11:12 10, 211, 214
  11:14 108
  11:17 35, 116
  11:18 24
  11:19 5
  11:21 16, 41, 227

  11:25 41–42, 54–55, 114, 128
  11:25–27 5, 23, 45
  11:26 5, 41
  11:27 41
  11:28 41, 61
  11:29 42–43
  11:30 42–43
  11:32 42
  11:33 24, 43
  11:34 37, 44, 50, 206
  12   15, 43–44
  12:1   43–44
  12:1–5 54
  12:2   54, 93, 96, 163
  12:3   222
  12:4   18, 54
  12:5   24–25, 43, 186
  12:6   54, 98, 223
  12:9   128, 223
  12:11 83
  12:12 17, 24, 44, 46, 56, 88, 188
  12:13 8, 18, 22, 227
  12:13–14 46, 50, 223
  12:15 46, 281
  12:16 98
  12:18 30, 49, 105
  13   48
  13:1   22, 43, 48
  13:2   22, 48, 90
  13:3   49
  13:5   38
  13:6   50, 82, 92, 115, 137, 216
  13:7   12, 36, 63, 90
  13:8   224
  13:9   38
  13:11 8
  13:12 29
  13:13 133
  13:16 22, 51
  13:17 22, 92, 107
  13:18 6, 14
  13:21 52
  13:22 29, 36, 52
  13:23 58–59, 82–83
  13:24 35
  13:25 30, 47, 87, 94
  13:26 22
  14   22
  14:1   80, 104, 114
  14:2   93
  14:3   33, 84, 96
  14:4   60
  14:5   54
  14:6   44, 96
  14:9   60
  14:10 53, 84, 86, 96, 120
  14:11 11
  14:12 47, 55, 98
  14:13 96
  14:14 128
  14:16 54
  14:20 56

  14:21 18, 57
  14:22 56
  14:23–25 56
  14:25 56
  14:27 231
  15:2   8, 102
  15:7   20, 57, 60
  15:8   43
  15:9   20, 56
  15:11 31, 74
  15:11–12 74
  15:12 25, 49, 52, 83, 232
  15:14 62, 95, 168
  15:15–17 59
  15:16 67
  15:18 90
  15:19 20, 90
  15:20 60, 66
  15:25 95
  16:1   61
  16:2   54, 63
  16:3   5, 23, 33, 41, 45, 52, 61, 95
  16:5   79
  16:7   145
  16:8   12
  16:10 24, 147, 156
  16:11 64, 76, 100, 138, 206
  16:15 64
  16:16 85, 209
  16:17 67
  16:18 67
  16:20 18
  16:22 59, 76, 90
  16:23 26
  16:24 18, 25, 94
  16:24–25 79
  16:25 46, 90, 170
  16:26 67, 74
  16:27 43
  18:32 32, 44
  19:2   24, 186
  19:3   14, 186
  19:16 231
  20:5   40
  20:8   208
  20:13 128
  20:27 231
  21:7   231
  21:20 130
  22:11 222
  22:14 186
  22:21 188
  22:22 186, 188, 224
  22:23 15, 186
  22:24 224
  22:25 224
  22:26 224
  22:27 224
  23:1   225
  23:2   225
  23:3   225
  23:4   225

Sirach (cont.)
- 23:5 181
- 23:6 225–226
- 23:7 226
- 23:8 226
- 23:9 226
- 23:11 98
- 23:16 46
- 23:27 243
- 24:9 58
- 24:27 117
- 24:30–33 67
- 25:1 31
- 25:18 35, 46
- 25:21–22 188
- 25:24 74
- 26:4 52
- 27:5–6 16, 259
- 27:5 30
- 27:6 30
- 27:16 15, 82, 224
- 27:16–17 247
- 27:17 191
- 28:13 10
- 28:14 10
- 28:15 10, 21
- 30:12 7, 24, 43, 89, 185
- 30:13 60
- 30:14–15 87
- 30:15 106
- 30:17 80, 82, 242
- 30:19 36, 50, 61, 176
- 30:20 46
- 30:21 14, 53–54, 104
- 30:22 108
- 30:23 53, 94, 104, 128, 186
- 30:24 41
- 30:25 52
- 31:1–2 41, 133
- 31:2 22, 86, 185, 224
- 31:3 82, 231
- 31:4 49, 82, 92, 115, 216
- 31:6 45
- 31:7 26–27, 67
- 31:10 84, 189
- 31:12 85
- 31:12–13 53
- 31:13 47, 84, 90, 96, 111
- 31:14 86
- 31:15 22, 86, 111
- 31:16 16, 29, 54, 86, 90, 120, 247
- 31:17 90
- 31:18 85
- 31:19 86, 88, 101–102
- 31:20 29, 52
- 31:21 88
- 31:22 25, 44, 46, 67, 88, 110, 210, 247
- 31:25 54
- 31:25–27 109
- 31:26 43
- 31:28 74, 146
- 31:29 119
- 31:30 54, 60
- 31:31 91, 247
- 32:1 29, 86, 211, 214
- 32:2 25, 49, 216
- 32:3 67
- 32:4 18, 48
- 32:5 58, 107, 215
- 32:7 25, 48–49, 82, 117
- 32:9 20
- 32:11 23, 84
- 32:12 53
- 32:14 25, 97
- 32:16 17, 94, 108, 215
- 32:17 25, 206
- 32:18 25, 94
- 32:20 52, 58
- 32:21 59, 61
- 32:22 50
- 32:23 210
- 32:24 231
- 33:3 39
- 33:7–15 227
- 33:9 208, 235
- 33:11 208
- 33:12 235
- 33:14 16, 39
- 33:16–18 79
- 33:20 54
- 33:21 47, 120
- 33:22 210
- 33:23 43, 148
- 33:25 133, 210
- 34:6 231
- 34:7 231
- 34:11 231
- 34:12 231
- 34:19 231
- 34:21 232
- 34:23 232
- 34:24 232
- 34:25 232
- 34:30 233
- 34:31 233
- 35 23, 59
- 35:5 233
- 35:6–7 233
- 35:11 22, 52, 210, 235
- 35:12 55, 98, 229, 235
- 35:13 44, 234–235
- 35:14 235
- 35:15 235
- 35:15–16 112, 131
- 35:16 9, 235
- 35:17 24, 52, 76, 237
- 35:20 93
- 35:22 47–48, 55, 237
- 35:23 33, 237
- 35:24 237
- 35:25 237
- 35:26 237
- 36 100
- 36:1–2 237
- 36:3 105
- 36:4 237
- 36:5 237, 249
- 36:6 63
- 36:6–7 237
- 36:7 100
- 36:8 237
- 36:9 100
- 36:10 41, 100, 239
- 36:12 100, 114, 237
- 36:13 239
- 36:17 149, 161, 239
- 36:18 239
- 36:19 239
- 36:20 74
- 36:21 239
- 36:22 239
- 36:23 239
- 36:24 87, 102, 124, 239
- 36:25 16, 239
- 36:26 96, 102, 239
- 36:27 239
- 36:28 98, 239
- 36:29 241
- 36:30 241
- 36:31 195
- 37:1 195
- 37:2 15, 22, 53, 82, 86
- 37:4 105
- 37:5 117, 126, 159
- 37:5–6 182
- 37:6 126, 241
- 37:8 25, 241
- 37:9 39
- 37:11 21, 106
- 37:12 107
- 37:13 92
- 37:14 115
- 37:16 2
- 37:17 17
- 37:18 39, 151, 231
- 37:19–20 40
- 37:22 200
- 37:25 128
- 37:26 58
- 37:27 18
- 38:1 25, 86
- 38:4 112
- 38:12 25, 49, 98
- 38:16 24, 147
- 38:17 35
- 38:18 38, 53, 104
- 38:23 67, 147
- 38:24 4, 18, 38
- 38:25 18, 107
- 38:25–27 50
- 39:16 25, 48–49, 60, 82, 117–118
- 39:18 39
- 39:20 55
- 39:21 25, 118
- 39:24 39, 124
- 39:25 39, 65, 74

Sirach (cont.)
  39:26   240–241
  39:27   241
  39:28   241
  39:29   241, 269
  39:30   25, 46, 117, 241
  39:32   74, 114
  39:33   25, 60
  39:34   117
  39:35   243
  40:1   4, 38, 65, 118
  40:4   37
  40:5   41, 90, 159
  40:6   122
  40:10   13, 243
  40:11   127, 243
  40:13   12, 127
  40:15   2, 82, 107, 121
  40:17   243
  40:18   128
  40:19   123, 270, 272
  40:21   231
  40:23   120
  40:24   120, 126
  40:25   123
  40:26–27   227
  40:27   126
  40:28   24, 35, 63, 117, 147
  40:29   102, 113, 141
  40:30   14, 28, 46, 87
  41:1   82
  41:2   38, 48, 90, 114, 123–124, 130, 274, 285
  41:2–3   150
  41:3   9, 125, 128
  41:4   41, 96
  41:5   126–127
  41:6   126
  41:7   37
  41:9   158
  41:9–22 158
  41:10   121, 124
  41:11   269
  41:11–13 58
  41:12   123, 128
  41:13   106, 128, 208
  41:14   80, 128
  41:16   33, 58, 84
  41:17   24, 134, 181
  41:17–19 128
  41:17–42:1d 128
  41:18   131, 271
  41:19   128, 130
  41:19–42:1 128
  41:20   14, 130
  41:21   49, 130
  41:22   5, 130
  42   245
  42:1   9, 15, 20, 96, 112, 146, 191
  42:1   128
  42:1–8 128
  42:2   35
  42:3   16, 22, 30
  42:4   16, 30
  42:5   106
  42:7   60
  42:8   26, 50, 54, 67, 206
  42:9   39, 41, 82
  42:10   24, 39, 136, 243
  42:11   19, 56, 85, 88, 126, 130, 136, 138, 140, 243, 245
  42:11–14 243
  42:12   20, 27, 168, 245
  42:13   245
  42:18   136, 265
  42:19   46, 67
  42:21   49, 51, 82, 105, 118, 132, 137
  42:22   43, 136
  42:23   25, 118, 137
  42:24   209, 142
  42:25   137, 134
  43:1   136–137, 176
  43:2   138, 142
  43:3   47, 142, 281
  43:4   64, 138
  43:5   92, 141
  43:6   41
  43:7   142
  43:8   16, 100, 253
  43:9   168, 265
  43:13   92, 139
  43:14   118, 143
  43:16   124, 141
  43:17   141, 161
  43:18   188
  43:20   32, 144
  43:21   16
  43:23   134, 138, 143
  43:25   63, 140, 144
  43:27   41
  43:31   144
  43:32   140
  44:1   65, 84, 227, 249
  44:1   249
  44:1–15 249
  44:2   65, 249
  44:3   78, 142, 249
  44:4   31, 145, 147, 249
  44:5   249
  44:6   125, 249
  44:7   145–146, 249
  44:7–14 58
  44:8–9 235
  44:9   114
  44:10   249
  44:11   107, 271, 274
  44:12   146
  44:13   148
  44:14   63, 150, 249
  44:15   24, 249
  44:16   150
  44:16–17 83
  44:17   41, 156, 163
  44:19   43, 210
  44:20   83, 144, 148
  44:21   146, 149
  44:23   159
  45:1   31
  45:4   146
  45:5   150, 152
  45:6   150
  45:7   126, 150
  45:9   152
  45:11   152
  45:12   119, 148
  45:13   154
  45:14   151–152
  45:15   150
  45:16   96
  45:17   150
  45:18   26, 34
  45:18–19 63
  45:20   23, 150
  45:21   150, 176
  45:23   63, 98, 152
  45:25–26 170
  46:4   154
  46:5   67, 154
  46:6   63
  46:7   31, 247
  46:8   51, 63
  46:12   158
  46:13   160
  46:15   181
  46:16   138, 148
  46:19   158–159
  46:19e–f 159
  46:20   41, 160
  47:2   34, 156
  47:6   37, 119, 149
  47:7   104, 158
  47:8   176
  47:9   156, 158
  47:11   156
  47:12   176
  47:13   162
  47:14   117
  47:15   160
  47:16   160
  47:17   98, 160
  47:19   109
  47:20   43, 97, 148
  47:22   24, 158
  47:23   31, 163
  48:1   28, 222
  48:7   8
  48:8   44, 148
  48:12   44, 186
  48:14   63
  48:15   33
  48:16   235
  48:23   163
  48:25   137
  49:7   138
  49:8   109
  49:14   64
  50   168

Sirach (cont.)
 50:4 59, 95
 50:5 134
 50:6 120
 50:7 141
 50:8 56
 50:11 17
 50:12k-l 176
 50:22 84, 231
 50:25 7
 50:26 208
 50:27 50, 67
 51 249
 51:1 7
 51:2 7, 23
 51:2 231
 51:3 58, 250
 51:5 249
 51:6 172, 231
 51:7 249
 51:8 250
 51:9 250
 51:10 7, 15, 250
 51:11 250
 51:12 98, 250–251, 253
 51:13 251
 51:14 281
 51:15 251
 51:19 137
 51:20 92, 251
 51:21 251
 51:21–22 251
 51:22 235, 251
 51:26 16
 51:30 65

Wisdom (Wis)
 8:2 8
 8:9 8

4 Dead Sea Scrolls

CD II 11–12 101
CD III 15 230
CD III 17 46
CD III 20 168
CD V 6 3
CD V 12 84
CD VI 15 12
CD VIII 5 12
CD XI 12 21
CD XI 20 4
CD XIII 14 133
CD XIV 2 7
CD XIV 15 99
CD XIX 17 12
CD XIX 35 24, 63, 147
CD XX 3, 6 47
CD XX 4 61
CD XX 14 24, 63, 147
1Q19 3 5 8

1Q20 XIII 13 57
1Q20 XX 29 60
1Q20 XXI 13 45
1Q20 XXII 27 13
1Q23 3 3 78
1Q23 26 2 36
1Q26 1 5, 8 19
1Q34bis 3 i 2 41
1QH^a 4 9 9
1QH^a IV 17 41
1QH^a IV 22 8
1QH^a IV 27 168
1QH^a IV 35 54
1QH^a IX 18 208
1QH^a IX 21 208
1QH^a IX 31 30
1QH^a V 16 138
1QH^a V 31 33
1QH^a X 14 19
1QH^a X 18 8
1QH^a X 22 16
1QH^a X 24 60
1QH^a XI 4 22
1QH^a XI 7 20
1QH^a XI 19–20 7, 23
1QH^a XI 23–24, 30 208
1QH^a XI 33–35 65
1QH^a XII 6 22
1QH^a XII 7 47
1QH^a XII 8 49
1QH^a XII 28 22
1QH^a XIII 7 99
1QH^a XIII 8 7, 23
1QH^a XIII 10 60
1QH^a XIII 12.29 59
1QH^a XIII 36 36
1QH^a XIV 8 60
1QH^a XIV 10–11 24, 63, 147
1QH^a XIV 18 57
1QH^a XIV 21 96, 112
1QH^a XIV 25 46
1QH^a XIX 6–8 208
1QH^a XIX 20 4
1QH^a XV 32 64
1QH^a XVI 24 7
1QH^a XVI 25–26 283
1QH^a XVI 29–30 7, 23
1QH^a XVI 33 109
1QH^a XVII 151
1QH^a XVII 24 64
1QH^a XVIII 28 150
1QH^a XX 32 32
1QH^a XXI 2 33
1QH^a XXIII 13–14 33
1QH^a XXVI 13–14 58
1QH^a XXVI 15 4
1QIsa^a 45, 79
1QIsa^a XXIV 7 80
1QIsa^a XLV:22 83
1QM I 10 19
1QM I 11–12 100
1QM III 4 131

1QM III 9 23
1QM VI 13 5
1QM X 13 32
1QM XI 6 101
1QM XII 4 4
1QM XII 14 33
1QM XV 9 63
1QM XV 11 90
1QpHab I 6 31
1QpHab IV 1, 3 72
1QpHab IV 1.3 36
1QpHab VII 7 100
1QpHab VIII 11 58
1QpHab XI 8 54
1QS I 4 18
1QS I 24 48
1QS III 24 54, 65
1QS III-IV 65
1QS IV 5 67
1QS IV 7 151
1QS IV 11 5
1QS IV 11–14 7, 23
1QS IV 19 46
1QS IV 23 168
1QS IX 4 31
1QS IX 24 20
1QS V 4 67
1QS VI 4 112
1QS VI 14 46
1QS VI 15 112
1QS VI 26 152
1QS VII 8 55
1QS VII 14 39
1QS VIII 2 67
1QS XI 2 106
1QS XI 12 54
1QS XI 13 7, 23
1QS XI 21 33
1QSa I 11 49
1QSa II 17 112
1QSb (1Q28b) I 5 8
1QSb (1Q28b) II 24, 25, 26 8
1QSb IV 23 39
1QSb IV 27 22
2Q18 2 3 16
2Q18 2 4–5 16
3Q5 1 3 24
3Q15 V 6, VII 4, X 5, XI 12 168
3Q15 X 10 60
3Q15 XI 7 60
4Q124 8 4 206
4Q138 1 33 88
4Q158 10–12 4 76
4Q158 10–12 6–7 14
4Q160 3–4 ii 3 101
4Q161 2–6 26 13
4Q166 ii 6 22
4Q169 3–4 ii 5 120
4Q169 3–4 iii 1–2 36
4Q169 3–4 iv 2 55
4Q171 1–10 I 6 90
4Q171 1–10 IV 16.18 23, 41

4Q174 1–2 i, 54	4Q372 1 11 99	4Q417 2 i 9 84, 215
4Q174 1–2 i 1 60	4Q372 1 17 82	4Q417 2 i 11 25
4Q174 21 8 54	4Q372 1 20 84	4Q417 2 i 19–21 26
4Q175 I 13 101	4Q372 8 4 8	4Q417 2 i 19–22 188
4Q176 8–11 12 96	4Q372 14 2 65	4Q417 2 i 24 4
4Q176 8 13 98	4Q374 2 ii 8 22	4Q417 2 ii + 23 5 4
4Q177 2 4 43	4Q379 22 ii 9 43	4Q417 2 ii + 23 8 4
4Q179 1 1 11	4Q380 1 i 7 90	4Q417 2 ii + 23 25 2
4Q179 1 ii, 3 30	4Q381 13 51	4Q417 4 ii 3 58
4Q183 1 ii 5 12	4Q384 C 2 50	4Q418 7b 7 4
4Q184 1 2, 13, 15 24, 181	4Q385 3 3 90	4Q418 8a,b,c,d 15 22, 185, 195
4Q184 1 3 86	4Q385 4 1 53	4Q418 8a–d 12 16, 102
4Q184 1 13 128	4Q385 4.2–3 100	4Q418 9+9a-c 18 88
4Q184 1 14 54	4Q385 4 6 101	4Q418 9 11 111
4Q185 1–2 ii 12 80	4Q385 6 8 108	4Q418 10ab 4 48
4Q196 18 2 60	4Q385a 17a-e ii 3 57	4Q418 43–45 i 9 4
4Q197 3 1 82	4Q386 1 ii 8 49	4Q418 69 ii 6 7, 23
4Q200 2 4 2	4Q389 6 1 166	4Q418 69 ii 8 60
4Q201 1 iii 18 60	4Q392 1 9 8	4Q418 69 ii 12 49
4Q202 1 ii 20 60	4Q393 3 5 22	4Q418 77 2 25
4Q204 1 v 8 180	4Q394 3–7 i 18 138	4Q418 167 6 109
4Q204 1 vi 12 20	4Q398 14–17 i 7 249	4Q418 168 2 94
4Q210 1 ii 18 141	4Q398 14–17 ii 5 18	4Q418 177 4 25
4Q214 2-6 5 169	4Q400 1 i 4 8	4Q418 197 3 25
4Q216 5 1 65	4Q400 1 i 16 48	4Q418 228 3 25
4Q216 5 9 65	4Q403 1 i 20 144	4Q418a 4 2 49
4Q216 VII 10–16 208	4Q403 1 i 28 98	4Q420 1a ii-b 2 13
4Q222 1 2 60	4Q399 1 ii 2 18	4Q421 1 a ii b 14 13
4Q222 1 3 23	4Q405 20 ii + 21–22 2 47	4Q423 4 1 19
4Q223–224 2 II 19 76	4Q405 20 ii-22 4, 9 18	4Q423 5 5 100
4Q223–224 2 V 21 42	4Q405 23 i 11 180	4Q424 1 4 96
4Q225 1 4 148	4Q409 1 i 6 98	4Q424 1 6 67
4Q242 1–3 2.6 13	4Q409 1 i 8 98	4Q424 1 10 84
4Q254a 1–2 2 30	4Q415 11 8 94	4Q424 3 7 8
4Q257 V 5 151	4Q416 1 11 46	4Q425 1+3 7 43
4Q266 2 i 5 4	4Q416 1 11–133 65	4Q427 1 1 4
4Q266 6 i 7 32	4Q416 1 12 186	4Q427 3 9 32
4Q266 10 i 8 99	4Q416 2 i 3–5 84, 215	4Q427 7 i 19 4
4Q266 11 9 145	4Q416 2 i 4 4, 39	4Q429 4 i 10 96
4Q266 11 10 8	4Q416 2 i 6 25	4Q431 1 2.3 49
4Q268 1 7 4	4Q416 2 ii 3–6 188	4Q433a 2 8 57
4Q269 9 8 2	4Q416 2 ii 3.18 26	4Q434 1 i 12, 2 2 23
4Q270 5 21 2	4Q416 2 ii 5–6 21	4Q436 1a,b 2 92
4Q271 3 14 2	4Q416 2 ii 6 4	4Q438 3 2 12
4Q271 3 15 42	4Q416 2 ii 6–9 188	4Q462 1 16 52
4Q271 5 i 13 4	4Q416 2 ii 10 211, 214	4Q468bb 1 2 206
4Q272 1 i 16 32	4Q416 2 ii 15 22, 185, 195	4Q470 3 4 60
4Q274 2 i 6 55	4Q416 2 ii 18 109	4Q482 1 4 33
4Q285 8 4 22	4Q416 2 ii 20 2, 4, 35	4Q491 11 i 8 49
4Q287 2 9 8	4Q416 2 ii 21 27	4Q491 11 ii 20 127
4Q302 2 ii 7 57	4Q416 2 iii 5–8 188	4Q498 1 i 1 22
4Q302 11 2 57	4Q416 2 iii 6 83	4Q501 1 5 33
4Q303 1 8	4Q416 2 iii 6.15.20 4	4Q502 95 1 22
4Q322 1 3a 89	4Q416 2 iii 7–8 58	4Q502 96 6 22
4Q324 1 6 89	4Q416 2 iii 10 64	4Q504 7 9 123
4Q324a 1 i 1 89	4Q416 2 iii 11 36, 105, 111	4Q509 12 i 13 54
4Q332 2:3 89	4Q416 2 iii 16 23, 41	4Q509 12 i-13 6 41
4Q333 1:3.7 89	4Q416 2 iii 17 88	4Q510 1 6 41
4Q347 1 6 129	4Q416 2 iii 21 22, 46, 48	4Q511 1 8 47, 60
4Q368 10 ii 5 82	4Q416 2 iv 5.13 27	4Q511 10 2 41
4Q371 1a-b 8 109	4Q417 1 i 11 4	4Q511 30 2 65
4Q371 1a-b 9 99	4Q417 1 ii 13, 14 19	4Q511 30, 4 143

4Q511 52+54-5+57-9 2 32
4Q512 1–6 17 15
4Q521 2 ii + 4, 13 283
4Q521 7+5 ii 3 118
4Q523 1 ii 9 123
4Q524 14 2 99
4Q525 2 ii 1 10
4Q525 2 ii + 3 3 46
4Q525 2 iii 4 49
4Q525 5 10 8, 94
4Q525 5 13 67
4Q525 13 2 84
4Q525 14 ii 6 96
4Q525 14 ii 6–7 6
4Q525 14 ii 18 18
4Q525 14 ii 19 8
4Q525 16 6 31
4Q525 21 6 46
4Q525 22 3 57
4Q525 25 4 186
4Q529 1 11 65
4Q531 1 5 60
4Q532 2 10 60
4Q533 3 3 13
4Q534 1 i 9–13 30
4Q546 13 4 13
4Q548 1 ii-2 13 151
4Q549 2 6 92
4Q550 1 6 13
4Q556a 5 i 7 13
4Q563 1 3 129
4Q580 4 3 87
4QHb 14 2 33
5Q13 1 2 98
11Q5 XXII 13–14 101
11Q10 XXV 6 52
11Q10 XXXV 3 113
11Q13 II 9 137
11Q14 1 ii 7 22
11Q17 VII 4 47
11Q19 LIX 5 80
11Q19 LXIV 9 76
11Q19 LVII 11 99
11Q19 XLVII 9 25
11Q19 LXIV 7 99
11Q20 16 2 27
11QPsa XXVIII 7–8 98
11QPsa XXVIII 9 188
11QPsa XXVIII (Ps 151A) 5–7 67
11QTgJob 9:1 = 24:24 206
11QTgJob 33:24 87
11QTgJob II 2 59
11QT XXV 12 40
11QT XXVII 7 40
11QT XXIX 9 65
11QT LIV 2 27
11QT LIX 5 46
Mur 22 6 80
Mur 31 21 80
Mur 46 2.6 82
Naḥal Ḥever 56 7 82

5 Rabbinic Literature

5.1 Mishnah

m. ʿAbod. Zar. 1:9 237
m. ʿAbod. Zar. 5:7 52
m. ʾAbot 1:1 25
m. ʾAbot 1:7 18
m. ʾAbot 1:9 50
m. ʾAbot 2:1 50
m. ʾAbot 2:7 53
m. ʾAbot 2:10 86
m. ʾAbot 4:4 20
m. ʾAbot 4:10 114
m. ʾAbot 4:11 182
m. ʾAbot 5:7 54
m. ʾAbot 5:7 37
m. ʾAbot 5:11 35
m. B. Bat. 5:3 48
m. B. Bat. 5:10 132
m. B. Meṣ. 2:5 48
m. B. Meṣ. 6:1 137
m. B. Qam. 1:1 14
m. Ber. 2:1 7
m. Ber. 3:1 112
m. Ber. 4:2 6
m. ʿErub. 6:1 137
m. Ketub. 1:5 200
m. Ketub. 3:4 28
m. Maʿaś. Š. 4:8 35
m. Menaḥ. 11:1 195
m. Naz. 9:8 56
m. Ned. 3:4 176
m. Ned. 9:10 36
m. Neg. 12:6 243
m. Neg. 14:3 138
m. ʿOr. 3:3 38
m. Parah 3:3 6
m. Peʾah 1:1 106
m. Šabb. 2:5 45
m. Sanh. 3:4 50
m. Soṭah 1:8 48
m. Soṭah 5:5 130
m. Soṭah 9:15 61
m. Yebam. 4:2 21
m. Yebam. 16:7 103

5.2 Tosefta

t. B. Qam. 7:8 13
t. Ber. 5:7 85, 86
t. Demai 6:4 116
t. Pesaḥ. 8:6 20
t. Soṭah 2:3 36
t. Soṭah 4:5 54

5.3 Jerusalem Talmud

y. Ber. 4:1 73
y. Ber. 7:2 36
y. Ber. 9:4 8
y. ʿErub. 5:1 49
y. Ḥag. 2:1, 77c 2
y. Ḥag 9b–10a,1 4
y. Ketub. 30a 237
y. Nid. 3:2, 50c 82
y. Sanh. 2a 10
y. Šabb. 1:1 87
y. Shek. 48d 158
y. Soṭah. 7b 26
y. Soṭah 9:10 130
y. Soṭah 9:24 130
y. Taʿan. 3:5 110

5.4 Babylonian Talmud

b. ʿArak. 15b 106
b. B. Bat. 16b 113
b. B. Bat. 98b 37
b. B. Bat. 146a 123
b. B. Bat. 153a 92
b. B. Meṣ 8b 132
b. B. Qam. 92b 50
b. Ber. 16a and 53b 52
b. Ber. 24a 87
b. Ber. 43a 20
b. Beṣah 32b 124
b. ʿErub. 54 54–56
b. ʿErub. 96b 21
b. Giṭ. 6b 11
b. Giṭ. 61b 250
b. Ḥag.12b 16
b. Ḥag 13a 4
b. Ḥag. 15a 209
b. Ḥag. 16a 12
b. Ketub. 8b 96
b. Ketub. 81b 21
b. Ketub. 110b 123
b. Mak. 10b 58
b. Meg. 9b 58
b. Meg. 14b 16
b. Meg. 15b 225
b. Meg. 27a 176
b. Menaḥ. 9a 168
b. Moʿed Qaṭ. 27b 114
b. Ned. 24a 6
b. Nid. 16b–17a 186
b. Pesaḥ. 28a 64
b. Pesaḥ. 181a 84
b. Šabb. 10a 188
b. Šabb. 41a 87
b. Šabb. 52b 16
b. Šabb. 88a 96
b. Šabb. 88b 28
b. Sanh. 38a 25, 209
b. Sanh. 65b 207
b. Sanh. 100b 14, 27–29, 39, 42–43, 53, 123, 133, 189, 191, 243
b. Sanh. 111b 225
b. Soṭah 12b 225

b. Soṭah 49b 61
b. Ta'an. 16a 233
b. Yeb. 63a 27
b. Yeb. 63b 14, 28–29, 42–43, 189, 191
b. Yeb. 121a 10
b. Yoma 28b 176
b. Zebaḥ. 88a 109

5.5 Targumic Texts

Frg. Tg. Gen 1:1 58
Frg. Tg. Gen 49:5 21

Sam. Tg. Gen 4:7 21
Sam. Tg. Gen 40:13 21

Tg. Esth II 1:2 138

Tg. Neof. Gen 1:1 58
Tg. Neof. Gen 3:16 143
Tg. Neof. Gen 18:12 89
Tg. Neof. Gen 44:18 6
Tg. Neof. Gen 49:5 21
Tg. Neof. Deut 29:18–19 12
Tg. Neof. Deut 32:15 24
Tg. Neof. Deut 33:3 22

Tg. Onq. Gen 3:15 61
Tg. Onq. Gen 31:31 73
Tg. Onq. Exod 14:27 87
Tg. Onq. Exod 20:21 172
Tg. Onq. Num 12:5 41
Tg. Onq. Num 12:8 231
Tg. Onq. Num 16:7 41
Tg. Onq. Num 16:26 110
Tg. Onq. Deut 14:1 114
Tg. Onq. Deut 32:11 100
Tg. Onq. Deut 33:3 22

Tg. Ps.-J. Gen 31:31 73
Tg. Ps.-J. Gen 49:5 21
Tg. Ps.-J. Exod 9:31 115
Tg. Ps.-J. Num 22:4 14
Tg. Ps.-J. Deut 22:29 28
Tg. Ps.-J. Deut 32:11 100

Tg. Judg 15:9 24
Tg. Judg 4:18 110
Tg. 1 Kgs 2:16 130
Tg. 2 Kgs 5:7 49
Tg. 1 Chr 28:12 49
Tg. Job 9:12 59
Tg. Job 19:8 211
Tg. Ps 52:6 172
Tg. Ps 72 100
Tg. Qoh 3:15 11
Tg. Song 1:16 57
Tg. Isa 9:4 112
Tg. Isa 10:15 98
Tg. Isa 41:16 60
Tg. Jer 14:22 49

Tg. Ezek 31:3 57
Tg. Zech 9:8 279

5.6 Midrash Rabbah

Gen. Rab. 1:4 101
Gen. Rab. 1:5 2
Gen. Rab. 8 4
Gen. Rab. 10:6 111–112
Gen. Rab. 22:8 18
Gen. Rab. 44 10
Gen. Rab. 45 72
Gen. Rab. 65:20; 73:5 53
Gen. Rab. 68:4 26
Gen. Rab. 73:12 52
Gen. Rab. 79:1 84
Exod. Rab. 21:7 110
Lev. Rab. 16:1 106
Lev. Rab. 16:2 106
Lev. Rab. 16:3 106
Lev. Rab. 4:8 87
Lev. Rab. 34:6 6
Num. Rab. 7:4 82
Deut. Rab. 2:2 96
Deut. Rab. 15 50
Deut. Rab. 17 96
Deut. Rab. 33
Qoh. Rab. 5:10 18
Qoh. Rab. 5:14 11
Qoh. Rab. 7:26 188

5.7 Other Rabbinic Works

'Abot R. Nat. 43 6
Alphabet of Ben Sira 14, 27–28, 43, 55
Amidah 101
Birkat Hamazon 101
Chuppah of Eliyahou 131 188
Chuppah of Eliyahou 201 187
Der. Er. Rab. 5:2 187
Der. Er. Rab. 7 86
Der. Er. Rab. 7 85
Der. Er. Zuṭ. 2.2 20
Der. Er. Zuṭ. 2:4 9
Der. Er. Zuṭ. 3:3 54
Eleazar HaQalîr 4, 6, 77, 78, 135, 146, 191, 243
Hekhalot Rabbati 1:2 48
Joseph Ibn Abitur 59, 106
Mekhilta de Rabbi Sime'on ben Yoḥaï
  12:12 60
Mekhilta Exod. 20:8 208
Mekhilta Exod. 21:13 58
Midr. Prov. 21 38
Midr. Psa. 27 65
Nissim, Ḥibbûr Yaphê 12
Pesikta Rabbati 25 110
Pirqoï ben Baboï 87
Sa'id Ibn Babshad 59
Saadia Gaon, Sefer HaGaluy 4, 12, 15, 42, 47, 50

Sefer Yetsira 60 209
Sem. 8:12 172
Shemuel bar Hosha'ana 106
Sipra Nedaba 1:1 80
Sipre Deut 48 41
Tanḥ. 18
Tanḥ. Meqitz 4:1 114
Tobiah ben Moshe 59
Qedoushta'ot 45
Yannaï 6, 45, 72, 78, 87, 104, 111

6 Other Sources

Aḥiqar syr. 2:43 10
Aḥiqar syr. 2:65 10
Aḥiqar syr. 2:72 28
Aḥiqar TAD C.1.1.3 132
Aḥiqar TAD C.1.1.19 132
Aḥiqar TAD C.1.1.90 61
Aḥiqar TAD C.1.1.94 51
Aḥiqar TAD C.1.1.99–100 26
Aḥiqar TAD C.1.1.112 45
Aḥiqar TAD C.1.1.130–131 26, 188
Aḥiqar TAD C.1.1.167–168 51
CTA 14 ii 50–51 142
CTA 14 iv 29 142
Epistle of Barnabas 4:3 100
Chronology of Elias of Nisibis 138
Ephrem, On Genesis and Exodus 54
Justin, Dial. 34:3–6 100
Justin, Dial. 64:6 100
KAI 121:1 22
KAI 124:4–6 22
KAI 162:3 22
KAI 181:9,23 168
KAI 226:9–10 5
Ketef Hinnom 2:5 79
Kuntillet 'Ajrud 19:7–8 79
LAB 19:13 100
Nerab Stele 2:5–6 114
Papyrus Insinger 10:12–13 50
Papyrus Insinger 25:2 36
Ps.-Phoc. 121 10
Pss. Sol. 17:26 100
Pss. Sol. 17:29–30 100
TAD A.2.4.7 76
TAD B.2.6.23 134
TAD B.2.6.27 134
TAD B.7.2.8 129
TAD B.7.2.10 129
Testament of Saint Ephrem XI 50
Theognis 499-502 88
T-S 8H18.12 96
T-S 12.863 38, 62
T-S 12.864 258
T-S AS 133.74 227
T-S AS 137.436 235, 243
T-S H.6.42 168
T-S H.15.75 106
T-S NS 93.80 116, 237
T-S NS 108.43 103, 230
T-S NS 193.99 235